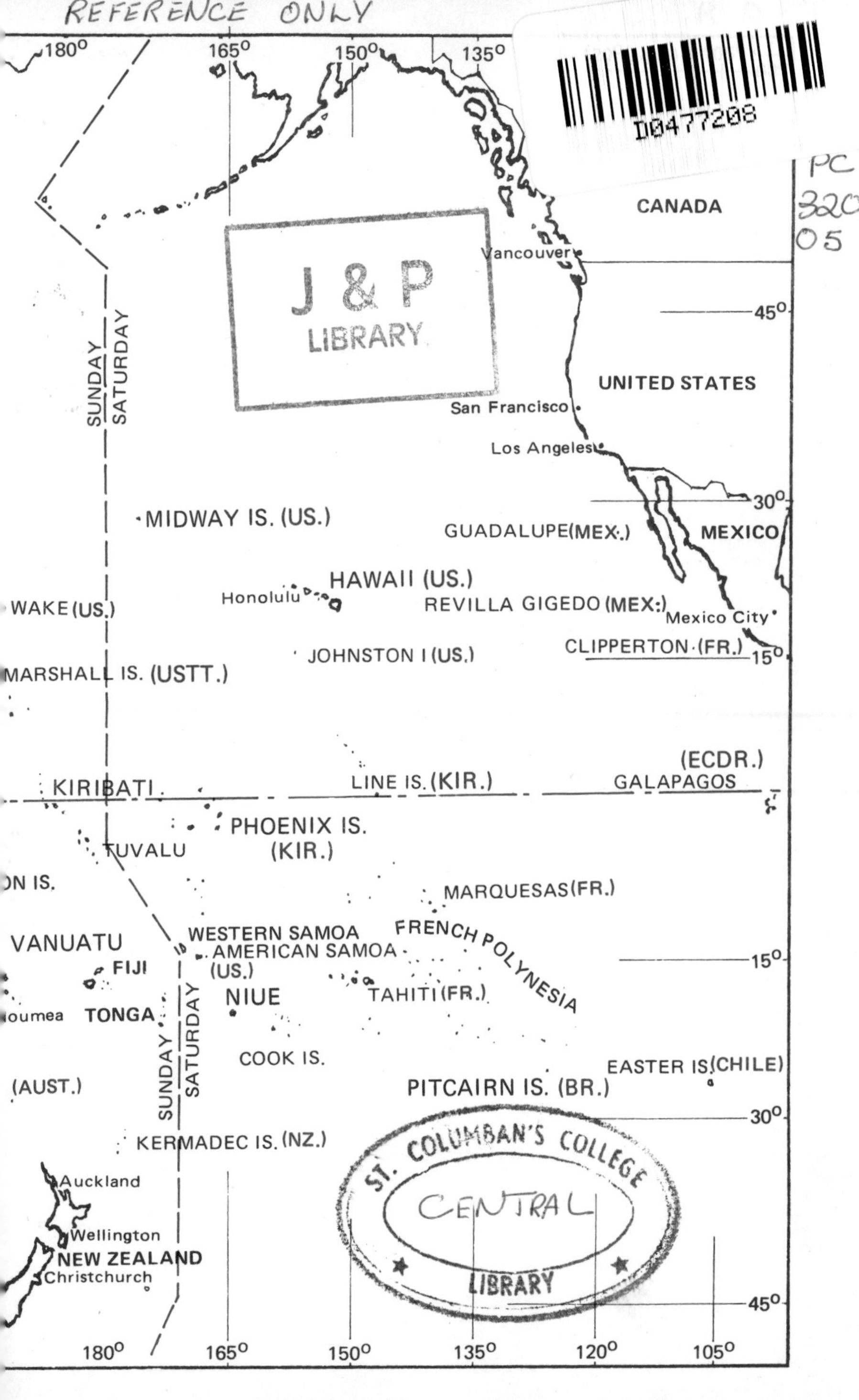
180°
165°
150°
135°
CANADA
Vancouver
45°
UNITED STATES
San Francisco
Los Angeles
SUNDAY
SATURDAY
30°
MIDWAY IS. (US.)
GUADALUPE(MEX.)
MEXICO
HAWAII (US.)
Honolulu
WAKE (US.)
REVILLA GIGEDO (MEX.)
Mexico City
JOHNSTON I (US.)
CLIPPERTON (FR.)
15°
MARSHALL IS. (USTT.)
(ECDR.)
GALAPAGOS
KIRIBATI
LINE IS. (KIR.)
PHOENIX IS.
(KIR.)
TUVALU
ON IS.
MARQUESAS(FR.)
VANUATU
WESTERN SAMOA
AMERICAN SAMOA
(US.)
FRENCH POLYNESIA
FIJI
15°
NIUE
TAHITI (FR.)
Noumea
TONGA
COOK IS.
EASTER IS.(CHILE)
(AUST.)
PITCAIRN IS. (BR.)
30°
KERMADEC IS. (NZ.)
Auckland
Wellington
NEW ZEALAND
Christchurch
45°
180°
165°
150°
135°
120°
105°

PACIFIC ISLANDS YEAR BOOK

PACIFIC ISLANDS YEAR BOOK

FOURTEENTH EDITION

EDITOR: JOHN CARTER

SYDNEY: NEW YORK

GENERAL EDITOR:
STUART INDER

Published by Pacific Publications (Aust.) Pty. Ltd.
76 Clarence Street, Sydney, N.S.W. 2000

Editor-in-chief:
John McDonald

First edition, 1932
Second edition, 1935
Third edition, 1939
Fourth edition, 1942
Fifth edition, 1944
Sixth edition, 1950
Seventh edition, 1956
Eighth edition, 1959
Ninth edition, 1963
Tenth edition, 1968
Eleventh edition, 1972
Twelfth edition, 1977
Thirteenth edition, 1978
Fourteenth edition, 1981

National Library of Australia Card Number
and ISBN 0 85807 049 9

Library of Congress Catalogue Card Number:
32-24429

Typeset by Keyset Phototype Pty. Ltd., Sydney
Printed by Hedges and Bell Ltd., Maryborough, Vic.

PREFACE

There have been, as usual, important political changes in the Island nations of the Pacific since the previous edition of the Pacific Islands Year Book appeared in 1978. This new 14th edition records the advent of independence for Kiribati (formerly the Gilbert Islands) and Vanuatu (formerly the New Hebrides) and notes the changes in the Trust Territory of the Pacific Islands as its various groups prepare for the dismantling of the Trusteeship agreement which will launch them into a life of their own. Some of them are already well advanced in exercising their new self-governing authority. But throughout the entire Pacific, there is hardly an Island group which has not changed in some significant fashion and this new edition attempts to keep abreast of developments, supplying the information in an easily accessible form.

If some statistics appear to be out of date it is because later figures were unavailable. The pressures placed upon some of the smaller Island States, as they face up to the many urgent problems that come with independence, has meant that the collection or analysis of data has sometimes had to be put aside for tasks considered to have higher priority. This is unfortunate, because, of course, forward planning depends on having accurate and up-to-date statistics. Nevertheless, despite their problems of time and staff, Island governments have continued to give us their utmost co-operation in supplying information, for which we are most grateful.

Without their goodwill, the Pacific Islands Year Book could not continue to play the vital part it has done for almost 50 years in disseminating impartial information on this important, and expanding region of the world.

THE PUBLISHERS

CONTENTS

SUMMARY OF ISLANDS

	Status	Capital or Administration Centre	Land Area (sq. km	Population	Local Time (GMT ±)	Exchange* (=$Aust.)
AMERICAN SAMOA	Unincorporated U.S. territory	Pago Pago	197	31,500	−11	$US1.1731
COOK ISLANDS	Self-governing in free association with New Zealand	Avarua	240	18,500	−10.30	$NZ1.1905
EASTER ISLAND	Dependency of Chile	Hanga Roa	117	2,000	−3	Peso 39.0
FIJI	Independent state, member of Commonwealth of Nations	Suva	18,272	601,000	+ 12	$F0.9187
FRENCH POLYNESIA	Overseas territory of France	Papeete	4,000	141,000	−10	CFP93
GALAPAGOS	Province of Ecuador	Puerto Baquerizo	7,700	6,000	−5	—
GUAM	Unincorporated U.S. territory	Agana	549	90,000	+ 10	$US1.1731
HAWAII	State of the U.S.	Honolulu	16,638	887,000	−10	$US1.1731
IRIAN JAYA	Province of the Republic of Indonesia	Jayapura	410,000	1,037,740	+ 9	R625
KIRIBATI	Independent republic, member of Commonwealth of Nations	Tarawa	719	56,452	+ 12	$Aust1.00
KOSRAE	[a] Member, Federated States of Micronesia	Kosrae	109.6	4,940	+ 10	$US1.1731
MARSHALL ISLANDS	[a] Self-governing but also part of Trust Territory of Pacific Islands	Majuro	171	29,670	+ 10	$US1.1731
LORD HOWE ISLAND	Australian sovereign territory, part of New South Wales		12.9	300	+ 10	$Aust1.00
NAURU	Independent republic, associate member of Commonwealth	Yaren	22	7 700	+ 12	$Aust1.00
NEW CALEDONIA	Overseas territory of France	Noumea	19,103	138,000	+ 11	CFP93
NIUE	Self-governing in free association with New Zealand	Alofi	258	3,578	−11	$NZ1.1905
NORFOLK ISLAND	Territory of Australia	Kingston	34.5	1,698	+ 11.30	$Aust1.00
NORTHERN MARIANA ISLANDS	[a] Commonwealth state in association with U.S. Also part of Trust Territory	Saipan	471	15,970	+ 10	$US1.1731

OGASAWARA ISLANDS	Japanese territory	Chichi-Jima	100	1,562	+9	Yen243.12
PALAU	[a†] Self-governing but also part of Trust Territory	Koror	460	14,800	+10	$US1.1731
PAPUA NEW GUINEA	Independent state, member of Commonwealth	Port Moresby	461,690	3,168,700	+10	K0.759
PITCAIRN	Dependency of Britain, administered by British High Commissioner in N.Z.	Adamstown	4.5	64	-8	—
PONAPE	[a] Member, Federated States of Micronesia also part of Trust Territory	Kolonia	375	23,140	+10	$US1.1731
SOLOMON ISLANDS	Independent state, member of Commonwealth	Honiara	29,785	196,823	+11	$SI.0.936
TOKELAU	Dependency of New Zealand		10.11	1,565	-11	$NZ1.1905
TONGA	Independent monarchy, member of Commonwealth	Nuku'alofa	671	92,000	+13	TP0.983
TORRES STRAIT ISLANDS	Australian possession administered by Australia	Thursday Is.	673 (approx.)	6,698	+10	$Aust1.00
TRUK	[a] Member, Federated States of Micronesia, also part of Trust Territory	Moen	118	38,650	+10	$US1.1731
TUVALU	Independent State and member Commonwealth of Nations	Funafuti	25.9	9,000	+12	$Aust1.00
VANUATU	Independent republic, also member of Commonwealth of Nations and Association de Co-operation Culturelle et Technique (France)	Vila	11,880	112,596	+11	NFH80
WALLIS AND FUTUNA	Overseas territory of France	Mata Utu	124	9,192	+12	CFP93
WESTERN SAMOA	Independent state, member of Commonwealth	Apia	2,934	151,515	-11	WST1.059

† at Oct. 10, 1980

[a]Change in political status will be complete on ending of Trusteeship Agreement, scheduled for 1981.

PACIFIC CHRONOLOGY

1506.— Alvaro Telez (Portuguese) visits Sumatra.

1509.— Diego Lopez de Sequeira (Portuguese) visits Sumatra and Malacca.

1511.— Antonio d' Abreu (Portuguese) sails as far east as Aru Islands and Irian Jaya, then to Moluccas. This is first visit to Spice Islands.

1513.— Vasco Nunez de Balboa (Spanish) crosses the Isthmus of Panama and sights the Pacific.

1517.— Fernando Perez de Andrada (Portuguese) in China.

1520-21.— Ferdinand Magellan (Spanish) discovers Magellan Strait and crosses Pacific to Guam and Philippines in ships 'Victoria' and 'Trinidad.' After Magellan's death in Philippines, Juan Sebastian Elcano returns to Spain in 'Victoria' with cargo of spices, reaching Seville on 9 September 1522.

1521.— Spanish conquest of Mexico.

1525-26.— Spanish monarch sends expedition under Garcia Jofre de Loaisa to East Indies for spices. Four ships enter Pacific, but are separated by storm. Only the flagship reaches Moluccas. Expedition becomes fiasco. One ship, caravel 'San Lesmes,' lost.

1526.— Jorge de Meneses (Portuguese) lands on Vogelkop (Irian Jaya) and names region Ilhas dos Papuas.

1527-29.— Alvaro de Saavedra (Spanish) sent from Mexico to trade with Spice Islands and ascertain fate of Loaisa expedition. Two of his three ships lost after becoming separated in the Marshall Islands. With cargo of spices, Saavedra makes two attempts to return to Mexico from Moluccas, but is defeated by contrary prevailing winds.

1529.— Spain cedes Moluccas to Portugal by Treaty of Zaragoza.

1531-35.— Spanish conquest of Peru.

1537-42.— Spaniards explore Pacific coasts of North and South America, reaching as far north as San Francisco.

1542-45.— Ruy Lopez de Villalobos (Spanish) crosses Pacific from Mexico to Philippines, where attempt to found colony fails. Villalobos' flagship 'San Juan' fails in two attempts to return to Mexico. On one, Inigo Ortiz de Retes skirts northern coast of New Guinea and names it Nueva Guinea.

1564-65.— Spanish colony founded in Philippines by Miguel Lopez de Legaspi. Two of Legaspi's ships return to Mexico by running north to 40th parallel and skirting North American coast. These voyages establish Spain's galleon route, in use between Mexico and Philippines for next 250 years.

1567-68.— Alvaro de Mendana crosses Pacific from Peru and discovers Guadalcanal, San Cristobal, Malaita and other islands in the Solomons.

1577-80.— Francis Drake enters Pacific and sails up coasts of South and North America, looting Spanish towns and capturing treasure ships. After crossing Pacific to East Indies, he becomes first British circumnavigator.

1595.— Mendana leaves Callao with four ships to colonise Solomon Islands. In May, he discovers group now known as Marquesas Islands. Later, one of his ships disappears near Santa Cruz Island (Ndeni), where settlement is established. However, after Mendana's death, expedition leaves for Philippines. Second and third ships disappear en route, leaving flagship alone.

1598-1600.— Beginnings of Dutch exploration of Pacific. Mahu and Van Noort expeditions.

1605-06.— Pedro Fernandez de Quiros, pilot on Mendana's second voyage, sails from Callao in search of supposed southern continent. After passing through the Tuamotu Archipelago, Quiros reaches the Duff Islands (north of Ndeni) and then sails south past the Banks Islands to the island which he calls La Austrialia del Espiritu Santo — now simply Espiritu Santo or Santo, New Hebrides now Vanuatu. After an abortive attempt to found a colony in

Big Bay, Quiros heads northward for the standard route home to Mexico. Eventually the second-in-command Luis Baez de Torres, reaches the Philippines through Torres Strait and the Spice Islands.

1606.— Willem Jansz (Dutch) reaches southern coast of Irian Jaya from East Indies.

1616.— Willem Cornelisz Schouten and Jacob Le Maire (Dutch) round Cape Horn for first time and cross the Pacific in search of the southern continent. They discover northern outliers of Tonga; Futuna and Alofi (which they called Hoorn Islands); and some of the New Guinea islands.

1642-43.— Abel Tasman (Dutch), on voyage from Java and Mauritius, discovers Tasmania, New Zealand, Tonga, some of the Fiji islands, New Ireland, New Britain etc.

1648.— Fedot Alexeev and Semen Dezhnev discover Bering Strait on voyage from Kolyma River, Siberia. (See also 1728).

1700.— William Dampier (British) discovers strait between New Britain and New Ireland, and sights southern end of New Ireland.

1722.— Jacob Roggeveen (Dutch) discovers Easter Island and Samoa.

1728.— Vitus Bering (Russian) rediscovers Bering Strait.

1742.— Commodore George Anson (British) captures Spanish treasure galleon.

1765.— Commodore John Byron crosses Pacific on first British attempt to discover the southern continent.

1767.— HMS 'Dolphin' (Captain Samuel Wallis) and 'Swallow' (Captain Philip Carteret) on new voyage in search of southern continent. After separation near Strait of Magellan, Wallis discovers several Tuamotuan atolls, Tahiti and Wallis Island (Uvea). Carteret discovers Pitcairn Island, crosses Pacific to Ndeni, and lands at Buka and New Britain.

1769-78.— Captain James Cook makes three voyages to the Pacific. On the first, he observes transit of Venus at Tahiti, charts and names the Society Islands, circumnavigates the North and South Islands of New Zealand, and skirts Australia's east coast. On the second voyage, which establishes beyond doubt that no southern continent exists, he discovers and/or explores several islands in the Cook group, Niue, Tonga, Norfolk Island, Vanuatu, New Caledonia, Easter Island and the Marquesas. On his last voyage, he adds more islands in the Cook group, plus the Hawaiian Islands to his list of discoveries before being killed at Kealakekua Bay, Hawaii, February 14, 1779.

1785-88.— La Perouse (French) explores Pacific in ships 'Astrolabe' and 'Boussole' which are both wrecked at Vanikoro. La Perouse's fate remains unknown for 37 years.

1788. — First British settlement in Australia — at Port Jackson (Sydney).

1789. — Mutiny on the "Bounty".

1791. — Captain Ingraham (American) discovers northern Marquesas Islands.

1791-1792. — Vancouver and Broughton (British) discover Chatham Islands and Rapa, and visit Hawaii and north-west coast of America.

1792-1793. — D'Entrecasteaux (French) visits many Pacific islands in searching for La Perouse.

1797. — London Missionary Society establishes stations in Tahiti and Tongatapu.

1815. — Christianity adopted in Tahiti and nearby islands.

1820. — Bellingshausen (Russian) makes extensive survey of Tuamotu Archipelago.

1823. — Rev. John Williams (LMS) takes native missionaries to Rarotonga and other islands in Cook group.

1830. — Williams takes Christianity to Samoa.

1834. — French Catholic missionaries occupy Mangareva.

1840. — British sovereignty proclaimed in New Zealand.

1842. — French annex Marquesas and proclaim protectorate over Tahiti.

1853. — French annex New Caledonia.

1856. — Representative of J. C. Godeffroy und Sohn, of Hamburg, arrives in Samoa.

1874. — Fiji ceded to Britain.

1875. — Tupou I of Tonga signs constitution guaranteeing freedom to all Tongans.

1876. — First LMS missionaries reach Papua.

1877. — Western Pacific High Commission created by Great Britain to deal with British affairs in parts of the Pacific having no established governments.

1883. — British Government repudiates Queensland's annexation of Papua.

1884. — Germany annexes New Britain, New Ireland, and north-east coast of New Guinea. Britain declares protectorate over Papua.

1888. — Cook Islands declared under British protection. Chile annexes Easter Island.

1892. — Britain declares protectorate over Gilbert and Ellice Islands.

1893. — British protectorate established over southern Solomon Islands.

1894. — Republic set up in Hawaii.

1898. — Philippines and Guam ceded to United States following war with Spain. US also annexes Hawaiian Islands.

1899. — Spain sells Caroline and Marshall Islands to Germany. Western Samoa becomes German colony. Eastern Samoa becomes a US territory. Phosphate discovered on Ocean Island and on Nauru, a German colony.

1900. — Niue declared a British possession.

1901. — Ocean Island added to Gilbert and Ellice Islands Protectorate.

1906. — Australia accepts control of Papua from Britain. New Hebrides becomes an Anglo-French condominium.

1914. — German New Guinea and Nauru occupied by Australians; Western Samoa by New Zealanders; and Caroline, Marshall and Mariana Islands by Japanese. Otherwise, World War I has little effect on Pacific affairs.

1915. — Gilbert and Ellice Islands Colony created.

1919-1920. — Former German colonies in Pacific become mandated territories of League of Nations — New Guinea to be administered by Australia, Western Samoa by New Zealand, Caroline, Mariana and Marshall Islands by Japan, and Nauru by Australia, Great Britain and New Zealand jointly.

1932. — Japan annexes Caroline, Marshall and Mariana Islands.

1935. — Philippines created a semi-independent commonwealth by the United States, to become independent republic in 1946.

1941-1945. — War in Pacific between United States, the Netherlands and British Empire on one side and Japan on the other. Japanese occupy Netherlands East Indies, Guam, Nauru, Gilbert Islands, Solomon Islands and some parts of New Guinea until driven out.

1946. — Former mandated territories of League of Nations become trust territories of United Nations under same administering countries, except that United States takes over Mariana, Marshall and Caroline Islands as the Trust Territories of the Pacific Islands from Japan. Holland surrenders East Indies to Javanese nationalists.

1947. — Agreement creating South Pacific Commission signed in Canberra, Australia.

1949. — Commonwealth Parliament of Australia approves administrative merger of Papua and New Guinea.

1950. — Independent state of Indonesia established.

1959. — Territory of Hawaii becomes 50th state of USA.

1962. — Western Samoa becomes independent sovereign state.

1963. — Dutch New Guinea (Irian Jaya) handed over to Indonesia which had claimed it since 1949.

1965. — Cook Islands attain self-government.

1968. — Nauru becomes an independent sovereign state.

1970. — Fiji becomes an independent state.

1971. — South Pacific Forum established.

1974. — Niue attains self-government.

1975. — Papua New Guinea becomes independent state.

1976. — Gilbert and Ellice Islands Colony, on January 1, become two colonies, Gilbert Islands and Tuvalu.

1978. — Solomon Islands (July 7) and Tuvulu (October 1) declare their independence.

1979. — The Gilbert Islands becomes an independent republic (July 12) under the name of Kiribati. The United States signs treaties of friendship with Tuvalu and Kiribati and abandons claims to islands in both groups.

1980. — The New Hebrides becomes independent (July 30) under the name of Vanuatu.

THE PACIFIC WAR

The Pacific War began on December 7, 1941 with attacks by Japan on British, American and Dutch territory and ended on August 14, 1945, with Japan's unconditional surrender. Following is a summary of the main actions of the war. During this time Japan was still fighting in China, which she had attacked in 1937, and also kept large numbers of troops in Manchuria to protect her borders with Russia, with whom she had signed a neutrality pact in April, 1941.

Japanese attack forces prepare. On November 26, 1941, Japan's Pearl Harbor Striking Force of 28 ships under Vice Admiral Chuichi Nagumo assembled in the Kurile Islands under great secrecy and headed south-east, blacked out and under strict radio silence. On December 2, Nagumo received confirmation from Admiral Isoroku Yamamoto, Commander-in-Chief of the Japanese Combined Fleet, that the Striking Force would attack the US base at Pearl Harbor on December 8 (Tokyo time, December 7 Hawaii time). Japanese forces meanwhile were being moved into attack positions in widely-scattered areas of the North Pacific and Asia, as Japan prepared for a seven-point simultaneous assault on British, American and Thai territory.

Japan strikes in seven places. In a period of less than 14 hours from December 7, the Japanese struck Malaya, Hawaii, Thailand, the Philippines, Guam, Hong Kong and Wake Island, in that order. The first Allied shots were fired near Kota Bharu, a small village on the east coast of Malaya, when a Japanese invasion force of Japanese transports with 5,500 men and naval escorts anchored offshore at 2200 hours on December 7 local time, and British shore batteries fired on them. The Japanese escorts replied and Japanese troops began landing at 0030 on the 8th. Hudson aircraft of the Royal Australian Air Force No. 1 Squadron attacked the force, thus striking the first air blows against Japan in the war. When the Japanese began their landing there was still an hour and a quarter to go in Honolulu before the Japanese attack began on Pearl Harbor. That same night the Japanese had landed in Thailand as a stepping stone to northern Malaya.

Pearl Harbor debacle. Japan's air attack, from Nagumo's carrier-based force, began on 0755 on December 7, achieving complete surprise. Total US losses were 2,341 servicemen killed and 1,143 wounded, and 68 civilians killed and 35 wounded. Of the service dead, more than 1,000 men were in the battleship 'Arizona' sunk at its moorings. Of eight battleships in port, four were sunk or capsized and four damaged. Of the 97 ships in port, 18 were sunk or damaged, and 188 aircraft destroyed. Japanese casualties were fewer than 100 killed or wounded, 29 aircraft and five midget submarines destroyed.

Guam falls quickly. Guam was attacked by air at 0830 on December 8 and invaded on December 10, surrendering the same day. It was the first US territory to be captured by the Japanese.

Wake Island surrenders. Japanese bombers began attacking US Wake Island, 2,092 km east of Guam, on December 8. A small invasion fleet was repelled on December 11, but arrival of a second invasion fleet on December 23 resulted in Wake's surrender that day.

Philippines attacked. Air attacks began on US airfields and installations in the Philippines on December 8 and within one week US air power there was rendered impotent and the harbour at Manila made untenable for shipping. Japanese landings also began on December 8.

Hong Kong falls. Japan had concentrated forces on the frontier opposite the New Territories by December 8 and immediately began attacking British territory by air and by land, advancing swiftly into Kowloon and assaulting Hong Kong island, which surrendered on December 25, 1941.

The fight for Singapore. The Japanese advanced swiftly down both coasts of Malaya, overcoming ground resistance and being little inconvenienced by an Allied air force which was seriously under strength with fewer than 160 first-line aircraft. British naval strength was decimated with the sinking by the Japanese of the battleship 'Prince of Wales' (35,700 tonnes) and battle-cruiser 'Repulse' (33,9000 tonnes) off Malaya on December 10, with the loss of 840 men from both ships. Allied troops were forced to withdraw to Singapore, which surrendered on February 15, 1942, after a Japanese Malayan campaign totalling 70 days, one month less than the Japanese had estimated. British losses totalled 138,708, of whom over 130,000 were taken prisoner. Japanese casualties were 9,824 dead.

Netherlands East Indies invaded. Attacks had earlier been made on Borneo, and stepping stones to Java – Amboina, Sumatra, Bali and Timor – were seized. The Japanese came ashore on the night of February 28, 1942, simultaneously in eastern and western Java, and Dutch and other Allied forces surrendered on March 12.

The Philippines fall. Meanwhile, the defence of the Philippines, under the control of Lieut.-General Douglas MacArthur, was going as badly for the Allies as had the campaign in Malaya. The Japanese made main landings at Davao in the south, and at several points in northern and southern Luzon, the main island. The Davao landings were meant to facilitate the invasion of Borneo and the Netherlands East Indies and played no part in the Luzon conquest. When MacArthur's plan to defeat the Japanese on the beaches failed, he withdrew to the Bataan Peninsula for a last ditch stand, with headquarters on Corregidor. Manila had been declared an open city on December 26, 1941. There was fierce fighting for the peninsula, and on March 12, 1942, MacArthur, with some of his officers, escaped from the Philippines under US Presidential order from Roosevelt, and reached Australia on the 17th. The Bataan defenders were defeated in April. On May 6 the Luzon force surrendered, and the US defenders of the Philippines were finally overcome.

Bataan death march. With the surrender of Bataan, about 64,000 Filipinos and about 12,000 Americans became Japanese prisoners, and on April 10 they were forced to begin an 88 km march from Mariveles to San Fernando, then by crowded rail truck to Capas, and a further 12 km march to POW compounds at Camp O'Donnell. This became known as the Bataan Death March, during which 7,000 to 10,000 men, including 2,330 Americans, died from disease, exhaustion or brutality.

The Fall of Burma. The British regarded Burma as a bastion against Japan's invasion of India's eastern frontiers. Through Burma also ran the Burma Road, by which China's armies were supplied and US air bases in China were maintained. If Burma were captured, China would be isolated and might collapse, thus releasing Japanese armies for use in the Pacific. Japan assigned its XV Army for the conquest of Burma. Small forces attacked as early as December 11, 1941, but the Japanese began to move into Burma in strength on January 20, 1942, and the capital, Rangoon, fell on March 8. By the end of May, Allied forces were in full retreat, although many Burmese personnel took to the hills and continued to wage war against the Japanese.

Further attacks on the Pacific Islands. After repeatedly bombing Rabaul, capital of Australia's mandated territory of New Guinea, Japanese forces landed in Rabaul on January 22-23, 1942, and soon overcame Australian resistance. New Ireland to the north was successfully occupied at the same time, and this was followed by heavy air raids on various New Guinea towns and on Port Moresby, capital of the Australian territory of Papua. Landings were also made on the New Guinea mainland. Rabaul was soon being developed as a Japanese naval base. The Japanese now laid plans to capture Port Moresby in May, Midway Island and the Aleutians in June and in July to move against Fiji, Samoa and New Caledonia. Meanwhile Nauru and Ocean Island were left undefended and were eventually occupied by the Japanese on August 26, 1942.

Australia reinforced. Australia was now quickly being built up as a base for Allied offensive operations in the South-West Pacific. Between January and mid-March, 1942, 90,000 US Army men were sent to the Pacific, 57,000 of them to Australia. To secure supply lines from the US to Australia, the US garrisoned Palmyra, Christmas Island, Canton Island, Bora Bora, the Samoas, Fiji, Tonga, New Caledonia and New Hebrides and smaller garrisons appeared on many other islands. In Australia the Japanese made nuisance air raids on Darwin, Townsville and Sydney. Following General MacArthur's arrival in Australia in March from the Philippines, he was appointed Supreme Commander of the South-West Pacific, which was henceforth an Army responsibility. Admiral Chester Nimitz, Commander-in-Chief, US Pacific Fleet, was appointed Commander-in-Chief Pacific Ocean area, which became a Navy responsibility. They were required to co-operate with one another. Allied forces operated under their direction. General MacArthur elected to call himself Commander-in-Chief rather than Supreme Commander.

Doolittle raid on Tokyo. During this period of Allied reverses, Allied morale was temporarily lifted through a daring raid on April 18, 1942, by 16 US Army Air Force B-25s on the Japanese mainland cities of Tokyo, Nagoya, Osaka and Kobe. The flight took off from the aircraft carrier 'Hornet', then 1,011 km east of the Japanese coast, and was led by Lt.-Col. J. H. Doolittle. The raids inflicted little material damage, but convinced Japan that it needed to seize Midway Island as a forward base from which to attack the US Pacific Fleet.

Tulagi captured. Japanese forces assigned to capture Tulagi, capital of the British Solomons, and Port Moresby in Papua, had assembled in Truk, in the Japanese mandated islands of the Carolines, and sailed south on April 30, one of its groups occupying Tulagi without opposition on May 3. On May 4 the force directed to land in Port Moresby sailed from Rabaul, and other Japanese naval groups planned to rendezvous with it in the Coral Sea for this attack. But the Allied navies now moved to meet them.

Battle of the Coral Sea. This took place on May 7, 1942, when US and Australian land-based aircraft sighted some of the Japanese ships and reported them to a combined US and Australian naval force nearby. In the subsequent attacks on each other's ships, only aircraft were used, and the Coral Sea battle was the first naval battle in history in which opposing ships never came within sight of one another. The Allies lost more ships than the Japanese, but fewer aircraft than the Japanese and had only half as many casualties, and they succeeded in turning back the Port Moresby invasion force. The Japanese had planned to seize Port Moresby so as to safeguard their flanks and provide a base for attacking Australia; this was the first check on Japan's advance towards Australia.

Battle of Midway. Large opposing naval forces under the commands of Admiral Yamamoto and Admiral Nimitz met off Midway on June 4, 1942, after the Japanese had made a carrier-borne airstrike on the American-held island, unaware that US naval forces were in the vicinity. The Japanese fleet suffered losses so severe that it never recovered, and Midway became a turning point in the war.

Aleutians occupied. As a by-product of their attempted occupation of Midway, Japanese forces successfully occupied Attu and Kiska, in the American-owned Aleutian Islands, on June 7.

Papua fighting. The Japanese made an overland bid to capture Port Moresby, having failed by sea in the Coral Sea battle. Landing at Buna on July 21, 1942, they fought their way across the Kokoda track to within 48 km of Port Moresby before being forced back, mainly by Australian forces, who also repulsed landings at Milne Bay. The Allies then began to fight their way up the north coast of Papua in a long campaign that did not end until January 1943 with the fall of Buna.

Guadalcanal offensive. While the Papua campaign waged and began extending into New Guinea, a large, mostly American force, launched the first big Allied offensive in the Pacific by landing more than 17,000 troops on Guadalcanal and the Tulagi area on August 7, 1942, taking the enemy by surprise. The battle for Guadalcanal soon developed into a struggle for possession of the partly built Japanese airfield, near Honiara, which the Americans named Henderson Field for a Marine Corps hero of the Battle of Midway. It was a war of supply, with the Allies bringing in supplies and reinforcements during the day, and the Japanese bringing them in at night aboard destroyer-transports which ran down 'The Slot' to Savo Sound with such regularity that the Americans called the operation the 'Tokyo Express'. Within two months there was especially bitter fighting as the Japanese developed an all-out offensive to recapture Guadalcanal. The tide was finally turned against the Japanese in November in a fierce three-day naval battle. By February 1943 the 'Tokyo Express' was running in reverse.

Battle of Savo. Two days after the Allied Guadalcanal landing in August 1942, Japanese and Allied naval forces met off Guadalcanal in what became known as the Battle of Savo Island. This resulted in the worst defeat ever suffered by a predominantly American force in a surface action, with the loss of 1,023 men, with 709 wounded. Among the ships lost was the Australian cruiser 'Canberra'.

Coastwatchers. During the Guadalcanal and Papua New Guinea campaigns the Allies were assisted by men, mostly Australians supported by Islanders, operating in Japanese-held territory and supplying valuable information on Japanese movements by portable radio. These men were directed by the Coast Watching Organisation, which had been developed and was administered by the Royal Australian Navy through the Naval Intelligence Division. Most Coastwatchers had lived in the islands before the war as planters, or plantation workers, government officers and small businessmen and were given naval rank for their operations. Many were killed or were posted missing during service.

Allied Pacific drive. Allied forces by mid-1943 had gone on the offensive everywhere in the Pacific against what had been developed as a purely defensive Japanese island perimeter. American aircraft struck an important blow to Japanese morale and planning capacity by ambushing and shooting down an aircraft carrying Admiral Yamamoto (Commander-in-Chief of the Japanese Combined Fleet) over Buin, Bougainville, on April 18, killing Yamamoto. The Americans had earlier cracked the Japanese naval code and knew his movements and many other Japanese key moves in the Pacific. The Allies occupied Papuan offshore islands and captured Salamaua and Lae, and continued to fight up the New Guinea coast. In the Solomons, they pushed the Japanese out of New Georgia, and began air attacks aimed at neutralising the vital Japanese base at Rabaul, New Guinea, in preparation for an island-hopping campaign.

Ellice Islands occupied. The Americans occupied the Ellice Islands, establishing a base at Funafuti, and developed other islands, including Baker Island.

Bougainville campaign. The Allies launched a campaign to recapture Bougainville on October 27, 1943, with the seizure of the nearby Treasury Islands, followed on November 1 by troop landings at Cape Torokina, in Emperor Augusta Bay. They were soon firmly established at Torokina. Important work was done here by the 1st Battalion of the Fiji Infantry Regiment.

Rabaul neutralised. A prolonged and crippling series of air raids on Rabaul in November finally resulted in the withdrawal to Truk of major Japanese naval forces that had been stationed there. Rabaul ceased from that time to be an offensive threat to the Allies, remaining only as a strong defensive position.

Central Pacific island-hopping. The Americans attacked the Gilbert Islands on November 20, the invasion of Betio, on Tarawa, being especially hard fought with the loss of 1,090 US Marines and 2,311 wounded, and the loss of the entire Japanese garrison of 4,690, except for 17 Japanese and 129 Korean labourers taken prisoner. Most of the US losses were due to the beach landing being made at unusually low tide, which stranded landing barges on the reef. Kwajalein, Japanese headquarters in the Marshalls, was attacked and in American hands by February 4, 1944, comparatively cheaply in US lives but not in Japanese, and Majuro and other Marshall Islands were also captured. This was followed by the capture of Eniwetok, and air attacks on Truk, where on February 18, American carrier-based aircraft sank most of the Japanese naval fleet in the lagoon. Truk was not invaded.

Two-pronged drive for the Philippines. Allied strategy was for a two-pronged drive against the Philippines, and to Japan itself, through the Central Pacific islands, and the South-west Pacific via the north coast of New Guinea and former Dutch territories. It was decided to by-pass a number of Japanese-held areas including Rabaul, Kavieng, Truk and Yap. The main Allied effort was to be made through the Central Pacific under Admiral Nimitz. With extended supply lines and a growing shortage of ships and aircraft, Japanese defences were now beginning to crumble. American submarines, which hitherto had had comparatively little effect, were beginning to sink an increasing number of Japanese warships and transports attempting to reinforce scattered, hard-pressed garrisons in many areas.

Dutch New Guinea campaign opens. In December 1943 the Allied South-west Pacific forces under General MacArthur landed in west New Britain, and in the first few months of 1944 the Allies fought up the north coast of New Guinea, capturing Madang and Aitape, and Hollandia in Dutch New Guinea. The landings at Aitape and Hollandia cut off 180,000 Japanese troops and 20,000 civilians, many of whom were later killed or died of starvation or disease. The New Guinea Admiralty Islands and Emirau Island were captured, and the Americans quickly developed Manus, in the Admiralties, into one of the largest naval bases in the Pacific.

Burma offensive. In early 1944 Allied forces went on the offensive in Burma at several points, and Japanese forces began to lose ground.

Fight for Biak. Airfields at Biak, Dutch New Guinea, were required so as to give support to the Central Pacific operations, but General MacArthur's forces met stiff resistance in the invasion of Biak on May 27, 1944, as the Japanese had dug into caves and cliffs. Not until mid-August were the last pockets overcome, with Japanese losses more than 4,700 killed.

Saipan invaded. Meanwhile Admiral Nimitz's Central Pacific forces had invaded Saipan on June 15, but not until August 10 was the island secured after some of the most bitter fighting of the war. More than 57,000 American troops were employed, of whom 3,426 were killed and 13,099 wounded. The Americans killed 23,811 Japanese, but many others died in the jungle. More than 14,000 civilians were captured, most of them Japanese. The nearby island of Tinian also fell. Admiral Chuichi Nagumo, who had led the Pearl Harbour Striking Force in 1941, committed suicide on Saipan.

Guam falls. American forces invaded Guam on July 21, 1944, after the most prolonged air and naval bombardment yet delivered in the Pacific. Guam was secured by August 12, but mopping up of Japanese guerillas continued until the end of the war. Almost 18,000 Japanese died in the fighting.

Morotai, Palaus, captured. Forces under General MacArthur secured Morotai Island, in the Dutch Halmaheras, on September 15, 1944, meeting no opposition on the beaches. In the Carolines, American forces assaulted the southern Palaus – Peleliu, Angaur and Ngesebus – at the same time. From the south and the east the Allies were now closing in on the Philippines. The Americans planned to take Peleliu in four days, but it did not fall until November 26, after one of the war's bloodiest encounters. The Americans lost 1,792 killed or missing and 8,011 wounded in the Palau operations, most of them on Peleliu; of 13,600 Japanese who died, about 11,000 died on Peleliu.

Assault on the Philippines. The Allied invasion of the Philippines was preceded by an intensive air campaign, begun in September 1944, to reduce Japanese air defences there. The largest convoy ever seen in Pacific waters – totalling 701 vessels – invaded the Leyte Gulf on October 20, and 200,000 men of the US Sixth Army were put ashore on beaches of Leyte's east coast, with only minor casualties. Japanese forces numbering 387,000 troops were distributed throughout the Philippines, under the command of General Yamashita, conqueror of Malaya and Singapore, but only some 22,000 were on Leyte. Japanese reinforcements were soon pressed into Leyte, which became the crucial battleground for possession of the Philippines. Outside the gulf there was fierce naval action – the Battle of Leyte Gulf – which virtually destroyed Japan's faded naval strength.

Kamikaze units formed. At Clark Field, Luzon, on October 20, 1944, the Japanese 1st Air Fleet formed the first unit of the Kamikaze Special Attack Corps, whose suicide pilots were to crash their bomb-laden Zeke aircraft on enemy installations or warships. The corps was sponsored by Vice-Admiral Takijiro Ohnishi and the first unit was commanded by Lieut. Yukio Seki. The first Kamikaze attack was on the Australian cruiser 'Australia' off the Leyte beaches on October 21, and killed 20 crew members and the captain, and so badly damaged the cruiser that she was forced to withdraw to Manus. Kamikaze attacks soon became commonplace, and probably more than 34 ships were sunk and 300 damaged by suicide pilots in different areas of the Pacific. Casualties from them in the US Navy alone exceeded 4,400 killed and 5,400 wounded.

Final Philippines operations. After heavy fighting, Leyte was finally secured by Christmas, 1944, and Luzon was assaulted in January 1945, with the immense amphibious fleet the target of many Kamikaze attacks. The repaired Australian cruiser 'Australia' was crashed by no less than five aircraft in three days with a further loss of 44 crew members killed. The Allied land forces captured Clark Field on February 1, but the fight for Manila was street by street, and the capital was reduced to rubble, the Japanese garrison dead almost to a man, before the city was taken on March 4, 1945. The Bataan Peninsula and Corregidor had meanwhile been attacked and subdued, but northern areas under the control of General Yamashita had still not been controlled by the time the war ended in August. A total of 114,011 Japanese in the Philippines surrendered on Japan's defeat, but in the fighting another 300,000 had died.

Iwo Jima won. Bombing of Tokyo from Saipan by B29s had begun in November, 1944, but the range was regarded as too great for effective attacks, and the Allies decided to secure closer bases occupying Iwo Jima, in the Bonin Islands, only 1,062 km south of Tokyo, and Okinawa, one of the Japanese home islands, which also could be used as a naval base if Japan had to be invaded. Iwo Jima, powerfully fortified and defended, was given the heaviest pre-invasion pounding of any island in the Pacific and invaded on February 19, 1945. Iwo Jima had to be won yard by yard over a month, with the loss of 6,812 Americans killed and 19,189 wounded and virtually the entire Japanese garrison of 22,000 killed.

Okinawa operation. Okinawa was attacked with an invasion fleet of 1,300 vessels and 183,000 assault troops on April 1, but was not secured until July 2, after more fierce fighting. Supporting naval forces were under continual attack by Kamikaze planes, 355 Kamikaze missions having set out on one single day, April 6. Okinawa was the costliest operation in the Central Pacific. American losses were 12,520 killed, 36,631 wounded; Japanese losses were 110,000 killed and 7,400 taken prisoner. The Allies had 36 ships sunk and 368 damaged at Okinawa.

Borneo, Burma operations. Allied forces captured Tarakan Island and other points on Borneo beginning in April and continuing through to July. The Japanese in Burma, exposed to increasing attack because of the fall of the Philippines, were driven back and the Allies re-occupied the capital, Rangoon, on May 3.

Japan bombed and blockaded. Tokyo and other Japanese cities came under increasing air attack from February, 1945. On March 10, over 300 B29s in the most destructive raid of either the European or Pacific wars, razed a quarter of Tokyo's buildings and killed more than 83,000 people, leaving more than 1,000,000 homeless. In the following months, about 66 cities were systematically burned out, with a paralysing effect on war production and civilian morale. Japan's depleted merchant shipping was further reduced by increased Allied air and sea attacks including extensive mining of Japanese home waters, thus effectively blockading her. Japan's imports of bulk commodities dropped from 22,039,000 metric tons in 1940 to 2,743,200 in 1945.

Peace-feelers. In February and March, and again in July, Japan put out peace-feelers through Russia in the hope of finding a face-saving formula to stop the war. Russia ignored these moves.

Atom bombs dropped. In July, 1945, the United States successfully tested the atom bomb, and on August 6 the first such bomb to be dropped was loaded into a B29 in secrecy at Tinian in the Marianas, and exploded that morning over the Japanese city of Hiroshima, burning out the city in extensive fires which burned for days, killing an estimated 71,379 people and injuring 68,023 others. On August 9 a second atom bomb was dropped on Nagasaki, causing less damage and killing, by Japanese estimates, 25,680 people and injuring 23,345. The bombs provided the face-saving pretext needed by the Japanese leaders for surrender, and Japan surrendered unconditionally on August 14.

Russia declares war. Russia, which had hitherto not intervened in the Pacific War, declared war on Japan on August 8 and on the 9th invaded Manchuria, Korea and southern Sakhalin, and later the Kuriles. She crushed the Japanese forces and continued the fighting for some days after Japan's formal surrender, capturing, among other material, 600 tanks.

Surrender signed. The formal instrument of surrender was signed aboard the US battleship 'Missouri' on September 2, 1945. Other ceremonies in other areas followed and for several years Japanese servicemen were still being repatriated to a shattered homeland.

THE LAW OF THE SEA IN THE SOUTH PACIFIC

*by Geoffrey Dabb**

It is obvious from a glance at a map that the land area of the islands of the South Pacific Ocean is insignificant compared with the vast ocean spaces in which they lie. Until recently, the resource areas under the control of Pacific island countries did indeed amount to only the few square miles formed by the area of the islands themselves. This has now changed. The new Law of the Sea recognises that small islands might be the basis for sea and seabed resources jurisdiction over hundreds of thousands of square miles. We have now entered the era of the 200-mile zone, and the map of the Pacific will not be the same again.

Some maps adopt a technique of framing lines to indicate the sovereignty position over islands and island groups. This was a legacy of the methods employed by colonial powers during the 19th century in making their claims to various island groups or in reaching agreement between themselves as to their respective limits of influence. These "picture-frames" did not pretend to indicate sovereignty or control over sea or seabed; they indicated only the sovereignty position – or perhaps the claimed sovereignty position – with regard to the enclosed islands. In the era of the 200-mile zone new maps must be drawn to show the limits of the new zones. The development that must necessarily follow from this is the drawing of true sea boundaries between neighbouring zones.

So far-reaching for the South Pacific are the implications of the new Law of the Sea that the background to these developments deserves some examination. The 200-mile zones were not invented by the maritime powers or the distant-water fishing states as an act of generosity to the South Pacific. How did it come about that the world community suddenly decided to recognise 200-mile jurisdiction? Why should general agreement have been reached on the distance of 200 miles and not 10 or 100 or 300? What are the restrictions on national jurisdiction in these new zones? What new problems and opportunities might they create?

THE NEW LAW

In general terms, the new Law of the Sea that has emerged is a compromise between the interests of developed states, with their ability to explore and exploit resources far afield, and the developing countries who lack such ability and who see a geographical extension of resources jurisdiction as offering one of few avenues for the promotion of their own development. "Resources" in this sense covers both the living (fish) and the non-living (oil and minerals).

International law is a body of rules – sometimes vague and often controversial – which is reflected in the common practice of individual states. "International law" at the beginning of this century recognised a limit of three nautical miles seaward from the coast as the extent of jurisdiction over the sea that might be exercised by a country. The last 30 years has seen the emergence of a variety of much more extensive national claims to jurisdiction over the sea and seabed. The result was a situation in which no one could confidently assert what the standard limits of jurisdiction might be without risk of challenge from one group of states or another.

A momentous assertion of jurisdiction came on September 28, 1945, when the United States proclaimed the exclusive right to exploit resources of the adjacent seabed in the extension of the land area known as the "continental shelf". This claim, if valid, clearly benefited states with broad continental shelves, particularly where those shelves contained offshore petroleum resources, but it was of

*** The author is the adviser on international law in the Department of Foreign Affairs and Trade of Papua New Guinea. The views expressed are those of the author and do not necessarily reflect those of the Department or of the Papua New Guinea Government.**

small value to states with little continental shelf, and of no benefit at all to land-locked states. It was partly as a response to the new continental shelf concept that some countries of Latin America proposed their own kind of extension of jurisdiction in the form of a 200-mile territorial sea, virtually a claim to be able to regulate all activities in that area.

The United States, and other states which had made continental shelf claims, had taken care to claim rights in the seabed only and not to change the status of the sea itself. They had also directed their claims towards resources so as not to affect uses of the sea by vessels, commercial or military. The 200-mile claims of Latin American states, therefore, were in sharp conflict with the position taken by maritime powers and distant-water fishing states, with the latter adopting a policy of non-recognition of the Latin claims.

A MATTER OF CONTROVERSY

The reasons for a 200-mile limit for these claims was associated roughly with the extent of continental shelf claims. While the proper limit of the continental shelf has been and remains a matter of controversy, a typical claim by a broad-shelf state might be of the order of 200 miles. This rough limit coincided also with the aspirations of states on the Pacific coast of South America who claimed the existence of a distinctive ecological system, influenced by cold coastal currents and dependent on nutrients from the land in the form of effluent from rivers. In the case of Peru, this claim to control the seas of the coastal zone was the basis for management of a highly lucrative industry harvesting anchovetta (a sardine-like species used for fishmeal) an industry which made Peru the world's leading fish exporter during its boom years.

As other Latin American countries followed suit in adopting a 200-mile nautical limit, the zone so claimed became a unifying cause for Latin America in its relations with the United States. The more that the United States contested the claim to the extended area of jurisdiction, the more united and spirited were the Latins in their defence of it.

In 1958 came the culmination of a United Nations-sponsored attempt to codify in treaty form existing international practice and consensus on the Law of the Sea. In order to foster wide acceptance of the treaty provisions, the texts were split into four different conventions which have gained varying degrees of endorsement, although none has been universally accepted. Even in 1958 it proved impossible to reach agreement on a standard maximum breadth of the territorial sea, although none of the parties which accepted the territorial sea convention would have claimed a greater limit than 12 miles, and many would have insisted on the traditional three.

Since 1958, international practice has gradually edged towards acceptance of broader and broader maritime limits. Australia, for example, by no means the most ambitious coastal state, claimed the right to exercise fisheries jurisdiction in the 12-mile zone (i.e. in a further 9-mile belt beyond the 3-mile territorial sea) in addition to its rights over the resources of a very extensive continental shelf. This kind of claim became fairly typical for coastal states by the mid-1960s.

THE LAW OF THE SEA CONFERENCE

The main stimulus to the convening of the Third United Nations Law of the Sea Conference, proposed in 1967, was only partly the need to rationalise claims to coastal state jurisdiction. A new issue had emerged with the discovery of seabed mineral riches on the deep ocean floors. These exist in the form of potato-sized pieces of rock which after recovery and processing yield several marketable metals. They are sometimes called "manganese nodules", because manganese is a constituent, but nickel, copper and cobalt may also be extracted from them. The deep ocean floor where the nodules occur is, for the most part, beyond national jurisdiction even on an extended view, but some deposits do occur within 200 miles of certain Pacific Islands – near the Cooks, for example.

The Conference held its first substantive session in Caracas, Venezuela, in 1974, after three years of disappointingly unproductive preparatory work. Although the central question, in which all participants were interested, concerned the establishment of machinery to regulate the exploitation of the seabed "beyond national jurisdiction", it had become clear that agreement on a comprehensive treaty could only be reached if acceptable compromises were developed on all other incidental questions.

Although no final treaty text has been agreed – indeed, some would say that the still-continuing Conference has already failed – the central compromise that has been embodied in the working document has profoundly affected international practice today. This central compromise calls for a territorial sea limit of 12 miles together with recognition of the resource rights of coastal states out to a distance of 200 miles. The name devised to describe the extended resource area is "the exclusive economic zone", a 188-mile zone measured from the 12-mile territorial sea which itself is usually measured from the low-water line along a coast.

Many other elements form essential parts of the package. Some of these deal with:

- rights of passage and overflight and rights of archipelagic states;
- the rights of states to regulate fisheries in the 200-mile zone and their obligations to fishing states;
- scientific research in the zone;
- control of marine pollution in the zone;
- the problem of the continental shelf where it extends beyond 200 miles;
- delimitation between the territorial seas,

200-mile zones and continental shelves of neighbouring states;

- the rights of land-locked and so-called "geographically disadvantaged" states;
- generally applicable dispute – settlement procedures.

The question that the Conference really started out to resolve, the terms of exploitation of the deep seabed beyond national jurisdiction, has proved to be the most difficult to settle and is now the main obstacle to adoption of a treaty text. This has come about because of the polarised positions of the highly-industrialised countries on the one hand and developing countries on the other. The industrialised countries have argued that machinery should not be set up that could have the effect of denying a country – or a nationally-sponsored mining company – from undertaking operations in the deep seabed if it is able and willing to do so.

The developing countries have taken the view that the resources of the deep seabed are the "common heritage of mankind" which should be exploited by the international community itself and mainly for the benefit of its poorer members. Although individual country positions vary, this view would tend to limit operations by individual countries or companies to those consistent with the resources policy and the financial terms determined by an international authority. Negotiations over the last two or three years have explored the possibility of a kind of dual system under which the "international area" would be divided in two, with a different system of exploitation applying in each part.

Although denying that their action indicates a failure of the Conference, the United States and some other industrialised countries have recently been preparing legislation providing for the mining of the deep seabed to take place in the absence of a treaty. The effect of this action on the future of the Conference is a matter for speculation, but it has been strongly condemned by the Third World.

The main fruit of the Conference up to this point, then, is the working document known as the "Informal Composite Negotiating Text" (ICNT). This has assumed importance because many countries have used the document as a guide in making new sea and seabed claims. Some of the document, but not all of it, states for practical purposes what international law now is. It therefore forms the starting point for any discussion of the current position in the South Pacific.

The largest single interest group concerned with the Law of the Sea is made up of coastal states, meaning states who benefit from the right to exercise rights over extended areas of sea and seabed. These should be distinguished from maritime powers, who might be mainly interested in freedom of navigation or access to resources, and from land-locked states (like Afghanistan or Switzerland), and states who do not gain much benefit in geographical terms (like Singapore or Poland). Among the coastal states, interests vary considerably. Some might attach greatest importance to securing rights to the outer continental shelf, while others might be pursuing an archipelagic claim or be affected by an international strait. Some might feel reluctant to abandon a 200-mile territorial sea claim, while others might feel that their interests are best served by a moderate stand on this point.

IS THERE A SOUTH PACIFIC APPROACH?

Although these kinds of considerations enable different interests to be identified among South Pacific countries, all of which are coastal states, it remains true that there is a great deal of common ground between them and certain particular interests that they might pursue to their mutual advantage.

For example, one point of controversy at the conference concerned whether very small islands should generate any 200-mile zone at all. Some countries, with small islands of another country off their coasts, argued that all islands did not automatically qualify for such a zone and they were supported by others on the more abstract ground that islands would cause a disproportionate amount of sea to fall under national jurisdiction. The possession of an uninhabited rock, say the result of an acquisition in the colonial era, would entitle the owner to jurisdiction over some 126,000 square miles of ocean.

On this point, South Pacific countries, although they were by no means equally affected, adopted a united stand in arguing for non-discriminatory treatment of islands. Subsequently, in the absence of a treaty, island-owning states have tended to develop a consistent self-serving policy of asserting zones around islands, a practice which has tended to undermine the case of island opponents. It might be argued at some future time, however, that the issue is not free of doubt, because the ICNT says that "rocks which cannot sustain human habitation or economic life of their own" do not have an economic zone.

In general terms, then, the countries of the South Pacific Forum comprise a group of fairly moderate coastal states. Although some have special individual interests as a result of geography, stage of development or other concerns, they share many interests, of which perhaps the best example is a common position on the small islands question.

Common interests in the region will be well-served by the adoption of a united approach to maritime powers or distant-water fishing countries or even towards the land-locked or geographically disadvantaged states who are still claiming preferential rights of access to the zones of coastal states.

Although the failure of the Conference is not certain, there is much pessimism among delegations about whether it will be possible to reach agreement on a comprehensive package. One possibility would be the splitting up of different issues into "mini-treaties", so as to enable agreement to be consolidated on the less controversial issues. However, many experts doubt whether this would have the effect of obtaining a generally applicable agreement, as countries will tend to want to participate only in those provisions which benefit them.

IF THE CONFERENCE FAILS

If there is no treaty, international law will be determined according to the prevailing view of what is lawful and what is not. Under this test, the content of international law has obviously changed dramatically in recent years as countries have taken unilateral action to establish zones of extended jurisdiction on the basis of the ICNT.

It is most unlikely, in view of prevailing practice, that the international court would now maintain its conservative attitude of 1974 when it was reluctant to uphold the extension of fishing jurisdiction by Iceland against the United Kingdom, and the Federal Republic of Germany. In fact, so many fishing states, including Japan, the Soviet Union and the United States, have now claimed 200-mile jurisdiction for themselves, that it is inconceivable that they should seriously challenge the assertion of the same kind of jurisdiction by a coastal non-fishing state. What might well be in doubt, though, are the exact limits of the powers of the coastal state in the zone. These are matters that are dealt with in detail in the ICNT, but which have not been generally confirmed by states in taking unilateral action.

It might well be argued also that some of the more novel parts of the ICNT that were negotiated at the Conference will not be binding in the absence of a treaty. For instance, this will leave open the possibility of disputes about the degree of control of certain states over their archipelagic waters. Indonesia, the Philippines, Fiji, Papua New Guinea and the Solomons either maintain or propose to put into effect special rules for the waters inside their respective archipelagos. Because archipelagic states are few in number it is less easy to base a case on general practice as might be done for the 200-mile zone.

With regard to the latest prospects for success at the Conference, hopes were fairly high among delegates at the start of the resumed 8th Session in New York in July, 1979. A determined – if not desperate – effort was being made by the moderates to achieve a compromise package on the deep seabed. However, even if a procedural means could be found for adopting a compromise text, real success will only come when all states with important interests express willingness to be bound by it. This will take a long time.

On the assumption that for the next few years the regime in the 200-mile zone should reflect the provisions of the ICNT, the powers of the coastal state will mainly be concerned with resources and not with other uses of the zone, such as transit passage through it. The coastal state will, however, hold certain powers with regard to control of the conduct of scientific research and the prevention of marine pollution.

At the Conference, some developing coastal states argued that they should have the right to formulate their own regulations about the passage of foreign vessels through the zone if they thought that certain standards were necessary to protect the environment. This was strongly resisted by maritime powers on the ground that it would lead to a mosaic of different requirements which would hamper international shipping or, at the very least, make rates much more expensive. This turned out to be a fairly convincing argument because many coastal states, even if possessing a large zone themselves, need to transit the zones of other states in order to reach distant destinations. This is true, for example, of most Pacific island countries, which are "zone-locked" in the sense that shipping passing to or from their ports must transit the zones of neighbouring states. This is one reason for a moderate stand on the question of coastal state jurisdiction by such states.

A COASTAL STATE'S POWERS

The main features of the fisheries package, which was agreed fairly early, are the principles of conservation and optimum utilisation. A coastal state has power to regulate the taking of fish within its zone, but it is under a duty to ensure that its resources are not endangered by over-exploitation. At the same time, it is under a duty to see that the resource does not go to waste. In theory, there is a determinable level at which fishing can take place in such a way that the maximum yield is taken each year without danger of permanently depleting the resource.

It is the duty of the coastal state to determine the allowable catch on the basis of the best scientific evidence available to it. It may also determine its own capacity to take fish in its own zone. Having done this, it should then enter into arrangements under which other countries may have access to the surplus. For example, State X might determine that the annual yield from a flounder resource in its zone is 10,000 tonnes and that its own vessels will take 3,000 tonnes. State X should then allow the vessels of other states to take the remaining 7,000 tonnes, but fishing by those other states may be made subject to conditions imposed by State X including payment of fees, the landing of the catch in its own ports, compliance with gear restrictions and so on. Some states have already adopted a policy of requiring as a condition of access that a bilateral fishing agreement be entered into in which they might insist on reciprocal access and other matters.

Obviously an important question is what would happen if the coastal state was accused of having made a mistake in determining the allowable catch or its own fishing capacity. Let us suppose that State Y said that no squid could be taken in its zone when it was clear that an unfished squid resource existed there. This could well lead to a dispute situation between State Y and one or more fishing states. As it happens, this is one of the unresolved areas of contention at the Law of the Sea Conference, namely the extent to which a coastal state might be liable to compulsory dispute-settlement procedures challenging the exercise of its discretion. Some fishing states would say that their acceptance of the fisheries provisions was conditional on compulsory dispute settlement. In the absence of a Convention, with fishing pressure increasing on scarce resources, this is a potential area of controversy in the future.

So far as seabed resources are concerned (including petroleum, minerals, and sedentary species such as shellfish), the concept of the new 200-mile economic zone introduces a novel concept. This is that the rights of the coastal state are not related directly to the configuration of the seabed. Under the concept of the continental shelf, the extent of the coastal states' jurisdiction depends on the depth of the adjacent seabed; if it forms part of a relatively shallow extension of the land area, it will probably qualify as a continental shelf and be made subject to control on that basis. Under the economic zone concept, the resources of the seabed of the whole of the zone would be subject to coastal state jurisdiction regardless of depth. A highly contentious issue remaining outstanding at the Law of the Sea Conference is what should happen to areas of continental shelf which extend beyond the 200-mile limit. Of the Forum countries, only Australia and New Zealand have this problem, because the island countries, for the most part, lack any physical continental shelf extending more than a few miles.

The resources of the seabed are subject to coastal state control in much the same way as resources on land. There is, however, an obligation not to use the seabed so as to interfere with navigation in the zone.

THE TUNA QUESTION

It has been widely accepted that there are some species of living marine resources which require special treatment. For example, anadromous species, such as salmon, which spawn in rivers but spend most of their life cycle at sea, are regarded as subject to the management of the state of origin, and fishing for them should not take place on the high seas. The theory is that only if salmon are about to enter their river of origin may a reliable determination be made of the level of the allowable catch.

Whales are sometimes regarded as an exception to the principle of optimum utilisation in view of the desire of some governments to give them absolute protection.

Some countries argue that so-called highly migratory species should be subject to special regime. This classification includes pelagic species of an oceanic distribution, the most important of which are the commercially valuable tuna: skipjack, yellowfin, bluefin and albacore. From the point of view of the United States, which has a distant-water fishing fleet designed to operate for long periods over an extended range, the best method of managing tuna fishing would be through an international body consisting of interested coastal states and fishing states. It is argued that only measures made through such a body can take account of the fishing pressure to which a particular stock might be subject over the whole of its range which might extend through several economic zones as well as the high seas. However, from the point of view of Pacific Island countries, tuna offer about the only immediately available prospect of winning any economic advantage from the 200-mile zone. As most Pacific islands are sea mounts rising from the deep ocean floor, these countries lack continental shelves providing a habitat for bottom-dwelling commercial species, such as cod, flat fish or prawns, which provide the basis for valuable commercial fisheries elsewhere.

Some islands are in a position to establish a fishery based on reef-dwelling species, but this is a sensitive environment which cannot withstand heavy fishing, and reef species are unlikely to support a fishing effort much above the level of subsistence fishing. On the other hand, tuna stocks not only offer the prospect of catches of many thousand tonnes per year, but an established and growing market exists on which the product commands rewarding prices except at times of periodic over-supply.

The three methods of taking tuna are, first, by long-line (which brings in a mixed catch of the larger species of relatively higher value), secondly, by pole and line fishing using live bait and, thirdly, by purse-seine netting from the specially designed larger and newer vessels. Because of high fuel and labour costs, the more sophisticated purse-seine technique has an economic advantage over the other methods. However, the important point is that economically feasible tuna fishing of any kind is ill-suited to a village level approach and requires finance and technology.

Pacific Island countries take the position that tuna, while in the 200-mile zone, are subject to coastal state jurisdiction in the same manner as other species; that is to say, foreign vessels may not take tuna without being licensed by, and complying with conditions imposed by, the coastal state.

The United States has adopted a quite different approach. Its 200-mile fishing law specifically does not apply to tuna and states further that the United States will not recognise the extended fishing jurisdiction of other countries unless they accept the principle that tuna fishing must be managed by an international organisation. This means that where the Magnuson Act (as the American law is called) applies, there is no regulation of tuna fishing at present, for example, around the Hawaiian islands or

American Samoa. This is consistent with the American view that the regulation of tuna fishing must await the establishment of an international body, tuna fishermen in the meantime being free of control by coastal states.

JAPAN'S VIEW

Although this is an official government position, the operators of tuna vessels are free to take a different view, and for some years American vessels have been buying licenses from Latin American states and have recently approached some Pacific Island countries, for example New Zealand and Papua New Guinea, with a view to making similar private arrangements. Japan, the major distant-water fishing power in the Western Pacific, does not share the American view and has been seeking access arrangements with Forum countries on the basis of acceptance of coastal state jurisdiction over tuna.

Although there has been much talk of the great potential value of the untapped tuna resources of the South Western Pacific, it is not quite so easy to see in practice how benefits might be channelled to individual coastal states. The two separate avenues that might be easily identified are, first, the taxing of foreign fishing in individual 200-mile zones and, second, participation by the coastal state itself in fishing or processing activities.

Both these approaches depend on the level of profitability of tuna fishing at a particular time. Obviously a tax or royalty cannot be set at a level which is uneconomic in view of anticipated profits, and the other participants in a joint venture will naturally expect a return on investment which will tend to determine what share of profit might be available for a participating state. It is true that some countries might be content with little or no financial return if they receive benefits from the venture in the form of employment opportunities, roads, wharves or other facilities. However, all these must ultimately be paid for from the profits of the venture.

Unfortunately for Pacific Island countries, the short-term prospects for negotiating fisheries agreements are currently unfavourable due to low market prices for tuna, accompanied by high fuel and labour costs.

The problem of gaining a worthwhile return from the tuna resource for Pacific Island countries is like many other negotiating situations involving access to resources. It has, however, the additional feature that the resource is a renewable one; if it is not taken it will go to waste. Further, there is the possibility that even if one or more states insist on terms unacceptable to the investor, the same resource might be taken by the investor in other waters. Whether or not this last proposition is generally sound is not yet known for certain, because scientists need to discover much more about the distribution, yield and habits of tuna stocks in the Western Pacific.

The idea of a regional fisheries organisation was informally discussed among South Pacific countries at the Law of the Sea Conference, the Forum countries together with Micronesia meeting as the "Oceania Group"

The main advantage of a regional organisation was the enhanced bargaining power of the group as against fishing powers if all the individual 200-mile zones could be lumped together. While a fishing country could afford to be deprived of access to the zone of one country, it could hardly risk exclusion from the whole area, which represented a sizeable proportion of the world's seas. Other advantages of an organisation approach to fisheries management were the need to co-operate with regard to migratory stocks, the benefits of a co-ordinated approach to research, the possibility of mutual assistance in surveillance and enforcement, and, for the smallest countries, the prospect of assistance, or even the provision of complete services, in all aspects of administering fishing policy.

At the political level, fisheries was regarded as a field in which regional solidarity could be developed in concrete terms. This led to the convening of a "mini-Forum" in Suva in October, 1976, specifically to discuss Law of the Sea questions. In the ensuing declaration, members decided "in principle" to establish a South Pacific Fisheries Agency "to promote the conservation and rational utilisation of the fish stocks of the region".

CONFUSION

It soon became apparent when the details came to be considered that members had different perspectives on the role that the organisation was to play. This has led to confusion which has so far prevented the development of an effective body. One group of countries believed that the organisation should be basically a "common interest body" that would aim primarily at the promotion of interests of coastal states as against fishing states, of which the most prominent were the United States and Japan.

A second point of view was that the organisation should be set up mainly to enable a co-operative approach to the management of highly-migratory species; under this view, all states through whose zones the fish migrate should be allowed in, as well as, logically, fishing states taking the stocks on the high seas. A third view seemed to attach more importance to political considerations rather than fisheries implications in proposing that the membership should be basically that of the South Pacific Commission. As this view would have allowed in one major fishing power, the United States, while excluding others as well as other states intimately concerned with the same fish stocks, it was regarded by some countries as a proposal for a political grouping rather than one likely to promote the fishing interests of the South Pacific.

In July, 1977, a meeting of officials failed to clear the air, with the result that the declaration of the

8th South Pacific Forum in Port Moresby in August was an ambiguous compromise. Because of this, the two rounds of treaty negotiations in November, 1977, and July, 1978, produced a document in which differences between the various points of view were papered over without really being resolved. Consequently, differences again emerged at the Niue Forum meeting in September, 1978, with the Forum adopting the lowest common denominator among all points of view: a fisheries agency based on Forum membership as at least a temporary expedient.

The Forum Fisheries Agency, as it is called, now has its own director, Mr. Philip Muller of Western Samoa, and has moved from SPEC Headquarters in Suva to new headquarters in Honiara. The question of a wider-based organisation remains outstanding, and is unlikely to be resolved until Forum members adopt a uniform view of the purposes and functions of the body. If it is accepted that the Forum Fisheries Agency is basically a common interest group, there would probably be no objection to eventual admission to membership of all Pacific territories having similar identifiable interests and fisheries management jurisdiction of their own. At the same time, there is scope for the establishment of a wider body consisting of all states with an interest in the management of Pacific tuna stocks which might have the important role of co-ordinating and promoting research aimed at producing recommendations as to levels of fishing effort across the whole region.

It is easy to be critical of Forum membership as a qualification for membership of a fisheries body. From the point of view of Papua New Guinea and the Solomons, for example, co-operation with the Philippines, Indonesia and Micronesia would probably be far more beneficial than collaboration with the Cook Islands or Tonga. This is because of shared stocks as a result of the pattern of tuna migration. However, in setting up any organisation it is obviously easier to build on an established relationship rather than to feel one's way towards a new working relationship where close ties do not exist. The Forum fisheries organisation is an interesting beginning for regional fisheries co-operation, but it is only one of a number of different possible groupings.

At their meeting in Honiara on July 10, 1979, Forum members agreed on the terms of a treaty between them formally establishing a Forum Fisheries Agency whose members affirm coastal state zonal management rights over tuna. This document is now gathering ratifications. At the same time the Forum recognised the need for a second, more broadly-based body that would co-exist with the Agency. The second body would provide an avenue for co-operation with fishing states (including the United States) in the management of the broader-ranging stocks, possibly throughout the whole of the Pacific. The method of establishing the second body is still under discussion.

DELIMITATION BETWEEN ZONES

A question asked by many people when they hear of zone boundaries being drawn 200 miles from land is: what happens when two countries are close together? What determines where the boundary runs between the two zones¿ There are, of course, scores of examples of situations throughout the world where such a boundary must be arrived at. While a few principles have emerged which are aids to resolving the problem, there are also many dispute situations where there is disagreement as to how the principles should be applied.

In relation to the territorial sea and continental shelf, before the development of the concept of the 200-mile zone, there were two principles to which parties could appeal depending on how their interests might be best served. The first was that of the "median" or "equidistance" line, which would run, in theory, exactly half-way between the nearest base points (usually the coastline at low water) of the two countries.

Obviously, this principle could lead to a strange result where country A happens to possess a small island just off the coast of country B. The median line in that situation would be very favourable to country A and unfavourable to country B. In such a situation, country B would argue that the second principle should be applied. It would argue that the most important factor was the need to produce a fair and equitable line, even if this meant abandoning the median line altogether.

Because of their respective situations, most countries with a delimitation problem tend to emphasise either the median line or equitable principles as the dominant factor. At the Law of the Sea Conference, the debate on this issue has led to a situation in which it will clearly not be possible to please everyone and a very general kind of formula will have to be negotiated which will leave all sides equally dissatisfied.

The United Kingdom, for example, has been a staunch advocate of the median line because this produced a favourable result both as against France (where the Channel Islands would influence the boundary) and against Ireland (where the possession of the small islet of Rockall would give the United Kingdom a large area of continental shelf). An arbitrator's decision has now settled the Channel dispute in a manner more favourable to France, and the outcome of the Rockall question might depend on what view is ultimately taken of the effect of islands classified as "rocks". Greece has also been a champion of the median line because this principle would ensure that virtually the whole of the Aegean Sea would be a Greek lake, this circumstance causing Turkey to be equally outspoken in favour of equitable principles.

Among Pacific countries, there is likely to be fairly widespread, but not unanimous, support for the median line. This follows from the argument advanced by these countries that small islands should

not be treated in any less favourable manner than continental territory, if only because of the economic dependence of the inhabitants on sea resources. However, special circumstances existing in some situations might call for a modification of the median line in order to produce an equitable result.

A COMPLICATED AFFAIR

Perhaps the most striking illustration of this is the negotiated boundary agreement between Australia and Papua New Guinea, signed on December 18, 1978. This was an immensely complicated affair with many political and geographical factors requiring attention. Both sides agreed at an early stage that an equitable solution should be reached through a process of friendly negotiation. The result is unique – for the present at any rate – because the median line has been abandoned to the extent that some Australian islands become enclaves in an area of Papua New Guinea sea and seabed jurisdiction.

The agreement has also recognised that the resources boundary for seabed purposes need not be the same as for fisheries, one line passing to the south of three inhabited Australian islands in the central strait and one to the north. In fact, the Torres Strait agreement does not just concern Torres Strait, but provides for a 1,200 mile boundary to separate resources jurisdiction from the Arafura Sea to the Coral Sea. It is a good example of a basic rule of international law that the best method of settling boundary differences is by a negotiated agreement in which the parties can make provision for their own special interests rather than having a result imposed from outside.

Apart from the variable weight that might be given to small islands, other factors might lead to a departure from the median line in particular circumstances. One of these is the configuration of the seabed. One party might be able to argue that its continental shelf extends well past the median line, while the opposite state has a very narrow shelf. This was the situation in the area between the north-west coast of Australia and the island of Timor where a negotiated settlement had to be reached between Australia and Indonesia for the purposes of the seabed. Another question is whether the seabed line in this situation should necessarily be the same as that for the sea, a question now outstanding between Australia and Indonesia in view of the need to fix a boundary between their 200-mile zones.

Another question might be whether the baselines drawn between islands in the case of an archipelagic state should influence the delimitation. Then there is the problem of "historic waters". It has been recognised that a bay or semi-enclosed area over which a country has exercised exclusive sovereignty might have the status of historic waters, but beyond this the claim is controversial. Tonga, like the Philippines, has claimed a "picture-frame" area of sea as historic waters. Unless neighbours respect this claim the delimitation is likely to be complicated.

The process of delimiting mutual boundaries has a forcing effect in relation to disputes or uncertainties concerning sovereignty over land territory. The question of which country owns a small uninhabited Pacific island might remain in abeyance for many years simply because there is no need for a claimant to actively assert its claim unless it is challenged to do so, and it is easy for other states to avoid expressing any position on the matter. All claimants can afford to defer a resolution of the dispute without the need for any action. The creation of 200-mile zones poses a dilemma.

If a country which declares 200-mile jurisdiction extends that jurisdiction to the area around a disputed island it will be creating a potential confrontation situation with another claimant. If it enforces jurisdiction by arresting another vessel the question of its sovereignty over the island will be directly raised. If, on the other hand, it does not extend jurisdiction to the area, or declines to enforce it, then the strength of its claim will be undermined over a period of time by its own course of conduct.

In the Pacific a number of small islands are the subject of competing claims by the United States on the one hand and, on the other, New Zealand, the United Kingdom or the Cook Islands. We have already seen in the recent Treaty of Friendship between the United States and Tuvalu the resolution of a contest over certain small islands. It is likely that the forcing effect of 200-mile jurisdiction, which creates a situation that might vary from awkward to intolerable, will cause the settlement of other claims.

Apart from the question of disputed territory, the negotiation of boundary settlements might imply a degree of respectability and permanence about the jurisdiction which is recognised. A good example of this is the current negotiations between Australia and Indonesia concerning the seabed near East Timor. For Australia, the negotiation of this boundary, which has been outstanding for some time, implies formal and unequivocal recognition of Indonesian sovereignty.

A similar kind of implication, but more subtle, occurs in fixing maritime boundaries in the Pacific between island nations and the territories of metropolitan powers. In the case of French territories for example, the fixing of boundaries confirms the legitimacy of French sovereignty in the region. There is no question, of course, about the legal situation – the islands are subject to French sovereignty – but the confirmation of mutual boundaries between island countries and France introduces colour of respectability and normality about France's place in the Pacific. This implication would be avoided if steps were taken to emphasise the involvement of peoples of the dependent territories in the negotiations. The negotiated arrangements, for instance, could be made subject to approval by some locally

representative body, as occurred in the case of pre-independence negotiations between Australia and Indonesia about Papua New Guinea's boundaries.

ISSUES FOR THE FUTURE

This article has summarised some of the main issues in the continuing story of the Law of the Sea as it affects the Pacific. We are, however, in only the early stages of a new era of development of a political, economic and legal kind. Over the next few years, these are some of the issues that will arise and the questions that will need to be answered:

• What will be the ultimate fate of the Law of the Sea Conference? The 8th Session in Geneva in March/April 1979 made sufficient progress to keep alive hopes for a successful outcome.

• Will workable machinery be established to control mining of the deep seabed? Even if there is general agreement on a text at the Conference, it is a separate question whether the convention will be widely accepted. An ambitious global project such as this will require the support of virtually all countries in order to function properly.

• How will seabed mining affect Pacific island countries? If international machinery is established, the headquarters of the organisation will probably be located in a developing country. Fiji is one of the possible venues under consideration. Even if the organisation is located elsewhere, the Pacific, and particularly the area from Hawaii to Mexico, will offer the most promising sites for the first mining operations. If seabed mining on a large scale proves profitable it is likely that promising sites in the South Pacific will come under examination. A few of these are close to island countries, with some nodule deposits occurring within 200 miles. Because of the difficulty in predicting the demand for minerals 20 years or more in the future, it is a matter for speculation at the present time what mineral deposits might attract large scale investment. Much will depend on new industrial requirements and the possibility of product substitution.

• What form will fisheries co-operation take in the South Pacific? At the present time the Forum Fisheries Agency is certain to play an important role. There remains a need for a more widely based body to promote co-operation in the management and conservation of tuna species. There might well be more than one such organisation depending on the ranges of stocks. This could bring together coastal states through whose zones fish migrate and states whose vessels fish on the high seas.

• What will be the pattern of distant-water fishing in the South Pacific? Because stocks here are among the last to be the subject of intensive fishing pressure it is likely that new flags will be seen in the region including the Soviet Union and the Republic of Korea as well as Japan and the United States. Much further research will be necessary before the optimum level of fishing can be established. As several countries have programmes for the construction of vessels to take tuna in tropical waters, competition for access to the allowable catch will become progressively more intense. At the same time, developing island states will be seeking to develop their own fishing industries which will necessarily involve the curtailment of some distant water operations.

CONCLUSION

Like any other field of international affairs, the relations between countries with regard to the Law of the Sea are continually changing. For the present, the reconciliation of interests that has led to recognition of 200-mile zones presents a new avenue of development for many small countries. There has been much rhetoric, as a result, about the new opportunities and the new bargaining power in the hands of these countries. The next few years will show whether the promises are as bright as they seem. Immediate prospects might well depend on trends in the market for tuna or the economic effects of increasing fuel prices. In the longer term it is conceivable that new sea or seabed resources will be discovered that will further enhance the value of extended jurisdiction. The world is a small place and its resources limited; the right to control access to the resources of any substantial part of it — even sea and seabed — is an asset of immense potential value.

SOUTH PACIFIC COMMISSION

The South Pacific Commission was founded on February 6, 1947, when representatives from six governments with dependencies in the South Pacific signed an agreement. The agreement, usually known as the Canberra Agreement, was signed in Canberra, Australia, by the governments of Australia, France, the Netherlands, New Zealand, the United Kingdom and the United States.

Since the agreement, one country, the Netherlands, has withdrawn from the commission (in 1962, when it ceased to administer the former colony of Dutch New Guinea, now known as Irian Jaya), but six independent Pacific states have now been admitted to membership.

Western Samoa became a member in October, 1964, the Republic of Nauru in October, 1969, the Dominion of Fiji in May, 1971, Papua New Guinea in September, 1975, the Solomon Islands and Tuvalu both in 1978, making a total membership of 11. Under an amendment to the Canberra Agreement, which provides for accession to the agreement of any self-governing country, not being independent but being in free association with a fully-independent government, the Cook Islands and Niue, both in free association with New Zealand, were preparing early in 1980 to accede to the agreement and become participating government members. Kiribati, which became an independent republic within the British Commonwealth of Nations in July, 1979, was expected to accede to the agreement in 1980.

The Kingdom of Tonga has always worked in close liaison with the commission; it makes a voluntary contribution to the commission's budget and benefits from its services, but is not a member, although entitled to membership.

Any country in the commission's area may apply for membership once it becomes independent or self-governing in free association with an independent member.

South Pacific Conference. Until 1974, commissioners from the then eight participating governments met in annual session. The South Pacific Conference, attended by delegates from the Pacific territories, first met in 1950: it provided an opportunity for representatives from the Pacific Islands to make known to the participating governments their territories' special needs and problems. From the first meeting of the conference in 1950, it was held every third year, but in 1967 it became an annual event. It met immediately before the commissioners' session and made recommendations to it.

At the 13th South Pacific Conference, which met in Guam in 1973, proposals were put forward by Australia for changes in the functioning of the commission. These proposals were studied at a meeting of participating governments in Wellington, New Zealand, in March, 1974. The result was a Memorandum of Understanding which was formally signed by representatives of the eight participating governments in Rarotonga, Cook Islands, in 1974, during the 14th South Pacific Conference.

The Memorandum provides for the South Pacific Commission and the South Pacific Conference to meet once a year in a joint session to be known as the South Pacific Conference. The conference examines and adopts the commission's work programme and budget for the coming year, and discusses any other matters within the commission's competence.

Each government and territorial administration has the right to send to the conference a Representative and Alternate, each of whom has the right to speak.

Another effect of the change brought about by the Memorandum of Understanding was the abolition of plurality voting by which each participating government had a vote for itself and one for each of its independent territories. With the change, each Representative, or in his absence an Alternate, has the right to cast one vote on behalf of the government or territorial administration which he represents.

To assist the conference in its work, the Memorandum provides for a Planning and Evaluation Committee which meets each year to evaluate the preceding year's work programme; to examine the draft work programme and budget for the coming year; to agree on two themes of regional interest (one social, one economic) to be discussed by the conference; and to report to the conference. The Memorandum also provides for a Committee of Representatives of Participating Governments which approves the administrative budget, nominates the commission's principal officers, and reports thereon to the conference.

Commission's Role. The South Pacific Commission's role is advisory and consultative. Its programmes are closely co-ordinated with those of the countries and territories of the Pacific in the three main fields in which it works: health, social development and economic development. The commission does not concern itself with the politics of the states and territories within the region, nor does it attempt to control their development programmes.

Finances. The commission's budget is derived from proportional contributions from participating governments which, in the past, had to reach unanimous agreement before contributions could be increased. Today, there is no ceiling. Any member wishing to increase its own contribution can do so by making additional contributions to specified projects. The agreed proportions for the 1980 budget were: Australia 33.60%; New Zealand 18%; United States 17%; France 14%; United Kingdom 12.30%; Fiji, Nauru, Papua New Guinea, Solomon Islands, Tuvalu and Western Samoa 0.85% each. In addition, Australia, New Zealand, France and the United States made contributions to stated projects.

Voluntary contributions are also made to the budget by territorial administrations which have not formally acceded to the Canberra Agreement, and through special grants for international organisations and institutions working in the Pacific region.

For 1980, the commission's total budget is CFP3,466,343 ($Aust. 3,948,300 approx).

Languages. The official working languages of the commission are English and French.

SPC publications. *South Pacific Bulletin* quarterly; English and French editions. *Technical Publications* are published as the need arises and include the following series: Technical papers; Handbooks; Information documents; Information circulars; Reports of meetings. These publications disseminate information on recent developments in the commission's field of work.

"South Pacific Conference Proceedings" and "SPC Annual Report".

Staff. Eighty-seven in Noumea, thirty in Fiji and five in Sydney.

Activities. The commission has a number of professional staff members under the direction of the Director of Programmes. He is responsible for ensuring the proper functioning of the work programme, for visiting countries and territories of the Pacific on request and acting as Secretary-General during the absence of that official.

The work of the commission is in three main fields:

HEALTH: Public health; environmental health and sanitation, including the recycling of waste matters; health education; maternal and child health; nutrition; epidemiology; mental health; dental health; research and training.

SOCIAL DEVELOPMENT: Education, language-teaching, including production of language-teaching materials; audio-visual aids; educational broadcasting; urban re-organisation and rural development; community education for women; social welfare; youth work; conservation and enhancement of culture; population and demograph.

ECONOMIC DEVELOPMENT: Improvement in plant and animal production; plant and animal quarantine and protection; agricultural extension; inshore and outer reef fisheries; economic affairs; statistics; research and training.

GENERAL: Special project on Conservation of Nature and Natural Resources, post of Regional Ecological Adviser; short-term specialist services, study visits and assistance to research in the fields of health and economic and social development; funds for regional travel by students; grant-in-aid towards South Pacific Festival of Arts.

The principal officers of the SPC at May, 1980, were: Secretary-General, Mr. M. Young Vivian; Director of Programmes, Mr. W. T. Brown; Director of Administration, Mr. D. W. J. Stewart; Sydney Representative, Mr. K. Earle.

SOUTH PACIFIC FORUM

The South Pacific Forum, an organisation of independent and self-governing countries of the South Pacific, was formed at a meeting in Wellington, New Zealand, in August, 1971. The meeting was attended by the President of Nauru (Chief Hammer DeRoburt), the Prime Minister of New Zealand (Sir Keith Holyoake), Prime Minister of Fiji (Ratu Sir Kamisese Mara), Prime Minister of Tonga (Prince Tu'ipelehake), Prime Minister of Western Samoa (Tupua Tamasese Lealofi IV), Premier of the Cook Islands (Mr. Albert Henry) and the Australian Minister for External Territories (Mr. C. E. Barnes).

The Forum was created out of a need by the newly-independent island countries of the South Pacific for an organisation through which to voice their joint political views, denied to them by the South Pacific Commission, which proscribes political expression.

Principal architect of the Forum, which meets annually, was Fiji Prime Minister Ratu Sir Kamisese Mara, who was also creator of the Forum's forerunner, the Pacific Islands Producers Secretariat (PIPS), later the Pacific Islands Producers Association (PIPA). The first meeting of PIPS was at Apia in 1965, with Fiji, Tonga and Western Samoa taking part. The Cook Islands and Niue joined later. With the change in name to PIPA, a full-time executive secretary was employed, with headquarters in Suva and Ratu Mara as its first president.

Originally a commercial pressure group aiming to find markets for the Islands' exports, it began to assume a political tinge by the beginning of the 1970s. Its sixth meeting, at Nukualofa in April, 1971, when the Gilbert and Ellice Islands Colony was admitted as a member, and 60 delegates and observers attended, saw an unofficial, private meeting between Ratu Mara, Prince Tu'ipelehake, Tamasese Lealofi and Mr. Albert Henry. The four leaders discussed the formation of the Forum. The result was a request to New Zealand to host a meeting of the independent South Pacific countries to form the South Pacific Forum. The meeting at Wellington was followed in February, 1972, by a second meeting at Canberra when the South Pacific Bureau for Economic Co-operation (SPEC) was established and became the Forum's secretariat. PIPA was still in existence but it voted for its own dissolution in 1974.

The Forum has continued to meet every year and, through its SPEC has co-operated on several projects with the South Pacific Commission. The Forum's most important decision was made at the 1977 meeting in Port Moresby when it moved to establish the South Pacific Regional Fisheries Agency and urged Forum members to claim a 200-mile economic and fishing zone in their national waters.

The headquarters of the South Pacific Regional Fisheries Agency is at Honiara, capital of the Solomons.

The Forum has also established a shipping line, The Forum Line, and the South Pacific Trade Commission, which has its offices in Sydney.

It has continued as a Heads of Government organisation with plenary powers and membership is confined to independent and self-governing countries in the South Pacific including Australia and New Zealand. Its boast has always been that, as its meetings are attended, in most cases, by government leaders, the Forum can make decisions on the spot whereas, in the South Pacific Conference, many matters have to be referred by delegates to their governments.

The Forum has given membership 'in an observer capacity' to non-self-governing states and also has placed the services of SPEC at the disposal of those states.

In 1980, the Forum was studying a SPEC report recommending a merger of SPEC and the South Pacific Commission to avoid duplication of effort.

The 11th meeting of the Forum, at Tarawa in July, 1980, admitted Vanuatu (New Hebrides) to full membership – 16 days before Vanuatu attained independence – and also admitted the Federated States of Micronesia as a member in an observer capacity.

CHURCHES CONFERENCE

The Pacific Conference of Churches (PCC) is an organisation embracing almost all the Christian denominations in an area which is, coincidentally, the same area covered by the South Pacific Commission outside Australia and New Zealand.

The Conference was inaugurated at a Pacific-wide Conference of Churches and Missions at Lifou in the Loyalty Islands (New Caledonia) in 1966 and was a merger of Pacific ecumenical bodies.

Member churches in 1979 were: Church of the Province of Melanesia; Anglican Diocese of Polynesia; Church of Christ in the New Hebrides (Vanuatu); Cook Islands Christian Church; Gilbert Islands (Kiribati) Protestant Church; Nauru Protestant Church; Ekalesia Niue; Congregational Christian Church in Samoa; Tuvalu Church; Evangelical Church of New Caledonia and Loyalty Islands; Evangelical Church of French Polynesia; Methodist Church in Fiji; Methodist Church of Samoa; Free Wesleyan Church of Tonga; Presbyterian Church of the New Hebrides (Vanuatu); United Church of Christ in Ponape; United Church of Christ in the Marshall Islands; the United Church in Papua New Guinea and the Solomon Islands; Fellowship of Christian Churches in Samoa; Solomon Islands Christian Association and the Episcopal Conference of the Pacific (RC) which includes the Archdioceses of Suva, Noumea and Papeete and the Dioceses of Samoa and Tokelau, Rarotonga, Tarawa, Tonga, Port Vila, Taiohae (Marquesas) and Wallis and Futuna.

The Conference describes itself as 'an organ of co-operation among the Churches and their associated mission boards in the Pacific within the framework of the wider ecumenical movement'.

The chairman is the Rt. Rev. Jabez Bryce, Anglican Bishop in Polynesia; the general secretary Mrs. Lorine Tevi and the treasurer Mr. Alfred Jack.

Headquarters are in Suva.

SATELLITE LINK

Hovering in space 35,780 km above the Pacific Ocean is a man-made satellite which has become an important link between the South Pacific island countries. It is one of 10 satellites orbiting the world and providing global communications for almost all the countries of the world through earth stations, of which the South Pacific island countries have a few.

The system is operated by the International Telecommunications Satellite Organisation (INTELSAT), which has headquarters in Washington (DC).

The INTELSAT global satellite system comprises two essential elements: the space segment, consisting of satellites owned by INTELSAT, and the ground segment, consisting of the earth stations, owned by telecommunications entities in the countries in which they are located.

In March, 1980, the space segment consisted of 10 satellites in synchronous orbit at an altitude of approximately 35,780 km (22,240 miles). Global service is provided through a combination of INTELSAT IV-A and INTELSAT IV satellites over the Atlantic, Indian and Pacific Ocean Regions.

The INTELSAT IV-A has a capacity of 6,000 voice circuits and two television channels, while the INTELSAT IV has a capacity of 4,000 voice circuits and two television channels. The future generation of satellites – the INTELSAT V – the first launch of which is scheduled for December, 1980, is designed for a capacity of 12,000 voice circuits and two television channels.

The ground segment of the global system consists of 274 communications antennas at 224 earth station sites in 125 countries and territories.

The combined system of satellites and earth stations provides more than 760 earth station-to-earth station communications pathways.

In addition to the international voice circuits in full-time use (now about 16,000), INTELSAT provides a wide variety of telecommunications services, including telegraph, telex, data and television to over 140 countries, territories and possessions.

INTELSAT now authorises two standards for earth stations that operate international services through its satellites: Standard A, with 30-metre (100 ft), or larger, dish antenna, 10 storeys tall, which can be rotated one degree per second and which can track to within a fraction of a degree a satellite stationed in synchronous orbit; and a smaller Standard B of 10 metres (33 ft).

Fiji, which has an earth station at Wailoku, near Suva, is a member country of INTELSAT together with Australia and New Zealand. INTELSAT non-signatory users include Kiribati, Nauru, the Solomon Islands and Tonga, among the independent countries. Vanuatu is now expected to join these countries. Other territory users are French Polynesia, Guam and New Caledonia.

DIRECTORY

The Pacific Island nations and territories, and the major islands which are not attached to a particular group, are listed in the following pages in alphabetical order, beginning with American Samoa and ending with Western Samoa.

The alphabetical listing is given in the content pages 6 and 7.

If you cannot find an island in the listing, refer to the general index, beginning on page 540, as it will be one of a group. For example, Tahiti is found in the directory under French Polynesia.

AMERICAN SAMOA

American Samoa consists of the six islands of the Samoan group east of the 171st meridian of west longitude. It is an unincorporated territory of the United States of America and, in 1978 had a population of 31 000 and a land area of 196 sq. km.

The main island is Tutuila (135 sq. km), which is about 3700 km south-west of Honolulu and 2575 km north-east of New Zealand. The other islands are Aunuu, Tau, Ofu, Olosega and the small isolated atoll Rose Island, in reality two small islets which are uninhabited. The administrative centre is Pago Pago on Tutuila and the local time is 11 hours behind GMT.

The currency, is that of the United States and the National Anthem is also the American National Anthem but there is also an official song, "Amerika Samoa" and two flags, the US Stars and Stripes and the territorial flag adopted in April, 1960 when a new constitution was approved. This flag consists of a large white triangle bordered in red and containing a white-headed eagle, all on a blue field. The American national bird bears in its claws a yellow 'uatogi' (a war club representing the power of the state) and a 'fue' a fly switch (signifying wisdom and the 'fono', the traditional Samoan council). The motto on the Territorial Seal is 'Samoa Muamua le atua' (Let God be first).

Public holidays include those traditional in the USA and also April 17 (Flag Day which commemorates the first raising of the US flag); and the second Sunday in October (White Sunday – a children's religious festival).

THE PEOPLE. In 1900, just after the US took over the territory of American Samoa, it was inhabited by 5698 Samoans, a Polynesian people. It took 70-odd years for the population to rise to the September 1974 census figure of 29 191, of whom the great majority were Samoan or part-Samoan. On February 1, 1977 a census sample survey indicated a population of 30 600. The birth rate has been falling steadily since 1968. In that year it was 41.3 per thousand, but it was only 34.1 in 1973, rising to 39.7 in 1975. In 1977, there were 1030 births representing a birthrate of 33.66 per thousand. In 1977, 45 per cent of the population was under 15 years of age.

Recent population growth is reflected in the following census figures of total population: April 1950 – 18 937, April 1960 – 20 051, April 1970 – 27 159, September 1974 – 29 191, 1977 – 30 600, 1978 – 31 000.

In 1976, there were 1336 aliens living in American Samoa. About two-thirds of these were Asians, predominantly Korean and Chinese working with the fishing fleets for the tuna canneries, in addition to about 500 Americans and a few New Zealanders, Australians and continental Europeans.

The bulk of the population lives on Tutuila which had 27 360 inhabitants in 1974, leaving only 1831 on Manu'a and Swain's islands.

The American Samoans live mostly in rural communities. These accounted for 16 573 inhabitants in 1974, while 10 706 were in the urban centre of Pago Pago and 1912 in the other town of Leone, about 20 km away.

Nationality. The American Samoans are nationals of the US, and have free entry to the US. After meeting the necessary requirements, they may become citizens of the US.

Language. The Samoan language is closely related to Hawaiian and other Polynesian languages. However most of the American Samoans also speak English, as bilingual education has been in effect for the greater part of this century.

In Samoan, the "g" is pronounced "ng" as in "English", so "Pago" is pronounced as "pahng-o".

Migration. Population figures remained static for some years due to substantial Samoan migration to Hawaii and the United States, but due to changed administrative policies since about 1963, this flow has considerably declined. In 1979, there were about 4500 Samoans (from both Samoas) living in Hawaii.

Religion. Most of the islanders (63 per cent) are members of the Christian Congregational Church, a result of the work of the London Missionary So-

ciety. There are about 19 per cent Roman Catholics, about 9 per cent Mormons, and about 5 per cent Methodists.

Lifestyle. The Samoan way of life is structured around a social system of clans, or extended family ("aiga") and their chiefs ("matai"). A village may have any number of chiefs, depending on the number of related families in the village. The "matai" is chosen by the family members and is responsible for the well-being of the "aiga", for the maintenance of family lands and the communal economy which still prevails in village life.

Recreation. Popular pastimes include many sports such as cricket, played Samoan style.

GOVERNMENT. The Government of American Samoa is composed of three branches: executive, legislative, and judicial.

Legislature. The legislature of American Samoa consists of an 18-member Senate and a 21-member House of Representatives. The legislature, under a revised constitution which came into force in 1967, has the sole authority to enact laws (subject always to the Governor's approval).

The new Fono (legislature) building at Fagatogo cost about $1 million to build. The opening ceremonies took place in October 1973, coinciding with the silver jubilee of the legislature.

Executive. The executive branch consists of the Governor, Lieut. Governor, and department and office heads. The Governor, as the chief executive (and the Lieutenant Governor) used to be appointed by the Secretary of the Interior and exercises his authority under the direction of the US Department of the Interior.

The Governor has the right to veto bills, from which there is then right of appeal to the Secretary of the Interior.

The Samoan people, three times, by popular vote, rejected proposals that they elect the Governor and Lieutenant-Governor.

But finally, in August 1976, in a fourth referendum on the question, the proposal to make these positions elective was carried.

The first such elections held on November 8 and 22, 1977, resulted in Peter Coleman becoming the first elected Governor. He assumed office on January 3, 1978, succeeding Governor H. Rex Lee.

Elections. Each of the 15 political counties in the territory elects one or more matai by Samoan custom to serve in the Senate for four years. The 20 voting members of the House of Representatives are elected by popular vote. The elected member from Swain's Island does not have voting rights. Members of the House of Representatives serve for two years. Legislation is debated in Samoan, and the debates are later translated to English.

Local government. The Office of Samoan Affairs, also known as the Office of Local Government, supervises operations carried out at the district, county and village level. The Office is a link between the Samoan people and territorial government officials.

The Secretary of Samoan Affairs is one of the traditional leading chiefs.

Within the Samoan administration are three district governors, 14 county chiefs and 53 pulenu'us (village mayors), six village police officers and three district clerks. The office of Samoan Affairs conducts elections, and concerns itself at the local level with village problems, such as water systems, roads, sanitation, agriculture, schools and land disputes.

Public service. As of September 30, 1978, the following was the breakdown of employees with the Government of American Samoa: 3,656 local hire employees; 181 contract employees of which 7 were American Samoans, 162 United States citizens and 12 other nationalities.

Co-operative union between Samoas. A co-operative association, established between the two Samoas, considers mutual problems such as immigration, agriculture, fisheries, crime, health and other matters. The joint meetings are chaired by the Governor of American Samoa and the Prime Minister of Western Samoa on a rotating basis.

Justice. The judicial branch consists of a High Court having territorial jurisdiction throughout the islands, a district court for each of the five judicial districts into which the islands are divided, a small claims court, a traffic court and a matai title court. The small claims, traffic and matai courts are comparatively new, and are presided over by Samoan judges.

The chief justice is appointed by the Secretary of the Interior, and the associate judges are appointed by the Governor on the recommendation of the chief justice but subject to confirmation by the Senate of American Samoa.

A law requiring that all disputes regarding matai titles and land registrations be arbitrated by the Office of Samoan Affairs has helped cut down the court's case-load in those areas. A new set of "Rules of Practice Governing Procedure in the High Court of American Samoa" was promulgated in 1974.

The court and the newly formed Bar Association are well catered for with legal literature. A compendium of all decisions handed down by the High Court since 1900 began publication in 1976 as the 'American Samoa Reporter and Digest System'. The Bar Association's Samoan Pacific Law Journal is available to the local legal community and is ordered by many law schools and libraries in the US and other parts of the world.

High Court proceedings on the trial level are generally conducted in Samoan and English before a panel composed of the chief justice or the associate justice and two associate judges. Matai cases are heard exclusively by a panel of three associate judges. Traffic courts are conducted by a single associate judge. Legislation was passed by the Fono in 1978 expanding membership of the Court of

Appeal to include judges from other United States territories, a principle which also operates in Fiji and other British Commonwealth countries. Judges from California, Hawaii and Guam assisted in the Appeal Court in 1978. The Office of Samoan Information reported that the inclusion of "off-island" judges ensured neutrality in the review of trial court decisions and had been "enthusiastically received by the bench and bar".

Another important innovation has been the introduction of the right of an accused to trial by jury in serious criminal cases. The new rules provide for unanimous verdicts by six-man juries.

LEGAL AFFAIRS. The Office of the Attorney-General provides legal services to the government and also prosecutes or defends all civil cases involving the government, prosecutes in all criminal cases and represents the government in administrative hearings. For the year ended September 30, 1978, the office handled 34 civil cases, 127 criminal cases, 1,495 immigration hearings, 37 juvenile cases and 116 other cases and hearings.

Immigration. In the same period, the Office of Immigration, which, together with the Office of the Attorney-General comes under the Department of Legal Affairs, dealt with 902 passports, 12,345 letters of identity, 2,798 non-immigrant visas and 567 immigrant visas. In the same period, 83,722 people visited the territory. Registered aliens residing in American Samoa in 1978 totalled 1,353.

Public safety. The Department of Public Safety is responsible for maintenance of law and order, fire protection and prisons. Crimes recorded in 1977-78 (1976-77 in brackets) were: assault 237(165); rape 25(12); homicide 5(8); theft 183(252); burglary 220(221); robbery 12(10); motor vehicle theft 20(16); arson 3(6); prostitution 0(1); sex offences 24(40); narcotics 1(6); juvenile offences 35(47).

Police. The bureau was reorganised in 1977 with Vaisa'u Sa'ilele as Police Chief and Captain Tulifua Siva as Assistant Police Chief. Newly-appointed division chiefs include officers trained by the FBI and at police academies in the United States.

Liquor laws. Local residents need a permit to obtain bottles of "hard" liquor from the government store.

DEFENCE. Until 1951, the territory had a US Naval Station on Pago Pago, between Fagatogo and Utulei. Pago Pago is regarded as one of the best natural anchorages in the South Pacific. The government maintains a coast guard of seven members.

EDUCATION. The education system is based on the American pattern of eight years elementary school and four years high school. During the sixties, television was the chief medium of instruction. However, in recent years this has changed, with greater weight being given to the role of the classroom teacher. By 1976 educational television was concentrating mainly on English teaching.

Greater attention is also being given to the Early Childhood Education Programme, with an ECE centre at Fagatogo.

The ECE programme serves 1,505 children, aged 3 to 5 at 135 centres in 57 villages. In addition, American Samoa has the following schools: 24 state elementary schools and four private; four state high schools and two private; and one Community College. In 1977-78, 7,468 students were carried by 25 school buses which travelled 440,000 km.

The Community College is in Mapusaga, about 14 km from town and the largest high school, Samoana H.S., is located in the Fagatogo area. Two other high schools are at Leone and Faga'itua on Tutuila; the fourth high school is on the island of Ta'u.

Enrolments in 1978 were 5,192 in state elementary schools and 1,272 in private ones; 2,170 in state secondary schools and 477 in private secondary schools, giving totals of 8,997 in the state schools and 1,749 in private schools. Enrolment in the American Samoa Community College in 1978 totalled 777. Dr. Saeu Scanlan, who became community school president in September, 1978, is the first Samoan to hold the position. There were 626 teachers (529 Samoans and 97 non-Samoans) employed by the Department of Education in 1978. Special Education classes catered for 221 handicapped pupils in 1978 with 28 teachers and 6 teacher trainers.

Community college. The American Samoan Community College includes the Mapusaga main campus, vocational trades facilities at Tafuna and a nursing complex at Faga'alu. Construction was begun in 1978 on five new buildings to cost $3.9 million.

Overseas studies. In 1978, there were 193 American Samoan students studying on government scholarship programmes. Most were either in Hawaii or on the US mainland. Financial assistance to each student was increased in 1978 to $3,000 per academic year. The total education budget for 1978 was $9,384,832, expenditure per pupil (excluding federal grants) amounting to $587.41.

LABOUR. The government service is the largest single employer of labour in American Samoa, the official payroll of 3,892 in 1978 representing about half the total workforce. Outside the government service, the two fish canning factories employ the most people. On the government payroll were 181 specialists on contract, 2 federal employees, 53 elected officials, 2,836 local care service employees and 820 employed under special public service programmes. The Department of Manpower Resources directs training and selection of government employees.

Private industry. The fishing industry is easily the biggest employer in the private sector. The payroll for the canneries and the Marine Railway totals 1,259.

Minimum wage rates under the Fair Labor Standard Act in 1979 ranged from $1.10 an hour for laundry and dry cleaning workers to $1.96 for workers in the fish canning factories, other levels depending on the type of industry. Following a review of blue-collar jobs within the government service, a new separate pay plan has been instituted which sets the minimum salary for blue-collar workers at $1.40 an hour.

Social security. By introducing a superannuation scheme for civil servants in 1972, the government set the pace for the rest of the territory's employers. The canneries followed suit and more than 60 per cent of all employees are now covered by a superannuation scheme. At the end of September, 1978, 22 ex-government employees were receiving retirement benefits. There is also legal machinery covering workmen's compensation claims.

Unemployment in 1978 was estimated at about 14 per cent, a drop of 4.5 per cent on the peak year of 1976. It is expected to drop to about 12 per cent in 1980. While these figures would be alarming in a metropolitan country, they have not the same significance in American Samoa and other South Pacific island countries because of family and village systems and subsistence economies. But there is another factor to unemployment in American Samoa. Some of those who could join the workforce prefer status employment in the limited fields of light assembly or light manufacture, where jobs are not always available, rather than in the wider area of fish packing.

Unions. The United Cannery and Industrial Workers of the Pacific Union of the USA entered the territory in 1975 to represent local cannery workers in Van Camp Co.

HEALTH. The main hospital is the Lyndon B. Johnson Tropical Medical Center which has 181 beds, including tuberculosis, leprosy and obstetrics units. Further extensions were completed in 1975. The hospital handled 108,778 out-patients in 1978.

The Department of Health also operates dispensaries throughout the territory. Overseas, the Tripler Army Hospital in Hawaii provides base-cost treatment for Samoan patients. The department's medical staff in 1978 consisted of 11 doctors, 3 dentists, 16 American Samoan medical officers, 4 Samoan dentists, 19 registered nurses, 156 licensed practical nurses and 14 nursing aides.

Family planning. There is an active Family Planning Clinic which encourages contraception and, a few years ago, advised Samoans to space their families as they did their coconut trees. The family planning campaign is producing results. The birth rate in 1975 was 40 per thousand of population. It had dropped to 33.66 in 1978.

Child care. One effort to improve family health, especially with regard to the children, is through the food service division of the Education Department which serves about 9,000 school lunches and about 7,250 breakfasts each day.

Diseases. The main health problems are venereal disease, infectious hepatitis, infantile diarrhoea, an "influenza-like illness" and "injuries caused by road traffic accidents". According to statistics, tuberculosis and filariasis have ceased to be health problems. In 1977 there were only 7 cases of pulmonary tuberculosis reported and no cases of filariasis. There has been a steady increase of cases of gonorrhea – 42 in 1975, 86 in 1976 and 89 in 1977 – but there have been no cases of syphilis reported in the last 8 years. There are a few cases of leprosy and

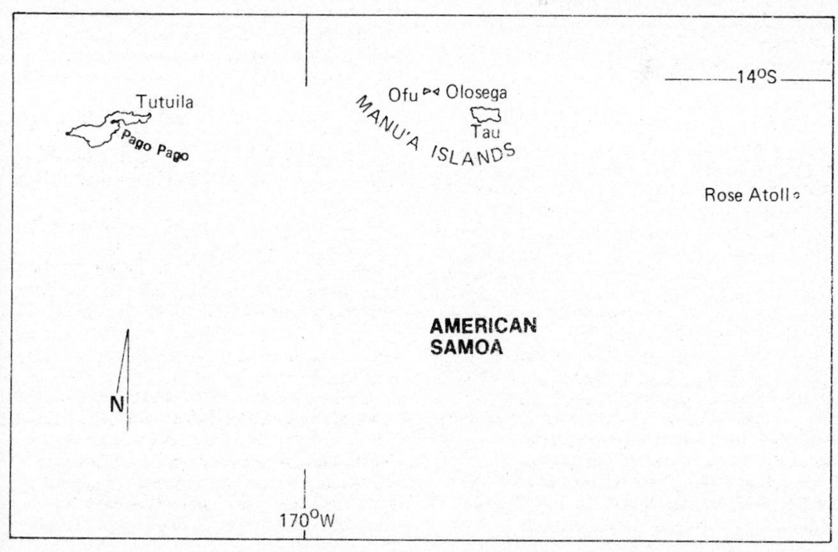

hepatitis remains endemic, 50 cases being reported in 1977. In 1978, there was an outbreak of typhoid fever when 23 cases were treated but the outbreak was controlled and there were no deaths.

The crude death rate in 1977 was 4.0 per one thousand of population against 4.4 in 1976. Heart diseases were responsible for 15.6 per cent of deaths in 1977 and cancer for 13.1 per cent.

THE LAND. The total land area of American Samoa is 197 sq. km. Tutuila, the largest of the seven islands in the group, is almost bisected by the harbour at Pago Pago and has an area of 145 sq. km. Aunu'u is a small island off the south-eastern tip of Tutuila. There are three Manu'a islands – Ta'u (39 sq. km), Olosega and Ofu (11 sq. km combined). They are about 100 km east of Tutuila. Swain's Island is a small privately-owned coral atoll, approximately 2 km in diameter and 450 km north of Tutuila. Rose Island, 400 km east of Tutuila is a tiny uninhabited atoll.

The island of Tutuila extends 30 km from east to west and is about 6 km wide. The whole group extends 500 km from Swain's in the north to Rose Island in the south.

The highest peak is Mount Matafao (702 m) on Tutuila, where Mount Pioa, known as "The Rainmaker" is 563 m.

Apart from the coral atolls of Swain's and Rose Islands, the territory is formed from the remains of extinct volcanoes, leaving central mountain ranges with only limited coastal plains.

Soil. Some 70 per cent of the group is forest. Of the remaining 30 per cent suitable for agriculture, about 4,800 ha are under cultivation.

Climate. Trade winds and frequent rains give American Samoa a pleasant climate. Pago Pago usually receives about 5,000 mm of rain a year, most of it falling between December and March. The average temperature ranges from 21 to 32 deg Celsius. Humidity averages 80 per cent.

Fauna and flora. The mountainous regions are characterised by rainforests with tall ferns and trees such as the Barringtonia.

Land tenure. Samoans own all the land with 596 ha belonging to the Government of American Samoa and only a small area owned in fee simple by individuals. As more than 96 per cent of the land is owned communally, its use and occupancy are regulated by traditional customs. All disputes over land registrations are arbitrated by the Office of Samoan Affairs before going on to the High Court.

The alienation of native land is prohibited, but lands can be leased for periods not exceeding 40 years, subject to approval by the Governor.

PRIMARY PRODUCTION. American Samoa, unlike most other island groups in the South Pacific, does not base its economy on copra. A thriving fish industry, with by-products, makes it relatively strong economically.

Crops. There are 70 semi-commercial farmers and about 10-15 of these produce wholly for the market. There are 36 licence holders who import produce from Western Samoa and Tonga.

Taro is the main import from Western Samoa but attempts are being made to make the territory self-sufficient in this root crop. The Tapitimu Experimental Farm was reactivated in January, 1977, with the planting of 3,000 taro tops, a gift from the Western Samoa Government. After the first harvest, 30,000 taro tops were provided for a local farmer.

The Manu'a Experimental Farm is conducting a crop propagation programme with Cavendish bananas and by mid-1978 about 1,000 plants had been sent for sale to farmers. The experimental farms also provided insecticide and fungicide treatment for farms. There is also a project to combat bunchytop in bananas, a disease which has reduced banana production by 50 per cent.

Late in 1977, the Department of Agriculture introduced a biological control programme against the African snail.

During the year ended September 30, 1978, local farmers provided a total of more than 47 tonnes of taro, 44 tonnes of bananas, 3.2 tonnes of fruits (mainly pineapples) and 408 kg of vegetables for the School Lunch Programme. Other crops grown locally are coconuts, breadfruit and yams but these are for local consumption.

Pests. Spraying has been carried out for leafhoppers and army worms in taro. Other pests include scab moth and black-leaf streak on bananas; nematodes; weevil borers; coconut beetles and stick insects.

Livestock. A recent survey indicates that there are 3,000 pigs, 3,000 chickens and 150-200 cattle.

Fisheries. The fishing industry is largely controlled by Van Camp, a big American corporation, which took over the Pago Pago fish factory in 1954, and Star Kist Inc, which went to American Samoa in 1963. Fishing boats from Korea and Taiwan supply the canneries.

The local dory fleet of a score or more small craft catches an estimated 100,000 kg of fish each year for local consumption.

The Department of Marine Resources operates a small boat-building and fisheries training programme.

In October, 1977, a project was launched to rid the reefs of Tutuila of the crown-of-thorns starfish. By June 21, 1978, 290,485 starfish had been collected and destroyed at a cost of $43,752. A further $30,000 was allocated to the project and by the end of 1978 an estimated 500,000 starfish had been destroyed. It was reported that one stretch of reef at Taema Bank had been completely destroyed by starfish.

A mariculture programme was also started to provide baitfish for tuna vessels operating out of Pago Pago and also to provide prawns. Experiments are also being conducted to establish an oyster farm.

AMERICAN SAMOA — EXPORTS
(in $'000)

	1974-75	1975-1976	1976-77	1977-78
Watches, clocks	4,706	2,542	2,415	318
Shark fins	263	75	94	—
Fish, fresh	242	464	134	57
Fish meal	138	322	281	534
Meat, canned	—	58	33	9
Pet food	3,481	2,414	4,589	5,584
Jewellery	88	767	584	806
Tuna, canned	73,600	58,244	73,098	96,823
Miscellaneous	469	—	3	3
Total exports	**82,934**	**64,893**	**81,232**	**104,134**

Local fishermen caught about 25 tonnes of fish for local consumption in 1978.

MANUFACTURING:. The Van Camp and Star Kist canneries are located side-by-side in Satala, across Pago Pago Bay from Fagatogo. There are several shark fin processing and export companies. Production of fish fluctuates considerably from year to year.

Tuna exports in 1978 were valued at $96,822,867; in 1977 at $73,098,222 and in 1976 at $58,244,373.

At the end of 1978 the two canneries were being supplied by 100 South Korean vessels and 83 Taiwanese vessels.

While recognising the importance of fishing in the economy, government policy is to diversify as much as possible. Sultan Jewellery Co, of Hawaii, has a small plant in American Samoa, and is training American Samoans as skilled operatives.

Other recent new enterprises include that of Meadowgold Milk's milk and ice cream plant, which provides fresh milk, some new local retail businesses, and a major bowling alley. A new gas plant was being built.

Further development to help diversification can be expected in an industrial park at Tafuna, close to the International Airport. By late-1977, 99 per cent of the industrial park had been completed.

TOURISM. Tourists visiting American Samoa in 1978 totalled 11,157, an increase of 2,801 over the previous year. The total of all arrivals in 1978 was 85,602 made up of 5,180 on business, 11,157 tourists, 22,436 in transit, 46,829 'others'. Departures totalled 70,335 consisting of 3,456 on business, 8,967 tourists, 20,674 in transit, 37,238 'others'.

The local Office of Tourism operated by the Government of American Samoa, is located in the Fagatogo area.

HOUSING. There are two Samoan-owned construction companies.

LOCAL COMMERCE. There are several large modern supermarkets plus a variety of general stores. A new shopping centre on the western side of the island has eight different shops. There is also a new furniture company, several US and Japanese auto-distributors and several wholesale distributors.

OVERSEAS TRADE. American Samoa enjoys a highly favourable trade balance, due to the prosperous fishing industry which accounts for over 90 per cent of the value of exports. The level of imports and exports has been as follows in recent years, values expressed in $'000:

	1974-5	1975-6	1976-77	1977-78
Imports	46,549	49,894	57,953	73,340
Exports	82,934	55,898	64,893	104,156

Main imports are food and drink, and oil fuel.

Some representative imports in recent years have been as shown in the accompanying table.

IMPORTS
(in $'000s)

	1974	1975	1976
Beer	484	585	627
Elec. Goods	1,273	1,305	1,608
Gasoline, motor	1,845	1,699	2,703
Machinery	722	588	936
Meat, preserved	487	764	1,181
Meat, fresh	624	694	1,178
Motor veh. & parts	1,901	2,028	1,513
Diesel fuel	7,446	9,456	8,778
Jet fuel	2,589	6,264	6,945
Poultry, fresh	989	882	973
Watches, clocks	2,334	1,796	1,798

The U.S. is the major supplier of imports. The figures in the accompanying table, which do not include government imports and fish tendered to local canneries, indicate the relative positions of major suppliers in recent fiscal years.

REPRESENTATIVE IMPORTS BY COUNTRY

Country	1977 $	1978 $
Australia	1,818,087	2,672,870
New Zealand	2,869,502	4,226,232
Fiji	875,751	1,583,448
Western Samoa	365,264	460,990
Japan	6,298,604	8,895,587
Great Britain	16,320	38,793
Canada	353,924	473,599
Germany	4,231	0
Korea	0	82,917
Hong Kong	454,566	498,466
Tonga	86,560	32,306
South Africa	21,640	0
Singapore	133,153	337,714
Republic of China	108,753	51,975
Pakistan	0	1,567
Switzerland	1,145,514	100,278
Scotland	84,852	0
United States	40,303,429	53,873,495
Philippines	898	0
Guam	0	9,500

CUSTOMS TARIFF. There are no import duties, but there are excise duties.

Main excise duties are: all liquor, 100 per cent. ad valorem; firearms, 75 per cent. ad valorem; motor vehicles for commercial use, 25 per cent. ad val.; if over 4,600 lb, 50 per cent. ad val.; motor vehicles for family use, 10 per cent. ad val.; petroleum, 8½ cents per US gal.; lubricating oils, greases, 15 per cent. ad val.; soft drinks, ½ cent per 8 fluid oz; sub-standard construction materials, as per list put out by govt., 20 per cent. ad val.

FINANCE. The government is financed by local revenue, grants-in-aid and special purpose grants from the United States. In 1978 local revenue from taxes was $10 million. The total budget revenue for 1979 was estimated at $50.8 million compared with $44.6 million in 1978. Grants from the United States amounted to $22.5 million. Port revenue in 1978 totalled $2,380,875.

Expenditure. The operating budget for the Public Works Department in 1978 was $25 million for capital improvement programmes. The department is responsible for major activities in construction and maintenance of all government facilities. Programmes for 1977-78 centred on new buildings for the Community College, a new highway, road maintenance, a new small boat harbour, airport terminal improvements, sewage system improvements and water and power system improvements.

Allocations for 1979 were as follows with percentage comparison for 1978 in brackets: Education, $9,925,757 (+17%); Higher Education, $1,819,000 (-6%); KVZK-TV, $852,112 (+5%); Vocational Education Advisory Council, $70,500 (+3%); Arts Council, $260,000 (+37%); Health, $6,090,600 (+5%); Administration on Aging, $1,777,825 (+57%); Health Council, $162,740 (+30%); Agriculture, $346,000 (+30%); Tourism, $189,000 (-45%); Development Planning, $149,500 (-37%); Marine Resources, $235,830 (+19%); CETA, $1,642,375 (-10%); Energy Office, $355,484 (-); Environmental Protection, $162,700 (+9%); Youth Conservation, $456,000 (+31%); Port Administration, $800,000 (-3%); Marine Rail (Tramway), $80,000 (+2%); Public Safety, $990,000 (-1%); Traffic Safety, $687,000 (+45%); Criminal Justice Planning, $429,721 (+5%); Governor's Office, $694,500 (+35%); High Court, $418,000 (+10%); Local Judiciary, $106,000 (+30%); Legislature, $1,112,500 (+15%); Administrative Services, $1,866,000 (+3%); Legal Affairs, $565,000 (+28%); Local Government, $486,000 (-5%); Material Management, $585,000 (+6%); Manpower Resources, $433,220 (+4%); Public Defender, $99,500 (+13%); Territorial Audit, $159,000 (+14%); Samoan Information, $92,000 (+1%); Planning & Budget, $170,000 (+20%).

Twenty-two capital projects were approved for 1979, requiring $8,027,958. The capital improvement budget for 1978 was $8,196,464. To finance 15 different special programme projects $3,342,000 was appropriated and enterprise and special revenue funds appropriated $8,098,500, 24 per cent more than the 1978 appropriation of $6,563,000.

Currency. Official currency is the US dollar.

Banks. The old Bank of American Samoa, a government institution, was sold to the Bank of Hawaii some years ago, thus establishing the first private bank in American Samoa. With the premium from that sale the Government of American Samoa established the Economic Development Bank of American Samoa, which issues loans for housing and business. The American Savings and Loan Corporation also opened at Pago Pago. There is also a branch of the First National City Bank in Fagatogo (Pago Pago) and banking hours at the two banks are from 9 a.m. to 4 p.m. Monday to Friday. The Savings and Loan Corporation which is in Pago Pago Park is open from 9 a.m. to 12 noon on Saturdays.

Overseas investment. The government's policy on development is to encourage overseas industry to invest in the territory, while at the same time ensuring that local people share in it, and protecting the local people from alienation of their lands as well as their culture and traditions.

The Development Planning Office in American Samoa provides basic data on the economy as well as related information and promotional services to investors. It is the main agency responsible for promoting industrial development in the Territory.

Incentives provided under the Industrial Incentives Act, 1963, are available equally to local and foreign investors, though the latter must satisfy certain government conditions over participation of Samoan labour and capital. Repatriation of capital and profit is freely permitted. Various tax incentives are allowed, while products processed in American Samoa are eligible for duty-free entry into the U.S., provided not more than 50 per cent of the cost of the finished item is of foreign material.

Development. American Samoa is pushing ahead with development although the pace has been reduced during recent years of world recession. Since 1974 many new schemes have been launched or completed. There has been heavy investment in roads, water projects, sewerage systems, power projects, airport and harbour construction, the telephone system, educational buildings, health services and other capital works.

In 1977-78, capital improvements costing more than $25 million were in progress. They included completion of air port runway improvements, road works including a new highway from Aoa to Amouli on Tutuila (cost $1,269,070), construction of a new conference convention centre and completion of improvements to water and power services.

TRANSPORT. Most of the formed roads, paved and unpaved, are on Tutuila. These roads are constantly being improved and new roads are opened where needed. A new road was completed in 1976 linking Fagasa Pass to the television transmitter on Mount Alava. A new mountain road links Afono and Vatia with the southern shore of Tutuila.

All buses are privately owned and licensed. The service stops generally after 5 p.m. and on Sundays and holidays. Transport by bus is relatively inexpensive and great fun as the routes meander to meet passengers' needs.

Vehicles. The total number of vehicles of all kinds in 1978 was 3,266, a drop of 90 on the previous year's total. The total included 2,488 cars, an increase of 94 on the 1977 total.

Airlines. International services are operated by Pan American using Boeing 747s to fly to Australia, New Zealand, Tahiti, Honolulu and the US mainland, Air New Zealand which uses DC8s and DC10s on routes to New Zealand and UTA French Airlines.

South Pacific Island Airways provides regularly scheduled flights to Western Samoa and the Manu'a Islands, and to Tonga and Niue. There are six flights daily between Pago and Apia and every-other-day services to Tonga. Niue is twice weekly. Twin Otter prop-jets and one Cessna 402B are used.

Polynesian Airlines, based in Apia, uses HS748 prop-jets to provide Apia-Pago inter-island services, and Otters to Tonga, Fiji and Niue.

Local airfields. The territory's international airport at Tafuna is about 15 km from Pago Pago by road. The runway is 2,700 m long and 45 m wide. Airport operations are under the control of the Airport Management Division of the Department of Port Administration. In the Manu'a group, the island of Ta'u has a small airport built by a private company, while there is a government airstrip on the island of Ofu, catering for small passenger aircraft.

Port facilities. Pago Pago, the main port of American Samoa, no longer handles as many ships as it did in the early seventies because of the introduction of LASH (lighter aboard ship) vessels and container ships.

Although the volume of trade dropped in 1976, dock facilities remained inadequate for large vessels. Both the main dock and oil dock are 120 m long but an extension of 180 m has been recommended.

To overcome the docking problem for inter-island traders, a floating dock of three 13-metre sections was installed in Pago harbour in 1975. A small boat dock and marina were completed in 1976 at Fagatogo.

At Ofu, a boat harbour was completed and work on Ta'u harbour was scheduled for completion in mid-1979. These are the first two harbours in the Manu'a group.

In late 1975 it was also announced that a boat harbour would be built on the reef area fronting Aunu'u Village. The plan provides for a revetted mole extending 66 m from the shore, with a concrete dock at the seaward end. There will be a 6.6 m deep turning and docking area, and a 2 m deep access channel next to the mole. South of the docking area there will be another revetted mole, 72 m long, to protect the harbour.

In 1978, 170 overseas vessels arrived and departed from Pago Pago. The total included 22 pleasure cruise ships. Pago Pago was also popular with cruise yachts, playing host to 275 yachts in 1978.

Shipping services. Farrell Lines offers a monthly LASH service between the USA and Australia via Pago Pago. The Daiwa Line and Kyowa Shipping Lines each provide a monthly service from Japan and the Far East. The Pacific Forum Line operates a fully containerised fortnightly service out of New Zealand and Australia. Pacific Islands Transport Lines serves the islands from the American west coast. Pacific Navigation of Tonga operates a general cargo/container service every five weeks; Karlander a monthly service; China Navigation's New Guinea Pacific Line (NGPL) from Far East ports and Warner Pacific Line from Honolulu monthly.

Within the Government of American Samoa, the Water Transportation Division operates a fleet of small craft, including tugs, launches and mobile cranes. A monthly shipping service to Swain's Island is provided.

COMMUNICATIONS. In 1978, an agreement was signed with Communications Satellite Corporation (COMSAT) to modernise and update the communications system by establishing a satellite earth station near Tafuna International Airport on

Tutuila. Initial communication will be to Hawaii and the U.S. mainland. Other Pacific services will follow. Tutuila's telephone system is automatic and caters for more than 4,570 subscribers and almost all are now on single lines instead of joint party lines. The service was extended to Ta'u in the Manu'a group in 1975 and microwave installation began operating on Tutuila in late 1975. Late in 1978 more than 20 subscribers in the remote islands of Ofu and Olosega were connected to a territory-wide telephone system.

The government operates a 24-hour continuous telephone service and maintains radio-telegraph circuits connecting American Samoa with relay and terminal facilities in Hawaii, Fiji and Western Samoa.

In 1978, the overseas telegram service handled 61,705 messages and 92,198 overseas telephone calls were made.

Telex. There were 30 local subscribers in 1978 and the number of calls made through the service totalled 18,098.

Radio and TV. The 10,000 watt radio station WVUV broadcasts Samoan and English programmes providing news and entertainment 24-hours-a-day.

The TV station KVZK began operating in October 1964. The transmitter on top of Mt Alava at the apex of Pago Pago Harbour sends out programmes to reach all over Tutuila and the Manu'a Islands, and is also received in Western Samoa. Two channels of news and entertainment broadcasts may be viewed from 3.30 p.m. to 11 p.m. The three channels of daytime programmes prepared for school classrooms have been greatly reduced in recent times, and in 1975 the KVZK-TV was separated from the Education Department to be placed under the control of a new entity, the Office of Television Operations.

Most programmes are in colour. An estimated 5,000 to 6,000 receivers are in private homes and about 20 per cent are colour sets.

Additional TV services will be available when the satellite earth station has been established. In 1978, TV broadcasts operated for about 263 hours a week of which 75 hours were occupied with the programmes for the schools. Wide coverage is now given to local events. For the Flag Day celebrations in April, 1978, the TV cameras operated for 14 hours.

Newspapers. In 1979, the press in American Samoa comprised the following publications: "Samoa News", edited by J. P. King, a weekly with 24-32 pages of local news in English and Samoan. The "News Bulletin" is a three-page daily in English published free by the government's Office of Samoan Information. Circulation in 1978 was 78,000. "Fa'a Samoan Pea", produced by the students at the Community Office, is a magazine of Samoan culture.

WATER, ELECTRICITY. To complement the supply from rainwater, a well-drilling programme is under way to tap underground reserves from such areas as the Tafuna plain. Extra pipelines and pumping stations have been built to bring much-needed supplies into the Pago Pago Harbour area.

Most villages have their own reticulated water supply.

Electric power of 110 volts is now supplied throughout Tutuila and on the Manu'a Islands of Ta'u, Ofu and Olosega. Main supplies on Tutuila came from the Satala and Tafuna Power Plants. Installed capacity in 1978 was 25mw with a maximum peak of 12.5mw. In an energy-saving drive 35 solar hot-water units were installed in the government housing at Tafuna and one unit was installed at Government House. Grants totalling $421,859 were made in 1978 by the United States to fund energy-saving projects and plans. A demonstration house was also opened for inspection of its energy conservation features.

PERSONALITIES AND ORGANISATIONS

Governor: Peter T. Coleman.
Lieutenant-Governor: Tufele Li'a.

SENATE

President and Speaker: S. P. Aumoeualogo Salanoa.
Members: Iosefa Sunia Fofo.
Peni P. Galea'i.
M. Tuiolosega Tagaloa.
Tamotu Mulitauaopele.
Suiaunoa Fa'amausili.
Steffany W. Alo.
Talio Magalei.
Sasa'e Pagofie.
Malama Le'oso.
Edward Meredith Amituana'i.
Solosolo Sao.
M. O. A. Mageo.
Tenari F. Lutu.
Gatta Gurr.
Letuli F. Olo.
Maiaua Hunkin.

HOUSE OF REPRESENTATIVES

Speaker: F. Tuia Tuana'Itau.
Members: J. Fuavai Te'o.
Suafanu'u T. Ale.
Falesigago Foutu'ua.
So'Oso'Oali'i Savali.
Vao Taipeaua.
Antonio Le'lato.
P. Mata'Utia Tuiafono.
Fiaaoga Siatu'u.
Fa'asuka Lutu.
Manaia E. Fruean.
Petelo Uti.
Va'aitautia Talamoni.
P. Soli'ai Suaavamuli.
Agaese A. Tago.
Iosefo K. Iuli.

Faiisiota Tauanu'u.
F. Pilitati Auono.
Frank Reed.
Edwin Gurr.
Jack Thompson.

HEADS OF GOVERNMENT DEPARTMENTS
Director of Education: Mrs. Mere T. Betham.
Secretary of Samoan Affairs: P. U. Fuimaono
Director of Agriculture: Tauili'ili Pemerika
Director, Administrative Services: Walter Jensen.
Director of Medical Services: Dr. R. Sumner A. Cheeseman.
Attorney-General: Lyle L. Richmond.
Director, Port Administration: Oliver Hunkin.
Director, Public Works Department: Al Pratt.
Commissioner, Public Safety: H. C. Letuli Toloa.
Assist. Comm. Public Safety: Lloyd Jackson.
Acting Treasurer: Ray Coston.

JUDICIAL BRANCH
Chief Justice: William K. O'Connor.
Associate Justice: Richard Miyamoto.
Chief Judge of Land & Title: Upuese Galoia.

CONSULAR REPRESENTATION
Australia: G. L. Urwin, Acting High Commissioner for Australia in Apia.
Western Samoa: Sala Suivai.

SCIENTIFIC INSTITUTIONS. Museum of American Samoa, in the old Navy Post Office in downtown Fagatogo. A good library service, with library extension facilities in the public high schools, satellite library buildings in various areas and a well-patronised mobile library controlled by Library Board of Trustees.

SPORTING FACILITIES.
Lava Lava golf course in Tafuna, 9-holes; a 12-lane bowling alley; Pago Pago Yacht Club; American Samoa Lawn Tennis Association.
Territorial Boxing Commission, Sports Commission.

CULTURAL ORGANISATIONS.
American Samoa Arts Council, Korea House, for recreation of fleet members.
American Samoa Historical Commission, East-West Center Selection Board.

ENVIRONMENTAL ASSOCIATIONS.
Environmental Quality Commission (government-sponsored), Board of Territorial Parks and Recreation.
National Parks, Rose Island National Wildlife Refuge.

YOUTH ORGANISATIONS.
Student members of Youth Conservation Corps and Neighbourhood Youth Corps work in the territory during summer vacation. A Director of Territorial Youth Activities was provided to the Training Division of the government Department of Manpower Resources in 1973.

OVERSEAS REPRESENTATION.
Hawaii Office of the Government of American Samoa. Sister city relationship with Oceanside, California. Delegate-at-large in Washington D.C.
Tourism (overseas): Hugh M. Birch, Australian Regional Director, 61 Cross St., Double Bay, N.S.W. (Tel. 32 0291).

PAGO PAGO BUSINESS DIRECTORY

Airlines:
Air France
Air New Zealand
Pan American
South Pacific Island Airways
Polynesian Airlines
UTA/French Airlines

Banks
Bank of Hawaii
Development Bank of American Samoa
American Savings & Loan Corporation

Canneries
Star Kist Samoa Inc
Van Camp Seafood Inc

Dairy Products
Meadow Gold Samoa Ltd

Duty-free Centres
Marcel Grisard Co Inc
Transpac Corporation

Food & General Merchandise
Burns Philp (SS) Co Ltd
Ho Ching Annesley Inc
B. F. Kneubuhl Inc
Nia Marie & Co
Olotoa Overland Inc
G. H. C. Reid Co
South Pacific Traders

Furniture
South Pacific Furniture and Appliances

Import & Export
Girdwood, Jones Co
Oceanic Systems Inc

Petroleum products
Standard Oil Co

Photography
M & M Photo Studio

Rental car & leasing
Avis
Hertz
Morris Scanlan
Pacific Services

Service Stations
Haleck's Service Centre
Double "O" Service

Travel bureaus
Samoa Tours & Travel Agency Inc.
Samoan Holiday & Travel Centre

HISTORY. No archaeological research has yet been carried out in American Samoa, but excavations in Western Samoa have revealed Lapita pottery dating back to about 800 B.C. It can probably be assumed from this that all of the Samoan Islands have been inhabited by man for well over 2,500 years.

In the centuries immediately preceding European contact, Tutuila, American Samoa's main island, was subordinate to the Atua district of Upolu, and was a place of banishment for troublesome Upolu chiefs. However, the people of Manua lived largely to themselves, under the leadership of a powerful chief, the Tui Manua.

The islands of American Samoa first became known to the western world in 1722 when the Dutch navigator Jacob Roggeveen sighted Tau, Ofu and Olosega in the Manua group, and had brief contact with the islanders. Forty-six years later, Bougainville, the French explorer, also touched at Ofu and Olosega and bartered trinkets for fresh food. At these and other islands in Western Samoa, Bougainville was struck by the islanders' skill in handling their canoes, and he accordingly named the two groups the Navigator Islands. In 1787, Bougainville's countryman La Perouse anchored near Aasu on the northern side of Tutuila. His second-in-command, de Langle, and 11 of his men were massacred when they went ashore for water. Four years later, Captain Edward Edwards of HMS 'Pandora' called at Tutuila on two occasions during his search for the 'Bounty' mutineers.

For nearly 40 years after news of the de Langle massacre reached Europe, most European navigators gave Samoa a wide berth. However, from about 1803 onwards runaway sailors and escaped convicts from New South Wales began to reach Samoa from Tonga and elsewhere. By 1830 several score had settled there. Some of these men, as well as a well-travelled Samoan named Siovili, introduced a form of Christianity to the Samoans. In addition, converts from Tonga and a Tahitian who drifted to Tau from Tubuai began teaching.

Missionaries arrive. The Samoans were therefore well prepared for the arrival in 1830 of the first Christian missionaries, John Williams and Charles Barff, of the London Missionary Society, who left Tahitian teachers ashore. In 1836, the Rev. A. W. Murray of the LMS settled on Tutuila where he remained for many years. He arrived only a few months after Captain Cuthbert of the British whaler 'Elizabeth' had discovered Pago Pago harbour. Most Tutuilans were soon under firm missionary influence, and within a year Island teachers had also carried the Gospel to Manua.

Meanwhile, word about Pago Pago's commodious harbour had spread, and soon it was a popular port of call for the whaling vessels of several nations. However, Pago Pago never experienced the activity that occurred in neighbouring Apia, particularly after the German firm of J. C. Godeffroy and Son began trading there in 1857. On the other hand, American shipping interests foresaw that Pago Pago could be of value to a proposed trans-Pacific steamship service and they took steps to obtain a foothold there. In 1872, Commander R. W. Meade of the USS 'Narrangansett' signed a treaty with the Mauga (high chief) of the Pago Pago area which gave the United States the exclusive right to build a naval station in return for US Government protection. Meade's treaty was never ratified, but in 1878 certain harbourside lands were transferred to the United States for a coaling depot.

The Big Powers are involved. During the next 20 years, the United States, Germany and Great Britain were deeply involved in the turbulent events that were played out in Western Samoa. The upshot of these events was that in 1899 a commission of the three powers recommended that the only means of providing stable government in Samoa was to partition the islands. Germany thereupon annexed Western Samoa; the United States accepted Tutuila and Manua; and Great Britain withdrew from the group in return for German concessions elsewhere.

The American territory was placed under the jurisdiction of the US Department of the Navy and designated a naval station. Commander B. F. Tilley, USN, became the first officer in charge. The US flag was formally raised on Tutuila on 17 April, 1900, following the receipt of a deed of cession from the chiefs of that island. The Manuan chiefs signed a deed of cession in 1904. The United States did not formally accept the two deeds until 1929. But even after it did so, the Samoans still had only the status of American-protected persons – not that of US citizens.

From 1905 onwards, commanders of what was then called the Tutuila Naval Station received appointment as governor rather than commandant; and in 1911 American Samoa was adopted as the name of the territory. Swains Island, 320 km north of Tutuila, which had been acquired by an American citizen, Eli Jennings, in 1876, was made an administrative part of American Samoa in 1925. The territory remained under naval administration until 30 June, 1951, when it was transferred to the jurisdiction of the US Department of the Interior. Mr Phelps became the first civilian governor.

First constitution. In 1960, after six years of discussion, a constitutional convention of American Samoans approved the territory's first constitution. This contained a bill of rights, granted law-making authority to the territorial legislature, and stated that it would be government policy 'to protect persons of Samoan ancestry against alienation of their lands and the destruction of the Samoan way of life and language contrary to their best interests'. At a ceremony commemorating the 60th anniversary of the raising of the American flag, the first flag of American Samoa was hoisted. The governor's report for that year stated that American Samoa was still an 18th century society, but that it was "trying to meet 20th century hopes and aspirations". The report warned that the people needed to exercise effort and restraint in trying to accomplish in a few years what Europe had achieved in 400.

In 1961, however, all ideas of administrative restraint were seemingly abandoned. With the appointment of Governor H. Rex Lee, it was decided to start forthwith on what was officially described as "a complete rehabilitation and development program to correct the lagging economic and social development". Special funds were obtained from the US Congress, and almost overnight a dynamic programme began that rocketed American Samoa into the 20th century. Governor Lee's term of office lasted six years. When it ended, American Samoa had many new roads, new harbour facilities, new houses, a new hospital, the massive Lee Auditorium, widespread electric light and sewerage schemes, fine schools, a luxurious hotel in Pago Pago, a jet airport with attractive terminal buildings, a growing tourist industry, thriving fish canneries and a TV system of education with programmes transmitted in English.

The innovations of the Lee era earned much praise from Western visitors. But many leading Samoans and others were dismayed by their destructive effect on the old social system, causing sharply increasing crime and juvenile delinquency. Just before Governor Lee left the territory in July 1967, one Samoan leader said: "We are now engaged in a battle for the survival of ourselves as a people, for the survival of the things that are dear to us, and for the preservation of the way of life that has sustained us well since the beginning of our history."

The tourist boom initiated under Governor Lee (and the accompanying Westernisation of the territory) surged on during the next few years. But the many Samoans who had been persuaded to invest in the hotel saw little in the way of dividends because of the massive cost of running it. Meanwhile, some of the magnificent enterprises of the Lee era began to falter. Frequent power and water shortages caused heavy losses to business people as well as irritation and inconvenience to tourists; the idea of trying to educate the Samoans in English rather than Samoan was abandoned as a failure; and TV education itself had to be curtailed because of its high cost and the inability to transmit lessons without power. Finally, in early 1975, many Samoans in government employment – American Samoa's largest industry since Lee's time – had to be laid off as funds from Washington dried up.

Governor John M. Haydon, who resigned in August 1974 after five controversial years in office, had hoped to be American Samoa's last appointed governor. But during his term the Samoans voted decisively against electing a governor from their own ranks.

However, after two further referendums resulted in rejection of Washington's attempt to bring some autonomy to territorial rule, the voters changed their minds and voted 'yes' with the fourth referendum. American Samoan Peter Tali Coleman, the only Samoan to be an appointed governor, who held office for 4½ years (Oct. 15, 1956 to May 24, 1961) and later served with distinction in Micronesia, won the contest for the first elected governor. He took office on January 3, 1978, from H. Rex Lee, who was brought back from Washington as caretaker governor on May 28, 1977. Tufele Li'a, Mr Coleman's running mate, became Lieutenant-Governor.

Civil governors

Governor Phelps Phelps
Feb 23, 1951–June 20, 1952
Governor John C. Elliott
July 16, 1952–Nov. 25, 1952
Governor James Arthur Ewing
Nov. 28, 1952–Mar. 4, 1953
Governor Lawrence M. Judd
Mar. 4 1953–Aug. 5, 1953
Governor Richard B. Lowe
Oct. 1 1953–Oct. 15, 1956
Governor Peter Tali Coleman
Oct. 15, 1956–May 24, 1961
Governor H. Rex Lee
May 24, 1961–July 31, 1967
Governor Owen S. Aspinall
Aug. 1, 1967–July 31, 1969
Governor John M. Haydon
Aug. 1, 1969–Oct. 15. 1974
Lt. Gov. Frank C. Mockler (Acting)
Oct. 15, 1974–Feb. 6, 1975
Governor Earl B. Ruth
Feb. 6, 1975–Sept. 30, 1976
Governor Frank Barnett
Oct. 1, 1976–May 27, 1977
Governor H. Rex Lee
May 28, 1977–Jan. 3, 1978
Governor Peter Tali Coleman
Jan 3. 1978– to Present

Further information: J. A. C. Gray, 'Amerika Samoa', Annapolis, Maryland, 1960; 'Pacific Islands Monthly'.

MAIN ISLANDS IN DETAIL

TUTUILA. Tutuila is about 30 km long, and ranges from about 3 to 9 m wide. A broken mountain range runs almost the whole length of the island, with numerous deep fertile valleys running down to the coast. The main villages are scattered along the level land near the west and south coasts and on the southern slopes. The settlement on the northern side of the island, which is rough and precipitous, is very small. The whole island, even to the tops of the peaks, is densely wooded and very beautiful. There are several outstanding peaks, notably, Matafao (702 m), near the centre of the island; northward and eastward are Mount Alava (485 m) and Mount Pioa; in the western part of the island is Mount Olotele (486 m). The best-known moun-

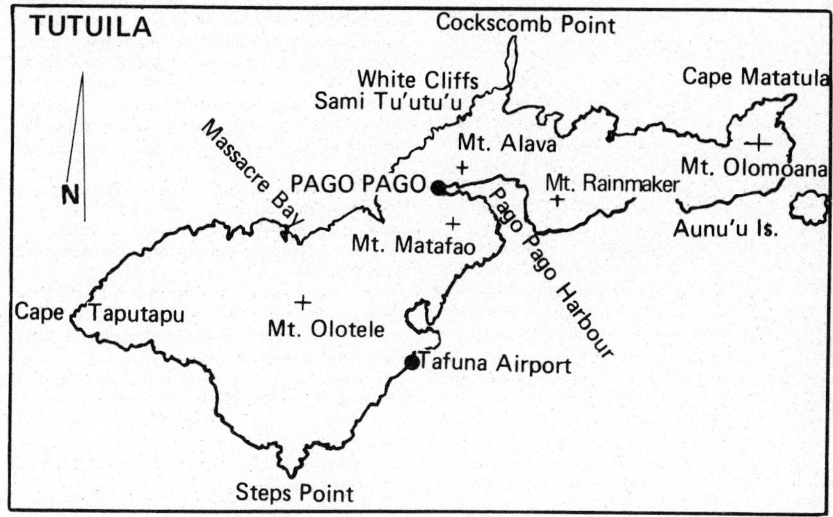

tain is the Rainmaker, a truncated cone seen across Pago Pago harbour from the Americana hotel, frequently wreathed in cloud. Because of the steep-sided nature of local mountains they appear to be much higher than they are.

There are several harbours in Tutuila, apart from Pago Pago, with villages of some importance. Leone, on the south coast, is the only harbour, besides Pago, which can accommodate other than small ships, but it is little used.

The Pago Pago Bay area is the centre of Tutuila (and, indeed, American Samoan), activity.

The town itself is scattered along several kilometres of foreshore on the deeply indented harbour, with the hotel and high school at one extremity, the Government Offices, Bank and businesses in the centre, and other stores and the canneries, etc., at the other extremity. What to the foreign visitor is known collectively as Pago Pago however, was originally a collection of villages, Pago Pago being one of them.

Between 1961 and 1966 there was considerable building activity in Pago Pago in connection with the tourist hotel and the introduction of TV education. The aerial tramway was installed at this time from Solo Hill across the harbour to Mt Alava.

The territory's internal airport at Tafuna is capable of taking Boeing 747 jet aircraft.

MANUA GROUP.

Ta'u, the chief island of the Manua Group, is conical in shape and rises to a central mount (1,000 m). The southern and eastern coasts are precipitous, but the land slopes gently to the westward and northward. The principal settlement is at Luma, on the west coast. There is a harbour scheduled for completion in 1979. Meanwhile there is a very good anchorage to the northward, in Faleasau Bay. The population of Ta'u is 1,300.

Olosega and Ofu are small islands about 11 km N.W. of Ta'u. They have a population of about 400 each. They are separated by a very narrow strait and both are enclosed by the same reef which dries out at low tide and obstructs the channel between them for anything but very small boats. Both islands have precipitous hills with small areas of flat land where soil is very fertile. Highest points are 500 m on Ofu and 600 m on Olosega. There is a small airstrip on Ofu.

SWAIN'S ISLAND. Swain's Island, which lies about 450 km north of Tutuila is an atoll about 2 km long by 1.7 km wide. The greatest elevation of the land is about 6 m. There is no entrance into the lagoon, which has brackish water.

The atoll was once thought to have been discovered in 1606 by the Spanish explorer Quiros and named Gente Hermosa because of its attractive people. However, recent research has established that Gente Hermosa was Rakahanga in the northern Cook Group, and that Swain's Island remained unknown to Europeans until well into the 19th century. It was named by Captain W. L. Hudson of the United States Exploring Expedition who learned of it in Samoa in 1841 from a whaling captain called Swain. Shortly afterwards, some islanders from Fakaofu (now in

Tokelau) formed a colony on the atoll, and three Frenchmen began exploiting it as a coconut plantation. The atoll was and is known to the Tokelau people as Olosenga.

In 1856, Eli Jennings, an American with a Samoan wife, claimed title to the island from an Englishman, Captain Turnbull, and took over the plantation and its Tokelauan labourers. The plantation has remained in the Jennings family ever since, producing up to 200 tonnes of copra a year.

Because of its closeness to the Tokelaus (about 175 km) and its cultural affinities with them, Swain's Island was included with those islands, then called the Union Group, when Britain incorporated them into the Gilbert and Ellice Islands Colony in 1916. However, in 1925, the island was annexed by the United States and placed under the administration of American Samoa. Control was more or less nominal until 1953-54 when labour disputes between the Jennings family and Tokelauan copra cutters resulted in a resident government representative being stationed on the island by US executive order. By traditional custom, the islanders choose a delegate to the House of Representatives in Pago Pago, but he has no vote in that assembly's proceedings. The population at the 1970 census was 74, compared with 125 in 1937.

FOR THE TOURIST. Information about the islands is provided by the Office of Tourism within the Government of American Samoa in Pago Pago. There is also a Visitor Industry Board, headed by a leading personality in the local travel trade. The country is most picturesque and Pago Harbour quite breathtaking in its dramatic beauty. Visitors should also take the opportunity of visiting nearby Western Samoa, which can be a day trip by air but should preferably be treated as a two-day visit.

American Samoa is a duty-free area with most stores carrying duty-free goods including cameras, tape recorders, jewellery, perfume, cosmetics, fabrics etc.

Business hours are from 8 am to 5 pm weekdays (banks 9-4 Mon. to Friday only), and 8 am to 12 noon on Saturdays. No stores open on Sundays or holidays except for the Airport duty-free shop which is open for all flights. None of the duty-free stores accepts credit cards – only cash or travellers' cheques.

Travellers should ensure that their travellers' cheques are endorsed for release by the financial authority of the country of issue, otherwise the banks in American Samoa will refuse to accept them. Tipping is not encouraged.

Entry formalities. US citizens do not require passport or visa but a US Government document showing place of birth. Resident aliens need an alien registration card and document allowing return to the US.

All other persons need a passport or identity certificate authorising return to country of origin or onward. Visitors must have a return or onward ticket and may stay up to 30 days without further permission.

All visitors must possess a valid international certificate of smallpox vaccination.

Sightseeing. The village of Pago Pago, nestling at the end of the bay, includes a cluster of traditional Samoan "fale" houses, offering indigenous handicrafts, while high school competitive sports can be

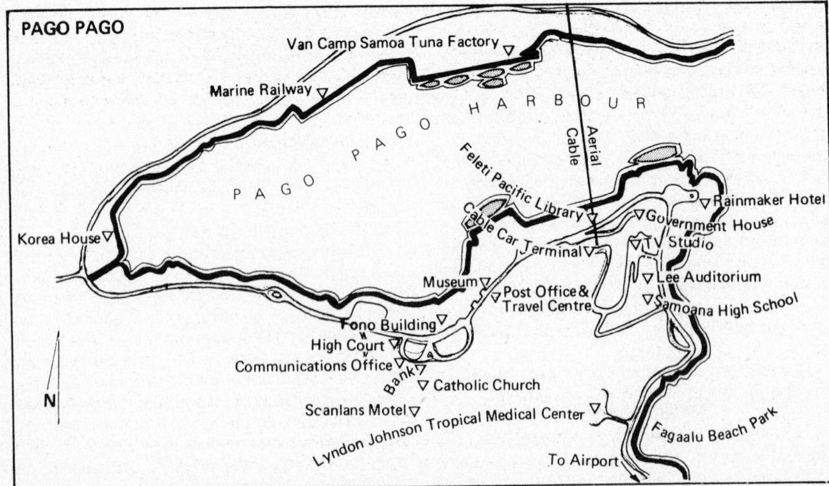

seen at the Sports Field and the American Samoan-Korea House, a recreation centre for fishing fleets, adds a touch of the Orient to this area.

Another Samoan village may be reached by taking a short, relatively easy hike along the Afona Trail, on the north shore of the harbour.

Around Fagatogo, the business and administrative centre, interesting points include the "malae" or village green, the new Fono (Legislature) Building, the white colonial-style courthouse, the new museum, the farmers' market – a centre of activity on Saturday mornings – and Sadie Thompson's Hotel (of Somerset Maugham's "Rain" fame), now the Max Haleck Store No. 3.

The Office of Tourism has established several additional attractions for sightseers. A botanical agriculture park was opened in Aloau village in July, 1978. Tourists can see the preparation of traditional Samoan foods, herbal medicines, tapa making and fine mat weaving. The village of Aoa features five 'fale' for camping, spaces for tents, barbecue pits, open showers and other facilities and sleeping mats, mosquito nets, canoes and fishing equipment are available for rental. The Amanave tourist village stages demonstrations of handicraft production by the women. Another attraction is the Jean P. Haydon Museum. A new programme "Home staying" has been introduced in the villages. The Office of Tourism has assigned certain village chiefs as hosts to tourists who rent guest fale. The tourists experience at first-hand what it is like to eat, sleep and live in a traditional Samoan house. The scheme is attracting many tourists.

Eleven fale have been provided for accommodation in the Manu'a group.

Four Office of Tourism information centres have been opened, at the transit lounge at the airport, in the lobby at the Rainmaker Hotel, at Aoa village and at the Convention Center at Utulei.

Three vantage points offer spectacular views over Pago Pago Bay. Solo Hill probably offers the best over-all view of the entire bay. It is the departure point for the aerial tramway which travels along one mile of cable to the summit of Mt Alava.

Blunt's Point, an old World War II look-out, may be reached by a short walk up a jeep road to the summit. Breaker's Point may also be reached by hiking up a jeep road.

Other walks lead to the Virgin Falls, in Faga'alu Valley and to Rainmaker Mountain, which is rather a tough climb.

Off the main island of Tutuila, visitors may go to the Manu'a Islands aboard commercial vessels at reasonable rates. On the island of Ta'u, there is the Niumata Mailo motel. There are several bush stores on each of the Manu'a Islands.

Festivals. American Samoa has three special festivals of interest to tourists.

These are Flag Day, April 17, which commemorates the first raising of the American flag in the islands; there are displays of Samoan dancing, singing, etc., on the Fagatogo "malae".

White Sunday – the second Sunday of October – is literally a "Children's Day" in the islands, with everyone dressed in white and the children leading church services and acting out religious plays.

Swarm of the Palolo: late October to early November. Islanders wade out to the reef to scoop up eggs of the mating coral worm (Palolo), considered a great delicacy.

Historic sites. Various local buildings, including the two-storey white colonial-style courthouse, are included in the National Register of Historic Buildings.

Representatives abroad. Delegate-at-large, Washington, D.C., U.S.A., Australia, Office of Tourism, Government of American Samoa: Hugh M. Birch, 61 Cross Street, Double Bay, NSW 2028 (tel. 02-32 0291).

ACCOMMODATION

Pago Pago

RAINMAKER HOTEL: 190 rooms, all air conditioned, located near town, restaurant, cocktail lounge, swimming pool and small private sandy beach. Organises "Fiafia" feast nights and entertainment.

HERB AND SIA'S MOTEL: 10 rooms, one meal included. In Fagatogo. A fiafia (Samoan feast and dancing) is held on Tues., Wed. and Fri. nights.

CLIPPERTON ISLAND

Clipperton Island, a lonely coral atoll at 10 deg 18 min N. latitude, 109 deg 13 min W. longitude, north-west of the Galapagos and 2,900 km due west of the Panama Canal, is a dependency of France. It is not part of French Polynesia. Clipperton was under the authority of the Governor of French Polynesia until 1979. Under a ministerial decree gazetted on February 2nd 1979 jurisdiction over the island was transferred direct to Paris.

In 1977 it was suggested that this island might be transferred to the jurisdiction of the French Antilles. Under the application of the 200 mile sea limit, Clipperton has a zone of economic interest extending to 324,000 sq. km.

It has a strange history. John Clipperton was mate on a ship of the English navigator, William Dampier. In 1704, he quarrelled with Dampier in the Gulf of Nicoya, and, with 21 other mutineers, seized a barque and roamed the eastern Pacific, as a pirate. They made the lonely, isolated atoll – originally discovered by the Spaniards – their hide-out in 1705; and the island thus was named after the pirate.

A reef, about 8 km in circumference, encloses a lagoon where small ships may once have sheltered, but which now is closed by the coral reef. It was listed as one of the United States guano islands under the Guano Act of 1856; but it was not occupied by Americans.

France had already annexed it in 1855 and, in 1897, it was seized by a Mexican garrison, and Mexico kept a garrison there for years. The opening of the Panama Canal gave the atoll new importance, and France asserted her prior claim. The question of ownership was submitted to the arbitration of King Victor Emmanuel of Italy; and, on January 31, 1930, he declared in favour of France. Mexico, announcing to the world that the Monroe Doctrine was being flouted, handed over the atoll to France in November, 1932.

Lieut. Gauthier in the 'Jeanne d'Arc' took possession in the name of France on January 26, 1935.

A British firm (Pacific Islands Company) worked phosphate deposits on Clipperton between 1906 and 1917. About 100 people, the phosphate settlers and a Mexican army garrison, regularly received supplies by ship from Mexico; then, at the outbreak of war in 1914, Clipperton was forgotten by the Mexican authorities.

During the three years that followed the arrival of the last supply ship, most of the people died from starvation and sickness. The garrison commander, Captain Ramon d'Arnaud, and a few others, set out in a small boat to intercept an imaginary passing ship, but were never heard of again. When most of the men had died, an immense negro (keeper of the lighthouse) murdered the remainder; he, in turn, was killed with an axe by one of the young women he tried to enslave. This happened on July 18, 1917, only a day before the US Navy vessel 'Yorktown' called at the island and rescued the surviving three women and eight children.

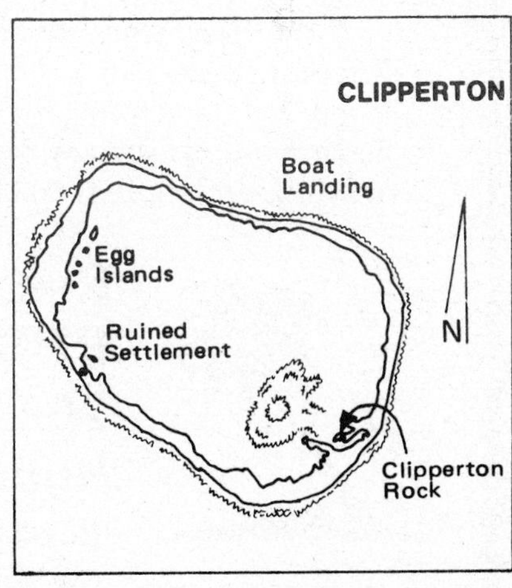

COOK ISLANDS

Located between 156 and 167 deg. W. longitude, and between 8 and 23 deg. S. latitude, the 15 islands of the Cooks are an internally self-governing state in free association with New Zealand. The population of the group in December 1976 was 18,128.

The main island is Rarotonga (67 sq km) which is 3,000 km north-east of Auckland. The administrative centre on that island, is Avarua. Local time is 10 hrs behind GMT but "Daylight saving", from January 1 to March 31, puts the Cook Islands 9 hrs behind GMT during that period.

The flag shows the Union Flag in the top pole corner and a ring of 15 white stars on a royal blue background. The stars represent the islands of the group. The National Anthem is "God Save the Queen", but there is also a Cook Islands national song "Te Atua Mou'e" (God is Truth). New Zealand currency, together with Cook Islands' coins, are legal tender.

Public holidays include: January 1, Good Friday, Easter Monday, April 25 (ANZAC day), early June (Queen's birthday), early August (Constitution day), late October (Gospel day), Christmas and Boxing day.

THE PEOPLE. The Cook Islands Maori is Polynesian and several tribes trace their ancestry back to Samoa and Raiatea (French Polynesia). By tradition there are also connections between the Rarotongans and the New Zealand Maori. The Cook Islands census of December 1, 1976 recorded a total population of 18,128, compared with 21,323 in 1971 and 19,247 in 1966. At the end of 1979, the population was estimated to be 19,200. About half are under 15 years of age.

The southern islands have the greater part of the population (89 per cent in 1976). The most populous islands are Rarotonga (9,802 in 1976), Aitutaki (2,423), Mangaia (1,530) and Atiu (1,312).

Nationality. Cook Islanders are British subjects and citizens of New Zealand through the New Zealand Citizenship Act 1948 and by the Constitution adopted in 1965.

Language. Most of the islanders are bilingual, using their own Polynesian dialect and English. The languages of Polynesia are all closely related and are of the Malay-Polynesian family. There is a strong similarity between the dialects of the NZ Maori, the Cook Island Maori and the Tahitian. If a NZ Maori speaks Maori in the Cook Islands, he is readily understood. If he goes to Tahiti, and speaks Maori without pronouncing his k's, he can still be understood.

Migration. Hundreds of Cook Islanders go to New Zealand to seek employment or trade skills. In 1977 there were about 20,000 in New Zealand, compared with 4,499 in 1961. The largest communities of islanders are in Auckland and timber mill towns.

Religion. The London Missionary Society was the pioneer in educational and missionary effort in the Cook Islands. The evangelisation of the people began at Aitutaki in 1821 and, with some setbacks, spread through the group, guided by Rev. John Williams. For many Cook Islanders the most respected early Christian teacher was Papeiha, a Raiatean, who introduced the gospel to Aitutaki in 1821, Rarotonga in 1823. Many Cook Islanders were sent away in the early days as native pastors to Samoa, the New Hebrides, Papua and elsewhere. The church is still a most powerful influence.

About 75 per cent belong to the Cook Is. Christian Church (formerly the LMS); about 12 per cent are Roman Catholic; and the remaining 13 per cent Seventh-day Adventist, Latter-day Saints, etc.

The exuberant church singing, in European and Maori styles, is a great joy to hear.

Lifestyle. Generally the islanders continue to live in extended families, with a tribal leader to whom they owe allegiance. In some cases, e.g. in Rarotonga, land is held under registered title and worked by families. In other areas, e.g. Pukapuka, the traditional communal pattern of livelihood is followed.

Recreation. Favourite pursuits in the Cooks follow Polynesian tradition and include feasting, music-making and dancing. There is also frequent

participation in church meetings.

Sports include cricket, tennis, rugby, lawn bowls, netball, boxing, golf, sailing and athletics. There is also a fishing club.

GOVERNMENT. The islands formally became part of New Zealand on June 11, 1901. They gained internal self-government in 1965, and after the first general elections held in April 1965, voted to remain in free association with New Zealand. The latter, with the Cook Islands government, assumes responsibilities in external affairs and defence.

Legislature. The Legislative Assembly of the Cook Islands, under the Cook Islands Constitution Act 1964, consists of 22 members representing the islands as follows: Rarotonga and Palmerston (nine members), Aitutaki and Manuae (three), Atiu and Mangaia (two each), Manihiki, Mauke, Mitiaro, Penrhyn and Rakahanga (one each), Pukapuka and Nassau (one).

The Constitution of the Cook Islands is the supreme law of the land and the Legislative Assembly alone has power to amend or repeal it, upon a two thirds majority vote.

Executive. Executive authority is vested in Her Majesty the Queen. However the office of the New Zealand High Commissioner was discontinued on October 15, 1975, the High Commissioner having acted as Cook Islands Head of State, as well as representing New Zealand.

In mid-1976, the Cook Islands Constitution had not yet been amended to separate these dual responsibilities of the New Zealand High Commissioner, the New Zealand Government indicating that it would be represented at the diplomatic level in the Cook Islands for the foreseeable future by a Representative rather than a High Commissioner. Both governments took the view that the best interests of each would be served if the Head of State was appointed by the Cook Islands government.

Executive government lies with a cabinet of ministers comprising the premier and six other ministers, chosen by the premier.

Elections. A general election, by universal suffrage, is held every four years. Governing party is the Democratic Party, with the Cook Islands Party in opposition.

Local government. Island councils have existed for many years on each of the main islands. They were reconstituted by the Local Government Act 1966 which provides for the chairman to be elected from among council members, instead of having the island Resident Agent in this post, as previously. The councils meet regularly to supervise various local activities, collect certain taxes and carry out various island works and services. In addition, each village has a village committee to maintain good order and help maintain roads.

House of Ariki. The House of Ariki of the Cook Islands consists of up to 15 Ariki, representing all islands in the group, and is required to meet at least once every 12 months. The House considers any matters submitted to it by the Legislative Assembly in relation to the welfare of the Cook Islands people. The Ariki are hereditary chiefs and are consulted mainly over land and islander customs.

Justice. An itinerant chief judge from New Zealand serves the Cook Islands and Niue.

The High Court deals with criminal and civil matters including inquests and valuations. Cases with a maximum fine of $200 or maximum sentence of six months are presided over by a Commissioner. Other cases are heard by the Chief Justice of the Cook Islands. The Land Court deals with land matters only and is presided over by a Judge of the Land Court. The Children's Court deals with juvenile crime and is presided over in the same way as the High Court.

In the High Court, a decision of the Commissioner can be appealed before the Chief Justice of the Cook Islands. An appeal against the latter's decision can be made to the New Zealand Supreme Court and in turn, a further appeal can be made to the New Zealand Appellate Court. The final court of appeal is the Privy Council in London. In the Land Court the only appeal against the Commissioner's decision is to the New Zealand Land Appellate Court which is presided over by two judges from the New Zealand Maori Land Court and the Chief Justice of the Cook Islands.

Liquor laws. The manufacturing of intoxicating liquor in the Cooks is illegal. The liquor is imported by the government and sold through the Cook Islands Liquor Supplies and various authorised stores. There are several licensed bars in Rarotonga, while the bowling, golf and sailing clubs have liquor licences to serve members and guests. It is an offence to drink in public places, such as outside dance halls.

Gambling. Licences are issued, under the Gaming Act 1967, to permit gambling by totalisator, housie, small raffles, lotteries. New Zealand horse races are followed keenly.

DEFENCE. Under the Cook Islands Constitution Act 1964, the New Zealand Government is responsible for the defence and international relations of the Cook Islands, in consultation with the C.I. government. On the New Zealand side, relations are handled by the Ministry of Foreign Affairs.

EDUCATION. Schools are operated by the government, the Roman Catholic Mission, and the Seventh-day Adventist Mission.

Under the Educational Act 1966, education is free and compulsory between the ages of six and 15 years.

There are 38 schools in the Cooks, including nine colleges, 26 primary schools and a teachers college. Pre-school centres are established on most islands. There is also an apprentice training scheme.

The Roman Catholic mission operates two primary schools, and Nukutere College at Avarua, Rarotonga. The Seventh-day Adventists operate two primary schools, Papaaroa Junior College, at

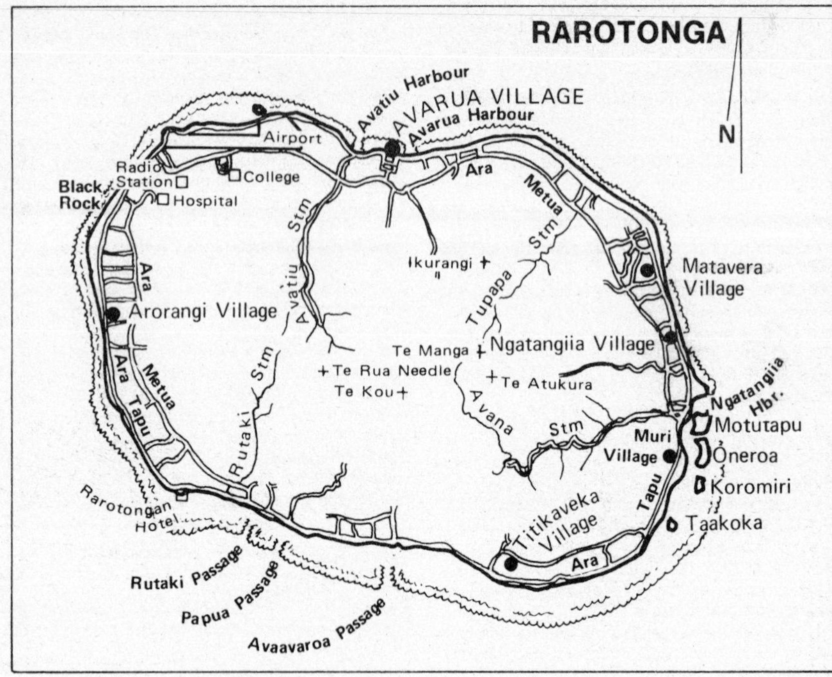

Titikaveka, Rarotonga and a college on Aitutaki.

Schools in 1977 recorded a total of 7,172 pupils. In government schools there were 4,414 in primary, 1,756 in colleges (Fi-U5), and 308 in high schools (Fl-L5). In the S.D.A. schools there were 161 in primary and 43 in high school. In the Roman Catholic schools there were 387 in primary and 103 in college. The government's Tereora College, Rarotonga, is the only secondary school catering for Form 6. Other government secondary schools are on Aitutaki, Mangaia and Atiu.

The Teachers' College completed at Tereora in 1970 had 48 students in 1977.

Students enrolled overseas are mainly in New Zealand and Fiji, with some in Western Samoa. Up to 100 students and trainees receive education or vocational training each year under the New Zealand Training Scheme.

LABOUR. In the northern atolls, people subsist largely on coconuts and fish. There is little economic opportunity other than making copra. In the Southern Group, many people work on their own plantations although in recent years there has been a noticeable shift into other forms of paid labour. In 1979, composition of the work force was:

Agriculture & Fishing	22.8%
Manufacturing & Construction	15.8%
Commerce, Transport & Services	54.4%

The government is a major employer with 900 casual workers in 1975, 1,200 local public servants, and 40 officers seconded from the New Zealand public service.

Wages. Basic wage rates for labour paid by the government in 1977 was 60 cents per hour. Wharf labour was then paid 63 cents per hour.

Unions. The Cook Islands Industrial Union of Waterside Workers is the only trade union in the group. There is also a powerful Public Service Association.

Social security. There is a superannuation fund for government employees. The idea of a national provident fund for other workers has been considered but no action had been taken by mid-1977. There is also an old age and destitute scheme, with pensions financed from stamps sold at the philatelic bureau. By late-1977, the old age pension was $5.00 weekly.

HEALTH. Free medical and surgical treatment is available for all Cook Islanders. School and preschool children also receive free dental treatment.

A general hospital equipped with dispensary, X-rays, and laboratory facilities is maintained in Rarotonga, on Sanatorium Hill. In addition an outpatient clinic at Tupapa and at Akaoa district caters for minor ailments, six days a week.

The office of the division of Public Health which

caters for disease control, environmental sanitation and mother and child health is situated in the Ministry of Health and Education at Tupapa.

Cottage hospitals (accommodating a few patients) have been built at Aitutaki, Atiu, Mauke, Penrhyn, Manihiki, Pukapuka, and Mangaia. They are managed by doctors.

On the islands of Mitiaro, Nassau, Rakahanga and Palmerston there are small dispensaries managed by dressers. Referral of cases to base hospital when required is by aircraft or boat; patients needing specialist treatment are referred to New Zealand.

The group is served by 21 doctors of whom three are in private practice. The dental service includes nine dental officers.

Diseases. The Cook Islands are generally free from common diseases prevalent in other tropical islands. Filariasis is endemic but active vector control and mass treatment of the population continues. Malaria does not exist. Metabolic disorders and hypertension are prevalent and venereal disease is increasing.

THE LAND. The total land area of the islands is 240 sq. km. situated in 2.2 million sq.km. of sea. The largest island is Rarotonga (65 sq. km), followed by Mangaia (51 sq. km). No other island is more than 30 sq. km. The other 13 islands are Aitutaki, Atiu, Mitiaro, Mauke, Manuae, Takutea and Palmerston in the Southern Group and Penrhyn, Manihiki, Rakahanga, Pukapuka, Nassau and Suwarrow in the Northern Group.

The islands extend 1,400 km from Penrhyn, situated 9 deg. south of the equator, to Mangaia, which is just north of the Tropic of Capricorn. The largest island, Rarotonga, is about 10 km wide, and some 32 km in circumference.

The highest peaks are Te Manga (652 m) and Te Atukura (639 m), both on Rarotonga.

A whole range of relief patterns is noted, from the submerged volcanic peaks of the northern atolls, covered with coral, to the steep, raised volcanic peaks of Rarotonga, with its narrow fringing reef. Mangaia and Atiu are both surrounded by a makatea – a raised, former coral reef, like castle walls, with limestone caves inside. Mitiaro has lower cliffs, with a lake inside as the beginning of a lagoon.

Natural features. All the islands of the Northern Group, as well as Manuae and Takutea in the south, are coral atolls, generally enclosing a lagoon. The remaining six islands of the Southern Group are more elevated. The lagoon of Aitutaki is regarded as one of the most beautiful in the Pacific.

Soil. The atoll soil permits only restricted growth, however the deeper volcanic soil in the Southern Group is more fertile and produces abundant supplies of tropical fruits.

Climate. From December to March the climate is warm and humid, with the possibility of serious storms, as all of the Cook Islands lie within the hurricane zone. Advance warning of tropical storms is given by a meteorological service with headquarters in Fiji. From April to November the climate in the Southern Group is mild and equable. The mean annual temperature in Rarotonga is 23.6 deg. C., and the average yearly rainfall is 2,030 mm.

Flora and fauna. The raised islands support casuarina, barringtonia, hibiscus, palms, frangipani, poinciana, and bougainvillea in abundance. Atoll vegetation is largely pandanus and coconuts.

Apart from pigs and fowls the fauna includes the great bird nesting sanctuary on Suwarrow, the pearl shell beds of Penrhyn and Manihiki, and beds of brilliantly-coloured clam shells in the Northern Group.

Land tenure. All the land in the group is owned by the Maoris, and their ownership is fully safeguarded. No Maori may sell or mortgage or otherwise dispose of his lands except that he can mortgage his lands to an authorised body to secure a housing loan. He can sell or lease to the Crown for more than 60 years for public purposes only, or to a religious body for more than 60 years for church purposes. The rental of land varies according to its value.

Changes to the law in 1970 now allow landowners to form a "body corporate" and to lease land for commercial purposes for a maximum of 60 years.

Under the Cook Islands customary land tenure system, it is not unusual for 120 persons to be owners of as little as one fifth of a hectare. The use to which this land was put was frequently bogged down in the inability of the owners to agree about it. The Land (Facilitation of Dealings) Bill provides a means of getting landowners to agree by imposing majority rule on their deliberations, but at the same time there is no compulsion upon landowners to form bodies corporate – the machinery is there if they want it.

Where land is leased for commercial purposes, the owners must be given shareholding rights of not less than 10 per cent of the equity capital, in addition to the land rental.

PRIMARY PRODUCTION. In the northern atolls, output is restricted mainly to coconuts and fish. In the fertile southern islands production is concentrated on bananas, citrus and pineapples.

The principal crops are planted in the following estimated areas: coconuts, 3,500 ha; citrus fruits 400 ha; taro 120 ha; bananas, 193 ha; tomatoes 11 ha; pineapples, 147 ha; maniota, 124 ha; kumaras (sweet potato), 60 ha; yams, 2 ha; and coffee, 10 ha.

The main citrus growing is on Rarotonga, Aitutaki, Atiu and Mauke. The chief banana growing islands are Rarotonga and Aitutaki, while commercial supplies of pineapple come from Mangaia and Atiu.

Livestock. Results of a survey on Rarotonga in April 1977 showed that the livestock population on that island was: cattle 207; pigs 6,498; goats 1,095.

Fisheries. Mother of pearl shell is collected according to overseas demand and the state of the local shell grounds.

MANUFACTURING. Secondary industries operating in Rarotonga include a fruit cannery, two clothing factories and production of local handicrafts.

LOCAL COMMERCE. Locally-produced vegetables and seafoods are sold at markets in Avarua, Rarotonga.

The Ministry of Agriculture and Fisheries was reorganised in 1978 and plans made to improve commercial production. Trading activities by the ministry were reduced considerably and the subsidies on fertilisers and chemicals sold by the government's Ngatipa Store were withdrawn. Produce growers decided in August, 1978, to establish a Cook Islands Primary Producers Federation.

The acompanying tables give details of agricultural and artisanal fisheries production for the year ended March 31, 1979.

AGRICULTURE

	'000kg	$'000
Citrus	2,858	342
Pineapple	1,312	197
Banana	417	51
Copra	771	187
Other fresh fruit	136	51
Vegetables	193	167
Total	**5,687**	**995**

FISHERIES (SOUTHERN GROUP)

	000kg	$'000
Rarotonga	171	301
Aitutaki	472	623
Mangaia	44	50
Atiu	17	19
Mauke	34	38
Mitiaro	25	28
Total	**763**	**1,059**

TOURISM. The government pursues a policy of "controlled tourism", aimed at ensuring a harmonious development with the rest of island life. In particular, the policy is that no hotels should be higher than the coconut palms. Impetus to development of the tourist industry came from the opening of the first Cook Island jet airport for full internatinal services in 1973, the opening of the Rarotongan Hotel in May 1977 and, a month later, commencement of a weekly Air New Zealand service between Rarotonga and Honolulu. Tourist development is promoted by the C.I. Tourist Authority.

The number of tourists and visitors arriving in the islands during the twelve months to June 1979 was 19,722 compared with 9,898 in 1976. New Zealanders formed the largest group in 1978 (10,981), followed by Cook Islands Maoris (2,614).

OVERSEAS TRADE. The Cook Islands suffer from an adverse balance of visible trade. The financing of imports double the value of local exports is made possible by aid from the New Zealand Government and funds transferred by Cook Islands workers in New Zealand.

About 80 per cent of Cook Islands exports go to New Zealand. Foodstuffs are the major class of imports.

New Zealand provides more than 80 per cent of the group's imports.

Customs tariff. There is free trade between the Cook Islands and New Zealand. Import licences are required for goods imported from countries other than New Zealand.

FINANCE. Revenue raised in the Cook Islands is supplemented by aid from New Zealand in the form of grants and loans. Recent budgetary figures are set out in the accompanying table.

For the financial year ending March 31, 1977 revenue included: import duty, $679,343; import levy, $1 million; income tax, $1.3 million; postal stamp sales, $27,168; overseas sales of stamps, $418,362.

Income tax is assessed on a sliding scale with rebates for a dependent wife, and for children. Superannuation contributions are not taxed. Company tax is 35 per cent.

External aid. The level of New Zealand aid is reviewed annually. The amount for the recurrent budget in financial year 1976-77 was $3.7 million. Grants are made for social services and ordinary administrative expenditure, plus grants and loans for capital works and economic development. In addition the Australian and the Netherlands governments and various International Agencies are providing assistance to encourage economic development in the Cook Islands.

Currency. New Zealand currency is used in the group. Besides the circulation of notes for 20, 10, 5, 2 and 1 dollar and New Zealand cents, there are Cook Island coins for $1 and 50, 20, 10, 5, 2 and 1 cent in silver and $100 in gold.

Banks. The National Bank of New Zealand and the government Post Office Savings Bank operate in the islands.

Development plan. The National Development Corporation Act was passed in 1975 to set up this new agency. Its purpose is to manage some of the existing trading departments and to help islanders and other residents establish small businesses and industries through loan finance and management advisory assistance. In 1977, Asian Development Bank aid was approved to help establish the N.D.C.

International organisations. At the beginning of 1980, the United Nations Development Programme was represented in Rarotonga by Mr. Don Hunter,

COOK ISLANDS — IMPORTS AND EXPORTS (In $'000)

	1970	1974	1978
Imports	5,766	n.a.	18,200
Exports	2,692	2,516	2,400

of New Zealand, Statistical Adviser, UNDP/UNFPA; Mr. P. Sirikige, of Thailand, civil engineer; Mr. K. G. J. de Silva and Mr. Ruwan R. Abeyratne, both of Sri Lanka, draftsmen/surveyors; Mr. W. Jonsay, of the Philippines, agricultural extension officer (UNDP/FAO); Mr. J. A. Gosselin, of New Zealand, Secretary of External Affairs; Mr. M. Mitchell, of New Zealand, Advocate-General; Mr. J. M. Dado, of the Philippines, Financial Secretary; Mr. A. B. Orth, of the United States, fisheries biologist; Mr. Y. Ogawa, of Japan, master fisherman; Mr. K. Kawasaki, bait specialist; Mr. Miles Nesbit, of the United States, captain/owner, fisheries resources feasibility study ship; Mr. T. Videnov, of Bulgaria, sanitary engineer, WHO; Mr. A. D. Fortes, of Tanzania, motor maintenance mechanic, UNDP/FAO; Mr. A. C. Ramachandran, of India, motor maintenance mechanic, UNDP/FAO.

Postage stamps. Sales of Cook Islands postage stamps are an important source of revenue. A philatelic bureau at Avarua handles sales to philatelists. Cook Islands coinage is also sought by collectors.

TRANSPORT. On Rarotonga, a 32 km sealed road, the Ara Tapu, encircles the island's coastline. In addition, a centuries-old stone roadway around the island, the Ara Metua, is sealed between Avatiu and Black Rock.

Local public transport includes hire cars, taxis, scooters, buses and horse and buggy rides.

Overseas airlines. Rarotonga is served by Air New Zealand which flies from Auckland, Nadi, Honolulu and Papeete, using DC 8 and DC 10 aircraft.

Domestic airline. Cook Islands Airways, owned by Air New Zealand and the Cook Islands Government, flies between Rarotonga, Aitutaki, Atiu, Mitiaro, Mauke and Mangaia, using Britten-Norman Islander aircraft and Cessna 337. There is also a flying school which owns a Cessna 172 and provides scenic flights.

Airfields. The jet airport, opened to international traffic in 1973, is on the western side of the town of Avarua, Rarotonga. It can take DC 10 aircraft and has a runway of 2,377 m, some of it built out into the lagoon. There are airstrips at Aitutaki and Penrhyn capable of handling large aircraft. New airstrips at Atiu (825 m, grass), Mitiaro (914 m, rolled coral) and Mangaia (792 m rolled coral) are used by the smaller inter-island services. An airstrip is

COOK ISLANDS — MAIN EXPORTS (In $'000)

	1971	1974	1976
Bananas	316	117	84
Copra	142	300	106
Fresh citrus	124	15	2
Pearl shell	6	46	81
Pineapple juice	108	107	154
Citrus juice	509	604	725
Other juice	23	—	4
Fruit, canned	86	397	189
Fruit pulp	93	112	39
Clothing	550	779	430
Handcrafts	42.1	91	41
Footwear	—	—	72

COOK ISLANDS — MAIN IMPORTS (In $'000)

	1969	1970	1973
Foodstuffs	817	1,360	1,089
Textiles	335	512	508
Oil, petrol, etc.	336	275	229
Tobacco, cigarettes	91	—	69
Vehicles, parts	144	—	195
Timber, cement, etc.	127	137	130

COOK ISLANDS — REVENUE AND EXPENDITURE (In $'000)

	Revenue	Expenditure	N.Z. Aid
1972	3,928	5,578	1,650
1974	4,348	7,442	1,838
1976-77	10,980	10,980	3,700
1977-78	12,515	12,135	3,350
1979-80	15,200(est)	16,200	n.a.

planned for Rakahanga.

Port facilities. The port of entry for the Cook Group is Rarotonga. Rarotonga has two harbours, Avatiu and Avarua. The roadstead off Avarua provides open anchorages for vessels of any size except in strong northerly winds. Loading is by lighters, which use a 20 m concrete wharf at Avarua.

Avatiu harbour has been widened and deepened in recent years to take vessels up to 75 m in length and up to 4.5 m draught at the eastern wharf. The western side of the basin takes yachts and fishing vessels. In June 1977 further work began on widening and deepening the access channel into the harbour.

The harbour at Mangaia is used mainly for the export of pineapples.

Apart from the substantial harbour improvements undertaken in recent years in Rarotonga, extra work has been carried out in the outer islands, particularly Aitutaki and Atiu. A new harbour was built at Atiu by the New Zealand Army.

In all the islands there is a problem from the shallow depth of water, which limits access to the lagoon to cargo-carrying lighters. It is possible for small to medium-sized vessels to enter the lagoons of Penrhyn and Suwarrow but a clearance should be sought and local advice obtained.

Shipping services. The NZ Shipping Corporation operates fortnightly cargo services from Auckland to Rarotonga and Aitutaki with two vessels.

Local shipping. Inter-island services are provided by two vessels operated by Silk and Boyd Ltd., the "Manutea" and "Mataora"; by the South Pacific Shipping Corporation's "Fetu Moana" and "Tiare Moana" and by a newcomer, SPINCO, wholesalers, of Rarotonga and Manu'ae, with the "Tokerau".

COMMUNICATIONS. There is a telephone service in Rarotonga. Smaller networks operate throughout the group. Overseas telephone calls are made direct through Cable & Wireless. Every inhabited island has a radio station, maintaining direct communication with Rarotonga, which in turn connects with all other countries. Postal and telegraph services are available on all the islands.

A telex service from Rarotonga operates worldwide via New Zealand.

Radio, TV. The government-owned radio station 1ZC, "The call of the Cook Islands", broadcasts daily in English and Maori. News programmes include bulletins from New Zealand and Australian national stations.

Newspapers. The "Cook Islands News" is government-owned and printed in English, with occasional Maori. It is issued daily, except Saturday and Sunday, by the Cook Islands Broadcasting and Newspaper Corporation. "Photo News" appears weekly.

There are two weekly newspapers published by the main political parties, "The Weekender" by the Democratic Party and "Te Akatauira" by the Cook Islands Party.

WATER, ELECTRICITY. Rarotonga has water galleries, and intakes direct from streams. Aitutaki is supplied by bores and tanks filled by rain from house roofs. All other islands use tanks.

Power is generated by diesel, supplying current of 240 volts AC in Rarotonga. Generators on Aitutaki, Mauke, Atiu and Rakahanga supply AC only.

PERSONALITIES AND ORGANISATIONS

GOVERNMENT LEADERS

Dr. Thomas R. A. H. Davis: Premier, Minister of Finance, Minister for External Affairs.

Dr. P. Robati: Deputy Premier, Minister of Health, Minister for Public Service, Postmaster-General.

I. Short: Minister of Agriculture and Fisheries, Minister for Tourism.

V. Ingram: Minister for Justice, Minister for Labour, Industries and Commerce.

T. Tangaroa: Minister for Internal Affairs and Outer Islands Affairs.

P. Pokino: Minister for Works, Electricity and Survey.

T. Simiona: Minister for Education and Leader of the Legislative Assembly.

COOK ISLANDS LEGISLATIVE ASSEMBLY

Speaker: David Hosking.
Clerk of the Assembly: Joe Caffery.

Aitutaki: Ngereteina Puna, Kura Strickland, Geoffrey Henry.
Atiu: Tangata Simiona, Vainerere Tangatapoto.
Mangaia: Matepi Matepi, Papamama Pokino.
Manihiki: George Ellis.
Mauke: Tupui Henry.
Mitiaro: Tiki Tetava.

Penrhyn: Tangaroa Tangaroa.
Pukapuka (and Nassau Is.): Inatio Akaruru.
Pualkura: Harry Napa, William Heather.
Rakahanga: Pupuke Robati.
Takitumu: Iaveta Short, Teariki Matenga.
Teautonga (and Palmerston Is.): Dr. T. Davis, Vincent Ingram, Teariki Piri, Fred Goodwin.

JUDICIARY

Chief Judge of the High Court: Sir Gaven Donne.
Judge of the Land Court: Judge Dillon (acting).

ADMINISTRATION OFFICIALS

Secretary to Cabinet and Clerk of the Executive Council: J. Cafferey (acting).
Advocate-General: M. Mitchell.

SECRETARIES TO THE PRINCIPAL MINISTRIES

Premier's Dept.: J. Caffery (acting).
Financial Secretary: M. Dado.
Health: Dr. G. Koteka.
Education: T. Short.
Supportive Services: G. Cowan (acting).
Justice and Lands: Nikau Tangaroa.
Internal Affairs: T. Manu.
Trade, Industries, Labour and Commerce: Richard Chapman.
Agriculture and Fisheries: K. Tama (acting)
Public Service Commission: J. Macauley
Survey and Physical Planning: George Cowan.
Electric Power Supply: T. Westbury (acting).
Superintendent of Police: J. Butterworth.
Collector of Customs: T. Tutaka.
Collector of Inland Revenue: J. Ditchburn (acting).
Government Anthropologist: R. Moekaa.
Cook Islands Broadcasting and News Corp: S. Sadaraka.
General Manager, Primary Produce Marketing Board: P. Joseph (acting).
Cook Islands Airways, General Manager: G. B. Ward.
General Manager, Tourist Authority: T. Okotai.

OUTER ISLANDS CHIEF ADMINISTRATION OFFICERS

(These were known formerly as Resident Agents or Clerks-in-charge).
Aitutaki: M. Simiona.
Atiu: N. Tearapo.
Mangaia: T. John.
Mauke: T. Ngaoire.
Mitiaro: R. Pokoam.
Palmerston: Bill Marsters.
Manihiki: S. Williams.
Rakahanga: T. Arahu.
Pukapuka: R. Tutar.
Penrhyn: W. Benetito.

CHURCH LEADERS

Cook Islands Christian Church: Rev. T. Teauariki. Roman Catholic Church: Bishop D. G. Browne. Seventh-day Adventists: Pastor G. Porter (President). Church of Latter Day Saints: President T. Strickland.

BUSINESS ASSOCIATIONS

Rarotonga Chamber of Commerce Inc., Public Service Association.

SERVICE CLUBS

Jaycees, Rotary, Returned Soldiers Association, Child Welfare Association, Crippled Children's Association, Hospital Comforts Fund, Hibiscus Club.

SCIENTIFIC INSTITUTIONS

Library and Museum Society.

SPORTING FACILITIES

Rarotonga Sailing Club, C. I. Sport Association, Rarotonga Bowling Club Inc., Rarotonga Golf Club (9-hole), Rarotonga Owners and Trainers Club (horse racing), Muri beach races every three months.

CULTURAL GROUPS

C.I. National Arts Theatre (dancing), Parent-Teacher Association, Women's Federation.

YOUTH ORGANISATIONS

C.I. Youth Organisation, Girl Guides, Boys Brigade (Protestant), Boy Scouts (Roman Catholic), Girls Brigade, Junior Missionary Volunteers (S.D.A.).

PARKS

A national park is pending for Rarotonga.

CONVENTION FACILITIES.

The Rarotongan Hotel conference room, capacity 200 people, sound system, projectors, typists facilities, etc.

RAROTONGA BUSINESS DIRECTORY

Duty free stores
Cook Island Trading Corp. Ltd.
J. & P. Ingram & Co.
Smugglers Hut.
South Seas International.
Johnsons Duty Free.

Clothing factories
Scott & Watson Ltd., at Avarua.
Cashmore McNicoll, at Arorangi.

Shipping & Airlines
Silk & Boyd, Inter-Island vessels.
Waterfront Commission, Agents NZ Shipping Corporation.
Union Citco Travel Ltd., Agents overseas lines.
Air New Zealand.
Cook Island Airways.

Travel agents and tour operators
Union Citco Travel Ltd.
Star Travel Ltd.
Tipani Tours Ltd.
Exham Wichman.

Motor vehicles
Cook Island Motor Centre, Panama.
Arorangi Auto Works Ltd., Arorangi.

Beco Ltd.
Auto Marine Services, Nikao.
Sam Rere.
Seaview Auto Works.
Auto Parts Ltd.
Fair Deal Panelbeaters.

Banks

National Bank of New Zealand Ltd., Avarua.
C.I. Post Office Savings Bank, Avarua.

Island curio manufacturers and retailers

Island Crafts Ltd.
Tiki Industries Ltd.
Cook Islands Women's Federation.
Cook Island Government, Cultural Division.

Photographic Studios

Rohea's Photography, Avarua.

Footwear

Winleigh Products Ltd.

Canning

Kia Orana Foods Ltd., Avarua.

Building Contractors

Mainline, Brown & Dogherty, Arorangi.
John Short Construction, Titekaveka.
Customline Finishes, Arorangi.
Errol Young Builders.
Rarotonga Concrete & Construction Ltd.
Teepee Homes Ltd.
Cook Island Government Housing Authority.

Plumbers

J. Estall & Sons.
M. Wilson.
Pacific Traders & Services Ltd.

Painters

Rarotonga Painters & Decorators Ltd.
Keil Painters & Paperhangers, Panama.

Plasterer

Owen Webb, Matavera.

Petroleum Importers

Shell Oil Co Ltd, Avatiu.
B.P. (South West Pacific) Ltd.
Mobil Oil (Australia) Ltd.

Liquor Wholesaler

CI Government, Liquor Supply, Avatiu.

Bakeries

Avarua Bakery.
Atua Bakery.
Blue & White Bakery.

Soft Drinks

Tropic Enterprises, Avatiu.
Rays & Co. Ltd.

Restaurants

Trailways Hotel, Kii Kii.
The Outrigger, Arorangi.
Jade Restaurant.
The Rarotongan.
Beach Hotel.
Vai-ma Steak House.
Happy Valley Restaurant.

Grocery Importers

Rusco Ltd.
Wholesale Rarotonga Ltd.
Spinco Ltd.

Supermarkets

Moneysaver — Leaders Ltd.

General merchants

Cook Islands Trading Corporation Ltd.
J. P. Ingram & Co.
Avatiu General Traders.

Laundry & drycleaners

Blue Pacific Laundry Ltd.

Rental operators

Cook Island Rental Car Ltd. — cars.
Stars Travel Ltd. — cars/motorbikes.
Polynesian Rentals Ltd. — cars.
Rarotonga Hire Centre — motorbikes.
Island Merchants Ltd. — motorbikes.
Johannasons Enterprises Ltd. — motorbikes.
Cycle Hires — bicycles.
Jay Bee Auto — bicycles.

Boiler makers

Rarotonga Welding & Steel Construction Ltd.

Barristers & solicitors

Short & Tylor.
Clarke & Co.
V. Ingram.
M. Turner

HISTORY. The Cook Islands did not exist as a political entity until European times. Although the people today are all of a common Maori ancestry, at the time when the first Europeans arrived, most islands were very much places unto themselves. Each island should be examined separately, particularly before New Zealand annexation in 1901, when the boundaries of what are now the Cook Islands were laid down. The history of each island is set out in the "Islands in Detail" section which follows this general history.

From 1823 onwards most of the islands came under the spiritual and, to a large extent, the temporal control of the LMS missionaries, who were stationed on Rarotonga and supervised the Hervey Islands Mission of the London Missionary Society.

It was during this time that the mission-inspired "blue" laws were codified on the islands, with many of their features remaining to this day in practice, if not by legal sanction. F. J. Moss, the British Resident in 1893, described the police appointed by the Church on Rarotonga, "This police, irresponsible and under no direct control, incessantly spied upon and harassed the people. The fines they could extract from the people formed their sole pay and were divided at stated times between the Ariki, the Judge and the police". The missionaries also sought to protect the islanders from the "evil" influences of Europeans by controlling the entry upon islands of traders and men from the ships, especially the whalers, which frequently called. The ariki in some cases also tried to stop young men from joining ships as crew members.

Protectorate declared. In the 1880s there was increasing concern about the possible intrusion by the French into the area and New Zealand began to take an interest in the group. A British Protectorate was declared on Rarotonga in October, 1888, by Captain Bourke, of HMS "Hyacinth". The protectorate was extended to include all the islands in the southern Cook group, and they became known as the Federation of the Cook Islands. During the period of the British Protectorate an elected federal parliament came into being, and made laws for the whole group, although each island had the right of self-government. A system of public schools was set up, a hospital board established and postage stamps issued.

Frederick J. Moss was appointed by the New Zealand Government to be the British Resident in the Cook Islands. In 1897, Moss drafted a bill to create a court having exclusive jurisdiction over cases involving foreign residents, with the British Resident to be the judge. The Cook Islands parliament refused to pass the bill and Moss dissolved the parliament, with the result that the ariki petitioned the Governor in New Zealand to remove Moss. Sir James Prendergast, the Chief Justice of New Zealand, conducted an enquiry into Cook Islands affairs and subsequently Moss was withdrawn and replaced by Lieutenant-Colonel W. E. Gudgeon.

New Zealand annexation. Annexation by New Zealand became an immediate goal and in 1900 the Rarotongan ariki were persuaded to petition New Zealand to annex the Cook Islands, and on 11 June, 1901, the Cook Islands formally became part of New Zealand, the boundaries being extended to include the northern islands. The British Resident became the Resident Commissioner and the old laws of the Cook Islands continued in force, subject to the provisions of the Cook Islands Act, which was passed in the same year.

In 1915, an act of the New Zealand Parliament consolidated the laws concerning the Cook Islands and provided for the appointment of a Minister for the Cook Islands, with the Resident Commissioner being responsible to the minister. The functions of the minister were later assumed by the Minister for Island Territories.

During World War I, many Cook Islands men served overseas and most of the islands have honour boards which list their names. In World War II, the New Zealand Government decided not to recruit Cook Islanders and only a handful served.

In 1946, a Legislative Council was set up, with the Resident Commissioner as President, with the members of the council representing all the islands and government departments. 1957 saw the creation of a Legislative Assembly, with extended powers and in 1962, as a first step towards self-government, an Executive Committee of the Legislative Assembly, to advise the government, was set up. The purpose of the Executive Committee was to advise on policy matters and to draw up proposals for the annual appropriations of funds by the assembly.

In December 1962, New Zealand's delegate to the United Nations told the Trusteeship Council that the Cook Islands would have internal self-government within three years. 1964 was marked by the withdrawal of the Resident Commissioner and all official members from the Legislative Assembly and the Executive Committee, under a Leader of Government Business, became a fully operative Cabinet. Provision was also made for the election, under universal suffrage, of a new Legislative Assembly of 22 members.

Self-government approaches. The New Zealand Parliament passed legislation in November 1964, granting a new constitution to the Cook Islands. Observers from the United Nations supervised the first general election for the Legislative Assembly on 20 April, 1965, with the Cook Islands Party, led by Mr. (later Sir) Albert Henry winning a substantial majority. However, although Mr. Henry led the party, he could not stand as a candidate because of residential qualifications.

One of the first acts of the new assembly was to amend the constitution by deleting the clause relating to the length of residence of electoral candidates. In June 1965, Mrs. Marguerite Story, the sister of Mr. Henry, resigned from her newly-won place in the assembly, a by-election was held and Mr. Henry upon his election became Premier of the Cook Islands. Mrs. Story became Speaker.

The Legislative Assembly had been offered the choice of four forms of self-determination for the Cook Islands – full independence; integration with some other Pacific Islands nation; full integration within New Zealand; and internal self-government. The assembly chose the last alternative and the Constitution as amended came into force on 4 August, 1965 giving the Cook Islands full responsibilities for internal affairs, New Zealand assumes responsibilities for external affairs and defence, New Zealand undertakes to provide the Cook Islands with financial support and Cook Islanders remain New Zealand citizens with unrestricted rights of entry into New Zealand.

In 1965, the constitution was also amended to provide for the establishment of a House of Ariki – an ariki being a paramount chief, there being several ariki on Rarotonga and a paramount ariki on each of the outer islands. The one exception is Penrhyn, where there is now no ariki, the line having been broken by the raid made upon the population there by Peruvian slave-raiders. The House of Ariki has no legislative powers – it considers any matters relating to the welfare of the people which the Legislative Assembly puts before it, and it gives its opinion and recommendations to the assembly. The House of Ariki also makes recommendations to the Assembly on the customs, traditions and land tenure. In short, the House of Ariki is a consultative body.

Under the constitution, the position of High Commissioner to the Cook Islands was created. The High Commissioner was to represent New Zealand in the Cook Islands and as the representative of the Queen he also filled the role of Head of State. It requires a two-thirds majority of the Legislative Assembly to amend the constitution. However, the office of New Zealand High Commissioner was discontinued in 1975. In 1974, Sir Albert Henry called a snap election with the intention of increasing his majority in the assembly, thereby ensuring himself of the numbers required to carry through amendments. In the result, the ruling Cook Islands Party lost one seat, thereby failing to achieve the required number of seats to bring into being any amendment.

The Cook Islands Party won its fifth successive election on March 30, 1978, but was unseated the following July by Chief Justice Gaven Doone for electoral corruption and the Democratic Party members, elected in March, became the government with Dr. Thomas Davis as Premier. Sir Albert Henry and seven of his fellow party polititians were arraigned on the corruption charges. Subsequently, the Queen deprived Sir Albert of his knighthood.

Population outflow. Since the end of World War II, Cook Islanders have been migrating to New Zealand in ever-increasing numbers. They have been able to find employment in hospitals, as drivers, and in large industries, especially the timber-milling plants. This loss of a very significant portion of the economically active section of the population was accelerated by the introduction by Air New Zealand in 1973 of scheduled services to New Zealand.

The Cook Islands Government has become very concerned about the effects upon the economy and social life of the country, and especially of some of the outer islands, of this continuing flow of Cook Islanders to New Zealand.

MAIN ISLANDS IN DETAIL

RAROTONGA. Rarotonga with its rugged, bush-clad hills and deep valleys, is often described as one of the most beautiful islands in the Pacific. Circular in shape, it is about 32 kilometres in circumference and has a total land area of 67 sq km. In most places the fringing reef is close to the shore and the lagoon is shallow. At Muri the lagoon widens out and the sailing boats of the Rarotonga Sailing Club race on its waters. There is a narrow band of coral debris beyond the beach. This is backed by fertile land, which is used for growing food crops, or for commercial citrus plantations.

Ancient taro beds, still in use, are to be found in several of the valleys which penetrate into the interior, with several streams, notably the Avana and Avatiu, making their way to the sea. Fresh water from the streams inhibits the growth of coral and has formed the openings in the reef at Avatiu, Avarua and Ngatangila. In earlier times ships were able to enter the lagoon at Ngatangila, but the entrance is now silted up. Legend has it that some Polynesians sailed to New Zealand from Ngatangila to form part of the Maori population there.

There are some most exciting climbs to be made in the hills, which rise to 652 metres at Te Magna, 638 metres at Te Atakura, 509 metres at Maungaroa and 485 metres at Ikurangi, an isolated and dominating peak behind Avarua.

Avarua was previously extensively used as a harbour for the lighters which worked overseas ships but now the harbour at Avatiu has been dredged, sheet piling walls installed and wharf sheds built. Sizable vessels now tie up at the wharf in Avatiu harbour, which is also a favourite haven for cruising yachts. There are ablution facilities available on the wharf for the crews of visiting yachts.

For many years the LMS missionary, Rev. John Williams, was credited with being the first European to "discover" Rarotonga on 25 July, 1823. However, historical reconstruction has shown that the mutineers on the 'Bounty' were at Rarotonga in 1789, but did not land.

The Sydney schooner 'Cumberland', Captain Philip Goodenough, was at Rarotonga in 1814, seeking a cargo of sandalwood. Violence broke out between the Maoris and the crew and several people from the schooner were killed.

When John Williams was off Rarotonga on the 'Endeavour' in 1823, Papeiha, who had previously worked as a Christain teacher on Aitutaki, volunteered to swim ashore and he is now revered as the first man to preach the doctrine in Rarotonga.

A tar-sealed coastal road encircles the island and inland the second circuminsular road, the Ara Metua is considered to have been built under the leadership of the chieftain Toi about the 11th century A.D.

During World War II an airstrip was constructed at Rarotonga and this has been progressively upgraded and is now the international airport.

According to legend, the present Rarotongan Maori population are the descendants of two Polynesian chiefs, Karika from Samoa, and Tangiia from Raiatea, who arrived at Rarotonga about the end of the 12th century and combined forces to conquer the earlier Polynesian inhabitants. The two invading parties were united through marriage of Tangiia to Karika's daughter. It is from these two parties that the present Rarotongan tribal divisions each with its paramount ariki, trace their descent. The ownership of land in Rarotonga remains in the hands of Rarotongans, but many of the people who live on the island today are from the outer islands, and most of these people do not have land tenure rights on Rarotonga.

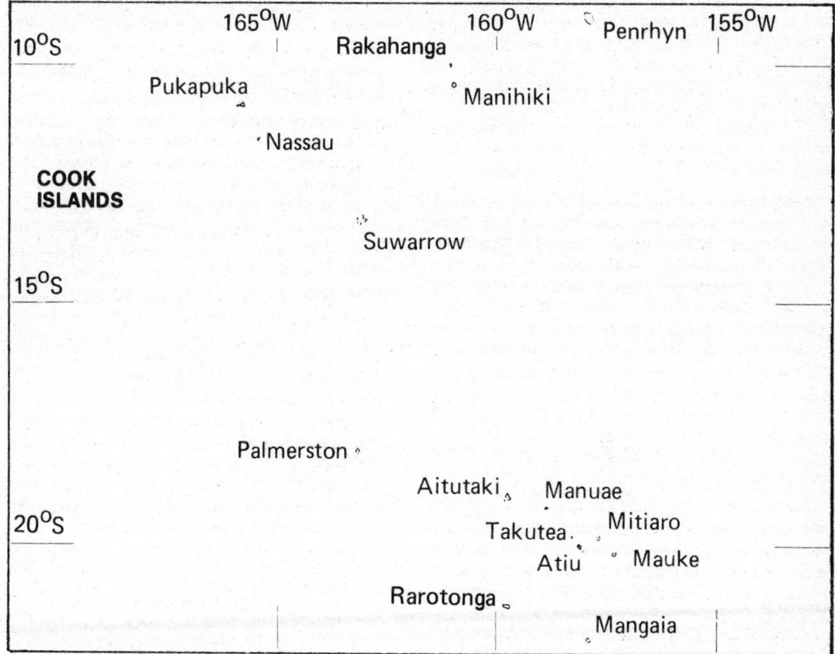

When the missionaries came to Rarotonga, the people were domiciled in the house-sites spread throughout the island and the missionaries were able to coerce the people into moving into villages which were set up around the early churches and Sunday schools. The people still retain land rights in their tapere, or land-holding units, but land rights have become very complex because of the registration of multiple inheritance.

Various export crops have been grown on Rarotonga since the mid 18th century, including cotton, copra, limes and oranges. The island once received many visits from whaling vessels seeking provisions or recruits for their crews.

It is estimated that in 1823 the population of Rarotonga numbered about 6,000, but as a result of the ravages of introduced diseases and other causes by 1893, F. J. Moss, the British Resident, stated that the population was probably less than 2,000.

Since World War II the greatest emphasis has been placed upon revitalising the citrus industry and today almost all of the fruit is processed at a factory at Avarua, which also processes citrus, pineapples and other fruit from the outer islands. There are two clothing factories and two handicraft workshops which provide some industrial work for people on Rarotonga but by far the largest employer is the Cook Islands Government.

There is a modern hospital situated on the site of the former turberculosis sanitorium on the hill overlooking Black Rock. There are eight primary schools in the villages and Tereora College and the Nikao Teachers' College are located at Nikao. The Catholic Church has St. Joseph's Primary School and Nukatere College at Avarua and the SDA Church has a small school at Titikaveka. The buildings of the Cook Islands Library and Museum Society occupy a most beautiful site to the rear of the old Avarua Church.

In the main settlement at Avarua the large stores are able to supply almost all requirements from stock, with meat and other perishables being supplied principally by the Government Freezer. A daily newspaper is published in Avarua, which is also the site of the studios of Radio Cook Islands.

Each of the villages is marked out by its coral limestone church of the Cook Islands Christian Church. Most of these buildings are over 100 years old and have been constructed in an intriguing variety of architectural styles. In each of the villages there are also large meeting halls, where dances and various meetings and ceremonial occasions take place. There are two large cinemas in Avarua.

Electricity and a continuous telephone service are available in all inhabited areas of the island. There are many sporting facilities and the Rarotonga Golf Course is unique in that its greens and fairways are scattered among the many masts and stays of the wireless station.

The people of Rarotonga and Palmerston Island are represented by nine members in the Legislative Assembly of the Cook Islands.

MAUKE. London Missionary Society missionary, Rev. John Williams, was on a voyage of exploration in 1823, in what is now the southern Cook Islands, on the British vessel 'Endeavour', Captain John Dibbs. They landed on Mauke on 23 July, 1823, when the work of converting the inhabitants to Christianity was begun. The people of Mauke, together with those of Mitiaro, had suffered over the years from raids by the warriors of Atiu. The Atiuans had established a form of sovereignty over Mauke, and after the appearance of the Europeans in the area, the Maukeans were able to enlist their aid to resist the incursions of the Atiuans.

Mauke is low-lying, with a land surface of 2,032 hectares, situated 241 kilometres north-east of Rarotonga. The geological formation of the island is similar to that of Atiu and Mangaia, with some fine caves located in the cliffs of the makatea.

Since the mid 1950s efforts have been made to expand the agricultural production of Mauke and plantings of citrus have been brought into production. Trial plots of peanuts, tobacco and ginger were also made but none of these led to further large-scale commercial exploitation. The ownership of land on part of Mauke has been consolidated and a small herd of shorthorn beef cattle is run there.

Landing on Mauke is difficult, as open boats have to use a boat passage, or at times land upon the open reef. The island has a 914 m airstrip.

All the people live in Areora, which has a school, hospital, government offices and store. There are two churches, belonging to the Catholic Church and the Cook Islands Christian Church. The latter church building is of great interest as, when it was built, the two principal groups in the congregation could not agree about the style of construction. As a consequence it was built in two distinct styles at either end, with the pulpit straddling the midpoint between the contending sides.

In the past, the children of secondary school age attended the Junior High School at Atiu, or Tereora College on Rarotonga. In 1975, Sir Albert Henry announced that in future most Mauke children would receive their secondary education on their home island. The people of Mauke are represented by a member in the Cook Islands Legislative Assembly.

The author Julian Dashwood (pseudonym Julian Hillas) lived on Mauke for many years and describes life there in his 'South Seas Paradise' (1964).

MITIARO. The London Mission Society missionary, Rev. John Williams, was on the first vessel to visit Mitiaro, the 'Endeavour', Captain John Dibbs, on 19 July, 1823. The island, which has an area of 2,455 hectares, is situated 229 kilometres north-east of Rarotonga. It is low-lying and much of the surface is taken up with a cliff of old coral, up to about six metres in height. The interior of the island is largely swampy and there is a brackish lake in which are found the itiki, or Mitiaro eels, which are regarded as a great delicacy in the Cook Islands. There are a few patches of fertile soil, in which the people grow bananas, which form the principal source of carbohydrates in the Mitiaro diet.

There has been little European exploitation of the island, as its commercial potential is very small. Attempts over the years to establish cash crops such as copra, pepper and allspice, have been marked by failure. The best known European resident on Mitiaro in earlier years was Viggo Rasmussen, a schooner skipper.

Landings are made by open boat through the boat passage in the reef near the settlement. The island has a 914 m airstrip.

The life style of Mitiaro is dominated by the food cycle. The men spend much time at sea in one-man canoes catching tuna and other large fish, or bringing bunches of bananas to their homes along the causeway, which has been constructed across the swamp.

Among the Cook Islanders, the people of Mitiaro are renowned for the manufacture of piere, or dried bananas, which are tightly packed in a wrapping of banana leaves.

There is a school on Mitiaro, a dispensary, a wireless station and government offices. Mitiaro is represented by a member in the Legislative Assembly of the Cook Islands.

TAKUTEA. Uninhabited, Takutea is a small island of 125 hectares, about 41 kilometres north-west of Atiu. James Cook sighted Tatutea and landed on the island on 31 March, 1777. In 1903, as Ngamaru, Ariki of Atiu, had presented the island to the Crown. W. E. Gudgeon, the Resident Commissioner, proposed that Takutea be made a penal colony for the Cook Islands. However, there were numerous claims by Atiuans to rights on Takutea and the Land Court of the Cook Islands awarded the island to the people of Atiu as a whole. An elected committee administers the island and, since 1955, parties of Atiuans have visited the island at about yearly intervals to gather copra and the red tail feathers of the frigate birds which nest there.

Takutea has no safe anchorages. The waters near the island are a bountiful fishing ground.

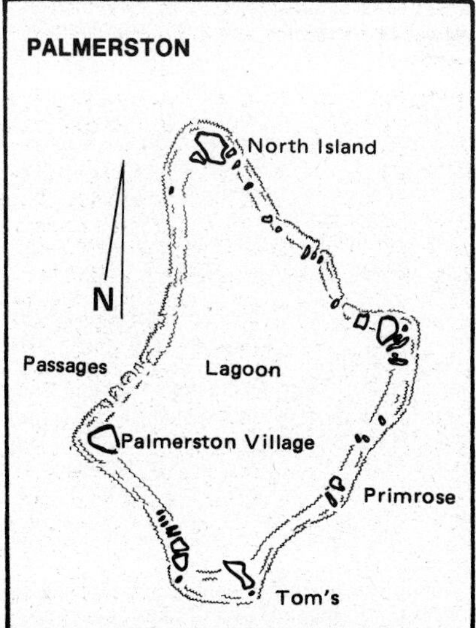

PALMERSTON ISLAND. Palmerston Island is a small coral atoll of about 225 hectares, situated 434 kilometres north-west of Rarotonga. It was uninhabited when it was discovered by James Cook on 16 June, 1774, during his second voyage of discovery. There is no evidence of any previous permanent occupation by Polynesians.

Several islets are situated on the fringing reef, with the present inhabitants residing on Home Islet. Several attempts were made to exploit Palmerston Island during the first half of the nineteenth century and one of these set up by Captain Michael Folger, of the Sydney vessel 'Daphne', in 1811, resulted in violence and murder among the Europeans placed on the island.

In 1862 an Englishman, William Marsters, took up residence on the atoll and eventually established there his family by three Polynesian wives. Marsters divided his family into three clans, the "head", the "middle" and the "tail", and drew up family laws, which forbade members of a clan marrying within the clan. The Marsters family, who speak a local form of English, have remained in occupation of the island.

In 1953, the license issued in 1888 to William Marsters, confirming his rights of occupation, expired and was not renewed. Instead, an amendment to the Cook Islands Act in 1954 vested the island in the inhabitants (that is, the Marsters' family) as customary land, except for 4.45 hectares set aside for Administration purposes.

Over the years a number of ships have been wrecked on Palmerston Island, and several of the major buildings, including the meeting house and church, are largely built of shipwreck timbers.

The Palmerston Island men are noted boatmen and boat-builders. Many of the Marsters people have moved away from their home island, and there are colonies of the family on Rarotonga, Aitutaki and Penrhyn Island.

The island is included in the Rarotonga electorate for the purposes of representation in the Cook Islands Legislative Assembly.

SUWARROW. Lieutenant Mikhail Lazarev, of the Russian vessel 'Suvarov' discovered the uninhabited coral atoll, now known as Suwarrow, on 28 September, 1814. H. B. Sterndale, who spent some time on the island later in the century, reported the existence of former coral limestone buildings, and this has led to debate as to whether or not Polynesians or earlier Europeans had been on Suwarrow before Lazarev landed there.

There have been several shipwrecks on the atoll and stories have been generated of buried pirate treasure and loot from shipwrecks. Various attempts were made to find treasure on Suwarrow during the nineteenth century and outbreaks of assault and murder ensued. The Auckland trading company of Henderson and Macfarlane made use of the island as a trading post during the latter part of last century.

The island was declared to be a British Protectorate on 22 April, 1889, and part of Anchorage Island, the principal islet, is still an Admiralty reserve. It was occupied for some time by Lever Bros. Company, when experiments with Torres Strait shell were carried on, unfortunately without success. There is some pearl-shell of good quality in the lagoon, but only a little sporadic div-

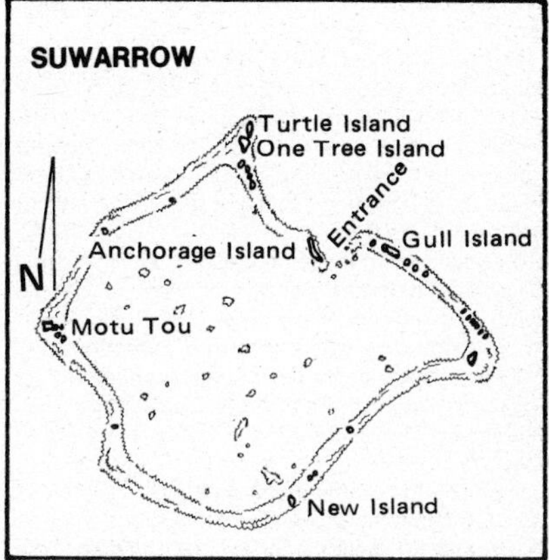

ing is done. Until the 1930s A. B. Donald Ltd. (Auckland) leased the island for copra-making but the ravages of termites have made it necessary to prohibit the export of copra from these islands.

Suwarrow has suffered severely from the effects of hurricanes and much of the atoll has been eroded away. During the 1942 hurricane the group of Europeans on the atoll were able to survive only by climbing into the branches of a large Barringtonia tree.

In more recent times Suwarrow has received some prominence because of the interest taken in the life-style of the late Mr Tom Neale, who lived there for long periods, often as a hermit. His adventures are told in the book 'An Island to Oneself'. He died at Rarotonga in December, 1977.

The atoll is a bird sanctuary and there are great flocks of tropical sea-birds, including terns, frigate birds and bosun birds.

Vessels may go through the passage and anchor in the lagoon near Anchorage Island, but this is not safe in northerly weather.

NASSAU. The first sighting of Nassau appears to have been made by Captain Louis Coutance, in the ship 'Adele,' owned by the Mauritius firm Merle, Cabot and Company, in 1803. The island, about 45 kilometres south-east of Pukapuka, is a coral outcrop of about 225 hectares, which has no lagoon. There are no safe anchorages and boat landings are made across the open reef.

The island was annexed for Great Britain in 1892 by Captain Gibson, of HMS 'Curacao'. On his third visit, in 1881, Rev. W. Wyatt Gill (LMS), of Rarotonga, found the island to be occupied by John Ellacott, an American, in charge of a few Pukapukans. Ellacott had registered, in 1873, a claim for protection of his occupation of the island with the US Consul in Tahiti. He sold Nassau to H. G. Moors in 1892, and Moors in turn sold it to Messrs. Rye and Stunzer; it later passed from them to Burns, Philp and Co.

There is evidence that in pre-contact times the Pukapukans made occasional visits to Nassau and in 1945 the island was purchased on behalf of the people of Pukapuka by the New Zealand Government for £2,000; the Pukapukans then raised £2,000 from the sale of copra from Nassau and repaid the amount.

It was intended that the people from Pukapuka would spend limited periods on Nassau, before being returned to the home island. However, many of the colonists expressed a desire to remain on Nassau and a permanent population has now been established, although fears have been expressed about the food resources available there.

A school has been built on Nassau, wireless links are established with Rarotonga and a medical dresser attends to health matters. The people on Nassau are represented in the Cook Islands Legislative Assembly by the member for Pukapuka.

MANIHIKI. The first European report of the existence of Manihiki is credited to Captain Patrickson, of the ship 'Good Hope' on 13 October, 1822, who named it Humphrey's Island. The atoll was declared to be a British Protectorate and the flag was hoisted by Commander A. C. Clarke, of H.M.S. 'Espeigle' in August, 1889.

Manihiki is a most beautiful coral island, with many motu, or islets, strung along the reef which fringes the lagoon. The total land area is about 140 hectares. Two settlements, Tauhunu and Tukao, have been set up on Manihiki since the advent of the missionaries, who discouraged the people from making frequent boat passages to Rakahanga, some 40 kilometres to the north. The people are said to be the descendants of migrants from Rarotonga, 1,675 kilometres to the south.

During the nineteenth century the population suffered from the activities of blackbirders and Peruvian slave-raiders. It was fitting perhaps, that Captain 'Bully' Hayes, Pacific blackbirder was shipwrecked on Manihiki.

The New Zealand Government blasted boat passages through the fringe reef opposite both villages and these are used for the handling of passengers and cargo. The island produces copra and at various times has been a wealthy source of pearl-shell. However, the pearl-shell trade has fallen away because of reduced prices for shell and as a result of the over-exploitation of the oyster-shell beds. The Manihiki men are skilled divers, both without artificial aids and with the conventional brass helmet diving suit.

For a number of years the Royal New Zealand Air Force maintained a landing area on the lagoon for its Sunderland flying-boats, and this island thus played a vital role in many search and rescue missions in the Pacific.

On a number of occasions, boatloads of Manihikians have been blown away from their island and there have been some remarkable survival voyages. In 1965 four survivors out of a crew of seven men reached Erromanga in the New Hebrides after spending 65 days at sea, with virtually no provisions.

The lagoon abounds with the paua (clam) and the Manihiki people send supplies of the salted shell-fish to friends and relatives on Rarotonga.

Experimental programmes with cultured pearls have been conducted in the lagoon for several years.

There is a hospital at Tauhunu, where the government offices and wireless station are situated, and there are primary schools in the two villages. The people are represented by a member in the Cook Islands Legislative Assembly.

RAKAHANGA. The first European to reach Rakahanga was Spaniard Pedro Fernandez de Quiros on March 2, 1606. One of the chroniclers of the expedition, Torquemada, was so taken with the appearance of the Rakahangans that he called it 'Isla de Gente Hermosa' (Island of the Handsome People).

There were no further European visitors until the Russian, Thaddeus Bellingshausen, called at Rakahanga on 7 August, 1820, and called the island Grand Duke Alexander Island. Rakahanga was declared to be a British protectorate in 1889 by Commander A. C. Clarke, of H.M.S. 'Espeigle'. The island, which has a land surface of 1,085 hectares, lies about 1,120 kilometres north-west of Rarotonga.

In pre-contact times the Maoris lived on Rakahanga and made occasional visits to Manihiki, about 40 kilometres to the south, to gather food and other items. The passage between the two islands has always been chancy and frequently boats have been lost. The missionaries were able to persuade some of the Rakahangan people to take up permanent residence on Manihiki.

The atoll is unusual in that the rather shallow lagoon is almost land-locked. The main boat passage is at the south-west corner, near the settlement. The main cash crop is copra, and the women of Rakahanga, like their kinswomen on Manihiki, are noted for their skill in weaving fine panama-style hats and mats from rito, the young leaves of the coconut palm. The people use coconuts and fish as their main food and they also have plantings of puraka, a coarse variety of taro.

Some attempts have been made to establish pearl-shell beds in the lagoon, but these have been largely unsuccessful, probably because of the unsuitable water conditions.

The burial grounds on Rakahanga are of interest as some of the dead have been placed in grave houses, that is, graves which have been roofed over and which have in them items such as sewing machines and kerosene lamps, which would be of use to the departed in the hereafter.

The island has a school, government offices and a dispensary. Secondary school age pupils attend either the Junior High School at Aitutaki, or Tereora College on Rarotonga. The Catholic priest at Manihiki makes use of any vessels travelling between Manihiki and Rakahanga to visit his congregation on the latter island. Rakahanga is represented by a member in the Cook Islands Legislative Assembly.

It was on the reef at Rakahanga that the Frenchman Eric de Bisschop lost his life after the completion of his epic raft voyage from Polynesia to South America and return. The wreck on Rakahanga is described in Bengt Danielsson's 'From Raft to Raft'.

PUKAPUKA. Pukapuka was the first island in the Cook Islands sighted by Europeans, the expedition of the Spaniard Alvaro de Mendana on 20 August, 1595. Mendana called the island San Bernando. The position of the atoll was confirmed by Commodore Byron on H.M.S. 'Dolphin' on 21 June, 1765, when he named it Isle of Danger. At various times Pukapuka has been known as Danger Island.

The atoll, which has a surface area of about 45 hectares, lies about 1,150 kilometres north-west of Rarotonga. It consists of three motu, or islets, Wale, Motu Ko and Motu Kotawa, each of which is situated at one of the corners of the triangular-shaped lagoon. The atoll has suffered severely from the visitations of hurricanes and a long submerged reef leads to the west to the Toka (sand bank), which appears to have been once part of the main island.

Christianity was established on the island at about the time of the visit there in 1857 of the L.M.S. missionary Rev. Aaron Buzacott. Peruvian slave raiders in 1863 abducted about 100 men and women. The Pukapukans are closely related to the Tokelauans and Samoans and there are marked dialectic differences between the Maori language spoken on Pukapuka and that of the other islands in the Cook group.

The three main tribal subdivisions all live on Wale, but each has planting and other rights to one of the motu, the planting lands being worked at times decreed by the elders of the island. Life is communal and work tasks and food are shared according to a person's status as a man, a woman or a child. Over the centuries the Pukapukans have created an extensive taro swamp on Wale, and all work in the swamp is reserved to the women. The main source of cash income is from the sale of copra and again the proceeds are shared on a communal basis. The Pukapukan men are skilled canoe builders and still use large canoes made from a number of small pieces of wood lashed together with sennit, (braided cordage).

An American expedition conducted solar eclipse observations on Motu Kotawa in 1958.

On the island there is a school, hospital, wireless station and government offices. The Catholic church is quite remarkable for its striking decoration in religious motifs formed by the use of thousands of cowrie shells. This was a labour of love carried out by the Dutch priest, Father Benetio, who was stationed on Pukapuka for many years.

The L.M.S. barque 'John Williams' was wrecked on Pukapuka on 15 May, 1864. The American author, Robert Dean Frisbie, lived on Pukapuka for many years, and he has written with great distinction about life on Pukapuka in 'The Book of Pukapuka', 'Mister Moonlight's Island' and 'The Island of Desire'.

Pukapuka has a representative in the Legislative Assembly. Many Pukapukans have migrated to Rarotonga and most are concentrated in the settlement at Pue, near Avarua.

MANGAIA. Mangaia, the southern-most of the Cook Islands, lies about 177 kilometres east by south-east of Rarotonga and has a total land area of 5,714 hectares. Its highest point, Rangimotia is 169 metres above sea level. The island is surrounded by a narrow fringing reef, backed by formidable cliffs of makatea, or coral limestone, which reach to heights of up to 60 metres, with breadth varying between 60 and 1,500 metres.

Much of the makatea is bare rock, which slopes into areas of sharp, closely packed pinnacles, which are almost impenetrable. Beyond the makatea the land is of red volcanic soil, formed into rolling hills, with several swamps and a small lake situated near the inner wall of the makatea.

In the old days the people had to make their way inland by means of steps cut into the makatea but there is now a road to Oneroa which passes through a cutting blasted through the makatea. The land on Mangaia has not been surveyed nor have land titles been registered with the Cook Islands Land Court and land is distributed among the Mangaian population according to traditional practices.

There are three villages on Mangaia, at Oneroa, Ivirua and Tamarua, and they are linked by a road which encircles the perimeter of the island.

James Cook was the first European visitor to Mangaia, on 29th March, 1777. He did not land as the people gave him a hostile reception. The LMS missionary Rev. John Williams failed also in his initial attempts to land Polynesian teachers on the island during his first visit there on 13th July, 1823. H. E. Maude, in his reconstruction of the voyages of the 'Bounty' after the mutiny, suggests that the ship called at Mangaia. Whaling ships called at Mangaia frequently during the early part of the nineteenth century to obtain provisions and to recruit crew members.

In earlier times the principal exports from Mangaia were copra, citrus fruits and tomatoes, but since the mid-1960s a flourishing pineapple industry has been created. The fruit is loaded on to lighters in a small harbour, which has been built in the reef near Oneroa, and then ferried out to the inter-island vessels which transport it to the canning factory at Rarotonga. Mangaia has a 792 m airstrip.

The work load imposed by the tasks of growing and harvesting the pineapples has greatly restricted the opportunities enjoyed by the Mangaians to grow other crops, such as coffee, or to engage in traditional subsistence tasks like taro growing and fishing.

Deposits of manganese have been found on the island but are not in sufficient quantity to warrant commercial exploitation. The makatea contains an extensive system of limestone caves, with stalactites and stalagmites and ancient subterranean burial sites. The Mangaians use the limestone from the stalactites and stalagmites to make multi-coloured food pounders. The women make gaily coloured hat bands and other decorative items from pupu, a small land snail, which emerges from the makatea after rain falls.

The Cook Islands Christian Church has a church at Oneroa of great artistic interest because of the intricate bindings in sennit which adorn the rafters and other interior timbers. The Mangaians cling to many traditional customs, such as those which accompany the choosing of a new paramount ariki, the ceremony combining elements of the traditional Polynesian practices and the pomp and circumstance of a coronation of British royalty.

The main government offices, stores, hospital, a primary school, and the Mangaia Junior High School are at Oneroa. There are also primary schools at Ivirua and Tamarua. Mangaia has two representatives in the Legislative Assembly.

MANU'AE. Captain James Cook was the first European to visit Manu'ae, on 23rd September, 1773 on HMS 'Resolution'. He named the atoll Hervey's Island in honour of Captain Hervey, one of the Lords of the Admiralty. The name Hervey Islands came to be used for what is now the southern Cook Islands for most of the nineteenth century.

Manu'ae is the only true coral atoll in the southern Cook Islands. It has a surface area of 680 hectares. It is 200 kilometres north-northeast of Rarotonga.

When Cook visited Manu'ae it was inhabited by Aitutakians, who had seized it from the Atiuans. The island was abandoned as a place of residence in the 1830s. Several Europeans were domiciled there under arrangements with the Aitutakian leaders until a legal lease for John Strickland was created in 1893.

The lagoon at Manu'ae encloses two islets, Manu'ae and Te Au o Tu. About 85,000 coconut palms have been planted on the two motus and for much of the present century the plantation was worked by Manu'ae Plantations, for whom A. B. Donald and Co. acted as managing agents. Well known managers on the island have been

Captain Andy Thompson, the renowned schooner skipper, and the Dane, Karlo Anderson. James Ullman, in his 'Where the Bong Tree Grows', described life on Manu'ae during Karlo Anderson's managership.

More recently the plantation has been worked by the Cook Island Co-operative Bank, which has maintained gangs of plantation workers on the island.

In 1965 an international expedition carried out solar eclipse observations on Manu'ae, commemorated by a special Cook Islands stamp.

ATIU. Atiu, which has an area of 1,483 hectares, lies 187 kilometres north-east of Rarotonga. It is of volcanic origin and beyond the cliffs of makatea the red volcanic soil is formed into rounded and flat-topped hills. The people all live in what appears to be one settlement at the centre of the island, but which is in fact seven contiguous villages, representing the pre-contact organization of the people into seven land-holding tapere. Each tapere was traditionally headed by a person of the chiefly rank of mataiapo or ariki.

James Cook was the European discoverer of Atiu, on 31 March, 1777, on HMS 'Resolution'. The Rev. John Williams, of the London Missionary Society, was at Atiu on the 'Endeavour', Captain John Dibbs, on 20th July, 1823, when the work of converting the Atiuans to Christianity began. At the time of European contact the ariki of Atiu had established sovereignty over the neighbouring islands of Mauke and Mitiaro, and the three islands are collectively known as Nga-Pu-Toru.

The cliffs of makatea on Atiu are noted for some extensive limestone caves, which contain stalagmites and stalactites.

The traditional leaders of the island retain much of their former powers and have been largely instrumental in encouraging the people to improve conditions on the island. The co-operative movement has played a significant role in the Atiuans' work of re-housing themselves. The citrus replanting scheme has enabled the growers to greatly reduce their indebtedness to the Cook Islands Government.

In recent years the Atiuans have consolidated ownership of some of the planting land and a valuable pineapple plantation been established. As the production of export crops has increased, so have the problems multiplied in transporting the fruit to the processing plant on Rarotonga. Formerly, cargo was landed through very difficult reef passages, but in 1974 and 1975, New Zealand Army engineers built a small harbour for the lighters that work the ships standing off the Atiu reef. The island has an 825 m airstrip.

Dr. Dennis McCarthy, a retired New Zealand doctor, has been responsible to a great extent for the implementation of a programme to control the incidence of filariasis and its advanced stage, elephantiasis, on the island. The disease has now been virtually eliminated.

The island has a primary school, junior high school, hospital, wireless station, government offices and stores. Atiu has two members in the Legislative Assembly.

AITUTAKI. The first European to discover Aitutaki was William Bligh, on HMS 'Bounty', on 11th April, 1789, not long before the famous mutiny. Captain Edward Edwards, of HMS 'Pandora', was there on 14th April, 1791, while searching for the mutineers. The London Missionary Society missionary, Rev. John Williams, visited Aitutaki in 1821, when he put ashore the Raiatean teachers Papeiha and Vahapata, this being the first work of Christian conversion in the Cook Islands.

The LMS missionary, Rev. Henry Royle, who arrived there in 1839 and remained working there until 1876 was an influential figure. Many whaling ships called at Aitutaki to obtain provisions and to recruit crew members.

The island is about 225 kilometres north of Rarotonga and has a total land area of 1,991 hectares. Its geological structure is unusual in that it is part volcanic island and part coral atoll. Its lagoon is generally considered to be one of the most beautiful in the Pacific and it was previously a favourite stop-over for the flying-boat service operated by Tasman Empire Airways Ltd. (now Air New Zealand). There is no deep boat passage into the lagoon and ships land their passengers and cargo through a reef passage opposite the settlement of Arutanga.

During World War II an American construction battalion was stationed on Aitutaki and a causeway was built to the edge of the reef near Aru-

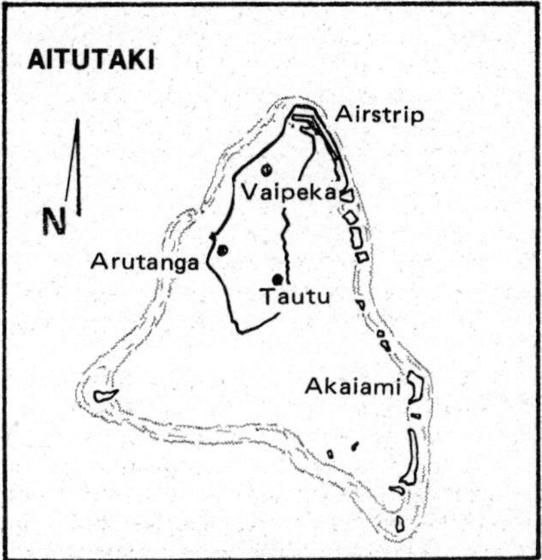

tanga, but this has been eroded away. The Americans also built an airstrip, which is still in use.

Earlier in this century Hansen's disease (leprosy) on Aitutaki was a serious problem and quarantine measures were enforced, but these were abandoned in the 1960s.

The Aitutakians are noted for the precision and vigour of their dancing. Their dancing teams have had much success in the Bastille Day celebrations in Tahiti.

A marine beacon was erected in 1954 on Maina Island, at the south-western end of Aitutaki, and it serves as a navigational aid. Aitutaki has an annual rainfall of about 2,350 mm, but there are long periods of dry weather when public supplies come from government tanks.

Aitutaki has a public electricity supply, primary schools, a junior high school, hospital, wireless station, government offices and stores.

PENRHYN. The 'Lady Penrhyn' was one of the ships in the first fleet which took convicts to Botany Bay, in the first settlement of Australia. On departure, she set sail for China, and on 8th August, 1788, Captain William Sever sighted and named an atoll Penrhyn's Island. The Maori name for the island is Tongareva, which has been translated as meaning either "floating Tonga" or "away from the south".

The atoll encloses a lagoon of 280 square kilometres, one of the largest of all the lagoons in the Pacific. 1,170 kilometres north-east of Rarotonga, Penrhyn has a total land area of 600 hectares, but much of it carries little vegetation.

With Suwarrow, Penrhyn is the only coral atoll in the Cook Islands where quite large vessels are able to enter the lagoon. There are three entrances, the most frequently used being that of the Taruia Passage near the village of Omoka. Te Tautua is the only other settlement, being on the opposite side of the lagoon from Omoka. Prior to the arrival of Europeans, the Penrhyn people lived on most of the motu on the fringing reef. There is a depth of about 6.5 metres of water in the Taruia Passage and inter-island vessels tie up at the wharf at Omoka.

Maori LMS pastors from Rarotonga introduced Christianity to the island in 1854 and the European missionaries visited their congregation on Penrhyn at infrequent intervals. Peruvian slave-raiders were largely responsible for depopulating Penrhyn during the 1860s when many of the people, including the Maori LMS pastors, were transported to South America, most to work in the saltpetre mines. It is estimated that there were about 2,000 people on Penrhyn in pre-European times and this figure fell to 326 in 1916.

The island was annexed by Britain in 1888. At the turn of the century, several European traders had set themselves up at Penrhyn and the Maori people owned their own trading schooners. The island was exploited for its pearl-shell beds and the Penrhyn men are justifiably noted for their prowess as divers. The production of shell has declined in quantity and value and it is now of little relative importance in the economy of the island. The island's principal export is copra. The people sail about the lagoon in English-style cutters about 6 metres long.

During World War II, the American forces built an airstrip on Penrhyn and it was re-activated in post-war years in connection with the American and British nuclear testing programmes. The airstrip is still maintained and is used infrequently. A Liberator bomber crashed on the island during the war and the duralium from the wreckage is still used by the people in the manufacture of artifacts such as combs and the barbs on fishing trolling hooks.

There are primary schools at Omoka and Te Tautua, with a hospital, wireless station and government offices being located at Omoka.

There have been several shipwrecks on Penrhyn, the most well-known being that of the 'Chatham' in 1853. E. H. Lamont, who survived the wreck and spent about eighteen months on Penrhyn, wrote one of the Pacific classics, 'Wild Life Among the Pacific Islanders', about his adventures on Penrhyn.

Earlier in this century, stern measures were imposed to control the spread of Hansen's disease (leprosy), which had been contracted by some Penrhyn Islanders, and some of the people were isolated on a motu at Penrhyn or sent to the leper station at Makogai, Fiji.

The people of Penrhyn are represented in the Cook Islands Legislative Assembly by the member for Penrhyn.

FOR THE TOURIST. The Cook Islands provide many delights for visitors who enjoy the relaxing atmosphere, walks, horse and buggy rides or travelling to outer islands by pineapple boat. Detailed information is provided by the Cook Islands Tourist Authority and by Air New Zealand. Visitor accommodation is mainly of the motel type, in single storey units. Islanders have insisted that nothing should be built higher than the coconut palms, so as to preserve the Island atmosphere.

Duty free facilities. There are several duty-free stores in Avarua, offering a variety of imported goods. In addition, there are attractive local handicrafts including woodcarvings following traditional patterns, delicately worked pearl shell, woven hats, baskets and broad mats as well as embroidery which has been popular since missionary days. A novel item is the ukelele made from a coconut shell by island craftsmen.

Entry formalities. Entry permits are not required by local people, permanent residents of the group, and visitors (other than those on business) whose stay does not exceed 30 days, provided they hold valid travel documents and ticket, with a confirmed booking for the outward or return journey. A passport is required for all visitors, except Cook Islanders who hold a certificate of identity.

Applications for permits are dealt with by the Premier's Department, Rarotonga; NZ Department of Foreign Affairs, Wellington and Auckland; A. B. Donald Ltd, Papeete; and NZ high commissions, embassies and consulates.

Persons arriving in Rarotonga from a stopover in Samoa, Fiji, Tahiti or any area where rhinoceros beetle is prevalent may be required to have their baggage fumigated.

Airport tax. There is no airport tax at Rarotonga airport.

Sightseeing. The coral reef and lagoon waters are a centre of interest for those who enjoy snorkeling, and shell collecting, especially in guided groups on the reef at night.

On land, the island may be toured along the Ara Tapu 33 km. sealed road which encircles Rarotonga. The visitor can see the green tropical growth which begins beside the beach and stretches across the coastal plain to the hills, broken by lines of citrus trees and small villages.

The Ara Metua is an historic road which still survives in broken stretches, slightly inland from the Ara Tapu. The origin of its stone paving is shrouded in legend dating back to about 900 A.D. Stone seats of earlier councils may be sighted near the road; many are sacred to the descendants of the earlier warriors.

Other touches of history can be seen in a walk around Avarua, including The Cook Islands Christian Church as well as the Mission House, restored as a Church Museum. Many old-time missionaries are buried in the church graveyards. The Roman Catholic cemetery at Nikao is colourfully bedecked with flowers for All Souls festivities in early November.

Other occasions of interest are the Constitution celebrations, August 1 - 10 with visitors from outer islands gathering in Rarotonga to compete in all manner of sports, dancing and traditional entertainment.

A popular event is a race day on Muri Beach, with the wild excitement of bareback riders wheeling their mounts around a marker in the sand. Needless to say, the atmosphere is rather far removed from that of the English Derby. Muri beach races are held about once a month, with betting on these and overseas races quite popular.

Other occasions for spontaneous enjoyment are the ever-frequent "umukai", traditional island feasts which include dishes cooked in a Maori earth oven, accompanied by great merriment.

Tourist representatives abroad. Detailed information is available from the Cook Islands Government Office, Communications House, 12 Heather Street, Parnell, Auckland, New Zealand, and from Air New Zealand offices.

Accommodation in Rarotonga

TRAILWAYS HOTEL — 40 rooms, all air-conditioned, restaurant, lounge bar, 24-hour bar and coffee service; dinner dance, floorshow Saturday; swimming pool; shorefront, no beach; at Kii Kii, 3 km. from township.

ARORANGI BEACH MOTEL — 20 self-contained apartments, some with kitchenettes; restaurant, bar, island food and dancing, swimming pool, boating; on beach front in palm grove, 5 min. from airport and township.

THE LITTLE POLYNESIAN — bungalow units with bath and kitchenette; licensed dining room; outrigger canoe, rental cars; swimming pool, lagoon swimming; directly on beach at Titikaveka Village, 15 km. from Avarua.

KII KII MOTEL — 12 self-contained apartments, 2 km. from town.

PUNAMAIA MOTEL — 12 self-contained units, 2 km. from town.

ACE MOTEL — 4 self-contained twin units, one unit for up to six people, all with kitchens and electric fans; 2 minutes from Avarua.

ARAMOANA FLATS — 4 self-contained units, 10 minutes from Avarua.

LAGOON LODGES — 4 2-bedroom air-conditioned houses; adjacent to beach at Arorangi, 10 km. from town; also single home on edge of Muri Lagoon, 11 km. from Avarua.

RAROTONGAN HOTEL — 150 rooms.

Aitutaki accommodation

RAPAI MOTEL — 12 twin, one family unit; dining room, bar, canoeing, snorkeling, lagoon tours. Only accommodation on Aitutaki, 5 km. from airport, on beach.

CORAL SEA ISLANDS TERRITORY

The Coral Sea Islands Territory is an Australian external territory. It comprises scattered reefs and islands, often little more than sandbanks, spread over a sea area of 1,035,995 sq. km with only a few square kilometres of actual land area. The sea area lies to the east of Queensland between the Great Barrier Reef, latitude 12 deg. S and longitude 157 deg. 10 min. E. There are no permanent inhabitants.

The islands were declared to be Australian territory by the Coral Sea Islands Act of 1969. This followed an exchange of letters between the governments of Australia and the United Kingdom in November 1968 in which Britain recognised Australian control over the islands. The exchange of letters merely confirmed that the Queen's sovereignty over the islands was exercised by the Australian and not the British Government.

Some of the better known islands are Cato, Chilcott islet in the Coringa group, and the Willis group. Others are Bird Islet, West Islet and others forming part of Wreck Reef; Herald Beacon Islet and others forming part of Mellish Reef; the Frederick Reef, Bougainville Reef and Lihou Reef islands; and the island known as Pocklington Reef.

There is no administration on the islands, but they are visited regularly by Royal Australian Navy vessels and Australia has control over the activities of any visitors. There is a manned weather station on Willis Island, about 483 km east of Cairns. A number of unmanned facilities, including a lighthouse on Bougainville Reef, a weather station on Cato Island and beacons on Frederick Reef and Lihou Reef, are also operated by the Australian Government.

The Minister for Administrative Services is responsible for the Territory, through the Department of Administrative Services in Canberra.

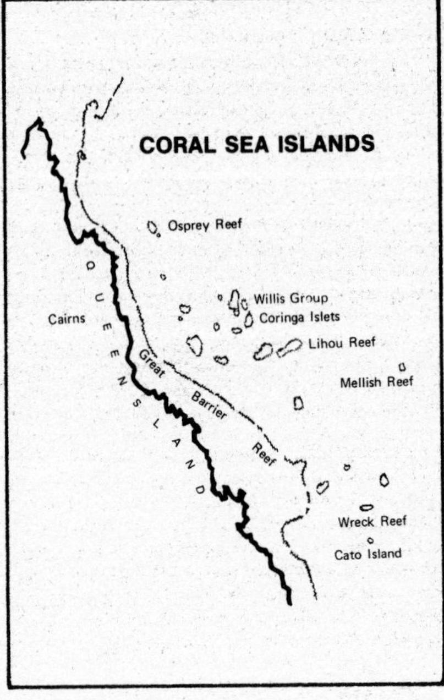

EASTER ISLAND

Easter Island, a dependency of Chile, lies in the great empty expanse of ocean between the west coast of South America and Pitcairn Island, its nearest inhabited neighbour. It is situated in approximately 27 deg. 10 min. S. lat. and 109 deg 30 min. W. long. Santiago, the Chilean capital, is 3,790 km eastward; Pitcairn is about 1,600 km westward. The official Spanish name for the island is Isla de Pascua. It is also known as Rapa-nui, a Polynesian name dating back to the 'sixties of last century, and as Te-Pito-O-Te-Henua (The navel of the World). The French call it Ile de Paques.

The island has an area of about 170 sq km. There are about 2,000 residents. The coastline is generally steep and the interior is chiefly composed of low hills and plateaus. Hanga Roa, on the west coast, and adjoining Mataveri are the only settlements. The island is administered by a governor appointed by the mainland. The Chilean peso is the official currency. The coat of arms, national anthem, flag and public holidays are also those of Chile. The only variation is that on September 9, the day when Chile annexed the island in 1888, a special Rapa-nui or Policarpo Toro Day is commemorated

THE PEOPLE. Of the estimated 2,000 residents (1977), about 800 are temporary residents from Chile – government and airline officials, members of the Chilean Air Force, Navy, hospital workers, police, nuns, etc. The remainder are native Easter Islanders, a Polynesian people speaking a language known locally as Rapa-nui. The islanders also speak Spanish, the official language. Residents of all descriptions in contact with tourists usually speak some English.

Citizenship. The islanders have Chilean citizenship. Almost all islanders over 15 have visited Chile, and some have lived there to go to secondary school or to work for several years. Roman Catholicism is the prevailing religion.

Life on the island is informal. More than 400 vehicles of various types are used on the rough dirt roads. Their houses and clothing are Chilean in style, and many of their customs, such as tea-drinking, the 'abrazo' (embrace), etc. are identical. On the other hand, many local customs are still in evidence but the making of string figures which was a popular diversion is dying out. Tamure-style dancing has been imported from Tahiti.

GOVERNMENT. The island is administered by a military governor appointed by the Chilean Government and a corps of Chilean officials. Formerly a department of the province of Valparaiso, Easter Island has now become a province of its own. There are 28 public services. Frequently, even minor details of administration have to be referred to Chile for decision. A local mayor appointed by the governor has a voice in local affairs, but his powers are limited because he has no means of raising revenue. Council elections have been suspended (Jany, 1979).

Justice. The legal system is the same as in Chile, operated on an island basis. There is a Chilean judge at the courthouse, who also acts as civil registrar and performs all legal functions. The National Police or "Carabineros" patrol the island and maintain the small gaol. There is petty crime such as cattle stealing, theft and family quarrels and occasionally rape and drunkeness.

Liquor and gambling. Liquor laws are the same as in Chile, though liberally interpreted. There is no formal gambling, but many invest in the weekly Chilean national soccer pool.

DEFENCE. The Chilean Air Force maintains a small base on the island at Mataveri, site of the airstrip. A Chilean warship or the Chilean naval training vessel "Esmeralda" usually pays an annual visit to the island . The Chilean Navy has a small base. However, the largest armed force is the National Police or "Carabineros".

EDUCATION. The Regional Department of Education in Valparaiso is responsible for education on the island. There is one school with just over 700 students run by the government under the same Regional Department and a kindergarten. There are eight years of primary school and four grades of secondary school, which is being extended. Pupils attend in two shifts, morning for grade 5 (primary) and secondary grades and afternoon for primary grades 1 to 4. The kindergarten has morning and afternoon sessions with different children. The nursery has 25 pupils. There are 27 teachers.

Scholarships from various sources are available to enable children to attend secondary school in Chile. Some islanders continue to post-secondary education in colleges and universities.

LABOUR. Work opportunities for the islanders exist in the Chilean administration and the tourist industry. About 80 government employees from Chile are on the island who, with about a third of the local population, provide the workforce. Most local adults work in fishing, agriculture, tourism or commercial stores. However, a growing number of more highly-qualified islanders join the Public Service and seek employment in Chile or elsewhere.

Wages. These are fixed according to Chilean standards and in 1980, were about $US150 a month.

HEALTH. Maternity patients or others needing surgery or casualty treatment can now be accommodated in a new hospital, completed in 1976. It opened with 20 beds but has the capacity for 20 more. There are two doctors, a dentist, chemist, midwife, two nurses with a university degree and auxiliary staff. There are two ambulances. The hospital is air-conditioned and was prefabricated in Miami. It is situated behind the church in Hanga Roa village.

THE LAND. The island is 22 km long by 11 km wide, with an area of 170 sq km. It is almost triangular in shape, having an extinct volcano near each corner. The highest of these is Mt Terevaka (506 m) in the NW. Its crater is called Rano Aroi. Lava flows from Terevaka spread over much of the island in ancient times to the other volcanoes. These have left the surface of the island exceedingly stony. There are numerous caves below the surface. High black cliffs, battered by a strong surf, make access to the island difficult from the sea. There are only three or four small sandy beaches. The main one is at Anakena, the legendary landing place of the culture hero of the Rapa-nui, "King" Hotu Matu'a.

The island has a semi-tropical climate, with trade winds blowing from the east and SE during most of the year. The annual rainfall varies considerably and there are occasional droughts. However, precipitation of 1,250 mm, mainly in winter (June-July), is about the average. The only surface water is in the crater lakes of the extinct volcanoes.

Grasses flourish on the island, which was once treeless but trees planted in recent years are now flourishing. The trees include pines, eucalypts and fruit trees. Seabirds, a small lizard and insects are the only indigenous fauna.

All Easter Islanders have lived in Hanga Roa for more than 100 years.

PRIMARY PRODUCTION. Plants cultivated by the pre-European inhabitants of the island are still cultivated today. They include bananas, sweet potatoes, yams, sugar cane and gourds. Food plants introduced since then include corn, melons, potatoes, beans, tomatoes, grapes, avocados, squash, pineapples, and fruit trees. Many islanders bring seeds and cuttings back from their travels and many of these have prospered.

Livestock in ancient times consisted of only the chicken and a native edible rat, the 'kio'e', now extinct. Sheep, horses, cattle, pigs, cats, dogs, pigeons, quail and ducks have been introduced in the past century or so. Sheep, first brought from Australia by John Brander of Tahiti in 1872, provide Easter Island with its only significant export, wool.

Livestock. Due to serious soil erosion, the sheep population of 60,000 in the early 1950s had to be drastically reduced. At the beginning of 1980 there were about 10,000. Most are corriedales but there are some merinos. At the annual shearing, each clip is about 2.8 kg and all wool is sent to Chile. The sheep also provide meat for local consumption.

There are also about 2,000 horses on the island which are mostly wild but are useful for keeping down the grass. About 280 farmers have mixed-breed cattle which provide beef. Late in 1976, 600 cows and 32 Hereford bulls were imported from Punta Arenas, southern Chile. They are maintained at a government station and bred with bulls from Australia and New Zealand. By late-1979, there were 1,600 head of cattle.

Fish and lobsters are caught locally including tuna and a local delicacy, nanue.

TOURISM. With an extension of Lan Chile flights, the number of tourists is growing and there were about 4,000 visitors in 1980. They came from Germany, France, North America, Brazil, Chile and Australia.

LOCAL COMMERCE. The two supermarkets obtain supplies from Chile and stock canned and frozen foods, wines and soft drinks. A small range of clothing and cosmetics can be bought from about 20 general stores. Fresh fruit and vegetables can be obtained at the local market which is open for five and a half days a week.

The two larger shops are owned by a governmental and private enterprise, although islanders control the small kiosks and bottle shops. An islander is the local baker.

FINANCE. The island is a financial drain on Chile, which spends much more on the island than is obtained from the sale of wool and from tourism, the only industries. Special postage stamps have not been exploited as a source of revenue, those in use being Chilean. However, the local post office has a special postmark. The Banco del Estado de Chile (the Chilean State Bank) has a branch on the island.

TRANSPORT. There are no bitumen roads, but about 60 families have vehicles, usually with 4-wheel drive. Horses are numerous and everything in Hanga Roa is within walking distance. Horses

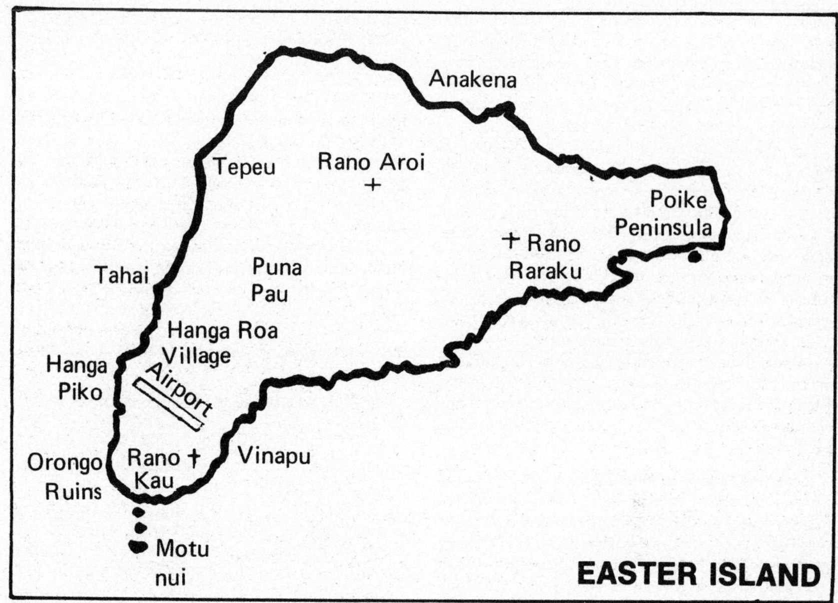

may be rented at the rate of $US5 daily. Weekly rates are also negotiable. Cars for rent, including a driver, are about $60 per day. There are also more than 100 motor cycles on the island.

Depending on the season, ships may anchor at almost any time in one or another of several indentations round the coast. The one most commonly used is Hanga Piko, on the west coast, a short distance south of Hanga Roa. Facilities include a stone quay, cranes, warehouses and electric light. The pier takes three 16 m landing craft used for unloading ships which anchor offshore. Other landing places are: Hanga Roa or Cook Bay; La Perouse Bay, NE coast; Hotuiti, SE coast and Vinapu, SE coast. Two cargo ships provide non-perishable foods, goods, machinery and equipment. They are supported by the Chilean Government.

The Chilean airline LAN-Chile, using a Boeing 707, calls at Easter Island on flights from Santiago to Tahiti and Nadi return. Flying time from Santiago is about five hours; and to Tahiti, four hours. Mataveri Airport, in the SW corner of the island, is of jet standard.

COMMUNICATIONS. Telephones are installed in all the public offices and in several dozen private homes. There are now 100 telephones. Calls to Chile may be made with little difficulty. International calls are made by satellite. Radio contact is maintained daily with Valparaiso by the government radio station. All-day radio programmes are transmitted from the local station Radio Manukena maintained by the Chilean Air Force. TV programmes on videotape from Chile are broadcast at night. Short wave and medium band radio reception is good. Chilean newspapers and magazines arrive each week. The local priest, Father David Reddy OFM, is the only licensed amateur radio operator. His call sign is CE 0 AE. He has contacted more than 40 000 hams throughout the world.

WATER AND ELECTRICITY. Most potable water, until recently, was obtained from masonry cisterns collected from iron roofs. Water is now pumped to Hanga Roa from wells on the north slope of Rano Kau. It is safe to drink. Electricity is 110 volts at the Hotel Hanga Roa. Elsewhere, the voltage is 220 (2-pin round plug).

PERSONALITIES

Governor: Capt Ariel Gonzalez Cornejo.
Mayor: Samuel Cardinale.
Chief of Police: Nelson Acevedo Navarrete.
Judge: Orasmin Gillies Gil.
Head of Port Authority: César Radic Guazzini.
LAN-Chile (airline) Manager: Fernando Mazo.
Curator of local museum: Sergio Rapu Haoa.
Priest: Father David L. Reddy, OFM.
Experts on local history and folklore: José Fati Puara Hey, 'Kiko' Pate Paoa, León Tuki Hey.

HISTORY. Recent research has shown that Easter Island was probably inhabited as far back as A.D. 400. Over the centuries, the islanders built large numbers of stone statues, temple platforms or 'ahus' and other stone works. These were distributed over much of the island. The tallest statue is about 10m high; some are 6 to 9m; most are from 3.5 to 6m.; and some are smaller. They were carved out of volcanic rock, and represent the upper portion of the human body. The latest theory is that they represent stylised portraits of significant ancestors.

The quarry and carving site for the statues was the crater slopes of the most easterly volcano, Rano Raraku. The sculptors apparently worked on them until they were attached to the living rock by only a slender keel running down the back. When freed, they were slid down the slopes and were stood up to be finished, then dragged by manpower to be erected on the 'ahu'. Many were crowned with topknots of red volcanic tuff. The statues were called 'moai'. About 1,000 of them were carved. The carving seems to have gone on for 1,000 years until, suddenly, it ceased. Work on some 'moai' at Rano Raraku was never completed; others were abandoned half-way down the slopes or en route to their platforms.

Roggeveen's arrival. One theory suggests that the carving era ended when a war broke out between two groups of islanders known as the Hanau Eepe (usually called the Long Ears) and the Hanau Momoko (Short Ears). This war apparently began just before or just after the arrival of the European discoverer of the island Jacob Roggeveen. Roggeveen, a Dutchman, came upon the island on Easter Day, 1722, and named it accordingly. His three ships remained off the island for three days, but he and his men made only one excursion ashore.

In 1770, a Spanish expedition under Captain Felipe Gonzalez visited the island from Peru and took possession of it for the King of Spain. A document was drawn up, and several of the islanders signed it with 'certain characters of their own form of script'. This was the first time that a version of the celebrated 'rongo-rongo' writing of Easter Island was seen.

Four years after the Spaniards' departure, Captain Cook visited the island briefly. Other explorers to call there over the next 60 years were: La Perouse (1786), Lisiansky (1804), Kotzebue (1816), Beechey (1825), and Du Petit-Thouars (1838). In 1806, Captain Benjamin Page took an islander to London where he sponsored his baptism in 1812. Nearly 50 ships, mostly whalers visited the island from 1792 onwards, but on average, probably never more frequently than once every two years.

Peruvian blackbirders. In 1862, when the island's population probably stood at about 3,000, a flotilla of Peruvian ships raided the island to get much-needed labour for Peru. There was a second raid in 1863. From 800 to 1,000 islanders are estimated to have been carried off. However, protests by diplomats and missionaries soon forced the Peruvian government to insist on the islanders being repatriated. Many died before arrangements could be made to send them home; others died on the way. Some of the few who did see their homeland again carried smallpox and tuberculosis germs with them which quickly wiped out many of those who had remained behind.

In 1864, while smallpox was still raging, a French religious missionary, Brother Eugene Eyraud of the Order of the Sacred Hearts, settled on the island. Two priests with assistants from Mangareva arrived with him on a second visit. These missionaries did all they could to alleviate the islanders' misery, but their numbers fell away rapidly during the next few years. Meanwhile, the missionaries discovered that many of the islanders had inscribed wooden boards called 'rongo-rongo' in their houses, and they succeeded in obtaining a few examples of this unique Polynesian writing before the tablets were all hidden or destroyed with the adoption of Christianity.

By 1868, when Eyraud died, the missionaries had baptised all the remaining islanders. In that same year, a French adventurer, Dutrou-Bornier, settled on the island. In an arrangement with John Brander, a merchant in Tahiti, Dutrou-Bornier began buying up the islanders' land with a view to establishing a sheep ranch. Conflict soon arose with both the islanders and the missionaries. The upshot was that the missionaries withdrew to Mangareva in 1871 taking some of the islanders with them, and other islanders were persuaded to leave the island to work on Brander's plantations in Tahiti. Six years later, Dutrou-Bornier himself was murdered, apparently because of brutality and overbearing conduct. By then, Easter Island's population had fallen to a record low of 110. All modern Easter Islanders are descended from 15 couples among those 110 people, plus a few outsiders who arrived on the island afterwards.

Chilean annexation. Until Chile annexed the island in 1888, Brander's sheep-raising interests were managed by a part-Tahitian, Alexander Salmon. Those interests were then taken over by a Chilean company, Compania Explotadora de la Isla de Pascua, a subsidiary of Williamson, Balfour Co., of London and Valparaiso. About 18,000 sheep had the run of the island, and the few islanders were confined to a small region round Hanga Roa on the west coast. Except that the islanders gradually increased in numbers, there was little of note in the island's history until World War I when, in October 1914, the German Pacific Squadron used Easter Island as a rendezvous and revictualling base.

While the squadron was at the island, an English archaeologist, Mrs Katherine Scoresby Routledge, was making the first serious attempt to unravel some of the mysteries of the island's past. She remained there nearly 17 months, and subsequently wrote a book, 'The Mystery of Easter Island'. Another important scientific expedition arrived in 1934 comprising a Belgian ethnologist, Henri Lavachery, a French archaeologist Alfred Metraux and a Chilean scientist, Israel Drapkin. The following year saw the ary, Father Sebastian Englert. He lived there until just before his death in 1969, and worked incessantly to improve the lot of the islanders and to record what he could of their language, history and traditions. In 1955, a large-scale scientific expedition under the leadership of the Norwegian explorer Thor Heyerdahl visited the island and carried out extensive archaeological research.

Recent history. Meanwhile, the island was under the administration of the Chilean Navy, which appointed a naval officer as governor. Apart from the occasional visits by scientists, and sporadic calls by yachts and liners, the islanders' only contact with the outside world was an annual visit by a Chilean naval vessel. However, about 1950, with the aim of opening the island to aviation, a rough 600m airstrip was built at Mataveri at the SW corner of the island. A Chilean Catalina amphibian aircraft piloted by Roberto Parrague of the Chilean air force landed there in 1951, but could not take off again with a load of fuel. When the plane attempted to take off from the sea, it crashed. Shortly afterwards, an Australian airman, the late Sir Gordon Taylor, called at the island on a trans-Pacific west to east survey flight in a Catalina flying-boat. Thereafter there were no significant developments in the aviation field until the 1960s.

In 1954, the Chilean government terminated its lease to the Compania Explotadora and turned the sheep ranch over to the naval administration. Its aim was to improve conditions for the islanders. However, as time passed the islanders grew increasingly discontented.

In 1965, their leaders wrote an open letter to the President of Chile complaining of the naval governor's treatment of them, of restrictions on their movements, and of their lack of a vote in Chilean elections. Soon afterwards, the naval administration was superseded by a civil administration, and the islanders obtained all the rights provided by Chilean citizenship.

In the early 1960s, the airstrip at Mataveri was lengthened and improved and new plans were afoot to bring Easter Island into the modern world. With a view to recording all they could about the physical conditions of the islanders before their age-old isolation was shattered, a Canadian medical expedition visited the island for two months in 1964 and examined every island resident.

In 1965 and 1966, Roberto Parrague made further proving flights to the island from Santiago and Tahiti. At the time of his second flight, the Mataveri strip had been lengthened to more than 1,800m and had been sealed. A fortnightly service between Santiago and Easter Island was inaugurated by LAN-Chile in April 1967 with a DC6B aircraft. The flight took nine hours. The service was extended to Tahiti at the beginning of 1968. By March 1970, the Mataveri airstrip had been further upgraded and LAN-Chile was able to begin a weekly jet service to Easter Island and Tahiti using 707 Boeing jets. There are now three flights a week in the summer (southern) and two during the remainder of the year. The link with Tahiti placed Easter Island within relatively easy reach of passengers from Australia, New Zealand and North America, as well as Chile and the Pacific Islands.

Origins of the people. The most hotly debated question of Easter Island history in recent years has been the origins of the people who inhabited the island when Roggeveen encountered it in 1722. The orthodox view has long been that the islanders of Roggeveen's time were simply Polynesians of South-East Asian origin who had reached the island, probably from the Marquesas, in the last phase of their exploratory voyages eastward. However, Thor Heyerdahl, of 'Kon-Tiki' fame, and some other scholars believe that the islanders of 1722 were a mixed people – that before that Polynesians arrived from the east, the island was settled by South American Indians and that it was they who were responsible for the statues and other stone works.

In 1975, Australian historian Robert Langdon gave the debate a new twist when he suggested in his book 'The Lost Caravel' that the islanders were actually an amalgam of three racial types: from South America, Polynesia and Europe – the latter including a Basque element from the Spanish caravel 'San Lesmes' which was lost in the eastern Pacific in 1526. Langdon brought forward evidence that some modern Basques and Easter Islanders of reputedly pure island descent share certain rare genetic characteristics which are unknown in most other people of the world.

Further information: Most of the ample literature on Easter Island is concerned with its ancient history rather than recent times. Among the few books in the latter category are Helen Reed's 'A World Away', Toronto, 1965, which tells of conditions at the time of the Canadian medical expedition's visit in 1964, and Bob Putigny, 'Easter Island', Papeete, 1976, an excellent tourist guide. A comprehensive account of the contact of Easter Is. with Europeans, and of contemporary life, is to be read in "Reaction to Disaster" by Grant McCall, New York, 1977. A recent book is Michel Rougie's 'Rapa Nui', in English, Spanish and French (Editions Delroisse, Paris, 1979) explores the island's archaeology, history and tourism, adding some beautiful photographs. Recent books dealing chiefly with the island's prehistory include: Alfred Metraux, 'Easter Island,' London, 1957; Thor Heyerdahl, 'Akuaku,' London, 1958; Thor Heyerdahl and Edwin Ferdon, eds., 'Archaeology of Easter Island,' Stockholm, 1961; Sebastian Englert, 'Island at the Centre of the World,' London, 1972; 'The Land of Hotu Matu'a,' Santiago, 1974; Peggy Mann 'Easter Island, Land of Mysteries', Holt, Rinehart & Winston, New York, 1976. Beautiful descriptions and illustrations of ancient and modern stone and wood artifacts from the island are in "The Art of Easter Island", Thor Heyerdahl, London 1976. The William Mully and

Gonzalo Figueroa's 'The Ahu Akivi-Vaiteka Complex and its Relationship to Easter Island Architectural Prehistory', Hawaii, 1978, is the most recent book on the island's treasures.

FOR THE TOURIST. The huge statues and other archaeological remains (see below under "Sightseeing") are the chief features most tourists wish to see. There are several organised day and half-day tours to the most interesting sites. Visitors may also fish, swim and ride horses. Because of the stony ground, sturdy walking shoes are advisable. The standard of food at hotels and private guest houses is high. Seafood, beautifully served, is a specialty. Souvenirs for sale include small stone 'moai' (statues), straw hats, shell necklaces, wood carvings and similar handicrafts.

Hotel Hanga Roa, the leading hotel, has 60 twin rooms (some triples). Facilities include room service, swimming pool, bar and lounge, and several shops.

Hotel Hotu Matu'a has a bar and restaurant.

There are 41 guest houses, including that of Rosita Cardinale. They are clean, have about six double or triple rooms and hot water. To experience the real island atmosphere, a stay at a guest house is recommended. Tariffs include meals.

There are several primitive, but interesting restaurants and night spots, such as "Piditi" near the airport, and "Toroko" adjacent to the fishermen's dock at Hanga Roa.

Islanders control local tours and can arrange excursions, "curantos" (feasts and parties) and other activities. The largest firm is Mahina Tours but similar facilities are offered by Martin Rapu, Daniel Tepano, Mana Ika, Aku Aku Tours and Archaeological Travel Service.

Entry formalities. For visitors staying less than three months, only a current passport is required for most nationalities, without the need of a visa. For further information contact the nearest Chilean Embassy or Consulate.

Airport tax. A tax of about $US1.50 per person is charged to visitors who make a stop-over on the island on flights from Santiago.

Sightseeing. Most visitors, long or short term, are interested in the stone statues and shrines. Visits are usually made to Ahu Tahai a reconstructed ceremony centre where three ahus have been restored and where Ko Te Riku, the only standing moai with a red top-knot, can be seen. Work of reconstruction is continuing. During reconstruction of an ahu at Anakena in 1978 under the supervision of the museum curator, Sergio Rapu Haoa, pieces of shaped white coral were discovered. It was found that they fitted into the eye sockets of the moai. They also discovered three layers of ahus, one on top of the other, coming from three civilisations.

Regarded as the leading archaeologist of Easter Island, Dr William Malloy, of the University of Wyoming, USA, died in 1978 and his ashes have been buried at Ahu Tahai on the island.

Other musts are: Akivi, where seven standing statues on the ahu were restored in 1960; Rano Raraku, where the statues were quarried and where many still lie on the slopes; Togariki, which had the biggest ahu of all, and where 15 moai once stood, but which was destroyed by a tidal wave in 1960; Poike, where two factions, the Long Ears and the Short Ears, are supposed to have fought their last battle in which the Long Ears were virtually exterminated; the crater, reed-covered lake in the middle of Rano Kau; and Orongo ceremonial village where there is an area of rock outcroppings covered with petroglyphs in high relief. Anakena, a very beautiful beach and the site of the residence of the ancient kings, exhibits an extraordinary, well-preserved "ahu", which was restored in 1978. Its statues have "pukao" or top-knot of red volcanic tuff.

FIJI

There are 320 islands in Fiji (18,376 sq. km) which is an independent country within the British Commonwealth. The group is located between 15 and 22 deg. S. latitude and 177 deg. W. and 175 deg. E. longitude. The capital, Suva, is on Viti Levu and is about 3,160 km north-east of Sydney and 2,120 km north of Auckland. Population of the group in 1976 was 588,068. Local time is 12 hours ahead of GMT.

Fiji's flag, flown for the first time on Independence Day, October 10, 1970, consists of the Union Flag of Britain in the top, left-hand corner and the shield with the Fiji Coat of Arms in the fly, all on a light-blue background. Ensigns flown on vessels are similar but with varying backgrounds – government ships with dark blue, merchant ships red and naval squadron white. The Governor-General's flag is the dark-blue Commonwealth flag with a centre crest of a crown with lion and the word 'Fiji' below the crest. The National Anthem, by Michael Prescott of Suva, is "God bless Fiji", which begins "Blessing grant, oh God of Nations, on the Isles of Fiji". The currency is the Fiji dollar divided into 100 cents. Its value against the Australian dollar in July, 1980, was $1.0637.

POPULATION. The indigenous Fijians are racially classed as Melanesians but they have a considerable admixture of Polynesian blood. At the time that the first Europeans arrived in Fiji, this Polynesian influence was greater in the Lau Islands (nearest to Tonga) and in the windward sides of the largest islands; while those people in the interiors of the large islands were more purely Melanesian.

The Fijians today are outnumbered by the Indians, the first of whom came from India as indentured labourers in 1879. The indenture system was abandoned in 1916 but by then 40,000 elected to remain as free settlers, and they have long since become part of the community as farmers, business or professional men, public servants, clerical workers, transport workers, etc.

The Europeans came first to Fiji in the early 19th Century in search of sandalwood. They were followed by missionaries and by settlers who wanted land and to trade.

Many of the 'other islanders' that now show up in the census figures are people such as the Banabans who originally came from Ocean Island and settled on Rabi Island which was purchased for them before the last war; or the people from Kioa Island where several hundred Ellice Islanders have been resettled. The people of Rotuma, which became a dependency of Fiji in 1881, are Polynesian. There are about 2,700 on the island itself plus about 4,000 in Fiji proper. The Chinese were comparative

	1936 census	1956 census	1966 census	1976	1978 (est.)
Europeans	4,028	6,402	6,590	4,929	3,393
Fijians	97,651	148,134	202,176	259,932	272,447
Part Europeans	4,574	7,810	9,697	10,276	10,721
Rotumans	2,816	4,422	5,797	6,822	7,619
Other Islanders	2,476	5,320	6,095	7,291	5,442
Indians	85,002	169,403	240,960	292,896	306,957
Chinese	1,751	4,155	5,149	4,652	4,633
Others	78	91	273	1,270	834
	198,376	345,737	476,737	588,068	612,046

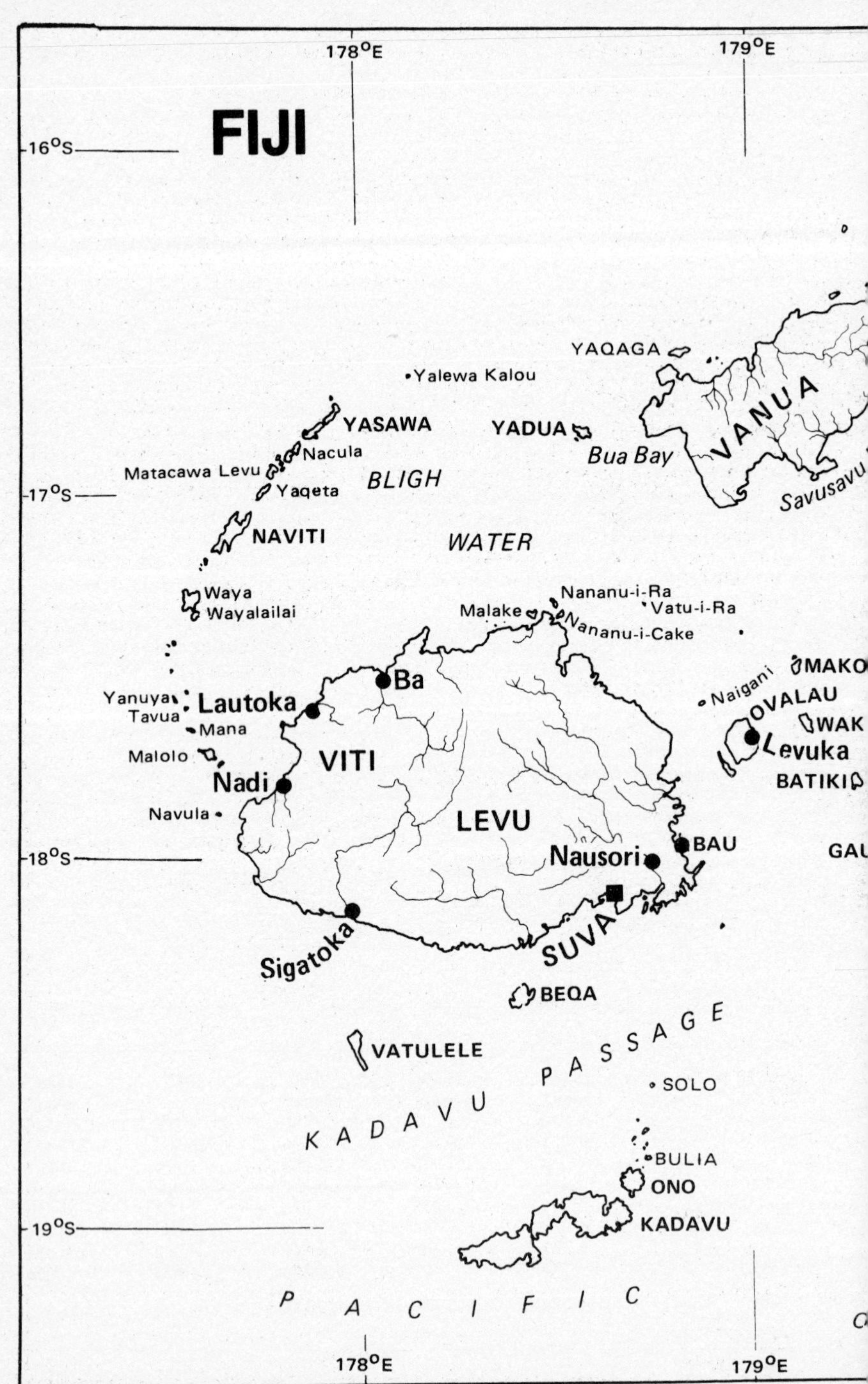
FIJI
178°E
179°E
16°S
17°S
18°S
19°S
YAQAGA
Yalewa Kalou
YASAWA
YADUA
Bua Bay
VANUA
Savusavu
Nacula
Matacawa Levu
Yaqeta
BLIGH
WATER
NAVITI
Waya
Wayalailai
Nananu-i-Ra
Vatu-i-Ra
Malake
Nananu-i-Cake
MAKO
Naigani
OVALAU
WAK
Levuka
BATIKI
Ba
Yanuya
Tavua
Lautoka
Mana
Malolo
VITI
Nadi
Navula
LEVU
BAU
GAU
Nausori
SUVA
Sigatoka
BEQA
VATULELE
PASSAGE
SOLO
KADAVU
BULIA
ONO
KADAVU
PACIFIC

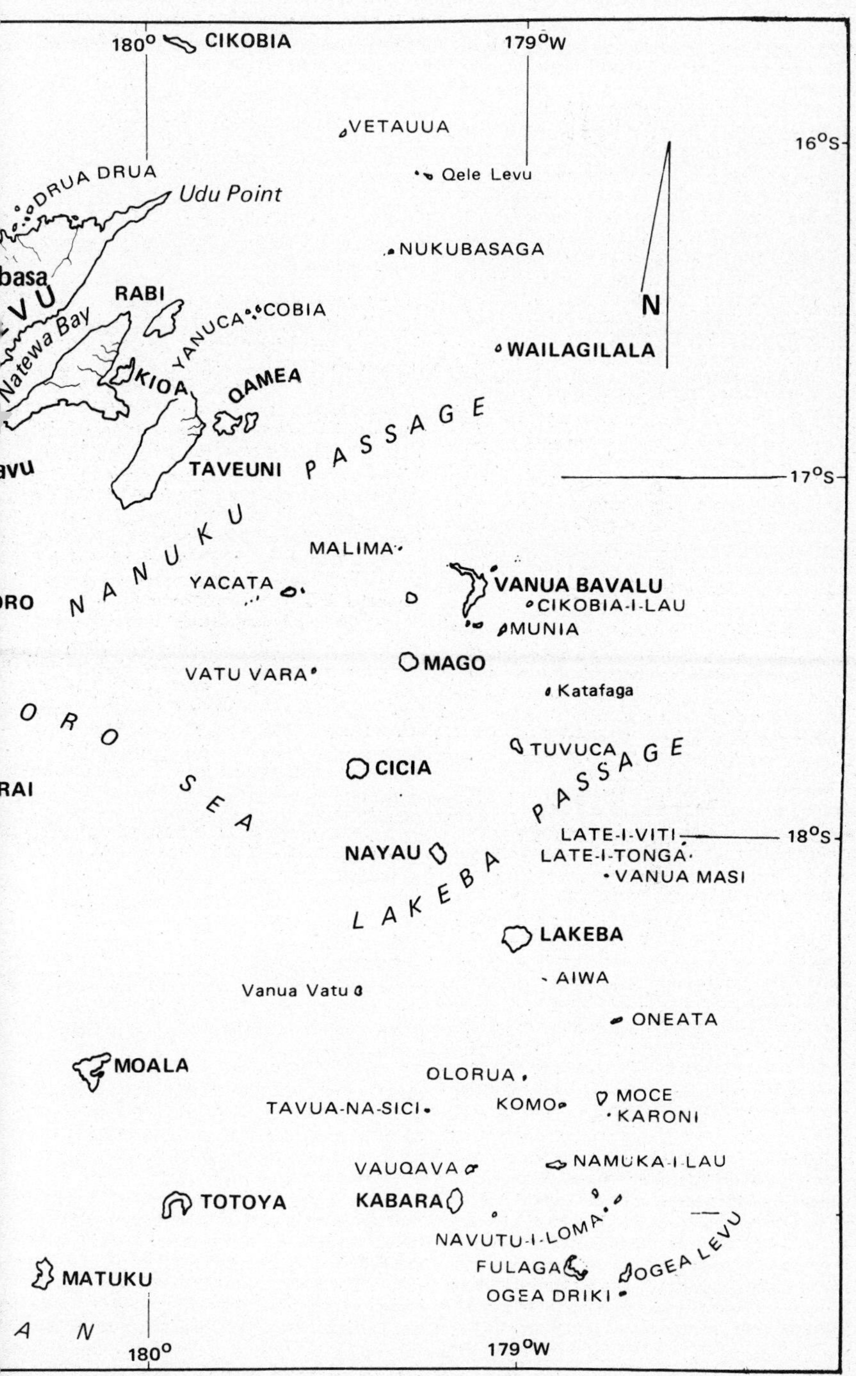

180°
CIKOBIA
179°W
VETAUUA
16°S
Qele Levu
DRUA DRUA
Udu Point
NUKUBASAGA
N
RABI
YANUCA
COBIA
Natewa Bay
WAILAGILALA
KIOA
QAMEA
NANUKU PASSAGE
TAVEUNI
17°S
MALIMA
YACATA
VANUA BAVALU
CIKOBIA-I-LAU
MUNIA
VATU VARA
MAGO
Katafaga
KORO SEA
TUVUCA
CICIA
LAKEBA PASSAGE
LATE-I-VITI
18°S
NAYAU
LATE-I-TONGA
VANUA MASI
LAKEBA
AIWA
Vanua Vatu
ONEATA
MOALA
OLORUA
TAVUA-NA-SICI
KOMO
MOCE
KARONI
VAUQAVA
NAMUKA-I-LAU
TOTOYA
KABARA
NAVUTU-I-LOMA
OGEA LEVU
FULAGA
MATUKU
OGEA DRIKI
180°
179°W

latecomers to Fiji, now mostly working as shopkeepers, merchants, tradesmen, etc. The first census to record Chinese was in 1911 when there were just over 300.

The current population density is about 32.3 people per square kilometre. Recent population forecasts were for 653,000 by 1980; 716,000 by 1985 – all assuming a stabilising fertility rate.

There is a marked drift of the rural population to urban areas, particularly Suva, Lautoka and Nadi. The 1978 census gave the following figures: Great Suva area 117,827; Lautoka 28,847; Ba 9,173; Labasa 12,956; Levuka 2,767; Nadi 12,995; Savusavu 2,295; Sigatoka 3,635; Nausori 12,821; Navua 2,568; Rakiraki 3,755; Tavua 2,144; Vatukoula 6,425.

Nationality. People born in Fiji are Fiji citizens and British subjects. Others may acquire citizenship under certain conditions, including renouncing of previous citizenship. Commonwealth born citizens must be residents for seven years. Non-Commonwealth people can only obtain Fiji nationality after nine years residence.

Language. English is the official language and the Bau dialect is the most widely adopted of the Fijian tongues. Hindustani is spoken by the majority of the Indians. Travellers to Fiji are sometimes puzzled when they seek to find on the map a place name they have heard or seen in print; this is because, in writing Fijian, certain letters of the English alphabet are used to represent certain sounds. The five main variations are: "c" is pronounced as "th" (as in "that"); "b" as "mb" (as in "number"); "d" as "nd" (as in "sand"); "g" as "ng" (as in "ring"); and "q" as "ng-g" (as in "linger").

Migration trends. Canada has been the main destination for emigrating Fiji Islanders, particularly for Indians and Chinese. Changes in Australian and New Zealand migration policies have halted the flow to those countries to a large extent. However both continue to accept skilled tradesmen. The drain of skilled people has caused the Fiji Government concern; in October, 1974, it said migration, particularly of skilled people, had reached a rate of 9,600 a year, or nearly one per cent of the population, after not exceeding 1,300 through the 1960s. Because of increased Fijian population and a shortage of employment, migration into Fiji is strictly controlled. Generally, permission to work in Fiji is given to non-Fijian citizens only when there are no qualified local personnel capable of doing the job.

Religion. The principal religious groups are Methodist (about 38 per cent); Hindu (40 per cent); Roman Catholic and Islam (about eight per cent). Other Christian groups include Church of England, Seventh-Day Adventist and Presbyterian.

Lifestyle. A large proportion of the people still live in villages, fully sharing the obligations and rewards of a community existence and led by a chief. However, under modern economic pressures, life for Fiji citizens is changing, with increasing numbers of people working for wages and, in cities like Suva, living far away from their family villages.

Recreation. Fiji offers a wide variety of sporting activity, including cricket, hockey, basketball, squash, tennis and bowls. The winter sports, Rugby football and soccer, easily command the biggest followings, both player and spectator. Water sports are popular throughout the group. Golf has made spectacular advances in recent years through private sponsorship of tournaments which have attracted leading overseas players.

GOVERNMENT. Since independence was gained on October 10, 1970, Fiji has been independent within the Commonwealth. It has a bicameral parliament consisting of a nominated Senate and an elected House of Representatives; with a Cabinet presided over by a Prime Minister. The constitution contains a statement of fundamental freedoms and rights. The Cabinet is directly responsible to parliament and consists of the Prime Minister and other Ministers appointed by the Governor-General on the PM's recommendation. There are 12 members (ministers) and seven ministers of state but the latter are not cabinet members. The constitution allows for an Ombudsman to investigate complaints about the actions of government authorities.

The 1970 constitution provides for the House of Representatives, in the first instance, to have 52 members – 12 Fijian, 12 Indian and three general members elected from communal rolls; and 10 Fijian, 10 Indian and five general members elected from national rolls. (The national rolls have members of all races who vote together.)

Members of the House elect a Speaker from among themselves and the Prime Minister chooses his own Cabinet. The constitution also provides for 22 members in the Senate, with eight members appointed by the Great Council of Chiefs; seven by the Prime Minister; six by the Leader of the Opposition; and one by the Council of Rotuma. Senators elect a President from among themselves.

The Queen is Head of State, and is represented in Fiji by the Governor-General.

The first general election after independence took place in April, 1972. The Alliance Party was returned to power, taking 33 seats. The National Federation Party won 19.

A Royal Commission on the electoral system reported in 1976 that the communal system should be retained for some time but with a reduction in the number of communal seats, and an increase in the number of national seats. This report was rejected by the Alliance Party.

An election was held in March-April 1977 and the National Federation Party gained 26 seats, the Alliance 24 with a seat each to the Fijian Nationalist Party and an independent. The NFP was unable to form a government and the Alliance was reappointed as a minority government. Another election was held in September 1977 and in this, the Alliance regained power with 36 seats. The NFP had 15 and one was taken by an independent

Local government. The district administration was retained when Fiji became independent. The four districts, each in charge of a commissioner are: Central (headquarters at Nausori), covering Tailevu, Naitasiri, Rewa, Serua and Namosi; Eastern (Levuka) covering Lau, Lomaiviti, Kadavu and Rotuma; Northern (Labasa) covering Bau, Macuata and Cakaudrove; and Western (Lautoka) covering Ba, Nadroga/Navosa and Ra.

The Fijians, while still subject to the central government, have their own administration which is based on the village (koro). The head of the village, usually nominated by the people, is the turaga-ni-koro, who directs the village's activities. Several koros are grouped to form a tikina (district), while a number of tikina, in turn, form a yasana (province).

There are 14 provinces: Nadroga/Navosa, Ba, Ra, Tailevu, Naitasiri, Rewa, Serua, and Namosi are all on Viti Levu and take in some islands adjacent to the coast. The others are Bau and Macuata (Vanua Levu), Cakaudrove (part of Vanua Levu, Taveuni, and adjacent islands), Lau (the Lau islands), Kadavu (the island of Kadavu and adjoining islands) and Lomaiviti (a number of islands in the Koro Sea).

Each province is governed by a council and a roko tui. The roko tui is executive head of the council and his appointment has to be approved by the Fijian Affairs Board. The councils deal with all matters affecting Fijians, impose rates and make by-laws which must have approval of the Fijian Affairs Board. Each year the annual meeting of the Great Council of Chiefs discusses proposed legislation which has a direct bearing on Fijians. The council is regarded as the keeper of Fijian tradition. A new function for the council is to elect eight senators.

Fijian Affairs Board. This is the authority under which the Fijian administration system functions. The board comprises the Minister for Fijian Affairs and Rural Development, eight members elected by the Fijian members of the House of Representatives, and two members elected by the Great Council of Chiefs. The board has a number of expert advisors. One of the board's main functions is to make recommendations to the government on matters which it feels will benefit Fijians. It also sees legislation which affects Fijians before it is submitted to Parliament

Rabi Island administration. This island is administered internally by the Rabi Island Council. The island is owned by the Banabans as a freehold property but is otherwise part of Fiji, and the islanders are Fiji citizens. In 1975 the Banabans announced that they wanted their original home, Ocean Island, to be granted independence from the Gilbert Islands as an associate state of Fiji, but this has been rejected by Kiribati with the agreement of Britain.

Town councils. Suva and Lautoka City Councils and eight town councils are regulated by the Local Government Act. The town councils are at Nadi, Ba, Sigatoka, Nausori, Labasa, Savusavu and Levuka. Lami, just to the west of Suva was declared a town in 1977. All council members are elected from common rolls.

Public Service. In 1979 the Fiji civil service totalled about 16,000 salaried staff. Of these about 700 were expatriate staff either engaged directly by the government, or seconded by Australia, New Zealand and Britain under various aid schemes. The Fiji Government also employs, as distinct from the established staff, a varying force of hourly paid employees, mainly in the Public Works Department. This totalled about 8,000 people.

Justice. Justice is administered by the Fiji Court of Appeal, the Supreme Court and the magistrates' courts. The judiciary comprises a Chief Justice, appointed by the Governor-General after consultation with the Prime Minister and Leader of opposition; and up to seven puisne judges, presided over by the Chief Justice who have jurisdiction to hear and determine appeals from the Supreme Court, which itself is an appellate court for decisions by magistrates' courts. Appeals from the Court of Appeal lie with the Privy Council in London. The Supreme Court is the superior court of record with unlimited criminal jurisdiction to hear and determine any civil or criminal cases including those involving interpretation of the Fiji constitution. In civil cases the jurisdiction of magistrates courts is limited to $2,000 for certain claims, but $3,000 in the case of motor accident cases.

Police. The strength of the Police Force is 1,426 including some 80 civilian employees. The force is controlled by a seconded British police officer.

Liquor laws. Public bars are closed on Sundays, but liquor can be served in licensed restaurants and hotels with a meal. Licensed night clubs can operate until 1 a.m. Most private social clubs have liquor licences for the benefit of members and guests. Consumption of liquor in public places is an offence in most Fiji towns.

Kava drinking. In Fiji kava is known as yaqona and it is one of Fiji's borrowings from Polynesia. The drink is prepared from the root of the yaqona plant and usually served from a large wooden bowl. Kava drinking is a ceremony both interesting and unique. It is one of the most ancient and honoured customs of the islands of Fiji, where it is probably taken more seriously than anywhere in the Pacific. It is associated with most of the religious and State functions, and also popularly drunk at feasts, etc. The effect of kava drinking has been much misrepresented and exaggerated. Unless taken in enormous doses, it has very little, if any, effect on the mind or body. Kava, or yaqona, is not an intoxicant but is a soporific and after a long drinking session an individual may appear heavy headed and dull.

Gambling. There is generally tight control on gambling in Fiji. Poker machines are illegal. Some dice games are also illegal. Betting on horses, etc., is legal and there are about 20 betting shops in the country. Betting is mainly on the results of Australian races. Lotteries can be conducted by charity and club organisations on permits obtained from the police. The Fiji Government has rejected propositions for the opening of gambling casinos in Fiji; however it is possible to play roulette and similar games at club and charity functions.

DEFENCE. A defence agreement with New Zealand continues. Men of the Royal Fiji Military Forces are trained in Australia, New Zealand and Sandhurst Academy in England.

In 1979 the strength of the regular force was about 630 men, including 57 officers. Two seconded RAN officers were serving with the naval squadron which has about 70 men. Fiji has a contingent of its regular soldiers serving in Lebanon. Several have been killed by terrorists. Fiji also supplied soilders for the U.N. force supervising the elections in Zimbabwe in 1980.

In 1974, the government decided to involve the army in civilian development projects. With New Zealand help a building school was built at Queen Elizabeth Barracks. Here up to 40 young men get training as building workers for a year, under military discipline. They get army pay and uniforms but at the end of the year they are free to return to civilian life as building workers.

The government also decided to establish a special construction corps of about 30 regulars for use on rural development projects, such as bridge and road building.

In 1975, as a special measure to relieve unemployment, the government recruited 200 men to serve with the RFMF for three years in a "conservation corps". After training, the men were to be employed on pine planting, road construction and other development schemes. They were not part of the regular army but were to work under military discipline, pay and other conditions.

New Zealand and British army units undergo jungle warfare training in Fiji regularly. The RFMF co-operate in these exercises which usually take place in Vitu Levu.

The government in 1975 decided to form a naval squadron as an arm of the Royal Fiji Military Forces. In 1976, it took delivery of three minesweepers from the United States Navy, which are now used to patrol Fiji waters and curb illegal fishing by Japanese, Korean and Taiwanese fishing boats. There is also a smaller ship transferred from the Marine Department.

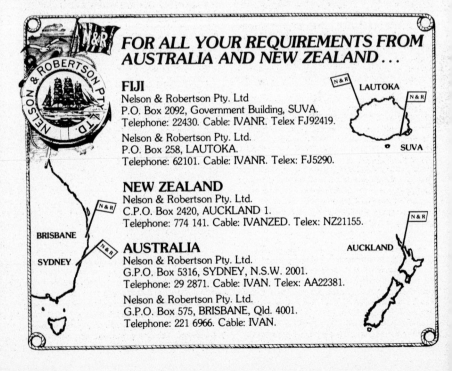

EDUCATION. The great majority of schools in Fiji are operated by local committees and these tend to be mono-racial. So while there is no government policy of racial segregation in school, considerable racial segregation has resulted because of different backgrounds and language, and because of the committee school system encouraging individual groups of people to establish a school. Of the total number of 804 schools in 1979, 35 were operated by the government, with the majority operated by committees and over 100 maintained by church missions. Estimated student enrolments in 1979 include 132,500 at primary schools, 32,995 in secondary schools, 1,678 in technical and vocational schools and 743 in primary teachers' colleges. A total of 804 schools included 646 primary, 128 secondary and 30 technical and vocational schools. The last-named were at Nasinu (government), Corpus Christi (Catholic) and Fulton College at Tailevu (Seventh-day Adventist).

Apart from the teacher training school, the 34 government schools included 21 primary, 6 secondary and 4 vocational. Construction of a new teacher training college at Lautoka was completed in 1978. Of 5,547 teachers, 4,229 were primary, 1,103 were secondary, 165 technical and 50 were at teacher training establishments.

Average government school fees were $12 a year at primary level and $36 a year at secondary school. The primary school course covers six years, followed by two years in junior secondary school, and four years at secondary school.

The government introduced free primary education in class 1 in 1973, and by 1978 all primary education (classes 1-6) was free. Free and partly-free places are available in secondary school for children with academic ability but unable to pay fees themselves. School attendance is not compulsory. In 1978 about 95.30 per cent in the 6-13 age group attended school, most of the 6,000 children not in school had been at school for varying periods but had left before reaching the age of 13 years. Primary class 7 will be fee-free in 1981 and class 8 in 1982.

Technical education. The government is giving special attention to increasing the provision of vocational and technical training at all levels and to encouraging secondary and higher education. Full-time vocational training is available at the Fiji Institute of Technology in Suva, with over 2,400 students in 1979; the School of Maritime Studies for Seamen, in Suva; and the School of Hotel and Catering Services in Suva.

The Western Division Technical Training Centre at Ba, opened in 1978, enables apprentice training to be decentralised.

University of the South Pacific. The university is at Laucala Bay, Suva, occupying buildings previously used by the Royal New Zealand Air Force. The first preliminary courses began in February, 1968, as a preparation for islanders wanting to proceed to degree and diploma courses. The university had 2,348 students in 1977 and they included degree courses – 461; Preliminary I – 85; Preliminary II – 234; Dip. Ed. – 396; Dip. Tropical Fisheries – 26. There were 280 part-time day students and 542 extension students.

Of the 276 government scholarships awarded for degree courses at U.S.P., 231 were by the Fiji Government, 6 by Australia, 30 by New Zealand, and 9 by Canada. A further 12 students were attending courses at U.S.P. with scholarships awarded by: Shell Oil 2; Adi Laisa Memorial 2; Morris Hedstrom 2; Narsey Memorial 4; Barclays 1; Suva City Council 1.

Dr. J. A. Maraj, a West Indian from Trinidad, assumed the post of Vice-Chancellor in July, 1975. Chancellor of the University is Ratu Sir Kamisese Mara, Prime Minister of Fiji. Countries represented on the University Council are Western Samoa, New Zealand, Australia, Fiji, Solomon Islands, Cook Islands, Gilbert Islands, Tuvalu, Nauru, Vanuatu, Tonga, United States of America. The South Pacific Commission is also represented.

Schools of the university are Education, Natural Resources, Social and Economic Development. A Chair of Agriculture was created in 1975. Under its extension programme the university has established extensions centres in Honiara, Tarawa, Nuku'alofa, Apia and Rarotonga with the help of $US464,000 in grants from the U.S. Carnegie Corporation.

The University of the South Pacific began offering external courses for its Diploma in Education in 1974 (students can study at home).

In 1975, the university agreed on establishment of a degree course in agriculture and in 1977 the Regional College of Tropical Agriculture in Western Samoa became the USP School of Agriculture. It introduced a new two-year degree course for Bachelor of Education in 1975, and a degree course in Accountancy. It plans to begin a degree course in Medicine through the Fiji School of Medicine.

The university depends on Pacific Islands governments for support. Governments make a basic grant plus tuition fees. Fiji in addition makes a special grant in respect of economic advantages derived from having the University of the South Pacific in its territory. Fiji's total contributions in 1979 were estimated at nearly $3 million – by far the largest of any single country. Australia, New Zealand and Britain provide other financial assistance. In 1974, Canada announced a $4.6 million grant for the construction of new buildings for the School of Natural Resources. Nauru made a special $200,000 grant in 1974 and in 1977, an Institute of Marine Resources was established at Suva with aid from the West German government.

The University of the South Pacific had planned capital developments costing $10.5 million during 1978-80. The 1977 recurrent budget was $4.244 million and $5.2 million in 1978. Fees provide $1.624 million. During 1978-80, contribution to the block grant was Fiji 74.1 per cent; Tonga 7 per cent; Western Samoa 5.6 per cent; Kiribati 4 per cent; Solomons 3.4 per cent; Cooks and New Hebrides 1.7 per cent each; Niue 1.2 per cent; Tuvalu and Nauru 0.6 per cent each; Tokelau 0.1 per cent.

Fiji School of Medicine, at Tamavua, Suva, trains medical practitioners who, since 1975, have been allowed to enter private practice in Fiji after six years' government service. In Fiji they are now addressed as "doctor". The school, which traces its early beginnings to 1878, has courses in medical, dental, and pharmaceutical services. It is associated with the University of the South Pacific and has its courses upgraded to full degree standard. In 1977, the first medical assistants graduated after a two-year course to equip them for limited duties in country areas. These 'barefoot' doctors are to relieve pressure on general practitioners. About 280 students were on the roll in 1979 including 42 from other South Pacific island countries.

Education budget. Fiji's budget for education in 1980 was $49,211,370. Fee-free education and remission of fees in 1979 was estimated at $2,335,700. Education costs claim more than 25 per cent of the operating budget.

Overseas studies. Apart from private students overseas, there were scholarship students on Fiji government grants in Australia, New Zealand, Britain and other countries.

LABOUR. An estimated 74,000 people were employed in Fiji in 1978. Employment figures covered wage and salary earners only and did not include thousands of self-employed farmers, fishermen and others. There were about 4,500 employers.

Of the total in employment, 29 per cent (21,760) were working in the community, social and personal service sector, including central and local government, medical, education, welfare, recreational and repair services. Manufacturing gave jobs to 18 per cent (13,494); wholesale and retail trades, hotels and restaurants, 16.6 per cent (12,422); construction 11 per cent (8,205); transport, storage and communications 10.6 per cent (7,914).

Wages and hours. Working hours are 44 to 48 weekly on five or six days although in the last three years there has been a tendency for more industries to switch to a five-day week of 40 to 45 hours. Wage rates were pushed up by inflation in 1977. In 1977 hourly minimum rates ranged from .72c to $1.12 an hour for workers represented by trade unions. In April, 1975, after the abolition of prices and incomes control policy, the government agreed to award civil servants regular cost of living pay increases based on increases in the consumer price index.

Wages for house servants range from $10-$20 or more a week. Many employers provide house-servants with accommodation, lighting, water and pay them less accordingly.

There is no general basic wage in Fiji. Wages are regulated by industry with five Wages Councils regulating the following trades: Building, civil engineering and electrical, wholesale and retail, hotel and catering, road and transport, and sawmilling. In 1979 there were 43 registered trade unions with a total membership of about 37,000. Most other workers were not organised but were covered by wages councils.

By 1977, average daily wage rates for respective industries were: agriculture $5.76; mining $7.01; manufacturing $6.87; construction $7.97; electricity $7.70; commerce $6.89; transport $7.69; service $7.16; all others $7.11. In 1979, rates for some unskilled workers rose to $1.50 on hour.

After independence Fiji became a full member of the International Labour Organisation and an ILO regional office was opened in Suva in 1975. Amendments to trade union legislation created an element of compulsory arbitration for the first time. The Minister of Labour was empowered to declare strikes illegal if they occurred in certain essential service industries without due notice, and to send disputes to be settled by binding arbitration if other means of solving them proved fruitless.

Fiji Trade Union Congress. This is the forum for united action by more than 30 significant unions. A rival body, the Fiji Council of Trade Unions, was formed in 1973.

Fiji National Provident Fund. To provide social security for employees, the Fiji National Provident Fund was set up in 1966 to pay members upon retirement either a lump sum, a pension, or a combination of both. Provision is also made for pension payments to widows. Since 1971 a members' insurance scheme is included in the fund, and in 1976 the government offered housing finance for fund members on condition that loans were repaid. Employers are responsible for paying into the fund for their employees, at the rate of 12 cents in the wages dollar, half of this payment being deducted from the employees' wages. The fund has about 100,000 members. The fund is now the largest single source of finance in Fiji. The 1978 advances by it totalled $117.5 million. Of this, 37.6 per cent was borrowed by government and 28.2 per cent by the private sector.

Fiji National Training Council. Created in 1974, this organises training programmes for commercial, industrial and technical workers throughout the country. From 1976 new schemes include overseas study grants and grants to employers in setting up training courses. Funds are obtained from employers who can each contribute 1 per cent of their annual payroll.

HEALTH. Medical services in Fiji are in charge of a Ministry of Health, and the permanent head of the Medical Department is Secretary for Health. Medical and dental treatment can be obtained at low charges from government hospitals and clinics covering most areas of Fiji.

As well as government doctors, in 1979 there were 20 private medical practitioners in Suva, seven in Lautoka, three in Labasa, six in Ba, four in Nausori, five in Nadi, three in Sigatoka and one in Kadavu. There were six dentists in Suva, three in Lautoka, two in Ba, and two in Nadi.

Plant Protection Equipment
Holder's large range of small sprayers
leading the field

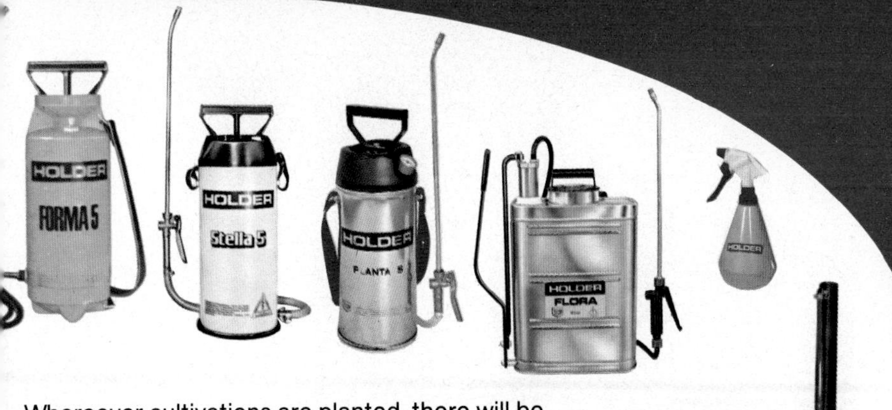

Whereever cultivations are planted, there will be inevitably dangerous insects and fungus. Therefore, if you want to harvest more than they leave, you have to fight them. For any size of garden, from the smallest flower bed, to the large orchard, Holder offers a suitable sprayer.

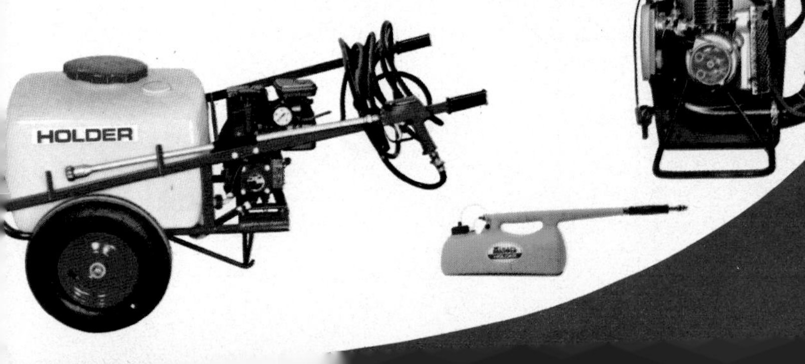

In 1975, the Medical and Dental Practitioners Act was amended to allow graduates of the Fiji School of Medicine to enter private practice after a minimum of six years' government service. Fiji's principal hospital is the Colonial War Memorial Hospital, Suva, with 337 beds. The 261-bed Lautoka Hospital, costing $7 million, opened in August, 1975. Other main hospitals are at Labasa and Levuka. In addition there are 14 sub-divisional hospitals, three area hospitals, four special hospitals and 45 health centres. Specialiast hospitals are Tamavua (tuberculosis), St. Giles (mental disorders) and the P. J. Twomey Memorial (leprosy). Fiji's infant and child mortality rates are low and average life expectancy is almost 70 years.

There is no serious drug problem in Fiji. Tuberculosis was once a major hazard but years of intensive effort brought the disease under control in 1972. The main health drive now concerns filariasis, which is prevalent in some areas of Fiji but is now close to being brought under control. There was an outbreak of dengue fever in 1980, as in other Pacific areas.

The health budget for 1980 is $18.67 million.

Family planning. Fiji's family planning programme has been described by several international authorities as one of the world's two most successful ones; the other being Singapore's. It cut the birth rate from 41.78 in 1959 to 27.81 in 1972. Target of the plan was 25 per 1,000 by 1975. Instead it rose to 29.9 per 1,000 by the end of 1976 and to 31.9 per 1,000 by the end of June 1977.The Medical Department attributes the increase to a larger number of women of child-bearing age. It expects the rate to begin falling again as older women in this category become less fertile. Young women are far more responsive to the concept of family planning and the campaign remains a key aspect of overall health planning. The eventual target is now set at 22 per 1,000. The Department says the success of the birth control compaign has saved millions of dollars in terms of a need for many thousands fewer school places. Another achievement is of a political significance; the Fijian birth rate was higher than the Indian rate in 1972, but in the early 1960s the reverse was the case.

Medical research. Fiji Medical Department hospitals have laboratories which do some research on local health problems. The Fiji School of Medicine does limited research, mainly in the form of surveys. The Colonial War Memorial Hospital in Suva also contains the Wellcome Virus Research Laboratory, set up by the Wellcome Trust of New Zealand. This concentrates on filariasis and other mosquito-borne diseases and works closely with the Otago University, New Zealand.

THE LAND. With a total area of 18,272 square kilometres, Fiji comprises some 320 islands of varying sizes, ranging from the great islands of Viti Levu, which covers 10,390 square kilometres, to mere rocks a few metres in circumference. About 150 islands are inhabited.

The distance from the Yasawa Group in the north-west to the Lau Group in the south-east, is about 480 km. The islands of Fiji have an obvious strategic importance for airlines, shipping and telecommunications.

The higest peak in the country is Mount Victoria, 1,424 metres. There are several other mountains in the vicinity of 1,000 metres. The larger islands, especially Viti Levu, Vanua Levu, Taveuni, Kadavu, and the Lomaiviti Group, are mountainous and of volcanic origin, rising more or less abruptly from the shore to a height of from 1,300 to 1,400 metres. The hills are generally of a grand and picturesque outline, being composed for the most part of old volcanic lavas. Upon the south-eastern or windward sides of the islands they are covered in dense forests.

Natural features. The country is well watered. Frequent rains keep alive the sources of the thousands of small streams feeding the main rivers. Of these rivers, the Rewa (on Viti Levu) is the biggest. It is navigable for 130 km from its mouth, with several large streams running into it. Besides, these the Sigatoka, the Nadi, and Ba Rivers, with many others, drain the principal watersheds of Viti Levu. In Vanua Levu the rivers are not so large, though they are nearly as numerous. The largest is the Dreketi River.

The lower lands are more lightly timbered, and apparantly have been under cultivation at some distant period. On these flats the soil is almost everywhere deep, easily worked, and especially rich in humic acid. The northern and north-western sides of the larger islands, or leeward sides, are characterised by a comparative absence of forest lands; and here hills or plains are covered with long reeds or grass, and dotted with clumps of casuarina and pandanus.

Fiji is rich in harbours and roadsteads as it is in rivers. Each island is surrounded by a barrier reef of coral, and, with few exceptions, is accessible through passages usually found opposite to the most considerable valley or river.

Climate. The climate is of the tropical oceanic type, but with the tempering influences of the prevalent south-east trade winds which control it. The hot months are December to April, when humidity is high.

In rainfall, clear demarcation is shown. The windward sides of the large islands are extremely wet, while on the lee sides, sheltered by the mountains, the annual precipation may be 1,640 mm more or less, with a well marked dry season favourable to sugar growing. But there is no month without some rain, while the abundant running streams assist both communnications and cultivation. Strong winds, excessive rainfall, and hurricanes, occasionally prove destructive to crops, but they are "planter's risk" in this part of the South Pacific.

Flora and fauna. Fiji wildlife extends from 68 species of land and freshwater birds (including brilliantly coloured parrots) to flying foxes, a small tree python and chamelon. The islands have approximately 3,000 species of plants, just over a third of them native to Fiji. They range from orchids to poinciana flame tree. The most famous is the fuchsia-like 'tagimaucia' which blooms in the high Taveuni jungle.

Resources. Fiji's main agricultural crops are sugar, coconuts, and root vegetables. The forest lands possess a wealth of hard and soft wood timbers. The geological structure favours the existance of minerals.

Land reclamation. The government is conducting experiments to reclaim agricultural land from mangrove swamps on the coast. A 280 hectare scheme is in progress at Ravivavi, near Lautoka, and two others at Rakiaraki on the north-east of Viti Levu on the coast. There are tens of thousands of hectares of mangrove swamp in some coastal areas, but the government does not plan to go too far as these areas are important for coastal protection and also as a food source for Fijians who have traditional fishing rights covering them. Much of downtown Suva is built on reclaimed land and both the government and city council have several small current projects under a way with the aim of using the land for industrial, commercial and civic uses. The experimental mangrove reclamations are under 800 hectares in total.

Land tenure. The arrival of European and Indian settlers with their desire for land has prompted various measures to protect Fijian land ownership. Before Cession to Britain in 1874, Europeans gained title to a considerable proportion of the easily cultivated land. Then when the chiefs of Fiji ceded the territory to Britain, one condition was that Fijian land rights should be protected. Shortly after, about 160,000 hectares of land were granted and registered as freehold while further alienation of Fijian land occurred in sales during 1905-09. Since 1909 there has been no further land alienated. Land holdings in 1979 were as in the accompanying table:

	Hectares
Fijian communally-owned land	1,520,775
Freehold (other than Crown)	181,035
Crown, freehold	35,640
Crown, Schedule A	59,940
Crown, Schedule B	31,185
Rotuman communal	4,455
	1,833,030

Crown land shown in the table has been purchased by the Crown from time to time. Some of this is land that has reverted to the Crown when the Fijian mataqali, or land-holding unit, has died out. Other Crown land is that for which no Fijian owners could be found at the time of Cession. Something like 116,00 hectares of Fijian land is leased, principally to non-Fijians.

Land Sales Act. A 1973 Land Sales Act aims at defeating speculation by restricting purchases of freehold land by non-residents. A resident is classed as a citizen or person who has lived in Fiji for at least seven years. Generally the consent of the Minister of Finance is needed before a non-resident can buy a large undeveloped parcel; if this is obtained and the land is subsequently resold at a profit without development, the seller is liable to tax on the profit at income tax rates.

Native Land Trust Board. With the agreement of the Fijian people, the government created the Native Land Trust Board in 1940 and gave it control of all native land on behalf of the Fijians. The board has three duties: to protect the interests of native owners by reserving ample lands for their present and future needs; to provide suitable land for settlement; and to secure continuity of policy and security of tenure. Certain land classified as native reserve may not be leased or otherwise disposed of, while all other native lands may be leased by the board to people of any race.

In 1975, the Native Land Trust Board set up a Native Land Development Corporation as a public company to develop Fijian land with maximum involvement of Fijian landowners as shareholders, managers, and businessmen. The company also takes an interest in general business ventures, and by 1979 had brought into several local businesses and was managing the new Seaqaqa sugar-cane estate on Vanau Levu.

The Department of Lands, Mines and Surveys administers Crown Lands and the leasing thereof. The position, since 1940, is that persons wishing to acquire land in Fiji must either (a) buy or lease from the owners or alienated, or freehold land; or (b) lease any available land from the Native Land Trust Board or from the Department of Lands, etc.

Landlord and Tennant Act. The Agricultural Landlord and Tennant Ordinance has operated since 1967 to help overcome the problem that most agricultural development in the country is on leased land. The legislation initially provided for tenancy over renewable 10-year periods, as well as five-yearly rent assessments if desired.

As a result of a committee appointed to review this ordinance, in 1976 an amendment was made which raised the minimum period for which an agricultural lease can be granted to 30 years. This gave tennants of Fijian land much greater security of tenure. Leasehold disputes can be decided by and independent tribunal; and rent revisions may be considered through an independent authority.

PRIMARY PRODUCTION. Fiji's chief export-earning industries are sugar, fishing, gold and copra. Banana exports, once a big earner of overseas exchange, ceased in 1974. Ginger became a new export and surpassed the value achieved by bananas. Industries which produce the most for home consumption are dairying, rice, fruit and vegetable growing.

Sugar. Sugar was grown commercially in Fiji as

far back as 1870 around what is now Suva. The industry was tenative until the Australian Colonial Sugar Refining Co. became interested in Fiji and built the first sugar mill at Nausori, by the Rewa River, about 22 km from Suva in 1882. The same company established mills at Rarawai, on the "dry" side of the island, at Labasa, on Vanau Levu, and a large mill at Lautoka in the north-west of Viti Levu.

About the same time that CSR was establishing itself on the Rewa, several other smaller mills were set up, but by 1926 the Australian company was the only sugar miller in the colony. The company closed down its Nausori mill in 1959. Originally sugar was grown on large estates in Fiji, mostly with indentured Indian labour, but when the indentured system ceased after 1916, the large sugar estates were gradually broken up and, instead, Fiji's sugar industry began to be worked on the present system of small holdings by tenant farmers.

Over the years there was a number of industrial disputes, and in the 1960s there were two important inquiries into the sugar industry. The CSR established a local subsidiary, South Pacific Sugar Mills Ltd., to operate the Fiji industry, but after the second inquiry, in 1969, the CSR announced that it was unprofitable for it to remain in the industry in Fiji and that it would withdraw – after the 1972 crushing season.

The Fiji Government on March 31, 1973, purchased the CSR Company's 36,199,300 shares in South Pacific Sugar Mills Ltd., at 27.625 cents a share. In addition the Fiji Government purchased CSR Company's freehold land for $3.75 million.

On April 1, 1973, the Fiji Sugar Corporation Ltd., (FSC) took over the assets of South Pacific Sugar Mills Ltd., except for the CSR freehold land which came under direct Fiji Government administration.

FSC was formed by the Government as a public company to run the milling on commercial lines. All but 2.2 per cent of its shares are owned by the government. The company has a board appointed by the government. Part of the agreement with CSR provided that CSR should continue as marketing agents for Fiji sugar, but in 1975, the government decided to undertake its own marketing. The Fiji Sugar Marketing Co. Ltd., was formed in 1976. In 1979 a new FSC subsidiary company, South Pacific Distillers Ltd., was formed to manufacture rum, gin, vodka, whisky, brandy and industrial alcohol with a factory at Lautoka. Chairman of the Fiji Sugar Corporation is Mr. A. D. Leys, a Suva lawyer. Mr. J. S. Thomson is Independent Chairman of the Sugar Board.

In March, 1976, the government announced it would restructure the organisation of the sugar industry. It said the Sugar Board and Advisory Council would be abolished and a statutory sugar authority created with production, marketing, research and other areas. These proposals were still under consideration in 1980.

Sugar production reached a peak of 400,000 tonnes in 1968, then began to decline for various reasons. After nationalisation, the government concentrated on modernisation, with new equipment in the flour mills, a bulk loading system at Lautoka and a new cane-growing project at Seaqaqa on Vanau Levu, which, in 1977, produced 105,667 tonnes of cane. Production began to rise and the industry broke all records for the 1979 season and the 1979/80 crush. The 4,058,251 tonnes of cane crushed in the season ending on February 7, 1980, beat the standing 1970 record by 1,172,000 tonnes, and the 473,181 tonnes of sugar made beat the 1968 record by 73,000 tonnes.

Sugar marketing. Following the expiry of the Commonwealth Sugar Agreement and United States Sugar Act in 1974, Fiji in 1975 concluded an agreement with the European Economic Community which ensured continued minimum sales of about 170,000 tonnes of sugar a year to the EEC (effectively Britain) at a guaranteed minimum price. Fiji also has long-term sugar supply agreements with New Zealand, Malaysia and Singapore. In 1977, under a new International Sugar Agreement, Fiji was given a world quota of 125,000 tonnes. As this does not include the EEC quota, Fiji can therefore sell all the sugar it produces.

For the year ended March 31, 1978, FSC reported a net profit of $6.69 million.

The Fiji Sugar Corporation provides about 50 field officers to advise and help farmers, undertake pest, weed and soil control, conduct research and plant breeding. The FSC also provides over 645 km of permanent railways and 240 km of temporary track to transport cut cane from the fields to the mills.

At the end of 1979, about 17,000 farmers were growing cane. About 3,800 people were employed by the sugar mills and related establishments and about 6,000 found seasonal work harvesting sugar.

Copra. The preparation and export of copra was Fiji's earliest industry, commencing with the first white population, and now, as an export earner, ranks after sugar. But the industry has been restricted to Vanua Levu and outer islands – initially because coconuts on the mainland of Viti Levu were completely controlled by a pest peculiar to Fiji, the purple moth *(Levuana iridescens),* and no attempt was made to cultivate coconut plantations there.

The Coconut Industry Ordinance provides for the development and control of the copra industry. It provides also for a Coconut Industries Board and a Coconut Advisory Council. The board is not a marketing organisation, as in some other Pacific islands, and does not compulsorily acquire all export copra but controls the industry by licensing buyers, processors etc.

About 50 per cent of Fiji copra is produced from Fijian native groves and subsidy payments for rehabilitation work and new plantings have in the past been big incentives for plantation improvements, but when the subsidy scheme started to tail off in 1969 most of this work tailed off also.

In addition, because of the combined effects of a series of hurricanes and droughts which damaged palms in the main coconut areas, coupled with the fact that more than half the palms are estimated to be well past their best bearing age, copra production has fallen each year.

The difficulties faced by the industry were made even worse by wildly fluctuating copra prices ranging from a low of $65.68 a tonne in June 1972 to a record peak of $585.78 a tonne in March 1974. In mid-1975 prices were again so depressed that for the first time the Fiji Government stepped in with a direct subsidy.

The Fiji Government subsidy maintains a price of Fiji 1 grade copra at $190 a tonne at Suva. Producers repay the subsidy when the actual market price exceeds $190. The repayment is the difference between $190 and the actual price. In 1977, the Government announced that it was preparing proposals for a copra price stabilisation scheme designed to replace the subsidy. In 1978, prices averaged $265.75 a tonne.

As plantations recover from the hurricane damage of the early 1970s, copra production has begun to rise after the low year of 1975. In 1976, production began to rise and reach 26,934 tonnes; in 1977 it was estimated to be 28,000 tonnes but fell to 25,606 tonnes in 1978.

In April, 1977, the Government opened a $2 million factory at Suva to make a range of coconut oil based foodstuffs, including margarine and other edible products. A company, Fiji Foods Ltd, has a government investment with lesser interests held by a British company and Fijian co-operatives. The year 1970 was the last year in which raw copra was exported by Fiji, since then all copra has gone to the local mills which nevertheless run at only about half their full capacity. Meal is also exported, but the amount is falling due to local needs. For nine months of 1978 to September 30, 7,000 tonnes of oil seed, copra and meal valued at $550,000 were exported. For the same period 23,000 tonnes of coconut oil valued at $11.19 million were exported.

Rhinoceros beetle. Experiments with an introduced virus had dramatically curbed the incidence of the palm-destroying beetle infection by the end of 1974. The government was so encouraged by this success that it wound up the Coconut Pests and Diseases Board, originally formed to fight the beetle, and transferred its functions to the Department of Agriculture.

Pineapples and citrus. In mid-1979, pineapples were grown in Fiji for local consumption. In 1978 120 ha were devoted to pineapple growing. A small quantity is exported.

In 1977, the Government announced that the National Marketing Authority, the British Commonwealth Development Corporation and groups from New Zealand and Hong Kong would join in a project to plant 100 ha of oranges. A canning factory would be built to process the juice for local and export sales.

Other fruits and vegetables. Exports of small quantities of fruit and vegetables such as yams, dalo, melons, beans, tomatoes, garlic and egg plant are being sold mainly to New Zealand. In 1974 a New Zealand-backed company, Votua Levu Farms Ltd., began airfreighting vegetables to New Zealand from a 16 ha irrigated farm it established at Nadi. This trade by mid-1977 was growing rapidly and was worth several hundred thousand dollars a year.

Ginger. Ginger has rapidly become an important export crop. In 1976, 1,026 tonnes were produced from 59 ha and were worth $635,000. Another 20 ha were planted in 1977 but in 1978 the total area planted fell to 75 ha. Several firms were planning to process ginger. Raw ginger was being exported to Asia, North America and Europe. In 1978 1,826 tonnes valued at $1,199 million were exported.

Passionfruit. After showing promise in the mid-1970s, this industry has declined and one of the two firms processing the fruit for export has left the Sigatoka Valley. However, efforts are being made to revive the industry and it showed an upward trend in 1978 when 369 tonnes were harvested compared with 229 tonnes in 1977. In 1979, there were 215 growers, 200 less than a few years ago, but the farmers are learning newer methods and yields of up to 39,774 kg per hectare have been achieved. Growers are under contract to South Pacific Foods, the only processor in the valley and a subsidiary of the Sydney firm Mangrove Mountain Juices Pty. Ltd. All the fruit is pulped and the bulk of it exported to the parent company, a small amount being sold in Fiji. Pawpaw, guava, mango and banana are also processed. In 1976 the exported juice was worth $61,837.

Rice. Fiji has abandoned hopes to be self-sufficient in rice by 1979-80 but still hopes to achieve this aim later. Main growing areas are the Rewa Valley near Suva, and the Navua district about 50 km from Suva. About 8,900 ha of double-cropped irrigated ricelands are planted annually and production in 1978 was 16,105 tonnes of paddy, equivalent to 10,951 tonnes of polished rice. Rice imports in the same year amounted to 16,416 tonnes worth $6,025,186. Main efforts are to increase yield rather than the area planted.

The rice schemes were launched with FAO/UNDP aid and now derive much support from Australia, which is supplying experts and equipment.

Cocoa. Cocoa development in Fiji has been slow due to problems with seed varieties. But the government has persevered with the crop as a money earner for small holders in country areas, partly as an alternative to copra. In 1975, the government said trials had appeared to overcome plant disease problems and the way seemed clear for a steady growth of the industry, although on a moderate scale. The variety Amelanado appears to be the answer. In 1976 estimates put the area of cocoa at 120 to 160 ha scattered through Taveuni, the Cakaudrove area of Vanua Levu, and south-eastern Viti Levu.

Total production in 1977 was 97 tonnes. It rose to 122 tonnes in 1978 and 144 tonnes in 1979, the increases coinciding with a rise in world prices. The National Marketing Authority paid $220,680 for 122.6 tonnes in 1978.

Tobacco. British Tobacco Ltd., and Carreras Ltd., now make cigarettes in a jointly-owned factory operated in the name of the Central Manufacturing Co. Ltd. In 1976, about 269 ha was devoted to commercial tobacco production which yielded 473,182 kg of tobacco. The 800 growers earned $580,000 in 1976 when the factory produced a record 600 million cigarettes. Production in 1978 was 12 tonnes of manufactured tobacco and 618 tonnes of cigarettes.

Tuna fishing. In partnership with the Japanese in a fish freezing and canning factory at Levuka, the government is the largest exporter of fish products in the South Pacific Islands. In 1977 Fiji exported 2,113 tonnes of fish products worth $4.68 million and in the nine months of 1978 to September 30, exports totalled 2,931 tonnes worth $6.22 million. The Pacific Fishing Co., owned by two Japanese companies, has operated a tuna freezing factory at Levuka since 1964. Fiji became a significant shareholder in 1975 when a canning factory was built for $1.3 million. This was followed by the opening of a can manufacturing plant in which the government has shares.

Korean and Taiwanese fish catchers supply the factory along with the Ika Corporation of Fiji, a government statutory authority, established in 1975. By March, 1979, Ika was operating six ships, three on charter from Hokuku Marine of Tokyo. In 1979, it employed 150 men, 101 of them Fijians. The total catch by Ika in 1978 was 2,524 tonnes, mainly skipjack with 15 per cent yellowfin. However, Fiji spent in 1978 in canned fish imports about as much as it had earned in fish exports, mainly because canned fish needs no refrigeration.

Other fishing. Fiji has a comparatively large fleet of fishing boats operated by local fishermen. Latest figures show that 2,830 fishermen are supplying the local fish markets and these are registered as: Central Division 40 per cent; Northern Division 20 per cent; Western Division 30 per cent and Eastern Division 10 per cent. In the past, coastal village and outer-island fishing has been mainly for subsistence although Suva Market has always seemed well supplied. An increasing number of fishermen are now turning to commercial fishing, as they are assured of marketing outlets through the National Marketing Authority and the fish carrier service of the Fisheries Division. More fishermen are being taught fishing methods and the correct use of nets. Local fish prices have been kept fairly stable by the National Marketing Authority and freezer capacity at local markets is increasing, making for greater production.

Fish retailed in Fiji in 1978 increased by 17.7 per cent in weight and 36.29 in value over the 1977 catch. Apart from municipal market sales, 99.4 tonnes were sold by the marketing authority and 1,024 tonnes in hotels, shops and other outlets. Subsistence fishermen caught 4,095 tonnes in 1978.

Other marine products. Efforts by the government in 1974 to encourage trading in beche-de-mere, shark fins and shells is paying off. Exports of shark fins, beche-de-mere, trochus, mother of pearl and turtle shells earned Fiji more than $587,000 in 1979. This included 32 tonnes of shark fins worth $284,000, 167 tonnes of trochus shells worth $165,000, 23 tonnes of mother of pearl shell worth $50,000 and 200 kg of turtle shell worth $8,000. Most of the marine products come from co-operatives in Bua, the Lau Group and the Yasawas.

Dairy farming. In 1978 there were some 280 registered dairy farmers who were milking about 13,000 cows. Forty-six farmers were supplying whole milk by retail. Local commercial production is about 450,000 kg butterfat a year. The large co-operative, Rewa Dairy Co. completed its modernisation programme in 1977. During the year 1976-77 it handled 4.8 million litres of milk and 190,000 kg of butter. It also produces powdered milk.

The emphasis is on whole milk production resulting in 1978 in an 11 per cent increase in butter-fat equivalent supplied to the Rewa Co-operative Dairy Co. by the farmers. But milk production per cow is poor, the result of inferior nutrition and poor stock management. There has been an improvement in access to farms and the farmers are getting better prices for their milk.

Local production had had little impact on imports, which have risen steadily over the last few years. Butter imports increased from $844,000 in 1975 to well over a million in 1978.

Beef. Fiji is striving for self-sufficiency in agricultural products but imports of farm produce are still high. There has been a big drive to increase beef production and two large beef development projects promise good results. The projects are the Uluisaivou Corporation scheme on 40,470 ha on Kadavu and the Yalavou project on 25,092 ha of hilly country along the upper reaches of the Sigatoka River. However, Fiji has problems, a shortage of female breeding cattle, a slow rate of development and competition from imported beef, comparatively cheap and of good quality. A private cannery produces corned beef.

Canned and fresh beef imports in 1977 reached nearly $3 million. Local cattle slaughtered in 1978 provided 2,755 tonnes of boneless beef, representing 43 per cent of beef consumption.

Goat meat helps to make up the gap in meat production and is essential to the Indian community. There are about 60 goat farmers producing about

260 tonnes of meat a year. The production of pig meat is improving and only 93 tonnes of pigmeat was imported in 1978. The local industry was expected to produce about 600 tonnes of pigmeat in 1979.

Poultry. Fiji is almost self-sufficient in eggs, producing more than 30 million in 1978 from flocks totalling nearly 155,000, but there was also a slight rise in imported eggs which represents 4 per cent of Fiji's egg consumption. Fiji produced 2,904 tonnes of poultry meat in 1978 and imported about 420 tonnes. Local hatcheries produced 119,000 layers and 1,322,000 meat chicks in the same year but also imported 32,000 layers and 885,000 meat chicks.

Timber. Fiji is pinning much faith in Caribbean Pine. By the 1980s the export of pine logs, chip and pulp is expected to be worth $50 million at present values, and could even replace sugar as No. 1 primary export. In 1973, the Government accepted an FAO recommendaton for a pine planting project to cover large areas of dry unused hill country in Viti Levu and Vanua Levu. Pilot plantations have indicated a dividend – soil under the pines is so improved by them that cattle can be grazed in the forests.

Up to the end of 1978 about 40,000 ha of pine had been planted and more than 11,000 ha of hardwood plantations had been established, with yearly plantings averaging 700 ha. Pine planting has been extended to some islands in Lau and Lomaiviti. Backing has come from New Zealand with over $2 million in aid, and in 1975 a $10 million loan from the Commonwealth Development Corporation was negotiated, for pine scheme purposes.

Mahogany planting was suspended in 1972 after trial plantations came under attack by a borer beetle. It is being continued on a limited scale, while attempts to control the beetle are made. Eucalyptus trials have started and are promising. Fiji still imports timber but the amount is static as use of local timber increases.

Production is only just beginning as the plantations are young. In 1978, of the 180,000 cubic metres of sawlogs produced, only two per cent came from the new plantations, but, by 1985, it is expected that sawlog production will have doubled to 300,000 cubic metres with plantation timber contributing 20 per cent. In addition, about 200,000 cubic metres of pine pulpwood or chips will be exported by 1985. By the year 2000, total production of sawlogs and pulpwood is expected to be about 1,500,000 cubic metres. Already there are signs that timber production is saving import costs. In 1974, Fiji spent $1,795,000 on imported timber. In 1978, imported timber cost only about $200,000. In 1979, Fiji had 14 sawmilling companies.

Years of research by the Forestry Department into the quality of local timbers has shown that properly worked and treated, they are acceptable and often superior substitutes for imports. Mill trials with coconut timber, a difficult log to saw, indicates even this could be put to large scale use.

In 1975 it was estimated that native forests would be the main supply for 10 to 15 years more before the new pine and other forests could be cut.

MINING. The ownership of all minerals in Fiji is vested in the Crown under legislation that goes back to 1908. A Mining Board has oversight of the industry. The most valuable mining in Fiji up to 1980 has been gold-mining, now confined to the mine operated by Emperor Gold Mining Co. Ltd. in the Vatukoula area near Tavua, in northern Viti Levu. In the past returns have been very rich and in 1977 nearly $7 million-worth of fine gold from Vatukoula was exported.

About a dozen major international companies – British, US, French, Canadian, South African, Australian – were actively prospecting in Fiji in 1979. The search was mainly for base metals, chiefly copper and oil. Four areas have been chosen for seabed drilling for oil.

When there was a rise in gold price several were giving attention to gold and Emperor was hopeful that the high gold prices of 1974-75 would make the exploration of low grade ores worthwhile The gold price boom, Emperor said, would extend the life of Vatukoula mine by 20 years or more since low grade ores in its depths had become worthwhile to mine. However, in January 1978, about 600 of the 1,300 workers were dismissed at Vatukoula, and it was uncertain whether the mine would continue operations.

Negotiations for purchase of the mine by the Fiji Government fell through in 1979. With the gold price boom, the company seemed to have entered a new era of prosperity and more miners were employed but in 1980 another miners' strike was creating difficulties.

Production at Vatukoula has dropped steadily, from 3,230 kg in 1970 to 2,146 kg in 1975, 2,035 kg in 1976, 1,519 kg in 1977 and about 1,000 kg in 1978. After experiments, Emperor began in 1974 to extract and refine tellurium in addition to gold. In 1976, tellurium worth $17,415 was recovered.

Apart from gold, no other minerals have been exported by Fiji for some time. After investing nearly $3 million in preparing to mine a low grade bauxite reserve at Wainunu, Vanua Levu, a Japanese consortium withdrew early in 1974, mainly because currency fluctuations had affected the viability of the project.

Copper. In 1975 interest was centred at Namosi, about 40 km inland north-west from Suva, where the giant Amax group, working with the Anglo-American group of South Africa, CRA and the Preussag group of West Germany were exploring copper deposits. In 1977 they announced that they would intensify work on the prospect which looked most promising. However, optimistic statements by Fiji Government ministers at the time indicated that a major copper mine was a strong possibility by the end of the 1970s. Amax was working in an area pinpointed by the Barringer group of Canada, whose Fiji interests it purchased.

Most of the areas licensed to Barringer had been surrendered by it in 1975, but several pinpointed areas, including Namosi, were being investigated more closely. Released areas were being taken up by other companies.

There was disappointment at the end of 1979 when the company reported that the deposits probed so far appeared to be marginal. Work was continuing, however, in 1980.

Other mining companies active in Fiji include Amoco, Metals Miniere Ltd of Australia, Melven Copper Ltd of Australia, Utah International Inc., and CRA Explorations Pty Ltd. In 1977, Pacific Energy & Minerals took over the Southern Pacific petroleum concession and Dakota Exploration (Fiji) had obtained a 7,620 sq. km concession near Lomaiviti. Pacific Energy and Minerals Ltd., and Mapco Inc., both of the United States, planned to begin drilling for oil in Bligh Waters in 1980.

MANUFACTURING. Three industrial subdivisions have been developed at Suva and industry is tending to move out in the direction of Nausori as land becomes scarce in the city area. Other industrial estates are at Lautoka, Nausori, Ba, Tavua, Labasa, Savusavu, Taveuni, Rakiraki and Levuka. The government has plans for estates in rural areas.

There is a wide range of local industries from agricultural equipment, building materials and containers to plastics, furniture, foodstuffs and clothing.

Established industries include:

Aluminium products, acetylene, adhesive, agricultural equipment, aquariums, barbed wire, batteries, beer, biscuits, boats, brooms, butter, bags (paper and plastic), baking powder, beverages (non-alcoholic and alcoholic), building materials, candles, cassette tapes, cement, ceiling installations, umbrellas, cigarettes, clothing, concrete products and ready mixed concrete, coconut products, confectionery, cordials, corrugated iron, cultured pearls, carbonic gas, ceilings, coatings, coir, yoghurt, conduits, containers (metal, paper board, plastic), curry powder, dairy products, detergents, disinfectants, doors, electroplated goods, fibreglass products, fibrous plaster products, fish meal, fruit and vegetable juices and pulp, furniture, fabrics, feeds (animal), flour and sharps, fishing equipment, food products, footwear, handicrafts, honey, hardware, ice cream, insulation and acoustic material, industrial gases, jelly crystals, jewellery, lead products, louvres, matches, meat products, motor bodies, nails, oils, oxygen, paper products, perfumery products, plastics, plywood, polyurethane foam, poultry feeds, packaging materials, paints, pegs, pipes, pool tables, pumps, putty, roll-formed roofing iron, roofing materials, salt, sand and gravel extraction, sauces, screens, shell products, soap products, solar water heaters, solder, solvents, species, staples, steel rolling, sugar (castor and icing), suitcases, switch boards (electric), tanks (metal), tapa cloth, tea packing, thinners, venetian blinds, water proofing materials and compounds, windows, wire (barbed, chain link, mesh-work), wood preservatives, wood products, wrought iron products, polyester fillers.

In addition there is a fisheries base with a cannery and freezing plant, rice milling, and a number of servicing industries including dry-cleaning, laundering, tyre retreading, electroplating, radio repairing, motor vehicle repairing and body building, printing, upholstering, general engineering, civil engineering and building, marine engineering and slipway management, real estate and advertising agencies, commercial colour film, processing and data processing by computer system.

Suva has three slipways and can take vessels from 250 to 1,000 tons and there are ship building and repair firms. The Fiji Sugar Corporation is also opening a distillery at Lautoka.

TOURISM. Fiji tourism showed phenomenal growth averaging 25 per cent in the late 1960s and early 1970s but this was halted by 1974 from the effects of a world-wide depression, coupled with increasing competition from Singapore and Hawaii. In 1975, the number of tourists (average stay 8.1 days) was 161,707, a drop of 10.7 per cent on the previous year. The slide stopped in 1976, with the total (168,665) increasing by 4.3 per cent. The total of 173,019 in 1977 represented a 2.6 per cent increase. The average length of stay rose to 8.4 days in 1977. The 1978 total was estimated to be about 186,000. In 1977, 57,101 sea cruise passengers stopped at Fiji and the total of similar visitors in 1978 was 57,940. These are not included in the visitor totals as many stay only a few hours. Hotel building slowed down with the slump in tourism but several new hotels have been opened since 1977. In 1977, hotel capacity was 1,224,554, more than four times the 1970 total. At the end of 1977, the number of rooms available was 3,562 in hotels with more than 30 beds. In 1976, the total was 3,313. By 1980, the estimated need is for more than 10,000 beds. Only sugar earns more than tourism but much of the revenue from tourism is hidden and the actual gain may be higher than that from sugar.

In 1976, the total turnover from hotels, which includes meals, accommodation and liquor receipts, was $30,592,000 and for 1977, $34,318,000. Total earnings, which include income from tours, duty-free shopping, etc., was estimated to be $70 million in 1977. At the end of 1977, 3,436 people were employed in the hotel industry.

The Fiji Visitors Bureau, with offices in Fiji and overseas, is financed from government and private enterprise to supply detailed information for visi-

FIJI — IMPORTS & EXPORTS
($000)

	1970	1975	1976	1977	1978
Imports	90.5	220.97	238.04	281.01	300.84
Exports	62.3	115.95	122.52	164.31	170.72

Note: Exports include re-exports.

tors, and to promote tourism in Fiji. The 1978 budget increased the Fiji Government contribution to $700,000 and $725,000 in 1979 to allow considerable increase of promotion in North America, Australia and New Zealand.

HOUSING. The authority provides subsidised accommodation for people earning a maximum of $140 weekly. The authority's 1977 budget was $10 million. By the end of 1978 the Housing Authority had provided 2,834 houses, 1,118 rental flats, 191 rental houses and 18 shops. Its 1976-80 plans call for the building of another 6,750 units at an estimated cost of $40 million.

LOCAL COMMERCE. Before they can engage in any business, individuals or companies must take out a licence and pay the necessary fee, ranging from a few dollars to a few hundred dollars. Persons engaging in the professions must also take out a licence and pay an annual fee. From 1977, all businesses in towns and cities had to pay an annual business licence fee to the municipal council. The amount of this fee depended on the classification of each business.

Other fees are paid to the Registrar of Titles, for the registration of companies.

OVERSEAS TRADE. Fiji's trade depends on four staple industries – sugar, coconut oil, gold and timber. In 1976 fish became significant, and a cannery was opened. In 1977, all types of fish exports earned $4,686,000. Other promising commodities are ginger and passionfruit. In recent years however, the tourist industry has earned more revenue than some of the above and is thus the most valuable "hidden export", helping to overcome the trade deficit.

The record deficit of $115.5 million in 1976 was increased to 116.7 million in 1977. Exports jumped from $74.26 million in 1973 to $123.74 million in 1974 due mainly to unusually high world prices for sugar, coconut oil and gold.

In recent years imports and exports have been as shown in accompanying tables.

In 1977, Britain was stil Fiji's best customer with most of its $67.45 million purchases (54.1 per cent of all Fiji exports) being sugar. Coconut oil sold to Britain in the same year was worth $6.76 million. Britain was the only EEC country which gave Fiji a favourable trade balance. It was $40.68 million in Fiji's favour. The United States bought sugar worth $5.62 million and other earnings from exports in 1977 included Australia $10.56 million, Malaysia (sugar) $11.65 million, Singapore $7.9 million and Canada $2 million. Western Samoa was Fiji's best neighbouring customer, buying Fiji goods worth $1.29 million. Fiji trades with almost all its island neighbours and has a favourable trade balance with them all. Fiji's world trade deficit in 1977 was $116.69 million. For nine months of 1978 to September 30 the deficit was $108.1 million.

Australia topped the list of Fiji's suppliers in 1977 with a total of $77.94 million. Japan was second with $45.57 million and New Zealand third with $39.1 million. Australia is Fiji's largest supplier of food, and exports from Japan are mainly motor vehicles and goods for the tourist trade. Exports from Britain, mainly machinery, cost $27.55 million. New Zealand supplied food which cost $16.1 million.

FIJI — MAIN IMPORTS
($000)

	1969	1973	1974	1975	1977
Food	15,282	33,909	41,302	38,504	53,829
Beverages and tobacco	1,684	2,961	2,943	2,988	4,532
Crude materials, ex. fuel	674	2,563	3,341	1,920	2,398
Mineral fuels	8,376	15,619	34,490	38,508	54,133
Animal-veg. oils	859	2,408	3,582	3,604	4,203
Chemicals	5,117	10,787	14,641	16,660	20,201
Manufactured goods	15,316	32,048	44,812	39,612	51,062
Machinery, transport equip,	16.761	41,150	35,220	44,734	51,507
Misc. manufactured articles	11,548	25,691	33,890	28,155	30,848
Misc. transactions	2,271	7,508	5,110	6,282	8,301
TOTAL	77,888	174,645	219,331	220,967	281,014

FIJI — ORIGIN OF IMPORTS ($000)

	From Britain	Other Commonwealth	Elsewhere
1969	15,457	37,736	24,587
1970	15,670	44,500	30,311
1975	29,561	119,610	71,796
1977	27,557	158,940	94,517

FIJI — DESTINATION OF EXPORTS ($ million)

	To Britain	Other Commonwealth	Elsewhere
1969	18.4	17.8	12.2
1973	21.7	24.5	18.5
1975	71.8	33.8	2.8
1977	67.4	46.8	11.08

Total imports in 1977 were $281.01 million, an increase of $42.97 million over 1976, and for the nine months of 1978 to September 30, the total was $215.43 million. Exports for 1977 of $164.31 million were $41.79 million more than in 1976. In 1977 sugar earned 75 per cent of exports; coconut products 7.49 per cent; gold 5.26 per cent and fish 3.76 per cent. Major imports in the same year were mineral fuels 19.26 per cent, food 19.15 per cent, machinery 18.32 per cent and manufactured goods 18.17 per cent.

Principal exports in 1977 were: 342,000 tonnes sugar, worth $93,576,000; 18,000 tonnes coconut oil, worth $8,865,000; 5,000 tonnes oil seed, cake and meal, worth $464,000; 1,519 kg gold, worth $6,559,000; 8,000 tonnes cement, worth $478,000; 1,866 tonnes prepared, preserved and canned fish, worth $3,728,000; 247 tonnes fresh, dried and smoked fish, worth $958,000; lumber, worth $724,000; 1,815 tonnes ginger, worth $1,415,000; 90,000 tonnes molasses, worth $1,942,000; 671,000 kg bakery products, worth $465,000; 17,000 kg cigarettes, worth $60,000; 151,000 litres paints, worth $310,000; 2,061,000 sq. m. veneer sheets, worth $801,000.

The following are selected goods imported in 1977 which are competitive with similar goods produced in Fiji: flour and sharps, worth $1,092,000; tea, $1,719,000; canned beef, $1,216,000; fresh beef, $1,615,000; canned fish, $3,677,000; butter, $1,002,000; rice, $5,236,000; beer, $280,000; unmanufactured tobacco, $935,000; clothing,

FIJI'S PRINCIPAL EXPORTS ($'000)

	1973	1975	1977	1978 (Jan-Sept prov.)
Sugar	34,280	94,717	93,756	43,905
Coconut oil	5,669	5,064	8,865	11,190
Oil seed, cake and meal	480	306	464	550
Gold	6,125	8,584	6,559	3,984
Cement	301	588	478	380
Fish — prep. preserved and canned	—	179	3,728	5,874
Fish — fresh, dried and smoked	—	34	958	349
Lumber	550	397	724	620
Ginger	610	607	1,415	639
Molasses	786	1,242	1,942	2,555
Bakery products	336	473	465	446
Cigarettes	95	19	60	49
Paints	275	190	310	258
Veneer sheets	745	597	801	433
Domestic exports	52,373	115,948	124,484	75,442
Re-exports	22,053	26,345	39,831	31,879
TOTAL EXPORTS	74,426	142,293	164,316	107,321

$6,024,000; paints, $375,000; lumber, $73,000. The list for 1980 is expected to show that Fiji is now self-sufficient in lumber.

Fiji co-operatives. About 1,100 co-operative societies of all types operated in Fiji in 1979 – with a total membership of more than 40,000. Most small towns and agricultural settlements have one or two for the purpose of marketing copra, and there are co-operative land, fishing and other ventures. The Fiji Co-operative Association has been developed as the central wholesale supplier for retail co-operatives throughout the country.

Co-operatives are supervised by the Department of Co-operatives. A co-operative training centre at Lami, Suva, is attended by co-op officials from many other Pacific Island countries. Most towns have a municipal market where local farmers sell vegetables, fruit, eggs and fish. Saturday is the main market day.

About 800 were of the village consumer-and-marketing type. There were 21 co-operative wholesale associates.

Customs tariff. Fiji uses the Brussels Nomenclature schedule for import duties. This is a very detailed system and breaks down the schedule into more than 1,200 individual items. Fiji also now uses the single-line system. The tariff rate is divided into fiscal duty and customs duty. There is an export tax on some primary products and minerals.

The import duties range from free on several staple food lines (incl. livestock, butter, cereals, flour, margarine), some plants, chemicals, pharmaceutical goods, and fertilisers, and up to a maximum of 70 per cent on a very few lines. Details of duties may be obtained from the Comptroller-General of Customs in Suva.

FINANCE. For budget purposes, Fiji divides its revenue and expenditure into "recurrent" and "capital". Its recurrent revenue comes from taxation, customs and excise duty, post office receipts, licence fees, etc. Its capital revenue comes mostly from raising loans; from grants and from appropriations from general revenue.

FIJI — RECURRENT BUDGET (in $ million)

	1977	1978	1979*	1980*
Revenue	151.7	160.35	192.46	223.54
Expenditure	155.07	172.76	196.6	223.54

*1979/80 figures are estimates.

Taking the capital revenue ($54.14 million) and capital expenditure ($54.46 million) into account, Fiji budgeted in 1980 for a small deficit of about $318,000. Main revenue estimated for 1979 included customs duty, $61.874 million; income tax and other internal taxes and licences, $94.879 million; fees, royalties, sales and reimbursements, $13,564 million; port dues and rent of government property, $2.139 million.

Operating expenditure for 1979 included $75.56 million for personal emoluments, $41.21 million for education, $16.16 million for health, $2.87 million for the University of the South Pacific, $15.65 million for economic services, $27.53 million for general administration, $5.09 million for pensions and $34.57 million for the public debt. Capital revenue for 1979 included $33.45 million from overseas loans and $3.95 million in grant aid. Capital expenditure included $1.33 million for prisons, $16.23 million for infrastructure, $6.41 million for social services, $6.43 million for rural infrastructure and $1.47 million for rural social development.

Tax system. The Department of Inland Revenue administers the laws relating to income taxation, estate and gift duties, and assesses and collects those duties. Both individuals and companies are liable to income tax. The tax year is the calendar year.

Income tax. The 1974 Income Tax Act came into force on January 1, 1974 and replaced the Income Tax Ordinance of 1965. It introduced a new scale for the taxation of incomes. The pay as you earn, and provisional tax systems still apply.

Basic tax is levied at the rate of 2.5 cents on every dollar of income of every resident whose income exceeds $600 a year; and on every dollar of chargeable income derived during the year by every company, except non-resident shipping companies.

In addition to basic tax, normal tax is levied on chargeable incomes, i.e. after deduction of the main allowances such as those for single people, widows and widowers with dependent child, non-employed spouse, working wife, child allowance, education, dependent blood relative, besides life insurance or provident fund payments, professional membership, subscriptions and journals.

As an example, normal tax on chargeable income between $8,000 and $10,000 is $1,970 plus 45 per cent of each dollar above $8,000.

Fiji citizens and residents pay a 5 per cent tax on company interest and dividends. Non-residents are liable to a 15 per cent dividend withholding tax. The former income tax surcharge has been abolished. Company tax is 35 per cent; for non-resident shipping companies it is 2 per cent; for non-resident life insurance companies 27.5 per cent; for other non-resident companies doing business in Fiji it is 42.5 per cent. Profits remitted out of Fiji by companies are not subject to withholding tax.

All Fiji employers are required to pay a levy of 1 per cent of their annual payroll to the Fiji National Training Council, but can claim grants from the council for the training of employees.

Fiji has arrangements for relief from double taxation of income with several countries including Britain, Australia and New Zealand.

Currency. Fiji's decimal currency has notes in denominations of 50 cents, $1, $2, $5, $10 and $20. Coins are 1c, 2c (bronze), 5c, 10c, 20c, and 50c (cupronickel). The 50c coin was added in 1975.

In 1974 the Fiji dollar's link with the pound sterling was broken and attached to the US dollar for the purposes of exchange transactions. In 1975 the government also ended the tie with the US dollar and in mid-1975 the Fiji dollar was "floating". The rate for exchange purposes is calculated by the Central Monetary Authority and is based on prevailing rates of currencies of several countries having major trade with Fiji. Fiji is a member of the International Monetary Fund, World Bank, and various other international finance agencies.

Banks. Trading banks in 1979 were Bank of New Zealand; Bank of New South Wales; Australia and New Zealand Banking Group Ltd; Bank of Baroda; Barclays Bank International Ltd and the National Bank of Fiji.

The National Bank of Fiji provides savings bank facilities at all post offices and postal agencies and in 1975 opened its first branches at Ba and at Walu Bay, Suva. It operates five and a half days a week. It is now a state-owned trading bank. Banking hours are 10 a.m. to 3 p.m. Monday to Thursday and 10 a.m. to 4 p.m. Friday; closed weekends. Head office and main branch are in Gordon Street, Suva.

Fiji Development Bank. This is a statutory body set up as a source of credit for agriculture, industrial and commercial ventures. Funds come from the government as grants and loans, and from the Asian Development Bank. In March, 1979 outstanding advances by it totalled $28,178,000. The bank also operates a Stock Exchange which opened in June, 1979.

Central Monetary Authority. The Fiji Government created the Central Monetary Authority in April, 1973 as its prime instrument for control of the monetary system. The authority will evolve into a full central bank. It succeeded the old Currency Board. Functions include the issue of currency, control of bank-lending interest rates, foreign exchange control, and acting as a banking institution for commercial banks.

Credit unions. At the end of 1978 there were 375 registered credit unions with a total membership of 56,762 and savings of $4,875,056. Outstanding loans totalled $4,481,249 and total assets were $5,447,002.

Investment incentives. Fiji welcomes investment in manufacturing industries and offers many incentives to foreign investors. But the government has a priority list and the Ministry of Commerce's policy is to see local participation in any foreign-sponsored undertaking when possible. Concessions include income tax concessions (up to five years free tax) reduced rates of withholding tax on interest and dividend paid to non-residents; accelerated depreciation relief; permit for primary industries to write off certain development costs in the year in which they occur and to carry losses forward until they have been fully recouped; duty concessions on imported plant, machinery, equipment and raw materials; protection against imports.

The extent of concessions depends on the benefits an industry is likely to give Fiji. Under Central Monetary Authority guidelines the equity capital and loans should be a ratio of one in three, but this formula can be varied in special cases.

Fiji has tax treaties with several countries, enabling many foreign investors to gain relief in their own country. Industries on the protection list include flour milling, tea blending, and steel rolling.

The government prefers local and foreign borrowing for setting up a new industry to be in the same ratio as the local and foreign shareholding in the company. Finance is available from the Fiji Development Bank, Fiji National Provident Fund, and normal local sources.

Businessmen seeking information about regulations covering foreign investment, establishment of new industries, business fees and licences, should in the first instance contact the Permanent Secretary for Commerce, Industry and Co-operatives, PO Box 2118, Suva, Fiji.

Development plans. The capital budget estimates are presented at the same time as the recurrent budget but this budget is part of a plan of development that covers a period of years, usually five.

As Fiji is now independent it does not qualify for CD and W grants, nonetheless capital aid and development grants are still promised by Britain for the years immediately ahead.

Revenue for the 1975 capital fund was estimated at $30 million. It included local loans of $5.6 million; overseas loans of $18 million; British, Australian, New Zealand and Canadian grants totalling $1.3 million; other aid in kind of $4.7 million.

A plan for the economic development of Fiji over the years 1976-80 was published by the Fiji Government at the end of 1975 and approved by both houses of Parliament. It is the seventh in a series of five year plans.

A total capital expenditure of $342,598,000 is envisaged. The breakdown of this is administrative services $29,547,000; agriculture $20,705,000; fisheries $6,398,000; forestry $14,500,000; sugar industry development $9,684,000; mineral resources $2,702,000; commerce and industry $3,416,000; education $17,782,000; youth and sport $900,000; health $14,109,000; housing $16,303,000; marine $7,037,000; civil aviation $5,628,000; posts and telecommunications $19,458,000; roads and bridges $29,725,000; sewerage $10,880,000; water supplies $38,104,000; hydro-electricity $59,800,000; public works $4,147,000; rural services $24,610,000; miscellaneous $3,770,000.

Target of the plans include a basic growth of 7% a year in the gross national product; the limitation of population growth to 2% a year; the creation of some 22,000 new jobs; the opening of large areas of land in Fiji which are still inaccessible and largely unused.

Other prime targets; to build some 1120 km of new roads; three outer island airstrips a year; three new outer island jetties a year; to restore sugar output from about 250,000-300,000 tonnes a year to 400,000 tonnes and possibly 600,000 tonnes; to develop hydro-electricity potential in the interior of Viti Levu; to continue the large scale pine planting scheme started in the late 1960s and planned to cover about 52,650 ha; to boost local beer, dairy pork and vegetable production; to build up a large local tuna fishing fleet; to improve water supplies and local radio telecommunications.,

The seventh plan covers every other aspect of economic happening in Fiji, including encouragement of local industry, financial institutions, and the creation of a local stock exchange. It aims to achieve free primary education and make a great improvement in secondary education facilities; health projects will largely centre on family planning and the prevention of disease, many traditional diseases having been eliminated or nearly so.

The plan will be financed by the government out of its own annual revenues; about 28% ($78,000,000) will be borrowed locally; cash grants, soft and commercial loans totalling $102,000,000 will be obtained from foreign sources; and foreign capital aid worth $35,000,000 is hoped for under this optimistic plan. A mid-term review of the plan was to be made in 1978.

TRANSPORT. Fiji is well supplied with public transport. Virtually every road capable of taking a bus has a bus service and there are well over 300 operators in the country with 700 vehicles. At least 3,000 passengers a day travel some section of the road between Suva and Lautoka by this means. In addition there are about 1,000 taxis. All bus and taxi fares are fixed by the Road Transport Authority, but some taxis in country areas do not have meters installed.

Roads. The longest road in the country is that around Viti Levu of 510 km. From Suva to Lautoka, west-about, it is called Queen's Road; and from Suva to Lautoka, east-about, it is King's Road.

There are 2,960 km of public roads in Fiji, of which 280 are bitumen surfaced. Work is under way on rebuilding the Suva-Nadi road which will add another 110 km of bitumen-sealed roads.

The 64 km Nadi-Sigatoka section and the 56 km Suva-Deuba section have been completed but floods created by hurricane Wally in March 1980, damaged the new road, obliterating it on some stretches. Savusavu and Labasa are linked by a gravel road completed in 1979. A considerable amount of feeder road construction is in constant progress in all parts of Fiji.

Vehicles. At December 31, 1978, there were 42,402 vehicles of all kinds registered in Fiji. This total includes 19,415 private cars, 11,978 goods vehicles and 2,022 motor cycles. As a fuel conservation measure the government has imposed restrictions on the import of private cars and the engine capacity.

In 1979, there were 889 buses operating under road service licences issued by the Transport Control Board which exercises strict supervision over the bus transport industry. Of the taxi fleet, which numbered 1,403 vehicles in 1979, 535 were based at Suva. Taxi meters are compulsory in Suva, Nausori, Nadi and Sigatoka. In 1979, there were 670 rental cars operating.

Overseas airlines. Qantas has four terminating flights a week (Sunday, Monday, Wednesday and Saturday) from Melbourne through Sydney to Nadi.

Pan American has four two-way flights a week through Nadi between Sydney and North America via Honolulu.

Air New Zealand has two terminating flights a week Auckland to Nadi (Wednesday and Sunday) until the end of October, 1980, after which there will be three terminating flights a week (Sunday, Monday and Wednesday). There is also a flight on Sundays from Nadi to Los Angeles via Honolulu.

CP-Air operates two flights a week (Friday and Sunday) through Nadi to Sydney and return.

Continental Airlines operates two flights a week (Tuesday and Saturday) Sydney to Nadi with return flights Thursday and Sunday.

Japan Airlines (DC8) operates twice-weekly flights Tokyo-Nadi-Auckland and return.

Air Nauru operates a two-way flight once a week between Nauru, Nadi and Nausori with connections at Nauru for Japan, Guam, Manila, Taipei, Okinawa and Hong Kong.

Polynesian Airlines operates twice weekly between Nadi and Apia.

Fiji-based Air Pacific uses BAC111 jets and HS748s to operate services to Tonga and New Zealand; to Western Samoa; to the Gilbert Islands, Tuvalu and Nauru; to the New Hebrides; and to Brisbane (Australia) via the Solomon Islands and also via New Caledonia.

Domestic airlines. Air Pacific has handed over most of its internal services to Fiji Air with the exception of Nausori to Nadi service and Nausori to Labasa. Over the years the Fiji Government has gradually increased its shareholding in Air Pacific and now holds 75 per cent. Air New Zealand and Qantas retain their stock but are no longer represented on the directorate.

Fiji Air Limited (formerly Air Pacific) operates all domestic routes in Fiji with the exception of Nadi-Nausori-Labasa. It has a fleet of DHC Twin Otter 200s and an amphibian plane. The company is a private one but the government holds about 16 per cent of issued stock.

Pacific Crown Aviation Ltd operates helicopters from a hangar and helicopter base at Lami. Charter work is undertaken for the mining industry, the Fiji Electricity Authority, government departments and private interests.

Turtle Island Airways Ltd operates amphibian planes from Nadi Airport on charter flights to island resorts and other destinations in Fiji. It is also available for "mercy missions".

Airports. Fiji's international airport is at Nadi, about 200 km from Suva by road. A multi-million dollar scheme to upgrade the airport for use by jumbo jets was completed in mid-1975. Improvements included an enlarged terminal building, strengthened runways and more parking aprons.

Apart from Nadi, the most important local airport is at Nausori, 22 km from Suva. It was, like Nadi, built during the war. It is subject to occasional flooding because of its proximity to the Rewa River. The 1,969 m main runway is sealed and has a flare path for night landings. A secondary runway is grass over gravel.

Domestic airstrips (in 1979) were at Ba, 730 m long; Bureta (Ovalau), 790 m; Bua, 1,060 m; Deuba, 760 m; Gau, 760 m; Koro, 760 m; Lakeba, 760 m; Labasa, 1070 m; Laucala Island, 820 m; Malololailai Island, 640 m; Matai, 910 m; Natadola, 595 m; Rabi, 660 m; Savusavu, 915 m; Vanuabalavu, 920 m; Vatukoula, 745 m; Wakaya Island, 730 m; Ono-i-Lau, 760 m.

Ports. The three ports of entry in Fiji are Suva, Lautoka and Levuka. All ports and wharves are under the jurisdiction of the Ports Authority of Fiji, which also assumes responsibility for stevedoring and the supply of cargo-handling machines. It is concerned with developing and expanding harbour and shore facilities to cater for the needs of overseas shipping.

The members of the authority are Messrs T. R. Vakatora (chairman), R. D. Dods, S. Siwatibau, Loh Heng-Kee, P. F. J. Corbett, E. Wong, W. Thompson and Ratu Jone Mataitini. The principal officers are Director-General, Mr. Loh Heng-Kee; Director of Administration, Mr. N. R. Singh; acting Secretary, Mr. Atama Beci; acting Port Accountant, Mr. Ram Pratap; Wharf Managers, Mr. H. L. Jones (Suva), Mr. Vinod Choy (Lautoka), Mr. C. Nilsen (Levuka, Officer-in-charge). Water and fuel oil can be obtained at all three ports. At Lautoka and Suva ships can be connected to telephone services. None of the ports has cranes; all cargo is discharged by ships' derricks. At Suva harbour tugs are available; they are of an ocean-going class, also suitable for salvage work.

Wharves. A new wharf was opened at Levuka in May, 1980. It will take ocean-going vessels drawing nearly 5 m. Lautoka wharf is L-shaped, 135 m long with 10 m alongside at low tide.

The main Suva wharf, King's Wharf, has a face of 484 m and can take vessels up to 42,000 tonnes (P&O Line "Oriana"). The Walu Bay face of the wharf is approx. 147 m.

As well as these main wharves there are smaller ones at Vatia and Pt. Ellington on Viti Levu; at Labasa and Savusavu, Vanua Levu and at Rotuma.

At Suva there are repair facilities for ships up to 1,000 tonnes needing slipping. Engineering facilities for a wide range of repairs for much larger ships also exist at Suva.

Fiji is also gaining a reputation for shipbuilding.

There are three ship repair and building yards at Suva, one government-owned equipped with a gantry crane. The Carpenter group has a new ship repair yard complete with a synchro-lift for vessels of up to 300 tonnes. The yard has capacity for five 300-tonne ships. Charles Whippy and Co. operate the third slip.

Harbour masters are located as follows: Suva Harbour Master's office, King's Wharf, Suva; Lautoka – Lautoka Harbour Master's office, Queen's Wharf, Lautoka; Levuka – Harbour Master and Chief Customs Officer at Customs Office, Levuka jetty, Levuka.

Shipping Services. International shipping services operate as follows:

PACIFIC FORUM LINE: Container, unitised/palletised and reefer cargo service from Melbourne and Sydney to Lautoka and Suva. Also similar from Lyttelton and Auckland to Suva.

PACIFIC NAVIGATION OF TONGA: A five-weekly refrigerated general cargo/container service from Sydney and Brisbane to Suva and Lautoka.

KARLANDER (AUST) PTY LTD: Monthly cargo service Sydney to Lautoka and Suva.

SOFRANA UNILINES (FIJI EXPRESS LINE): To Suva and Lautoka every three weeks from the main ports on the east coast of Australia and monthly to Lautoka from Melbourne and Sydney.

NEW ZEALAND UNIT EXPRESS (NZUE): A fortnightly palletised cargo service from Manila, Keelung, Kaoshiung and Hong Kong to Lautoka and Suva, thence to New Zealand.

NEDLLOYD: Bi-weekly cargo service from Sourabaya, Jakarta, Bangkok, Port Kelang and Singapore to Suva, thence to NZ. Also regular cargo from Northern Europe and UK to Fiji.

CHINA NAVIGATION: Monthly service from main ports Japan to Suva and Lautoka, thence Noumea and NZ.

KYOWA SHIPPING LTD: Monthly from Hong Kong, Taiwan, South Korea and Japan to Fiji.

DAIWA LINE: A 30-day service from Moji, Kobe, Nagoya, Yokohama to Suva and Lautoka. Monthly cargo service from Japan via Guam to Suva and Lautoka.

PAD LINE: Approx three-weekly RO-RO service from Suva to Honolulu, US West Coast and Canadian ports, and back to Suva.

BLUE STAR LINE LTD: Container service direct to and from New Zealand calling at Suva and Honolulu on NZ-US west coast voyages.

REEF SHIPPING: An 18-day service from Auckland to Suva and Lautoka.

PACIFIC LINE: A fortnightly RO-RO cargo service from NZ to Lautoka and Suva.

UNION STEAM SHIP CO. OF NZ LTD: A

RO-RO container/unitised from Auckland to Lautoka and Suva on a 14-day frequency.

BANK LINE: Direct fast monthly service from Hull, Hamburg, Bremen, Antwerp and Rotterdam to Suva and Lautoka.

BANK AND SAVILL LINE LTD: Regular cargo services from US Gulf ports to Australia and NZ call, on demand, at Suva and Lautoka.

WARNER PACIFIC LINE: Unitised/palletised and reefer cargo services every 45 days Honolulu-Pago Pago-Apia-Nukualofa will call, by inducement, at Suva.

SITMAR CRUISES: A year-round cruise programme to South Pacific Islands includes Fiji.

P & O: Liners on cruises from Australia call at Lautoka, Savusavu and Suva. Also liners call at Suva on all eastbound and westbound voyages between Sydney and the US.

ROYAL VIKING STAR LINE: Makes infrequent cruise calls at Suva.

Inter-island shipping. The small, inter-island ship is disappearing from the scene and is being replaced by barges towed by tugs. About 120 local ships are registered with the Fiji Marine Department. The department is being called upon increasingly to use its vessels to maintain communications with some of the outer islands which were formerly served by local shipping companies. When space permits, the department's vessels carry passengers and cargo at normal commercial rates.

COMMUNICATIONS. Internal telephone and radio telephone services are being continually extended in Fiji. Practically all inhabited islands can be contacted by telephone or radio telephone services. There are automatic exchanges in most large towns on Viti Levu with direct dialling between Suva, Lautoka, Nadi, Ba, Nausori, Deuba, Labasa, Levuka, Navua, Rakiraki and Sigatoka.

Fiji is a telecommunications centre for the South Pacific region and is linked by the Commonwealth Pacific Telephone Cable (COMPAC) with Australia, New Zealand, and the international telecommunications network. A satellite earth receiving station, built by Cable and Wireless Company Ltd, operates at Wailoku, Suva.

The telex system, with international subscriber dialling to most world-wide destinations is growing fast and is used extensively by airlines, travel agents, hotels, banks and business concerns.

Radio. Radio broadcasting services are in the sole hands of the Fiji Broadcasting Commission, which broadcasts programmes over three stations daily in Fijian, English and Hindi.

Television. Fiji does not have a public television service, but there is increasing use of television receivers geared to showing pre-recorded video cassettes.

Newspapers. There is a large range of newspapers, the oldest of which is 'The Fiji Times' (established 1869), morning daily based at Suva. Others published by The Fiji Times and Herald Ltd. are the 'Sunday Times' (1979); 'Shanti Dutt', (1935) Hindi weekly; 'Nai Lalakai' (1962), a Fijian weekly; 'Fiji Holiday' (1968), a monthly free newspaper concentrating on the tourists for the tourist industry.

Other newspapers and periodicals are:

'Fiji Beach Press', a bi-monthly in English on the tourist industry, published by News (South Pacific) Ltd of Suva (1969).

'Business News', a monthly business journal published at Suva by the News (South Pacific) Ltd which also publishes 'Air Pacific News', a monthly newspaper and 'Fiji Medical Journal'.

'Contact', a religious weekly (1978), published by the RC Archdiocese of Suva in English and Fijian.

'Fiji', a magazine published by Suva every two months by the Fiji Ministry of Information (March/April 1978).

'Fiji Royal Gazette', official gazette of the Fiji Government published in Suva weekly (1872).

'Fiji Sun', a daily newspaper in English published by Newspapers of Fiji Ltd in Suva (1974).

'Nai Tukuni', a Fijian weekly published in Suva.

The 'Sunday Sun', a weekly newspaper published on Sundays by Newspapers of Fiji Ltd in Suva.

'Jai Fiji', a weekly newspaper in Hindi published in Lautoka (1959).

'Na Mata', a monthly magazine in Fijian published by the Fiji Ministry of Information in Suva (1970).

'Davui', a Fijian monthly, and 'Shankh', a Hindustani monthly, both published by the Ministry of Information.

'Vanua', a newsletter published every two months in English by the Native Land Trust Board (1976).

"The Coconut Telegraph', a newsletter published monthly at Savusavu, Vanua Levu, for the General Electors Association.

'Fiji Sugar', a monthly magazine issued from the office of the Independent Chairman of the Sugar Industry.

'News and Views' published monthly at Lautoka by the Fiji Red Cross Society (1955).

ELECTRICITY. The Fiji Electricity Authority owns all power stations in Fiji except at Vatukoula, where it is owned by the mining company. A $10 million power house has been built at Vuda Point near Nadi and serves most of western Viti Levu. Sixty per cent of Fiji's population lives within the supply areas of the authority's network.

The power supply is generally 230v AC.

The Fiji Government is planning a major hydroelectric power project centred on the Nadrau Plateau in central Viti Levu. Work on the scheme, costing an estimated $125 million, began in 1977 and power generation is expected to begin in 1981.

WATER. Water supplies are provided to all main towns. Vatukoula has a private supply. The Suva, Ba, Lautoka, Nadi, Nausori and Tavua supplies are fully treated. The Labasa, Levuka, Navua, Savusavu, Sigatoka and Vaileka supplies are partly treated or just chlorinated. Many villages, schools, hospitals and government stations in rural areas have untreated supplies. Special treated supplies go to the tourist areas at Korotogo and Pacific Harbour.

PERSONALITIES AND ORGANISATIONS

Governor-General: Ratu Sir George Cakobau.
Prime Minister: Ratu Sir Kamisese Mara.

MEMBERS OF THE SENATE:

Prime Minister's nominees: Sir Robert Munro (President), Andrew Deoki, Ramanlal I. Kapadia, Akanisi Dreunimisimisi, Dr. Sevanaia B. Tabua, Faiz Sherani, Wesley Barrett.
Great Council of Chiefs' nominees: Ratu Livai Volavola, (Vice-President); Inoke Tabua, Ratu Glanville W. Lalabalavu, Ratu Jone Mataitini, Ratu Tevita Vakalalabure, Ratu Meli Loki, Joeli Sereki, Ratu Tevita Latianara.
Leader of the Opposition's nominees: Kaur Battan Singh, Suman Shiromaniam Madhavan, Chandra Prakash Bidesi, Bakshi Balwant Singh Mal, Colin Stanley Weaver, Subramani Basawaiya.
Council of Rotuma's Nominee: Wilson Inia.

MINISTERS

Prime Minister: Ratu Sir Kamisese Mara.
Deputy Prime Minister, Minister for Fijian Affairs and Rural Development: Ratu Sir Penaia K. Ganilau.
Attorney-General: Andrew Deoki
Minister for Agriculture and Fisheries: Jonati Mavoa.
Minister for Commerce and Industry: M. Ramzan
Minister for Labour, Industrial Relations and Immigration: Ratu David Toganivalu.
Minister for Health: E. J. Beddoes.
Minister for Finance: Charles Walker.
Minister for Education: Semesa K. Sikivou.
Minister for Tourism, Transport and Civil Aviation: Tomasi R. Vakatora.
Minister for Urban Development, Housing and Social Welfare: M. V. Leweniqila.
Minister for Works and Communications: L. L. Nasilivata.
MINISTERS, but not in Cabinet, are:
Minister of State for Home Affairs: Ratu W. B. Toganivalu.
Minister of State for Information: S. S. Momoivalu.
Minister of State for Forests: Ratu J. Tavaiqia.
Minister of State for Co-operatives: I. P. Bajpai.
Minister of State for Youth and Sport: S. N. Waqanivavalagi.
Minister of State for Lands and Mineral Resources: W. J. Clark.

HOUSE OF REPRESENTATIVES at December, 1977

Speaker: Mr M. Qionibaravi.

Government Backbenchers: S. Waquanivavalagi (National, North Eastern); Ratu Serupepeli Naivalu (National, North Central); Ratu Josefa Iloilo (National, Vanua Levu North and West); K. R. Latchan (National, East Central); Iqbal Mohammed (National, North Central); S. Ramlu (National, Vanua Levu North and South); P. K. Bhindi (National South Central/Suva West); K. S. Reddy (National South Eastern); Mr W. Clark (National, Western); Mr D. Costello (National, Northern); Ratu N. Dawai (Fijian, Ba/Nadi); Mr J. Banuve (Fijian, Ra/Samabula/Suva); Ratu Seci Nawalowalo (Fijian, Kadavu/Tamavua/Suva Suburban); Mr J. Naisara (Fijian, Cakaudrove); Mr H. Thaggard (General, Northern and Eastern); Mr F. Caine (General, Western); Mr W. Yee (General, Suva and Central).

Opposition: J. Ram Reddy (Leader of the Opposition); Mr Harish Sharma (Indian, Sigatoka); Dr Santa Singh (Indian, Savusavu/Macuata); Mr H. M. Lodhia (Indian, Nadi); Mr S. N. Kanhai (Indian, Nasinu/Vunidawa); Mr K. C. Ramrakha (Indian, Nausori/Levuka); Mrs Irene Narayan (Indian, Suva City); Mr Navind Patel (Indian, Ba/Lautoka Rural); Mr K. N. Rao (Indian, Ba); Mr R. S. Gounder (Indian, Tavua/Vaileka); Mr Mohammed Sadiq (Indian, Labasa/Bua); Mr Jai Raj Singh (National-North Western); Mr I. Nadalo (National, South Western); Mr V. Parmanadam (Indian, Suva Rural); Mr K. Matatolu (National, North Western).
Independent: Ratu Osea Gavidi (Fijian, Nadroga/Navosa).

JUDICIARY

Chief Justice, Timoci U. Tuivaga. **Puisne Judges,** Sir M. Tikaram, G. Mishra, J. T. Williams, R. G. Kermode, G. O. L. Dyke. Note: Justice Sir Moti Tikaram has been seconded to act as full-time Ombudsman.

HEADS OF GOVERNMENT DEPARTMENTS

Secretary to the Cabinet: Dr. Isireli Lasaqa.
Secretary for Foreign Affairs: J. Kotobalavu.
Secretary for Home Affairs: Lt.-Col. M. Buadromo.
Secretary for the Public Service: U. Chandra.
Director for Information: D. Diment.
Commissioner of Police: J. E. Orme.
Government Printer: I Ravutu.
Solicitor-General: H. Picton-Smith.

Director of Public Prosecutions: Kulen Ratneser.
Administrator-General/Registrar-General: M. Gardiner.
Secretary for Finance: W. Thompson.
Comptroller of Customs: L. Gardiner.
Commissioner of Inland Revenue: S. Singh.
Controller of Supplies: S. Narain.
Secretary for Fijian Affairs and Rural Development: Ratu E. Kanaimawi.
Commissioner of Native Lands: G. S. Mate.
Secretary for Agriculture: R. Yarrow.
Conservator of Forests: G. H. D. Williams.
Director of Lands & Surveyor-General: T. Rupene (acting)
Director of Mineral Development: R. N. Richmond.
Secretary for Health: Dr. J. Senilagakali.
Principal of Fiji School of Medicine: Dr B. Pathik.
Secretary for Education: E. Kacimaiwai.
Controller of Prisons: Major B. Masi (acting).
Auditor-General: T. Bhim.
Clerk to Parliament: Mrs Lavinia Ah Koy.
Chairman Public Service Commission: J. Sykes.
Ombudsman: Justice Sir Moti Tikaram.
Supervisor of Elections: P. Howard.
Secretary for Urban Development and Housing: B. Dutt.
Secretary for Social Welfare: V. Liga.
Secretary for Commerce and Industry: L. Qarase
Secretary for Co-operatives: J. Nacoke.
Secretary of Labour: Satyanand.
Principal Immigration Officer: P. Gounder.
Director of Marine: M. M. Joy.
Suva Harbour Master: Captain A. Foster.
Secretary Post and Telecommunications: J. Manikiam.
Director Civil Aviation: M. Varley.
Director Meteorology: J. Waygood.
Secretary Transport, Civil Aviation and Tourism: B. Vunibobo.
Secretary Liquor Board: J. Tukuna.

FIJI DIPLOMATS ABROAD
High Commissioner to Britain: Mr Joseph Gibson.
High Commissioner to Australia: Major J. Takala.
High Commissioner to New Zealand: Ratu Josua Toganivalu.
Permanent Representative at United Nations, High Commissioner to Canada and Ambassador to the US: Mr F. Bole.
Ambassador in Brussels (for EEC affairs): Mr Satya Nandan.
Ambassador to South Pacific Forum Countries: Mr J. Cavalevu.

DIPLOMATIC MISSIONS IN FIJI
EEC delegate to Fiji, Tonga, Western Samoa: E. Stahn.
British High Commissioner: Lord Dunrossil.
Indian High Commissioner: Mrs S. Kochar.
Australian High Commissioner: R. Greet.
Papua New Guinea High Commissioner: Dr Ako Toua
Australian Trade Commissioner for Pacific Islands: J. B. White.
New Zealand High Commissioner: M. J. Powles.
People's Republic of China Ambassador: Mi Guojun.
United States Ambassador: William J. Bodde Jr.
Tuvaluan High Commissioner: K. Latasi.
Hon. Consul for Sweden: A. Katonivualiku.
Hon. Consul for Netherlands: R. J. Woodman.
Hon. Consul for Norway: Sir Robert Munro.
France, Ambassador: R. Puissant
Ambassador for Japan: H. Ohtaka
Consul for Nauru: L. Stevens.
Hon. Consul for West Germany: P. Erbsleben.
South Pacific Bureau for Economic Co-operation: Dr. G. Gris.
W.H.O., Programme Co-ordinator for South Pacific: Dr C. J. Ross-Smith.

(Note: Since independence in 1970, Fiji has established diplomatic relations with a number of countries, which have designated their ambassadors to Australia or New Zealand, based in Canberra or Wellington, as ambassadors also to Fiji. These diplomats make occasional visits to Fiji.)

HEADS OF ORGANISATIONS
Commander Royal Fiji Military Forces: Colonel R. I. Thorpe.
Commander, Naval Squadron: Commander Stan Brown.
Ports Authority of Fiji, Director: Mr Loh Heng Kee.
University of the South Pacific, Vice-Chancellor: Dr J. A. Maraj.
Fiji National Training Council, Acting-Director: Jamal ud-Din.
Fiji Consumer Council, Chairman: S. Ali.
Fiji Broadcasting Commission, Chairman: Vacant.
Fiji Sugar Corporation, Chairman: A. D. Leys.
Fiji Museum: F. Clunie.

CHURCH DIGNITARIES:
Roman Catholic Church: Archbishop of Suva: Archbishop Petero Mataca.
Anglican Church: Bishop in Polynesia: Right Reverend Jabez Bryce.
Methodist Church in Fiji: President: Rev. Daniel Mastapha.

Presbyterian Church: Rev. L. R. Miller.
Seventh-day Adventist Church: President: F. K. Bera.
Assemblies of God of Fiji: General Superintendent: Rev. Alipate Cakau.
Church of Jesus Christ of Latter-Day Saints: President: Georges L. Bourget.
Salvation Army: Regional Officers: Capt. & Mrs D. Major.
Pacific Theological College: Principal: Dr. S. A. Havea.

PROFESSIONAL AND BUSINESS ASSOCIATIONS: Fiji Employers' Consultative Association (represents about 100 of Fiji's largest companies); Fiji Master Builders Association; Fiji Association of Architects; Fiji Institute of Draughtsmen; Fiji Master Printers Association; Fiji Association of Electrical and Mechanical Engineers; Fiji Medical Association; Fiji Law Society; Fiji Association of Manufacturers; Fiji Hotel Association. Fiji Trades Union Congress (supported by majority of trade unions); Fiji Council of Trade Unions.

Significant Trade Unions: Building Workers Union; Fiji Hotel and Catering Workers Union; Fiji Oil and Allied Workers Union; Public Employees Union; National Union of Factory and Commercial Workers; Fiji Sugar and General Workers Union; Fiji Sugar Tradesmen's Union; Fijian Mineworkers Union; Public Service Association; Fiji Transport Workers Union; Telecommunications Employees Union; Fiji Teachers Union; Fijian Teachers Association, Federated Airline Employees Association; Fiji Nurses' Assocation; Pastoral Employees' Union; Bank Officers' Association; Maritime Officers' and Engineers' Association; Insurance Officers' Association; Fiji Hotel and Catering Employees' Union; Air Pacific Employees' Association; Fiji Electricity Authority Staff Association; Fiji Local Government Officers Association; Sugar Milling Staff Officers Association; Housing Authority Employees' Union; Copra Plantation Workers' Association; Fijian Affairs Board and Provincial Councils Employees' Association; Fiji Sugar Clerks'/Supervisors' Association; University of the South Pacific Staff Union; Fiji Electricity Authority Employees' Union; Fiji Electricity Authority Executive Officers' Association; Fiji National Training Council Staff Association; Burns Philp (SS) Co Ltd & W. R. Carpenter Group Salaried Staff Association; The Association of the University of the South Pacific Staff; National Union of Municipal Workers; Fiji Waterfront Workers' and Seamen's Union; Union of Trades Union Employees; National Union of Timber Workers; Emperor Group Salaried Staff Association; Fiji Miscellaneous Employees' Union.

Chambers of Commerce: Association of Fiji Chambers of Commerce; Suva Chamber of Commerce; Suva Indian Chamber of Commerce; Lautoka Chamber of Commerce; Sigatoka Chamber of Commerce.
Junior Chambers of Commerce: Suva, Lautoka, Nadi, Ba, Sigatoka, Labasa, Nausori, Pacific Harbour.
Rotary clubs: Suva; Suva North; Lautoka and Nadi.
Lions clubs: Suva, Lautoka. Nadi, Labasa, Sigatoka.
Apex clubs: Suva, Lautoka, Nadi, Sigatoka. Labasa, Ba.

ARCHIVES, LIBRARIES, MUSEUM
The National Archives of Fiji are housed in buildings in the Thurston Gardens, Suva. The documents preserved there mainly concern the British administration of Fiji, but there are other important collections, such as the records of the Methodist Church in Fiji. Attached is the Sir Alport Barker Library, an extensive collection of books on the Pacific bequeathed to Fiji by a former owner of the 'Fiji Times.'

The Fiji Museum is in the same area and has an extensive display of Fiji and Pacific artifacts, including war canoes and the rudder from the 'Bounty'.

SPORTING FACILITIES
Nearly all sports are catered for in Fiji. Organised clubs in the main centres provide for football, cricket, tennis, bowls and hockey.

Yacht and power boat races are held by the Royal Suva Yacht Club and the Lautoka Yacht Club.

18-hole golf courses are situated at the Fiji Golf Club in Suva and the Pacific Harbour resort at Deuba, 56 km from Suva.

Suva has several squash courts. There is a flying club, with members getting instruction to private pilots licence level.

Game fishing boats are based at Lautoka, Yanuca Island near Sigatoka (Fijian Hotel) and Korolevu Beach Hotel.

CULTURAL GROUPS
Fiji Arts Club, headquarters at the Playhouse, Suva, (active drama, photographic, dance, music and painting sections).

The Indian Government cultural centre, Suva, specialises in dancing.

The Fiji Dance Theatre (developing as Fiji's national theatre, preserving Fijian dances and customs).

The Fiji Craft Association, Suva; The Fiji Society (meets regularly to hear members' papers on a wide range of mainly local affairs); Suva YWCA (various cultural activities); Soqosoqo Vakamarama — Fiji Women's Organisation with craft shop.

ENVIRONMENTAL ASSOCIATIONS
The National Trust of Fiji, Chairman: Mr. Faiz

Sherani (to hold property of national interest and protect lands, reefs etc). ATOM at University of the South Pacific, (mainly to agitate against nuclear tests in the Pacific).

NATIONAL PARKS

The Thurston Gardens (formerly the Botanic gardens) adjacent to grounds of Government House; a small aquarium in Suva, operated by tropical fish export company; Suva City Council hopes to establish a zoo eventually as part of large new botanic garden to be developed in Flagstaff area, Suva. There's an 800 ha recreational park at Colo-i-Suva forest near Suva, with trails etc. The National Trust also plans marine national parks covering defined areas of coral reefs and islets.

INTERNATIONAL ORGANISATIONS

Fiji Red Cross (branches in most towns).

St. John Ambulance Association (branches in most towns).

YWCA in Suva and Lautoka.

YMCA in Suva Youth Centre.

Salvation Army — hostel at Raiwaqa, Suva.

International Labour Organisation, regional office in Suva.

World Health Organisation — South Pacific regional office in Suva.

United Nations Development Programme — regional HQ in Suva.

South Pacific Bureau for Economic Cooperation, Suva.

YOUTH ORGANISATIONS

YWCA; YMCA; Fiji National Council of Youth (coordinating body for all youth groups); Fiji Scouts; Fiji Guides; Young Farmers' Club; Suva Youth Centre, a multi-racial club and Charman's All Races' Club, boxing, body-building and associated pursuits for boys.

Fiji does not have any youth hostels, although the Suva YWCA sometimes has spare accommodation available temporarily in its Suva hostel.

CLUBS

There is a very wide range of clubs, social or devoted to specific interests such as sport, shell collecting, etc., throughout Fiji.

HISTORY. Man first arrived in the Fiji group more than 3,000 years ago. Archaeologists distinguish three types of pottery made by the early inhabitants. These are called Lapita, paddle-impressed and plain ware. Lapita pottery found in the Sigatoka area of Viti Levu has been dated back as far as 1290 BC, and on Yanuca Island, a date of 1030 BC has been established. Paddle-impressed pottery was also made on Yanuca Island at least as far back as 710 BC. Similar pottery found at Navatu and Vuda is estimated to have been made from 100 BC to AD 1100. A subsequent plain pottery-making phase at Vuda is thought to have lasted from AD 1250 to European times. Such pottery is also still made in the Sigatoka valley and elsewhere.

Besides ancient pottery, archaeologists have found numerous fortified sites in Fiji that date back to early times. Two types, 'ring ditch' and ridge forts, are extremely common on Viti Levu, particularly the windward side, and also on Wakaya Island. Both types were still in use when the first Europeans arrived.

European discovery. The European discoverer of Fiji was the Dutch navigator Abel Janzsoon Tasman who got among some of the north-eastern reefs in 1643, in his vessel, 'Heemskerck', and named them Prins Willem's Islands. Captain Cook sighted the small island of Vatoa in the south-eastern corner of the group in 1774. But it was not until 1789 that the main islands were seen. This was when William Bligh and some of his crew were making their celebrated open boat voyage from Tonga to Timor following the mutiny in the 'Bounty'. A Fijian canoe chased them near the Yasawas.

Bligh took the opportunity to examine the islands more thoroughly when he returned to the Pacific in 1792 in HMS 'Providence' to make a second attempt to obtain breadfruit from Tahiti. In 1797, some of the northern islands were reported by Captain James Wilson of the missionary ship 'Duff'.

Sandalwooders began operating in the area in the early years of the 19th century. But it was left to the official exploring expeditions to complete the discovery and charting of the group. In 1820, two Russian ships under Thaddeus von Bellingshausen examined Ono-i-Lau and its two southerly neighbours, Tuvana-i-Ra and Tuvana-i-Colo. In 1827 and again in 1838, the French explorer J. S. C. Dumont d'Urville carried out some extensive surveys; HMS 'Victor' did the same in 1836; and in 1840, the first really reliable chart of the group was made by Commodore Charles Wilkes of the United States Exploring Expedition.

Sandalwood trade. The discovery of Fiji's sandalwood was made by a survivor of the schooner 'Argo', which was wrecked near Lakeba about 1800. Soon there was a scramble to obtain cargoes of the precious wood from Bua Bay, Vanua Levu, to be taken to the Far East. The trade lasted until 1814, by which time all the accessible sandalwood had been cut out. It brought the first white settlers to the group. One of these, a Swede named Charles Savage, gained considerable influence in Bau. He was the chief's favourite, had numerous wives, and was of great service to the Fijians because of his knowledge of firearms. Another early beachcomber, Paddy Connel, was in high favour at Rewa.

After the departure of the last sandalwooders from Fiji, there was a lull in western contact with the group until the early 1820s when American and other ships began calling in search of beche-de-mer. Their success depended on the ability of the captains to maintain good relations with the chiefs, as it was necessary to have a large corps of Fijians to work as labourers, as well as land to erect boiling and drying houses, and a trade store.

The beachcombers. Such beachcombers as were already in the group became important as intermediaries and interpreters, and others soon joined them. Some were deserters from whalers. The most notable was David Whippy, a young American from New Hampshire, who settled at Levuka in 1822. Like the others, he married a Fijian and became one of the pioneers of the mixed-blood community that has existed at Levuka ever since. Commodore Wilkes met Whippy in 1840 and had him appointed vice-consul for the United States soon after his return to that country.

The missionaries. Meanwhile, the first Christian missionaries – two Tahitians – arrived in the group. They had been sent to Lakeba from Tahiti in 1826, but were detained in Tonga and did not reach their destination until 1830. Five years later, they were joined by two European evangelists, David Cross and William Cargill, of the Wesleyan Church. Although the local chief, Tui Nayau, made the missionaries welcome, he showed little interest in their doctrine, and for some time they made few Fijian converts.

The many Tongans who lived in Lakeba, however, were more amenable; and all the islanders, both Fijians and Tongans, were eager to learn to read and write. Cross and Cargill tried to simplify things in this respect by using a single letter to represent each Fijian sound. Thus it was that the letters b, c, d, g, and eventually q were given the values that they still have today, namely mb; th (as in 'that'); nd; ng (as in 'sing'); and ngg (as in 'younger') respectively.

Although the European missionaries had entered Fiji from the east, they soon realised that the most important and populous centre in the group lay in the west – in the SE corner of Viti Levu. Cross tried to obtain a foothold on Bau, a small island off that coast in 1838. Unsuccessful, he went to Rewa where a printing press was set up in 1839. Later, a mission station was also opened on Viwa Island, two miles from Bau.

Still, the missionaries made few converts. Yet little by little their pacifism and good example caused the Fijians to question their own customs.

Cakobau. Meanwhile, Cakobau, the chief of Bau, had had considerable success in extending his influence to the coastal villages of Viti Levu, to the islands of Lomaiviti, to Taveuni, and to Lau. By 1850, foreigners were beginning to address him as Tui Viti (King of Fiji). But about this time, there was a revolt against him among his conquered subjects because of his heavy demands on them that had no sanction in local custom.

Faced with repeated defeats in battle, Cakobau decided on 28 April, 1854 to embrace Christianity. A series of events soon afterwards enabled Cakobau to re-establish his fortunes; and by the late 1850s the whole of Fiji had taken sides either with Cakobau or with Ma'afu, a chief of Tongan origin, who had gained considerable power and prestige among the Lau islands. The scene was set for a showdown between Cakobau and Ma'afu when W. T. Pritchard, the first British consul to be appointed to Fiji, arrived in Levuka in 1858.

International rivalries. Pritchard's appointment followed a period in which several French and American warships had visited Fiji. This had made Britain afraid that one or other of the two powers might try to annex the islands. As it turned out, however, an opportunity soon arose which led Britain to annex the islands herself. Cakobau was being pressed to settle a claim by various American residents for $45,000, and as he had no money, he turned to Pritchard for help. Claiming to have 'full and exclusive sovereignty and dominion' in the group, he offered to cede Fiji to Britain provided Britain would pay his debts. Pritchard took a document to this effect to London, but the government was preoccupied with other matters, and when he returned to Fiji 12 months later he could only report that the offer of cession was being considered.

In the following year Col. W. T. Smythe, representing the British Government, was sent to Fiji to ascertain whether it would be expedient for Britain to accept the offer of cession. At the same time, a botanist, Dr. Berthold Seemann, was commissioned to report on Fiji's potential for tropical agriculture. The arrival of Smythe and Seemann caused rumours to spread that Fiji would, in fact, become British, and many Britons flocked to the group from Australia and New Zealand to become settlers. When the American Civil War began shortly afterwards, causing a world-wide shortage of raw cotton, the new settlers took to growing cotton on a large scale.

Although Smythe advised Britain not to accept Cakobau's offer of cession, the large influx of British settlers made it inevitable that Britain would eventually be forced to intervene. Meanwhile, various attempts were made at the instigation of the European residents to establish a regular form of government. Although some reforms were made, all attempts ended in failure because of the jealousy and hostility of the leading chiefs. Finally, in 1873, the acting British consul, J. B. Thurston, again asked the Foreign Office if Britain would be prepared to annex Fiji.

As the 'blackbirding' of Pacific Islanders to work in Fiji had been causing increasing concern to Britain for several years, the government took the opportunity to appoint a new commission of inquiry. The commission comprised Commodore J. G. Goodenough, commanding the Australian naval station, and E. L. Layard, newly appointed consul in Fiji. On March 21, 1874 these commissioners reported that the offer of cession should be accepted.

Cession. In September of that year, 1874, Sir

Hercules Robinson, Governor of New South Wales, arrived to determine the terms of cession. A formal Deed of Cession was signed at Levuka on 10 October. Its signatories were Cakobau (Tui Viti and Vunivalu, or war lord), Ma'afu (chief of the Lau confederacy, including Taveuni and much of Vanua Levu), and 11 other principal chiefs. Sir Hercules Robinson, who became provisional Governor, announced that all lands that could be shown to have been fairly and honestly acquired by Europeans would be secured to them; that all lands that were in actual use or occupation by any tribe would be set apart for them; and that all the residue of the land would go to the government for the general good.

Measles epidemic. The first substantive Governor, Sir Arthur Gordon, arrived in the colony in June 1875 and established his headquarters at Levuka. His regime began at an unpropitious time. Earlier in the year, a measles epidemic had raged through the Fijian villages and had wiped out a third of the native population. Moreover, the cotton market slumped due to the recovery of cotton planting in the United States at the end of the Civil War.

It was soon obvious that one of Gordon's chief problems was to revive the colony's economy. Copra and sugar seemed to offer the best possibilities, but these crops required large labour forces, and Gordon was opposed to Fijians working for Europeans in their own country. It was in these circumstances that Gordon authorised the importation of labourers from India under a five-year indenture system. At the end of five years, the Indians were to be free to return home at their own expense; but if they chose to remain for a second term, the Fiji Government was to pay their passages. However, at the end of 10 years they could elect to remain in Fiji.

Indians arrive. The first shipload of 498 labourers reached Fiji on 14 May 1879, and from then until 1916 there were about 2,000 such immigrants each year. Although the Indian Government originally insisted that there should be a ratio of 40 women to every 100 men, this ratio was not maintained. As a result, there were frequent fights among the male immigrants over women, and other evils and abuses. Yet despite everything, many of the Indians felt they were in a better situation in Fiji than they would have been at home, and they remained in the colony to become independent farmers, on land leased from the Fijians.

Sugar industry. Meanwhile, sugar had become by far the most important industry in Fiji. Although there were a number of small companies and individuals with interests in sugar production before the turn of the century, eventually they were all swallowed up by the Colonial Sugar Refining Company of Australia. The CSR moved into Fiji in 1881 – the year before the colony's capital was moved to Suva from Levuka (which had severely limited possibilities for development). The CSR established its first mill on the banks of the Rewa River, where the town of Nausori soon sprang up. Its first sugar was exported from there in 1883.

That same year, CSR decided to open another mill at Rarawai on the Ba River on the dry side of Viti Levu, following the success of another company's mill opened at Raki-raki, Ra, in 1881. During the next few years mills were also opened at Labasa, Vanua Levu, and Lautoka.

Although Gordon laid some of the foundations for the development of a highly successful sugar industry during his five years in Fiji, his principal achievement was the introduction of a system of administration whereby Fijian institutions were developed to provide a chain of authority extending from the village headman to the Governor. This system, in its main essentials, remained operative throughout Fiji's 96 years as a British colony.

Another area in which there was little change was the system of land ownership. Following its policy of protecting the Fijians' land rights, the British administration insisted that all foreign claims to land dating back to before Cession had to be submitted to a Land Commission for adjudication. Claims to about 162,000 ha were finally substantiated. On the other hand, the sale of Fijian land to foreigners was forbidden, although for four years from 1905, land sales were again permitted, and during that time about 8,000 additional ha were alienated.

Constitutional changes. The depressed economic situation of Gordon's time did not improve until after the turn of the century, by which time both the sugar and copra industries were getting on their feet. Even so, many of the European settlers felt dissatisfied with their lot; and when, in 1900, the Premier of New Zealand, R. J. Seddon, visited the colony, they agitated for federation with New Zealand. Although this move failed, it did produce some constitutional concessions. In 1904, the colony's Legislative Council, which had previously been all-European and entirely nominated by the Governor, was made more representative, through the election of six Europeans and the nomination of two Fijian members from the Council of Chiefs. In 1916, one Indian member – nominated by the Governor – sat in the council for the first time; but it was not until 1929 that the first elected Indian members took their seats. Some Indians later agitated for a 'common roll' and this led, in 1937, to the introduction of a partly-elected, partly-nominated council that was somewhat larger than before. It now consisted of the Governor, 16 official members, five European members (three elected, two nominated), five Fijian members nominated from the Council of Chiefs, and five Indian members (three elected, two nominated). Thereafter, the council's composition remained unchanged until 1963 when it was enlarged to a membership of 38 – a nominated speaker, 19 official members and 18 unofficial members. The latter were divided equally on racial lines – four elected Fijians, four elected Indians and four elected Europeans, plus two Europeans and two Indians nominated by the Governor, and two Fijians nominated from the Council of Chiefs.

In the 1963 election, women of all races voted for the first time, but each community voted from separate rolls. In 1964, the executive council was enlarged and, in effect, became a cabinet. Its 'Ministers' were called 'Members' but were responsible for specific portfolios.

In 1965, a conference in London led to the adoption of the constitution of 1966 which enlarged the Legislative Council to 40 members. Of these, four were official members and the rest were elected. Fourteen of the elected members were Fijians, 12 were Indians, and 10 (called General members) were Europeans or individuals from other minority racial groups. Nine Fijians, nine Indians and seven General members were elected from separate communal rolls, and the remainder – except two Fijians chosen by the Council of Chiefs – were elected under a system of cross-voting.

The 1966 constitution was not destined to last for long. In April 1970, after the abatement of several years of antagonism between Fiji's two main political parties, another constitutional conference was held in London. It was then agreed that Fiji should become independent on October 10 that year – 96 years after the signing of the Deed of Cession. The 1970 conference was attended by the Governor of Fiji, all 40 members of the Legislative Council, and senior British officials.

Fiji independence. Prince Charles represented Queen Elizabeth II at ceremonies to mark Fiji's change of status. Ratu Sir Kamisese Mara, who had previously been Chief Minister, became the first Prime Minister; and the former Governor, Sir Robert Foster, become the first Governor-General. Sir Robert Foster was succeeded in January 1973 by Ratu Sir George Cakobau, great-grandson of the Cakobau who had signed the Deed of Cession.

The most important development in Fiji since independence has been the nationalisation of the sugar industry. Negotiations for the purchase of South Pacific Sugar Mills Ltd., the Fiji interests of the Colonial Sugar Refining Company were concluded in 1971; and on April 1, 1973, control of the sugar industry passed to the Fiji Sugar Corporation, a limited liability company set up by the government.

Further information: No comprehensive history of Fiji has yet been published. Probably the most reliable and useful of the brief histories is contained in Sir Alan Burns' book 'Fiji' (London, 1963). R.A. Derrick's 'A History of Fiji', first published in 1946, takes the story only as far as Cession. A proposed second volume was not completed. Other useful books covering aspects of Fiji's history are: Peter France, 'The Charter of the Land' (Melbourne, 1969); J. D. Legge, 'Britain in Fiji, 1858-1880' (London, 1958); K. L. Gillion, 'Fiji's Indian Migrants' (Melbourne, 1962); and Deryck Scarr, 'I, The Very Bayonet: A Life of Sir John Thurston, (Canberra, 1973). Designed for school use, but useful generally is 'Fiji in the Pacific: A History and Geography of Fiji', by G. J. A. Kerr and T. A. Donnelly (Brisbane, 1969). Also available is 'Bibliography of Fiji, Tonga and Rotuma', by Philip A. Snow (Canberra 1969). 'Fijian Way of Life' by G. K. Roth (Melbourne, 1973), 'Race and Politics in Fiji' by Robert Norton (Univ. of Q'l'd Press, 1977).

SMALLER ISLANDS IN DETAIL

Most people get a wrong impression of Fiji because, in addition to some 300 small islands, it includes the very large islands of Viti Levu and Vanua Levu, and the large islands of Taveuni and Kadavu. As Viti Levu, especially, and Vanua Levu and Taveuni to a lesser degree, contain practically all the population, and the developed economic wealth, people look upon those islands as Fiji, and forget that, hidden behind them, there is a great archipelago that equals in beauty, fertility, interest and general attractiveness any other group in the Pacific.

With the exception of a few coral atolls, chiefly in the Ringgold, Exploring and Lakeba groups, the islands of Fiji are of volcanic and sedimentary materials deposited on a vast platform that was probably once part of a continental land mass that extended north to the Philippines and south to Australia.

The Fiji Islands may be divided into seven sub-groups. These sub-groups, working from east to west, are:—

EASTERN or LAU Group, of 57 islands of which 26 are inhabited.

The MOALA Group, which is included with the Lau Group for administration purposes and consists of three volcanic islands.

VANUA LEVU (5534 sq km), TAVEUNI (435 sq km) and the adjacent islands.

LOMAIVITI (or Inner Fiji), about 12 islands, scattered about in the Koro Sea (which is the section of ocean enclosed by the Lau Group on the east, Vanua Levu, on the north, and Viti Levu and Kadavu on the west).

VITI LEVU (10,389 sq km) and adjacent islands.

KADAVU Group, which lies between 89 and 97 km south of Suva and includes, besides the large island of Kadavu (407 sq km), the island of Ono (30 sq km) and numerous small islands lying within the Astrolabe Reefs.

THE YASAWA ISLANDS, an almost continuous chain of about 20 large and small islands, running generally north and south, and forming the western portion of Fiji.

THE LAU ISLANDS. The islands of Lau can most conveniently be divided into four groups:

NORTHERN LAU – The Exploring Isles (which

include Vanua Balavu, Namalata, Susui, Munia, Cikobia, Sovu Islets, Avea, Qilaqila, Adavaci, and Yanucoloa); Wailagilala; Naitauba; Malima; Kibobo; Kanacea; Mago; Yacata; Kaibu; Nukutolu; Vatu Vara; Katafaga; Vekei; Tuvuca; and Cicia.

CENTRAL LAU — Lakeba, Nayau, Oneata; Aiwa; and Vanua Vatu.

SOUTHERN LAU — Moce; Karoni; Olorua; Komo; Namuka; Yagasa cluster; Kabara; Marabo; Waqava; Fulaga; Ogea; Ogea Driki; Vatoa; Ono-i-Lau; Tuvana.

MOALA GROUP — Moala; Totoya; and Matuku.

The islands of Lau are scattered over 113,900 sq km of ocean, but the aggregate area of the islands is 460 sq km. The southern islands are nearer to Tonga than to Suva and the Tongan influence on the group has been great in the past. In 1855, Ma'afu, a Tongan chief, established himself at Lomaloma and encouraged European settlement, particularly on the northern islands, where cotton was grown. In those days Lomaloma was a much more important centre than it is today.

The structure of the Lau islands is mainly raised limestone — peaks reach 305 m on some islands. But eight of the 29 inhabited islands are partly volcanic — the volcanic rock having in places burst through the limestone. Three islands are purely volcanic (Moce, Komo and Olorua).

THE EXPLORING ISLES. These were named by Wilkes in 1840 after the official title of his expedition (United States Exploring Expedition). They consist of seven islands and numerous islets scattered around the margins of a lagoon about 518 sq km in area and enclosed by a barrier reef 130 km in circuit. The reef is roughly triangular and has five navigable entrances. The island of Vanua Balavu takes up most of the western end of the lagoon and is the largest island of the group. It is of composite formation (limestone and volcanic) and is 52 sq km in area. Lomaloma, once an important centre in cotton-growing days, is in the south of the island. It was once a port of entry for Fiji. It was the headquarters of the Hennings Brothers, then the largest trading firm in the Fiji Islands.

The northern part of Vanua Balavu is heavily indented, affording numerous good anchorages. It is also scenically beautiful. Munia is about 3 km long and rises to 290 m. Its volcanic soil is very fertile. It is privately owned. The local Fijians were removed to Avea in Ma'afu's time.

NAITAUBA is of composite construction, lies 32 km west of Vanua Balavu, has an area of about 8 sq km and is roughly circular in shape. From the flat land on the south-west, the island rises steeply to 186 m. The north coast rises straight out of the sea in 34 m high cliffs. It was privately owned by the Hennings family for many years and worked as a copra plantation. Since 1966, it has been owned by Mr. Raymond Burr.

WAILAGILALA is a true atoll, 34 km NW of Naitauba. It is only 1006 m long and 640 m wide and is no more than 4.6 m above sea level. It has a lighthouse which marks the eastern side of the northern entrance to the Fiji archipelago.

KANACEA is 12 km west of Vanua Balavu, is 244 m high and has an area of 13 sq km. It is privately owned and worked as a copra plantation.

MAGO. Height, 270 m, is saucer-shaped, 2 sq km, and the interior plain is immensely fertile. Cultivation is carried on to perfection here, and all tropical fruits flourish and produce abundantly. The "Sea Island" cotton produced by Mago became world-famous. Later, sugar was grown there, and now it is worked as a copra plantation. Mago, in the early days, belonged to the Somosomo chiefs, and when they adopted Christianity, they agreed to sell the island and remove the population, and Mago became the exclusive property of a family named Ryder. It is now owned by the Borron family.

VATU VARA, or Hat Island, is 32 km west of Mago and because of its distinctive shape, is one of the best known islands of the group. The crown of the hat is a truncated pyramid rising over 305 m. It is the highest point to which limestone has been elevated in the group. The brim of the hat is a wide belt of gently sloping land not more than 7.5 m above sea level. It is usually uninhabited although at one time an American seaman named Joe Thompson lived there. He seemed to have a supply of gold coins and the legend grew that treasure was buried there. Thompson died insane and his secret (if any) died with him. Vatu Vara is visible for 56 km and serves as a guide to ships.

KATAFAGA is a small composite island 40 km south east of Vanua Balavu. There are no Fijian villages and it is owned privately, and worked as a copra plantation.

CICIA is 27 km SSW of Mago and has an area of 34 sq km. It is of composite formation and has five villages and several privately owned coconut plantations.

LAKEBA (villages: Tubou, Waciwaci, Waitabu, Nukunuku, Vakano, Yadrana, Nasagalau). This is a rounded, volcanic island, of 54 sq km area with several summits in the centre. The highest is Mt Goodenough, a twin peak, 220 m high. Coastal lands are immensely fertile, but the interior is poor, and covered with grass and screw pines. Yams, kumalas, coconuts and all tropical plants grow most profusely on the coastal belt and this probably is the most productive of all the rich islands of the south-east. Lakeba was an important meeting place between Fijians and Tongans,

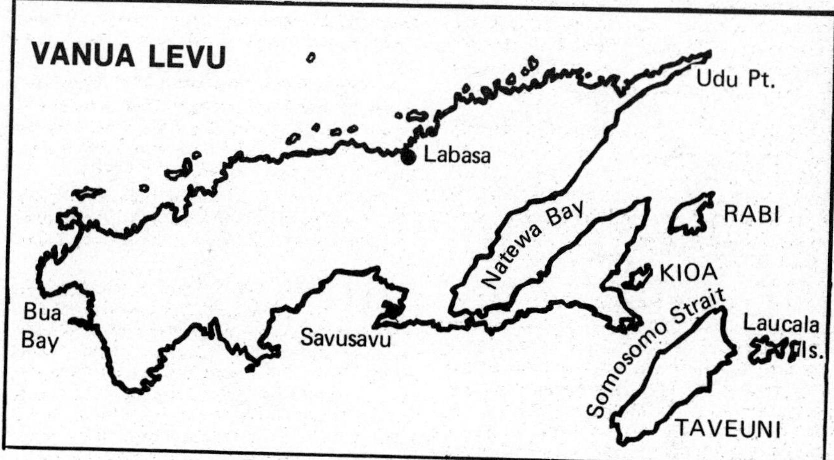

all through their history. The first Wesleyan missionaries settled here in 1835. It was the place most frequently visited by Europeans before they settled in Levuka. It has an airstrip.

THE MOALA GROUP. Moala, Totoya and Matuku — structurally have nothing to do with the Lau group. They are submerged volcano cones. The people trace their descent from people who came from Viti Levu. Copra and bananas are produced and, as they lie only a night's sail from Suva, foodstuffs are disposed of at that port. They are 97 to 113 km S-W from Lakeba.

OTHER ISLANDS. The islands south of Lakeba have a purely Fijian economy. On the inhabited islands copra and all the Fijian foodstuffs are produced.

The southernmost outliers of the Fiji Archipelago are the two Tuvana Islands, 32 km south of Ono-i-Lau. They are densely wooded sand-cays used by Ono people for agriculture.

The total population of Lau, including the three Moala islands, in the census of 1976 was 14,452.

ISLANDS OFF VANUA LEVU AND TAVEUNI: Starting in the west, and proceeding along the north coast of VANUA LEVU, and thence down the east coast, the chief offshore islands are:—

YADUA.

YAGANA, NUKUIRA, TEVEA, VEDRALA, GALOA, NADOGO, VATUKA — All close together off the north-west coast.

MACUATA, TALAILAU, NAGANO, NUKUNUKU, CUKINI — Clustered together off the northern coast.

VOROVORO.

KIA.

MALI.

MATAIVAI.

TUTU, KAVEWA, DRUADRUA, NAMUKALAU and BEKANA — Along the north-east coast.

RABI, 472 m high, and KIOA, two large islands lying between NATEWA PENINSULA (VANUA LEVU) and TAVEUNI. RABI, at one time owned by Lever Bros., is now the home of more than 2,000 Banabans from OCEAN ISLAND and GILBERTESE. KIOA was bought for surplus population from what is now TUVALU. On RABI there has been considerable development by the Banabans.

YABU, YANUCA, COBIA, NUKUBASAGA, QELELEVU — Small islands, lying well out to the north-east of TAVEUNI and known as the RINGGOLD ISLANDS, or Islands of BUDD REEF.

VETAUUA.

CIKOBIA-I-RA, most northerly of the FIJI GROUP.

QAMEA, LAUCALA, MATAGI — Fairly large islands, lying close to TAVEUNI, on the north-east. MATAGI is worked as a copra plantation. There is an airstrip on LAUCALA, which is privately owned.

TAVEUNI: Taveuni (the old name was Somosomo, from its town of that name, being the residence of the ruling chiefs), ranks fourth in size, and is one of the finest islands of Fiji.

Lying south-east of Natewa Peninsula, Vanua Levu, it is 42 km long, an average 11 km wide, and rises symmetrically on both sides to a backbone ridge, at the highest point of which Mt. Uluigalau (1,231 m) is notable because it is exactly under the 180th meridian, twelve hours east and west from Greenwich.

In the mountains behind Somosomo there is

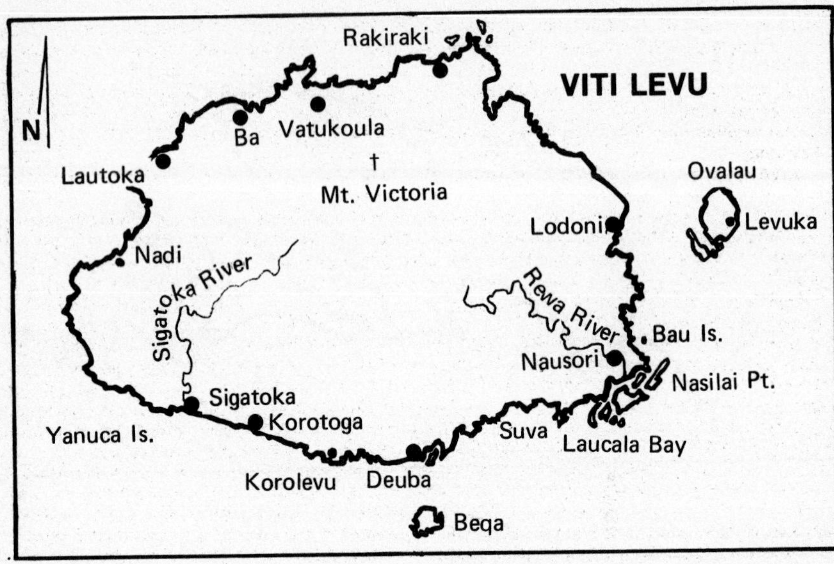

a lake of considerable size that provides Somosomo with a water supply. Fiji's most beautiful wildflower, the tagimaucia, grows only on the shores of this lake.

Somosomo is on the trunk road that runs from Ura in the south to Qeleni in the north of the island. It also has a pleasant modern hotel.

The island has a heavy rainfall in the higher ranges and is densely wooded. Virtually all tropical produce will grow and at one time Sea Island cotton was cultivated. Its main product is now copra.

There were two airstrips on the island — Matei at the northern end of the island which is government owned and a privately owned strip at Ura which is now unused.

ISLANDS OFF VITI LEVU: BAU — Its importance as the old native capital centres in the past. It is built on a tiny island only about 15 m above sea-level, connected with Viti Levu's eastern coast, at low water, by a narrow causeway of coral formation, about 1.5 km in length. Formerly it was the stronghold and home of the great chief Cakobau, and of all his family, and of the nobles before whom the tribes of other districts owed subjection, and to whom they granted special privileges. Its chief took precedence over all other chiefs; the language of Bau was to the islands of Fiji as the Latin tongue was to the civilised world; and to come from Bau was to give a man a definite status.

The island has an area of only 8 ha, but at one time an estimated 3,000 or 4,000 lived there. At present there are between 200 and 300. A mission house and school occupy the highest point — a 15 m soapstone rise — and the three villages occupy the flat land — Bau being the home of the high chiefs; Soso that of the craftsmen and Lasakau that of the fishermen. The south end of the village green is occupied by the Cakobau Memorial Church; the north end by the Council House.

Bau is still the home of the highest chiefs in Fiji — many of whom now go forth to other parts of the country as administrative officers.

BEQA ISLAND, which is separated from the southernmost point of Viti Levu by the Beqa Passage, is 6 km in breadth, and has several peaks, the highest being 340 m above the sea. Portions of the island are under cultivation, and lemons and shaddocks grow wild in large quantities on the hills. The appearance of Beqa is beautiful from all points of view, as it is clothed in foliage from the summit of the hills to the water-line.

The fire-walking ceremony is performed by the people of this island, and the Fijian name for it is Vilavilairevo, which means "Jumping into the Ovens", and this is literally what occurs. The men prepare the ovens by placing big stones in a fire pit. After the fire has been burning for some time and the stones have become white hot, firewalkers jump onto the stones and, stepping from one to another, walk around in the oven in a circle. When they come out no trace of burns can be seen on their feet. Although the ceremony has been closely followed by scientific men, no satisfactory explanation of the feat has yet been offered.

YANUCA is a small island on the same encircling reef as Beqa.

Other islands off the Viti Levu coast include the following:

VIWA, small inhabited, about three km north of Bau.

QOMA, off the mid-eastern coast and the largest of a cluster of small inhabited islands.

NANANU GROUP, off Port Ellington on the North Coast; and MALAKE further east, both groups frequently have been used for grazing goats and even sheep.

MAMANUCA GROUP, 13 small volcanic islands off west coast and south of the Yasawas — only two of them inhabited, but favourite cruising grounds for yachts and pleasure craft; MALOLO GROUP of three small islands south of Mamanuca and closer to the Viti Levu coast. There are tourist resorts on some islands.

VATULELE, a large island of 31 sq km about 32 km S.E. of Sigatoka; several villages and a lighthouse.

SERUA, small and close inshore off most southerly part of Viti Levu coast. The seat of local paramount chief, and of considerable Fijian importance. The island consists of a hill at each end and a low saddle in the middle.

NAQARA and NAMAKA are privately owned small islands between Serua and Suva. Right at the entrance to Suva Harbour, and favourite picnic spots, are the small coral islands of NUKULAU and MAKULUVA.

KADAVU: The high island of Kadavu is generally the first landmark seen by travellers coming from the south. Next to Taveuni, it is considered one of the finest in the group. It is about 48 km in length, and varies in breadth from 400 m to 13 km. At the Namalata isthmus it is nearly divided into two separate islands, the backbone range of hills entirely disappearing; and at Daku isthmus it is only 1 km broad where the range is only 61 m. Total area is 411 sq km.

Kadavu is of volcanic origin, and has some high mountains, of which Mount Washington (Buke Levu, or "the great yam heap") is most conspicuous, rising to a height of 838 m above the sea. From a high central ridge the land falls away gradually. All the lower parts of the island are well watered, and a white sandy beach skirts the coastline. There are numerous sheltered bays and harbours.

The population, 1976, was 8,699, almost entirely Fijian. The Government Station and hospital are at Vunisea, at the east end of the Namalata isthmus. There are mission stations at Richmond and Naidiri. Small amounts of copra are produced, also bananas and timber.

The north coast of Kadavu is about 80 km south of Suva; the island and its smaller outliers lie within the Great Astrolabe Reef — the islands being themselves volcanic. The most important of the lesser islands is ONO, with an area of 30 sq km and a central peak of 35 m. There are several villages. North of Ono are BULIA, DRAVUNI and SOLO (which has a lighthouse and nothing else).

GREAT ASTROLABE is a 50 km loop of coral separated from the North Astrolabe ring by a channel of clear water about a km wide.

LOMAIVITI. Lomaiviti, or Central Fiji, consists of seven large islands and a few small ones, situated in or near the Koro Sea. They have an aggregate area of 410 sq km. The large islands are (from W to E) Ovalau, Makogai, Wakaya, Batiki, Gau, Koro and Nairai. Moturiki (about 10 sq km) lies close to Ovalau.

The islands are volcanic, and Ovalau (nearest the mainland of Viti Levu) is separated from that island by 16 km of shallow sea. Population of the Lomaiviti area was 13,568 in 1976, predominantly Fijian, except for the townspeople of Levuka, a few planters and storekeepers.

Communications in Lomaiviti are centred on Levuka.

OVALAU ranks first in point of importance, from the fact that its chief town, Levuka, was the capital of Fiji until the seat of government was removed to Suva in 1882. In 1976 the population totalled 1,397 and of Ovalau 6,513.

The island, 13 km by 11 km, is of volcanic formation. It is high and rugged, consisting of very steep hills rising to a height of 626 m, crowned with great crags and by deep gorges, formerly densely wooded.

A tuna fishing enterprise was established there in 1964-65 and as a result there is now more commercial activity in the town. The fish are caught by Japanese, Korean and Taiwanese fishing boats engaged under contract and are frozen at shore installations and shipped abroad.

The town has a good water supply from the dammed waters of Totoga Creek in the gorge above and a very pleasant swimming pool from the same source. The business section runs along the very narrow coastal flat but the residential area straggles up the steep hills and some of Levuka's streets are, in fact, long flights of steps.

It has a hotel, shops, a club, several schools and some pleasant scenery. A large smooth stone at Nasova, at the edge of the town, marks the spot where the Deed of Cession was signed in 1874 and the Union Jack hoisted.

Levuka is a port of entry for overseas ships. Regular communication with the mainland is by launch to Natovi on Viti Levu and then by bus to Suva, or by light aircraft which run a regular

WILLIAMS &
GOSLING LTD
BUT SERIOUSLY
We specialise in:
CUSTOMS CLEARANCE
HOUSEHOLD REMOVALS AND PACKING
AIR FREIGHT (WE ARE IATA AGENTS)
SHIPS' AGENCY
ROAD HAULAGE
SUVA LAUTOKA AND NADI AIRPORT
P.O. Box 79, Suva. Telex: FJ2163. Tel: 31 2633

daily service from an airstrip some kilometres out of Levuka.

NAIRAI, about 23 sq km in area, was famous in old times for the manufacture of its mats, baskets, etc., and, like Batiki, was subject to Bau.

Population is about 707 (1976).

BATIKI produces all the fruits and roots common in Fiji, and sustains a community of four villages. It has no protected anchorage. It is surrounded by reefs extending up to more than a kilometre from shore and through which there are only narrow passages. It is 30 km south-east of Ovalau and about 9 sq km in area.

KORO is shaped like a shark's tooth, being 8 km wide at the north coast and converging at the south in Muanivanua Point (in Fijian meaning "end of the land"). There is a lighthouse on the point. Total area is 104 sq km. The island is rugged, the centre being a plateau of broken country where there are several peaks from 300 to 520 m. The highest peak, 650 m, is in the western range. The island is well-watered by short streams. The plateau has fertile land suitable for planting. The population of 3,199 in 1976 was almost all Fijian.

GAU, the most southern of the Lomaiviti islands, is 140 sq km in extent. Highest peaks are over 700 m. Population is about 2,600.

WAKAYA and MAKOGAI lie to the north-east of Ovalau, and, although several kilometres apart, they are situated within the same reef. There is a remarkable shelf formed near the centre of Wakaya, which goes by the name of the "Chieftain's Leap", from a tragedy of the long past.

In September, 1917, von Luckner, commander of the German raider "Sea Adler" that had been wrecked in French Polynesia landed with a party on Wakaya while trying to escape in a launch. They were captured by a party of police.

Makogai has an area of 8 sq km and with its smaller outlier, Makodroga, was used as a settlement and hospital for the treatment of leprosy patients from Fiji and other parts of the South Pacific until 1969.

The highest point on the island is about 275 m and Makogai has fertile soil and a pleasant climate. There is an anchorage in Dalice Bay in the north-west; the old hospital installations are at the southern end of the bay.

HORSESHOE REEF is a ring of dangerous reef 1.5 km in diameter 20 km NE from the lighthouses on Wakaya Reef and Batiki Island. It is in the main seaway, and there have been several wrecks on it.

YASAWA GROUP. The Western, or Yasawa group (charted on old maps as the Ba or Leeward Islands) extends in a north-north-easterly and south-south-westerly direction, forming a comparatively narrow chain, for a distance of 80 km, north-westward of the north-west coast of Viti Levu. In number, there are 16 definite islands, with numerous islets and rocks.

In 1976, the group's population totalled 4,372.

NAVITI, 34 sq km, is the largest of the group, next to which, in size, is YASAWA, 28 sq km.

Thirteen km from Naviti are the seven islands constituting the WAYA group, including Eld, Fox, Agate and Sinclair Islands. Waya Island has several singularly sharp peaks, the highest being 570 m above the sea, and it is covered with vegetation from summit to water-line.

Other islands include: ALEWA KALOU (or Round), NACULA, TAVEWA, YAQETA and VIWA.

ROTUMA. Rotuma is the principal island of a small group which lies about 390 km N.N.W. of Fiji, in lat. 12.27 S., and long. 177.7 E. Rotuma is 13 km long and has a maximum width of 4 km. Geographically and ethnically it has little to do with Fiji but is, politically, part of the dominion.

N.N.W. of Rotuma is the small inhabited island of Uea (260 m high), and westward of Uea are two islets, Hatana and Hofliua. The latter is otherwise known as the singularly-formed Split Island, which looks as if it has been cleanly split with an axe. Altogether, eight small islands surround Rotuma, the others being Solnahu, Solkope, Afnaha and Hauatiu.

Population at 1976 census was 2,805 on Rotuma and 4,064 living elsewhere in Fiji. It is administered by a District Officer, who is responsible to the Commissioner, Eastern at Ovalau. The Government station is at Ahau; Motusa, situated on a narrow neck of land at the western end of the island, is also important. Chief industries are copra production and the making of finely-plaited mats, which are much in demand.

Small inter-island vessels from Suva call every few months with passengers and stores and to lift copra.

An airstrip was scheduled to open in 1980.

There is a wireless station on Rotuma. A medical officer supervises the public health service.

Rotuma's volcanic soil grows practically anything in the way of tropical fruit and vegetables — yams, tapioca, pawpaw, taro.

An excellent highway encircles the main island; and there are a number of cars and trucks in use. The Rotuman Sports Club has a large, modern club house, tennis court, golf course, etc.

Chief villages are Motusa, Ahau (Government Station, with the Residency, hospital and Courthouse), Sumi (R.C. Mission), and Lau. Hilly landmarks on the main island are Suelhof (255 m), Soloroa (220 m), and Satarua (167 m). An unusual feature seen on the 27 km drive around the island is the large number of graveyards, with an array of elaborate tombstones.

The island was discovered in August, 1791, by Captain Edwards, in the frigate 'Pandora', when searching for the 'Bounty' mutineers, and named by him Grenville Island. Captain Wilson visited it in the missionary ship 'Duff' in September, 1797. French and British navigators wrote accounts of it in 1824 (M. Duperrey), 1827 (Captain Dillon), 1828 (M. Legoarat) and 1841 (Lucet).

Almost from the time of its discovery Rotuma was a favourite resort for escaped convicts and runaway sailors. Duperrey, in 1824, found there four English sailors who had deserted from the ship 'Rochester'.

About 1840 the Roman Catholics and the Wesleyans started missions there. In later years a series of wars commenced between the adherents of the different religious sects, and the distracted chiefs, in 1879, asked that Britain annex the group. This was done on May 13, 1881. The laws are the laws of Fiji, with some local variations, especially in relation to land. The land belongs to the Rotumans; it may not be sold to non-natives, but may be leased for not more than 21 years.

The Rotumans, unlike the Fijians, are Polynesians, and mostly resemble the Tahitians, Hawaiians, and Maoris; but in the last few decades, much "foreign" blood has been mixed with that of Rotuma. The Rotumans speak a language that includes words found in the dialects of almost all the adjacent Pacific Groups. The Rotumans have always been great wanderers and before the European era regularly visited Fiji, Tonga, the Gilbert Islands and even the New Hebrides in their large canoes.

The group is divided into seven districts over each of which there is a chief who is responsible to the District Officer. Districts are Naotau, Itumutu, Itutiu, Mulahaha, Juju, Oonafa and Pepsei. The Rotuman Council, whose members are nominated, meets once a month.

No Rotuman member is sent to the House of Representatives as such, Rotuma being part of a Fijian constituency; but a Rotuman Senator is nominated.

FOR THE TOURIST. The Fiji Visitors Bureau supplies detailed information to visitors, but is not a booking agency. It is financed by the government and donations from local business firms. The Fiji Visitors Bureau has overseas offices in Sydney, Melbourne and Auckland and is represented by an agent in San Francisco.

The general manager is Mr Malakai Gucake.

There are numerous local travel agents, including: Burns Philp Travel, Suva, Lautoka, Nadi Airport and Travelodge Hotels; Campbell's Travel Service, Suva; Fiji Tours Ltd., Nadi Airport; Fiji Travel Service Ltd., Suva; Hunts Travel Service, Suva, Nadi Airport, Lautoka (agents for Thomas Cook, American Express); Lodhia and Co., Nadi; Macquarie Travel Service, Suva, Nadi Airport; Menan Taxi and Travel Agency, Ba; Tapa Tours Ltd., Suva, Nadi Airport; M. H. Travel Service, Lautoka, Nadi Airport; Nishant Trading Co., Suva; Pacific Travel Service, Suva, Ba, Nadi; Senirosi Travel Agency, Suva; United Travel Service, Ba; Union Steam Ship Co., Suva; Victory Travel Agency, Nadi. Bank of N.S.W. Suva.

Entry formalities: Visitors may be issued with permits to stay for one month. These can be extended to six months on arrival. Visitors must have valid passports, onward or return tickets and adequate funds for their support.

Visas are not needed by nationals or citizens of Commonwealth countries, most West European and South East Asian countries, USA etc. There is a long list of these countries, but nationals of other countries need a visa unless their stay in Fiji is less than three hours, so if in doubt visitors should enquire before attempting to enter Fiji. Passports and visas are not needed by people who transit Fiji by the same ship or aircraft, but 'ship' does not include a private yacht.

People arriving by air must have a valid international smallpox certificate unless they have been in Australia, New Zealand or specified nearby Pacific Islands for at least 14 days before arrival on Fiji. Travellers arriving by sea do not need vaccination certificates unless they came through India or any other country infected by smallpox.

Travellers over one year of age arriving by air must have cholera and yellow fever vaccination certificates if arriving from countries infected by these diseases.

Airport tax: $5.00 per passenger departure on all international travellers.

Duty free shopping: Most of the goods sold in Fiji under the 'duty free' label are not completely so, as they bear a 10 per cent fiscal tax. However they are still usually much cheaper to buy than in Australia, New Zealand or the US and Britain.

The following items in this class can be bought over the counter: Watches and bands, including those with diamonds and other precious stones; radios; record players; tape recorders; television sets; electric razors; cameras and accessories; movie cameras; projectors to 8mm; slide viewers; film for still and movie cameras; portable typewriters; all jewellery including pearls, diamonds and other precious stones set or unset; telescopes; binoculars; perfume, but not other cosmetics; furs and fur clothing; sporting goods including golf clubs. Golf bags are duty free if delivered direct to a ship or aircraft.

Nadi Airport duty free shop sells duty free liquor and cigarettes to departing and transit passengers. At Suva, passengers on cruise ships can arrange for shops to deliver duty free liquor to them aboard ship.

Other items that make good "buys" are Indian silk saris, scarves, silver and tortoiseshell jewellery, woven baskets, mats, tapa cloth, Fijian dolls. Locally made clothes from imported fabrics are also attractive.

Suva's busy general market is situated near King's Wharf. It is notable not only for the variety of goods sold but for the opportunity it gives of studying the several races of people who make up Fiji's population. Stallholders sell not only fruit, vegetables, fish and sea foods, but every variety of woven mat, bag, shell necklace and other curios.

Popular resorts: Fiji's main holiday areas are the sunny west side of Viti Levu and the cooler but still sunny 'Coral Coast' section along the south Viti Levu coast between Sigatoka and Deuba. The Nadi area has a number of hotels catering for all tastes; it offers interesting tours to the highlands in the interior, through the sugar-cane districts, the sugar mills and a number of small outlying islands.

Several get-away-from-it style resorts in the Mananucas and near Lautoka and Nadi include the Castaway Resort at Qalito Island, the luxury Mana Island Resort and the Etai and Treasure Island resorts. A three-day cruise through the adjacent Yasawa Islands is another major attraction.

Some people who wish to visit Suva from Nadi, take a taxi around Queen's Road one way and fly back to pick up planes again at Nadi.

Along the Coral Coast the main resort hotels are the Fijian at Yanuca; the Reef Hotel; Korolevu Beach Hotel and at Pacific Harbour, the Beachcomber Hotel. Small self-contained chalets are also available in these areas at reasonable rates. There are several good hotels in Suva, but the city is mainly a commercial, shopping and administrative centre, with no resort hotels. The drive around the north of Viti Levu between Lautoka and Suva via Rakiraki, Ba and Tavua is worthwhile, with a stop at Rakiraki, but the Rakiraki-Suva section, while scenically spectacular, is still untouched as a resort area.

Visitors should make the effort to get away from the main island. Savusavu, in the centre of the coconut growing area, is worth a stay of a couple of days and has several small hotels. Likewise Taveuni, the large island just across from Savusavu, where there are two hotels. But these two areas are very quiet, as is Levuka, Fiji's old capital on Ovalau Island. But it is well worth a visit, because of its charm.

The Lau group, although remote, geographically, is easy of reach these days as there are airstrips on Lakeba, Vanuabulavu and Ono-i-Lau with regular flights from Nausori. There are no hotels in the Lau or Lomaiviti groups but accommodation can usually be found in a Fijian village for those prepared to rough it.

Wakaya Island, a private island in Lomaiviti, is being developed by a major international company as a residential park for the very wealthy and will have limited accommodation for casual visitors also. But it will be some years before this island is really opened up to tourists.

Archaeological and historical locations: The Fiji Museum has undertaken limited archaeological exploration. Many areas of Fiji, the Rewa River Delta especially, are pocked with ring forts, relics of the days when villages had to be fortified against attacks by cannibal neighbours. There are large terrace forts on the sides of the Sigatoka Valley and elsewhere. Large earth forts exist on Wakaya Island.

On the north end of Taveuni, at a height of about 300 m there are mysterious earth works of a large scale; the origin and purpose a mystery. In several areas of Fiji there are petroglyphs (rock carvings): at Dakuniba in southern Vanua Levu; at Sawailau in the Yasawas; Vola Creek, Savusavu Bay; Taveuni; and Beqa and Yanuca are the best known.

The museum has dated pottery fragments from sand dunes at the mouth of the Sigatoka River as being about 2,000 years old.

On Bau Island, home of the great chief Cakobau who ceded Fiji to Britain, the government is restoring some of the old chiefly buildings. Serua Island – just off the coast of south Viti Levu – is another interesting example of a fortified islet. A stone monument in Suva marks the site of land auctions after cession. Levuka town on Ovalau Island, once Fiji's capital, has not changed much from how it looked in the 1880s. It contains many charming old wooden buildings. Some Fiji towns have colonial-style wooden houses perhaps 100 or so years old. They are still private homes and not open to the public. The National Trust of Fiji hopes to eventually acquire examples of such buildings.

It has already acquired Burns Philp's old building in Levuka.

Suva – capital, chief port. The city of Suva, as we see it today bears little resemblance to the then new capital of the 1880s. The whole foreshore area to the seaward of Victoria Parade, from Nubukalou Creek to the point where the Thurston Gardens run up to Government House, has been reclaimed by draining former mangrove swamps and cutting down the natural soapstone knolls and ridges to make filling. Further reclamation has made way for a broad roadway along the waterfront.

At the eastern end of Victoria Parade most of the buildings on the reclaimed land are set in green lawns and gardens; huge, spreading trees shade the footpath and altogether make up one of the most charming streets in the South Pacific.

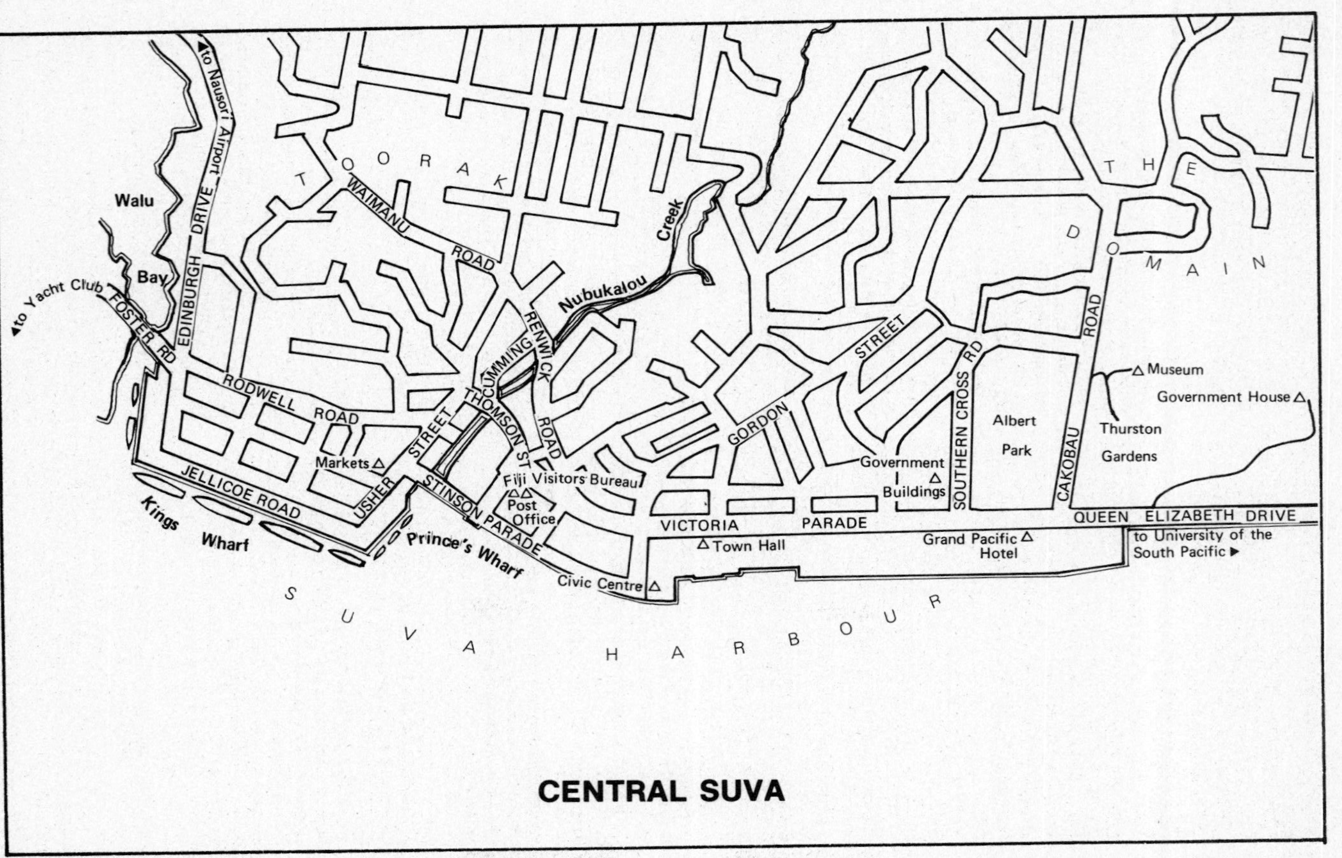

CENTRAL SUVA

Also at the eastern end of Victoria Parade are the Government Offices, Native Land Trust Board building and Broadcasting House, one street back; alongside is Albert Park where many of the big sporting fixtures are held; and opposite Albert Park, is the Grand Pacific Hotel, a Travelodge Hotel. East of Albert Park, on the other side of Cakabou Road, the Thurston Gardens wiht the Fiji Museum in the grounds, lead to the brow of the hill and Government House which is backed by a residential area, called the Domain. The business area of Suva is westward of MacArthur Street in Victoria Parade and in the clusters of streets that run on both sides of Nubukalou Creek. The General Post Office, banks, newspaper offices, departmental stores and streets of Indian tailor and curio shops are all in this area.

Like the tenement area of Toorak, residential Suva is built on rising ground behind the foreshore of the harbour but post-war expansion has resulted in housing development also at Suva Point, and on the slopes looking down on Laucala Bay.

In the opposite direction – westward from the city, beyond Walu Bay – there has been considerable residential development at Lami which is now a town in its own right. A steep road, a little west of King's Wharf, runs north through the self-contained suburb of Samabula and turns west again to the pleasant residential area along the Prince's Road, Tamavau which has excellent views over Suva Harbour, Lami and the mountains beyond.

Suva has the highest concentration of Europeans and Indians in Fiji and Fijians are increasingly attracted to the bright lights of the city. This fact, with a large Chinese community – mostly merchants – Polynesians, other islanders and part-Europeans, makes a walk in Suva's streets an ethnological object lesson and adds considerably to its attraction for tourists.

Here is a selection of hotels and other accommodation in Suva, and other main areas of Fiji:

ACCOMMODATION

Suva Hotels

GRAND PACIFIC HOTEL, Victoria Parade, Suva, situated in 1 ha of garden at edge of harbour. Swimming pool. All rooms air-conditioned, with private bathroom or shower.

OUTRIGGER MOTEL, on sea front, Queen Elizabeth Drive, Suva. Swimming pool, licenced. All rooms air-conditioned with private shower and toilet.

HOTEL SUVA, Waimanu Road, Suva. Bedrooms are air-conditioned and half have private shower and toilet.

HOTEL METROPOLE, Princes Street, Suva. Bed and breakfast.

HOTEL ISA LEI, facing harbour, Lami, approximately 10 minutes from city centre. Swimming pool, all rooms air-conditioned with private facilities.

TRADE WINDS HOTEL, facing harbour, Bay of Islands, approximately 10 minutes drive from city centre. Swimming pool, all rooms air-conditioned with private shower, toilet and balcony.

TRAVELODGE HOTEL, on harbour-side, on Victoria Parade. 139 rooms, air-conditioned with private bath, refrigerator. Swimming pool.

CAPRICORN APARTMENT HOTEL, in city two minutes from main shops. 25 self-contained apartments with kitchenettes, showers and toilets, air-conditioned. Swimming pool.

SOUTHERN CROSS. 30 air-conditioned units, private facilities, swimming pool, restaurant.

HILLCREST HOTEL. 32 twin rooms, eight self-contained suites, air-conditioned, swimming pool, restaurant.

COURTESY INN, Gordon Street, 52 rooms, air-conditioned, private facilities.

Suva, Other Accommmodation

TOWN HOUSE SERVICED APPARTMENTS, Fisher Street. 28 self-contained apartments with cooking facilities. Coffee shop, liquor bar.

WAIMANU GUEST HOUSE, Marks Street. Bed and breakfast.

TROPIC TOWERS. 30 self-contained apartments, swimming pool, dial-a-meal service.

TANOA GUEST HOUSE, Princes Road. Bed and breakfast, liquor licence, swimming pool,

LOLOMA HOTEL, Gorrie Street, 14 apartments.

SOUTH PACIFIC GUEST HOUSE, Victoria Parade. Bed and breakfast.

SUNSET APARTMENTS, Corner Murray and Gordon Streets. 12 self-contained apartments with maid service.

SUVA APARTMENTS, Flagstaff. 11 self-contained apartments.

TALEI MOTEL, Kimberley Street. 4 units.

DOMAIN LODGE. Fully furnished flats with all facilities.

Viti Levu

TROPIC SANDS RESORT, Deuba, 56 km from Suva on Queen's Road. Apartment units with private facilities.

BEACHCOMBER. Modern resort hotel operated by Travelodge, on the site of the old Beachcomber at Deuba, 56 km from Suva. Air-conditioned, swimming pool.

PACIFIC HARBOUR, Deuba. Pacific Harbour villas. Self-contained villas, two to four bedrooms, maid service, some with pool. These are run in association with the Beachcomber.

MAN FRIDAY RESORT, off Queen's Road, 88 km from Suva. Self-contained bures near beach with everything supplied except food which can be bought on site.

KOROLEVU BEACH HOTEL, Queen's Road, 104 km from Suva. Resort hotel, all rooms and bures with private shower and toilets, swimming pool.

TUBAKULA BEACH APPARTMENT HOTEL, on Queen's Road, Korotogo, 134 km from Suva. Self-contained two bedroom, A-line chalet-type bungalows. Swimming pool.'

SANDY POINT COTTAGES, Queen's Road, Korotogo, 135 km from Suva. Self-contained cottages, maid service, swimming pool.

PARADISE POINT RESORT, next to Korolevu Beach Resort, 90 rooms, restaurant, room service, swimming pool.

NAVITI RESORT, 122 km from Nadi, in the Korolevu area. 144 air-conditioned rooms, swimming pool, restaurant, all normal resort facilities.

THE REEF HOTEL, Queen's Road, Korotogo, near Sigatoka, 135 km from Suva. Air-conditioned, all with private bath, etc., swimming pool.

HYATT REGENCY HOTEL, Coral Coast: air-conditioned with restaurant, coffee shop, 3 bars, pool with swim-in bar.

WARATAH LODGE, Queen's Road, Korotogo. 5 self-contained A-line cottages accommodating six, swimming pool.

VAKAVITI CABINS AND UNITS, Korotogo. 4-roomed motel; 2 cabins. Swimming pool.

KOROTOGO BEACH COTTAGES, at Korotogo. 4 beach cottages each accommodating 4 persons. Bungalow, accommodating 6-8 persons.

SIGATOKA HOTEL, Sigatoka, 82 km from Nadi airport. A country-style hotel, with bar trade.

THE FIJIAN HOTEL, Yanuca Island, connected by causeway to Queen's Road, near Sigatoka. Resort hotel with luxury accommodation; air-conditioned. Swimming pool; excellent beach.

NADI HOTEL, Queen's Road, 6 km from Nadi airport. Single rooms, without air-conditioning, and sharing bathroom.

HIBISCUS HOTEL, midway between Nadi airort and Nadi town. Swimming pool; rooms with private showers and toilets. Air-conditioning.

SUNLOVER HOTEL, 80 air-conditioned rooms, restaurant, pool, about 6 km from Nadi airport.

DOMINION INTERNATIONAL HOTEL, midway between airport and Nadi town, air-conditioned rooms, pool.

REGENT OF FIJI. International luxury beach resort at Denarau Beach, about 8 km from Nadi airport. 300 rooms, air-conditioned, convention pavilion, pool.

SUNNYSIDE GUEST HOUSE, Nadi. Bed and breakfast.

MOTEL TABUA, between airport and Nadi town. Self-contained rooms. Bed and breakfast.

SUNHAVEN PRIVATE HOTEL, 6 km from Nadi airport, 14 rooms, bed and breakfast.

MELANESIAN HOTEL, 2 km from Nadi airport. 18 rooms with privte shower/toilet. Swimming pool, liquor licence.

MOCAMBO HOTEL, Namaka Hill, overlooking Nadi airport. All rooms air-conditioned with private shower and toilet; swimming pool.

HOTEL TANOA, on hill above Nadi airport; swimming pool; rooms with shower/toilet; air-conditioning.

FIJI GATEWAY HOTEL, at entrance to Nadi International Airport; 103 air-conditioned and sound-proofed rooms, private shower/toilet; swimming pool.

NADI TRAVELODGE, on hill overlooking Nadi International Airport. 81 air-conditioned suites with bath/shower/toilet, refrig., swimming pool.

NA BURE VUDA BEACHSIDE RESORT, between Nadi Airport and Lautoka; 7 self-contained cottages; 10 fully-serviced flats. Shop, dining room service, swimming pool.

SEABREEZE MOTEL, Lautoka. 12 rooms with shower/toilet; bar. $5 B & B.

LAUTOKA HOTEL, 26 km from Nadi airport. Rooms vary from standard single room in the main hotel to air-conditioning, private bathroom, in detached Namoli House.

CATHAY HOTEL, Lautoka. Swimming pool; rooms air-conditioned with private bathrooms.

BA HOTEL, 39 km from Lautoka, on King's Road, Swimming pool; rooms air-conditioned, with private bathrooms.

TAVUA HOTEL, 200 km from Suva, King's Road (64 km from Lautoka). Swimming pool; rooms with shower/toilet.

RAKIRAKI HOTEL, 156 km from Suva on King's Road. Rooms with shower/toilet. Swimming pool, bar.

TAILEVU HOTEL, Korovou. 48 km from Suva, in centre of dairy country. Rooms with shower and toilet.

HOTEL FIJI, Nausori. On banks of Rewa River, near Nausori airport and 23 km from Suva.

Other Islands

CASTAWAY ISLANDS RESORT, on 31 ha island in Malolo Group, 23 km of Viti Levu coast at Nadi. Accommodaion in bures and rooms.

GRAND EASTERN HOTEL, Labasa, north coast of Vanau Levu. Private swimming pool; all rooms with private bathroom and fan, some with air-conditioning.

BEACHCOMBER ISLAND BURES, Tal Island, Mamanuca Group, off Nadi Bay, daily connection by launch from Lautoka. Accommodation in Bures, self-contained with cooking facilities, smaller Bures for two, inc. meals.

PLANTATION VILLAGE, on Malolo Lailai Is., 8 km from Castaway Is. resort. There is a bar/grill and 25 large bures each accommodating six, with fully equipped kitchen and housegirl to take care of cooking, etc. Transport from Lautoka daily.

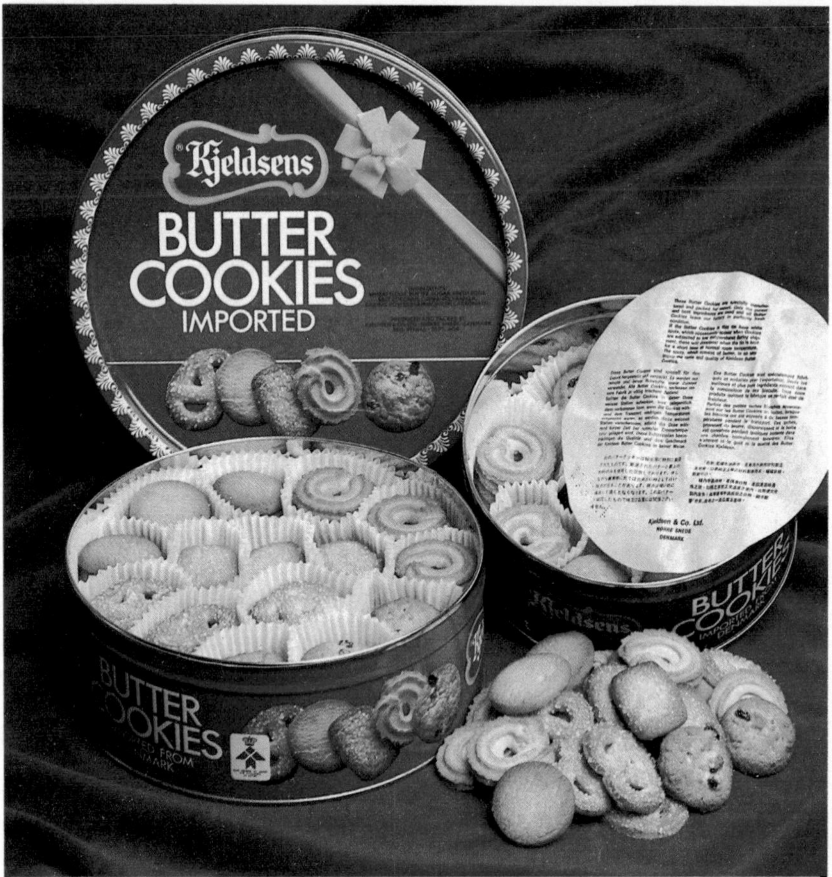
Kjeldsens
BUTTER
COOKIES
IMPORTED

Komatsu Makes a Difference

In critical areas like reliability and performance, Komatsu products and systems are making a significant difference at mining and construction sites around the world.

In the USA, for example, Komatsu's largest and most powerful work machine — the D455A bulldozer — is establishing a superior record of reliability and productivity at mining sites that virtually no other machine in its class can match.

And in another critical area, technology, Komatsu is also making a difference — in responding to market demands for improved product quality, and for new and original product innovations. Consider our new computerized seabed robot system.

Operating on the ocean floor, it can relay TV pictures of the seabed to a mother ship, or perform man-like boring, drilling and piling operations down to planned depths of 500 meters.*

Discover the Komatsu difference — above sea level, or down to depths of 500 meters. Komatsu — a name you can build on.

* The Komatsu seabed robot system is currently operating in the Japan Inland Sea at depths down to a maximum of 70 meters, in a government-sponsored bridge works program.

KOMATSU LTD.

Tokyo, Japan

Komatsu overseas offices: Singapore, Jakarta, Manila, Bangkok, Bangalore, Karachi, Beijing, Seoul, Sydney, Ankara, Cairo, Alger, Dubai, Teheran, Baghdad, Jeddah, Riyadh, Ad Damman, Nairobi, Abidjan, Lagos, Johannesburg, Moscow, Warszawa, Brussels, Paris, Madrid, Düsseldorf, Stuttgart, London, Habana, Buenos Aires, Panamá, Caracas, São Paulo, Mexico City, San Francisco, Oakland, Philadelphia, Detroit, Dallas, Atlanta, Chicago, Toronto, Vancouver, and distributors in over 100 countries around the world.

TREASURE ISLAND RESORT in Yasawas, about 19 km from Lautoka; air-conditioned rooms with private facilities and tea and coffee making facilities; pool; restaurant.

MANA ISLAND RESORT, on Mana Island, about 24 km from Lautoka; hotel with luxury resort facilities.

SAVUSAVU TRAVELODGE, at Savusavu, south coast of Vanau Levu, 48 suites, with air-conditioning, private bath, shower, toitel. Swimming pool.

SAVUSAVU TOWN HOUSE, in township area, 18 air-conditioned rooms, bar, dining room.

NAMALI ESTATE RESORT, 10 km from Savusavu township, overlooking bay, 4 rooms, 2 bures.

ROYAL HOTEL, Levuka. On the island of Ovalau, off Viti Levu eash coast (Levuka was the old capital of Fiji). 14 rooms iwth shower/toilet. Air and launch connections wiht the mainland of Viti Levu.

RUKURUKU HOLIDAY RESORT, on Ovalau. 3 cottages, 2 bures, with cooking facilities or with meals.

TAVEUNI TRAVELODGE, at Waiyevo, 23 km from Matei airport on the west coast of Taveuni overlooking Somosomo Strait. 33 air-conditioned suites with bath/shower/toilet. Swimming pool.

TOBERUA ISLAND RESORT, on 1.5 ha island off SE point of Viti Levu but within barrier reef. 16 large luxury bures, with private facilities; swimming pool.

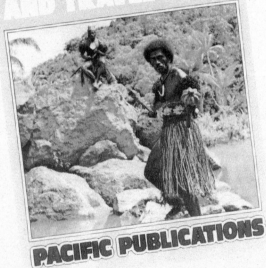

FRENCH POLYNESIA

French Polynesia, an overseas territory of France, consists of five main groups containing some 130 islands. They have a land area of 4,000 sq. km in an area of four million square kilometres of ocean. They extend from 7 to 29 deg. S. latitude and from 131 to 156 deg. W longitude. Papeete, the capital, is on the island of Tahiti which is about 5,390 km east of Sydney and about 6,520 km south-west of California. Local time is 10 hours behind GMT.

The population was 137,382 in April 1977.

The national anthem and flag are those of France. The red and white Tahitian flag is also widely used.

The currency is the French Pacific franc (Cours du Franc Pacifique-CFP) with a 1977 exchange rate of CFP 18.18 to the French franc and 93 to the A$1.00.

Public holidays include the traditional French ones: January 1, Easter Monday, May 1 (Labour Day), Ascension (39 days after Easter Sunday). Monday after Pentecost (about 10 days after Ascension), July 14 (Bastille Day), August 15 (Assumption), November 1 (All Saints), November 11 (Armistice Day) and Christmas Day.

THE PEOPLE. At the last official census in April 1977, the total population of French Polynesia numbered 137,382. Tahiti had 95,604 inhabitants of whom 22,967 were in Papeete. Polynesians represent 75 per cent of the population, Europeans 9 per cent, half-European 7 per cent, Chinese 7 per cent, half-Chinese 1 per cent and others 1 per cent. The continuing growth of the population on Tahiti, especially around Papeete, contributes to the Windward Islands' total of 101,392 followed by the Leeward Islands (16,311), the Marquesas (5,419), Austral Island (5,208) and the Tuamotu-Gambier group (9,052).

Nationality. French Polynesians are French citizens.

Language. The official language is French. Tahitian is widely used among the islanders.

Religion. In their religious beliefs, more than half the population is Protestant, with about one third Roman Catholic, 6% Mormon, 2% Seventh-day Adventists and others being Jehovah's Witnesses and Buddhists.

Lifestyle. The lifestyle varies considerably from urban Papeete with its large population concentrating on business and administrative activity, tourist facilities and French legionnaires, to the rural life on outer islands.

All Tahitians share the same generous love of hospitality, feasting, dancing and a warm response to the natural beauty which surrounds them.

GOVERNMENT. As an overseas territory of the French Republic, French Polynesia elects the thirty members of its Territorial Assembly by popular vote, every five years. The Assembly members in turn elect the seven members of the Government Council (Conseil de Gouvernement) which is presided over by the High Commissioner who is a public servant appointed by the French Government in Paris. He is the chief executive of the territory, in charge of the public service and holding considerable power. French Polynesia is also represented in Paris by a senator and, from March 1978, two deputies who are all elected.

Internal self-government. The last elections for the Territorial Assembly were held in May 1977. Political parties are popularly divided into so-called "autonomist" and "anti-autonomist", the distinction being rather a question of degree of collaboration with the French public servants representing the Paris government. The islanders' demands for internal self-government, some even calling for independence, have been strongly resisted by the French authorities who have emphasized the economic advantages of co-operation with France. However, under new political status introduced in July 1977, wider powers (locally called "internal autonomy") were given to the Government Council which has an elected vice-president.

Local government. Municipal government is an important arm of administration with responsibility for local schools, roads, water supplies, bridges and other capital works. The mayor and council of each municipality or commune are elected. Under the French system, however, real authority lies with the Chefs de Subdivision, (district officers) public servants appointed by and responsible to the French governor. There are five such administrative subdivisions, representing the five island groups.

Over recent years, Paris policy has been to increase the financial resources and fields of activity of the municipalities. This has met considerable opposition from the Territorial Assembly which sees such division of power as a lessening of the Assembly's influence and a counter-move to internal self-government.

JUSTICE. There are lower and higher courts (Tribunal de Premiere Instance and Tribunal Superieur d'Appel). There is a President and Vice President (equivalent of judges) of each but, in the lower court, cases are also presided over by magistrates. At the head of the judiciary department is Chief of the Judiciary Service, equivalent to an Attorney-General. Other officers of this department include prosecutors, examining magistrates, etc. Most of the judiciary officials are stationed in Papeete but in Raiatea there is a judge of the lower court.

Law and order is kept by the gendarmerie, which is part of the French National Gendarmerie whose members are recruited in France. They have locally hired assistants. The police corps, on the other hand, is locally recruited and paid by a municipality or commune and act within a commune's limits.

The basic laws in force are those of France, made applicable as occasion may demand by promulgations; plus ordinances, laws, etc., passed by the Assembly, that have a completely local application.

Liquor laws. Liquor is sold in bars, restaurants and cafes from 7 a.m. to 1.00 a.m. seven days a week. In certain bars outside Papeete closing time is not till 2 a.m. It is illegal to sell liquor to anyone under the age of 18 but there are no other restrictions.

There is little public drunkenness in French Polynesia. The local people usually drink local beer or punch made with red wine, local limes and sugar. Even more popular are soft-drinks.

Gambling. There is no official, legalised gambling.

DEFENCE. In 1963 French Polynesia became a nuclear test base – Centre d'Experimentation du Pacifique (CEP). By 1975 this consisted of a command base at Pirae in Papeete, accommodating all the essential services; a logistic support base at Hao, in the Tuamotus 900 km from Papeete, with an air strip and deep sea port; and the actual nuclear testing facilities on the atolls of Mururoa and Fangataufa, near Hao.

The installation of the CEP brought considerable changes to the Polynesian economy, increasing trade, building, and administrative personnel. This was accompanied by rapid inflation and a drift of workers from traditional agriculture and fishing.

Total expenditure on the CEP in 1974, plus that of the Atomic Energy Commission (CEA) and defence forces reached some CFP 11,100 million. Of this, about CFP 8,000 million provided wages for the 11,500 people employed.

Nuclear explosions. The first nuclear device was exploded at Mururoa in July 1966.

Protests followed, and grew, from Pacific countries, resulting in several years' boycott of various French trade, aircraft and shipping activities. In 1975 France announced that atmospheric tests were suspended and the first underground explosions then began on Fangataufa atoll.

The numbers of military personnel concerned with the experiments fluctuate. According to official reports the CEP reduced its staff in 1975 and again in 1976. As a result, about 3,000 civilian and military staff were located at Mururoa while only a few hundred were left at Hao. The military strength at Tahiti was also reduced.

EDUCATION. At the primary level, education is financed from the territorial budget while secondary and technical education is conducted with State funds. Private schools are operated by church missions with the State financing running costs.

There were 179 government primary schools with 30,396 pupils in 1979, together with 8,340 in 16 private primary schools. There were then 5,603 students in 13 government secondary schools and 3,273 in six private ones.

Technical training was being taken by 1,996 students in government schools and 607 in private ones.

State secondary schools include the Lycee Paul Gauguin in Papeete which has annexes in other districts and outer islands; the high school at Uturoa (Raiatea Is.) and the new Taaone Technical High School at Pirae in Papeete which has a course in Tourism.

Church secondary schools in Tahiti include the College Pomare IV (Protestant) and the College La Mennais (Roman Catholic). These schools have accommodation for boarders and prepare students for the baccalaureat or university entrance.

Other specialised education is available through the Teachers' Training College (120 students). The Chamber of Commerce in Papeete conducts courses in business English, shorthand, typing etc.

Scholarships for higher education and for French Universities are made possible by government grants. In 1979 there were about 200 scholarship students studying in metropolitan France.

Education is compulsory. It is free of charge in the government schools for day pupils; 14 is the legal school leaving age.

LABOUR. Information on the employment situation in French Polynesia is not readily available. Latest estimates indicate an active labour force of 44,000, including self-employed and about 25,500

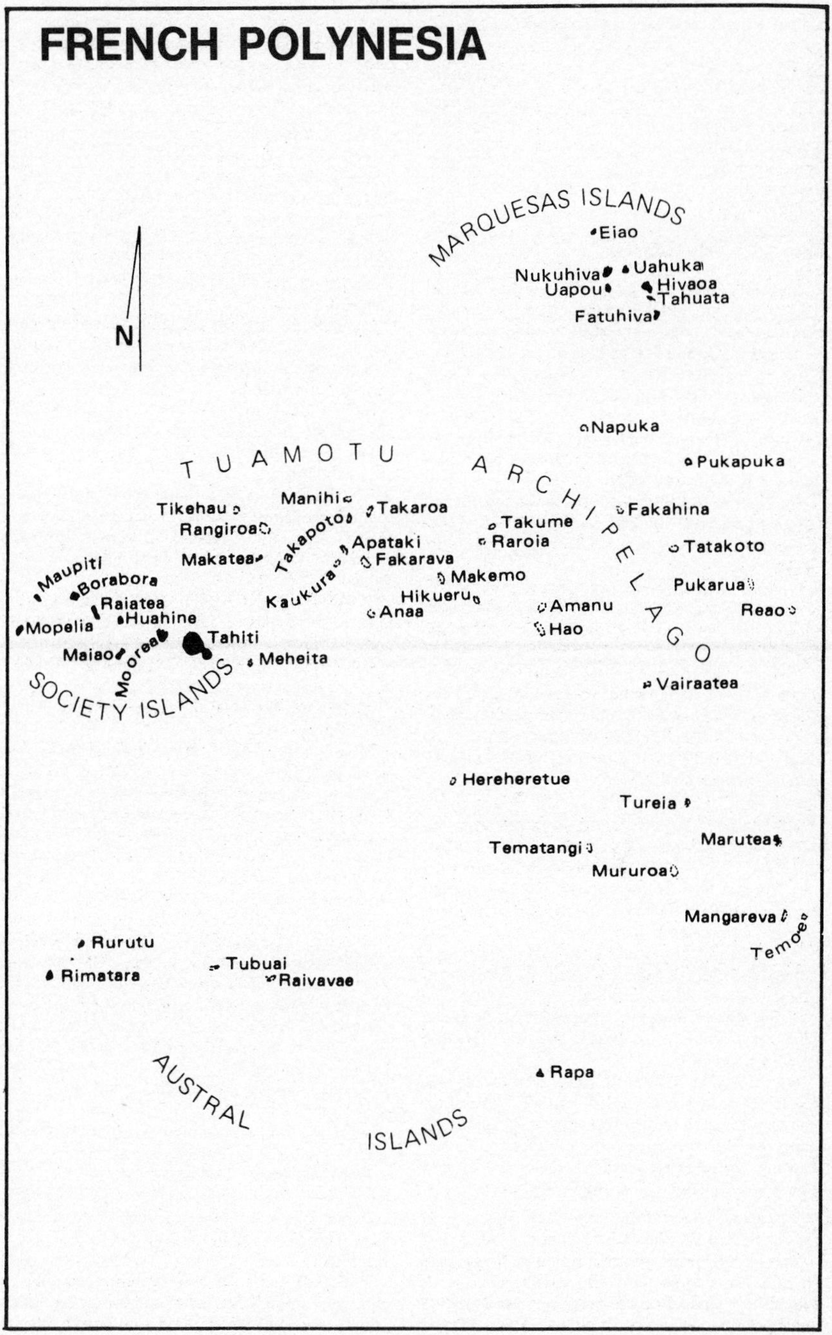

FRENCH POLYNESIA

N

MARQUESAS ISLANDS
Eiao
Nukuhiva
Uahuka
Uapou
Hivaoa
Tahuata
Fatuhiva

Napuka
Pukapuka

TUAMOTU ARCHIPELAGO
Manihi
Tikehau
Takaroa
Rangiroa
Takapoto
Takume
Fakahina
Apataki
Raroia
Tatakoto
Makatea
Fakarava
Makemo
Pukarua
Kaukura
Hikueru
Amanu
Reao
Anaa
Hao
Vairaatea

Maupiti
Borabora
Raiatea
Huahine
Mopelia
Tahiti
Maiao
Moorea
Meheita
SOCIETY ISLANDS

Hereheretue
Tureia
Tematangi
Maruteas
Mururoa
Mangareva
Temoe

Rurutu
Rimatara
Tubuai
Raivavae
Rapa
AUSTRAL ISLANDS

civilian employees. Main employee sectors are:

Banks, commerce	over 3,850
Building const.	about 3,000
Hotels	over 2,600
Transp., services	2,500
Manuf. industry	1,550
Domestic help	1,000
Professions	650
Primary ind.	about 400
Public service	5,370
Army, CEA, CEP civilians	2,500

The installation of the nuclear testing centre (CEP) has greatly influenced the territory's employment situation, bringing a shift of workers away from agriculture and fishing towards tertiary activities.

The initial construction of CEP facilities also affected the building industry.

Wages. The minimum wage rate (SMIG) increased from CFP62 per hour in December 1973 to CFP101 at the end of 1977.

The total payroll of employees in the territory is estimated to have doubled from about CFP5,500 million in 1973 to an annual CFP11,300 million in 1975.

Workers' accident compensation and other social benefits are financed through payroll tax paid to the Caisse de prevoyance sociale de la Polynesie Française.

Unions. These include the Federation des Syndicats de la Polynesie Française (general) Cartel des Syndicats des Dockers, Syndicat des Cadres de la Fonction Publique (Public Service), and the Syndicat Territorial des Instituteures et Institutrices Publics (State school teachers).

HEALTH. Health services are well provided for. More than 20 doctors are available for the civilian population in Tahiti, while military specialists with the CEP may be called in emergencies. The Mamao Hospital in Papeete, with 400 beds and modern equipment, opened in 1970.

There is a small hospital staffed by doctors in each group of the outer islands as well as dispensaries attended by travelling doctors.

Tahiti also has doctors operating private hospitals (cliniques), while about sixteen dentists serve the civilian population.

Research. The Institut de Recherches Medicales Louis Malarde, set up in 1947 with US assistance conducts research into endemic diseases. Under US and French doctors, the Institut has brought the disfiguring disease of elephantiasis under control and now concentrates more on fish toxicity.

Diseases. Tuberculosis has been the biggest health hazard for the local Polynesians in recent times but vigorous vaccination and X-ray programmes have been undertaken. Filariasis and its end result, elephantiasis, are regarded as now being under control. Diabetes, rheumatic fever, dengue fever and fish poisoning are major problems.

Certain local food habits can cause Tahitian meningitis from eating uncooked prawns, or fish poisoning from eating certain fish.

THE LAND. The five archipelagoes forming French Polynesia are scattered across 4 million square kilometres of ocean, although their actual land area is only 4,000 sq. km. Tahiti (1,042 sq. km.) is the largest island. The Tuamotu archipelago, by contrast, is composed of 76 islands, mostly atolls, with an average surface of 10 sq. km above sea level. These include the nuclear test sites of Mururoa and Fangataufa.

Islands at the opposite extremities of the territory are as far as 2,000 km apart, while the capital Papeete, on the island of Tahiti, is 1,500 km from various outer islands.

Highest mountain peaks are Mt. Orohena (2,237 m.) and Mt. Aorai (2,068 m.) on Tahiti.

The five archipelagoes, listing the main islands, are as follows:

SOCIETY ISLANDS. The Windward Group, comprising Tahiti, Moorea, Mehetia, Tetiaroa and Maiao. And the Leeward Group, comprising Huahine, Raiatea, Bora Bora, Maupiti and Tahaa.

TUAMOTU ARCHIPELAGO. Anaa, Makemo, Hao, Reao, Napuka, Mururoa, Rangiroa, Apataki and Fakarava.

GAMBIER ISLANDS. Mangareva, Taravai, Aukena, Akamaru and Temoe.

AUSTRAL ISLANDS. Tubuai, Rurutu, Rimatara, Raivavae and Rapa.

MARQUESAS ISLANDS. Hivaoa, Nukuhiva, Fatuhiva, Eiao, Uapou, Uahuka, Fatuhuku, Tahuata, Motane and Hatutu.

Most of these archipelagoes are composed of now-extinct volcanoes, with high mountainous formations and deep well-watered valleys. Such islands are generally surrounded by a coral reef forming sheltered lagoons. Islands like the Tuamotus, however, are small, flat coral atolls.

Climate. The climate is tropical, but moderate – average temperature being 27 deg C., falling to 21 deg C. during July and August. In January and February, hottest months of the year, the thermometer at Papeete registers 32 deg C. maximum. Rain falls through the year but mostly between November and March.

Average rainfall in Papeete is 1,750 mm. annually.

Humidity is generally high especially in the wet season. Cyclones have been experienced.

Flora and fauna. The islands of volcanic origin have fertile soil producing prolific vegetation including magnificent flowers, such as the Tahitian tiare. This is a fragrant gardenia, worn in leis or in the hair.

The local fauna on land is mainly introduced, with wild animals limited to some pigs and fowls. Ninety species of birds are present, most being visible around the shores of Tahiti. The greatest variety and abundance of fauna is found, in the sea with its fish and crustaceans.

Land reclamation. On the Papeete foreshore land reclamation has provided 14 hectares at Fare Ute for industrial and military purposes. An adjacent 14-ha strip of coral reef was reclaimed to provide extra berthing and storage facilities in the port of Papeete.

Land tenure. It is extremely difficult for foreigners to obtain land in French Polynesia although there is still provision for the Governor to authorise the transfer "under certain circumstances". The "circumstances" are, however, rare. Nonetheless, since the hotel-building boom some large parcels of privately owned land have changed hands. In the case of approved businesses wanting to establish themselves, the government will do its best to find suitable land.

Over 85 per cent of the land is in Polynesian hands although a considerable amount of this is leased to aliens, notably to the Chinese.

It is calculated that 35 per cent of the Chinese population lives by agriculture and only in a minority of cases is the land they work their own.

PRIMARY PRODUCTION: Efforts are being made to extend agricultural output in French Polynesia.

Copra. Still the main agricultural product despite fluctuations in world prices, recent output has been:

COPRA PRODUCTION
(in tonnes)

	1975	1976	1977
Windward Is. incl. Tahiti	1,063	1,200	1,070
Tuamotu-Gambier	11,287	9,550	7,635
Total inc. other is.	22,348	19,505	14,949

Coconut oil. The Territory's total copra output is used by the Tahiti Oil Co. (Huilerie de Tahiti) to be processed into coconut oil for export, and into coconut meal for use as cattle feed by the local beef industry, although some is also exported.

COCONUT PRODUCT EXPORTS
(in tonnes)

	1975	1976	1977
Coconut oil	11,147	13,341	9,657
Coconut meal	2,200	1,015	—

Vanilla. This crop has also declined through disinterest by growers. Vanilla exports have dropped from 28 tonnes in 1970 to 12 tonnes in 1974 and only 9 tonnes estimated in 1977.

Coffee. Grown in small plots for the local market, output was 160 tonnes in 1975, 102 tonnes in 1976 and 84 tonnes (est.) in 1977.

Vegetables. Produced mainly on the plains of Tahiti, vegetable output was about 4,500 tonnes in 1977. This necessitated imports of 5,000 tonnes of fresh vegetables. The 250 ha devoted to vegetables are cultivated by some 300 producers, mostly of Chinese origin.

Fruit. Local marketed production is over 4,000 tonnes. Of this, 111 tonnes were exported in 1977. This was only 5 per cent of the value of imported fruit.

Livestock. While efforts continue to increase the existing cattle herds, imported stock has enabled much of the local demand for milk, chickens and eggs to be satisfied.

Pork production in 1977 was 650 tonnes while imports were 250 tonnes.

In the same year, locally produced beef sales reached 378 tonnes while imports were 2,424 tonnes. Some 700 cows produced 1.6 million litres of milk. Three local companies make yoghurt, butter and cheese, but their output is insufficient to meet all the local demand.

Table poultry production was 360 tonnes in 1977 and 1,445 tonnes had to be imported. Few eggs were imported in that year as local production from 20 poultry farms exceeded 1 million dozen.

Fish. Application of the 200-mile economic zone gives French Polynesia over four million square km of sea and encourages the fishing industry. The tuna catch by Oriental boats totalled 12,000 tonnes in 1977 of which 8,000 tonnes went for processing in Pago Pago. An extra 2,869 tonnes of fish was sold in Tahiti markets.

Shrimp farms. The fisheries office CNEXO with territory finance built 5 ha of ponds for farming fresh water shrimps in 1976. Over five tonnes was sold in Tahiti in 1977. The COP centre at Vairao produces salt water shrimps.

Oysters. About 100 oyster growers in the Leeward Islands harvested about 25 tonnes of oysters in 1976 compared with 30 tonnes in 1975. Local consumption is about 70 tonnes annually.

Pearl Culture. In the Tuamotu and Gambier islands eight co-operatives and five private companies cultivate pearls, including the "black" pearl. In 1977 production included about 28,000 round pearls. Export of round and half pearls was 26,000 carats valued at CFP 18 million. Output for 1978 was expected to be 50,000 pearls i.e. about 7 kg.

MANUFACTURING AND MINING. Other industries include textile fashion goods, handicrafts, foodstuffs and a brewery.

There are no mineral ventures on land, but surveys of the sea bed seeking deposits of manganese nodules are conducted by the National Marine Research Centre (CNEXO).

Until recent times phosphate was the territory's main export with 368,780 tons shipped out in 1961 from the island of Makatea in the Tuamotus. But the workings were closed in 1966, as they were no longer economical.

TOURISM. Tourist traffic is shown in the table.

	1975	1976	1977	1978
Tourists	82,822	91,993	91,475	93,941

This included 718 ship arrivals in 1978. The number of hotel rooms at the beginning of 1979 was 2,059, including 1,126 on Tahiti, 572 on Moorea and 211 on Bora Bora.

The Tahiti Tourist Development Board is the instrumentality charged with the orderly development of tourism. It is financed by a percentage of some taxes and its functions are widespread. It is not a tourist agency. It has several sections – promotion and planning, visitor facilities, statistics and research, and administration and finance.

HOUSING. The Territory's building industry is determined considerably by the level of activity in the two main sectors of the economy – the CEP nuclear test programme and tourism.

In the construction of dwellings, figures from the Department of Urbanism reflect activity in the Windward group (Tahiti and neighbouring islands). New dwelling units built there have been as follows: 1,033 (1970), 908 (1973), 1,134 (1974), 1,005 (1975) 971 (1976) and 992 (1977).

LOCAL COMMERCE. Local commerce is conducted by French, Polynesian and Chinese businessmen. Island produce is offered for sale in markets such as those in the centre of Papeete.

OVERSEAS TRADE. The rapid growth of Polynesian trade in recent years has mainly been due to the needs of the CEP nuclear test centre, as well as the pressures of inflation.

In recent years, exports and imports have been as in the table (values expressed in CFP millions).

	1973	1975	1976	1977
Imports	16,898	22,317	25,699	29,186
Exports	394	398	470	548
Re-exports	1,103	1,571	1,441	916
Total exports	1,497	1,969	1,911	1,464

EXPORTS
(In CFP million)

	1975	1976	1977
Coconut oil	312	392	445
Coconut cake	15	6	–
Vanilla	17	13	18
Fresh fruit	7	5	8
M.O.P.	2	2	1
Trocus	–	1	7
Pearls	9	15	18
Others	36	36	51
Total local products	398	470	548
Re-exports	1,571	1,441	916
Total	**1,969**	**1,911**	**1,464**

Customers. In 1977, 66 per cent of all exports from French Polynesia went to France and the franc zone compared with 85 per cent in 1975.

IMPORTS
(In CFP million)

	1976	1977
Foodstuffs	5,419	6,628
Petrol products	2,101	2,352
Raw mats (cement, wood etc.)	2,047	2,745
Equipment	9,151	10,760
Consumer goods (textiles, cars etc.)	6,981	6,701
Total	**25,699**	**29,186**

Suppliers. Most imports were obtained from France (50 per cent in 1977), U.S.A. (19 per cent), New Zealand and West Germany (4 per cent each).

Customs tariff. Imports are subject to the various port and customs levies, giving preference to goods from France and the E.E.C. These taxes include:
Customs duty on goods coming from countries outside the E.E.C. (average rate of 10%);
Import duty imposed on all imports except for certain basic necessities and various material for the CEP (from 1 to 32%);

An additional, temporary import duty of 5 per cent on certain grounds was introduced in 1975 and maintained in 1976.

Sales tax on various products, especially petroleum products, tobacco and alcohol (various fixed charges).

Export taxes are imposed at the following rates: MOP (2.5%); copra (20%); pearls (2.5%) and movie films (CFP2 per metre of film).

FINANCE. The annual territorial budget for French Polynesia is funded from local (mainly indirect) taxes, certain public service contributions from France and loan monies. Budget expenditure is divided into four sections: the operation of the public service; subsidies and funds given e.g. to the municipalities; infrastructure, and loan repayments.

In addition to the territorial budget, overseas funds are granted as follows: to account for public service departments maintained by France; French grants for capital works (FIDES); and capital works grants from the European Development Fund (FED).

The territorial budget and overseas funds in recent years are summarised in the accompanying table, values in millions of francs CFP:

REVENUE	1976	1977
Tax receipts	7,659	8,354
French contribs.	1,159	942
Loans	1,079	1,416
Total	**9,897**	**10,712**

EXPENDITURE		
Public service	4,541	4,678
Subsidies (communes etc.)	3,223	3,896
Infrastructure	1,320	1,928
Loan repayments	530	563
Total	**9,614**	**11,065**

EXTERNAL AID		
French contribs. above	1,159	1,051
French public service	11,227	12,382
Fr. capital grants (FIDES)	156	278
FED grants	68	68
Total	**12,610**	**13,779**

Taxation. Due to the absence of personal income tax in French Polynesia, about 75% of local tax revenue is derived from sales tax and import and export dues. Other taxes include the business licence fee ("patente"), company tax, land tax and transfer fees.

Currency. The overseas note issuing authority or reserve bank (Institut d'Emission d'Outre-Mer), circulates notes in the following denominations: CFP100, 500, 1,000 and 5,000. Coins are for CFP1, 2, 5, 10, 20, 50 and 100.

Banks. Three banks in the territory operate about 20 branches. They are the Banque de l'Indochine et de Suez (Indo-Suez), the Banque de Tahiti and the Banque de Polynesie.

There are also two finance companies – Credit Caledonien et Tahitien, and Credit du Pacifique. Three additional credit institutions with offices in Papeete are the Caisse Centrale de Cooperation Economique; the Societe de Credit et de Developpement de l'Oceanie (SOCREDO); and the Societe d'Expansion et de Developpement du Pacifique.

Investment incentives. Under investment incentives offered by the territory and the French government, cash premiums may be granted for investment in agriculture, fishing, food production, transport, hotels, health clinics and crafts, provided certain minimum criteria are met concerning jobs created and level of funds invested. Full details of conditions required and application forms are contained in "Investments in French Polynesia", a booklet issued by the Tahiti Tourist Development Board in Papeete.

Development Plans. As a part of France, the territory has its economic development plotted within the national 5-year plans. The 6th Plan covered 1971-1975, so the 7th Plan covers the next 5 years, setting new targets in the fields of agriculture, fisheries, tourism and energy sources.

TRANSPORT. Public transport on Tahiti is by local bus, called "le truck", which is cheap and picturesque, leaving from the central market of Papeete. There are over 200 km of roads on Tahiti, mostly following the coastline. On Moorea there are about 100 km of roads, as well as some 60 km on Raiatea and 30 on Bora Bora.

About a dozen firms in Tahiti and several on Moorea hire out cars, motorbikes and air conditioned buses. There are also local taxis.

Vehicles. There is a high rate of motor vehicle ownership. New vehicle registrations are shown in the accompanying table.

Vehicle Registrations

	1977	1978
Private cars	1,984	2,351
Commercial, Ind., Agric	1,246	1,283

Overseas airlines. The following international airlines serve French Polynesia through the Faaa international airport on Tahiti:

UTA – French Airlines use DC10s on eastbound flights to and from Los Angeles, via Honolulu as well as westbound flights to and from Paris via Nadi (Fiji), Noumea (New Caledonia), Sydney (Australia), S.E. Asia and the Middle East.

Air New Zealand flies in from Auckland direct or via Nadi and Rarotonga, then on to Los Angeles.

LAN-Chile makes a weekly flight to and from Santiago via Easter Island, using a 707.

Domestic airlines. Three local groups operate flights to 19 islands, from Papeete. Seats are available on scheduled or charter flights. Shortest trip is 7 minutes to Moorea; the longest is 8 hours to the Marquesas. Air Polynesie, a UTA subsidiary, uses F-27 turbo-prop, Britten-Norman and Twin Otter. Air Tahiti flies Britten-Norman, Cessna 206 and Piper Aztec. It operates a continuous daily airbridge between Papeete and Moorea. Tahiti Air Tour Service combines bus and boat excursions with flights aboard 2-engine Beechcraft.

Airports. The international airport for French Polynesia is at Faaa, about 5 km from Papeete. It began operating in late 1960 and has a 3,937 metre runway. A modern passenger terminal was opened in 1963.

The 26 commercial airfields operated away from Tahiti are as follows:

Windward Islands (off Tahiti): an 880 m airstrip on Moorea, and a short airstrip on Tetiaroa which takes Twin Otters.

Leeward Islands: F-27 fly to Bora Bora (which will take a jet in an emergency) and to Raiatea (which will take up to an Electra) and Huahine. Maupiti sealed airstrip was being extended to 875 m in 1977.

Austral Islands: F-27 fly to both Tubuai and Rurutu.

Marquesas: Twin Otter fly to Hiva Oa and Ua Huka (853 m. airstrip). On Ua-Pou there is a strip for light aircraft.

On Nuku Hiva a 1,500 m airstrip was opened in December 1979. Other airfields are on Mataiva,

Tikenau, Kaukura, Apataki, Fakarava and Arutua.

Tuamotus: On Rangiroa a 2,297 m airstrip is served by F-27, while Twin Otter fly to Manihi and Takapoto. In addition, for operations at the nuclear test sites, there are large airfields at Mururoa and Fangataufa atolls, while the jet airstrip at Hao is serviced by regular commercial flights. Airfields opended in 1976 on Makemo, Anaa and Napuka.

Gambier: There is a new airfield at Totegegie on Mangareva.

Port facilities: The port of Papeete is protected by a 1,500 m seawall built on a coral reef. The port opens to the sea through a deep water passage. To handle the great increase in traffic caused by the nuclear test base, the berthing and storage facilities were considerably extended over the two years to 1966. This involved the reclamation of about 14 ha. of coral reef from the sea. This strip was linked to another reclaimed area of 14 ha. at Fare Ute providing industrial and military land.

The harbour installations have separate areas for local small craft, for warships and for cargo vessels. They can accommodate ships up to 35,000 tons and have a depth in parts of 11.5 m. alongside at low tide.

Length and depth of the wharves is as follows: Main wharf – 450 m., 11.3 m.; inter-island traders – 280 m., 6.6 m.; transit wharf – 129 m., 10 m.; oil wharf – 105 m., 11 m.; passenger liners – 233 m., 9 m; wharf for Moorea – 100 m long; fishing wharf – 90 m; deep sea fishing – 200 m; pleasure craft – 360 m; also naval wharves, and slip-yards.

Overseas shipping. Chandris Lines maintains a twice-monthly passenger service from Sydney via N.Z., Suva or Papeete.

Union Steam Ship Co. of NZ operates a monthly service from Auckland to Papeete, Apia and Nukualofa; Bank Line operates a monthly service from Europe via the Panama Canal to Papeete, other Pacific ports and return; it also operates from US Gulf ports to Australia and NZ with calls at Papeete on demand.

Farrell Lines operate LASH vessels from US west coast and Canada to Papeete etc. Nedloyd offers regular cargo services from northern Europe and UK to Papeete etc.

Pacific Islands Transport Line operates a five/six weekly container service from North American west coast ports to Papeete and beyond; Polynesia Line operates container and general cargo service from US west coast to Papeete etc.; Daiwa Line has direct regular sailings from Japan to Tarawa, Papeete etc. Kyowa Shipping Lines have monthly services from Japan through Asian ports to Guam, Pacific islands including Tahiti.

China Navigation Co. operates from Oriental ports via the Pacific Islands. From Europe, Hamburg-Sued operates monthly our of Hamburg and France; Campagnie Generale Maritime has three services monthly from north European and Mediterranean ports. CGM also has a four-weekly service from Sydney. Passenger liners of the Pacific Far East Line take cargo from the US west coast.

Inter-island shipping. Copra boats and schooners connect Tahiti with the neighbouring islands and the remote archipelagos. At least ten of these boats have either cabin or deck facilities for passengers. Several daily trips to Moorea take from 55 to 75 minutes. There are also scheduled trips to Huahine, Raiatea and Bora Bora, some operated by the Ets. Donald company, which also operates to the Marquesas on a 4-week round trip. The Papeete Port Authority in 1979 had 28 vessels registered on inter-island routes.

Yachts. Crew and passengers must be in possession of passports, and upon arrival in Papeete must contact the Customs or Gendarmerie. Crew list changes are only permitted in harbours where gendarme approval can be obtained. Prior to departure, yachts must obtain permission to leave from the port captain. Besides Papeete, formalities can be accomplished at other points of entry: Marquesas – Taiohae (Nuku Hiva), Ua Pou, Hiva Oa; Austral Islands – Tubuai, Rurutu, Raivavae; Tuamotu/Gambier – Mangareva; Leeward Islands – Raiatea, Huahine, Bora Bora; Windward Islands – Moorea.

Note: For further entry requirements see Tourism section.

It is illegal for owners of visiting yachts to charter them locally or to use them for trading or carrying passengers or freight, without the prior permission of the government.

COMMUNICATIONS. There are post offices in Tahiti (Papeete, Pirae, Faaa, Paea, Taravao), Moorea, Huahine, Raiatea-Tahaa, Bora Bora, Maupiti, Rangiroa, Marquesas and Austral islands.

Office hours: Mon. to Fri. 07.30 to 11.30 and 13.30 to 16.30 (17.00 for cables); Sat. and Sun. 08.00 to 10.00 (cables, mailing letters).

Tahiti has an automatic telephone network, with manual services inter-island. For international telephone calls, sample rates in 1975 for three minutes with proportionate increases per minute were: France, (CFP 595), W/Germany (955), USA (1,190), Mexico (1,515), Australia, Fiji, New Zealand (530) and Japan (1,485).

Telex messages may be sent from the Chamber of Commerce – Mon.-Fri. 0730 to noon and 1330 to 1700; Sat. 8 to 10 a.m.; Táharaa Hotel – Mon.-Fri. 0800 to noon and 1300 to 1630, Sat. 0800 to noon; Beachcomber Hotel – Mon. to Sun. 0800 to 2200.

For telex messages, sample rates in 1975 for three minutes with proportionate increases per minute were: France (CFP 495), Australia, New Zealand, Fiji (529), Western Europe, Japan, Canada, USA, Mexico (910).

For cables, normal rates per word were France (CFP 27), Western Europe (60), North America (38 to 52), South America (65 to 80), New Zealand, Fiji (33), Australia (49), Honolulu (71), Japan (83).

Radio and TV. Radio-Tele-Tahiti is government-controlled and operated through FR3, the overseas arm of the French broadcasting service. Television began in 1965 and includes colour.

Press. Tahiti has three daily newspapers in the French language. The widest-circulating is "La Depeche de Tahiti", followed by "Les Nouvelles".

There is also a number of weekly and monthly publications including an English language weekly "Tahiti Sun Press", which is free and caters for the tourist industry.

WATER AND ELECTRICITY. Electricity voltage in Tahiti is 220. There is 110 in certain areas. Water is abundant on the mountainous islands such as Tahiti, where it is reticulated. The drinking of imported mineral water is also popular.

PERSONALITIES AND ORGANISATIONS

Governor:
Monsieur Paul Cousseran
Chief of the Judiciary Service (Attorney-General):
M. Roland Girard
Rear Admiral, Regional Commander of the Armed Forces (Commander of the C.E.P.):
M. le Contre-Amiral Yves Leenhardt

HEADS OF GOVERNMENT DEPARTMENTS:

Cultural Information: M. J-P. Perea (adjoint)
Posts and Telecommunications: M. Francois Audibert
Economic Affairs: M. Louis Savoie
Health: Professeur Henri Revil
Mines and Public Works: M. Alban Ellacott
Civil Aviation: M. Guy Yeung
Education: M. J-M Barre
Customs: M. Bernard Paoletti
Rural Economy: M. Andre Chochin
FR3 (Radio-TV): M. Henri Sire
Lands: M. Yvonnic Allain
Port Captain: M. Louis Le Caill

DISTRICT ADMINISTRATORS:

Windward Islands: M. Jacques Dewatra
Leeward Islands: M. Yann Zebrowski
Tuamotu-Gambier: M. Philippe Berges
Marquesas: M. Andre Pouillet
Austral Islands: M. Roger Gloaguen

STATUTORY BODIES

Tourist Development Board:
M. Patrick Leboucher
ORSTOM:
M. Jean Fages (Scientific Research Centre)
CNEXO Station:
M. Jean de Chazeaux (Oceanographic Research)

POLITICAL REPRESENTATIVES

Two Deputies to France: M. Gaston Flosse; M. Jean Juventin
Senator to France: M. Daniel Millaud
Social and Economic Counsellor: M. Eric Lequerre

GOVERNMENT COUNCIL

Vice President: M. Francis Sanford
Councillors: Marc Tevane, Jean Amaru, Hans Carlson, Emile Le Caill, Tinomana Milou Ebb, Alexandre Ata

TERRITORIAL ASSEMBLY 1979

President: Frantz Vanizette
Members: Messiurs John Teariki, Roger Amiot, Joel Buillard, Leon Lichtie, Marc Davio, Taratua Teriirere, Arthur Chung, Franklin Brotherson, Philippe Brotherson, Gaston Flosse, Marcel Hart, Pierre Hunter, Michel Law, Alexandre Leontieff, Andre Lorfevre, Pupure Maiarii, Henri Marere, Jean Juventin, Paul Pietri, Andre Porlier, Guy Rauzy, Tama Teriivaetua, Charles Taufa, Jacques Tehiura, Jacques Teuira, Andre Toomaru, Mme. Emilienne Jouette and Mme. Tuianu Le Gayic

MAYORS

Papeete: M. Jean Juventin
Faaa: M. Alfred Helme
Pirae: M. Gaston Flosse
Moorea Maiao: M. John Teariki

CONSULAR CORPS

Honorary Consul for Austria: M. Marcel Krainer
Honorary Consul for Sweden: M Michel Solari
Honorary Consul for Norway: M. Victor Siu, B.P. 306
Honorary Consul for Holland: M E. J. den Breejen
Honorary Consul for Denmark: M. Robert Herve, B.P. 42
Honorary Consul for Chile: M. Jean Arbelot, B.P. 1350
Honorary Consul for Belgium: M. Rudolf Bambridge
Honorary Consul for Monaco: M. Paul Emile Victor
Honorary Consul for Germany: Mme. Claude Weinmann
Honorary Consul for Finland: Mme. Janine Laguesse

CHURCH DIGNITARIES

Polynesian Evangelical Church (Protestant): M. le Pasteur Marurai Utia.
Roman Catholic: Archbishop Mgr. Michel Coppenrath.
Church of the Latter Day Saints, (Mormon) President: Mr Golden Wayne Mack.
Seventh-day Adventist, President: M. Lazare Doom.

Sanito, President: M. Etienne Vanaa.

BUSINESS ASSOCIATIONS

Chambre de Commerce et d'Industrie de la Polynesie Francaise, Papeete; Union Patronale (Employers' Federation).

SERVICE CLUBS

Rotary Club, Lions Club in Papeete.

SCIENTIFIC INSTITUTIONS

CNEXO (National Oceanographic research centre), ORSTOM (Scientific research centre) in Tahiti, Musee de la Decouverte (Captain Cook museum) Papeete; headquarters for the territory's library services is in the "Maison de Jeunes et de la Culture", Papeete; Musee Gaugin, Musee de Tahiti et des iles.

SPORTING FACILITIES

Olympic pool, stadium, boxing, basketball, horse racing, golf course, tennis, bowling; Tahiti Aero Club at Faaa; Chasse Sous-Marine Club (underwater spear fishing) in Papeete, Yacht Club de Tahiti at Arue, Club Nautique at Moorea and Club Nautique at Raiatea, Haura Club, Surf Club, Club Alpin, Club des Archers, Club de Tir aux Pigeons, Club de Squash, Societe Canine de P.F., Judo Club, Club des Parachutistes, Club Gnunsu (Kung Fu). The "Comite Territorial des Sports (CTS)" controls the main sporting activities.

CULTURAL GROUPS

Numerous artists' studios; "Maison de Jeunes — Maison de la Culture de Polynesie Francaise" a striking architectural complex accommodating a theatre, library and conference rooms; various dance groups, etc. Youth organisations include Protestant and Roman Catholic scouts and girl guides; "Maison de Jeunes" (see above) youth complex.

TRADE DIRECTORY OF PAPEETE

Airlines

U.T.A. French Airlines, Boulevard Pomare.
Air New Zealand, rue du General de Gaulle.
Air Polynesie, C/– U.T.A., Bld. Pomare.
Air Tahiti, Faaa Airport, Tahiti.
Lan Chile Air Line, C/– U.T.A.

Doctors

Dr. Sylvain Boschi, Clinique Cardella, rue A.M. Javouhey.
Dr. Armand Cauret, Clinique Cardella.
Dr. Charles Fichter, Rue Colette.
Dr. Pierre Harmann, Clinique Cardella.
Dr. Yen Howan, Clinique Cardella.
Dr. J. C. Laspeyres, rue Dumont D'Urville.
Dr. J. Louis Meunier, Clinique Cardella.
Dr. Raymond Ott, rue Colette.
Dr. Francoise Parc, rue Colette.
Dr. Michel Tauzin, Clinique Cardella.
Dr. Alain Temple, Clinique Cardella.
Dr. Paul Zumbiehl, Clinique Cardella.

Dentists

Gil Akrich/A. Pariente, Quartier du Commerce.
F. Bonnet/B. Colney, Quartier du Commerce.
J. Dubouch, rue Leboucher.
B. Kany, rue du Marechal Foch.
Le Caill/Kirgus, Quai du Commerce.
M. F. Raoult, rue du Marechal Foch.
P. Rallier, rue Colette.

Customs agents, transport

Entreprise J. A. Cowan et Fils, Motu Uta
S.F.T./Gondrand Freres, rue des Remparts.
Tahiti Transit, Motu Uta.
C.A.P. (Cie d'Acconage Polynesien), Motu Uta.
S.A.T.-Nui, Fare Ute.

Construction

C.G.E.E./Alsthom, rue Tefaatau, Pirae.
A. Herbreteau, Vallee de Tipaerui.
SOTACO, Fariimata/Mission.
SOGECO, Passage Gardella.
Alphonse Sun, Pirae.
Sin Tung Hing, Fare Ute.
S.M.P.P., Vallee de Tipaerui.
Entreprise Jean Tellier, rue Paul Gauguin.

Underwater Work

Marine Corail ETSMP, Fare Ute.

Importers

Morgan Vernex, Fare Ute.
Shields Tahiti Imports, Passage Gardella.
Arupa Import, rue des Remparts.
Wan Distributions, Arue.
Etc. Oceania, Fare Ute.
CIDA, Fare Ute.
COMIMPEX, Faaa.
Etc. Farnham, Rue Clappier.
Poly Import, Fare Ute.

Printers

Imprimerie Multipress Les Nouvelles, Fare Ute.
Imp. Juventin & Fils, Ave. Bruat.
Imprimerie Peaucellier, Ave. du Prince Hinoi.
Imprimerie Polytram, Vallee de Tipaerui.
Imprimerie Ferrand, rue du General de Castelnau.

Stationery

Metagraph, rue des Remparts.
Luciani, Place Notre Dame.
Polygraph, Face Temple Paofai.
Hachette Pacifique, Ave., Bruat.

Photographics

Terii Photo, rue Paul Gauguin.
SOUNAM, rue Edouard Ahnne.
Studio Te Pari, rue Paul Gauguin.
Studio Vaininiore, Boulevard Pomare.
Photo Flore, rue Albert Leboucher.

Architects

Raymond Chansay, rue Paul Gauguin.
Michel Prevot, Ave. Bruat.
Christian Regaud, Ave. Bruat.

J. Hughes Ricard, rue Colette.
Rodolph Weimann, rue Tefaatau, Pirae.

Supermarkets
Bon Marche Paofai, rue du Lieut. Varney.
Cecile, Ave. du Cdt. Chesse.
FANAO, Ave. Prince Hinoi.
HAMUTA, Ave. Pomare, Pirae.
Liou Fong, Ave. Prince Hinoi.
PARE, Ave. Pomare, Pirae.

Boating equipment
Comptoir Polynesien, Fare Ute.
Marine Corail, Fare Ute.
Nauti Sport, Fare Ute.
Sin Tung Hing, Fare Ute.
Tahiti Marine, Boulevard Pomare.

HISTORY. Archaeological evidence indicates that the Marquesas Islands were inhabited at least as far back as A.D. 300 and that there were people on Maupiti, at the western end of the Society Islands, by A.D. 860. However, archaeological research in French Polynesia is still in its infancy, and no clear picture has yet emerged concerning prehistoric settlement patterns.

Magellan's visit. The first European to set eyes on any part of the territory was Magellan who discovered Pukapuka in the north-eastern corner of the Tuamotus in 1521 during the first voyage round the world. The Spanish navigator Mendana discovered the southern group of the Marquesas in 1595; and other islands of the Tuamotus were seen by Quiros in 1606. Schouten and Le Maire in 1616, Roggeveen in 1772 and Byron in 1765. However, European interest in the area was not aroused until 1767 when Captain Samuel Wallis of HMS 'Dolphin' discovered Tahiti and took possession of it in the name of King George III. In the following year, Bougainville, the French navigator, also chanced on Tahiti in the course of a world voyage. He named it La Nouvelle Cythere because it reminded him of Cythera, birthplace of the Greek goddess of love. He later published a glowing account of it.

Cook's visit. Tahiti's third European visitor was Lieut. James Cook, who reached the island in 1769 in HMS 'Endeavour'. His visit was inspired by Wallis' discovery and sponsored by Britain's Royal Society. Its purpose was to make accurate observations of the transit of the planet Venus across the sun with the object of simplifying the determination of longitude at sea. Cook anchored at Matavai Bay, eastward of Papeete, and made his observations on the spit since known as Point Venus.

He later took the opportunity to travel round Tahiti and to visit or reconnoitre the neighbouring islands of Huahine, Raiatea, Tahaa and Bora Bora. He named these latter islands the Society Islands because they lay 'contiguous to one another'. (Cook's name has since been extended in meaning to include Tahiti, Moorea and other islands to windward and leeward.)

News of Wallis' discovery had caused considerable alarm in Spain because the Spaniards feared that the British might establish a base on Tahiti from which to attack Spain's South American possessions. An expedition under Domingo Boenechea was therefore fitted out in Peru to go to Tahiti to investigate. It visited Tahiti in 1772 and returned to report that nothing was amiss.

"Noble savage". In 1773, Cook visited Tahiti and the other Society Islands in the course of his second voyage to the Pacific in the ships 'Resolution' and 'Adventure'. He was there again in 1774. One of the consequences of these visits was that an islander called Omai was carried back to England, where he became a celebrity as a 'noble savage'. After much had been written about him, Cook returned him to his home island, Huahine, on his third voyage in 1777. Meanwhile, in 1774, the Spaniards in Peru had sent a second expedition to Tahiti to land two Franciscan friars to work as missionaries. The friars, however, were poorly fitted for their task, and when a ship came with provisions for them in the following year, they begged to be allowed to return to Peru.

After Cook's last visit in 1777, 11 years passed before Tahiti again saw a European ship. This was the 'Lady Penrhyn', which put into the island for provisions after depositing convicts at Botany Bay.

Mutiny on the 'Bounty'. In the following year, 1789, HMS 'Bounty' arrived under Lieut. William Bligh to obtain a cargo of breadfruit plants for the West Indies. Bligh anchored in Matavai Bay, and waited five months until the plants he wanted were ready for transporting. Meanwhile, there was loss of discipline on board his ship and some amorous attachments were formed on shore – two factors that led to the famous mutiny in Tongan waters in April 1789. Bligh was subsequently cast adrift in an open boat with 18 companions, and the mutineers under Fletcher Christian sailed back to the eastern Pacific in the 'Bounty', intent on settling there. After obtaining livestock in Tahiti, the mutineers tried to form a settlement on Tubuai, about 500 km south of that island. When this failed, Christian returned to Tahiti to land 16 men who did not wish to remain with him. Then he sailed off to search for another island to settle on.

Meanwhile, Bligh in the open boat had reached Timor, from where he returned to England. When news of the mutiny reached the Admiralty, Captain Edward Edwards was sent to the Pacific in HMS 'Pandora' to find and arrest the mutineers. He headed straight for Tahiti, arrested the mutineers in residence there in March 1791, and continued onwards to a disastrous shipwreck on Australia's Great Barrier Reef. In the following year, Bligh returned to Tahiti in the ships 'Providence' and 'Assistant' on a second attempt to transplant breadfruit to the West Indies, which he completed without difficulty.

First missionaries. So much had now been written about the South Sea Islands, particularly Tahiti, that the newly-formed London Missionary Society decided to send missionaries there in the ship 'Duff'. The evangalists reached Tahiti on March 5, 1797, and 18 of them were landed at Matavai Bay. Although they had the protection of a prominent local chief, they made little progress. Several of them abandoned the mission in 1799 and went to Sydney; and most of the remainder followed in 1809 after a fierce civil war broke out. However, a number of the latter drifted back a year or two later, and established new headquarters at Papetoai Bay, Moorea. In 1815, their endeavours were finally rewarded when the Tahitian chief Pomare II adopted Christianity and routed a rival heathen clan in battle. From then on, Christianity spread rapidly throughout the Society Islands as well as to the Austral group and Tuamotu Archipelago.

French interest. After the death of Pomare II in 1821, the LMS missionaries became increasingly influential in political affairs. Meanwhile, more and more ships visited the islands, as the Pacific whaling industry got into full swing. In 1836, two French priests from a Catholic mission opened on Mangareva in 1834 were sent to Tahiti to try to establish a foothold. The Tahitians, under the influence of the LMS missionaries, drove them away.

In 1838, a French naval officer, Captain Du Petit-Thouars, arrived in Papeete and demanded 'reparations' for the priests' ill-treatment, otherwise he would bombard the island. His demands, which included the payment of 2,000 dollars and a gun salute to the French flag, were met. A year later another French commander, La Place, threatened to fire on Papeete unless Tahiti's sovereign, Queen Pomare IV, allowed Frenchmen and others the free exercise of the Catholic religion in Tahiti and her other possessions. The Queen, protestingly, agreed.

Meanwhile, the Queen and principal chiefs of Tahiti had written to Queen Victoria asking that their islands be placed under British protection. Their request was rejected: the British were too busy elsewhere. The French, however, were interested in the islands, as they needed a base in the eastern Pacific for their whalers, gunboats and merchant ships. In 1841, the French consul in Tahiti, J. A. Moerenhout, deceived four of the principal chiefs into signing a document asking for French protection. About the same time, the French Government decided to take possession of the Marquesas Islands, and Du Petit-Thouars, now an admiral, was sent to the Pacific again for that purpose. Several months later, in August 1842, he returned to Tahiti where Moerenhout's document provided him with a pretext for seizing that island as well. After a fortnight of threats and bluff, the Queen and principal chiefs signed a protectorate treaty, and Du Petit-Thouars appointed a provisional government to regulate the affairs of foreigners.

A few months later, George Pritchard, the British consul, who had been on leave in England, returned to Tahiti in a British warship, HMS 'Vindictive'. Both he and the warship's commander, Toup Nicholas, were astonished at the French proceedings. Nicholas, for his part, told the provisional government that he could not accept the protectorate, and he took it on himself to remain in Tahiti for several months to protect the Queen's interests. He also wrote to the British Admiralty protesting at the 'unprecedented' and 'dishonest' actions of the French.

Protectorate. Nicholas' sentiments had not reached England when the British Foreign Secretary announced that Britain had accepted the protectorate. On the other hand, news of Britain's decision had not reached Tahiti when Du Petit-Thouars arrived there a third time to inform Queen Pomare that France had ratified his treaty and that it was therefore 'definite and irrevocable'. Inevitably, there was trouble. Pritchard protested that the Queen had never willingly sought French protection and the Queen refused to strike her personal flag. The upshot was that French troops landed to occupy Papeete and replace the Queen's flag with the French Tricolor; Pritchard struck his flag on the ground that he was not accredited to a French colony; and the Queen fled to the safety of a British warship then in harbour.

Several months later, Pritchard was arrested and deported for provoking Tahitian resistance to the French; and Queen Pomare fled to Raiatea. When news of all this reached Europe, feeling ran high both in England and France and the two countries almost reached the brink of war. Hostilities were averted when the French King, Louis Phillipe, offered to pay Pritchard an indemnity from his own purse for the treatment he had suffered. In fact, the King was overthrown in 1848 before the amount of the indemnity could be agreed upon, and it was never paid.

Meanwhile, the French had consolidated their position in Tahiti; and in February 1847 Queen Pomare finally accepted the protectorate and returned to Papeete from her self-imposed exile on Raiatea. Under a treaty with Great Britain in that year, France agreed that Raiatea and the other leeward islands of the Society Group, which had fought against French rule, should remain independent. This meant that the French protectorate was confined only to those islands considered to be Queen Pomare's domains. These were: Tahiti, Moorea, Tetiaroa, the Tuamotu Archipelago, and Tubuai and Raivavae in the Austral Group.

Cotton plantation. During the next 25 years, the only outstanding event was the establishment of a huge cotton plantation at Atimaono on Tahiti's southern coast. The plantation was run by an Irish adventurer, William Stewart. It sought to cash in on the world-wide shortage of cotton caused by the American Civil War. Because of a shortage of local labour, Stewart persuaded the authorities to allow him to import 1,000 Chinese coolies from Hong Kong. These arrived in 1865-66. The plantation went bankrupt in 1873 and some of the Chinese were never repatriated. They thus became the nucleus of French Polynesia's large Chinese population of today.

Following the death of Queen Pomare in 1877, the French took steps to convert their protectorate into a colony. Survey work on the proposed Panama Canal had just begun and it seemed likely that Tahiti would become an important refuelling depot for trans-Pacific shipping. In 1880, the Queen's successor, Pomare V, was persuaded to abdicate and to declare Tahiti and its dependencies 'united to France'. The leeward islands of the Society Group remained independent until 1888 when they were annexed to the new colony, following the abrogation of the 1847 treaty with Great Britain. In the following year, France declared a protectorate over Rimatara and Rurutu (Australs) and they were annexed in 1901.

The only noteworthy event from the turn of the century to the beginning of World War I was the bombardment of Papeete in 1914 by the German raiders 'Scharnhorst' and 'Gneisenau'. Forty-nine shells were fired on the town, which was considerably damaged.

Tahiti goes "Free French". In June, 1940, after France capitulated to Germany, Tahiti's governor, J. Chastenet de Gery, remained loyal to the Vichy Government of Marshal Petain. However, in a referendum held two months later, only 18 Tahitians opted to remain under Petain while 5,564 voted for the Free French Government of General de Gaulle. This opened the way for close co-operation between French Oceania and the Allies. Hundreds of islanders enlisted to fight overseas, and Bora Bora was made available to the Americans as a military and seaplane base.

The trauma of the war years and new ideas picked up at Bora Bora and overseas promoted a more aggressive, nationalistic spirit among many islanders after the war. By mid-1947, 26 trade unions had been formed and a committee had been set up under a Huahine-born man, Pouvanaa a Oopa, to 'conduct Tahiti and its archipelagoes towards more political economic, administrative and cultural freedom'. The Pouvanaa committee showed its strength when it led a huge crowd to oppose the landing of three newly-arrived officials from France. However, Pouvanaa and his associates were arrested and held in custody for five months before being tried on charges of challenging governmental authority. They were acquitted. Pouvanaa's popularity greatly increased after this, and he went on to be elected as French Oceania's representative in the French parliament. He also formed a political party which gained a majority of seats in the local Territorial Assembly in 1953 and 1957.

Becomes French Polynesia. In August 1957, the territory was reconstituted as French Polynesia; the powers of its Territorial Assembly to make laws were considerably extended; and a council of government was created with local people holding ministerial posts. Pouvanaa became vice-president of the new council, with the governor ex-officio president. In April 1958, Pouvanaa announced a plan to secede from France and form an independent Tahitian republic. Soon afterwards, his party introduced an income tax law in the Assembly designed to raise revenue from the (mainly Chinese) traders.

After opponents of the tax law stoned the Assembly building, causing the law to be abrogated, the Territory's conservative politicians and other cabled Paris rejecting the proposed republic. At this point, General de Gaulle resumed control of the tottery French Government and offered French colonies around the world the chance to become independent by voting for it. In French Polynesia 36 per cent of the people voted for independence. A few days later, Pouvanaa, who had campaigned vigorously on the issue, was arrested and eventually charged with attempted murder, arson and the illegal possession of arms. In October 1959, he was found guilty and sentenced to eight years imprisonment and 15 years exile from Papeete. Fifteen associates received lesser sentences. No one said so publicly at the time, but it was widely felt that Pouvanaa and company had been 'framed'.

After Pouvanaa was spirited out of Tahiti to France, the Tahitian political scene became much quieter, and as the council of government was suspended, the islanders were again without executive power in their own government. Meanwhile, work had begun on an international airport at Faaa, Tahiti, with the aim of developing the tourist industry in French Polynesia. The airport was opened for passenger traffic in October 1960. Among the first to make use of it were actors and film technicians, including Marlon Brando, for a new film version of 'Mutiny on the Bounty'.

Nuclear tests. In April, 1963, the French Government announced plans to use Mururoa and several other atolls in the Tuamotu Archipelago for a nuclear testing project. Plans were also announced to modernise and enlarge the port of Papeete to cope with maritime traffic connected with the project. Soon afterwards, French technicians and troops began arriving in Tahiti in large numbers. After Pouvanaa's old party and another protested about this. President de Gaulle outlawed them both. Despite this, the territory's radical politicians continued to oppose the nuclear project at every opportunity, as they have ever since. On the other hand, employment opportunities created by the project, plus a spectacular growth in tourism, brought unprecedented prosperity to Tahiti throughout the 1960s and early 1970s, and many outer islanders flocked to the 'bright lights'.

The first of a series of nuclear devices was exploded in the atmosphere at Mururoa in September

1966. Further tests have been held in most years since then. However, in 1975, world-wide opposition to the atmospheric tests forced the French to begin testing underground at Fangataufa Atoll.

Since 1967, the territory's radical politicians, led in recent years by Francis Sanford, have kept up constant pressure on France for internal self-government (autonomie interne). The autonomists had a significant victory in November 1968 when, after considerable pressure from them, Pouvanaa a Oopa was pardoned and allowed to return to Tahiti. He became the territory's representative in the French Senate in 1971. Pouvanaa died in 1977.

In 1975-76, French Polynesia was experiencing a recession and was having difficulty in balancing its budget due to a lull in the tourist industry and a big drop in the number of jobs associated with the nuclear testing project.

Further information. Robert Langdon's 'Tahiti: Island of Love' (4th edn, Sydney, 1972) outlines the main events in Tahiti's history to the date of publication. Since that book was first published in 1959, several detailed studies and accounts of particular periods have appeared. They include: John Davies, 'The History of the Tahitian Mission, 1799-1830' (Cambridge, 1961); Douglas Oliver, 'Ancient Tahitian Society' (Honolulu, 1974); articles by Colin Newbury in the 'Journal of the Polynesian Society', 1967 and 1973; J. Chastenet de Gery, 'Les Derniers Jours de la Troisieme Republique a Tahiti, 1938-1940' in 'Bulletin de la Societe des Etudes Oceaniennes, vol. 16 No. 2, 1974; and Emile de Curton, 'Tahiti 40' (Paris, 1973).

ISLANDS IN DETAIL

THE SOCIETY ISLANDS

The Society Islands are made up of two groups — the Windward Islands (Iles du Vent, in French) and the Leeward Islands (Iles sous le Vent). The Windward Islands consist of Tahiti (the largest), Moorea, Maiao, Tetiaroa and Mehetia. The Leeward Islands comprise the twin islands of Raietea and Tahaa, Huahine, Borabora, Maupiti and the atolls of Tupai, Mopelia, Motu One (or Bellingshausen) and Manuae (Fenua Ura or Scilly).

WINDWARD ISLANDS

Tahiti. Tahiti, the largest of the Windward Islands and commercially the most important in the territory, was formed by two long-extinct volcanoes. The two sections are joined by the narrow isthmus of Taravao. Tahiti thus has the shape of the figure eight. The larger portion, Tahiti-nui, which is almost circular, is about 120 km in circumference. The smaller portion, Tahiti-iti, also called the Taiarapu Peninsula, is more flattened and is about 20 km long by 13 km broad.

The island is encircled by a reef, broken in parts where fresh water streams enter the sea. The breaks or passes allow entrance to the coastal lagoon. The most important pass, commercially, is that into Papeete harbour. The best natural harbour is Port Phaeton on the southern side of the Isthmus of Taravao. However, prevailing moisture-laden winds and high mountains nearby make this part of the island much wetter than Papeete.

The total area of Tahiti is 1,042 sq km and the population is close to 100,000. Papeete's geographical position is 17 deg. 32 min. S. lat. and 149 deg. 34 min. W. long.

The interior of Tahiti is an uninhabited and trackless upland of jagged peaks and steep gorges from which many rivers and streams run to the sea. Between the hills and shore is an alluvial belt of great fertility. The Tahitians are natural coastal dwellers, but they go to the lush river valleys to fish, to gather food and firewood and to bathe in the rivers and under the innumerable waterfalls.

Ever since the exploration of the Society Islands by the early navigators, writers and travellers have vied with each other in giving to tired humanity picturesque and delightful descriptions of the Society Islands; until Tahiti has come to be known, throughout the world, as the place above all others which most truly presents the beauty, charm and romance of the South Seas.

The main peaks on Tahiti are Mt. Orohena (2,237 m), Mt. Aorai (2,064 m), Mt. Maiao, usually called 'Le Diademe' (1,310 m), and Mt. Roniu (1,323 m) on Taiarapu Peninsula. Mt. Orohena was climbed for the first time by Europeans in September 1953.

Tahiti has one lake, Lake Vaihiria, imprisoned in an old crater about 458 m above sea level and surrounded by precipitous mountains. It can only be reached on foot by a trail that goes in from the coast in the Mataiea district. Numerous rivers and streams have to be forded.

At the time of the island's discovery by Europeans there were no villages as such, habitation being strung out right around the coastal belt. This is still more or less the case, the island being divided into districts rather than villages. The districts are very often natural divisions, being segments of the island, or valleys each separated from the next by the spiny ridges on each side.

Tahiti is divided into 19 districts — 14 for Tahiti-Nui and five for Tahiti-Iti (the peninsula).

Travelling north then east are the following districts, starting from Papeete; Pirae, Arue, Mahina, Papenoo, Tiarei, Mahaena, Hitiaa and Faaone.

Going south and east, also starting from Papeete, are the following: Faaa, Punaauia, Paea, Papara, Mataiea, Papeari.

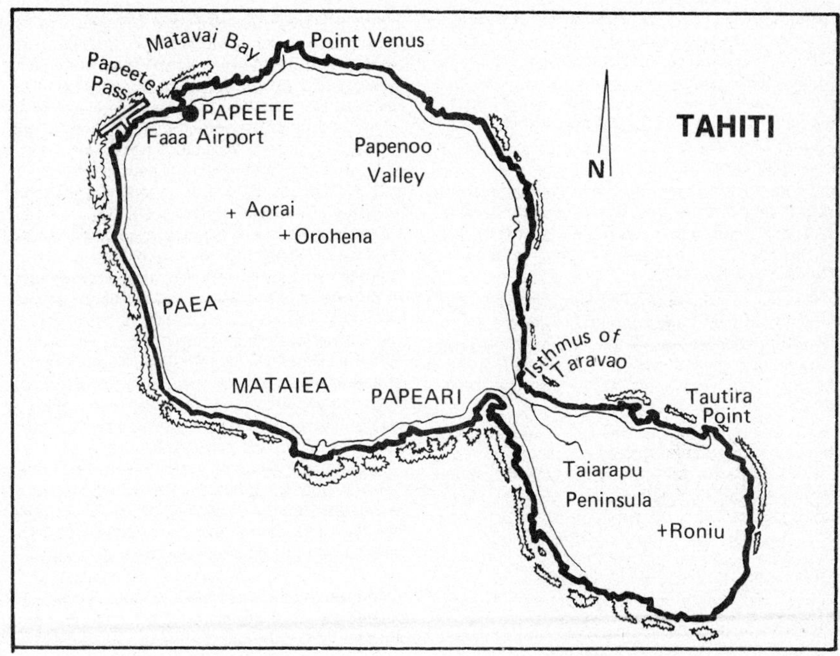

In the peninsula are the following districts: Afaahiti, Pueu, Tautira, Teahupoo, Vairao.

A good tar-sealed road of about 120 km completely encircles Tahiti-Nui and two arms of road go up each side of Taiarapu Peninsula — the north arm ending at Tautira Point and the southern arm at Teahupoo. It was at Tautira that Robert Louis Stevenson lived for some months in 1888. It is now a well-populated centre, with schools, shops, etc. The road has been reconstructed in parts and Tautira is something of a tourist attraction as it is from this point that excursions are made in big canoes to the islets near the Pari — the steep cliffs that form the coast at the tip of the Peninsula and prevent the construction of an encircling road on Tahiti-Iti.

At a point near where the Tautiri road joins the main highway at Taravao, a road leads up to a temperate plateau, site of a stock-breeding station.

The road skirts the coastline, at times on the north coast being only a narrow shelf cut in the cliff. The coastal belt widens in the south-west but nowhere is it very extensive.

The barrier reef-enclosed coastal lagoon provides a waterway for canoes and small craft and safe fishing. Although the Tahitians have forsaken much of the traditional Polynesian way of life, dugout canoes with outriggers (called pirogues locally) are in use everywhere. The beaches of Tahiti are predominantly black sand and are less attractive than some in the other islands for that reason.

Matavai Bay, at the NW corner of Tahiti, was the usual anchorage for the early European visitors to the island. But the bay is exposed to westerly winds for several months of the year, whereas Papeete harbour is safe throughout.

It was for this reason that Papeete developed as Tahiti's capital — from about 1818 when the Rev. William Pascoe Crook established the first mission station there. The town has now spread eastward to Pirae and westward to Faaa, which are communes or municipalities in their own right. The combined population of Papeete, Pirae and Faaa at the 1977 census was 51,987 — more than half of Tahiti's total of 95,604. Faaa is the site of Tahiti's international airport, while the port of Papeete is the chief shipping and distribution centre in the territory. The port can handle vessels up to 35,000 tonnes.

Between 1962 and 1964 about 14 hectares of land were reclaimed at the northern point of Papeete harbour and this, Fare Ute, is now used as an industrial and military area. In 1963 work commenced on an extension of Fare Ute, a project that has given Papeete a completely new harbour.

Between 1967 and 1970, reclaimed waterfront land was turned into pleasant gardens, and a waterside boulevard with double carriage-way was constructed. A new ships' passenger terminal was also built and nearby the architecturally striking Fare Manihini, home of the Tahiti Tourist Development Board, on the new Boulevard Pomare.

There are many new buildings facing the boulevard, others have been renovated or painted and thus within a few years the old ramshackle appearance of the waterfront has been completely changed.

The main business area is along the waterfront — just over the street from the cruise ship wharf and the yacht harbour — but commerce is now extending east and west and behind the quays as well, with, in places, some fine new buildings.

The days of division of business between large, European-owned enterprises and small Chinese-owned shops are now gone. There are still plenty of the typical "Chinatown" stores of jumbled merchandise with no attempt at display but Chinese also own modern supermarkets and department stores. Some Europeans, on the other hand, now run small attractive specialty shops that would not disgrace the Champs Elysees.

It is planned, eventually, to build a new yacht harbour and a club house, but in the meantime the yachts still tie up along the quay and look picturesque.

One of the most modern streets is Avenue Bruat, tree-lined, with good buildings and the new government offices. Since 1967 the new residence of the High Commissioner has been built in the park-like area between Rues General de Gaulle and Dumont d'Urville. Next to it is the new Territorial Assembly building which includes a separate convention facility. This building is on the site of the old queen's palace which was demolished in 1967. Another recent addition to Papeete is the Olympic swimming pool on the harbour side just west of the Tipaerui stream.

Papeete has an attractive post office and radio communications centre on the Boulevard Pomare, one block away from the new fashion hub of town, the Vaima Centre. The Bank of Indo-Suez in Rue de General de Gaulle, opposite the cathedral, is also a fine building.

Papeete and its Polynesian inhabitants have become much more sophisticated since the end of the war, and life has lost much of its former simplicity. Purists even look back to the pre-1920 days for the "real" Tahiti — the days when the Tiare Hotel was the centre of social activity.

The municipal market and bus and taxi station takes up one whole town block, one block back from the Quai de Commerce in Rue Bonnard.

The best time to visit the market is between 5.30 a.m. and 7.30 a.m., any Sunday. Young people who have obviously been dancing all night, meet, mingle and gossip with the older, harder working fraternity who have come in to sell produce or to buy the week's provisions.

Most offices and shops in Papeete open at 7.30 a.m. and close for a long lunch period at 11 a.m. or 11.30 a.m. In the afternoon they open from 1 or 1.30 p.m. till 5.30 p.m. Some shops open Saturday afternoons; some close.

Boat-day when the overseas passenger ships are in port, has long been a big occasion in Papeete. Tourists throng the streets, cafes and shops and take tours around the island, and at night most of the tourist hotels put on special floor-shows and Tahitian dances.

To the boat-days, since the opening of the big jet airport at Faaa, had been added plane days, when the air terminal is crowded with Tahitian sellers of leis and throbs with the easy laughter and tears of arrivals and departures.

Evening is a pleasant time in Papeete. Lone men in canoes go quietly out to fish in the lagoon; youngsters play and swim off the beaches; the bars and cafes along the quais are crowded with sailors and their girls drinking beer or coffee.

Moorea. Moorea (formerly called Eimeo) is situated about 17 km from Tahiti. It has an area of about 13,237 hectares. It is the remains of a huge volcano, of which about half has been eroded away. Spectacular scenery is one of its chief attractions. Two fiord-like bays on the northern side are the remains of the old crater. They are Paopao Bay (or Cook's Bay) and Opunohu (or Papetoai) Bay, which are separated by majestic Mt. Rotui, 899 m high. The islands highest peak, Mt. Tohivea, is 1,207 m. Another remarkable peak, Mt. Muaputa, 880 m, overlooking the village of Afareaitu has a hole through its summit. Population at the 1977 census was 5,826.

The island is a favourite resort, for a short stay, for discriminating travellers who want a glimpse of 'unspoiled Tahiti'. It may be reached from Tahiti by light aircraft which land at an airstrip at Tamae, at its NE corner. Launches operating between the two islands take about one and a half hours each way. A road, about 60 km long, has been built round Moorea's narrow coastal strip. Motor vehicles and bicycles are available for hire at some of the hotels. Details of the hotels are given elsewhere.

Moorea is interesting historically as the centre from which Christianity spread throughout the Society Islands and to the rest of the Pacific. It also has other associations with the early missionaries.

few of the early explorers visited Moorea because they believed it had no good anchorages. However, Cook discovered otherwise in 1777 and wrote that the 'romantic cast' of Opunohu

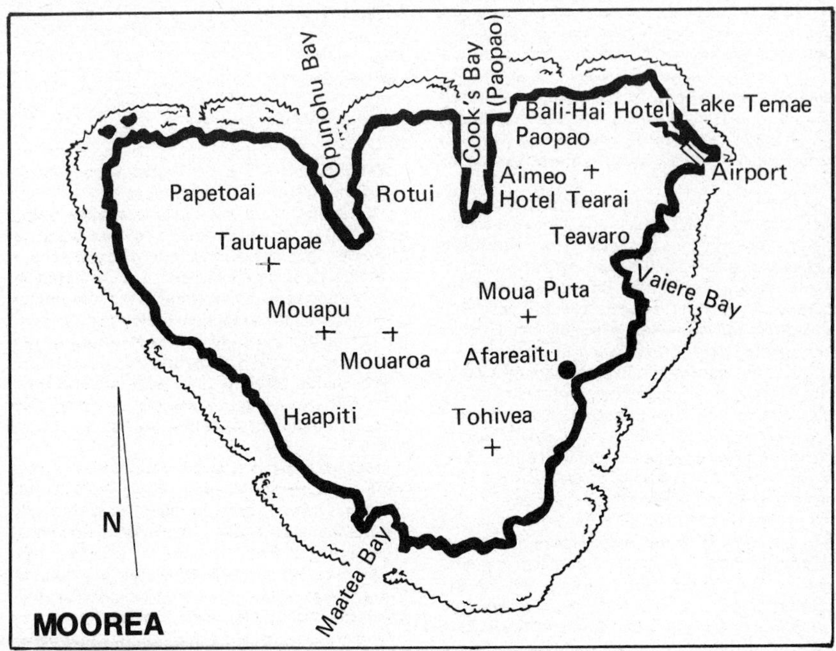

Bay rendered it 'a prospect superior' to anything in Tahiti.

The village of Papetoai at the western entrance to Opunohu Bay became the headquarters of the LMS missionaries in the Pacific in 1811 and they were there when the Tahitians adopted Christianity in 1815. In 1817, Papetoai was the missionaries' dispersal point for other stations. An octagonal church built there between 1822 and 1829 has the distinction of being the oldest European building still in use in the South Pacific.

At the head of Opunohu Bay is an extensive valley where the LMS tried unsuccessfully to establish a sugar plantation in 1818. The project failed because the islanders feared they would become slaves. A scheme to grow cotton also failed. The property subsequently had a succession of owners, including the German company, Societe Commercial de l'Oceanie, from 1904 to 1914. It is now owned by the French Administration which has an agricultural training school there.

Besides its scenic attractions, neighbouring Cook's Bay is interesting because Cook himself never anchored there. His name was apparently applied to the bay mistakenly in the early 19th century. Several villages on the island's east coast, namely Temae, Afareaitu and Maatea, figure prominently in Herman Melville's semi-factual novel 'Omoo' — as Tamai, Afrehitoo and Martair.

Temae, situated on a lake of the same name, is one of the few villages in Polynesia not situated on the sea. Afareaitu was once the site of the famous LMS school, the South Seas Academy, which was opened for the missionaries' children in the early 1820's. It was also at Afareaitu that the pages of the first book to be printed in the South Seas were pulled in 1817.

Maiao. Maiao, known also as Maiao-iti, Tapuamanu and Tubuai Manu, is a small, little-known island about 105 km due west of Tahiti and 64 km WSW of Moorea. It combines the physical characteristics of a high and low island. There is a weathered mountain ridge of volcanic origin (maximum elevation, 170 m), encircled by low coral flats which contain two shallow lakes. Around all this is a lagoon enclosed by a barrier reef. The total land area is about 9 sq. km. Some of this is barren sand and swamp — breeding grounds for numerous mosquitoes and sandflies.

Small vessels can anchor about 300 m from the southern reef. But the two passes into the lagoon are navigable only by canoes and very small boats. Communication with the island is therefore difficult.

At the 1971 census, Maiao had a population of 216. The only village is on the south-eastern side. The island is unique in the Society group in that no Europeans or Chinese are allowed to live there permanently. Copra is the chief source of income, having ousted yams and manioc for which the island was once noted. Small trading vessels call at Maiao about once every two or three weeks.

Until the French annexation of the leeward Society Islands in 1888, Maiao was under the sovereignty of Huahine. Wallis, its European discoverer, passed it after leaving Tahiti in 1767 and named it Sir Charles Saunders Island. No European is known to have landed on it until 1809 when two LMS missionaries, sailing from Moorea to Huahine, were forced to put in there.

The Maiao people adopted Christianity without any European missionary being present. During the whaling era, they traded occasionally with passing ships. A Scotsman who lived there in those days may have been chiefly responsible for the occasional occurrence of red hair and light skins among the Maiao people of today.

An Englishman, Eric Trower, tried to obtain sole possession of the island in the late 1920s and early 1930s in the belief that Maiao might be rich in phosphate. His activities led to the present-day ban on non-Polynesian residents.

Further information: Ben Finney, 'Polynesian Peasants and Proletarians', Cambridge, Mass., 1973.

Tetiaroa. Tetiaroa, 42 km north of Tahiti, is the only atoll in that vicinity. It comprises 13 islets, the largest of which is about 3.25 km long. The total land area is about 640 hectares, most of which has been planted with coconuts. Large colonies of terns, boobies and other sea birds inhabit the atoll, and there is good fishing both inside and outside the lagoon.

In the heyday of the royal Pomare family, Tetiaroa was used as a pleasure resort and as a refuge during political disturbances. The site of the royal residence on Rimatuu islet is still marked by enormous tuu trees, which were apparently planted in very ancient times. The trees cover about 1 hectare with much-appreciated shade. The remains of several ancient 'marae' may still be seen. Female members of chiefly families used to go to Tetiaroa for fattening before marriage, and to live in the shade of the tuu trees so that their skins would become fair.

Until 1790, Tetiaroa was known as Teturoa — recorded as Tethuroa by some of the early European explorers. The only such explorer to visit the atoll was Captain Bligh, who went there in quest of three deserters from the 'Bounty' in January 1789.

In 1904, the Pomare family gave Tetiaroa to Dr. W. J. Williams, a Canadian dentist, in recompense for his dental services to them. Dr. Williams, who was British consul in Tahiti from 1916 to 1935, died at Tetiaroa in 1937. His stepdaughter sold the island to the American film actor Marlon Brando in 1966.

Marlon Brando has built the Tetiaroa Village on the atoll with bungalows and A-frame huts for visitors.

Mehetia. This is an extinct volcanic cone rising steeply from the sea to a height of about 430 m. It is the easternmost of the Society Islands, being about 100 km due east of the south-eastern end of Tahiti. The island is roughly circular, about 20 km in circumference, and 240 hectares in area. Its northern side is so steep that only about a third of its total area is suitable for crops and human habitation. There is no anchorage and the only landing place is hazardous.

The name Mehetia, which has become established by usage, is actually an error. The correct name is Me'etia, as is explained below.

In pre-European and early European times, trading canoes proceeding from Tahiti to the Tuamotus (Anaa) used to make for Mehetia to await a favourable wind. The Tuamotuans knew the island as Meketu, whereas to the k-less Tahitians it was Me'etu. However, after Tu (Pomare II) was invested as paramount chief of Tahiti in 1790, the syllable 'tu' in all Tahitian words was changed to 'tia' and Me'etu thus became Me'etia. This is why, in early European times, the island was variously recorded as Maitoo, Maitu and Myetoo as well as Maeatea, Maitea, Myetea, Maitia, etc. Historians have frequently confused Mehetia with the Tuamotuan island of Makatea, which, to the Tahitians, is Ma'atea.

The European discoverer of Mehetia was Captain Wallis, who called it Osnaburg Island. It then had about 100 inhabitants. Bougainville, in 1768, called the island Le Boudoir and Pic de la Boudeuse; and it was known as Todos los Santos to the early Spanish explorers. About 1806, the Mehetia people were driven out by warriors from Anaa, and it was uninhabited for some years.

In 1835, it was used as a penal settlement. Nowadays, the island is privately owned and uninhabited, but visited periodically by copra cutters. A Frenchwoman, Mrs Janine Rouillere, gave the island some notoriety in 1967 when she spent 37 days alone there as a female Robinson Crusoe.

Raiatea and Tahaa. These are two high islands lying about 32 km westward of Huahine. They stand on the same submarine base and are encircled by a single barrier reef. Once inside the reef, it is possible to sail right round the two islands without leaving the lagoon. Tahaa, the more northerly island, is separated from its neighbour by a channel about 3 km wide. The islands have a total length of about 36 km. In general physical characteristics, in productions and in scenic attractions, they conform very closely to the description of Tahiti. Raiatea's population at the 1971 census was 6,406; that of Tahaa, 3,539.

Raiatea is the second largest of the Society Islands. It has the shape of an isosceles triangle and is about 48 km in circumference. A range of mountains runs north and south from which numerous spurs extend to the coast. The highest point is Mt. Toomaru, 1,032 m. The mountains become lower at the northern end of the island. The extensive Temehani Plateau is in this area.

Uturoa, situated on the NE tip of Raiatea opposite Tahaa, is the principal port for the two islands and administrative centre for the Leeward Islands. It has been a commune (municipality) since 1945 and has all the facilities of a town of its size and importance. An airstrip, is situated 2 km northward of Uturoa. Light planes link it with Tahiti. Uturoa's population in 1971 was 2,681.

A road suitable only for four-wheel drive vehicles provides access to the Tapioi lookout behind Utoroa from which the island's mountains and lagoon, and the surroundingg islands may be clearly seen. There is a good road, 32 km long, down Raiatea's eastern coast to Opoa, the religious centre of the Society Islands in pre-European times. Near the Bali Hai Hotel, 2 km south of Uturoa, is the village of Apooiti, the only place on Raiatea where firewalking is still practised.

The next village, about 7 km further on, is Avera, scene of a battle with the French in 1897. There are no other villages until Opoa (population: about 900) is reached. On a point a little eastward of the village is the celebrated Taputapuatea marae, once the most sacred religious site in eastern Polynesia. The marae, restored in 1968-69, is made of enormous slabs of coral.

There is no road along the rugged southern coast of Raiatea. But Tautara, the southernmost village on the western side of the island, may be reached by road from Uturoa, a distance of about 43 km. The road takes in the villages of Tevaitoa, Tehurui, Vaiaau and Fetuna. Near Tevaitoa is the Tainuu marae, also made of coral slabs.

Tahaa, roughly circular in shape, is about 11 km in diameter. It was once a symmetrical cone, but it is now deeply dissected by broad valleys radiating out from a central mass of peaks. The highest point is Mt. Ohiri, 590 m. Vaitoare on the south coast opposite Uturoa is the chief settlement. A launch links the two towns each Wednesday, market day. A road of sorts encircles the island.

Historically, Raiatea and Tahaa are of considerable interest. They have apparently been inhabited for many hundreds of years, but it is not yet clear where the original inhabitants came

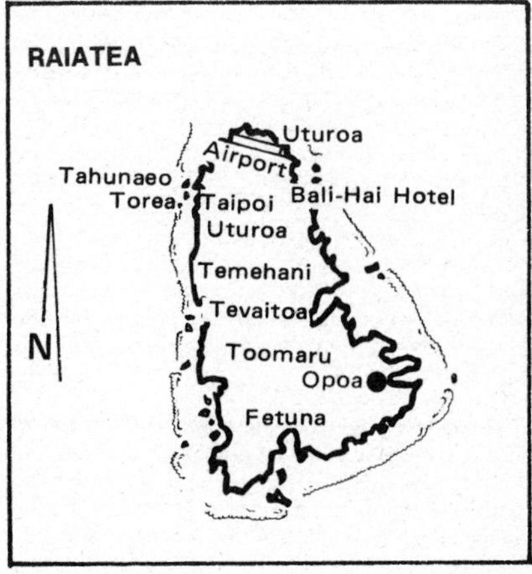

from. At some stage, however, immigrants appear to have arrived from Samoa. They called Raiatea Havaiki or Havaii after Savaii in their homeland, while Tahaa received the name Kuporu or Uporu after Savaii's sister island, Upolu. The best known figure in the prehistory of the two islands was Hiro. He is said to have been Raiatea's first king and to have been the founder of two dynasties which lasted down to European times.

Australian historian Robert Langdon has postulated in his book 'The Lost Caravel' (Sydney, 1975) that Hiro was the leader of a band of Spanish castaways from the caravel 'San Lesmes' that had been wrecked on Amanu Atoll, Tuamotu Archipelago, in 1526. Tradition says that Hiro and his associates built a great 'pahi' or canoe on Raiatea in which they eventually sailed away — apparently to Rarotonga and New Zealand. Two of Hiro's sons remained behind. One succeeded him as King of Raiatea; the other assumed sovereignty over Bora Bora.

When Captain Cook visited Raiatea in 1769, the chief of Bora Bora had conquered Raiatea and had driven many of the Raiatean chiefs to other islands. One, who was then living in Tahiti, was the sage Tupaia who accompanied Cook as far as the East Indies, where he died. Cook also called at Raiatea in 1773, 1774 and 1777.

Christianity was adopted in Raiatea and Tahaa soon after the Tahitians accepted it in 1815. The first LMS missionaries to settle on Raiatea were the Revs. John Williams and Lancelot Threlkeld who arrived in 1818. The Rev. Robert Bourne went to Tahaa in 1822. It was from Raiatea that Williams and Bourne carried the Gospel to Rarotonga in 1823, and that Williams made his famous voyage to Samoa in 1830. Raiatea thus figures prominently in Williams' book, 'A Narrative of Missionary Enterprises . . .'

After France declared a protectorate over Tahiti in 1842, there was a long struggle for the sovereignty of Raiatea. Tamatoa, a son of Queen Pomare of Tahiti, was crowned king in 1857. France annexed Raiatea and Tahaa in 1888, but a chief called Teraupoo resisted French rule from the Avera valley. Finally, in 1897, the French sent troops to the island to put down the rebellion. After a six-week struggle, Teraupoo and his associates were arrested and deported. Teraupoo was exiled to New Caledonia until 1905; his associates were banished to Eiao in the Marquesas. Raiatea's history has been uneventful since then.

Huahine. Huahine, lying about 130 km NW of Tahiti, consists of two mountainous masses that form virtually two islands. At one point, the two parts are joined by an isthmus about 100 m long which is exposed at low water. A bridge connects the two parts at this point. The northern, larger portion is called Huahine-nui (great Huahine), and the other Huahine-iti (little Huahine). The highest peaks are Mt. Turi, 680 m, on Huahine-nui, and Mt. Moufene, 457 m, on Huahine-iti.

The island generally is fertile and rich in all the usual productions of the high volcanic islands of the Society Group. Large areas have been planted with coconuts. The principal village and harbour is Fare-nui-atea, usually known as Fare, on the NW coast. There are two passes into the harbour. Yachtsmen are advised to obtain the services of a pilot before entering them. A road, mainly along the coast, links Fare with the villages of Fitii, Faaua, Haapu (west coast), Parea (south coast), Maeva (NE coast), Faie (east coast) and Maroe (north coast of Huahine-iti).

Maeva, on the corner of a lake of the same name, is built out over the water on stilts. It is reputed to be the only village of its kind in Polynesia. The lake is famed for its fish and crabs. Near the western end of the lake is an airstrip used for regular services to and from Tahiti. About 2 km from the airstrip, just northward of Fare, are the Hotel Bali Hai and the Hotel Huahine. Huahine's population in 1977 was 3,140. The Fitii district (666 people) was the most heavily populated.

A whalebone 'patu' (Maori-style hand weapon) found at Huahine in 1972 indicates that the island has been inhabited for at least 1,100 years. There are, indeed, many archaeological relics on the island, including more than two dozen maraes near Lake Maeva, some of which have been restored. The lake itself contains fish traps that date back several hundred years.

The first European to give an account of Huahine was Captain Cook who visited it briefly in 1769, 1774 and 1777. Thereafter, the island saw few Europeans until 1808-09 when a party of LMS missionaries, who had fled from Tahiti because of civil war, made it their headquarters for nearly a year. In 1818, after the adoption of Christianity in Tahiti, the LMS reopened a station on the island. One of the missionaries was the Rev. William Ellis, author of the famous 'Polynesian Researches' (London, 1829), which describes life on Huahine at length. As a result of early LMS influence, Huahineans are still largely Protestant.

Huahine resisted French rule in 1846, and did not come under French control until 1888. One of the most notable Polynesians of recent times, the political leader Pouvanaa a Oopa, was born on Huahine in 1895.

Bora Bora. Bora Bora (sometimes written Borabora) is one of the most picturesque islands of the Society Group. It lies about 16 km WNW of Tahaa and 270 km NW of Tahiti. It is primarily of volcanic origin. The main island is nearly 10 km long by 4 km wide. There are two smaller ones, Toopua and Toopua-iti (sometimes written Tupua and Tupua-iti), which are separated from it by a channel on its western side.

All three islands are encircled by a barrier reef on which are a number of low islets. The three volcanic islands are the remains of an ancient crater. The main island is dominated by several peaks, of which the highest are Mt. Otemanu, 727 m, and double-peaked Mt. Pahia, 658 m. The eastern side of this island has a barren appearance. The western side is fertile. Copra and vanilla are the chief agricultural crops, but tourism is the main industry. The population in 1971 was 2,196.

Between the main island and Toopua is a commodious, well-protected harbour called Te Ava Nui (the big harbour). It is about 2 km long by the same distance broad. A pass through the reef into the harbour is north-east of Toopua. Vaitape, the principal settlement and administrative centre, is on the main island opposite the northern part of Toopua. Two hotels, Noa Noa-Club Mediterranee and the Maitai are situated to the northward of Vaitape. Another, the Hotel Bora Bora, is on Raititi Point, the south-western horn of the island.

North of Vaitape, on the NW shore of Faanui Bay, there is a yacht basin. Just off the bay, an area has been set aside for water-skiing, etc. An airstrip on Motu Mute, on the reef north of the main island, is used by small aircraft to link Bora Bora with Tahiti and other islands in the group. However, it is also operational for aircraft up to Electra and DC7 size, and in an emergency a jet can land there and take off again unloaded.

The remains of more than 40 marae, built by Bora Bora's ancient population, are still to be seen on the island. They are of coral slabs rather than volcanic rocks as in Tahiti. Another relic of ancient times is the 'turtle stone', a petroglyph with representations of several turtles.

Bora Bora was known anciently as Vavau, which suggests that it was once colonised by people arriving from the island of that name in Tonga. Tradition also records the arrival of a 'prince' from Rotuma. Another noted personage in Bora Bora's prehistory was Hiro (see under Raiatea), who is said to have had a hiding place near the southern tip of Toopua, and to have performed various remarkable feats in that vicinity. Several landmarks still bear his name. A rock in the interior of Toopua which rings like a bell when struck is called the Bell of Hiro. Some rocks between Toopua and Toopua-iti are known as Hiro's canoe; and others that Hiro is reputed to have played with are called the 'timoraa o Hiro'. Hiro's son Ohatatama is said to have been the first king of Bora Bora.

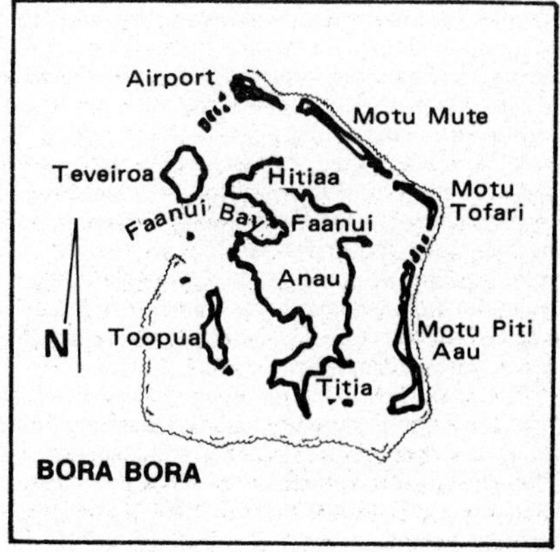

Bora Bora's European discoverer was Captain Cook. He sighted it on his first voyage in 1769, and made a brief visit to the island in 1777.

Cook and his companions rendered the island's name either as Bola Bola or Bora Bora, but it should, in fact, be Pora Pora as the Tahitian language has neither the 'b' nor 'l'.

The first European to live on the island seems to have been James Connor from the British whaler 'Matilda', which was wrecked on Mururoa Atoll in 1792. After the crew sailed back to Tahiti in the ship's boats, Connor married a Huahine woman and went to live on the southernmost point of Bora Bora, which he called Point Matilda, now corrupted to Point Matira. Numerous Society Islanders today, particularly the Bambridge family of Tahiti, are descended from Connor, the earliest known European progenitor in the group.

The Rev. J. M. Orsmond established the first LMS mission station on Bora Bora in 1820 and remained until 1824. He was succeeded by the Rev. George Platt who remained until 1830. The islanders have been largely Protestant ever since.

As with the other leeward islands of the Society Group, Bora Bora did not accept French sovereignty when Tahiti became a protectorate in 1842. It remained independent with its own sovereign until France annexed it in 1888. Terii-Maevarua II, the last queen of Bora Bora, died in Tahiti in 1932. She was a grand-daughter of Queen Pomare IV of Tahiti.

In 1928-29, one of the last and most notable silent movies was shot at Bora Bora. This was 'Tabu', the story of the tragic love affair of a Polynesian couple who had broken the ancient 'tabu' laws. The stars and cast were Bora Borans. The noted French yachtsman Alain Gerbault stayed at Bora Bora for long periods during his two voyages round the world in the 'twenties and 'thirties. In 1948, his remains were transferred to Bora Bora from Timor where he died in 1941, and a monument was later erected to him.

During World War II, Bora Bora was an American air and naval base. The first troops arrived on 23 February, 1942, and for the next four years up to 6,000 men were stationed on the island. The naval base, built at Faanui Bay, serviced ships on their way to the Solomons. The present-day airstrip on Motu Mutu was completed in April 1943 after less than four months' work. Some Quonset huts and anti-aircraft guns still remain on the island as reminders of the American presence — besides several dozen islanders with American genes. The principal French representative on the island during the war was Francis Sanford, who later became one of Tahiti's leading politicians.

The airstrip on Motu Mute was restored and put into service again in 1951. Until the international airport at Faaa, Tahiti, was opened in 1961, it was the only commercial airfield in French Polynesia. Until then, Bora Bora was also a base for flying boats. Population in 1977 was 2,572.

Maupiti. Maupiti (formerly Maurua) is situated about 40 km westward of Bora Bora. The island is of volcanic origin and has some remarkable castle-like cliffs. The maximum elevation is about 370 m. A barrier reef encircling a wide lagoon surrounds the island, which is about 10 km in circumference. The reef extends from 3 to 5 km on all sides. Two large reef islands form a semicircle on the northern part of the reef. A pass on the south side gives access to the sheltered water within the reef. The entrance is intricate and often dangerous. Visiting yachtsmen are advised to secure the services of a pilot.

Vaitea on the northern side of the main island is the only settlement. At the 1977 census, the population was 710. Copra and vanilla are the chief sources of income. Production is limited by the lack of cultivable land. Water is obtained from springs, as there are no streams. A visitor to Maupiti in the early 'fifties noted that the islanders were more industrious than elsewhere in the Society Group, and it is said that their dialect differs considerably.

Artifacts unearthed on the island in 1962 were quite different from those of the Polynesians of historical times, and were thought to have much in common with those of the ancient Moa-hunters of the South Island of New Zealand. The artifacts included pendants, adzes and fish-hooks. The remains of ancient marae and pig fences are commonplace on the island.

Roggeveen in 1722 is thought to have been the first European to sight Maupiti. But Cook in 1769 was the first to record its name. The island was little visited by Europeans until after Christianity was adopted in Tahiti in 1815. The islanders are still Protestants.

Deposits of a black basaltic rock, capable of taking a fine polish, are a feature of Maupiti. An umete, or food bowl, made from this rock was taken to Peru in 1775 by Maximo Rodriguez, the interpreter with the Spanish mission at Tautira, Tahiti. The bowl, the only one of its kind known, is now in the Archaeological Museum, Madrid.

Maupiti is well worth a visit to see a local fish drive. About 300 people and a fleet of canoes take part.

Tupai. Tupai (otherwise known as Motu-iti and Tubai) is a small atoll about 13 km north by west of Bora Bora, of which it was formerly a dependency. There is a narrow passage through the reef at the NW end of the island, and three passages on the eastern side. The atoll is entirely covered with coconut trees — about 150,000 of them. It abounds with sea-birds, and turtles breed there.

In former times, the Bora Bora people used to visit Tupai to fish. In the sixties of last century, the king of Bora Bora leased the atoll to a Nova Scotian called Stackett, who made coconut oil with an ingenious steam engine. It has been privately owned for many years. In 1971, there were 19 inhabitants. Copra production in 1970 was 85 tonnes. Legend has it that a Peruvian treasure is buried on Tupai.

Mopelia, Manuae, Motu One. These three islands, all of atoll formation, are the westernmost islands of the Society Group. They are leased until 1999 to the Compagnie francaise de Tahiti and have been planted in coconuts. Copra cutters visit them periodically; otherwise they are uninhabited.

Mopelia, also known as Maupihaa or Mopihaa, lies about 160 km WSW of Maupiti. It is roughly circular and about 8 km in diameter. Wallis in 1767 called it Lord Howe Island. Vessels up to 200 tonnes may enter its pass. The atoll is famous as the resting place of Count von Luckner's raider "Seeadler", which was wrecked there by high seas while being careened during World War 1. A few relics of the vessel still remain.

Manuae, otherwise Scilly Island or Fenua Ura, is about 64 km WNW of Mopelia. It was also a discovery of Captain Wallis. It is about 11 km long by 9 km wide. The three-masted vessel 'Julia Ann' was wrecked there in 1855. Her complement, which included 24 women and children, remained on the atoll for two months until they built a boat and sailed to Raiatea.

Motu One (meaning 'sandy island') is also known as Bellingshausen, Temiromiro. It consists of four low coral islands, covered with coconut palms and other trees, on a triangular reef. There is no entrance into the lagoon. The Russian explorer Kotzebue discovered the island in 1824.

AUSTRAL ISLANDS. The Austral Islands comprise the five inhabited islands of Rurutu, Tubuai, Rimatara, Raivavae and Rapa as well as the uninhabited Marotiri (or Bass) Rocks and Maria (or Hull) Island. The islands lie to the southward of the Society Islands. The nearest to Tahiti is Rurutu, about 500 km SSW. Geologically, the Australs appear to be a south-easterly extension of the Cook Islands, representing all that now remains above water of a vast submerged mountain chain. Following is a detailed description:

Rurutu. Rurutu, an island of volcanic origin, resembles some of the islands of the southern Cook group. Its interior is mountainous. The highest peak, Mt. Manureva (Soaring Bird), reaches an elevation of 400 m. A coastal strip of land is protected by a continuous coral reef.

Moerai, in a small bay on the western side, is the principal village. The government agent resides there. Other villages are Hauti, south of Moerai, and Avera on the eastern side. The total population in 1977 was 1,555.

If the weather prevents anchorage opposite Moerai, Avera is usually sheltered. The two villages are about 5 km apart, and it is practicable to walk from one to the other across the central uplands. The uplands are clothed in grass and fern, with thick undergrowth in the ravines.

The villages are well laid out, and the people are intelligent and industrious — and mostly prosperous. They build and operate their own schooners, and carry their produce to Papeete. The also call at Tubuai and Raivavae, and sometimes Rapa.

The chief exports are arrowroot, hats, mats, pigs, cattle, copra and vanilla. Tropical fruits are not as plentiful as on some of the other islands. The chief vegetable crop is taro, which the islanders prefer to breadfruit. In recent years, the French Administration has encouraged the islanders to grow European vegetables such as carrots and potatoes. The climate is temperate, especially in the winter months.

Rurutu was discovered by Captain Cook on his first voyage in 1769. He was under the erroneous impression that it was called Ohitiroa. Until the second decade of the 19th Century, the island had little contact with Europeans.

A significant event occurred in 1821 when a large Rurutuan canoe was drifted to Raiatea. LMS missionaries on Raiatea provided its occupants with the means of returning home, with two native teachers.

Christianity was adopted on Rurutu soon afterwards. An English visitor to Rurutu in 1828 reported that about 10 years previously a strange disorder had attacked the people, killing about 2,500 and reducing the population to about 350. Only two people were then above 25 years of age.

The French established a protectorate over Rurutu in 1889. It was annexed to France in 1900.

Tubuai. This is an oval-shaped island about 460 km due south of Tahiti. It is about 10 km long by 5 km wide. Mt Taita (400 m) is its highest point. A barrier reef encircles the island. The only reliable entrance is at Mataura on the north side near a village of the same name where the French gendarme resides. There is an airstrip for light planes linking the island with Tahiti.

The climate is healthy and temperate. Oranges of fine quality, coffee, coconuts, and arrowroot are grown. The population in 1977 was 1,549.

Tubuai is thought to have been inhabited for only a few generations when Captain Cook discovered it in 1777. In 1789, the mutineers of the 'Bounty' attempted to make a settlement there after obtaining livestock from Tahiti. The remains of a fort that they built near the NE corner of the island may still be seen. The mutineers abandoned Tubai after an affray in which 66 of the islanders were wounded. After returning to Tahiti, some of the mutineers eventually sailed to Pitcairn Island.

Ships sailing between NSW and Tahiti occasionally touched at Tubuai from 1814 onwards. Pomare II of Tahiti visited the island in 1819 when its government was formally delivered to him.

In 1822, the LMS missionaries in Tahiti sent two native teachers to the island at the Tubuaians' request. Many of the islanders were then afflicted by a mysterious disease which had been brought to the island by the survivors of a canoe that had drifted there from Anaa Atoll in the Tuamotu Archipelago. A visitor in 1828 reported that the population had dropped in 10 years from about 3,000 to 230, of whom about two-thirds were males. By 1831, the number had fallen to 182.

By virtue of the cession of the island to Pomare II in 1819, Tubuai became a French protectorate in 1842 when Tahiti and its dependencies came under French control. It was annexed to France in 1880.

Rimatara. Rimatara, the westernmost of the inhabited islands in the Austral group, lies about 120 km WSW of Rurutu. It is roughly circular in shape and about 4 km across. Its highest point is about 80 m above sea level.

Rimatara is well wooded, well watered and very fertile. It is surrounded by a coral reef which runs close to the shore in most places. Two passages exist near the NE point of the island, and there are four boat landings.

There are three villages, Amaru, Anapoto and Motu Ura, which are connected by road. The total population in 1971 was 738. Taro is grown extensively, and oranges, bananas, breadfruit and pigs are plentiful. Fish, however, are scarce.

Rimatara remained undiscovered by Europeans until 1821 when Captain Samuel Pinder Henry of Tahiti visited it. LMS missionaries from Tahiti left two native teachers there the following year; and almost the entire population of about 300 was found to be under religious instruction in 1823. There has been little of note in Rimataran history since then.

The island became a French protectorate in 1889, and was annexed to France in 1900.

Raivavae. Raivavae, described as one of the most beautiful islands in the eastern Pacific, lies about 155 km ESE of Tubuai. It is about 8 km long and 4 km wide. Its rugged moutains and hills slope gently to the coast. Mt. Hiro, the highest point, is about 440 m high.

The island is surrounded by a barrier reef on which are about two dozen wooded islets. There are two passages through the reef on the northern side. Of these, Tetobe, on the NW side, is practicable for small ships. Raiurua Bay at the western end of the island offers an excellent anchorage at all times. There is a jetty at which vessels drawing up to 3 m can lie alongside.

Raivavae has five villages, Matotea, Rairua, Mahanatoa, Anatonu and Vaiuru. Their total population in 1971 was 1,021. Coffee, arrowroot, livestock and a little copra are exported. Oranges and other citrus fruits, bananas and breadfruit grow well. But the island is not commercially important.

Some interesting old marae and hill terraces were investigated in 1956 by members of the Norwegian Archaeological Expedition to Easter Island and the East Pacific. A considerable number of large and small stone statues, reminiscent of those of Easter Island, once existed on the island, but most have now been removed. Two of the largest are now in the grounds of the Gauguin Museum in Tahiti.

The European discoverer of Raivavae was Captain Thomas Gayangos, of the Spanish frigate 'Aguila', who called there briefly in 1775 while sailing southward from Tahiti to pick up a wind for Peru. Captain W. R. Broughton of HMS 'Chatham' sighted the island again in 1791 and named it High Island, by which it was known for many years. In the early 19th century, several European vessels visited Raivavae for sandalwood. When Pomare II of Tahiti called there in the ship 'Arab' in 1819, the island's chiefs formally ceded the government to him. Raivavae thus became a French protectorate in 1842 when Tahiti and its dependencies came under French control. France annexed the island in 1880.

An old name for Raivavae is Vavitao.

Further information: Donald Stanley Marshall, 'Island of Passion (Ra'ivavae)', London 1962.

Rapa. Rapa, sometimes known as Rapa-iti (Little Rapa) to distinguish it from Rapa-nui (Big Rapa), one of the native names for Easter Island, lies some 1,130 km SE of the Society Islands. It is roughly horshoe-shaped with a deeply indented coastline. The island is the remains of an ancient volcano, whose crater, now open to the sea, is the present Ahurei Bay. Rapa is roughly 30 km in circumference and ruggedly mountainous. Its highest peak, Perahu, has an elevation of more than 600 m.

Rapa is in approximately the same latitude as Norfolk Island and, being well out of the tropics, it has no barrier or fringing reef, although patches of coral occur. Ahurei Bay, which is on the eastern side, is the best anchorage. It is about 1,000 m wide, but the entrance to it is narrow with much foul ground. Yachts wishing to enter should avail themselves of a pilot.

The village of Ahurei, on the shores of the bay, is the main settlement. Most of the houses are of coral blocks, but the villagers sometimes prefer to live in reed houses with thatched roofs, as these are believed to be cosier. A church occupies a cleared space in the centre of the village.

The flora of Rapa is stunted compared with that of the warmer, more northerly islands. Coconuts do not thrive and breadfruit and papaws are lacking. However, oranges, mangoes, bananas, taro, tomatoes and coffee do well, and some produce is exported to Tahiti. The population in 1971 was 368.

The prehistoric population of Rapa was apparently much larger than at any time since. This is evident from the well-constructed forts on all accessible mountain summits and in the principal passes from one valley to another. The forts are in the form of flat terraces, usually overlooked in each case by a tower. Similar constructions are uncommon in Polynesia. An archaelogical expedition under Thor Heyerdahl investigated the forts in 1956.

The European discoverer of Rapa was Captain George Vancouver of HMS 'Discovery' in 1791. The island then had no European visitors until 1816. Ten years later, six Tahitians were sent there as missionaries, and within two or three years the entire population of about 2,000 had adopted Christianity. Thereafter, as contact with the outside world increased, new diseases caused many deaths. By 1867, about four years after Peruvian slavers had raided the island, the population had dropped to 120.

France declared a protectorate over the island in 1867 when it seemed likely that it would become an important coaling station between Panama and New Zealand. It was annexed to France in 1900.

In the 19th Century, the Rapan men were much sought after as seamen and pearlshell divers. As a result, the island usually had a heavy surplus of women. This situation still exists to some extent. In 1967, when the total population stood at 363, there were only 18 males on the island between the ages of 15 and 19 compared with 30 females.

The French administration maintains a school and a weather station on the island, and there is a reticulated water supply to the main village.

Further information: F. Allan Hanson, 'Rapan Lifeways', Boston 1970.

Maria. Maria Island is the westernmost of the Austral group, being about 200 km NW of Rimatara. It is a typical atoll, composed of four islets on a triangular reef. It is uninhabited but is visited occasionally by people from Rimatara on fishing and copra-cutting expeditions.

The island takes its name from the whaler 'Maria' (Captain George W. Gardner) from which it was sighted in 1824. Other names that have been applied to it are Hull, Sands and Nororutu. The island was annexed by France in 1901. Lever's Pacific Plantations Ltd., are said to have been granted a lease to it in 1902, but the company made no use of the island.

Marotiri (Bass) Islands. The Bass or Marotiri Islands lie about 75 km east by south of Rapa. They are nine in number, of which eight are little more than rock pinnacles rising sheer from the sea. The ninth has two pinnacles with a saddle in between. The saddle contains some stone platforms and towers similar to those on Rapa. The highest pinnacle in the group is just over 100 m.

Why the islands are called Bass is unknown, although there may be a link with George Bass, the discoverer of Bass Strait between Victoria and Tasmania, who visited parts of eastern Polynesia in 1802 in quest of salted pork for the infant colony of NSW. He did not, however, leave any record of sighting the pinnacles.

The islands are seldom visited except by people from Rapa who go in long-boats to fish there. An expedition under Thor Heyerdahl examined the archaeological remains in 1956.

TUAMOTU ARCHIPELAGO

The Tuamotu Archipelago, excluding the high volcanic cluster of Mangareva and its neighbour, Temoe Atoll, consists of 76 islands situated between 14 and 24 deg. S. lat. and 135 and 149 deg. W. long. It is also called the Paumotu, Low or Dangerous Archipelago. With a few exceptions, all the islands are low-lying coral atolls — rings of coral enclosing salt-water lagoons. The chief exception is the upraised island of Makatea, formerly noted for its phosphate deposits, now exhausted. In the few other islands that are not atolls, the central lagoons that once existed have dried or silted up. The largest atolls are Rangiroa, Fakarava, Makemo and Hao, all about 50 km long. The smallest, such as Pinaki and Taiaro, are barely 1½ km in diameter. The total land area is about 900 sq. km.

The archipelago is remote from all continents and is little known to Europeans. Its low, sometimes badly charted reefs make it hazardous to navigators; and at most atolls only small craft can negotiate the reef passages and find anchorages in the lagoons. Moreover, as coconuts and pearlshell are the only commercial resources, the archipelago is unattractive to all but a few traders. However, since the early 1960s, several atolls, notably Mururoa, Fangataufa and Hao, have figured prominently in the French Government's nuclear testing programme in the Pacific.

The climate of the archipelago is hot, with the period from May to October slightly cooler than the rest of the year. The trade winds blow throughout, most rain falls during the warmer period. Hurricanes are sometimes experienced, usually between December and February. The most notable on record were in 1877, 1878, 1903 and 1906 when villages were destroyed; boats, vegetation, and soil washed away; and many lives lost. The supply of fresh water is a problem throughout the archipelago, as the porous ground absorbs the rain, and there are no streams or springs. Fresh coconut 'milk' is often used for drinking.

Pisonia, Cordia, Morinda citrifolia, Erythrina, and types of hibiscus are the only native trees in the Tuamotus apart from the coconut palm, which was probably introduced by man. There are also a few bushes and grasses. Lizards and rats are the only indigenous animals. Land birds are also scarce, but there is a variety of seabirds. Fish and shellfish are plentiful, and sharks and turtle common.

A census in 1971 revealed that the total population of the archipelago was 7,660. Seven atolls had a population of more than 200. They were: Hao (1,268), Rangiroa (937), Tureia (848), Anaa (375), Reao (256), Makemo (243) and Napuka (203). Nineteen atolls had more than 100 inhabitants at the 1971 census; 13 had up to 100; and the rest were uninhabited. Three religious groups are well represented in the Tuamotus — the Roman Catholics, Mormons and 'Kanitos', the local name for adherents to the Reorganised Church of Jesus Christ of Latter Day Saints.

No archaeological information is yet available on how long the archipelago is likely to have been inhabited by man. However, research carried out in 1929-30 and 1934 by expeditions of the Bishop Museum, Honolulu, revealed striking differences in Tuamotuan physical types, language and culture. Some of the stone 'marae' of the eastern part of the archipelago were found to have much in common with the stone remains of Niihau and Necker Islands in the Hawaiian group and with those of the interior of Tahiti and Moorea. This has led some specialists to think that they may be relics of an early wave of migrants who differed substantially from Polynesians of the Tonga/Samoa area who arrived later. Moreover, as the Tuamotuan dialects contain many words that are not found in Tongan and Samoan, it has been suggested that the first Tuamotuans may have been South American Indians.

Pukapuka Atoll, on the north-eastern margin of the archipelago, was the first island in the Tuamotus — and also the first in the Pacific — to be seen by Europeans. Its discoverer was Fernao Magalhaes (Ferdinand Magellan), who crossed the Pacific in 1521 in the Spanish ships 'Victoria' and 'Trinidad'. About four and a half years later, another Spanish ship, the caravel 'San Lesmes', apparently ran aground on Amanu Atoll in the central part of the archipelago. The caravel became separated from three other vessels in June 1526, shortly after entering the Pacific from the Strait of Magellan en route to the Moluccas. Evidence suggesting that an early European ship had come to grief on Amanu came to light in 1929 when four iron cannon, heavily encrusted with coral, were found near Amanu's north-eastern tip. One was recovered at that time, and two others in 1969. The latter are now at Point Venus, Tahiti. Their recovery followed the publication of an article by an Australian historian, Robert Langdon, in which he speculated that the cannon may have come from the 'San Lesmes'. Langdon later published a book, 'The Lost Caravel' (Pacific Publications, Sydney, 1975) in which he expounded the theory that the caravel's crew had survived shipwreck to intermarry with Polynesian women; that they and their descendants had spread to many Polynesian islands, including New Zealand and Easter Island; and that they had strongly influenced Polynesian culture.

In 1606, 80 years after the disappearance of the 'San Lesmes', the Spanish explorer Quiros

passed through the Tuamotu Archipelago and some of his men landed on Hao Atoll. Ten years later, the Schouten and Le Maire expedition (Dutch) landed on Pukapuka and later touched at Takaroa, Takapoto, Manihi and Rangiroa. More than a century then passed before the Roggeveen expedition (also Dutch) got among the Tuamotus. Roggeveen lost one of his three ships, the 'African Galley', on Takapoto in April 1722 and five of his men deserted there. Roggeveen later sailed past Manihi, Apataki, Arutua and Rangiroa before getting some much-needed refreshments at Makatea.

For about 10 years in the third quarter of the eighteenth century, European ships were in the Tuamotus in a constant succession. In 1765, an Englishman, Commodore John Byron, sailed along the archipelago's northern fringe in HMS 'Dolphin'. He discovered Napuka and Tepoto, and later landed on Takaroa, Takapoto's near neighbour, where he found relics of the 'African Galley'.

Two years later, the 'Dolphin', on a new voyage under Captain Samuel Wallis, discovered some of the small atolls in the SE corner of the archipelago as well as Paraoa, Manuhangi and Nengonengo. Meanwhile, HMS 'Swallow' (Captain Carteret), which had become separated from the 'Dolphin' near the Strait of Magellan, became the first European ship to encounter Mururoa, Nukutipipi and Anuanuraro.

In 1768, Bougainville, the French explorer, discovered several of the eastern and central atolls, and coined the name 'Dangerous Archipelago'. Cook passed the same way about a year later, making the important discovery of Anaa, which he called Chain Island.

In 1772, a Spanish explorer, Domingo Boenechea, discovered Tauere and Haraiki, and called at Anaa, in sailing to Tahiti in the ship 'Aguila'. A year later, Captain Cook, on his second voyage to the Pacific, discovered three more atolls in the south-central part of the archipelago. On a subsequent visit to the Tuamotus on the same voyage, some of his men landed at Takaroa, and Cook gave the name Palliser's Islands to the four large atolls of Apataki, Toau, Kaukura and Arutua. In 1774, Boenechea made a second voyage to Tahiti from Peru which resulted in the discovery of Tatakoto and Amanu.

For nearly 20 years after this, there were no more European visitors to the Tuamotus. Then several more came in a bunch. In 1791, Captain Edward Edwards in HMS 'Pandora' discovered (South) Marutea and Tureia; in 1792, Captain William Bligh discovered Tematangi in HMS 'Providence', and the British whaler 'Matilda' was wrecked on Mururoa; and five years later, Captain James Wilson of the missionary ship 'Duff', added Pukarua to the charts following his discovery of Mangareva and Temoe.

The first European attempt to exploit the resources of the group was made in 1802 after Captain John Buyers of the British ship 'Margaret' saw islanders at previously undiscovered Makemo wearing pearl shells around their necks. He fitted out his ship for a pearling voyage in Tahiti, but was wrecked on Arutua within a few days of returning to the Tuamotus.

Captain William Campbell of the Sydney brig 'Hibernia' obtained some beche-de-mer and pearl shell in some of the north-western atolls in 1809. This encouraged about a dozen other ships to make voyages to the same islands for the same purpose during the next five years. However, news of the discovery of sandalwood in the Marquesas in 1814 caused the pearling trade to be abandoned abruptly, and it was not resumed until the early 1820s.

Meanwhile, two Russian exploring expeditions were in the Tuamotus. In 1816, Otto von Kotzebue sailed along the archipelago's northern fringe in the ships 'Rurick' and 'Nadeshda' and made detailed surveys of some atolls. Four years later, after 300 years of European contact, Thaddeus von Bellingshausen in the ships 'Vostok' and 'Mirnyi' made the first thorough examination of the archipelago. He sighted and often closely examined 20 atolls, of which about half had previously been unknown to Europeans. His charts were published in 1823 by his hydrographer countryman A. J. Krusenstern in an 'Atlas de l'Ocean Pacifique' — the first volume of charts devoted solely to the Pacific. This was accompanied by a 'Receuil de Memoires Hydrographiques' which critically examined and systematised the hydrographic knowledge acquired in the Pacific over the previous three centuries.

Within a few years of Bellingshausen's Tuamotuan survey, European ships began to appear in the archipelago with much greater frequency than they had ever done before. There were reasons for this. The development of trade between New South Wales and British India on the one hand and Chile on the other opened a new shipping lane through that part of the Pacific in 1819; the pearlshell trade based on Sydney was resumed in 1822; the exploring vessels 'Coquille' (French) and 'Blossom' (British) arrived to make detailed surveys; and an occasional whaler skirted the archipelago. This increased activity resulted in the discovery of several more atolls and the proliferation of names for both new and old discoveries.

The pearlers who returned to the archipelago in 1822 confined their activities to the north-western atolls, which they described collectively as the Palliser Islands. However, in 1823, an Englishman, Captain Richard Charlton, was tempted to try his luck at Hao Atoll, and from then on the search for pearlshell was chiefly centred on the more easterly atolls. Valparaiso, Chile, became the capital for the pearling industry after adventurers from that port made their first voyage to the archipelago in 1825 and ships from Sydney ceased to participate. In the early years, the pearlers hired islanders from the Society Islands and Anaa to dive for them. But later on the more tractable Rapa Islanders were used.

A survey in 1826 by Captain F. W. Beechey, of HMS 'Blossom', which took in 28 atolls and added three new ones to the charts, completed the primary exploration of the archipelago. Thereafter, only a handful of atolls remained to be discovered. The last of them, Taiaro and Kauehi, were sighted by Captain Robert Fitzroy of HMS 'Beagle' in 1835. The first chart depicting all 76 islands of the archipelago was published in 1845 by Commodore Charles Wilkes, of the United States Exploring Expedition, who had made an extensive survey of the Tuamotus in 1839-40. The chart assigned native names to more than 60 of the islands; but for most of those to the north and east of Hao, the names were later found to be inaccurate or assigned to the wrong islands.

Christianity was first taken to the Tuamotus — to Anaa — in 1817 by an Anaan who had been to a school on Moorea run by missionaries of the London Missionary Society. By 1821, Anaa and several neighbouring atolls were all said to have renounced their old gods. However, Christianity did not prosper in those islands. By 1845, Anaa was reportedly in a state of disorder and confusion, with the people frequently quarrelling among themselves. It was at that point that an American Mormon missionary, Benjamin Grouard, settled on Anaa and won 600 islanders to his faith. More than 100 were later baptised on other atolls in the Western Tuamotus.

Meanwhile, in 1842, Tahiti, Moorea and 'dependencies' had become a French protectorate, and in 1849 a French Catholic bishop was installed in Tahiti. News of the progress of Mormonism on Anaa and elsewhere prompted the bishop to send two priests from Mangareva (where a Catholic mission had been established since 1834) to open a mission station in the Tuamotus. The priests began their work on Faaite, but moved to Anaa in 1851. Their arrival provoked violence on the part of the Anaans, which led the French authorities in Tahiti to ban the Mormons from their protectorate. However, Mormon influence persisted and spread through the work of native converts, and it retarded the work of the Catholic missionaries for almost two decades.

The French authorities in Tahiti had first made it known in 1849 that they considered the Tuamotus to be among the dependencies of Tahiti and Moorea, and therefore part of their protectorate. However, it was not until October 1853 that they formally extended their administration to the archipelago. They did this by appointing a leading Anaan chief, Paiore, as regent for Queen Pomare of Tahiti. They also sent a French naval officer, Xavier Caillet, to Anaa as special commissioner. French rule was then gradually extended to other atolls by vesting authority in the local chiefs. By the end of 1858, 46 islands in the western and central part of the archipelago were reported to have 'received and fully accepted the protectorate flag'. The inhabitants of the remaining islands were still looked on as 'cannibals and savages' and navigators were warned to treat them with the 'greatest prudence'.

An abortive attempt to bring some of the eastern atolls under French control was made in 1860. Thereafter, the 'conquest' of the remaining atolls was left to the Catholic missionaries. Pakarua was the first to feel their influence. In 1865, the entire population was persuaded to go to Mangareva to be indoctrinated in the Catholic faith. They were repatriated about a year later.

Most of the remaining heathen islands were evangelised by personal visits from two missionaries stationed on Anaa, Fathers Albert Montiton and Germain Fierens. These priests made several arduous voyages to the eastern islands beginning in 1869. By 1883, all islands in the archipelago were considered Christianised.

After the introduction of Christianity, many atolls that were previously bare or almost bare of coconuts were heavily planted, often under the guidance of missionaries, and a reasonably prosperous copra industry developed. Meanwhile, the pearlshell industry continued, with ships operating out of Tahiti. In recent years, pearl diving has been strictly controlled to prevent lagoons becoming exhausted. Experiments have also been carried out to try to develop an industry in cultured pearls.

Neither of the two world wars had much impact on life in the Tuamotus, and the islanders largely retained their own distinctive speech habits and ways of doing things. But two developments since the 1950s have tended to obliterate most of the old culture. The first was the introduction of daily radio broadcasts from Tahiti; the second, the inauguration of the French Government's nuclear testing programme. The latter, which was first announced in 1963, has brought thousands of foreigners to the atolls, caused some atolls to be evacuated, and has completely altered the islanders' economy. Hao Atoll, in the central part of the archipelago, now has an international airstrip more than 3,000 m long. Airstrips have also been built at Rangiroa and Manihi, thus placing the people of those areas within easy reach of Tahiti.

There are few books entirely devoted to the Tuamotus. Two of the most readable and informative are Clifford Gessler's 'The Dangerous Islands' (London, 1937), published in New York as 'The Road My Body Goes'; and Bengt Danielsson's 'The Happy Island' (London, 1952). Scientific studies on the archipelago by Kenneth P. Emory, J. Frank Stimson and Edwin G. Burrows have been published by the Bishop Museum, Honolulu.

Atolls with more than 100 inhabitants at the 1971 census are described below in alphabetical order. Mururoa and Fangataufa, which figure prominently in the nuclear testing project, are also included in this section, although they have no permanent inhabitants. Fangataufa is described under the heading 'Mururoa'.

AHE. Ahe is a well-wooded atoll with fine coconut plantations in the north-western corner of the archipelago. It is about 16 km long and about 13 km westward of Manihi. Its lagoon is accessible to small vessels with a draught of less than four metres. The village of Tenukupara is on the south-eastern side. In 1971, the atoll's population was 121.

Schouten and LeMaire in 1616 and Roggeveen in 1722 probably sighted Ahe. But the question of Ahe's European discovery is obscure because of its nearness and similarity to Manihi. The US Exploring Expedition surveyed Ahe in 1839 and named it Peacock Island.

AMANU. Amanu, an oval-shaped atoll, lies about 800 km due east of Tahiti. It is about 29 km long from SW to NE. A channel about 14.5 km wide separates it from the NE end of the Hao Atoll. There are two small passes through the reef on the western side. The village of Ikitake is near the more southerly (and principal) pass. The population in 1971 was 104.

Amanu was first reported by the Spanish explorer Andia y Varela in 1774. Bellingshausen, the Russian explorer, charted it in 1820 and named it Moller Island. The islanders in those days were reputed to be cannibals.

In 1929, the Administrator of the Taumotus, Captain Francois Herve, found four ancient cannon near the north-eastern tip of Amanu. They were in shallow water and heavily encrusted with coral. One cannon was recovered and later placed in the museum in Papeete, but it has since been lost. The present wherea•outs of one of the others is also unknown. However, the remaining two are now in the Museum of the Discoverers at Point Venus, Tahiti, having been recovered from Amanu by a French naval officer in 1969. The Amanu cannon figure prominently in Robert Langdon's book 'The Lost Caravel', described in the introduction to the Tuamotus.

ANAA. Anaa, once the most important and populous atoll in the archipelago, lies about 350 km east of Tahiti and 56 km SW of Faaite. It is composed of 11 islets and is elliptical in shape. It is about 30 km long by 10 wide. The lagoon is shallow and has no entrance, but approach to the atoll is easy on the lee side where the reef is steep-to. There are five villages, of which the chief one is Tuuhora. The population in 1971 was 375 compared with about 2,000 in the mid-19th century.

Anaa was formerly inhabited by hardy, warlike, heavily tattooed islanders who roamed over much of the archipelago in huge double-hulled canoes called 'pahi'. They called themselves Parata, meaning sharks, and were much feared by the other atoll dwellers. Many of the atolls had been conquered by them.

The first European to sight Anaa was Captain Cook in 1769. He called it Chain Island because of the chain-like appearance of its 11 islets. However, Europeans learned little of the Anaans until 1806 when three of their 'pahi' were blown to Tahiti in a storm. It was then noted that their language differed considerably from that of Tahiti.

Anaa was the first atoll of the Tuamotus to adopt Christianity — in about 1821. It later played an important role in supplying divers for the pearl shell trade; and it was also an important source, first of coconut oil, then of copra. Anaa was the gateway through which Mormonism was introduced to the Tuamotus in the 'forties of last century; and it was there, too, that Roman Catholic missionaries established a base in 1851 from which they evangelised the rest of the archipelago.

In 1853, when France extended its administration to the Tuamotus, Anaa was chosen as the seat of government. However, a devastating hurricane in 1878 resulted in Fakarava usurping Anaa's position. Another hurricane in 1906 further damaged the atoll, and by 1911 its population had dropped to 199. In 1936, the population stood at 371, in 1951 at 481, and in 1956 at 508. The decline since then is attributable to immigration to Tahiti, where the tourist industry and the nuclear testing project offer better employment opportunities.

Anaa's soil is much deeper than that of most atolls and it is heavily planted with coconuts. In certain conditions, its shallow lagoon reflects a clear green image in the sky which may be seen from a great distance.

APATAKI. Apataki Atoll, about 30 km long by 24 kmwide, was formerly the headquarters of the administrator of the Tuamotu Archipelago. It is one of a group of four atolls — the others being Toau, Arutua and Kaukura — which Captain Cook named the Palliser Islands in 1774. The group is roughly 300 km northwest of Tahiti.

Apataki is well-wooded except on its southern

side, where the reef is submerged and dangerous. Three passes on the western side give access to the lagoon. Tehere, the northernmost, is the only practicable one for large vessels. Pakaka, the southernmost, is used by local schooners. The village of Niutahi is on the south side of Pakaka pass. The population of the atoll in 1971 was 118.

The Dutch explorer Roggeveen sighted Apataki in 1722 and named it Avondstond (Evening). Hagermeister, a Russian navigator, examined it in 1830. It was shown on maps for many years as Hagermeister Island.

ARUTUA. Arutua, lying about 14.5 km west of the north end of Apataki, is roughly circular in shape, with a diameter of some 29 km. It is planted with coconuts on its northern side, but much of its reef on the south side is submerged. Porofai pass, near the southern end of the east side, provides an entrance to the lagoon for very small vessels. The nearby village is called Rautini. Arutua's population in 1971 was 188.

Roggeveen, the first European to sight Arutua, named it Meerder Zorg (More Trouble) because of its dangerous reefs. To Cook, it was one of the Palliser Islands — (see Apataki above). The British merchant ship 'Margaret' (Captain John Buyers) was wrecked there in 1803 on the first pearling voyage to the Tuamotus.

FAAITE. Faaite, oval in shape, lies between Fakarava to the NW and Tahanea to the east. Tahanea, the nearer of the two, is about 11 km away. Faaite is lightly wooded and about 25 km long. Vessels of up to 60 tons may enter the lagoon by a passage at the NW end. Nearby is Hitianau village, with a population, in 1971, of 141. Bellingshausen, Faaite's European discoverer, named it Admiral Chichagov Island. The first Roman Catholic mission station in the Tuamotus was established there in 1849.

FAKARAVA. Fakarava, lying about 400 km ENE of Tahiti and 72 km northward of Anaa, is the second largest atoll in the archipelago. It is rectangular in shape, about 65 km long and 24 km broad. The western side is bare reef; but the other three sides, consisting of some long stretches of land and a number of islets, are well wooded, mostly with coconut trees. Ngarue pass, on the northern side, is the best of three entrances into the lagoon. It is nearly 1 km wide, has a depth of nine metres, and is suitable for large vessels. The village of Rotoava, formerly administrative headquarters for the archipelago, stands at the NE extremity of the atoll. It consists of a long avenue bordered by bungalows. Most of the population (167 in 1971) lives there. Another village, Tetamanu, diagonally opposite across the lagoon, was in ruins at last report.

Fakarava is usually said to have been discovered in 1820 by the Russian navigator Bellingshausen, who named it Count Wittgenstein Island. However, seven years before that, eight members of the crew of the British ship 'Daphne' were marooned there after the crew mutinied and killed the captain and two other men.

The atoll became the seat of the French Resident in the Tuamotus following a hurricane and tidal wave which devastated Anaa in 1878. Robert Louis Stevenson, who visited Fakarava in 1888, published an account of his sojourn in his book 'In the South Seas'. Headquarters for the archipelago were later transferred to Apataki because conditions there were more favourable for experiments on pearl culture.

FANGATAU. Fangatau Atoll (also written Fagatau and Angatau) lies about 62 km WNW of Fakahina. It is roughly triangular in shape and only 40 km in circuit. There is no entrance into the lagoon, but landings can be made on the western point where the village of Marupua stands. Fangatau's soil is loose and sandy, and vegetation is more abundant than on most atolls. The local coconuts are renowned for their flavour. The population in 1971 was 114.

Fangatau was known to the ancient Tahitians as Marupua, but it was not sighted by Europeans until 1820. Its discoverer, Bellingshausen, named it Count Arakcheev Island, usually abbreviated to Arakcheev on 19th century charts.

In pre-European times, the Fangatauans were skilled canoe builders and navigators. The atoll still contains many well-preserved marae. A Bishop Museum expedition made a study of the Fangatauans and their culture in 1929. The islanders were then found to have 'an extraordinary Caucasian cast of features' and to have philosophical ideas embodied in their chants that seemed to be derived from some 'highly developed ancient civilisation'. Robert Langdon's book 'The Lost Caravel' devotes a long chapter to Fangatau.

HAO. Hao Atoll, a forward base for the French nuclear tests at Mururoa and Fangataufa, lies 14.5 km south of Amanu and about 800 km east of Tahiti. It is roughly wedge-shaped and a little more than 50 km long. On the north and eastern sides, there are several long stretches of land; but on the southern and SW sides, the reef is so low in places that the sea washes into the lagoon. Kaki pass, in the middle of the northern end of the atoll, is practicable for vessels with a draught of up to 5.5 m. The fairway, which is about 400 m long, has been swept in recent years to a depth of 7 m over a width of about 100 m. There is an anchorage with 22 m depth westward of Otepa, the principal settlement, which is about 8 km from Kaki pass on the NE side of the lagoon. The land at Otepa is somewhat elevated — 'almost a hill', according to one writer. Hao's population in 1971 was 1,268. This compared with only 194 in 1962 and 448 in 1967.

The facilities built for the nuclear testing project include a 3 300 m airstrip, radio masts, hangars, workshops, port facilities, offices and accommodation for up to 2,000 men. Many of the numerous coral heads in the northern part of the lagoon have been marked by buoys and beacons.

Hao was the first atoll in the Tuamotus on which Europeans are recorded to have made a landing. In February 1606, a boat party from the Quiros expedition went ashore there in search of water. Quiros named the atoll La Conversion de San Pablo (St. Paul's Conversion). More than 160 years then passed before Bougainville sighted Hao and named it La Harpe. In the following year, 1769, Cook also sighted it from HMS 'Endeavour' and named it Bow Island. Bellingshausen made the first chart of it in 1820, and about three years later European pearlers found the passage into its lagoon. From then on, Hao was an important source of pearl shell and also a base for pearlers operating at other atolls in the eastern part of the archipelago.

A visitor to Hao in 1894 reported that the islanders spoke a completely different language from that of Tahiti. If this was so, little is now known of it. In 1903, virtually the whole of Hao's population was wiped out when 261 islanders, who had gone to Hikueru Atoll for the diving season, were carried off by a tidal wave.

KATIU. Katiu, about 24 km long, lies between Raraka and Makemo in the centre of the archipelago. Coconuts cover its NE side, where the village of Toini stands. The southern side is completely bare. Two passes into the lagoon are practicable for small vessels. The population in 1971 was 113.

Bellingshausen discovered Katiu in 1820 and named it General Osten-Saken Island. It is shown on some old maps as Saken Island.

KAUEHI. Kauehi, a nearly circular atoll about 24 km across, lies about 40 km NE of Fakarava and about 18 km NW of Raraka. It is very low-lying, but is well-planted with coconut trees. A pass on the SW side gives access to the lagoon. The village of Tearavero was the home of 115 islanders in 1971.

Kauehi, discovered by FitzRoy in 1835 and recorded by him as Cavahi, was one of the last atolls in the archipelago to be seen by Europeans. Wilkes, unaware of FitzRoy's discovery, named it Vincennes Island in 1839.

KAUKURA. Kaukura Atoll (like Apataki and Arutua, above) was one of the four Palliser Islands of Captain Cook. It is an oval-shaped atoll about 40 km long. It is well planted in coconuts, particularly on its NE side. Only small vessels can enter its shallow lagoon. The population in 1971 was 131. Rahitahiti is the only permanently inhabited village.

Europeans had some unhappy experiences with the Kaukurans in the early days. In 1803, a party of Kaukurans attacked the crew of the British ship 'Margaret' after she was wrecked on neighbouring Arutua; and in 1831, the master and mate of the British ship 'Truro' were murdered after being inveigled ashore at Kaukura.

Kaukura was severely damaged in the hurricane of 1878.

MAKEMO. Makemo, a narrow atoll about 64 km long, lies in the central part of the archipelago. It is one of the most productive and populous atolls. The northern side is well wooded, but the southern side is bare and dangerous to approach. There are passes into the lagoon at the NW extremity and about 16 km from the eastern extremity on the northern side. Near the latter is Pukeva village, the only permanent settlement. Many of the inhabitants are expert divers. The population in 1971 was 243.

The sight of islanders wearing pearl shells in 1802 inspired Makemo's European discoverer, John Buyers, to fit out the first pearling expedition to the Tuamotus. He called the atoll Phillips Island. Bellingshausen, who visited it in 1820, saw only two people on shore and concluded that it was not regularly inhabited. He named it Prince Golenitschev-Kutuzov-Smolenski Island.

The atoll has since had its attraction for Europeans. In 1883, an Englishman was reported to have lived there for 40 years; and in 1926, Alain Gerbault met a Dane there who had acted as pilot for Robert Louis Stevenson in 1888.

MANIHI. Manihi, the sister atoll of Ahe, lies in the NW corner of the archipelago. It is about 22 km long by 9.5 km broad, with a pass suitable for small craft at its SW end. Except on the NW side, the whole atoll is thickly planted with coconuts. As pearl shell also abounds, Manihi is one of the most productive atolls in the archipelago. The 1971 census revealed a population of 163.

An airstrip at Manihi is used by small chartered planes.

Manihi was probably discovered by the Dutch expedition of Schouten and Le Maire in 1616 (see under Ahe). It was one of the first atolls to be exploited by Europeans for pearl shell. An early pearling vessel, the 'Venus', of Sydney, was wrecked there in 1811. The atoll was later known as Wilson Island.

MATAHIVA. Matahiva (also written Mataiva) is the westernmost of the Tuamotu atolls. It is circular and about 8 km in diameter. The only pass is a boat entrance on the NW side. Coconuts thrive there.

Before World War II, Matahiva was not permanently inhabited, but was visited periodically from neighbouring Tikehau. The census of 1971 recorded 151 permanent inhabitants.

Matahiva was known to the ancient Tahitians and was recorded by Europeans as far back as 1774. However, Bellingshausen, in 1820, was the first European to set eyes on it. It was then uninhabited.

Several 18th century visitors to the Society Islands recorded seeing Matahivans in those islands who had been driven there in storms. In 1806, warriors from Kaukura drove all the Matahivans out. Several canoe-loads of them reached Tahiti.

MURUROA. Mururoa, one of the most southerly atolls, has become world famous since the French Government announced in 1963 that it intended to use it for nuclear tests. The first of a series of nuclear devices was exploded in the atmosphere there in mid-1966; and each year, for the next eight years, there was generally a similar series. Then, following world-wide protests, the tests were conducted underground at Fangataufa, 32 km southward.

Mururoa, which is about 27 km long by 13 km wide, is the only atoll in the SE part of the Tuamotus with an entrance for ships into its lagoon. The pass is about 1 km SW of the atoll's northernmost point. It has been dredged to a depth of seven metres. A quay about 45 m long has been constructed on the NE side of the lagoon. Seaplanes can land nearby. There is also an airstrip for land planes. Buildings that have been constructed for the nuclear tests include a group of radio masts near the eastern point, a tall tower on the southern side, and concrete buildings on the northern and western points.

Carteret, the European discoverer of Mururoa, named it Bishop of Osnaburg Island in 1767. It became known as Matilda's Rocks after the British whaler 'Matilda' was wrecked there in 1792. Beechey, who visited it in 1826, found no trace of its ever having been inhabited.

Mururoa was planted with coconuts by a Papeete firm to which it was assigned in 1876, and pearl diving was also carried on there. However, no permanent settlement was ever established on the atoll.

Fangataufa is much smaller than Mururoa. It is roughly rectangular in shape, about 8 km long by 5 km wide. There is no entrance into the lagoon. The atoll served as an observation post for the atmospheric tests at Mururoa.

Beechey, Fangataufa's European discoverer, named it Cockburn Island.

French Polynesia's Territorial Assembly ceded both Mururoa and Fangataufa to France in 1964.

NAPUKA AND TEPOTO. Napuka and its sister island Tepoto are the most northerly of the Tuamotu group. They are separated from their nearest neighbours by more than 160 km, and being away from the main shipping lanes, they have had relatively little contact with outsiders. Byron, in 1765, named them the Disappointment Islands because a heavy surf and the apparent hostility of the islanders prevented him from obtaining badly-needed fresh food.

Napuka, known locally as Te Puka a Maruia, is an atoll shaped roughly like a triangle. It is about 7 km by 3.25 km wide. The eastern and western sides are well wooded, but the southern side is bare. The population in 1967 was 362 — the third highest figure in the archipelago. However, by 1971, it had dropped to only 203. Copra provides the islanders with a cash income.

Tepoto, which may be seen from Napuka, is an upraised coral island. A lagoon that once existed has dried up. The island is covered with coconut palms. The inhabitants communicate regularly with Napuka by canoe and send urgent messages by smoke signal. They numbered 69 in 1971.

Until 1870, when a Catholic missionary visited Napuka for the first time, the people of both islands had had virtually no contact with Europeans. Even in 1934, when a Bishop Museum expedition spent several weeks there, they could still claim that no Europeans other than missionaries had ever lived ashore. One of the discoveries of the Bishop Museum team was that the Napukan language contained many words that bore no apparent resemblance to those of other Polynesian languages.

Clifford Gessler's book 'The Dangerous Islands' (London 1937) gives a vivid picture of Napukan life.

NIAU. Niau, an atoll of elliptical shape, is about 10 km long and 8 km wide. Its nearest neighbours are Kaukura and Toau. Niau is unusually high — about 7.5 m above sea level — and its lagoon is completely enclosed from the sea. The lagoon, which is brackish, contains an excellent fish known as ava, which tastes like salmon.

Deposits of phosphate are found on both the beach and lagoon floor, but they are of poor quality and have not been exploited. However, the land is unusually fertile. Coconuts, oranges, limes, bananas and even breadfruit grow freely. The 1971 population was 107.

Niau was uninhabited when Bellingshausen discovered it in 1820 and named it Greig Island. However, traces of human habitation were seen on shore. The 1878 hurricane severely damaged the atoll.

An old Polynesian name for Niau has been variously recorded as Faau, Fakau, and Fakaau.

NUKUTAVAKE, PINAKI, VAIRAATEA. Nukutavake is one of a group of three small islands in the SE corner of the archipelago which are inhabited in turn by the same people. The others are Pinaki and Vairaatea. Nukutavake is unusual for the Tuamotus in that, although it is flat and of coral formation, it has no lagoon nor evidence of a former one. It is about 8 km from NE to SW, and about 1 km wide. Except near its eastern extremity, it is well wooded. Many of the inhabitants (125 in 1971) migrate to Vairaatea from May to July, and to Pinaki in August. Vairaatea is about 35 km westward; Pinaki is about 13 km SE. Vairaatea, by far the larger of the two, is about 4.5 km at its greatest width.

Wallis, in 1767, was the first European to see the three islands of the Nukutavake people; but Quiros had discovered Vairaatea in 1606. The Nukutavake people were formerly skilled boatbuilders whose keeled, single-hulled vessels were made of many small pieces of timber sewn together with sinnet. Their ancient culture was little changed until well into the 20th century.

PUKAPUKA. Pukapuka, not to be confused with an island of that name in the Cook group, is situated at the NE corner of the archipelago. It is an atoll with a total land and sea area of about 4 sq km. Its nearest neighbour is Fakahina, about 160 km SW.

The atoll, seen by Magellan in 1521, was the first island in the Pacific to be discovered by Europeans. It was then uninhabited. But when the Schouten and Le Maire expedition called there in 1616, they found three dogs on shore. For this reason, the atoll was named Honden Eylandt (Dog Island), and it was so known for almost two centuries. When the US Exploring Expedition called there in 1839, birds as tame as barnyard fowls were seen in "incredible" numbers.

A visitor in 1904 reported that wild cats were common on some islets. About 100 islanders from other atolls were diving for pearlshell. A few years later, the people of Fakahina — at the suggestion of a French Catholic priest — planted the atoll with more than 35,000 coconut trees. A combination of sun, phosphate, humus and guano brought the trees on remarkably quickly, and the Fakahinans established a permanent settlement. The population in 1971 was 111.

PUKARUA. This is an elliptical atoll in the eastern sector of the archipelago, about 48 km WNW of Reao. The lagoon has no entrance, but boats can land on the western side opposite the village of Marautaora, and also north of the NW point. The population in 1971 was 196.

Captain James Wilson of the 'Duff' who discovered Pukarua in 1797 named it Serle's Island. It was then uninhabitated, but traces of former human occupants were seen. Beechey, in 1826, found about 100 people there — 'of the same dark swarthy colour' as the islanders of Reao. In 1865, more than 50 Pukaruans were taken to Mangareva to be indoctrinated in the Catholic faith.

A Japanese anthropologist, Sachiko Hatanaka, made a socio-economic study of Pukarua in 1961-64.

RANGIROA. Rangiroa, about 70 km long and with an extreme width of 22 km, is the largest atoll in the archipelago. It lies between Tikehau and Arutua, some 320 km NE of Tahiti. The atoll is well wooded all round. Two passes on the northern side lead into the lagoon. Nearby are two villages with the same names as the passes — Tiputa and Avatoru. Their total population in 1977 was 1002. The lagoon, once of considerable importance as a pearling centre, is particularly safe. Large vessels can sail between the two villages without difficulty. Air Polynesie (formerly RAI) runs a daily air service to the atoll from Tahiti.

Rangiroa was well known to the ancient Tahitians as Rairoa. Schouten and Le Maire, who touched there in 1616, called it Vlieghen Eylandt because of its troublesome flies. Roggeveen in 1722, called it Goede Verwaghting (Good Expectations). Another early name for it was Dean's Island. Until quite recent years, it was shown as Nairsa on some maps — including one in this Year Book — because of a mistranscription of the name Rairoa in the mid-19th century.

REAO. Reao, the easternmost inhabited atoll in the archipelago, lies about 48 km ESE of Pukarua and some 215 km east of Vahitahi. It is about 16 km long and well wooded, but with no entrance into its lagoon. The population in 1971 was 256.

Reao is remote from regular shipping lanes and remained undiscovered by Europeans until 1822. The first to sight it was Captain John Bell of the British ship 'Minerva.' In the same year, the French explorer Duperrey also sighted it and named it Clermont Tonnere. This name remained in use for many years.

Some Reao islanders were taken to Mangareva in 1865 to be taught the Christian faith, and in 1874 a Catholic missionary lived on their island for several months. The Catholic church in Tahiti has taken a close interest in the atoll ever since; otherwise it has had little contact with the outside world.

After cases of leprosy were discovered on Reao in the 1920s, Father Paul Maze (later Archbishop of Tahiti) urged the French administration to establish a leprosarium on the atoll. This was done in 1936; but leprosy cases from all parts of French Polynesia are now treated at Orofara, Tahiti.

The Reao islanders are intimately connected with the inhabitants of Pukarua. They are of particular interest to Polynesian scholars. This is because they are unusually dark-skinned and non-Polynesian in appearance; because their language contains many words and forms that are foreign to other Polynesian languages; and because their island is noted for numerous ancient marae which have much in common with some of the stone structures of Easter Island. An expedition organised by a Japanese anthropologist, Miss Sachiko Hatanaka, visited Reao in 1976.

TAKAPOTO AND TAKAROA. Takapoto and Takaroa, lying about 8 km apart in the NW corner of the archipelago, were named the King George Islands by Byron in 1765. Takapoto, which lies SE of its neighbour, is about 16 km long and well-wooded. The lagoon has no entrance, but boats can land easily near the SW extremity. The population in 1971 was 108.

Takaroa, about 24 km long and 8 km wide, has an entrance for vessels of up to 3 m draught. Anchorages are good in all parts of the lagoon. The convenience of the lagoon made Takaroa popular with the early pearlers. The 1971 population was 150.

The Dutch explorers Schouten and Le Maire discovered the two atolls in 1615, but, unaware of their duality, they gave them a single name — Zondergrondt Eylandt (Bottomless Island). In 1722, the 'African Galley', one of Roggeveen's three vessels, was wrecked at Takapoto and five of his men deserted there. Iron from the wreck was taken to Tahiti before Europeans reached that island in 1767. Byron found other relics on Takaroa in 1765.

Takapoto and Takaroa came under the influence of the Latter-day Saints in 1851. The village on Takaroa, called Teavaroa, has long attracted favourable comment for its lay-out and pleasant houses. Cultured pearls of excellent quality have been produced at the two atolls in recent years in experiments financed by FIDES.

TATAKOTO. Tatakoto (also written Takoto), about 145 km NW of Pukarua, is a bean-shaped atoll about 14.5 km long. Its northern side is well-planted with coconut trees. There is no entrance into the lagoon. The 1971 population was 144.

The Spanish explorers Boenechea and Andia y Varela discovered Tatakoto independently of each other on the same day in 1774. Boenechea called it San Narcisco. Duperrey in 1822 called it Ile Daugier.

A Frenchman, Albert Javelot, became the atoll's chief about 1900 and held the post until he died in 1927. He planted the island with coconut trees and developed a copra industry.

Dr K. P. Emory of the Bishop Museum reported in 1931 that the people of Tatakoto were 'distinct in language, physical type and culture' and thAt they deserved a special study. No such study has since been made.

TIKEHAU. Tikehau Atoll, about 13 km westward of Rangiroa, is a roughly circular atoll, about 26 km across. It consists of a chain of wooded islets. There is a pass into the lagoon for small vessels at the western extremity. The population in 1971 was 164. The atoll was discovered by Kotzbue in 1815 and named Krusenstern Island.

Other Tuamotu inhabited atolls. The following inhabited atolls and islands had populations of fewer than 100 at the 1971 census: **Marokau** (93), **Hikueru** (91), **Fakahina** (85), **Makatea** (78), **Tepoto** (69), **Vahitahi** (65), **Raroia** (63), **Vairaatea** (60), **Taenga** (44), **Raraka** (34), **Nihiru** (30), **Takume** (22) and **Hereheretue** (3). Tepoto and Vairaatea have been described above under Napuka and Nukutavake respectively. Of the others, Marokau, Hikueru, Makatea and Raroia merit brief comment.

Marokau and Hikueru, two centrally situated atolls about 25 km apart, have both yielded rich harvests of pearshell over the years. Both were swamped by tidal waves during a hurricane in 1903. Nearly 100 people perished at Marokau, and 379 lost their lives at Hikueru, including 261 islanders from Hao. Jack London, in his 'South Sea Tales,' has left a vivid description of the hurricane, based on eye-witness accounts.

Makatea, an upraised coral island which rises to a height of about 100 m, was formerly noted for its phosphate. It lies about 192 km NE of Papeete. In 1962, when its phosphate was still being worked, the population stood at 2,273. Only 55 remained in 1967. The phosphate was discovered in the first decade of the 20th century, and was worked until September 1966 by the Compagnie Francaise des Phosphates de l'Oceanie. During World War II, more than 200,000 tons were exported annually.

Raroia is the atoll where the 'Kon-Tiki' raft was washed up in 1947 after its voyage from Peru. One of the raftsmen, Bengt Danielsson, later spent 18 months on the atoll and published two books about it.

UNINHABITED ATOLLS. Many of the 37 Tuamotuan atolls that were uninhabited at the 1971 census have been planted with coconuts and are visited periodically by copra cutters. The 37 atolls are: Ahunui, Akiaki, Anuanuraro, Anuanurunga, Fangataufa, Haraiki, Hiti, Manuhangi, Maria, Marutea North, Marutea South, Maturei-Vavao, Morane, Motutunga, Mururoa, Nengonengo, Nukutipipi, Paraoa, Pinaki, Ravahere, Reitoru, Rekareka, Tahanea, Taiaro, Tauere, Tekokoto, Tematangi, Tenararo, Tenarunga, Tepoto, Tikei, Toau, Tuanake, Vahanga, and Vanavana.

Ten of the uninhabited atolls, all very small, make up three groups — Duke of Gloucester (Anuanuraro, Anuanurunga and Nukutipipi); Raevski (Hiti, Tepoto and Tuanake); and Actaeon (Maturei-Vavao, Tenararo, Tenarunga and Vahanga).

MANGAREVA ISLANDS. The islands of Mangareva (formerly known as the Gambier Islands) are a volcanic cluster within a large lagoon at the

SE corner of the Tuamotu Archipelago, some 1,450 km SE of Tahiti. A small atoll, Temoe, lies about 40 km SE of the group.

The four largest islands in the group are Mangareva, Taravai, Aukena and Akamaru. There are several others that are little more than rocks. Mangareva, the largest island, is roughly like a reversed L in shape. It is about 6.5 km long with a maximum width of a little over 1.5 km. Mt Duff (440 m) is its highest point. Rikitea, the main settlement in the group and the seat of the local administrator, is at the foot of Mt Duff. The total population in 1971 was 566.

Three passes into Mangareva's lagoon give access to an inner channel to Rikitea. Vessels up to 50 m in length and with a draught of up to 4 m can use the channel.

The reef surrounding the Mangarevan islands is several kilometres distant from them, so the islands are well protected from the main force of the ocean. On the reef are many coral islets, seldom more than 100 m wide. One of these, Totegegie, is the site of an airstrip built in 1967-68 capable of handling international aircraft.

Mangareva has a mild climate except in midsummer. Its annual average rainfall is more than 2,000 mm, but as there are no permanent streams, the islanders must rely on springs or cisterns for their water supplies. A high grass called aeho, which goes brown during the dry seasons, gives the islands a barren appearance at that time. But in the folds in the hills there is rich soil where fruits and vegetables thrive.

The earliest settlers of Mangareva appear to have been castaways from the Tuamotu Archipelago, the Marquesas and Rarotonga. The buccaneer Edward Davis may have been the first European to sight Temoe and Mangareva — in 1687. But the first positive report of them was from Captain James Wilson of the 'Duff' in 1797. In 1826, Captain F. W. Beechey of HMS 'Blossom' became the first to enter the lagoon and give an account of the inhabitants. In the next few years, pearlers from Valparaiso and Tahiti found their way to Mangareva.

A band of Catholic missionaries who arrived in the group in 1834 soon converted the islanders to Christianity. The most notable of these was Father Honore Laval who remained in the group until 1871. He was responsible for constructing the huge church of St. Michel at Rikitea capable of seating 1,200 people (which is still in good repair) as well as a convent for Mangarevan girls (now a roofless ruin) and a number of other buildings. The building work was on a scale hitherto unknown in that part of the world. Because the islanders were unaccustomed to the labour demanded, Mangareva's population fell rapidly from more than 2,000 in 1840 to a few hundred. Complaints about Laval's activities finally led to his being removed to Tahiti. Ten years later, in 1881, France annexed Mangareva.

The atoll of Temoe, which has some interesting archaeological remains, has not been inhabited since the Catholic missionaries moved its people to Mangareva in 1838.

Peter Buck and K. P. Emory of the Bishop Museum carried out archaeological and ethnological work at Mangareva and Temoe in 1934. In that same year, the Tahiti schooner 'Pro Patria' was wrecked on Temoe with the American writer James Norman Hall on board. Hall wrote an account of his experiences in 'Shipwreck' (London, 1935).

MARQUESAS ISLANDS

The Marquesas Islands, consisting of 10 volcanic islands and a few small islets, are situated between 7 deg. 50 min. and 10 deg. 35 min. S. latitude and 138 deg. 25 min. and 140 deg. 50 min. W. longitude. The total land area is estimated at slightly more than 1,000 sq. km. The population of 5,419 at the 1977 census was only a fraction of what it was a century and a half ago.

The six largest islands are Hivaoa, Nukuhiva, Uapou, Uahuka, Tahuata and Fatuhiva. Hivaoa, the greatest in length, is about 40 km long and 16 km at its widest. All the volcanic islands are extremely rugged owing to erosion and faulting. There is generally a central mountain range from which ridges fall abruptly to the coast, sometimes in precipices more than 300 m high. Between the ridges are deep, fertile valleys. Flat land is scarce, as there are no coastal plains. The maximum elevation in the six largest islands ranges from 850 to 1,200 m.

The forbidding appearance of the coastline of most islands is redeemed by many deep bays. On the western sides of the islands, these are reasonably well sheltered. A feature of the group is that although it lies within the tropics, there is very little coral and no barrier reefs. Even fringing reefs are rare.

Although there is generally a high degree of humidity, the climate of the Marquesas is healthy and fairly pleasant. From April to October, the trade winds prevail from between east and SE. Less regular winds blow from between east and NNE during the rest of the year when there are some hot, calm days. There is little range in temperature throughout the year. The mean annual temperature at Atuona, Hivaoa, is about 25 deg. Celsius (78.4 deg Fahr.). The annual rainfall varies greatly and is unevenly distributed. In wet years, precipitation is well over 2,540 mm; in dry years, it is less than half that figure. The heaviest rainfall is on the windward sides of the islands, particularly the larger ones. On Hivaoa and Nukuhiva, for example, the flora becomes less luxuriant from east to west.

Lack of labour has retarded the economic development of the Marquesas. Although land is plentiful and many crops grow well, copra is the only significant export. Vanilla, cotton, sugar-cane, taro, coffee, manioc, oranges and other fruits are other agricultural items that could be developed. There is also ample potential for the raising of cattle.

Taiohae on Nukuhiva is the administrative centre and port of entry for the group. It is about 1,200 km NE of Tahiti. The population in 1971 census was 819. The administrator has the title of 'chef de circonscription' and receives instructions from the governor in Tahiti. The Marquesas Islands have two elected representatives in the Territorial Assembly of French Polynesia.

It should be noted that no standardised form has been adopted for the rendering of place names in the Marquesas. Thus, the main island of the group is variously written Nukuhiva, Nuku-Hiva, Nuku-hiva and Nuku Hiva. In this year book the first form has been used in all cases.

HISTORY OF MARQUESAS: Archaeologists believe that the Marquesas Islands were inhabited by man at least as early as 300 A.D., and probably several centuries earlier. However, they are not yet unanimous as to where the people came from. Pieces of pottery and adze types have suggested Samoa to some researchers; others think in terms of Fiji or Tonga, while Thor Heyerdahl has insisted that at least some of the ancient Marquesans originated in South America.

In modern times, the Marquesans had no migration traditions concerning their ancestors, and their culture seemed to be one of long development with no recent innovations from the outside world. Nevertheless, evidence from physical anthropology indicates that the Marquesas were settled by people of two distinct racial types and linguists have established clear-cut dialectical differences between the northern and southern islands. For example, the word for 'moon' was 'ma'ama' in the north and 'mahina' in the south — words that crop up elsewhere in Polynesia, but usually in separate regions.

The Marquesans of the past were skilled wood carvers and workers in stone. Their stone work included images in human form; house platforms; places for ceremonial use like the 'marae' of eastern and central Polynesia; and places of public assembly, with dance floors. The house platforms, called 'paepae', are still to be found everywhere, mute memorials of the great population that once existed in the group. They are built of large blocks of unhewn stone, cleverly fitted together and making almost a solid mass. The places of public assembly ranged downwards in size from about 60 m square. One behind Taiohae is 90 m by 24 m.

The European discoverer of the Marquesas Islands was the Spanish explorer Alvaro de Mendana. In July 1595, on a voyage from Peru in search of the supposed southern continent, he came upon the islands of Fatuhiva, Motane, Tahuata and Hivaoa, which he named collectively after the Marques de Mendoza, viceroy of Peru.

No Europeans visited the group again until Captain Cook called there in 1774. Cook added tiny Fatuuku, north of Hivaoa, to the charts. But he missed seeing the seven other islands of the group still further north. Six of the northern islands were discovered by Joseph Ingraham, of the American trading ship 'Hope' in April 1791. However, as no account of his discoveries was published until 1810, the credit for discovering them was long given to Etienne Marchand, of the French trading ship 'Solide', who passed through the group in June 1791. Motuiti was, in fact, Marchand's only genuine discovery.

William Pascoe Crook, of the London Missionary Society, made a lone but unsuccessful attempt to convert the people of Tahuata after being landed there from the missionary ship 'Duff' in 1797. He later went to Nukuhiva; but failing there, too, he returned to England in a whaler in 1799.

Fourteen years later, during the war between Great Britain and the United States, Nukuhiva became the first island in the Pacific to be annexed by the United States — an act that was never ratified. The act was performed by Captain David Porter of the US frigate 'Essex', who had been sent to the Pacific to harass and capture British shipping.

Having captured 12 such ships off the South American coast and in the Galapagos Islands, Porter sailed for the Marquesas. Arriving at Taiohae, Nukuhiva, in October 1813 with several of his prizes, Porter made friends with the local people through a tattooed Englishman, Wilson, who had lived there for several years. He then established a camp on shore to revictual his fleet, but was soon induced to assist the Taiohae tribes in a war against the neighbouring Haapas.

After the Haapas were subjugated, friction developed towards another tribe, the Taipi, and they, too, were conquered. Porter then decided to take possession of Nukuhiva for the United States. On November 19, 1813, he read a formal proclamation, and ran up the American flag to the accompaniment of a 17-gun salute. Then, having buried a copy of his proclamation on what he had renamed Madison's Island, Porter sailed away to continue his war against British shipping. However, Porter's career as a raider was soon terminated, for a few months later he was outmanoeuvred and outgunned by two British warships outside Valparaiso.

Meanwhile, Porter's activities at Nukuhiva had led to a new development in the history of the Marquesas. Soon after his departure, a group of British prisoners-of-war, whom he had left in the care of some of his men, escaped from the island and sailed for Sydney in one of Porter's prizes. They reached Sydney in June 1814, bringing news that the Marquesas Islands contained valuable stands of sandalwood.

Within a few weeks, the first of several Sydney ships set out for the Marquesas in quest for this commodity, and for four or five years some profitable cargoes were obtained. Then, as the sandalwood trade petered out, the islands became an increasingly popular calling place for the American whalers which began visiting the Pacific in large numbers. The whalers generally remained in port for three or four weeks, and scenes of drunkenness and licentiousness were commonplace.

The LMS missionaries in Tahiti took a few native teachers to the Marquesas between 1825 and 1831. But these men accomplished little because of internal wars. A second attempt to establish a European mission was made in 1834 when the Revs. George Stallworthy and John Rodgerson of the LMS settled on Tahuata. Stallworthy remained there until 1841, while other missionaries came and went. But again little headway was made. Meanwhile, in 1838, two French priests were landed at Tahuata from the French naval vessel 'Reine Blanche', whose commander, Captain Du Petit-Thouars, had been sent to the Pacific to investigate the potential for French commerce.

In 1842, Du Petit-Thouars paid a second visit to the Marquesas and annexed the group to provide a base for French warships, whalers and merchant vessels. After leaving a detachment of troops at Taiohae, Du Petit-Thouars sailed for Tahiti where he found a pretext to establish a French protectorate. This development made the Marquesas unnecessary to France as a base, and twice during the next 17 years the troops were withdrawn. However, France retained jurisdiction over the group and established a civil administration there in 1881, the year after Tahiti became a French colony.

In 1853, the American Board of Commissioners for Foreign Missions in Honolulu sent some Hawaiian Protestant missionaries to the group. Several such missionaries were still there well into this century. But the French Catholic mission, having the backing of the Administration, made the greatest headway. Meanwhile, the native population was dwindling alarmingly due to the introduction of foreign diseases, drunkenness, prostitution, murder, human sacrifice, cannibalism and warfare.

No reliable figures are available for the 18th century, but it has been estimated that the population stood at approximately 50,000 in Captain Porter's time. By 1842, according to an estimate by Du Petit-Thouars, it had fallen to about 20,000; and 30 years later it was only about 6,200. The figures continued to decline in the 20th century and reached a record low of 2,225 (including 131 non-natives) in 1926. Since then, there has been a slow, but steady recovery. In 1946, the figure was 2,802; by the census of 1962, it had increased to 4,838; and at the 1977 census, it stood at 5,419.

During the American Civil War, the growing of cotton was instituted in the Marquesas, and about 50 Chinese were taken to the group from Tahiti to work as labourers. The cotton venture was short-lived, but there has been a Chinese community there ever since. The most significant attempt to exploit the economic resources of the group in the past 100 years was made by a German firm, the Societe Commerciale de l'Oceanie, which flourished there from the last quarter of the 19th century until its property was sequestrated during World War I. The German company had several warehouses and maintained a fleet of schooners for the collection of produce, which was taken to Tahiti.

Since World War II, the Marquesas have been popular with yachtsmen sailing between California or Panama and Tahiti. The most important event of recent years was the inauguration of an 800 m airstrip on Uahuka. This was opened in 1970, enabling small aircraft to fly to the Marquesas for the first time. Plans to build a major airport on Nukuhiva were announced in 1976.

No history of the Marquesas has yet been published. But a good deal of historical information will be found in Louis Rollin's 'Les Iles Marquises', Paris, 1929, and Bengt Danielsson's 'Forgotten Islands of the South Seas', London, 1957.

Details of the islands from south to north are:

FATUHIVA: Fatuhiva, the southernmost island of the group, is about 13 km long by 6.5 wide. It is crescent shaped, with a rugged coastline. The highest peak is about 950 m above sea level. The island is the remains of two volcanoes, one of which grew up within the crater of the other. Eventually about half of each slipped into the sea. Most of the remains of the outer side of the larger cone face eastward, falling in serrated, razor-backed sections to the sea. The inner cone is separated from the outer by a moat-like depression. In this are two streams which drain into the sea on the island's western side — at Hanavave Bay in the north and Omoa Bay in the south.

Fatuhiva is the wettest of the Marquesas Islands. Both Hanavave and Omoa Bays have luxuriant vegetation. These two bays, and Uia on

Make sure. Make it a Yanmar.

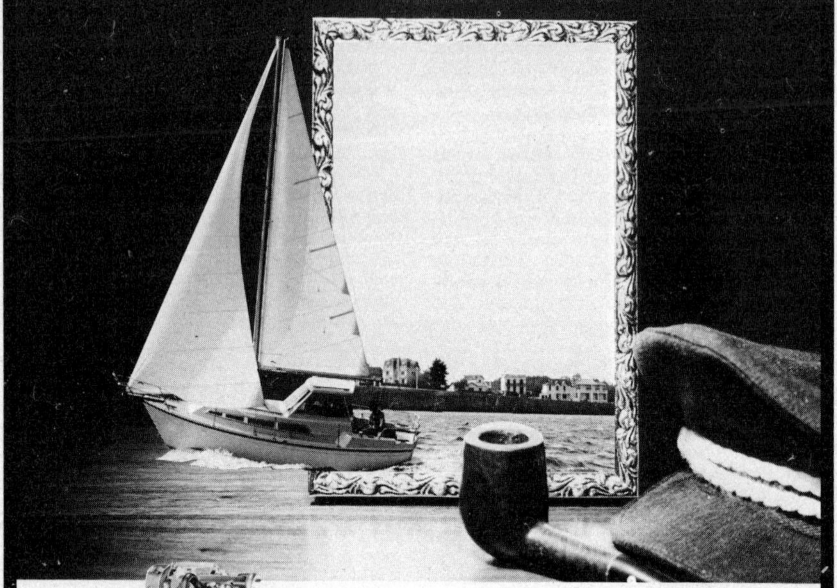

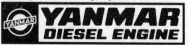

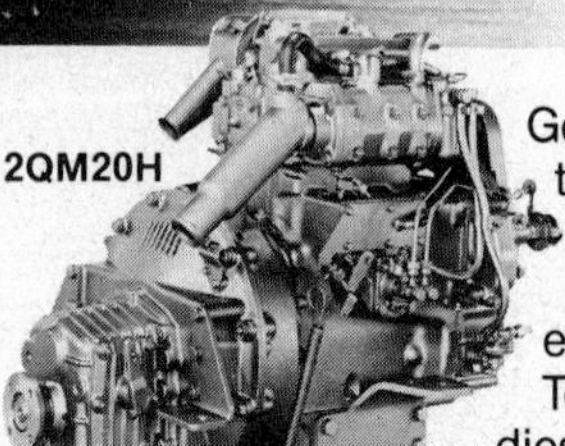

2QM20H

Getting a new boat can be an exciting adventure, but selecting its engine shouldn't be. To make sure you're buying and installing proven engine dependability, listen to the voices of experience.

Today they are saying Yanmar, because our diesels have become a boatyard byword for reliability. And for good reason. They are being installed in the thousands this year and every year in boats, like yours, by builders who know their business, and who know the numerous demands placed on seagoing machinery. Everytime, anytime sure starting. Simple, routine maintenance. Easy operation. Handy servicing. Maximum safety and economy. Quiet, vibration-free, fuss-free motoring. All popularity winning points for Yanmar diesels. In the Yanmar range there's a quality engine that's practically tailor-made to suit your boat. Make sure to inspect the full range, a good boat deserves it.

(DIN. B)

Model	YSM8	YSM12	SB8	SB12	2QM15	2QM20H	3QM30H
PS/rpm	8/3200	12/3000	8/3200	12/3000	15/3000	22/2800	33/2800

Today is the Day of the Diesel...

YANMAR DIESEL ENGINE

YANMAR DIESEL ENGINE CO.,LTD.

1-1, 2-chome, Yaesu, Chuo-ku, Tokyo 104, Japan Cable: YANMAR TOKYO Telex: 0222-2310, 0222-4733

the east coast, are the sites of the only settlements. The total population in 1977 was 386, compared with 198 in 1926 and 324 in 1956.

Mendana landed at Omoa Bay in 1595. He named the island Magdalena. The inhabitants were the last in the Marquesas to come completely under French control. They were expert wood carvers and tattoo artists. Much of their ancient culture persisted well into the present century.

The Norwegian ethnologist Thor Heyerdahl lived on Fatuhiva just before World War II. He has described his experiences in a book called 'Fatu-Hiva' (London, 1974).

MOHOTANI. Mohotani (or Motane) is a banana-shaped island, 8 km by 2.5 km, lying about 26 km south of Atuona on Hivaoa. It rises to a height of 520 m in its southern part, becoming gradually lower towards the north. The central part of the island contains a narrow plateau covered by a forest of large trees. The island is uninhabited. In 1971 it was declared a protected site by the French Administration because of the interest to science of its birds and vegetation. However, these are menaced to a considerable extent by sheep and wild cats (originally domesticated) which were introduced to the island last century.

Ancient 'paepae' and stone tools found on the island indicate that it was inhabited in pre-European times. When Mendana discovered it in 1595, he named it San Pedro. The Compagnie Coloniale de l'Oceanie held a lease to the island in 1927 and some of its workers then lived there.

TAHUATA. South of Hivaoa and separated from it by the Bordelais Channel, is the island of Tahuata, formerly known as Santa Cristina. It is about 13 km long, 7 km at its widest part, and 50 km in circumference. It is clearly the remains of a huge volcano. What is left of the crater forms the eastern part. The highest point on the crater rim is about 1,000 m above sea level. Towards the south end of the island, the slope from the rim to the coast is very steep, with high cliffs at the ends of buttress-like spurs. In the north, the slope is more gradual. Porous rocks and a low rainfall make it necessary for the inhabitants (477 in 1977) to get their water from springs near the coast.

Vaitahu Bay, formerly known as Resolution Bay, is the best of three anchorages on the west side. It was the most commonly used haven of the early European visitors to the Marquesas. Mendana, who called it Madre de Dios, anchored there in 1595. Cook, in HMS 'Resolution', was the next visitor in 1774. Both Cook and Mendana's pilot, Quiros, remarked on the light skins and splendid physiques of the islanders.

In 1797, William Pascoe Crook, the first Protestant missionary to reside in the Marquesas, was landed at Vaitahu Bay from the 'Duff'. Vaitahu was also the first station of the French Catholic priests who arrived in 1838; and it was there that the first French naval garrison was established after French annexation in 1842. The French lost 26 men in a battle with the islanders on 17 September 1842. The garrison was withdrawn in 1847. The native population in those days was about 700. It had fallen to 250 by 1926.

A few decaying buildings, a ruined church and refectory are about all that remain of the European activity at Vaitahu in the first half of last century.

HIVAOA. Hivaoa, the largest and most fertile of the Marquesas, is about 37 km long with a maximum width of 16 km. It is extremely rugged in its higher parts, with deep gullies alternating between razor-backed ridges. Mt. Temetiu, about 1,200 m, is the highest point on the island. Another lofty peak is Mt. Heani, 1,072 m, which towers behind Atuona, the chief settlement, at the mouth of the picturesque Atuona Valley on the Bay of Traitors.

Like the other islands, Hivaoa has a forbidding, iron-bound coast. Along the south and southwest coast and along much of the north coast there are many cliffs from 150 to 300 m high. The best anchorages are on the northern side, but because of lack of supplies and the difficulty of communicating with Atuona, they are little used.

Taahuku Bay, just eastward of Atuona, provides a sheltered anchorage for vessels up to almost 100 m in length and 6.75 m in draught. In fine weather, landings can be made near Point Feki. Atuona Bay affords an anchorage for local schooners. Cargo and passengers are carried ashore in whaleboats.

Atuona was formerly the seat of the French administration in the Marquesas. It is still the headquarters of the Catholic bishop and Hivaoa's largest populated centre. Among its facilities are a radio station, concrete wharf, hospital and Chinese stores. Other villages on the island are Taaoa (south coast) and Hanaiapa and Puamau (north coast). The total population in 1971 was 1,115, several hundred fewer than Nukuhiva and Uapou. However, in 1956, Hivaoa was the most populous island in the group.

Traditions recorded in the 1920s claimed that some valleys on the southern coast of Hivaoa were the first places to be settled by the Marquesans. The number and extent of archaeological remains found in all parts of the island indicate that it was once densely inhabited. The Puamau valley at the north-eastern end of the island contains the best and largest stone images.

Mendana sighted Hivaoa in 1595 and called it Dominica, which the French convert to

Dominique. When more or less continuous European contact with the Marquesas began in the nineteenth century, Hivaoa was generally avoided because of the islanders' reputation for aggression, and constant wars between two tribes called Pepane and Nuku. Roman Catholic missionaries who were stationed on the island after French annexation in 1842 made few converts for many years, and were constantly robbed and threatened with death.

Despite the internal strife, an American, John Hart, began growing cotton near Atuona in the 1870s, but the project failed within a few years. In 1880, following the murder of a European, the French sent three warships to the island in a determined effort to bring the islanders under control. Peace has reigned there since then.

Atuona became the seat of the Catholic vicariate of the Marquesas under Bishop Joseph Martin in 1893. The church was soon the island's biggest landowner. It was from the bishop that the French painter Paul Gauguin bought a plot of land when he settled on Atuona in 1901. Gauguin died at Atuona two years later and is buried there.

Atuona became the headquarters of the French administration in the Marquesas in 1904 because sandflies had made Taiohae, Nukuhiva, an unpleasant place to live. The headquarters were re-established at Taiohae in the 1940s.

FATUHUKU. Fatuhuku, called Hood Island by Cook, lies about 25 km north of Hivaoa. It is only about 2 km long and less than 1 km wide. Its highest elevation is about 360 m. The island is bounded on all sides by vertical cliffs or steep slopes and is difficult of access. It seems never to have been permanently inhabited, but fishermen from Hivaoa visited it in ancient times, as their descendants still do. Numerous frigate birds, boobies and terns nest on the island.

UAPOU. Uapou, the third largest and most heavily populated island in the group, lies 37 km south of Nukuhiva and about 88 km WNW of Hivaoa. It is about 14.5 km long from north to south and 13 km wide, with a central ridge running lengthwise which reaches a height of 1,232 m. There are a number of secondary ridges. Among the ridges rises a series of spectacular pinnacles like towers and spires. Several small bays on the western side provide anchorages for vessels of schooner size and sometimes larger vessels. The eastern side is exposed to wind and sea.

The main settlements are at Hakahau on a small bay on the NE side and at Hakamai on the west. Hakahau Bay is the only possible anchorage on the eastern side. The total population in 1971 was 1,590, compared with only 322 in 1926 and an estimated 2,000 in 1842. Just over 1,000 of the present inhabitants live in the Hakahau district.

The remains of numerous stone fortifications, temples and house platforms are still to be found on Uapou. The European discoverer of the island was Ingraham in 1791. Marchand also sighted it in 1791. Old names for it are Marchand and Adams.

Polynesian missionaries from the Society Islands were taken to Uapou in 1826. But neither they nor later missionaries accomplished much. Even as late as the turn of the present century, the islanders were still said to be practising cannibals. About a quarter of the population was wiped out by smallpox in the 1860s.

Motuoa, a small flat-topped islet off the south coast, is the home of millions of sea birds. It is about 120 m high.

UAHUKA. Uahuka, lying 37 km east of Nukuhiva, is the remains of a volcano of which the southern half has disappeared. It is about 14.5 km from east to west and about 8 km at its widest part. A semi-circular ridge, the rim of the old volcano, divides the island in two. Its greatest height is 550 m. This is much lower than in other islands. The rainfall is consequently smaller and the vegetation less luxuriant. The chief settlements, Vaipaee, Hane and Hokatu. are all on the south coast. The population in 1977 was 350, compared with 139 in 1926 and 300 in 1856. The island was probably never of great importance in ancient times.

An airstrip 490 m long was built on Uahuka in 1970. It can only be used by light planes, and is incapable of being lengthened because of mountains at both ends. Communication with Nukuhiva and other islands is by launch.

Uahuka has also been known as Ile Solide and Washington Island. These names date back to Marchand and Ingraham who both discovered the island in 1791.

NUKUHIVA. Nukuhiva, lying about 112 km north of Hivaoa and 37 km west of Uahuka, is the principal island in the northern Marquesas. It is about 32 km long by 19 km wide. Like Fatuhiva it consists of an outer cone within which a later volcano built up. The southern side of both cones have now disappeared. The highest peaks are about 1,200 m above sea level.

On the western side of the island is a plateau some 830 to 860 m high. The two principal valleys are Hakaui, narrow and canyon-like, and Taipi, which is much broader. There is a good anchorage in Controleur (Comptroller) Bay at the mouth of the Taipi valley. Another, smaller valley opens into Taiohae Bay, a port of call for overseas ships. On this bay is the village of Taiohae, the principal settlement on the island and seat of the administration for the Marquesas. Other settlements are at Hakaui, Taipivai and Hooumi on the south coast and at Hatiheu and Hakapa in the north.

The island's total population in 1977 was 1,553 of whom 819 were in the Taiohae district. Copra is the chief export. Taiohae is the port of entry for the Marquesas and foreign visitors must obtain permission from the Administration before landing at other islands. An airport was opened on Nukuhiva in December 1979, with an airstrip of 1,500 m.

Nukuhiva, once heavily populated, was unknown to Europeans until the French navigator Etienne Marchand sighted it from a distance in 1791 and named it Baux Island. The first European to put into it was Lieut. Hergest of HMS 'Daedalus' in 1792. The LMS missionary William Pascoe Crook, who had been landed on Tahuata in 1797, moved to Nukuhiva in 1798. One of the earliest beachcombers, Edward Robarts, was there for eight years from 1800. An account he wrote of the Marquesas was published in Canberra in 1974.

After two Russian explorers, Krusenstern and Langsdorff, visited Nukuhiva in 1804, the island ousted Tahuata as the most common calling place for ships passing through the group. The Porter affair of 1813-14 (see under History) put Nukuhiva firmly on the map. For several years thereafter, the island was visited for its sandalwood. In 1829, the US warship 'Vincennes' called at Nukuhiva to try to assure a hospitable reception for all American ships, chiefly whalers, which were visiting the Marquesas in increasing numbers. Missionaries sent from Hawaii arrived in August 1833, but vacated the field to the LMS in the following year.

The French took formal possession of Nukuhiva in 1838 and three French Catholic priests established a mission station there in 1839. In 1842 the French occupied the island. The remains of Fort Collet, built at that time and named after the first French commandant, are still to be seen on a promontory at the eastern end of Taiohae Bay. The American novelist Herman Melville, then a seaman, deserted from the American whaler 'Acushnet' in Controleur Bay during the French occupation and spent some time in Taipi valley. His experiences were the basis for his semi-fictional book 'Typee'.

The French garrison was withdrawn from Taiohae in 1849, but re-established there soon afterwards. In 1862, two Peruvian slavers called at Nukuhiva and other islands in the group and kidnapped more than 30 men. Some of these were brought back from Peru in the following year, afflicted with smallpox. Although an attempt was made to isolate them in Taiohae, the disease soon spread and within six months a quarter of Nukuhiva's population had been wiped out.

A year or two later, the administration granted William Stewart, of Tahiti, 4,000 hectares of the Taipi valley for the growing of cotton, and 31 Chinese were brought in as labourers. After Stewart's company went bankrupt in the early 1870s, the Chinese dispersed and took to growing opium.

After the French annexation of Tahiti in 1881, a civil administration replaced the military regime in Taiohae. However, in 1904 the administration transferred its headquarters to Atuona on Hivaoa because sandflies in plague proportions had made life at Taiohae unbearable. The administration returned to Taiohae in the 1940s.

During World War I, the German cruisers 'Scharnhorst' and 'Gneisenau', which bombarded Papeete, used Controleur Bay as a base. Czech settlers made a shortlived attempt to form a colony in the interior of Nukuhiva between the wars.

The remains of numerous 'paepae' (stone foundations on which the ancient Marquesans built their houses), 'tohua' (dancing areas), 'akaua' (fortifications) and 'meae' (temples) are to be found on Nukuhiva — testimony to the large population that once flourished there.

EIAO. Eiao, formerly called Masse Island, is 90 km NW of Nukuhiva and uninhabited. It is about 10 km long by 5 km at its greatest width. The highest point is about 600 m. Most of the eastern side is a precipitous slope. The only anchorage is at Vaituha on the NW side.

The island suffers periodic droughts and was probably not inhabited permanently in pre-European times. However, it was used for making stone adzes from a hard grey phonolite that occurs there. Numerous finished and unfinished adzes and other stone relics of ancient times have been found on the island.

Eiao was used as a convict settlement and place of exile until the turn of the century and was subsequently leased for some years to the Compagnie Navale de l'Oceanie. Sheep, cattle, pigs and donkeys introduced to the island in former times have since multiplied into thousands. In the mid-1960s, they were reported to have eaten almost every growing thing on the island and are dying out themselves from starvation. Their depredations have caused serious soil erosion. In 1972, Eiao was reported to have been investigated as a possible site for underground nuclear tests.

HATUTU. Hatutu, the most northerly of the Marquesas Islands, is separated from Eiao by a channel a few kilometres wide. It is about 6.5 km by 1.5 km. Its highest point is about 330 m above the sea. The island is uninhabited but is visited for its good fishing.

Thousands of ground doves of a species unknown elsewhere in the Pacific are to be found on the island. They are said to have a close resemblance to a South American species.

MOTU ONE. About 18 km ENE of Hatutu are two small islets on a shoal on which the sea

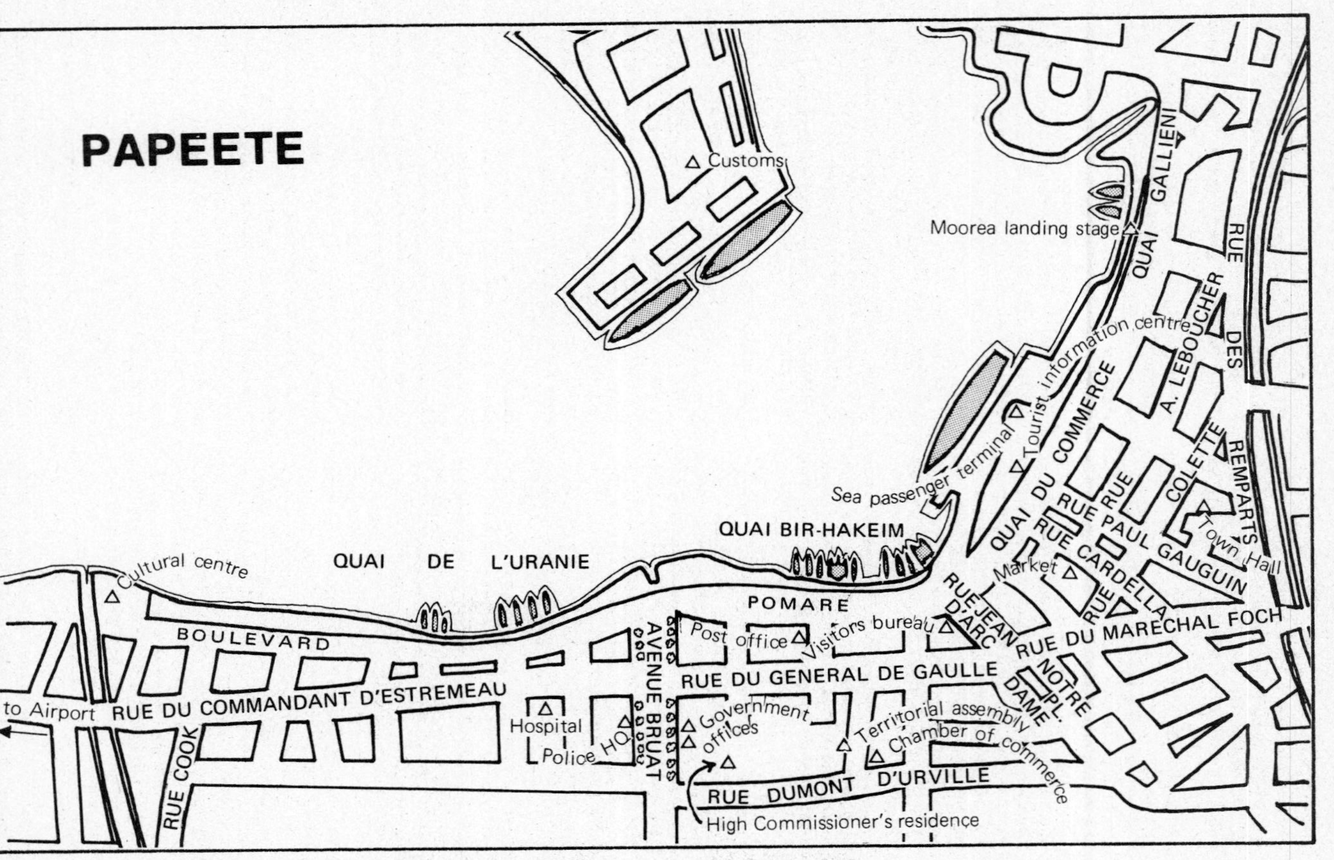
PAPEETE
Customs
Moorea landing stage
QUAI GALLIENI
RUE DES REMPARTS
A. LEBOUCHER
Tourist information centre
QUAI DU COMMERCE
COLETTE
Town Hall
RUE
RUE PAUL GAUGUIN
RUE CARDELLA
RUE
Sea passenger terminal
QUAI BIR-HAKEIM
Market
RUE JEAN D'ARC
RUE DU MARECHAL FOCH
NOTRE DAME PL.
QUAI DE L'URANIE
Cultural centre
POMARE
BOULEVARD
Post office
Visitors bureau
AVENUE BRUAT
RUE DU GENERAL DE GAULLE
to Airport
RUE DU COMMANDANT D'ESTREMEAU
Hospital
Police HQ
Government offices
Territorial assembly
Chamber of commerce
RUE COOK
RUE DUMONT D'URVILLE
High Commissioner's residence

breaks heavily. The islets, known as Motu One or Ile de Sable, are from 1.8 m to 3 m high. Shoals are common in this vicinity and navigators are advised to give the area a wide berth.

FOR THE TOURIST. The Tahiti Tourist Board (Office de Developpement du Tourisme) is located on the Papeete waterfront, in the Fare Manihini. This office publishes detailed information on French Polynesia, besides facilitating tourist planning and promotion and sponsoring festivals etc. In addition, the Syndicat d'Initiative provides local information on the spot.

There are also various tour agencies, including Tahiti Nui Travel, Tahiti Tours, Tahiti Voyage, Kia Ora Tours, Pacific Travel, Tahiti Poroi, Voyagence Tahiti, Tahiti Holidays, Marama Tours and Manureva Tours. See also the section on transport earlier in this French Polynesia section of the yearbook.

Bernard Covit's "Official Directory and Guide Book for Tahiti", written in English and French, is a most comprehensive source of information on these islands, and is obtainable in Papeete.

Entry formalities. All visitors must have a valid passport and a return ticket or a document of outward transportation, failing which they must make a deposit equivalent to the return air fare to their place of origin.

No visa is required by French nationals, citizens of Common Market and certain other countries on visits not exceeding three months, and for citizens of most other countries on visits not exceeding one month (from Australia, Canada, New Zealand, Singapore, U.S.A., etc.).

A foreigner may stay up to six months by having his visa renewed in Tahiti. He may be also granted a second six month period. For longer stays a permit must be obtained from the High Commissioner.

Persons entering the territory as tourists are not allowed to take employment, even of a temporary nature. A "work permit" from the authorities is required for employment.

Smallpox vaccination is required of passengers arriving from infected areas, while those embarked in Fiji and Samoa must have all baggage except hand luggage fumigated at Faaa Airport. This process takes about two hours and is designed to prevent the entry of pests in the coconut industry.

Foreign currency may be taken into the territory and there is no difficulty in changing Australian banknotes, for example, in Tahiti, although the rate is usually slightly below that for travellers cheques. CFP may be reconverted on leaving and CFP notes may also be converted outside the country, e.g., at the French bank in Sydney.

Customs regulations permit a passenger to bring in 400 cigarettes and 1 litre of alcoholic beverages, duty free.

Airport tax. There is no airport tax.

Duty-free facilities. The Tahiti Duty Free shop is in the Vaima Centre in Papeete. Luxury imports, including French specialities, are sold at the Faaa international airport and in Papeete boutiques. They include French wines, silks, perfumes and tableware. Many prices reflect high French living costs.

Most interesting local items are the colourful and versatile "pareu" cloth and dresses; pearl jewellery, Marquesan wood carvings, shell necklaces, woven hats, baskets and mats.

Sightseeing. Tahiti is probably the most famous island in the South Pacific, and it will continue to attract large numbers of tourists who will, as always, be charmed by its spectacular scenery and its atmosphere. They will make 120 km round-island excursions, and short boat and air trips to nearby Moorea, and farther afield to Bora Bora. Some of the more popular sights are listed, but other more detailed information on Tahiti and other islands is to be found under Islands in Detail.

Point Venus. A drive 6.5 km eastward from Papeete brings you, after a short detour, to the tomb of Pomare V, last king of Tahiti, who was interred there in 1891. Further on, the road runs by Matavai Bay, the anchorage of the early explorers. About 13 km from Papeete, there is a side road to Point Venus where Cook observed the transit of Venus in 1769. An old monument marks the spot. Also in the vicinity is a monument to Wallis, Bougainville and Cook, Tahiti's first three European visitors; and a monument to the pioneer LMS missionaries who arrived in the 'Duff' in 1797. Two other points of interest are the lighthouse and the Museum of Discovery. The lighthouse, which is 25 m high has been in service since 1868. The museum was established in 1969. Outside the museum entrance and two 'built-up' iron cannons of the 16th century which were recovered from Amanu Atoll, Tuamotu Archipelago, about the time the museum was opened. Robert Langdon in his book 'The Lost Caravel' has put forward the theory that they are relics of the Spanish ship 'San Lesmes' which disappeared near the Strait of Magellan in 1526 en route to the East Indies.

Fautaua Gorge is quite close to Papeete and may be visited on foot or by car. The road leaves the east coast road about 2.5 km from the town and follows the Fautaua River. A short distance up the valley is Pierre Loti's Pool (where there is a monument to this celebrated French author). As the road dwindles in the gorge, it is necessary to go afoot, the distance from the fall being about 10 km. Tracks lead both to the top and the base of the fall, the latter being rough and entailing some walking in the stream; but there are good bathing pools. At the top of the fall is an old fort, a relic of the fighting between French and Tahitians in the 1840s.

Tautira: When making the round-the-island trip many visitors like to take the side trip up Tahiti-Iti, the smaller of Tahiti's two parts, to Tautira. It was there that Robert Louis Stevenson lived for about three months in 1888 and wrote part of "The Master of Ballantrae". Tautira was also the location of the first Catholic mission house in Tahiti – that of some Spanish priests who arrived in 1774. A sign now marks the spot. There is a country-style hotel.

Lake Vaihiria – up in the mountains in the centre of Tahiti, lies deep Lake Vaihiria, surrounded by tremendous peaks. The trip is best made from Maitiea district with guides and takes 1½ days, the night being spent under an improvised shelter. Some wading in Vaihiria River is involved and the ascent to the lake, about 450 m altitude, is rough but not beyond a good walker.

Papara is a district on the south coast that is important in Tahitian history. There, in ancient times, stood the great 'marae' (temple) of Mahaiatea – largest and most important single relic of the pagan religion yet discovered in Polynesia. It has been partly restored.

Gauguin Museum and botanical gardens. The museum is in the Gardens, at Papeari, about 50 km from Papeete. The entire life of the painter is depicted in a striking building which was financed by the Singer-Palignac foundation of France. Most of the documents came from Europe. In the grounds there are two ancient stone tikis from Raivave.

Golf course. An 18-hole golf course was opened at Atimaono, 40 km from Papeete, on the east coast, in 1970.

In the 1860s, Atimaono was the site of a huge cotton plantation, for which Tahiti's first Chinese residents were imported as labourers.

Other things to do or see: Papeete Municipal Market on a Sunday morning early, when the local people do their shopping; water-skiing; big-game fishing; glass-bottom boat excursions to the reefs; scuba-diving; floor shows in the main hotels; the Olympic swimming pool on the harbour front at Tipaerui; the Museum of Tahiti and its Islands, 16 km from Papeete at Punaauia.

Lookouts. A magnificent view of the coast and town can be got from Fare Rau Ape, about 550 m above sea level. It is 1.5 km out of Papeete, east bound and 7 km up a steep, narrow road into the mountains. A country style restaurant perches on the side of the mountain.

Other high view points are at Pamatai, reached by a few kilometres of road inland from a point just on the Papeete side of Faaa airport; and from the Taravao Plateau.

Bastille Day fete. Bastille Day (July 14) is extended in Papeete to a week of festivities – and these are sometimes prolonged over the second weekend following.

Dancing and other competitions between district teams are held; side-shows and stalls are erected along Papeete waterfront and few Tahitians seem to sleep during the entire period of the festival.

Restaurants. Local fruits and seafoods, besides imports, contribute to the interesting variety of French, Chinese and Polynesian cuisine. Among the choicest, outside hotel restaurants, are "Le Belvedere" at an altitude of 600 m behind Papeete; "Le Dragon d'Or", "Le Jade Palace", "Le Mandarin", "La Soupe Chinoise" and "Te Hoa" for Chinese dishes; European meals – "Michel et Eliane", "Ma Maison", "Aeafore", "Moana Iti", "Vaima" and "Le Lagoonarium"; also the "Pitate" night club and bar adjacent.

Convention facilities. Papeete Cultural Centre. This is situated on the Papeete waterfront, within walking distance of the centre of the city. The Cultural Centre offers an 865-seat theatre with sound and projection equipment as well as simultaneous translation facilities. An additional auditorium has 120 seats. Accommodation for visiting sports teams or students is provided in 22 rooms.

There is also the Convention Hall of the Territorial Assembly. This is situated in the heart of Papeete, opposite the Post Office. The hall has 463 seats, sound and projection equipment and simultaneous translation facilities. Post office, telephone and telex installations are available on request.

The Museum of Tahiti and its Islands, 16 km from Papeete at Punaauia, has an airconditioned conference room seating 208 persons with writing table, light and ashtray; podium seats eight people; four lecturers' microphones and 26 mobile ones; two tape recorders in sound cabin; 16 mm movie projector, slide projector.

ACCOMMODATION

Tahiti — Central Papeete

KONTIKI — 45 rooms, de luxe, air conditioned rooms, private balconies and bathroom, on waterfront.

MATAVAI — HOLIDAY INN — 138 rooms.

ROYAL PAPEETE — 35 rooms, on Papeete waterfront, air conditioned, all amenities.

MAHINA TEA — 14 rooms, family style, above Ave. Bruat.

Point Venus: 10 km east of Papeete

ROYAL TAHITIEN — 40 rooms, 5 bungalows, air conditioned, on black sand beach.

PRINCESS HEIATA — 34 rooms, restaurant, Polynesian-style, gardens, pool.

TAHARAA — 199 rooms, pool, access to beach, 9-hole golf.

70 km from Papeete:

TE ANUANUA — 12 bungalows in Pueu village.

West towards Faaa Airport within 10 km of Papeete:

TAHITI — 88 rooms and 18 bungalows on edge of lagoon, swimming pool.

BEACHCOMBER — 183 rooms, 17 bungalows, air conditioned, beach, pool side bar.

TE PUNA BEL AIR — 48 rooms, 29 bungalows, white sand beach, natural spring swimming pool.

MAEVA BEACH — 223 rooms, white sand beach, swimming pool.

15 km from Papeete:

TAHITI VILLAGE — 9 rooms, 23 bungalows, white sand beach.

Moorea:

AIMEO — 26 rooms, 19 bungalows, situated on Cook's Bay, fine cuisine.

BALI HAI — 12 rooms, 41 bungalows.

CLUB MEDITERRANEE — 265 bungalows.

HIBISCUS — 30 rooms, 30 bungalows.

KIAORA VILLAGE — 50 bungalows.

MOOREA LAGON — 45 bungalows.

MOOREA VILLAGE — 48 bungalows.

TIPANIE — 19 bungalows.

CAPITAINE COOK BEACH H. — 24 rooms, 20 bungalows.

Bora Bora

BORA BORA — 80 bungalows, incl. 15 de luxe, built on stilts over lagoon.

NOANOA — 10 rooms, 41 bungalows (a Club Mediterranee village).

OAOA YACHT — 8 rooms, 16 bungalows on Vaitape Lagoon.

B. MATIRA — 12 bungalows.

MARARA — 44 bungalows.

Huahine Island

BALI HAI — 10 rooms, 34 bungalows.

Raiatea Island

BALI HAI — 16 rooms, 16 bungalows.

Rangiroa Atoll

KIAORA — 25 bungalows.

Tetiaroa Island

TETIAROA VILLAGE — 10 rooms, 17 bungalows.

Kaurura Atoll

PATAMURE VILLAGE

Manihi Atoll

KAINA VILLAGE — 7 rooms, 14 bungalows.

GALAPAGOS

These islands straddle the Equator about 970 km west of the coast of Ecuador. They lie between 1 deg. 30 min. N. and 1 deg. 30 min. S. lat., and at 90 deg. 30 min. W. long. The group is volcanic origin. It takes its name from the Spanish word for the numerous huge tortoises originally found there, but now reduced to comparatively few in the highlands of some of the islands. There are 13 large islands, 6 smaller ones and 42 rocky outcrops. Most of them have a Spanish and an English name. The land area is about 7,700 sq. km; the population a little over 4,000. Today tourism provides most of the jobs in the Galapagos. The islands are a province of Ecuador, divided into three cantons, and administered by a naval governor. The capital is Puerto Baquerizo (formerly called Puerto Chico) on San Cristobal (Chatham Island). Ecuadorean currency, the sucre, is used, and other Ecuadorean usages prevail.

Population. At end of 1978 it was about 6,000 with more males than females but the present ratio is not known. In mid-1975, of a population of 4,058, 2,363 were males. The people are mainly Ecuadoreans. Since 1959, Ecuadorean policy has limited the number of permanent non-Ecuadorean residents, but this appears to have been relaxed in the last few years. In 1975, the permanent foreign residents, mostly from northern Europe, numbered about 100. By the end of 1978 the number of foreign settlers had increased to 300, many of them from the United States. There is a closely-knit colony of German settlers on Santa Cruz. They left Germany for Galapagos to escape the hazards of life in war-torn Europe. About half the population lives at Puerto Baquerizo and there are sizeable settlements at Progreso in the hills about 5 km from Puerto Baquerizo (San Cristobal) and at Puerto Ayora and Bella Vista on Santa Cruz. Spanish is the official language and most of the people are Roman Catholics.

THE LAND. The principal islands from west to east are: Fernandina (Narborough); Isabela (Albemarle); Pinta (Abingdon); Marchena; Santiago or San Salvador (James); Rabida (Jervis); Pinzon (Duncan); Baltra (South Seymour); Santa Cruz (Indefatigable); Floreana, originally Santa Maria (Charles); Genovesa (Tower); Santa Fe (Barrington); San Cristobal (Chatham); and Espanola (Hood). Other smaller ones are Bartolome, Sombrero Chino, Daphne and North Seymour. Isabela, the largest island, is about 100 km long by 25 km broad. Its five highest peaks range in height from 1,690 metres to 1,175 metres. Fernandina, San Salvador, Santa Cruz and San Cristobal, the next largest islands, range from 8 to 20 sq. km.

The Galapagos are along the dividing line between the cold Peruvian or Humboldt Current from the south, and the warm South Equatorial Current from the north. These currents here curve to flow side by side in a west-north-westerly direction, but the borderline varies. Often the southern coasts and islands have sea-water temperatures of 15 deg. C while the northern coasts of islands have temperatures of 27 deg. C.

Soil. The soil of the principal islands, particularly of San Cristobal and Santa Cruz, is rich and supports flourishing agricultural and horticultural industries. Production has increased over the years, both in dairy and beef cattle, and there are good yields of fruit, mainly oranges, avocados and pineapples. The Progreso area of San Cristobal is particularly important and has an increasing number of small agricultural holdings, some of which are coffee plantations.

Climate. The climate of the islands is mainly influenced by the prevailing cold, dry, south-east wind which brings drought conditions, sometimes for a year or more. What little rain there is falls mainly on the higher levels of the larger islands where the annual average is estimated at about 1,219 mm, with wide variations. The vegetation in areas of heavier rainfall is lush and dense compared with the barren low-lying coastal regions. Most rainfall is in the form of thundershowers between November and March. At other times some fog and drizzle is experienced at lower levels. Fresh water is thus very scarce on all islands and absent on many, and fertile land is all at higher levels on the weather or south-east sides of the main islands.

Flora and fauna. Isolation combined with a tropical location in the plankton-rich Humboldt Current, have resulted in the evolution of a unique variety of flora and fauna. This has attracted many scientific expeditions to the islands and has resulted in the establishment of research facilities.

Seals and sea-lions abound in the warm waters and large sharks are common as are tuna, crabs and lobsters. Pelicans, boobies, frigate birds and others nest on many islands while penguins and albatrosses occur in isolated colonies on some of the smaller islands. Flamingos can be seen on Santiago, Rabida, Isabela and Floreana where they live in brackish lagoons. Darwin's finches are present on most islands and these species were one of the phenomena which inspired Darwin's theory of evolution.

Marine and land iguanas are found in large numbers on most islands, as are the small lava lizards. And, of course, there are the world's largest tortoises (See also "History").

TRANSPORT. On Baltra Island, north of Santa Cruz, is a 3 km airstrip built by the Americans during World War II. An airstrip built by the Americans during World War II. An airstrip for small planes has been in service on San Cristobal since early 1974.

From January, 1979, TAME (Transportes Aereos Militares Ecuatorianos) has operated flights almost daily to Galapagos from Quito and Guayaquil on the Ecuadorian mainland but the only weekly scheduled flight by TAME is on Fridays. On other days the flights are chartered by the various tour operators to link with their cruising vessels in the islands.

The cost of a single air fare from Guayaquil to Baltra Airport on Santa Cruz at January, 1979, was $US90.00 plus 4 per cent tax. As the sea cruises between the islands from the mainland are so popular, it is advisable to book a flight well in advance, and it is absolutely essential to reconfirm bookings and departure times on several occasions as the charter services can be erratic and timetables are 'elastic'.

HISTORY. The Galapagos Islands were uninhabited by man when Europeans first visited them in the 16th century. However, pieces of pottery found there in 1953 by a team of investigators led by Thor Heyerdahl indicate that American Indian fishermen visited the islands before the Spanish conquest of South America. The fishermen were probably from Ecuador and northern Peru. They probably used rafts of the type in use off the Ecuadorean and Peruvian coasts until the end of the 19th century. The evidence of their visits to the Galapagos has been seen, even by Heyerdahl's severest critics, as lending weight to his theory that, American Indians reached Polynesia in prehistoric times.

The European discoverer of the Galapagos was Tomas de Berlanga, third bishop of Panama. He landed in the group in 1535 after having been carried there by strong currents while sailing from Panama to Peru. The islands were referred to as the Galapagos on a map published by Ortelius in 1570. But no one visited them much until British buccaneers began using them as hide-outs towards the end of the 17th century. The English names for the islands date from that period.

The buccaner William Dampier who visted the group in 1684 left one of the earliest accounts of the iguanas and huge tortoises that could then be counted in thousands. The buccaneers made good use of the tortoises as food, as did the whalers and other visitors of the 19th century, Captain David Porter, of the US frigate 'Essex', for example, took on about 500 of the creatures at San Salvador (James Island) in 1813.

In 1832, General Jose Villamil took possession of the Galapagos for Ecuador. He used Floreana (Charles Island) as a colony for political prisoners, military delinquents and criminals sent from Ecuador. The colonists farmed, fished and caught tortoises to supply produce to visiting whalers. When HMS 'Beagle' visited the islands in 1835, the naturalist Charles Darwin recorded that there were between 200 and 300 colonists. Darwin's observations on the unique bird and animal life of the Galapagos provided important proof in his later studies on evolution.

By 1849, only 25 settlers remained in the group, as the tortoises had been wiped out on Floreana and whalers had stopped calling. However, various other attempts at colonisation were made over the next 80 years. One of the most successful was made on San Cristobal where the Cobos family established extensive sugar cane, fruit and vegetable plantations at Progreso. In 1914, Progreso had a population of 300.

Another successful settlement, first established on Floreana in 1893 and transferred to Isabela four years later, exported sulphur and plantation produce. In 1924 about 200 Norwegians settled on Santa Cruz and Floreana. But their settlement was unsuccessful.

In the 1930s, the Galapagos received some sensational publicity when an Austrian baroness, Eloise Bosquet de Wagner Wehrborn, took up residence on Floreana with two German male companions. The baroness set herself up as 'empress' of the island, bullying a few other European settlers already there and making free use of a pistol to keep off new arrivals. She and one of here male companions were apparently murdered in March 1934 by her second companion. Alfred Rudolph Lorenz. Lorenz then fled the island in a passing launch. Eight months later the launch was found wrecked on Marchena (Bindloe) Island. Lorenz and the launch owner apparently died of thirst after reaching the shore.

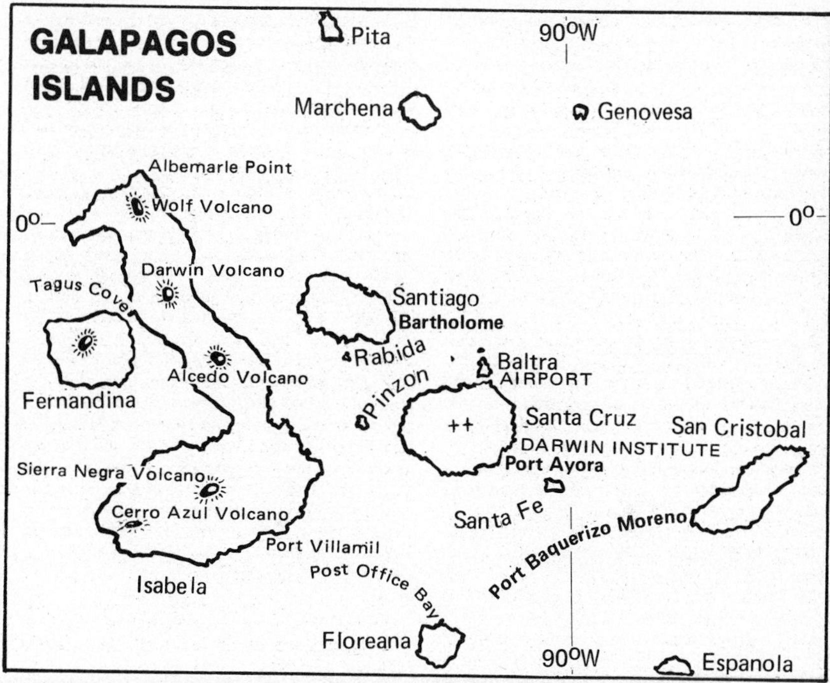

During World War II, the US Army and Navy had a base on Baltra Island. Water was brought to the island from nearby Santa Cruz (Indefatigable) Island. in 1959, exactly a century after the appearance of Darwin's 'The Origin of Species,' plans were laid for the establishment of the Charles Darwin Research Station at Academy Bay on Santa Cruz. The station was built with international help. It was opened officially in 1964, and has quarters and facilities for more than 50 scientists. Among its many projects is one to raise the rarer species of tortoise under controlled conditions with a view to restocking individual islands. The station is also concerned with controlling and exterminating predatory animals.

Originally there were 15 sub-species of tortoise on the islands of the group; of these, four are now extinct; four are seriously threatened with extinction; four are in reasonable numbers but much reduced from former times; and two are still numerous. The 15th sub-species is regarded as a mystery as only one animal has been seen in modern times. This was in 1906 on Fernandina (Narborough) where tortoises had not been known previously. Many searches have since been made without result although it is considered possible, if not probable, that some may survive on the remote southern slope of the island's volcano. This island is uninhabited by man or animal.

In 1968, the Parque Nacional de Galapagos (Galapagos National Park) was inaugurated with help and advice from the Darwin station. In 1977, the DRS enlarged its facilities and began active marine studies.

Work is going very well on developing a marine national park and plans are complete for a Marine Science Centre on Santa Cruz. It all augurs well for the future of the islands' natural environment and, at the beginning of 1979, 80 people were working at the national park and 20 more were permanently employed at the Charles Darwin Station. There is a constant stream of eminent biologists and zoologists staying as guests at the centre and the national park. The Ecuadorian government continues to assist the work with generous funding, following its grant of nearly $US150,000 in 1977 to the Charles Darwin Station, and donations are being received from the National Park as well as from individuals and organisations all over the world.

Visitors to the park are asked to observe strict rules of behaviour to ensure the survival of the unique flora and fauna which includes giant cacti, masked parrots, seals and giant tortoises. Much of this is seriously threatened by feral pigs, dogs, cats, rats, donkeys, cattle and exotic plants that have been introduced since the 17th century.

ISLANDS IN DETAIL. The three cantons forming the Province of Galapagos are: Isabela, San Cristobal and Santa Cruz. Each includes the island named and several others. Isabela, whose chief settlement is Villamil, includes the islands of Fernandina, Charles Darwin and Teodoro Wolf. San Cristobal, site of the capital, Puerto Baquerizo (or, in full Puerto Baquerizo Moreno), takes in the islands of Santa Maria, Espanola, Genovesa and Sante Fe. Santa Cruz, of which Puerto Ayora is the chief centre, has the islands of Baltra, Marchena, Pita, Pinzon, Rabida and Santiago under its jurisdiction.

Puerto Baquerizo, on San Cristobal, is the residence of the naval governor, who, in mid-1977 was Comandante Murillo. It is the port of entry for the group and the site of naval installations. It has schools, a Catholic Church, cinema, hospital, water supply, electricity and radio services. There is a direct telephone link with Guayaquil and Quito. A wharf is available for small craft. A road links Puerto Baquerizo with Progreso. Originally rough, it has been considerably improved in recent years. A fish freezing plant at Puerto Baquerizo is no longer in use.

On Santa Cruz, there has been considerable development since 1960. The island now has a hospital, schools, telecommunications, post office, restaurants, hotels, cinema and other services on a par with Puerto Baquerizo. The branch office of TAME airlines is located at Puerto Ayora. It should be noted that aircraft arriving from the South American mainland land at Puerto Ayora on Santa Cruz rather than the capital, Puerto Baquerizo on San Cristobal Island. A road, completed in 1975, crosses the island from Academy Bay to Baltra Channel and provides a link with the airfield on Baltra island. The cross-island trip takes one and a half hours and costs $US7.00 in 1979.

Isabela Island had a volcanic eruption in 1957. Most of the islands are uninhabited by people and are now protected as part of the national park.

FOR THE TOURIST. The Galapagos Islands have increased in popularity with the tourist in the last few years and several new hotels have greatly improved tour facilities and now attract increasing numbers of tourists. Late 1977 saw the opening of the Hotel Delfin, the biggest hotel on Santa Cruz and regarded as the leading establishment with accommodation for 36 people – 16 twin-bedded rooms and an A-frame with accommodation for four. The hotel is part of a package deal by Metropolitan Touring of Quito. It provides the accommodation for the passengers cruising on the yacht Delfin, but it also receives regular guests. All rooms are fully carpeted with private showers and other facilities. Another new hotel on Santa Cruz is the Hotel Galapagos, with 14 twin-bedded rooms plus private facilities, and also rated as 'first class'. The Hotel Sol y Mar comes next with accommodation for 26 people. The hotels El Pacifico and Colon are rated 'third class' and there are also several smaller pensions offering lower-cost accommodation of a lesser standard.

On Floreana Island, the Pension Wittmer is rated "second class". There is also a good seafood restaurant near the wharf.

There are also "floating hotels" or tourist vessels operating on a fly-cruise basis. Aircraft make two-hour flights between the islands and the Ecuador mainland. The vessels and their capacities are "Iguana"-68 passengers; "Delfin"-38; "Isabela"-16. An important addition to the fleet in November, 1979, was the 1000 tonne luxury vessel "Santa Cruz" built exclusively for Galapagos Islands cruising with accommodation for 90 passengers in 45 staterooms with private baths. The top price for the 1979 programmes is $US620.00 (seven nights) on the Iguana, and the lowest $US260.00 (four days/three nights) on Delfin. The prices do not include air fares. There are also five smaller yachts for charter ranging from $US2,500.00 a week (six passengers) to $US5,800.00 a week (10 passengers), all plus air fares. There are two scheduled week-long cruises for the charter yachts, but the period can be extended by arrangement.
ment.

On such ships, tourists have the services of experienced island guides and there is ample time to spend ashore at the various islands visited by these ships. Photographic slide shows and talks are also provided for passengers.

At Puerto Ayora it is possible for small groups of visitors to hire converted fishing boats in which they may cruise around the islands at their leisure. The cost of hiring a boat and the services of a captain and mate varies between boats.

The Galapagos are a favourite calling place for American and European cruising yachtsmen, who frequently make it their first call after the Panama Canal and before crossing the Pacific. Tagus Cove, Santa Cruz, is considered the best anchorage for yachts, but there are many others. It is stressed that no vessel can visit Galapagos without first obtaining a permit from the Direccion De Marina Mercante (Director of Merchant Marine).

Post Office Bay, on the north coast of Floreana (Charles or Santa Maria), was a famous crossroads in the old whaling days. An ancient barrel in which whalers put letters to be picked up later by homeward-bound vessels is still used by cruising yachtsmen.

A fee of $US6.00 is charged to each visitor to the Galapagos National Park but this is expected to rise to $US25.00 by the end of 1979. The increase will help to finance the National Park's programmes.

Camping is not permitted on any of the islands. Information on each island is available from the Park Headquarters at Puerto Ayora. Also provided is a copy of the regulations which visitors are asked to observe so that the unique heritage of the islands may be preserved.

Further information. This may be obtained from: Ecuadorian Department of Tourism, Direccion Nacional de Turismo, Reina Victoria 514 y Roca, Quito, Ecuador. Telephone Quito 239 044.

TAME Airlines are at Avenida 10 de Agosto 239, Quito, Ecuador. Telephone: 510 211.

For information on Galapagos cruises and accommodation: Metropolitan Touring, Avenida Amazonas 239, Quito, Ecuador. Telephone 524 400. Telex 2482 Metour ed.

GUADALUPE

Guadalupe is a mountainous island of volcanic origin lying at 29 deg 11 min N. latitude and 118 deg 17 min W. longitude, 380 km west of the American continent at Baya, California. It is a possession of Mexico.

The island is 264 sq km in area. It rises to 1,220 m at its northern end, where there are some fertile valleys, and is 33 km long and 12 km wide.

The southern part of the island is barren, and the cliffs on the western side are almost perpendicular. The eastern side has a more gentle slope. The island is surrounded by cliffs of lava and is extremely rugged. The best anchorage is at Melpomene Cove at the southern end, where the water is about 18 m deep. There is a good landing place at the western end of the cove.

The island is uninhabited, except for a small garrison maintained by the Mexican Government.

The island is noted for the Guadalupe seal, which is protected by Mexican law. Guadalupe is treated as a nature reserve, and unauthorised landing is prohibited.

Mean annual precipitation on Guadalupe is 290 mm. Rain falls mainly in the winter. Mean annual temperature range is 14-21 deg C.

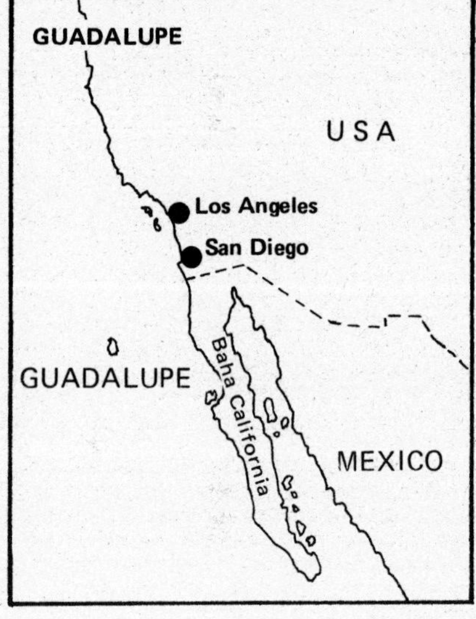

GUAM

Guam, a 549 sq. km island at the southern extremity of the Mariana archipelago, is an unincorporated territory of the USA. Its location is 13 deg. 26 min. N. latitude and 144 deg. 43 min. E. longitude. Local time is 10 hours ahead of GMT.

The capital of Guam is Agana which is about 2,170 km south of Tokyo and 5,300 km west of Honolulu. The population estimate in 1978 was 109,000.

The official flag and national anthem are those of the USA. The great seal of Guam depicts a sailboat near a coconut palm on the shore. Currency is the US dollar.

Official holidays include: January 1, Washington's birthday, Good Friday, Memorial Day, July 4, July 21 (Liberation Day), Labour Day, Columbus Day, Veterans Day, Thanksgiving, Feast of the Immaculate Conception and Christmas Day.

THE PEOPLE. Estimated 1978 population was 109,000 including 20,000 US military personnel and dependants. Guam's ethnic composition can best be described as cosmopolitan. Approximately 62% of the people trace their ancestry to the island's natives, the Chamorros, and 21% to the Philippines. Other areas of cultural influence are Japan, Korea, China, Mexico, Polynesia and Micronesia. The average family size is five persons with a median age of 19 years, almost 10 years below the national average.

Nationality. Guam had been a territory of the US since 1898. Full US citizenship was granted in 1950 to persons born in Guam. Residents do not have the right to vote in national elections, however.

Language. English is the official language. Chamorro is widely spoken by the Guamanian people. Many stores have Japanese and a few Tagalog-speaking clerks.

Migration. Population variations in recent years have occurred through the intake of Asian construction workers and transient military personnel and their dependants. Slow but continuing migration comes from the US mainland and Hawaii. Also, Chamorros continually emigrate to the mainland.

Religion. The local population is predominantly Roman Catholic. Other faiths are Episcopalian, Baptist, Seventh-day Adventist, Mormon, Jewish, Baha'i, Nichiren Shoshu Buddhist and Jehovah's Witnesses.

Lifestyle. The Guamanian people developed a lifestyle influenced especially by Spanish Catholic colonialism, giving closer ties to the Filipino or Mexican than the Micronesians further east. Today, however, American customs are predominant. For example, the 'ngingi' or kissing of an elder's hand to show respect is inevitably being replaced with either a handshake or by both the 'ngingi' and a kiss on the cheek. The Chamorro language and 'old ways' are being revitalised through the Chamorro Bicultural Bilingual Programme in elementary schools.

Islanders live in a variety of European-style houses, made of either wood and tin, or, increasingly more common, typhoon-proof concrete. Social life on the island centres on the family, the church, weddings, christenings, wakes, and politics, a large extended family being an important factor in the lives of most Guamanians. Fiestas honouring the patron saint of each village are held at least once each year to which the entire island is invited for food and merriment.

GOVERNMENT. Guam is an unincorporated territory, administered under the Organic Act of Guam, 1950, as amended. The government of Guam consists of an executive, a judicial and a legislative branch. This provides legislative local autonomy. Guam's relationship with the United States Government comes under the general supervision of the Department of the Interior.

While Guamanians are highly patriotic, increased experience at self-government and a developing economy are causing the people to question the role of the US Government in Guam's affairs. In September, 1976, a referendum sponsored by the Guam Political Status Commission was held to 'improve Guam's status with the United States'. A proposal to seek independence was rejected. Steps toward the adoption of a locally-written and ratified Constitution were taken during 1977. A Constitutional Convention was authorised by Federal Congressional legislation in October, 1976. A general election was held in April, 1977, to elect 32 delegates to the convention, the purpose of which was to draft a constitution for the people of Guam by the end of the year. It was presented to and approved by Congress and the President, but in a referendum held on August 4, 1979, the constitution was overwhelmingly rejected.

Executive. The executive head is the Governor, previously appointed by the US President but in late 1970 elected for the first time by voters at large. The Governor and Lieutenant-Governor are elected for four-year terms.

Legislature. Since 1950, Guam has had a unicameral legislature consisting of 21 senators elected by legislative districts for two-year terms.

Judicial. The District Court of Guam, with a judge appointed by the President of the United States for a term of eight years, serves as the Federal court of Guam. Like a US district court, it has jurisdiction over all cases arising under the Constitution, treaties, and laws of the United States. The Superior Court of Guam handles all other cases arising under the laws of Guam.

Elections. The last election for Governor and Legislature was held in November, 1978. There are two parties, Republican and Democratic, both affiliated with their US counterparts. The island has a non-voting delegate to the US House of Representatives, with an office in Washington (DC).

Local government. The island is divided into 19 municipalities or villages. There is no local government at this level. Elected commissioners, who have no legal authority, carry out varied functions on a village level ranging from ombudsman to social chairman.

Public service. In March, 1977, there were 13,915 public servants in Guam compared with the highest level of 17,095 in 1973. Twenty percent of all civilian employment is within the federal government and 25% is in the territorial government.

Gambling. Cockfighting is an approved sport, and each Saturday, Sunday and public holiday the Sport-O-Drome in Tamuning, really comes alive from 10 am to midnight. As much as $US9,000 has been wagered on a single match. Greyhound racing with parimutuel betting takes place three times a week on a multi-million dollar track opened in 1976. Bingo is popular and is held nightly at the Guam Recreation Center. Casino gambling was rejected by a public referendum in April, 1977, following the lead of the Catholic Church.

DEFENCE. Units of the US Air Force and Navy are stationed on Guam, and defence installations take up 35% of Guam's land. Defence expenditures, amounting to $US286 million in 1978, dominate the economy.

As part of the Strategic Air Command's global force for deterrence, the Third Air Division, with headquarters at Andersen Air Force Base, is concerned with SAC operations in the Pacific area west of the International Date-Line and in the Far East and Southeast Asia. From 1965 to mid-1969, B-52 bombing missions, nicknamed ARC LIGHT, were flown to South Vietnam targets. From April to August, 1975, the division and its subordinate units played a major role in Operation New Life, the evacuation of refugees from Southeast Asia. The 54th Weather Reconnaissance Squadron has been active in Guam since 1947. Its primary mission is to provide aerial weather reconnaissance of tropical cyclones throughout an 18 million sq. km area of the Western Pacific. Special aircraft allow data to be collected from the eye of these storms. Because of constant surveillance people can be forewarned of impending destructive weather. Air Force personnel on Guam in July, 1978, numbered 2,592 plus 4,172 dependants.

Repair and maintenance of the US Seventh Fleet is accomplished by the US Naval Station at Apra Harbour. The Naval Station is also a repair and provisioning base for nuclear Polaris submarines, which the US regards as deterrent weapons of prime importance. The Naval Air Station owns and operates the island's commercial airfield and shares its use in a joint-use agreement with the civilian government. Navy personnel totalled 5,703 active duty personnel plus 4,790 dependants as of July, 1978.

EDUCATION. There is a well-organised public school system. Education is compulsory for children from six to 16 years of age. There are 37 public schools, 28 of them elementary, five junior high, two senior high, one trade and technical school and a school for the handicapped. Other schools are operated by religious organisations.

SCHOOL ENROLMENT 1978-79

	Public	Private
Kindergarten	—	280
Elementary (grades 1-6)	15,850	2,590
Junior High (grades 7-9)	5,934	1,227
Senior High (grades 10-12)	4,277	1,126
Guam Community College	2,468	—
Total	28,529	5,223

The University of Guam, which opened as the territorial College of Guam in 1952, had a total enrolment of 3,104 students for the autumn term, 1978. These included 854 part-time students.

The New Guam Community College was established by public law in 1977, with classes beginning in August, 1978. It offers high-school programmes from grades 10-12, apprenticeship training and adult high school education in addition to job and higher education preparation.

LABOUR. The number of civilian employees on payrolls in March, 1977, was 30,816, of whom 21,851

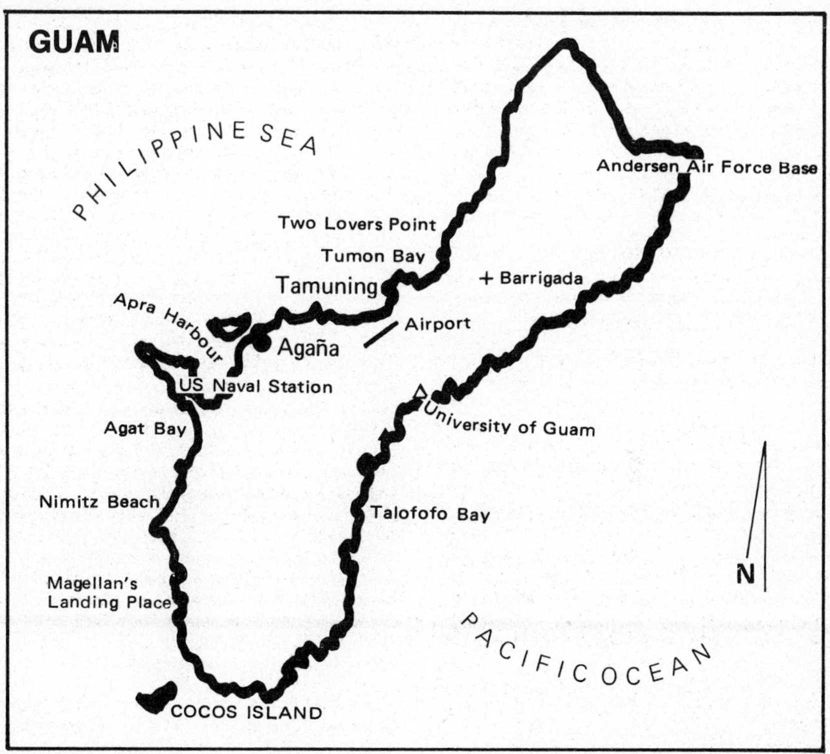

were US citizens, 5,027 were immigrant aliens and 3,938 were aliens admitted temporarily. The last-named made up 64% of agricultural and 74% of construction workers.

The military establishment is, by far, the largest single income-generating sector. Employees in 1978 consisted of 9,204 active duty personnel and 5,419 civilians. Of the latter, 93% were hired locally.

CIVILIAN EMPLOYEES BY INDUSTRY

	1975	1976	1977
Agriculture	111	131	147
Construction	5,388	3,319	4,019
Manufacturing	1,211	1,045	977
Transport, public utilities	1,587	1,417	1,476
Trade	5,541	4,872	5,411
Finance, insurance, real estate	1,363	1,295	1,268
Service, tourism	4,040	3,536	3,603
Federal government	6,681	6,014	6,318
Territorial government	9,016	8,431	7,597
Total	34,938	30,060	30,816

Wages. The minimum wage laws applicable to US also apply to Guam. The average hourly earnings of production and non-supervisory workers on private payrolls was $US3.94 in January, 1978. The average mean income of the 16,800 families on Guam, who average five members per family, was $US16,405 in March, 1978.

HEALTH. Medical care is of a high standard. A new 200-bed Guam Memorial Hospital was opened in late 1976. Excellent out-patient care is available at the Catholic Medical Center and the Seventh-day Adventist Clinic. Physicians number one per thousand civilian population. There is also an 89-bed navy hospital and four out-patient clinics for all service patients. Generally health conditions are good. Malaria, yellow fever and cholera are unknown.

Disease research. The National Institute of Neurological Disease and Stroke (N.I.N.D.S.), has been on Guam since 1956 with specialists from Japan and the US working on two serious local diseases, amyotrophic lateral sclerosis and parkinsonism-dementia, known locally as letico and bodig. These involve a gradual paralysis of the entire body and are caused by a viral infection of the nervous system.

LIVESTOCK POPULATION

	Poultry[1]	Carabaos	Cattle	Goats	Pigs	Horses
1974	139,110	256	2,771	537	10,463	118
1975	142,537	259	2,502	492	11,726	126
1976	91,360	247	1,829	504	8,442	120
1977	95,928	235	1,647	455	10,130	123
1978	147,875	314	1,493	432	10,637	135

[1] Laying birds only

THE LAND. Guam has an area of 549 sq. km. The island is about 51 km long and varies from six to 14 km in width. It is the peak of a submerged mountain located in the Marianas Trench, the deepest known part of the ocean. The northern part of the island is a relatively flat limestone plateau, 150 m above sea level, with cliffs that drop precipitously into the ocean. The southern part of the island is volcanic in origin with hills and mountains rising to 396 m.

Climate. The tropical climate is healthy and on the whole, pleasant, uniformly warm and humid. The east and east-north-east trade winds prevail for six months of the year, from December to May, during which time it is cooler and there is less rain. The driest month is generally April. From June to November winds become gustier with frequently occurring squalls during the rainy season yielding up to 30 cm of rain per month. Average annual rainfall is 200 to 250 cm. Daily temperatures are usually between 24 and 30 deg. C with mean annual temperature of 27 deg. C. Night-time temperatures are about 4 deg. C lower.

Tropical cyclones or typhoons form to the southeast of Guam and pass on their way to the Philippines or Japan. Winds of up to 322 km an hour have been recorded inside these storms. Fortunately, storms of this magnitude strike the island only infrequently. Today, the population has access to cyclone-proof shelters, and supplies and communications can be re-established immediately. The last major cyclones (or typhoons) were Supertyphoon Karen in 1962 and Supertyphoon Pamela in May, 1976.

Fauna and flora. Main native animals are fruit bats (fanihi) and lizards. Animals now found on the island include wild deer, doves and other birds, and coconut crabs. Flowers include poinciana (flame tree), *Ixora, plumeria* (frangipani), orchids, lilies, allamanda and bougainvillaea creepers. Trees include *Laucaena glauca* (tangantangan), casuarinas, coconuts and pines.

Resources. Chief resources lie in the sea, the tropical climate and tropical vegetation.

Land tenure. About 35% of the land in Guam is owned by the federal government, about 45%, or 24,984 hectares is privately owned, and 20% is owned by the Government of Guam. Most private land holdings are small and of 10,038 private owners, 94% have 2 ha or less.

AGRICULTURAL PRODUCTION. Since the end of World War II Guam has imported most of its food. Agriculture currently employs fewer than 200 persons although many families cultivate garden plots and raise small animals for personal consumption. It is estimated that imports of fruits and vegetables are 80% of consumption, imported meat is 90% and imported fish is 95%. The military presence especially has drawn local people away from cultivating their land, while more islanders are going into business, from small shops to elaborate department stores. To become a major sector, commercial agriculture on a larger, more capital intensive scale is being encouraged.

AGRICULTURAL PRODUCTION (tonnes)

	1976	1977	1978
Fruits and Vegetables	544	1,671	3,000
Poultry	54	54	56
Pork	233	279	475
Beef	54	34	33
Eggs (million dozen)	2.0	2.1	2.3

Fruits and Vegetables. A major agricultural endeavour in 1977 was the establishment of a new hydroponic farm. Hydroponics had great potential in Guam because it is less land and labour-intensive than traditional field farming and because it offers better environmental protection from cyclones and tropical plant pests and diseases. Farming in Guam had reached 120 hectares under cultivation by May, 1976 when a supercyclone destroyed all crops and caused losses of more than $US3.5 million. By 1978 total production had increased to 520 hectares and 3,000 tonnes. Watermelon is the island's largest crop with 1,500 tonnes produced on 83 hectares.

Livestock. While commercial beef and poultry production exist on Guam, pork has the greatest potential for expansion. Efforts are now being made to construct a slaughterhouse facility to encourage pork production, which reached a high of 475 tonnes in 1978. Beef is thought to be too land-intensive and poultry meat too expensive in terms of imported chickenfeed to be viable commercial investments. Eggs, on the other hand, are being produced in sufficient quantities to meet local demand, with a surplus being exported to neighbouring islands. A high of 2.3 million dozen was produced in 1978.

Fisheries. Aquaculture and mariculture are especially suitable for Guam's warm climate. A fresh-water experimental fish farm, owned and staffed by the Government of Guam, is currently operating in Talofono. It consists of two ponds, one of which is devoted to raising shrimp brought in from Hawaii, and the other for eels (from Taiwan), milkfish (bangus) and talpia, a local fresh-water fish. The vast resources of the Pacific constitute another area to explore. Local fish production of 94 tonnes in 1977-78 was mainly from boat operators, net fishermen and fish weir operators. The Pacific Tuna Development Foundation has instituted research projects into tuna resources development. Limited scale production had begun for prawns, catfish, carp and eels.

MANUFACTURING. Manufacturing activities on Guam include oil refining, rock and concrete production, printing and publishing, food processing, and a few export-oriented firms whose main products are garments and watches. This sector employs only 3.2% of the total labour force, or about 1,000 to 1,200 persons.

Plans for substantial diversification of Guam's manufacturing sector are hindered by lack of raw materials and a trained labour force; however, the potential for moderate expansion of light industry exist based on Guam's role as the urban centre of the Western Pacific.

LOCAL COMMERCE. Wholesale and retail trade accounted for 40% of the total gross business receipts in 1978. Most trading firms are concentrated in the northern section of the island, particularly Tamuning and Agana, ranging from small "Mom and Pop" stores to large shopping centres and grocery stores, and smaller specialty shops. Because of Guam's duty-free port status, many items may be purchased at a lower cost than in the US or even Hong Kong, such as watches, cameras, perfume, designer fashions, and jewelery.

OVERSEAS TRADE. Statistics on international trade show that Guam continually relies on imports, which accounted for 91% of the total value of trade in 1975-76.

Values of exports and imports in recent fiscal years are shown in the accompanying table.

EXPORTS AND IMPORTS
($ millions)

	1975	1976	1977[e]	1978[e]
Exports	28.5	25.2	30.7	34.2
Imports	266.2	267.6	269.0	272.0

[e]Estimates

Chief imports are fuel, machinery and transport equipment, manufactures and food. The importance of major trading partners is shown in the accompanying table:

TRADING PARTNERS
($ millions)

		1975	1976
Australia	**Export**	–	–
	Import	3.7	2.4
Hong Kong	**Export**	1.3	1.2
	Import	11.3	5.9
Japan	**Export**	0.9	0.4
	Import	17.2	13.0
New Zealand	**Export**	–	–
	Import	1.4	0.8
Philippines	**Export**	0.6	0.5
	Import	8.0	6.3
Taiwan	**Export**	0.7	8.8
	Import	5.3	7.3
USA	**Export**	15.9	5.4
	Import	109.7	86.9
Trust Territory	**Export**	8.6	6.2
	Import	0.7	0.8

Customs tariff. Guam is a free port. However, import duties are levied on alcoholic beverages, tobacco and fuel.

Guam's exports, which reached nearly $US47 million in 1979, are largely re-exports, many cargoes reaching Guam being for transshipment, mainly to the United States and to the Trust Territory, with the exception of eggs, iron and steel scrap and crude petroleum and petroleum products.

Exports in 1979 were: food and live animals $3.3 million; beverages and tobacco $5.3 million; crude, inedible materials (except fuels) including scrap metal $1.1 million; mineral fuels, lubricants and related materials $16.4 million; animal and vegetable oils and fats $1.06 million; manufactured goods, chiefly materials, $1.8 million; machinery and transport equipment $3.7 million; miscellaneous manufactured articles $7.9 million; special unclassified transactions $5.8 million

TOURISM. Since 1967, Guam has seen spectacular development in the building of hotels, with an accompanying rapid growth in the tourist industry. Tourism is believed to offer the greatest immediate potential for economic development, with Guam becoming to Japan what Bermuda is to New England, USA. The number of visitors in recent years is shown in the accompanying table.

Japanese tourists far outnumber those from elsewhere by as much as 75% in any one year and the industry has become geared to catering for their special wants.

Guam Visitors Bureau reported that the industry showed few surprises in 1978 concluding the year with a 4% drop in total arrivals but substantial gains in the main markets of Japan and North America. Of real importance was a healthy 19% gain in hotel room occupancy tax collections, an indication of increased island income in all areas of tourism spending assisted by cheaper dollars for Japanese.

Visitor profiles altered slightly. Statistical

measurements showed slightly longer lengths of stay, a wider age spread (more families, more older people), somewhat more people visiting friends and relatives. In short, the beginnings of a more balanced market segmentation not entirely to Guam's credit as Hawaii captured a good share of the traditional honeymoon market.

VISITOR ARRIVALS BY AIR

Year	Total	Japan	North America/ Hawaii
1967	6,000 (est)	66%	na%
1968	18,000 (est)	35%	38%
1969	58,265	50%	32%
1970	73,723	60%	24%
1971	119,124	71%	17%
1972	185,399	75%	16%
1973	241,146	70%	15%
1974	260,568	66%	11%
1975	239,695	67%	9%
1976	201,344	69%	9%
1977	240,467	63%	13%
1978	231,975	70%	14%

Arrivals by cruise ships totalled 3,752 in 1976; 5,361 in 1977 and 6,843 in 1978. Air arrivals for the first quarter of 1979 totalled 67,966, 50,380 of that total coming from Japan.

FINANCE. Public revenue for general government operations is raised through local income tax, property tax, a 4% gross business receipt tax, business licence fees and turn-over tax, and excise duties on alcoholic beverages, tobacco and fuel. In addition, various autonomous and semi-autonomous agencies, such as the public utilities, airport, commercial port, and hospital, collect revenues for services rendered. Guam also receives federal grants-in-aid.

The Government of Guam general fund statement of revenue and expenditure excluding the self-financing agencies has been shown in the accompanying table:

REVENUE AND EXPENDITURE (\$millions)

	Local revenue	Expenditure	US grants-in-aid
1976	84.2	121.0	21.0
1977	83.7	123.5	33.8
1978	94.2	143.3	39.6
1980	178.6	–	47.6

Income Tax system. Income tax was introduced to Guam under the Organic Act of 1950 which applied to Guam the income tax laws enforced in the US. Taxes are levied only by the Government of Guam. Rebates on income tax are available to approved ventures in agriculture, manufacturing, commercial fishing, services and the improvement of real property, under the Guam Economic Development Authority (GEDA) Public Law 8-80 and amendments. Qualifying Certificates are issued by the Governor upon recommendation of the GEDA which receives applications. Other concessions include assistance with credit, site, labour and management.

Military expenditure. Significant items of military expenditure in recent fiscal years may be summarised as in the accompanying table. Income taxes collected from military salaries are kept by the local government, amounting to more than 25% of all income tax collected.

Currency. United States currency of dollars and cents are used in Guam.

Banks. There are branches of three national banks: Citibank, Bank of America, and Chase Manhattan Bank; state banks: Bank of Hawaii, First Hawaiian Bank, Hongkong Bank, Bank of California, and California First Bank; on territorial bank: Bank of Guam; and two savings and loan associations: Guam Savings and Loan Association, and American Savings and Loan Association.

TRANSPORT. Guam has excellent sealed roads across the island, with 640 km of all-weather roads reaching virtually the entire population. There is no mass public transport system, but taxis and rental cars are plentiful. Private automobiles are the primary mode of land transportation.

Vehicles. There were 57,779 licensed motor vehicles on Guam in 1977. They included 40,648 private cars, 14,691 freight, 1,278 military and 1,162 motorcycles.

Overseas Airlines. Guam is rapidly beoming the transport hub of the Western Pacific. Hongkong, Taipei, Okinawa, Manila, Osaka, and Tokyo are served by Japan Air Lines, Pan American World Airways, Continental/Air Micronesia, and Singapore Airlines. Direct service to Honolulu is provided by Pan-American and Continental Airlines. Air Micronesia includes links between nine islands in the Trust Territory and Honolulu. Points south,

MILITARY EXPENDITURE (\$ millions)

	Military pay	Civilian pay	Military construction	Other	Total expenditure
1976	78.3	69.1	21.3	28.6	197.3
1977	79.2	58.1	24.3	50.5	212.0
1978	84.4	78.4	70.3	52.9	286.4

including Nauru, Noumea and Australia may be reached on Air Nauru. Air Pacific International, Island Air, Fox Air, Transmicronesian Airlines, and Continental/Air Micronesia operate daily scheduled passenger service between the Northern Marianas and Guam as well as flights to the Trust Territory. Braniff Airlines planned to begin service to Manila and Honolulu in July, 1979, and other airlines are seeking permission to fly the Pacific route as well.

The Guam International Airport services more than 600,000 passengers a year. A modern civilian air terminal opened in 1967 with four million dollars in terminal and aircraft related improvements added in 1976. Two runways 2,411 m and 3,047 m in length are capable of handling the largest commercial jets. The airport operates under a Joint Use Agreement through which runway crash, fire, and rescue facilities are provided by the United States Navy. The Andersen Air Force Base is on the northeast corner of the island for military flights only.

Port facilities. The harbour and port of entry is Apra Harbour, the largest harbour in the Pacific. The harbour is partly man-made; a protective curve extending five km from Cabras Island forms the Glass Breakwater, named for Captain Henry Glass who made a bloodless capture of Guam from the Spanish in the American-Spanish war. (The Spaniards on the island did not know they were at war with America.)

Apra Harbour is controlled by the Navy except for the Commercial Port, a 13.35 ha facility opened in 1969. It has modern facilities for handling either containerised or conventional cargo, including concrete warehouses and docks and paved container yards. Ships up to 233 metres can be accommodated. Cargo is carried from Japan and the Far East by the Daiwa Line and Kyowa Shipping Lines. Nauru Pacific Line operates out of Australia via Papua New Guinea to Guam and Micronesia. The United States Lines is the major cargo carrier between Guam and the US.

COMMUNICATIONS. Guam is included in the domestic postal service of the US. On April 24, 1978, a new $US4 million 8,091 sq.m. Main Postal Facility began operations. The postal system is excellent although delivery service is limited due to the absence of street names and house numbers throughout most of the island. There are now eight branch post offices and 10 contract stations in less populous areas.

The RCA Global Communications and Western Union feature overseas telephone and telex, telegram, satellite, and data communications transmission facilities to almost anywhere in the world. There are more than 12,300 telephones on the island, plus 6,300 extensions, provided by the Guam Telephone Authority, Government of Guam.

Commercial radio and television (including colour TV) are provided by radio stations KATB and KSTO and radio and television station KUAM, which derive revenue from advertisements. Guam Cable TV, a five-channel subscription service, offers television programmes from Los Angeles, California. Two new "premium movie" channels have been recently added. Television Station KGTF is what, in the United States, is called "public TV". It is largely educational or cultural, and depends for its revenue on grants and donations.

There is one daily newspaper, the "Pacific Daily News" (morning). In addition, the Air Force has a weekly paper called "Tropic Topic" and the Navy has the bi-weekly "Guam Report" and the monthly "Crossroads".

Water, electricity. Guam generally has an abundant water supply from its heavy rainfall and underground water wells. The islandwide power system is jointly operated by the Guam Power Authority (Government of Guam) and the United States Navy, with a total capacity of 307 megawatts and a peak demand of 156 megawatts. Transmission is being improved through the installation of typhoon-resistant concrete utility poles. Most electric outlets are 110 and 220 AC; normal wall outlets are 120 volts, 60 cycles.

PERSONALITIES AND ORGANISATIONS

Governor: Paul Calvo
Lieutenant-Governor: Joseph F. Ada
Military: Rear Admiral Robert R. Fountain Jnr., Commander US Naval Fleet Marianas, FPO San Francisco. Major General Andrew Pringle Jnr., Commander HQ 3rd Air Division, Andersen Air Force Base.

LEGISLATURE

Speaker: Thomas Tanaka
Minority Leader: Richard Taitano
Senators: Catherine Aguon, Celia Bamba, Frank Blas, Edward Charfauros, Thomas Crisostomo, Edward Duenas, Ernesto Espaldon, Carmen Kasperbaurer, Alberto Lamorena III, Antonio Palomo, Benigno Palomo, Peter Perez Jr., John Quan, Franklin Quitugua, Joe San Augustin, Francisco R. Santos, Raymond Sudo, James Underwood, Antonio Unpingco.

MUNICIPAL COMMISSIONERS

Chief Comissioner: Enrique S.M. Aflague
Agana: Thomas F. Mendiola
Agana Heights: Frank M. Portusach
Agat: Antonio Terlaje
Asan-Maina: Jose S. Quitugua
Barrigada: Raymond S. Laguana
Chalan Pago-Ordot: Vicente S. San Nicolas
Dededo: Jose M Garrido
Inarajan: Alfred S. N. Flores
Mangilao: Nicolas D. Francisco
Merizo: Joaquin Q. Acfalle
Mongmong-Toto-Maite: Norberto F. Ungacta
Piti: David B. Salas
Santa Rita: Juan M. Perez

Sinajana: Ignacio N. Sablan
Talofofo: Ramon L. G. Quinata
Tamuning: Gregorio A. Calvo
Umatac: Albert T. Topasna
Yigo: Antonio A. Calvo
Yona: Vicente C. Bernardo

JUDICIARY

Chief Justice, Superior Court: Judge Cristobal C. Duenas
Presiding Judge: Judge Paul J. Abbate
Judge Janet H. Weeks
Judge Richard Benson
Judge John Raker
Judge Joaquin V. E. Manibusan

GOVERNMENT SERVICE

Executive Assistant to the Governor: Matt Lonac
Press Secretary to the Governor: Ron Tangy

DIRECTORS OF GOVERNMENT DEPARTMENTS:

Administration: Frank G. Blas
Agency for Human Resources and Development: Joe R. San Augustin
Agriculture: Antonio Quitugua
Bureau of Budget and Management Research: Alfred B. Pangelinan
Bureau of Planning: Betty Guererro
Chief Commissioner: Enrique S. M. Aflague
Civil Defence: Pedro L. G. Roberto
Civil Service Commission: David Flores
Commerce: Jose D. Diego
Corrections: James Miles
Criminal Justice Planning Agency: Thomas Duke
Education: Elaine S. M. Cadigan
Guam Airport Authority: Manuel F. L. Guererro
Guam Community College: John Salas
Guam Economic Development Authority: David D. L. Flores
Guam Education Telecommunication Corp. (KGTF): Iris Muna
Guam Election Commission: Joseph Mesa
Guam Energy Office: Jesus San Augustin
Guam Environmental Protection Agency: Mr. Natarajan
Guam Health Planning and Development Agency: Cerila Rapadas
Guam Housing Corporation: Rufo Taitano
Guam Housing and Urban Renewal Authority: Pedro G. Cruz, Jr.
Guam Memorial Hospital: Mike Henroid
Guam Power Authority: Paul Cavote
Guam Telephone Authority: John T. San Sugustin
Guam Visitors Bureau: Martin Pray
Insular Arts Council: Sister Mary Calista
Labour: Jose R. Rivera
Land Management: Dometrio R. Pablo
Attorney-General: Kenneth North
Library (Nieves M. Flores): Magdalena Taitano
Mental Health and Substance Abuse Agency: Peter A. San Nicolas
Parks and Recreation: Felix L. Crisostomo
Port Authority: Gregorio C. Sanchez
Public Defender: Alexander M. Loebig, Jr.
Public Health and Social Services: Franklin Cruz
Public Safety: Jose R. Mariano
Public Utility Agency of Guam: Antonio Salas
Public Works: Jose E. Gutierrez
Revenue and Taxation: Ignacio Borja
University of Guam: Dr. Rosa Carter
Veterans' Affairs Officer: Francisco Perez
Vocational Rehabilitation: Lourdes D. Camacho
Youth Affairs: Arthur Jackson

CONSULAR CORPS:

Consul-General of the Republic of the Philippines: Lucilo A. Purugganan
Consul-General of the Republic of Korea: Hang Kyung Kim (acting)
Consul-General of Japan: Hiroshi Ohi

BUSINESS AND PROFESSIONAL ASSOCIATIONS

Guam Chamber of Commerce, Pacific Jaycees, Guam Federation of Teachers, Guam Teachers' Association, American Association of University Women, Guam Business and Professional Women's Club, Guam Press Association, Guam Employers' Council, Guam Board of Realtors, Guam Contractors' Association, Guam Society of Professional Engineers, Guam Association of Secondary Principals, Guam Medical Society, Guam Nurses Association, Guam Pharmaceutical Association.

SERVICE CLUBS

Marianas Lions Club, Rotary Club of Guam, Guam Women's Club, American Cancer Society, Guam Tuberculosis and Respiratory Association, American Civil Liberties Union, Boy Scouts of America, B.P.O. Elks Lodge, Faith Hospitality House, Filipino Ladies Association of Guam, Four-H Youth Development, Guam Association of Retired Persons, Guam Dental Study Group, Guam Girl Scout Council, Knights of Columbus, Kiwanis Club of Guam, Marianas Association for Retarded Citizens, Order of Eastern Star, Chapter No. 1, Ordot Community Advancement Association, Sanctuary, Teen Challenge Guam, United Service Organisation, United Seamen's Service, American Red Cross.

SPORTING FACILITIES

Bike Pedalers, Guam Fishing and Boating Association, Guam Shell Club, Marianas Skin Divers' Club, Marianas Yacht Club, Country Club of the Pacific and Windward Hills Golf and Country Club (two 18-hole golf courses), MJ

Riding Academy, Agana Swimming Pool, Bowling Alleys, Tennis Courts, Surfing Locations.

CULTURAL GROUPS
Guam Symphony Society, Million Dollar Players, Guam Theater Guild, Guam Choral Society, Fine Arts Gallery (University of Guam), Insular Arts Council.

SCIENTIFIC INSTITUTIONS
Micronesian Research Center, National Institute of Neurological Disease and Stroke (NINDS), Guam Museum, University of Guam Marine Laboratory.

PARKS
Tarzan Falls, Umatac Bay Park, Saluglula Pool, Adelup (Rota) Park, Puntan Dos Amantes, Cetti Bay Overlook, Fort Soledad Overlook, Talofofo Surfing Beach Park, Ipan Beach Park, Ipao Beach Park, Merizo Pier Park.

BUSINESS DIRECTORY

Building Contractors
Black Construction Corporation, Box 6548, Tamuning
Hawaiian Dredging & Construction Corporation, Box 2328, Agana
Investment Overseas Corporation, Box 6427, Tamuning
Oripac Painting Company, Box 1221, Agana
Pacific Construction Company, Box EM, Agana
RSEA (Guam) International Corporation, Box 1930, Agana

Construction Equipment
Bard Universal (Guam) Ltd., Box 7627, Tamuning
Benson Guam Enterprises, Inc., Box 7408, Tamuning
Guam Hardwood Construction Supply, Inc., Box 8779, Tamuning
International Equipment of Guam, Box 6548, Tamuning
Mid-Pac Far East Inc., Box 7420, Tamuning
Oceanic Lumber, Box 7448, Tamuning
Pacific Machinery Inc., Box DT, Agana

General Merchants
Atkins Kroll (Guam) Ltd., Box 6428, Tamuning
Atlantica Guam Corp., Box 8229, Tamuning
Calvo Enterprises Inc., Box 7899, Tamuning
Duty Free Shoppers Ltd., Box 7746, Tamuning
Guam Marketing, Box T, Agana
IBM Corp., Box BC, Agana
Island Equipment Company Inc., Box 3040, Agana
Jones and Guerrero Company Inc., Box 7, Agana
F. L. Moylan Company Inc., Box DF, Agana
Pacific International Company, Box AT, Agana
Xerox Corporation, Box ES, Agana

Shipping Agencies
International Navigation Company, Box 2712, Agana
United States Lines, Box 8897, Tamuning
Pacific Navigation System, Box 7, Agana
Seatrain Lines California, Box FO, Agana
Atkins Kroll (Guam) Ltd., Box 6428, Tamuning
Maritime Agencies of the Pacific Ltd., Box 3488, Tamuning

HISTORY. Archaeological excavations on Guam have revealed that the island was inhabited at least as early as 1320 BC. Two separate prehistoric cultures have been distinguished. One, called pre-Latte, was characterised by redware pottery, a lime-filled impressed ware, shell and stone adzes, shell beads and pendants. The Latte culture is associated with a later people who built their houses ('latte') on large stone pillars called 'halege'. Some of these pillars, arranged in double rows, are still to be found on Guam.

When the first Europeans reached Guam in the first quarter of the 16th century, the people of Guam, called Chamorros, were apparently of mixed origins. Rank and class consciousness were important factors in their lives. There were three classes – the 'matua' (nobles), 'atchaot' (middle class) and 'manachang' (commoners). They were organised in matrilineal clans and lived in villages on the coast, near rivers, or on hill-tops for their own protection. They built their houses and canoes with great skill, and were ingenious in making stone axes, chisels, knives, spearheads, hammers, mortars, pestles and slingstones. Their small outrigger canoes could travel at a great speed and were known to the early visitors as 'flying proas'. The Chamorros themselves were tall, well-built and robust, and wore few if any clothes. They are thought to have been of Malaysian origin.

European discovery. The European discoverer of Guam was Ferdinand Magellan who reached the island on March 6, 1521 after a hungry voyage of 98 days from the Strait of Magellan. He also sighted Rota and possibly Saipan. Tradition has it that he anchored at Umatac Bay on the southwest side of Guam where he traded with the islanders for food and water. When the islanders stole a skiff, Magellan sent an armed party ashore to recover it and to punish them. Seven Chamorros were killed and 40 or 50 of their houses burned. The thieving propensities of the islanders prompted the Spaniards to call Guam and its neighbours Islas de los Ladrones (Islands of Thieves). Another more flattering name – a tribute to the Chamorro canoes – was Islands of Lateen Sails.

Guam was one of the first islands in the Pacific to have a resident European. In 1526, when the flagship of Garcia Jofre de Loaisa called at Guam en route to the East Indies, a Spaniard called Gonzalo de Vigo was found to be living there. He had deserted from Magellan's ship 'Trinidad' at an island northward of Guam when that ship, having obtained a cargo of spices in the Moluccas, was trying vainly to pick up a favourable wind for Mexico.

Spain takes possession. In 1565, an expedition under Miguel Lopez de Legaspi, who had been sent from Mexico to colonise the Philippines, called at Guam and took possession of it for the King of Spain. Later, after reaching the Philippines, two of Legaspi's ships became the first to return to Mexico across the Pacific. The route they took was to the north of Hawaii and then down the coast of California. The practicability of return voyages to Mexico was thereby established, and for the next two and a half centuries Spanish galleons plied annually between the two countries, carrying silver ingots from Mexico to pay for the luxuries of the Orient in Manila.

Although the westward-bound galleons passed among the Ladrone Islands (or Marianas, as they were later known), it was not until the latter half of the 17th century that it became customary for them to call at Guam. In 1668, a group of Jesuit missionaries led by Diego Luis de Sanvitores settled on Guam, protected by a garrison of Spanish and Filipino soldiers. In the same year, a royal order required all galleons to put in at Guam; and soon the Spanish military commandant was given the rank of governor.

The Jesuit missionaries were at first well received by the Chamorros, about 13,000 of them being baptised during the first year. However, the islanders soon realised that the Spaniards were a threat to their way of life, and in July 1670 they rose in open rebellion against them. This was the beginning of 25 years of sporadic warfare. Some of the Spanish governors were particularly repressive, vengeful and brutal, while the Chamorros seized many opportunities to hit back.

One early historian, who has been much quoted, claimed that in only two years of fighting, the Chamorros were reduced from 40,000 to 5,000. However, it is probable that, as in other parts of the Pacific, unfamiliar diseases were the principal killers among the Chamorros. Smallpox, for example, ravaged the island in 1688. Many lives were also lost in devastating typhoons that struck the island in 1671 and 1693.

Chamorro resistance to Spanish rule was finally crushed in 1695 after a party of islanders who attacked the Spaniards and then fled to one of the northern islands were hunted down and routed. The islanders then agreed to return peaceably to Guam and become loyal subjects of the Spanish Crown. No Chamorros lived in the northern islands from that time onwards.

During the next 200 years, Guam was a sleepy backwater of the Spanish Empire in which Catholicism permeated most aspects of life. Until 1815, the only events to disturb the island's calm were the annual visits of the galleons, a periodic typhoon, and the occasional appearance of some unexpected foreigner. Among the foreign visitors were two English buccaneers, Woodes Rogers (1710) and John Clipperton (1721). There were also exploring expeditions headed by Crozet (1772) and Malaspina (1792). Crozet, who arrived during the energetic and enlightened governorship of Mariano Tobias, described Guam as 'the only island in the vast extent of the South Sea . . . which has a European-built town, a church, fortifications, and a civilised population.'

In 1815, some seven years after Spain's defeat at the hands of Napoleon, the galleon trade between Mexico and the Philippines ceased, and Guam fell on hard times. There was little improvement in the remaining eight decades of Spanish rule. However, from that time onwards, foreign vessels put into Guam with much greater frequency, and the islanders derived some benefit from their demands for victuals and repairs. Notable visitors included Kotzebue (1817), Freycinet (1819) and Dumont d'Urville (1828 and 1839).

There were also occasional American vessels trading with the Far East, and for about 30 years from 1823 some 30 whalers called at Guam each year. By 1855, Guam had become sufficiently important to American commerce for the United States to establish a consulate there. But there was a serious setback in the following year. A smallpox epidemic wiped out 3,644 Guamanians, which so reduced the population that the government permitted many Carolinians and later Japanese to settle on the island to replace them.

American possession. After the Spanish-American War broke out in 1898, four American ships under Captain Henry Glass, USN, were ordered to capture Guam on their way to the Philippines. This order was carried out without bloodshed, and the American flag was raised on the island for the first time on June 21. Two months later when Spain sued for peace, Guam was ceded to the United States together with the Philippines for $US20 million. A census, two years later revealed that the island's population was 9,676, of whom all but 46 were Guamanians.

Captain Richard P. Leary, USN, took over as the first American governor of Guam in August 1899 after President McKinley had decreed that the island should be placed under the control of the US Navy. It became primarily a coaling station and, later, a naval base in the Western Pacific. Leary and his successors faced many problems created by the last Spanish governors. Principal among these were illiteracy, disease and unsanitary conditions. By World War I, considerable progress had been made in combating these problems as well as in the fields of agriculture, land management and public works.

During the war, the German cruiser 'Cormoran' was interned in Apra Harbor and eventually scuttled there by her crew.

In 1917, the First Congress, an advisory council of 34 nominated Guamanian leaders, was convened to give them experience with the problems of government. Fourteen years later, an elected congress, consisting of two houses with a total of 43 members, was introduced. Although neither congress could initiate legislation, both were important stepping stones towards Guam's self-government of today.

Pacific War. On November 3, 1940, one of the most severe typhoons in the island's history spread destruction everywhere. Just over a year later, on December 8, 1941, Japanese aircraft attacked the island from neighbouring Saipan. Within two days, thousands of Japanese troops invaded the island, and the Americans, who numbered less than 400, surrendered. For the next 31 months, the Guamanians were subject to stern, often harsh, military rule. Then, an American force of 55,000 men landed and recaptured the island after several weeks of bitter fighting. Nearly 1,300 Americans and 11,000 Japanese were killed.

An American military government ruled Guam until the end of May 1946, after which the naval administration was re-established. For the next four years, the Navy had the task of rehabilitating an island that had been almost completely devastated by war. Agana, the capital, was cleared of its ruins and a completely new town was laid out. Other district centres were also recreated. Meanwhile, employment was plentiful, business boomed, and within a few years the Guamanians were enjoying one of the highest living standards in the Pacific.

On June 1, 1950, an Organic Act signed by President Truman made Guam an unincorporated territory of the United States and gave its people American citizenship. The Act also brought an end to naval administration and turned over responsibility for the island to the Department of the Interior. Carleton S. Skinner was appointed the first civilian governor. By June 1960, Guam had its first appointed Guamanian governor, Joseph Flores. Meanwhile, its chief industry was the US defence establishment, which played an important part in the prosecution of the Vietnam war.

In 1962, security measures were rescinded to permit American tourists to visit Guam without formal clearances. This move was designed to facilitate the development of a tourist industry and so reduce the territory's dependence on military expenditure.

The numbers of visitors grew from 300 in 1964 to 50,000 in 1970 and soon there was a hotel-building boom and related growth. The Organic Act was amended by Congress to allow for election of a governor and in 1971, Carlos G. Camacho was inaugurated as Guam's first elected governor.

After the Vietnam war ended on April 30, thousands of refugees were flown to temporary quarters on Guam before being transferred to the United States. At one point there were more refugees on the island than residents. In August, 1975, the Fifth South Pacific Games were held on Guam.

Further information: Paul Carano and Pedro C. Sanchez, 'A Complete History of Guam,' Rutland, Vermont, 4th printing, 1968. Charles Beardsley, 'Guam, Past and Present,' Rutland, Vermont, 1964. M. Cook, 'The Island of Guam,' 1917.

FOR THE TOURIST. Guam has witnessed a sensational development in tourism: the 10 years to 1974 registered a jump from 300 to 234,000 visitors per year. Even the names of the numerous hotels, restaurants and shopping plazas give an immediate indication of the Japanese, Guamanian and American interest in providing facilities to please visitors. Guam is especially popular among Japanese honeymooners.

The Guam Visitors' Bureau publishes colourful descriptive data in both English and Japanese. In addition, there are various local travel agencies and tour operators, including: American Express Inc, Marianas Travel Agency; and in nearby Tamuning – Micronesia Tours Inc, Turtle Tours, Getz International Travel Agency, and Guam International Travel Agency.

Duty-free facilities. Guam is a duty-free port, and its many shops offer a wide range of luxury goods from Japan, Europe, China, Thailand, India and the Philippines. Shops are open daily until 9 pm.

The four main shopping areas are: Tumon Bay with a new public market and shopping centre opened in December 1977; Tamuning, which features major department stores; Agana, the capital, with supermarkets and department stores; and Dededo, a typical American suburban shopping centre.

Entry formalities. Non-United States citizens visiting Guam must have a valid passport and US visa. US citizens entering Guam need proof of citizenship.

Smallpox immunisation is no longer required. Immunisation against cholera and yellow fever is required if a visitor arrives from an infected area.

Sightseeing. Guam abounds with relics of prehistoric times, Spanish rule and World War II battles. All this, together with the village life of present day Chamorros, may be seen on a drive around the island's 90 km coastal highway.

The modern government and commercial buildings of Agana itself are also interspersed with colourful reminders of former times, and reflect very well the melting pot of influences to which Guam has been subject since the war.

Agana Cathedral (Dulce Nombre de Maria), the largest church in Guam, is built on the site of a church destroyed in World War II. A block away is Skinner Plaza, dedicated to the first civilian governor of Guam, Carleton Skinner. Yet another block away is one of the historic Spanish bridges which has been preserved in a park-like setting.

Some of the best examples of Spanish architecture remaining on Guam are in Plaza de Espana, a beautifully kept park next to Agana Cathedral. For more than 230 years the plaza was the seat of government for Guam and the adjoining Mariana Islands. The Azotea is the only remaining piece of the original governor's palace, and is still used today for special occasions. A small, round building with wrought ironwork nearby is the original "Chocolate House", where wives of the Spanish governors served cups of chocolate to guests. The remains date back to 1736.

Behind the Azotea is a small building housing the Guam Museum, packed with artifacts and relics of the Pacific War battles in Guam. Close to the museum is Latte Stone Park, with ancient latte stones (pronounced lah-tee) dating from prehistoric times. The stones have become a symbol for Guam, but no one is sure of their original use. Many archaeologists and historians consider they were used as foundations for houses. Some were carved from rock and others from natural limestone mortar. Those in the park were found near the Fena River in south-central Guam. There are many original latte sites scattered in remote spots throughout the island.

At the top of the hill close to the park is Government House, next to the remains of Fort Apugan, also known as Fort Santa Agueda, a Spanish-built fortress. This spot offers a commanding view of Agana and its bay.

Some 50 restaurants around Agana reflect the local cultural heritage – sushi and yakitori from Japan, tortilla and hot peppers from Mexico, fish, coconut and taro from Chamorro ancestors and ice cream and hamburgers from the U.S.A.

Five new tourist attractions were opened on Tumon Bay late in 1979 including a public market, a $100,000 complex in traditional Spanish style, the Tumon Bay Shopping Center consisting of a large gift and souvenir store and flower shop and a restaurant-snack bar the Carl Rose Gift Center and the Tumon MOPed Rental Center, where tourists can hire motorised bicycles, which don't require licences. The hire charge of $4.50 an hour or $15 a day include insurance and petrol. New tennis courts have also been installed at the Guam Dai-Ichi Hotel on Tumon Bay.

A start has also been made on a new Guam International Airport Terminal to cost $45 million. The terminal, which will include a maintenance hangar and cargo operation, six aircraft aprons and remodelled terminal buildings, will be completed in 1981.

In dress, elderly women use the Filipino mestiza. Young and old wear the Japanese zori sandals. Young people have also adopted the latest in Western attire.

Guam offers superb skin and scuba diving, water skiing, deep-sea fishing and two golf courses.

One of the biggest annual events in a Guamanian village is the celebration of the feast of the patron saint, which is both a religious and social event. All day Saturday, the women prepare their best Chamorro foods for the Sunday feast. On the Saturday evening there is a sunset procession in the streets around the church.

Tourist representatives abroad. Guam Visitors Bureau, Tokyo; Guam Delegate to Congress, Washington D.C.

Most resort accommodation is on Tumon Bay, adjacent to Agana Bay and within 10 minutes of the airport.

ACCOMMODATION

Agana and Tumon Bay:

CASA DE FLORES, 50 rooms, 2 4-bedroom suites; restaurant, cocktail lounge.

FUJITA GUAM TUMON BEACH HOTEL, 300 rooms, incl. 45 family rooms with kitchenette; completely air-conditioned; dining room "Latte" serving Japanese and Western cuisine, coffee shop, snack bar, nightclub, sushi bar, Japanese restaurant, cocktail lounge, swimming pool, barbecue, game centre, tennis court.

GUAM CONTINENTAL, 203 units; suites in Japanese, American, Filipino style; completely air-conditioned, restaurant, 24-hour coffee shop, lounge with nightly entertainment, shops, fishing boats, sailboats, outrigger canoes, scuba equipment, swimming pool; on Tumon Bay beach.

GUAM DAI-ICHI HOTEL, 202 rooms, suites; central air-conditioning, dining room, Japanese and Chinese restaurant, bar, cocktail lounge, theatre nightclub, sailboats, outrigger canoes, swimming pool.

GUAM DAI-ICHI ANNEX, 200 rooms, dining room, meeting room, lounge, gift shop, bars.

GUAM HILTON, 375 rooms, completely air-conditioned, 3 dining rooms, 24-hour coffee shop, snack bar, 2 bars, cocktail lounge, nightclub; fishing boats, scuba instruction, swimming pool, indoor games, tennis courts, sauna; 400-seat meeting room; beach resort.

GUAM HOTEL OKURA, 230 rooms with ocean view, suite; completely air-conditioned, dining room, Chinese restaurant, Teppanyaki Corner, Terrace Restaurant, bar, cocktail lounge, 24-hour coffee shop, nightly entertainment; swimming pool, tennis courts, game room, water sports; on Tumon Bay beach.

MENDIOLA APARTMENT HOTEL, 78 units.

TUMON VIEW APARTMENTS, two-bedroom units with kitchenettes.

PACIFIC ISLANDS VILLAGE. All facilities including sports centre.

GUAM REEF HOTEL, 300 rooms, suite; air-conditioned, 3 restaurants, 3 lounges, swimming pool, beach resort with fishing boats, coral viewing, sailboats, scuba facilities; 4 meeting rooms up to 150 seats; at Tumon Beach.

MAGELLAN HOTEL, 30 rooms, has community kitchen; near business centre.

MICRONESIAN HOTEL, 100 rooms, with/

without private bath, some with kitchenettes; air-conditioning available, dining room, basketball court.

GUAMERICA HOTEL, 78 rooms.

JOINUS HOTEL, 40 rooms, cafe, shops, two Japanese restaurants, bar.

SUEHIRO HOTEL, 28 rooms, Japanese restaurant.

TERRAZA TUMON VILLA. Rooms and kitchenettes.

GUAM HORIZON. 104 units in an apartment complex.

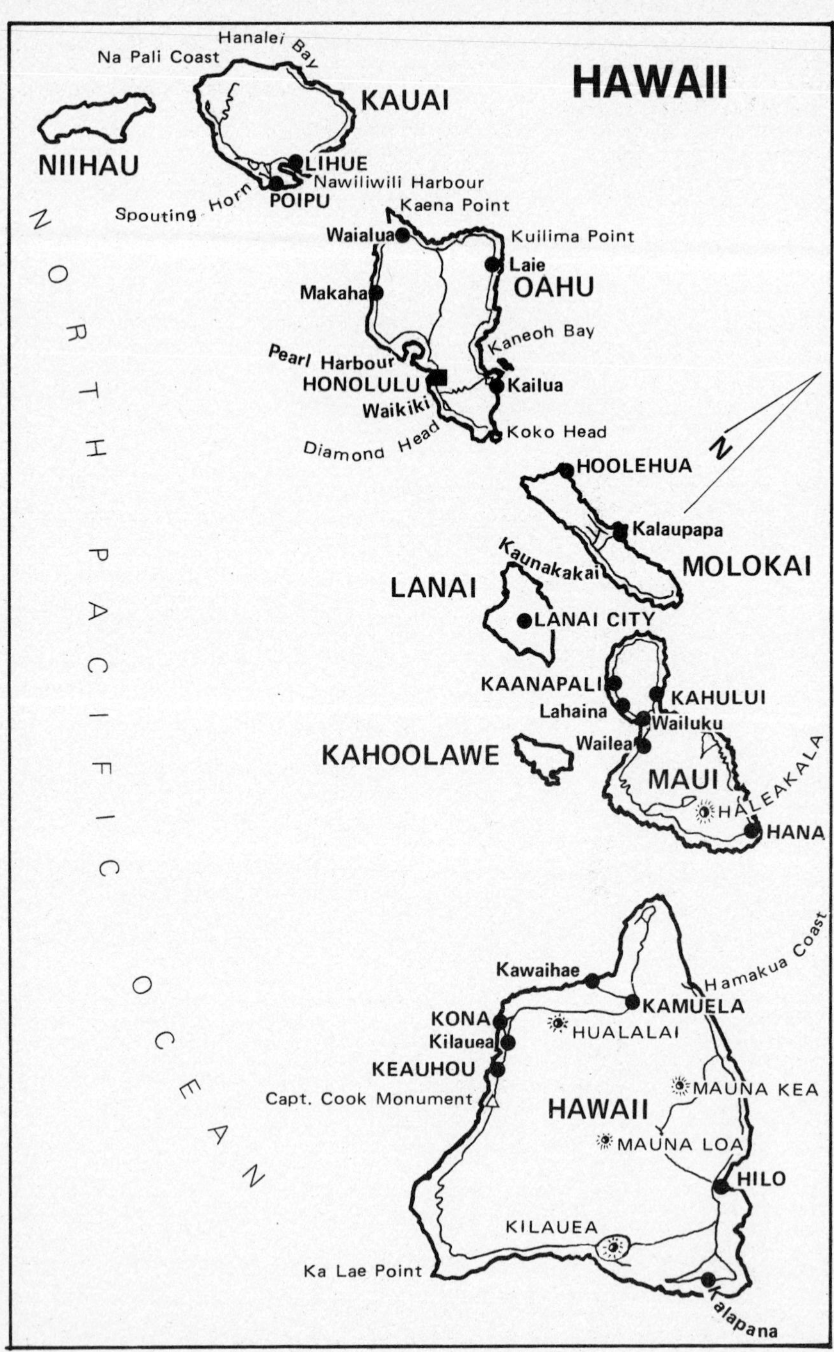
HAWAII
Hanalei Bay
Na Pali Coast
KAUAI
NIIHAU
LIHUE
Nawiliwili Harbour
POIPU
Spouting Horn
Kaena Point
Waialua
Kuilima Point
Laie
OAHU
Makaha
Kaneoh Bay
Pearl Harbour
HONOLULU
Kailua
Waikiki
Koko Head
Diamond Head
N
HOOLEHUA
Kalaupapa
Kaunakakai
MOLOKAI
LANAI
LANAI CITY
KAANAPALI
KAHULUI
Lahaina
Wailuku
Wailea
KAHOOLAWE
MAUI
HALEAKALA
HANA
NORTH PACIFIC OCEAN
Kawaihae
Hamakua Coast
KAMUELA
KONA
HUALALAI
Kilauea
KEAUHOU
MAUNA KEA
Capt. Cook Monument
HAWAII
MAUNA LOA
HILO
KILAUEA
Ka Lae Point
Kalapana

HAWAII

Hawaii, a state of the United States of America, consists of eight major inhabited islands and 124 minor ones (land area 16,638 sq. km) located between 18 deg. 50 min. and 28 deg. 15 min. N. latitude and 154 deg. 40 min. and 178 deg. 15 min. W. longitude. The capital is Honolulu on Oahu, which is about 6,200 km south-west of San Francisco. Local time is 10 hours behind GMT. Estimated population in 1976 was 887,000.

The state anthem is "Hawaii Ponoi"; the state flag consists of eight horizontal stripes (alternatively red, white and blue) representing the eight islands, with the British Union Flag in the upper left corner. The presence of the Union Flag commemorate's the British "connection" in the late 18th and early 19th centuries when the group was called the Sandwich Islands. The currency is the US dollar.

Public Holidays are: January 1, third Monday in February (President's Day), March 26 (Kuhio Day), Good Friday, the last Monday in May (Memorial Day), June 11 (Kamehameha Day), July 4, third Friday in August (Admission day), first Monday in September (Labor Day), second Monday in October (Columbus Day), fourth Monday in October (Veterans' Day), Christmas Day, Thanksgiving Day and all election days except primary election day.

THE PEOPLE. At the last decennial census in 1970, the total population of the state was 769,913. The estimated population in 1978 was 896,600.

The State's total population includes 58,100 members of the US armed forces and 61,000 of their dependants. Most of them live on the main island of Oahu where the capital, the city of Honolulu, has 352,100 people.

The population is young – the median age in 1977 was 28.3 years – and racially diversified. The major unmixed ethnic groups in 1977 were Caucasians (27.5 per cent of the non-barracks, non-institutional population) and Japanese (25.9 per cent). In addition, 25.7 per cent were of mixed race, primarily part-Hawaiian.

Migration. Migration has been a major factor in the growth of the population: between 1970 and 1978 there was a net immigration (excluding military personnel and dependants) of 55,700, accounting for almost half of the total civilian population growth during that time. Intended residents arriving aboard westbound civilian carriers in fiscal 1978 numbered 47,300, of whom 27,600 were military personnel and dependants and 19,700 were other civilians. Immigrants arrival in fiscal 1977 totalled 7,800, mostly from the Philippines and Korea.

Religion. Numerous religious groups are represented in the state with almost half the population belonging to Christian Churches, and principally Roman Catholic; Buddhist sects claim about a sixth of the population as members, with Shinto having the next largest number of adherents. Hawaii's many beautiful church buildings include the Mormon temple of Laie. Our Lady of Peace Cathedral, St Andrew's Cathedral, Central Union Church, and Kawaiahao Church on Oahu; Kaahumanu Church, Maui; St Benedicts, Hawaii; and Waioli Church, Kauai. There are many contemporary churches as well as Buddhist temples and ancient Hawaiian heiaus.

Lifestyle. Hawaii, particularly Oahu, is the most densely built-up of all the Pacific Islands; the archipelago has been developed as a tropical island playground and holiday resort for tourists, particularly Americans and Japanese. Rapid development has resulted in controversy with residents who want to preserve more of the traditional island lifestyles.

GOVERNMENT. Executive powers are vested in a governor and lieutenant governor elected every four years. The State has a bicameral legislature; 51 Representatives are elected from 25 Districts for two-year terms, and 25 Senators are elected from eight Districts for four-year terms, the legislature meets annually in Honolulu, the capital city.

Hawaii, as a State, elects a delegation to the US Congress – two Senators and two members of the House of Representatives.

Official election results are published by the office of the Lieutenant-Governor.

Local Government. Local Government is vested in one combined city-county (Honolulu, i.e. Island of Oahu and several outlying islets), three non-metropolitan counties (Hawaii, Kauai and Maui), and one area (Kalawao County) administered by the State Department of Health.

Justice. The State Judiciary includes a five member Supreme Court and four Circuit Courts with judges appointed by the governor with the consent of the State Senate. The State also has four District Courts whose judges are appointed by the Chief Justice of the Supreme Court.

Statistics on law enforcement, courts and correction in Hawaii appear in the annual reports of the county police departments, the State Judiciary, and the Department of Social Services and Housing.

DEFENCE. There are 110 military installations in the State of Hawaii, including the Commander-in-Chief Pacific whose command encompasses nearly 60 per cent of the earth's surface. Other major military bases include Pearl Harbor, Hickman Air Force base, Schofield Barracks, Kaneohe Marine Corps Air Station, and Barbers Point Naval Air Station.

The military controls 90,300 ha of land in Hawaii, including the entire island of Kaho'olawe and 25 per cent of Oahu. There are growing controversies over the military's bombing range on Kaho'olawe, the storage of nuclear weapons near residential communities on Oahu, and the potential radiation dangers from nuclear-powered warships operating out of Pearl Harbor. The State Health Department is beginning a programme to independently monitor marine life in and around Pearl Harbor for possible accumulation of radioactivity.

On July 1, 1978, military forces and dependants in Hawaii numbered 119,000. The Navy alone accounted for about half the total. In addition, 19,100 civilians were employed by the military. Total federal military expenditure in the state in 1978 was $US1,160 million, the second-largest source of income in the Hawaiian economy.

EDUCATION. The Hawaii State Department of Education supervises local teaching facilities. Enrolment in elementary, intermediate and high schools in 1978-1979 totalled 206,812. There were 229 public schools and 136 private schools in 1978 with 170,515 students and 36,297 students respectively. Some 49,736 students attended colleges and universities in the State in 1978-1979, chiefly the Manoa (Honolulu) campus of the University of Hawaii. The Hawaii State Library System has 45 locations with an annual circulation of 4.86 million. The University also maintains a second four-year campus in Hilo on the island of Hawaii, West Oahu College at Ewa, and a statewide community college system composed of seven two-year colleges. There are also four private four-year colleges.

East-West Center. This organisation for cultural and technical interchange between East and West is located at the University of Hawaii. It provides specialised and advanced academic courses and technical training for more than 1,500 students who each year are chosen from Pacific and Asian countries and from mainland USA.

Chief studies are in the Communication Institute, Food Technology and the Culture Learning Institute. An environment and policy Institute was established in 1977.

LABOUR. Details of employment and wage levels are collected by the Hawaii Employers Council and the Hawaii State Department of Labor and Industrial Relations.

The civilian labour force averaged 398,000 in 1978. The unemployment rate averaged 7.8 per cent. Activities with especially large numbers of employees include government (87,000 in 1978, about 34 per cent of them in federal jobs), services (89,000), and retail trade (79,000). The average annual earnings of wage and salary workers under the Hawaii Employment Security Law reached $10,903 in 1977. Specific industries include: government $13,768, construction $16,541, services $8,879. Classified by occupation group, average pay rates in 1978 ranged from $660 monthly for junior typist to $970 for secretary and $1,000 for entry level civil engineer.

Average weekly hours worked in 1978 ranged from 31.4 (for retail trade) to 44.4 (for communications and utilities). Labour union membership was estimated at 140,000 in 1976. Work stoppages in 1978 involved 1,800 workers. Hawaii's minimum wage under the State's Wage and Hour Law in 1979 was $2.90 per hour.

HEALTH. Major data on vital statistics and health come from the Hawaii State Department of Health and the US Public Health Service. Vital indices generally reflect the high health standards in the islands. The State had 22 acute care civilian hospitals (with 2,241 beds), 32 skilled nursing and intermediate care facilities (with 2,133 beds), and 253 care homes (with 1,666 beds) in 1977. There were 1,500 physicians and surgeons, 594 dentists, 5,127 professional nurses, and 340 pharmacists licensed and living in Hawaii in 1978.

Generally, causes of death in Hawaii now follow the mainland pattern with heart diseases accounting for one third all deaths in recent years and cancer, one fifth.

THE LAND. The State consists of eight major islands and 124 minor ones with a total land area of 16,638 square kilometres.

Honolulu, on the island of Oahu, is 342 km from the second largest city, Hilo, on the largest island, Hawaii. Triangular in shape, Hawaii is 150 km long by 120 km wide. The archipelago extends 2,560 km. Highest mountains are Mauna Kea (4,206 m) and Mauna Loa (4,170 m) which are both on the island of Hawaii.

The Hawaii Islands are mountainous, of volcanic origin, with extensive coastal plains and cool plateaux, as on Hawaii itself.

Natural features. The longest stream is

Kaukonahua Stream (Oahu), 53 km in length; the biggest lake is Halaii, 336 hectares, on Niihau Is; and the biggest named waterfall is Kahiwa, a 574-metre cascade, on Molokai. Daily information for best volcanic viewing areas and any earthquake activity is provided by the Hawaii Volcanoes National Park telephone service. Further detailed geographical data are given in "Hawaii, the Natural Environment", published by the State Department of Planning and Economic Development.

Climate. The islands have remarkably balmy temperatures and wide variations in rainfall. The all-time temperature range in down-town Honolulu, for example, is from 14-31 deg. C. Normal precipitation, however, ranges from 140 mm near Kawaihae to 13.28 m atop Waialeale. The islands are not subject to typhoons.

Flora and fauna. Official flowers have been established for each of the eight main islands. The State flower is the hibiscus and the State tree is the candlenut *(Aleurites moluccana)*. Local plantings include orchids and other exotica besides the street displays of magnificent tropical flowering trees. Among local wild life, the Hawaiian goose is the State bird emblem.

The fertile volcanic soil produces abundantly, with tropical fruits and forests.

Land tenure. Land ownership in Hawaii puts 58 per cent of property in private hands with 35 per cent owned by the state and 7 per cent belonging to the federal government.

PRIMARY PRODUCTION. Statistics on Hawaiian agriculture exclude *pakalolo* (marijuana) and other illicit plants. Some authorities have speculated that the income from such illegal production may exceed that from more traditional forms of diversified agriculture. Annual income from pakalolo in Hawaii has been estimated at $1 billion.

Sugar is Hawaii's main legal crop and all production, less local requirements, goes to the United States mainland.

Hawaii is not self-sufficient in food production. In 1978, Hawaii produced 41 per cent of the fresh market vegetables consumed locally, 28 per cent of the chickens, none of the rice, and 90 per cent of the eggs.

The total value of crop sales in 1978 was $306 million. Major crops in 1978 were sugar ($183 million in sales), pineapple ($63 million), and flowers and nursery products ($17 million). Livestock sales in 1978 amounted to $73 million.

The total areas planted in 1978 were: sugar 89,400 ha; pineapples 17,800 ha; macadamia nuts 4,100 ha; coffee 1,000 ha; other fruits and vegetables 6,600 ha.

The commercial fish catch in fiscal 1978 was 6.2 million kg. Skipjack (Aku) accounted for 35 per cent of the total. Commercial fishermen numbered 2,574; they operated 1,437 fishing vessels serving 44 fishery wholesaling and processing establishments.

Forest products harvested in 1977 had a value of $3.5 million.

MANUFACTURING AND MINING. Mineral production in 1978 totalled US$51 million, most of it in cement and stone, with small quantities of sand, gravel, pumice, volcanic cinder and lime.

The value added by manufacture rose from $326 million in 1967 to $700 million in 1976. About 72 per cent of all manufacturing activity in the State was on Oahu in 1976. Food processing – mostly sugar and pineapple – accounted for more than half of the value added by manufacture in that year.

Hawaii has more than 700 companies engaged in manufacturing. Heavy manufacturing includes an oil refinery that turns out all petroleum products; two cement plants; a steel mill manufacturing reinforcing rods; an aluminium extrusion plant and a concrete pipe plant.

Light manufacturing includes 70 garment factories that produce Hawaiian-type sportswear and other clothing, much of it from textiles screen-

HAWAII — CROP SALES
(In US$'000)

	1968	1978
Sugar, unprocessed cane (1,000 tons)	11,280	9,263
Pineapples, fresh ('000 tons)	921	675
Macadamia nuts in shell ('000 kg)	4,741	9,988
Coffee parchment ('000 kg)	2,588	808
Vegetables, melons, taro (1,000 tons)	97,073	157,890

Hawaii — Crop Sales
(In US$'000)

	1968	1978
Sugar, unprocessed cane	111,200	182,700
Pineapple fresh equivalent	35,900	63,000
Macadamia nuts in shell	2,381	10,714
Coffee parchment	1,471	2,072
Vegetables, melons, taro	10,463	30,325
	161,415	288,811

printed in Hawaii; home and office furniture; plastics; adhesives; pumping equipment, handicrafts and apart from sugar mills and fruit and fish canneries a variety of food and drink products such as nuts, fruit, candies, jams and jellies, beer, sake, rum and most brands of soft-drinks known on the U.S. mainland.

TOURISM. Tourism has shown rapid growth in recent years. It represents the largest source of income in the Hawaiian economy. Approximately 3,670,000 visitors stayed overnight or longer in Hawaii during 1978, compared with 1,315,000 in 1968 and only 172,000 in 1958. The average number of visitors present at any given time in 1978 was 96,000. Total visitor expenditures (exclusive of trans-Pacific fares) in 1978 amounted to $2.2 billion compared with $440 million a decade earlier. The 1978 visitor total included 2,500,000 from the U.S. mainland, 315,000 from Canada, and 470,000 from Japan. Expenditures per visitor day in 1977 averaged $54.62 for westbound visitors and $146.85 for the Japanese.

Information on tourism and recreation is issued by the Hawaiian Visitors Bureau, the State Parks Division of the Department of Land and Natural Resources, the U.S. National Park Service etc.

LOCAL COMMERCE. By mid-1979, more than 31,000 corporations and partnerships were registered to do business in Hawaii: 21,088 local ("domestic") corporations; 3,149 out-of-state ("foreign") corporations; and 6,965 partnerships. Business units with one or more employees as of 1977 numbered 18,660, including 257 with 100 or more employees. During fiscal year 1979, 3,233 new local corporations were formed and 1,168 existing local corporations were dissolved or merged.

Business receipts of corporations approached $9.1 billion in 1975; business receipts of proprietorships in the same year amounted to $660 million. Hawaii's largest corporation, Amfac, Inc., reported 1978 sales of $1.5 billion, with a net profit of $42 million.

Prices. In April, 1979, the Honolulu all-items consumer price index for all urban consumers stood at 200.7, with the 1967 level equal to 100. The index had increased 10.6 per cent in the preceding 12 months, 45.8 per cent since April, 1974, and 87.2 per cent since April, 1969.

An "intermediate" budget for a four-person family living on Oahu was estimated at $23,099 as of 1978. This family budget was 24 per cent higher than the corresponding urban United States average, and was second only to Anchorage, Alaska, among major American metropolitan areas. Hawaii-U.S. mainland differentials were greatest for rents and least for clothing.

Housing. The number of housing units in the State in 1979 numbered 287,000. Less than half are owner occupied. The average selling price of single family homes on Oahu during the year ending February 28, 1979, was $114,000. The median gross monthly rent for Oahu rose from $140 in 1970 to $234 in 1976.

Income, expenditures, and wealth. The gross state product in 1976 amounted to approximately $7.4 billion. Per capita income in 1978 was $8,437. This exceeded the national average by 8 per cent, and thus failed to compensate for the Islands' 24-30 per cent higher cost of living. Top wealthholders in Hawaii – those with gross assets of $60,000 or more numbered 53,700 in 1972. Total assets of this group amounted to $7.9 billion, 40 per cent of which was in real estate.

OVERSEAS TRADE. Most of Hawaii's trade is with the U.S. mainland but, due to geographical location, there is a growing trade with Asia. Among the foreign nations, Hawaii's leading trading partners in 1977 were Indonesia for imports and Australia for exports. Imports from Indonesia amounted to $257 million, or 26 per cent of the total, while exports to Australia reached $23 million, or 24 per cent of all foreign exports. The Indonesian imports consisted mostly of crude oil.

Imports to Hawaii from foreign nations totalled $1.1 billion in 1978. Exports to foreign countries in 1978 totalled $137 million. Merchandise received from the U.S. mainland totalled $1.8 billion in 1976, the most recent year available. Merchandise exported to the mainland totalled $415 million in 1976.

Foreign-owned U.S. firms in Hawaii operated 138 establishments in 1976, and employed 7,729 persons with an annual payroll of $71 million. Out of 39,782 hotel rooms in the State as of July, 1978, 8,381 (or 21.1 per cent) were foreign owned.

HAWAII — OVERSEAS TRADE
($US million)

	Imports foreign	**Exports** foreign
1968	139	49
1978	1,100	137
	Imports U.S.	**Exports** U.S.
1966	689	311
1972	1,220	350
1976	1,800	415

Overseas Investment. The Department of Planning and Economic Development provides assistance with business information and trends, contact, etc. to foreign investors.

Imports. Of the imports from foreign countries in 1978, the main source was again Indonesia, followed by Japan, Singapore, Brunei, Taiwan, Malaysia, Oman, the Bahamas, Hong Kong and West Germany. Indonesian imports to Hawaii totalled $246,609,000 in 1978, mainly in the form of petroleum products.

FINANCE. The total public revenue collected in 1978 amounted to $2,229 million derived by U.S. government tax ($1.2 billion), Hawaii State ($996 million), and county tax (434 million). Individual income taxes accounted for 85 per cent of Federal collections and 23 per cent of State collections. State revenue receipts totalled $1,421 million, chiefly from the General Excise and Use Tax ($368 million) and Federal grants-in-aid ($376 million). The largest expenditure item in the State accounts for 1978 was education – $450 million.

In June, 1978, there were eight banks with 171 branches, 10 savings and loan associations with 115 branches, three trust companies, and 238 industrial loan or small loan licensees in Hawaii. Deposits in island banks totalled $3.6 billion in 1978. Assets of savings and loan associations stood at $2.9 billion in mid-1978. There were 158 credit unions with combined assets of $704 million at the end of 1978.

Further details on Hawaii government statistics are supplied by the Hawaii State Departments of Accounting and General Services, Budget and Finance and Taxation.

Currency. Hawaii uses U.S. dollars and cents.

TRANSPORT. Most local travel in Hawaii is by private car, resulting in major traffic congestion in recent years. The State had 6220 km of public streets and highways; 580,000 registered motor vehicles, and 81,000 registered bicycles at the end of 1978. Hawaii residents purchased 45,993 new passenger cars in 1978. Revenue from local bus service in Honolulu during 1978 amounted to $9.7 million. Honolulu bus fare increased from 25c to 50c in 1979. Bus passengers carried by Honolulu Mass Transit lines in 1978 totalled 67.7 million.

The State has 11 commercial airports, 49 general aviation, military or private airports, 14 civilian heliports, 3,586 active pilots, and 541 active civil aircraft.

Air services. Hawaii is served by regular international flights in many directions, including Pan AM and Qantas. There are eight Air New Zealand flights each week through Honolulu linking Los Angeles, Nadi, Rarotonga, Auckland and Australia. Most scheduled inter-island domestic travel is now by air. In 1977 there were a number of air taxis and two major airlines – Aloha Airlines and Hawaiian Air. Using DC9 aircraft, Hawaiian Air flies to 7 airports from Honolulu – Hilo, Waimea-Kohala, Keahole, Kahului, Molokai, Lanai and Lihue.

There are 50 airfields, 14 being state-operated, 6 for the military and 30 private airstrips, mostly on sugar plantations. The main airports are as follows: Honolulu International Airport (Oahu Is.); General Lyman Field at Hilo, Upolu, Waimea-Kohala and Ke-ahole (Hawaii); Hana, Kahului and Kaanapali (Maui); Lihue (Kauai); Kalaupapa and Molokai (Molokai); Lanai.

Port Facilities. There are three ports of entry in the Hawaiian Group – Honolulu, on Oahu; Hilo, on the island of Hawaii; and Kahului, on Maui Island.

Ports are under the control of the Department of Transportation, Harbours Division. Harbour Masters are in charge. After the usual quarantine and migration formalities cruising yachtsmen will be advised where they can tie up.

There are two yacht harbours in Honolulu – one in Honolulu Harbour proper and the other, Ala Wai Yacht Harbour, at Waikiki. For obvious reasons the latter is mostly favoured by yachtsmen; however, accommodation is strictly limited as all but a few berths are permanently occupied by local yachts.

Yachts also anchor off Diamond Head, near the Kahala Hilton Hotel etc.

Ships arriving in the main port of Honolulu in 1978 totalled 1,651 overseas vessels and 1,981 interisland.

The other main harbours, by volume of cargo handled are: Barbers Point (petroleum), Kahului (sugar), Hilo, Kaunakakai (fruits), Pearl Harbor (fuel), Nawiliwili, Kawaihae, Kaumalapau, Port Allen and Kalaupapa.

Shipping Services. Hawaii is well provided with local and overseas shipping links, particularly with the US mainland.

The chief source for transportation statistics is the Hawaii State Department of Transportation and its Highways, Harbors, and Airports Divisions.

Communications. Telephone service in the Hawaii group is operated by the Hawaiian Telephone Company which has over 659,000 telephones in service.

The company is a wholly owned subsidiary of the General Telephone and Electronics Corporation, one of the top industrial corporations of the United States.

Two undersea cables link Hawaii with the west coast of USA; other cables link Hawaii with Japan; and the British-Commonwealth COMPAC cable, which passes through Honolulu, is also in use.

The Hawaiian Telephone Co. participates in the Communications Satellite Corporation (COMSAT).

At the initiative of the University of Hawaii, the PEACESAT satellite is used for communication, particularly of a scientific, medical or general education manner, around the islands of the South Pacific.

Radio and television. There were 34 commercial and educational radio stations in the islands early in 1979. This included 25 on the regular broadcast band and nine FM stations. The State also had 15 television stations (13 commercial and two educational), including satellites but excluding translators. Ten cable TV companies served 97,000 subscribers. More than 96 per cent of all households had television sets, and half of the adults surveyed watched three or more hours daily.

Newspapers. Island publishers printed seven daily newspapers, numerous magazines and other periodicals, and a wide diversity of books. Newspaper circulation reported by the three English-language dailies averaged 215,400 in 1978. The major dailies are the "Honolulu Advertiser" and the "Honolulu

Star-Bulletin". There are also various ethnic papers, in Japanese, Filipino etc.

Of special interest to tourists are the "Waikiki Beach Press" and "Tourist News". All local entertainment facilities are described in the weekly booklet "This Week on Oahu".

Water, electricity, gas. Data on these facilities are available from the Hawaii State Public Utilities Commission. Electric current is 110-120 volts.

PERSONALITIES AND ORGANISATIONS

Governor: George R. Ariyoshi.
Lieutenant Governor: Jean S. King.
Senate, President: Richard S. H. Wong.
House of Representatives: Speaker James H. Wakatsuki.
Two Hawaii members of U.S. Senate: Spark M. Matsunga, Daniel K. Inouye.
Two Hawaii members of U.S. House of Reps.: Daniel K. Akaka, Cecil Heftel.

HEADS OF GOVERNMENT DEPARTMENTS

Director of Planning and Economic Development: Director Hideto Kono.
Director of Education: Charles Clark.
Director, Social Services and Housing Dept.: Andrew Chang.
Director, Health Department: George A. L. Yuen.
Chairman, Agriculture Department: John Farias
Director, Transportation Dept.: Ryokichi Higashionna.
Chief Justice: William S. Richardson.
Head of Military Forces, Commander-in-Chief, Pacific: Admiral R. L. J. Long.
Harbourmaster, Honolulu: Captain Donald Gately, P.O. Box 397, Honolulu, Hawaii 96809 (for commercial transport only.)
Hawaii Visitors Bureau: President, John G. Simpson, 2270 Kaiakaua Avenue, Honolulu, Hawaii 96815.

SPORTING FACILITIES. Hawaii has 1,600 recognised surfing locations and about 40 km of sandy, accessible beaches. Skin-diving and yachting are popular. There are 46 golf courses, 317 tennis courts and facilities for baseball, basketball and football.

CULTURAL GROUPS.

Commedia Repertory Co.: Hawaii Performing Arts Co.; Honolulu Community Theater; Honolulu Theater for Youth; University Theater; Univ of Hawaii; U.S. Army Recreation Services Theater Guild, Honolulu Symphony Orchestra.

SCIENTIFIC INSTITUTIONS, MUSEUMS AND OTHER CULTURAL ATTRACTIONS.

Oahu: Bernice P. Bishop Museum; Foster Botanical Gardens; Honolulu Academy of Arts; Iolani Palace; Kahuku Sugar Mill; Mission Houses Museum; Mormon Temple Grounds; National Memorial Cemetery; Pacific Submarine museum; Paradise Park; Polynesian Cultural Center; Queen Emma Summer Palace; Royal Mausoleum State Monument; Sea Life Park; U.S.S. Arizona; Wahiawa Botanical Gardens; Waikiki Aquarium; Waimea Falls.

Hawaii: Hulihee Palace; Kamuela Museum; Kilauea Visitor Center; Lyman House Memorial Museum.

Maui: Baldwin Home Missionary Museum; Hale Hoikeike; Halekii-Pihana State Monument.

Kauai: Hanalei Museum; Kauai Museum; Kokee Natural History Museum; Waioli Mission House.

Molokai: Kalaupapa Settlement.

ZOO.

Honolulu Zoo in Waikiki.

PARKS.

National: Haleakala, Hawaii Volcanoes, Kaloko-Honokohau National Cultural Park, Pu'uhonua o Honaunau National Historical Park, Puukohola Heiau National Historic Site.
State and County: There are altogether 61 state and 590 county parks.

HISTORY. The Hawaiian Islands are believed to have first been settled from the Marquesas Islands about 650 A.D. Artefacts found at several sites on the island of Hawaii and also at Bellows Beach, Oahu, are similar to artefacts found in the Marquesas. A second migration probably reached the islands from Tahiti some centuries later and overcame the original inhabitants, known in tradition as dwarfs called 'menehune'. Close resemblances between the languages of Hawaii and Tahiti, and Hawaiian traditions of an island called Kahiki (i.e. Tahiti) lend weight to theories of a migration from Tahiti. Whatever the precise truth was, Hawaii's migrants brought with them breadfruit, bananas, yams, sugar cane, taro, the sweet potato, dogs, pigs and chickens. The presence of the sweet potato among their food plants indicates contact of some kind with South America at some period.

Spanish Visits. Historical research has refuted old claims that the Hawaiian Islands were discovered in 1555 by a Spaniard named Juan Gaetan or Gaetano. However, survivors from one or more of the Spanish galleons that disappeared in the 16th and 17th centuries on voyages between the Philippines and Mexico may have reached the islands. Evidence suggesting this came to light in the early 'sixties when scientists at the Bishop Museum, Honolulu, found a piece of iron and a length of woven cloth (probably sail cloth) in the burial casket of a deified Hawaiian chief. The chief is reputed to have lived on the island of Hawaii in about the 16th century. Moreover, tradition has it that a number of white men once came ashore at Kealakekua Bay, Hawaii; that they were given wives, became chiefs and left light-skinned descendants. The elaborate helmets and feather capes that were worn by chiefly Hawaiians in the latter part of the 18th century may be further evidence of the arrival of castaway Spaniards. A few pieces of iron were also found in their possession at that time.

Cook's Discovery. To the outside world, the Hawaiian islands remained unknown until Captain James Cook discovered them on January 18, 1778. Cook was then on his third voyage to the Pacific, and was sailing northwards in search of the North-West Passage. At that time, he touched only at the north-westerly islands of Kauai and Niihau. But about 12 months later, in returning from the north-west coast of America, he also called at Maui and Hawaii. He was killed at Kealakekua Bay on February 14, 1779, when the Hawaiians apparently mistook him for the god Lono.

Cook's visit to the American coast resulted in the discovery of the sea otter whose fur was much in demand in China. This soon brought adventurers from Europe and the United States to the same area, and in crossing the Pacific to China to sell their furs, they generally put into Hawaii. The first ships to call were the British vessels 'King George' and 'Queen Charlotte' in 1786. Their commanders had both been on Cook's last voyage. The first American ship, 'Columbia', arrived in 1789.

Kamehamea I. The coming of the fur traders coincided with the rise of Kamehamea I, a member of a chiefly family of the island of Hawaii. After a series of fierce wars, Kamehamea unified all the Hawaiian islands under him and created a kingdom which lasted until 1893. He won a great naval victory in 1793 with cannon supplied by Europeans. Three years later, he sought help in his wars from the British explorer Captain George Vancouver, who misinterpreted his request, raised the British flag and took possession of the islands for the British Crown. Vancouver's proceedings were never ratified.

But Kamehamea's conquests continued. By 1795 Maui, Molokai, Oahu and Hawaii were under his control. Kauai submitted in 1810.

Disease Strikes. Meanwhile, visiting European and American ships, including numerous whalers from 1819 onwards, brought in new diseases that caused a rapid decline in the islands' native population. From perhaps as many as 300,000 in Cook's time, the numbers fell away to about 135,000 in 1820, about 85,000 in 1850, and 40,000 in 1890. The heavy mortality was accompanied by orgies of drunkenness, prostitution, gambling and other excesses. In 1819 there was a climax to this when the newly-installed Kamehamea II abolished the 'kapu' (tabu) system that had previously ruled the lives of the commoners. He also ordered the destruction of the ancient idols and places of worship.

First Missionaries. When the first European missionaries reached Hawaii in 1820, they were appalled by the disorder and demoralisation among the islanders. Some wondered whether it was really possible to civilise and Christianise such people. The missionaries were Calvinists from New England, sponsored by the American Board of Commissioners for Foreign Missions. Despite their misgivings, they and their wives quickly learned Hawaiian and concentrated their attention on the chiefs. While the women taught needlework, the male missionaries won many friends by treating the sick. They produced their first printed work in Hawaiian in 1822 and conducted their first baptism the following year. Meanwhile, the Hawaiian chiefess Kaahumanu, who acted as regent following the death of Kamehamea II in 1824, did much to bring about the formal conversion of the islands to Christianity. First, she ordered strict observance of the Sabbath; and later, in co-operation with the other chiefs, she decreed a code of laws against murder, theft, fighting and the breaking of the Sabbath. She also ordered the establishment of schools. The number of schools grew rapidly. By 1831, they had 50,000 students.

Christianity suffered a temporary setback after Kaahumanu's death in 1832. The young king Kamehamea III was a lukewarm convert. However, by 1835, another woman, the king's half-sister Kinau, had gained control of political affairs, and, through her, as one observer put it, the American missionaries could 'govern the islands with unlimited sway.' In 1838, under their influence, strict liquor laws were introduced, and four years later there were temperance laws. Increasingly, the missionaries, particularly those in Honolulu, became involved in the government. Some actually resigned from the mission and joined the government. Among those who exerted considerable influence were William Richards, Hiram Bingham, and Gerrit P. Judd. Judd was virtual dictator of Hawaii during a series of events that led Captain Lord George Paulet, of HMS 'Carysfort', to annex the islands for Great Britain on 25th February 1843. However, Hawaiian independence was restored by Paulet's commanding officer, Rear-Admiral Richard Thomas, five months later.

Annexation Efforts. In 1854, Judd, who had then been dismissed from office, pressed the United States to annex Hawaii. The proposal was strongly supported by American residents. But with the accession of Kamehamea IV, who had once been mistaken for, and was victimised as, a Negro in the United States, all hope of annexation vanished for the time being. It was during the reign of Kamehamea IV (1854-63) that the first successful oil well was drilled in the United States – at Philadelphia in 1859. This event and the outbreak of the American Civil War caused a rapid decline in the Pacific whaling industry that had been the basis of Hawaii's economy for many years. (By 1830, 150 ships had been visiting Hawaii annually; in 1846, there was a peak of 596; and even in 1859, the annual average was still over 500.)

With the loss of revenue from the sale of provisions and other goods to the whalers, Hawaii experienced hard times for several years. Then a new industry developed: sugar. This required plenty of labour, a commodity that Hawaii could not supply. As a result, many thousands of Islanders, Chinese, Japanese and Portuguese were imported. It was in this way that Hawaii's multi-racial population of today came into being.

With the development of the sugar industry and the decline in numbers of the Hawaiian population, the American Calvinist missionaries lost their predominance, and newer American settlers began to exert considerable influence. Among these was the unscrupulous Walter Murray Gibson, originally a Mormon missionary. Other settlers married into the Hawaiian royal family and thus gained an interest in large tracts of land. A well-known example of this was Charles Reed Bishop, a banker and statesman in the Hawaiian Government, who married the chiefess Bernice Pauahi, the last direct descendant of Kamehamea I. (In 1889, after her death, Bishop founded the Bernice Pauahi Bishop Museum as a memorial to her.)

Hawaii Becomes Republic. The last four monarchs of the Hawaiian kingdom were Kamehamea V (1863-72), Lunalilo (1873-74), Kalakaua (1874-91) and Queen Liliuokalani (1891-93). During Kalakaua's reign, Hawaii signed a reciprocity treaty with the United States that laid the foundation for the eventual annexation of the islands by the United States. The treaty was precipitated by political instability and corruption, and was followed by a revolution that broke out in 1893. An American move for annexation failed at that time because President Cleveland opposed it. The result was that Hawaii became a republic with Sanford B. Dole as president. However, agitation for annexation continued, and a resolution approving this was passed by the US Congress in June and July 1898.

US Flag Raised. On August 12 of that year, the American flag was raised in Hawaii and President Dole transferred jurisdiction to the United States. The islands were formally constituted as the Territory of Hawaii on June 14, 1900. Dole was appointed first governor.

The years from 1900 to 1940 were chiefly remarkable for the growth of the sugar industry and of the islands' multi-racial population. The area devoted to sugar increased from about 51,000 to 95,000 ha, while production increased from around 153,000 tonnes to well over one million tonnes annually. Pineapple-growing also thrived. At the same time, the total population of Hawaii increased from 154,000 to more than 423,000. The Japanese, with 61,116 in 1900 and 157,905 in 1940, were by far the largest ethnic group. Their percentage of the population remained more or less constant at about 40. Caucasians, with 26,252 in 1900 and 103,791 in 1940, became an increasingly larger percentage of the total – 17 per cent in 1900 and 24.5 per cent in 1940. Hawaiians and part-Hawaiians, on the other hand, declined percentagewise from nearly 25 to 15, although their numbers increased from 38,254 to 64,310. The fourth largest ethnic group in 1940 were the Filipinos. Their numbers then stood at 52,569, or 12.4 per cent of the whole population, compared with nil at the turn of the century.

Pacific War. World War II came to Hawaii with horrifying suddenness on 7 December 1941 when aircraft from a large Japanese armada bombed the naval base at Pearl Harbor on Oahu. Eighteen of the 96 ships in the harbour were either sunk or severely damaged, 2,403 Americans were killed, and 1,178 wounded. The attack brought the United States into the war and galvanised it into retaliatory action. Soon Oahu had become a huge staging centre for fighting the Japanese both in Asia and the Pacific Islands. Camps for basic and special training were set up, as well as hospitals, intelligence and operations centres. More than a million men passed through the Schofield Barracks during the war, and at its end there were 253,000 troops on Oahu, compared with only 43,000 when Pearl Harbour was bombed. Martial law prevailed until October 1944.

Postwar Development. After the war, Hawaii was faced with exceptional problems of readjusting to peace. Despite this, its two largest industries, sugar and pineapple-growing, grew apace, while beef, dairy milk, vegetables, eggs, coffee, poultry, tropical fruits and nuts became increasingly important money-earners. However, the most spectacular growth was experienced in the tourist industry. Large and lavish hotels sprang up throughout the group, and especially on the outer islands. Tourist numbers grew from 46,000 in 1950 to 243,000 in 1959, and then the figures began to soar to spectacular heights. The reason for this was Hawaii's emergence as the 50th state of the United States. The news coverage of this development had the effect of a multi-million dollar advertising campaign for the tourist industry. People in the mainland United States suddenly discovered where Hawaii was.

Statehood. An official proclamation declaring Hawaii a state was issued by President Eisenhower on August 21, 1959. It ended a long struggle in Hawaii to attain first-class American citizenship. Significantly, Hawaii's first representatives in the US Congress were drawn from three different ethnic groups – Caucasian, Japanese and Chinese. At that time, the number of Caucasians in Hawaii (202,000) almost matched the number of Japanese (203,000), due to heavy post-war migration. Each represented about a third of the total population. Since then, the number of Caucasians has surged well ahead. By 1967, for example, they represented 37 per cent of the total while the Japanese had dropped to 28 per cent.

During Hawaii's first decade of statehood, sugar and pineapples declined in economic importance while the tourist industry grew phenomenally. In 1966, for the first time, income from tourism passed the combined value of sugar and pineapples shipped to the mainland. That same year, almost a million tourists visited Hawaii, among whom were tens of thousands of GI's from Vietnam. During the next year or two, government spending associated with the Vietnam War was the state's biggest source of income.

As less than 20 per cent of Hawaii's total land area is suitable for intensive cultivation, the proliferation of hotels and the rapid growth in the permanent population has produced some weighty political problems. For example, should farmland be rezoned for urban use? Which natural and historic sites should be protected and preserved? Where and how high should hotel and apartment buildings rise? There are also serious environmental problems. An inquiry in 1971 revealed that 55 million gallons of untreated sewage were released from Honolulu each day into the ocean near Waikiki Beach; that Waikiki itself was overcrowded with tourist hotels; that Hawaii's air and water were polluted; and that the use of pesticides by the sugar and pineapple industries was ten times greater per hectare than on the mainland.

Despite facts such as these, the tourists have continued to come. By 1973, the yearly total was in the vicinity of two million, of whom about one-eighth were from Japan. The Japanese were also investing in the tourist industry, and had financial control of about 11 per cent of the 36,000 hotel rooms in the state. The permanent population in 1974 was estimated at 846,000, or almost twice the figure of 1940. By then, probably few if any residents of Hawaii could be described as pure-blooded Hawaiians, but a sizeable percentage still looked on themselves as ethnically Hawaiian. In 1974, these people demanded reparations from the United States for land appropriated from their ancestors in the 19th century, or, alternatively, the return of such land.

Further Information: Gerrit P. Judd, 'Hawaii: An Informal History', New York, 1961; Gavan Daws, 'Shoal of Time: a History of the Hawaiian Islands', Honolulu, 1968.

ISLANDS IN DETAIL

The eight major Hawaiian Islands are of volcanic origin, with coral reefs partly encircling most of them, but fully encircling none.

From south-east to north-west they are Hawaii, Maui and Kahoolawe, Lanai and Molokai. Oahu, Kauai, Niihau, and the North-West Islets that in all amount to 13 sq km. The archipelago is 2,560 km long and is situated between 18 deg, 50 min and 28 deg, 15 min. North latitude and 154 deg, 40 min and 178 deg, 15 min. West longitude. Total land area is 16,638 sq km and includes 130 atolls, islets, reefs and pinnacles.

The best harbours are at Honolulu and Pearl on Oahu; but there are deep water ports at Hilo and Kawaihae, on Hawaii (with container service available at Hilo); and at Kahului. Maui: barge facilities are available on Molokai, Lanai and at Hana on Maui. Ocean freighters can be berthed at all but Molokai; and Hilo and Honolulu can take large passenger liners.

HAWAII. With an area of 10,456 sq km, Hawaii is the largest island and also has the two highest mountains — Mauna Kea (4,206 m) and Mauna Loa (4,170 m) which are snow-capped in winter. There is also Kilauea, an active volcano and others which are dormant. The island is traversed by other mountains which give it a rugged and picturesque appearance. In places, cliffs rise boldly up to 900 m above the sea.

Hawaii, triangular in shape, is 150 km long by 170 km wide. There are cool plateaus on Hawaii, and thousands of sheep are grazed on Mauna Kea foothills. Several small rivers (the biggest being the Wailuku, which flows into Hilo Bay, through the city of Hilo) run off the slopes of Manua Kea on to the eastern coast.

Principal industries are sugar-growing and milling (13 mills), coffee production, beef cattle raising (Hawaii is responsible for half the beef produced in the state), and the growing and processing of macadamia nuts at Honokaa. Orchids are produced for export to the mainland and there is a growing tourist industry to this island with its diversity of terrain and climate from beachside to mountainside. Hilo airport will take large commercial jets but Honolulu on Oahu is the international terminal.

MAUI, the second largest island with an area of 1,886 sq km, is 89 km long and 40 km wide. It is divided into two masses by a low sandy isthmus. The eastern part consists of Haleakala ("House of the Sun"), a volcanic dome 3,056 m high with a crater-like depression in its summit, measuring 6.4 km by 11.2 km with walls up to 900 m deep, and cinder cones up to 300 m high looking like ant hills on its 65 sq km floor.

West Maui mountains result from an older, much eroded volcanic dome (1,765 m high), cut by great valleys. Rainfall here approaches 10,200 mm a year.

The low isthmus is dry, but the soil is fertile and is suitable for sugar cane when irrigated. Water is brought from the wet windward slopes of Haleakala in ditches which run through tunnels. On slopes above, pineapples and a variety of truck crops are grown on homesteads. Cattle graze on lush grasslands.

Pineapple and sugar cultivation are the main industries on Maui but there is also a rum distillery, food processing and garment manufacture. Tourism and scientific research are also

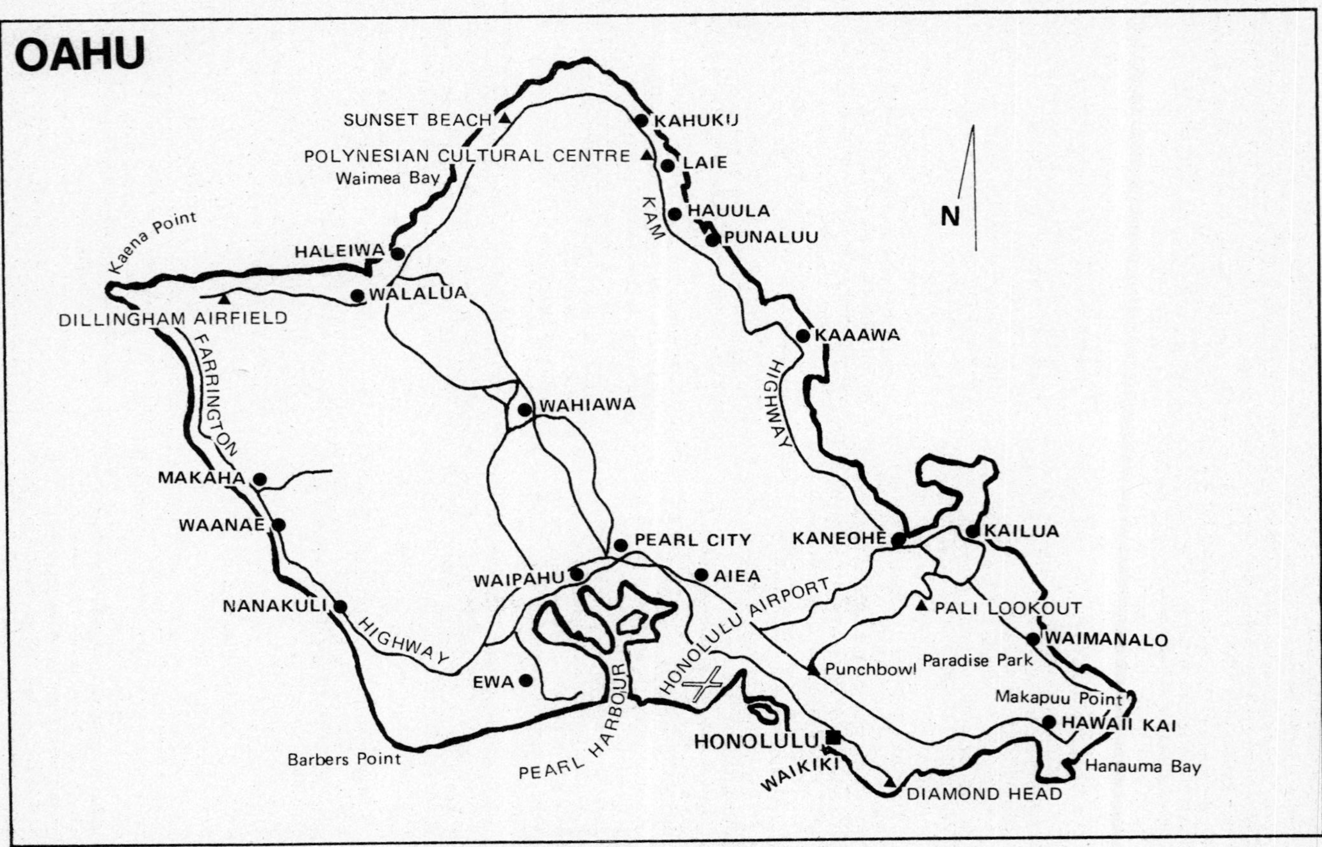
OAHU
N
SUNSET BEACH
KAHUKU
POLYNESIAN CULTURAL CENTRE
LAIE
Waimea Bay
KAM
HAUULA
PUNALUU
Kaena Point
HALEIWA
WALALUA
DILLINGHAM AIRFIELD
KAAAWA
FARRINGTON
HIGHWAY
WAHIAWA
MAKAHA
WAANAE
PEARL CITY
KANEOHE
KAILUA
WAIPAHU
AIEA
NANAKULI
HONOLULU AIRPORT
PALI LOOKOUT
WAIMANALO
HIGHWAY
Punchbowl
Paradise Park
EWA
PEARL HARBOUR
Makapuu Point
HAWAII KAI
HONOLULU
Barbers Point
Hanauma Bay
WAIKIKI
DIAMOND HEAD

important sources of revenue.

Scientific laboratories are located on the rim of the Haleakala Crater where a $US5 million infra-red tracking station and astro-physical observatory was completed for the US Department of Defense in 1965. The observatory houses a 152.4 mm reflector telescope and two 122 mm infra-red telescopes. The station is operated by the University of Michigan and the University of Hawaii.

The Institute of Geophysics of the University of Hawaii also has observatories on Haleakala — a solar laboratory and an air-glow zodiacal light observatory. The Smithsonian Institution has a satellite tracking station nearby. The US Air Force and the Federal Aviation Agency also have facilities there. Haleakala is part of the Hawaii Volcanoes National Park. There are airports at Kahului, Hana and Kaanapali.

MOLOKAI (676 sq km) is the main pineapple-growing area and it is also a cattle raising location. There is a leprosy hospital on an isolated peninsula of the north coast and there is also an airport. From the Sheraton-Molokai Hotel at the western end of the island, visitors can see African and other exotic animals on Molokai Ranch where they are bred and raised for sale to zoos.

KAHOOLAWE (116.6 sq km), just south of Maui, is barren and uninhabited. It is used as a target island for gunnery and other practice by the U.S. armed forces.

LANAI (361 sq km), a hilly island with a peak of 1,027 m is south of the passage between Molokai and Maui. Its people are mostly pineapple growers. This island has an airport.

OAHU with the city of Honolulu (''Fair Haven'' — originally known as Brown's Harbour), is intensively developed and has a very large population. It is the third largest island (64 km long and 42 km across) and the two mountain ranges have altitudes up to 1,500 metres, but are eroded into ridges and valleys. Pearl Harbor, a naval base, is situated on the southern coast of Oahu.

The City of Honolulu and, in effect, the whole island of Oahu is the centre of business, government and tourism for the State of Hawaii. Although it is the smallest area of the four counties into which the state is divided, it had 38 per cent of the state's population (about 886,000 including military personnel) in 1976. Total area of Oahu is 1,535 sq km.

Pineapples, sugar and diversified crops are grown in the rural areas but there are also heavy and light manufacturing industries and rapidly expanding research and development activities, especially in the fields of oceanography, astrophysics, geogphysics and biomedicine. In addition to governmental organisations engaged in research, the Oceanic Institute, the Bishop Museum, the Pineapple Research Institute and the Hawaiian Sugar Planters' Experiment Station are among the private research organisations.

Waikiki is the primary destination of many thousands of tourists who visit Hawaii each year. Most pass through Honolulu's $25 million international airport.

Apart from the beaches, hotels restaurants and night-life, tourists find much to interest them in Honolulu and its environs. It is the academic centre of the state, has the State Library, the Academy of Arts and historical buildings like the Iolani Palace, (once the residence of Hawaiian royalty) and the State Capitol built in 1969. The National Memorial Cemetery is located in Punchbowl, an extinct volcano crater and there lie thousands of the dead of the Pacific War.

The island has a first-class highway system (exceeding 1600 km of high quality roads) and some spectacular scenery. At Makaha on the west or windward coast, a spectacular surf provides the venue for international surfing competitions. At Laie, on the north-east corner of Oahu, is the Polynesian Cultural Plaza where the cultures of Hawaii, Tahiti, Tonga, Samoa, Fiji and the New Zealand Maori are displayed in a natural setting.

The rainfall on Oahu varies with location in relation to the prevailing winds and the mountains. Honolulu City itself receives about 700 mm a year but the rainfall a few kilometres away in the hills can be many times this amount.

Average annual temperature in Honolulu is 24 deg C. with little seasonal variation.

KAUAI (1,421 sq km) is fourth in size and has an oval shape roughly 48 km by 41.5 km. It is considered by many visitors to be the most beautiful island of the group. Its high interior (up to 1,598 m) has heavy rainfall, up to 11.5 metres a year, which forms numerous rivers, rushing down fertile valleys to glistening white beaches. The slopes are well forested and plantations of sugar cane and pineapples are established on the coastal plains. The largest town on Kauai is Lihue; most people live on the south east and north coastal plains.

Growing and processing sugar cane is the main industry but tourism has now become a significant influence on the economy. Hotel building has been booming and as the island is only 166 km from Honolulu, day trips by air are feasible.

There is excellent swimming at beaches and freshwater pools, good hunting and fishing. There are many camping grounds, picnic facilities and playgrounds. The airport at Lihue is capable of taking short range jets. There are 480 km of roads.

Kauai is the main island in Kauai County which also includes the 180 sq km of Niihau and the two small uninhabited islands of Kaula and Lehua (less than 1.5 sq km each). Niihau is privately owned and not accessible to the public.

FOR THE TOURIST. Hawaii's fame as an international pleasure destination hardly needs describing. Most of its claims are true. The exhilarations of nature burst from its surf, there are volcanoes, luxuriant flowers and fruits. Lessons in human communications flow from its East-West Center, the Bishop Museum, Polynesian Cultural Center, or even Sea Life Park but, mostly from Hawaii's unique cultural mixture and the aloha spirit of its people. For tourists who need any stores, there is the vast Ala Moana Shopping Center near Waikiki Beach.

Hotels. There is ample publicity material to guide the visitor through Hawaii, and to offer visitors a wide choice of hotels and accommodations. On the main island of Oahu, in the Waikiki-Honolulu area there were 133 hotels in 1979. Maui island has 115 as of 1979; Kauai – 46; Hawaii – 61; Molokai – 5; and Lanai – 1.

Duty-free. These facilities are available at the Honolulu international airport. Shopping centres around Honolulu are designed in very attractive fashion with all manner of imported goods from the U.S. mainland and Asia as well as offering local fruits and flowers, "Aloha" shirts and other casual wear.

Airport Tax. There is no airport tax.

Sightseeing. The two remaining centres of volcanic activity in the Hawaiian islands, Mauna Loa and Kilauea, lie within the Hawaii Volcanoes National Park, covering 92,000 hectares, on the island of Hawaii. Each of these has a caldera (or super-crater), within which there are periodic outbreaks of molten lava.

The volcanoes park conserves the most representative areas of volcanic interest in the United States. Its craters, active and dormant, are among the most important in the entire world and even the active ones may be visited with reasonable safety.

State Monuments. On Oahu Is.: Diamond Head State Mon.: Iolani Palace: Puu O Mahuka: Royal Mausoleum: Ulu Po Heiau. Washington Place: U.S.S. Arizona Memorial.

Hawaii: Hikiau Heiau State Mon., Lava Tree:
Maui: Hale Kii-Pihana State Mon.:
Kauai: Russian Fort State Mon.

Bernice P. Bishop Museum. Honolulu is the home of one of the most important scientific and cultural institutions in the Pacific – the Bernice P. Bishop Museum. Its field workers have carried out exacting ethnological and natural history research in almost every group of South Pacific islands and its ancient Polynesia collections and present-day specimens are world famous. The Museum is a memorial to the Princess Bernice Pauahi, last of the Kamehamea family of Hawaii chiefs, and was founded in 1889 by her husband, Charles Reed Bishop, who was prominent for 50 years in the public and business affairs of Hawaii.

Visitors' Bureau. The Hawaii Visitors Bureau at 2270 Kalakaua Avenue, Honolulu is responsible for overseas promotion of the islands and has offices in Tokyo and throughout the U.S. mainland. Other overseas representation includes Hawaiian Air at 75 Miller Street, North Sydney, Australia.

HOWLAND AND BAKER ISLANDS

These two islands, both American possessions, are almost on the Equator some 1,100 km due east of Kiribati and about 600 km NW of Kanton and Enderbury Islands in the Phoenix group. They are about 56 km apart. With Jarvis Island in the Line group Howland and Baker were declared to be American possessions by Presidential order in 1936 when various islands in the Central Pacific seemed potentially valuable to trans-Pacific aviation. The United States claim to the three islands was based on the Guano Act of 1856 which had listed them as American possessions. Earlier, in May 1935, several American colonists were landed on each island. They were evacuated after Japan entered World War II.

HOWLAND ISLAND. Howland is about 2.5 km long by a little less than 1 km wide. It is low and sandy, with one patch of trees about three metres high. A fringing reef surrounds it. Vegetation is sparse, but there is a large bird population, of which the most common species is the blue-faced booby.

Captain Daniel Smith of the New Bedford whaler 'Minerva' discovered the island in 1828 and named it after his ship's owner. American then British interests worked the island's guano between 1858 and 1890. Thereafter, the island was deserted until American colonists were landed there in 1935. Two years later, an airfield was hurriedly constructed for the US fliers Amelia Earhart and Fred J. Noonan who were attempting to fly around the world. However, the pair disappeared after leaving Lae, PNG, on July 2, 1937. A beacon there is now called the Amelia Earhart Light.

BAKER ISLAND. Baker Island is about 1.5 km long and a little less wide. It is about eight metres above sea level, and treeless.

Captain Obed Starbuck of the whaler 'Loper' discovered the island in 1825 and named it New Nantucket. It takes its present name from Captain Michael Baker, another American, who visited it in 1832 and again in 1839 to bury a member of his crew. On the second occasion, he was struck by the curious nature of the soil, and suspecting it to be guano, raised the American flag. After analysis of samples taken to the United States confirmed his suspicions, he sold his claim to the American Guano Co.

Representatives of the American Guano Co. landed on the island in February 1857, and a US naval vessel called there in the following August to survey the island and take official possession in the name of the United States. The company worked the deposits from 1859 to 1878. John T. Arundel & Co., of London, did the same from 1886 to 1891.

American colonists landed on the island in April 1935 and built a lighthouse and several substantial dwellings. The island is said to be visited annually by the US Coast Guard.

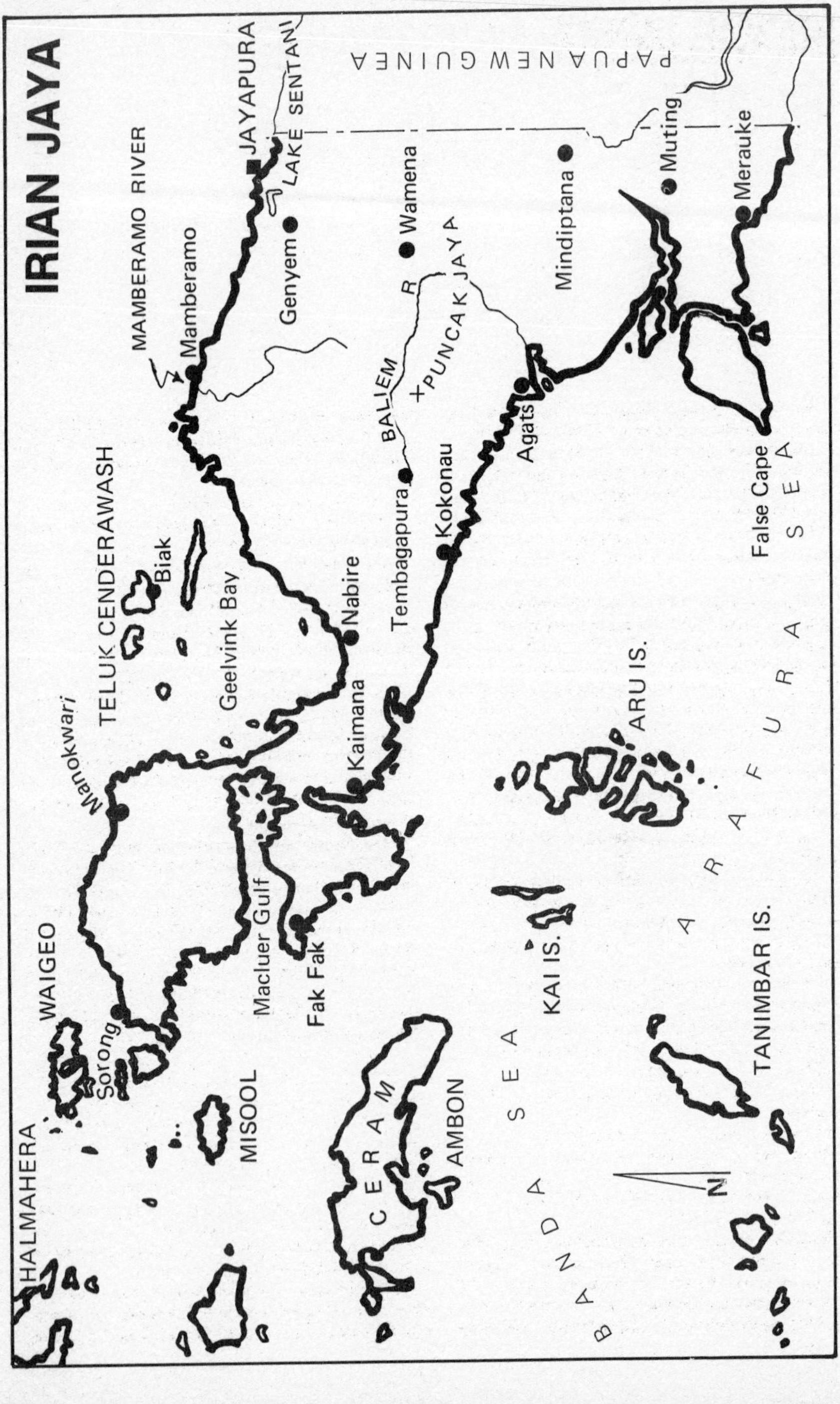

IRIAN JAYA
MAMBERAMO RIVER
JAYAPURA
LAKE SENTANI
PAPUA NEW GUINEA
Mamberamo
Genyem
Wamena
BALIEM R
PUNCAK JAYA
Mindiptana
Muting
Merauke
TELUK CENDERAWASH
Biak
Geelvink Bay
Nabire
Tembagapura
Kokonau
Agats
Manokwari
Kaimana
WAIGEO
Sorong
Macluer Gulf
Fak Fak
HALMAHERA
MISOOL
CERAM
AMBON
BANDA SEA
KAI IS.
ARU IS.
TANIMBAR IS.
ARAFURA SEA
False Cape
N

IRIAN JAYA

Irian Jaya, the easternmost province of the Republic of Indonesia, consists of that half of New Guinea west of the 141 deg. E. longitude, and certain offshore islands. The capital of the province is Jayapura and local time is 9 hours ahead of GMT. Population was estimated at 1,037,740 in 1977.

The national anthem and flag are those of Indonesia, as are the public holidays. The currency is the rupiah.

THE PEOPLE. The 1,037,740 inhabitants of Irian Jaya in 1977 were composed of various tribes, such as the Mukoko of Baliem Valley, the Ekari of the Wissel Lakes region, the Arfak at Kepala Burung, the Muju of Merauke District, and so forth. Each tribe is broken down again into still smaller units. Because of the harshness of the terrain, they are spread over a large area in small groups, kept apart by such other factors as dialect and customs. The various races evident in West Irian are Australoid, Melanesoid, Pygmoid, Weddoid and Paleo-Mongoloid according to anthropologist Professor Kleiweg de Zwaan.

The people inhabiting the coastal areas consist mostly of overseas aliens and emigrant families from the interior living in mixed villages.

The Papuan population is estimated at approximately 925,000.

There were an estimated 4,800 foreigners living in Irian Jaya in 1971, of whom the most numerous were Chinese (2,810), followed by Americans (679), and Dutch (358). Some 250 missionaries are included in the total number of foreigners.

Indonesians from other provinces make up the remainder.

Urban population is estimated at 260,480.

Irian Jaya's largest town is the provincial capital, Jayapura, with some 47,400 inhabitants. The next biggest are Sorong (44,900), Manokwari (27,500) and Merauke (21,366).

Nationality. All original inhabitants of Irian Jaya are "Indonesians" and "Indonesian citizens" ("warga negara") by law. Terminologies used by the Indonesians with reference to Irian Jayan people included "penduduk asli" (autochthones). Now the more prestigious term "putra daerah" (son of the region) is more commonly used to contrast with the immigrant group referred to as "pendatang" (newcomers).

Although the younger generation call themselves "orang Irian" (Irianese), the older generation refer to themselves as "orang Papua" (Papuans).

Irian Jaya has its representation in Jakarta, the SEKUIB ("Sekretariat Urusan Irian Barat" – Secretariat for West Irian Affairs) which until 1969 – the year of the Act of Free Choice – was part of the Ministry of Internal Affairs but was later transferred to the Ministry of Foreign Affairs.

There is also a club House for the Irianese community and guests, located at Tanah Abang in Jakarta bearing the name of "Wisma Koreri" (Koreri House) where students, teachers, public servants and policemen from Irian Jaya who come to Jakarta for schooling, training and conferences, are accommodated.

Language. Melanesian languages are restricted in Irian Jaya to a few coastal districts, where they appear strongly mixed with Papuan elements. Outside the central mountain country there are only a few areas in which more than a few thousand people speak the same language. The structure of these small language territories reflects the isolation in which the people lived, divided into an endless variety of small groups. There are at least 250 main languages spoken daily by as many tribes.

Malay has become the lingua franca of contemporary Irian Jaya but government long-term policy is the universal use of Bahasa-Indonesian.

Migration. Migration – or more particularly transmigration – has considerable significance in the development of Irian Jaya.

Contact with the outside world has occurred in Irian Jaya for several centuries. To appreciate this, one has only to observe the many mixed Melanesian-Malay types among the coastal people in Sorang, Biak, Merauke and Fakfak.

Transmigration – a temporary or permanent resettlement of people within the boundaries of the same State – was practised in what was the Dutch

East Indies well before World War II, when the Dutch imported indentured Javanese labourers for their coconut plantations in the Merauke district. Their descendants today are rice farmers around Merauke.

Tanah Merah, more inland at the Digul river, was made a punitive asylum for hundreds of Indonesians, (among them the former Vice-President Hatta), who were against Dutch colonial policy. Many of their descendants now live in Merauke.

Also before the war, the Dutch missions, due to shortage of their own personnel, imported native missionaries into Dutch New Guinea from Christianised areas, such as the Minahasa in the northern Celebes, the Kai islands and Ambon. They held church services in Malay.

Shortly before the Indonesian take-over, the Dutch initiated yet another form of transmigration: they imported into Dutch New Guinea large numbers of their mixed-race descendants in Java and Sumatra who, according to Dutch law, enjoyed Dutch rights and privileges. This venture proved a total failure since the migrants were not professional agriculturists and expected to find their old socio-political privileges in their new "home".

Irian Jaya has never been a prime choice for human resettlement in Indonesia. Its coastal areas are malaria-infested, and local traditions are too remote from those that the average Indonesian finds acceptable. Nevertheless, immigration into the territory continues, and is steadily on the increase. Domestic pressures in towns such as Surabaya, Unjung Pandang, Manado, Ambon and Ternate are forcing people to migrate to places where earning a living presents fewer difficulties. This coincides with Indonesian government policy of "promoting the social and economic life of the people in order to establish the solid foundation of social and economic development, so that within a relatively short period Irian Jaya will arrive at a relatively similar level of development to the other regions of Indonesia" (from the Five-year Development Plan, "Repelita").

So far, in the farming sector, farmers or farm labourers, mainly from Central and East Java, have been recruited and sent in small contingents to Irian Jaya on a government-subsidised migration scheme.

From 1964-75, 824 families totalling 3,372 people were transmigrated to several locations, i.e. Sobron-Dosay (1964-72) and Karyabumi (1975-76) both in the Jayapura district; Kumbe (1964), Kurik (1966-67) and Kuprik (1967) in the Merauke district; Nabire (1968-75) in the Paniai district; and Oransbari and Warmare (1971-73) in the Manokwari district. These groups of migrants had grown to 854 families totalling 4,032 (2,167 males and 1,865 females) by March 31, 1977. During 1976-77, another 110 families (478 people) from Central Java were scheduled to be resettled; 60 families in Klasaman (Sorong district); and 50 families in Karya Bumi (Jayapura district).

On 30 October 1972 the following land-areas were selected for resettling transmigrants:

	ha.
Jayapura district	10,000
Manokwari district	40,000
Sorong district	40,000
Paniai district	50,000
Fakfak district	10,000
Merauke district	20,000
TOTAL	170,000

Of these the following areas had been allocated to the settlers:

Sorong district	10,500 in 1975
Manokwari district	10,000 in 1974
Paniai district	15,000 in 1974
Jayapura district	3,065 in 1976
Merauke district	27,400 in 1975
TOTAL	65,965

With local village communities already established, new land for cultivation has to be wrested from the jungle through slash-and-burn methods. In the close contacts between migrants and local villagers, it is hoped that the latter will learn of new food plants and cultivation techniques, and acquire an eagerness to earn money, through mere imitation.

Most of the non-subsidised immigrants coming from neighbouring provinces are not farming in Irian Jaya, but join the labour force in the urban centres along the coast, mainly Jayapura, Sorong and Merauke, taking what manual, semi-skilled, or secretarial work is available. It is often hard for the local Irianese to compete with these dynamic, frontier-type immigrants.

The transmigration policy in Irian Jaya is only part of the government's internal policies of bringing the big province, which makes up 21.6 per cent of Indonesia's total land area, into the mainstream of an "Indonesia Raya (Greater Indonesia), stretching from Sabang at Sumatra's northern tip, to Merauke in the south-east corner of Irian Jaya".

A reverse flow – although negligible in numbers, and designed only for short periods – of Irianese visiting other parts of Indonesia, mainly Java, is also subsidised by the Indonesian government. Irianese public servants, members of the local House of Representatives, students, sports teams, village chiefs and action group leaders, including women, are regularly sent to Jakarta and other big towns to give them a first-hand impression of Indonesia's technical advancements, and to imbue them with "the feeling of pride to belong to the Indonesian nation". Marriages of Irianese with Indonesians are encouraged.

Religion. Statistics published by Christian religions in Irian Jaya claim that 93 per cent of the people profess the Christian faith. Of these people, the Catholics claim 30 per cent and the rest are split between two Protestant groups: the G.K.I (Gereja Kristen Injili), and the T.M.F. (The Mission Fellowship). TMF members are A.P.C.M. (Asian Pacific

Christian Mission), A.B.M.S. (Australian Baptist Missionary Society), N.R.C. (Netherlands Reformed Congregation), R.B.M.U. (Region Beyond Missionary Union), T.E.A.M. (The Evangelical Alliance Mission) and ZGK (Zending Gereformeerde Kerk). The G.K.I., T.M.F. and Catholic missions have their main headquarters in Jayapura.

The affairs of the minority Moslem congregation (about 8 per cent of the population) are managed by the Department of Religion in Jayapura.

The Christian missions in Irian Jaya run their own schools, hospitals, transport and agricultural projects. They receive some subsidies from the Indonesian government and from supporters overseas. Especially in the interior, they also assist the government and the general public by providing air transport: the Mission Fellowship with its M.A.F. (Missionary Aviation Fellowship); and the Catholic Mission with its A.M.A. (Associated Mission Aviation) aircraft. Both M.A.F. and A.M.A. have ticket offices at Sentani airport, Jayapura.

However, many people still adhere to the traditional New Guinea religious belief, which may be termed dynamic-animism.

GOVERNMENT. Following the pattern of Indonesian administration, the province ("propinsi") of Irian Jaya, is divided into nine administrative districts ("kabupaten"). These are the border districts of Jayapura and Merauke, the highland districts of Jayawijaya and Paniai, the island district of Teluk Cenderawasih (Bird of Paradise Bay), and the coastal districts of Yapen-Waropen, Manokwari, Sorong and Fakfak, with their capitals respectively Jayapura, Merauke, Wamena, Nabire, Biak, Serui, Manokwari, Sorong and Fakfak. Jayapura is also the provincial capital of Irian Jaya.

The chief administrator of the province is the governor ("gubernur"), who is appointed by Jakarta. This post has been held since 1975 to the present by Sutran, assisted by his deputy ("wakil"), an Irianese, E. Paprindej. Sutran, a brigadier general with long experience in West Irian, replaced former governor Acub Zainal in March 1975.

The nine districts are further divided into 116 sub-districts ("kecamatan"), each administered by a "camat". Each sub-district is made up of a number of administrative villages ("desa") headed by a village chief ("kepala desa"). While both Irianese and non-Irianese are represented in the ranks of "camat", the post of village chief appears to be exclusively reserved for Irianese.

In the interior, however, many tribes still live in a neolithic state as nomadic hunters and practising agriculture mainly as slash-and-burn cultivation of their foods. There are tribes – living deep in the jungle – who may not have heard of the Indonesian government and never seen the world beyond their villages. These nomads are commonly called "suku terasing" (an Indonesian term meaning isolated tribes). Exercising administration over them cannot be effective unless they can be persuaded to change their transient hunter's life into that of settled farmers. The Indonesians believe that rural development can be achieved only by resettling these "isolated tribes" along roads which link their new villages with towns. It is hoped that the tribes will have more frequent contact with the other tribes and townspeople, and thus accelerate their social, economic and cultural assimilation with other tribes and people. Also, in time it is intended that the villages will serve as food production areas for the towns, and thus reduce the quantity of imported food.

It is intended that in this process, the tribes would increasingly participate in the cash economy which should stimulate them to produce surplus crops to earn cash. In turn, this should enable them to abandon their present subsistence economy. It is anticipated that with these expectations of development, the economic life of the villagers can be improved, and their villages can be better administered.

The creation of the "desa" – the new administrative village – will bring drastic changes in village authority as the requirements for becoming a new-style village "chief" include possession of a primary school certificate, or knowledge of reading and writing, and the ability to speak Bahasa Indonesia, Indonesia's national language. Previously, in villages of Irain Jaya, the traditional leaders gained authority through superior performance in fighting (or as strategists and negotiators) in tribal wars. Now the village head has to be elected from several eligible candidates who, in the final choice, need to be sanctioned by the "bupati" (district administrator). This is necessary to comply with legal provisions and regulation which are also applicable elsewhere in Indonesia.

Since West Irian – now Irian Jaya – was declared autonomous by President Suharto on September 16, 1969, the province gained the status of "daerah" (autonomous region). The province is further referred to as a First Level – and the district as a Second Level – autonomous region, with the governor and the "bupati" as their respective heads. Regional autonomy in Indonesia does not extend to the sub-districts, hence the "camut" (sub-district administrator) functions mainly as a liaison between the "bupati" and the villages.

Legislature. The governor as chief executive of the autonomous province makes legislation together with his House of Representatives. While legislative initiatives may emanate from the House of Representatives, final legislative authority nevertheless resides with the governor at the provincial level, and the "bupati" at the district level.

The dual function of the governor of Irian Jaya as the Chief Executive in the province and, at the same time, the most senior public servant in Irian Jaya, responsible to the President and Minister of Home Affairs, indicates that Indonesia's policy toward Irian Jaya is one of increasingly strengthening its ties with Jakarta rather than lessening them.

Although Jayapura is the provincial capital and the seat of the provincial government, the offices of the governor and his staff, together with the various departments, were moved in 1974 to Kotaraja, 10 km from Jayapura on the Sentani highway.

Composition of public service. Most of the top functions in the public service in Irian Jaya are held by non-Irianese. Recently, certain positions, such as the post of Chief of the Jayapura Traffic Police Department, were given to Irianese.

Four positions of district administrators ("bupati") were held in 1979 by Irianese. They held office in Jayapura, Merauke, Jayawijaya, and Manokwari. In the other districts (Biak, Paniai, Sorong, Yapen-Waropen and Fakfak) the posts were held by non-Irianese.

Highest military rank held by an Irianese in 1976 was that of major.

Figures for 1971 showed a total of 15,480 civil servants in Irian Jaya.

Liquor laws: Before 1963, the Dutch Liquor Ordinance allowed a maximum of five bottles of beer to be sold to adults (over 21 years) while restaurants could serve beer only with a meal.

During a ban on beer imports from 1963-66, people drank "saguwer" brewed locally from fermented palm wine; and "sopi", a wine imported from Manado (Northern Celebes); and whisky from Ujung Padang.

The ordinance was finally abolished and beer is now freely available. It is supplied by breweries in Java and augmented by imports from Holland, Australia and Singapore. Bars, restaurants and hotels in Jayapura, Biak and Sorong serve most types of liquor.

The "Rukum Kampung" and "Rukun Tetangga" (neighbourhood organisations) deal with drunkards in their respective regions. Habitual drunkards can face disciplinary measures and discharge from employment, or resettlement in a "dry" area where liquor is not available.

Sport: Western sports have only recently been introduced into Irian Jaya, particularly soccer and boxing designed to serve as a means of neutralising tribal conflict, especially in the highlands and the interior. The idea has been to channel the warrior spirit into the peaceful pursuits of contact games. Other popular recreations are water skiing, spear fishing, yachting and tennis but these are mainly confined to the expatriates and upper classes.

Gambling: Games played with cards and dominoes – indeed all forms of gambling – are strictly forbidden in Irian Jaya. People found guilty of gambling by the police face a trial and their names may be published in the Jayapura newspaper.

Prostitution. Although officially prohibited in Irian Jaya and elsewhere in Indonesia, prostitution is practised in Jakarta, Surabaya and Medan and has spread to Jayapura, Biak and Sorong. Although the term "night club" is prohibited, "Bars" and "Discotheques" employ "hostesses" and conduct a thriving business in such commercial and administrative centres. The hostesses are imported from Java, Ujung Pandang (South Sulawesi) and Manado (North Sulawesi).

DEFENCE: The province of Irian Jaya is grouped with Maluku to form the Seventh Military Region of Indonesia. It is commanded by a navy general based at Biak.

The estimated number of military personnel stationed in Irian Jaya is 25,000 men. The headquarters for army, navy and police are at Jayapura; that for the air force is at Biak; ;and the marine corps are based at Manokwari.

The 17th army "Cenderawasih" (Bird of Paradise) Division is stationed in Irian Jaya and is subdivided into regiments, battalions, companies, platoons and sections.

EDUCATION. Irian Jaya has an education system embracing kindergarten, primary, junior high school and senior high school systems.

There are also a teacher-training school system and two tertiary institutions.

The first university in the history of the area, Cenderawasih University, was established in 1962.

The public education policy of the government is to harmonise the school system and curricula in Irian Jaya with the rest of Indonesia. One difference is that the medium of instruction, "Bahasa Indonesia", the national language of Indonesia, is taught from Grade 1 onwards, whereas in the other provinces of Indonesia the first three years of instruction at primary school level are given in the local vernaculars.

From statistics available in 1977, it was estimated that due to lack of available finance, 16 per cent of youngsters entitled to receive primary education would be unable to receive any. A year earlier, the number of primary pupils in Irian Jaya was 132,772 and there were 18,633 pupils in secondary school.

Nevertheless, the Indonesian government claimed that most villages possessed a primary school and in several sub-districts, there were junior high schools.

By 1977, the Indonesian government had established Vocational Training centres in several district capitals in Irian Jaya. Their instructions included automobile and machinery techniques, building construction, radio techniques etc.

The premier institution of tertiary education, the Universitas Cenderawasih, now provides courses the Master of Arts degree. Other tertiary studies may be pursued through the Academy of Administration and Accountancy in Jayapura. There was also the college for Local Administration where some subdistrict administrators for Irian Jaya have been trained.

Roman Catholic and Protestant Academies of Theology were opened in Alepura and there is a branch of the California-based Summer Institute of Linguistics (SIL) in Jayapura. Activities of the SIL include bible translation into Irian Jayan languages and English classes at Cenderawasih University. It also organises evening classes in English for government officials in Jayapura.

By 1977, the Indonesian government had established Vocational Training centres in several district capitals in Irian Jaya. Their instructions included automobile and machinery techniques, building construction, radio techniques etc.

The premier institution of tertiary education, the Universitas Cenderawasih, now provides courses for the Master of Arts degree. Other tertiary studies may be pursued through the Academy of Administration and Accountancy in Jayapura. There was also the college for Local Administration where some subdistrict administrators for Irian Jaya have been trained.

Recently Roman Catholic and Protestant Academies of Theology were opened in Alepura and there is a branch of the California-based Summer Institute of Linguistics (SIL) in Jayapura. Activities of the SIL include bible translation into Irian Jayan languages and English classes at Cenderawasih University. It also organises evening classes in English for government officials in Jayapura.

CENDERAWASIH UNIVERSITY STAFF, ENROLMENTS AND GRADUATIONS

	Lecturers		Students		
	Full time	Part time	Total	New	Graduates (B.A. or B.S.)
1970	60	104	573	163	26
1971	53	102	519	160	37
1972	68	54	n.a.	194	33
1973	74	46	658	175	63
1974	56	84	572	165	50
1975	69	98	650	178	64

IRIAN JAYA — ACADEMY OF LOCAL GOVERNMENT

Students and Graduates

	Public servants	Study assignment	Graduates B.A.
1971	58	48	20
1972	62	44	30
1974	81	38	45

IRIAN JAYA — THEOLOGY STUDENTS AT ALEPURA

	Lecturers		Students
	Full time	Part time	
1973	4	3	27
1974	5	6	38
1975	5	6	52

LABOUR. Of Irian Jaya's population, 80 per cent or 820,000 people lived in the interior in 1977 and of them, about 534,000 were aged between 10 and 69 years and lived by subsistence farming. It was estimated that of some 20,000 students who had attended secondary schools, 60 per cent had attended non-vocational establishments. This resulted in a difficulty for Irian Jayan students to get jobs either through lack of experience, or through lack of job vacancies.

In 1975-76, it was estimated that the highest percentage of job seekers (who had attended primary and/or secondary schools), 86 per cent in 1975 and 97.6 per cent in 1976 were aged between 20 and 29.

One problem faced by the government is the disproportionate number of jobs held by non-Irianese. For every three non-Irians holding technical positions, only one Irianese is employed in a similar capacity.

The situation is worse in administration where Irianese hold only 20 per cent of the jobs; only in unskilled work as manual labourers do Irianese hold four jobs to each held by an outside Indonesian.

The number of unskilled vacancies on multimillion dollar enterprises (such as oil drilling and copper mining) is high only in the initial stages of construction when roads and buildings must be established. Once the base facilities are provided, local workers are dismissed and more sophisticated outsiders are employed to handle the machinery.

Another problem is that of Indonesian transmigrants. Most have equal or superior technical or non-technical training to that of the Irianese. In coastal areas, where most development projects have been conducted, local Irianese have found it hard to compete for jobs against transmigrants, even when the local people possess competitive diplomas or other qualifications.

In 1975, 763 business enterprises and corporations in Irian Jaya employed 38,452 labourers — an increase of 2,926 over requirements in 1971. Net increase of transmigrants to Irian Jaya during the same period was 29,403 people who mostly settled in urban areas. There is also an urban drift from villages and the intensity of this is impeded only because of the roadless terrain of the interior.

HEALTH. In 1978, each of the nine "kabupaten" (districts) of Irian Jaya had its own government health office and its own district hospital. Total beds in these establishments were 823. There were also five hospitals for special diseases, a psychiatric institution (75 beds) at Abepura, and leprosy rehabilita-

IRIAN JAYA — SCHOOLS 1976

	Number	Enrolment	Teachers
Primary schools	1,303	132,772	n.a.
Junior high schools	234	16,361	367
Senior high schools	13	2,272	132
Senior technical high schools	35	5,384	257

tion centres (235 beds) at Sorong, Kaimana, Merauke and Yapen.

The 116 "kecamaten" (sub-districts) had 110 community health centres and of these, four had hospital facilities (68 beds). There were also 61 mother-and-child care centres, mostly located in the interior. There were also two hospitals for the armed forces (154 beds), 7 health care centres (85 beds), 23 polyclinics and 17 mother-and-child care centres in the district capitals or other urban centres.

IRIAN JAYA — HOSPITALS AND BEDS 1978

	Hospitals No.	Beds No.
Jayapura	3	451
Teluk Cenderawasih	2	165
Yapen Waropen	1	75
Manokwari	1	104
Sorong	4	220
Fak-Fak	1 — 1(M)	44 — 12
Merauke	1	106
Paniai	1 — 1(M)	40 — 12
Jayawijaya	1 — 1(M)	25 — 25

Note: (M) indicates Mission hospitals.

Christian missions and the Muslim Muhamadiah were responsible for a further six hospitals, a 16-bed leprosy hospital, 70 polyclinics and 11 mother-and-child care centres.

In 1978, the government health department staff in Irian Jaya was 2,430 including 64 general practitioners, 4 medical specialists, 9 dentists, 11 health inspectors, 95 midwives, 346 nurses, 3 chemists, 33 malaria controllers and 1 nutritionist.

Health care is included as one of the priorities in the Repelita II (1974-79) programme for developing the source of human labour, but in 1978-79, only 8.4 per cent of the provincial budget (3.18 per cent in 1976-77) was devoted to health care, and of this, 47.8 per cent (58 per cent 1976-77) was allocated for salaries.

However, INPRES (presidential decrees) provided further sums for medicines, equipment, construction of houses for professional staff and other matters. INPRES grants enabled 40 health centres to be built in 1976-77. It has been estimated that between 1976 and 1978 203,161 residents were protected from malaria by DDT spraying; 522,581 received BCG vaccination; 750,109 received primary smallpox vaccination and 5,711 received medical help for leprosy.

Foreign enterprises in Irian Jaya which run their own hospitals, mainly for their own workers, are Freeport Sulphur and Pacific Nickel; and the domestic Pertamina national oil company, the state electricity Company, the Irian Bhakti enterprise and the Bank of Indonesia.

Diseases. It has been estimated that 14.69 per cent of the people are affected by skin and subcutaneous tissue diseases (including scabies); 14.59 per cent are suffering from malaria and the yearly average for influenza is 11.04 per cent.

Since 1971, aid from a U.N. Development Programme and the WHO has enabled a systematic malaria eradication scheme to be initiated in the larger towns by spraying twice a year. Only at Biak and Merauke are the results considered satisfactory. In 1978 there were 754 patients with tuberculosis but only 524 were in hospitals.

Yaws (framboesia) which is still present in the interior and in isolated coastal areas claimed 78,741 victims in 1978 but only 993 were in hospitals, and 1285 people were vaccinated against the disease. A cholera epidemic occurred in 1979 from October 14 to 23. There were 85 cases reported in Jayapura.

Mortality rates from influenza and pertussis (whooping cough) were high in 1978. Venereal disease is mainly confined to towns where there is prostitution. Jayawijaya reported 219 cases of gonorrhoea in 1977.

THE LAND. Irian Jaya has an area of 410,660 sq. km including 54,668 sq. km of rivers and lakes. Mainland Irian Jaya is approximately 1,130 km in length and 724 km at its broadest.

The highest peak, which is also the highest in the whole island of New Guinea, is Puncak Jaya in the Sudirman Range, which rises to 5,093 m. Ten other peaks in this range exceed 4,880 m. Although Irian Jaya lies close to the equator, some mountain tops are perpetually snow-capped.

The interior is mostly a heavy rainforest rising in great, ragged ridges, pock-marked by villages and patches of cultivation. The rest of the land is coastal, holding vast sago and mangrove swamps. The configuration of the country is thus one of extremes: endless swamps and gigantic massifs. The swamps are among the most extensive in the world, and the mountains are so high they make possible the existence of glaciers.

The climate is equatorial, except in the highlands where the temperature can fall to freezing.

Rainfall varies between an average of 2,000 to 3,000 mm per annum in most coastal areas to between 3,000 and 4,000 mm in the uplands.

Irian Jaya's largest rivers are the Mamberamo and Digul. Only the Mamberamo is navigable as far as Marine Falls by ships with a draught of 2 m.

Irian Jaya's interior is characterised by huge lake systems, among the largest of which is the Wissel Lakes area. Other mountain lakes are found near Baliem (Archbold and Habbema), between Habbema and Wissel (Hagers), and in the Vogelkop (Bird's Head) area (Ajamaroe and Anggi).

Islands close to the coast of Irian Jaya are included therein; but the small groups of Aru, Kai and Tanimbar, in the Arafura Sea, just north of Australia, have always been part of Indonesia.

Islands of Irian Jaya. There are several groups of islands of which the island groups in Teluk Cenderawasih or Bird of Paradise Bay (formerly the Schouten Islands), and Yapen are the most significant. Each of these groups represents an administrative district ("kabupaten"). The first group consists of two main islands, Supiori and Biak, and the Padaido islands. As these islands have been in contact with the outside world for several centuries, one can see Melanesian and Malay mixtures among their people.

During World War II Biak was of strategic importance and both Japanese and the Allies used the coral island as a springboard for further operations in the south-west Pacific.

Biak is now an important transit station for ships and aircraft. The runway of Mokmer airport at Biak was built by the Americans during the War and has remained the best in Irian Jaya. Biak is now also the headquarters of the Supreme Commander of all Indonesian military forces in Irian Jaya. Travel between Indonesia and Irian Jaya has substantially increased and the development of Biak is geared to provide this transit traffic with facilities such as offices, hotels, stores, restaurants and entertainment.

The Biak district administration has also established an agricultural experimental station at Wirmaker – 40 kilometres north of Biak town, where new fruits imported from other parts of Indonesia are tested and established. Biak people are considered to be the most advanced of those in Irian Jaya and some occupy top positions in politics, education, the public service and administration in Irian Jaya. There has always been a regular flow of Biak people leaving their island to work elsewhere.

Yapen islands are rather isolated, and rely heavily on trade from Biak. Now that Nabire has developed into an agricultural hinterland, Yapen island (with Serui as its capital) serves as transit station for the export of soya beans and cassava (manioc) from Nabire to Biak. Imports include construction materials and household goods from Biak for distribution to Yapen, Waropen, Manokwari and Paniai.

Serui is where Indonesian nationalists including Dr Sam Ratulangi were exiled by the Dutch. The exiles lived among the local people and some pro-Indonesian Irianese leaders including Silas Papare, are from Serui.

Were it not for the discovery of oil and minerals in the Bird Head area (Vogelkop) around Sorong, such islands as Gag (where nickel has been found) would remain undeveloped, like those groups in the South – Kai and Aru. During the past decades, there was a tendency among job-seeking islanders to migrate to the mainland and a large contingent of Kai islanders now live in Merauke. The people on the many tiny islands in Yos Sudarso (formerly Humboldt) Bay are mainly fishermen. Close to Jayapura, these people were strongly influenced by Dutch politics and education, especially from 1945-62. The people near Jayapura have always been noted for accelerated social and economic transition, and it has been the breeding place for West Irianese regionalism. It was mainly from this area – including bay islands such as Tobati – that discontented elements among the West Irianese crossed the border into PNG as political refugees. It is estimated that 5,000 Irianese have been given permissive residence in Papua New Guinea. After Independence in 1975, many of these refugees became Papua New Guinea citizens.

Flora and fauna. The flora is a mixture of Indo-Malayan and Australian types. For centuries the highland peoples burnt forests to flush game and make room for agriculture. This has created the great highland grass plains of the Baliem Valley and Wissel Lakes country, both large centres of populations.

The native plant with the widest variety of uses is the coconut, which provides food, drink, oil, wood, leaves for thatching, fibre for matting, and shells for water vessels. Nipa and areca palm leaves are also used for thatching. Other plants mainly used for food are: sugar cane, banana, sweet potato, sago palm, taro, papaw, yam and the breadfruit. Other varieties of trees of high economic value are also found, such as copal and rattan.

There are many known species of birds, mostly related to Australian types, though a few, such as the hornbill, are exclusively Asian. However, the high mountains limit the range of birds. Important groups are the birds of paradise, of which there are many varieties; kingfishers, flycatchers, parrots and honeyeaters; pigeons and doves including goura, the largest pigeon in the world; the flightless cassowary which provides the natives with food, plumes for head-dresses and sharp bones for daggers; and many water birds, including pelicans, cranes, cormorants, ducks, herons, storks and ibises.

Irian Jaya is the home of many marsupials, including several species of wallaby and the tree kangaroo, a native cat and various bandicoots, pouched mice and possums. Possums vary in size from mouse-like gliding possums to the cuscus, the largest of the possum family. Also found are wild pigs, wild dogs, several species of fruit bats or flying foxes, and the world's largest tree-climbing water rats. Large mammals are not found on the island except for those imported from other regions, such as livestock (oxen, horses, etc.). Marine mammals include the dugong and dolphin.

The reptiles are generally related to Australian species. Of the venomous type are death adders, whip snakes and banded sea snakes. Also found are big monitor lizards, the oceanic gecko, the giant skink, crocodiles, turtles, the Pacific boa and the scrub python.

Land use. It was estimated in 1977 that only 200,000 ha (0.5 per cent) of the land in Irian Jaya is considered favourable for agricultural development. A further million hectares (2.5 per cent) could be available if the primary forest was cleared. There is also 265,000 ha of sago palm growing in swampy coastal regions which provides staple food for people in those areas.

PRIMARY PRODUCTION. Irian Jaya's main food crops are sweet potatoes, taros, yams, cassava (tapioca) and vegetables. These have long been the staples for the local people.

FOOD CROP PRODUCTION IRIAN JAYA — 1978

	Acreage (hectares)	Tonnes
Rice	1,709	3,349
Corn	2,616	2588
Cassava	4,593	22,715
Sweet potato	36,221	211,319
Taro	7,701	33,909
Other tubers	142	771
Sago	4,477	17,501
Peanuts	1,785	1,595
Mung bean	374	251
Soya bean	1,374	1,331
Other bean	53	63
Vegetables	3,413	7,392
Fruit	6,978	18,970

Cash crops. Cultivation of cash crops for export is still limited to specific areas. The main export crops and their areas of cultivation are:

Copra: Merauke, Raja Ampat Is (Sorong), Sarmi, Kaimana, Numfor and Biak
Nutmeg; Fakfak and Kaimana
Cocoa: Serui-Yapen Waropen, Manokwari, Genyem, Sentani, Sarmi
Rubber: Merauke district (Digul, Mindiptana, Bada, Kepi, Muting) Ransiki, Timika, Kokonau
Coffee: Enarotali, Serui, Bokondini

Feasibility studies are being pursued by the Horticulture department to cultivate cloves, tobacco, cashew nuts, kapok, sugar cane and pepper. However, during 1976-77, total exports of cash crops from Irian Jaya were worth $US 1.9 million or 0.5 per cent of total export earnings.

CASH CROP EXPORTS — IRIAN JAYA ($US)

	1974-75	1976-77
Nutmeg	812,820	842,810
Mace	823,120	368,090
Copra	n.a.	603,490
Cocoa	n.a.	20,960
Rubber	8,470	83,500

CASH CROP PRODUCTION

	1977	1978
Coconuts (t.)*	7,121	N.A.
(ha)*	16,464	16,504
Nutmeg (t.)	860	490
(ha)	4,918	4,931
Cocoa (t.)	335	18
(ha)	1467	1416
Coffee (t.)	56	N.A.
(ha)	392	392
Rubber (t.)	171	N.A.
(ha)	1334	1334
Cloves (t.)	1.3	N.A.
(ha)	1370	1376

* (t) — tonnes * (ha) — hectares

CASH CROP EXPORTS

	1976 tonnes	1977 tonnes	1978 tonnes
Copra	2436	2883	596
Nutmeg	457	796	269
Mace	155	157	220
Cocoa	29	33	5.5
Coffee	N.A.	14	N.A.
Rubber	155	103	112

Livestock. As a potential source of income for the people, most types of livestock have been introduced experimentally to Irian Jaya. Except for the ubiquitous pigs, the areas most suitable are considered to be:

Grime (1,200 ha) and Sekoli plains (3,500 ha)
Nabire plain (1,200 ha)
Near Manokwari (300 ha) and Ransiki (2,000 ha)
Digul and near Merauke (5,000 ha)
Plains in the Balim highlands, Enarotali, Kebar and other areas (14,000 ha)

IRIAN JAYA — LIVESTOCK POPULATION

	1976	1977
Cattle	8,512	9,226
Water Buffalo	21	27
Horses	1,642	1,684
Sheep	9,226	10,162
Goats	763	1,090
Pigs	189,715	196,617
Poultry	330,454	391,254
Ducks	24,819	26,416
Rabbits	6,422	N.A

Fisheries. Around Sorong, Merauke, Jayapura and elsewhere along the coast of Irian Jaya, fishing represents the main source of income for the local population. Freshwater fisheries in ponds, rivers and lakes cover 800,000 ha.

The production of fish, both freshwater and sea, increased from 14,341 tonnes in 1976 to 17,028 tonnes in 1977, an increase of 17.1 per cent. Exports of all sea products in 1977 increased by 933.5 tonnes

(26.8 per cent) over the previous year's total representing a price increase of US $5,065,767. Total value of exports in 1977 was $US18,849,219.60. At Sorong, cold storage rooms with 250 tonnes capacity have been built by the West Irian Fishing Industry and Maviva Product Development. Surveys for upgrading the fisheries industry have been carried out by the Fund for West Irian/United Nations Development Programme (FUNDI/UNDP).

SEA FOOD EXPORTS

Export realisation of prawns and some other sea products in 1977 was:

	Kg	$US
Prawns	1,558,060	5,946,016
Tuna	137,400	512,400
Crocodile skins	35,000	381,937
Pearl shell	4,490	1,796
Shark fins	900	721
Total	1,735,850	6,842,870

MEAT AND EGG PRODUCTION (In tonnes)

	1976	1977
Beef	125.14	125.5
Mutton	10.7	15.9
Pork	3,646	4,375.2
Goat	0.2	0.4
Chicken	144.3	287.7
Game (Deer etc)	640	500
Eggs	583.3	707.7

The greatest government investment in a fishing enterprise is the Usaha Mina Ltd Co. which has 30 fishing boats, each of 30 tonnes and cold storage facilities with a capacity of 1,300 tonnes. Its base equipment includes a 300 tonne capacity dockyard, instrument workshop, radio station and housing for its administrative personnel. Total staff is about 700.

There are five other private fishing companies operating in Irian Jaya waters and their catch includes prawns and other fish. There are ice factories at Jayapura (two), Biak (one) and Sorong (two). Their main task is to supply ice to fishing vessels but they also sell it to the general public.

Indonesian government policy for Irian Jaya's agriculture was, in the first instance, to introduce new food crops in order to improve the nutritional value of the local staple foods – which consist mainly of carbohydrates such as sweet potatoes, taro, yam and sago – and, secondly, to encourage production for the cash market in order to raise per capita income.

But the achievement of these aims faces formidable obstacles, not the least of which is the reluctance of the Irianese to change their methods of farming which have been practised on their land from time immemorial.

So, in 1977, agriculture in Irian Jaya still presented a picture of predominantly subsistence farming.

The development of food resources for domestic consumption has thus been slow, occurring mainly in the transmigration centres where the migrants from other provinces have started rice and vegetable cultivation.

The government has succeeded in developing some fish-breeding, and in introducing some new plant foods in the highlands. However, the bulk of food, if it is not grown locally (sweet potatoes, yam, etc.), must still be imported.

Forestry. Although 75 per cent of the entire surface of Irian Jaya is covered with forest, only 100,000 ha of productive forests are at present being exploited.

Current estimates are that there could be a further 650,000 ha of accessible productive forests not yet in use; and in those areas still inaccessible to transport, there may be a further 3.75 million ha of productive forests.

At present, the main export commodities are logs ($US 442,300 in 1976). Another important forestry byproduct is copal, a resin used in varnish manufacture. Exports of copal in 1976 were worth $US 41,120.

MINING AND OIL. Although some initial assays have indicated that Irian Jaya may possess substantial deposits of minerals, the main income producers to date are oil and copper.

Export income from minerals is as follows:

IRIAN JAYA – MINERAL EXPORTS (in $US million)

	1974-75	1975-76	1976-77
Oil	134.1	257.8	335.9
Copper	116.3	77.9	101.2

The main mining operations are the following:

Tembagapura (Ertsberg) Copper Project. Discovered in 1936, Ertsberg (Ore Mountain) represents possibly the largest base metal outcrop in the world, and was developed in the '70s by Freeport Indonesia Inc, a subsidiary of Freeport MINERALS Company. It rises 2,800 m above sea level in Irian Jaya's primitive interior. A three-unit tramway – claimed to be the world's largest – and a 104 km long pipeline – said to be the longest copper concentrate pipe in the world – developed by Bechtel-Pomeroy of San Francisco, delivers the copper concentrate slurry through 38 km of rugged mountain terrain and 62 km of mangrove swamp and tropical rainforest to the port of Kokonau on the Arafura Sea. The US$163 million project, completed and in service in 1973, handles 250,000 tonnes annually, opening the 35-million-tonne Ertsberg deposit to international markets.

Damage assessed at $US 1 million was caused to this project in July 1977 when sabotage was directed at the pipeline carrying copper concentrate from the mine to the coast, and at a parallel fuel pipeline which supplies the mine machinery. The damage was the result of raids by the Irian Jaya liberation movement, the so-called Provisional Revolutionary Government of West Papua New Guinea, which is fighting against Indonesian control.

P.T. Pacific Nickel Indonesia. Since February 17, 1969 this consortium of American, Canadian and Dutch companies has been working under contract with the Indonesian government. In 1971, the company discovered nickel laterite layers on the island of Gag in the Waigeo area of the Sorong district.

In 1972 a feasibility study by Bechtel Corporation was aimed at establishing development facilities on Gag Island for producing 52,000 tonnes of nickel annually, and the Indonesian government assigned the company to build the mining and processing facilities. US$550 million has been invested in the project while another US$15 million was spent on survey and research.

With world-wide over-production of nickel, work on Gag Island was deferred during 1977. However, mineral prospecting by the consortium was being continued elsewhere in Indonesia. The plan to erect a smelter costing $US 1,000 million was still "active" with a completion date set for 1983. In 1974 the Indonesian Government decided to provide 20 per cent of the capital needed.

Petroleum Industry. After oil exploration in the Bird's Head area of Sorong by the Netherlands New Guinea Petroleum Company ceased in 1959, a 10-year period of inactivity ensued. Oil production by Pertamina, Indonesia's state-owned oil company, was limited to the Klamono area. After 1966 there was some rehabilitation of the Sele oilfields.

Offshore exploration was renewed by AGIP and Phillips Petroleum, both functioning as contractors of Pertamina, in mid-1969, and there was more inland in the Bomberei and Kasim areas at the end of 1971 by Gulf and Petromer Trend.

Further exploration was conducted in the Mogoi and Wasian locations in 1972, and in the Klamono and Bintuni areas in August 1973, by the *Compagnie Générale de Géophysique,* another contractor of Pertamina. Using the seismic method, oil was found in substantial production quantities in the Kasim area by Petromer Trend in the first quarter of 1973.

By 1977, three companies were conducting active drilling programmes and in 1976, 28 holes were drilled. Of these, eight revealed oil and/or gas. Two other companies were conducting geophysical exploration.

At Sele and Kasim about 175-200 foreigners, mostly Americans, are working on contracts, earning net salaries of about $US2,000 a month with free food and accommodation. After every four weeks, they are entitled to two weeks' leave with return air transport free to the places of their recruitment (Singapore and Bangkok).

The Indonesian labourers earn above-local salaries and are entitled to a week's holiday after every four weeks of work. This is mostly spent in Sorong. This situation has sent local food prices skyrocketing and makes Sorong the most expensive place to live in the province.

With the oil boom, the district capital of Sorong was transformed into a busy town with an increasing immigrant population coming from outside Irian Jaya, mainly from the Moluccas and Celebes, to work as labourers on the oilfields.

In 1976, downtown Sorong was teeming with inns, bars and restaurants. Non-Indonesian personnel of the oil industries are not permitted to spend their holidays there.

TOURISM. With a need for accommodation for visitors to the administrative centre of Jayapura, the business centre of Biak and the oil industry at Sorong, there has been a rapid increase in numbers of hotels, guest houses, travel agencies and restaurants in Irian Jaya. In 1972 BAPPARDA (Body for Developing Local Tourism) was established, but in most places, the standards of accommodation are below international levels and prices are high.

Some indication of the rise in tourism may be gained from the following table.

IRIAN JAYA — TOURIST EXPENDITURE

	Indonesian tourists No.	Overseas tourists No.	Total spending ($US million)
1970	48,967	4,105	5.3
1972	59,250	16,562	7.6
1974	71,692	20,040	9.2
1976	86,747	24,428	11.1

The average stay of a foreign tourist is five days with a daily expenditure of $US20.00. Foreign tourists to Irian Jaya came from the USA, Japan, Holland, Germany, France, Switzerland, Italy and other west-European countries.

LOCAL COMMERCE. The local Irianese mostly lack any tradition of commercial activity. This fact, coupled with the presence of commercially active migrant elements from other provinces and of Chinese, makes it extremely difficult for them to develop business talents and initiatives.

Only a small number of Irianese are to be seen selling inside the recently inaugurated concrete "Pasar Sentral" (Central Market) in Jayapura's Hamada district. Mostly, they are still in their traditional places, squatting outside the building to sell their simple produce.

Retail stores, repair shops, eating stalls, restaurants, bars, nightclubs, minibus transport, small hotels and inns are all owned either by Indonesians from outside the province or by Chinese.

In an effort to cope with this situation the West Irian Joint Development Foundation lends money, with preference to Irianese, to finance small-scale enterprises such as crop-growing and cattle-breeding. Loans are also made to Irianese fishermen for the purchase of outboard motors to be attached to their outrigger canoes to help them increase their catches.

Industry and Labour. At the close of the fiscal year 1978/79 there were listed 453 licensed industries employing 13,318 workers. It was estimated that these industries represented an investment of Rp3,450,098,000 compared with an investment in 1977/78 of Rp3,089,912,000 in 423 industries employing 3,220 workers, an increase of 7.8 per cent in the number of industries, 3.4 per cent in the workforce and 11.6 per cent in investment value.

INDUSTRY AND LABOUR

Type	Total	Capital investment (in 1000 rupiahs)	Labour
Food and drink	142	668,240	706
Building	56	419,047	1,336
Manufacturing	17	23,292	46
Chemical products	5	14,918	48
Services	233	2,324,601	1,182
Total	453	3,450,098	3,318

OVERSEAS TRADE. The value of Irian Jaya's exports and imports for the years 1971-76 and detailed exports for 1974-77 are shown in the accompanying tables:

IRIAN JAYA — EXPORTS AND IMPORTS (in $US'000)

	Exports	Imports	Balance of trade
1971	1,841	7,500	−5,659
1972	7,306	3,000	+4,306
1973	68,227	2,500	+65,727
1974	190,378	8,103	+182,266
1975	214,277	1,270	+213,008
1976	358,932	1,014	+357,918

IRIAN JAYA — EXPORTS (in $US'000)

	1974-75	1975-76	1976-77
Oil and gas	134,137	257,813	335,924
Copper	116,250	77,936	101,151
Prawns	8,901	9,013	16,834
Spices	1,635	818	1,211
Fresh and frozen fish	—	—	806
Copra	—	—	603
Crocodile skins	752	146	601
Trepang	—	—	492
Timber, logs	—	—	442
Crabs, frozen	—	—	132
Rubber	8	28	84
Copal	—	—	41
Cocoa	—	—	21

FINANCE. No recent figures are available showing the budgetary situation in Irian Jaya. The first five year development programme from 1969-74 ("Repelita I") was followed by "Repelita II".

However, development programmes have been impeded by major earthquakes in June and October 1976.

Taxes. Neither government personnel nor members of the Indonesian armed forces have to pay taxes; the only deduction from their monthly wages is 7 to 12 per cent as a contribution to pension funds. Revenues are derived from imports and exports. The Indonesian State Navigation "Pelni" in Jayapura handles all foreign imports which come mostly from Singapore and Hong Kong. All exports from Irian Jaya also pass through this Department and they include oil, copper, crocodile skins, timber, mace etc.

All revenues from exports and imports are sent to Jakarta where the central government then allocates funds for the provincial budget. The provincial government then distributes such funds to the districts.

For the autonomous province of Irian Jaya, the only internal taxes levied are automobile registration fees. Eventually, for the administrative districts ("kabupaten"), sales tax will represent their main source of revenue.

IRIAN JAYA — ANNUAL BUDGET (in Rp million)

1969-70	3.48
1970-71	3.56
1971-72	3.70
1972-73	5.55
1973-74	6.63
1974-75	13.43
1975-76	12.93
1976-77	12.77

Source: BAPPEDA (Regional Executive Body for Development)

Currency. The same notes and coins are circulated in Irian Jaya as in other parts of Indonesia. The denominations of the notes in rupiah (Rp) are Rp 25, Rp 50, Rp 100, Rp 500, Rp 1,000, Rp 5,000 and Rp 10,000. For coins the denominations are Rp 1, Rp 5, Rp 10, Rp 25, and Rp 100. Since the "Act of free Choice" in 1969 the rupiah ($ 1.00) = Rp 415) has been the only currency permitted in Irian Jaya.

After November 15, 1978, the Indonesian rupiah was allowed to float but was linked to the US dollar with an exchange value of US$1.00 = Rp 625. Before the change the rate was $US1.00 = Rp 425.

TRANSPORT. Road-building work of recent years has included construction of roads connecting food-producing hinterlands with provincial capitals, such as the Genyem-Jayapura and Wirmaker-Biak roads, and roads linking towns with transmigration centres such as the Sobron-Dosai-Jayapura and Kuprik-Merauke roads. Work has been in progress for several years to build a 150 km highway from Nabire to Enaratoli in the Paniai highlands. The longest overland route passable to cars in Irian Jaya is less than 200 km, but over the last couple of years to mid-1979 seven overland roads had been constructed. These are: Sentani-Boroway-Genyem (Jayapura district); Sentani-Doyo-Depapre

(Jayapura district); Biak-Korem (Teluk Cenderawasih district); Manokwari-Warmare (Manokwari district); Sorong-Klamono (Sorong district); Tanah Merah-Mindiptana (Merauke district); Teminabuan-Ayamaru (Sorong district).

Some short-distance roads have been made to give access to natural resources such as oil, copper, nickel and timber, but these are not considered to be public roads.

Airlines. Ten airlines the majority belonging to religious missions, were operating inside Irian Jaya in 1979. Air Niugini, Papua New Guinea's flag carrier flies between PNG and Irian Jaya. The two national airlines are Garuda Indonesian Airways (GIA) which operates daily and Merpati Nusantara Airlines (MNA) three times a week. The routes are – GIA; Jakarta-Ujung Pandang-Sorong-Biak-Jayapura and return and also Jakarta direct to Ujung Pandang. MNA: Jayapura-Biak-Ujung Pandang-Surubaya-Jakarta.

Airlines are: Merpati Nusantara Airlines, 13 aircraft; Garuda Indonesian Airways, 2 aircraft; Missionary Aviation Fellowship, 16; Associated Mission Aviation, 4; Seventh-day Adventist, 2; Region Beyond Missionary Union, 2; Summer Institute of Linguistics, 2; Air Niuguini, 1; Pelita Air Service (Pertamina), 10; Nation Utility Helicopters, 7.

The two mission airlines, Missionary Aviation Fellowship (Protestant) and Associated Mission Aviation (Roman Catholic), operate charter and passenger and cargo flights inside Irian Jaya at fares similar to those of MNA.

The Indonesian Air Force (AURI) is based at Biak, and besides providing regular military transport, it also provides Dakotas for air-drops of food in remote locations, or in disaster areas.

The only Indonesian airline maintaining regular flights to South-East Asia i.e. Singapore and Bangkok, is Pelita Air Service – owned by the Indonesian State Oil Industry (Pertamina) – to fly expatriate personnel from the oilfields to places of recruitment and recreation.

The only foreign airline operating in Irian Jaya is Air Niugini, Papua New Guinea's state airline which has weekly flights from Lae to Jayapura with Fokker F-28 jets. These aircraft land only at Sentani airport (35 km from Jayapura), refuel and return immediately to P.N.G. A few years ago, Garuda organised return flights from Jayapura to Lae, but the service was discontinued due to shortage of passengers.

To reach Tembagapura (Ertsberg copper mine), Merpati have flights to Kokonau where passengers transfer to helicopters for Tembagapura. With the exception of Biak, built during World War II by the U.S.A.F. and capable of taking DC-8 aircraft, the largest airfields in Irian Jaya at December 1976 were Jayapura (F-28 jet) and Sorong (F-28 jet). Airfields capable of accommodating the Fokker F-27 "Friendship" were Merauke, Piniai, Manokwari and Wamena. There were only Twin Otter facilities at Fakfak and Yapen.

All these strips (excepting Yapen) have an asphalt landing area. Other asphalt strips include Boruku (Indonesian Air force) suitable for Hercules; Numfor and Kemiri are capable of taking DC-3s. These latter airfields are all in the Cenderawasih Bay area.

AIRPORTS/AIRSTRIPS

	Owned and managed by				
District	Govt.	MAF	AMA	Private	Total
Jayapura	13	29	5	1	48
Jayawijaya	3	71	6	2	82
Teluk Cenderawasih	3	–	–	–	3
Manokwari	7	19	4	–	30
Sorong	3	3	–	1	7
Piniai	5	23	11	–	39
Merauke	7	12	7	–	26
Japen Waropen	2	–	–	–	2
Fakfak	4	3	3	2	12
Total	**47**	**160**	**36**	**6**	**249**

Port facilities. Much of the rehabilitation work done on harbours and docks in recent years has been directly related to economic development projects such as the oil and prawn-freezing industries in Sorong, and the timber export industry in Jayapura and Manokwari.

Under the auspices of the United Nations Joint Development Foundation – which has its headquarters at Jayapura (Jalan Percetakan Negara 4–6) – the building of 20-tonne ferrocement workboats was started in 1977 in the Waena area near Abepura. The boats are engaged in picking up copra and other produce from harbours such as Sarmi and taking the cargo along the coast or, even, outside Irian Jaya (e.g. to Halmahera).

COMMUNICATIONS. Since the launching of the "Palapa" satellite in July 1976, Indonesia has had domestic satellite communication linking all parts of the nation with direct telephone, telegraph and telex systems. The satellite is also used to transmit television programmes and it is planned to include television for educational purposes. All transmissions are in "Bahasa Indonesia", the national language.

In 1977, eight of the 40 earth stations in Indonesia were located in Irian Jaya. They were at Jayapura, Biak, Manokwari, Fakfak, Sorong, Merauke, Tembagapura (for the Ertsberg copper mine) and Gag Island (for the nickel project). Television reception in Irian Jaya is limited to Jayapura and Biak and only between 6.30 p.m. and 12.30 a.m.

Internal radio network. When Irian Jaya was transferred to Indonesia in 1963, there were radio stations at Jayapura and Biak. Others have since been opened at Sorong, Manokwari, Fakfak, Merauke, Serui, Nabire, and Wamena with the

R.R.I. Jayapura being the central transmitter.

Public information. "Kantor Wilayah" or 'Kanwil", the Regional Office of Information, is directly controlled by the Department of Information in Jakarta and has been established to disseminate policies of the central government. Its information programmes include election campaigns and the "Repelita" (five-year national development programmes).

All forms of media are used for public information including press, pamphlets, photo exhibits, public lectures, radio, film and television. Lack of transport and shortage of funds prevents information projects from being sent to many villages in the interior where illiteracy is also a problem.

Films exhibited in Irian Jaya are censored. They are imported from Jakarta, Hong Kong and the USA.

Director, Irian Jaya Office of Information, Head Office, Jayapura S. Ohei (Irianese); Deputy: W. F. Wanma (Irianese).

Newspapers. There are five publications with regular circulation in Irian Jaya. They are:

"Berita Karya", a newspaper supporting present government policy and widely read by public servants, members of the armed forces.

"Cenderawasih", a newspaper claiming to be independent but strongly oriented towards the government.

"Tifa Irian", (Irian Drum) representing opinions of Catholics in Irian Jaya.

"Mingguan Teropong" (Observer) an independent weekly with Islamic affiliations.

"Bulletin Antara", publicity outlet for the Irian branch of the National Antara headquarters in Jakarta.

WATER. Jayapura has a reticulated water supply, originally constructed by the Dutch, and supplied from a rain-filled reservoir at Angkasa. The water is not treated with caporite. Sentani, 35 km from Jayapura obtains its supplies from the Kemiri reservoir which is also used for swimming and other recreational pursuits by Jayapura residents. Similar supplies are provided at Manokwari, Sorong, Fak Fak, Nabire and Wamena. Biak, an arid coral island, obtains its water from Sorido dam. This water is scarce, and brackish. At Merauke, water is obtained from neighbouring swamps. With the possible exception of Wamena, **all** water in Irian Jaya should be boiled before drinking in any form.

ELECTRICITY. Generation of electricity in Irian Jaya is powered entirely by diesel engines, some installed as early as 1953. Under Indonesian administration, there has been rehabilitation or replacement of some generators and installation of new ones, mostly at airports.

Electric power stations in Irian Jaya are located at Jayapura, Sentani, Ifar, Sarmi, Biak, Serui, Manokwari, Sorong, Jefman Is (Sorong airport), Doom Is (near Sorong), Fak Fak, Tanah Merah and Merauke. A scheme has been proposed to utilise the waters of Lake Sentani for generation of hydroelectricity.

PERSONALITIES AND ORGANISATIONS

Governor: Brigadier-General Soetran
Deputy-Governor: E. Paprindej
Secretary: Mohamad Rusli
Regional Army Commander: Brig. Gen. C. I. Santoso
Regional Navy Commander: Admiral Mohamad Jafar
Regional Air Force Commander: Air Marshal I. Suyitno
Provincial Police Head: Brig. Gen. Sudarmaji
Public Prosecutor: B. M. Harahap
Chancellor of the University of Cendarwasih: Professor Tarumengkeng
Chairman of Provincial Representative Council: Rev. W. Maloali
Vice-chairman of Provincial Rep. Council: Colonel Noorcahyo
2nd. Vice-chairman: Dr Sumarto
Bupati (District Commissioner) of Jayapura: Th. Meset
Mayor of Jayapura: F. Imbiri
Bupatis: A. S. Onim (Manokwari); Wanma (Paniai); Andreas Karma (Yapen-Waropen); Albert Dien (Jayawijaya); J. Patippi (Merauke); Lieut. Col. Sukamto (Fakfak); Lieut. Col. Sutaji (Sorong)
Dean of Agriculture Faculty in Manokwari: Makbon
Head of Chamber of Commerce: Elpo M. Zein
Chairman of All-Indonesian Union of Importers: Indrabuchari
Chairman of Indonesian Exporters: Nazir Syafri

ASSISTANT SECRETARIES

Administration: S. Thamrin
Economic Development and Public Welfare: I. Made Marta
General Affairs: Samilan

HEADS OF GOVERNMENT DEPARTMENTS

Forestry: Purba
Agriculture: Bas Youwe
Social Affairs: S. Rumbiak
Health: Dr Suriadi Gunawan
Education and Culture: F. K. T. Poana
Fisheries: R. Soeprapto
Regional Income: B. Suradi
Inspectorate of Provincial Regions: W. Hadi
Directorate of Social and Political Affairs: Suhardi
Directorate of Village Development: I. Gondodipuro
Directorate of Agriculture: Hardjono
Planning and Regional Development (BAPPEDA): Sareco
Secretariat of Council of Local Representatives: Sihotang
Headquarters of Civil Defence (HANSIP): Lt. Col. Satam Judo Atmodjo

Academy of Administration: Samiyana
Harbour Master (Jalan Koti Harbour Complex): S. da Silva
Head of Customs and Duties: Rasikin Amin
Head of Harbour Formalities: Lewerisa

HISTORY. Writing in the Indonesian archipelago developed only after considerable contact had been enjoyed with Indian traders, and then only in the courts. Therefore, although the coasts of Irian Jaya were known from early times at least within the archipelago, there is no written proof of it. We must look to foreign sources for records referring to the existence of the island and its relationship with other peoples of the area in which it was located during the early period.

Because of the spices which grow abundantly in the eastern islands of the Indonesian archipelago – the Moluccas, Irian Jaya and adjacent islands – they could not long remain isolated from the rest of the world. Early Indian traders at the beginning of the Christian era gave the area the name of Samudranta or the Sea's Edge. It was written that at one end of Samudranta was located the island of Dwipanta or Islands' End since it was situated farthest east of the islands in the archipelago. The Indian poet Walmiki, in his epic Ramayana, wrote that in eastern Yawadwipa were located the Sjisjira Hills (Snowy Hills). Prof. H. Kern, Sanskrit scholar, and later Prof. N. J. Krom, historian, found evidence that Yawadwipa designated the Indonesian archipelago and that the Sjisjira Hills were the snowy peaks of Irian Jaya.

The great Sriwijaya empire of South Sumatra was a centre of Buddhistic learning during the first millennium of the Christian era. It was also the centre of a bustling sea trade in goods from China and India and indigenous produce including spices, aromatics, pearls, coral and jet, mother-of-pearl, and bird-of-paradise plumes.

In the seventh century, enterprising merchants from Sriwijaya arrived at the island of Irian, which they called Janggi and claimed it as part of the empire.

In the eighth century a Chinese traveller in his annals referred to Irian as Tung Ki and stated that it was part of the Moluccas.

The Javanese poet Prapantja in his work Nagarakertagama (AD 1365) mentioned that Irian formed a part of the Majapahit empire of East Java.

The Batjan chronicles relate that in 1512 a younger brother of the sultan, one Kaitjil Jelman, became ruler of the sub-kingdom of Misool and the first Islamic ruler in the region.

In the 16th century the islands of Irian, more popularly known as the Four Kings Island Group (Waigamo, Misool, Waigeo, Salawati) were brought under the authority of the Moluccan sultans. The Kingdoms of the Waigama and Misool became part of the Batjan sultanate while the sultans of Ternate and Tidore fought over the Kingdoms of Waigeo and Salawati. The wars which often erupted in this area due to the territorial expansionistic ambitions of the two sultans resulted in a re-arrangement of their authority: Ternate extended its power over the Celebes and those islands west of Halmahera; Tidore gained the area south to East Ceram and east to and including West Irian. Early in the 17th century, Tidore subjugated the Batjan sub-kingdom of Misool, thereby gaining control of the islands of the Four Kings Island Group, including East Ceram and West Irian.

The coming of the Europeans. By the 16th century, spices had become a necessity to Europeans, Asians and Africans alike, not only for food but also for medicinal purposes. The arrival back of Magellan's ship 'Victoria' in a Spanish port on Sunday, September 6, 1522, the first ship to have circumnavigated the world, brought a shipload of spices and a diary describing the area from which the spices came. This diary, belonging to an Italian passenger, is the first known European reference to the islands of Irian, making mention of a pagan King of Papua. However, he mislocated Papua.

Energetic Europeans saw a way of making a goodly profit, by transporting spices and other valuable produce – pearls, sandalwood, bird-of-paradise plumes – themselves, instead of depending on others. Such things being light took little space and brought in rich rewards. And so began the race to the Spice Islands.

The Spanish. After the first Spanish ship touched at Tidore in the year 1521 (the 'Victoria'), many Spanish ships visited it, travelling to and from Mexico. Some had to lay over in the islands awaiting favourable winds, and so discovered new islands, for example Alvaro de Saavedra in 1528 on his way to Tidor from Mexico. On June, 20 1545, the Spaniard Ortiz Retez on his way to Panama landed and, finding no hindrance, took the island of Irian in the name of the Spanish King, calling it "Nueva Guinea". However, the Spanish never again returned to take actual possession and with the Utrecht Agreement in 1714 Spain lost any rights it may have had to the island.

Of the Spanish sailors who travelled this area, it is necessary to mention one Luis Baez de Torres, who in 1606 had completely navigated the south coast of Irian and found a passage for ships in between the islands and coral reefs, that is the Torres Strait which separates the island of New Guinea from the Australian continent. This adventure remained unknown to many other European sailors for some time. In the 18th century, one-and-a-half centuries later, a map of "Nova Guinea" pictured it as an extension of "Nova Hollandia" (Australia).

Torres also visited "Onin" peninsula where he met with merchants professing the Islamic faith. They divided their time between trading and propagating Islam among the natives.

The Dutch. The first Dutchman to visit Irian, Willem Jansz, in his ship the 'Duyfken' in 1606, also touched at Kai and Aru islands and the southwestern coast of Irian where he found the land covered with dense forestation and scattered settlements of people "wild, savage, black and uncivilised," who had "murdered several of the ship's hands". Jansz was searching for new areas of trade for the Netherlands' Indies Company, however what he found was far from encouraging. The Dutch thereafter evidenced little interest in the island until it seemed that another European power had plans for opening trade stations and building a fort on the island. Dutch knowledge of Irian and adjacent islands remained slim until the beginning of the 20th century.

The British. In 1761 news reached Europe that English ships had entered the Moluccas and built a fort at Salawati. The Netherlands' Indies Company, having no idea as to whether the Company had any legal title to the area, whether spices coming under the Dutch monopoly were to be found there, or even where Salawati was exactly, established a committee, comprising two extraordinary members of the Netherlands' Indies Council and Council secretary to look into the matter. After several months of studying all available material, on November 23, 1761 a thick report of findings was submitted, containing all evidence relating to the Company's 'legal title' over the entire Great East (Groote Oost) which included West Irian.

In 1774 another Englishman succeeded in breaking the Dutch monopoly in the Moluccas. On November 9, Captain Forrest sailed out of Balambangan, an island north of British North Borneo, heading for the northern Moluccas and Irian on British East-Indies Company business. For five months he explored the northeastern seas in his ship 'La Tartare'. From January 27 to February 18, 1775 he anchored at Dore Bay (Manokwari) where he took 100 nutmeg seedlings for planting in North Borneo.

Fifteen years later the British East-Indies Company ordered Captain MacCluer to explore and map carefully the coastline of any islands around Irian Jaya. Based on MacCluer's findings, the British built a fort at Dore (Manokwari) with the permission and guidance of Nuku, a prince of Tidore governing West Irian and adjacent islands who had no love for the Dutch.

At the insistence of the Dutch Governor at Ternate, Sultan Kamaludin Sjah of Tidore registered a strong protest at this unlawful occupation of his sovereign territory. In his letter of protest dated September 15, 1794, the Sultan stated that Irian and adjacent islands had always been part of the Tidore Sultanate and demanded the immediate and absolute withdrawal of the British from the area. The English did relinquish their post by early 1795, but more probably from lack of food and resulting incidences of beriberi than as a result of Sultan Kamaludin's protest.

Twice during the early part of the 19th century the English wrested the Moluccas from the Dutch and twice they were returned with the signing of peace treaties, the last in 1814 in London. However, the return of the Moluccas as well as Irian was not de facto until 1817.

The Dutch take permanent possession. Regaining possession, the Dutch guarded their monopoly more closely than ever; the Government worried very much lest a foreigner come to occupy any part of the islands in order to break the monopoly. They would have enlarged their possessions on more than one occasion, but had not the military strength to do so. So weak were they, in fact, that when the Sultan of Sarawak requested assistance in his struggle with Brunei in 1838, the Batavian Government had to refuse, thereby losing all the North Borneo colonies (British North Borneo, Sarawak and Brunei).

During the 19th century Irian was frequently visited by European sailors and natural scientists. Among others Durmont d'Urville, the Frenchman who circumnavigated the globe in 1826-28, searching for places yet unknown to Europeans, put in at Irian at the Mamberamo estuary. There were so many visitors, some claiming parts of the island for their country, that the Dutch Government felt the need to build a fort as a sign of their legal title to Irian and to place markers on those parts of the coast which came under its law.

The first Dutch fort to be built in Irian Jaya was Fort Du Bus, erected near the Lobo settlement on Lobo Bay (Triton Bay) in 1828. Fort Du Bus suffered an unhappy history over the next eight years. Many of its residents succumbed to malaria and beriberi. The Irianese living in its vicinity persisted in their unfriendliness. Several times the fort was attacked by land and by sea by armadas from Seramlaut and Gorong in league with warriors from the local tribes. For as long as the fort remained standing with its complement of Dutch soldiers, they were not free to trade as they wished. (Note that from the 16th century the south-western coast had been monopolised at various times by rulers of Seramlaut, Geser, Gorong and Keffing.) After obtaining the authority and permission of the Dutch King, the fort was torn down and left behind forever on February 22, 1836.

Meanwhile, on August 24, 1828 it was proclaimed with ceremony that 'West Irian from 141 degrees East longitude on the south coast to the west, northwest and north up to Jamurseba, excepting that part already under the suzerainty of the Sultan of Tidore' was taken as a possession in the name of the Dutch King. It is noteworthy that from Jamurseba Point eastwards to Humboldt Bay, the region including Amberbaken, Dore, Wandamen, Great Irian Bay, Waropen, Tanah Merah, did not have to be claimed since it was part of Tidore which was already under Dutch rule.

The boundary is defined. In 1836 an extremely difficult question was put to the Dutch Government by the British Government. Exactly which areas came under Dutch authority; a question which was raised after the Dutch protested that the English had illegally entered Dutch territory, when British ships attacked a nest of pirates on Galang Island, a Dutch holding in the Riau group northeast of Bintan Island. An article in the "Singapore Free Press" a few years later to the effect that Lt. Yule of the British Navy had hoisted the Union Jack on the south coast of Irian added to the pressure on the Dutch to formulate a list of possessions.

The Colonial Government at The Hague found itself unable to come up with a satisfactory reply and in 1843 it instructed the Governor-General to prepare a detailed list of all areas considered to be directly or indirectly under the sovereignty or the influence of the Netherlands' Indies Administration. Should he come up with any 'vacancy', he was to fill in said 'vacancy' immediately by "conducting some act of sovereignty or by making some agreement (with the princes) which would include articles confirming sovereignty". It was necessary to conduct an accurate examination of all factors, which duty was allocated to the Governor in Borneo, A. L. Weddik.

In a note concerning the administrative connection of the Moluccas, Weddik reported, after his study had been completed, that in the year 1678 the west coast, the southwest coast and a large part of the northern coast of Irian were already under the suzerainty of Tidore. Based on this, the Netherlands' Indies Government issued a classified decree dated July 30, 1848 in which it was noted that the authority of the Sultan of Tidore over Irian covered the area "beginning from the tip Saprop Maneh 140 degrees 47' meridian on the northern coast, along the coastline, from Wandamen Bay to Kainkain Beba (Jamurseba) and further west, south and southeast as far as the border line stipulated ad interim in the proclamation dated August 24, 1828, that is the 141st meridian on the south coast; including also the interior as far as it seemed that that region was considered a part of the Netherlands' Indies after further exploration which would be held concerning the condition of nature of the area and the arrangement of administration of its inhabitants". Further, it was stipulated that included in the referenced area were all adjacent islands. In brief, the whole of Irian Jaya which formed an area of dispute or which the Dutch had disputed was recognised as part of the Tidore Sultanate.

Britain and Germany set up colonies. The interest of other nations in Irian was aroused. Natural scientists, sailors and travellers visited the island in considerable numbers. Warships from Italy, Russia, Britain and Germany often put in, especially at the eastern end (Papua New Guinea) whose status had not yet been defined, all contending for its ownership.

On November 27, 1882, a German reporter, Emil Deckert, outlined in the "Augsburger Allgemeine Zeitung" deliberately and with feeling the case for Germany's occupation of the eastern half of the island. The Germans reacted by collecting funds and setting up a trading company, the "Neu-Guinea Compagnie". The Australians reacted by registering a strong protest at the German plans. "The peace and security of Australia and its national importance will be threatened should a foreign nation, strong and powerful, occupy an area so close to Australia. Therefore, it is of the utmost importance that the entire east end should be immediately annexed." Not waiting for the go-ahead from the British Government in London, the Colonial Administration in Queensland proclaimed that East Irian was a possession of the Crown of England. The proclamation was dated April 4, 1883. It was not ratified by the British Government and was therefore declared null and void on June 11, 1883.

The Germans were so active in Papua New Guinea that on July 7, 1884 the British Government proclaimed its intention to occupy that part of Irian running from the 141st meridian on the south coast, eastwards to the farthest point and from there westwards to the 145th meridian East longitude. On September 18, 1884 official notification was made to the German Government with the implication that the north coast between the 141st and 145th meridians East longitude was available should somebody wish to avail themselves of the opportunity. The Kaiser needed colonies for economic reasons and did not therefore look well upon the statement from Great Britain. He took possession of the entire northern coast of New Guinea from the 141st meridian East longitude to the most eastern tip. Fortunately, the two countries were able to come to an agreement in 1885 on the boundaries of their respective colonies: a broken line beginning from the point cutting through 141 degrees East longitude and 5 degrees South latitude to 8 degrees South latitude at Mitrarock near Hercules Bay, the northeast coast at Mitrarock being dissected by the 8 degrees South latitude, which parallel also served as the borderline between the islands located on the east side of Irian.

By this agreement a strip of the north coast with a width of 0 degrees 13' without protest by the parties involved (Germany and Great Britain) was considered to be a part of the Tidore Sultanate, at that time itself being a part of the Netherlands' Indies Colonies. The boundary with West Irian, although never stipulated in any agreement, was respected by Germany and later also by Australia to whom the German colony was passed as a mandate territory at the end of World War I.

In 1901 the south coast of Irian was brought under the direct authority of the Netherlands as an assistant residency with its capital at Merauke. The rights of Tidore were exchanged with a reparations payment. Then Irian Jaya was made respectively a part of the Ternate Residency, a separate residency (1920-1924), and finally an assistant residency to the Ternate Residency which was, in turn, a part of the Great East Province (Gouvernement Groote Oost). With the division of West Irian regions within the Province of the Great East, the Netherlands' Indies authorities thereby did not treat Irian Jaya as anything other than an integral part of the Tidore Sultanate.

After the capitulation of Japan at the end of the Pacific War, Irian Jaya was given the status of a full residency.

During the Japanese occupation several underground movements had sprouted up, including the Jajabaya movement under the leadership of Martin Indey, the Manseri Mangundi movement at Biak, the Simson movement at Jayapura and various others. At the end of the Pacific War, Silas Papare, a guerilla leader against the Japanese, was awarded the Bronze Cross by the Allied Forces, who were in Irian at the time. The Allies then turned the island over to the Dutch colonial administration, irrespective of the Proclamation of Indonesian Independence of August 17, 1945.

The Proclamation of Indonesian Independence encouraged the continued opposition of the West Irianese against the Dutch Administration. Guerilla headquarters were found, among other places, in Sorong, Jayapura, Merauke and Manokwari. The Independent Indonesia Party, led by Silas Papare was established on November 30, 1945 at Serui.

Round Table Agreement. The Round Table Agreement of 1950 stipulated that the Residency of Irian Jaya would be handed over to the United States of Indonesia within one year.

On August 17, 1950, the United States of Indonesia became the Unitary Republic of Indonesia. Immediately the leaders of the West Irianese declared their loyalty to the Republic. Meanwhile the continuation of Dutch colonialism in West Irian Jaya ran unchecked. So as not to lose hold of their last colony in the area, the Dutch claimed that they wished only to bring advancement and betterment to the people.

One year passed and no settlement had been reached which accorded to the wishes of the West Irianese and the Republic. Opposition in the form of guerilla warfare increased in intensity. Efforts to settle the question through diplomatic channels on the part of the Republic also failed. In 1956 the Republic of Indonesia therefore announced that the Round Table Agreement had been unilaterally voided.

On August 16, 1956 the Republic of Indonesia formed the autonomous province of West Irian with the interim capital at Soa Siu on Tidore Island. Simultaneously, the Dutch formulated the plan to set up a separate state of Papua.

The President of the Republic of Indonesia delivered the Trikora Command on December 19, 1961, a three-pointed order to: (1) Fly the Indonesian flag in West Irian; (2) Defeat the formation of the Papuan state by the Dutch, and (3) Have the Indonesian armed forces ready to liberate West Irian. The first clash took place on January 15, 1962 in what is now known as the Aru Bay Incident. One by one the Dutch strongholds fell into the hands of the Volunteers for the Freedom of West Irian.

As a result, the Dutch took the question to the United Nations. With Ellsworth Bunker acting as intermediary, the New York Agreement of August 1962 was reached, in which it was aspired that the Dutch surrender West Irian into the hands of the United Nations Temporary Executive Authority, which action was finalised on October 6, 1962.

On November 10, 1962, with the knowledge of UNTEA, the University of Cenderawasih was established at the capital city of Jayapura with two faculties, covering the fields of Pedagogy and Law Administration.

Indonesian control. Mutual understanding was carefully nurtured between the UNTEA and the official Indonesian mission right up to the handing over of West Irian to the Republic on May 15, 1963.

In 1969 there took place the process known as "PePeRa", an Indonesian acronym for "Penentuan Pendapat Rakya", or "Determination of People's Opinion", which is commonly referred to as the "Act of Free Choice", and Indonesia took full control over West Irian.

In September 1969 President Suharto proclaimed West Irian an autonomous province of Indonesia.

The province was renamed Irian Jaya in 1973.

Various rebel movements based on the ideas of Papuan identity, and opposition to incorporation into Indonesia, have troubled the Indonesian authorities in Irian Jaya in the intervening years. The latest form taken by this opposition is the so-called Provisional Revolutionary Government of West Papua New Guinea, which claimed responsibility for the sabotage of the Ertsberg copper project. Closely associated with the existence of this movement are the delicate problems which have arisen in relations between Indonesia and Papua New Guinea over the sometimes large numbers of Irian Jayans who have crossed the border to seek refuge in PNG.

FOR THE TOURIST. Accommodation and tourist services are relatively expensive in Irian Jaya and rarely reach international standards.

Although Irian Jaya can be reached via Jakarta on the Garuda and Merpati airlines, or via Papua New Guinea aboard Air Niugini aircraft, there are no currency exchange facilities at Irian Jaya airports. A foreign tourist must obtain Indonesian rupiahs either before leaving Jakarta or at the Bank EXIM (Export and Import Bank). As Indonesian currency is linked to the $US, United States currency or travellers cheques will probably gain the most advantageous exchange rates. Papua New Guinea currency (the Kina) is not accepted in Indonesia or Irian Jaya.

Although there are plans to include Irian Jaya in the international Jakarta, Biak, Guam, Honolulu, San Francisco air route, at present there is no US-Asian-Australian or Pacific airline with direct access to Irian Jaya airports.

Internally, scheduled Merpati or MAF (Missionary Aviation Fellowship) flights are available to most centres. Garuda is equipped with Fokker F-28 aircraft; Merpati with the F-27, the Twin Otter and Cessna aircraft.

Accommodation in 1978 ranged from $US22.32 (Rp 9000) per day with meals to $US30.00 (Rp 12,000) but, in addition, there is a service charge ranging from 10 per cent to 21 per cent and a government tax, usually 10 per cent.

In the more expensive hotels and restaurants, there may be a choice of Indonesian, Chinese or European cuisine. Although 20 hotels are officially listed, only five have air conditioning. These are:

BIAK – Mapia and Titawaka

SORONG – Sorong and Utama

JAYAPURA – Dafonsoro.

Elsewhere, electric fans are available.

Television programmes, relayed from Jakarta via the national Palapa satellite, can be seen each evening after 6.30 p.m. at hotels in Jayapura and Biak.

Hotels and inns. Jayapura has eight hotels and inns listed as follows (Jalan means a street): Hotel Dafansoro in Jalan Percetakan Negara; Hotel Numbay in Jalan Trikora; Hotel Sederhana in Jalan Halmahera; Hotel Lawu in Jalan Sulawesi; Hamadi Inn in Jalan Hamadi; Mess G.K.I. in Jalan Sam Ratulangi; Guesthouse JDF in Jalan Angkasa Yoyo; Wismapraja in Jalan Tugu A.P.O. (Army Post Office).

Restaurants. Jayapura has several good restaurants supplying a wide range of Chinese and Indonesian dishes. They are: Chinese food – Restaurant Majestic, Restaurant Jakarta, Restaurant Eskimo. Mandonese (North Sulawesi) food – Restaurant Minahasa. Macasarese (South Sulawesi) food – Coto Gembira. Javanese food – Gudeg Bu Pawiro.

Shopping centres. Jayapura is now well-served by several modern shopping centres. They are: Imbi Centre in Jalan Taman Imbi; Irian Indah Centre in Jalan Ahmad Yani; Pasar Sentral Hamadi in Jalan Hamadi; Pasar Abepura in Abepura; Pasar Jaya in Jalan Koti (opposite Post Office); Pasar Ampera in Jalan Matahari.

The city has two swimming pools, the Cenderawasih in Jalan Gurabesi and Yoyo Swimming Pool in Jalan Angkasa Pura.

Sightseeing. Tourist attractions include:

Jayapura: Along the waterfront, the $US15 million new Provincial Government Office; the Sports Arena; Parliament Building; the Yos Sudarso and Act of Free Choice monuments; a Javanese theatre in the Ampera Night Bazaar; swimming at Base-G (Besji) beach; Loka Budaya Museum annex, Cenderawasih University (15 kilometres from Jayapura on the Sentani Highway) with a large collection of local art; the MacArthur monument at the Cyclops (Ifar) mountains, and his temporary World War II headquarters in Jayapura town; traditional life at Lake Sentani and the Skyline Heights overlooking the lake; and Angkasa residential area overlooking Jayapura Bay, with the dividing range between Irian Jaya and Papua New Guinea in the far east. There are at least 10 nightclubs in Jayapura of which "Scorpio" is the best known. Shops are open from 9 a.m.-2 p.m. and reopen from 5 p.m. until 9 p.m. Authentic Sentani carvings and other artefacts may be purchased at the Loka Budaya Museum of Anthropology.

Biak: World War II remains at Bosnik beach; the Japanese Dead Soldiers Monument in the subterranean lime caves; local village life along the coast; and agricultural projects in Sarwom and Wiermaker. There are three nightclubs in Biak of which the "Martini" is the most popular among foreign visitors.

Wamena: Dani tribes of the Baliem valley around Wamena, pig festivities and primitive dances, and magnificent highland sceneries.

Merauke: Attractions include majestic peaks, snowcapped all year round, on the flight from Jayapura to Merauke; and a visit to the Asmat tribe, whose woodcarving is considered the finest in Irian Jaya. The Asmat live around Agats village which can be reached by boat from Merauke. At the Asmat Museum of the Catholic Mission young artists can be seen carving artifacts.

Service clubs. In Irian Jaya, clubs such as the Rotary are non-existent. The public servants are united in the KORPRI (Korps Pegawai Republik Indonesia) – the Indonesian Public Service Corps. The wives of the Police and Armed Forces personnel have their own clubs, e.g. Bhayangkari (Police), Kartika Candra Kirana (Land Forces), Jalasenastri (Navy) and Adya Garini (Air Force). Each pursues objectives such as: supporting their husbands in their work; education of their children; promoting family health; and assisting social work for the hospitals.

JOHNSTON ISLAND

This is an atoll, 25 km in circumference, about 1,130 km WSW of Honolulu. It lies in 16 deg. 44 min. N. lat. and 169 deg. 17 min. W. long. Its height varies from about 4 metres in the west to 13 metres at Summit Peak at the eastern end.

The island was barren and uninhabited when Captain C. J. Johnston of HMS 'Cornwallis' discovered it in 1807. Both the United States and the Kingdom of Hawaii annexed it in 1858. In the next 50 years, a quantity of guano was removed. The atoll was taken over, for defensive purposes, by the United States Navy in 1934, and a seaplane base was built. Jurisdiction was transferred to the US Air Force in 1948 and since then, during nuclear testing and later, its facilities have been actively used, expanded and many improvements made. A landing field takes up almost the full length of Johnston islet.

Less than 3 km north-west of Johnston lies Sand (or Agnes) Island, which is only 2.5 metres high and 180 metres in diameter. A semi-circular reef, encloses both islands.

Johnston Island is serviced by Air Micronesia which provides four flights a week out of Honolulu, Monday, Wednesday, Thursday, Saturday. The U.S. army controls the island which is used as a storage site for chemical munitions which may still include poison gas transferred there from Okinawa.

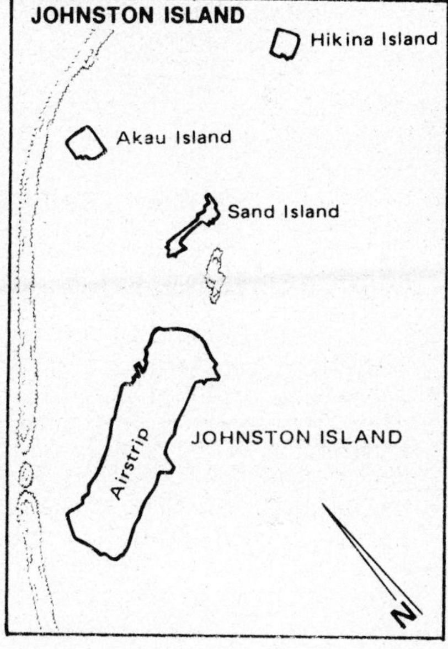

JUAN FERNANDEZ ISLANDS

The Juan Fernandez Islands, three small islands of volcanic origin, lie at a distance of 667 km and more west of Valparaiso. They are Chilean possessions. The largest, most important and nearest to Chile was formerly known as Mas a Tierra (Nearer to Land) and is now officially designated Robinson Crusoe's Island. It has an area of 93 sq. km. Just off the southwest tip of this is Santa Clara Island, otherwise known as Goat Island because it is inhabited only by wild goats. This island has a maximum height of 375 m above sea level. Heavy seas make access to the coast difficult and dangerous. About 170 km further west is Mas Afuera (Further Away), which the Chilean Government has called Alexander Selkirk's Island since 1966. It has an area of 85 sq. km and the highest point is 1,836 m. These are volcanic islands and all are mountainous and rugged.

The climate is mild with an annual average temperature of 18 deg. C. Regular year-round air services link Robinson Crusoe Island with Santiago and Valparaiso, and in the summer a monthly boat service operates between the islands and Valparaiso.

There are many sporting activities to be enjoyed with skindiving in the clear warm waters (constant at 22 deg C) a popular pursuit for visitors. The beautiful lobsters, which are plentiful in the surrounding waters and are served in a variety of ways in the restaurants, are said to be the largest in the world.

Hotels on Robinson Crusoe are the Hosteria Robinson Crusoe, Cabanas Daniel Defoe, El Pangal, Renaldo Green Pension, and many islanders rent low-cost accommodation to visitors.

The islands were uninhabited in pre-European times. Their European discoverer, Juan Fernandez, came upon them in 1574 on a voyage to Valparaiso from Callao, Peru. Spanish fishermen first settled them in 1591 and introduced the first goats. This and subsequent settlements, such as one by Jesuits from Chile in the 1660s, were shortlived. However, passing ships, particularly those of English buccaneers, found the islands useful sources for water and provisions. In 1681, the English buccaneer Bartholomew Sharp left a Mosquito (Panama) Indian on shore when he was surprised by the arrival of three Spanish men-of-war. The Indian lived there for three years and served eventually as the model for Friday in Daniel Defoe's novel 'Robinson Crusoe'. The model for Crusoe himself was Alexander Selkirk, a Scotsman, who was landed in the group at his own request, and taken off five years later.

The cave and lookout post said to be used by Selkirk can still be seen on the island.

After Commodore Anson visited the islands in 1740 and went on to capture a Spanish galleon, the Spaniards in Chile sent several hundred men and women to occupy Juan Fernandez and build a fort. Their settlement eventually became a penal settlement, but was abandoned in 1814. Between 1797 and 1808, a number of American and British sealing vessels made profitable visits to Mas Afuera; and for much of the rest of the century numerous whalers, particularly from the United States, fished in the vicinity and called at Mas-a-Tierra for provisions.

Juan Fernandez came under Chilean control after Chile achieved independence in 1819. From then onwards, the islands were occupied almost continually either as a penal settlement, place of exile for political prisoners, or for fishing and agriculture. The development of steam navigation and the opening of the Panama Canal in 1914 reduced the group's importance to shipping. But in 1915, Cumberland Bay on Mas-a-Tierra was the scene of an engagement between the German warship "Dresden" and H.M.S. "Glasgow" in which the Germans blew their own vessel up after a few shots had been fired.

Growing concern by scientists over the destruction of the natural resources of Juan Fernandez led President Alessandri of Chile to decree the islands a national park in 1935. Meanwhile, the number of colonists had increased from the few score of most of the 19th century to more than 400, and by 1978 the population stood at 800. Most of the residents of recent years have been associated directly or indirectly with the crayfishing industry. The village of San Juan Bautista on Cumberland Bay is their chief settlement. Yachts and fishing boats anchor in the bay.

Further Information: Ralph Lee Woodward, Jr. 'Robinson Crusoe's Island', Chapel Hill, North Carolina, 1969.

KERMADEC ISLANDS

The Kermadec Islands are a rocky group lying 965 km northwards of Auckland, between S Lat 29 deg 10 min. and 31 deg. 30 min. They are a New Zealand dependency administered by the New Zealand Land and Survey Department for the preservation of indigenous flora and fauna. The only present inhabitants are 10 New Zealand personnel on Raoul Island, who man the meteorological station which is maintained there by the NZ Ministry of Transport.

The principal islands are: Raoul (or Sunday) Island, 2 916 ha; Macauley Island, 309 ha; Herald group, 34 ha; Curtis Island, 59 ha; L'Esperance (French Rock), 5 ha.

The islands are volcanic, and thermal activity is present on Raoul, which is 32 km in circumference. There is plentiful rainfall and the climate is mild and pleasant. Total land area of the group is 33 sq. km.

Raoul Island is thickly wooded, triangular in shape, and rises towards one end to a height of 525m. It is very fertile, and almost every kind of tropical and sub-tropical plant will grow on it. There are four crater lakes or swamps, and at least two of them contain fresh water, which is not potable.

Raoul is the island regarded as most habitable. Communication is difficult – there is no sheltered anchorage, and ships cannot land a boat in rough weather. There is no public passenger service to the islands.

In 1936, as trans-Pacific aviation plans developed, the group attained a new significance, because it is about halfway betwen Tonga and New Zealand. In July, 1937, a meteorological reporting station was established on a plateau 40m above sea level on the north coast of Raoul, just off Fleetwood Bluff and across the island from the former Denham Bay settlement.

The prevailing wind is easterly and light. The mean annual temperature is about 19 deg C, with extremes of about 28 deg C and 9 deg C. Rainfall averages about 1 450 mm annually. In good weather there is a fair yacht anchorage at Boat Cove.

Landings in the Kermadecs are permitted only with special permission because the islands are an important nature reserve.

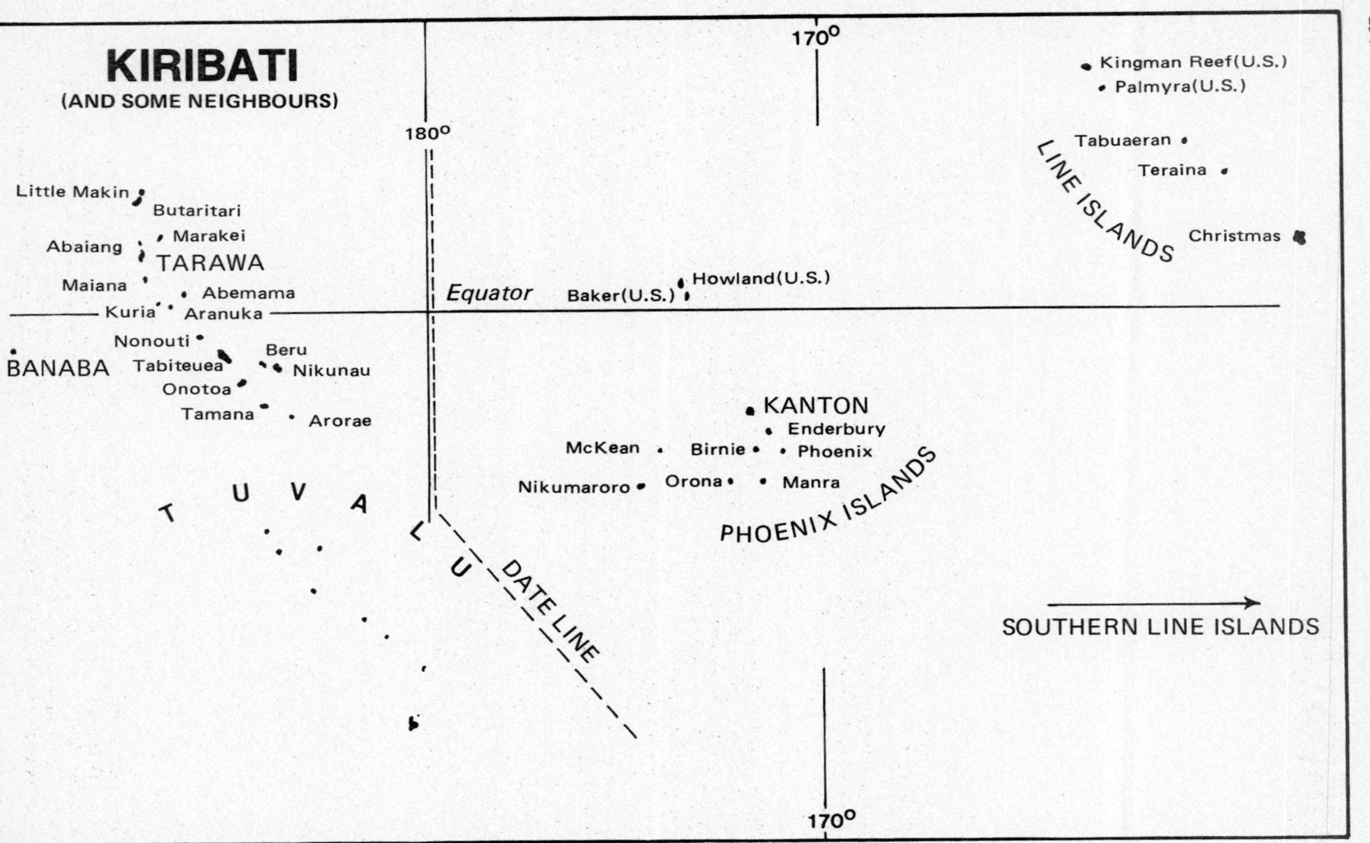
KIRIBATI
(AND SOME NEIGHBOURS)
180°
170°
Little Makin
Butaritari
Abaiang
Marakei
TARAWA
Maiana
Abemama
Kuria
Aranuka
Nonouti
BANABA
Tabiteuea
Beru
Nikunau
Onotoa
Tamana
Arorae
TUVALU
Equator
Baker(U.S.)
Howland(U.S.)
KANTON
Enderbury
McKean
Birnie
Phoenix
Nikumaroro
Orona
Manra
PHOENIX ISLANDS
DATE LINE
Kingman Reef(U.S.)
Palmyra(U.S.)
Tabuaeran
Teraina
LINE ISLANDS
Christmas
SOUTHERN LINE ISLANDS
170°

KIRIBATI

This group of 33 islands, lying astride of the equator over an area of five million sq. km. of ocean, was named the Gilbert Islands in the 1820s and was administered by Britain from 1892 until July 12, 1979, when it became an independent republic with the name of Kiribati (pron. Kiribas, the nearest pronunciation in the indigenous tongue to the word 'Gilberts').

The country, a member of the Commonwealth of Nations, consists of three main groups – the Gilberts proper, Phoenix, Northern and Southern Line Islands with Ocean Island. They are situated between 4 deg. N. and 3 deg. S. latitude and 172 to 177 deg. E. longitude. The most populous island, Tarawa, is about 1,800 km north of Suva, Fiji. The administrative centre, Bairiki, is on Tarawa. Local time is 12 hours ahead of GMT. The population, according to the 1978 provisional census figures, was 56,452.

Kiribati has retained the original design of the flag of the former British Colony of the Gilbert and Ellice Islands. The flag depicts a frigate bird poised in flight over a sun on the horizon. Three wavy lines underneath the sun represent the three island groups, the Gilberts, the Line Islands and the Phoenix Islands. The country's motto under the Coat of Arms is "Te Mauri, Te Raoi, Te Tabomoa (Health, Peace and Honour), a traditional phrase formerly used for toasts, good wishes and for ending speeches. The National Anthem is "Teirake Kain Kiribati" (Stand Kiribati).

The Gilbert group of islands was formerly known as Tungaru in the Micronesian language but, as other islands now forming part of Kiribati were not known by that name and were not a part of the original group, it was decided, in the interests of unity, to adhere to the name Gilberts bestowed on the whole group by the Russian hydrographer A. I. Krusenstern in the 1820s and retained by Britain.

The people are now known as I Kiribati. As there are only 13 letters in the language, and 'S' is not one of them, Kiribati is the nearest one can get to the phonetic sound of Gilberts. A 'T' followed by 'I' becomes an 'S', hence Kiribas. The final 'I' is not sounded unless followed by another word beginning with a consonant. In any event a 'T' cannot end a word.

Australian currency is legal tender but it is expected that Kiribati will, eventually, have its own currency.

Local public holidays are January 1, Good Friday, Easter Monday, Queen's Birthday, August bank holiday (a British institution), Independence Day (July 12), the Prince of Wales' birthday, Christmas Day and Boxing Day.

THE PEOPLE. Until October 1, 1975, the Gilbert Islands were joined with the Ellice Islands in a single British colony. On that date the Polynesian inhabitants of the Ellice Islands seceded to form Tuvalu (see entry under that name). The Gilbert Islanders (I Kiribati) are Micronesians.

The last census was held in December, 1978, at which time the total population (not including people on ships) was provisionally estimated at 56,452. An ethnic breakdown was not available but the 1973 count gave the total for the Gilbert and Ellice as 57,813, of which 47,711 were resident in the Gilbert Islands, consisting of 43,996 Micronesians, 1,215 Polynesians and 2,125 other Pacific Islanders including people of Micronesian-Polynesian descent.

Population distribution. There were in December, 1978, 18,116 people in urban Tarawa, forming 32 per cent of the total for the republic. Christmas Island, on which several development projects have started or are planned, had the most rapid population growth. In 1976 there were 674 people on the island and, according to the 1978 census estimate, this total had grown to 1,288 by the end of 1978.

The 1978 census indicated a fall in the growth rate of urban Tarawa from 6.7 per cent per year for 1968 to 1973 to 4.3 per cent for 1973-78. The departure of Tuvaluan civil servants after Tuvalu separated from the Gilberts in 1975 would have an affect on the growth statistics.

Demographic projections indicate that, with a

growth rate of 4.3 per cent per year for the 15 years to 1993, the Tarawa urban population would increase by 15,950 to a total of 34,066 at which level the density would be 4,705 persons per sq. km. against the existing density figure of 2,502. Hong Kong's population density in the mid-1970s was 4,062 persons per sq. km.

The population of the rural islands was virtually static from 1968 to 1973 but preliminary returns from the 1978 census suggested an increase from 1973 to 1978 of about 1,500, or 0.8 per cent per year. With the end of phosphate mining on Ocean Island (Banaba) at the close of 1979, about 1,270 I Kiribati were expected to leave the island for their home islands.

The population in the outer islands in December, 1978, was: Makin 1,421; Butaritari 3,164; Marakei 2,312; Abaiang 3,608; Maiana 1,685; Kuria 862; Aranuka 852; Abemama 2,402; Nonouti 2,293; Tabiteuea North 2,995; Tabiteuea South 1,295; Beru 2,216; Onotoa 2,043; Nikunau 1,741; Tamana 1,351; Arorae 1,527; Fanning 434; Christmas 1,288; Washington 417; Banaba 2,000 (approx.).

Population age structure. The following table gives the population age structure in 1973 with projections for 1978 and 1988.

Age	1973	%	1978	%	1988	%
0-14	22,383	43.8	23,311	40.9	29,201	40.1
15-54	24,367	47.6	28,909	50.7	37,864	51.9
Over 54	4,412	8.6	4,758	8.4	5,818	8.0
Total	**51,162**	**100**	**56,978**	**100**	**72,883**	**100**

Nationality. On independence (July 12, 1979), all persons of Kiribati descent automatically became citizens of Kiribati. Those born in Kiribati but not of Kiribati descent also became citizens at independence. Wives of I-Kiribati are also eligible for citizenship. Dual nationality is prohibited. Banabans automatically became citizens and the Constitution also safeguards other rights with regard to representation in the House of Assembly, Banaba land and entry into Banaba.

Language. The people speak a Micronesian dialect and English, which is used in official communications. The Constitution is silent on the question of a change in the official language with independence.

Migration. As a marine training school has operated successfully for several years in Tarawa, several hundred Kiribati men are crewing overseas ships and have acquired an excellent reputation. Their earnings, sent home for support of their families, play an important part in the country's economy. Others are working in other South Pacific countries but the end of phosphate mining on Banaba has forced more than a thousand to return to their home islands. Nearly two thousand are still employed in the phosphate workings in Nauru.

Religion. The main Christian denominations are Roman Catholic and the Gilbert Islands Protestant Church (Congregational). There are small numbers of Seventh-day Adventists and Baha'i.

Lifestyle. The Gilbertese are very much men of the sea, surrounded as they are by the waters between their numerous small islands. Traditional skills include cultivating babai (taro), fishing, making and sailing canoes. Outer island life is essentially affluent-subsistence with cash income from copra and some remittances. On South Tarawa the cash economy prevails and population pressure has resulted in a dependence on imported foods.

Recreation. Islanders' main interests are dancing, canoe-racing, volleyball and traditional games.

GOVERNMENT. From November, 1976, to July 12, 1979, Kiribati had internal self-government. It was originally decided that the country would gain its independence in June, 1978, but the protracted bid by the Banabans to secede and seek to have their island placed under the protection of Fiji as their "other" island of Rabi is in Fiji, caused a postponement. The date was eventually set after the British Government had ruled against the Banabans' claim.

The government consists of the President (Beretitenti), who is Head of State and Head of Government, a Cabinet composed of the President, the Vice-President (Kauoman-ni-Beretitenti), not more than eight other ministers from among the elected members of the House of Assembly and the Attorney-General. The President appoints his own Cabinet.

The President is elected nationally from among members of the House of Assembly (Maneaba-ni-Maungatabu) which nominates not less than three or not more than four as candidates. No one other than an elected member of the Assembly can be a presidential candidate. In the event of parliament's dissolution as a result of the President ceasing to hold office following a vote of no confidence, the Constitution provides for a Council of State, composed of the Chairman of the Public Service Commission, the Chief Justice and Speaker of the House of Assembly, which carries out the functions of president and government until an election has been held.

The term of office for both the president (Beretitenti) and the House of Assembly is four years. A president can be re-elected for two more terms. A vice-president, who assumes the office of president before the president's full term has expired, can serve only two further terms in the office of president.

Presidential powers include the granting of pardons, on the advice of Cabinet, to persons convicted of offences in law, or remit or substitute punishment ordered by the courts.

With regard to the House of Assembly, the president can withhold assent to a Bill if he is of the opinion that the Bill would be inconsistent with the Constitution. In such a case, the Bill is returned to parliament. If parliament again presents the same Bill to the president and he is still of his original opinion, he then refers it to the High Court. If the High Court declares that the Bill is not inconsistent with the Constitution, it is returned to the president who must then assent to it. A contrary decision by the High Court means that the Bill must go back to parliament. Parliament can alter provisions of the Constitution by an Act of Parliament subject to certain limitations with one exception – the provisions protecting the fundamental rights and freedoms of the individual. An act to alter any of these provisions must have the consent of not less than two-thirds of the electorate voting in a referendum.

The single-chamber legislature consists of 35 elected members, a representative of the Banabans nominated by the Rabi (Fiji) Island Council and the Attorney-General as an ex officio member. If the president is the elected representative of a constituency entitled to only one member of the assembly, a by-election is held in that constituency for the election of an additional member.

So far as the Banabans are concerned, the Constitution gives them a seat in the House of Assembly, returns to them land on Banaba acquired by the government for phosphate mining, and the right of any Banaban to enter and reside in Banaba. Banaba land can only be compulsorily acquired by leasehold and only then after consultation with the Banaban Island Council.

The Constitution also provides for the establishment of a Banaba Island Council and the appointment of a Commission of Inquiry three years after independence to review the special arrangements made by the Constitution for the Banabans. Any constitutional provision relating to the Banabans can only be amended if the Banabans' nominated representative does not vote against any amendment.

Residence of any Banaban on Rabi Island in Fiji, does not affect his rights or interest in any land on Banaba.

Local government. Island Councils are established on all permanently inhabited islands.

Since 1958 Island Councils have been able to make their own estimates of revenue and expenditure. Because of the scattered nature of the territory, the Councils have considerable freedom from direct supervision.

By 1970 councils on all the islands were functioning with elected members only.

For administrative purposes, since 1976 the islands have been divided into six districts, each in charge of a District Officer. The districts are: Tarawa, Northern, Southern, Central, Ocean Island and Line Islands.

Justice. The constitutional provisions governing justice are similar to those in force in other former British possessions. There is a High Court, which is a superior court of record with a chief justice and such number of other judges, if any, which might be prescribed. The chief justice is appointed by the president acting on the advice of the Cabinet tendered after consultation with the Public Service Commission. Other judges are appointed by the president on the advice of the chief justice sitting with the Public Service Commission. To qualify as a judge, a person must have held office as a judge in any country or has been qualified for not less than five years to practise as a barrister or solicitor. Judges can only be removed from office by the president and such removal must be by parliamentary resolution with parliament acting on the advice of a tribunal.

The High Court has original jurisdiction to hear and decide questions relating to interpretation of the Constitution and to hear and decide on any civil or criminal proceedings including those in any subordinate court.

There is a Court of Appeal for Kiribati which has jurisdiction and powers to hear and determine appeals as may be conferred on it by any law in force in Kiribati. The judges of the Court of Appeal are the chief justice and other high court judges and any other qualified persons who may be appointed by the president on the advice of the chief justice and the Public Service Commission.

The Constitution makes no mention of any referral to the Privy Council in London as is the case in some former British possessions. There are magistrates' courts as main courts of first instance on each inhabited island with five on Tarawa. Three magistrates sit together to try criminal and civil cases and five to hear lands cases. Their jurisdiction in land matters is unlimited but their criminal jurisdiction is limited to cases carrying a punishment of up to five years imprisonment and a fine of up to $500. Their maximum civil jurisdiction is $3,000.

Police. As well as having the responsibility for the maintenance of law and order, the Kiribati Police Force has responsibility for fire fighting services at airports and for domestic fire services in the urban area of South Tarawa. For police purposes, the country is divided into seven districts: Northern, Tarawa, Central, Southern, South Eastern, Banaba and the Line Group. Each district is commanded by an assistant inspector with the exception of Tarawa district, which is commanded by an assistant superintendent. In January, 1978, the force consisted of 177 men, 74 on South Tarawa, 12 on Banaba, 13 in the Line Group and between one and five in the rural islands. The ratio of police to population was 1:245 for Urban Tarawa, and between 1:431 and 1:2,402 for the rural islands of the Gilbert Group. There were also 77 special constables.

The total number of cases reported under the Penal Code rose from 3,468 in 1976 to 3,476 in 1977 and dropped to 2,451 in 1978. Police stations linked by radio in 1978 were Betio, Bairiki, Bikenibeu, Abaokoro, Banaba, Police HQ (Betio) and the airport fire tender. The rest are in contact through the normal radio telephone service.

Prisons. There are several prisons and lock-ups and work was continuing in 1979 on a new central prison on Tarawa to be opened in 1980. The average prison population in 1978-79 was 57 in five prisons. The Community Affairs Division of the Ministry of Health and Community Affairs concentrates on employing prison labour for public benefit and as part of a rehabilitation programme.

Liquor laws. The islanders may drink beer or liquor but have to get a licence to drink sour toddy on certain islands, where the Councils have by-laws to that effect.

DEFENCE. It was decided in December, 1975, to create a defence force, which would also be employed on development projects. A force of about 170 men was suggested. However, the plans were not proceeded with and the National Development Plan of 1979-82 makes no mention of a defence force.

EDUCATION. There has been no basic change in educational policy with the coming of independence, the National Development Plan of 1979-82 announcing that no fundamental change in policy was envisaged for the plan period, the policies being closely in accord with the objectives framed in December, 1975, which were listed as:

- To provide free and compulsory primary education by 1980 for classes 1 to 6;
- Improve the present standard of primary education;
- Integrate as far as possible all primary schools into a unified system;
- Establish post-primary 'Community High Schools' with a curriculum in accord with the rural environment;
- Provide, in association with the missions and churches, sufficient places in academic secondary schools to produce the students needed to meet requirements for skilled technical, professional and administrative manpower;
- Involve schools, both staff and pupils, in the total rural development programme.

Primary education. So far as primary education is concerned, there is a shortage of qualified teachers. In 1978, 122 of the 414 teachers in the government primary schools were completely untrained while a further 139 were only partly trained on various short courses.

At March 1, 1978, there were 13,236 primary pupils at government schools giving a ratio of 32 pupils to one teacher. At the same date, more than 12 per cent of all classes contained more than 40 pupils and some classes were very large. The ratio of 1:32 is expected to remain until some time after 1983.

Legislation was scheduled for January 1, 1980, making attendance at school compulsory for all children aged 6; in 1981 for all children aged 6 or 7 years; in 1982 for all children aged 6, 7 or 8. School fees were abolished in January, 1977, for all pupils in classes 1 to 6 in the government primary schools, except those on South Tarawa, Banaba and in the Line Group. Further abolition of fees was planned for all aged 6 in 1980, aged 6 and 7 in 1981 and all aged 6, 7 or 8 in 1982.

In 1977, most former mission schools, together with the mission teachers, were absorbed into the government primary school system. In 1978, five primary schools operated by religious organisations remained registered as private schools with a total of 245 pupils and 15 teachers. The government indicated its willingness to absorb them all if the schools sought it. Although primary school education was not compulsory at March 1, 1978, of an estimated population aged 6-11 of 9,500, 9,453 were enrolled in primary classes. Primary school enrolment and staffing at March 1, 1978, is tabled here:

	Number of Schools	Pupils	Teachers
Govt. Schools	79	13,236	414
Pte. Schools	5	245	15
All Schools	**84**	**13,481**	**429**

The development plan projected enrolments in government primary schools to total 12,737 with 439 teachers in 1979, 12,408 with 433 teachers in 1980, 12,000 with 423 teachers in 1981 and 11,418 with 408 teachers in 1982.

A survey of primary school classrooms in 1977 revealed that, of 392 classrooms in government primary schools, 132 were of temporary construction in local materials and 141 were in need of replacement or extensive repair. It was planned to construct and furnish 20 new classrooms a year from 1979 to 1982.

Community High Schools. These are intended to offer a type of education suited to the rural environment in which most would live and, at the same time, develop attainments and skills beyond those achieved at the primary level. The schools are not aimed, primarily, at preparing pupils for formal employment but to raise the educational quality of the intake at such institutions as the Marine Training School and the Tarawa Technical Institute and, also, in the general labour force. The schools are also intended to involve the whole surrounding community in a wide range of activities.

Four Community High Schools were established as a pilot project in 1977 on the islands of Makin, Maiana, North Tabiteuea and Tamana. At March, 1978, there were 384 students at the schools, 95 at Makin, 50 at Maiana, 162 at Tabiteuea North and 77 at Tamana. The projected output from these schools was 182 in 1979, 239 in 1980, 227 in 1981 and 206 in 1982. Further training in specialist skills was needed for teachers in such subjects as manual arts, home science, commerce and language.

Academic secondary schools. These schools are intended to provide manpower in the technical, professional and administrative fields. There are five secondary schools with a total enrolment of 873, 437 boys and 436 girls at March 1, 1978 – the government's King George V and Elaine Bernacchi School on Tarawa with 393 students; the Catholic Senior

College, North Tarawa, with 56; the Catholic Junior College at Abaiang with 170; the Hiram Bingham School at Beru with 152 and the Seventh-day Adventist High School at Abemama with 102. They are all co-educational boarding schools. All these schools, with the exception of the Catholic Senior College, provide a three-year course to the Kiribati Junior Certificate Examination. The best performers in the junior certificate examination may be selected to continue academic education in forms 4 and 5 at the KGV and EBS or the Catholic Senior College. A sixth form was established at KGV and EBS in 1978 and the Catholic Senior College for those successful in the fifth form course at KGV and EBS and the Catholic Senior College who wanted to take degree or diploma courses overseas after passing the Cambridge Overseas School Certificate Examination. Projected enrolments in the academic secondary schools were: 1979, 924 pupils; 1980, 972; 1981, 995 and 1982, 1,002.

Overseas studies. At the end of 1978, there were 88 students overseas on higher education courses, 65 pre-service students and 23 in-service. Thirty were on pre-degree or pre-diploma courses, 35 on degree courses and 23 on diploma courses. The majority were in Fiji, others being in New Zealand, Australia, the United Kingdom and elsewhere. The duration of the courses varied from one to three years for a diploma and from three to seven years for a degree. High wastage rates had been experienced in higher education, due mainly to deficiencies in the quality of local school education. Most of the in-service training was for short, upgrading courses, mainly involving teachers. Nine primary teachers are sent each year on a one-year diploma course to the United Kingdom. Planning required a total of 325 persons with higher educational qualifications by 1988.

Technical training. The Tarawa Technical Institute on Betio provides all "short" full-time, part-time and evening courses in English, Kiribati, typing, shorthand, carpentry, commerce, prison warder training, magistrates' clerks training, first-aid, civil service training and clerical, but the only full year, full-time course is for telecommunications technicians. Fourteen were enrolled for this course in 1978, and there were 593 students taking the short-term courses. The development plan will result in an extension of courses to include management training, plumbing, concrete practice, block-laying, accounting, business administration, office procedures, small business accounting, trade testing and licensing, teacher training in industrial arts and intensified civil service training. Adult Education evening classes will be extended and courses will also be offered in new annexes at Bairiki and Bikenibeu and at the Community High Schools on outer islands.

Teacher training. The Tarawa Teachers College is responsible for all basic primary teacher training in Kiribati. The total roll in 1979 was 114 on a two-year primary course. The intake is 45 per year. Developments planned include upgrading courses for inadequately training teachers, a three-year course, in-service training in specific fields such as language teaching and training additional teachers for the new Community High Schools.

Marine training. The Marine Training School conducts one-year courses in basic seamanship with three courses starting each year. The course intake was increased from 60 to 70 in 1977 and 210 trainees entered the three courses which began in 1978. The success rate for the previous three courses completed was 78 per cent, giving an output of about 164 on an intake of 210.

The school also conducts a short upgrading course for able seamen, engine-room greasers and stewards, who have returned from periods of contract service overseas. The success rate for these courses was 80 per cent in 1978 when 37 such courses were held for an enrolment of 359 trainees.

The school was started by John Swire of Hong Kong and the then Resident Commissioner, Mr V. J. Andersen. The Merchant Marine Training School opened in 1967 with the purchase from Europe of the vessel 'Teraaka'. In 1976 more than 800 qualified I Kiribati were employed on overseas ships, mainly those of China Navigation and Columbus Lines.

Almost the entire output of the school is now employed by the South Pacific Marine Service, a consortium of German shipping lines. Attempts to find employment for I Kiribati outside the consortium are frustrated by overseas maritime unions which impose wages and service conditions without any prior discussion with I Kiribati. The Pacific Forum Line is seen as a possible source of employment for Kiribati seamen. Until other sources of employment become available, the school plans no further expansion.

LABOUR. Because the concept of formal employment is unfamiliar to many I-Kiribati, information concerning the strength of the labour force is sparse, the only reliable figures available being from the 1973 Census. At that time the total workforce, including Tuvaluans, was 24,059 (11,616 males and 12,443 females) composed of 10,127 active in the villages, 5,062 wage employees, 732 seeking work and 8,138 not active. The principal occupations in Kiribati are provided by the copra plantations, particularly in the Line Islands, central and local government, the co-operatives, missions and private companies. Distribution of wage employees in 1973 was Tarawa 61 per cent, other areas 39 per cent. The figures have been affected by the shut-down of the phosphate mining on Banaba. At the end of 1976, the mines employed 336 I-Kiribati, 137 Tuvaluans, 13 Banabans and 17 Chinese. All the I-Kiribati were to return to their home islands at the beginning of 1980. In 1976, 418 I-Kiribati were employed by the Nauru Phosphate Corporation on Nauru and 81 by the Nauru Local Government Council. As development progresses on Christmas Island, more workers are finding jobs there. In 1976 there were 275 I-Kiribati and 13 Tuvaluans on the island's copra plantation, 61 I-Kiribati and one Tuvaluan on Fanning Island and 64 I-Kiribati and five Tuvaluans on Washington Island. The Tuvaluans are now being replaced by I-Kiribati. In the same year, 1,113 I-Kiribati and 56 Tuvaluans were in full-time employment in the New Hebrides, most on contract terms in government employment. The Kiribati Co-operative Federation employed 101 I-Kiribati in 1976. Until it was liquidated in 1977, the Gilbert Islands Development Authority employed nearly 1,200 I-Kiribati who continued in employment after the liquidation as the authority's functions were taken over by the government, which took over its public works functions, and the National Loans Board which absorbed the trading companies.

The seamen. In 1976, there were 871 trained seamen in the labour force, most of them working on overseas ships and sending home cash remittances totalling $800,000 a year. South Pacific Marine Service ships take the bulk of the I-Kiribati seamen – 633 in 1976. Nauru Pacific Line had 58 in the same year. It is hoped that there will be employment for graduates of the Marine Training School with the Pacific Forum Line, now moving into top gear.

Wages. The minimum wage level early in 1976 was 39 cents an hour with persons under 18 years of age on 30 cents an hour. Some government wage earners were getting 67 cents an hour. Seamen overseas are on considerably more, but figures are not available to give a clear picture of the more up-to-date earning capacity of the people. However, National Income figures suggest an increase in personal incomes of about 6 per cent a year. The retail price index is moving at about 9 per cent a year.

Trade unions. Trade unions have developed in association with particular companies or the government service and just before and after independence some unions became more militant, particularly the Public Employees' Union and the BKATM, and there have been some strikes. The latter union, which was formed by the employees of the now-defunct Gilbert Islands Development Association (GIDA), amalgamated in 1979 with the Banaba Phosphate General Workers' Union and the Line Islands International Union. Another union, the Kiribati General Workers' Union, appeared on the scene in 1979. Government plans to promote increased understanding and co-operation between the unions, employers and the government.

HEALTH. The Ministry of Health and Community Affairs is responsible for health services, which include village work in sanitation and water supplies, disease control and family planning.

Hospitals. There are two major hospitals in the Gilberts: the Tungaru Central Hospital at Bikenibeu, Tarawa (135 beds), and the Betio Hospital, both including dental clinics. They are supported by a number of rural hospitals and dispensaries.

Valuable assistance is received from organisations such as UNICEF, WHO, SPC, New Zealand foundations and the Red Cross, as well as from the medical profession in overseas countries.

Diseases. Diarrhoeal disease is very common and can only be reduced as safe water supplies and better waste disposal are provided. Programmes underway for the control of tuberculosis and leprosy resulted in a fall in the registration of new TB cases from 433 in 1961 to 158 in 1974. At the same time new cases of leprosy fell from 75 to 9, with 120 cases still under treatment in 1974. After 18 deaths from cholera in 1977, a WHO team was brought to the islands to supervise the implementation of stricter measures for water control and sanitation.

An environmental health programme has provided protected water supplies and sanitary latrines and the effect of these has been to lower the rate of child morbidity. Child health is one of the areas in which the latest development plan is concentrating and a programme covering the three contributing factors, nutrition, sanitation and social factors, has been developed to tackle the problems. The report on which the development plan is based reveals that special studies of child health show that at least 10 per cent of Kiribati children under five years of age suffer from malnutrition. In some areas the level is as high as 30 per cent.

Family planning. This policy has been actively pursued so that by 1976, 25 per cent of the female population concerned was using reliable methods of birth control. The urgency of the matter is underlined by the fact that real national income is not likely to grow at the rate of population increase which would have occurred if the average of five or six children per family had been allowed to continue.

Reports in 1979 indicated that the total number of users of family planning systems continued to increase but there was a movement away from the use of intra-uterine devices in favour of the pill or injection.

THE LAND. The land area of Kiribati is 822.76 sq. km with sea limits enclosing 3,000,000 sq. km, although with Kiribati's declaration of a 200-mile economic and fisheries zone the area will be much greater. The country consists of the Gilberts Group, 278.35 sq. km; the Line Group, 515.71 sq. km, and the Phoenix Group, 28.70 sq. km. Some of the islands have reverted in the official list to their local name.

The official estimate of Kiribati's land area is 719 sq. km., but this figure does not include the uninhabited islands of Malden (81 sq. km.), Starbuck (16.20 sq. km.), Caroline (2.27 sq. km.), Vostock (0.66 sq. km.) and Flint (3.24 sq. km.).

There are 17 islands in the Gilberts Group, Banaba (Ocean Island) now being officially claimed as part of the group, which consists of: Makin,

Butaritari, Marakei, Abaiang, Tarawa, Maiana, Abemama, Kuria, Aranuka, Nonouti, Tabiteuea (North and South), Beru, Nikunau, Onotoa, Tamana, Arorae, Banaba.

The Line Group: Tabuaeran (Washington), Teraina (Fanning), Christmas (the Northern Line Group), Malden, Starbuck (the Central Line Group), Vostok, Caroline, Flint (Southern Line Group).

The Phoenix Group: Canton, Orona (Hull), Nikumaroro (Gardner), Manra (Sydney). Phoenix, Birnie, McKean, Enderbury.

Christmas Island – locally Kiritimati (Kirisimas) – is the largest island with an area of 363.65 sq. km. The largest in the Gilberts Group is Tabiteuea (38.01 sq. km), and the smallest Tamana (only 4.81 sq. km) Kiribati extends about 3,870 km from Banaba in the west to Christmas Island in the east, and 2,050 km from Washington Island in the north to Flint Island in the south. The country stretches from 4 deg. 43 min. E to 11 deg. 25 min. S and from 169 deg. 32 min. E to 150 deg. 14 min. W. The islands are all low-lying atolls except for Banaba which is 87 m above sea level.

Natural features. With the atoll terrain, the coral rock is covered with only about 2.5 m of hard sand and scanty soil. There are no rivers but most islands enclose a lagoon.

Resources. Only Ocean Island is endowed with natural resources, in the form of once enormous and rich deposits of phosphatic rock.

Climate. The climate of the groups is not unduly trying, particularly during the season of the north-easterly trade winds (March-October). But it becomes enervating during the season of rains and westerly gales (October-March). The thermometer varies little, the lowest reading being 22 deg. C and the highest 37 deg. C in the shade – but usually it is between 26 and 32 degrees C.

Rainfall varies considerably, not only between the islands, but also from year to year. In an average year annual rainfall in the Gilberts ranges from 1,000 mm in the vicinity of the equator, including over 1,500 mm at Tarawa, to 3,000 mm in those islands furthest to the north. In the Phoenix Islands between 1,000 and 1,500 mm in one year is a good figure, whilst the Line Islands' average varies from about 700 mm at Christmas Island to more than 4,000 mm at Washington Island 400 km away. Ocean Island, the central and southern Gilberts, the Phoenix Islands and Christmas Island are subject to severe droughts lasting many months. At such times as little as 200 mm of rain may fall in a year.

Flora and fauna. The thin layer of soil on the atolls supports little growth, apart from seaside scrub, pandanus and coconuts. Native land fauna is limited to the Polynesian rat. Sea life is considerably richer, with its birds, fish and coral.

Land reclamation. On urban Tarawa the Temaiku Reclamation Scheme in 1970 retrieved almost three sq. km of land from the lagoon adjacent to the airport runway. There is often a need for sea walls to protect land from further invasion by the sea.

Land tenure. Most of the land in the Gilberts is owned by islanders in small peasant holdings. The sale of land by locals to non-nationals has been prohibited since 1917. Only an insignificant area remains alienated, mostly owned by missions. Land affairs are supervised by the Ministry of Home Affairs.

Washington and most of Fanning Island in the Line Group are the freehold property of a subsidiary of Burns Philp and Co. Ltd.; and Christmas Island is owned and worked as a plantation by the Government. Negotiations were being held in 1980 for the government to buy back Washington and Fanning Islands.

Land ownership in customary law, which has been codified, does not include unrestricted right of disposal. Tenure is a form of limited entail and generally speaking, the owner is regarded as having no more than a life interest and is required to pass-on the land to his next-of-kin at his death.

There are a few circumstances, however, under which an owner may dispose of land to other than his next-of-kin and these circumstances account for most of the incessant land litigation which is so marked a feature of life in Kiribati.

The customary inheritance law whereby each child receives a share of the parents' lands has led to continuous sub-division so that some holdings now consist of only three or four coconut trees.

As is to be expected, this form of sub-division is accompanied by widespread fragmentation of the holdings of individuals, both on one island and between several islands. The result is the anomaly that despite such land-hunger, the general standard of cultivation and development is low.

The Administration has tried to contend with these twin problems by encouraging owners to consolidate their holdings by exchange or leasing, and by advising Lands Courts when distributing estates to avoid the customary practice of sub-dividing every plot of land and instead to share the plots between the next-of-kin. In addition, following the Neglected Lands Ordinance of 1959, the government redistributed considerable holdings.

Main problems in recent times, apart from land ownership, have centred on the adequate supply of development land in urban Tarawa, which the government is seeking to provide under leasing arrangements.

PRIMARY PRODUCTION. The islands' only exported agricultural produce is copra. During the 'sixties, production averaged roughly 7,400 tonnes per annum, with little or no investment taking place. Most output was from Gilberts farmers (5,400 tonnes) with an additional 2,000 tonnes from Line Islands plantations. During the 'seventies incentives were being provided by the government to promote new planting and improve existing coconut groves.

Production has continued to fluctuate, however, as the accompanying table shows.

COPRA PRODUCTION

	Small-Holders	Plantations	Total
1970	5,106	1,868	6,974
1971	6,457	2,451	8,908
1972	3,208	1,903	5,111
1973	7,115	1,464	8,579
1974	9,540	2,663	12,203
1975	2,287	1,646	3,933
1976	6,215	2,152	8,367
1977	6,420	1,473	7,893
1978	8,258	1,999	10,257

New plantings in the Line Islands could result in higher production over a longer period.

Fruit. Food crops for local consumption are mainly babai (taro), coconuts, bananas, pandanus, breadfruit and papaw. Tomato growing is also being encouraged.

Livestock. Efforts are being made to establish strains of pigs and poultry suitable for local breeding. Imports of poultry, eggs and frozen meat were worth about $150,000 in 1972 and it is hoped local farming efforts can reduce such imports. In 1977 food accounted for 27 per cent of imports.

Fisheries. Locally caught fish form the staple of the islanders' diet. Kingfish, snapper and tuna are the main varieties caught by netting, trolling, on lines or in fish traps.

Considerable hopes are placed on development of marine resources. These centre on yellowfin and skipjack tuna and, more especially, the lagoon-farming of brine shrimp, pennaeid shrimp and fish. The chief areas of interest for lagoon-farming and aquaculture are around Tarawa and on Christmas Island, in the Line Islands. By 1977, the only project that was successful was the bait fish ponds. It was still hoped that the tuna and brine shrimp fisheries could be developed.

Efforts have continued and fishing trials by Japanese experts using the cultured baitfish between December, 1977, and February, 1978, were reported as being highly successful for both skipjack and yellowfin tuna. Sufficient quantities of baitfish are being produced on 40 ha of ponds at Temaiku, South Tarawa for the early stages of a commercial tuna fishing operation. The maximum yield of baitfish so far has been 2,820 kg per hectare per year. Catch trials in 1979 by a government-owned ship have been successful.

Fisheries zone. Kiribati declared a 200 mile fisheries and economic zone in April, 1978, giving the country potential control of a sea area of about 1,061,300 sq. km, but this was confined to the Gilberts Group. As Kiribati has now resolved the question of the American claims to 14 islands in the Line and Phoenix groups with a pact with the United States under which the United States relinquishes all claims, creation of further fishery zones in those groups will not be long delayed.

Licensing. Kiribati concluded an agreement with Japan for licensing Japanese ships to fish in its 200-mile zone, the Japanese agreeing to pay Kiribati $A520,000 a year in 1980 and 1981 and to provide a further $300,000 "in kind" for development projects. According to Minister of Finance Tiwau Awira in his 1980 budget speech, the amount Kiribati will get initially from Japan and Korea is about $675,000 less than expected. Korea will pay $163,000 for an annual licence and Kiribati was hoping at the end of 1979 to reach agreement with Taiwanese fishing interests. Towards the end of 1979, a Japanese survey team was in Tarawa to plan details of fisheries projects which the Japanese have promised to finance to the tune of $2 million. Kiribati has also asked Japan for a fishing ship similar to 'Nei Tewenei', a fish catcher provided under the Australian Aid programme.

Fish farming. I-Kiribati have placed great hopes on development of marine resources on Christmas Island particularly with regard to the brine shrimp and milkfish projects. The former project is expected to contribute at least $1 million a year to Kiribati's income and later the figure could reach $4 million a year. Early in 1980, Christmas Island was exporting 1½ tonnes of milkfish to Nauru and **half a tonne of lobsters to Honolulu each week and** expected this trade to earn $350,000 in 1980.

Training. A fisheries training section has been formed by the Fisheries Division to train technicians and some fisheries staff have attended courses in Japan, Israel and the Solomons.

Local fishing industry. There are plans to establish a tuna fishing company in partnership with an established company with Butaritari as the base and to establish a long-line fishing fleet in the Line and Phoenix groups. It is also hoped to improve subsistence fishing in the outer islands.

Forestry. Trial plantings of local and imported trees being conducted in collaboration with CSIRO, Melbourne, had achieved little success. The aim is to encourage local production and reduce timber imports which have been costing some $150,000 annually. Research is proceeding on growing types of timber in an atoll environment. It is intended to concentrate trials on Christmas Island where there is adequate land. Attention is also being paid to the opportunities for producing workable timber from old coconut trees felled and left to rot as a result of the coconut replanting programme. A mobile sawmill was scheduled to be in operation before the end of 1979.

Pests. A survey of insect pests was undertaken at the end of 1977. It was noted that there were relatively few insect pests in Kiribati, the main ones being the stick insect and the taro beetle. There are, however, very few of these. Quarantine facilities are being installed at the main ports of entry.

A poisoning campaign funded by the New

Zealand Government is being carried on to rid three rat-infested islands, Tarawa, Abaiang and Butaritari, of the ship rat.

MANUFACTURING AND MINING. Local industry is confined to small operations such as handicrafts, the salting of fish and kamaimai, biscuit and soft drink plants, and small boat building. The handicrafts (fans, mats, bags) are made principally from the pandanus leaf and have particularly intricate and colourful designs.

Most private businesses are centred on South Tarawa, but the government, using the National Loans Board, plans to assist private enterprise to increase the number of small businesses offering employment opportunities. Licensed businesses on South Tarawa at the end of 1978 totalled 280 consisting of furniture and carpentry 3, bakery 5, sour toddy 22, biscuit manufacture 1, clothing manufacture 1, construction and maintenance 31, bus operators 12, taxi/vehicle hire 17, stores and shops 108, hawkers 26, restaurants and cafes 17, hotel 1, entertainment 9, fishermen 13, farm 1, services (vehicle repair, insurance, laundry) 13.

MINERALS. The phosphate mining industry will disappear from the records as from 1980, the mining operations on Banaba closing down at the end of 1979.

Although there are no other proven commercial mineral resources, Kiribati is hoping that mineral wealth on the seabed may make a valuable contribution to the country's income in the future. Research carried out in the early 1970s indicated that there were offshore phosphate deposits in a region extending from Nauru through to Kiribati and Tuvalu, but the reserves are small and should have a relatively short life. There is more optimism displayed over manganese nodules on the seabed. Geologists at Columbia (USA) University's Lamount-Doherty Geological Observatory have identified an area of manganese nodules which stretches to Kiribati waters around the Line Group, and is described by the geologists as the best nodule field in the world.

PHOSPHATE INCOME

The income from phosphate exports and taxation since 1970 is shown in the accompanying table.

	Exports		Tax
	$'000	tons '000	$'000
1970	5,338.1	500.8	2,290.2
1971	7,510.2	625.8	2,690.9
1972	6,042.6	503.6	2,652.7
1973	10,637.4	730.3	2,909.9
1974	18,851.1	521.5	10,603.4
1975	26,745.0	521.4	22,783.4
1976	17,154.6	420.1	9,566.2
1977	15,741.2	418.6	8,301.3
1978	17,849.6	855.5	8,010.0[a]
1979	n.a.	n.a.	6,642.5[a]

a. Official Estimates

TOURISM. War relics on Betio, scene of one of the bloodiest battles of the Pacific War, and the attractions of visiting places off the beaten tourist track, are to be exploited by a newly-formed Kiribati Visitors Bureau in an attempt to attract tourists, insignificant in numbers up to the present. The Development Plan 1979-82 aims to develop a tourist industry which should play a significant role in the country's future. A tourist promotion film has been commissioned and a travel brochure produced, and Kiribati has joined the Pacific Area Travel Association (PATA). Visitors in 1976 totalled 614 and, in 1977, 796, but the figures do not distinguish true tourists. However, they included 60 Japanese in 1976 and 70 in 1977, and, with Japanese tourists pouring into the South Pacific in increasing numbers, many to visit the Pacific War theatres, Kiribati hopes to make a viable tourist industry. Difficulties to surmount include Kiribati's isolation, high air fares and lack of facilities.

At the end of 1979, Kiribati had three hotels, the Otintai on South Tarawa (26 rooms), which doubled its accommodation in 1979, the Captain Cook on Christmas Island (24 rooms) and the Abemama on Abemama Atoll (8 rooms). The Otintai and the Cook are operated by the government-owned Atoll Hotels Ltd. and the Abemama by private enterprise for the Abemama Island Council. In addition, each outer island has a rest house which is available for rent. Average room occupancy in the Otintai in 1977 was 48 per cent and in the Captain Cook 40 per cent. The latter was originally built to provide accommodation for the technicians working on the Japanese Downrange Tracking Station installed on the island by the Japanese National Space Development Agency.

It is planned to expand regular air services between Tarawa and Honolulu through Christmas Island which began in 1980, and to increase hotel accommodation by nearly 100 rooms. A second hotel will be built on South Tarawa and another on Christmas Island.

LOCAL COMMERCE. Local retail trade is dominated by co-operative societies. The movement has the major share of trading in Tarawa and a virtual monopoly outside the capital, except for Ocean Island and Christmas Island.

The co-operative movement had nearly 100 retail outlets in 1976 when there were 35 primary co-operatives with a total membership of 20,445, more than a third of the population.

Wholesale supplies for the co-operatives used to be imported by the government-owned Wholesale Society but this was absorbed in January 1972 into the Development Authority (dissolved in December 1977).

In addition, several private trading firms based on Betio operate retail stores there and elsewhere.

OVERSEAS TRADE. In 1974, value of exports rose dramatically compared with those for 1973 because prices for phosphate from Ocean Island almost quadrupled. This was because the price there is linked with that on Nauru where the president, DeRoburt, insisted on parity with the top world phosphate prices. However, since then, world prices have dropped. Phosphate from Ocean Island and copra accounted for 99 per cent of export earnings.

As phosphate mining ended in 1979, export totals will drop dramatically from 1980, but Kiribati has known for some time that the income from the Banaba operations would end in 1979 and has endeavoured to lessen the impact the end of mining will have on the economy. Attempts have been made to increase copra output but the industry relies very much on the weather. The accompanying table shows exports from 1974 to 1978 with a forecast of the 1982 figures.

EXPORTS
$'000 fob

	1976	1977	1978	Forecast 1982
Phosphate	17,155	15,741	17,849	—
Copra	956	2,432	2,513[a]	2,600
Handicrafts	36	30	na	100
Fisheries	—	—	na	300
Brine Shrimp	—	—	na	100
Other Commodities	—	9	na	100
Total Exports	18,147	18,212	na	3,200

a. Provisional

The 1979 totals are not available.

Imports. Imports consist mainly of food, fuel and manufactured goods and have increased by about 17 per cent yearly since 1970. The growth of machinery and transport equipment in recent years reflects acceleration in development, but the most rapid growth in import values has been in fuel oil caused by price increases levied by the oil-producing countries. In the accompanying table, the totals for 1975 include Tuvalu imports.

IMPORTS
$'000 cdv/cif

	1975	1976	1977	Forecast 1982
Food	3,030	2,943	3,207	5,000
Fuel	941	1,360	2,111	4,000
Manufactured Goods[a]	3,979	14,130	4,721	7,600
Other Imports	1,331	1,629	1,654	2,500
Total Imports[b] (cdv)	9,281	10,062	11,693	19,100
Total adjusted to cif basis	11,137	12,074	14,031	22,920

a. including machinery and transport equipment

b. imports are recorded on a 'current domestic value' basis. It is estimated that the equivalent cif value is about 20-25 per cent higher.

Suppliers. Australia provided 54.9 per cent of imports in 1975. Other sources included Britain (11.5 per cent), Japan (7 per cent), Fiji (5.3 per cent), New Zealand (3.6 per cent), Singapore (3.2 per cent) and Hong Kong (3.1 per cent).

Handicrafts and local produce such as shark fins and beche-de-mer are seen as affording opportunities for increasing the export trade to offset, as far as possible, the demise of the phosphate trade and the development plan provides for programmes to increase vegetables, poultry and egg production and cut exports and for developing handicraft production. Islanders are to be encouraged to acquire new skills in making jewellery from coral and shells. As shown in the export table (left), handicrafts earned $36,000 in exports in 1976 and $30,000 in 1977. The United States, which already takes a share of Kiribati production of handicrafts, Australia and New Zealand will be the main targets for the export drive. With the end of the phosphate, which was

LOCAL PRODUCE PRODUCTION

		Northern $	Central $	South Eastern $	Southern $	Total $
1975	**Handicrafts**	1,147	3,478	19,734	6,764	31,123
	Produce	39,499	41,086	10,946	14,252	105,783
	Total	40,646	44,564	30,680	21,016	136,906
1976	**Handicrafts**	40	1,225	10,460	7,783	19,508
	Produce	32,762	20,609	19,486	7,773	80,630
	Total	32,802	21,834	29,946	15,556	100,138
1977	**Total**	60,144	14,116	35,737	21,610	131,607
1978[a]	**Handicrafts**	2,946	265	2,493	5,351	11,055
	Produce	42,367	30,702	11,887	4,788	89,744
	Total	45,313	30,967	14,380	10,139	100,799

a. November

RECURRENT EXPENDITURE
($'000)

	Recurrent Budget Total	Allocation to RERF	Special Items	Contribution to Dev. Fund	Net Recurrent Expenditure
1973	7,793	1,039	—	8	6,746
1974	12,702	6,889	—	548	5,265
1975	30,404	19,526	3,535	549	6,794
1976	12,251	2,705	2,117	512	6,917
1977	12,442	1,555	1,712	1,517	7,658
1978	13,951	—	1,495	1,462	10,994

INTERNAL REVENUE 1977-1982
($'000)

	1977	1978	Est 1979	1980	Forecast 1981	1982
Direct taxes	885	880	1,060	820	880	935
Indirect taxes	2,818	2,510	2,553	2,370	2,410	2,520
Phosphate taxes	8,301	8,082	6,544	—	—	—
PWD overheads[a]	—	450	300	320	340	360
Tuna licences	—	259	1,000	1,360	1,430	1,500
Other income	1,947	2,807	3,140	3,390	3,630	3,850
Total revenue	13,951	14,938	14,597	8,260	8,690	9,165

a PWD overheads is the amount of administrative costs on public works projects financed by aid donors.

bought mainly by Australia and New Zealand, Britain will head the list of best customers as the copra buyer.

Customs tariff. A single-line metricated tariff structure was introduced in 1975, thereby eliminating Commonwealth preference tariffs.

Tariff matters are handled by the Division of Customs and Excise within the Ministry of Finance.

FINANCE. Tax on phosphate for Ocean Island has been providing more than half of the total revenue derived by the Gilbert Islands. Additionally, overseas aid was providing over 10 per cent of revenue and funding most of the budget for capital expenditure.

Through a Revenue Equalisation Reserve Fund (RERF), government savings have been used to acquire an investment portfolio to help overcome the budget deficit expected when phosphate revenue ceased in 1980 for which year the income from phosphate tax is shown as a token figure of $1,000. The 1979 phosphate income was more than $7 million. RERF's value at the end of October, 1979, was $68 million and was expected to total $70 million by the end of 1979. The fund is managed by a London stockbroking firm and is invested in the United Kingdom, the United States, Japan and Germany. At the end of 1973, the fund totalled a mere $6 million but, with the high prices in the mid-1970s it has built up rapidly. The EEC's STABEX Fund, which compensates developing countries for losses on the export earnings of certain primary products exported to Europe such as copra, has benefited Kiribati to the tune of $3 million for the poor copra years of 1975 and 1976. However, this is a loan which has to be repaid. But the EEC agreed in October, 1979, that any future STABEX payments would be in the form of grants and not loans.

The Budget. The 1980 Budget, the first to tackle the problems arising from the end of phosphate income, was presented in the House of Assembly late in 1979 by Finance Minister Tiwau Awira with the comment: "I doubt if there have been many other ministers of finance who have had the doubtful honour of declaring the country's main economic asset officially dead." The budget provides for a revenue from all sources of $13,099,020 of which $10,443,460 comes from the Ministry of Finance. Increased revenue was expected from the sale of stamps to collectors. Total estimated expenditure for 1980 was $13,086,470, which was nearly $1.5 million less than the total expenditure permitted for 1980 under the terms of Britain's Independence Financial Settlement, and $977,000 less than the approved estimates for 1979. Under the settlement, Britain's "farewell" present to the I-Kiribati, Britain gives Kiribati in budgetary aid $2 million in 1980, $3.1 million in 1981 and $4 million in 1982. Under the same settlement, Kiribati has to contribute to the budget from RERF $4.25 million for each of the three years of the settlement period. As Kiribati expected an income from RERF investment dividends for 1980 of at least $5 million, the surplus of $750,000 would be reinvested.

External aid. Most aid comes from the United Kingdom, Kiribati having, with Tuvalu, formed the British Colony of the Gilbert and Ellice Islands. The United Kingdom funded nearly half of the 1978 development expenditure of $6,420,000, and a considerably higher proportion in earlier years. Other donors include Australia, New Zealand, the EEC and the various United Nations agencies. Aid is in three kinds – capital aid in actual finance for construction or engineering projects; aid in kind, equipment materials; technical aid, the provision of personnel for particular positions and provision of finance and facilities for training and higher education. From independence in 1979 to the end of 1982 Britain's assistance will total about $40 million, including the $9.1 million in budgetary aid and $15.5 million in development aid for various projects including fisheries, technical training, engineering schemes and the redevelopment of Banaba. Other aid will be for continuation of the Technical Co-operation Programme, additional support for emergencies, joint venture financing and other sound development projects. Australian aid for a sewerage scheme, new machinery and transport will total about $4 million and New Zealand aid from 1978 to 1981 amounts to $1,256,000. The United Nations Development Programme (UNDP) amounts to $673,000 over the same period. From the European Development Fund comes $4,150,000.

Tax system. Past reliance on phosphate earning resulted in the phosphate tax providing more than half of locally-derived revenue. Import duty accounts for more than one tenth of local revenue while less than 10 per cent comes from personal and company tax.

Import duties, many of which were increased in the 1980 Budget, will remain the major source of local revenue. The government is hoping that fishing licences taken out by the distant fishing nations will help to bridge the massive gap caused by the Banaba mine closure. There was no increase in income tax under the 1980 Budget as the government was waiting to assess the amount of wage and salary increases expected to apply in the first full financial year after independence.

Revenue and expenditure is shown in the accompanying tables.

Currency. Australian currency is legal tender. Sterling coins are accepted but circulate at par with Australian coins. American dollars are used at Canton and are accepted elsewhere.

Banks. Most local savings are deposited with the Bank of New South Wales which operates agencies on most islands. This bank entered the territory in 1970 and took over the operations of the government savings bank and many functions of the government treasury.

Overseas investment. The government welcomes investment from overseas sources as in the case of shipping companies supporting the Marine Training School, and fish farming projects at Christmas Island.

Development Plan. Planning since 1973 has concentrated on creating a new economic foundation needed with the end of phosphate mining on Banaba. The current plan, 1979-82, has been framed very much with external aid in mind as Kiribati cannot hope to continue as a viable country, especially as it is now independent, without a considerable amount of external aid at the outset. However, all the projects outlined in the plan, the fourth in a series beginning in 1970, aim to bridge the gap created by the loss of income from phosphate, raise living standards in the outer islands and, at the same time, preserve the 'distinctive culture' of I-Kiribati. The tuna fishing industry is seen as the major national asset for economic development, but efforts will also concentrate on tourism, fish farming, the copra industry and growth in air transport to strengthen links with the outside world. Christmas Island, which is over half the area of Kiribati, is planned as an alternative growth centre to Tarawa. External aid will play a big part in the plan. Christ-

DEVELOPMENT EXPENDITURE
($'000)

	Gilberts Group (Rural)	Line and Phoenix Groups	Urban Tarawa	Mixed/ undeterminate Location	Total
Agriculture	952	581	41	101	1,675
Fisheries	413	345	1,600	587	2,945
Urban Works	—	—	4,406	—	4,406
Urban Amenities	—	—	6,875	—	6,875
Air and Sea Communications	1,480	1,500	2,114	871	5,965
Rural Infrastructure	944	1,213	—	1,135	3,292
Commerce and Industry	130	1,175	668	150	2,123
Health	1,391	—	341	1,745	3,477
Education	250	—	682	7,473	8,405
Administration and Law	223	1,555	1,107	683	3,568
Miscellaneous	—	—	—	2,225	2,225
TOTAL	5,783	6,369	17,834	14,970	44,956

mas Island represents a very promising asset as it is wholly owned by the government.

Development expenditure for 1977 totalled $3,565,800 and for 1978 $6,420,400.

Postage stamps. Kiribati is hoping to increase its income from its postage stamps and in 1979 the government joined forces with an important philatelic firm in Bristol, England, in a joint commercial venture with the UK firm directing sales. Philatelic sales in 1976 totalled $173,611 but, although later figures are not available, this total was well exceeded in 1978 and 1979.

TRANSPORT. The high cost of transport and Kiribati's remoteness are significant factors in the high price of imports. Local transport is mainly via the lagoons and by air.

Roads. There is a reasonably good road running the length of South Tarawa from Bonriki through to Bairiki and work on sealing this road on its entire length was carried out in 1979. There were high hopes that communications would improve with the building of a four-kilometre causeway between Bairiki and Betio which are linked by launch service but engineering problems which surfaced after the work was started caused what is hoped will be only temporary abandonment of the project. A loan worth $1.15 million was obtained from the Asian Development Bank to build the causeway but, when work stopped, only $30,000 had been spent. Each island has roads suitable for bicycles and motor cycles and, usually, there is a road running alongside the lagoon.

Vehicles. There are about 2,000 vehicles in Kiribati of which nearly three-quarters are motor cycles. There are several bus companies.

Overseas airlines. Air Pacific and Air Nauru have regular services connecting Tarawa with Nauru and Suva, where other connections can be made.

An additional weekly flight (Tuesdays) by a Norfolk Island Airlines 10-seat plane began in July, 1980 between Suva and Tarawa.

In 1976 Mercer Airlines of California, USA, began to operate an air service between Tarawa and Christmas Island, 2,812 km to the east.

Domestic airline. The internal Air Tungaru Corporation operates from Tarawa to Abemama, Tabiteuea, Butaritari, Nonouti, Marakei, Maiana, Nikunau, Onotoa and Beru, at least twice a week. There is also a service to Christmas Island.

Kiribati has obtained from the United States a permit to operate a service by Air Tungaru from Tarawa to Honolulu via Christmas Island, taking in Kanton Island to service the American base on that island, served in the past by charter plane. The inaugural flight was early in 1980.

The internal air service carried 14,593 passengers in 1978 and, as the service operates at a loss, it is subsidised to the extent of about $6.30 per passenger.

Local airfields. International flights operate through Tarawa at Bonriki Airport which has new terminal buildings opened in 1979. A re-constructed and wider runway costing $1.2 million is planned for 1980-82.

Domestic airfields are at Abemama, Tabiteuea, Butaritari, Nikunau, Onotoa, Nonouti, Marakei, Maiana, Beru and Christmas Island.

Port facilities. The main overseas port in the country is on Betio, Tarawa. The wharf has a frontage of 92 m. There are three cranes in operation. There are three warehouses with a total floor space of 1,205 sq. m. Night operations are hampered by inadequate lighting.

All overseas vessels are worked by tugs and barges from anchorages off shore, since neither the length of the wharf nor the depth of the harbour are adequate to accommodate overseas vessels. Three tugs and five barges are in operation. The port is equipped to handle container traffic.

The construction of wharves and ports elsewhere in the country is made difficult by the extensive reef areas, nearly dry at low tide, which surround most of the islands. The lagoons, however, offer safe anchorages. The lagoon at Butaritari is of a depth and size which make it a natural harbour and it is proposed as the location for a shore based tuna fishing operation.

The reef flats around the islands constitute a major constraint on development, since they severely limit access by boat to the islands for passengers and cargo. A programme of reef blasting by a team of New Zealand experts has cleared channels on some islands and facilitated access for fishermen and workboats of larger vessels anchored off the reefs. There are requirements on some islands for blasting of passages for larger vessels. Dredging of passages is also sought on some islands.

A shipyard is located in the harbour basin at Betio. The yard has carried out construction of the 23 m landing craft Nei Nimanoa, a 12 m tug and a number of barges. The yard also carries out repairs to government and other vessels. The yard was formerly part of GIDA but was placed under the control of the Ministry of Communications and Works on liquidation of GIDA.

Ports of entry are Banaba, Tarawa, Fanning and Christmas islands. There is a customs officer and an immigration officer at each of these ports, and medical officers at all ports except Fanning. Banaba Island and Tarawa have harbour masters and pilots. It is likely that Banaba's port will be downgraded. In 1976, 227 vessels including 44 overseas ships, were handled at Betio.

Shipping services. Kiribati has difficulty in attracting shipping lines because of its remoteness. In 1979, Bank Line, which regularly serviced the Line Islands picking up copra, announced its withdrawal, but Warner Pacific agreed to take over the service. Nauru Pacific Line operates a regular cargo/passenger service from Melbourne to Nauru and Tarawa, and the Japanese Daiwa Line operates a container service every 30 days from Sydney

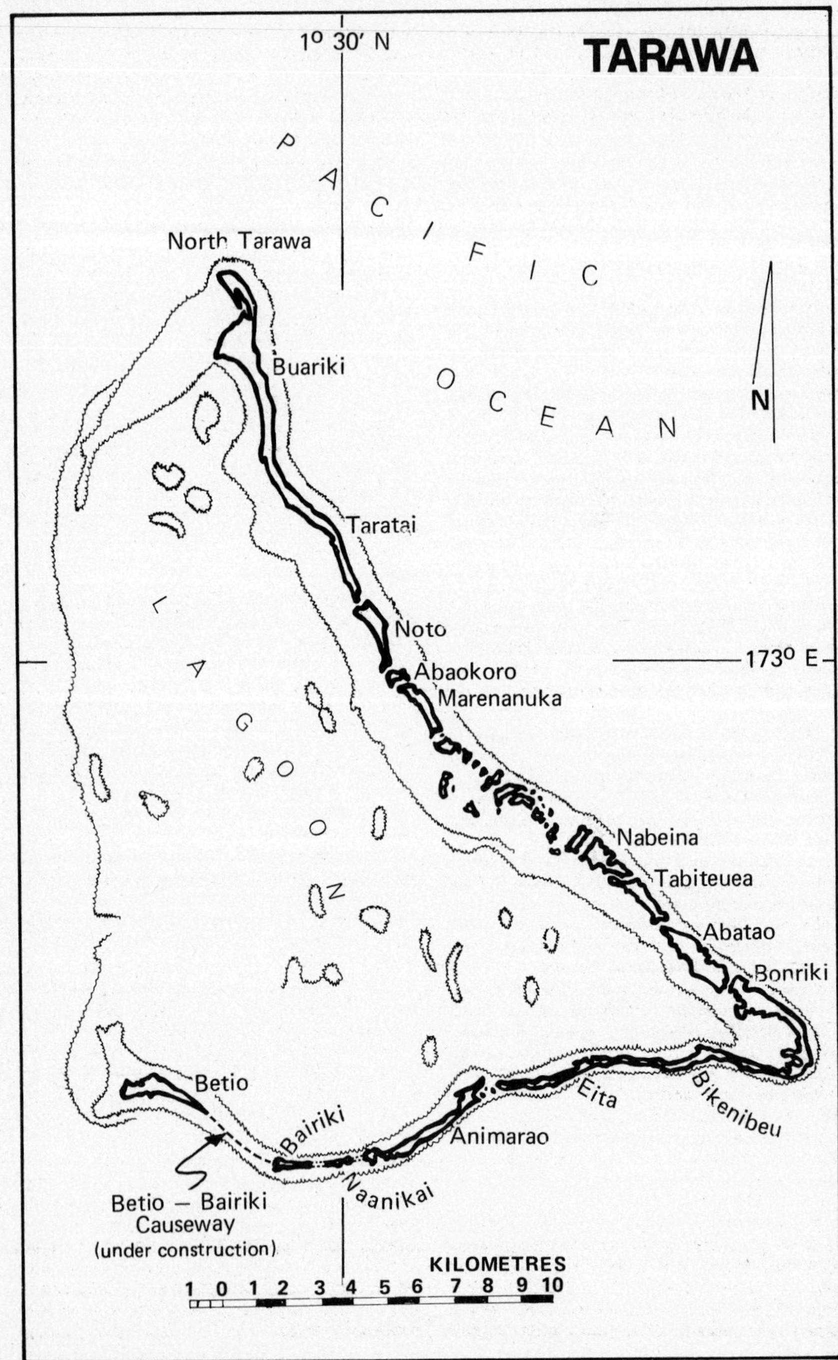
TARAWA
1° 30′ N
173° E
PACIFIC OCEAN
LAGOON
N
North Tarawa
Buariki
Taratai
Noto
Abaokoro
Marenanuka
Nabeina
Tabiteuea
Abatao
Bonriki
Bikenibeu
Eita
Animarao
Bairiki
Naanikai
Betio
Betio – Bairiki
Causeway
(under construction)
KILOMETRES
1 0 1 2 3 4 5 6 7 8 9 10

through Honiara and Kieta to Tarawa and also a monthly cargo service from Japan through Guam, Fiji, Tahiti, the Samoas, New Caledonia and Honiara to Tarawa and then on to Guam.

Internal shipping services are operated by the Kiribati Shipping Corporation (KSC) and two small private operators. The Corporation was established following the liquidation of the Gilbert Islands Development Authority, which was previously responsible for the operation of shipping services. The corporation operates inter-island services and various ferry services, including the service between Betio and Bairiki.

Over the three years 1976-78 an annual average of 8,000 freight tons of general cargo and 600 freight tons of fuel have been shipped to outer islands from Betio. From the outer islands to Tarawa the loading has been 2,000 freight tons of general cargo and about 13,500 freight tons of copra. About 9,100 passengers are carried from Tarawa to outer islands and back each year. Carriage of both cargo and passengers between outer islands is very small.

The inter-island fleet operated by the KSC consists of three motor vessels and two landing craft and two private vessels, of 12 and 8 tonnes are operated by Compass Rose Enterprises and Teikaraoi Co. respectively. The training ship 'Teraaka' has also provided freight and passenger services to the outer islands in the course of its marine training schedule. A landing craft and four launches are used between Betio and Bairiki and a twice-weekly ferry service operates between North and South Tarawa.

COMMUNICATIONS. The Telecommunications Division of the Ministry of Communications and Works is responsible for telecommunications throughout Kiribati and maintains the following services: high frequency radio links to all except the Line Islands; Tarawa and international telephone services; internal and external telegraphic services; internal teleprinter circuits; ship-to-shore communications and marine safety network; ground-to-air and air-navigation systems and specialist communications for ministries and statutory authorities. Improvements to all these services are foreshadowed in the Development Plan including the installation of manual telephone exchanges on outer islands when justified by subscriber demand and the creation of a link of international standard between South Tarawa and Christmas Island, with HF radio links between the three main Line islands. Commercial radio-telegraph services are provided to Suva and Nauru, and there is an international radio telephone through Suva. Eight trans-receiver sets, costing $1,000 each, were installed in outer islands in March, 1980.

Radio. The Broadcasting and Publications Authority (BPA) was established by law and began operations in January, 1979, replacing the Broadcasting and Publications Division of the Chief Minister's Office. The authority has a chairman and not less than five members appointed by the Minister of Home Affairs, and has a monopoly of broadcasting in Kiribati. It is financed by government grant and revenue from radio and publications advertising. Radio Kiribati has good reception throughout the Gilberts Group but not in the Line Group which, it was anticipated, would be included by late 1980 as a new and more powerful transmitter has been acquired. Radio Kiribati is on the air from 0600 to 2200 Monday to Friday, from 1200 to 2200 on Saturdays and from 1100 to 2200 on Sundays.

Newspapers. BPA also produces a weekly newspaper, "Atoll Pioneer" in English and a monthly "Te Uekera" in the Kiribati language. There are also monthly newspapers in the vernacular published by the churches. Tarawa is on the Peacesat network which is used for educational transmissions through the University of the Pacific centre at Suva.

WATER AND ELECTRICITY. Water supplies come from wells, roof catchments and galleries on urban Tarawa and from wells and some roof catchments in the rural areas. Drinking water from the galleries is piped along South Tarawa to fill communal tanks and storage tanks, the latter being filled by tanker delivery in times of drought. Roof catchments are mainly on private houses. No charges are made for water supplies except for bulk delivery by tankers when the rate is $3.25 per 1,273 litres. Following the cholera outbreak in 1977, it is planned to provide all households with access to protected supplies of drinking water and upgrade the water supply system on Tarawa.

A power house on Betio supplies electricity to the whole of South Tarawa and there are a number of small private and local government-owned generators in the outer islands.

PERSONALITIES AND ORGANISATIONS

Beretitenti (President) and Head of Government: Hon. Ieremia Tabai

CABINET

The Beretitenti: Ieremia Tabai
Kauoman-ni-Beretitenti (Vice-President) and Minister of Home Affairs: Teatao Teanaki
Minister of Trade, Industry and Labour: Taomati T. Iuta
Minister of Finance: Tiwau Awira
Minister of Health and Community Affairs: Abete Merang
Minister of National Resources and Development: Roniti Teiwaki
Minister of Education, Training and Culture: Ieremia Tata
Minister of Communications and Works: Babera Kirata
Minister for Line and Phoenix Groups: Teewe Arobati
Note: The Constitution requires the name of the Beretitenti (President) to be in the form of the Kiribati language.

Members of the House of Assembly (Maneaba-ni-Maungatabu)
Speaker: Rota Onorio, M.B.E.
Abete Merang: Tarawa Urban
Babera Kirata: Onotoa
Baraniko Raaba: Tabiteuea North
Binata Tetaeka: Makin
Boanareke Boanareke: Tamana
Bwebwentaratai Benson: Betio
Beiaiti Highland: Maiana
Etekia Batiua: Nonouti
Ieremia Tabai: Nonouti
Ieremia Tata: Butaritari
Ioane Benna: Aranuka
Karawaiti Taraia: Tarawa Urban
Leo T. Ubaitoi: Tabiteuea North
Moiaua Toariri: Christmas
Naboua T. Ratieta: Marakei
Otiuea Tanentoa: Beru
Roniti Teiwaki: Betio
Tabeata Tamaiti: Marakei
Tabuarorae Taniera: Banaba
Taniera Kautoa: Abaiang
Taomati T. Iuta: Beru
Teatao Teannaki: Abaiang
Teburea T. Bakaoti: Betio
Teeta Ioran: Arorae
Teewe Arobati: Abemama
Teitintau Teitiaua: Tabiteuea South
Tekinaiti Kaiteie: Abemama
Tenanoa Kanono: Tarawa Rural
Tetaake Eria: Washington
Tetimra Taie: Kuria
Teweia Uaruta: Tarawa Rural
Tiwau Awira: Nikunau
Toanimatang Teraoi: Butaritari
Toia Taruru: Tarawa Urban
Willie Yee On: Fanning

MINISTERIAL OFFICERS
Office of the Beretitenti
Secretary to Cabinet: Ata Teaotai
Secretary for Foreign Affairs: Atanraoi Baiteke
Ministry of Home Affairs
Secretary: Nakibae Teuatabu
Government Printer: Toon Amanu
Manager Broadcasting and Publication Authority: Keith Daniels
Broadcasting Engineer: Bill Reiher
Commissioner of Police: Beretitara Neeti
Ministry of Trade, Industry and Labour
Secretary: Pete Bokai
Registrar of Co-operatives: George Kwong
Secretary to the Copra Society: Binatake Tawaia
Manager Otintal Hotel: Borerei Uriam
Ministry of Finance
Secretary: Tony Davis
Chief Accountant: Iaremako Teoiaki
Chief Customs Officer: Viane Taoaba
Ministry of Health and Community Affairs
Secretary: Dr Tawita Tira
Chief Medical Officer: Dr Taketiau Beriki
Head of Community Affairs: Nanimatang Karoua
Ministry of Natural Resource Development
Secretary: Tion Otanga
Chief Agriculture Officer: Koraobara Tetabea
Chief Fisheries Officer: Brendan Dally
Ministry of Education, Training and Culture
Secretary: Hugh A. S. McLelland
Principle Tarawa Teacher's College: Titi Rimon
Headmaster King George V and Elaine Bernacchi Schools: Ronald Walter Wareham
Principle Tarawa Technical Institute: Morris R. Franklin
Superintendent Marine Training School: Capt. Herbert Rau
Ministry of Communication and Works
Secretary and Director of Civil Aviation: A. R. Tailor
Controller of Postal Services: Bitamatang Kiboboua
Controller of Telecommunications: Ken Stevenson
Marine Superintendent: Capt. Willie Schutz
Chief Engineer Public Works Department: Ian Grainger
Senior Construction Engineer: Iain H. Macgee
Manager Public Utilities Board: N. T. Biribo
General Manager Shipping Corporation: Capt. Tom Murdoch
Marine Engineering Manager: Jack Muller
Ministry for Line and Phoenix Groups
Secretary: John Ikakeau Tonganibeia
The Chief Justice: O'Brien Quinn
The Attorney General: Michael Jennings
Chairman Public Service Commission: Capt. Teitia Redfern
Manager Housing Corporation: Tiaon Tira
Director of Audit: Tim Ioteba
Public Service Commission
Chairman: Capt. Teitia Redfern
Members: Bishop Paul Mea, Rev. Koae Taburimai, Sam Highland
Diplomatic Representatives
American Ambassador: Mr. W. J. Bodde (in Suva)
British High Commission: Mr. Donald H. G. Rose
New Zealand High Commission: Mr. M. Bowles (in Suva)

GOVERNMENT CORPORATIONS & SUBSIDIARIES
Atoll Auto Store (Betio and Bairiki): manager, George Kum Kee
Atoll Products and Freezer (Betio): manager, Tara
Atoll Hotels Ltd.
Otintai Hotel (Bikenibeu): manager, Borerei Uriam

Capt. Cook Hotel (Christmas Is.): manager, Andrew Barty-King
Atoll Soft Drinks (Butaritari): manager, Tamuera Taniera
Atoll Plantations Ltd. (Christmas Is.): manager, P. E. Langston
Kiribati Co-operative Federation Ltd.
General manager: Ienraoi Kamoriki
Asst. general manager: Willie S. Tokatake
Secretary: Kiakia Tarau
Chief executive officer: James Warren
Sales development manager: Robuti Teaeki
Personnel manager: Kautu Kamoriki
Chief accountant: Timeon Teem
Senior buying officer: Willie H. Reiher
Merchandise manager: Teiwaki Reretake
Local produce & handicraft manager: Nawere Tebutei
Biscuit factory manager: Bruno Reiher
AIR TUNGARU CORPORATION
Chairman: vacant
General manager: Scotty Watson
Operations manager: Gilbert Butler
Chief pilot: John Nash
Engineering manager: J. R. Norton
Traffic supervisor: Ioakim Timon
Tarawa travel service manager: Kiriata Taaram
SHIPPING CORPORATION OF KIRIBATI
General manager: Capt. Tom Murduch
Operations manager: Capt. Taniera Naaua
Ports manager: Kokoria B. Etuare
Marine engineering manager: Jack Muller
Personnel officer: Teibuako Burentarawa
CHRISTMAS ISLAND
Secretary to Minister: John Ikakeau Tonganibeia
Project development officer: Patrick Lawrence
Senior fisheries officer: Jan Hoogestieger
Public works manager: Kara Iererua

BUSINESS DIRECTORY

All these private businesses are registered on South Tarawa. The owner's name in each case is in brackets, followed by the place-name.

Teinainano Urban Council area:
Nei Karikiraoi, store, cafe, bar (Beniana Roaia) Bairiki
Uen Te Mauri, store, cafe, taxi, bus service (Borata Kiaua) Bairiki
Bairiki Trading Co., store, bakery, bus service, taxi (Bong Kum Kee) Bairiki
Taraia's Store (Taraia Kauongo) Nanikai
Willie's Store (Willie Lee) Teaoraereke
Suzie's, store, cafe, bar (Susana Kum Kee) Bairiki
Taotin Trading Co., store, bakery, cinema (Kataotao Amitong) Teaoraereke
Temanna and Tamane Store (Betero and Kaitanga) Teaoraereke
Aue Store (Kabwebwenikua Aran) Taborio
Manoraki Trading Co., store, cinema (Teroata O'Brian) Bikenibeu
Biken Nei Meri Store (Roaia Temate) Bikenibeu
Temare and Sons, store, construction, cinema (Temare Tokaruru) Bikenibeu
Kaunaa Store (Ruaia Ambo) Bikenibeu
Marenaua, store, cinema (Tebeua O'Conner) Bikenibeu
Tabokai Brothers' Store (Tekinene and Brothers) Bikenibeu
Nei Tati, store, cinema (Maretati Ioteba) Bikenibeu
Butiraoi, store, bar (Simon Edward) Bikenibeu
EKK Trading Co., store (Elizabeth Kum Kee) Bikenibeu
Marenauan Bikenibeu West, store, cafe (Leisi Tofinga) Bikenibeu
Bairiki Holdings Pty. Ltd., Kiribati Supermarket, Tarawa Motors (N. J. Lieven) Antenon
A. T. Brothers Enterprise, taxi, rental cars, cinema (A. T. Brothers) Taborio
Fakaofo Nemia Construction Co. (Fakaofo Nemia) Banraeaba
I. Orma Construction (Ioane Ormaa) Teaoraereke
Kiba Construction (Eni, Salanoa and Papua Brothers) Eita
Uen Tarawa Bus Lines (Waysang Kum Kee) Bairiki
Uen Te Mauri Bus Service (Borata Kiaua) Bairiki
Coconut Express (Billy Schultz) Taborio
Coral Island Tours (David Edward) Bikenibeu

Betio Town Council area (Island of Betio)
Teikaraoi Fishing Co., Yamaha Centre (Mrs Teroata Ball)
D. K. Construction (David Murdoch and Tekerewa Banaua)
Evening in Betio, store, cafe, bakery (Eone Murdoch)
Gilbert Island Enterprises, store, cafe, cinema (Simon Edward)
Hibiscus Enterprises, store, cafe, bus service (Kwong Kwong)
Ivy's Tailor Shop (Ivy Pine)
Kong Kum Kee Brothers, store, cafe, bakery (Bongand Mosie Kum Kee)
Kirabun Beru, cafe (People of Beru)
Oten Trading Co., store (Oten Kwong)
Rotin Onotoa, store (People of Onotoa)
Fern Store, store, bus service (Taam Redfern)
Tamoaieta Electrical Repairs (Tamoaieta Wirama)
Tangiraki Trading Co., store, cafe, bar, bakery (Sam Highland)
United Sisters, tailor shop (Charlotte Murdoch)
Maribo Investments Ltd., store, shopping centre (People of Nikunau)
A. A. Brothers Trading Co., store (Teiwaki Reretake)

Kekeiaki Island Trading Store (People of Tamana)
F. & I. Pine Brothers, store (Ivy Pine)
Meria Cinemas (Schutz and Wilder)
Merikora's, store, cafe (Merikora Teibuako)

CO-OPERATIVE SOCIETIES

In each case the name of the island is given followed in some cases by the name of the society in brackets, the last name being the name of the manager.

Makin, manager Koneteti
Butaritari, Mabutonga
Marakei (Koubabati) Nikora
Abaiang (Tangitang) Teaoti
Tarawa Rural (Marewentarawa) Obeta
Bairiki (Nano-Tasi) Tio
Bikenibeu (Inanoi) Uriam Ioteba
Betio (Nano Lelei) Kirabuke Maio
Betio (Nikon-Boon) Kaere
Maiana (Ekonikara) Katiua
Kuria (Teiraoi) Tutime
Aranuka (Riki) Iete
Abemama (Tangiraoi) Akau
Nonouti, Mikaere
Tabiteuea North (Tanaeang) Kobebe
Tabiteuea (Utiroa) Tiben
Tabiteuea South, Tabomao
Onotoa, Taioti
Beru, Bentara
Nikunau, Taniara
Tamana, Nataera
Arorae, Teruro
Bikenibeu (Nei Tewenei) Betero
Buariki (Eutan Karawa) Bubutei

HISTORY: The I-Kiribati (Gilbert Islanders) are of Micronesian stock but recent archaelogical discoveries suggest that the islands were first settled by Austronesian-speaking people long before the birth of Christ. A subsequent invasion of Fijians and Tongans about the 14th century A.D., resulted in a merging of the older and newer groups through inter-marriage. The result, by the time Europeans first began describing the islanders in detail in the early 19th century, was that the population was reasonably homogeneous in appearance and in traditions.

Although the Gilbertese people have many common traditions, social organisation was not uniform throughout the group. Social units in the north tended to be larger than those in the south and on most islands, there were at any time, several leaders competing for dominance. In some instances (for example Butaritari-Makin and Abemama-Kuria-Aranuka), paramount chief, emerged. With European contact, firearms and sometimes trading monopolies, these men were able to consolidate their position.

In contrast, authority in the southern islands was vested in "maneaba" (meeting house) councils of old men and each was the leader of his own "kainga" or clan hamlet. Most of the islands were divided into several competing "maneaba" districts and throughout the group, "maneaba" has remained the focal point of all social and political activity.

European discovery. The Gilbert Islands may have been sighted by the crew of a ship originally commanded by Hernando de Grijalva which crossed the Pacific from Mexico in 1537. However, details of that voyage are too vague for any positive identifications to be made. The first undoubted European discovery in the Gilberts was that of the Spanish explorer Quiros who sighted Butaritari in 1606 and named it Buen Viaje (Good Voyage).

A local tradition that appears to date from about that time tells of a white-skinned, red-haired, red-bearded man who drifted ashore at Beru in a boat shaped like a box, who took eight sisters as wives, and who had 23 children. The descendants of that stranger are now supposed to be scattered throughout the group. The tradition has never been thoroughly investigated. But it has been suggested that the red-bearded man may have been a survivor of one of the lost ships of the Mendana expedition to the Pacific of 1595.

The modern discovery and exploration of the Gilbert Islands began in 1765 when Commodore John Byron discovered Nikunau in HMS 'Dolphin'. In 1788, Captain Thomas Gilbert of the ship 'Charlotte' and Captain John Marshall of the 'Scarborough' discovered several more islands when sailing from Sydney to China. The remaining islands were discovered by Europeans between 1799 and 1826. Those concerned were two British merchant captains, a French explorer and an American whaler.

Gilberts named. The name Gilbert Islands was given to the group by the Russian hydrographer A. I. Krusenstern in the 1820s. From that time until about 1870, many British and American whaling vessels sought sperm whales in Gilbertese waters. Seamen from some of these vessels occassionally deserted in the islands and became beachcombers, while adventurous Gilbertese were taken on as crewmen. The first European to live in the group landed there in 1837. After trading vessels began visiting the group from about 1850, some of the beachcombers became traders and agents for firms in Australia, Germany and the United States. Other traders were sent there by their firms. Coconut oil was the chief commodity of trade until copra completely replaced it about 1870-1880.

Labour recruiting. In the second half of the 19th century about 9,000 Gilbertese worked overseas, especially on plantations. In the 1860s the Peruvian recruiters were virtually slave-traders and islanders later learned to fear the 'men-stealing ships' from Tahiti. Nevertheless, many Gilbertese were willing, even eager, recruits, especially in times of drought.

The main destinations of these labourers were Fiji, Samoa, Tahiti, Hawaii and, towards the end of the century, Central America. The recruiting at this time established a pattern of 'family' migration which was most unusual for the labour trade in the 19th century. It also established patterns for 20th century migration to Ocean Island and Nauru.

The first European missionary to live and work in the Gilberts was the Rev. Hiram Bingham, a Protestant, of the American Board of Commissioners for Foreign Missions. He established a mission on Abaiang in 1857, and with the help of Hawaiian Pastors spread Christianity throughout the northern islands. In 1870, after Polynesian teachers of the London Missionary Society had established missions in the Ellice Islands (now Tuvalu), the Rev. S. J. Whitmee of the LMS brought Samoan pastors to Arorae, Tamana, Onotoa and Beru. From those islands, the LMS continued to spread northwards until, in 1917, the American Board agreed to withdraw from the group. In the islands north of the equator, however, the LMS never enjoyed the same success that it had in the south, and Roman Catholicism tended to become the dominant religion in those islands.

Catholic priests of the Sacred Heart order began work in the Gilberts in 1888, using Nonouti as their first base. Missionaries from the Seventh-day Adventist Church, the Baha'i faith, and the Church of God have also gained adherents since World War II.

British interest. The first attempt by Europeans to exert formal authority in the group followed the appointment in 1877 of the Governor of Fiji as High Commissioner for the Western Pacific. This gave the Governor jurisdiction over British subjects, and his authority was exercised through British naval commanders who were made deputy commissioners. In 1892, Captain E. H. M. Davis of HMS 'Royalist' visited the group and proclaimed it a British protectorate in a ceremony at Abemama. After the British flag was also raised over the Ellice Islands, headquarters for the new protectorates were established at Butaritari and in 1896 at Tarawa. At first the administration consisted only of the British Resident; later, district magistrates were appointed. Councils of island elders, known as native governments, were set up to administer a simple code of laws based as far as possible on traditional forms of government and laws, often modified by mission and other foreign influences.

In 1900, following the discovery of phosphate there, Ocean Island was annexed by Great Britain and placed under the Resident Commissioner's jurisdiction. Seven years later, the exploitation of Ocean Island phosphate had become so important that the protectorate's headquarters were transferred to that island.

British annexation. In 1915, after obtaining the formal approval of the native governments, Britain annexed the Gilbert and Ellice Islands by an Order-in-Council. The order came into effect on January 12, 1916, from which date the two groups became the Gilbert and Ellice Islands Colony.

In that same year, Ocean Island and also Fanning and Washington Islands (which Britain had annexed in 1888 and 1889 respectively) were incorporated within the colony, as were the three Tokelau Islands (then known as the Union Group), which had been a British protectorate since 1889. Christmas Island (which had been annexed in 1888) was added to the colony in 1919. But the Tokelau Islands were transferred to New Zealand administration in 1925 because of the difficulty of communicating with them from Ocean Island. The uninhabited Phoenix Islands became part of the colony by an Order-in-Council of March 18, 1937. Three of the Phoenix Islands, Gardner, Hull and Sydney, were colonised in 1938 by land-hungry islanders from the southern Gilberts. By 1940, 600 Gilbertese had settled there. Meanwhile, in 1939, the British Government had agreed that two of the Phoenix Islands, Canton and Enderbury, should be administered jointly with the United States. The two islands were of interest to the Americans because of their value in trans-Pacific aviation.

Pacific War. In December 1941, within two days of the Japanese raid on Pearl Harbour, Japanese aircraft bombed Ocean Island and reconnaissance parties landed briefly on Tarawa and Butaritari. A few months later, most Europeans on Tarawa and Ocean Island were evacuated. Some government officials and missionaries elected to stay and were joined by coastwatchers sent from New Zealand. Twenty-two Europeans, most of them coastwatchers, were subsequently killed by the Japanese.

Meanwhile, temporary headquarters for the administration of those parts of the colony not in enemy hands were established in Sydney. It remained there until November 1943 when American forces drove the Japanese from the Gilberts. New headquarters were then set up on Tarawa, where they have remained.

When Ocean Island was reoccupied in 1945, it was found that the Japanese had recently massacred all but one man (who had miraculously escaped) of the Gilbertese labour force, and that the native inhabitants, the Banabans, had been deported to Nauru and Kusaie in the Caroline Islands. On being rescued, the Banabans elected to live on Rabi Island, Fiji, which had earlier been bought for them.

Resettlement. Within a few years of the war, the authorities concluded that Sydney Island in the Phoenix Group could not support a permanent population, and arrangements were made to resettle that island's colonists at Gizo in the Solomon Islands. Later, to suit administrative convenience and overcome the difficulties of communication with the Phoenix group (reinforced by a prolonged drought on Hull and Gardner Islands) it was decided to transfer the remaining Phoenix Islands settlers to Wagina in the Solomon Islands. The transfer was made in 1963-64.

One of the most important post-war moves in the main islands was the strengthening of the co-operatives that had been established before the war. This made it unprofitable for any overseas trading firm to return to the group. There were also moves to give the islanders a more active role in their own government. In 1951, the first of three biennial conferences for magistrates was held. These meetings led to the inauguration of annual Colony Conferences (from 1956 to 1962) at which nominated representatives met to discuss the colony's affairs.

In 1963, an Executive Council and an Advisory Council were created to give the islanders an advisory role in government. Membership of both bodies was by nomination of the Resident Commissioner. In 1967, the Advisory Council was replaced by a House of Representatives had no legislative powers, but could make recommendations to the Governing Council.

Legislative Council. In 1971, further constitutional developments took place. The House of Representatives was replaced by a Legislative Council of 23 elected members, three ex-officio members and two public service members; and the Governing Council was superseded by an Executive Council. The elected members of the Legislative Council had the right to elect a Leader of Government Business to act as their chief spokesman, but the Council's legislative functions were limited. As for the Executive Council, its powers were advisory, but the Resident Commissioner could assign members to formulate policy on various subjects.

On January 1, 1972, the colony ceased to come under the jurisdiction of the Western Pacific High Commission, as it had done for the previous 80 years, and the Resident Commissioner, Sir John Field, was sworn in as Governor.

At the end of 1972 the colony became responsible for the Southern Line Islands.

In 1974, the colony moved forward to a ministerial form of government. The Legislative Council was replaced by an elected House of Assembly, and a Chief Minister. Later that year, the Ellice Islanders, by an overwhelming majority, voted in a referendum to secede from the colony. The separation took place on October 1, 1975, although joint administration from Tarawa continued until January 1, 1976.

On November 1, 1976, another stage in the progression to independence came with the appointment of a Minister of Finance and full internal self-government was attained on January 1, 1977, when the Council of Ministers became entirely "localised" with the exception of the position of the Attorney-General. In April/May, 1977, more than 200 representatives of local government councils, churches, traditional leaders, women's clubs and co-operative societies met on Tarawa and made recommendations for a new Constitution. Independence came on July 12, 1979, when Princess Anne, daughter of Queen Elizabeth II, who was accompanied by her husband, Captain Mark Phillips, presented the Letters Patent formally declaring the country's independence from Britain. With independence, the name Kiribati was adopted.

In September, 1979, a treaty of friendship was signed between the Republic of Kiribati and the United States. Under the treaty, the United States relinquished all claims, made under the Guano Act of 1856, to 14 islands in the Line and Phoenix groups. For practical purposes, however, Kiribati agreed to joint administration of Canton Island (now Kanton Island), on which the United States has a space tracking station.

Banaban case. In February 1975, the Banabans initiated a suit in the High Court, London, against the British Government and British Phosphate Commissioners, claiming more than seven million pounds for back royalties on phosphate mined from Ocean Island and unspecified recompense for damage to that island. Later, a party of 36 Banabans landed on Ocean Island from Rabi in support of their claim that Ocean Island should be granted independence from the Gilbert and Ellice Islands Colony. Towards the end of the year, talks on the subject were held in Tarawa between the Banabans and the Gilbert Islanders, but nothing was resolved.

Late in 1977, the Gilbert Islands Council of Ministers and the Rabi Council of Leaders signed eleven Resolutions to be known as the Bairiki Resolution concerning the relationship between the Banabans and the Gilbert Islands government and the future of Ocean Island, which would henceforth be called only by its Gilbertese name 'Banaba'.

Three of the Resolutions agree that a referendum be held to determine the future of Banaba and what would be the status of phosphate revenue, employment, access, etc., whether the outcome be in favour of the status quo or in favour of separation.

Both parties agreed that the British Government should be bound to honour the outcome of the referendum, when deciding on the future of Banaba at the Gilbert Islands Independence Constitutional Conference.

Other Resolutions concerned financial arrangements, the rehabilitation of Banaba and the management of the phosphate industry.

The parties also resolved to continue discussions on matters of common interest and to be united in their submissions to the British of other governments.

Meanwhile, the case in the High Court continued until June 1976 – the longest case in British history.

In his judgement Justice Megarry found against **the Banabans on the royalties case but found that,** under a 1913 agreement, the B.P.C. was obliged to replace certain portions of Ocean Island. Damages for this breach were to be negotiated by the parties. He also found that the British Government had, in some ways, failed to fulfil its colonial trust but pointed out that in such matters the Court had no power. Subsequently the British, Australian and New Zealand Governments offered the Banabans an *ex gratia* payment of $10 million in addition to any damages decided upon.

Banaban rights. Mining on Banaba finished at the end of 1979. The Banabans, however, failed to persuade Britain or I-Kiribati to allow them to cecede with their island, and the island continues to be part of Kiribati. The Kiribati Constitution, makes special provision for the Banabans, ensuring them a seat in the House of Assembly, the return of the land on Banaba acquired by the government for phosphate mining and the right of every Banaban to enter and live in Banaba. Banaban land can only be compulsorily acquired by leasehold and only after consultation with the Banaban Island Council. The Constitution also provides for a Commission of Inquiry which, three years after independence, will review the special arrangements made for the Banabans in the Constitution. Any amendment to the provisions in the Constitution relating to the Banabans can only be effected if their nominated representative in the House of Assembly does not vote against such amendment. In all other respects, Banaba will be treated as any other outer island of Kiribati.

British aid to Kiribati will include an allocation for the redevelopment of Banaba.

COMMISSIONERS

Only 14 men held the office of Resident Commissioner or Governor of the Gilbert and Ellice Islands colony in the 84 years from 1892 to 1976 when the Ellice Islands, as Tuvalu, became a separate dependency. They were:

- 1893–C. R. Swayne.
- 1895–W. Telfer Campbell.
- 1909–Captain J. Quayle Dickson.
- 1913–E. C. Eliot (later C.B.E.)
- 1922–H. R. McClure.
- 1926–A. F. Grimble MA (later Sir Arthur Grimble, K.C.M.G.).
- 1933–J. C. Barley.
- 1942–V. Fox-Strangways.
- 1946–H. E. Maude, MA, M.B.E. (later O.B.E.).
- 1949–W. J. Peel, B.A.
- 1952–M. L. Bernacchi, C.M.G.
- 1962–V. J. Andersen, O.B.E., V.R.D.
- 1970–Sir John Field, K.B.E., C.M.G. (Governor from 1972).
- 1973–J. H. Smith, C.B.E.
- 1978–R. O. Wallace.

Mr Wallace continued as Governor until Independence.

Further information. No complete history of the Gilbert Islands has been published. Some of the early history is covered in H. E. Maude's "Of Islands and Men" (Melbourne, 1968). This also gives an account of the Phoenix Islands Settlement Scheme. Sir Arthur Grimble's "A Pattern of Islands" (John Murray, London 1952) is based on his period as governor and his early writings on the group were collated by his daughter Rosemary Grimble in "Migrations Myth and Magic from the Gilbert Islands" (Routledge and Kegan Paul, London 1972). This contains descriptions of the prehistoric astronomy and navigation of the people. A history of the Roman Catholic Mission in the Gilberts is to be found in Ernest Sabatier's "Sous l'equateur du Pacifique" (Editions Dillon, Paris, 1939). Austin Coates "Islands in the South" offers an interesting hypothesis on prehistoric migration by Austronesians which is contrary to most accepted theories, and which makes many references to the Gilbertese as navigators. Edwin H. Bryan Jnr's "American Polynesia and the Hawaiian Chain" (Honolulu, 1942), gives histories of the Line and Phoenix Islands. Details of Ocean Island history is to be found in Albert F. Ellis' "Ocean Island and Nauru" (Sydney, 1936) and in articles by Robert Langdon and Stuart Inder in "New Guinea", Vol. 1, No. 4, (Sydney, 1966). In 1979, to mark Independence Year, the Kiribati Ministry of Education, Training and Culture with the Institute of Pacific Studies and Extension Services of the University of the South Pacific published "Kiribati-Aspects of History" (Fiji Times & Herald Ltd. Suva) both in English and the Kiribati language. Twenty-five I-Kiribati were the authors.

ISLANDS IN DETAIL

BANABA. Banaba, which is now the name of Ocean Island on official lists, is situated just south of the Equator some 260 km east of Nauru and 400 km west of the Gilbert Islands. It has the shape of a pearl oyster shell, and is about 10 km in circumference with a maximum elevation of about 78 m. The island may have been first settled, like the Gilbert Islands, by migrants coming via Micronesia. It later had continuing contact with the islands of the Gilbert group. The Banaban language is a variant of Gilbertese. Ocean Island's modern history is completely intertwined with the exploitation of its phosphate deposits. The industry closed down at the end of 1979.

The phosphate deposits were worked on behalf of the British, Australian and New Zealand Governments by the British Phosphate Commissioners (BPC). The key personnel were Europeans. The labouring work was done by Gilbertese, Tuvaluans and Chinese.

Ocean Island was first reported to the western world by Captain Jered Gardner of the American ship 'Diana', who sighted it on January 3, 1801 and named it Rodman's Island. The name Ocean Island is due to Captain John Mertho of the ship 'Ocean' who came upon the island in 1804 and thought he was the first European to sight the island.

Except for occasional visits by whalers and traders from the 1820s onwards, Ocean Island had little contact with the outside world until phosphate was discovered there in 1900. Although it came within the British sphere of influence when Britain signed an agreement with Germany in 1886 partitioning the Western Pacific, Britain did not formally annex it or make it part of the Gilbert or Ellice Islands Protectorates when those governments were proclaimed in 1892.

The phosphate was discovered by Albert F. Ellis, an employee in the Sydney office of the Pacific Islands Company, of London. The discovery was made after Ellis analysed a strange piece of stone, thought to be fossilised wood, that had been bought to Sydney from Nauru. In May 1900, he negotiated an agreement with the Banabans which gave his company the sole right to work the phosphate deposits for 999 years for an annual payment of £50.

Meanwhile, the company obtained a licence from the British Colonial Office which stated among other things that Ocean Island was a British posession and that the licences had exclusive right to occupy the island from January 1, 1901 and to display the British flag in token of occupation. The British High Commissioner for the Western Pacific in Fiji was later instructed to issue a proclamation to make Ocean Island part of the Gilbert and Ellice Islands Protectorate. The High Commissioner, however, declared that the island had been annexed because the licence issued by the British Government had referred to the island as a "posession" of Her Majesty. The matter was further confused when the commander of the HMS 'Pylades' hoisted the British flag at Ocean Island on September 28, 1901.

Meanwhile, the Pacific Islands Company (reconstituted in 1903 as the Pacific Phosphate Company) had organised the exploitation of the phosphate, and by about 1909 about two million tonnes had been exported. Apart from their annual fee of £50, the only financial benefit that accrued to the Banabans was about £20 an acre for mining land bought from them, plus compensation for fruit trees destroyed.

These ungenerous terms eventually provoked numerous questions in the House of Commons and made the Banabans so bitter that they refused to sell any more land to the phosphate company. The impasse was resolved in 1913 when the company agreed to pay the Banabans a royalty of 6d. a ton on all phosphate mined. The activities of the Company continued to attract unfavourable press and parliamentary comment and partly to insure against future embarrassment, and partly to tidy up the various legal entities all administered by the Resident Commissioner, steps were taken to establish the Gilbert and Ellice Islands Colony.

After World War I, when Britain, Australia and New Zealand were given a League of Nations mandate over nearby phosphate-producing Nauru, the governments of those three countries bought out the Pacific Phosphate Company for £3½ million. The British Phosphate Commissioners (BPC) were then appointed to exploit the phosphate deposits of the two islands on behalf of the three governments.

When the Banabans refused to sell more land in the late 1920s, the government compulsorily acquired what it wanted, but paid for it at a price that it considered reasonable. At the same time, the royalty rate was increased to 10½d. per ton but this remained unchanged until 1942. Further land was compulsorily acquired in 1931, but the royalty remained unchanged until 1942. However, since 1913 the government had also been putting money away on the Banabans' behalf against the day when Ocean Island was mined out. In 1942, after the Japanese had occupied Ocean Island, some of this money was used to buy Rabi Island for them.

The Japanese occupation began in August 1942. Most Europeans had then been evacuated, but there were about 700 Banabans on the island, plus 800 Gilbertese labourers and their wives and children. The Banabans and some of the Gilbertese were deported to Kusaie, in the Carolines. Other Gilbertese were sent to Nauru and Tarawa, but 200 were retained on Ocean Island to work as fishermen. All were treated badly and some died.

After news of the Japanese capitulation reached Ocean Island in August 1945, the Japanese massacred all the remaining Gilbertese except one who escaped miraculously. This sole survivor later gave evidence at a war crimes trial at which the Japanese garrison commander and the quartermaster were sentenced to death.

In September 1945, the Banabans and Gilbertese on Kusaie, then numbering 1,003, were brought to Tarawa. As Ocean Island was still a shambles, they elected to live on Rabi Island where they have since remained. They are Fiji citizens. Meanwhile the BPC re-established itself on Ocean Island, and in 1947 exported 120,360 tonnes of phosphate. The tonnage had more than doubled by 1950. In 1965, the export figure was 350,000, and in 1969 it was well over 500,000 tonnes. The royalty paid to the Banabans was

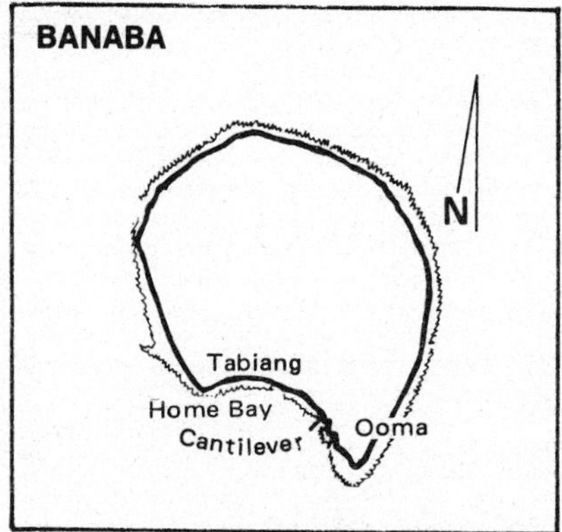

1/3d. a ton from 1947 to 1958; 1/9d. a ton from 1958 to 1964; then 2/8d. a ton. When the last named figure was adopted, the BPC was also paying a royalty on Ocean Island phosphate of 23/-d. to the Gilbert and Ellice Islands Colony. Meanwhile, the Nauruans were receiving 13/6d. a ton for their phosphate.

Banaban resentment, anger and bitterness over the comparatively poor deal they were getting almost led to violence on Rabi in April 1965. Thereafter, the British Government treated them with much more consideration and their share in the phosphate revenue was increased from time to time. In 1968, the government also made an ex-gratia payment to them 'in consideration of the effects of phosphate mining upon Ocean Island since 1900.' But the Banabans were not satisfied. They employed public relations advisers to publicise their cause, and economic and legal advisers to help them take their case to the United Nations. Finally, in February 1975, the Banabans sued the British Government in the High Court of Great Britain, claiming £7 million for back royalties and an unspecified amount as recompense for damage to Ocean Island. Meanwhile, with the Gilbert and Ellice Islanders moving towards separation and independence, and Ocean Island's phosphate due to run out in 1979, the Banabans sought independence for their original homeland.

Despite protests, demonstrations and a petrol bomb attack on mining plant on Banaba early in 1979, the Banabans were unable to obtain separation from Kiribati, but certain rights with regard to land ownership and representation in the Kiribati House of Assembly were reserved for the Banabans in the Kiribati Constitution.

(LITTLE) MAKIN. This, the northernmost of the Gilbert Islands, is only about 4.5 km long and 1.5 km wide. When the wind is NNE to ESE, there is a sheltered anchorage for small craft. The government station is at the village of Makin on the main islet. Rainfall is heavy. In pre-colonial times this island was ruled, with Butaritari, by a single paramount chief.

BUTARITARI (MAKIN). This is a roughly triangular atoll measuring about 17 km from east to west. Its fine deep lagoon has three entrances for ships and provides good anchorage. From the mid-19th century until World War II it was the main trading centre within the Gilbert group. Robert Louis Stevenson lived there for a short time in the 1880s.

Most of the land is on the south side of the lagoon, and the principal villages are on the two main islets, Butaritari and Kuma. Other islets are: Ubantakoto, Namoka, Natata, Kotabu, Tukerere, Nabuni, Otearíki and Bikati. The south side of the atoll is a continuous grove of coconuts and pandanus.

The principal settlement is also called Butaritari, near the SW corner of the westernmost islet, which is nearly 13 km long.

Butaritari was occupied by Japanese forces in 1942 and, shortly afterwards, was attacked by allied forces in the 'Carlson Raid'. Partly as a consequence of this raid Betio islet on Tarawa was fortified. After the Battle of Tarawa, Butaritari was captured by the Americans who used it as a naval and air base (1943-45). The airstrip has been restored for regular air services from Tarawa.

The European discoverer of Butaritari was the Spaniard Quiros who sighted it in 1606 and named it Buen Viaje. It was rediscovered in 1788 when Captain Thomas Gilbert in the 'Charlotte' and Captain John Marshall in the 'Scarborough' were sailing to Canton from Botany Bay. Marshall gave the names Allen's, Gillespie's, Touching's, Clarke's, Smith's and Scarborough to the principal islets.

MARAKEI. Marakei is about 8 km by 5 km. The government station is at the village of Rawannawi. Marakei is a "classical" atoll; Two islets, north and south, almost completely enclose a small lagoon, leaving only a boat entrance. Sponges are plentiful in the surrounding waters.

Captain L. I. Duperrey of the French exploring vessel 'Coquille' is credited with the European discovery of Marakei in 1824. However, he was under the impression it was Abaiang — the Matthew's Island of Captain Gilbert.

ABAIANG. This atoll is about 25 km long by 8 km wide. Six islets ring the lagoon — Teirio, Nuotaea, Nanikirata, Twin Tree, Ribono and Iku. The land is continuous on the eastern side. Vessels drawing up to 4.8 metres can enter the lagoon, which provides a sheltered anchorage.

Captain Thomas Gilbert, its European discoverer in 1788, named it Matthew's Island, after the owner of his ship, the 'Charlotte'. He called the lagoon Charlotte Bay and the main island

Point Charlotte. Subsequent errors in identification led to the island being known as Charlotte Island. Its local name is sometimes written Apaiang.

The first Protestant missionaries to the Gilberts, led by the Rev. Hiram Bingham, settled on Abaiang in 1857.

TARAWA. This atoll is shaped like an isosceles triangle. It has islets on its southern and eastern reefs, but not on its western reef. The islets, in total, extend over 64 km and have an area of 920 hectares. The principal ones are: Betio, Bairiki, Eita, Buota, Taritai, Abaokoro, Noto, Buariki, Teaoraereke, Nabeina, and Bikenibeu.

Tarawa is a port of entry and the main centre of the group. The lagoon has one navigable entrance. At Tarawa are the government headquarters, central hospital, government secondary schools, teacher training college, etc. All are situated on the islets of Bairiki, Betio and Bikenibeu.

Betio in the south-west corner, was the scene of one of the fiercest American landing-assaults during the Pacific war, when, on November 24, 1943, U.S. Marines captured it from a strongly-entrenched Japanese garrison after a grim five days' battle.

Until 1942, the Administration office was in Betio. After the recapture, the settlement and Administration offices were established in Bairiki which, in turn, became headquarters for the Gilbert and Ellice Islands Colony. In 1954 new permanent buildings for the District Office and station establishments were constructed on Betio, where the Wholesale Society installations are also situated. Betio harbour has been reconstructed and developed as the main Tarawa port. Also on Betio are a club, a public bar and cafe, cinemas, a small slipway, workshops and a fuel depot.

The government residency is situated on nearby Bairiki, as is Tarawa's main "maneaba" (community centre and meeting-place). About 18 km to the NE is Bikenibeu, where the Central Hospital, secondary schools, teachers' training college and hotel are situated.

Bonriki, in the SE corner of the atoll, is the site of the atoll's airstrip. In 1963 two causeways were completed, linking the southern islets and a motor road now extends some 32 km from Bonriki to Bairiki. A further causeway to link Bairiki and Betio, should be completed in 1979.

The headquarters of the Roman Catholic Church in the colony is at Teaoraereke and that of the Protestant Church at Tangintibu.

In 1788, Captain Thomas Gilbert of the 'Charlotte' became the first European to sight any part of Tarawa. He called three of the northernmost islets Gilbert's, Marshall's and Knox's Islands. A later navigator called it Cook's Isle.

MAIANA. Maiana is roughly oblong, measuring about 14 km by 9 km. Its eastern side is a single long island. There are a few smaller islets on the northwest and southwest. The lagoon is studded with coral heads and ships cannot enter it. The principal villages are: Tebangetua (government station), Bubutei, Temangaua, Tebiauea, Tebanga and Temantongo. Although near Tarawa, inaccessibility of the lagoon resulted in Maiana being visited infrequently until an airstrip was completed in 1976.

The atoll's European discoverer was Captain Patterson of the brig 'Elizabeth' in 1809. He called it Hall's Island.

ABEMAMA. Abemama is 19 km by 8 km. Its chief villages are Tabontebike (government station), Tebanga, Tabiang and Baretoa. Vessels up to 500 tonnes can enter its lagoon where there is good anchorage. Tabiang-Binoinano Islet occupies the northern and NE sides of the atoll. In the SE and SW are Tabonua, Kabaungaki, Bike and Abatiku.

Abemama's European discoveror was Captain Charles Bishop of the brig 'Nautilus'. He came upon it in 1799 and named it Roger Simpson's Island after an associate who was on board. The native name is also written Apemama and Apamama.

During the 19th century, Abemama, Kuria and Aranuka were united by a line of paramount chiefs. Of these, Tem Binoka (described by Stevenson in "In the South Seas") became the best known and, probably the most despotic. It was here that Commander H. M. Davis, of HMS 'Royalist' proclaimed the Gilbert Islands a British protectorate on May 2, 1892.

Abemama was occupied by the Japanese during the whole of 1942, but was retaken by the Americans and used as a supply and air base until the end of the Pacific war. The wartime airstrip has been restored for services connecting it with Tarawa and other islands.

Towards the end of the war, it was proposed that Abemama should be the post-war capital for the Gilbert and Ellice Islands Colony. This proposal was abandoned in 1947 because of the better passage into Tarawa's lagoon.

Abemama is the headquarters for the SDA church in the colony.

KURIA. Kuria, some 6 km by 3 km, has only one important village — Buariki — which is the site of the government station. It has no lagoon. To the north of it, separated by a narrow passage, is the islet of Oneke. Kuria was another of the discoveries of Captains Gilbert and Marshall in 1788. They named it Woodle's Island. In precolonial times Kuria was "ruled" by the chiefs of Abermama.

ARANUKA. Aranuka consists of two islets on a triangular reef about 9 km long. The islands are at the eastern and western ends, with some very small islets in between, in the north. The government station is at Buariki village. The land area is about 1,500 hectares. The small lagoon has no ship passage.

In 1788, Captain Marshall of the 'Scarborough' called the eastern and western portions of Aranuka Hopper's and Henderville's Islands respectively. This later led to the belief that Marshall had discovered Abemama and that his name for it was Hopper's Island. In pre-colonial times Aranuka was included within the domain of the chief of Abemama.

NONOUTI. This atoll is 39 km by about 16 km. The government station is at Matang Village. The lagoon has an entrance for small vessels and though the channel is long and difficult there is a good anchorage. The eastern side is one long strip of land cut by a few narrow passages and at north and south are small islets separated by long gaps from the main strip of land.

Nonouti was first recorded by Captain Charles Bishop of the 'Nautilus'' in 1799, who named it Sidenham Teast's Island after the owner of his ship. In 1888, the first Roman Catholic mission group was established on the island.

TABITEUEA. After Tarawa, this atoll is the most populous in the group. The government station is at the village of Utiroa. Other villages are Eita, Tanaeang and Teuabu.

The two largest islands are Buariki-Taku in the SE and Eanikai-Utiroa on the NE side of the reef's northern end. A string of small islets separates them. A long, tortuous ship channel gives access to the southern part of the lagoon.

This is the largest island and once had the largest population. For administration and elections it is divided into north and south; the government station in the north is at Utiroa (a location shelled by the Wilkes expedition in 1841 after a seaman was killed); and the station in the south is at Buariki.

In the early 1880s the northern "christian armies" led by Hawaiian pastors massacred the "Pagans" of the south (in the name of "The Book" and in pursuit of land) and killed about 1000.

The nave Tabiteuea (Tapu-te-uea) means "chiefs are forbidden". The society is egalitarian and there are no "noble" families. Elders met in *maneaba* (meeting houses) and controlled district affairs. These traditions are still strong.

Captain Charles Bishop of the "Nautilus" was its discoverer in 1799. He named it after himself, while he called Eanikai, the main islet, Drummond's Island.

Nearby Bishop charted a shoal which he called Nautilus Shoal. The whaler 'Corsair' is reputed to be wrecked on it in 1835. But in 1966, Captain E. V. Ward, an experienced local mariner, cast doubt on its existence.

BERU. Beru, which is about 18 km long, was the headquarters in the GEIC of the London Missionary Society for 60 years until they were shifted to Tangintebu, Tarawa, in 1960. The mission's printing press followed shortly afterwards, but a post-primary school for girls and boys has remained on Beru.

The government station on the atoll is at the village of Tanukinberu. Other villages are Tabiang and Taboiaki.

Captain J. Clerk of the whaler 'John Palmer' was the European discoverer of the atoll in 1826. He named it Maria Island. Peru, Francis, Sunday, Eliza and Peroat are other names that have been applied to it.

NIKUNAU (formerly Nukunau) is an island about 13 km long and 2.5 km broad. Its chief villages are Rungata (government station), Muribenua, and Nukumanau. There is a small land-locked lagoon in the north. Small vessels anchor just off Rungata and larger vessels about 1 km to the north.

The island was once known as Byron Island because Commodore John Byron of HMS 'Dolphin' discovered it in 1765.

ONOTOA. Onotoa is about 19 km long and has no sheltered anchorage. The villages are Buariki (government station), Tabuarorae and Aiaki. The lagoon is bordered by a reef on the western side, with a good boat channel near the centre. Its islets are: Tanyah, Bowerick, Sand, Otoeie, Hack, Tabuaroarae, Onutu, and Temuah.

The honour of being the first European to sight Onotoa belongs to Captain J. Clerk of the 'John Palmer' in 1826. He called it Eliza Island, but it also came to be known as Clerk Island.

TAMANA. This is a small island about 5 km long and by 1.25 km wide. The government station is at the village of Bakaka. Thamana was one known as Rotch's Island, the name given it by its European discoverer, Captain J. Clerk in 1826.

ARORAE. This island, the southernmost of the Gilbert group, is about 6.5 km by 3.25 km. Its villages are Tamaroa and Roreti. The government station divides them. Captain Patterson of the brig 'Elizabeth' named it Hope Island in 1809. This was later changed to Hurd Island by the hydrographer John Purdy.

PHOENIX ISLANDS. The Phoenix group consists of eight scattered islands located between 2 deg. 30 min. and 4 deg. 30 min. S. lat. and between 170 deg. 30 min. and 174 deg. 30 min. W. long. The islands are Kanton (now with a 'K' as there is no 'C' in the Kiribati language), Enderbury, McKean, Birnie, Phoenix, Nukumaroro (Gardner), Orona (Hull) and Manra (Sydney). Kanton and Enderbury have been jointly administered by Britain and the United States until Kiribati independence when they became part of Kiribati, the United States relinquishing all claim to them and other islands in Kiribati and Tuvalu. The United States however has an agreement with Kiribati to maintain a space tracking station on Kanton and share administration and future development with Kiribati. Total land area of the Phoenix Group is 28.70 sq. km. All the islands are low atolls enclosing lagoons. Only Kanton is inhabited.

Archaelogical evidence indicates that Manra, Orona and Nikumaroro were inhabited by man in pre-European times. However, all were without people when the first European whalers visited the group, probably in the early 1820s. Between 1859 and 1877, Enderbury,McKean and Phoenix Islands were worked for their guano by an American firm, the Phoenix Guano Company.

A British subject, John T. Arundel, acquired rights to all the islands in 1881 and obtained leases to them from the British Government. He worked the guano on some and planted them and others with coconut trees. In 1889, most of the islands were annexed to Great Britain by Commander Oldham of HMS 'Egeria'. Captain H. W. S. Gibson of HMS 'Curacoa' annexed Nikumaroro Island in 1892.

After the guano deposits were exhausted, Orona and Manra developed into successful coconut plantations and the other islands were neglected. Nevertheless, during the years leases to all the islands, except Enderbury and McKean, passed from one company to another — from J. T. Arundel & Co. to the Pacific Islands Company Ltd., to Lever's Pacific Plantations Ltd., to the Samoa Shipping and Trading Co. Ltd., and finally to Burns Philp (South Sea) Co. Ltd. In 1937, the eight islands were included within the boundaries of the Gilbert and Ellice Islands Colony, and administration officials were stationed on Kanton and Hull. A little later, the GEIC government bought the islands from Burns Philp to resettle land-hungry Gilbertese. Settlement began on Hull, Sydney and Gardner that same year, and within a few years more than 1,000 islanders were living there.

Meanwhile, in 1938, the United States sent small parties of men to occupy Kanton and Enderbury Islands because of their potential value in trans-Pacific aviation. In the following year, the British and United States Governments signed a 50-year agreement for the joint administration of Kanton and Enderbury. The Americans immediately began to build aviation facilities on Kanton. These remained in use until 1967. As for the colonialisation scheme, this was abandonded in 1963 following a prolonged drought and difficulties in maintaining communication. All Gilbertese residents were resettled in the Solomons.

Details of the six islands administered solely from Tarawa are:

McKean Island. This is an almost circular island with a diameter of little more than 1 km. It has a shallow lagoon. Captain Henry Barber of the 'Arthur' discovered it in 1794 and named it Drummond's Island. Its present name is that of a member of the United States Exploring Expedition who was first to sight it during a survey in 1840. The island has not been occupied since American guano interest ceased operations there some time between 1859 and 1871.

Birnie Island. Birnie is the smallest of the Phoenix group, being only about 1.25 km long and about 500 metres wide and enclosing a salt water lagoon. A whaler, Captain Emment, discovered it about 1820. Its name is that of a well-known British shipowner of that time. The commander of HMS 'Egeria' annexed the island for Great Britain in 1889, but no use was ever made of it.

Phoenix Island. Phoenix is a pear-shaped island less than 1.25 km long and 1 km wide. A plateau at one end of the island, about six metres above sea level, slopes away to a shallow lagoon. The island is uninhabited and was reported to be overrun with rabbits. There are also many thousands of sea birds.

The European discoverer of Phoenix Island is unknown. It was probably the captain of a whaler of that name who came upon it some time before 1828. Between 1862 and 1872, the island was worked by the Phoenix Guano Company. It has not been used since. The commander of HMS 'Egeria' took possesion of it for Great Britain in 1889.

Nikumaroro (Gardner Island). This is an atoll about 6.5 km by 2 km, enclosing an ample lagoon. The width of the land varies from about 100 metres on the east and north-east side to about 1 km on the west. There are two narrow passages into the lagoon. The island has a brown, peat-like soil that is very fertile. Puka trees *(Pisonia grandis)* and *Cordia subcordata* grew prolifically in the 1930s.

The island's European discoverer was Captain Kemin in 1824. But the atoll is said to take its name from Gideon Gardner, owner of the ship 'Ganges' in which a Captain Coffin sighted it in 1828. J. T. Arundel planted part of the island with coconuts in 1892, the years in which Captain H. W. S. Gibson of HMS 'Curacoa' annexed it for the British Crown.

Because of a drought in the 1890s, Arundel's coconuts did not thrive, and the island was not further utilised until Gilbertese colonists went there in 1938-39. The Gilbertese called the island Nikumaroro. All the settlers were removed to Wagina Island, Solomons, in 1963.

Orona (Hull Island). This atoll, which lies eastward of Nukumaroro, is about 11 km long by 5 km wide. There are numerous small islets on the reef and many entrances into the big lagoon.

Stone structures found on the island in 1933 indicate that it was inhabitated long before it became known to Europeans in the 1820s. The island was named and first chartered by Commodore Charles Wilkes of the United States Exploring Expedition in 1840; but a Frenchman and 10 Tahitians were then living ashore.

J. T. Arundel & Co. started planting the island with coconuts in 1887, two years before the commander of the HMS 'Egeria' proclaimed it a British posession. The British companies that subsequently leased the island shipped some copra from it. The Burns Philp ship 'Makoa' was wrecked there in 1937.

After Gilbertese settlers went there in 1938, the island's population grew to 610. The Gilbertese were resettled at Wagina, Solomon Islands, in 1963. Since then the U.S. has built a radar station on the island.

MANRA (SYDNEY ISLAND). Manra is roughly circular, and encloses a land-locked lagoon. It measures about 3.25 km from west to east and 2.5 km from north to south. Fish traps in the lagoon indicate that this was once open to the sea and that the island supported a pre-European population. Numerous ancient stone structures have also been found there.

Like Birnie Island, Sydney was discovered by Captain Emment about 1820. J. T. Arundel & Co. shipped guano from the island between 1882 and 1885, and planted it with coconuts. The British companies that subsequently leased the island exported copra.

The island was annexed for Great Britain by the commander of HMS 'Egeria' in 1889. Gilbertese colonists went there in 1938 and within two years they numbered 260. However, by 1950 the authorities had decided that the island could not properly support a permanent population. In 1958, the entire population was evacuated and most of them resettled at Gizo, Solomon Islands. Since then the island's coconut plantations have been worked by the Phoenix Islands Cooperative Society.

LINE ISLANDS DISTRICT. The Line islands administrative district of the Gilbert Islands is made up of three northern islands, Tabuaeran (Washington), Teraina (Fanning) and Christmas, and five southern islands, Malden, Starbuck, Vostok, Caroline and Flint. The northern, inhabited islands, lie a few degrees north of the Equator some 15 to 20 degrees south of the Hawaiian chain and nearly 30 degrees eastward of the Gilberts. With Kingman Reef and Palmyra Island (two United States possessions), all the islands form a chain running in a NW to SE direction. Washington is about 190 km SE of Palmyra and about 120 km NW of Fanning. Christmas Island is about 245 km SE of Fanning.

TABUAERAN (WASHINGTON ISLAND) which has also been called Prospect Island and New York Island, is about 4 km long by 2 km wide. It is about 3 m above sea level and has a large fresh water late at its eastern end. A fast-multiplying fish, tilapia, has been introduced in the lake in recent years. The island has been described as 'the most difficult and dangerous loading port in the Pacific'. An anchorage at the west point may be used only in calm weather.

The island is owned by Fanning Island Plantations Ltd., a subsidiary of Burns Philp & Co. Ltd., of Sydney. It is completely covered with coconut palms — some 200,000 of them. I-Kiribati are employed in copra-making. There were no indigenous inhabitants in historical times; but archaeological discoveries on the island suggest that it was reached or visited in the past by mariners from Tonga.

Captain Edmund Fanning who discovered the island in 1798 named it after the United States President. The United States Exploring Expedition visited it in 1840. Its history, since then, has been closely linked with Fanning Island's. Britain annexed it in 1889.

TERAINA (FANNING ISLAND) is an atoll about 50 km in circumference. The land area is 34.54 sq. km; that of the lagoon about 110 sq. km. The land is never more than 1 km wide.

Most of the land is owned by Fanning Island Plantations Ltd., a subsidiary of Burns Philp & Co. Ltd., Sydney. Somewhat more than a third of its holdings is under coconuts. Labour for the plantations is imported from the Gilbert Islands.

English Harbour provides a sheltered anchorage for vessels up to about 1,000 tonnes. There is also a calm weather port known as Whaler's Anchorage, but as this is too far from the lagoon entrance for easy cargo handling, vessels usually drift off the entrance.

Provisions for Fanning Island and the other islands in the administrative district are carried by copra and colony vessels, and by vessels used for the recruitment and repatriation of plantation labour.

The island was discovered by Captain Edmund Fanning of the American ship 'Betsey' in 1798. By 1850, a Captain Henry English was conducting valuable trade in coconut oil from the island. He was followed by William Greig (British) and George Bicknell of Hawaii. These men also planted Washington Island. About the turn of the century, their interests were acquired by Father Emmanuel Rougier of Fiji, later Tahiti. Three after Rougier's death in 1932, the island was bought by Fanning Island Plantations Ltd.

Captain Sir William Wiseman of HMS 'Caroline' annexed the island to Great Britain in 1888 after

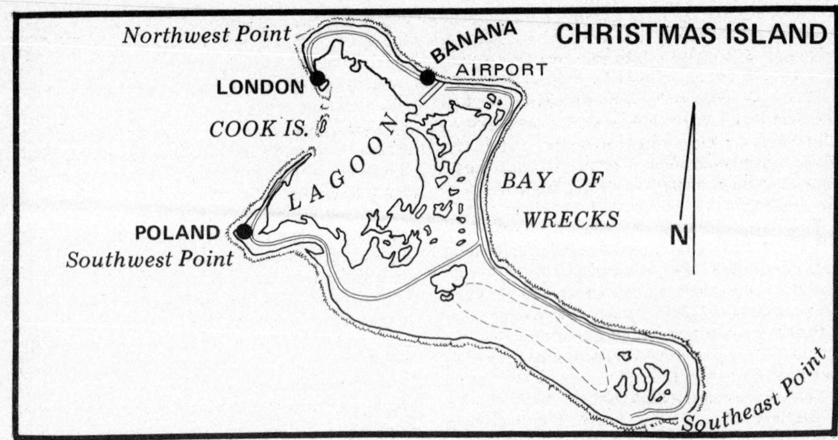

it was found that it lay in the line of the proposed trans-Pacific cable. From 1902 to 1963, the island was the connecting link for the cable between Bamfield, Canada, and Suva, Fiji. Then the new British Commonwealth coaxial cable was opened, and the cable station on Fanning, operated by Cable and Wireless Ltd., was closed.

CHRISTMAS ISLAND. Christmas Island, in about 1 deg. 59 min. N. lat. and 157 deg. 30 min. W. long., is about 160 km in circumference. It is the largest island of purely coral formation in the world. In shape, it resembles a chop. It stretches from NW to SE. The larger portion is in the NW and encloses a spacious lagoon. The interior of the land area is remarkable in being dotted with more than 100 sheets of water. Some of these are lakes several kilometres in diameter. A large bay exposed to winds and currents from the east is known as the Bay of Wrecks because of the large number of ships that have come to grief there.

Coconuts have been planted north and south of the lagoon. There is a good anchorage off Cook Island near the entrance. Only fairly small craft can enter the lagoon safely, as there are many coral patches and not much depth. There are two settlements, London, to the north of Cook Island and Paris, to the south of it.

Pre-European artifacts of different periods and a number of stone structures have been found on the island. But the island was uninhabited when Captain Cook discovered it on December 24, 1777, and spent Christmas Day there. However, the Spaniards might have been there before Cook's voyage. The first ship known to have been wrecked there was the 'Briton' in 1836.

The island was examined for guano in the 1850s, and an American, Captain J. L. Pendleton, of the ship 'John Marshall', took possession of it in 1857. The US Guano Company worked the island for several years after November 1858. Subsequently, the British Government leased the island to the Anglo-Australian Guano Co. and Alfred Houlder. But when a representative of the latter visited it in 1872, he found it occupied by three men working for a Honolulu man. Moreover, the USS 'Narrangansett' had just been there and had taken formal possession for the United States. Despite this and an American protest, Captain William Wiseman of HMS 'Caroline' annexed the island to Great Britain in 1888.

Lever's Pacific Plantations Ltd. leased the island from the British Government in 1902 for 99 years and planted it with nearly 73,000 coconuts. The lease was taken over by Father Emmanuel Rougier in 1913 and worked in the name of Central Pacific Coconut Plantations Ltd. from 1914. After Rougier died in 1932, his nephew took charge of the plantation, but abandoned it during the Depression.

With the development of aviation in the mid-1930s, Christmas Island began to attract attention as a possible refuelling base for trans-Pacific aircraft. The British Government forestalled any new American claim to the island by sending representatives there in 1937. However, during World War II both American and New Zealand troops garrisoned it and it was used as an air base to link Honolulu with the US base at Bora Bora. The Americans did not leave until 1948. Meanwhile, the Rougier lease was deemed to have terminated, and the Gilbert and Ellice Islands Colony took over the running of the coconut plantation.

In 1956-58, Britain used Christmas Island as a base for nuclear experiments. The United States did the same in 1962. As a result, more than 100 km of sealed roads were made, but they have not been maintained.

As the island, wholly owned by the government, has more than half the total land area of Kiribati, the government plans to develop it into an alternative economic centre to South Tarawa. Already fish farms have been established, the island is linked by air with Tarawa and Honolulu, and there is a hotel, the Captain Cook with 24 rooms. Another hotel is planned and the copra industry will be developed. By December, 1978, the population had grown to 1,288.

MALDEN ISLAND. This island lies about 386 km south of the equator in 155 deg. W. long. It is flat and triangular, on a reef measuring about 6.5 km by 8 km and enclosing a large lagoon. Only stunted vegetation grows there.

Stone-faced platforms and graves found on Malden indicate that Polynesians lived there for several generations before Europeans discovered it. It was then uninhabited. K. P. Emory, of the Bishop Museum of Honolulu, estimated in 1924 that the pre-European population must have reached from 100 to 200. The occupation of the island was known in tradition to the people of Manihiki, Northern Cook Islands.

The European discoverer of Malden was Lord Byron of HMS 'Blonde', who came upon it in 1825 after conveying the remains of the king and queen of Hawaii from England to Honolulu. Byron named it after his surveying officer.

Guano deposits were discovered on the island about 1849, and a series of Australian guano enterprises worked them profitably for about 70 years. About 1889, Grice, Sumner & Co., of Melbourne, had about eight Europeans working there with 150 Polynesians from Niue and Aitutaki. In 1922, the island was leased to Malden Island Pty. Ltd., of Melbourne, a successor of Grice, Sumner. But this firm did not exercise its lease after 1929. From 1956 to 1964, the island was used as a base for members of the British armed services during nuclear tests at Christmas Island.

STARBUCK ISLAND. Starbuck Island lies about 540 km south of the equator and 174 km SSW of Malden Island in 155 deg. W. long. It is barely 4.5 metres at its highest point. 10 km long and about 3 km wide. It is barren and treeless, with a shallow lagoon.

Captain Obed Starbuck of the US whaler 'Hero' discovered it in 1823, but it was named after his namesake, Captain Valentine Starbuck, who sighted it three months after its discoverer. Captain William Swinburne of HMS 'Mutine' annexed it for Great Britain in 1866.

Houlder Bros. and Co. of London began digging guano from the island about 1870 and, during this period, an opening for small boats was made in the reef on the north-west. The island was worked for some years by J. T. Arundel & Co. and later by the Malden Island guano-seekers. It has been unoccupied and unworked since 1920. Attempts to plant coconuts on the island failed.

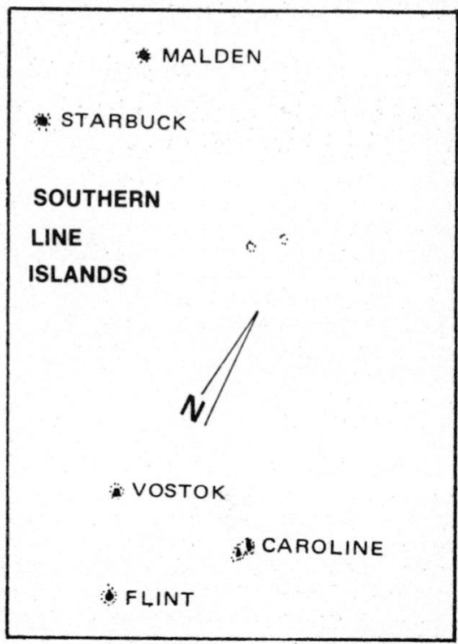

The British built a beacon on the western end as a warning to shipping. Starbuck has been called also Low, Starve, Hero, Barren, Coral Queen and Volunteer.

CAROLINE ISLAND. This island measures about 10 km north and south, by about 1 km wide. There are over 20 islets strung along the reef enclosing a shallow lagoon, which is closed against anything larger than a ship's boat. Some of the islets are 4.5 to 6 metres high, and most are covered with coconut palms, pandanus and similar growth. There is no anchorage, and approach to the wooded shores is difficult. Water can be had by digging.

Graves containing adzes and 'marae' platforms have been found on the island, indicating that Polynesians once inhabited it. Its European discoverer was Captain W. R. Broughton, of HMS 'Providence' in 1795. Several British and American captains subsequently gave it different names.

The British firm of Collie and Lucett, of Tahiti, formed a small stock-raising settlement there in 1846. In 1868, Captain Edward Nares of HMS 'Reindeer' took possession of it and reported that 27 people were living there, raising pigs and poultry, salting fish, and planting coconuts. In 1872, the island was leased to Houlder Bros. and Company, of London. Some guano was extracted.

J. T. Arundel & Co. took over the Houlder Bros. lease in 1881 and planted numerous coconuts. A total eclipse of the sun was observed there in

1883. In 1910, the island was leased to S. R. Maxwell & Co., of Auckland, for coconut growing. After World War II, leases to it were held by Mr M. P. A. Bambridge, and, later, Captain Omer Darr, both of Tahiti.

The island has also been called Thornton, Hirst, Clark, Independence and Carolina.

VOSTOK ISLAND. This is a low, uninhabited, triangular coral lump less than 2 km sqaure. A central clump of puka trees, about 25 metres high, is its principal feature. At the south-west corner is a boat passage through the reef, but there is no anchorage.

The Russian explorer Bellingshausen discovered it in 1820 and named it after his ship. It later acquired the names Stavers, Reaper, Leavitts and Anne. The United States claimed it under the Guano Act of 1856, but the claim was never pressed. In 1873, Mr J. T. Arundel of Houlder Bros. and Co., London, took possession of it for the British Crown. It is not known whether it was worked for guano. Although subsequently leased to various companies none of them made use of it. Captain Omer Darr, of Tahiti, acquired the lease in 1964.

FLINT ISLAND. Flint Island is situated in 11 deg. 25 min. S. lat. and 151 deg. 48 min. W. long. It is about 5 km long by one broad, flat, and with a maximum height of about 7.5 metres. It is well-wooded and entirely surrounded by a coral reef, through which a boat passage has been blasted. The passage leads to a landing place on the western side.

The European discovery of the island is said to date back to 1801, but the name of its discoverer is unknown. A vessel of the US Exploring Expedition surveyed it in 1841, and it was claimed as an American possession under the US Guano Act of 1856. However, the island was occupied by Mr J. T. Arundel of Houlder Bros. and Co., London, in 1872, for the purpose of exporting guano. Coconuts were planted there from 1875, and the island was solely used as a coconut plantation after the export of guano ceased in 1893. A lease that J. T. Arundel & Co. had had from 1885 was acquired by the Pacific Islands Co. Ltd. in 1897, and later by Lever's Pacific Plantations Ltd. S. R. Maxwell & Co. Ltd., of Tahiti and Auckland, held the lease from 1910 to 1934. In 1922, 30,000 palms were growing on the island. From 1951 to 1964, the island was leased to Mr M. P. A. Bambridge of Tahiti, and subsequently to Captain Omer Darr of Tahiti.

KANTON ISLAND (CANTON). As there is no letter C in Gilbertese, the letter K has been substituted for the initial capital letter C — Kanton — in official lists. Canton Island is about halfway between Honolulu and Noumea, a distance of 5,400 km. It is an atoll enclosing a chop-shaped lagoon about 11 km long and about 5 km broad. There are several entrances into the lagoon, and the atoll offers the best anchorage in the Phoenix group. The land is merely a coral sandbank about 14½ k long and seldom more than 600 metres wide. Except where trees have been planted in recent times, the vegetation is low and stunted.

Canton was named after a New Bedford whaler that was wrecked there in 1854. It was known previously as Mary and Mary Balcout Island, but its discoverer is unknown. The island was worked for its guano between 1881 and 1891 by J. T. Arundel & Co., of London, who obtained a lease to the island from the British Government. The lease was subsequently transferred to other British companies. A party from HMS 'Leith' erected a sign asserting British sovereignty over the island in August 1936. In the following year, the boundaries of the Gilbert and Ellice Islands Colony were extended to include all the Phoenix Islands and the rights to those islands were bought by the colony from Burns Philp (South Sea) Co. Ltd. Two British officials were stationed on Canton in August 1937, and some Americans arrived in the following March. Just over a year later, the UK and US Governments signed the treaty providing for the joint administration of both Canton and Enderbury.

During 1938-39, Pan American Airways developed an airport and cleared the lagoon of coral heads. When war came to the Pacific in December 1941, the airport came under military control and the US Air Force built an airfield for land planes on the north-western rim. From 1945 to 1958, the airfield was regularly used by the trans-Pacific airlines, Qantas and PAA. The development of long-range aircraft then made the airfield superfluous except in emergencies.

In the early 1960s, a satellite tracking station was established on Canton for the Project Mercury space research programme. Meanwhile, the United States Federal Aviation Agency continued to maintain landing facilities and navigational aids. More than 60 Gilbert and Ellice (Tuvalu) Islanders were employed on the island on various installations and both the US and Britain continued to maintain administrative officers there until 1968. They were then withdrawn, and in October 1970 it was officially stated that the island was uninhabited. However, early in 1971 it was revealed that in 1970 Canton had become a United States tracking station for anti-ballistic missiles and that it was serviced by US and American Samoan personnel. It is understood that ballistic missiles are fired from the United States across the Pacific towards Guam. They are intercepted by anti-missiles from the US base at Kwajalein, but to gauge recovery effectively the US has a series of tracking stations, of which Canton is one. Enderbury (see below) and Hull and Birnie are also used.

ENDERBURY ISLAND. Enderbury Island lies about 60 km ESE of Canton Island. It is about 4½ km long by 1½ km wide. The lagoon that once existed is now only a shallow puddle. Slabs of compact coral rock make up much of the land area. Grasses, low bushes and a few small trees are the only vegetation.

The island is said to have been discovered by Captain James J. Coffin of the British whaler 'Transit' in 1823. The name is thought to be a corruption of Enderby, the British whaling house. The island was surveyed by vessels of the United States Exploring Expedition in 1840 and 1841.

The Phoenix Guano Company, an American concern, worked the island's guano deposits between 1859 and 1877. J. T. Arundel & Co., of London, did likewise for several years after 1881. Thereafter, no one troubled about Enderbury until 1937 when, with other islands in the Phoenix group, it was investigated as a place of settlement for land-hungry Gilbertese.

Although the island came under Anglo-American administration in 1939, it has been little utilised since then. In the 1960s, scientists of the Smithsonian Institution set up camps there during bird-tagging expeditions connected with their study of migratory birds in the Pacific. More recently, it has had a part in the United States' anti-ballistic missile programme.

FOR THE TOURIST. The very remoteness of the islanders and their adaptation to atoll existence can tempt the traveller seeking a really new experience. The remaining scars of the Battle of Tarawa in the Pacific War are of interest to those who study war relics. While there are no regularly scheduled excursions for tourists, visitors can organise fishing trips, swimming, picnicking and shelling excursions by launch from Tarawa. Boat trips can also be made to other islands. Air flights operate to Butaritari, one of the first islands to be colonised, Christmas Island, North Tabiteuea, Abemama, Marakei, Nonouti, Beru, Maiana, Nikunau and Onotoa. Other airfields planned for 1979 were Tamana, Arorae, Makin and Banaba. Abemama was the home of Robert Louis Stevenson in 1889, and Tabiteuea is well known for its dances. Christmas Island is well known for its distinctive bird life and there are facilities for game fishing.

Accommodation. The Otintai Hotel at Bikenibeu has 26 rooms and faces the lagoon. Traditional dancing (some of the best in the Pacific) can be arranged and other attractions include deep-sea fishing, sailing, excursions, skin-diving, clamshell and octopus fishing, hotel-sponsored picnics and barbecues.

Christmas Island has one hotel, the Captain Cook with 24 bedrooms and there is a privately-owned hotel on Abemama Island with eight rooms constructed of local materials. All other islands have a rest house.

Visitors need a passport or equivalent travel document and an onward ticket.

Details can be had from the Kiribati Visitors Bureau, Tarawa, Kiribati, Central Pacific.

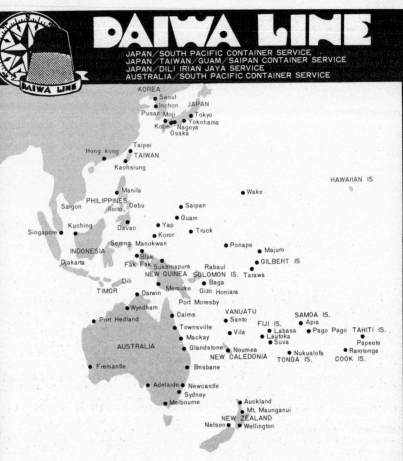

LINE ISLANDS

Beginning about 1,500 kilometres south of the Hawaiian group is a string of small, low, semi-barren islands known as the Line Islands. They run in a SSE direction towards French Polynesia. From north to south, they are: Kingman Reef and Palmyra, Washington, Fanning, Christmas, Jarvis, Malden, Starbuck, Caroline, Vostok and Flint Islands. Kingman, Palmyra and Jarvis are US possessions; the rest are in Kiribati.

Guano was extracted from some of the islands late last century and early this century; some have been planted with coconuts.

All the islands are of coral formation, but only six – Caroline, Malden, Christmas, Fanning, Palmyra and Kingman – have interior lagoons and so qualify to be called atolls. Most of the lagoons are shallow. Washington is unusual in having a large fresh water lake. In the others, the lagoons that once existed have dried up.

Accounts of each island to 1942 will be found in Edwin H. Bryan Jr., "American Polynesia and the Hawaiian Chain", Honolulu, 1942.

KINGMAN REEF. Kingman Reef is 1,480 km south of Honolulu in 6 deg. 23 min. N. lat. and 162 deg. 25 min. W. long. It is a bare, triangular reef, about 15 km long by 8 km wide, sheltering a lagoon with considerable depths. Captain Edmund Fanning, of the American trading ship 'Betsey', discovered it in 1798. Captain W. E. Kingman described it in 1853. It was annexed to the United States on May 10, 1922; and in 1934 when trans-Pacific aviation was under discussion, the reef was placed under the control of the US Navy.

In 1937, Pan American Airways, pioneering the new airmail service with flying-boats between Hawaii and New Zealand, used its sheltered lagoon as a half-way station between Honolulu and Pago Pago. The route was abandoned after a flying-boat was lost off Pago Pago in January 1938. Kingman is still under the control of the US Department of the Navy.

PALMYRA ISLAND. Palmyra Island is located at 5 deg. 53 min. N. lat. and 162 deg. 5 min. W. long. It consists of about 50 islets totalling some 1,190 hectares. The island was discovered by Captain Sawle, of the American ship 'Palmyra', in 1802. It has also been known as Samarang.

The Kingdom of Hawaii annexed it in 1862; Britain did the same in 1889; and the United States included it among the Hawaiian Islands by Congressional Act of 1898. The US cruiser 'West Virginia' took formal possession in 1912. It was excluded from the boundaries of Hawaii by the Hawaii Statehood Act, and is now the responsibility of the US Department of the Interior. Judge Cooper, of Honolulu, acquired title to the island in 1911, and used it for growing coconuts. He sold all but two islets to Leslie and Ellen Fullard-Leo. When Cooper died in 1929, the other two islets (Home Islands) passed to his heirs.

Palmyra's central lagoon was originally divided into three by coral reefs. During World War II, the US Navy had 6,000 men on the island, and they dredged a seaplane runway that merged the two western lagoons into one. A causeway was built on the remaining reef. At the same time the Navy joined three of the former islets into one. They built a landplane runway of about 1,800 metres which was used by the US Air Force until 1961. It is now unserviceable.

The main harbour is West Lagoon, which is entered by a channel on the SW side of the atoll. Both the channel and harbour will accommodate vessels drawing four metres of water. The atoll is only about two metres above sea level, but as it has a high annual rainfall – about 4,400 millimetres – the islets are covered in dense vegetation. many of the roads and causeways built during the war have become unserviceable and overgrown.

In 1962, a Californian firm tried to promote Palmyra as a resort and tourist area, but it did not eventuate.

Ownership of Palmyra is (1979) shared by Fullard-Leo's three sons, Leslie, Dudley and Ainslie who live in Hawaii. The US Government announced in 1979 that it was considering buying Palmyra to use as a nuclear waste dump, a proposal which the South Pacific Forum decided at its 1979 meeting to oppose. The Fullard-Leo brothers also said they would refuse to sell the atoll for that purpose.

Twenty five people were living on Palmyra in 1979.

JARVIS ISLAND. Jarvis Island is a small, bleak bowl-shaped place, about 3 × 1.5 km lying by itself just south of the equator, in 160 deg. W. long. It was first reported by Captain Browne of the British ship 'Eliza Francis', in 1821, and has been called Bunker, Volunteer, Jervis and Brook. The American Guano Co. claimed it in 1857, and from then until 1879, when it was abandoned, large quantities of guano were removed. It was annexed by Britain in 1889, and in 1906 leased to the Pacific Phosphate Co., but apparently never worked. When United States officials occupied and claimed the island in 1935, Britain offered no objection; and at various times since that date it has been used as a weather station. Millersville, the settlement on the western side of the island, consisted of several wood and stone houses, with a radio-shack and towers. It was occupied for a time during the International Geophysical Year. It is now under the control of the US Department of the Interior and uninhabited.

WASHINGTON, FANNING, CHRISTMAS, MALDEN, STARBUCK, VOSTOK, CAROLINE and **FLINT.** See under Kiribati.

NORTHERN LINE ISLANDS

Kingman Reef
160°
Palmyra Is.
5°
Tabuaeran Is.
Teraina Is.
N
Christmas Is.
0°
Jarvis Is.

LORD HOWE ISLAND

Lord Howe Island is a dependency of New South Wales, lying about 500 km off the Australian coast. Its position is 30 deg. 30 min. S. lat. 159 deg. 50 min. W. long. It is 670 km north-east of Sydney. The population in 1977 was about 300 permanent residents.

The island is volcanic in origin and covers about 1,288 hectares. It is very beautiful and covered with luxuriant vegetation, dominated by two mountain peaks. The island is included in the Phillip electorate for the New South Wales State Parliament and is managed by the Lord Howe Island Board, located in the Lands Department, Sydney.

Island time is 10 hours ahead of G.M.T.

THE PEOPLE. Today's islanders generally were born on Lord Howe, although mostly their families originally came from Australia. The quiet isolation of the island produces a lifestyle as if the 1950s stood still. It is almost impossible to migrate to Lord Howe. Short term visitors must have return tickets and accommodation booked in advance.

Favourite recreations on the island consist of fishing, swimming and exploring by bicycle or minimoke, bowls and golf.

GOVERNMENT. By the Lord Howe Act of 1953, the island was vested in the Crown, freed and discharged from the estate of any person. The act provides for leases in perpetuity for "Islanders" (as defined by the act) but there is provision for transfer of a lease to a non-islander where it is established that there is no islander willing or able to take it on.

In 1954 the former Board of Control was reconstituted as the Lord Howe Island Board. This Board, with offices at 23-33 Bridge Street, Sydney is charged with the care, control and management of the island. One member is a Lord Howe Islander, elected by the residents, for a term of three years.

An Island Committee of four members, elected by islanders, makes recommendations to the board and carries out such duties as the board authorises it to perform. The board is represented at Lord Howe Island by a Superintendent. Besides a road-grading plant (with tractors), the board provides motor transport, an artificial insemination service for cattle and, with the advice of the Federal Transport Department, conducts the airfield. The board normally meets three times a year, twice on the island and once in Sydney.

A new Lord Howe Island Act has been tabled in parliament on the status of islanders, who can live, vote and hold land there, etc. but it had not been enacted by early-1978.

Police. There are two special constables on the island, but there is little or no crime.

Liquor. The board conducts a public liquor store, where liquor is retailed at Sydney prices, plus freight. The board issues licences for retailing liquor. Applicants state their requirements, which are considered by the board, which then fixes the conditions for the licences.

EDUCATION. The school has an enrolment of 40-50 pupils and is staffed by three teachers, provided by the NSW Education Department. After completing primary levels, students may study to School Certificate level by correspondence, under the supervision of the teachers. Only 10 students do secondary education study on the island. Most students go to the mainland for secondary education.

LABOUR. The workforce consists of 80 people and of these, about half work for the government. The remainder are engaged mainly in providing services for tourists. The Board has 20 employees, including three who work at the airport. Practically all fit men turn out to help unload the monthly cargo ship. A number of islanders help to collect palm seed for export.

HEALTH. The Gower Wilson Memorial Hospital, with three beds, which is in charge of a doctor and a full-time nurse, caters for most medical needs of the people. It has modern equipment. The hospital is able to cater for most cases, but some patients, who are seriously ill, are sent to the mainland. A dentist visits the island at six-monthly intervals.

THE LAND. The island is crescent-shaped, about 11 km long and from one to three km in width, with an area of 1,288 ha. The two peaks covering about two-thirds of the island are Mt. Gower 932 m and Mt. Lidgbird 822 m. Mt Gower is usually capped with cloud. Mt. Lidgbird rises in a succession of steep terraces, and is pyramidal in shape.

Because of the peculiar boulder formation, the island has scarcely more than 120 ha suitable for agriculture. However this land is extremely rich, and will produce almost any type of sub-tropical vegetation. A flora and fauna reserve controlled by the Board covers about 70 per cent of the island.

The climate is mild and the rainfall abundant.

A coral reef on the western side of Lord Howe is the most southerly in the world. It encloses a broad lagoon, about 6 km long by 2 km wide.

Only islanders are granted perpetual leases of land, at nominal rents of $2 per year. Any houses for sale must be sold at the Board's valuation and islander residents have first preference for purchase.

Flora and fauna. There are many rare and beautiful plants. The forests comprise mostly the unique Kentia palms and huge banyans.

At first settlement there were neither mammals nor snakes on the island (but cats, pigs and rats were subsequently introduced).

The slopes of the mountain are honeycombed with the burrows of the rare Bighill muttonbirds, that make this island their home.The commoner species of muttonbirds occupy the dense palm forest on the eastern side of the island – it is one huge muttonbird rookery.

Other birds include the strong-billed magpie, the kingfisher, and the rare woodhen which lives at the top of the mountains. The woodhen is one of the rarest birds in the world. Scientific study in recent years suggest that the tiny woodhen population is stable with about 23 birds, all tagged.

The sea birds are protected, as are certain fish which must not be taken from the lagoon or Ned's Beach where tame fish are fed by hand. A comprehensive environmental survey of the island was made in 1974 by Dr Harry F. Recher of the Australian Museum, Sydney.

PRIMARY PRODUCTION. The island's only export is world-famous Kentia palm seeds. The seed of the island's four varieties of Kentia or Howea palm is gathered by islanders and shipped to Sydney and then exported to all parts of the world.

Several hundred bushels of seed are exported each year. In addition, the palm trees are a prized souvenir for garden-lovers to take home. The income varies according to demand.

Lord Howe Island provides some of its own food, including beef, and its own milk. Produce grows well in the good agricultural soil. The islanders are able to provide a good proportion of their own vegetables.

TOURISM. The board has not published figures of revenue derived from tourism. The number of tourists staying in guest houses was 5,582 in the financial year to June 1978 and about another 1,000 stayed privately. The number of visitors is increasing with the establishment in 1974 of the air service.

Development plan. In 1976 the board drew a planning scheme for land use on the whole island. A building code was also adopted to encourage an attractive development which would preserve the island's natural attractions including its beautiful trees.

LOCAL COMMERCE. There are three local shops – Thompson's Store, Lagoon Store and Nick's Trading Post. There is a film show twice weekly in the public hall. There is a post office, the Commonwealth Bank and Bank of N.S.W. agencies.

FINANCE. Lord Howe Island derives its income from a number of sources, including the sale of palm seed, liquor sales, a tourist charge of 20c a day and charges for services. The NSW Government provides a subsidy to run the hospital and also provides financial assistance for road work. The Federal Government gives assistance to maintain the airport.

For the financial year 1979/80 the board has budgeted for the expenditure of about $1 million, which includes wages, etc. $345,000; administration expenses $50,000; plant $100,000; materials $60,000; health $50,000; liquor purchases $195,000; miscellaneous $300,000.

TRANSPORT. There are about 16 km of road, the major sections of which are sealed and lit at night. There are about 180 vehicles on the island, including motor cycles. The most popular and convenient forms of transport are bicycle and Mini-moke which can be hired locally.

Airlines. An airstrip was built on the island and came into use in November 1974. Previously the island had been served by Sandringham flying-boats from Sydney, landing in the lagoon. The airstrip is approx. 1,000 metres long.

The licensed air carrier is Advance Airlines, which operates from Mascot, Sydney. There is another service from Brisbane operated twice weekly by Norfolk Island Airlines. It returns to Brisbane via Norfolk Island. Oxley Airlines operates periodically from Port Macquarie, and North Coast Airlines flies an occasional service from Coffs Harbour. Oxley Airlines and North Coast Airlines use light aircraft, carrying 7-8 passengers. Advance Airlines operates a daily return service during winter, but in summer, especially during school holidays, operates up to five services a day, using two aircraft. The Advance Airlines' flights take about 1 hour 40 minutes.

Shipping. Cargo is shipped by the French Compagnie des Chargeurs Caledoniens (CCC), based in

Noumea and operating out of Sydney. The agents are Hetherington Kingsbury.

COMMUNICATIONS. There is no local telephone network, but since August 1975 the island has been linked with Australia by radio telephone. Cables and Telex messages can be sent. A roneod news sheet, "The Signal", is published privately each fortnight.

Radio. A local radio station began broadcasting in early 1976, with contributions from the Island Board and staffed by volunteers. The radio uses the old flying-boat terminal building. Programmes include music and discussions, broadcast daily during daylight as volunteers are available. At night, islanders can listen to radio programmes from Sydney. A radio beacon on the island is an important navigational aid to trans-Pacific aircraft.

Weather station. The Lord Howe Island meteorological station is an important link in Pacific sea and air navigation.

WATER AND ELECTRICITY. The Department of Transport runs a diesel-operated generator producing 240 volts, for all island needs. Rainwater is collected in tanks; other supplies are sold from chemically treated wells.

PERSONALITIES

Lord Howe Island Board (Members as at September, 1980).

P. D. Hills, MLA, Member for Lord Howe Island (Phillip electorate)

A. E. Llewellyn, Director of Crown Lands in NSW, Acting Chairman

D. B. McFadyen, Island Member

M. A. Morris, MP, Member

R. J. Morgan, Secretary.

Superintendent on Lord Howe Island: Leonard Judd

Chairman, Island committee: D. B. McFadyen.

HISTORY. Lord Howe Island was uninhabited when it was first seen by a European, Lieut. H. Lidgbird Ball, of HMS 'Supply', on February 17, 1788. Lieut. Ball was en route to Norfolk Island, with Lieut. P. G. King, to found a settlement there, and named the island Lord Howe's Island after the First Sea Lord of the Admiralty. Lieut. Ball named the nearby rock tower Ball's Pyramid, after himself. The ship did not put in to Lord Howe Island on this sighting, but a boat was sent ashore to investigate on the return journey from Norfolk Island on March 13, when Ball formally took possession of the island for Britain.

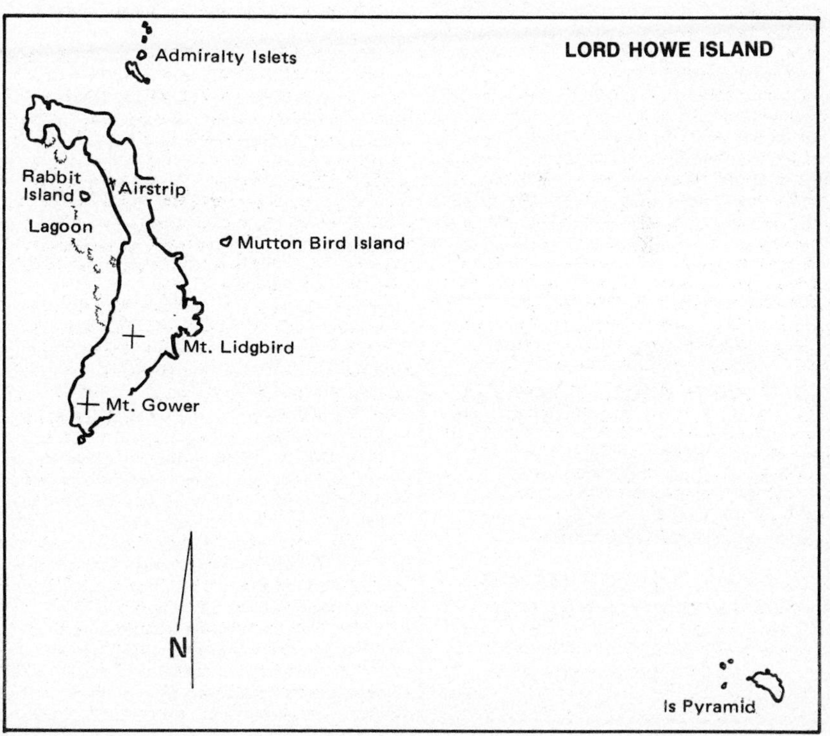

It was visited regularly by ships during the next two years or so, but after the novelty wore off and the infant colony at Port Jackson became more involved in its own affairs, the island was neglected again.

It was not until 1834 that it got its first settlers when three men, their Maori wives and two Maori boys, arrived in the whaler "Caroline" and were put ashore probably at what is now known as Blinky's Beach. Master of the whaler was Captain John Blenkinthorpe.

These settlers left after about seven years, and over the next 40 or 50 years other settlers drifted in and established themselves. Some were families from Sydney who grew produce and raised pigs. Some were stranded by shipwreck, or else were ships' deserters. Some made a good living by selling provisions to whaling vessels. The settlers had no legal right of occupancy, but they were not interfered with.

Several proposals to make the island a penal colony, like Norfolk Island, came to nothing during the early years of that century.

The NSW Government placed Captain Richard Armstrong as Resident Magistrate on the island in 1879, and Captain Armstrong virtually became island leader, helping to develop among other things an export business in Kentia palm seeds. He was also responsible for attracting a schoolteacher to the island, Thomas Wilson, who remained there for many years, although after he left the school remained closed until 1922.

Captain Armstrong's administration, in 1882 resulted in a Commission of Inquiry which was critical of him, but the captain fought the commissioner's findings on appeal and won. He afterwards left the island.

There were further royal commissions in 1911 and 1912, mainly to inquire into complications surrounding the palm seed industry, which was out of control, and the land situation, which was equally unsatisfactory. Settlers had "permissive occupancy", but no real title to land.

The findings of the commissions resulted in establishment in 1913 of the Lord Howe Island Board of Control, which not only controlled the now declining seed industry but also involved itself with most other aspects of island life. The days of laissez-faire were at an end.

However it was not until after World War II, in 1953, that the vague land situation was got into some sort of order. This was when NSW brought into force, on April 23, 1953, the Lord Howe Island Act, which put the NSW Government in firm control of island affairs.

In the intervening years, life on Lord Howe Island went on quietly, broken only occasionally by an unusual event such as the unexpected landing in 1931 of a tiny seaplane flown solo from New Zealand via Norfolk Island by Captain Francis Chichester, who many years later was to be knighted for his equally courageous solo sailing exploits. Chichester's plane was severely damaged after his landing – the first of any aircraft on Lord Howe – and he remained on the island for nine weeks while he and the islanders repaired the aircraft for its final successful flight to Australia.

In September 1948, an RAAF crew were not so lucky when their Catalina crashed into the bush while attempting to land at Lord Howe and seven of them were killed.

An important change in Lord Howe's lifestyle followed the advent of the flying-boat service in 1947, because the island became more accessible. The service finished after the opening of the airport in 1974.

OTHER ISLANDS

Outlying Islands. A group of rocky islets, called the Admiralties, lie on the north-east side of Lord Howe and are difficult to approach, except in calm weather. They are the nesting-place of myriads of sea-birds. Ball's Pyramid about 20 km S.E. of Lord Howe, was named after Lieut. Ball of "Supply". It is a spectacular, 560 m pinnacle of rock, rising out of the sea.

FOR THE TOURIST. Virtually all the tourists to the island are Australians. They number about 5,000 each year. Guest houses and flats have sufficient facilities to accommodate a total of over 300 people at a time. Bookings can be made through the NSW Government Travel Centre, 16 Spring St, Sydney or the Lord Howe Island Tourist Centre, 275 George Street, Sydney.

Pastimes available on the island include fishing, swimming, scuba diving, bush walking, and bicycle rides. A golf course and tennis courts may be used by visitors. Swimming is possible throughout the year.

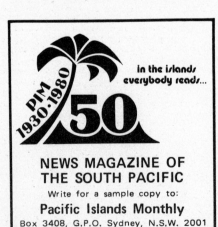

Dress on the island is informal and in the evenings, men wear short-sleeve shirts, shorts and long socks. Ties need not be worn.

There are clubs for bowls, and a 9-hole golf course, overlooking mountains and lagoon, all clubs with liquor licence.

The Seventh-day Adventists and Church of England each has a church on the island.

Lord Howe Island has a tranquil and friendly atmosphere. Visitors are fascinated by the hand feeding of tame fish at Ned's beach. Schools of mullet, parrotfish and silver drummer are fed by people who go into the water to knee depth.

Parties who go fishing in boats may be assured of a catch, mostly kingfish. Lodges have packs of locally frozen fish available to take back to Australia.

ACCOMMODATION

Lodges with full board:

PINE TREES, 22 suites, 6 bungalows, licensed to serve liquor (56 people).
OCEAN VIEW, 9 suites, 9 bungalows, licensed (40 people).
BLUE LAGOON, 15 suites, licensed (40 people).
CORAL COURT, 4 suites (8 people).
SEA BREEZE, 9 suites, licensed (20 people).
BEACHCOMBER, 3 suites, licensed (5 people).
LORHITI, 6 suites, licensed (18 people).
Suites are fully self-contained with private facilities; a bungalow is room only, share facilities.

Holiday flats and cottages:

All equipped with linen etc.
LEANDA LEI APARTMENTS, 11 flats (39 people).
TRADER NICK'S COTTAGE, 5 suites (15 people).
EBB TIDE FLATS, 2 flats (6 people).
AGGIE'S FLAT, (2 people).
PACIFIC PALMS, 12 flats (48 people).
BROKEN BANYAN, 6 flats (12 people).

MIDWAY ISLAND

Midway is about 1,900 km from Honolulu at the end of the chain of rocks and atolls extending to the north-west of Hawaii. It is an atoll about 25 km in circumference and an American possession. The entrance into the lagoon is on the south side, between the two islets of Eastern and Sand.

Midway was discovered in 1859 by Captain N. C. Brooks of the Hawaiian barque 'Gambia'. For some time it was referred to as Brooks Island. Captain William Reynolds of the USS 'Lackawanna' took possession of it for the United States on August 28, 1867. It had no indigenous population.

The atoll was placed under the jurisdiction of the US Navy in 1903, and is still under naval jurisdiction. In the thirties a hostel was built on Sand Island for overnighting plane passengers. Later, in 1939, hundreds of men were camped on Eastern Island to convert it into a submarine and air base. The air station was completed in August, 1941, and attacked on December 7, 1941 by the Japanese on their return from bombing Pearl Harbor. The Japanese tried hard to capture Midway, but failed. The sea battle off Midway against U.S. naval forces, June 3-5, 1942, was one of the turning points of the Pacific war. The defeat of the Japanese forces gave the United States Navy control of the Pacific.

In 1978, Eastern and Sand Islands were still serving as a naval station and air facility for the Navy. Midway is also a World Meteorological Organisation Upper-Air Observatory Station, which is operated by the Naval Weather Service. This service provides data on upper level winds and temperatures to worldwide users who utilise the data in current analysis, as well as for research purposes.

The islands are also classified as a National Wildlife Reserve to protect the bird life of the islands. This includes the laysan albatross (gooney bird), the frigate bird, the fairy tern and the bosun bird. This facet of the islands falls under federal statutes as set forth by the U.S. Department of Interior.

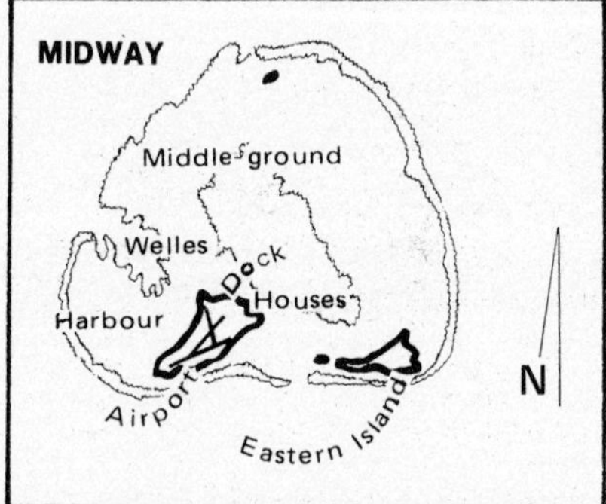

NAURU

Nauru, a single raised atoll of 22 sq. km with a circumference of 19 km, is an independent republic and an associate member of the British Commonwealth. It is located about 42 km south of the equator at 166 deg. 56 min. E. longitude. It is about 4,000 km north of Sydney and 4,160 km west of Honolulu. Local time is 12 hours ahead of GMT.

The population in 1979 was estimated at 7,700. The administrative centre is in the Yaren district.

The national anthem is "Nauru Ubwema" (Nauru, Our Homeland) and the flag is royal blue, divided by a narrow horizontal gold band with a 12-pointed star in the lower left quarter. Australian currency is used.

THE PEOPLE. Of a total estimated population on Nauru of 7,700 people in March 1979, 4,600 were Nauruan. The others include 450 Europeans employed in the government or with the Nauruan Phosphate Corporation, and 1,900 Gilbertese, Tuvaluans and other Pacific islanders, 650 Chinese working for the NPC together with their families and 200 Filipinos.

The Nauruan population is widely scattered along the coastal fringe of the island (the centre has no permanent inhabitants), but the migrant workers are concentrated in dormitory apartment blocks in the NPC area on the waterfront near the loading cantilevers.

What can loosely be described as the "town centre" of the island is situated between the airport and the cantilevers, where the post office and the modern civic or conference centre are situated. The main government offices are near the airport.

Citizenship. Nauruans are Nauruan citizens.

Language. The national language is Nauruan but English is widely understood and spoken.

Religion. The Nauruans are Christian and adhere either to the Nauruan Congregational Church, the Nauru Independent Church or the Catholic Church. Most Nauruans are Protestant.

Lifestyle. Because of a high income from phosphate royalties, the lack of taxes and the provision of many free services by the government, most Nauruans are well provided with material things such as radios, car, refrigerators, etc. But they are not a people who flaunt their comparative wealth, and Nauruans live a fairly simple, island-style of life, enjoying the modern conveniences without feeling overwhelmed by them.

They are strongly sports-minded, and follow all kinds of sports but especially Australian Rules football and softball.

GOVERNMENT. The Republic of Nauru is governed by the Nauruan Parliament of 18 members elected by common roll every three years. For electoral purposes the island is divided into districts, most districts electing two members. After each election the parliament elects the republic's President, who chooses a Cabinet of five or six members led by himself, to act as executive. The President is thus both head of state and de facto prime minister. Voting is compulsory for all Nauruans over 20. There are no organised political parties.

Nauru is an Associate member of the British Commonwealth, which means that the republic has all the benefits of Commonwealth status except the right to attend the Prime Ministers' conferences.

Local government. The Nauru Local Government Council has both important responsibilities and a large income (mainly through phosphate royalties). The Head Chief of the NLGC also happens to be President of the republic, and for many years members of Nauru's Cabinet have also been elected councillors. This development has resulted in a two-tier system of government, with responsibilities for some Nauru affairs being divided between the council and the government. As an example, Nauru's shipping line is operated by the Nauru Local Government Council, but Nauru's airline is operated by the Nauru Government, although both can be important instruments of national policy.

Justice. The judicial arm of government is composed of the Supreme Court of Nauru, presided over by a Chief Justice, the District Court, presided over by a Resident Magistrate, and the Family Court. All are courts of record.

The Supreme Court exercises both original and appellate jurisdiction. The practice and procedure

Discover the Pacific with Air Nauru. We fly to almost all of it.

KAGOSHIMA
HONG KONG TAIPEI OKINAWA
PONAPE
MAJURO
SINGAPORE MANILA GUAM
NAURU TARAWA
HONIARA
VILA NADI SUVA APIA
NOUMEA NUKUALOFA
MELBOURNE AUCKLAND

Whether you are traveling for pleasure or for business, discovering the Pacific with Air Nauru is truly a unique experience.

As the first and only airline to link the major Pacific ethnic regions of Micronesia, Melanesia and Polynesia with Asia and Australia, we can show you a diversity of geography and culture that is at once stunning and unforgettable.

With 45,000 unduplicated flying miles, we can move you faster and easier from one island to another – like no other airline can.

And, with our all-Boeing fleet, we can move you in the kind of comfort and superb style that you have come to expect from the largest of the world airlines.

Discover the Pacific with Air Nauru.

Nobody flies to more of it than we do.

For ticketing, reservations and flight information, telephone: 740 in Apia, Western Samoa; 477-7106 in Guam; 595 or 727 in Honiara, Solomon Islands; 229 in Majuro, Marshall Islands; 312-377 in Suva, 72795 in Nadi, Fiji 448 in Tarawa, Kiribati; and 653-5709 in Melbourne, Australia.

of the Supreme Court was regulated by the Rules of the Court of the Supreme Court of Queensland, but is now governed by several local statutes and regulations. The Chief Justice lives in Melbourne and goes to Nauru about four times a year. The Family Court consists of the Resident Magistrate and, at least two lay members, and deals with family matters and child welfare.

By legislation of Nauru and Australia and at Nauru's request, appeals lie in most cases with leave of the High Court of Australia or the Supreme Court of Nauru, to the High Court of Australia.

Public Service. Most departmental heads in the Nauru public service are expatriate. The government follows a policy of employing specialists from outside in the absence of suitably-qualified Nauruans, although Nauruans have employment preference. Only Nauruans may become permanent public officers.

Police. The police force of about 57 is under a local director. Most members of the force are Nauruans. All are recruited on Nauru, including those who come from other Pacific Islands.

Liquor laws. The legal age for drinking liquor is 21. The only prohibition on Nauruan and Island women is that they may not drink outside their homes without a legal permit. Hotel bar trading hours are 5.00 p.m. to 10.00 p.m., Monday to Friday, 10.00 a.m. to 10.00 p.m., Saturday.

DEFENCE. Nauru does not have any defence pacts or treaties. Her defence is assured by Australia but no formal agreement to this effect exists.

EDUCATION. Education is free and compulsory for Nauruan children from six to 16 years. In 1979, the government had five infant schools, one primary school and one secondary school. These schools catered for 1,400 pupils at primary level and 500 at secondary level. The Sacred Heart of Jesus Mission had one infants' school, a primary school and a secondary school, all in the same establishment. There were about 175 primary pupils and 139 secondary pupils.

In the government primary school, Aiwo District, European and Nauruan children are taught together in English. The second government primary school is the Location School, which cater for about 420 children of phosphate workers – mainly Gilbertese, Chinese, Tuvaluans and a number of Nauruan scholarship children.

Overseas study. Most European children go to boarding school in Australia or New Zealand for education at secondary level. The government makes a grant towards the cost.

Nauruans studying at secondary and tertiary level overseas totalled 95. Most of them were in Australia. There were some in Papua New Guinea, Fiji and New Zealand. Others were studying privately overseas.

The teaching staff in all schools comprises about 80 Nauruans and 50 expatriates. For teacher-training, cadetships are offered in Australia. This is supplementary to local teacher-training.

LABOUR. As the local labour force is insufficient to meet requirements of the phosphate industry the Nauru Phosphate Corporation (NPC) recruits workers from Kiribati, Tuvalu, Hong Kong and the Philippines. The normal labour contract is for 12 months but these may be renewed each year. As at January 31, 1979, NPC employed 99 Nauruans, 92 Europeans, 226 Chinese, 14 Filipinos, 831 Kiribati, Tuvaluan and other Pacific Islanders.

Unskilled phosphate workers earn a minimum wage of $3.20 per day plus free food and accommodation. Paid overtime is a significant factor. Nauruans are not provided with food and accommodation and received a basic wage of $3,800 a year.

Nauruans are employed on various positions in the phosphate industry ranging from labourers to junior engineering positions. There are 16 who are employed as apprentices in various trades and several have been taken on as trainee supervisors. While the percentage of Nauruans employed is not high, opportunities are there for those who are willing and able to work.

Through their own housing scheme, they have a good standard of accommodation. The NPC provides houses for contract workers and dependants.

While there are no trade unions as such in the industry each of the ethnic groups have their own Workers' Committee who have regular meetings with management.

HEALTH. Nauru has a modern health service, which includes two well-equipped hospitals. No fees are charged for medical or dental services. If specialist treatment is necessary, the patient is sent to Australia. The government bears the cost in the case of Nauruans. The estimated cost of health services for 1978/79 was $1,138,560.

The fight against disease has been largely successful. With the exception of filaria, other tropical diseases of the Pacific are either of rare incidence or have been completely eliminated. Typical examples are tropical ulcers and yaws, which are now nonexistent. Tuberculosis is also well under control. All new arrivals on the island must be X-rayed before entry, or within 24 hours of arrival.

The government operates one hospital, and the NPC the other. Both are staffed by fully-trained doctors, sisters and nurses. The government maintains 11 maternity and child welfare clinics. TB, dental and diabetes clinics are maintained at the government hospital.

THE LAND. The ground rises from a sandy beach to form a fairly fertile belt, 150 to 300 m wide, encircling the island. Further inland the coral cliffs rise to a central plateau about 30 m above sea level. The plateau is composed largely of phosphate-bearing rock, which covers about three-fifths of the entire area. Highest point is 70 m.

Because of the generally poor, highly porous soil and irregular rainfall, cultivation is restricted to the coastal belt, where coconut palms and pandanus

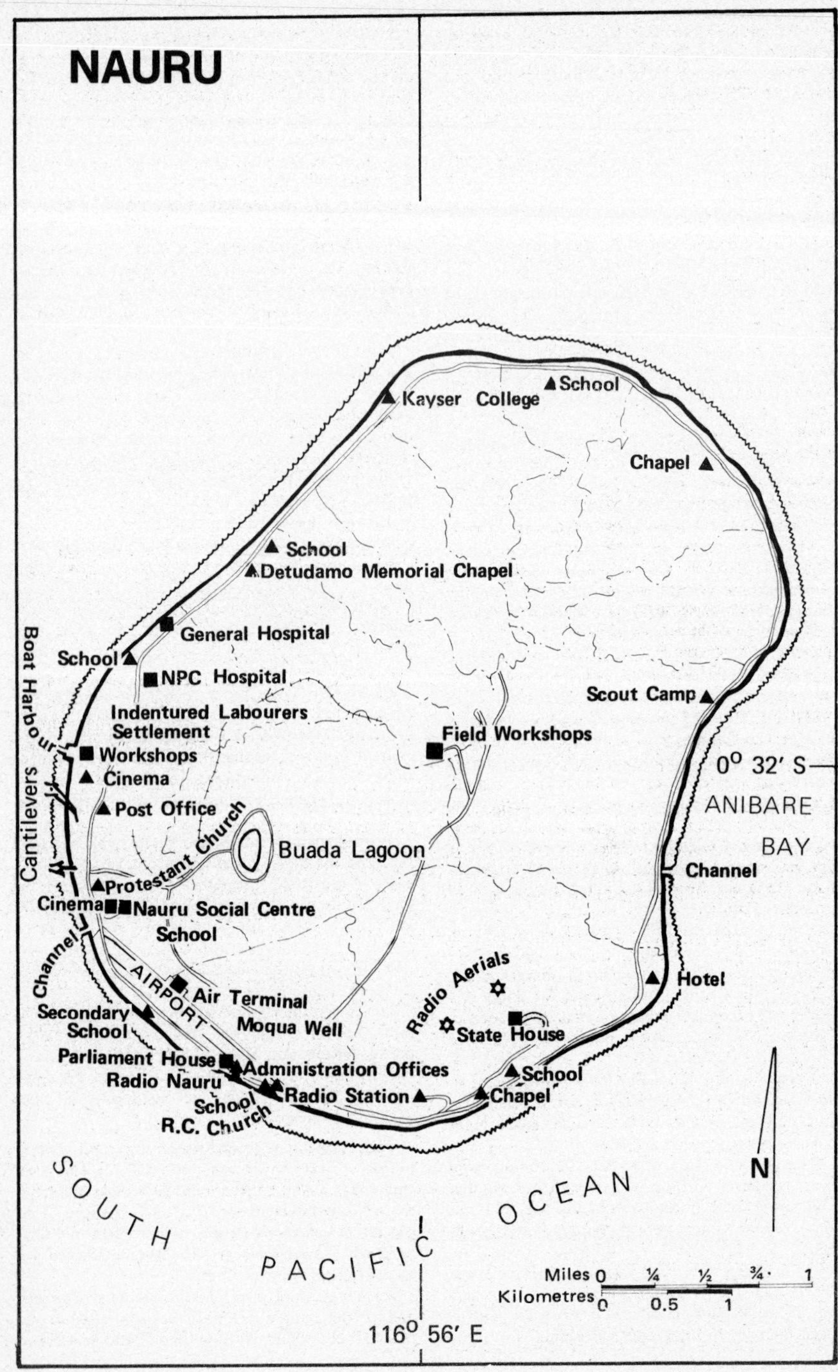
NAURU
School
Kayser College
Chapel
School
Detudamo Memorial Chapel
General Hospital
School
NPC Hospital
Scout Camp
Indentured Labourers Settlement
Field Workshops
Boat Harbour
Workshops
Cinema
0° 32′ S
ANIBARE BAY
Post Office
Cantilevers
Protestant Church
Buada Lagoon
Channel
Cinema
Nauru Social Centre
School
Channel
AIRPORT
Air Terminal
Radio Aerials
Hotel
Secondary School
Moqua Well
State House
Parliament House
Administration Offices
School
Radio Nauru
Radio Station
Chapel
School
R.C. Church
SOUTH PACIFIC OCEAN
N
Miles 0 ¼ ½ ¾ 1
Kilometres 0 0.5 1
116° 56′ E

grow, and to the fringe of land surrounding the shallow Buada Lagoon, where bananas, pineapples and some vegetables are grown. One of the owners of the lagoon has established a fish farm in his section of the lagoon.

There are 179 varieties of plants and trees and many species of moths, butterflies and dragonflies.

There are no rivers.

With the exception of small allotments held by the government, the NPC and missions, the island is owned by individual Nauruans.

Climate. The climate is tropical, and tempered by sea breezes with a day temperature of 30 deg. C. The average annual rainfall is 203 mm, but actual rainfall is extremely variable – it has been as low as 104 mm, and as high as 4,572 mm in a year. The wettest period is during the westerly monsoon season, from November to February. For the rest of the year easterly trade winds prevail.

Reclamation. At various times the Nauru Government has investigated the possibility of reclaiming or otherwise making use of the worked-out phosphate land in the centre of the island. One possibility, not yet abandoned, is that an international airstrip be built across the coral pinnacles with the dual purpose of it serving as a rain catchment area. Rainwater would be run off into underground reservoirs to eliminate the island's regular water shortages. Because of a reclamation programme using garbage and other waste as filling, large areas of worked-out land have reverted to bush.

PRIMARY PRODUCTION. Primary production is confined to fruit and vegetables, livestock and fish. Coconuts are the main crop. The seas around the island teem with fish, but the people are content to catch only enough for their own use. Any surplus is stored in the Co-operative cool store. The people keep pigs and chickens, which provide some fresh meat. Otherwise all food requirements come from overseas.

MINING. The economy of Nauru is based on the phosphate industry. The beginnings and later development of this industry are outlined under the section on Nauru's History. The phosphate is mined and marketed by the Nauru Phosphate Corporation, which was incorporated in June, 1969 and which assumed full control of the industry from the British Phosphate Commissioners on July 1, 1970. The corporation is an instrumentality of the Government of Nauru.

Nauruan phosphate is the highest grade in the world, 84 per cent BPL guaranteed, with rock treated in Nauru's modern calcination plant as high as 91 BPL.

After the scrub and overburden are removed by bulldozers, the alluvial phosphate and the large lumps of rock phosphate are removed from around the coral pinnacles by mechanical extractors with clam-shell buckets.

The phosphate is trucked to the railhead for primary crushing and reduced to less than 2". A narrow gauge railway system transports the crushed material to the treatment plant where it is dried to 3.0% water before further crushing to less than ½" (run of mine).

A proportion of the fine material is further upgraded by high temperature calcination to remove organic carbon and cadmium. This product is marketed as Nauru Calcined Rock (NCR). Ships up to 36,000 tonnes dwt. are loaded by cantilever loading systems while moored to buoys in an open water port.

Recent shipments were as follows:

	Run of Mine (tonnes)	**NCR (tonnes)**
1977/78	**1,486,956**	**8,500**
1978/79	**2,200,000**	**30,000**

Maximum production was 2,394,000 tonnes in 1973/74.

In 1979, it was officially estimated on Nauru that the island had reserves of about 38.8 million tonnes of phosphate, which based on present production should last until the end of the century.

TOURISM. Nauru has not been developed as a destination point but it possesses a hotel, the Menen Hotel, which is up to international standard. Most guests are transit passengers but in recent years there has been an increase in Japanese visitors touring the Pacific War battle-grounds.

LOCAL COMMERCE. The Nauru Co-operative Society, operated by the Nauru Local Government Council, runs two general stores and a liquor store. The Local Government Council also operates the hotel and hotel hire car service, the Nauru Pacific Line and the Nauru Insurance Corporation. There is a large number of small Chinese-operated food and general stores, together with two cinemas and small cafes. There is not a wide variety of other small businesses or repair services.

OVERSEAS TRADE. Nauru does not publish import and trade statistics. The sole export is phosphate.

Customs tariff. There are no import duties except on tobacco and alcoholic beverages. These are at very low, almost nominal rates. However, there is a prohibition on the import of firearms, ammunition, and animals, including domestic pets.

FINANCE. The 1978/79 Budget provided for expenditure of $40,611,850 against estimated revenues of $35,015,350 plus a credit balance from the previous year of $5,760,649.

Main revenue comes from phosphate sales, with the government taking about half the profits per tonne, but the amount varies from year to year. The rest is paid out to Nauruan land-owners, a royalties long term trust fund and the Nauru Local Government Council. The government also has a considerable income from overseas investments, such as the 52-storey Nauru House in Melbourne, hotels in Apia and Majuro and the Saipan Building in Saipan.

Main budget expenditures for 1978/79 (estimated) were: Health $1,138,560; Education $1,636,800; Works and Community Services $3,700,000; Civil Aviation $15,900,000; Justice and Police $339,000; Finance $1,317,000; Island Development and Industry $114,000; Telecommunications $1,050,000; Lands and Survey $584,000; Chief Secretary's Office $553,000; External Afairs and Overseas Offices $1,909,000; Judiciary $92,000; Public Debt $4,974,500.

Revenues for the year ended June 30, 1978 were: Civil Aviation $6,018,104; Telecommunications $104,308; Interest on investments $212,108; Philatelic Bureau $101,178; Revenue from Loans $26,791,458; Customs and Excise $30,721; Corporate fees and licences $32,885.

The 1980/81 budget earmarked $29.4 million for Air Nauru out of a budget total estimated expenditure of $59 million. Fuel costs were expected to be $11 million. Estimated revenue for the same period was $11 million.

Other large sums are also received and expended by the Nauru Local Government Council, some of the expenditure being on items which otherwise would have to be met by the government. The council's balance sheet is not a public document.

Taxation. There is no income tax or direct tax in Nauru.

Banking. The Bank of Nauru was established in October, 1976, taking over the operations of the Bank of NSW, which had operated on the island for a number of years. Since March, 1977, the Bank of Nauru has been wholly owned and guaranteed by the government. The General Manager is Mr. R. Devenish.

By special arrangement with Australia, Nauru has remained within the Australian monetary system and Australian banknotes and coins are legal tender on Nauru.

Company registration. The Nauru Government receives registration fees for the registration in Nauru of overseas corporations which use the island for tax planning purposes.

Licence fees are: trading licence for main store or store without branches $100 a year; branch store $50; explosives import licence $50; dog licence $10.

TRANSPORT. There is an excellent wide, sealed coastal road right around the island, linking all villages. The Buada district inland is also linked by sealed road with the coast, and other sealed roads connect residential areas of the NPC and government. Vehicular traffic is heavy on Nauru, as a high proportion of Nauruans own cars or motor cycles, and there are also drive-yourself facilities. In late-1979, the motor vehicles registered consisted of 640 motor cycles and 1,200 cars, trucks and other vehicles. Driving licences were held in 1980 by 3,040 persons.

The NPC operates about 6 km of 3'0" gauge railway line in connection with phosphate recovery.

Aviation. The republic has its own airline, Air Nauru, which operates scheduled services from Nauru to Japan, Taipei, Hong Kong, the Philippines, Guam and Micronesia, the Solomon Islands, Western Samoa, Tonga, Kiribati, Vanuatu, New Caledonia, Fiji, Australia and New Zealand.

Air Nauru operates five jet aircraft. Servicing is done outside of Nauru.

Nauru international airport has a single sealed 1708m runway, and a modern terminal building.

Shipping. The Nauru Pacific Line operates vessels servicing the island, and also offers regular commercial cargo services to other users. Services include regular cargo-passenger service from Melbourne to Nauru and Tarawa (Kiribati), a container service from Melbourne to Micronesia including Guam and a conventional/container and passenger service from San Francisco and Honolulu to Majuro, Ponape, Truk and Saipan. The line is wholly owned by the Nauru Local Government Council. The Nauru Phosphate Corporation also charters vessels for its special needs.

In 1979, Nauru Pacific Line ships were Eigamoiya (4,497 tonnes), Enna G (9,490 tonnes), Kolle D (19,812 tonnes), Rosie D II and Charter Fentress.

Nauru has no wharves. Passenger and cargo handling is by barge, operating between a small artificial boat harbour and the vessels are usually tied to deep-sea moorings near the phosphate loading cantilevers.

COMMUNICATIONS. A satellite/earth receiving station was installed in 1975, giving Nauru worldwide telephone communication. There is also a telex system with the number 775 and with eight subscribers. There is a modern internal telephone service on Nauru.

A medium-frequency shipping watch is maintained on the international distress frequency; two high-frequency schedules for shipping are observed at 0015 and 0830 GMT.

A broadcasting station maintains a restricted local service. There is a small government news sheet, the Nauru Bulletin published fortnightly and The Nauru Post, a privately-owned weekly newspaper.

WATER AND ELECTRICITY. Nauru has full electricity services, supplied by engines of the Nauru Phosphate Corporation. Voltage is 240v 50 cycle AC.

Water supplies are mainly from roof storage tanks, and in prolonged dry periods water is imported as ballast in the regular shipping which calls at the island, pumped ashore into cement storage tanks, and distributed to houses by tanker. This operation is handled by the NPC.

PERSONALITIES AND ORGANISATIONS

President of the Republic, Minister for External Affairs, Island Development and Industry, Minister for the Public Service, Minister for Civil Aviation Authority: H. E. Hammer DeRoburt, OBE

OTHER CABINET MINISTERS

Minister for Finance: K. N. T. Aroi

Minister for Health and Education: J. D. Audoa

Minister for Justice: L. D. Keke
Minister for Works and Community Services: B. Detudamo
NAURU PARLIAMENT
Speaker: D. P. Gadaraoa
Deputy Speaker: J. A. Bop
MEMBERS OF PARLIAMENT
Aiwo District: Rene Harris; David Agir
Anetan/Ewa Districts: Roy Degoregore; Bucky Ika
Anabar/Anibare/Ijuw Districts: David Gadaraoa; Obeira Menke
Boe District: Hammer DeRoburt; Kenas Aroi
Buada District: Ruben Kun; Totowa Depaune
Meneng District: James Bop; Bobby Eoe
Ubenide District: Bernard Dowiyogo; Lagumot Harris; Buraro Detudamo; Derog Gioura
Yaren District: Joseph D. Audoa; Leo D. Keke
HEADS OF DEPARTMENTS
Chief Secretary: Vacant
Senior Administrative Officer: I. S. Watson
Administrative Officer: G. Degiodoa
Secretary for Island Development & Industry: Kinza G. Clodumar
Secretary for Justice: D. Lang
Secretary for Health and Education: L. R. Newby
Secretary for Finance: J. R. Phillips
Secretary for External Affairs: Vacant
Director of Education: A. E. Howley
Director of Medical Services: Dr. K. Thoma (Acting)
Director of Works and Community Services: R. Garvin
Director of Police: D. Daniel
Director of Lands & Survey: Vacant
Director of Civil Aviation: Felix Kun (Acting)
Director of Telecommunications: G. R. Peterkon
Director of Audit: J. Shuttleworth
Chief Justice: Hon. I. R. Thompson
MELBOURNE ESTABLISHMENT:
Consul-General: T. W. Starr
Senior Administrative Officer & Legal Adviser: K. Whitcombe
Finance Officer: Vacant
Personnel Officer: W. Grundy
Nauruan Welfare Officer: D. Dowabobo
Accountant: Vacant
Nauru Phosphate Royalties Trust: Chairman: T. W. Starr
Travel Manager: K. Anderton
Chief Buyer: W. Pickering
AIR NAURU:
Chief Pilot: P. Lavender
NAURU PHOSPHATE CORPORATION:
General Manager: B. Blundell
Operations Manager: G. Gersbach
Personnel Manager: T. Rockell
Melbourne Manager: J. Blackburn
BANK OF NAURU:
General Manager: R. H. Devenish
NAURU INSURANCE CORPORATION:
Managing Director: N. Welsh
POST OFFICE:
Postmaster: F. Smith
DIPLOMATIC POSTS:
Nauru: Australian High Commissioner: Oliver Cordell
W. Samoa: Hon. Consul: John Willis
Melbourne: Consul-General: T. W. Starr
London: Nauru Representative: Q. V. L. Weston
Hong Kong: Consul: Charles Cheung
Auckland: Consul-General: L. T. Davis
Tokyo: Consul: R. Tom
Taipei: Consul: Kelly Emiu
Suva: Hon. Consul: Lawrence Stephen
Guam: Hon. Consul: David Orlans
Honolulu: Hon. Consul: K. Char
NAURU LOCAL GOVERNMENT COUNCIL:
Head Chief: Hammer DeRoburt.
Councillors: Buraro Detudamo (Secretary), James A. Bop (Treasurer), Joseph D. Audoa, Roy Degoregore, Deang Detabene, James Doguape and Edwin Tsitsi.
Principal Finance Officer: A. Ironmonger
Administrative Officer: J. Cokonasiga.

HISTORY. Nauru has been inhabited by man for an unknown number of centuries. The original inhabitants were undoubtedly castaways who drifted there from some other island. The Nauruan language is said to be "absolutely distinct" from all other Pacific languages, being a fusion of elements from the Gilberts, Carolines, Marshalls and Solomons. Early this century, people of distinct racial types were to be seen on the island. Those of the south had curly, but not woolly hair. Those on the western side had very straight hair, suggesting Gilbertese descent. And elsewhere they appeared to be of mixed origins. The islanders were divided into twelve clans and spoke different dialects. But after European missionaries fixed on the principal dialect for Bible translation work early this century, the others gradually became obsolete.

The European discoverer of Nauru was Captain John Fearn of the British ship 'Hunter' in 1798. He named it Pleasant Island because of its attractive appearance, and it was thus known to Europeans for the next 90 years. However, there was little contact with Europeans until the 1830s when whalers operating in the Line whaling grounds called there for food and water. It was then that Nauru received the first of its many beachcombers.

One of these, John Jones, an Irish convict, poisoned seven and shot four of his fellow beachcombers in October 1841 because he feared they would usurp his influence over the Nauruans. The evil influence of such men spread to the Nauruans, who then numbered about 1,400. In 1852, some of them were involved in the massacre of part of the crew of the American brig 'Inga', and shortly afterwards they tried to cut off two other American ships.

Beachcombers. Most beachcombers, of course, were not as bad as Jones and conformed to the social patterns of the island. Two whose descendants still live on Nauru were William Harris, who settled there in 1842, and Ernest M. H. Stephen, who was left there by a ship's captain in 1881 when only 13 years old. The beachcombers were useful to the Nauruans in acting as intermediaries with visiting ships. They thus helped them to obtain steel tools, firearms, alcohol and other white men's goods. They were also useful in repairing weapons and as allies in the clan warfare that had always been an essential part of Nauruan life.

Clan warfare became deadlier and more frequent as the Nauruans' stock of firearms increased, and for 10 years from 1878 it was virtually incessant. Meanwhile, some German traders who had settled on the island requested that it be incorporated within Germany's Marshall Islands Protectorate. This was done formally in October 1888 when the German gunboat 'Eber' landed an imperial commissioner on the island who marched around it with a small armed force. The island had the appearance of a battlefield. The commissioner therefore arrested all 12 chiefs and threatened to deport them to Jaluit unless all firearms on the islands were surrendered. During the next two days, 765 weapons were handed in. This represented almost one firearm for every adult, as the population then stood at about 1,300, of whom about 300 were children. Because of the recent carnage, women outnumbered men by 30 per cent.

German administration. After the German flag had been raised on October 2, a German trader was placed in provisional charge of the island's administration and the gunboat left. Traders generally doubled as administrators until 1905. Meanwhile, in 1899, the first Western missionary arrived on the island. This was the Rev. P. A. Delaporte, a German-born American Protestant. He took up the work of several earlier Gilbertese pastors, soon had a large following, and was exerting considerable influence. A German Roman Catholic missionary, Father Kayser, settled on the island in 1903. Although conflict ensued between the two missionaries, they both did valuable work in reducing the Nauruan language to writing.

A development of a different kind was then in the making. In 1898, H. E. Denson, manager of the Pacific Islands Company, Sydney, had made an interesting discovery. During a tour of the Western Pacific on behalf of his company, which had planting, trading and guano interests, he had called at Nauru and had become fascinated by what he thought was a fossilised tree. He took two specimens of the "tree" back to Sydney. A year or so later, one of these attracted the attention of Albert F. Ellis, a company employee with wide experience on the guano islands of the Central Pacific. Thinking that it resembled rock guano, Ellis analysed it and found it to contain 78 per cent phosphate of lime. This led to the realisation that the phosphate deposits on Nauru were "simply enormous" because, as Denson put it, the whole island was "one mass of rock" of the same nature.

Phosphate. As the Jaluit Gesellschaft had the sole right to work any guano deposits in the Marshall Islands Protectorate, the London board of the Pacific Islands Company began delicate negotiations with it in the hope of exploiting the new discovery. Meanwhile, Ellis was sent to Ocean Island, Nauru's nearest neighbour, to see if it, too, contained high quality phosphatic rock, as its geological formation was known to be the same. He reached that island in May 1900 and found that it did indeed contain vast deposits. He then got two local chiefs to put their marks to a document granting his company the right to mine the deposits for 999 years for an annual royalty of £50. Later, at Nauru, he confirmed the existence of that island's huge deposits.

Ellis' company was able to start exploiting the Ocean Island phosphate almost immediately. This was because, according to an agreement between Great Britain and Germany of 1886, which had divided the Western Pacific between them, Ocean Island was in the British sphere of influence. By 1906, there was a thriving industry on Ocean Island. That same year, the Pacific Phosphate Company (which had grown out of the Pacific Islands Company) concluded an agreement with the German Government and the Jaluit Gesellschaft. This enabled it to begin operating on Nauru with a part-British, part-German staff. The Gesellschaft was given a share in the company plus a royalty for every ton of phosphate that it mined on Nauru, Ocean Island, or elsewhere. On the other hand, there were no direct benefits for the Nauruans. In fact, it was not even thought necessary to negotiate for rights to mine their land.

By the end of 1907, 11,630 tons of Nauruan phosphate had been exported to Australia. Over the next six years, a total of about 630,000 tons were shipped. Caroline Islanders and Chinese were imported to work the deposits. Some brought dysentery, infantile paralysis and tuberculosis which caused many Nauruan deaths.

World War I. When World War I broke out in Europe on August 4, 1914, the Germans placed Nauru under martial law. A month later, the many British subjects on the island were shipped to Ocean Island. However, in November, an Australian force of 60 men under Major-General W. Holmes was sent from Rabaul in the phosphate company's ship 'Messina' to take possession of Nauru. Holmes' orders were to embark the deported Britons at Ocean Island and take them back to Nauru, establishing them there through the use of force if necessary. However, as the Germans on Nauru offered no resistance, the orders were carried out without difficulty. The Germans were then deported to Australia, and the phosphate industry carried on under the protection of an Australian garrison.

Soon after the British were re-established on Nauru, a Japanese warship and troopship arrived to take possession of the island in the same way as other Japanese forces had already taken over the Marshalls, Marianas and Carolines. When they found the Australians in possession they left.

For the next five years, Nauru continued to be garrisoned by Australian troops and phosphate mining went on. In 1919, a mandate for the island's administration was conferred jointly on Great Britain, Australia and New Zealand by the League of Nations. But, for convenience, Australia continued in sole administrative control. At the same time, the Pacific Phosphate Company was bought out on both Ocean Island and Nauru at a cost £3,500,000, and all titles to the phosphate deposits, etc. were vested in a board representing the three powers, known as the British Phosphate Commissioners. By agreement, the phosphate was to be distributed for home consumption in the proportion that the three governments had compensated the phosphate company. This was 42 per cent each to both Great Britain and Australia, and 16 per cent to New Zealand. An agreement of the three powers made it clear that Nauru's phosphate was a government-owned monopoly. There was nothing in any agreement about royalties for the Nauruans.

Royalties. Through the intervention of the first Australian Administrator, General T. Griffiths, the Nauruans were paid a royalty of 2d per ton (compared with ½d per ton previously) and another 1d per ton was set aside "for the benefit of the natives as a whole". In addition, £20 per acre was paid in advance to Nauruan land-owners when their phosphate land was taken over. The royalty rate remained in force until 1927. By 1939, the Nauruans were getting 8d per ton. Meanwhile, phosphate exports rose from 182,170 tons in 1922 to 932,100 tons in 1939. In 1940 there was a drop to 808,400 tons due to the fact that war had again come to Nauru.

Early in December 1940, a westerly gale lashed the island, and seven ships which arrived to load phosphate could not get alongside the cantilever, but lay off and on. It was then that two German raiders arrived. They were the 'Komet' and 'Orion', disguised as 'Nanyo Maru' and 'Narvik'. The phosphate ships were "sitting shots" for the raiders. Five of them – 'Triona' (4,413 tons), 'Vinni' (5,181), 'Komata' (3,900), 'Triadic' (6,378) and 'Triaster' (6,032) – were sunk.

The Germans took the survivors from these and from other ships they had sunk south to Emirau Island, near Kavieng, New Ireland, and put them ashore on December 21, 1940. Then the 'Komet' went back to Nauru and shelled the cantilever loading gear and some other phosphate installations. However, the damage inflicted was not enough to dislocate the phosphate workings, and no one was killed.

A year later, Nauru was attacked again. On December 9, 1941, two days after Pearl Harbour, Japanese planes appeared from the north and dropped bombs. Further bombing attacks occurred later. Meanwhile, all Europeans on the island were evacuated except seven who insisted on remaining to care for the Nauruans. They included the Australian Administrator, Lieut.-Colonel F. R. Chalmers, and two missionaries.

Japanese occupation. The Japanese occupied Nauru in August 1942. In the following year, 1,200 Nauruans and the two missionaries were deported to Truk, Caroline Islands, to work as labourers. Meanwhile, the Japanese had built an airstrip on Nauru. By January 1943, their bombers could make use of it. This provoked an American bombing raid on the island on March 25, 1943, in which eight Japanese bombers and seven fighters were caught on the airstrip and destroyed. The Japanese retaliated by executing the five Europeans still on the island.

American bombing attacks continued throughout 1943 and became more frequent after the Americans recaptured the Gilbert Islands in November that year and occupied the Marshalls in February 1944. The attacks foiled Japanese plans to export phosphate. Australian forces re-occupied Nauru on September 13, 1945. Four and a half months later, on January 31, 1946, 737 Nauruans were returned to their home in the BPC ship 'Trienza'. The 500 others had died of starvation, disease and Japanese brutality.

Trust territory. With the end of World War II, Nauru was made a United Nations trust territory, with Australia, Great Britain and New Zealand as the trust powers. Australia again provided the administration. Meanwhile, the BPC moved quickly to reorganise the phosphate industry. In 1950, exports exceeded one million tons for the first time. Except in the following year, the annual figure was well above the million mark – generally from 1½ million to 2 million tons – until the Nauruans became independent in 1968. Two and a half years later, they gained full control of the phosphate industry.

The political advancement of the Nauruans began in December 1951 when the Nauru Local Government Council replaced a Council of Chiefs, a largely hereditary body with no powers. The formation of the council and the emergence of strong leaders, particularly Timothy Detudamo and Hammer DeRoburt, accelerated the Nauruans' desire to control their own affairs. Visits to the island by United Nations missions gave them opportunities to voice their views. The leaders also addressed the United Nations in New York and employed economic advisers to help them negotiate with the partner governments.

The Nauruans made a significant step forward in 1965 when they obtained an increase in their phosphate royalties from 37 cents to $1.75 per tonne. In 1966, this was increased to $4.50; and in 1967, it was agreed that the phosphate would be purchased at $11 per tonne for the next three years, subject to world price adjustments. Much more importantly, the partner governments agreed to hand over control of the phosphate industry from 1970. In return, the Nauruans were to pay the BPC $21 million for its capital assets. An agreement granting the Nauruans independence was signed on October 24, 1967.

Republic of Nauru. The date chosen for the inauguration of the Republic of Nauru – 31 January, 1968 – was the 22nd anniversary of the return from Truk of the islanders deported by the Japanese. Head Chief Hammer DeRoburt, soon after independence was elected first president.

Since independence, Nauru has started its own shipping line and international airline, Air Nauru. It has also invested heavily in real estate and various business enterprises in Australia and elsewhere. The phosphate industry has been run since July 1, 1970, by the Nauru Phosphate Corporation. Much development has gone on in the island.

In December 1976, Bernard Dowiyogo was elected President but eleven months later, he dissolved Parliament on October 7, 1977 to seek a mandate for his government. This was because ex-President Hammer DeRoburt had refused to accept the 1976 election as constitutional.

However, Dowiyogo's period of control was limited. On April 19, 1978, Chief Hammer DeRoburt's supporters forced the resignation of Dowiyogo by defeating a bill in Parliament dealing with phosphate royalties.

Mr Lagumot Harris succeeded Mr Dowiyogo but he resigned after only a week or two in office when Parliament rejected an appropriations bill designed to finance the republic until the end of the year.

In the ballot that followed, Chief Hammer DeRoburt was elected.

Further information. Nancy Viviani, 'Nauru: Phosphate and Political Progress', Canberra, 1970; Maslyn Williams, 'Three Islands', Melbourne, 1971 (gives a history of phosphate mining on Nauru, Ocean Island and Christmas Island).

FOR THE TOURIST. Nauru is no tourist "destination", but anybody who has the opportunity to fly through Nauru using one of the many excellent Air Nauru jet flights which connect various points in the north and south Pacific should spend at least a few days on the island. The government-owned 58-room Menen Hotel, not far from the airport, is modern and comfortable. Its rooms and suites are air-conditioned. General manager is Tony Ashbridge.

Nauruans are friendly and sophisticated. The moon-like landscape of the worked-out phosphate diggings is both eerie and fascinating. There are still the remains of wartime pill-boxes along some beaches; some pleasant swimming and fishing. Because Nauru is duty-free, liquor and electrical goods are cheap.

There are a number of interesting Chinese shops in the "Chinatown" section of Nauru. There is a nine-hole golf course, tennis courts and several picture theatres.

Entry formalities. Visitors planning to stay need to apply for visas before arrival, either through Nauru or one of several overseas offices. Nothing is required by transit passengers catching the next available flight.

Outsiders cannot obtain residential status.

Visas permit a stay of no more than one month, even for non-Nauruan husbands or wives of Nauruans, who have to apply each subsequent month for a new visa, if wishing to stay in Nauru.

NEW CALEDONIA

New Caledonia consists of one large and one small island, and the Loyalty and Huon groups. The largest island has an area of 16,118 sq. km and is one of the largest in the Pacific. The group is located between 19 and 23 deg. S. latitude and 163 and 168 deg. E. longitude. The main island, New Caledonia and the other groups form a French overseas territory.

The capital is Noumea, on New Caledonia, and is about 1,850 km north-east of Sydney. Local time is 11 hours ahead of GMT.

In January 1979, the estimated population of the group was 137,000.

The national anthem and flag are those of France. Currency is the French Pacific franc (Cours du Franc Pacifique – CFP) which in 1980 had an exchange rate of CFP 18.18 to the French franc and 93 to the A$1.00.

Public holidays are: January 1, Easter Monday, May 1 (Labour Day), Ascension (39 days after Easter Sunday), Monday after Pentecost (about 10 days after Ascension), July 14 (Bastille day), September 24 (Anniversary of French Possession), November 1 (All Saints), November 11 (Armistice Day), Christmas Day.

THE PEOPLE. The indigenous people of New Caledonia are Melanesians. Before European annexation they are estimated to have numbered between 50,000 and 70,000. They lived a fairly typical Melanesian existence of subsistence agriculture. The political unit was the village or a loosely knit group of villages; a multiplicity of dialects was spoken and intertribal wars and family feuds were common. Some groups practised cannibalism.

Evidence of the former large populations is seen throughout New Caledonia even today in the evenly terraced mountainsides which are all that remain of irrigation systems for the cultivation of taro. (Some examples can be observed from the road between Noumea and Tontouta international airport.)

For many years after annexation the Melanesians bitterly resisted the French but gradually they were forced to submit, with the usual result – the population began to decline, probably as a result of disruption of cultural patterns and introduced diseases. The Melanesian population reached its lowest point shortly after World War I and has since increased fairly steadily. The census of 1963 showed approx. 42,000 Melanesians; that of 1976, 55,598.

Census. At the 1976 census, Noumea's population totalled 56,078 and nearby Mt Dore, 10,659 with a total of 87,429 people in the territory's southern subdivision. There were 16,977 in the west subdivision, including Bourail (3,149). The east subdivision had 14,309, including Poindimie (3,010). The Loyalty Islands had a population of 14,518.

Divisions of the population may be seen from the following census results:

	March 1969	April 1976
Melanesians	47,300	55,598
Europeans	36,900	50,757
Wallisians	6,220	9,571
Tahitians	3,370	6,391
*Others	6,790	10,916
Total	100,580	133,233

* Includes about 5,000 Indonesians and 2,000 Vietnamese.

Of the estimated population of 137,000 in January 1979, 49% were believed to be under 20 years of age.

Nationality. The territory's Melanesian population have full French citizenship. Members of foreign communities, such as the Vietnamese and Indonesians who were originally brought to the island for labour purposes, may acquire French citizenship; many have done so and have also gallicised their names.

Language. Many languages are spoken in New Caledonia, reflecting different ethnic origins, but the official language, spoken by all, is French.

Migration. The rapid development around Noumea since the late 'sixties has been through a shift of population from rural areas as well as immigration from France, North Africa, New Hebrides, Wallis Is., French Caribbean and Tahiti. This was prompted by the planned massive expansion of the nickel industry.

Religion. The population is divided between the Roman Catholic and Protestant churches. Protestant teachers of the L.M.S. particularly influenced the Loyalty Islands and east coast of the mainland. Noumea also has small communities of Mormons, Bahai and Seventh-day Adventists.

Lifestyle. Noumea, with its nickel works, is the most industrialised city in the South Pacific islands and life in this urban centre with the numerous services and social activities offered is markedly different from the rural lifestyle. Many Melanesian communities still remain relatively isolated, living by fishing and subsistence agriculture, although health and education facilities are available to all.

Recreation. Among favourite recreations are water sports and hunting (deer, bird game) petanque (bowls), cycling, football and tennis.

GOVERNMENT. New Caledonia is an Overseas Territory of France, with executive control vested in the High Commissioner, who is a public servant appointed by the government in Paris.

Legislature. There is a 36-member Territorial Assembly, elected by universal suffrage to debate and approve the territorial budget submitted by the Administration. In addition the Assembly may express its "desires" on policy matters outside its jurisdiction and controlled from Paris.

Executive. In his role as executive head of the territory, the High Commissioner meets with his Government Council (Conseil de Gouvernement) of which he is President, the other members being elected by the Territorial Assembly.

Autonomie interne. Throughout the many years of agitation for internal self-government in the territory (autonomie interne), debate has centred on the powers of the High Commissioner and his council.

The French Government has continually insisted it will not grant the territory internal self-government. Instead, France has offered decentralisation. Under new statutes applied from September 1977, the Government Council was enlarged from five to seven elected members. The High Commissioner retains executive control. Under the French system, public servants do not answer to the Territorial Assembly but to the High Commissioner who answers to Paris. Paris government control of the Caledonian nickel industry ensures effective control of the territory as a whole.

Electoral system. Two deputies represent New Caledonia and French residents of the New Hebrides in the French National Assembly and are elected by universal suffrage in New Caledonia and French voters in the New Hebrides. A senator to represent New Caledonia in the French senate is voted by an electoral college of representatives from municipal councils and all members of the Territorial Assembly.

The 36 members of the New Caledonian Territorial Assembly are elected for a five-year term under universal suffrage. The last elections were in July 1979 and saw a reduction in splinter parties, with three political parties being elected: two pro-French administration parties, the Lafleur-Laroque group's Rassemblement Pour la Caledonie dans la Republique (15 seats) and Lionel Cherrier's Federation pour une Nouvelle Societe Caledonienne (7) seats); and the independence-seeking Pidjot-Lenormand-Uregei group, Front Independantiste (14 seats), combining the Union Caledonienne, PALIKA and FULK (Kanakas), Socialists and Multiracials (UPM).

For general electoral purposes, the territory is divided into four electorates – south (including Noumea), west, east and Loyalty Islands.

Local government. The above names, but with different boundaries, are used to describe the four administrative subdivisions in the territory. The headquarters of these subdivisions are La Foa (south), Kone (west), Poindimie (east) and We on Lifou Is. (Loyalty group). Each subdivision is headed by a "chef de subdivision", a public servant from France. The municipality of Noumea is administered separately, under the territory's secretary-general, second-in-command to the governor.

The administrative subdivisions are further divided into 32 communes or municipalities, each with an elected municipal council and mayor. Final authority rests with the public servant at the head of each subdivision who must approve all mayoral decisions.

Public service. The top echelon of most government departments in New Caledonia consists of metropolitan French public servants, many of them trained in leading French schools for administrators and engineers. Since France is governed by its bureaucracy rather than political parties which are constantly splitting and re-grouping, the public service is regarded as a highly-trained elite. Very few Caledonians have been appointed as departmental heads.

Justice. The laws generally are the laws of France plus such subsidiary legislation and decrees by the Governor that pertain specifically to New Caledonia.

The principal officers of the courts are appointed by the Minister of Justice in France and include the President of the Court of Appeal, the President of the Civil Court, the President of the Court of First Instance, Attorney-General, Magistrates, etc.

A division of the National Gendarmerie is stationed in the territory. Officers of this force are recruited in France although there is an auxiliary gendarmerie of Melanesians. The service includes a Maritime Gendarmerie and a Riot Squad (Gardes Mobiles). The police force, as distinct from the gendarmerie, is locally recruited and operates in the city of Noumea, under a French officer.

The territory's prison, Camp Est, is at Nouville, opposite the harbour from Noumea, and dates from times of the penal settlement.

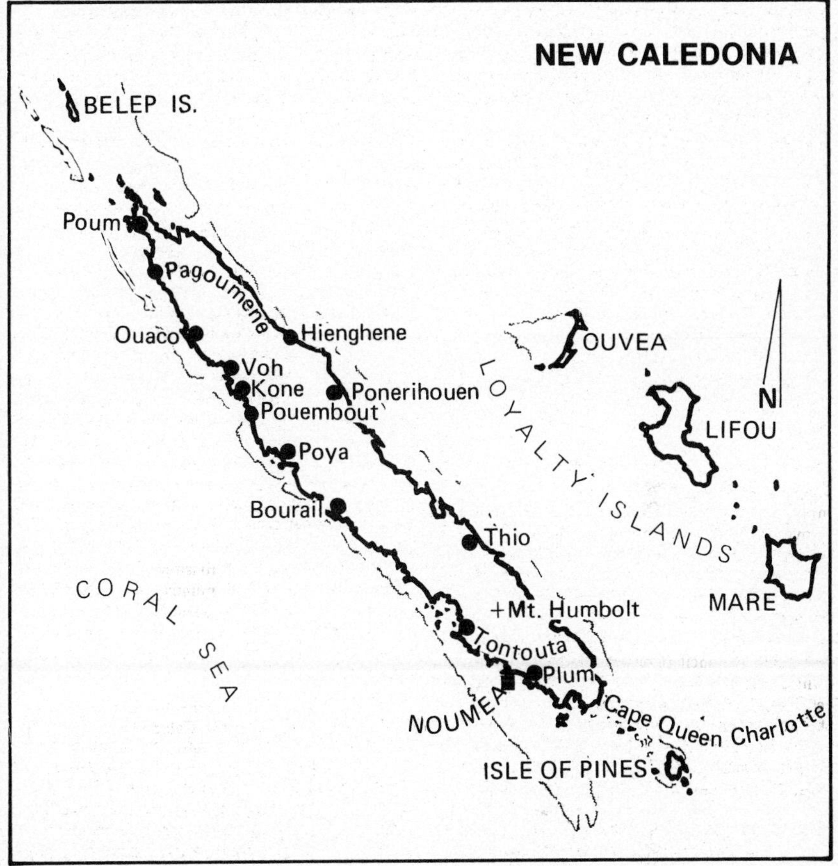

Liquor laws. Liquor is obtained from bars, cafes, restaurants or from liquor stores. Bars are open from early morning to 11 p.m. Although it was previously forbidden, the French aperitif pastis has been allowed in the territory since 1975.

Gambling. The Casino Royal opened at the Chateau Royal Hotel in December 1974 and offers games such as roulette, baccarat and chemin de fer. Visitors must be adequately dressed and show their passport. A more casual atmosphere pervades in the poker machine saloon. Changed ownership of the hotel in 1979 is expected to cause a re-location of the casino.

DEFENCE. Since Noumea was an important base for US and Allied forces in the Pacific War, France has emphasised the strategic necessity of maintaining troops in New Caledonia. Their role is to help assure the defence of French territories in the Pacific and to render service locally in case of natural disasters or possible disorders.

Under the French national budget, military expenditure in New Caledonia in 1975 for running expenses was allocated CFP 1,980 million together with CFP 181 million for capital expenditure.

Various bases for marines, paratroopers, etc., are located in Noumea, Plum and Bourail. The naval installations are at Pointe Chaleix, Noumea, adjacent to the main yacht club.

In 1976 a new air force base was built at Tontouta, and an army helicopter landing site in Noumea. The first Puma helicopter for the rapid transport of fully armed men arrived in April 1976.

Military personnel stationed in New Caledonia were estimated to number 3,500-5,000 in late 1979. They included regular army, paratroopers and gendarmerie, navy and air force. About 200 of the young Caledonians undergoing compulsory military service were then training in France.

EDUCATION. Schools are operated by both the state and churches under the supervision of the

Department of Education. France finances the state secondary system and in 1975 offered to take over the primary sector also from the territorial budget: the change-over applied from 1978.

At the primary level in 1975 there were 235 schools, of which 142 were state and 93 private. At the secondary level, there were 20 schools of which 8 were state-operated and 12 private. There were also 12 technical schools, 4 being state and 8 private. Three establishments, one of them private, offered courses either in teacher training or in technology, and preliminary law and economics courses towards a French university degree.

Student enrolment is summarised in the accompanying table:

SCHOOL ENROLMENTS — 1977

	State	Private	Total
Primary	20,557	12,209	32,766
Secondary	3,993	3,275	7,268
Technical	1,746	715	2,461
Higher	501	60	561
Total	26,797	16,259	43,056

In 1979 student enrolments totalled 45,637.

Overseas studies. To further their studies overseas, about 100 students attend universities in France and a small number enrol in Australian private schools.

Ever since 1966 when De Gaulle promised New Caledonia a University, plans have been discussed. It has been intended to encourage foreign students to come to Noumea as a centre of French culture in the Pacific. At the same time the local population would be served by courses of a technological nature. The embryo of such an institution could be seen in courses started in 1977 in association with the National Institute of Technology (Centre National des Arts et Metiers-CNAM).

In the meantime, each January the French Government organises a Summer School in Noumea for teachers of the French language from New Zealand, Fiji, and Australia. This is accompanied by a Summer Festival presenting French art, music and drama. Numerous French language student groups visit Noumea each year to improve their knowledge of living French.

The language laboratories at the Chamber of Commerce in Noumea are used by visiting students in addition to providing English instruction for young Caledonians. The Chamber of Commerce also conducts business courses in shorthand, typing etc.

LABOUR. The total workforce in New Caledonia is about 46,000 people. The chief source of labour statistics is the social service organisation, CAFAT, which records the number of employers paying payroll tax and the number of employees thus covered for social service benefits. In addition, there are the self-employed persons who may be traced through those paying a business licence or "patente".

NEW CALEDONIA — WORKFORCE (as at April 1976)

Agriculture	13,564
Mining	2,110
Industry, incl. smelting	5,469
Construction	4,475
Water, elec.	547
Transp., telecomm.	2,632
Commerce, bank, real estate	6,458
Services	11,338
Others	96
Total	46,689

Reflecting the overall world recession, the mining sector workforce dropped from 2,103 in December 1977 to 1,438 in December 1978.

Foreigners at the end of 1975 comprised 3 per cent of employees; all others were of French nationality. Europeans accounted for 46 per cent of all employees, Melanesians 28 per cent, Polynesians 7 per cent, Wallis Islanders 7 per cent, New Hebrideans 2 per cent and "other French" 11 per cent.

Wages. Wage levels, as recorded by the Labour Inspector, grew from the end of 1972 to the end of 1978 so that the minimum basic rate (SMIG) rose from CFP 92 to 164 per hour. During that period, the locally calculated cost of living index rose 16 per cent through the 1974 calendar year and 6.1 per cent in 1977.

Total wages and salaries for employees were CFP 17,060 million in 1977, compared to CFP 17,434 million in 1976, according to CAFAT.

Social security. Through the CAFAT social service organisation employees receive benefits derived from a payroll tax paid by employers. This payroll tax is about 25 per cent. Among the benefits are ante-natal and maternity leave for working mothers, and child endowment. Endowment at the end of 1974 amounted to a maximum of CFP 4,050 per month per child.

HEALTH. Government health services in New Caledonia are administered by military personnel. This ensures that medical facilities are available throughout the territory even in areas where private doctors may not choose to reside. The Department of Health thus employed 65 doctors in 1979, compared with 55 practising privately. There were 5 government dentists and 18 in private practice. Government pharmacists numbered 4, with 26 in the private sector.

Noumea's main hospital is the Hopital Gaston Bourret, dating from early colonial days, with 508 beds. Plans for a new hospital to provide more modern accommodation have been under discussion for several years, .

There are several private clinics, including the Clinique Magnin (in Vallee des Colons) and the Polyclinique (Anse Vata), with 112 beds between them, besides the Clinique de Noumea (Magenta) opened in 1975 (176 beds).

For the inland areas there are 17 medical centres

with 278 beds, 13 nursing centres with 91 beds, and 25 dispensaries.

Many cases requiring emergency or highly specialised treatment are flown for hospitalisation to Australia.

For TB patients, the La Pirogue Sanatorium, just outside Noumea, has 34 beds.

Leprosy patients are treated at the Raoul Follereau centre at Ducos, in Noumea, which receives assistance from the New Zealand Lepers Board. In 1975, 27 new leprosy cases were detected bringing the total number of cases to 563 at the end of the year.

There is one home for the aged, Ma Maison, operated by Roman Catholic mission sisters including Australians and other foreigners.

Research Institute. Medical research into local health problems is carried out by the Institut Pasteur, adjacent to the Gaston Bourret public hospital.

Diseases. Intestinal parasites and enteric-type diseases are fairly common. There is no malaria. With two widespread epidemics of dengue fever in the Pacific Islands in recent years, strict measures are taken to combat the mosquito vector of this disease. Fish poisoning, from the eating of certain fish, is another local health hazard. Respiratory infections and VD are significant problems, and cancer, alcoholism and traffic accidents are increasing.

THE LAND. The territory of New Caledonia and dependencies has a total land area of 19,103 sq. km. The New Caledonian mainland is extended cigar-shape, about 400 km long and 50 km across giving a total area of 16,750 sq. km. Lying in the same axis as the mainland are the Isle of Pines and Walpole Is. in the south, together with the Belep, Surprise and Huon islands in the north.

The Loyalty Islands, about 100 km to the east consist of Lifou, Mare and Ouvea in addition to several small islands, the only inhabited one being Tiga. The Loyalties have a land area of 1,970 sq km.

The third group of islands in the territory is the Chesterfields, which lie 400 km north-west of the mainland and are uninhabited.

From the Huon group in the north to Walpole in the south, the territory extends 900 km. From the Chesterfields in the west to Mare in the east is a distance of 1,000 km.

The chain of mountains extending along the centre of the mainland divides the island into two distinctly different areas – the lush east coast, and the broad cattle plains of the west coast.

The highest mountain peak is Mont Panie of 1,628 metres, in the north of the mainland.

Natural features. The Diahot river, in the north of the mainland, is the longest in the territory, extending for 90 km. In addition, 10 rivers flow to the east coast and 13 to the west coast, but there are no rivers on the other islands.

There are thermal springs in the central mountains, at La Crouen, where a health centre and guest house are located.

The islands are surrounded by coral reefs, enclosing calm lagoon waters.

Soil resources. The main richness of the Caledonian soil lies in its mineral wealth – iron, chrome, cobalt and, especially, nickel. The open-cut mining of this wealth has very much over-shadowed agricultural development.

Climate. New Caledonia's tropical climate produces an average annual temperature of 23 deg. C. with little variation – only 6 or 7 degs. C. – in monthly averages throughout the year. The island is cooled by the south-east trade winds.

During the wet season, December to March, cyclones can occur, sometimes bringing heavy rains. The east coast receives about twice the rainfall of the west coast, an average of 2,000 mm in the east, compared with 1,000mm in the west, including Noumea.

Fauna and flora. Local flora is of considerable interest to botanists because of the many endemic varieties. One local specimen which can be noted by casual observers is the sentinel-style pine, the *Araucaria cookii* sighted by Captain Cook. On the west coast, the sparsely-wooded plains with *Melaleuca leucadendron* paper bark trees remind visitors of inland Australian landscapes.

The most interesting of local fauna is the cagou bird, with a prominent white crest. This bird does not fly but runs along the ground and makes a sound like the barking of a dog. It can be seen tame in captivity.

Land reclamation. There has been considerable land reclamation around Noumea. The city was actually built on a marshy harbourside, which necessitated the filling of large areas, especially around the Quartier Latin. Recent extensions have been the new car park built on the shores of the Baie de la Moselle in 1973, as well as the massive new port extensions built across the main harbour.

Land Tenure. When France took possession of the islands, all land was taken over by the state which subsequently made grants to individual settlers besides allocating areas for Melanesian reserves.

The Loyalty Islands, Belep group and Isle of Pines are almost exclusively Melanesian reserves. Missions throughout the territory own about 2,000 ha. and Melanesian reserves over 372,509 ha.

There is a high degree of privately owned land on the mainland. In 1960 this was:

	ha
Privately owned	344,000
Rented from state	157,000
Melanesian reserve	142,000
State land	1,032,000
Total	1,675,000

The law forbids the alienation of Melanesian reserves other than to the state. Foreigners may acquire land with the approval of the Governor.

Since 1978 the state has been purchasing private land for re-allocation to Melanesian reserves on the east and west coasts.

PRIMARY PRODUCTION. In an economy very much pivoting around nickel production, labour costs and the poor organisation of distribution circuits have kept agricultural production at a relatively low level.

The Department of Agriculture estimated 1975 production of fruit and vegetables, including tribal gardens, at just over 30,000 tonnes. As this is quite inadequate for local needs, 1975 imports of fruit and vegetables reached a value of CFP697 million.

Coffee and copra. The only agricultural exports from New Caledonia are coffee and copra. However quantities remain insignificant: 538 tonnes of coffee was marketed in 1976-77 compared with 663 tonnes in 1974-75. The crop is mostly robusta, with a small quantity of arabica.

The volume of copra marketed in 1977 amounted to 1,388 tonnes, compared with 735 tonnes in 1972. Most copra comes from the Loyalty Islands. About one thirds of production goes to the local oil mill while the rest is exported to France.

Livestock. Some 588 cattle properties in New Caledonia utilise 280,000 hectares of grazing land of which only 6,300 ha. is improved pasture. There are also 155 piggeries.

There were about 120,000 cattle at the end of 1976, the 1973 drought having reduced the herds evaluated at 160,000 in 1972. This caused an increase in meat imports, while the locally-killed meat remained static at 2,454 tonnes in 1976. Local pork production was 258 tonnes, imports 396 tonnes (1974). Poultry production in 1975 met 20 per cent of local requirements, the rest being imported (1,997 tonnes in 1975). Locally marketed eggs were sufficient to meet demand by 1976.

Fisheries. Commercial fishing has remained at a fairly low level, with about 27 professional fishermen selling 205 tonnes of fish worth CFP41 million in 1976.

Main interest in fisheries in recent years has been in the cultivation of oysters as well as the large aquaculture project involving shrimps, all on the Baie de St. Vincent, some 30 km out of Noumea. The aquaculture ponds were created with the aid of South Pacific Commission and United Nations finance and personnel.

The trochus industry was revived in 1975 and 1976.

Forestry. Forest land in New Caledonia is estimated at 250,000 hectares. In addition there are 800,000 ha. of melaleuca plains, 300,000 ha. of scrubland as well as mangrove swamps etc.

The Forestry Commission has almost 70,000 ha. under its control including re-afforestation projects and a Centre Technique Forestier Tropical is located at Port Laguerre near Noumea.

Timber production in 1976 was about 9,743 cubic metres. Imports were 10,268 tonnes, about half those for 1973.

MINING. New Caledonia has immense mineral resources. Apart from nickel and chrome, there are large deposits of iron, manganese and cobalt. Antimony, mercury, copper, silver, lead and gold have also been found.

Nickel. The nickel mines are generally worked by bulldozers from the mountain tops with the ore being carried down to the coast by various mechanised systems or by truck. From the coast it is shipped to the smelters in Noumea or exported to Japan.

New Caledonia is the world's second largest producer of nickel ore, after Canada.

Mines Department figures show that peak production was reached in 1971, but dropped thereafter due to low demand. France maintains a strict control over the new Caledonian mining industry and has declared nickel to be a strategic material. France thus controls the granting of prospecting and extraction permits, and the possible entry of non-French smelting companies, as well as deciding which persons may export what quantity of ore to what destination at what price.

NICKEL ORE PRODUCTION
(In '000 tonnes)

year	gross wet tonnes	Ni - Co content
1971	7,722	151
1975	6,692	133
1976	5,900	116
1977	8,820	116
1978	3,279	N.A.

There are about 15 persons and companies, including the so-called "petits mineurs" (independent miners), who hold the rights to export Caledonian nickel ore, shipped only to Japan. The average nickel content of exported ore is 2.46 per cent.

The chief mining towns, operated by the island's sole smelting company (SLN), are at Thio, Kouaoua and Poro on the east coast and at Nepoui on the west coast.

Chrome. Once an important industry in New Caledonia, chrome mining ceased about 1960. However in 1975 the Tiebaghi mine on the island's west coast shipped about 18,000 tonnes of ore. Owner of the mine, INCO of Canada, embarked upon a two-year exploration programme in 1976, estimated to cost more than $US3 million.

Iron. Iron ore has not been exported since 1968.

Smelting. In 1980 the SLN mining company was still the only company smelting nickel in the territory, despite plans announced in 1969 for Canadian INCO, US AMAX and Patino to build new factories and raise output to as much as 200,000 tonnes by 1976.

Discussions have continued with the Paris government over the entry of non-French mining companies, but projects have been delayed by soaring costs, unavailability of matching French finance, and more competitive operating terms in countries such as Indonesia.

In the meantime, the SLN (Societe Le Nickel) has

NEW CALEDONIA NICKEL METAL PRODUCTION
(In tonnes of nickel content)

	1972	1973	1974	1975	1976	1977	1978	1979 (est.)
Ferro-nickel	34,050	35,759	48,533	52,802	38,152	28,283	19,889	
Mattes	20,199	21,476	18,837	18,266	23,759	23,038	17,103	
Total	54,249	57,235	67,370	71,068	61,911	51,321	36,992	42,000

improved its efficiency, increased production capacity at its Noumea smelters and re-organised its legal and financial structure.

At the end of 1974, the SLN transferred all its nickel assets – in New Caledonia and at its Le Havre factory in France – to a new company named "Societe metallurgique Le Nickel – SLN", still commonly known as "SLN". The old SLN company then became a holding company of the new concern and was re-named "IMETAL".

At the same time, the US AMAX bought a 10.7 per cent interest in IMETAL, while the new SLN received a boost in finance as half its shares were taken up by SNPA (Aquitaine Petroleum), the French state oil company.

With this new financial backing, the SLN plans to streamline its smelting operations and raise the capacity of its electric furnaces to 90,000 tonnes per annum by the early 1980s.

Production at the Noumea smelters of the SLN in recent years has been shown in the table.

All the smelted nickel is exported, more than half going to France, the remainder to North America and Japan. Exports in 1978 totalled 41,751 tonnes.

New nickel projects. Foreign companies have for many years held talks with the French Government, ever since it announced in 1966 that a second company would be authorised to smelt nickel in New Caledonia. Under the French Sixth Plan it was envisaged that by 1976 the territory would be producing up to 200,000 tonnes of nickel metal per year. However, new factories were still only a matter of discussion early in 1980.

The project for the north of New Caledonia is centred on Poum and Koumac, where there are extensive reserves of garnieritic nickel ore. The companies interested in this area have been US AMAX, as well as Patino with its subsidiaries COFREMMI and SOMMENI. The latter included French Pechney-Ugine-Kuhlmann and the Swedish Grangesberg.

The project for the south of New Caledonia is centred on Goro and Port Boise, with their extensive reserves of low-grade, lateritic nickel ore.

The first company prospecting in this area – COFIMPAC – grouped INCO and a French consortium, but ceased operations in 1971. The US Freeport Minerals associated with French SNPA to survey this area, while AMAX joined with Pennaroya to also consider a project here.

One of the problems in expanding the industrialisation of New Caledonia is the financing of the immense infrastructure necessary – port facilities, roadworks, energy supplies. Although the new factories have not yet materialised, Paris has encouraged the territory to undertake considerable loan raisings in order to build up the infrastructure.

In a further bid to encourage new nickel investment, the territory's tax laws were changed in 1975 so that future exporters would be taxed not just on the value of nickel shipments but on company profits. Export tax levied on SLN nickel metal in 1974 was CFP1,079 million.

Other industries. The chief industrial area of Noumea is at Ducos, which has numerous warehouses and workshops.

Chief items of production in 1978 were 50,801 tonnes of cement from the Numbo Cement Works, 29,767 hectolitres of soft drinks; 300 tonnes of soap from local copra and 2.4 million plastic bottles. In addition, 21,480 hectolitres of beer were produced by the island's brewery, the Grande Brasserie de Nouvelle Caledonie, at Magenta.

TOURISM. Tourism is New Caledonia's second major industry, after nickel. Main innovations in late 1979 were the beginning of the Club Med. resort (former Chateau Royal hotel) and the opening of the Maison du Tourisme booking and service complex, both on Anse Vata beach.

The local high cost of living and preoccupation with the nickel industry have tended at times to pose problems for tourism. In periods of a nickel slump, however, the authorities give greater encouragement to the tourist industry.

Growth in the tourist industry is reflected in the following figures showing the number of visitors to New Caledonia:

1974	1976	1977	1978
24,000	34,983	40,369	51,491

Over the past few years, visitors aboard cruise ships averaged 37,000 annually.

Overall expenditure by tourists in 1974 was estimated at CFP800 million, compared with CFP 380 million in 1973.

Information for visitors is provided by the Government-financed Office du Tourisme, 27 rue de Sebastopol, and by the Syndicat d'Initiative, in the old Town Hall, facing the central square, this office being organised by local community leaders.

LOCAL COMMERCE. The three largest importing firms with retail stores are Ets. Ballande, Maison Barrau and Prisunic.

The largest export firm is the nickel smelter SLN which is also the largest exporter of nickel ore. It is a member of the New Caledonian Nickel Ore Producers and Exporters Association.

Local agricultural produce is marketed partly through the wholesale market opened at Ducos in Noumea in late 1974. Municipal markets operate near the Noumea central square.

OVERSEAS TRADE. The value of exports published by the Customs Department differs from that of the Mines Dept. who record the final accounts in nickel transactions.

Exports. New Caledonia's exports are composed almost entirely of nickel. The value of exports in recent years has been as shown in the table.

The "other" products are mainly re-exports, especially scrap metal, also mining and construction equipment. Later figures include re-exports to Wallis and Fortuna and the New Hebrides.

Customers. France has always been New Caledonia's main client, taking 47 per cent of exports in 1978. Japan remains in second place (29 per cent of exports) taking all the nickel ore and some metal. The other main clients have been the USA and Canada which also buy Caledonian smelted nickel.

Imports. New Caledonia imports 90 per cent of its capital goods and the major share of consumption goods. Imports since 1969, especially, have reflected the build up as well as the slump in nickel developments.

Suppliers. France remains New Caledonia's chief source of imports, although her share dropped from 52 to 44 per cent between 1972 and 1978. Second largest single supplier is Australia (10 per cent). The EEC countries supplied 10 per cent in 1978, Japan 5 per cent, New Zealand and USA 4 per cent each.

Customs tariff. Import taxes are imposed at several levels and include: Customs duty levied on goods from foreign countries, excluding the EEC (average rate 10%); Taxes imposed on all imports: general import tax (average 17%). Finally, consumption tax on various items, particularly petroleum products, sugar, tobacco and alcohol.

Copies of customs schedules are sold by the Chamber of Commerce in Noumea.

FINANCE. Locally-derived revenue finances the so-called territorial budget, which is spent on maintaining public service departments such as social services, public works, and supplying municipal budgets.

In addition the French national budget finances such state government services as education, civil aviation, military, etc.

Expenditure in New Caledonia through the territorial budget, the national budget and FIDES (French government grants) in recent years has been as shown in the accompanying table.

These figures include amounts transferred from "running expenses" to "investment" and thus counted twice; they also include the credits which are carried forward from year to year and thus counted more than once without being spent.

Also included in the table figures are loan repayments which totalled CFP71 million in 1970, 361 million (1973) 961 million (1976), and 1,094 million (1977).

Local tax system. The first stages of personal income tax were introduced to the territory at the beginning of 1980. Other significant sources of government revenue are import and export duties, and indirect taxes. Tax laws were changed in late 1975 so that in future the nickel industry would be

EXPORTS
(In CFP million)

Product	1973	1975	1976	1977	1978
Nickel ore	3,578	4,827	6,492	6,451	2,597
Nickel metal	11,434	19,461	18,888	19,836	12,663
Coffee	28	23	30	37	N.A.
Copra	6	—	6	11	N.A.
Other	709	1,181	1,272	1,489	2,224
Total	15,755	25,492	26,688	27,824	17,484

IMPORTS
(In francs million)

Products	1973	1975	1976	1977	1978
Foodstuffs	4,288	5,139	5,172	5,545	5,519
Textiles	1,403	1,400	1,116	1,456	1,309
Coal, petrol	1,904	5,822	6,043	6,270	4,509
Raw mats & ind. products	4,656	6,159	5,033	5,540	4,848
Mach., transp.	4,474	6,877	5,490	5,911	5,337
Other	1,023	1,652	1,325	1,310	2,404
Total	17,748	27,049	24,179	26,032	23,926

BUDGET ALLOCATION
(in CFP million)

Year	Terr. budget running exp.	Terr. budget investment	Nat. budget running exp.	Nat. budget investment	FIDES
1972	7,686	3,637	3,833	680	506
1973	6,711	1,954	4,615	614	198
1974	8,040	1,579	7,061	608	276
1975	9,832	1,295	6,809	887	353
1978	12,956	176	9,009	959	N.A.

taxed not simply on the volume of metal exports but rather on company profits.

Currency. Local currency is the franc CFP (Cours du Franc Pacifique) tied to the French Franc with IFF = 18.18 CFP. Local banknotes are issued by the Institut d'Emission d'Outre-Mer. Denominations are 5,000, 1,000, 500 and 100 CFP. Coins circulate for 1, 2, 5, 10, 20, 50 and 100 francs CFP.

Banks. There are five banks installed in New Caledonia, four of which have opened since 1967.

The oldest bank in the territory, the Bank of Indochina, amalgamated in 1975 with the Bank of Suez to be renamed Banque de l'Indochine et Suez or, more commonly, Indo-Suez.

Other banks are the Banque Nationale de Paris (BNP), the Societe Generale, the Banque de Paris et des Pays-Bas (PARIBAS). The fifth bank, Banque de Nouvelle-Caledonie, opened in September 1974. Its shareholders are Credit Lyonnais, the Bank of Hawaii, Mr. Jean Breaud and local investors.

Overseas Investment. The investment of foreign funds in New Caledonia is strictly controlled by the French Government, which insists that 50 per cent of any such enterprise should be French-owned. The only area of active encouragement is the tourist field. Funds from EEC countries have greater facility of entry.

Certain tax benefits are granted to approved companies planning investment which would promote local agricultural, industrial or hotel sectors. Upon approval from Paris or the High Commissioner such companies avoid certain import duties, business licence fees and land tax.

Development Plans. Under the French Sixth Plan (1971-75) it was aimed to increase New Caledonia's nickel output to 200,000 tonnes of metal per year.

Under the Seventh Plan (1976-80), target for nickel metal production capacity was reduced to 90,000 tonnes. Actual production was about 42,000 tonnes in 1979. In 1980 discussions were still underway with the US and Canadian companies AMAX and INCO over possible development of nickel deposits in the north and south of the island. A new ten-year plan (1980-1990) was launched in 1979 providing broad outlines for development of agriculture, nickel, tourism, social welfare and cultural interests. Paris indicated that about 130,000 million CFP credits and loans could be available in this ten-year contract, with the island remaining a territory of France.

TRANSPORT. Coastal roads permit a complete driving circuit of New Caledonia. In addition there are several cross roads into the centre of the island. Some of their side roads would only be suitable for heavy mining trucks or adventurous drivers in the territory's various motor rallies.

Noumea itself boasts various scenic promenades as well as a 7 kilometre expressway leading out of town. Altogether the mainland has 364 km sealed road and 808 km unsealed, as well as 1,055 km partly sealed municipal roads and 2,485 km country tracks. Outer islands have 471 km roads and bush tracks.

VEHICLES. The importance of motor traffic may be gauged by new vehicle registrations which have shown the largest increase in the years of greatest nickel development:

	1970	1973	1974	1975	1978
passenger	5,489	3,623	4,066	4,894	2,988
service	2,438	1,221	1,266	1,274	834

These figures exclude two-wheeled vehicles which numbered 752 new registrations in 1978.

Overseas Airlines. New Caledonia is served by UTA French Airlines which includes the island on its flights across the Pacific to Los Angeles and through India to Paris, using DC8 aircraft. UTA also flies from New Caledonia to the New Hebrides and Wallis Island.

Air New Zealand operates to the territory from Auckland, using DC10s.

Qantas Airways fly in from Sydney with Boeing 747s.

Air Pacific flies through Noumea from Fiji to Brisbane, Australia, using BAC 111s.

Domestic Airlines. The territory's internal airline is Air Caledonie, formerly known as TRANSPAC. It operates from Noumea's domestic airport at Magenta to Houailou, Touho, Kone, Mueo and Koumac on the mainland, as well as the Isle of Pines, and islands of Ouen, Art, Lifou, Ouvea, Mare and Tiga. Air Caledonie uses Twin Otter and Britten-Norman Islanders.

Pentecost Aviation and Taxical, both based at Magenta Aerodrome, have helicopters for charter.

Airfleet. The territory's airfleet at the beginning of 1978 numbered 79 aircraft, divided as follows: public transport (15), French Navy (4), private and Gendarmerie helicopters (11), private planes (47), Air Force planes (2).

Local Airfields. New Caledonia has 12 commercial airfields as well as a number of private airstrips. The international airport at Tontouta is 53 km from Noumea and had a new international passenger terminal opened in 1972. The runway measured 3,250 m by 45 m in 1978.

Apart from Tontouta international airport and various private airstrips, New Caledonia has the following airfields:

Magenta (Noumea) sealed airstrip, 1,100 metres long;
Houailou, east coast, 1,000 m, sealed;
Touhou, east coast, 1,100 m, sealed;
Kone, west coast, 1,000 m, sealed;
Koumac, west coast, 1,450 m, compacted soil;
Plaine des Gaiacs, west coast, 1,400 m, compacted soil;
Ile des Pins (Isle of Pines), 1,100 m, sealed;
Art (Belep Is.), 500 m, compacted soil surface;
Lifou Is., 1,100 m, sealed;
Ouvea Is. (at Ouloup), 1,100 m, sealed;
Mare Is. (at La Roche), 1,100 m, compacted coral;
Tiga Is., 1,100 m, compacted coral and soil;
Hienghene, east coast, 800 m, grass;
Ile Ouen, 460 m, compacted soil;
Mueo, west coast, 700 m, sealed;
Voh, west coast, 600 m, compacted schist;
Poindimie, east coast, 500 m, sand and grass.

Ports. Most traffic is through the Port of Noumea and nearby wharves of the nickel company. Completely new installations were built across the harbour in the early 'seventies, including a causeway which linked Noumea to what was formerly the island of Nou, in 1972.

Shipping has thus been taken away from the old wharves along rue Jules Ferry and instead uses the following new facilities:

Deep sea wharves, 1,120 m long with depths of 6 to 10 m;
Island traders' wharf, 340 m long with depths of 3 to 5 m;
SLN nickel company wharves, 530 m long with depths of 8 to 9 m;
Floating pontoon with 10 m depth at Baie de Numbo cement works.

Elsewhere on the mainland, ore carriers load nickel at harbour installations such as those at Nepoui and Thio, while using barges at Houailou, Kouaoua and elsewhere.

Small coastal vessels ship supplies through wharves at the following points: Isle of Pines, and the Loyalty Islands of Lifou, Ouvea, Mare and Tiga, also Belep Is.

Shipping Services. Shipping companies serving New Caledonia include Karlander, Daiwa, Compagnie Generale Maritime, Compagnie des Chargeurs Caledoniens (CCC) and SOFRANA-Unilines, which operate out of Australia and New Zealand.

From Japan, Hong Kong and other Far East ports cargo services are operated by Daiwa and Kyowa.

Services from Europe are operated by Bank Line, Nedlloyd, and CGM.

PAD operates from the U.S. west coast.

Local Vessels. Locally registered vessels at the end of 1974 included one freighter, 3 island traders, 10 inter-island vessels and 1 large fishing vessel. In addition there were 145 small craft, mainly pleasure boats, compared with only 88 in 1972.

COMMUNICATIONS. Telephone services connect Noumea with most centres on the mainland and outer islands. The automatic service extends from Noumea as far as Tontouta international airport. At the end of 1978 there were 20,612 telephone subscribers throughout the territory, of whom 18,238 were in Noumea.

For overseas calls, most radio-telephone communications are with Paris, Sydney and Auckland for which there is a 24-hour continuous service.

A new "Telspace" antenna installed at Nouville in December 1975 has considerably improved telephone, telex, radio and TV links with New Caledonia, allowing satellite transmission.

Telex. Noumea is served by telex and businessmen may put messages through the Chamber of Commerce.

Radio and Television. Local radio and Tele-Noumea are French Government-controlled and operated through FR3, the overseas arm of the French broadcasting service, formerly known as ORTF.

Tele-Noumea has been operating since 1965 and extends through most of the mainland and, since late 1975, to the Loyalty Islands. It transmits in colour.

Many of the programmes for radio and most of those for television are dispatched from metropolitan France. All programmes are in French.

Newspapers. New Caledonia has one daily newspaper – "Les Nouvelle Caledoniennes".

WATER AND ELECTRICITY. Noumea has a good water supply provided by the Dumbea Dam outside the capital.

The local electricity authority UNELCO supplies power for Noumea and its surrounding area from the hydro-electric installations at Yate Dam as well as from diesel-operated generators shared with the SLN at its nickel factory in Noumea. Inland electricity supplies come from municipal and private generators. In Noumea, the voltage is 220.

PERSONALITIES AND ORGANISATIONS

Chief Executive of the Territory: Monsieur Claude Charbonniaud, High Commissioner for France in the Pacific.

GOVERNMENT COUNCIL (CONSEIL DE GOUVERNEMENT)

President: High Commissioner for France.
Vice-President: M. Dick Ukeiwe.
Members: Messieurs Stanley Camerlynck, Pierre Maresca, Albert Etuve, Franck Wahuzue, Pierre Frogier and Georges Nagle.

TERRITORIAL ASSEMBLY

Members: Messieurs Roger Laroque, Jacques Lafleur, Jean Leques, Andre Caillard, Rene de St. Quentin, Petelo Manuofiua, Max Frouin, Georges Faure, Auguste Parawi-Reybas, Justin Guillemard, Jean Delouvrier, Yves de Villelongue, Lionel Cherrier, Jean-Pierre Aifa, Gaston Morlet, Gerald Meyer, Christian Boissery, Melito Finau, Gabriel Paita, Jean-Marie Tjibaou, Francois Burck, Maurice Lenormand, Roch Pidjot, Francois Poadouy, Y. Yeiwene, Yann Celene Uregei, Nidoish Naisseline, Jacques Moureu, Jacques Violette, Edouard Wapae, Andre Gopea, Paul Napoarea, Eloi Machoro and Madame Marie-Paule Serve.

REPRESENTATIVES IN FRANCE

Deputies: M. Roch Pidjot, Jacques Lafleur.
Senator: M. Lionel Cherrier.
Conseiller Economique et Social: M. Roger Laroque.

CHIEF GOVERNMENT OFFICIALS

Secretary-General of the Territory: M. Rene Laufenburger.
Commander, French Pacific Troops: General Jean Barthelemy.
Naval Commander: Capitaine Ct. Mioche

STATE OFFICERS

Exterior Commerce: M. Colombani.
Police: M. Mao.
Posts and Telecommunications: Gilbert Ancian.
Merchant Marine: M. Munch.
Port Captain: Commandant J. L. Boglio.
Education: Roland Bruel.
Mines: Alain Bocaille.
Civil Aviation: J. P. Forlon.
Customs: J. Le Louarn.

OFFICES OF TERRITORIAL GOVERNMENT

Topographical Services: M. Michaut.
Finance: M. R. Berthomier.
Statistics: M. J. P. Colliez.
Youth and Sport: Jacques Eyssartier.
Health: Colonel S. Petit.
Livestock: M. Chabeuf.
Public Works: M. Chmutz.
Labour and Social Security: R. Visticot.
Office du Tourisme de N-C, director: Bruno Tabuteau.

CHURCH DIGNITARIES

Roman Catholic: Msgr. Klein, Archbishop of Noumea.
Protestant Mission: M. Kaen Ihage, Secretary.

BUSINESS, PROFESSIONAL AND CULTURAL ASSOCIATIONS

Chambre de Commerce et d'Industrie, Chambre d'Agriculture, Federation Patronale (Employers' Federation), Jeune Chambre Economique (Jaycees), SOENC (trade union), Association des Producteurs et Exportateurs de Nickel (nickel exporters).

Service Clubs

Rotary, Lions, Kiwanis, Federation Feminine de N-C.

Scientific Institutions

Musee de Noumea (museum), Bibliotheque Bernheim (Public Library), ORSTOM (marine and botanical research).

Cultural groups

Amis de la Musique, Jeunesses Musicales de France, Ecole de Musique, Josy Miller Ballet School, Federation des Oeuvres Laiques, Centre Culturel, Gemmanick artist/painter, Patrice Nielly art studio, numerous ethnic associations but no English-speaking clubs; Societe d'Etudes Historiques.

Environment

Association pour la Sauvegarde de l'Environnement, Jardin botanique et zoologique (Noumea botanical gardens), Societe d'Ornithologie (bird-lovers), Aquarium de Noumea.

Sports

Comite Territorial des Sports (Territorial Government Sports Commmittee which includes representatives of all the territory's sporting leagues from cycling to judo and soccer); Club des Nageurs Caledonien (swimming club), Tennis Club du Mont Coffyn, Cercle Nautique Caledonien (yacht club), Nautile Club (sailing club), Club des Chasseurs Sous-Marin (underwater fishing), Etrier (horse riding club), Melanesian Cricket Club (for women only), Dumbea Golf Course is planned, Aero Club Caledonien, Para Club Caledonien (parachuting), ASACNC (automobile club), Espadon Club (deep sea fishing).

International organisations

Red Cross, South Pacific Commission headquarters.

Youth organisations

Boy Scouts and Girl Guides of Roman Catholic and Protestant Churches, respectively; Auberge de Jeunesse (youth hostel) in Noumea; Comite territorial de la jeunesse (territorial government youth committee).

Convention Facilities

South Pacific Commission (international organisation), ORSTOM, (French governmment research institute).

DIPLOMATIC POSTS IN NOUMEA

Australian Consul-General, Mr. M. A. Leader, Trade Representative Mr. P. Appleton, B.P. 22 (P.O. Box); B.I.S. Bank Bldg., cnr. rue Jean-Jaures and Ave. Foch.

Indonesian Consul, Drs. S. N. Padmonegoro, B.P. 26; 4 rue de Strasbourg, Faubourg Blanchot.

New Zealand Consul-General, Mr. Derek Morris, B.P. 2219; Boulevard Vauban.

Honorary Consul for Belgium, Mr. Jean-Pierre Faget, B.P. 2683, 13 rue Jules Ferry.
Honorary Consul for Italy, Mr. Andrea Benazzo, C.G.M. Bldg., rue Gallieni. B.P. 144.

NOUMEA BUSINESS DIRECTORY

Agents, Customs
Agence Jean Brock, B.P. 122.
Agence Roger Busiau, B.P. 144.
Compagnie de Transit Caledonien (COTRANS), B.P. 2520.
Peschaud Pacifique, B.P. 1319.
Societe du Chalandage, B.P. 97.

Airlines
Air Caledonie (AIRCAL), 6 rue de Verdun.
Air New Zealand, B.P. 122.
Qantas, 29 rue Jean-Jaures.
UTA, 12 rue de Sebastopol.
Air Noumea, Magenta Aerodrome, B.P. 4131.
Pentecost Aviation, Magenta Aerodrome.

Architects
Allegre, Gilbert, 13 rue Colnett.
Cayrol, Gabriel, B.P. 177.
Perm, Vladimir, 27 rue de Sebastopol.
Rampal, Jacques, B.P. 194.

Auto Sales
Agence Alma (Citroen), B.P. A3 Noumea Cedex.
Agence Automobile (Fiat), B.P. 842.
AUTOCAL (Simca, Chrysler), B.P. 843.
Johnston et Cie (Ford), B.P. 52.
SCET (Daihatsu, Lancia), B.P. M4 Noumea Cedex.
Menard Freres (Peugeot), B.P. h 2 Noumea Cedex.
Pacific Auto (Alfa-Romeo), B.P. 471.
Renault New Caledonia, B.P. D4 Noumea Cedex.
SATMA (British models), B.P. 91.
Ste. Importation Auto (SIA) (Volkswagen, Porsche), B.P. 2245.
Ste. J. Cheval et Cie (Opel, Magirus Deutz), B.P. 100.
CIMAC (Volvo), B.P. 1320.
Suzuki, Cite Industrielle, Ducos.

Bookshops
Ets. Ballande, rue de l'Alma.
J.P.L., 32 rue de la Republique.
Librairie Pentecost, 34 rue de l'Alma.
Librairie Montaigne, 27 rue de Sebastopol.
4 Zarts, 21-ter, rue Jean Jaures.
Librairie Hachette, 11 Ave. Foch.
La Diffusion Caledonienne du Livre, 12 Ave. Brun, Quatier Latin.

Builders, Construction
Bernard, Roger, B.P. 665.
Entreprise Raymond Frere, B.P. 596, 5 rue Renoir, Lotis. Veyret.
Leconte, Andre, Cite Industrielle, Ducos.
Entreprise Vilabat, B.P. 921.
Entreprise Louis Duffieux, 3 rue Louis Catalan.
Societe Constructal, rue Taragnat, Vallee des Colons.
UNIBAT, B.P. 2233.
Solia, Roger, 15 rue Bon.
SOGECO, rue Ampere, Lot 183 Cite Industrielle, Ducos.

Doctors
Agez, Yves, 5 rue Guynemer.
Armand, Paul, 27 rue de Sebastopol.
Beretti, Jean, B.P. 414.
Caillard, Edmond, B.P. 457.
Dubois, Andre, Jeanine, and Claude, B.P. 844.
Guegan, Francois, B.P. 1055.
Tollinchi, Guillaume and Paul, 14 rue de Sebastopol.
Ulveling, Claude, B.P. 382.

Dentists
Artagnan, Pierre, 27 rue de Sebastopol.
Dano, Francois, B.P. 242.
Mura, Dr. Raymond, B.P. 1201.
Tivollier, Jean-Paul, B.P. 563.
Verges, Jean, B.P. 279.

Hospitals, private
Clinique Magnin, Route Territoriale No. 13.
Polyclinique de l'Anse Vata.
Clinique de Noumea, Magenta.

Importers — Exporters
Ets. Ballande, B.P. C4 Noumea Cedex.
Maison Barrau, B.P. A4 Noumea Cedex.
Prisunic, B.P. L4 Noumea Cedex.
Johnston et Cie, B.P. 52.
La Cote d'Argent, B.P. 738.
Siber Hegner (Const. Mat.) B.P. 1054.
CRIMEC (Agric. & Mining), B.P. 196.
C. Itoh et Cie Ltd., B.P. 632.
Kanematsu-Gosho Ltd., B.P. 2373.
Mitsui et Cie. Ltd., B.P. 37.
Mitsubishi Corp., B.P. 1056.
Nippon Yakin Kogyo Co. Ltd., B.P. 805.
Pentecost Group, B.P. H5 Noumea Cedex.
Ste. Le Nickel B.P. E5 Noumea Cedex.
Sumitomo Shoji Kaisha Ltd., B.P. 1615.
Rabot, Edouard, B.P. 113.
Sauvan, Guy, B.P. 561.
REPREX, B.P. 1572.

Lawyers
Chatenay-Reuter, B.P. 276.
Dunoyer, Jean, 24 rue de l'Alma.
Leder, Jean, B.P. 361.
Lomont, Jean, B.P. 629.
Louisia, Yves, 8 Ave. Marechal Foch.
Solier, Elie, 43 rue de l'Alma.

Manufacturers
Ste. Le Nickel, B.P. E5 Noumea Cedex.
Grande Brasserie de N-C (brewer, soda), Magenta.
Gratian, Lucien (ice cream), 11 rue Bourarate.
Ciment de Numbo (cement), B.P. 310.
Ste. Le Froid (coca-cola), Montravel.

Mining Coys. & Representatives
Berton, Jean-Claude, 6th Km.
B.R.G.M., B.P. 56
COMICA, B.P. 597.
Galliot, Roger, 1 rue de Sebastopol.

Lafleur, Jacques, B.P. 37.
Mines Pentecost, B.P. H5 Noumea Cedex.
Montagnat, Georges, B.P. 166.
Mouledous, Andre, B.P. 55.
Porcheron, Ernest, B.P. 124.
S.L.N. Public Relations Office, B.P. 1166.
S.L.N., B.P. E5 Noumea Cedex.
de Rouvray et Cie., B.P. 545.
Ste. Nationale des Petroles d'Aquitaine (SNPA), C/- S.L.N. incl., also Japanese importers, above.

Pharmacies

Pharmacie Caledonienne, B.P. 3877.
Pharmacie Centrale, B.P. 1317.
Pharmacie Commerciale, B.P. 92.
Pharmacie Blanchet, B.P. 146.
Pharmacie Normale, B.P. 406.
Pharmacie, Tonnelier, B.P. 101.

Printers

Artypo, 8 rue Bichat, Quatier Latin.
Imprimeries Reunies de Noumea, 45 rue de Sebastopol.
Societe Caledonienne d'Editions, B.P. 25.
Imprimerie I.C.P., rue Edouard Mercier.
J.P.L., 34 rue de la Republique.
Imprimerie du Pacifique, 10 rue Papin, Ducos.

Shipping companies

Agence Maritime Johnston, B.P. 449.
A.M.A.C.-Pentecost, B.P. A3 Noumea Cedex.
Ets. Ballande. B.P. C4 Noumea Cedex.
Ste. du Chalandage, B.P. 97.
Compagnie des Chargeurs Caledoniens (CCC) B.P. 833.
COFRANA, B.P. 1407.
C.G.M., B.P. F5 Noumea Cedex.
Hanner, Simon, B.P. 220.
Pantaloni, Honore, 12 rue Duquesne.
SOMACAL, B.P. 286.
SOFRANA-Unilines, B.P. 1602.
Ste. Leeman Navigation.

HISTORY. New Caledonia was evidently populated many hundreds of years before being discovered by Europeans, with probable migrations from Papua and certainly Polynesian settlers who landed in the Loyalty Islands.

Bougainville, sailing south from the New Hebrides in 1768, noted signs of nearby land; and when Captain James Cook came into these seas six years later, he made a search and discovered an island which he named New Caledonia because the pine-clad ridges suggested a resemblance to Scotland. He landed at Balade, on the north-east coast, on September 4, 1774, remained several days and before leaving, marked on a tree the name of his ship, date, etc., to show that the British were the first to arrive.

Cook tried to sail round to the west, but could not get outside the encircling coral reef on the west coast, so he doubled back along the east coast and, coming south, discovered and named the Isle of Pines, on September 20, 1774.

Searching for the lost La Perouse, a French expedition, under D'Entrecasteaux and De Kermadec, arrived at Isle of Pines on June 16, 1792, and sailed along the east coast of New Caledonia, which they very thoroughly explored.

During the next 50 years, the great island was visited by various navigators, explorers, sandalwood traders and runaway seamen, and convicts from New South Wales. Among them, English trader James Paddon settled on the Isle of Nou, in Noumea harbour. Missionaries from the London Missionary Society then the Marist Brothers arrived from 1840.

Penal settlement. Both Britain and France coveted the big island and its smaller outliers of the three Loyalty Islands and the Isle of Pines but were reluctant to come to the point of upsetting the existing status quo. Towards the mid-19th century, however, the French began to see the island as a penal settlement and also as a naval and mercantile base close to Australia, from which there was already beginning a promising trade with Europe. At the same time there was agitation from within France for annexation in order to protect French missionaries who were occasionally attacked by the natives, killed and eaten.

The final decision was probably taken in 1850, following a native attack on a French survey ship "Alcmene" when the entire crew was eaten at Paaba, but it was not until 1853 that Admiral Febvrier-Despointes raised the French flag – at Balade on September 24 and on the Isle of Pines on September 29.

At the time, Captain Denham of the "Herald" was there from the Sydney station, surveying the coastline. The British were incensed at the French annexation but not sufficiently so to do anything about it.

In 1854 Captain Tardy de Montravel selected the site for a capital and construction began – it was called Port-de France – known since 1866 as Noumea.

The use of New Caledonia as a penal settlement was commenced in 1864, and the history of the place, for forty years thereafter, is associated with the stories of penal island horrors, common to such establishments. About 40,000 prisoners were transported there, the headquarters of the system being the notorious Ile Nou.

Most of France's long-term political prisoners were sent to New Caledonia, particularly socialists, in the round-up which followed the Franco-German War.

These political deportees were imprisoned at Ducos, near Noumea, and on the Isle of Pines.

Transportation ceased in 1897, but a large section of the European population for years afterwards were long-term prisoners and their descendants.

From 1853 until 1884 New Caledonia was administered by military governors; in 1885, a civilian governor was placed in charge, assisted by a Conseil-General (elected advisory council).

Other than turn it into a penal settlement, the

French were able to do little with their new colony initially. They tried to encourage colonists to take up land but in the face of native hostility, few newomers were prepared to try it although a number of individualists, English, Irish, Scandinavian, had dug themselves in long before annexation. In their early years, the French were continually suppressing native risings, the bloodiest of them in 1878 and the last skirmish only in 1917.

The colony's economic development was marked by the discovery of nickel by Jules Garnier in 1863, and the "gold rush" beginning in 1870. John Higginson spearheaded the development of the Caledonian nickel industry.

In the first half of the twentieth century, the Caledonians proved their valour fighting for France in two world wars. In World War I the islanders joined the Tahitians to form the Bataillon du Pacifique (Pacific Battalion) and fought in France. In World War II, the Caledonians were among the first overseas French to respond to General de Gaulle's appeal to fight as "Free French" after Paris fell to the Germans. The islanders served mainly in North Africa.

In the Pacific War. US General Patch arrived in New Caledonia in March 1942 with the first contingent of men, to turn the island into a great US military base for operations against the Japanese.

The Americans built four airfields, impressive roads and launched the territory into the modern era.

Political development progressed in 1958 when the new Loi-Cadre (law) allowed the election of ministers in charge of different sectors of territorial activity and all sitting as members of the Conseil de Gouvernement (Governor's Council). The High Commissioner, representing the central government, remained as Governor and chief executive.

In December 1963 the ministerial posts in the governor's council were abolished by Paris, thereby giving rise to a strong local campaign for internal self-government.

NEW CALEDONIA'S ISLANDS IN DETAIL

NEW CALEDONIA. Known as "la grande terre", the Caledonian mainland is about 400 km long by 50 km wide. With an area of 16,750 sq. km it is the largest island in the South Pacific after New Zealand. It is surrounded about 10 km offshore by a barrier reef measuring 1,600 km in length.

The mainland is cigar-shaped and divided by a central mountain chain from which numerous rivers make their way to the sea, particularly on the east coast. They cause sudden dangerous floods in the wet season. The island's capital, Noumea, is situated at the south-west tip. Other centres are Bourail, Kone and Koumac, travelling north along the west coast, and Thio, Houailou and Poindimie along the east coast.

ISLE OF PINES. Known in French as Ile des Pins and in Melanesian as Kunie, it is situated at 22 deg. S. lat. and 165 deg. E. long, about 50 km SE of Cape Queen Charlotte on the mainland. Navigation through the reefs is via the Havannah and Sarcelle passes.

The island has an area of 134 sq. km and extends about 17 km north-south and 15 km east-west. It was named in 1774 by its discoverer, Captain Cook, who noted its tall, narrow pine trees which now bear his name — Araucaria Cookii. The first Protestant missionaries arrived there in 1841, followed in 1848 by the Roman Catholic mission which continues today at Vao, in the south east. Seven kilometres west is the harbour of Kuto, the administrative centre, and near it the famous Kanumera holiday resort. Five kilometres inland towards the aerodrome are the remains of the prison and graveyard for French political deportees who were kept on the island from 1872 to 1900. The chief settlement in the north is around the anchorage at Gadji.

BELEP ISLANDS. This archipelago is situated about 50 km north west of the northern tip of the mainland, in 19 deg. 41 S. lat. and 163 deg. 19 E. long. It comprises Art Is. (5,560 ha), Pott Is. (1,184 ha), Nienane Is. (245 ha) and the northern and southern Daos (55 ha).

According to tradition, Belep was the name of a mainland chief who settled there ten generations before the missionaries arrived in 1856. The chief centre is Uala, on Art Is. The islands are a Melanesian reserve, with a Catholic mission established there.

HUON AND SURPRISE ISLANDS. These are among a cluster of small sandy phosphate formations which surround the d'Entrecasteaux Reef, north of the Belep group. Huon is 260 km northwest of the northern tip of the mainland. Surprise, to the south-west, has a good anchorage on the leeward side and is 60 ha in area.

LOYALTY ISLANDS. These lie parallel to the east coast of the mainland, about 100 km offshore. From south to north, the three main islands of Mare, Lifou and Ouvea are about 50 km one from the next. They are formed of upraised coral forming low plateaux never reaching 100 m above sea level, often falling straight into the sea or bordered by a narrow, flat coastal plain. In early times, Polynesian migrations mingled with the Loyalties' Melanesians. The islands are treated largely as Melanesian reserves, with both Roman Catholic and Protestant missions present. There are no rivers in the Loyalty Islands.

Mare Is. is located on 21 deg. 30 S. lat. and 168 deg. E. long. It has a maximum length of 40 km and an area of 650 sq. km. It is shaped like an irregular hexagon, with its rocky cliffs surrounding the island like a fortress. Inland are the two small volcanic hills of Rava and Peorawa, rising 10 to 15 m above the coral plateau. The chief centre is Tadine on the west coast. Other centres are La Roche, on the north coast, Netche on the west, and Penelo on the east coast.

Lifou Is., like Mare, is a plateau bordered by high cliffs along a coastline indented with deep bays, such as Sandal Bay, bordered by the town of Chepenehe in the west, and Chateaubriand Bay in the east with the town of We. We is the administrative headquarters of the Loyalty Islands subdivision. Limestone rocks on Lifou have numerous caves, the most beautiful being perhaps Tinge-ting, about 6 km north of Nathalo, in the north east. Lifou Is. is situated in 21 deg. S. lat. and 167 deg. E. long. It is the largest of the Loyalty Islands, with an area of 1,150 sq. km. It extends about 60 km in length and 50 km wide.

Ouvea Is. is an atoll situated 20 deg. 30 S. lat. and 166 deg. 30 E. long. and has an area of 160 sq. km. The main island, to the east, is composed of two segments connected by a band of coral barely 40 m wide in places. The lagoon is enclosed on the western side by a string of islets. The chief centre, with holiday resort, is Fayaoue, on the south west of the main island.

Tiga Is. lies between Lifou and Mare, about 30 km north of Mare. It is about 6 km long and 2 km wide.

WALPOLE ISLAND is in line with the Loyalty Islands at their southern tip, about 150 km east of the Isle of Pines and the same distance SE of Mare, i.e., about 22 deg. 30 S. lat. and 168 deg. 40 E. long. Walpole is about 1 sq. km in area formed of limestone strata up to 70 m high. The island is surrounded by steep cliffs and is very difficult of access as it has no protective barrier reef. Durand Reef lies to its north west. The exploitation of phosphate from 1910 to 1936 has left the island barren of trees. It is believed to have been discovered in 1800 by Captain Butler who named it after his ship, the 'Walpole'.

MATTHEW ISLAND. Situated about 450 km due east of the southern tip of the New Caledonian mainland, and 350 km SE of Aneityum in the New Hebrides. The island is conical in shape, of volcanic origin. It is 500 m in diameter and up to 177 m high. It is uninhabited.

CHESTERFIELD ARCHIPELAGO. This lies about 600 km west of the northern tip of the Caledonian mainland and extends about 500 km north-south. The group includes several small atolls of 15 to 20 ha. They are inhabited by numerous seabirds, and guano was worked there around 1879 by Austral Guano. The main atolls are Long, Brampton Passage, Mouillage (Anchorage), Reynard, Loop and Avon.

The archipelago was discovered in 1793 by the ship 'Chesterfield'. The French took possession officially in 1877, although an Englishman, Captain North, had previously occupied these islands. Their main interest now lies in resources of the seabed with oil leases taken out in the area.

FOR THE TOURIST. New Caledonia has something for everyone – lush tropical landscapes and harsh mining terrain, from rugged mountain to soothing lagoon. Noumea, the capital, is fast developing as a showcase of the French way of life, with lavish restaurants or delicious take-away food from the supermarkets; sophisticated dressing in the Paris-style boutiques or chic Tahitian pareos worn on the beach. There are multi-storied hotels and seaside thatch bungalows or camping areas throughout the mainland, for anyone who really likes to rough it. Those who get upset by misunderstandings with the French, may be advised to take a dose of good humour with their cognac.

Noumea transport ranges from taxis and rental cars to the "baby-car" small buses which run through all the suburbs from a new parking lot between the central square and the Baie de la Moselle.

Duty free shopping. Under a system introduced in 1975, certain stores displaying the "DUTY FREE from NOUMEA" sign will allow a 20 per cent discount on certain items on a minimum bill of CFP 2,000 when visitors produce their passport. The purchases involved must be handy for Customs inspection in hand luggage on departure at the airport, bottles sealed etc. Relevant receipts must be handed to Customs so the storekeeper may be officially reimbursed. Failure to surrender receipts means a loss for the storekeepers.

There is also a Duty Free shop in the departure lounge of Tontouta airport. Cruise ship passengers have duty-free purchases in town delivered to their ship. There is also a boutique in the shipping passenger lounge where black coral jewellery, local handicrafts and styles of clothing can be bought.

Entry formalities. All visitors must hold a valid passport and have an onward or return ticket. Foreigners do not require a visa for stays of less than 30 days.

Visiting yachts must report to the Port Captain in Noumea who will also kindly call upon yachts at the Cercle Nautique yacht club in the Baie des Pecheurs to complete formalities.

Airport tax. This is not levied in New Caledonia.

Sightseeing. City tours of Noumea include hilltop lookouts, the museum and the world-famed aquarium with its fluorescent corals.

Nouville, the former island now linked by causeway across Noumea harbour, retains many old buildings from early convict days, including a disused chapel which has been converted into a theatre "le Theatre de l'Ile".

The small zoo and botanical gardens near Mont Te on the outskirts of Noumea contain local wildlife. They are open to the public at specified hours.

Visitors travelling inland may see the New Zealand War Cemetery at Bourail. By proceeding further, across the central mountains, one may drive along the lush East Coast with numerous Melanesian villages.

An interesting circuit closer to Noumea takes one from Boulouparis across the central mountains to the nickel centre of Thio on the East Coast then through rural Canala to La Crouen spa and on to Melanesian villages at Couli before returning via the Relais Melanesian restaurant at La Foa and back to Noumea.

After sampling the feasts for the eye, one finds eating is a major pleasure in Noumea where the diversity of the local population offers all manner of cuisine from Indonesian and Vietnamese specialties to dishes from North Africa and all the regions of France, as well as local mangrove oysters, heart of coconut palm and Tahitian fish salad.

Tourist representatives abroad. U.S.A. – Mrs. Charlotte Hyde, T.C.I., 700 South Flower Street, Los Angeles; Australia – Mrs. D. Gubbay, New Caledonia Tourist Office, 12 Castlereagh St., Sydney; New Zealand – Mr. Stuart Robertson, Caledonia Tourist Bureau, P.O. Box 3647, Auckland.

ACCOMMODATION

Noumea Town centre

PARADISE PART MOTEL – 64 units, air-conditioned, private facilities, kitchenette; two swimming pools, restaurant/bar; set in 3 acres gardens in Vallee des Colons suburb, with free bus to heart of town 5 mins. away.

CALEDONIA HOTEL – 25 rooms incl. 16 with private toilet and cooking facilities, air-conditioning, bar and restaurant.

HOTEL LA PEROUSE – 30 rooms incl. 18 with private facilities, air-conditioning, snack-type restaurant and bar adjacent.

HOTEL SEBASTOPOL – 36 rooms all with private bathroom, bar, breakfast room, boutique.

YOUTH HOSTEL – (Auberge de Jeunesse) for members of National Youth Hostel Organisation, on hill directly above city, 52 bunk beds in dormitory-style rooms, all with communal bathroom facilities, common kitchen; Central A-frame building houses lounge, dining room and recreation centre.

Anse Vata beach 10 mins. by bus from Noumea

CLUB MEDITERRANEE – 250 rooms, air-conditioned, own balcony, private facilities, on beach; swimming pool, tennis, sailing and other sports; bar, all meals; formerly Chateau Royal hotel.

HOTEL ISLE DE FRANCE – near beach, 103 rooms incl. 7 suites, private bathroom, refrigerator, tea facilities, telephone, radio; also pool and snackbar, restaurant and bar.

NOUVATA – opposite beach, rooms with private bathroom, air-conditioning, swimming pool, bar, restaurant.

HOTEL LE LAGON – 3 mins. from beach, 60 rooms, mostly air-conditioned, telephone; radio and TV on request; bar, lounge and restaurant.

MOTEL ANSE VATA – 23 rooms with private bath, air-conditioned, fully equipped mod. kitchens.

Bale des Citrons beach, 8 mins. from Noumea.

NOUMEA HOTEL – opposite beach, 46 rooms, private facilities, bar, lounge, restaurant, TV room.

HOTEL RESIDENCE – 1 block from beach, 30 rooms, private facilities, refrigerator, restaurant, bar, TV room; specialises in school groups.

HOTEL MOCAMBO – near beach and yacht club, 35 rooms, air-conditioned, radio, telephone, TV, tea facilities, private bathroom, bar and lounge with restaurant adjacent.

East Coast, mainland.

CHEZ MAITRE PIERRE – lush riverside gardens, 11 native style bungalows and 25 rooms with private facilities; plus two dormitories; bar, lounge, restaurant; family-style, at Hienghene, 392 km from Noumea.

RELAIS DE KOULNOUE – facing sea, 16 native style bungalows, bar, restaurant, dance floor, swimming pool, at Hienghene.

RELAIS D'AMOA – on beachfront, 5 rooms and 4 bungalows; restaurant, bar, dance floor, swimming pool, at Poindimie, 317 km from Noumea.

HOTEL DE LA PLAGE – facing beachfront, 4 comfortable upstairs rooms, 11 at rear; restaurant and bar; at Poindimie.

HOTEL LA CROUEN – spa resort in mountains by river with mineral pool for guests; 9 cabins incl. 6 with private facilities; restaurant, bar and terrace; at La Crouen, 100 km from Noumea.

HOTEL SANTACROCE – 10 rooms with private facilities, some air-conditioned; at Thio, nickel centre, 130 km from Noumea.

HOTEL BEL AIR – 11 units with private facilities, bar and restaurant; at Houailou, 241 km from Noumea.

West Coast mainland

TONTOUTEL – 32 rooms, next to Tontouta international airport, 50 km from Noumea.

RELAIS MELANESIAN – 10 native-style bungalows with private facilities, restaurant, bar, lounge with TV; at La Foa, 118 km from Noumea.

EVASION 130 – chalet-style with 8 bedsitters and facilities; restaurant, bar, swimming pool, outdoor barbecue; at Sarramea, behind La Foa.

EL KANTARA – near beach, 15 units with private facilities, TV, radio and telephone; 2 restaurants, bus trips to New Zealand War Cemetery; at Bourail, 170 km from Noumea.

TROPICAL HOTEL – 10 air-conditioned rooms with private facilities, restaurant and bar; at

Kone, 280 km from Noumea.

HOTEL KONIAMBO — with 10 carpeted log cabins, air-conditioned, private facilities, bar, restaurant; at Kone.

HOTEL COPPELIA — 10 air-conditioned rooms with private facilities; restaurant; at Koumac, 384 km from Noumea.

HOTEL MADONA — 13 air conditioned rooms with private facilities, restaurant and bar; at Koumac.

HOTEL PASSIFLORE — 9 rooms, half with private facilities, restaurant and bar; at Koumac.

OUTER ISLANDS

Isle of Pines (30 mins. flight from Noumea)

RELAIS DE KANUMERA — closed as at early 1980.

Ile Ouen (20 mins. flight from Noumea)

TURTLE CLUB — 14 native-style bungalows with private facilities; bar, restaurant and lounge.

LOYALTY GROUP

Ouvea Is. (45 mins. flight from Noumea)

RELAIS DE FAYAQUE — on coral island, 10 native-style bungalows with private facilities, bar, restaurant, lounge and TV.

Lifou Is. (45 mins. flight from Noumea)

RELAIS DE WE — 8 native-style small bungalows, restaurant and bar.

NIUE

Niue, an uplifted coral island of 258 sq. km and located at 19 deg. S. latitude and 169 deg. W. longitude, is about 480 km east of Tonga and about 560 km south-east of Samoa. It is a self-governing Commonwealth country in free association with New Zealand.

The administration centre is Alofi, on the West coast. Local time is 11 hr. 20 min. behind GMT. The population in 1979 was 3,578.

The flag is yellow with the Union Flag in the top left quarter. New Zealand currency is used.

Public holidays are those observed in New Zealand plus: Peniamina Day (a religious celebration of the anniversary when the first missionaries arrived); Annexation Day which celebrates the day that the island was annexed by New Zealand; and Takai, during the first week of the year.

THE PEOPLE. The Niueans are Polynesians. The mini-census conducted on March 10, 1979, gave a total population of 3,578 comprising 1,823 males and 1,755 females. This was approximately seven per cent below the 1976 Census and the drop is attributed once again to out-going migration, mainly to New Zealand where the numbers of Niueans are about treble those resident on the island. There were also 244 people classified as non-Niueans and this number represents Europeans, Samoans and Tongans including short-term visitors at the time of census. Population of Alofi was 960 – 10 less than at the 1976 census.

Citizenship. Under the 1974 constitution the Niueans remain British subjects and New Zealand citizens.

Language. While the indigenous language is a Polynesian tongue closely related to Tongan and Samoan, the islanders also use English because of their long attachment to New Zealand.

Migration. The restricted nature of local resources has led many Niueans to migrate to New Zealand. Although the population continues to decrease, the level of migration is not as high as in previous years. The loss of 133 persons by migration since March, 1979, has been significantly offset by the natural increase of 55.

Religion. Most of the population (75 per cent) belongs to the Ekalesia Niue, which has evolved from initial contact with the L.M.S. under Samoan influence. Latter Day Saints (Mormon) account for 10 per cent of the population, Roman Catholics for 5 per cent, while Jehovah's Witnesses and Seventh-day Adventists are also represented.

Lifestyle. While the Niueans are Polynesians, there are no chiefs or tribal system and hereditary rank is of no importance. The head of each extended-family has a voice in land matters only, while the elders of each community have a voice in matters affecting each village.

GOVERNMENT. Niue was granted self-government by New Zealand on October 19, 1974. Previously the island had been represented in Alofi by a Resident Commissioner who acted as President of the Niue Islands Assembly of 14 elected members. The Resident Commissioner was also Chairman of the Executive Committee which consisted of four members elected by the Assembly.

Under self-government the new constitution provides for Niue to continue in free association with New Zealand which remains responsible for defence and foreign affairs and ready to provide necessary economic and administrative assistance. The islanders also remain protected as New Zealand citizens.

Legislature. The new constitution provides for a Legislative Assembly consisting of 20 members, fourteen to be elected from village constituencies and six from a common roll.

Executive. The constitution provides for the general direction and control of the island to be in the hands of a Cabinet of four members – the Premier, elected by the Assembly and three other ministers, chosen by the Premier from among Assembly members.

Local Government. This takes the form of Village Councils, first set up in 1967. There are 14 councils and councillors are elected for a 3-year term.

Justice. Serious crime on Niue is rare – the Court has to deal mainly with cases of disturbance, making and consuming liquor, petty theft, etc. For example, the total number of criminal cases dealt with for the 12 months ending March 31, 1980, was 311 and more than 50 per cent of those cases were traffic offences.

Courts. There is a High Court under the control of a Chief Justice and in his absence a Commissioner and Justices of the Peace, with right of appeal to the N.Z. Supreme Court. The Land Court has jurisdiction over land disputes.

Liquor laws. Persons under 20 years are prohibited from drinking in public places, while all drinking is prohibited on roads, thoroughfares or greens. The Liquor Board controls licensed premises.

DEFENCE. Under the 1974 constitution, defence and international relations remain the responsibility of the New Zealand Government.

EDUCATION. All schools are under the control of the government.

Education is compulsory between the ages of five and 14, and educational facilities are rapidly expanding.

There were eight primary schools on Niue in 1980. The overall school intake for 1979 totalled 1,179. Pupils registered on school rolls were Primary 694 and Side School 51. There was one secondary school, the co-educational Niue High School, with 434 students, and 26 teachers.

In 1979, three students were attending secondary schools in New Zealand and 11 attended the University of the South Pacific in Fiji. Also training in New Zealand and Fiji were four teachers, three university students, four nurse-trainees and 16 others doing trade or professional courses in the Solomon Islands and elsewhere.

Teaching staff on Niue is predominantly local but in any year there are from 12 to 15 seconded teachers from N.Z.

Education cost the government an estimated $607,517 in 1979.

LABOUR. Opportunities for paid work exist only within the government services and in small industries such as those organised by the Niue Development Board. With 62 per cent of the population aged under 15 years, at the 1976 census, 33 per cent of residents were of working age, between 15 and 59 years. Most islanders who do not work for wages are engaged in their family plantations.

Wages. Basic wage rates in 1979 were 96 cents per hour for unskilled labour and $1.45 per hour for skilled workers.

There are no industrial unions.

Social security. The scheme introduced by the Niue Government in 1974 has been up-graded and persons now 60 years of age and over are entitled to a pension at the rate of $4 a week.

HEALTH. All medical and dental treatment, including hospital services, is provided free of charge, subsidised by New Zealand government grants. Visitors unattached to the local public service pay medical and dental charges at the rate fixed by the government. There are no private practitioners. There is a 30-bed hospital at Alofi where new wards and an operating theatre were completed in 1962. A new 10-bed maternity unit was completed in 1976. Attached to the hospital are outpatients' departments, X-ray unit, laboratory and dispensary. Clinics operate in three large villages. In 1979, 438 patients were admitted to the hospital and 10,804 received outpatient treatment; 66 major and 185 minor operations were performed. There were 95 births, 80 of which were hospital deliveries. Birth rate per 1000 population for the same period was 17.14 and crude death rate was 6.0.

The amount spent on public health has grown from $237,266 in 1975 to $402,428 in 1978. The amount spent in 1979 is estimated at $430,428. Hospital fees brought in $3,292 in 1978 and an estimated $6,000 in 1979.

Disease. The Niuean standard of general hygiene is high by Pacific standards, and although situated in the tropics, Niue is largely free from diseases often found in tropical areas. However, there have been outbreaks of dengue fever over the years, the worst occurring in 1980. At its peak in March, 1980, a third of the population was reported to be suffering from the disease which caused four deaths

THE LAND. The island of Niue has an area of 258 square kilometres, with a circumference of over 60 km by road. The island extends 19 km from north to south.

In general formation, the island takes the shape of two terraces, the lower being 27 metres above sea level and the upper saucer-shaped plateau rising to 65 metres.

Natural features. Niue is a raised coral outcrop and is probably the result of a series of tectonic upheavals, indicated by many deep chasms, especially those of Vailoa and Matapa. A coral reef encircles a precipitous and broken coastline. The soil, composed of worn-down coral, is fertile but not abundant and this factor, combined with the rocky and broken terrain, makes cultivation difficult. Most people live in villages on the western side of the island.

Climate. Situated just inside the tropics, Niue has a pleasant climate, fanned by the south east trade winds. The island is on the edge of the hurricane belt and the last major disturbance of this sort was in 1968. The mean annual temperature is 24.7 deg. C. and the average rainfall is 217.7 cm.

Land tenure. As the Niuean's livelihood depends on his family lands, alienation is forbidden, so that there are no landowners apart from the Niueans and the government.

PRIMARY PRODUCTION. Productive ventures in agriculture and livestock are carried out by the Niue Development Board, under the guidance of the Agricultural Department. The board, which is responsible for planning and financing schemes, produces lime juice, passionfruit pulp and juice, honey, copra and reconstituted milk.

Crops. Of the total area of about 26,000 hectares, about 20,400 ha are available for agriculture. The Development Board has encouraged increased

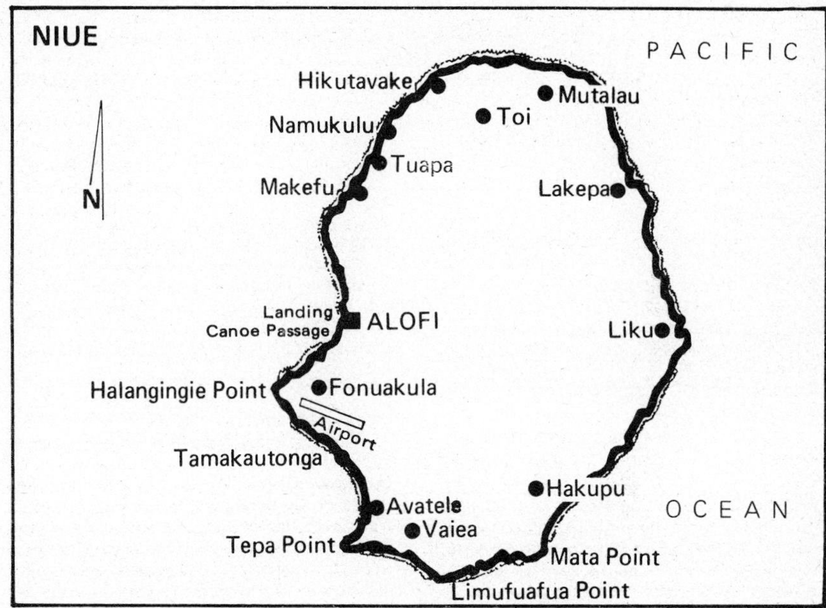

planting of lime trees and passionfruit vines. At the same time the agricultural authorities have a programme for soil study and improvement of stock, including coconuts and pasture grasses.

Honey. Bee-keeping has been a minor industry for some years and the honey produced is of high quality. It is exported.

Livestock. The main livestock owned by islanders are pigs and poultry. In addition, progress has been made in grazing cattle under coconut trees, thereby serving the dual process of keeping the plantations clear of undergrowth. This programme has been assisted by the provision of deep bores to help overcome the water problem. These cattle, many of them Friesians, are used for beef and milk production. In March 1979, there were 649 cattle.

Timber. About 5,400 ha of land is forest, containing some good millable timber. In 1970, for example, the government sawmill produced 378.68 cu. metres of timber for local building.

MANUFACTURING. Main activity centres on food processing for export, with lime juice extraction, preparation of passionfruit juice and pulp and honey. The Development Board has also assisted in establishing other small industries such as building and joinery, garage, local fishery, etc.

TOURISM. The island's first hotel was completed in 1975 after difficulties in obtaining equipment had prolonged its construction for more than two years. The first wing of 20 beds was completed in time to accommodate guests at the island's self-government celebrations in October, 1974. Since then a second wing has raised capacity to 40 beds. There is also a swimming pool. All guests' rooms have panoramic views of Alofi Bay.

In 1977, there were 925 visitors, 467 from New Zealand, 91 from Fiji and 53 from the United States. More than 400 were there for business reasons. In 1979, there were 2,135 departures and 1,936 arrivals, indicating that the hotel was not left idle.

NIUE — PRODUCTION AND LIVESTOCK
(in tonnes)

Year ending March 31	**1976**	**1977**	**1978**	**1979**	**1980**
Copra	236	339	170	354	334
Passionfruit and pulp	272	190	217	222	360
Limes (fruit)	133	176	223	334	350
Honey	31	25	38	31	32
Beef	12	103	164	65	n.a.
Pork	1	n.a.	n.a.	n.a.	n.a.
Cattle (number)	824	824	644	649	n.a.

NIUE — CHIEF EXPORT COMMODITIES
(In $'000)

	Copra	Plaited Ware	Passionfruit	Honey	Limes and juice
1975	74	21	83	13	6
1976	24	28	67	9	23
1977	23	36	103	14	17
1978	38	28	87	21	22

CO-OPERATIVES. There are two co-operative societies – Niue Handicrafts and the Public Service Savings and Loan Society. Niue Handicrafts was financed by the Niue Development Board to handle the marketing and production of the very fine ware plaited from pandanus and coconut palm leaf.

OVERSEAS TRADE. Most of Niue's trade, exports and imports, is with New Zealand. The value of exports and imports has been as follows in recent years,(in $'000):

	1976	1977	1978
Imports	2,102	2,530	2,780
Exports	153	255	240

Imports. Most items come from New Zealand which supplied 80 per cent of the $2,780,000-worth imports in 1978. Other imports come from Japan, then Singapore, Fiji, and, more recently, the Samoas.

Exports. Exports go mainly to New Zealand, then to Fiji and Australia. See the accompanying table for details of the value of various export commodities over recent years.

Customs tariff. The New Zealand Customs Tariff is in force, modified by the Niue Customs Tariff Order 1969.

This provides for a port and service tax of two and a half per cent, levied on all goods landed, as well as a five per cent export tax on copra and kumaras. There is a general five to ten per cent tax on certain "luxury" manufactured goods, including motor vehicles.

There is free trade between the island and New Zealand.

FINANCE. Total revenue from all sources does not cover expenditure and the NZ Government makes up the deficit with grants which are fixed three-yearly in advance but subject to an annual review by a NZ foreign aid team.

Budget. A comparative statement of receipts and expenditure in recent years appears in the accompanying table:

Taxes. Local revenue is raised mainly from income tax, (including "aid to revenue" tax), customs duty and manufactured goods tax.

External Aid. Under the Constitution Bill 1974, New Zealand undertook to supply necessary economic and administrative assistance. Thus, as noted above, budget deficits are met by grants and loans from New Zealand.

Currency. Niue uses New Zealand currency in dollars and cents.

There are no trading banks, but there is a Post Office Savings Bank at Alofi. The Treasury Department handles foreign exchange, travellers' cheques and other banking business.

Development Plans. For the first time the Niue Government has introduced its Five Year National Development Plan covering the period 1980/81 to 1984/85. It sets out, basically, to increase Niue's degree of self-reliance materially and to create self-confidence in the country's ability to meet a substantial share of the cost of maintaining a modern Niue. Planning and financing of development projects are carried out by the Niue Development Board and the agriculture sector continues to act as agency for the board and provide technical advice and operate pest control in the cash crop industry. (See sub-heading under the title Primary Production.)

Postage Stamps. The sale of postage stamps makes a significant contribution to local revenue and amounted to $111,840 in the year ended March 31, 1979.

TRANSPORT. There are approximately 128 km of all-weather roads plus 96 km of bush tracks negotiable by heavy trucks and four-wheel-drive vehicles. The main 60 km road circles the island but cross-island roads exist between Alofi and Lakepa, Alofi and Liku and Alofi and Hakupu. Considerable work has been done in recent years in improving the first two cross-island roads.

Vehicles. There were 999 registered motor vehicles at March 31, 1979, compared with 789 in 1976. Of these, 160 were classified as government vehicles and 839 privately-owned. There were 612 motor cycles compared with 497 in 1976.

NIUE — BUDGET FIGURES
(In $'000)

Year	Receipts	Expenditure	N.Z. Grants
1977/78	3,139	5,276	2,332
1978/79	2,985	5,363	3,161
1979/80	3,654	6,149	2,300
1980/81 (est.)	2,736	4,684	1,947

Overseas Airlines. Niue is served by Polynesian Airlines with three flights a week on the return leg of the Apia-Tonga-Niue-Apia route. The flight from Niue to Apia takes 1 hour 50 mins. An additional flight Apia-Niue-Rarotonga and return was introduced in 1978. Polynesian Airlines uses a Hawker-Siddeley 748 prop jet on the route. South Pacific Island Airways has a twice-weekly service from its base, Pago Pago, to Niue.

Local Airfield. Hanan international airport has a sealed runway of 1,647 m. It was completed in October 1970 and became fully operational for commercial air services in 1971. Proposals to extend the runway were being considered in mid-1980.

Port Facilities. The port of Alofi is an open roadstead. Vessels anchor offshore or cruise about off and on, and cargo is brought ashore by launches towing lighters through a natural passage in the reef that has been widened from time to time but on which coral is still encroaching. There is no alternative safe anchorage on the island but there are landings, of a sort, at Tuapa and Avatele.

In 1975 there were plans to widen the access channel of Alofi as well as undertake harbour development.

The Niue Island and Blue Water Yacht Club provides all facilities and a warm welcome to visiting yachtsmen.

Shipping Services. A four-weekly shipping service is operated by the New Zealand Shipping Corporation, from New Zealand to Niue and the Cook Islands.

COMMUNICATIONS. A single-line telephone system connects all villages on the island. A radio station is maintained by the government for overseas communication.

Radio. Broadcasts from Radio Niue, "Radio Sunshine" are made on a part-time basis, providing local and overseas news, notices, advertisements and light entertainment. Programmes are broadcast six mornings and evenings and five afternoons a week.

Newspaper. The island's weekly newspaper is "Tohi Tala Niue" which is published in English and Niuean by the Information Office of the Cental Office, Government of Niue.

WATER AND ELECTRICITY. There is no surface water, but pure drinking water is drawn from deep wells in the coral. An electrical power reticulation round the island was completed in 1977 and all 13 villages had been linked to the service.

PERSONALITIES

Hon. R. R. Rex, Premier, who is also Minister for Finance, Minister for Inland Revenue, including Customs and Trade, Minister of Transport (Shipping and Civil Aviation), Minister of Government Administration including Housing and Information Services, Minister of Police, Immigration and Emigration.

Hon Dr Enetama: Minister for Economic Developments, Minister for Education, Minister of Works, Minister of Justice, Lands and Survey including Local Affairs.

Hon. F. Lui, Minister of Agriculture including Forestry, Minister for Post Office and Minister for Tourism.

Hon R. R. Rex, Jnr, Minister for Health, Minister for Fisheries, Minister for Tele-communications and Minister for Youth, Cultural Affairs and Sports.

New Zealand Representative. T. Baker

Niue Tourist Board, Chairman. Hon. F. F. Lui

Secretary to Government. Terry M. Chapman

Financial Secretary, N. Verner

Director of Works, B. Waden

Registrar of Justice, S. Kalauni

Judge of High Court, Judge Sir Gaven Donne

Director of Education, H. Vilitama

Director of Agriculture, Morris H. Tafatu

Chief Officer of Police, S. Tohovaka

Director of Health, Dr H. Nemaia

Radio Superintendent, J. Gill

Postmaster, F. Ikimotu

BUSINESS DIRECTORY.

Burns Philp, Manager, Mr G. Chapman

R. R. Rex & Sons Ltd., Managing Director, Mr R. R. Rex

Niue Industries, Mr G. Cooper

General merchant, M. T. Nicholas

General merchant, Russel L. Kars

Niue Island Enterprises, Mr B. L. Nicholas

Village Restaurant, Manager, Mr R. R. Rex Jnr.

Polynesian Airlines, General Manager, Mr T. Bethan

HISTORY. A detailed archaeological survey was carried out on Niue in 1974 and the island is believed to have been inhabited for more than 1,000 years. The origin of the first migrants was probably Samoa or one of the islands of eastern Polynesia. A second migration, according to tradition, was a war expedition from Tonga about the beginning of the 16th century. A third, led by a Tongan chief of part-Niuean descent, resulted in the chief's assuming power over the whole island. Other contacts with Tonga seem to have been fairly frequent, and usually hostile.

Two distinct dialects are still spoken on Niue. One called Motu, meaning 'the people of the island', is used in the north. The other, Tafiti, meaning 'the strangers' or 'people from a distance', is used in the south. Tradition has it that the Tafiti district was more affected by Tongan immigrants than the other. The Niuean vocabulary generally resembles Tongan. However, it contains many words that are absent in Tongan but are common to Samoan, the eastern Polynesian languages, or both.

European Discovery. The European discoverer of Niue was Captain James Cook who made three landings on the west coast on June 20, 1774. Because of the fierce appearance and hostile conduct of the islanders, he called it Savage Island. This name persisted for more than a century, but has now fallen into disuse.

In 1830, two LMS missionaries, the Revs. John Williams and Charles Barff, called at the island in the 'Messenger of Peace' and tried to land two Polynesian teachers. They were repulsed. A similar thing happened in 1842. However, in 1846, the Revs. W. Gill and H. Nisbet landed a Niuean on the island who had lived in Samoa for some years and had been trained at the LMS seminary at Malua. This man, Peniamina, was eventually accepted by his people, and he persuaded them to allow a Samoan missionary, Paulo, to settle on the island in 1849. By 1852, between 200 and 300 Niueans had accepted Christianity; and by 1854, when the first books in Niuean were brought to the island from Samoa, heathenism had been virtually abandoned.

First resident Missionary. In 1861, the Rev. W. G. Lawes became the first resident English missionary. He was joined in 1868 by his brother, the Rev. F. E. Lawes, who remained on the island until his retirement in 1910. W. G. Lawes left in 1872. A census in 1861 revealed a population of 4,700, compared with the highest known figure of 5,070 in 1884 and a record low of 3,578 in 1979. However, during the second half of the 19th century, large numbers of able-bodied men were frequently absent from the island. Some never returned. In 1863, a Peruvian slaving vessel carried off about 130 men, most of whom died of disease in the Kermadecs. In 1868, the notorious 'Bully' Hayes kidnapped about 60 men and 30 women, and took them to Tahiti. Many others later went voluntarily to work on phosphate islands in the eastern Pacific. In 1899, for example, 561 Niueans were away.

The absence of so many men from the work-force retarded economic development, but there were some advances in this direction. In 1872, for example, 85,000 lb of hand-picked cotton was exported, as well as large quantities of arrowroot, coconut fibre and fungus. Trade was fostered by several Europeans who settled on the island. Among these was an Englishman, Henry Head, who was shipwrecked there in 1867. He married the high chief's daughter, had 15 children, and became the most influential person on the island, apart from the resident missionary.

A King elected. In 1876, the Niueans elected a king, Mataio Tuitoga. Under Head's influence, his successor, Fataaiki, petitioned Queen Victoria to take Niue under her protection. This, and similar requests in 1898 and 1899 were refused. But in April 1900, the Union Flag was hoisted over the island and a British official, Basil Thomson, declared it a British protectorate. (Thomson, later Sir Basil Thomson, who, in 1890, was Assistant Premier of Tonga later a magistrate in Fiji, head of the British Secret Service in World War I and after the war Governor of Dartmoor Prison in Devon.) British sovereignty was proclaimed on October 10, 1900, when the Earl of Ranfurly, Governor of New Zealand, visited the island.

Annexation. Niue was formally annexed to New Zealand as part of the Cook Islands in September 1901, and S. Percy Smith became the first government resident. The island was made a separate administration with its own resident commissioner and island council in 1904. Apart from occasional hurricanes, there were few outstanding events in the history of the island during the next 50 years.

One such was the murder of the resident commissioner, C. H. W. Larsen, in August, 1953.

Until 1960, there were no constitutional changes on Niue. Then the first Niue Assembly was established with an elected representative from each of the island's 13 villages, under the presidency of the resident commissioner. In 1966, some of the resident commissioner's powers were delegated to the Assembly following the introduction of the member system of government and the designation of Mr. R. R. Rex as leader of government business. Further constitutional advances were made in 1968 and 1972.

Self-government. Then, on October 19, 1974, Niue attained the status of 'self-government in free association with New Zealand' when the Niue Constitution Act 1974 came into force. This was exactly 74 years after the proclamation of British sovereignty. Celebrations to mark the occasion were attended by distinguished visitors from several Pacific Islands countries as well as New Zealand, Australia and the United Kingdom. Mr. R. R. Rex headed the first government as Premier, with a cabinet of three.

FOR THE TOURIST. The Niue Islands Hotel, overlooking Alofi Bay, opened in late 1974. The 40 bed hotel has a swimming pool and regular "island nights" and is just over a kilometre from the main shopping in Alofi. There is an early-morning market in Alofi, which should be visited before 7.30 a.m.

The island offers deep-sea fishing for tuna etc. as well as surprisingly clear water for skindiving and spearfishing over the reefs and pools. There are numerous limestone caves, some of them unexplored. Visits can be arranged to the juicing factory where limes and passionfruit are processed.

Archaeological Sites. Research excavations of ancient burial caves have been carried out by a New Zealand university, investigating bones found in limestone caves. For information on this survey see a publication entitled 'Niue Island Archaeological Survey'; Canterbury Museum (N.Z.) Bulletin Number 7, 1979, by Michael M. Trotter.

Further details of the island are available from the Niue Tourist Board.

NORFOLK ISLAND

Norfolk Island, a territory of Australia, is located at 29 deg. 02 min. S. latitude and 167 deg. 57 min. E. longitude. Its area is 34.5 sq. km and it is 1,676 km east-north-east of Sydney and 1,065 km north of Auckland. The resident population in a 1978 census was 1,698, including 460 persons holding temporary entry permits allowing them to reside on the island for six months.

Kingston, on the south coast, is the administrative centre and Burnt Pine, in the centre of the island, is the commercial and shopping centre. Local time is 11 hours 30 minutes ahead of GMT.

The Australian flag is flown, and "God Save Our Queen" is the anthem played at civic occasions. The island also has its own flag (a stylised Norfolk pine tree between two green bars) and a traditional choral work, the Pitcairn Anthem.

In addition to major Australian holidays which are observed on the island, Norfolk celebrates the anniversary of the arrival of the Pitcaimers on June 8, and Thanksgiving Day, usually on the last Wednesday in November.

THE PEOPLE. Norfolk Island is populated partly by the descendants of the 'Bounty' mutiny families, who moved there from Pitcairn Island in 1856, and partly by more recent settlers, mainly from Australia and New Zealand.

Migration is carefully controlled. Visitors may stay for 30 days without a written permit and may apply to stay an additional 30 days. Permits for longer stays are normally issued only to persons who have been employed to fill positions which residents are unable to fill. These permits expire after six months but may be renewed. No permits allowing outsiders to remain permanently on the island have been issued since 1974.

Ownership of land on the island carries no automatic residence rights with it.

By Australian law all persons born on Norfolk are Australian citizens, and travel under Australian passports.

In local parlance "Islanders" of Pitcairn descent are distinguished from "mainlanders" who have migrated to the island or are visiting there.

English is the official language. The Islanders speak their own language as well, called "Norfolk". It is evolved from Pitcairnese, a combination of ancient Tahitian and 18th century English.

A gradual influx of outsiders came to live on Norfolk following World War II, most of them adapting their former lifestyles to that of the Islanders. In more recent years, with increasing prosperity based on tourism, a "mainland" outlook and aspirations have begun displacing some of the older island ways. While more than half of Norfolk's 630 households produce at least some of their own food, only 157 of them are now on agricultural or pastoral land.

Religion. Resident clergymen conduct regular services in four Norfolk churches, the Church of England, Roman Catholic Church, Uniting Church in Australia, and the Seventh-day Adventist Church. Services are occasionally held in St. Barnabas Chapel, built when the Melanesian Mission was headquartered on Norfolk.

GOVERNMENT. The island has an Australian-appointed Administrator and a locally-elected Legislative Assembly.

The laws prevailing in Norfolk include certain Australian laws, which apply at the discretion of the Australian Parliament, and a range of local ordinances and acts governing essentially local matters. In any matters of law that are not covered either by Commonwealth or Norfolk laws, the English common law as it existed in 1828 applies.

Under the Norfolk Island Act 1979, Australia established the Norfolk Island Legislative Assembly and gave it executive and legislative authority in certain Island matters, mostly of a municipal nature. Enactments of the Assembly become law only when they have been assented to by the Administrator or by Australia's Governor-General.

Authority for larger-scale legislative and executive matters remains with the Commonwealth. Australia's present policy is to allow Norfolk to move toward self-government as a territory under the authority of Australia, and a review of the island's local powers is to be made by mid-1984.

The Commonwealth's executive powers over Norfolk are held by the Minister for Home Affairs. The resident Administrator represents the Commonwealth on the island, and is appointed by the Governor-General.

The Legislative Assembly consists of nine members elected for three-year terms, although the Administrator may direct that a new election be held at any time. The Assembly elects from its members a president and deputy president, and such executive ministers as it chooses to.

Day-to-day administration of the island's government is carried out by the Norfolk Island public service, which numbers about 140 persons. It is headed by a Chief Administrative Officer appointed by the Assembly, who is in effect the island manager.

Justice. The judicial system consists of a Supreme Court and a court of petty sessions. The Supreme Court is the highest judicial authority on the island and is a superior court of record with original, civil and criminal jurisdiction. Its two judges are not resident on the island. The court, other than in its criminal jurisdiction, may sit in NSW, Victoria or the Australian Capital Territory. Criminal cases are heard with juries.

The High Court of Australia has jurisdiction, with some exceptions, to hear and decide appeals from all judgments, decrees, orders and sentences of the Norfolk Island Supreme Court.

The jurisdiction of the court of petty sessions is exercised by a Chief Magistrate, or any three magistrates other than the Chief Magistrate. It deals with summary matters, civil and criminal. Appeals may be made to the Supreme Court against petty sessions decisions. The Chief Magistrate is stationed in Canberra and goes to the island when required.

Police. The approved full-time police establishment is one sergeant and two constables, seconded from Australia; with assistance from part-time local special constables when required.

The incidence of crime is low. Most matters dealt with in the Norfolk court of petty sessions are for traffic breaches. The island has no real gaol.

Liquor. A three-man Liquor Licensing Board hears applications for licences to serve liquor in hotels, guest houses or restaurants. Bars normally trade till 10 pm, but may get licences for later closing on special occasions. All liquor is imported by the Administration, which supplies it in bottles to individual purchasers or licence holders through the island's bond store between set hours. The Administration applies import duty, and other charges, to liquor sales, and also levies licence fees.

EDUCATION. Education is free and compulsory for all children between six and 15. The Norfolk Island Central School follows the NSW system of education, and teaches to Form IV, or 10th year level.

The New South Wales State Education Department, under an agreement between the Australian Government and NSW, seconds the teaching staff at Norfolk Island's expense. The Administration is responsible for maintenance and construction of buildings.

In August 1977, school enrolments were: Infant, 104; primary, 100; secondary, 100.

Administration bursaries are available for pupils wanting higher school or tertiary education on the mainland, and trainee scholarships are available for school leavers who want to take up technical training.

LABOUR AND SOCIAL SERVICE. For many years a system of "public work" required male residents to offer their labour free for work on the roads, or for other public work, for a certain number of days per year, or pay a set sum in lieu. The system developed from the early Pitcairn origins of the island people. In 1976 this option was replaced, and residents who are in employment and over the age of 18 now pay a twice yearly "public works levy", which in fact is a personal tax.

Australia's social services system of pensions, endowments and other benefits does not apply on Norfolk Island, although some residents do benefit from it, having qualified in Australia before migrating to the island. Volunteer organisations and the local government provide a range of help for residents in need, including weekly cash payments and free medical and hospital care. Burials and funeral services are free for everyone. There is virtually no unemployment on Norfolk Island and severe poverty is unknown.

HEALTH. Norfolk Island Public Hospital is under the control of a medical superintendent who is also the island's Government Medical Officer. The hospital is administered by a local board, which sets fees for medical and hospital services. The hospital is also supported by a subsidy from the island's revenues.

Hospital and medical services are free to certain classes of residents, notably the old or invalid.

There are 17 beds in the hospital, which handles both major and minor operations. Specialists from Australia and New Zealand visit the hospital.

A district nursing service operates under the supervision of the medical superintendent. The Administration meets the cost of this service.

The Government Dental Officer provides a free dental service for children and expectant mothers.

THE LAND. Norfolk Island is of volcanic origin, about 8 km by 5 km with an area of 3,455 ha.

The coastline of 32 km consists chiefly of high cliffs, but the land slopes down to the sea at one small area in the south side, where Kingston is situated, on Sydney Bay. Average elevation of the island is 110 m. Two peaks, Mt Pitt and Mt Bates, rise to about 305 metres on the north-west corner of the island. There is a large number of small streams.

Within sight of the southern shore are two small islands, both uninhabited. Nepean, the smallest and closest, is about 31 m high. Philip Island, 6 km from shore, has an altitude of 280 m.

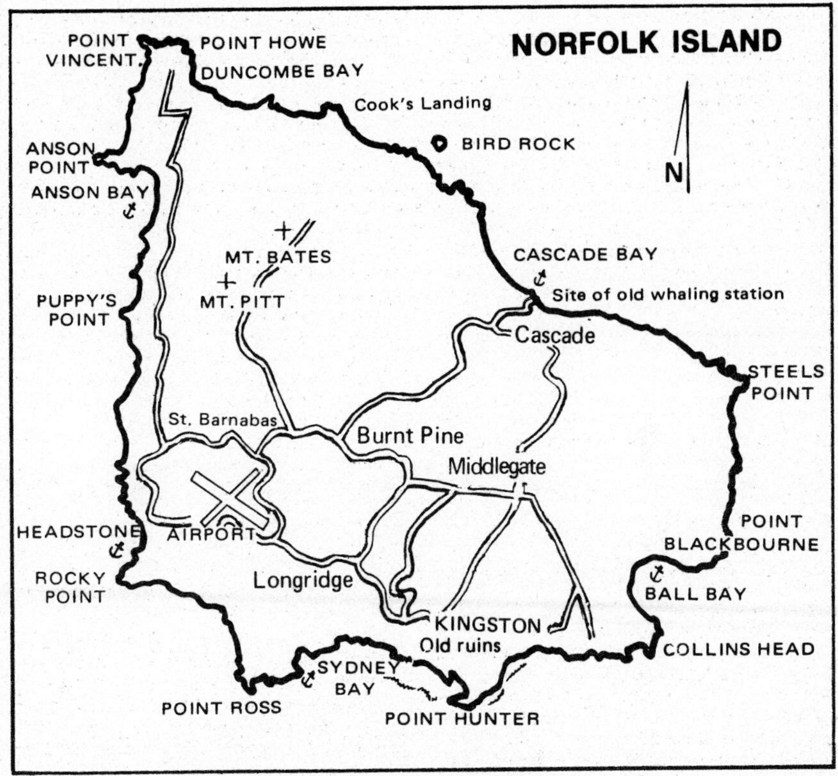

Climate. The climate is mild and sub-tropical. The average daily maximum temperature during the year varies from 15.8 deg. C to 26.5 deg. C, and the average daily minimum from 11 deg. C to 23.4 deg. C. The annual average rainfall is about 1,320 mm, fairly well distributed.

The climate is suitable for cultivating a variety of crops, and for grazing. The volcanic soil is friable and chemically rich. Restrictions are imposed by the limited land area, the steep terrain, the porosity of the soil and the depth of any basic water table. The top soil too is well drained. Water for irrigation and for stock is drawn from streams and subterranean sources.

Flora and fauna. The stately Norfolk Island pine *(Araucaria heterophylla)* which is endemic to the island grows to a height of 55 m and has been exported to many countries. A flowering white oak, its growth often shaped by the wind, is prevalent. The seed of Kentia palms form a small commercial crop. A sub-tropical rainforest on Mt Pitt includes palms and giant ferns. Introduced kikuyu grass covers many slopes, while various ornamental shrubs and trees have also been introduced. They include hibiscus, wild lemon, macadamia nut, red and yellow guava and avocado trees.

The island has no reptiles and no spiders dangerous to man but its insect population includes many varieties of butterflies and moths. There are 55 species of birds including white terns, vivid parrots and the endemic and rare green parrot. Philip Island, now almost denuded of vegetation by a colony of introduced rabbits, is a major nesting location for sea birds.

Land tenure. Of the total area of 3,455 ha, about 1,700 ha are held on freehold, 1,010 ha are Crown leasehold and 745 ha are designated roads, commons and public reserves.

The present system of land tenure was developed directly from the system established when the Pitcairn Islanders were settled on Norfolk Island in 1856, when the head of each family was granted a 20 ha block, or a 10 ha block was granted to males on marriage after settlement. The descendants of the original grantees sub-divided the freeholds many times, and thus many of the present small holdings are suitable only for residential or purely commercial non-agricultural uses.

Freehold land may still be purchased, but there are controls over sub-division.

Lands not granted to the original Pitcairn Island settlers and their descendants were at the time set aside as public reserves and commons. Most commons are now used for grazing and afforestation. Crown leases are used for grazing, agriculture and housing.

Under the Norfolk Island Act 1979, Australia retains full control over land policies and Crown land usage. Leases of Crown land, at moderate rentals for 28-year periods, are available or transferable only to residents.

PRIMARY PRODUCTION. Fragmentary subdivision of land hampers its use for commercially viable agriculture. Farming is generally a part-time occupation.

Supplies of local beef, poultry and eggs are inadequate for the island's needs, but commercial market gardening and poultry production have both expanded as the important tourist industry continues to develop. Development costs are high.

For export, the island produces seed from Norfolk pines and small quantities of avocados.

Although big catches of fish may be made in the surrounding sea, the establishment of a large-scale fishing industry is inhibited by the vagaries of the weather and lack of a harbour. Fishing boats are limited to a size which can be lifted by crane and moved by trailer. Trumpeter, kingfish, trevally, snapper and hapuku are most commonly caught, and sold locally.

Hardwoods from natural forests are negligible. Softwood from the Norfolk Island pine, the only local timber used for building, is now limited. A programme for the cultivation of eucalyptus and Norfolk Island pine on government reserves is being pursued.

TOURISM. During 1978-79, 21,000 tourists visited the island more than half from Australia and the rest mainly from New Zealand. Their average stay was just under 10 days. The number of visitors on the island varies from about 200 in "winter" to about 1,200 in the mid-summer peak.

Tourism is Norfolk Island's principal economic support. Visitors are attracted by the island's historic colonial buildings and ruins, scenery, peaceful atmosphere and low-duty shopping. In 1977-78, tourism brought about $9 million into Norfolk's economy, allowing the island to have a favourable balance of trade in its dealings with the outside world.

LOCAL COMMERCE. Because of its remoteness, small size and lack of a harbour, Norfolk Island was for generations unable to develop any significant, steady local industry until increased tourism was made possible by the construction of an airstrip during World War II. Tourism has brought Norfolk a level of prosperity which is unusual among the Pacific Islands, with local disposable annual income per capita of $7,421 in 1977-78.

Various small industries have flourished for a time and then waned, including whaling, bananas, bean seeds and passionfruit. Efforts to develop new industries are made from time to time despite the lack of need for new jobs. A pilot development of growing cut flowers for Australian and other overseas markets was started in 1979.

For several years starting in the late 1960s the island attracted some notoriety as a tax haven for Australians, and there was a boom in the registration of newly-formed companies. Changes in Australian law and closer attention from the Australian tax authorities brought the boom to an abrupt end in 1973.

OVERSEAS TRADE. A special aspect of Norfolk's economy is that a large quantity of the island's imports are "invisible exports" comprising cameras, radios, watches, jewellery, musical instruments and liquor etc, which enter the island at a low rate of Customs duty and are sold to tourists returning to higher duty areas, mainly to Australia and New Zealand.

The value of imports and exports in recent years has been:

Year	Imports $	Exports $
1970-71	3,678,270	278,599
1971-72	3,905,606	385,536
1972-73	4,719,161	475,002
1973-74	6,107,751	542,558
1974-75	6,172,174	621,017
1975-76	6,472,200	602,628
1976-77	6,930,456	800,912
1977-78	7,773,537	933,087
1978-79	8,986,898	1,168,347

Sources of imports in 1978-79 were:

Australia & Pacific Islands	$4,248,979
New Zealand	1,266,537
Asia	1,781,099
Europe	1,690,283

Exports in 1978-79 went to:

Australia & Pacific Islands	$567,385
New Zealand	346,621
Asia	16,333
Europe	238,008

Main imports in 1978-79 were:

Drapery and piece goods $1,076,974; motor vehicles, $585,397; beer, wine & spirits $509,054; jewellery $490,773; footwear $481,103; fancy goods $425,727; building materials $410,147; groceries $374,012; musical accessories $239,023; photographic goods $235,583; watches $226,687; cosmetics $205,236.

Customs. Norfolk Island has its own customs law, the island being outside Australian customs. Duties are levied on a wide range of goods, mostly at 5 per cent, though motor vehicles attract 15 per cent duty and clocks and watches 17 per cent. Customs officials attend the arrival of ships and aircraft and make such inspections as they feel are necessary. The import of fruit is prohibited because the island is free of fruit-fly. Passengers' effects of a normal nature are duty-free.

FINANCE. Norfolk Island is a separate and distinct financial entity, expected to support itself without any grants or aid from Australia. The Commonwealth pays for its own direct operations on the island, including the salaries of the Administrator and his staff of some four persons, the cost of operating the Australian-owned airport on the island, and the expense of a programme of restoring and maintaining historic Crown buildings in Kingston. In recent years Australia has also provided Norfolk with an increasing range of technical assistance and expert advice in conservation, quarantine and health, and other administrative matters.

Norfolk Island's own public revenues in the financial year ended June 30, 1979, were $2,283,951. Administration expenditures were $2,109,315, leaving a surplus for the year of $174,636. This was added to the island's Revenue Fund of surpluses from past years, which totalled $915,394 at the year's end.

The principal sources of revenue during the year were the sale of Norfolk postage stamps, $613,152; customs duties, $566,233; income from the Administration's monopoly on importing beer, wine and spirits, $285,017; company fees, $186,622.

Administrative expenses were the largest item of expenditure at $786,209, followed by the cost of the island's school, $321,923; repairs and maintenance of roads, buildings and other plant, $302,459; health and social welfare services, $275,180. Capital expenditures, charged fully as expense in the year in which they are made, were $252,043.

In August, 1979, the new Legislative Assembly assumed responsibility for the island's budget. It expected Norfolk's revenues to remain at the level of the previous year, but budgeted for higher expenditure and expected a deficit for the 1979-80 year of about $300,000. Additional sources of revenue, to balance the budget once again, were being examined.

Taxes. Norfolk Island has no income tax, death duties, property tax or stamp duties. There is a "public works levy" on residents, in reality a personal tax (see Labour and Social Service), a $2 departure fee for visitors, and an absentee landowner's tax.

Currency. The legal currency is Australian bank notes and coins.

Banks. The Bank of N.S.W. and the Commonwealth Bank of Australia have full-service branches on the island. Major international credit cards are honoured by many shops and restaurants, many of which also accept Australian or New Zealand cheques.

TRANSPORT. The island has about 80 km of roads, all of which except for about 8 km may be used by motor vehicles. About 48 km of roads are sealed. The rest are either earth-formed or coral surfaced.

There were 1,872 vehicles registered at June 30, 1979. Of these, cars, trucks, utilities, tractors, numbered 1,562; motor-cycles and scooters, 201; buses, 8; trailers, 52; and Administration vehicles, 49.

A private bus service operates between some hotels, the shopping centre and the beach at Kingston. There are hire services for motor cars, bikes and scooters. Bus tours of the island are provided for visitors.

Aviation. The airport is controlled by the Australian Department of Transport. There are two runways, one about 1,700 m, grass surfaced, and the other about 1,550 m, coral surfaced. East West Airlines, with Fokker Friendship F27-500s, provides services from Sydney. Air New Zealand, with a Fokker Friendship F27, operates from Auckland. Both airlines provide extra flights during holiday periods. Norfolk Island Airlines, owned on the island, operates four Beech King Air aircraft to Brisbane and Lord Howe Island and has a marketing link with Ansett Airlines of Australia.

Upgrading of the airport to accommodate medium-sized jets such as the Fokker F-28 or the BA 146 was approved by the Australian government late in 1979. The work is expected to take more than a year to complete. It will not involve any runway extensions beyond the existing airport boundaries.

Regular shipping services to Norfolk Island are provided from Australia and New Zealand by Compagnie des Chargeurs Caledoniens. Because there is no harbour where ships can berth, ships must stand off, and all cargo and passengers are carried between ship and shore by lighter, operated by the Administration. Loading jetties are at Kingston in the south, and Cascade, in the north. The weather and state of the sea determine which jetty is used.

The difficulties of sea access are one reason why development costs on the island are high. There are limits on what may be carried by sea and by air.

Various investigations have been made over the years about the possibility of building a harbour, but they have come to nothing largely because of the high costs likely to be involved.

COMMUNICATIONS. The automatic telephone exchange has a capacity of 400 lines. There is an international telephone service, connected to Sydney via radio link, and telephone calls may be made to most overseas countries and to ships at sea.

Plans for a proposed new trans-Pacific cable being considered by Australia include a repeater station on Norfolk, from which direct lines would run to Fiji and North America, Australia, and New Zealand. If the plan is carried out, it would give the island all-weather telephone and telex cable connections with the rest of the world, replacing the present radio link to Sydney, probably in 1984.

Overseas Telecommunications Commission (Australia) provides an overseas telegram service. OTC also provides an "on demand" coast radio station for shipping by radio telephone.

The Department of Transport and the local meteorological office of the Department of Science have radio communication with Australia. The Department of Transport also operates a medium-frequency non-directional beacon service, call sign NF with a range of 725 km, a high-frequency point-to-point communication service, and a very high-frequency air-ground-air service.

The Administration operates a radio transmitter for local broadcasts, providing about 85 hours a week of regular programmes of news, announcements and music.

There are two news publications, "The Norfolk Islander", published weekly, and the "Norfolk Island News", published monthly. The official "Norfolk Island Government Gazette" is produced weekly, or as the occasion demands.

WATER AND ELECTRICITY. There is no public water supply or sewage disposal. Water is available from roof catchments or wells and bores. The Australian Department of Transport operates the power station and 240v power is distributed by the Administration. It is available to most parts of the island.

PERSONALITIES

Administrator: Mr W. P. Coleman
Official Secretary: Mr. I. Hutchinson
Chief Minister and President of the Legislative Assembly: D. E. Buffett
Deputy Chief Minister and Deputy President of the Legislative Assembly: W. A. Blucher
Chief Administrative Officer: Mr Malcolm Bains
Medical Officer: Dr M. F. H. Sexton
Members of the Legislative Assembly: (elected July 1979 for three years): David Buffett, William Blucher, Ed Howard, Gilbert Jackson, Bruce MacKenzie, Duncan McIntyre, Bryan Nunn, John Ryves, Kevin Williams.

HISTORY. Norfolk Island is the second oldest British settlement in the South Seas, having been occupied within a few weeks of the first British settlement at what is now Sydney in 1788. It is the oldest of Australia's external territories.

Its European discoverer was Captain James Cook, on October 10, 1774 who landed at Duncombe Bay, where today a monument stands. He found the island uninhabited. He took possession of it for Britain and named it Norfolk Isle, "after the noble family of Howard", to which the Duke of Norfolk belonged. Little is known of the island's previous history, although there is evidence that it may have been inhabited for a brief period in earlier times.

Cook was impressed by the Norfolk Island pines and the wild flax plant growing in abundance, and felt the British Navy could use them for spars and masts, and for sail-making. As a result of his report, Captain Arthur Phillip some years later was instructed to send a detachment to occupy the island after having established a British colony in New South Wales. The Sydney colony was established on January 26, 1788, and on February 14 the armed tender 'Supply', carrying Lieut. Philip Gidley King and commanded by Lieut. Henry Lidgbird Ball, and with a party of convicts set sail for Norfolk. They came ashore in what is now the Kingston area on March 6, 1788, after some difficulty finding a suitable landing site. King had been appointed Superintendent and Commandant of Norfolk.

First Settlement. As it happened, the timber and the flax were unsuited to the navy's needs, and the early days of settlement were difficult, especially because of the amount of heavy clearing that had to be done before crops could be planted. This period has become known as the First Settlement.

Lieut. King spent two terms on the island, and when he left in 1796 the settlement was still a developing community of nearly 900 people with many public buildings. By 1804 the population, both settlers and convicts, had reached 1100 and by 1810 over a quarter of the island had been cleared.

But the long sea connection to Sydney, and the general difficulties and expense of keeping the Norfolk Island settlement going (it was never self-supporting and it lacked a harbour) resulted in the settlement gradually being run down and abandoned. Some of the people were moved to Van Diemen's Land (Tasmania). The last inhabitants left in 1814, and the island was deserted for the next 11 years, apart from occasional calls by whalers and other seamen.

Second Settlement. On June 6, 1825, Captain Turton, of the 40th Regiment, with a detachment of soldiers and convicts, landed at Kingston to begin the Second Settlement.

This was a penal settlement, and the prisoners were the worst of those from the gaols of New South Wales and Tasmania, usually those convicted of further offences, or considered intractable. The island prison was officially described as being meant as "a place of the extremest punishment, short of death". No private settlers were allowed. The many stories of brutality and sometimes rebellion date from this period. "I wish it to be understood that the felon who is sent there is for ever excluded from all hope of return," wrote Governor Brisbane of NSW.

There were both mild and harsh periods of this Second Settlement, but generally, during this time, Norfolk Island deservedly earned itself the name of "Hell on earth". Rumours of brutality and inhumane treatment continually reached the mainland, and there was growing agitation in some quarters to have the penal settlement closed. But the decision to cease using Norfolk Island as a penal colony was not made until 1852, and the last of the convicts did not leave until 1856.

The colonial stone buildings standing today date from this harsh Second Settlement. They were convict-built in local stone and consist of houses, gaols (these are mostly razed), stores, military barracks, a mill, grain silos, bridges and the fine old Government House. Settlements were made at Kingston, Cascade and Longridge, and joined by an extensive road system. (There are no buildings remaining of the First Settlement, as these were mainly built in timber, or in stone later used to build the Second Settlement.)

Pitcairners arrive. Meanwhile the people of Pitcairn Island had been looking for a new home. Most of the population in this small island east of Tahiti were descendants of the mutineers of the 'Bounty', who had scuttled their ship and hidden on the island in 1790. Their population was increasing on Pitcairn, and it was feared they would become short of land. One attempt at wholesale immigration, to Tahiti in 1831, had proved a failure, and they felt strongly that if they were compelled to immigrate a second time it should be to an uninhabited island.

The entire population of Pitcairn, 194 persons, landed on Norfolk from the 'Morayshire' on June 8, 1856 (the date is observed today as Bounty Day or Anniversary Day). Those few prisoners remaining on Norfolk Island had gone by the end of the month.

For the benefit of the Pitcairners, the island was created a "distinct and separate settlement" on June 24, 1856. The governor of New South Wales was appointed Governor of Norfolk Island as well, but his powers were limited to acting as a link between the island and the British Crown. The Pitcairners established the same kind of land tenure and community disciplines they had had at home, and these have left an indelible mark that can still be observed on Norfolk.

Some of the island's governors, notably Sir William Denison (1856-61), Sir John Young, (1861-67) and Viscount Hampden (1895-97) exceeded the limitations that Britain had placed on their powers concerning Norfolk Island. This was resented by many islanders and two small groups of families (possibly motivated by homesickness too) returned to Pitcairn in 1858 and 1863, leaving the majority of the Pitcairners to settle peacefully on Norfolk, where the old 'Bounty' names of Quintal, Young, Adams, Christian and McCoy are still prominent.

Melanesian Mission. The Melanesian Mission established a missionary training school, and headquarters for the Bishop of Melanesia, on the island in October 1866, after having been granted, free, by the British Government 99 acres of land and purchasing a further 933 acres. The station was named St Barnabas, on whose feast day the site was selected. The beautiful St Barnabas Chapel was completed in 1880. From this base on Norfolk Island the mission did important work in taking Christianity to the islands in the Western Pacific until 1920, when mission headquarters was moved north to the Solomon Islands and Norfolk affairs terminated.

Further political developments. During the 1880s, Sydney-based Governors of Norfolk became concerned at the island's resistance to outside authority, its inability to develop commercial trade, and its unwillingness to enforce strict standards of law and propriety. In 1896, Governor Viscount Hampden proclaimed the end of the islanders' right to govern themselves, and sent an appointed Chief Magistrate to administer the island.

Although the islanders protested, the British government upheld the Governor's action, and in 1897 Norfolk became a dependency of New South Wales, although legally remaining a distinct and separate colony. In 1914, again over the protests of many on the island, a British Order in Council placed Norfolk under the authority of the Commonwealth of Australia. Annexation to Australia, which had been discussed in 1897, has never been carried out.

From 1897 until 1979, various forms of locally-elected representative bodies were established on the island by Australia, but were given little more than advisory powers. During those eight decades the island developed what has been called "a rich history of disputation" with Australian authorities. This has included Royal Commissions, delegations of protest, petitions to English monarchs, numerous inquiries, and approaches to the United Nations.

The most exhaustive inquiry was conducted in 1975-76 by Sir John Nimmo, a judge of the Australian Industrial Court, and former Chief Justice of Fiji. His report was tabled in the Australian Parliament in November 1976.

Royal Commission. The Nimmo Report made 74 recommendations on a wide range of topics. Its essential four proposals were that Norfolk Island should be integrated into the Australian political system of laws, social benefits and taxes, with the island becoming part of the electorate of Canberra. It recommended against holding a local referendum on the island's future status, saying that if Australia is to be responsible for Norfolk Island's financial affairs, Australia should determine its form of government.

The report precipitated intense controversy. The eight elected members of the Norfolk Island Council unanimously opposed the proposal that the island should lose its separate political status and, in February 1977, acting as private citizens, they appealed to the United Nations to protect Norfolk Island from being integrated into Australia without the consent of the electors. A petition signed by 158 residents favouring the Nimmo Report was cited by the Australian Minister for Administrative services as an indication of feelings on the island. The petition was countered by more than 600 signed "solemn declarations" from more than two-thirds of

Norfolk Island's electors who supported the local council and wanted separate status to continue.

In May 1978, the Australian Minister for Home Affairs, Mr R.J. Ellicott, announced that the government had decided that Norfolk Island did not have to be governed by the same laws that apply in the rest of Australia. While insisting that the island was part of Australia, he said the government was prepared to see whether a form of self-government could be developed, with Norfolk taking responsibility for its own finances and controlling a range of municipal matters. In discussion with the council he said that the proposed new arrangements would operate on a basis of consensus between the island and the Commonwealth, but that self-determination for the island was out of the question.

The new administrative arrangements were embodied in the Norfolk Island Act 1979, which was passed by the Australian Parliament in May of that year. It created the Legislative Assembly, which has the right to introduce legislation on almost any subject related to Norfolk. its legislation does not become law unless approved by Australian authorities. The Assembly's powers are to be reviewed, and possibly increased, within five years.

The election of the first Assembly was affected by Australia's requirement that Norfolk's traditional first-past-the-post voting system be changed to one of proportional representation. The election was based on the new system despite bitter objections from the council, and despite the imminence of a referendum on the issue which had been petitioned by electors. The referendum, held some five months later, rejected the proportional method by a 58%-42% vote and led to controversy about whether the Assembly membership should submit themselves for re-election under the traditional voting system.

NORFOLK AND THE PACIFIC. The Pitcairners, who came into existence as a people because of the mutiny on the "Bounty", were for generations an inward-looking race, secluding themselves from the outside world. In recent years, however, they have begun reaching out to re-establish their ancestral connections with other Pacific islands. In 1979, the island sent its first team to participate in the South Pacific Games at Suva, where it won several medals. Later that year Norfolk's Chief Minister attended the South Pacific Conference at Tahiti, and was warmly welcomed as the island's first representative there. While he took part only as an adviser to the Australian delegation, it appeared likely that Norfolk would be attending future conferences in its own right.

Further reading: Merval Hoare, 'Norfolk Island: An Outline of Its History 1774-1968', Brisbane, 1969; Merval Hoare, 'Rambler's Guide to Norfolk Island', Sydney, 1965 and subsequent revised editions (this booklet, containing many maps, describes in detail the various places of historic interest on the island); R. Nixon Dalkin, 'Colonial Era Cemetery of Norfolk Island', Sydney, 1974 (contains chart, inscriptions and notes on the burials in Kingston cemetery); Philip Cox and Wesley Stacey, 'Building Norfolk Island', Sydney, 1971 (photographs, plans and charts, showing the architectural development of the island during its various periods).

FOR THE TOURIST. Casual clothing is the general rule. Warmer, but not heavy clothing, is needed for June, July and August. Visitors need stout shoes, a raincoat and an electric torch (there is only one street light).

There is a variety of activity on the island, including swimming, scuba-diving, fishing, walking, horseriding, and all manner of sports. The island's historic buildings offer the greatest fascination for visitors, and much work has been done in recent years in restoring or preserving them.

Visitors, whether arriving by ship or air, pay a government "visiting fee" of $2 a person, which is collected on departure.

Entry requirements. Australian and New Zealand citizens require onward or return tickets. Visitors from elsewhere must have any necessary visas. There are no special health requirements.

Sightseeing. Things of interest on the island include: a tour of Kingston, where most of the prisons and administrative buildings of the penal days stood. Some of these buildings have been restored, and all are of great historic interest. Nearby is the old cemetery, with its early tombstones, many of these marking the graves of convicts.

The Melanesian Mission area, on the Uplands was once a thriving settlement, but little remains now but the attractive vicarage and the beautiful old St. Barnabas Chapel. Nearby is the old mission cemetery not now in use.

Near the airport can be found the remnants of beautiful old Pine Avenue, and remnants of a small convict settlement identified by nothing more than stone arches.

There are superb views of the island after an easy climb of Mt Pitt and Mt Bates.

There is accommodation for more than 1,000 visitors at any one time in licensed hotels, motels, guest houses and self-contained flats.

ACCOMMODATION

AUNT EM'S ISLAND HOME — twin or single standard, twin or double ensuite.

BLIGHT COURT — twin units.

BOUNTY LODGE — twin or single units.

BUMBORA APARTMENTS — twin or single units.

CASCADE GARDENS — double or twin units.

CASTAWAY HOTEL (licensed) — multiple, double, single ensuite or executive; dinner/bed/breakfast.

CHANNERS CORNER — double or twin units.

COLONY LODGE — double or twin units.

CREST APARTMENTS — double or twin.

DOLPHIN INN — double, twin or studio-type units.

FLETCHER CHRISTIAN — double or twin.

HIBISCUS APARTMENTS — double or twin units.

HIGHLAND AIRTEL — double or twin ensuite; dinner/bed/breakfast.

HILLCREST HOTEL (licensed) — multiple, double, single or penthouse.

HOTEL NORFOLK (licensed) — double or single ensuite, double or twin deluxe; dinner/bed/breakfast.

ISLANDER LODGE — double or twin.

MOKUTU INN (licensed) — double, twin or single ensuite, dinner/bed/breakfast included.

MORNING-SIDE FLATS — double or twin.

NOBBS APARTMENTS — double or twin.

NORFOLK WHITE HERON (licensed) — double, twin or triple ensuite; dinner/bed/breakfast.

PAMS PLACE — double or twin units.

PANORAMA COURT — double or twin units.

PARADISE HOTEL (licensed) — double or twin standard or ensuite; all meals included.

PINE VALLEY APARTMENTS — double or twin units.

POLYNESIAN MOTOR HOTEL (licensed) — double or twin ensuite; dinner/bed/breakfast.

PONDEROSA — double or twin.

SOUTH PACIFIC HOTEL (licensed) — single, double, twin or triple ensuite, deluxe twin or double; dinner, bed, breakfast.

SUNHAVEN COUNTRY LODGE — double or twin standard or ensuite; all meals.

SIANANAS ISLAND HOME — double or twin ensuite or standard; dinner/bed/breakfast included.

VILLAS — double or twin units.

NORTHERN MARIANA ISLANDS

The Northern Marianas are a chain of 16 islands extending for some 480 km from north to south, the main island, Saipan, is towards the south of the group, at 15 deg. 12 min. N. lat. and 145 deg. 43 min. E. long.

The 16 islands include a group of three tiny islands known collectively as Maug. The islands in the group from north to south are Farallon de Pajaros, Maug, Asuncion, Agrihan, Pagan, Alamagan, Guguan, Sarigan, Anatahan, Farallon de Medinilla, Saipan, Tinian, Agiguan and Rota.

Their total land surface is approximately 471 sq. km. The three principal islands, Saipan (122 sq km), Tinian (101 sq km) and Rota (83 sq km) form two-thirds of the land area of the group. Only these three and the islands of Alamagan, Agrihan and Pagan are inhabited.

The population at the last census, 1973, was 14,335, with 12,366 people living on Saipan, 1,104 on Rota and 714 on Tinian, the remainder being on the islands of Alamagan, Agrihan and Pagan. The estimated population in mid-1978 was 14,850. Projections give a total population in 1980 of 15,970, in 1985 of 19,360, in 1990 of 23,320 and in 2000 of 33,130.

The people are divided into two main communities – three quarters of the population are Chamorro, descendants of the indigenous Mariana people, and the remainder are Carolinians, descendants of people originally from the Eastern Carolines who migrated during the 19th century.

In the interim, before the political union of the United States and the Northern Marianas is complete, the people are 'temporary citizens' of the United States but still carry the Trust Territory passport.

It is estimated that the Chamorros in the Northern Marianas and Guam number 60,000.

The Northern Marianas is now a Commonwealth in association with the United States, but until, the termination of the UN Trusteeship Agreement, scheduled for 1981, the territory is still, technically, part of the Trust Territory of the Pacific Islands, as is the remainder, the Marshalls and the Carolines, which have also changed their political status. Therefore, some of the Marianas statistics and history are to be found under the Trust Territory of the Pacific Islands section in this edition of the Year Book, as separate statistics have not been available.

On June 17, 1975, 78 per cent of the people of the Northern Marianas voted to become a Commonwealth of the United States rather than continuing with the Carolines and Marshalls in the Trusteeship, and on March 24, 1976, US President Ford signed the commonwealth covenant giving the Marianas internal self government, with the United States controlling defence and foreign relations with the right to maintain military bases in the territory. The new Constitution came into effect on January 9, 1978, the voters having, in December, 1977, elected a governor, lieutenant-governor and members of a bicameral legislature for the new government.

Elections. In the first elections in the new commonwealth, in December, 1977, Carlos S. Camacho, a public health physician and a former Member of the Congress of Micronesia, was elected as the first governor, with Francisco C. Ada, former executive officer to the Resident commissioner, Erwin D. Canham, as the lieutenant-governor.

EMPLOYMENT. As is the case in many developing countries, the government is the largest employer of labour in the Northern Marianas. When the territory became a commonwealth, it was decided to move the Trust Territory Government headquarters to Ponape but at the end of 1979, only the financial audit department had gone to Kolonia. Consequently, Marianas people continued to work for the Trust Territory Government. In 1977, of the 7,007 people working in the territory, 1,411 were employed by the T.T. government, 1,716 by the district legislature and 200 with government agencies. General merchandising employed 773, hotels and other catering services 733, construction companies 714 and transportation and stevedoring 323. Wages paid in 1977 totalled $US25,695,864, the T.T. government's share being $US8,015,710, and the

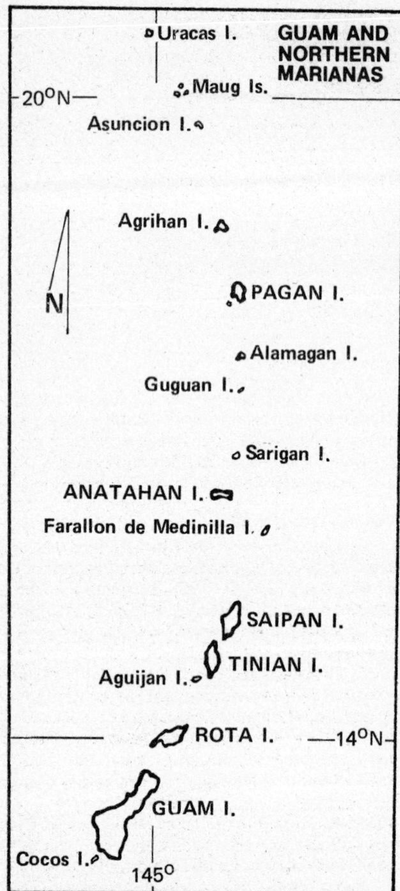

district legislature $6,998,092.

Efforts are being made to develop a maritime industry and manufacturing but there is a shortage of intensive labour.

The minimum wage in 1979 was $1.35 an hour. At December 31, 1978, there were 1,726 expatriates working in the country, 1,344 of them from the Philippines and 235 from Japan.

TAXATION. The Legislature established an income tax system in 1978 in accordance with its new political status as a commonwealth separated from the rest of the Trust Territory.

Tax is not payable on incomes of less than $5,000 a year. The wage and salary tax rates are:

"(a) Not over $5,000, No tax.

"(b) Over $5,000 but not over $7,000, 3% of amount over $5,000.

"(c) Over $7,000 but not over $15,000, tax computed in accordance with (b) plus 4% of amount over $7,000.

"(d) Over $15,000 but not over $22,000, tax computed in accordance with (b) and (c) plus 5% of amount over $15,000.

"(e) Over $22,000, tax computed in accordance with (b), (c) and (d) plus 6% of amount over $22,000."

Tax rates on gross revenue from business operations are:

"(a) Not over $5,000, No tax.

"(b) Over $5,000 but not over $50,000, 1% of amount over $5,000.

"(c) Over $50,000 but not over $100,000, tax computed in accordance with (b) plus 2% of amount over $50,000.

"(d) Over $100,000 but not over $250,000, tax computed in accordance with (b) and (c) plus 3% of amount over $100,000.

"(e) Over $250,000 but not over $500,000, tax computed in accordance with (b), (c) and (d) plus 4% of amount over $250,000."

"(f) Over $500,000, tax computed in accordance with (b), (c), (d) and (e) plus 5% of amount over $500,000."

SHIPPING. Most of the cargoes for the Northern Marianas are transshipped at Guam but Nauru Pacific Line operates a regular container service from Melbourne to Saipan via Majuro, Kosrae, Ponape, Truk and Guam. Kyowa Shipping Ltd. operates monthly services from Hong Kong and Far Eastern ports to Guam and Saipan, while Nauru Pacific has a regular conventional/container and passenger service from San Francisco and Honolulu to Saipan via Majuro, Ponape and Truk. The Philippines, Micronesia and Orient Navigation Co. (PM&O Lines) operates a regular container service on self-sustained ships with ro-ro capabilities from the United States through Honolulu to Saipan via Majuro, Kosrae, Ponape and Truk. Cargoes reaching the Marianas in 1978 totalled 53,640 revenue tons, only 8,669 tons being loaded in the Marianas for other ports.

TOURISM. The Northern Marianas saw much of the fighting in the Pacific War and because of the existence of so many battlegrounds and other relics of the Japanese presence, the Marianas is planning to develop its tourist industry. Already the country attracts more than twice the number of tourists visiting the rest of Micronesia. In 1977, 58,103 visitors came to the Marianas compared with 22,260 visiting the rest of the Trust Territories. Of the total, 33,396 were from Japan and 21, 744 from the United States. In 1978, there were 91,372 visitors of whom 62,189 were from Japan and 26,288 from the United States.

PERSONALITIES

Governor: Carlos S. Camacho
Lieutenant-Governor: Francisco C. Ada
Attorney-General: Vacant

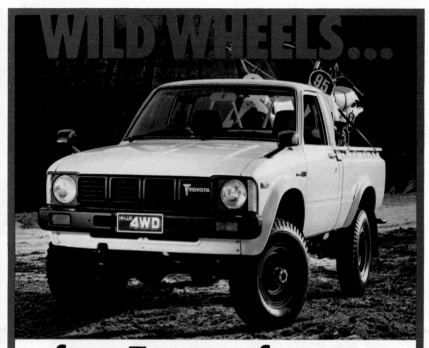

9 ways to put
DeZURIK quality
and reliability
to work for you.
1
2
PERMASEAL
3
4
5
DEZURIK
DEZURIK
6
7
8
9

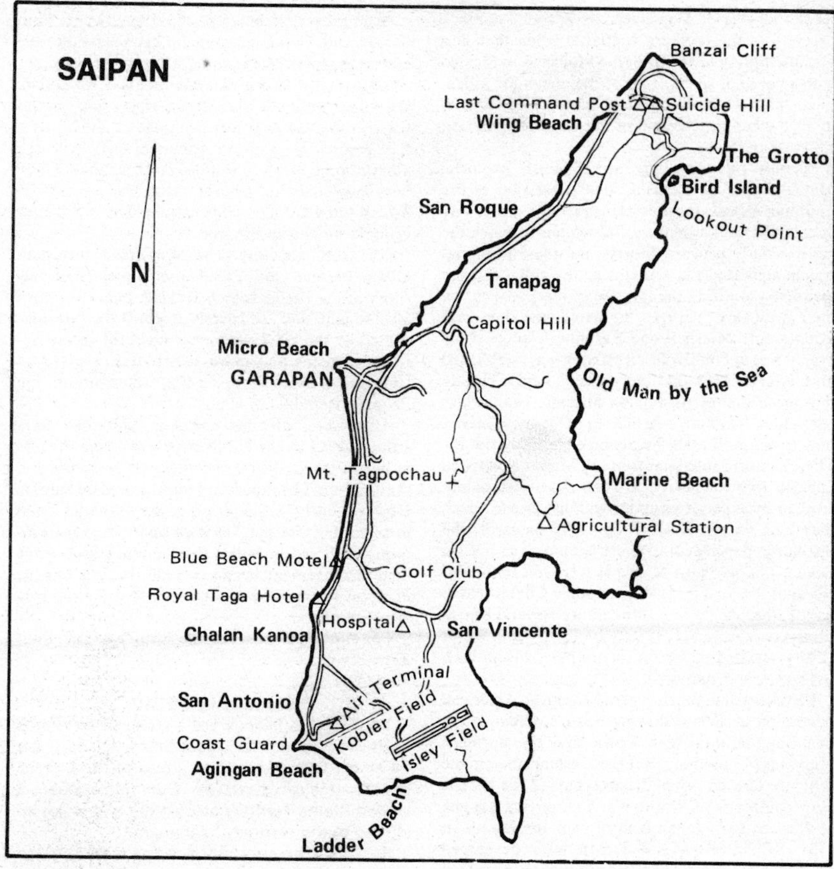

SENATE
Saipan: L. Guererro, P. R. Tenorio, Herman R. Guererro
Rota: J. Calvo, J. Inos, B. Manglona
Tinian: S. de la Cruz, H. Diaz, J. Hofschneider
HOUSE OF REPRESENTATIVES
P. Nakatsukasa, J. Villanueva, P. Tagabuel, A. Guererro, J. Sonoda, M. Borja, A. Igisomar, M. Kileliman, F. Ogomuro, O. Rasa, J. Lifoifoi, J. della Guererro, S. King, M. Ogo
MAYORS
Saipan: Francisco C. Diaz
Tinian: Felipe Mendiola
Northern Islands (Pagan, Alamagan and Agrihan): Daniel Castro
Rota: Prudencio Manglona
PUBLIC BODIES
Marianas Visitors Bureau, Managing Director: J. M. Guerrero
Director of Commerce & Labour: David Cahn
Public Information Officer: Mrs. Elfrida Craddock

HISTORY. Archaeological excavations in the Mariana Islands have revealed that man had inhabited the archipelago at least 3,500 years ago. The earliest radiocarbon date so far obtained is from Saipan – 1527 B.C. Two separate culture periods have been identified and named pre-Latte and Latte. The Latte period was characterised by the erection of double rows of capped, short, stone pillars as foundations for important houses. The making of redware pottery was a feature of the pre-Latte period. Impressions of rice husks on potsherds dating back to A.D. 1335 indicate that rice was cultivated in the Marianas before the arrival of Europeans.

Three of the Mariana Islands, Saipan, Rota and Guam, were discovered by Magellan in 1521 and named the Ladrones Islands. A year or so later, three men from one of Magellan's ships, the 'Trinidad', deserted in the northern Marianas when that ship was attempting to sail from the Moluccas to Mexico with a cargo of spices. Two of the men were killed, but a third, Gonzalo de Vigo, was found at Guam in 1526 when the flagship of the Loaisa expedition called there.

Spanish rule. In 1565, the Spanish explorer, Miguel Lopez de Legaspi, took possession of the Ladrones Islands for the Spanish Crown on his way to colonise the Philippines. Subsequently, when the galleon trade between Mexico and the Philippines was inaugurated the captains of the galleons were instructed to sail in the latitude of the Ladrones on their westward voyages to avoid the low and troublesome Marshall and Caroline Islands. However, it was not until a Jesuit mission was established on Guam in 1668 that the galleons began putting into those islands. The name Mariana Islands was adopted at that time – in honour of Queen Mariana of Austria (mother of the Spanish king, Charles II). The Chamorro inhabitants of the Marianas resisted Spanish rule for nearly 30 years, but were finally crushed by superior weapons and diseases to which they had no resistance. From 1695 onwards, the Spaniards persuaded all the Chamorros to live on Guam. The northern Marianas were left uninhabited until the Spaniards allowed some Chamorros to resettle there in the late 18th century. Several British explorers – Anson (1742), Byron (1765) and Wallis (1767) – called at Tinian for supplies during their voyages round the world.

US possession. When Guam became an American possession in 1898 following Spain's defeat in the Spanish-American War, Spain sold the northern Marianas to Germany. But the Germans had made little use of them when Japan occupied the islands at the outbreak of World War I. After the League of Nations gave Japan control over the islands in 1921, Saipan, Rota and Tinian were developed extensively as centres of sugar production. Fourteen years later, following Japan's withdrawal from the League of Nations, Saipan and Tinian were also developed as naval and air bases which the Japanese used to capture Guam about the same time as they attacked Pearl Harbor.

After American forces occupied Kwajalein and other islands in the Marshalls in February, 1944, they made heavy bombing raids on Guam, Saipan and Tinian. These culminated in the invasion of Tinian and Saipan in June, 1944 and Guam in July. During the bombing and the heavy fighting that followed, there was so much devastation that, later, the seeds of quick-growing tropical scrub had to be sown from the air to prevent erosion. The Americans lost 3,144 dead and 13,448 wounded in the fighting, and the Japanese garrisons were virtually exterminated. Many of the Japanese survivors jumped to their deaths from Mt. Marpi or from the cliffs on the north of Saipan into the sea. On Tinian 5,000 Japanese were killed, 380 surrendered and another 3,000 either died in caves or committed suicide.

After their occupation, the Americans built Saipan and Tinian into huge military bases for the attack on Japan. There were 200,000 invasion troops on Saipan in 1945. Five kilometres away, on Tinian, the Americans built what were then the longest runways in the world. It was from one of them that a B29 bomber took off on August 6, 1945, with the atomic bomb that was dropped on Hiroshima. Three days later a second nuclear bomb was flown from Tinian to be dropped on Nagasaki. The two bombs brought an end to the war.

US Trust Territory. The Marianas, other than Guam, became part of the United States Trust Territory of the Pacific Islands in 1947. However, from 1953 to mid-1962, all islands except Rota were controlled by the US Navy Department for special security purposes. Saipan was used to train Nationalist Chinese (Taiwanese) guerrillas to infiltrate the People's Republic of China.

After that, all the northern Marianas were administered by the US Department of the Interior as one of the six districts of the Trust Territory, and the Territory's headquarters were located on Saipan. However, in 1975, the people of the Marianas voted to separate from the Territory and to accept commonwealth status within the United States. A de facto arrangement began in 1976, but the change of status is expected to take several years to bring into full effect.

For further details, see the history of the Trust Territory.

ISLANDS IN DETAIL

The Mariana Islands are a chain that extends north from Guam for about 560 km. There are 14 single islands and one group of three small islands (Maug): however, Guam has been a United States Territory since 1898 and is not included in the Northern Marianas.

SAIPAN. The area of the island is 122 sq. km which is the largest in the group. There is a lagoon along its west coast and a range of hills extend from north to south for about two-thirds of its length. Mt Tagpochau (474 m) is the highest point. The Japanese had sugar plantations on the flat land at the north of the island below Mt Marpi. Later, they extended down the west coast and around the south coast. Nothing remains of these plantations, the mills or other installations.

The people of Saipan live a peasant-type of existence, or go into business to work for wages either in Government or for other Chamorros. They have lost their original culture and their mode of life is Spanish Catholic colonial rather than that of Pacific Islanders.

The Germans established a base at Garapan, on Tanapag harbour on the west coast where the present port and wharf are situated. The Japanese extended Garapan into a town of 10,000-20,000 people (estimates vary) overflowing around Mutcho Point. This town was completely obliterated in the fighting of 1944 and nothing remains today. The Chamorros and the Carolinians live in villages. The largest Chamorro village is Chalan Kanoa which has now developed into the shopping centre for the whole island.

The headquarters of the Mariana District was at Susupe, just north of Chalan Kanoa. The headquarters for the whole of the Trust Territory is still on Saipan — on Capitol Hill which is built in a recess in the hills about 300 metres above sea level and looking out over the western lagoon. This area of green lawns, modern staff bungalows, post-office and government offices was built during the time that the Mariana Islands (except Rota) were taken back into Navy jurisdiction between January 1953 and 1962.

Good roads link all the villages, airport, etc. and Capitol Hill is at the highest point of the cross island road.

After the Americans had occupied Saipan in 1944, several air bases were built — on Kagman Pt on the east coast; and Isley and Kobler Fields on the south of the island. Few of these airstrips remain in use. Kobler is the commercial airport.

TINIAN is separated from Saipan by a strait about 4.8 km wide. The total area of the island is 101 sq. km.

Tinian's most noted historical monuments are the huge runways built by the Americans after 1944 and from which the bombers took off on August 6 and 9, 1945, to drop the first atomic bombs on Hiroshima and Nagasaki. Plaques mark the place where the bombs were loaded.

Tinian has no lagoon and most of its shores are steep. The Japanese utilised the interior plateau to grow sugar-cane and pineapples and vegetables for home consumption.

When the Americans had gone after the war, the island quickly reverted to scrub and secondary growth. Even the huge airstrips remain unused except by an occasional charter flight.

Vegetable gardening is now the main occupation of the people but in the 1960s one quarter of the whole island was leased to a company as a ranch and by 1967 about 1,500 Angus cattle had been imported. The Northern Marianas had 7,196 cattle in 1976 while there were only 129 in the Trust Territories.

ROTA (Luta or Zarpane) has an area of 83 sq. km. Vegetable raising is the main occupation of the people in the southwest. Just north of Rota village, a peak 491 metres high is said to be an extinct volcano. The people of Rota speak purer Chamorro than those elsewhere in the Northern Marianas and are believed to be of purer stock. Throughout the Spanish purges during the late 18th century many Rota people hid in caves and escaped death or deportation to Guam.

ANATAHAN has an area of 31 sq. km. It is an extinct crater, elongated into two peaks, 714 m and 782 m high.

PAGAN (San Ignacio), largest of the purely volcanic islands is 13.6 km long by 5.6 km wide. Mt Oagan (574 metres) in the north-east, last erupted in 1922; the volcanic peaks in the southwest corner periodically emit steam. An airstrip was opened in 1967.

AGRIHAN is a volcanic island 9.6 km long by 5.6 km wide and 965 metres high. In 1810, Captain Brown and other Americans, with several families of Hawaiians, formed a colony on this island, but it was dispersed by the Spaniards, who destroyed the plantations. The Chamorros made their last stand against the Spaniards on the terraces of Agrihan, above the vertical cliffs.

FARALLON DE PAJAROS, northernmost of the Marianas, is known also as Uracas. It is an active volcano 319 metres high.

MAUG ISLANDS are a group of three steep peaks surrounding a lagoon, which is a sunken crater. There was once a Japanese weather station on this uninhabited island.

FOR THE TOURIST. From exploring the battle-scarred relics on land and in the lagoon to discovering jungle waterfalls or spear fishing in the lagoon, the tiny islands of the Northern Marianas offer new attractions for the adventurous traveller who is prepared to endure occasional inconvenience.

The scenic beauty of the islands, with the unaffected culture of their people is combined with historic battle sites.

Information is available from the tourist commission in Saipan and especially from the offices of Continental Airlines operating with Air Micronesia.

Tour operators include Micronesia Tours, Inc. and Saipan Kanko Service, in Saipan (Marianas).

Entry formalities. United States citizens need proof of citizenship to visit the territory, such as a driver's licence. No visa, passport, or advance entry permit are needed unless the stay is for longer than 30 days, or the visit is for some purpose, other than tourism, in which case an entry permit is required in advance.

Citizens of countries other than the US require both a visa and a passport. Smallpox immunisation is required unless the visitor starts from the US or one of its territories or possessions. Cholera and yellow fever immunisation are required if the visitor is from an infected area. Typhoid, para-typhoid and tetanus shots are recommended.

Sightseeing. Much intensive fighting took place in the Northern Marianas during World War II and many visitors go there to see the former battlegrounds. The area is also renowned for its reefs and lagoons and the pastimes associated with them. Particular attractions include:

Saipan: Suicide Cliff, the old Japanese gaol, the last Japanese command post, old Japanese hospital,

Peace Memorial, Sugar King monument, blue grotto, Bird Island.

Tinian: Atomic bomb loading sites; Japanese command post, House of Taga.

Rota: Latte stones, swimming hole, Wedding Cake Mountain, Japanese cannon site.

ACCOMMODATION

Saipan

SAIPAN CONTINENTAL HOTEL — Seven-storey unit on Micro Beach in Garapan; 191 air-conditioned rooms, restaurants, cocktail lounge, function room, swimming pool, shops, games and car rental.

HAFA ADAI BEACH HOTEL — One- and two-storey units on beach at Garapan; 58 twins, air-conditioned, restaurant and outdoor dining, cocktail lounge, gift shop, swimming pool.

HAMILTON'S APARTMENTS — Single-storey unit in Garapan Heights; eight air-conditioned rooms, restaurant, cocktail lounge, function room.

SAIPAN BEACH INTER-CONTINENTAL INN — Three-storey L-shaped unit on Micro Beach; 200 air-conditioned rooms, restaurant, cocktail lounge, swimming pool, duty-free shop, tennis courts, Japanese restaurant.

MARIANA HOTEL — Single-storey building on hillside overlooking Tanapag Harbor; 10 air-conditioned rooms, restaurant, cocktail lounge, swimming pool.

ROYAL TAGA HOTEL — Three-storey building on beach at Susupe; 73 air-conditioned rooms, restaurant, cocktail lounge, gift shop, swimming pool.

SAIPAN GRAND HOTEL — Five-storey unit in the business centre of Saipan; 120 air-conditioned rooms, restaurant, cocktail lounge, snack shop, gift shop, swimming pool.

Rota

BLUE PENINSULA HOTEL — Two-storey building in Song Song Village; 23 air-conditioned rooms, restaurant.

ROTA HOTEL — In Song Song Village; two-storey unit, 15 rooms (11 air-conditioned), restaurant, cocktail lounge, barbecue on beach.

ROTA PAU PAU HOTEL — Two-storey unit; 50 air-conditioned rooms, restaurant, cocktail lounge, gift shop, swimming pool, sport fishing, snorkeling, boat, bicycle and motor-cycle rental, scuba diving equipment.

Tinian

TINIAN CENTER — Single-storey unit; eight rooms (four air-conditioned), restaurant, cocktail lounge.

FLEMING HOTEL — Single-storey unit; seven air-conditioned rooms, restaurant, cocktail lounge.

ORINESIA HOTEL — In San Jose Village; single-storey building, eight rooms with shared bath, Japanese-style accommodation, boat rental.

OGASAWARA ISLANDS

These islands, almost 30 of them, are 1,000 km south of Tokyo. They are also known as the Bonin Islands. They are named after the Japanese Ogasawara who discovered them in 1593. In 1876 they were internationally admitted as part of Japanese territory. They came under the control of the US army in 1946, and reverted to Japan in 1968.

The main islands, Chichi-jima and Haha-jima mean Papa Island, Mama Island, etc., including Elder Brother, Little Brother, Bride, Matchmaker, etc.

The islands may be classified into five groups, and those having an area above 1 sq km are indicated:

Muko-jima (3 sq km), Nakodo-jima (1.58), Yome-jima, Kitano-shima.

Immediately to their south are the Chichi-jima or Beechey Islands – Chichi-jima (23.95), Ani-jima (7.85), Ototo-jima (5.30), Mago-jima, Nishi-jima, Hyotan-jima, Hitomaru-jima, Nishi-jima, Higashi-jima, Minami-jima.

The third group comprises the Haha-jima or Bailey Islands – Haha-jima (20.8), Muko-jima (1.45), Katsuotori-shima, Hira-jima, Futago-jima, Maru-jima, Ane-jima (1.67), Imoto-jima (1.36), Mei-jima (1.13).

Further south again are the Volcano Islands of Iwo-jima (22.36), Kitaiwo-jima (5.52), Minamiiwo-jima (3.67).

The other three islands, located at the north west, south west and eastern extremities respectively are Nishino-shima, Minamitori-shima (1.1) and Okinotori-shima. The last-named is the newest of the islands, formed by the explosion of a submarine volcano. All the Ogasawara islands are protrusions caused by submarine volcanic activity.

The islands are quite mountainous with many cliffs and there are no beaches except on Iwo-jima. The highest mountains are Chibusayama (462 m) on Haha-jima and Chuouzan (321 m) on Chichi-jima.

The islands have a total population of 1,546 including 1,243 on Chichi-jima and 303 on Haha-jima as at February, 1979. They are a municipal unit of Tokyo, with a mayor appointed by the Tokyo governor.

Schools on the two main islands had 55 primary level students on Chichi-jima and 17 on Haha-jima, while in Junior High School there were 28 and 6 students on the two islands respectively, in 1979. There is a senior high school on Chichi-jima with 30 students. Doctors from Tokyo serve in medical centres on Chichi and Haha.

The islands are served by a regular weekly ship from Tokyo to Chichi-jima, taking 26 hours for the trip. There are three regular services a week between Chichi-jima and Haha-jima.

The main harbour is Futami at Chichi-jima. Both islands have a general port and Chichi-jima also has a fishing wharf. In 1976 a feasibility study was under way to construct an airport at Ani-jima but the plan was abandoned.

Telecommunications are established between the main island of Japan and Chichi-jima where there are 444 local telephones. There were three public telephones on Haha-jima in 1978.

The main production in the group centres on vegetables for local and mainland consumption, as well as fishing for tuna, crayfish, prawns and turtles.

The natural beauty of the islands is expected to encourage their development for tourism. The sub-tropical climate produces an average temperature of 17 deg C. in winter and 27 deg C. in summer. Annual rainfall is 1,600 mm and typhoons occur in the area.

Wildlife includes the Ogasawara big bat, Ogasawara dragonfly, scorpion, big centipede, wild goats and cattle besides marine animals, coral and tropical fish. local fruits include banana, orange, pawpaw and mango.

The Ogasawara islands were designated as a National Park in 1972. There are 26 inns, at Chichi-jima, and a hostel for fishermen on Haha-jima. The biggest inns include Ogasawara Kanko Hotel, Mikazuki-so, Agasawara Kaikan and Green Villa.

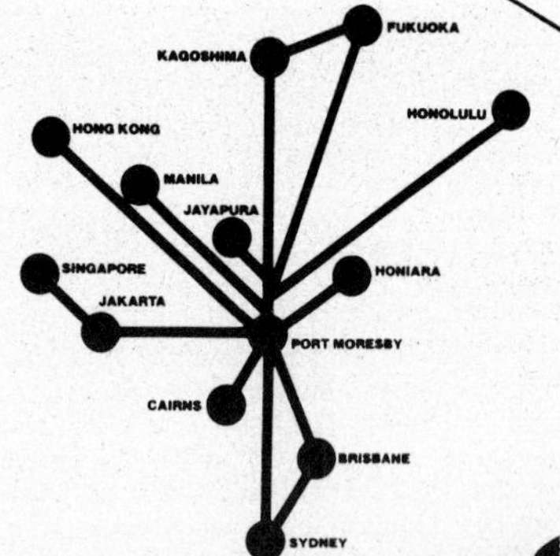

FUKUOKA
KAGOSHIMA
HONOLULU
HONG KONG
MANILA
JAYAPURA
SINGAPORE
HONIARA
JAKARTA
PORT MORESBY
CAIRNS
BRISBANE
SYDNEY

PAPUA NEW GUINEA

Papua New Guinea is an independent state and a member of the British Commonwealth. It consists of the eastern half of the island of New Guinea and many offshore islands including New Britain, New Ireland and Bougainville.

The nation extends from the equator to 12 deg. S. latitude and from 141 to 160 deg. E. longitude. Port Moresby, the national capital, is 3,900 km north of Sydney. Local time is 10 hours ahead of GMT.

The estimated population in June 1980 was 3,168,700.

The national flag is divided diagonally with a red upper right triangle on which is superimposed a yellow bird of paradise. The lower left is black with five white stars representing the Southern Cross. The national song is "Oh arise, all you sons".

Currency is the kina, which is divided into 100 toea.

THE PEOPLE. The inhabitants include a large diversity of types although some ethnologists made a distinction between the Papuan type people, who are believed to have been the first arrivals and who now tend to inhabit the interiors of the mainland and big islands; and the Melanesians who are the people of the coasts and offshore islands.

But, there had been much mixing of people long before Europeans made their first contacts, and the indigenous people of PNG can be considered to be related with those other Melanesians who occupy the greater part of the Western Pacific.

In the 1971 census the total population was 2,435,409 indigenous plus 47,157 Europeans and 3,600 Asians and peoples of other races. Estimated population in 1980 was 3,139,700 indigenous plus 29,000 people of other races. A national census is due in 1980.

There are a few groups of people in the Central Province and on the Upper Ramu, around Aiome, in Madang who have sometimes been described as pygmies or Negritos but this is probably incorrect. Although of very short stature they are similar in other respects to other local people and it could be that they are not the remnants of a separate migration at all but a development from people similar to neighbouring stock.

The people of the North-Western Islands of the Manus Province (which are closest to the Caroline Islands) are basically Micronesian although they now have been subjected to incursions of Melanesian blood. The people of Takau (Mortlock) and the Nukumanu (Tasman) Islands, are predominantly Polynesian but mixed now with New Britain, Manus and Caroline Islands blood. The people on the Nukumanu Islands are practically pure Polynesian and there is occasional immigration from Polynesian Ontong Java, a Solomon Islands outlier.

However, the above people are very tiny minorities in the predominantly Melanesian scene, which also contains such diverse types as the black-skinned people of Buka and the tallish, light-skinned people of the Trobriand Islands and the coast near Port Moresby.

The European population of Papua New Guinea continued to grow until 1971 when it was more than 47,000. The estimated expatriate population in June 1980 of 29,000 was a drop of about 1,000 compared with 12 months earlier.

Europeans who go to work in PNG today usually have short-term contracts and stay only a few years. Current Public Service contracts are for a maximum period of 3 years.

The Asian population in PNG established itself because the German New Guinea Company which administered New Guinea under charter for the first 15 years after German annexation in 1884 found New Guinea labour initially unsatisfactory and introduced Chinese, Malays and Ambonese. By the time Germany took over administration from the company the Asian population was between 300 and 400. Thenceforth labour was brought mostly from Hong Kong. At the time Australia began civil administration in 1921 there were 1,424 Chinese and 163 Ambonese and Malays.

The Chinese ultimately became the small shopkeepers and artisans of Papua New Guinea.

The population is scattered widely throughout the

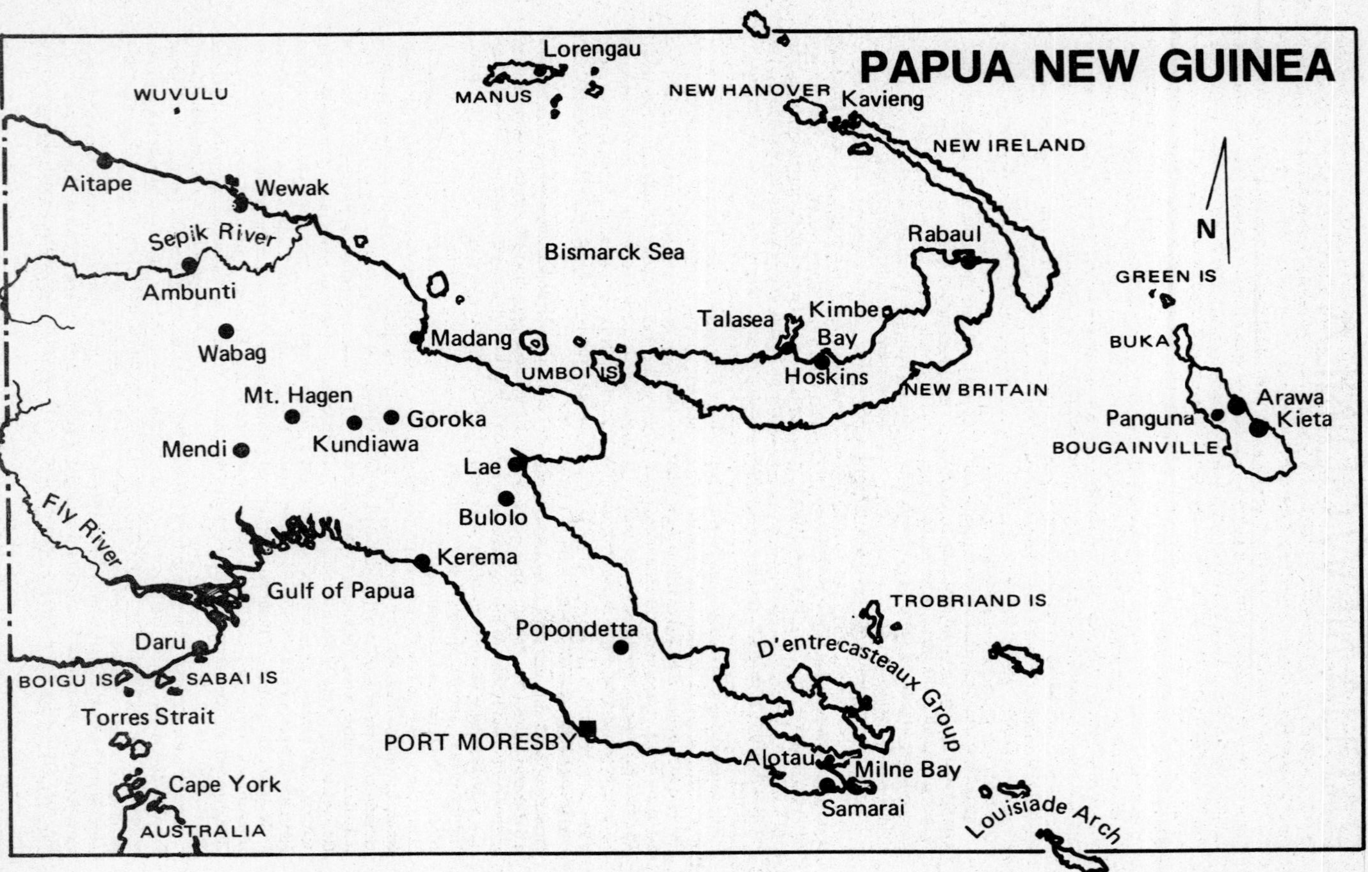
PAPUA NEW GUINEA
N
WUVULU
MANUS
Lorengau
NEW HANOVER
Kavieng
NEW IRELAND
Aitape
Wewak
Sepik River
Ambunti
Bismarck Sea
Rabaul
GREEN IS
Wabag
Madang
UMBOI IS
Talasea
Kimbe Bay
Hoskins
NEW BRITAIN
BUKA
Mt. Hagen
Goroka
Kundiawa
Mendi
Arawa
Kieta
Panguna
BOUGAINVILLE
Lae
Bulolo
Fly River
Kerema
Gulf of Papua
TROBRIAND IS
Popondetta
Daru
BOIGU IS
SABAI IS
D'entrecasteaux Group
Torres Strait
PORT MORESBY
Alotau
Milne Bay
Samarai
Cape York
AUSTRALIA
Louisiade Arch

country, but the greatest concentrations are in the Highlands provinces. Population of the Central Province, including the National Capital District of Port Moresby, was estimated in 1980 as 275,900 with 130,200 of these being in Port Moresby. The other provinces had the following estimated populations in June 1980: Western (headquarters at Daru) 94,150; Gulf (Kerema) 73,100; Milne Bay (Alotau) 139,600; Northern (Popondetta) 88,850; Southern Highlands (Mendi) 227,200; Enga (Wabag) 167,200; Western Highlands (Mt Hagen) 273,350; Chimbu (Kundiawa) 170,900; Eastern Highlands (Goroka) 301,500; Morobe (Lae) 331,000; Madang (Madang) 213,800; East Sepik (Wewak) 214,200; West Sepik (Vanimo) 109,900; Manus (Lorengau) 36,750; New Ireland (Kavieng) 77,050; East New Britain (Rabaul) 129,000; West New Britain (Kimbe) 100,100; North Solomons (Arawa) 136,600.

Citizenship. At the time of independence, September 16, 1975, anyone who had had two Papua New Guinean grandparents and did not hold foreign citizenship automatically became a citizen of Papua New Guinea. Others who had lived for over eight years in the country could apply for naturalisation but had to do it within two months after independence day. If the eight years falls after independence day, application must be made within two months of the date it falls due. One of the qualifications for naturalisation is that the applicant must be able to talk and understand Pidgin or Motu.

The citizens of Papua New Guinea are known as Papua New Guineans.

Languages. The great differences between the peoples of Papua New Guinea are brought into focus in the multiplicity of languages which are found within the country. There is one language for each 14,000 sq. km. In practice, of course, the languages change more often than this, in the thickly populated areas, to compensate for areas where there is sparse population, or none at all. In all there are probably about 700-800 languages.

Various attempts to cope with the language problem have been tried, including the use of Police Motu as a lingua franca in Papua before World War II, and the use of Pidgin English in New Guinea from the German era onwards. Pidgin has tended to supplant Motu in recent years.

Religion. The people had their own religions strongly influenced by a belief in magic, spells and sorcery. Although many now claim to be Christian, superstition is still prevalent.

Religious beliefs that embrace magic are an integral part of all Papua New Guinea native cultures. These beliefs and practices differ in detail from area to area but they are based largely on a form of ancestor and spirit worship. Most of the emphasis is on pleasing and propitiating spirits – some of relatives who are still remembered, some from the remote past.

Lifestyle. Changes in the social structure have come as a result of contact with outside influences but the social set-up in native life is still as varied as the people themselves. In some communities there is a form of matrilineal inheritance of land and other property; others follow a patrilineal system.

The community unit is the village (which is generally of from 50 to 300 people but may be either larger or smaller) although in some communities people live in smaller hamlets or even individual homesteads.

Dwellings are often made of local materials and therefore vary in type, size and material according to environment, although this, like everything else, is being modified by European contact.

There was not, as in Fiji and Polynesia, any system of hereditary leadership. Men in their own lifetime rose to be leaders because they had more energy than their fellow men and generally they acquired status by giving feasts and through a complex sequence of gift exchanges.

The life was completely communal, the economy subsistence, and allegiance never extended beyond the village or the collection of hamlets that made up the community unit. This exclusiveness is breaking down slowly but is still an obstacle to the concept of a national identity of the country as a whole.

In the cities, such as Port Moresby and Lae, the lifestyle is quickly becoming Westernised, with the people living in Western style housing, driving their own cars and shopping at supermarkets.

Recreations. Papua New Guinea is very sports minded, and most sports are played by all races. Football is a national enthusiasm. There are some excellent playing fields, sports grounds and golf courses, probably the finest golf course being the one at Lae. Bowling clubs flourish, as do clubs for yachting and power-boating. Because of off-shore reefs, there is rarely any opportunity for surfing, and the better beaches are in the remoter areas of the islands.

GOVERNMENT. Papua New Guinea became an independent state within the British Commonwealth on September 16, 1975, with Queen Elizabeth II as Head of State. She is represented in PNG by a Governor-General who is appointed by the Queen acting with the National Executive Council. In practice, the person to be Governor-General, whose term of office is six years, is nominated by parliament after a secret ballot.

The first Governor-General of Papua New Guinea was Sir John Guise who was appointed on September 16, 1975. He resigned to return to politics on February 28, 1977 and was replaced by Sir Tore Lokololo who remains in office.

The constitution provides for the parliament, the judiciary, the public service, the Governor-General and sets out the requirements for citizenship. Leader of the government is the Prime Minister.

National Parliament. During the transition period before and after independence, the National Parliament elected in 1972 remained in office until June – July 1977. At the 1977 election, the National Parliament was enlarged to 109 members – 20 representing Provincial seats and 89 representing Open electorates. The voting system was also changed to "first-past-the-post" in place of the previous modified preferential system. Seven parties contested the 1977 election, the major ones being the Pangu Pati, the People's Progress Party and the United Party.

Mr Michael Somare was re-elected Prime Minister when the new National Parliament met. As leader of the Pangu Pati, he formed a coalition government mainly with the support of the People's Progress Party.

Parliament elected Mr Kingsford Dibela as Speaker and Sir Tei Abal, leader of the United Party, became leader of the Opposition. He was replaced in May 1978, by Mr Iambakey Okuk.

After three unsuccessful attempts the Okuk opposition finally won a no-confidence motion which unseated the Somare government in March, 1980. Mr Okuk deferred to the popularity of Sir Julius Chan (Peoples Progress Party) who became Prime Minister in a five-party coalition. The coalition made Mr Okuk Deputy Prime Minister and Parliament elected Mr Sevese Morea as Speaker. Mr Somare became Leader of the Opposition.

The National Executive Council consists of all the Ministers with the Prime Minister acting as chairman. This council is responsible for the executive government of PNG.

In 1980 there were 24 portfolios.

Local government. There is a developing system of local government which in recent years has been widened to Area Authorities and Provincial Government, depending on the requirements and stage of development of various areas.

The system introduced in 1950 provided for indigenous local government bodies with authority to keep law and order; financing, organising or engaging in any business enterprise for the good of the community; carrying out works or providing any public or social service for the good of the community.

Later legislation provided for multi-racial councils with wider scope in the fields of health, education, commercial enterprises and in the collection of local taxes. The first multi-racial council was elected in 1965 and in the next four years most councils became multi-racial.

City and town councils came into operation in 1971 and in 1980 there were city councils for Port Moresby and Lae and urban councils at Madang, Rabaul and Arawa. However, these may be changed from their present form and replaced by "community governments" established under the aegis of provincial governments. Such a change was occurring in Rabaul.

Council members are elected from wards; there are Lord Mayors in Port Moresby and Lae; the others usually have presidents.

These urban councils raise revenue by various means including head taxes, rates on alienated land, entertainment taxes and grants from central government.

In 1980 there were 164 local government councils of all types including the urban councils, and these covered 92 per cent of the total PNG population.

Area Authorities and Provincial Government. Area Authorities were established as a means of giving each of the provinces a greater say in planning of the province.

They have now been replaced, in each province by Provincial Governments about half of which are 'interim', the rest fully elected. All Interim Provincial Governments will eventually be fully elected.

The central government has begun decentralising administration and is transferring specified functions at regular intervals, following these basic principles:

There will be one national public service; there will be minimum duplication of activities; there will be a clear division of responsibilities between national and provincial levels; financial powers will be delegated in step with responsibilities.

Some planning decisions have yet to be taken on the details of achieving these objectives.

The provincial governments will be given revenue grants, and may apply provincial taxes.

All local and provincial government is the responsibility of the Department of Decentralisation.

Public service. The Papua New Guinea Public Service is under the control of the Department of the Public Services Commission. The department also recruits overseas officers needed to meet the shortage of some specialised manpower.

In February 1980 total Public Service strength was 52,862 (including trainees and volunteers but excluding teachers).

Ombudsman commission. This is provided for in the constitution. A Chief Ombudsman and two Ombudsmen were appointed in December 1975.

Justice. The source of the laws of Papua New Guinea is the PNG constitution.

A new, unified Criminal Code came into force on November 1, 1975. The new code has been brought up to date, doing away with the death penalty except for treason, introducing among other items, crimes involving aircraft (e.g. hijacking) and increasing fines in line with present-day economic realities.

The Chief Justice is appointed by the Head of State acting with the National Executive Council. The other judges are appointed by the Judicial and Legal Services Commission.

The Courts. It is likely that, as time goes on, there will be considerable reorganisation in the instrumentalities concerned with legal matters, which prior to independence were set up in traditional Australian fashion. But in 1980 the courts that exercised jurisdiction in Papua New Guinea were: (a) National Court; (b) District Courts; (c) Local Courts; (d) Village Courts; (e) Children's Courts; and (f) Warden's Courts.

There is also a Court of Appeal called the Supreme Court.

Village Court decisions can be reviewed by Local or District Courts. Appeals from Local and District Courts go to the National Court and then to the Supreme Court, which is the last court of appeal.

Only the National Court has unlimited jurisdiction. It is presided over by the Chief Justice, or other judges, who also comprise the full bench of the Supreme Court for appeals.

PNG does not, as yet, have a jury system but it is planned that assessors will sit with judges to give an opinion on fact and traditional PNG customs.

In recent years a scheme to train local magistrates for work in lower courts has been in operation. They graduate as Assistant Magistrates and after a year, during which they sit with the court and perform other functions ancillary to the administration of justice, become full magistrates.

Legal Aid. This is available to people irrespective of race who do not have the money to assist themselves.

Legal practitioners are both barristers and solicitors in Papua New Guinea, instead of practising as one or the other as in some Australian States and in Britain.

Police. Law and order are maintained by the Royal Papua New Guinea Constabulary, divided into two branches: Regular Constabulary and Field Constabulary, of the Department of Police.

The Regular Constabulary carries out general and specialised police duties within the country. The Field Constabulary consists of delegated officers of the Department of the Prime Minister with ex-officio police powers in areas where there are no commissioned officers of the Regular Constabulary.

Local police officers are graduates of the Police College, at Bomana, outside Port Moresby.

The initial year of the 2-year course is conducted at the Joint Services College, 19AM Barracks, Lae.

For police recruited as other ranks there is no set period of service but policemen may retire on pension after 20 years.

At the head of the Constabulary is the Commissioner of Police with headquarters at Port Moresby. The Constabulary is responsible direct to the Minister for Police.

In December 1979 there were 4344 members of PNG Police. There were 326 officers (including 29 non-nationals) and 4018 other ranks.

Gaols. Prisons in PNG are called corrective institutions.

The main institution for long-term prisoners is at Bomana, near Port Moresby. There are subsidiary institutions near Lae, Wewak, Rabaul and Mount Hagen, plus smaller institutions in other provincial centres.

Liquor laws. Control of liquor licensing is through the Liquor Licensing Commission, which has power to grant the following 12 classes of licence: Publicans; tavern; limited hotel licence; dealers; storekeepers; booth; bottle shop; restaurant; packet; club; occasional; or canteen.

Hours for hotels, taverns and clubs are: 11 a.m. to 2 p.m. and 4 p.m. to 8 p.m., Monday to Thursday; on Friday the sale of liquor in hotels, taverns and clubs is permitted only between the hours of 12-1 p.m. and 6.30-9.30 p.m.; 10 a.m. to 2 p.m. and 4 p.m. to 8 p.m. Saturday; and 11 a.m. to 1 p.m. and 5 p.m. to 7 p.m. on Sundays.

Liquor sales are further restricted on pay-days.

Licensed stores must close at 6 p.m. or one hour before hotels, whichever is earlier. Bottle shops close two hours before hotels.

Customers must be off licensed premises 15 minutes after closing time; club members and guests may stay after trading hours although they cannot drink liquor.

There are restrictions on what type of liquor may be sold in public bars.

Liquor cannot be consumed in a bottle shop, store, in a moving vehicle, or in a street, road or any public place.

All advertising of spirits and wines is banned except in licensed premises or the vehicles owned by the licensee.

Gambling. No poker machines or gambling devices are permitted. However, playing cards is allowed. In 1977, 18 licensed bookmakers were operating. Their turnover for the first 13 months of operation since betting shops were legalised was K26 million which provided some K200,000 in stamp duty. A turnover tax on bookmakers was instituted in 1978. It is 1 per cent.

DEFENCE: Papua New Guinea assumed responsibility for defence from the Australian Government on March 6, 1975, by January, 1980 there were 3,655 national members including 298 national officers. By this time, only 134 Australians remained on loan to the PNG Defence Force.

The fully integrated units consist of a land element with three battalions (two of the Pacific Islands Regiment at Wewak and one Pacific Islands Regiment at Port Moresby; and an Engineer Battalion). The maritime element is equipped with five Attack class patrol boats based at Lombrum, Manus Island, and with heavy landing craft based at Port Moresby. The air element has four DC-3 and three Nomad aircraft.

As a part of national policy, the PNG Defence Force has been allocated practical work which contributes to national objectives; and of these, civic action is the most important.

It includes the use of soldiers, sailors and airmen for road and bridge building, airstrip construction, mapping, medical and health projects, fisheries surveillance, help in civil disasters and in search-and-rescue operations. Australia also provides practical assistance of this nature, in national aerial mapping, engineering works in the Southern Highlands Province, and advice to the Police.

At the end of 1979 there were 20 PNG Defence Force officers trained as pilots and from January 1978, PNG pilots and loadmasters began training at Port Moresby. Other officers are trained at the Joint Services college at Lae while specialists, such as legal officers, medical orderlies and dentists receive their training in Australia.

Under the PNG Constitution, the Defence Force is an arm of the government and is controlled, through its headquarters at Murray Barracks, Port Moresby, as part of the Ministry for Defence.

It is under the control of the Minister for Defence through the Secretary for Defence at Waigani and the Commander of the Defence Force at Murray Barracks.

EDUCATION. Education in Papua New Guinea is controlled by the government through the Department of Education, with the missions and churches playing an important part, especially at primary level. The total amount spent by government on education in 1979 was K63.5 million. In February 1976, a Five-Year Education Plan was adopted, providing for 6 years of primary and four to six years of secondary education. Targets have been only partly met.

The education system includes government schools and schools nominated by other education agencies which meet prescribed conditions. There is a National Education Board, consisting of the Director of Education and members representing the government, churches and missions, local government, teachers, commercial interests and tertiary institutions. A Papua New Guinea Teaching Service includes teachers in government schools and those teachers in agency schools which have been brought within the education system; and there is a Teaching Service Commission which determines service conditions for teachers. On January 1, 1980, the commission employed 11,364 teachers, of whom 1,319 were overseas staff.

All government schools are full members of the education system. Other education agencies, virtually all of them church or mission bodies, may nominate their schools as member schools, associate member schools or affiliated schools, if they meet the prescribed conditions. Only the Seventh-day Adventists have elected to stay outside the system while co-operating and remaining consistent with it in some respects. The majority of non-government schools have been accepted as full members of the education system. The government pays the salaries of qualified teachers in agency schools which have been accepted into the system; these schools also receive classroom materials; there is a subsidy for approved building programmes for high schools, technical colleges and teachers' colleges; maintenance and boarding grants for secondary school boarders, and grants for some other agency education personnel in secondary schools.

Expatriate Education. There is a marked division between general schooling in PNG and schooling for expatriates. The system is geared to concentrate resources on schools for Papua New Guineans, but the government has agreed to continue to provide a metropolitan type education for children of expatriates who need to be equipped for their eventual departure, provided they pay an economic fee. This education is available at both primary and high school level. The schools are known as 'International' schools.

In 1979 the total enrolment in this expatriate education system was 7,325 and there was a total of 50 schools. It should be noted that PNG children can attend these schools if the parents can afford the relatively high fees charged – K800 for primary schools and K1300 for high schools per annum. An increasing number of PNG children do attend.

Primary Education. Primary schools on a PNG curriculum are called community schools. The government's aim is to provide primary, or community, education for all children and it plans that 92 per cent of all seven-year-olds will be enrolled by 1985.

Total community school enrolment in 1979 was 277,301 with a staff of 9,092.

Secondary Education. There are four national high schools (previously called senior high schools), at Sogeri, Keravat and Aiyura, and at Passam. Students are selected from all provinces, and each school has a potential enrolment of 400.

In 1979 there were 94 high schools in PNG, with a total student enrolment of 34,624 and a staff of 1,299. The government aims to correct the imbalance and put more high schools in disadvantaged provinces.

School fees. Originally tuition for all pupils and students was free. However, in recent years charges have crept into the system, including charges for equipment. Charges at high schools are also made and vary from area to area. The maximum community or primary school fee in 1979 was K20, and for provincial high schools was K150.

Technical education. Technical education and training is provided for in technical colleges and schools, commercial training centres and vocational training centres. Continuous training courses are offered to students who have successfully completed Form II at a high school.

People who enter apprenticeships straight from high school at Form II level, attend technical courses on a block release system – i.e. they spend up to 10 full weeks at a technical college during the year and supplement this with training on the job, night classes or correspondence courses.

Commercial and secretarial training is available at Port Moresby, Lae and Rabaul and vocational training centres have been developed in many areas to provide full-time basic training for students who have completed primary school.

There are nine technical colleges including the

secretarial colleges, with a total enrolment in 1979 of 2,607 students.

Teacher training. The training of local community school teachers is undertaken in nine teachers' colleges. Two are run by the government and seven by church organisations. Secondary school teachers are trained locally at the Goroka Secondary Teachers' College which is part of the University of Papua New Guinea.

In 1979 there was a total of 2,101 student places in all teachers' colleges.

In the past, teachers at all levels have also been recruited in Australia, but by 1973 teachers' colleges in PNG were training sufficient primary school teachers to staff existing primary schools. The Goroka Secondary Teachers' College was not able to supply all the secondary teachers needed and a shortfall in graduates is expected until 1980.

Grants, scholarships. Although the government provides secondary education for children of all races through the multi-racial high schools, subsidies are being paid to expatriate parents who wish their children to go to secondary schools in Australia.

A bursary system also operates, subject to a means test. Expatriate public servants are entitled to an education allowance in lieu of a subsidy.

Tertiary education. The University of Papua New Guinea was established in mid-1965 and enrolled its first students in February 1966.

The faculties are Medicine, Arts, Science, Agriculture, Education and Law. The degrees of MB., BA., BSc., LL.B., B.Agr. B.Ec., B.Med. Sc., B.S. and B.Ed. are offered. In the post-graduate field the degrees offered are Diploma of Teaching English as a Second Language, Child Health, Obstetrics and Gynaecology, and Education in Developing Countries; BA(Hons), BEc(Hons), MA (Qualifying), MEcQ, MELQ, MScQ, LL.MQ, MA, MEc, M.Ed., MSc, LL.M, Ph.D

There is a number of sub-graduate courses, including Mass Communication and Land Administration.

University entrance is a minimum of five credit passes in the School Certificate, after which students do a preliminary year at the university before starting degree courses. The first students graduated at the end of 1970.

In 1979 there were 1,126 male students full-time, and 307 part-time; and 189 female students full-time, 60 part-time. Most were Papua New Guineans with others from neighbouring Pacific countries. All full-time students live on campus. The university has its own buildings, in landscaped gardens, at Waigani, Port Moresby.

What began as the Institute of Higher Technical Education, at Lae, later renamed the Institute of Technology and, since September 1973, the University of Technology, gave its first courses in 1967 with an enrolment of 31 students. It has an elaborate establishment close to Lae. It includes halls of residence for students, all of whom live on campus.

Students, who numbered 1,205 in 1979, are offered degree courses in Engineering, Business Administration, Commerce, Architecture, Building Economics, Surveying, Forestry and Chemical Technology. Diploma courses are offered in Cartography, Communications, Fisheries Technology and Valuation; and certificate courses in Surveying and Drafting.

Students are usually sponsored by a company organisation or attend on government scholarships. The students are Papua New Guineans except for a small number from adjacent Pacific Islands.

Other institutions of higher learning in PNG are the Vudal Agricultural College at Keravat, East New Britain, where there is a three year course leading to a Diploma of Agriculture; (one year of the course is spent at a field station in the Western Highlands), and the Bulolo Forestry College at Bulolo, in Morobe.

Vocational education. There are various vocational, adult education and correspondence courses in operation. Vocational centres offer a wide range of short term courses open to village groups, but these are in the development stage. There are adult education officers at most provincial headquarters.

LABOUR. Regulations fix minimum wage rates in various centres, and there are a number of awards in industry also setting minimum rates. General labourers in main towns get anything from K30.96 to K45 weekly. Since September 1, 1977, wages have been subject to half-yearly adjustments based on movements of the consumer Price Index. Urban rates are not binding on employers of domestic servants. At September 1, 1979, the minimum urban wage rose to K30.96 and at the same time the wages for rural primary workers was K11.96.

Social security. There are plans for a National Provident Fund to be established, initially for urban workers. With workers making compulsory contributions as well as employers. The scheme is to provide a lump sum for those covered at the age of 55. At February, 1980 this scheme had not been introduced.

HEALTH. The Papua New Guinea Department of Health provides hospitals, dispensaries and public health facilities for all Papua New Guinea. In addition, dental and ancillary services are provided and the department undertakes the training of nursing, some medical and other public health personnel.

The various Christian church bodies operating in Papua New Guinea all undertake health services, providing hospitals, nursing staff and medical officers. The PHD maintains close contact with the church missions in order to co-ordinate activities.

Hospitals. Hospital charges are based on ability to pay, and vary. Most people are treated free or for a nominal sum. Higher fees are charged in the intermediate wards to be found in major hospitals.

There are four base hospitals which provide specialist services for the four geographical regions of Papua New Guinea. They are at Port Moresby, Lae, Rabaul and Goroka. In addition there are district hospitals in those provinces which do not have a base hospital. The big copper project in Bougainville is served by a hospital at Arawa which replaced the old Kieta district hospital in 1972. New hospitals for Kimbe, West New Britain, and at Mendi, Southern Highlands were completed in 1975, and the new Kavieng and Maprik hospitals have been completed.

The Lutheran Mission hospital at Mambisanda serves as district hospital for Enga Province. There are over 50 less developed sub-district hospitals in PNG now called Rural Health Centres, as well as Maternal and Child Health clinics, rural health centres and dispensaries. In December, 1979, there were a total of 161 health centres, 209 sub-centres and 1,788 aid posts in Papua New Guinea.

Specialist hospitals include the Laloki Psychiatric Hospital, near Port Moresby. The four base hospitals have either psychiatric wards or clinics.

The Health Department is responsible for training staff other than medical officers. The trainees include health inspectors, health extension officers, medical technologists, radiologists, nurses and nursing aides, the latter being trained in most of the larger hospitals.

The PNG Institute of Medical Research, at Goroka, under the control of the Health Minister, undertakes research into PNG's health problems.

The Papuan Medical College was established in 1959 and became the Faculty of Medicine at the University of Papua New Guinea in 1971. This institution awards the degree of MB. Minimum education requirement for entrance is matriculation.

Although all members of the community may avail themselves of government medical services, there are also medical practitioners and dentists in private practice throughout Papua New Guinea.

Diseases. Malaria control is one of the prime aims of the Department of Health. This disease is now regarded as an entirely preventable disease, but it is still the major health problem among the indigenous population, mostly because of its secondary debilitating effect and accounts for approximately 10 per cent of the national health budget.

It is calculated that populations would double in a few years if malaria could be eradicated. To this end, special malaria-control areas have been established where mass treatment and preventive measures have been carried out including complete spraying, usually with DDT, of the inside of houses. The complete eradication of this disease will require the co-operation of the people, and this has not always been forthcoming. The malaria control programme reaches about 58 per cent of the people of PNG.

Pneumonia, usually a secondary result of some other disease, is the greatest cause of death in PNG hospitals and also the greatest cause of hospitalisation.

Tropical ulcers are prevalent.

Child mortality rate is high and to combat this Maternity and Child Health Clinics (including mobile clinics) have been set up and special efforts are made to educate people in these matters.

Venereal disease is on the increase, but cases of TB and leprosy under treatment are dropping.

THE LAND. Papua New Guinea lies wholly within the southern tropics. Its territorial boundaries stretch from the equator, in the north, to 12 deg. S. lat. in the south; from 141 deg. E. long. in the west to 160 deg. E. long. in the east. However the boundaries are irregular – for example, they exclude the Torres Strait Islands which go right up to the coast of western Papua New Guinea, but include the bulge of the Fly River into Irian Jaya in the east, the islands of Bougainville, Buka and other smaller groups, which geographically are part of the Solomon Islands.

The total land area is 461,690.33 sq. km. The land area includes the eastern half of the New Guinea mainland, (Indonesia's province of Irian Jaya occupying the western half); the Bismarck Archipelago, the main islands of which are Manus, New Ireland and New Britain; the northernmost Solomon Islands of Bougainville and Buka; and the groups of islands of the easternmost part of the mainland (Trobriands, D'Entrecasteaux, etc).

All the above groupings include their innumerable offshore islands which range in size from small islets to islands as large as Lavongai (New Hanover, which is 1,544 sq. km in area).

Natural features. The central core of the main island of New Guinea is a massive cordillera 2,500 km long that stretches from one end of the big island to the other. It is one of the world's great mountain systems and forms a drainage divide between rivers that, so far as Papua New Guinea is concerned, flow north into the sea off the north coast and those that flow south into the Gulf of Papua.

The mountains do not, however, consist of a single chain but rather a complex of ranges interspersed by wide valleys.

The principal units of the main mountain system in PNG, from west to east, are the Star Mountains (which extend across the Irian Jaya border), the Hindenburg, Muller, Kubor, Schrader and Bismarck Ranges each of which has peaks of over 3280 m, and the Owen Stanley Range with peaks of over 4265 m. Some of the highest peaks in PNG are: Mt. Wilhelm (4,697 m), Mt. Hagen (3,778 m); Mt. Michael (3,750 m); Mt. Bangeta (4,425 m); Mt. Giluwe (4,361 m); Mt. Victoria (4,037 m); and Mt. Albert Edward (3,990 m).

The islands of New Britain, New Ireland and Bougainville are also characterised by the typical central chain of mountains. In New Britain they reach a height of 2295 m, in Bougainville of over 2630 m, but in New Ireland the highest range is the Rossel Mts in the south, the highest peak of which is 2108 m.

West of the head of the Gulf of Papua, there are large areas of foothills between the central mountain chain and the swampy coastline. The foothill country has some ancient volcanic peaks which, though worn, still attain considerable heights – the Bosavi Mountains over 2600 m, Mt. Murray, 2432 m and Mt. Sisa, 2902 m.

Volcanoes. A line of volcanoes stretches along the northern coast of the mainland, crosses Vitiaz Strait, goes along the north coast of New Britain into the Gazelle Peninsula where Rabaul is situated, and then on through Bougainville. On the mainland south of this line there is little volcanic activity although there are many signs that there have been eruptions in the past. There was a serious eruption in what was regarded as an extinct volcano, at Mt Lamington, near Popondetta in 1951.

Most of the islands of the D'Entrecasteaux and Louisiade Archipelago are of volcanic origin and represent the peaks of a submerged mountain range. There are hot springs and other signs of volcanic activity at Fergusson Island.

A distinctive feature of the mainland is that within the interior there is a vast series of wide, well-watered valleys, stretching from the headwaters of the Markham River to the Irian Jaya border, and on both sides of the mountain divide. These valleys, with an average elevation of 1640 m, are clear of jungle, have a cool climate and support large native populations.

As this is a region of high rainfall there are a number of very large rivers on the mainland, notably the Fly, Purari, Kikori, Markham, Ramu and Sepik. The Sepik, Ramu and Markham drain the N.E. side of the mainland, and the others the southern side. There are hundreds of rivers of lesser size.

There are no comparable rivers in the big islands of New Britain, New Ireland or Bougainville. The drainage of these is taken care of by innumerable, small, rapid rivers flowing down from the mountains.

The north-eastern coastal areas of the mainland are believed to be rising while those of the south-east are continually sinking. For this reason coral reefs are not continuous along the coasts. Raised reefs do extend from the Sepik River mouth to Cape Cretin but from Salamaua, on the Morobe coast, to Goodenough Bay in Milne Bay Province, the coast is of drowned littoral type and there are no reefs.

Coral reefs are, however, an outstanding feature of the islands off the eastern tip of the mainland, and the coasts of New Britain, New Ireland and east and south coasts of Bougainville have fringing or barrier reefs.

Because of the character of the whole region, there are very few deep, landlocked harbours – exceptions being Port Moresby, Rabaul and Madang.

Climate. Apart from the Port Moresby area, which is in the "rain shadow" of the Owen Stanley Range and consequently has a dry climate, there is a regular and generally high annual rainfall in Papua New Guinea. The average is about 2,000 mm per year but there are wide variations – from 1195 mm per annum in Port Moresby to 5080 mm at Kikori on the Gulf of Papua.

There are two seasons – the south-east, or trade winds season, which lasts from May to October; and the monsoon, or north-west season which lasts from December through March. In the intervening periods the winds are variable, or there can be periods of unpleasant doldrums.

Although rain tends to be heavier in the monsoon season, rain can occur at any time in most places. Port Moresby is the only place in the country where the weather can be reasonably predicted into wet and dry seasons.

Because of the configuration of the mountains behind Huon Gulf, Lae city has its wettest season during the period of south-east trades.

Temperatures vary little throughout the year, the average coastal readings being between 21.1 deg. C min. and 32.2 deg. C max.

Temperature varies with altitude and the highland areas can be cool to miserably cold.

The country is not subject to hurricanes but is subject to earthquakes, which are much more frequent north of the Sepik River and in New Britain.

Flora and fauna. Dense jungles are a striking characteristic of a large part of Papua New Guinea. In most areas from sea level to 980 m, the rainforests grow in profusion.

Various types of indigenous sugarcane have been found for example, and some of them have enriched the world's sugar plantations.

The fauna of Papua New Guinea is closely related to that of Australia. Of the 100 species of mammals found, marsupials predominate and only a native cat is carnivorous.

There are wallabies, several species of the phalanger family (sometimes called gliding possums in Australia), the cuscus and the red bandicoot. There are spiny anteaters, bats, rats and mice and the southern coast has a native dog now very rare, apparently related to the Australian dingo.

There are 70 species of snakes some of which are not venomous (such as the python and some water-snakes) but the majority are. Lizards of all sizes including the giant monitor are present; tortoises and crocodiles are found in the rivers and sea and there are 1400 species of fish which contribute largely to the diet of coastal people.

There are over 650 species of birds that inhabit the mainland alone, including the glorious Birds of Paradise and the cassowary which are indigenous.

The most harmful of the insects are the malaria-carrying mosquito and the scrub typhus (or Japanese River fever) carrying tick or mite. The most beautiful of the insects are the huge and often vividly coloured moths and butterflies.

Land tenure: The total area of Papua New Guinea is 46,169,033 hectares. According to the latest figures available, 43,966,077 ha. of this is unalienated land; 216,628 ha. freehold land owned by non-indigenes; 3,747 ha. are held under tenure conversion; 1,982,581 ha. are government land (407,167 ha. of which are under leases; 38,070 ha. are native reserve; and 1,537,344 ha. designated "other", including land held for public purposes, for leasing, etc.).

Of the 407,167 ha. of land let out by the government under lease, 256,900 ha. are used for agriculture, 814 ha. for dairying, 81,433 ha. for pastoral, 16,287 ha. for residential and business purposes, 40,717 ha. for other leases, 10,179 ha. for missions and 837 ha. for town sub-divisions.

The ownership of land and the use of available land are subjects of much importance in Papua New Guinea and widespread changes in tenure are planned.

All unalienated land is deemed to be native-owned until proved otherwise. This protects the interests of the indigenous people until the ownership position is clarified by the Lands Titles Commission.

Customary land is land possessed or owned by an indigenous person or community by virtue of rights of a proprietary or possessory kind which arises from, and is regulated by, native custom.

Freehold land is of two kinds: (a) that which originated during the German administration, prior to 1914, in New Guinea and prior to 1906 in Papua; and (b) that which has, in recent years, been tenure converted by individual indigenes from customary ownership. Legislation was being drafted early in 1980 aimed at the eventual replacement of all existing freehold titles by leasehold titles.

After Papua became an Australian territory and when New Guinea became a mandated territory after World War I, the principle was accepted that no further freehold land was to be granted to non-indigenes. Freehold land that existed at that time continued to be freely bought, sold or leased. However, since World War II ownership of some of the permanently alienated land has been challenged by national groups. In other cases freehold land held by Europeans has been purchased back by government and restored to local groups or cut up for small holdings.

The 1973 Land Commission Report made many recommendations including:

All freehold and leasehold titles should be statutorially converted into government-guaranteed leaseholds. No compensation should be paid to freeholders and the government should be protected from compensation claims; however, freeholders who have their titles changed to leaseholds should have a five year "holiday" before rents are charged and in the case where the property is mortgaged they should be able to appeal to the Minister for special consideration.

Freeholds now held by Papua New Guineans should be converted into group titles, conditional freeholds used for unregistered customary land, or into government leases.

Government leases should be for 60 years with right of renewal, for PNG citizens; but for 40 years, with no automatic right of renewal, for non-citizens. (Non-citizens who involve substantial citizen ownership in their leases to have leases of 60 years duration.)

Present government leases which have less than 40 years to run (or 60 years for citizens) should continue to expiry; where the leases are for more than 40 years (or 60 years for citizens) they should be reduced to the appropriate term.

A government lease should be the only way a non-citizen can hold land, although a citizen should be able to grant or take a small area of land on direct lease, subject to certain conditions.

In areas where most of the rural land has been alienated and people are seriously short of land and where the return of undeveloped alienated land does not sufficiently relieve the shortage of land for cash cropping as well as subsistence, the government should take steps to recover developed land nearby, by compulsory process if necessary, and return it to the land-short people. Compensation paid to the holders of the former developed land should be limited to the unexhausted improvements on the land.

In line with these recommendations, the government has passed legislation to help transfer expatriate-owned plantations to Papua New Guinean groups. A special fund to help in the purchase of these plantations has been set up and is administered by the Department of Natural Resources.

So far 68 European plantations had been bought for redistribution under the Plantation Redistribution Scheme. However, redistribution has been slower than acquisition and further outright purchases have been suspended pending a review. An attempt will also be made to purchase a part-equity in some of the larger European and company-owned plantations.

The government will continue working on the proposals for legislation to provide for the registration of national land, the conversion of freehold to leaseholds, and for legislation to enable the registration of customary land.

Government land is land that has come into the hands of government through purchase or as successor to the German administration through mandatory powers after World War I, or through acquisition for public purposes.

Only the government, through the Department of Natural Resources has power to purchase land from the indigenes and this it does only after all the present and future needs of the owners and the best economic use of the land are taken into consideration.

Apart from comparatively small areas of land acquired for public purposes such as roads, airports, defence, and public safety, the land purchased from indigenous owners by the government is for the purpose of leasing to individuals or organisations of all races in line with the planned economic development of the country.

Native land systems: There is considerable variation in indigenous inheritance systems of land or use of land. Rights of ownership are normally acquired through birth but acquisition by purchase, once unknown is now an established custom in some places. Land use must also be distinguished from land ownership. Some communities still practise a system of shifting cultivation and they may, for a time, use the land of one or two individuals for gardens and then move on to land owned by some other individual or group.

This type of customary land tenure is not considered satisfactory for economic progress as it lacks flexibility.

In November, 1973 a Commission of Inquiry into PNG Land Matters issued a vital report, and many of its proposals are being put into effect by the PNG Government in stages.

The commission stated that four main aims were to return land to land-short New Guineans; to provide a system of land holding that would promote good race relations; to treat land as a national resource and emphasise the need to use it properly; and to discourage speculation in land.

A considerable part of the report dealt with customary land. The commission recommended that there should only be cautious alteration of some features of the customary system, which accounts for about 97 per cent of all PNG land; and that individualism in native land matters should not be encouraged. However, it believed that registration of some customary land is required and that provision should be made for various kinds of title, but only where the people understand and want it.

The commission suggested four kinds of titles for customary land: (a) group titles; (b) customary rights – under which clan leaders declare a named member of the clan has sole rights to any given portion of land for commercial purposes for a given time; (c) subsidiary rights, which individuals or groups may hold in land over which another group has the main rights (such as right to gather fruit, or basic materials for building); and (d) conditional freeholds which are suitable for groups, such as a family, to hold land in common.

One of the more important recommendations of the Land Commission Report was that all land laws in force in PNG be repealed and replaced by new legislation enacted by the National Parliament. Work has been proceeding on the drafting of such legislation for a considerable time but in February, 1980 the legislation had not been enacted.

PRIMARY PRODUCTION. Until 1972 Papua New Guinea's most important industries were agricultural. However, Bougainville Copper Ltd. began producing in 1972 and by 1973-74 was responsible for approximately 64 per cent of the total value of PNG exports. With the drop in copper prices, this was down 37 per cent in the year ended June 1977. Results improved in 1978, and Bougainville Copper made a strong recovery in 1979 with the dramatic increases in world prices for copper and gold.

Primary industries are still, however, the largest market for labour. Since 1972 palm oil has also entered the export field and exports from this industry were valued at K14 million in the 12 months to September, 1979.

Apart from copper and concentrates Papua New Guinea's main export industries now are coconut planting (copra and coconut oil, animal foodstuffs); cocoa; coffee; palm oil and palm kernels; rubber; timber milling; plywood and veneer manufacture; passionfruit planting (juice and pulp); tea planting; gold mining, pyrethrum (producing an extract used in insecticide).

Primary industries that produce for local consumption are vegetable growing, cattle raising, dairying and sawmilling.

Here are details of the major items of primary production:

Copra. Papua New Guinea is the biggest producer of copra and coconut oil in the South Pacific. The most important coconut plantation areas are the Gazelle Peninsula in New Britain, New Ireland, N.E. coast of Bougainville, Madang coast, parts of West New Britain and Manus, and the Milne Bay and Central provinces. Today, most of the country's export copra is dried in modern hot-air mechanical driers that produce a better quality product than the old village sun-dried or smoke-dried copra.

Part of PNG's coconut products is now exported in the form of coconut-oil.

About 50 per cent of all copra is produced from village groves and plantations; the rest from large scale plantations owned by individuals or companies, which are now being resumed by government for redistribution to Papua New Guineans under a scheme which is designed to place the whole coconut industry in indigenous hands by the 1980's.

Prices for copra (and hence coconut oil and other coconut products) fluctuate widely.

PNG exported copra worth K44 million in 1974-75 but sales totalled only K19 million in 1975-76 and an estimated K32.6 million in 1976-77 because of a marked fluctuation in prices after the boom years of 1972-73. During the 12 months to September, 1979, copra, copra expeller pellets and coconut oil worth K60.6 million were exported. In mid-1979 prices soared to US$750 per tonne of copra but by early 1980 had dropped to K600, still a good price.

All copra is marketed through the Papua New Guinea Copra Marketing Board which is a corporate body with power of succession and a common seal. The board consists of a chairman and members representing producers, and the Department of Primary Industry.

Copra is purchased by the board under a system of grade and ownership markings. A modified pool principle is employed, tentative purchase prices being declared and then, after the end of the trading period, final prices are determined in the light of actual trading results, and final payments made.

Palm oil. In 1967 the Papua New Guinea government and a British firm, Harrisons and Crossfield, with oil palm know-how, set up New Britain Oil Palm Development Ltd., on a 50/50 ownership basis. The idea was for a balance between a company plantation and adjacent local smallholders, who would have their crop processed in a factory built by the company; the government would be responsible for roads, and an overseas wharf at Kimbe.

Smallholders from all over Papua New Guinea were assisted to establish themselves by loans from the PNG Development Bank.

A K7 million factory was completed in 1971 and is being progressively enlarged until the whole available planting area comes into bearing. A second oil factory is under construction at Kumbango and will commence production in September, 1980. The company, at the end of 1976, had a planted area of 2,800 ha. and, in addition, there were 1,580 smallholders and 200 village plots with a total area of 7,940 ha. At June 30, 1979, the company had increased its planting to 3,700 ha and in addition there were 1,590 smallholders and 200 village blocks with a total area of 6,480 ha.

Production from the Hoskins factory for the year ended June 30, 1979, was 32,400 tonnes of oil and 4,600 tonnes of kernel. Value of palm oil exports for the 12 months to September, 1979, was K14 million.

In 1977 the government had also established another palm oil project at Sangara in the Northern Province, based largely on the redevelopment of unsuccessful smallholder cocoa blocks. Production should begin in April 1980. Another oil palm scheme at Bialla West New Britain is also scheduled for initial production in mid-1980.

Cocoa was planted as an alternative to copra before the Pacific War but plantations were all wiped out during the Japanese occupation 1942-45. After the war high prices for cocoa gave the industry a boost and there was vigorous planting either interplanted between coconuts, or on its own, especially in New Britain.

By the mid-1960's there were about 64,800 ha. under cocoa in Papua New Guinea and the economic development plan called for an increase to 91,125 ha. and a production of 35,560 tonnes. However this target was not achieved. Exports for 1978-79 was about 29,193 tonnes, a decline due to the age of the trees and reduced production from estates. About 50 per cent of the production comes from plantings by Papua New Guineans.

Most districts produce some cocoa but the most important production areas are in East New Britain, Bougainville, New Ireland and Madang.

PNG cocoa is of good quality and finds markets in West Germany, Netherlands, U.S.A., UK etc. as well as Australia. Estimated value of exports for the 12 months to September, 1979, was K61.3 million.

A Cocoa Industry Board was established in Rabaul in 1974. In 1976-77 it began to compile a register of fermentaries and it established a stabilisation fund in 1977. This stood at K67.5 million by late 1979.

Coffee. A little Arabica coffee was grown near Wau before World War II and some Robusta in New Britain and Bougainville, but the big increase in coffee production came after the New Guinea Highlands were opened for settlement in the early 1950's. It is now the country's largest agricultural export earner and there are in excess of 200,000 smallholder growers who produce 70 per cent of the total crop.

In the year ended October, 1979 about 48,520 tonnes of coffee beans valued at K118,243,807 million were exported.

Although coffee was originally grown by European planters, most production is now in the hands of Papua New Guineans.

The most important Arabica coffee growing areas in Papua New Guinea are Eastern and Western Highlands and Chimbu provinces and the high elevation areas of Morobe province. However, Robusta coffee is grown in Central, Milne Bay and Northern provinces and to a more limited degree in most of the other provinces. PNG coffee is exported to Germany, Netherlands, Australia, South Africa, UK and elsewhere.

Rubber. This is mostly confined to the Port Moresby side of Papua New Guinea.

The Australian Government made substantial grants to encourage rubber planting and the industry was well established by the 1920's.

In the 1950's special marketing arrangements were made by the Australian government for an assured market for PNG rubber in Australia which now takes the whole production. There are about 16,000 ha. under rubber and production was 4,069.5 tonnes in 1979.

Indigenous production is still negligible although smallholder interest has been fostered in Western Province at Cape Rodney and Bailebo in Central Province and at Gavien, East Sepik.

There are approximately 3,700 smallholders and in 1978 their prodcon amounted to only 432 tonnes. However, 80 per cent of their rubber trees have yet to come into tap.

The sale of rubber in Australia has been through a rubber pool since the 1950's and this has been continued since PNG independence. Towards the end of each year the rubber pool negotiates with Australian manufacturers for the sale of all PNG rubber in the following year. Prices are tied to world price for RSS No. 1 grade. For this concession the manufacturers are able to import all their other rubber requirements from non-PNG sources duty free. Estimated export value of rubber for the 12 months ending September, 1979 was K3.1 million.

Tea. The possibilities of tea growing were discussed in New Guinea in the late 1930's but only a few experimental plots were grown until the late 1940's when the goverot selected Garaina, in the Morobe district, at an elevation of 600m for large scale experiments. It was not until late 1962 that a tea factory was built at Garaina. Although Garaina tea was mid-level it was of good quality; moreover the yield per acre was about 80 per cent more than expected, and New Guinea labour, especially the women of the Waria valley in which the plantation is situated, took to picking easily.

Tea growing did not extend in that area but all commercial plantations were subsequently established in the Highlands, notably the Western Highlands and to a minor degree in Southern Highlands. From 1966 all production from Garaina was used as seed tea for the Highlands plantations. Garaina was put up for sale in 1973 but failed to attract a buyer. It has now been closed.

The first private tea estates were established in 1963-64 when several lots averaging 400 ha. each were put up for tender in the Wahgi Valley near Mount Hagen. By 1973 there were eight major non-indigenous estates in Western Highlands and four tea factories had been built. Two tea estates were then being developed in Southern Highlands.

In the 12 months ending September 1979 the export of 7,457 tonnes of tea was worth K8.2 million.

Passionfruit. Passionfruit juice and pulp have been exported from Papua New Guinea to cordial processors in Australia since a modest processing factory was set up near Goroka about 20 years ago. Growing the fruit is entirely in the hands of Papua New Guineans who sell the fresh fruit to the factory which has been purchased by the PNG Government. Production varies from year to year. At the end of 1977, 11,759 ha were planted with passionfruit including 100,000 vines planted in 1977. The 1976 harvest was 34,000 kg and production has steadily declined since then. High prevailing prices for coffee makes the production of passionfruit unattractive to the villager.

Pyrethrum. Pyrethrum, an ingredient of some insecticides, is extracted from a daisy-like plant. *Chrysanthemum cinerariaefolium,* which grows in the tropics at altitudes over 1800m. Varieties that would grow well in the PNG highlands were selected in the 1950's but the industry did not progress until a British firm, established an extraction factory near Mount Hagen.

Some thousands of hectares were planted by New Guineans in the Highlands provinces but the industry has not grown much since the mid-1960's. Growers have found returns too small for the work involved. In 1973 the factory was taken over by the government as the Kagamuga Natural Products Co. Ltd. Pyrethrum is now obtained from 830 ha in Enga province where there are some 30,000 smallholder growers. Production in 1979 was 170 tonnes. A shortage of natural pyrethrum pushed prices up to K1 per kilo in 1979 and this has led to renewed interest in the crop. 1980 production is expected to reach 250 tonnes.

OTHER AGRICULTURAL INDUSTRIES. Vegetable growing is very important to the economy and it has been estimated that possibly 80 per cent of the people rely on the vegetables they grow for food. It has been estimated that probably four or five million tonnes of vegetables and fruit are produced each year from some 250,000 ha.

The greatest output is of sweet potatoes which may represent 40 per cent of total vegetable production. Other important food crops include bananas, taro, yams, sugar-cane and coconuts. Up to 150,000 people who live near the great rivers and swamps, rely on the sago palm to provide the major part of their diets.

The people use an estimated 500 species of native fruits, vegetables and leaves. They also plant introduced varieties including tomatoes, maize, citrus fruit, papaw and peanuts. Cold climate vegetables including cabbage and potatoes are grown in some Highland areas.

All major vegetables are sold in town and country markets. The quantities are not recorded but may amount to 150,000 tonnes worth, perhaps, K30 million. Despite the large quantities of vegetables produced, a large and growing amount of food is imported. In an effort to encourage local production, a customs tariff of 30 per cent ad valoı was recently introduced on all imported frozen, canned or fresh vegetables.

The Government is encouraging increased production of vegetables in an attempt to reduce the imports. It is providing advice and assistance to smallholders and is building or improving roads to enable crops to be taken to sales outlets. Miscellaneous cash crops include peanuts for processing into roasted peanuts and peanut butter; tobacco for blending with imported leaf; and rice. However, all are produced only in small quantities.

Rice is grown in Central, Gulf, Madang, Milne Bay, Morobe and East and West Sepik provinces but on a very small scale. Production rose from 1,133 tonnes in year ended June 1974 to 1,610 tonnes by June 1976. Production has steadily declined since then. The largest harvests were 410 tonnes from the Mekeo area of Central province, 881 tonnes from East Sepik, and 199 tonnes from West Sepik. These quantities are minimal compared with PNG imports of rice which were 80,000 tonnes in 1978.

FOOD MARKETING CORPORATION. The Food Marketing Corporation Pty Ltd, a registered company fully owned by the PNG government with an authorised capital of K3 million, operates from headquarters in Port Moresby to handle distribution of fruit and vegetables throughout Papua New Guinea. It was established in 1976 with the aim of encouraging vegetable and fruit growing throughout the country, and arranging effective distribution. The corporation is also interested in exporting produce, although its main objective is to increase local production and distribution so that fruit and vegetables imports may be reduced.

The corporation is undertaking research into improved processing methods and is developing a number of new products. The corporation has branches in Lae, Kainantu, Goroka and Mt Hagen but plans to be represented eventually in every province.

The corporation operates the passionfruit processing plant in Goroka, which in 1976 produced 18,000 litres of pulp, and 9,100 litres of single-strength juice. There are plans to double the current passionfruit crop but grower interest is not high, and it is doubtful whether there will be any substantial increase in production.

Cattle raising and dairying. The long-range plan of the government is to make Papua New Guinea self-sufficient in meat, however this had not been achieved by 1979 although the progress in the last decade has been considerable.

In most localities, crosses with tropical breeds have proved superior to pure British breeds, and the majority of cattle in PNG would now be crossbreeds.

There were about 140,000 cattle in PNG in 1979, Morobe province is still the most important cattle area. After Morobe, in order of cattle importance, come the Central province and Madang and Western Highlands although all provinces have some cattle.

Indigenous farmers, especially in the Highlands areas, are being encouraged to develop an interest in cattle raising, by having a nucleus of 15 breeding cows and a bull. These smallholder cattle ventures are being financed by a World Bank loan of $US5 million and administered through the PNG Development Bank.

In January, 1979, the number of cattle owned by smallholders was approx. 46,264.

About 42 per cent of fresh, chilled or frozen beef is supplied locally but when canned and other meat are taken into consideration local supplies amount to only one-sixth of requirements.

Dairy cattle number less than 3,000 and dairying is carried on notably at Port Moresby, Lae, Goroka, Mount Hagen, Minj and Banz only in proximity to towns. Production of milk does not meet demand.

There is a central abattoir controlled by the government in Lae and there are smaller abattoirs in other cattle producing districts.

Other livestock. Experiments have been made from time to time with sheep, notably the Nondugl experiment with Romney Marsh sheep immediately after the war. But in large herds they have been unsuccessful. Some success is being achieved with experimental flocks in the Highlands which are partly financed with New Zealand aid.

The most important animal in the native economy is the pig. Pigs in most communities are primarily an indication of individual or village wealth, used for ceremonial purposes. In native life, pig meat contributes little to the diet of the people. However, efforts are being made by government to improve the quality of local pigs through extension work. Commercial piggeries operate near the towns and local supplies to these areas are adequate and of good quality. However, production is only 100 tonnes of carcass compared with imports of 550 tonnes.

Poultry are also a part of village life. But commercial poultry is still handled mostly by expatriates.

Some 60 per cent of poultry meat consumed is locally produced, and almost all the eggs.

Donkeys, goats and horses are also kept in Papua New Guinea but not in sufficient numbers to be economically important.

Marine industries. Traditionally coastal villages have always fished for food and this has remained largely unchanged except for the introduction of modern aids such as outboard motors and imported nets. In recent years villagers have been encouraged to preserve their surplus catch either by drying, smoking, or by the use of small freezers that have been established in strategic localities and from which fish are distributed to local markets.

Local fishermen have also participated in some commercial fishing, for example, in the Western Province where barramundi is caught in season in the estuaries of the large rivers. In the 12 months to September, 1979, barramundi worth K109,434 was exported.

A fleet of 47 tuna boats based at Kavieng, Rabaul and Manus caught tuna worth K18.5 million in the 12 months to September, 1979.

A fleet of 15 trawlers was working the Gulf of Papua for prawns. The catch of prawns and crayfish was valued at K5.7 million.

The PNG Government in 1977 was reorganising fishing activities under the Division of Fisheries with the aim of promoting local fishing and controlling resources. It was recruiting professional development officers for the provinces and planned to increase substantially over the next few years the export of tuna and prawns.

Training of inspecting officers was through the Fisheries School, Madang. In mid-1977, training in fisheries skills was provided by the new National Fisheries College at Kavieng, with one-, two- and three-year courses in commercial fisheries techniques. Up to 100 residential students per annum can be trained at the College which was funded with a grant of K1.65 million provided by Japan.

PNG reefs abound in trochus and green snail shell, beche-de-mer and pearl shell and all three products were exported in 1977.

Cultured pearls. Samarai Pearls Ltd. produces half-pearls from local MOP near Samarai.

Forestry and timber industry. Forestry products are expected to become one of the country's main export income earners. In the year ended December, 1978, export of forest products in the form of logs, sawn timber, plywood, veneer, woodchips, chopsticks and sandalwood realised a value of K24.85 million.

Some 17,870 ha. of forest have been replanted to 1980, two thirds of it in pine at Wau-Bulolo where natural hoop and klinkii pines are being cut for the manufacture of plywood at the Commonwealth New Guinea Timbers factory at Bulolo.

Currently about 680 ha. are being replanted per annum. Policy now favours big timber companies who can utilise the total produce of forests – timber, wood chips and pulp – and who can create a permanent industry through reafforestation. Small operators who worked timber leases for export logs, the land then being used for agriculture, are being phased out.

The oldest established timber enterprise in PNG is that of Commonwealth New Guinea Timbers which was set up in 1954 as a joint effort on behalf of the Australian Government and what was then Bulolo Gold Dredging. (Since 1973 the BGD share has been owned by Japanese interests and in 1979 the PNG Government bought control.) By reafforestation the klinkii and hoop pine forests have been maintained while the trees that are cut are turned into plywood and veneer at a factory at Bulolo.

Another important timber area, the Madang forest, is located about 40km from Madang town and, including the Gogol forest, has a total area of 83,000 ha. Right to exploit this forest is held by Jant Pty. Ltd., a Japanese company. The company produces woodchips and QUILA Logs. A sawmill at Binnen Harbour, Madang, with a chip mill to take care of waste, are in operation. Total investment is K10 million.

In 1973 rights to a 183,000 ha. forest at Open Bay, East New Britain, were let to the Open Bay Timber Co. Ltd., which is owned by Thiess Bros. of Australia, the Japanese Sobu Adachi (which has a major shareholding in Commonwealth New Guinea Timbers), and the Papua New Guinea Development Corporation. A sawmill and a wood chip mill have been established at Powell Harbour, to be wholly export-oriented, with a capacity of 84,000 cu m of sawn timber each year. Total investment is K15 million. In 1979 the woodchip mill was destroyed by fire. Another is to be constructed.

A large development on the Port Moresby side of the country is the ANG Timber Corporation which operates in the Marshall Lagoon-Cape Rodney area of Central Province. The company originally aimed at producing sawn timber, logs and woodchips and the development stage including a considerable amount of road building between the forest and the mill at Cape Rodney, harbour dredging, wharf building etc. is operated by Associated Pulp and Paper Mills Ltd, of Australia.

Smaller projects proposed as development are a K7 million enterprise in New Ireland: a K300 million scheme at Vanimo and a K5 million scheme for Umboi.

Other development areas were becoming available.

MANUFACTURING AND MINING. Excluding the panguna copper mining activities, the main secondary industries producing for export are the copra crushing mill at Rabaul, owned by a W. R. Carpenter and Co. Ltd subsidiary; the plywood factory at Bulolo, owned by Commonwealth New Guinea Timbers; and the oil-palm processing factory near Kimbe, West New Britain and the factory under construction at Higaturu. They are not labour intensive.

There are several large tea factories in the Wahgi Valley, but these are processing units rather than secondary industries in the usual sense.

Apart from secondary export industries there are a large number that produce for the local market with a minor export to neighbouring territories.

These include: Aerated water; biscuits; baskets; batteries; beer (two breweries in Port Moresby); glass bottles and containers; steel drums and metal buckets; canvas goods; chemicals for agricultural, industrial and domestic use, including detergents; cigarettes (one factory in Goroka and one in Madang); concrete blocks and components; clothing, fibre board containers and packaging material; paper towels and toilet rolls; ice cream; metal decking and roofing; galvanised iron sheets; fencing material; fibreglass; marine products; bottled gas; louvre windows; paint (three factories); joinery, timber and pre-fabricated buildings; radio assembly; refrigerators; sheetmetal work and water tanks; meat smallgoods; stationery and printing; stock food; cooking stoves; polythene bags; plastic containers; etc.

Gold mining. Papua New Guinea has had a long and lucrative history of gold mining, but the golden days of Wau and Bulolo and the big companies are now over.

Bulolo Gold Dredging closed down the last of its dredges in 1965. Placer Development Ltd took over BGD interests at the end of the 1960's, but sold its goldmining and other PNG interests to a Japanese company in 1973. New Guinea Goldfields has continued to work open-cut at Golden Ridges.

Virtually all individual mining by outsiders has now gone but indigenous miners are operating in Morobe, East and West Highlands, Sepik and Northern Provinces.

There are large-scale company investigations proceeding at Pongera and Yerikai.

In 1979 gold and silver production, EXCLUDING Bougainville Copper Ltd, was worth K2,372,548. Bougainville Copper production of gold and silver was valued at K167,152,000 gross.

Gold is not separated from the copper concentrate in the North Solomons. This is done at refineries in Japan, Germany and Spain where the concentrates are sent.

Copper mining. The most promising future copper development on the PNG mainland is in the Star Mountains area of Western Province where Kennecott Explorations (Aust.) Pty Ltd completed preliminary drilling in 1973 at a cost of $16 million. The deposits are believed rich enough to be economically viable despite transportation problems in such a remote area but in late 1973 Kennecott asked the PNG government for certain concessions before it proceeded further. Negotiations broke down, and the PNG government decided to pay for the final exploration itself and in 1975 set up the government-owned Ok Tedi Development Company to do the work. Drilling began again in 1976, and mid-year it was reported that there are at least 250 million tonnes of ore which could be recovered by open pit methods. The ore averaged 0.852 per cent total copper and contained 0.653 grams of gold per tonne. The government has entered into an agreement with the Australian BHP Co. for a further investigation of the prospect.

A decision is expected to be announced during 1980.

The copper success story has been at Panguna, Bougainville, in the Crown Prince Range behind Kieta, where Bougainville Copper Ltd went into production in 1972. The parent company, Conzinc Riotinto, had begun prospecting the area in 1964 following a government examination in 1960. Reserves are at least 944 million tonnes of ore with a copper content of 0.48 per cent, and 15.83 gm of gold to the tonne. Markets are assured for many years.

In the calendar year 1979, 584,692 tonnes of dry concentrate were produced. Consolidated net earnings of the company were K83.9 million.

The value of the Bougainville copper project is thus a vital part of Papua New Guinea's economy. In addition the company provides job opportunities on a larger scale than any other enterprise in PNG (except the government).

In addition to the mine site and town of Panguna up in the ranges, a coastal satellite town, Arawa, has been established on the coast. Arawa was built by the company and the PNG government on the site of a former plantation. Present population of the KIETA/Arawa/Panguna region is estimated as 18,000. Over the headland at Loloho, on Anewa Bay, is the port for the whole project, with wharf, power station, bulk loading equipment and ore driers.

The copper/gold/silver is mined at Panguna, about 25 km from the coast by all-weather road that goes over the Crown Prince Range at an altitude of 1037m. The mine is worked by open cut methods, the ore being crushed, ground and piped down to Loloho in the form of slurry where it is filtered and dried and exported as dry concentrate. It is shipped abroad for refining.

It cost over $A400 million to establish the Panguna-Arawa-Loloho complex.

Apart from Bougainville and Ok Tedi, other deposits are being investigated at Frieda in West Sepik, and at Yandera in Madang Province.

Petroleum. Petroleum policy was a major area of government interest in 1980. There have been no commercial oil discoveries in Papua New Guinea, although there are proven gas fields, some of them offshore in the Papuan Gulf. Exploration work is continuing.

TOURISM. PNG has had casual visitors for almost a century but only in recent years has it become interested in organised tourism and even now, with so many other important industries, this still has a minor place in the economy.

VALUE OF MAIN COMMODITIES EXPORTED — RANDOM YEARS

	1974-75 K'000	1976-77 K'000	1978 K'000	1979 (to Sept) K'000
Copra	29,411	191,187	23,023	29,569
Cocoa	39,127	55,131	62,955	49,266
Coffee	33,544	132,619	107,225	96,575
Rubber	2,584	3,128	2,630	2,409
Tea	3,848	8,001	7,833	6,555
Timber, logs	7,458	11,678	11,946	13,192
Timber, sawn	2,891	7,317	4,171	4,581
Plywood	2,572	2,887	2,858	2,415
Tuna	7,897	13,564	20,457	11,214
Crayfish, prawns	3,449	5,103	4,130	4,988
Copra oil	13,778	12,160	12,449	19,787
Other coconut products	1,061	1,291	1,060	1,177
Palm oil	6,785	8,535	10,483	11,851
Copper ore & concentrates	236,659	191,488	217,238	232,377

The Office of Tourism, headed by a Director of Tourism, comes within the Ministry of Commerce, Tourism and Industry financed through the departmental budget allocated by Central Government.

In the last few years, there has been a great improvement in the standard of facilities provided for travellers, both in hotels and air transport.

There were 26,374 short-term arrivals in Papua New Guinea in 1976. Of these 14,493 stated on arrival that they were on holiday. This represents an 18.8 per cent decrease from the previous year, though the current statistics do not include cruise ship passengers who have not been required to complete Customs documents as their visit does not extend beyond 24 hours.

The tourist industry represented K12.7 million in revenue to Papua New Guinea in 1975-76.

Airline operators arrange conducted tours or travel on an individual basis at an all-in charge. American tourists visit parts of the country as part of Pacific circle tours and there was increasing interest from Japanese tour groups in 1977.

OVERSEAS TRADE. For many years Papua New Guinea had an imbalance of trade, with imports being considerably higher than exports, but this has now changed because of the export of copper ore and concentrates from the giant Panguna copper mine on Bougainville. The accompanying table gives comparisons.

	Kina	
Year to June 30	**Exports**	**Imports**
1972	127,181,000	256,386,000
1973	229,614,000	228,997,000
1974	483,731,000	228,875,000
1975	427,472,000	393,997,000
1976	363,750,000	346,397,000
1977 (prov.)	517,408,000	393,249,000
1978 (prov.)	570,586,000	478,449,000

In 1979, the price of copper was increasing considerably after a drop, and other export commodities, particularly coffee and copra, were improving. The accompanying tables show the main exports and imports and their destination or origin.

Exports — Main Countries of Destination
9 months to Sept. 1979

	K
Australia	41,414
Japan	162,307
United Kingdom	32,788
U.S.A.	28,892
West Germany	125,472
Other	2,037
Total	**497,139**

NOTE: Copper/gold concentrate is exported to Japan and West Germany for refining. This accounts for the steep rise in total value of exports to these countries.

Quantities of Main Exports

	1978	1979 (to Sept)
	Tonnes	**Tonnes**
Copra	92,164	69,063
Cocoa	27,129	22,300
Coffee	46,125	40,276
Rubber	4,135	2,841
Tea	6,980	5,825
Copra Oil	29,088	29,452
Other coconut products	15,650	12,450
Palm oil	28,413	28,177
Copper ore & concentrates	655,638	477,561
	Cubic metres	**Cubic metres**
Timber, logs	440,200	331,050
Timber, sawn	42,100	41,522
Plywood	7,600	5,986

VALUE OF MAIN IMPORT CATEGORIES — RANDOM YEARS

	1967-68	1970-71	1973-74	1975-76
	K'000	K'000	K'000	K'000
Food and live animals	29,988	41,474	57,404	73,088
Beverages & tobacco	4,330	6,304	4,289	5,810
Inedible crude materials, except fuel	854	1,008	769	1,109
Mineral fuels, lubricants, etc.	5,366	8,655	9,642	47,220
Animal & vegetable oils, fats	150	258	471	846
Chemicals & chemical products	7,641	11,417	13,624	18,945
Manufactured goods, classified by material	23,286	45,787	38,964	48,051
Machinery & transport equipment	45,663	101,417	61,666	109,192
Misc. manufactured articles	17,838	25,427	22,202	27,992
Miscellaneous transactions	8,395	9,817	6,950	10,748
Outside packages	1,793	3,030	2,893	3,397
TOTAL	**145,304**	**254,594**	**218,874**	**346,398**

Imports — Main Countries of Origin 1975-76

	K
Australia	161,413
Japan	49,980
U.S.A.	24,368
Britain	18,327
Hong Kong	8,959
West Germany	4,956
Netherlands	2,487
All other	75,907
Total	**346,397**

Customs Tariff. Import duties are levied on a wide range of goods, and there is in addition a 2½ per cent general import levy imposed on the f.o.b. value of all goods except for some basic items such as rice, sugar, flour, tinned fish and tinned meat. Some examples of import tariffs are firearms and ammunition and playing cards, all 50%; buses, trucks and trailers, 10%; tea 45%. These charges are estimated to provide K52 million in 1980.

There are export duties on a wide range of items, mostly agricultural, including logs, and minerals. These charges are estimated to bring K7.8 million in 1980.

FINANCE. Papua New Guinea derives its public revenue mainly from three sources – locally raised revenue, grants from the Australian Government, and public loans. For many years before Papua New Guinea independence Australian grants provided about two-thirds of total revenue, but the proportion has gradually diminished as local revenues have increased. Main sources of internal revenue are from Customs (mainly import and excise duties), personal and company income tax, stamp duties, licence fees and public utilities.

Budget. The accompanying table shows comparative revenue figures of recent random years and their source. The 1976-77 budget, brought down in August 1976, cannot easily be compared with these figures because there have been some important changes in the method of financing, and in the application of grants, and also because the Papua New Guinea kina is not on a par with the Australian dollar, and exchange has to be allowed for. As from January 1, 1978, PNG moved to a financial year of January 1 to December 31. The first budget under this scheme was announced on February 21, 1978.

The Australian Government in 1976 guaranteed Papua New Guinea a five-year economic assistance commitment totalling at least $A830 million and untied. The first instalment, for 1976-77, totalled K175.9 million. Estimated total receipts for 1980 are (in K. million).

	K
Australian aid	182
Loans	72.5
Internal revenue	307.3
TOTAL	561.8

The loan receipts for the 1980 budget comprise concessional loans K32.8 million and other borrowings of K39.7 million.

The internal revenue is composed of K190.4 million in direct taxation (K69.3 million personal tax, K41.2 million company tax, K4 million in dividend withholding tax); plus indirect taxation of K102.6 million (including K52 million import duties), K42.7 million excise, K7.8 million export tax, plus other charges).

Expenditure. Highest expenditure for 1980 was K187.7 million for departmental activities.

Expenditure for the National Parliament for the year was estimated to be K2 million; Department of Defence, K22.5 million; Education, K27 million; Foreign Affairs, K7.3 million; Health, K37.1 million; Police, K19.7 million; Primary Industry, K20.7 million; Office of Implementation, K62 million; Transport & Civil Aviation, K23 million; Works & Supply, K8.5 million; Public Services Commission, K9.8 million.

REVENUE — COMPARISON BY RANDOM YEARS

Year ending June 30	Aust Grants K	Internal Receipts K	Loans K	Total Receipts K
1946	505,480	130,642		636,322
1950	8,368,908	2,801,040		11,169,948
1958	21,592,982	0,450,062		31,043,044
1960	25,616,564	13,187,856	246,390	39,050,810
1964	50,498,616	22,753,758	3,368,262	76,620,636
1968	77,594,251	47,766,375	8,397,214	133,757,840
1970	99,270,921	72,442,220	32,519,901	204,233,042
1974	140,450,000	109,500,000	54,500,000	304,450,000
1975	156,282,000	177,585,000	50,328,000	402,973,000
1976	127,000,000	223,566,000	40,140,000	429,467,000
1977	175,900,000	224,700,000	31,500,000	432,144,000
1978	171,939,019	288,419,909	28,620,531	488,979,459

For the calendar year 1978, the PNG Government estimates total expenditure of K485.8 million and revenue of K476.2 million.

Tax system. Papua New Guinea has a pay-as-you-earn income tax system. Wage earners have their taxes deducted at source and they are required to submit income tax returns only if they earn money other than by salary and wages. Tax is set on a sliding scale, with 4 per cent of tax on incomes of less than K1000 and 50 per cent of incomes over K30,000 a year.

Company taxation is at the rate of 36.5 per cent on taxable income, and 45 per cent on foreign companies not incorporated in Papua New Guinea and operating through branches within the country.

There is a dividend withholding tax of 15 per cent, which applies to non-resident shareholders in local companies.

Foreign aid. A major part of PNG's government revenue is aid from abroad. Direct aid comes from Australia, New Zealand, Japan and the United Nations Agencies and the Commonwealth Fund for Technical Co-operation. In 1979-80 Australian aid totalled K182 million (A$232 million). Japan, in the same year provided assistance with the hydro scheme survey for the Purari, and in providing a fisheries college at Kavieng. The Commonwealth Fund provides technical assistance awards. Other assistance, principally in the form of training, comes from some other countries.

Main international organisations giving aid to PNG are the UNDP, WHO, the World Bank, the Asian Development Bank, and the Commonwealth Fund for Technical Co-operation. The UNDP, WHO and CFTC provide grant aid for specific purposes. The World Bank and Asian Development Bank provide loans. Grant aid is mainly for providing expert personnel; the bank loans have been used for road construction, telecommunications development and other schemes requiring large capital sums.

Currency. Until April 19, 1975, Papua New Guinea used Australian currency, but since then it has used its own currency, which is not tied to the Australian dollar. The main unit is called a kina, made up of 100 toea. Kina notes are issued in denominations of K2, K5, K10 and K20. Coins are in denominations of K1, 20t, 10t, 5t, 2t and 1t. On February 1, 1980, K1 = A1.3091.

Banks. Banks operating in Papua New Guinea are the Bank of Papua New Guinea (which is the central bank), the Papua New Guinea Banking Corporation, the Papua New Guinea Development Bank, the Bank of New South Wales (PNG) Ltd, Australia and New Zealand Banking Group (PNG) Ltd and the Bank of South Pacific Ltd. On December 10, 1979, the first Merchant Bank in PNG commenced operations. It is called Resources and Investment Finance Ltd. and operates out of Port Moresby.

Investment controls, guidelines. The National Investment and Development Authority (NIDA) is a government agency responsible for collecting information on foreign investment within PNG, and for controlling investment activities. All foreign businesses must register with NIDA, and provide information on their foreign exchange arrangements. Foreign nationals must notify NIDA before they take up shares in established business, or otherwise become involved. NIDA seeks to identify businesses which will make best use of PNG resources and/or will give Papua New Guinean participation.

The government has set guidelines for foreign investment, and publishes lists of activities reserved for Papua New Guinean investment, and others in which overseas investment is encouraged. These vary from time to time and inquiries should be made to NIDA, Port Moresby.

The Investment Corporation of Papua New Guinea is a government corporation which buys shares in operating companies and sells them to Papua New Guineans either directly or indirectly through a mutual fund. In December, 1979 the corporation was represented on the boards of 48 companies.

The Papua New Guinea Government also has equity in a number of important foreign-owned enterprises and reserves the right to seek this participation where it considers it necessary.

TRANSPORT. Since the end of the Pacific war, Papua New Guinea has known a period of active road-building. There are good roads around towns, extending along the coasts and a developing system of interior roads.

Total length of roads in all provinces at the last formal listing was 17,241 km, but the actual total is certainly higher – the shortest length being in Manus (147 km) and the longest in the Central Province (1,753 km). The major highways extend from Lae to Mt. Hagen and on to Mendi in the Southern Highlands; from Wewak to Nuku in the Sepik; and between Kieta-Arawa-Panguna, on Bougainville. There is an important network of roads in the Gazelle Peninsula and, since 1975, a link between Lae and Madang.

A sum of K17 million was provided for roads in the 1980 budget.

Of the 43,763 motor vehicles registered as at December 31, 1977, (latest available figures) 13,933 were private vehicles owned by expatriates, 10,707 were private vehicles owned by PNG nationals and 12,664 were owned by corporate bodies and institutions. Of the 6,459 government vehicles, 5,120 were owned by the PNG Govt. and 1,339 by statutory authorities.

Overseas airlines. Early in 1978, Papua New Guinea was serviced by two international airlines, Air Niugini and Qantas, and one regional line, Air Pacific. Philippine Air Lines and Cathay were both operating flights through Port Moresby.

Services in March 1978 were:

AIR NIUGINI. Port Moresby-Sydney-Port Moresby, 707, three a week. Port Moresby-Brisbane-

Sydney-Brisbane-Port Moresby, 707, four a week. Port Moresby-Brisbane-Port Moresby, 707, one a week. Port Moresby-Cairns-Port Moresby, Fokker F-28, four a week. Port Moresby-Manila-Port Moresby, 707, one a week. Port Moresby-Kagoshima-Port Moresby, 707, one a week. Port Moresby - Madang - Wewak - Jayapura - Madang - Port Moresby, Fokker F-28, one a week. Port Moresby-Honiara-Port Moresby, Fokker F-28, two a week. (This service connects with Air Pacific at Honiara for Fiji.)

On February 2, 1980 Air Niugini and Cathay Pacific began operating a weekly joint service non-stop to Hong Kong every Saturday.

QANTAS. Sydney-Port Moresby-Sydney, 707, four a week. Sydney - Brisbane - Port Moresby-Brisbane-Sydney, 707, two a week.

Domestic airlines. Papua New Guinea registers three types of operators. 1st and 2nd level operators can run international routes (1st level) and main trunk routes (2nd level). 3rd level operators run feeder services. First, second and third level operators all must run regular services, although they may also run charters. All other operators have charter licences, which restricts them as to passengers and freight.

1st and 2nd level operations were in the hands of Air Niugini. There were two 3rd level operators and a large number of charter operators.

Airports. The two main airports in Papua New Guinea are Jackson's at Port Moresby, and Nadzab, 40 km from Lae. At Jackson's a new runway and taxiway have been built on the existing site, 2,750 metres long and 45 metres wide and thus capable of taking wide-bodied aircraft (e.g. Boeing 747 and DC10). New taxiways and a high-strength apron have also been built.

It was considered that Lae airport had reached the limit of development. Nadzab, an old wartime airstrip about 40 km up the Markham Valley, has been developed and operations began on October 29, 1977. An air conditioned bus takes passengers from Lae airport to Nadzab.

There are hundreds of small airstrips throughout Papua New Guinea, many of them privately owned.

Apart from Jackson's (Port Moresby) and Nadzab, the following are major airstrips which take regular scheduled services:

Daru, Buka, Goroka, Kavieng, Kieta, Madang, Momote, Mount Hagen, Rabaul, Wewak, Vanimo.

Ports. The Papua New Guinea Harbours Board is responsible for the ports of Aitape, Alotau, Lorengau, Vanimo, Port Moresby, Samarai, Rabaul, Lae, Madang, Kavieng, Kieta, Wewak, Oro Bay and Kimbe. The Board has a full-time chairman and a full-time secretary. Main ports are in charge of port managers. The board is financed by port and harbour charges and in addition can raise loans.

Ports of entry. Ports of entry are Port Moresby, Samarai, Lae, Rabaul, Madang, Wewak, Lorengau, Oro Bay, Kavieng, Kieta, Alotau and Kimbe.

Customs officers are stationed at main ports but for others notice of arrival is necessary so that a Customs officer can be sent.

Wharves. The following are the main wharves in use in 1980:

	Length m	Depth Alongside m
Aitape	18.3	4.3
Alotau	93	10
Buka	31.4	3.65
Daru	29.6	2.4
Kavieng	93.8	7
Kieta	122	7.5
Kimbe	60.9	10.7
Lae—old section	246	11
new section	184	11
Lorengau (Nabu)	15.2	5.1
Madang	137.1	10.1
Oro Bay	60.3	11.4
Port Moresby	213.3	7.6
NE berth	118	4.6
SW berth	67	3.8
Rabaul		
Bay Rd.	152.4	10.2
Blanche St.	121.9	7.9
Samarai	93.2	7.8
Vanimo	18.7	4.9
Wewak	73.1	6.7

The overseas wharf at Loloho, Anewa Bay, is privately owned by Bougainville Copper Ltd. In addition to the above main wharves, there are small ships or coastal wharves at Alotau, Kieta, Lae, Lorengau, Madang, Port Moresby, Rabaul, Samarai and Wewak. Pilots are stationed at Kieta, Lae, Madang, Port Moresby, Rabaul and Samarai. Pilotage can be arranged in advance at other ports.

Shipping services. Vessels trading from overseas ports to Papua New Guinea are primarily cargo carriers although some take passengers. The following services were operating on a regular basis in 1978:

FROM AUSTRALIAN PORTS: Containers Pacific Express (Burns Philp and AWP Line), New Guinea Australia Line/PNG Shipping Corporation operate three container vessels on a 28-day turnaround every nine days from Melbourne, Sydney and Brisbane to Port Moresby, Lae, Madang, Wewak, Rabaul, Kavieng, Kieta and Honiara (Solomon Islands).

New Guinea Express Lines operates three-weekly conventional and container services from Melbourne, Sydney and Brisbane to Port Moresby, Lae and Rabaul.

Karlander New Guinea Lines operates from Melbourne and Sydney to Port Moresby, Lae, Madang, Wewak, Manus, Kimbe, and Rabaul.

FROM FAR EAST: China Navigation Ltd operates regular cargo service from Japan, Hong Kong,

Taiwan and Singapore to Rabaul, Wewak, Madang, Lae and Port Moresby.

FROM NEW ZEALAND: Forum Pacific Line operates 30-day service from Auckland to Lae and Rabaul.

Sofrana-Unilines operates from Auckland to PNG, via Vila, Santo, Honiara, returning via Noumea.

FROM US: Karlander operates regular services from US west coast ports to Lae and Rabaul, and LASH ships to PNG, via Pago Pago, Auckland and Australia.

FROM BRITAIN AND EUROPE: Bank Line operates regular cargo service from Hull, Hamburg, Bremen, Antwerp and Rotterdam to Port Moresby, Lae, Madang, Kimbe, Rabaul and Kieta, returning via North America.

PNG Shipping Corporation: In 1977, the government-owned Papua New Guinea Shipping Corporation was formed and will trade under the name, PNG Line (PNGL). Its initial operations were co-operation in a joint service with NGAL and CONPAC to provide a container service between Australia and PNG. Three new ships, built in Japan and launched between April and June 1977, are used on the run.

Cruise ships. Cruise ships from various lines occasionally include Papua New Guinea ports in their itineraries.

Local shipping. Over 100 coastal vessels ranging in size from five tonnes to 1,000 tonnes provide cargo and limited passenger services between PNG main ports, outports, plantations and missions.

COMMUNICATIONS. Papua New Guinea is linked via the Seacom coaxial international cable to Guam, Jesselton in Sabah State, Hong Kong and Singapore in the northern hemisphere and to Australia in the south. Further connections can be made to New Zealand, Canada and Britain via the Compac cable. This is effected at the Sydney terminal.

Transmission levels are of a high quality.

International telecommunications are part of the services provided by the PNG Department of Public Utilities. The Coastal Radio Service, with two stations (Port Moresby and Rabaul), which provides communication with ships at sea, is also administered by the Department of Public Utilities.

Internal links from the Seacom cable are by very high frequency (VHF) and microwave radio circuits between Madang and Lae and between Lae and Port Moresby and other centres.

PNG subscribers connected to all automatic exchanges except Alotau and Samarai can dial their own calls to subscribers in most Australian States through International Subscriber Dialling (ISD) and Australian Subscriber Trunk Dialling (STD).

Within Papua New Guinea, STD calls may be made between subscribers in most areas.

A large section of the trunk telecommunications system has its electricity provided from solar power. This makes PNG the first country in the world to power its trunk system in this way.

PNG telex subscribers are connected to telex services throughout the world via the automatic exchanges in Port Moresby and Lae.

Internal radio network. Internal radio communication is provided by the Public Utilities Department through a system of zone centres which are linked to government or privately operated H.F. outstations. Communication between the outstations and the zone centre to which each is attached is by radio telephone. There are well over 1,000 of these outstations on isolated missions, timber camps, mineral survey camps, plantations and government posts.

Radio. The National Broadcasting Commission came into operation on December 1, 1973. The commission combines the functions of the Australian Broadcasting Commission which had operated in PNG since the end of World War II, and the 17 regional radio stations which had previously been run by the PNG Government. The NBC stations accept commercial advertising.

Generally the national stations are designed to serve the better educated Papua New Guineans, expatriates and the schools. The provincial short wave stations are designed exclusively for the local people they serve in the areas where they are located.

NBC medium wave stations are located at Port Moresby, Rabaul, Madang, Goroka, and Wewak although the national programmes originate in Port Moresby. NBC short wave stations which also carry the national programme are located in Port Moresby, Rabaul and Wewak.

Provincial short wave stations that cater only for their immediate areas are located at Kimbe, Kundiawa, Goroka, Kavieng, Mount Hagen, Popondetta, Lae, Kerema, Madang, Mendi, Port Moresby, Daru, Wewak, Kieta, Alotau Vanimo, Rabaul, Corengais and Wabag.

Newspapers. Papua New Guinea has two national morning newspapers the 'Papua New Guinea Post Courier' which is produced five days a week Monday to Friday, in Port Moresby, and the 'Niugini News', published in Lae Tuesday to Friday inclusive. Both are airfreighted to other areas of the country.

The first issue by Wantok Publications of a weekly newspaper 'The Times of Papua New Guinea' appeared on September 12, 1980.

Numerous smaller newspapers and news-sheets, covering regional areas, are produced. Churches, educational and professional bodies produce various periodicals, and the Papua New Guinea Office of Information produces a variety of publications.

WATER. Port Moresby and suburbs have a fully reticulated water supply which is filtered and treated to be safe for drinking. Some other towns have a partially reticulated supply and where reticulated water is available there are usually sewerage works. Some towns – such as Rabaul – are in a difficult position because there are no adequate rivers in the vicinity. In villages, people draw their water from adjacent streams except where villages have become part of towns.

ELECTRICITY. The Papua New Guinea Electricity Commission operates generating stations in the main centres and maintains numerous small stations on behalf of the government. In some industrial areas, notably the copper mining operations in Bougainville, town supplies are made available by private enterprise. All PNG centres have some electricity supply, although in the remoter areas the supply is restricted to certain hours. Distribution voltages are 240/415 volts 50 cycles alternating current.

PERSONALITIES AND ORGANISATIONS

Governor-General: Sir Tore Lokoloko, G.C.M.G.

CABINET MINISTERS

Prime Minister: Sir Julius Chan
Deputy P.M. and Transport and Civil Aviation: Mr Iambakey Okuk
Finance: Mr John Kaputin
National Planning and Development: Mr Galeva Kwarara
Primary Industry: Mr Roy Evara
Foreign Affairs and Trade: Mr Noel Levi
Lands: Mr Thomas Kavali
Urban Development: Mr Goasa Damena
Decentralisation: Fr. John Momis
Forests: Mr Joseph Aoae
Police: Mr Warren Dutton
Works and Supply: Mr Mark Ipuia
Minerals and Energy: Mr Gabriel Bakani
Education: Mr Sam Tulo
Commerce and Industry: Mr Opai Kunangel
Public Utilities: Mr Wiwa Korowi
Corrective Institutions and Liquor Licensing: Mr Akepa Miakwe
Justice: Mr Paul Torato
Health: Mr John Jaminan
Labour and Employment: Mr Jacob Lemeki
Media: Mr Clement Poye
Defence: Mr Gerega Pepena
Environment and Conservation: Mr Ibne Kor
Home Affairs: Mr Zibang Zurecnuoc
Science, Culture and Tourism: Mr Stephen Tago

DEPARTMENTAL HEADS

Prime Minister: B. Kidu
Defence: V. Eri
Education Science & Culture: P. Songo
Finance: M. Morauta
Foreign Affairs and Trade: A. M. Siaguru
Health: A. Tarutia
Justice: K. Los
Labour and Employment: K. Uiari
Commerce Industry & Tourism: W. Wekina
Minerals and Energy: N. Agonia
Lands: J. Genia
Works and Supply: J. Kairi
Transport and Civil Aviation: J. Tauvaga
Police Commissioner: P. Bouraga
Primary Industry: W. Lawrence

Public Utilities: I. Edoni
Chairman Public Service Commission: A. Tololo, O.B.E.

JUDICIARY

Chief Justice: The Hon. Mr Buri Kidu
Deputy Chief Justice: E. P. T. Raine
Justices: W. J. F. Kearney; A. B. C. Wilson; J. G. Smith; W. J. Andrew; M. Kapi and N. Pratt. Of these, Justices Prentice, Rain and Wilson had submitted their resignations to take effect early in 1980.

CHURCH LEADERS

Anglican Bishop of Papua New Guinea: Rt Rev David Hand, Port Moresby
Roman Catholic Archdiocese of Port Moresby: Archbishop Herman Paivu
Roman Catholic Archdiocese of Madang: Archbishop L. Arkfield
Roman Catholic Archdiocese of Rabaul: Deceased: no replacement, Feb. 1980.
Moderator, United Church: Rev L. Boseto, Port Moresby
Bishop, Evangelical Lutheran Church of New Guinea: Bishop Zurewe Zurenuo, Lae
President, Seventh-day Adventist Mission: Pastor L. A. Smith, Lae

PNG DIPLOMATS ABROAD

High Commissioner, Australia: Austin Sapias.
Deputy H.C.: D. Gamiandu
Ambassador to US and the UN: Paulias Matane
Ambassador to Indonesia and the Philippines: Dominic Diya
Acting High Commissioner to Britain: Fred Reiher
Consul-General, Sydney: Appointment to be made (Acting, Harold Ara'a)
Ambassador to Japan: A. Farapo
High Commissioner, Fiji: Dr. A. Toua
High Commissioner, New Zealand: I. Tarua

ELECTORATES AND MEMBERS OF THE PNG NATIONAL PARLIAMENT 1977-82

Speaker: Sevese Morea

Bougainville Provincial .... John Momis
Central Bougainville .... Raphael Bele
North Bougainville .... Sam Tulo
South Bougainville .... Anthony Anugu
Central Provincial .... James Mopio
Abau Open .... Gerega Pepena
Goilala Open .... Louis Mona
Kairuku-Hiri .... Joseph Aoae
Rigo Open .... Galeva Kwarate
Chimbu Provincial .... Iambakey Okuk
Chuave Open .... Robert Yabara
Gumine Open .... Delba Biri
Karimui-Nomane .... Nebare Kamun
Kerowagi Open .... Waguo Goiye
Kundiawa Open .... Konia Dewe
Sinasina-Yonggamugl .... Clement Poye
East New Britain Provincial .... Damien Kereku
Gazelle Open .... Martin ToVadek
Kokopo Open .... Oscar Tammur
Pomio Open .... Koriam Urekit
Rabaul .... John Kaputin
East Sepik Provincial .... Michael Somare
Ambunti-Drekikir .... Asimbiro Ston
Angoram Open .... William Eichhorn
Maprik Open .... Pita Lus
Wewak Open .... Anthony Bais
Wosera-Gaui .... Yambumbe Matias
Yangoru-Saussia .... John Jaminan
Eastern Highlands Provincial .... Barry Holloway
Daulo Open .... Gai Duwabane
Goroka Open .... Sailas Atopare
Henganofi Open .... Sununku Kroki'e
Kainantu Open .... Yubiti Yulaki
Lufa Open .... Suinavi Otio
Obura-Wonenara .... Undapmaina Kalagune
Okapa Open .... Billy Hai
Unggai-Bena .... Akepa Miakwe
Enga Provincial .... Paul Torato
Kandep Open .... John Yaka
Kompiam Ambum .... Tom Amaiu
Lagaip-Porgera .... Mark Ipuia
Wabag Open .... Tei Abal
Wapenamanda .... Pato Kakarya
Gulf Provincial .... Tom Koraea
Kerema Open .... Aron Oeaka
Kikori Open .... Roy Evara
Madang Provincial .... Bruce Jephcott
Bogia Open .... Caspar Anggua
Madang Open .... Angmai Bilas
Middle Ramu .... Wokam Rem
Rai Coast .... Mafuk Gainda
Sumkar Open .... Kare Maor
Usino-Bundi .... Opotio Rimoru
Manus Provincial .... Michael Pondros
Manus Open .... Nahau Rooney
Milne Bay Provincial .... John Guise
Alotau Open .... Kingsford Dibela
Esa'ala Open .... Justin Edimani
Kiriwina-Goodenough .... John Noel
Samarai-Murua Open .... Jacob Lemeki
Morobe Provincial .... Boyamo Sali
Bulolo Open .... Mathew Bendumb
Finschhafen Open .... Zibang Zure Zurenuoc
Huon Gulf Open .... Nagibo Seregi
Kabwum Open .... Tani Kungo
Lae Open .... Toni Ila
Markham Open .... Giri Yaru
Menyamya Open .... Neville Bourne
Nawae Open .... Silingi Kapalik
Tewai-Siassi .... Johnny Onzenga
National Capital District .... Josephine Abaijah
Moresby North-East .... Goasa Damena
Moresby North-West .... Mahuru Rarua-Rarua
Moresby South .... Sevese Morea
New Ireland Provincial .... Noel Levi
Kavieng Open .... Walla Gukguk
Namatanai Open .... Julius Chan
Northern Provincial .... Wesley Embahe
Ijivitari Open .... Akoka Doi
Sohe Open .... Stephen Tago
Southern Highlands Provincial .... Wiwa Korowi

Ialibu-Pangia Open .... Pundia Kange
Imbonggu Open .... Glaimi Warena
Kagua-Erave Open .... Yano Belo
Komo-Margarima .... Dambali Habe
Koroba-Lake Kopiago .... Paiale Elo
Mendi Open .... Posu Ank
Nipa-Kutubu Open .... Ibne Kor
Tari Open .... Matiabe Yuwi
West New Britain Provincial .... Lukas Waka
Kandrian-Gloucester .... Galopo Masa
Talasea Open .... Gabriel Bakani
West Sepik Provincial .... Karl Kitchens
Aitape-Lumi Open .... Stephen Sio
Nuku Open .... Christopher Sambre
Telefomin Open .... Wesani Iwoksim
Vanimo-Green River .... Wap Yawo
Western Provincial .... Kala Swokin
Middle Fly Open .... Waliyato Clowes
North Fly Open .... Warren Dutton
South Fly Open .... Ebia Olewale
Western Highlands Provincial .... Raphael Doa
Angalimp-South Wahgi .... Opai Kunangel
Baiyer-Mul Open .... Mek Ugints
Dei Open .... Parua Kuri
Hagen Open .... Pius Wingti
Jimi Open .... Thomas Kavali
North Wahgi Open .... Talu Bolt
Tambul Nebilyer .... Puliwa Mapikon

HISTORY. Until recently, little was known about the pre-history of Papua New Guinea, and a great deal has yet to be discovered. But modern scientific methods have established that man was in the New Guinea highlands at least by 8,000 BC, and it is probable that the first arrival of man in New Guinea was as early as 30,000 years ago.

There appear to have been several migrations, from Asia by way of Indonesia over a great length of time – the first ones at a time when sea levels were considerably lower than they are today, and New Guinea and Australia were joined.

The eastward movement from Asia and Indonesia continued on to other islands, including the Solomons, the New Hebrides, New Caledonia and Fiji.

The early people were hunters, not agriculturalists, who used bone and stone tools and weapons. Later migrations introduced agriculture, plants such as yams, taro, green vegetables and fruit, and pigs and dogs. Along the coast the sago palm and the coconut were bountiful providers, together with seafood.

There was no central government. Each community was virtually its own government, with little contact with other areas except through certain trade links.

The island of New Guinea, especially the part now known as Irian Jaya, was known to seamen and adventurers from Indonesia and the Asian mainland centuries before the first documented sightings. Antonio d'Abreu of Portugal, sailed as far east as the Aru islands on the south coast of what is now Irian Jaya, in 1511, but the first definite recorded landing of a European was in 1526, when another Portuguese, Jorge de Meneses, made a landing on the north-west coast and named it Ilhas dos Papuas. Papuas came from the Malay word Papuwah, meaning frizzy-haired, and Meneses is generally credited with being the actual European discoverer of New Guinea.

New Guinea named. The name New Guinea was coined in 1545 by the Spaniard Ortiz Retes, who while attempting to return from the Moluccas to Mexico, sailed along the north coast. The name appeared for the first time in print on Mercator's world map of 1569. Retes thought the people reminded him of those of the Guinea coast of Africa.

Torres arrived from the New Hebrides in 1606, examined the Louisiade Archipelago and the entire southern coast of Papua and Irian Jaya, passing through Torres Strait and sighting Cape York, in the course of his discoveries.

Dutch vessels also made visits about this time, followed by the English and French up to the 19th century. Among the visitors were Willem Janz, Le Maire and Schouten, Carstenz, Tasman, Dampier, Carteret, Bougainville (who left his name on Bougainville Island), Cook, and Captains Owen Stanley, John Moresby and Blackwood (in the 'Fly', in which he discovered the mouth of the great river that now bears the ship's name).

The first Englishman to claim any part of New Guinea for Britain was Captain Phillip Carteret at New Ireland in 1767. The next was Lieut. Yule in the 'Bramble' in 1846 at Cape Possession. Captain Moresby, who named Port Moresby, did so again in 1873 – but no action was taken by Britain, although in the Australian colonies there was considerable interest developing in the political future of the islands.

In 1828, when the Dutch had annexed the Western half of New Guinea (now Irian Jaya), Australia was still a penal settlement, but within the next 50 years Australia went a long way towards nationhood and was more closely concerned with events in the area.

Germany, after the end of the Franco-Prussian war 1870-71, precipitated a scramble by the Big Powers in the South Pacific and caused considerable alarm in Australia and New Zealand, in regard to her intentions in New Guinea. They were concerned about their own security.

The Australian colonies became so agitated in 1883 that the Premier of the day in Queensland, sent the police magistrate at Thursday Island, Henry M. Chester, to Port Moresby, to take possession of South-East New Guinea in the name of Queen Victoria. Chester raised the flag at Port Moresby, then the headquarters of the London Missionary Society and one European trader, on April 4, 1883. It was hoped that Britain, presented with a fait accompli, would ratify Chester's act, but Britain decided against this.

Australia and New Zealand continued to urge

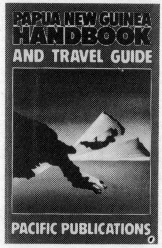

ONQUER ANY TERRAIN N GRAND STYLE.

ARDTOP

ALL NEW

hink of all the places you can go with ease style. The new-breed 4WD Nissan Patrol es in city traffic, at conquering wild terrain water up to 600mm deep.

you want multi-role utility no other 4-wheel e can deliver, you'll find the Nissan Patrol eatable. Because it is like no other 4WD icle.

onsider the passenger car elegance inside out. Beneath the smart styling is superged durability. And you've an impressive ice of deluxe options, economical gasoline liesel engines, too.

The new-breed 4WD Nissan Patrol.
Simply unbeatable!

PICKUP

WD NISSAN PATROL

an **Samoa:** B.F. KNEUBUHL INC. Pago Pago/**Cook Islands:** COOK ISLANDS MOTOR CENTRE LTD., Rarotonga/**Fiji:** CARPENTERS MOTORS. Suva/**Guam:** DATSUN MOTOR . Agana/**Hawaii:** NISSAN MOTOR CORPORATION IN HAWAII LTD., Honolulu/**Kiribati:** ATOLL AUTO STORES. Tarawa/**Nauru:** JACOB ENTERPRISES LTD./**New Caledonia:** CE ALMA S.A. Noumea/**Vanuatu:** PENTECOST S.A. Port Vila and Santo/**Norfolk Islands:** SIRIUS MOTORS/**Papua New Guinea:** BOROKO MOTORS LTD., Port Moresby/**Saipan:** N MOTOR COMPANY INC./**Solomon Islands:** UNITED ENTERPRISES LTD., Honiara/**Tahiti:** TAHITIBULL S.A.R.L., Papeete/**Western Samoa:** MORRIS HEDSTROM LTD., Apia

SANSUI DRAMATIZES ITS TECHNOLOGICAL LEADERSHIP AGAIN!

Super Compo Series 900 System III

Shown with optional AT-15S Audio Timer and AX-3S Sound Consolette. (Matching Speaker System: S-50)

THE AUDIBLE EDGE SUPERCOMPO

The superb sound quality of the top-of-the-line SUPER COMPO system will impress dedicated audiophiles. And the unique visual displays combined with easy operation will please music lovers. Only Sansui's proven advanced technology could offer both benefits.

The C-77 is the first preamplifier in audio history to have a built-in auto/manual fader for sound versatility. The B-77 "Linear A" DC-Servo power amplifier is a DC configuration that eliminates switching distortion. Peak power display and spectrum analyzer are "pictures" of the pure music. And pre-set 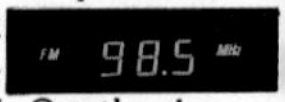 auto tuning is perfectly accurate with the T-77 Digital Quartz PLL Synthesizer tuner.

Superior technology. Super sound quality. Sansui SUPER COMPO.

SANSUI ELECTRIC CO., LTD. 14-1 Izumi 2-chome, Suginami-ku, Tokyo 168 Japan

Honda Accord... a natural choice when quality is the criterion.

The Honda Accord is an amazing blend of ingenious automotive and human engineering. It's compact, of course, to suit today's motoring conditions. Yet it's so roomy inside — and whisper-quiet. In fact, the whole interior atmosphere *tells* you you're in a superior type of car — a car whose silent, smooth and pleasant ride may even make BMW and Mercedes sit up and take notice.

And not forgetting the most fundamental part of the automobile: the engine. The Accord's is a flat-torque 1.6-liter type featuring transistorized ignition, meaning it's great for city and highway duty as well as durable. And it's not a thirsty brute, either, tending to be rather miserly in its consumption of fuel.

The Honda Accord comes superbly equipped — so many features are supplied as standard equipment that just about the only extras you would really like to have are the unique Honda power steering and Hondamatic transmission with overdrive.

So you see, if quality is your criterion in selecting a car, you're in luck. Because there's the Honda Accord. And it's the natural choice.

HONDA ACCORD

4-door Sedan / 2-door Hatchback

Equipment may vary in some countries.

Britain to annex that part of New Guinea not already claimed by the Dutch, and finally, in September, 1884, Britain officially informed Germany that she planned to establish a protectorate.

Germany urgently asked that no further action be taken pending clarification of certain points, and while these discussions were continuing, Germany formally hoisted the German flag at three points in north-east New Guinea and the Bismarck Archipelago, and proclaimed a protectorate on November 3, 1884.

Britain on November 6, 1884, proclaimed a protectorate over the south-east coast and the islands to the east, with an expedition by Commodore Erskine. This area became known as British New Guinea. The borders between British and German New Guinea were officially defined in 1885.

German administration. The German Government exercised authority in its new possession through the South Seas Syndicate, which on May 15, 1885, became the New Guinea Company. The company was controlled by a board in Berlin, and the head of administration in New Guinea was a governor.

It sought to operate plantations and trading stations, but it was unsuccessful, and after 15 years of muddle and heavy loss the charter of the New Guinea Company was cancelled, and in 1889 the administration of the colony was taken over directly by the German Government. Earlier, the company had administered the colony's affairs from Finschhafen, then had moved to Stephansort (Bogadjim) and finally to Madang.

The new Governor, Rudolph von Benningsen, shifted headquarters to Herbertshohe, now Kokopo, near Rabaul, and arrangements were much better as the Germans began building up a system of village administration.

Queen Emma. Among the planters and traders who lived under the German administration in those days was Mrs Emma Forsayth, known as "Queen Emma", who had arrived from Samoa in the late 1870s to become New Guinea's first planter. She and others were established around the Gazelle Peninsula and the Duke of York Islands nearby.

In October, 1899, the Germans incorporated the Marianas, Carolines and Marshall Islands (the three groups of Micronesia) into the administration, and on November 8, Bougainville and Buka were included as a result of an agreement with the US and Britain. Nauru was included later.

With the New Guinea Company concentrating on commerce, and a final shift of headquarters from Herbertshohe to Rabaul in 1910, the German colony began to make progress.

Britain and Germany at War. When World War I began in August, 1914, an Australian Expeditionary Force was sent to German New Guinea. It landed near Kokopo on September 11, 1914, and on the following day, after a brief battle with German forces, seized the German radio station at Bita Paka. The German administration surrendered on September 14, and for the next seven years German New Guinea was under an Australian military administration. Few changes were made in the German administrative system.

At the end of the war, all German properties were "expropriated", and control was vested in the New Guinea Expropriation Board. The properties, mostly plantations, were later put up for tender to private individuals.

The arrangement was that Germany would later repay the value of the properties to those who had lost them and returned to Germany. This was done, but acute inflation in Germany made the payments virtually worthless and the former owners were ruined.

League of Nations' Mandate. On December 17, 1920, the council of the League of Nations gave Australia a "C" class mandate to govern the former German colony (but not Nauru or Micronesia) and to report regularly. This administration under the mandate remained in force until the Japanese invaded Rabaul on January 21, 1942. The whole of the Mandated Territory of New Guinea thereafter became a theatre of war.

British New Guinea. Meanwhile the protectorate over British New Guinea of 1884 made little progress until 1888, when Dr (later Sir) William MacGregor headed a new administration with greater powers, the responsibility being shared by Britain and Queensland (acting on behalf of the other Australian colonies). The protectorate gave way to annexation the same year.

Administrator MacGregor was an explorer who did much to establish government influence through his travels. He also set up a Legislative Council and established a police force and a system of administration controlled by Resident Magistrates and village constables in various districts.

He wrote a series of reports during his 10 years in office in an effort to prove the country fit for commercial development. But the only outstanding development until 1900 was the discovery of several goldfields – Misima and adjacent islands proclaimed in 1889; Woodlark Island proclaimed in 1895; Gira, 1889, and Yodda, 1900. Neither these nor others proclaimed later were very rich and they did little to promote British New Guinea.

The title of Administrator was changed to that of Lieutenant-Governor in March, 1895, and MacGregor retired from his post in 1898.

Papua created. The Australian States federated in 1901. The new federal government of the Commonwealth of Australia agreed to take responsibility for British New Guinea. But it was several years before it formally did so, through the Papua Act of 1905, which also changed the name of the new Australian possession to the Territory of Papua. The Papua Act came into force on September 1, 1906, and provided a constitution under which Papua would be governed by a lieutenant-governor, executive council and Legislative Council.

But meanwhile, on March 18, 1902, the authority

exercised by the Governor of Queensland on behalf of the other former colonies had been transferred to the Governor-General and the new Australian Commonwealth, so there was a period of administrative inactivity and confusion.

The constitutional machinery established by the Papua Act continued right up to 1949, although because of the Japanese invasion of New Guinea in 1942, a military government took over in Port Moresby on February 12, 1942, and civil administration was suspended.

Pacific War. A Japanese force landed at Rabaul on January 23, 1942. It soon overwhelmed the small Australian garrison and volunteers. About 300 civilians and 900 soldiers were captured and later lost their lives when their prison ship, 'Montevideo Maru', was torpedoed en route to Japan.

The Japanese made Rabaul their forward base but went on to establish themselves on the mainland of New Guinea and on the coast of Papua. From there they pushed inland, to Kokoda and across the Owen Stanley mountains with the idea of taking Port Moresby from the rear. This plan did not succeed, and by September 1942, the Japanese advance had been halted by American and Australian forces under the command of General Douglas MacArthur; and thenceforward north-eastern Papua, and all of New Guinea, were recovered from the Japanese, district by district.

The Australian New Guinea Administrative Unit was formed in 1942, staffed mostly by experienced former officers of the Papua and New Guinea administrations. Its job was to take over administration of the districts as they were progressively cleared, and by 1944 the Allies were in control of both territories, although some Japanese forces did not surrender until 1945.

ANGAU administered all that part of Papua and New Guinea south of the Markham River until October 31, 1945, when civil administration took over. ANGAU continued to administer the rest until June 24, 1946, when all of the country was put under civil administration.

Administrative union. By this time it had become apparent that it was possible to administer both Papua and New Guinea jointly, and not as separate administrations as happened before the war. By means of the Papua-New Guinea Provisional Administration Act of 1945/46, and the Papua New Guinea Act 1949, and other legislation, the governments of the Australian Territory of Papua and the Trust Territory of New Guinea were gradually integrated, and the new structure functioned as the Administration of Papua and New Guinea.

The League of Nations had meanwhile been replaced by the United Nations Organisation, and Australia's mandate to continue to administer New Guinea under trusteeship was approved by the UN in December, 1946.

First Administrator of the combined territories was Colonel J. K. Murray, who remained in office until June, 1952.

The decades of the 1950s and 1960s saw great commercial and agricultural development in the combined territory, a similar increase in the numbers in the public service and an eight-fold increase in the non-indigenous population of Papua and New Guinea in comparison with the pre-war figures.

A great deal of the development and increased activity was from the non-indigenous sector, but from the resumption of civil administration it was made clear that the New Guineans were to be encouraged to take an increasing part in the development of the country.

Parliamentary development: Before the war, both Papua and New Guinea had separate Legislative Councils. In 1951, the first Legislative Council for the combined territories was inaugurated. It had 16 official members, three elected Europeans, and nine nominated members. The Administrator was the president. The council had little authority.

An enlarged council came into being in 1960, but the first big constitutional step did not come until 1964 when a House of Assembly of 64 members came into being. It consisted of 10 official members, 44 members elected from open electorates, and 10 members from reserved electorates for which only non-indigenes could stand. Everyone over 21 was entitled to a vote and for the first time the legislative body had a preponderance of indigenous members.

The House of Assembly was enlarged to 94 in 1968 and a Ministerial Member system introduced. It was further enlarged for the elections of 1972 to a House of 100 elected members, 82 from open electorates and 18 from regional electorates where candidates were required to have certain educational qualifications. Voting age was reduced to 18.

Self-Government and Independence. This House of Assembly had the task of preparing the country for self-government, which was declared on December 1, 1973, and for full independence, which came into effect on September 16, 1975. PNG then became a sovereign state within the British Commonwealth.

The National Identity Bill which was promulgated on July 1, 1971, established the name of the country as Papua New Guinea – thus doing away with the old title of 'Territory' and the 'and' that linked the two names.

Further Information. There is a wealth of material on Papua New Guinea, covering many aspects of the country. Among the most useful are Gavin Souter, 'New Guinea: The Last Unknown' (Sydney, 1963); C. D. Rowley, 'The New Guinea Villager' (Melbourne, 1965); Albert Maori Kiki, 'Kiki: Ten Thousand Years in a Lifetime' (Melbourne, 1968); Peter Hastings, 'New Guinea: Problems and Prospects' (Melbourne, 1969); Paul Hasluck, 'A Time for Building' (Melbourne, 1976). Current information is available in the 'Papua New Guinea Handbook and Travel Guide' (Pacific Publications, Sydney).

PAPUA NEW GUINEA ISLANDS IN DETAIL

ISLANDS OF MILNE BAY PROVINCE

TROBRIAND ISLANDS: The Trobriand Group lies to the north of the D'Entrecasteaux Islands. There are four main islands, and several islets. The islands are all of coral, some rise abruptly from the shore to a height of about 30 m, forming coral cliffs. Others are only just above the surface of the water. They were named after Denis de Trobriand, an officer of the D'Entrecasteaux expedition. The people are more like Polynesians than Melanesians, both in appearance and disposition, and are hospitable. They were made famous to the rest of the world through the work of the anthropologist Malinowski, between 1915-18. Trobriand carvings are exported to centres like Port Moresby and Lae where they are much sought after by tourists. The people practise a trade and exchange system called Kula. The Trobrianders are considered some of the best gardeners in Papua New Guinea. The soil on some of the coral islands is very rich. This area was the most important in the old Territory of Papua for mother-of-pearl and beche-de-mer fishing but there is little exported these days. An Assistant Commissioner is stationed at Losuia, on the main island, Kiriwina, where there is also a hospital. There is an airstrip and on Kiriwina lagoon, a hotel which is popular with tourists and weekending Port Moresby residents. The population of the Trobriands is approximately 17,173 (estimated).

WOODLARK: Woodlark Island — or Murua, to give it its native name — was at one time the chief goldfield of Papua. It was here that the first payable goldfield was worked. Estimated population is 3,117. It received its name from Captain Grimes of the "Woodlark", of Sydney, around 1836. The island, which is situated north of the Louisiade Archipelago is about 60 km in length from east to west. There are good anchorages on the south coast, including Guasopa Harbour and Suloga Harbour. The main centre was Kulumadau on the south coast. There is a subdistrict office at Guasopa where there is an airstrip. The island comprises a succession of hills and valleys and is covered in parts by dense tropical jungle. The people are Melanesians like those on the east coast of the mainland. The island has been thoroughly prospected. It produced over $1,400,000 worth of gold in the days when price of gold was far below present price. From Woodlark Island was obtained so-called "greenstone" for axes, adzes, chisels and ceremonial stones. The stone is an impure serpentine, almost as hard as the nephrite (jade or greenstone) of New Zealand. For administrative purposes, Woodlark is included in the Losuia district.

LAUGHLAN GROUP. The Laughlan Group consists of five islands and several islets and rocks, and is some 64 km to the east of Woodlark. Population is about 160. The largest island, Abomat, is located at latitude 9 deg 17 min S. and longitude 153 deg 17 min E. The lagoon of this is from 12 to 21 metres deep and is a secure anchorage, there is a plentiful supply of fresh water. The group is composed of coral and sand and only coconuts grow there, with the exception of small patches of sweet potatoes and bananas. There is generally a strong sea running between this group and Woodlark, but provided the weather is favourable they are in constant communication with each other. At present there is a small export trade in ebony.

D'ENTRECASTEAUX GROUP

Fergusson Island. Fergusson Island is the central island of the D'Entrecasteaux Group, with Normanby Island to the southward and Goodenough to the north-west.

Fergusson Is. is 60 km long in a NW and SE direction, with an average width of 25 km and an area of 1,345 sq km. There are three groups of mountains — Mt Kilkerran, 1375 m; Mt Euagwaba, 1220 m to 1525 m and Mt Maybole, 760 m.

From these mountains flow many small rivers and creeks, the principal being the Salamo River, running southerly into Dawson Strait, the Auwopal River, easterly into Hygeia Bay, and the Nuitala River into Hughes Bay, on the north coast. Good anchorages may be obtained at all times at the head of Dawson Strait, Hygeia Bay, and usually along the western coastline.

There is a large population distributed over Fergusson Island, particularly along the southern coastline, where numerous gardens cover a large area of the steep mountain slopes. There are several lakes, the largest of which is Lake Lavu. They are saline, and where evaporation has taken place a white deposit of soluble salts is often seen.

The most interesting features on Fergusson Island are the numbers of extinct volcanoes, hot springs, geysers, fumaroles, and the magnificent deposits of sulphur and geyserite. The geyserite, in parts, has formed beautiful white terraces. Thermal springs occur at Iamalele (Yamalele) and Deidei. Many of these contain sulphur, carbonic acid, gas, iron, alkalis, lithium, etc.

Population is an estimated 14,939 all nationals.

Normanby Island: Normanby Island is about 72 km in length and from 19 km to 24 km at its greatest breadth. It has an area of 1,036 sq km. There is a range of mountains (Prevost) whose highest peak is 1,098 m.

The island is surrounded by deep water and there are some safe harbours — Sewa being the best on the west coast. It was used during World War II by Allied naval vessels. It is a port of call for inter-island small ships.

There is also good anchorage at Maiobari Bay,

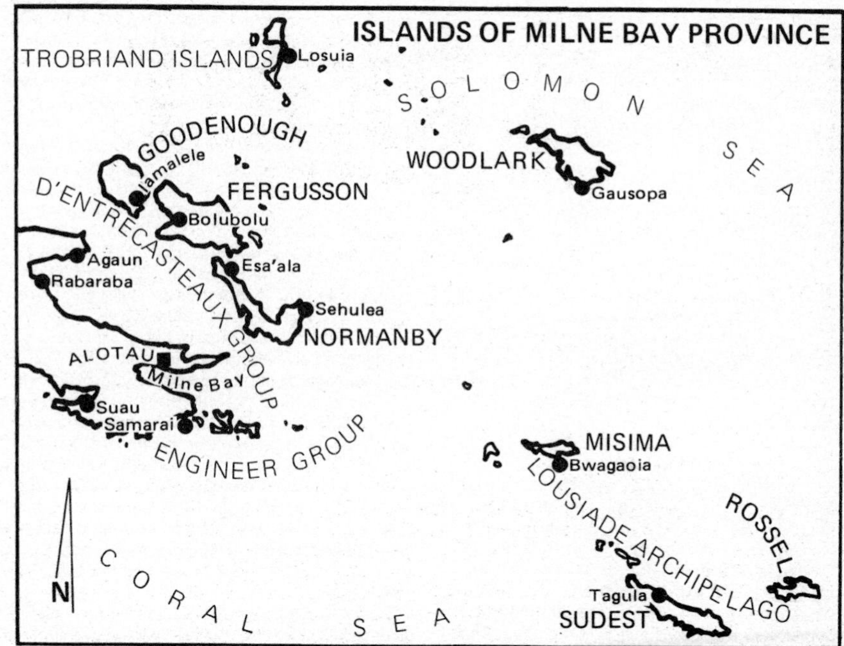

north of Sewa, where the bay is sheltered by Duchess Island. There is an excellent anchorage just north again where at Ubuia, the United Church has a Hansenide settlement.

Rock carvings in Sewa Bay are of unknown origin but are said to resemble others in Irian Jaya.

The population is an estimated 13,429 (Normanby and Dobu).

Goodenough Is. — Dobu Passage: Goodenough Island is separated from the western end of Fergusson Island by Moresby Strait. A mountain range, extending through almost the whole length of the island, culminates in two rugged peaks of about 2,440 m. The range is flanked by an extensive plain, which is studded with native groves. Part of the mountain slopes are occupied by terraced gardens, planted with yams. Limestone caves exist on the mountain spurs. Indications of gold have been found in several of the creeks.

Population is about 13,076, all nationals.

In the interior of Goodenough Island is a large rock, covered with paintings in black and white. It is regarded by the people with veneration because of its supposed mystical powers over the yam crops. An anthropologist has remarked that the nearest parallel to this rock is found in Central Australia.

Vivigani airstrip on the east coast of Goodenough Island was an Allied airfield developed during the war with Japan. It is used by a scheduled service.

There is a road from Wailagi to Nuatutu to Vivigani and on to Wataluma on the North Coast.

Dobu is a very fertile islet between Normanby and Fergusson Islands, and was originally the headquarters of the Methodist Mission. There is beautiful scenery in the little known Dobu Passage, with ranges rising to 1,653 m and 1,830 m. Behind these are mountains of 2,440 m.

Welle, or Samaroa Island, lies to the east of Fergusson Island, and is of volcanic origin. It contains an area of about 64 sq km. It is low-lying, its height in any place not exceeding 90 m.

LOUISIADE ARCHIPELAGO.

Louis Vaez de Torres is credited with being the European discoverer of this archipelago in August, 1606. He also spent 14 days in a bay on the south coast of Sideia Island just east of Samarai. In 1793 Joseph D'Entrecasteaux passed through these waters, and the northern group received his name.

It has been suggested that the Malays and the Chinese knew of the existence of these islands and visited them prior to Europeans.

The archipelago was rich in gold, and up to the Pacific War produced about 4,500 kg.

Sudest, or Tagula Island: Sudest is the largest

island in the group. It is about 80 km in length and 24 km at its greatest breadth. The island is formed by a succession of irregular hills and mountains. The highest point is Mt Rattlesnake, 915 m. Gold has been found in nearly all the watercourses. The rush was at its height in 1889, when many diggers worked the island quite profitably.

Sudest is known also as Tagula. It has an area of 802 sq km and an approximate population of 2,173. There is a sub-district office at Tagula on the NSW coast.

Rossel Island and others nearby: Rossel Island, situated 25 km to the east of Sudest, is 39 km in length and possesses a most irregular and tortuous coastline. This terminates in the east in Rossel Spit, which has been made famous by the many tales of shipwreck and danger emanating from there. There are traces of gold on the island.

Around Rossel Island are High Heron and Adele (the most easterly island in PNG). Estimated population is 3,060. Joannet, about 40 km north of Sudest, contains an area of about 65 sq km. It is well watered and there are indications of gold. There is a patrol port at Pambwa.

Misima Island: Misima (or St. Aignan) is situated in the NW extreme of the Louisiade Archipelago and has an area of between 233 sq km and 259 sq km. The island extends about 40 km in an east and west direction, being irregular in width, varying from 10 km to 11 km, in the eastern portion and tapering suddenly from near the centre of the island to a narrow strip about two or three km wide in the western portion. Bwagaoia is the largest harbour, situated on the south-eastern extreme, and is sheltered by a fringing coral reef, adjacent to a shallow lagoon with an extremely small entrance, but quite suitable for craft up to 500 tonnes. The island is very mountainous, particularly in the western narrow portions.

Mount Oiatau 1,037 m, is the highest point to a steep range trending parallel with the island.

There is little swampy country on the island, and consequently few mosquitoes. Gold has been found in many parts of the island, the main fields being near Bwagaoia, in the vicinity of Mt Sisa, with which it was connected by an old steam tramway and at present a ring road servicing the eastern half of the island approximately 40 miles in length, linking Bwagoia with Liak on the North Coast and Eiavs on the south Coast.

An important gold mining industry was established on Misima between the World Wars and two companies were operating there. There was a township and port at Bwagaoia. The evacuation of these islands by the Europeans when the Japanese invaded in 1942 caused the abandonment of these gold-mines, and the industry was not re-established after the war. The most valuable property, Cuthbert's Misima Goldmines Ltd., which had earned fantastic profits in the thirties, liquidated. A new company, Pacific Island Mines Ltd., was successfully floated in Australia in 1959 but by 1969 its interest on Misima had turned from gold to copper. The estimated population is 8,088

Calvados Chain: Included in the Louisiade Archipelago is the long string of islands known as the Calvados Chain, comprising: Mabui, Panasagusagu, Utian (Brooker), Rara, No Ina, Moturina, Basses, Panaroa, Panasia (Real), Vanariwa, Bushy, Leiga, Sabari (Owen Stanley), Laiwan, Bobo Ema, Bonawan, Bagaman (Stanton), Mabneian, Pananumara, Panakrusima (Earle), Abaga Gaheia, Hemenahei, Wanim, Nimoa (Pig), Iyin (Garden), and Ululina. The estimated Calvalos population is 2,175.

Population of the Louisiades is approximately 17,316, about half of it on Misima.

CONFLICT: The Conflict Group is about 113 km eastward of Samarai, and is well planted with coconuts. The group consists of more than 20 small islands on a large oval atoll and was named after HMS "Conflict" in 1880. Largest island is Irai, about 5 km long. There have been recent plans to develop the group as a tourist resort. To the west is the Engineer Group, comprising three main islands.

Samarai: A small island of about 24 ha is a port of entry. As a commercial centre it is being superseded by Alotau, on the mainland. It remains a port of entry, but it has also been eclipsed by Alstau as a shipping centre. The island is situated 5 km from the mainland. Captain Moresby in 1873 named it Dinner Island, and in 1878 it was made chief missionary station in south-east Papua for the LMS.

It is in regular shipping communication with Port Moresby 400 km to the west, and is also a regular port of call for ships passing through China Strait. Gurney airstrip, at the head of Milne Bay, is the nearest airport. There are regular air services from Port Moresby to Gurney, and a connecting launch to Samarai from the mainland for passengers, mail and freight.

Samarai, one of the most attractive settlements in Papua pre-war, was burned out by Japanese air raids in 1942. The township and wharf were rebuilt.

The islet is picturesque and beautifully situated, with views up and down China Strait out along the Eastern Passage and across the water to the mountains of the mainland. Post-war growth made it crowded — hence the decision to establish headquarters on the mainland at Alotau. There is a roadway round Samarai and it can be walked in 20 minutes.

Among the islands within sight of Samarai are Logeia, Sariba, Doini and Kwato. Stretching south-east from the Samarai group of islands lie the following: Dumoulin, Wari, Imbert, Stuers, Quessant, Sable, Kosmann, Lejeune, Duperre,

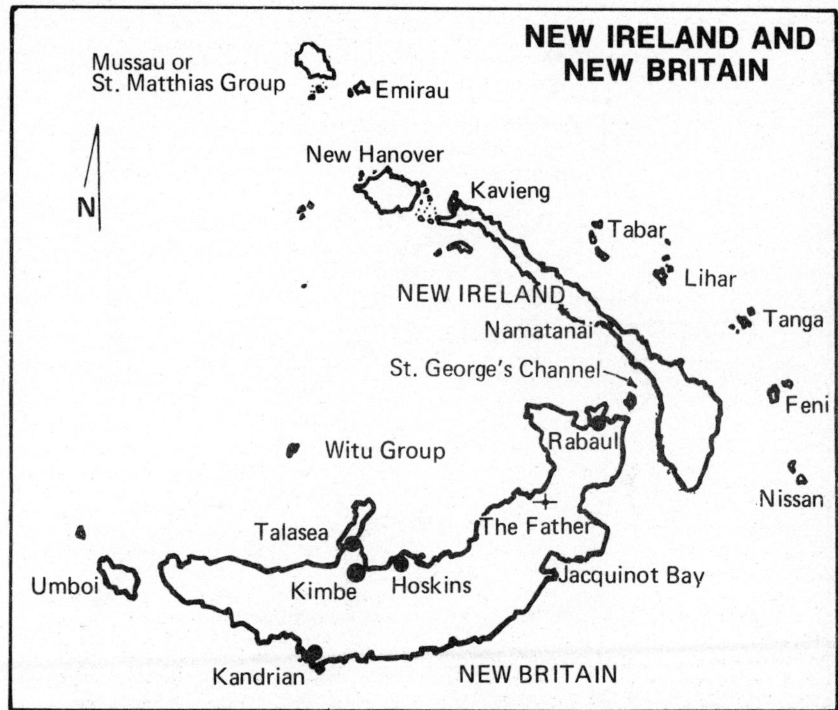

Jomard, Pana Waipona, Montemount and Duchateau.

ISLANDS OFF NEW BRITAIN

WITU ISLANDS. These are a group of volcanic origin about 80 km off the north coast, opposite the Talasea Peninsula. The largest are Garove (or Deslacs) about 67 sq km in area; Unea (or Merite) 28 sq km; Mundua, three sq km; and there are five other smaller islands. There are several extinct volcanoes, all densely forested. The highest is on Unea, 783 m. There are a number of very good coconut and cocoa plantations in this group, and an excellent harbour in Garove — a beautiful, landlocked bay apparently formed when the sea broke into a crater. There once was a very large population in this group but it was decimated by a smallpox epidemic in the first decade of the century. The population has increased steadily in recent years, and now numbers 6,750. There are airstrips for light aircraft on Unea and Garove.

DUKE OF YORKS. The Duke of York group consists of Duke of York Island (8 km by 8 km) and a number of small islands — notably Makada, Ulu (or Mouke, or Pig), Kabakon, Kerawara and Mioko. This group is low, thickly wooded, well populated, contains several plantations, and has a total area of 60 sq km. Population approximately 6,100. The group is situated in St. George's Channel, near Rabaul. The Duke of York group had an important part in the first colonisation of New Guinea. The first Methodist Mission station was located here, at "Port Hunter", in 1875. Various traders and planters established themselves there about the same time (including Mrs Forsayth, or "Queen Emma"); and from here they gradually colonised the adjoining Kokopo area of New Britain, then inhabited by formidable savages. The first beginnings of the afterwards powerful German firms of Godeffroy and Hernsheim were placed here. Kabakon, in 1903, was selected by a man named Engelhardt as the scene of a notable — but vain — attempt to establish a sunworshipping cult. Other off-shore islands of New Britain (East and West Provinces) are:

Off north coast, west to east — Jamalaure, Galimaruhe, Poi, Nusasi, Talangonai, Kautagi, Tuare, Garua, Banban, Lolobau, Tiwongo, Kakolan, Talele, Lolonakuka.

Off south coast, west to east — Arawe Group (Kaptimati, Marklo, Kumbum, Arawe, Angup, Ablaugi, Pileto), Ganglo, Bugi, Geglep, Aweleng, Amge, Alago, Abungi, Ampul, Lakei, Melinglo, Ayet, Ablingi, Agur, Gasmata, Dililo, Awrin,

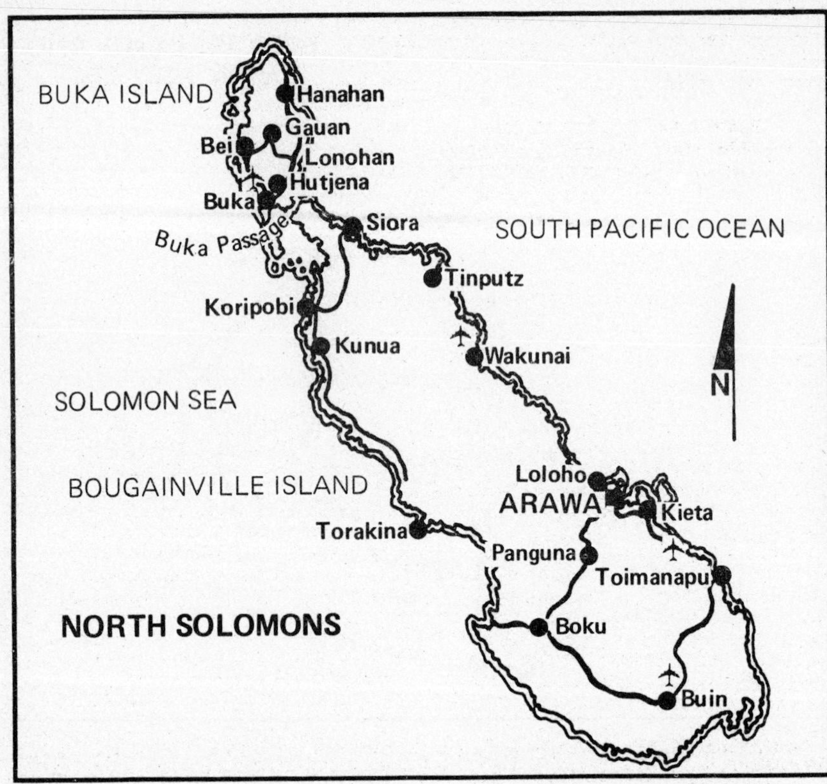

Amerer, Kiwok, Siwot, Walanguo, Lue, Lilum, Baronga, Kaskas, Mangrove, Kawauwu, Mockton.

Off Gazelle Peninsula — Watom, Urara.

NEW BRITAIN itself a narrow, crescent-shaped island, is the largest and most important unit of the archipelago. It is about 600 km long. The most important town, Rabaul, is situated on the north-east coast.

The total area of the island is estimated at 37,736 sq km and as the main breadth is only 80 km, its extreme narrowness can be easily realised. A high and very rugged range of mountains runs from one end of New Britain to the other.

The highest peak in New Britain is an active volcano, The Father, 2,284 m high, on the north-west coast, near which are the two mountains, the North and South Son. Close to Rabaul are three peaks, the Mother and the South and North Daughter, the first named being an extinct volcano.

Volcanic action is very evident throughout New Britain.

NEW IRELAND AND ITS ISLANDS

NEW IRELAND, like Manus, is also a province. It consists of the long narrow island of New Ireland, the fairly large island of Lavongai, which is better known as New Hanover, and which has its own offshore islands and islets; the Saint Matthias Group, which is NNW of New Hanover, and groups of small islands that lie east of New Ireland — Tabar, Lihar, Tanga and Feni. Some other islands off the south coast are described under Bougainville. The offshore islands of Lavongai include Mussau, Emirau, Tingwon, and Tench.

New Ireland itself lies at right-angles to the northern end of New Britain. It is 320 km long with an average width of 11 km except in the south where it expands to 50 km and is very mountainous without any rivers of size. Its coastline is fairly broken and its best harbours are at Kavieng, (the chief town) Namatanai, Muliana and Kalili. There are more than 400 km of roads down the east coast, and 300 km along the west coast. A large part of the island is under cultivation, particularly on the east coast.

The southern tip of New Ireland was the scene of a French "South Sea Bubble," when a Frenchman, Marquis de Rays set up a colony at Port Breton, which failed.

ISLANDS OFF BOUGAINVILLE

NUKUMANU (TASMAN) ISLANDS lie about 400 km to the north-east of Bougainville, in 4 deg 35 min South lat and 159 deg 25 min East long, on a reef measuring 11 km by 18 km, and on which there are some 40 small islands. The largest is Nukumanu with an area of 2.6 sq km. The population of 300 is almost pure Polynesian stock. There is immigration and inter-marriage from Ontong Java just to the south in the Solomon Islands.

TAKAU (MARQUEEN OR MORTLOCK) GROUP is about 195 km north-east of Bougainville, in 4 deg 50 min South lat, and 157 deg East long. This group also is a ring-shaped reef, on which there are about 20 islands with a total area of 85 ha. The largest is Takau. The population is about 500, the main strain being Polynesian, with an admixture of New Britain, Manus and Caroline Islands natives.

KILINAILAU (CARTERET) GROUP is about 70 km north-east of Buka, in 4 deg 45 min South lat and 155 deg 20 min East long. There are six islands which form an almost circular atoll about 16 km in diameter. There is a trading station. The population consists of about 1,011 people from Buka, who have apparently displaced a Polynesian population. The islands are planted with coconuts.

NISSAN OR GREEN ISLANDS (SIR CHARLES HARDY) are coral islands in 4 deg 30 min South lat and 154 deg 15 min East long. The atoll is elliptical, and measures about 16 km by 8 km and contains three islands. The greatest height does not exceed 60 metres. Coconuts, native fruit trees and ivory nuts are grown. The population is about 3,100. There is a trading station on the chief island (Nissan). The other islands are Barahun and Sirot. Within the centre of the atoll is Han Island.

Pinpill, a coral island a little to the north-west of the Nissan Group, is included with the latter for administration purposes. It is planted with coconuts. One of the important landings of the war in the Southwest Pacific took place on Nissan, which is also known as Green Is. There is an airstrip.

NUGURIA (OR FEAD) GROUP is about 200 km east of New Ireland and the same distance north of Bougainville, in 3 deg 15 min South lat and 154 deg 45 min East long. It consists of two atolls with some 50 islands, the total of which is only about 5 sq km. There are coconut plantations on the group. The population, which is mostly Polynesian, numbers about 300.

BOUGAINVILLE ISLAND itself is about 120 km long and varies in width from 65 km to 97 km. The Emperor Range (highest point Mount Balbi, 2,745 m), occupies the northern half, and the Crown Prince Range (200 m), the southern half. The interior is wild and broken, jungle clad and inaccessible. Balbi and Bagana (2,000 m) are active volcanoes and well-known landmarks. There are numerous small islands along the NE coast and off the NW coast.

There are a few good harbours, the best being at Kieta, Anewa Bay, Tonolei and Buka Passage. Other harbours on the east coast suitable for small craft are Raua, Tinputz, Tiop, Inus, Numa Numa.

On the west coast there is a safe anchorage for small ships at Banoni, and a fair anchorage for small craft at Mamaregu in Gazelle Harbour (Empress Augusta Bay).

BUKA ISLAND, to Bougainville's north, is hilly in the southern portion, the highest point reaching to about 400 m. In the south-west there is a mountain range of volcanic origin, and to the north and east the island is of raised coral rock. The interior, except in the south-west, is a lowland of level and undulating country.

Buka is separated from Bougainville by the very narrow Buka Passage.

Along the coast there are large areas of mangroves, and in the interior of Buka, dense forest, with some areas of grass. A great number of low coral islands lie off the south and west coast, and on them, and on the west coast, there are several plantations. The principal harbour is Queen Carola Harbour on the west coast.

Buka and its adjacent islands have a population of about 20,000 nationals.

ISLANDS OFF MOROBE

The main islands included in the Morobe Province are the large island of Umboi (Rooke) and the smaller islands of Tolokiwa and Sakar. All are in Vitiaz Strait between the mainland and New Britain. Umboi, 43 km by 24 km, is of volcanic origin, is up to 1,370 m high and has an area of 777 sq km, is well cultivated, populated in parts and has two good anchorages — Marien Harbour and Luther. Sakar is volcanic and very high, is 34 sq km in area and has at times been in violent eruption. Tolokiwa, wooded and inhabited, is 39 sq km in area, and has a conical volcanic peak 1,377 m high.

ISLANDS OFF MADANG

Off the coast of Madang Province are three large islands, each running up to a high peak — Manam Island (1,800 m), Karkar Island (1,835 m) and Long Is (1,305 m). Manam or Vulcan Is is 83 sq km in area and 15 km offshore. It is inhabited but the volcano that forms practically the whole island, is frequently in eruption and at times the whole population has had to be evacuated.

Aris is a small island off the western extremity of Manam.

Karkar or Dampier, is 362 km in area, is thickly

wooded and fertile. It is extensively planted in coconuts.

Bagabag an outlier of Karkar, is a sunken crater with an area of 36 sq km. It is wooded and inhabited. Long Is is 48 km from the mainland coast, 414 sq km in area and has two cone-shaped active craters, in one of which is a lake.

ISLANDS OFF THE SEPIK

Off the coast of the East Sepik Province are the islands of Kairiru, Mushu, Schouten Group, Tendanye, Valif and a number of small islets of little consequence. The islands of Aua and Wuvulu are also administered from Wewak. These islands, on the extreme north-western ocean fringe of Papua New Guinea, are officially part of the Manus Province.

The islands off the East Sepik coast range from upthrust coral islands to volcanic islands, some with active and others with dormant craters. They are all thickly populated and some support coconut plantations.

MANUS AND ITS ISLANDS

MANUS consists of a scattered province stretching between the Equator and 3 deg S Lat; and between 143 deg E long and 149 deg E long. The islands consist of Admiralty, Hermit, Ninigo, Anchorite, Pelleluhu and Nauma groups. Manus, the largest in the group is 96 km long by 32 km wide. Most of the population lives on Manus Island. It is heavily timbered and has a poor agricultural potential due to the broken nature of the region and generally low fertility of the soil. A central range of hills rises to 720 m.

Lou Island, some 32 km due south of Los Negros Island, is notably more fertile; this is due to its volcanic origin.

Nearly all of the small islands are low-lying atolls. They are covered with a very shallow topsoil in which coconuts, but little else will grow.

The Hermits and Ninigo atolls, about 320 km north-west of Manus Island, have a population of about 700.

At the eastern end of Manus is Los Negros Island, separated from the main island by extremely narrow Loniu Passage, the northern end of which runs into Seeadler Harbour. Lorengau is on the western side of Seeadler Harbour. Lorengau, Seeadler Harbour, Loniu Passage and Los Negros Island together provided the site for the huge Manus naval and air base built by the Americans at great cost during the Pacific war, and later abandoned.

Manus is closest to Micronesia and the old names of the many small islands that surround Manus Is within a radius of 60 km are all that remain to indicate that the Spanish saw some of them several centuries ago. Their official names and those by which they were originally known are: Sabben; Alim (Elizabeth); Baluan (St Patrick); Sivesa (Fedarb, Seppressa); Horno; Los Reyes; Pak (San Gabriel); Mbuke (Sugarloaf); St Andrew; Lou (St George); Rambutyo (Jesu Maria); Johnston; Pam (Maitland); Lambutin (San Miguel); Ton (San Rafael).

The North Western Islands lie from 290 to 320 km north-west of Lorengau and are atolls. The islands of Wuvulu and Aua are much closer to Wewak, in East Sepik Province.

The main atolls in this North Western group are Anchorites or Kaniet — five large islets scattered along the reef, at 0 deg. 55 min. S. latitude 145 deg. 30 min. E. longitude. Sae or Commerson, a large atoll with two islets, is at 0 deg. 45 min. S. latitude 145 deg. 15 min. E. longitude.

The Hermits is a large atoll supporting four large islets. Djalon, Maron, Akib and Luf, and a number of small islets. There was a famous plantation and home established at Maron in German times but the home has been demolished. Ninigo Group consists of large islets scattered over half a dozen atolls.

There has been much settlement and planting of these atolls from earliest European times and they also supported a healthy Micronesian population, but contact with Europeans almost depopulated the group in the early years of this century. Population is now increasing, although the people are no longer pure Micronesian.

Manu or Allison, Aua or Durour, and Wuvulu or Maty, are about 50 to 65 km west of the Ninigos, and are now administered from Wewak, for convenience.

In recent years there have been plans for developing Wuvulu, which has an indigenous population, as a tourist resort. It has an airstrip.

FOR THE TOURIST. Papua New Guinea is no Pacific atoll. With its mainland, archipelagoes and offshore islands it is continental in scope and presents vast contrasts in climate, scenery and terrain. Every province has its own attractions. The Papua New Guinea Office of Tourism, Box 773 Port Moresby, has extensive literature available to intending visitors, and the Papua New Guinea Handbook, published annually by Pacific Publications, Box 3408 GPO Sydney, has full details of all aspects of the country, including a special section for travellers.

Entry formalities. Anyone visiting Papua New Guinea requires an entry permit, or a valid passport endorsed for entry into the country. However in July, 1979, an 'easy visa' system was introduced, which has been extended until December 31, 1980. Under this system, bona-fide tourists from most of the world outside the Communist regimes and the Middle East are, granted a visa upon arrival in Port Moresby provided their stay in PNG does not exceed 30 days, and they have return air fares & sufficient funds for their support while in PNG. Vaccinations and inoculations are optional for travellers arriving in PNG from Australia. Visitors are advised to take anti-malarial tablets before arriving in the country and during their stay, as a precautionary measure.

Airport tax. Departing travellers pay an airport tax of K5.

Duty-free facilities. A very limited range of duty-free goods are available at Jackson's Airport, Port Moresby, and at a store in Port Moresby.

Shows. Most of the provinces of Papua New Guinea have an occasional "show". These were originally designed to exhibit the local produce of primary and secondary industry, however, they also have all the elements of a country fair where thousands of Papua New Guineans gather to dance, sing and feast and hundreds of visitors arrive to watch and to photograph.

The shows that attract the biggest attendance and world-wide publicity are those held at Goroka, Eastern Highlands, and Mount Hagen, Western Highlands. The shows are usually held in each place on alternate years – it was at Mount Hagen in 1977 and will be held at Goroka in 1980.

Ten thousand local people and more turn out for these occasions plus thousands of visitors, many from overseas. These shows are the mecca of professional and amateur photographers and miles of colour film are shot of the dancing, yelling mass of people, wearing their fantastic headdresses of bird-of-paradise and other plumes and their own style of dress which usually amounts to very little. Their energy seems inexhaustible although they may have been walking for days to get there and, when it is all over, must walk for a similar period to return to their villages.

Hotels are booked out a year in advance and so are airline seats. But some sort of dormitory accommodation is usually provided and there are charter flights from coastal towns.

Other dancing and feasts, generally known as "sing-sings" are organised for special local occasions; or smaller versions can be arranged for large groups of tourists or cruise ships.

War cemeteries. Three war cemeteries in Papua New Guinea are much visited by touring parties. The Commonwealth War Graves Commission, which is charged under Royal Charter with the permanent construction of British war cemeteries throughout the world, and which is administered in Australia by the Department of Administrative Services, is in charge of the war cemeteries.

The cemeteries are at Bomana, near Port Moresby; at Lae; and at Bita Paka not far from Rabaul.

Each of the three cemeteries is of individual plan, designed to make best use of local surroundings, but all are, in fact, beautifully kept parks, characterised by dignified stonework – in gateways, entrances, memorials and pavilions – and in green lawns and brilliant flowers, shrubs and trees.

Port Moresby and the National Capital District. Papua New Guinea has its capital at Port Moresby which, since 1945, has grown from a sleepy little tropical port to a busy city that has sprawled into new suburbs beyond the adjacent hills.

Until 1974 the city was part of Central District but was then excised from it and now functions as the National Capital Province.

With its good climate, splendid harbour and blue water on both sides, Port Moresby is attractive, except at the end of the dry season when it can be dusty, brown and parched. Most of the amenities of civilisation can now be purchased in Port Moresby, where there are department stores, hotels, cinemas, clubs and adequate taxi services.

There is a drive-in movie theatre and there are several small licensed restaurants where meals are served until a late hour as well as the restaurants attached to the hotels.

A number of firms run full or half day tours in Port Moresby, around the city itself or to points of interest in the surrounding countryside. Alternatively, visitors can hire rental cars from several firms in Port Moresby and suburbs. North-westward around the harbour is Konedobu, the area once reserved for government departments, but these are now also erected elsewhere. Behind Konedobu, on a low hill, and with a good view over the harbour is Government House. On the harbour side, close to Konedobu is the village of Hanuabada which, before the war, was a typical coastal Papuan one of thatched houses built out over the sea on thin stilts.

Some of the houses are still built over the sea but they are no longer of native materials – it is now necessary to go further out along the coast for that. Hanuabada has lost its former picturesque charm, but it is worth visiting.

A few minutes walk out of the shopping centre at Port Moresby to the eastern side of Paga Point, good swimming may be had at Ela Beach, an attractive stretch of sand bordered with pines. Two kilometres further on along the road bordering the sea is Koki, where hundreds of islanders live permanently on their big double-canoes which are mostly drawn up on the isthmus. There is a market nearby which is being developed as a major attraction.

From Koki the road winds over low hills to many growing suburbs, to the airport and beyond. From Boroko two roads lead to the left – the first to the low-cost housing development of Hohola and the second to the showground, drive-in cinema, and the University of Papua New Guinea.

In this area, on what was a wartime airstrip known as Wards, an increasing number of high-rise office buildings are being erected. The area is the city's new government and civic centre. It is also the site of modern Supreme Court and Arts Theatre buildings. There's an olympic size swimming pool at Taurama.

Outside National Capital limits, longer trips can be taken to Bomana War Cemetery, about 16 km out of Port Moresby, or to Rouna Falls, the Sogeri Tableland, and Variarata National Park. Rouna Falls are large and spectacular in the wetter times

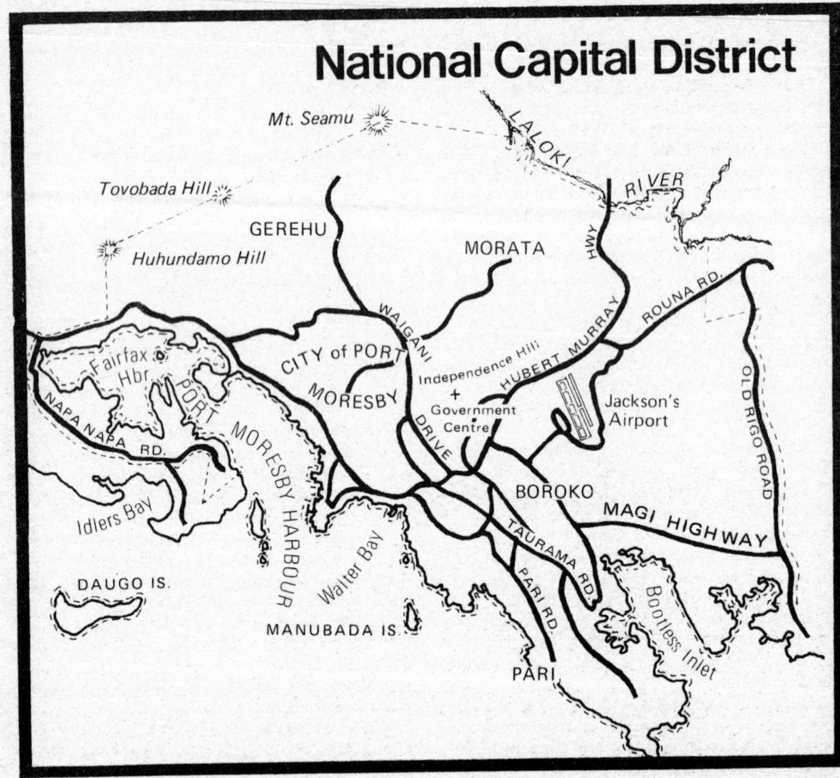

of the year, and accessible. They occur where the Laloki River plunges off the tableland that forms the foothills of the Owen Stanley Range, and a steep road winds up above the falls to the monument that marks the start of the wartime Kokoda Trail and from there on, the area is devoted to rubber plantations.

There are several travel agencies in Port Moresby plus the travel departments of the big firms, shipping companies, airline offices and hotels.

There are also many hotels and guest houses, and the following list is only a selection of those available in the National Capital District and in provinces throughout Papua New Guinea, and is not meant to be exhaustive.

ACCOMMODATION

National Capital District and Central Province

BOROKO HOTEL — Okari Street, Boroko. Number of Rooms, 8 Single, 29 Twin, 4 Family. Tel. 252677.

DAVARA MOTEL, Ela Beach Road, Port Moresby. Number of Rooms, 73 Twin, 6 Suites. Tel. 212100.

DEVON LODGE APARTMENTS, Kermadec Street, Ela Beach. Number of Rooms, 24 Double. Tel. 211722.

PORT MORESBY TRAVELODGE, Hunter Street, Pt. Moresby. International-Class. Tel. 214068. Multi-story Hotel.

GATEWAY HOTEL, 11 km from city, at airport. Number of Rooms, 1 single, 1 Double, 31 Twin, 2 Suites. Tel. 253855.

HOTEL MORESBY, Musgrave Street, Port Moresby. Number of Rooms, 7 Twin, 6 Family. Tel. 212266.

ISLANDER HOTEL, Cnr. Wards Road, Waigani Drive, Hohola. Number of Rooms, 46 Double, 34 Twin, 6 Suites, 2 Family. Tel. 255955.

PAPUA HOTEL, Musgrave Street, Port Moresby. Number of Rooms, 15 Single, 2 Double, 27 Twin, 2 Family. Tel. 212622.

SALVATION ARMY HOSTEL, Badili. Number of Rooms, 11 Double, 3 Family. Tel. 253744.

YWCA HOSTEL, 3 Mile Hill, Boroko. Number of Rooms, 4 Single, 2 Double. Tel. 256604.

OUTRIGGER MOTEL, Vanama Cres., Sunam, Port Moresby. Number of Rooms, 40 Double, 16 Twin, 1 Suite. Tel. 212088.

ROUNA HOTEL, Rouna Falls, 35 km by road

from Port Moresby. Tel. 281146.

TAPINI HOTEL, Tapini. Number of Rooms, 7 Double. Tel. Tapini 29.

LOLOATA ISLAND RESORT, 23 km from Port Moresby, offshore from Bogaro Inlet. Number of Rooms, 7 Family. VHF 240118.

KOKODA TRAIL MOTEL, Sogeri, 48 km from Port Moresby in the Owen Stanley Ranges. Number of Rooms, 2 Double, 1 Twin, 3 Family. Tel. 282256.

SALVATION ARMY COTTAGE, Sogeri, 50 km from Port Moresby on Owers Corner, ideal for weekends away. Tel. 253744.

ORORO GUEST HOUSE, Woitape. Number of Rooms, 6 Double. No phone facilities.

East New Britain

HOTEL ASCOT, Mango Avenue, Rabaul. Number of Rooms, 25 Single, 17 Twin. Tel. 921999.

MOTEL KAIVUNA, Mango Avenue, Rabaul. Number of Rooms, 7 Single, 1 Double, 24 Twin. Tel. 921766.

KALAU LODGE, 10 km from Rabaul. Number of Rooms, 5 Units. Tel. 922667.

RABAUL COMMUNITY HOSTEL, Cleland

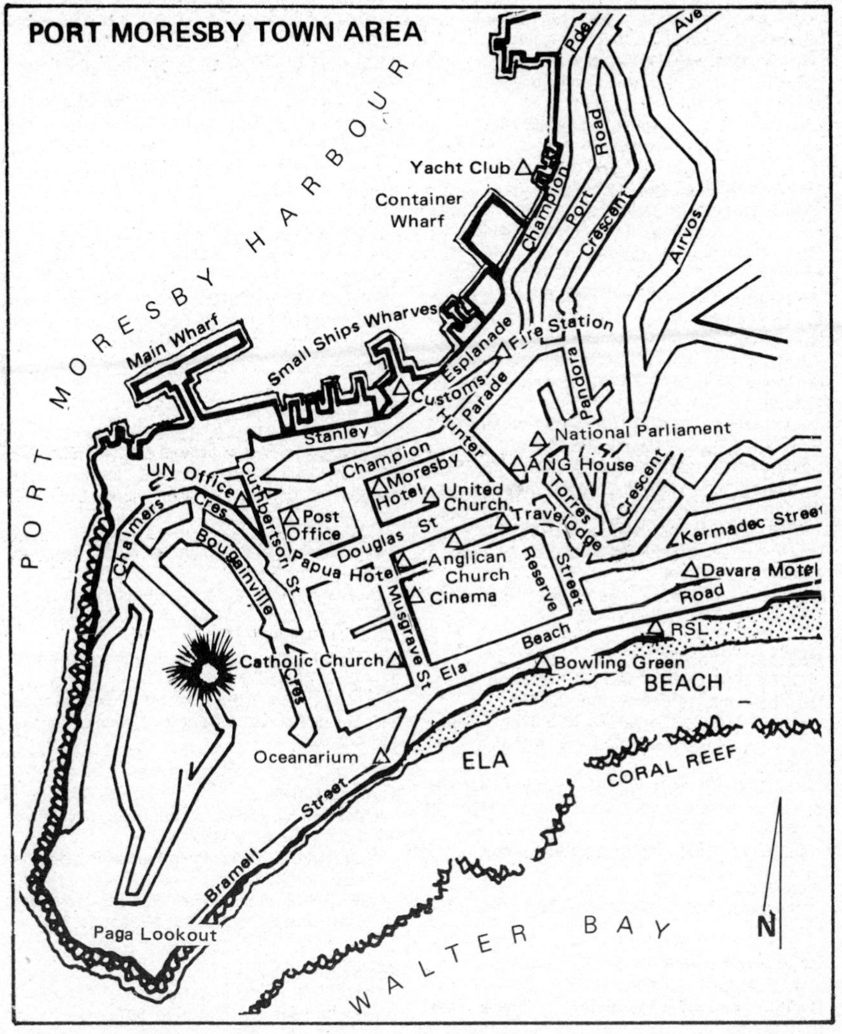

Drive, Rabaul. Number of Rooms, 4 Single, 46 Double, 15 Family. Tel. 922325.

TRAVELODGE, Mango Avenue, Rabaul. Number of Rooms, 40 Family (1 Double and 1 Single Bed). Tel. 922111.

East Sepik

SEPIK MOTEL, Wewak. Number of Rooms, 15 Twin. Tel. 862422.

WEWAK HOTEL, Wewak. 16 Single and 22 Twin Rooms. Tel. 862155.

WINDJAMMER MOTEL, Mission Point, Wewak. Number of Rooms, 4 Double, 14 Twin, 4 Suites. Tel. 86119.

KARAWARI LODGE, Amboin. Number of Rooms, 20 Double. No telephone.

ANGORAM HOTEL, Angoram. Number of Rooms, 2 Single, 10 Twin, 1 Suite, 1 Family. Tel. 521589.

MAPRIK WAKEN HOTEL, Maprik. Number of Rooms, 6 Twin. Tel. 891221.

Eastern Highlands and Chimbu

BIRD OF PARADISE HOTEL, Goroka. Number of Rooms, 16 Double, 37 Twin. Tel. 721144.

LANTERN LODGE, Goroka. 9 twin rooms. Tel. 721776.

MINOGERE MOTEL/HOSTEL, Goroka. Number of Rooms, 4 Single, 10 Double, 42 Twin, 13 Family. Tel. 721009.

SALVATION ARMY FLATS, Goroka. Number of Rooms, 4 Twin, 2 Family, (2 bedroom). Tel. 721218.

KAINANTU LODGE, Kainantu. Number of Rooms, 12 Twin, 7 Family. Tel. 771021.

SALVATION ARMY FLATS, Kainantu. Self-contained units with all cooking facilities. Tel. 771130

CHIMBU LODGE, Kundiawa, Chimbu Province. Number of Rooms, 2 Double, 17 Twin, 1 Family. Tel. 751144.

KUNDIAWA HOTEL, Kundiawa. Number of Rooms, 10 Twin. Tel. 751033.

Madang

COASTWATCHERS MOTEL, Madang. Number of Rooms, 14 Family. Tel. 822684.

HOTEL MADANG, Madang. Number of Rooms, 17 Single, 4 Double, 17 Twin, 4 Family. Tel. 822655.

SMUGGLERS INN MOTEL, Madang. Number of Rooms, 6 Double, 23 Twin, 2 Suites, 18 Family, 1 Single. Tel. 822744.

SIMBAI LODGE, Simbai. No telephone.

Manus

There is no tourist accommodation in this province.

Milne Bay Province

MASURINA LODGE, Alotau. Number of Rooms, 3 Single, 6 Twin, 1 Family. Tel. 611349.

SAMARAI GUEST HOUSE, Samarai. Number of Rooms, 2 Single, 2 Double, 1 Twin, 1 Suite, 1 Family. Tel. Samarai 258.

KIRIWINA LODGE, Losuia (Trobriand Islands). Number of Rooms, 9 Double. Phone outstations.

Morobe Province

BUABLUNG HAUS, Lae. Number of Rooms, 44 Single. Tel. 424412.

HOTEL CECIL, Markham Road, Lae. Number of Rooms, 16 Single, 1 Double, 12 Twin, 1 Family. Tel. 423674.

HUON GULF MOTEL, Markham Road, Lae. Number of Rooms, 27 Twin, 3 Family. Tel. 424844.

KLINKII LODGE, Klinkii Street, Lae. Number of Rooms, 20 Twin. Tel. 421281.

MELANESIAN HOTEL, First Street, Lae. Number of Rooms, 4 Double, 64 Twin, 2 Suites. Tel. 422487.

PINE LODGE HOTEL, Bulolo. Number of Rooms, 4 Single, 4 Double, 4 Twin. Tel. 445220.

WAU HOTEL, Wau. Number of Rooms, 4 Single, 3 Double, 4 Twin, 1 Family. Tel. 446233.

PARADISE SPRINGS INN, Sialum, near Finschhafen. Number of Rooms, 7 Units (each can accommodate four people). Phone outstations

New Ireland Province

KAVIENG HOTEL, Kavieng. Number of Rooms, 18 Twin. Tel. 941448.

MALANGAN GUEST HOUSE, Kavieng. Tel. 942093.

North Solomons Province (formerly Bougainville).

DAVARA MOTEL, Toniva Beach, near Kieta. Number of Rooms, 21 Twin, 21 Double, 2 Suites, 2 Family. Tel. 456175.

HOTEL KIETA, Kieta town. Number of Rooms, 27 Twin. Tel. 456277.

BUKA LUMAN GUEST HOUSE, Buka Passage. Number of Rooms, 1 Double, 2 Twin, 1 Family. Tel. 966057.

Northern Province

LAMINGTON HOTEL, Popondetta. Number of Rooms, 14 Twin. Tel. 297152.

WUJUGA PARK, Wanigela. Number of Rooms, 19 Twin. No telephone.

KOFURE VILLAGE GUEST HOUSE, Tufi. Number of Rooms, 6 Double. No telephone.

Southern Highlands

HOTEL MENDI, Mendi. Number of Rooms, 10 Double, 9 Twin, 1 Family. Tel. 591188.

West New Britain

PALM LODGE MOTEL, Kimbe. Number of Rooms, 4 Single, 5 Double, 25 Twin, 1 Family. Tel. 935001.

HOSKINS HOTEL, at airport, Hoskins. Number of Rooms, 9 Twin. Tel. VHF930145.

West Sepik

NARIMO HOTEL, Vanimo. Number of Rooms, 4 Single, 10 Double. Tel. 871113

Western & Gulf

DARU GUEST HOUSE, Daru, 4 Twin. Tel. 659104.

BENSBACH WILDLIFE LODGE, Western Province, West of Daru. Number of Rooms, 8 Twin. Tel. 521438.

HOTEL KEREMA, Kerema. Tel. 681041.

Western Highlands and Enga

RAMADA INN, Minj. Number of Rooms, 12 Twin. Tel. 565538.

AIRPORT HOTEL, Mt. Hagen. Number of Rooms, 4 Double, 11 Twin, 1 Family. Tel. 551326.

HAGEN PARK MOTEL, Mt. Hagen. Number of Rooms, 1 Double, 26 Twin, 5 Family. Tel. 521388.

HIGHLANDER HOTEL, Mt. Hagen. Number of Rooms, 35 Twin, 3 Family. Tel. 521355.

BANZ HOTEL/MOTEL, Banz. Number of Rooms, 12 Twin. Tel. 562245.

WABAG LODGE, Wabag. Number of Rooms, 15 Twin. Tel. 571069.

PITCAIRN ISLANDS

This is a British dependency, Pitcairn Island itself being a small irregular-shaped island only 3 km long by 1.5 km wide, with a total land area of about 450 ha. Included in the district are three uninhabited islands, Oeno, Ducie and Henderson, which is why the group is called Pitcairn Islands. Pitcairn is about 2160 km south-east of Tahiti, at 25.04 deg. S. Lat. and 130.06 deg. W. Long.

Population is about 70. An Island Council manages local affairs and there is also a Governor, based in New Zealand. New Zealand dollars and cents are official currency.

THE PEOPLE. Today's inhabitants are mostly the descendants of the 'Bounty' mutineers and of a few men who joined them on Pitcairn early in the nineteenth century.

Of the 57 local people and seven "outsiders" on the island in January, 1979, most were in the 16-55 age group. Many of the community have migrated over the years, particularly to New Zealand, where they have easy access, and the population has been steadily dropping.

Adamstown is the main settlement, consisting of a scattering of houses, many of them now abandoned as a result of the decreasing population, and some public buildings, including a school. The settlement is the original home of the mutineers, and is well situated on a northerly slope about 130 m above sea level, and covers about 25 ha of park-like land. There are many paths and lanes.

English is the official language and is taught in the school, but the dialect of Pitcairn is a mixture of English and Tahitian, with the former predominating. Visitors may hear a softly-slurred English which is perfectly comprehensible, but among themselves the islanders may lapse into speech which is hard to understand. They also use unusual local place names in conversation, such as John Catch a Cow, Where Tom Off, Timiti's Crack, Up in Ti, Down Cask, Up the Beans.

The islanders are firm adherents of the Seventh-day Adventist faith. An SDA pastor is permanently stationed on the island.

One of the highlights of community life is the ringing of different peals of bells to mark such events as times of worship, public entertainment, participation in public work, or occasionally to signal the approach of a ship, when everybody hastens to the landing.

The public square is the heart of Pitcairn. Here there are buildings which serve as courthouse, Island Magistrate's office, community hall, church, dispensary, library and post office. Outside the court house stands one of the anchors from the 'Bounty'. In the church is kept the famous Bible from the 'Bounty', on permanent loan to Pitcairn from the Connecticut Historical Society.

Pitcairners have only two meals a day, a late breakfast and late afternoon tea.

Community recreation is not deeply rooted in the island, partly because of the individual character of the people, and perhaps because an active outdoor life tends to send people to bed early. But there are occasional picnics, frequent birthday parties, fishing and goat hunting, basket-weaving, surfing in Bounty Bay or children's games around the landing, film-going or community cricket games with local rules and many players a side.

GOVERNMENT. Management of internal affairs is in charge of an Island Council, normally meeting monthly under the chairmanship of the Island Magistrate, in whom are vested executive as well as judicial powers.

The council is composed of the Magistrate, two councillors, the Chairman of the Internal Committee, the Island Secretary, three nominated members (one appointed by the Governor and two by the elected members), and two advisory members (one appointed by the Governor and one by the council). The Island Education Officer also acts as Government adviser but has no vote on the council.

Elections for the Island Council are held annually on Christmas Day, but the Island Magistrate is elected on a three-year term. Residents aged 18 or over, and who have lived three years on the island, are entitled to vote. Candidates for the post of Magistrate must have had 21 years' residence, and councillors five years.

Posts of Island Secretary and other local government officials, such as Postmaster, Radio Officer and Police Officer, are appointed by the Governor after consultation with the council. They are part-time posts. For the size of the Pitcairn population the number on the council and those holding official posts is probably large, but this is traditional to Pitcairn because of the family-type organisation begun in earliest times.

The council is empowered to enact regulations, but the Governor may revoke or alter them. In practice, there is rarely alteration to council decisions, apart possibly from the technical wording of by-laws.

The Internal Committee of the council comprises a chairman and other members, which the council may appoint, and its principal task is directing the local work programme.

The Governor of Pitcairn is the British High Commissioner to New Zealand, based in Wellington.

Justice. There is an Island Court consisting of the Island Magistrate and two councillors. Its jurisdiction is limited to offences under the island code, really local by-laws, and to civil actions. Its ability to gaol or fine is limited. The Island Magistrate also has summary jurisdiction of his own, which is further limited.

There is provision for a Supreme Court of Pitcairn, and for another court subordinate to the Supreme Court but distinct from the Island Court. But these are provisions only, for the Island Court itself is rarely required to sit.

Liquor and Gambling. There are no liquor regulations, or liquor sales, on the island, which is traditionally "dry". Nor is there any gambling.

EDUCATION. Education is free and compulsory. Schooling for children between 6 and 16 was in the hands of the SDA church until 1948, when a schoolteacher was seconded from the New Zealand Department of Education, teaching to the NZ syllabus. There have been education officers appointed on the same basis ever since. The teacher also acts as Government Adviser. Free secondary education for those over the age of 15 is available in New Zealand. Management of the Pitcairn School is in the hands of the Education Officer and a local committee.

LABOUR. There are few paid government jobs available on Pitcairn, and there is no business community in the usual sense, although the manufacture of carvings and other artefacts for sale to passengers on passing ships or through mail orders provides many people with an income.

The law requires all men between 16 and 65 to make themselves available for public work. This is directed by the Island Council and might necessitate building repairs, road work or the maintenance of the all-important boats at Bounty Bay. This form of labour is typical of small isolated communities living on little better than a subsistence economy, for in these conditions co-operative action is essential.

HEALTH. There is no permanent doctor on Pitcairn. There is a well-stocked dispensary and nursing assistance. Occasionally medical help is received from passing ships, and medical advice in an emergency has also been received from overseas via the two-way radio. Surgical cases have sometimes been evacuated to New Zealand. The general health of the population is good.

THE LAND. Pitcairn is a steep island, with a rugged coastline. Highest point is about 350 m above sea level. There are no streams, but abundant rainfall ensures fresh water, and the island is most productive. Soil is volcanic and very fertile. The islanders grow many fruits and vegetables, including citrus, sugarcane, watermelons, bananas, yams, taro, beans, pumpkin and coconuts. The fruit trees usually have large crops. The island is well stocked with wild goats and poultry.

Most of the gardens lie on the more gentle slopes to the south and west of Adamstown, although fruit trees are everywhere.

When Carteret sighted the island in 1767 he reported it was mostly entirely covered with trees, but clearing and burning which followed settlement has resulted in there being only a remnant of the original forest at the western tip of the island. Some steps towards forest regeneration have been taken. Miro *(Thespesia populnea)* is one of the more useful timbers, being used for building and for woodcarving.

Fish are plentiful and fishing is a popular pursuit.

Climate. This is most equable, with mean monthly temperatures varying from 18 deg. C in August to 24 deg. C in February, the absolute range being from about 11 to 33 deg C. Average rainfall is about 2000 millimetres annually, fairly evenly spread through the year. July and August are the driest months, and November the wettest.

The year 1976 was very dry, with rainfall of 668 mm.

Fauna and Flora. There is no especially distinctive flora on the island, and the only native mammal is the Polynesian rat. Other animals, such as cats, dogs and goats, have been introduced, but there are no pigs or cattle. Most of Pitcairn's birds are oceanic and migrant, and of the land birds most are to be found on the outlying islands of Henderson, Oeno and Ducie. Henderson has a unique flightless chicken bird. Of the birds breeding on Pitcairn the best known are the Fairy Tern and the Common Noddy. Pitcairn's bird life is protected by legislation.

Land tenure. Land is held under a system of family ownership based on the original division of the island by Fletcher Christian but modified over the years. There were important new divisions, perhaps better described as acquisitions, following the return of some few families to Pitcairn after the wholesale move to Norfolk Island in 1856 (see history of Pitcairn).

Under a system of bilateral inheritance, a wife's

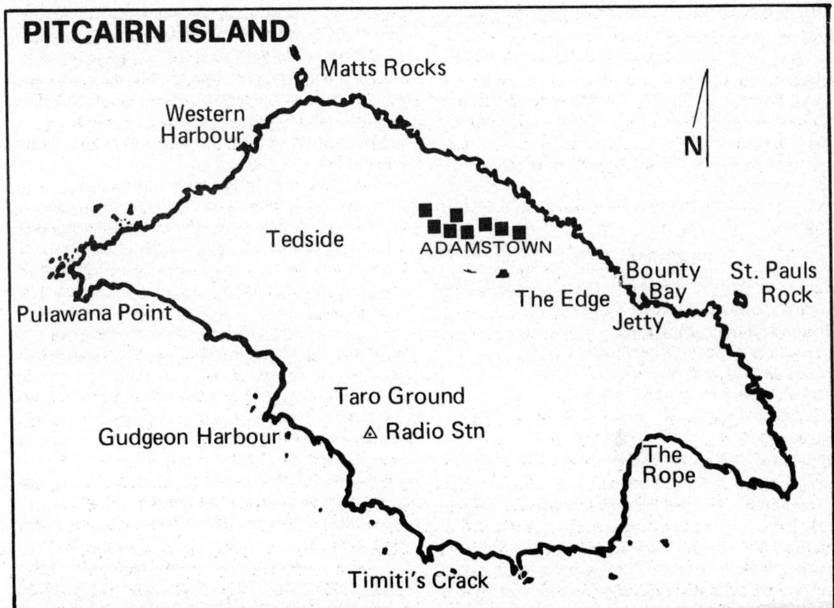

land passes to her husband, and ownership of land on the island is thus something of a patchwork quilt, with many scattered small holdings by families. Because of the falling population there has not been any pressure to implement land legislation to rationalise the situation. Any temporary scarcity of good land (premium is placed on flattish land near Adamstown) is taken care of by a system of "borrowing", under which an owner grants rights to a borrower for food gardens or housing for as long as he remains on Pitcairn.

There is no legislation to prevent land alienation to foreigners, but in fact this does not happen.

TRADE AND FINANCE. Pitcairn's revenue is derived mainly from the sale of postage stamps overseas, interest from investments, and from irregular British development grants. Government expenditure is on Administration services, such as radio communications and agriculture, and on education, health, works and the post office. Postal expenses for many years have been the largest single expenditure, but stamp sales have also been recorded as the major single source of revenue.

There are no records of the total income earned by Islanders from curio sales.

Bartering is an important part of Pitcairn life, either among individuals or on behalf of the whole community when fruit and vegetables are exchanged for other goods with visiting ships or yachts.

Postage Stamps. Pitcairn went without stamps, and finally used New Zealand postage stamps until October 1940, when it established its own post office and issued its own stamp series and thus established its most important revenue-earner.

Taxes. There is no income taxes, tariffs or duties. There are some minor licence fees.

TRANSPORT. There is no airstrip on the island and the number of visiting ships has declined in recent years. In 1978, 26 vessels called, compared with 52 in 1972. There are about four scheduled supply vessels calling each year, from New Zealand and other vessels call occasionally. Some of these visiting ships may fail to make contact with the shore if the weather is bad, for Pitcairn has no wharf and overseas ships must wait in the open sea. Bad weather can prevent the islanders from launching their boats from the jetty at Bounty Bay and getting out through the surf.

The facilities at the jetty include boat repair sheds, a slipway, a winch and a flying fox to take goods up the steep slope above the bay to what is called The Edge. Harbour improvements were made in 1976 by a team of British Army Engineers.

There are dirt roads linking Adamstown with most frequented parts of the island. These are used by the few bicycles, motor cycles and light vehicles on the island, but one special feature of Pitcairn's transport is the number of unusually-designed timber and steel wheelbarrows, widely used to move supplies.

COMMUNICATIONS. Pitcairn keeps regular radio schedules with the outside world through its radio station on a high location known locally as "Taro Ground". The radio officer is assisted by several islanders with training. Single side-band equipment is to be installed in 1980.

There is a party-line telephone service on the island.

A roneoed news-sheet called "Pitcairn Miscellany" is published monthly. It contains local news but it has many overseas subscribers.

WATER, ELECTRICITY. Tank water is used on the island and there are storage wells. Light and power is provided in Adamstown by a diesel generator.

PERSONALITIES

Governor: Mr. R. Stratton, British High COmmission, Wellington, New Zealand.
Commissioner: Mr G. D. Harraway, British Consulate-General, Auckland.
Island Magistrate: Mr. Ivan Christian.
SDA Pastor: Mr. Oliver Stimpson
Education Officer: Mr. Allen K. Cox.
Radio Operator: Mr. Tom Christian.
Internal Committee Chairman: Mr. Charles Christian.

HISTORY. Pitcairn Island was inhabited by man long before Europeans discovered it. Evidence of this has been found in the form of burial sites containing human skeletons, petroglyphs, earth ovens, stone adzes, gouges and other artefacts as well as breadfruit and coconut trees that were almost certainly planted by man. However, archaeologists have not determined where and when the first Pitcairners came from or why; or when they died out or went away.

The European discoverer of Pitcairn was Captain Philip Carteret who passed it in HMS 'Swallow' in 1767 and named it after the midshipman who first sighted it. An account of the 'Swallow's' voyage, with a description of Pitcairn, was among the books on board HMS 'Bounty' when she sailed from England in 1787 to obtain a cargo of breadfruit in Tahiti. Under the command of Lieutenant William Bligh, the 'Bounty' was to transport the breadfruit to the West Indies for replanting in the hope that it would become a staple diet for slaves employed on British plantations.

Because the 'Bounty' reached Tahiti at the wrong season for taking in young breadfruit plants, Bligh had to stay there for about five months before he could complete his cargo. This long soujourn resulted in loss of discipline among his crew and the formation of some amorous attachments with the Tahitian women. These two factors undoubtedly contributed to the mutiny which occurred on the 'Bounty' on April 28, 1789, three weeks after her departure from Tahiti.

Bligh and 18 others were cast adrift in an open boat near the Tongan Island of Tofua, while the 'Bounty' under Fletcher Christian was put about to sail back towards Tahiti. Bligh and his companions succeeded in reaching Timor, from where they returned to England. Meanwhile Christian and his fellow mutineers had tried to form a settlement on Tubuai, an island about 480 km south of Tahiti. When this failed, Christian returned to Tahiti, left 16 of his companions there, then sailed in search of a more suitable place to live. He had with him eight mutineers, six Polynesian men, 12 Polynesian women, and a small girl.

Mutineers search for a home. Christian's search for a home occupied about four months. He first sailed, via Rarotonga, probably Mangaia, and Tongatapu to the eastern outliers of Fiji. Then, because he had been impressed by Carteret's description of Pitcairn, he resolved to seek out that isolated island. Pitcairn was sighted on the evening of January 15, 1790, and the 'Bounty' was anchored in what is now called Bounty Bay.

After Christian had satisfied himself of the island's suitability for a settlement, the 'Bounty' was stripped of her contents and everyone moved ashore. On the 23rd the ship was burned to the waterline so that no clue to the mutineers' whereabouts would be visible from the sea. The mutineers were not heard of again for 18 years.

There was much violence in the meantime. About a month after their arrival, the Polynesian wife of one of the mutineers (John Williams) was killed while searching for birds' eggs. After about two years, Williams demanded the wife of one of the Polynesian men. This demand outraged the Polynesians and led to orgies of slaughter in which five mutineers, including Christian, and all the Polynesian men, were killed. The last massacre took place on October 2, 1793, when the mutineers left alive were Edward Young (a midshipman), William McCoy, Matthew Quintal and Alexander Smith, alias John Adams (seamen). There were also 10 women and a number of children.

In 1796, McCoy threw himself off a cliff in a delirious fit after producing an intoxicating liquor from the ti-root. Several years later, another woman, Quintal's wife, was killed while searching for birds' eggs, and Quintal went mad and threatened to kill both Adams and Young. The latter therefore felt justified in doing away with him before he could kill them, and did so with an axe. After Young died of asthma in 1800, Adams was the only man left alive, became a community husband to the nine remaining women. With the help of books taken from the 'Bounty', he set about educating the mutineers' 19 children and bringing them up according to strict moral standards.

Hideout discovered. When Captain Mayhew Folger of the American sealing vessel 'Topaz' put into Pitcairn in February 1808, he was surprised to see smoke ascending from an island that he thought was uninhabited. His surprise turned to astonishment when some of the mutineers' part-Polynesian sons rowed out to his ship and greeted him in English.

Although a report from Folger reached the British Admiralty, few people learned of the Pitcairn community until after the island was visited by two British warships, HMS 'Tagus' and 'Briton', in 1814.

From then until Adams died in 1829, about three dozen ships are known to have called there. Accounts which they carried back to Europe, India and the United States attracted the interest and benevolence of missionary societies and others.

As a result, Pitcairn received many gifts of Bibles, prayer books, spelling books, seeds, tools, crockery, cutlery, etc. Meanwhile, three new settlers arrived on the island – John Buffett, John Evans and George Hunn Nobbs. Nobbs became the pastor to the little community.

Moved to Tahiti. Concern over the Pitcairners' increasing numbers prompted the British Government to transfer them to Tahiti in March 1831. Although the Tahitians welcomed them and provided land for them, the Pitcairners were unhappy in their new environment. After 12 had died of unfamiliar diseases, a fund was raised to send the remaining 65 back to Pitcairn. They returned in the American brig 'Charles Doggett' (Captain William Driver) in September 1831.

In 1832, a strange, domineering, half-mad personage called Joshua Hill settled on Pitcairn, claiming to represent the British Government. Before long he had assumed the role of dictator, had expelled Nobbs and others, and had instituted a repressive regime. His rule lasted until 1838 when he was forcibly removed from the island. At the same time, Captain Russell Elliott of HMS 'Fly' drew up a simple constitution and code of laws for the Pitcairners. The constitution was dated November 30, 1838. It provided for the annual election by universal suffrage of a native-born magistrate to govern the island with a council of two, and for compulsory schooling.

Apart from a devastating storm in 1845, the next 18 years were fairly uneventful. As American whalers were now calling at the island in substantial numbers, the islanders developed a profitable trade in island produce. Meanwhile, their numbers grew apace and fears were again expressed that they would outstrip their island's resources. Finally, in 1856, the Pitcairners agreed to a British Government proposal that the entire community – then numbering 194 – should be transferred to uninhabited Norfolk Island.

Transfer to Norfolk Island. The transfer was carried out in the British merchant ship 'Morayshire'. Most of the islanders soon settled down in the new and much larger home. But some pined for Pitcairn. Two families named Young, 16 people in all, seized an opportunity to return in 1858, and four more families followed in 1864. This brought Pitcairn's population to 43. They shared five surnames – Christian, Young, McCoy, Buffett and Warren (that of an American newcomer). The male lines of the McCoys and Buffetts have since died out.

In March 1883, the Pitcairners adopted a resolution which has affected their lives ever since. Abandoning the Church of England, of which they had been nominal adherents since Adams' time, they became Seventh-day Adventists. This meant that Saturday became their day of rest; they became teetotallers (if they were not already); and they gave up eating pork, to which end they killed all pigs on Pitcairn. An SDA pastor has generally resided on the island since then.

In 1893, Captain Rooke of HMS 'Champion' introduced parliamentary government to Pitcairn – an elected council of seven with a president at its head. This, however, proved too cumbersome for such a small community, and a magisterial form of government was reintroduced after the British High Commissioner for the Western Pacific became responsible for Pitcairn's administration in 1898.

The change was made in 1904 by the British consul in Tahiti, R. T. Simons, acting on the High Commissioner's behalf. With some amendments, Simons' constitution remained in force until 1940 when H. E. Maude, also representing the High Commissioner, introduced the present system of government. At the same time a post office was established on the island, and Pitcairners began using their own postage stamps for the first time.

In 1938, two American philanthropists gave Pitcairn its first radio transmitting and receiving station. This was superseded during World War II when much improved facilities were introduced and a small team of New Zealand radio operators was stationed on the island. The wartime radio station has since been rebuilt.

Modern developments. There have been many innovations on Pitcairn since the war. In 1948, a prefabricated school was erected, with electric light and modern equipment; and a schoolmaster, on loan from the New Zealand Education Department, was sent to the island. New Zealand has supplied Pitcairn's teaching needs ever since. In 1959, the teacher and the SDA pastor began a monthly newsheet, 'Pitcairn Miscellany', which is now distributed to many interested people throughout the world. In 1965, earth roads were constructed between Adamstown and the most frequented parts of the island with two tractors provided by the British Government. Subsequently, bicycles, light motor cycles and even Mini-mokes were introduced. Other public works projects included the improvement of shore facilities, the erection of a prefabricated hostel for official visitors, and the introduction of a diesel generating plant to provide light and power to Adamstown.

However, the quality of life on Pitcairn has also regressed in some respects. In 1968, Shaw Savill passenger ships stopped calling at Pitcairn on voyages between Panama and New Zealand. This meant that the Pitcairners had less opportunities to sell their curios, and so personal incomes dropped. As a result, and also because of the attractions of the big cities, many of the young people left the island. A population of just over 60 in 1979 could be compared with 136 20 years earlier and a peak of 233 in 1937.

In early 1975 one of the islanders, Tom Christian appealed to Pitcairners abroad to come and 'repopulate a dying land'. But he warned that some young people still wanted to leave, that the ocean swells were heavy for those who manned the island's longboat, that shipping and mail services were extremely poor, and that earning a living could be difficult. On the other hand, he said Pitcairn was still free of crime, vice and drugs. Tom Christian's appeal was heeded. Later in the year, six young Pitcairners returned from New Zealand. This averted the immediate possibility that Pitcairn would have to be abandoned as a 'Bounty' settlement for lack of viable numbers.

When Fiji became independent on October 10, 1970, Pitcairn Island and its dependencies were put under the administrative control of the British High Commissioner in New Zealand. Previously, the Islands had been the responsibility of the Governor of Fiji who took over from the British High Commissioner for the Western Pacific after the posts of Governor and High Commissioner were separated in 1952. The British High Commissioner in New Zealand has the title of Governor of Pitcairn.

Further information. Numerous books and articles covering Pitcairn's history or aspects of it have been published. The most reliable is H. E. Maude's "The History of Pitcairn Island" in 'The Pitcairnese Language', A. S. C. Ross and A. W. Moverley, Eds., London 1964, David Silverman's 'Pitcairn Island', Cleveland, 1967, covers the island's history by topic.

PITCAIRN'S DEPENDENCIES. Oeno, Henderson and Ducie Islands, all of which are uninhabited, are Pitcairn Island's nearest neighbours. They were annexed by the British Crown in 1902 when the British consul in Tahiti sent Captain G. F. Jones to visit them. Jones placed a board on each inscribed with the words: 'This island is a dependency of Pitcairn and is the property of the British Government.' In 1937 when the Pacific Islands attained new values as aviation stations, the three islands were visited by HMS 'Leander' and new signboards were erected to reaffirm British sovereignty. They were made part of the Pitcairn Island Colony in 1938. Since a post office was opened on Pitcairn in 1940, the island's stamps have borne the words 'Pitcairn Islands' to cover its three dependencies.

Oeno Island. Oeno Island, about 120 km NW of Pitcairn, is a low atoll some 3.5 km in diameter. On the reef, which completely surrounds the lagoon, is a substantial sandy islet on which coconut trees, pandanus and other vegetation grow well. Water may be had by scooping sand from a depression in the centre of the islet. A boat passage on the northern side gives access to the lagoon.

Oeno was discovered by Captain James Henderson of the 'Hercules' in 1819, but it takes its name from the American whaler 'Oeno' (Captain George Worth) which was in the area in 1822.

About once every two years the Pitcairners visit Oeno for a working holiday when, besides enjoying the change of scenery, they fish, collect shells and coral for curios and pandanus leaves for basket-making.

Henderson Island. Henderson Island, lying about 168 km. ENE of Pitcairn, is formed of upraised coral limestone. It is roughly rectangular in shape, some 7 km long by 5 km wide. Except in the north where a fringing reef runs into a sandy beach, it is bounded on all sides by perpendicular cliffs considerably undermined by the sea. The island as a whole is about 30 m high, flat-topped, and covered with dense bush.

Quiros discovered Henderson Island in 1606 and named it San Juan Bautista. Its present name is that of the captain of the British merchant ship 'Hercules' who rediscovered it in January 1819. It was also known as Elizabeth Island last century from a ship of that name, Captain Henry King, which visited it in February 1819.

In 1820-21, some sailors from the American whaleship 'Essex', which was stove in by a whale, lived on Henderson for several months after reaching it in an open boat from the vicinity of the Marquesas. The 'Essex' men found eight skeletons in a cave; others have been found there since. It is not known whether the skeletons were those of islanders or Europeans, but it is thought likely they were of shipwrecked mariners of last century.

The Pitcairners visit Henderson Island occasionally to collect miro wood for curio-making. The island received considerable publicity in 1957 when an American citizen at his own request was put ashore there for a time with a chimpanzee.

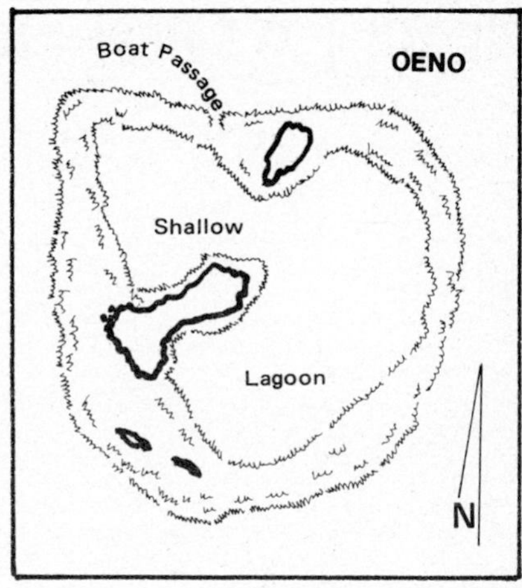

Ducie Island. This island, an atoll, is the most easterly of the Pitcairn group. It lies about 300 km, east of Henderson and some 470 km east of Pitcairn. There is a low islet covered with trees on the northern and NE part of the reef and several smaller ones on the southern side. The lagoon has no entrance and landing on the island can be difficult. Sharks are said to be dangerous.

Quiros, who discovered the atoll in 1606, named it Encarnacion. Its present name was bestowed on it by Captain Edwards of HMS 'Pandora' who passed it in 1791.

REVILLA GIGEDO

Revilla Gigedo consists of three islands and a large rock. The group lies at 18 deg 29 min – 19 deg 20 min N. latitude and 110 deg 45 min – 114 deg 50 min W. longitude, about 550 km from the coast of Mexico. It is a Mexican possession.

Socorro, or Santo Tomas, the largest island, is 107 sq km in area, and about 13 km long by 10 km wide. Its single volcanic peak is 1,051 m above sea level.

Clarion, or Santa Rosa Island, which is about 8 km long by 3 km wide, is 345 km to the west of Socorro, and is about 335 m at its highest point, Cerro Gallegos.

San Benedicto, which is about 5 km long and 1 km wide, is 50 km to the north of Socorro. About 297 m at its highest point, the island's surface is marked by cinder cones and deep ravines.

Roca Partida, a rock about 90 m long and 45 m wide, is 33.5 m high and lies about 11 km west of Socorro.

From sea level to 500 m, rainfall is less than 600 mm, and the temperature has a mean of 25 deg C.

From 600 m to 1,000 m, rainfall averages from 600 to 1,000 mm.

SOLOMON ISLANDS

The Solomon Islands, which became an independent member of the British Commonwealth on July 7, 1978, consist of a double chain of six large islands and many smaller ones including those of the Lord Howe, Santa Cruz, Duff and Reef groups. The total land area is 29,785 sq. km and the islands are located between 5 and 12 deg. S. latitude and 155 and 170 deg. E. longitude.

The major island is Guadalcanal with the capital Honiara (population 18,346) which is about 2,575 km north-east of Sydney and 1,600 km east of Port Moresby.

The other major islands are Choiseul, Santa Isabel, New Georgia, Malaita and San Cristobal. These main islands are mountainous, heavily wooded and thinly populated.

Local time is 11 hours ahead of GMT.

Solomon Islands currency was introduced in 1977 and circulated along with Australian currency until into 1979. The dollar rate is floating and related to a 'trade-weighted basket' of other currencies. In July, 1980, the exchange rate in relation to the Australian dollar was $A1.00 = $S.I.0.93. Coinage consists of 1c, 2c, 5c, 10c, 20c, $1, $5, $10. The $10 coin was introduced in 1979 and features the frigate bird which appears in the national crest.

The new flag, flown for the first time on Independence Day, June 7, 1978, is green and blue halved diagonally by a thin, gold stripe and has five white stars clustered at the hoist representing the four districts and the outliers. The coat of arms includes a crocodile, shark, two frigate birds, an eagle, spears with shield and a turtle. The birds, spears and turtle represent the four districts. The motto is 'To Lead is to Serve'. The National Anthem is 'God save our Solomon Islands'.

THE PEOPLE. The first full census taken in February 1970 showed a total population of 160,998, of whom 94 per cent were Melanesians. The next largest group are the Polynesians who have mainly settled on small offshore islands or atolls such as Ontong Java, Sikaiana, Rennell, Bellona, the Reef Islands and Tikopia.

Population breakdown in the 1970 and 1976 censuses are shown in the accompanying table. The 1976 census gave the total population as 196,823.

The estimated population in 1979 was 217,000 and the projection is for a population of 268,500 in 1985.

	1970	1976
Melanesian	149,667	183,665
Polynesian	6,399	7,821
Micronesian	2,362	2,753
European	1,280	1,359
Chinese	577	452
Others	713	773
TOTAL	**160,998**	**196,823**

The most heavily populated island is Malaita, with about one third of the group's population, almost all Melanesians (over 60,000 in 1976). Next most populated island is Guadalcanal, (inc. Honiara) with 46,619 people in 1976, compared with 35,187 in 1970.

Honiara, the capital, was built at the end of the Pacific War. Its population has grown from 11,191 in 1970 to 18,346 in October, 1979.

Citizenship. After Independence on July 7, 1978, the following categories applied for a person automatically to become a citizen, or who could apply for citizenship.

Automatic citizenship applied to anyone whose parents are or were British Protected persons and of a group, tribe or line indigenous to the Solomon Islands; or if they were born in the Solomon Islands and had two grandparents who were members of a group, tribe or line indigenous to Papua New Guinea or the New Hebrides.

Citizenship was also granted on application to all others who had been resident in the Solomon Islands for seven years during which any periods of absence had not totalled more than 18 months.

Further information is available from: The Citizenship Committee, P.O. Box C.L., Honiara, Guadalcanal, Solomon Islands.

Language. The official language is English, which is widely spoken throughout the islands, although

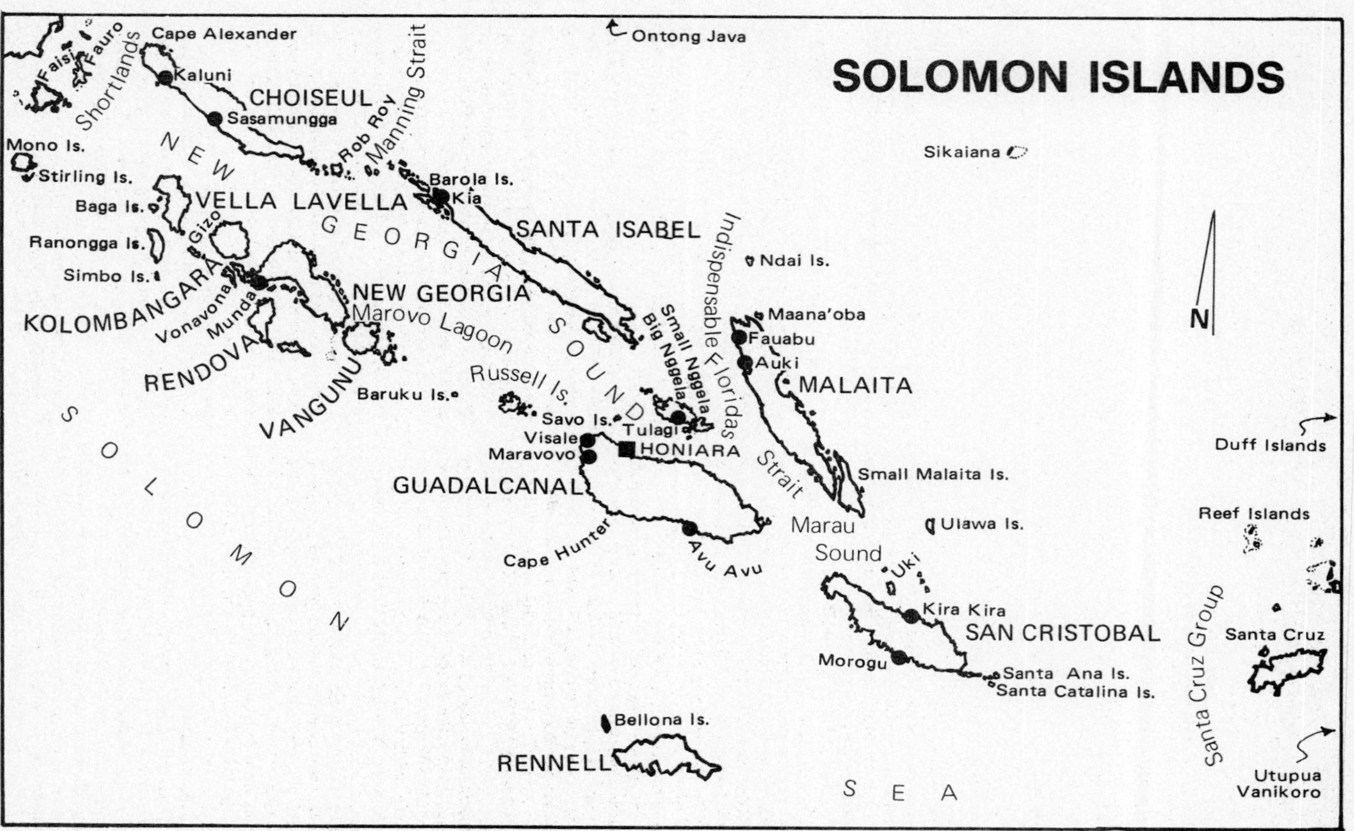
SOLOMON ISLANDS
Ontong Java
Cape Alexander
Shortlands
Fauro
Faisi
Kaluni
CHOISEUL
Sasamungga
Rob Roy
Manning Strait
Mono Is.
Stirling Is.
NEW GEORGIA SOUND
Baga Is.
VELLA LAVELLA
Barola Is.
Kia
SANTA ISABEL
Sikaiana
Ranongga Is.
Gizo
Simbo Is.
KOLOMBANGARA
Vonavona
Munda
NEW GEORGIA
Marovo Lagoon
RENDOVA
VANGUNU
Baruku Is.
Russell Is.
Savo Is.
Visale
Maravovo
Tulagi
HONIARA
GUADALCANAL
Cape Hunter
Avu Avu
Small Nggela
Big Nggela
Indispensable Strait
Floridas
Ndai Is.
Maana'oba
Fauabu
Auki
MALAITA
N
Small Malaita Is.
Marau Sound
Ulawa Is.
Uki
Kira Kira
SAN CRISTOBAL
Morogu
Santa Ana Is.
Santa Catalina Is.
Duff Islands
Reef Islands
Santa Cruz Group
Santa Cruz
Utupua
Vanikoro
Bellona Is.
RENNELL
SOLOMON SEA

the most effective lingua franca is Pidgin. In addition about 87 different vernacular forms of speech are used, with Melanesians living in villages only a few miles apart frequently unable to understand each other's tongue. There is no vernacular common to the whole country.

Religion. More than 95 per cent of the inhabitants are Christian. More than a third of the population belongs to the Anglican Diocese of Melanesia, while 19 per cent belong to the Roman Catholic church; 17 per cent to the South Sea Evangelical church; 11 per cent to the United Church, 10 per cent to the Seventh-day Adventist; other churches are also represented.

Lifestyle. Most islanders continue to follow the traditional village life where every family produces its own food and builds its own house.

Recreation. A major source of recreation for the islanders is the sea, where their big, black, sea-going canoes may still be seen among motorised boats. The traditional canoe is made of bent planks with stern and sometimes bow carried high and decorative. There is often much inlay work done with mother-of-pearl.

The people also take their soccer, rugby, tennis, cricket, athletics and basketball competitions seriously and the Solomon Islanders always feature in the South Pacific Games.

GOVERNMENT. The Solomons is a constitutional monarchy with the British monarch as Head of State and represented in the Solomons by a Governor-General appointed, on the recommendation of the legislature, every five years.

Legislature. It is a single-chamber National Parliament composed of 38 elected members. The normal life of parliament is four years. General elections were due on August 6, 1980.

Executive. The executive arm of government is the National Cabinet headed by the Prime Minister, who chooses his ministers, limited to 12 ministers.

Elections. Voting for the Legislative Assembly is by universal suffrage; the voting age was reduced from 21 to 18 years for the 1976 elections.

Main political parties are the People's Progress Party, the United Solomon Islands Party and the Nationalist Party.

Local Government. Since 1974 local government reform has aimed at increasing responsibility at the local level, with the financial support of the central government. The Solomons are administered through four districts, divided into eight local councils. The four districts are Malaita, Eastern, Western and Central districts.

The local councils, elected by universal adult suffrage, operate a wide range of facilities including communications, rural health services and schools. Many such projects, including roads, bridges and road transport are wholly subsidised by the government. Education and health facilities co-ordinate with the churches and central government.

Public service. Independence has seen a rapid replacement of expatriate public servants by Solomon Islanders wherever possible, although a number of overseas officers have remained on contract. The total employed in the Public Service in 1978 was 6,072 of which 302 were expatriates in established posts and 67 expatriates in technical assistance.

Justice. The English system of justice is administered through the High Court, consisting of a Chief Justice, usually resident in the Solomons, and a Puisne Judge, usually in the Anglo-French condominium of New Hebrides. In addition, magistrates courts operate in the four administrative districts together with local courts whose cases include customary titles to land. The right of appeal may take cases to the High Court or to the Fiji Court of Appeal or even the Privy Council in England.

Police. The Solomon Islands police force, headed by the Commissioner of Police, has its headquarters in Honiara, together with the Police Training School and the HQ of the Police Mobile Unit. The force includes 16 officers, 19 inspectors and 388 NCOs and other ranks. A radio network connects Honiara to 14 police stations in the islands. Training courses at home and abroad are held in co-operation with the police of the New Hebrides, Gilbert Islands, Papua New Guinea and Britain.

Liquor laws. Liquor is sold in hotel bars, clubs and licensed stores. Hotel hours, when liquor may be sold, are from 10 a.m. to 10.30 p.m. weekdays, and on Sundays 12 midday to 10 p.m. but restricted to hotel residents from 2 p.m. to 7 p.m.

EDUCATION. Organised schools provide for about two-thirds of the school-age children. Since independence, emphasis has been on providing a co-ordinated system of primary, secondary and tertiary education with two aims – to meet the need for skilled manpower as quickly as possible and to provide a basic education for all suited to the environment in which they will live and work as adults. Government policy is to mobilise all resources, government, churches, parents and children to achieve the national aim, which is to seek a compromise between an expensively, highly-educated elite needed in certain sectors and the needs of a rural-based economy. Government spending on education has grown from $1.28 million in 1973 to $4.68 million in 1978, representing 11.99 per cent of the government budget for 1978. Capital expenditure in 1978 was $1.013 million. The national system is wholly financed by central government. Private educational agencies like the churches can operate outside the national system but can expect only limited financial help from the government.

Aiming at decentralisation of government, responsibility for running primary and certain secondary schools has been handed over to local councils. The government gives grants to primary schools for equipment and pays teachers' salaries. Secondary schools controlled by local authorities receive grants for boarding, equipment, building maintenance and pupils' travel costs. Capital aid is available for primary and secondary schools.

There are about 300 primary schools within the national system operated by the local councils and about 50 primary schools run by the churches. Local councils employ 980 teachers for the primary schools.

The secondary system is composed of former National and New Secondary schools operating on different lines. The former runs a five-year course for children who have completed the six-year primary course and are selected by examination at primary standard six for secondary education. The New Secondary School, which replaces the former rural training centres, has a curriculum aimed at imparting knowledge useful in a rural environment, and teaches, among other things, the running of co-operatives, house building and farming. From 1979, the 'New' schools introduced a three-year course combining the academic with the technical. At the end of the course, after a national examination, certain pupils are selected to transfer to fourth form in a 'National' school. There are five aided former National Secondary schools and one administered by a voluntary agency. There are also eight New Secondary schools.

Another move to introduce the 'Island' environment into education has been the replacement of the Cambridge School Certificate examination (established in 1950) by the Solomon Islands School Certificate examination introduced with the help of the universities of Papua New Guinea and the South Pacific (Suva). The Teachers' Training College at Honiara provided 97 certificated teachers in 1977. Secondary school teachers are still being trained overseas. The government secondary school in Honiara runs a one-year sixth form to prepare about 30 students a year for university study abroad.

In 1978, there were 26,749 pupils at primary schools, 1,610 at National Secondary Schools and 1,374 at Provincial Secondary Schools. The National Secondary Schools are King George VI (Honiara), Betikama, Selwyn and St. Joseph's, Tenaru, all on Guadalcanal, Goldie (Western) and Su'u (Malaita). Students at the Honiara Technical Institute in 1978 totalled 374 on full-time courses and 372 at part-time/evening and other classes. There were 86 overseas students at the full-time courses. About 160 Solomons' students were studying overseas in 1976.

The Ministry of Education added "cultural affairs" to its title in 1974, thereby encompassing the library, museum and fostering of National Archives, local custom and Church Affairs and Tourism. On November 4, 1977, the Pro-Chancellor of the University of the South Pacific, Dr S. Langi Kavaliku, formally opened the first permanent buildings of the Solomons Islands' Centre of the University at Honiara. The new complex cost more than $A100,000 and was funded by grants from the Australian and New Zealand governments.

The Centre was established in November 1971.

LABOUR. The active labour force grew from 13,690 in 1970 to 14,454 in 1972, dropped back to 14,184 in 1974 and rose to 17,678 in 1978, 6,022 being in Honiara.

The dramatic rise in copra prices in 1974, followed by a drop in 1975-76 and coupled with a decline in the world market for timber, resulted in some employment shifts.

The labour force consists largely of unskilled men, with a keen shortage of skilled islanders for supervisory posts. Employers engaging overseas workers are urged to train locals at the same time. Efforts at localisation led to the number of expatriates in employment falling. Total number of non-Solomon Islanders in the work force in 1978 (December) was 1,034.

Officially sponsored overseas volunteers from Britain, New Zealand and USA numbered 67 in 1978.

Most were assigned to work with the malaria eradication programme, public health, broadcasting, library, fisheries, engineering, women's interests, small business, co-operative development and rural secondary school teaching. Those assigned to Government Ministries were mainly involved in specific projects relating to the implementation of the National Development Plan.

Few workers are able to bring their families to their place of work although employers are improving this situation, especially in urban areas.

In 1978, 1,545 island women were registered as employed. Of the total workforce of 18,478 in 1978, agriculture, forestry and fisheries employed 5,876; construction, manufacturing and mining employed 2,462, services such as utilities, commerce, transport and finance employed 3,409, while the administration and social services employed 5,931. Private business employed the most, 8,502.

More detailed information concerning working conditions can be obtained from the Annual Abstract of Statistics or from the Labour division, Ministry of Trade, Industry and Labour, Honiara.

Wages. The Wages Advisory Board regulates minimum wages and housing facilities for workers. The minimum wage for most workers in Honiara on June 1, 1976 was 16 cents per hour for a 45 hour week, with housing and 18.4 cents without housing. Unskilled daily paid workers employed by the government in December, 1978 received a basic wage of $3.04 per day for a five-day week of 40 hours. Skilled daily paid government workers received up to $6.96 a day. Annual salaries of Public Service established staff ranged from $1,296 to $9,780 at December 31, 1978.

Unions. There were four trade unions – the National Unions of Workers, the Solomon Islands Plantations Workers, Solomon Islands Public Servants Association and the Government Non-Established Workers' Union. There are four employer associations – the Primary Producers' and Trade Associaton of the Western Solomons, the Solomon Islands Plantations and Farmers' Association, the Chinese Association and the Chamber of Commerce. In the absence of further trade unions, the government encourages joint consultation to solve problems.

Social security. Social security legislation provides for the payment of workers' compensation for accidents at work.

There is now a National Provident Fund to which contributions for the year ended June 30, 1979, totalled $2 million.

HEALTH. The Ministry of Health and Welfare is responsible for government health programmes. Hospitals maintained by the government include the Central Hospital in Honiara with 158 beds, as well as three district hospitals with 222 beds and three rural hospitals, each with 32 beds, one at Malu'u including a 20-bed tuberculosis annexe. Roman Catholic nursing sisters staff the government leprosarium on Guadalcanal; extra beds are provided by three church hospitals maintained by the Church of Melanesia (Anglican), United Church (Methodist) and the Seventh-day Adventist Church. Many other church centres provide a variety of medical services.

The School of Nursing at Central Hospital had 56 students in 1977, while 14 islanders were studying at the Fiji School of Medicine and elsewhere.

The government health budget for 1978 was $2.21 million.

Diseases. Problems include malaria, tuberculosis and leprosy.

The Malaria Eradication Programme has been intensified in recent years, with frequent DDT sprayings to eliminate mosquitoes from dwellings. There were 19,987 cases treated in 1978, Central being the main problem area. Among tuberculosis sufferers, 455 cases were treated in 1978. BCG vaccination appears to have reduced pulmonary cases while the apparent increase in non-pulmonary forms probably reflects better public awareness and detection techniques.

Concerning leprosy, 32 cases were treated in 1978, compared with 144 active cases 12 years earlier. Surveys of the disease have been made by the WHO and the NZ Lepers Trust Board.

THE LAND. The Solomon Islands extend over some 600,000 sq. km of sea, lying as a scattered archipelago in a south-easterly direction from off Bougainville to Santa Cruz Is. The group has a total land area of 28,530 sq. km.

The six major islands are Choiseul, New Georgia, Santa Isabel, Guadalcanal, Malaita and San Cristobal. They vary in length between 145 and 200 km and in width between 30 and 50 km. The largest, Guadalcanal, has an area of approx. 5,650 sq. km.

The group is stretched over 1,400 km from one extremity to the other.

The main islands are rugged and mountainous, the highest named peak is Mt. Makarakombou (2,447 m) on Guadalcanal. Most islands are of igneous and metamorphic rocks, overlaid with considerable layers of marine sediments. The only extensive coastal plains are on the north-east coast of Guadalcanal.

Many outer islands are coral atolls and raised coral reefs.

Climate. The tropical climate is modified by the surrounding sea. Late April to November is the season of south-east trade winds. The highest temperature and rainfall are usually recorded from November to April, when cyclones may also occur.

Rainfall generally averages 3,000-3,500 mm a year, while reaching as high as 8,000 mm in some parts and averaging 2,250 mm in Honiara. Daytime temperatures are usually above 26 deg. C.

All the larger islands are well watered by rivers, with steep courses over most of their length and many of them have a significant energy potential.

There are four volcanoes: one on the island of Savo 30 km off Honiara, which has hot springs but has not erupted since 1840; Tinakula, in the far east of the Solomons, which has been active from time to time; one on the island of Simbo near the New Georgia group, together with Kavachi, a submarine volcano in the same area.

Flora and Fauna. Vegetation on the large islands is mainly dense rain forest.

There are few endemic animals – phalangers and bush mice, as well as a large skink, equipped with a prehensile tail and believed to be unique to the Solomons. There is a great variety of bird life while crocodiles are also present.

Resources. Many regard the seas as the most reliable area of future development, although mineral prospecting continues and bauxite exists in large deposits on Rennell Island.

Good agricultural land is limited, except on the Guadalcanal coastal plains. Main resources thus comprise the coconut and oil palms, forests, minerals and fisheries.

Land tenure. The registration of land titles was introduced in 1963, under the Land and Titles Ordinance 1959. Subsequent legislation provided three distinct systems of land tenure.

Initially, land is either held under the islanders' customary system or is alienated, i.e. unregistered land sold or leased by islanders to non-islanders. The third category is land now under registered title. The law protects customary land from being acquired by non-Solomon Islanders.

At the office of the Registrar of Titles, there were 4,600 titles registered by 1976, covering 332,753 hectares.

Land legislation is comprehensive and provides for perpetual estates, fixed term estates, leases etc. Customary land may be registered by the system of "land settlement" supervised by the Lands Office. The whole policy of creating a sound system of land tenure is in the charge of the Lands Division of the Ministry of Agriculture and Rural Economy.

PRIMARY PRODUCTION. In the chief primary industry of copra production, 1978 output was 27,529 tonnes. The figures compared with 29,205 tonnes in 1977 and 23,810 tonnes in 1976. Production by Solomon Islanders totalled 17,657 tonnes while plantation output was 9,871 tonnes. Marketing is handled by the Copra Board.

The Department of Agriculture and Lever's Pacific Plantations Pty. Ltd. continued the Joint Coconut Research Scheme on high-yielding coconut types.

Cocoa. The production of dried cocoa beans reached 234.5 tonnes in 1978, also stimulated by good prices. This compared with 162.6 tonnes in 1977 and 114.3 tonnes in 1976. Guadalcanal produced 29 per cent of the total in 1978; Central Islands 27 per cent; Malaita 24 per cent and the Western District 12 per cent.

The Dala Research Station continued basic investigation into cocoa agronomy. Control of fungus diseases and experimentation with new hybrids are important tasks.

Rice. An American irrigated rice project on Guadalcanal had 834 ha under irrigation at the end of 1976. Production in that year was 1,850 tonnes, but it rose to 3,345 tonnes in 1977. In 1978 production for all areas totalled 7,658 tonnes.

Oil palm. The first palm oil mill in this new industry began operating in 1976. Solomon Islands Plantations Ltd. had planted 3,626 ha on the Guadalcanal Plains, with improved seeds coming from Malaysia. In 1977, palm oil exported was worth $2.89 million and 1978 production was 10,334 tonnes of oil and 2,050 tonnes of kernels.

Other crops. In areas less interested in copra, cocoa or cattle, production continues in spices such as turmeric, ginger, cinnamon, tabasco and allspice.

Cattle. Keen interest in cattle has continued and herds were estimated to total 25,185 head in 1978. British, New Zealand and Australian funds were then available for pasture improvement and further cattle imports. Most of the stock was on expatriate plantations (12,006). Smallholders accounted for 9,441.

About 4,419 cattle were slaughtered for local consumption in 1977.

Fisheries. Solomon Taiyo fishing company, based at Tulagi and jointly owned by the government and Japanese interests, landed 18,204 tonnes of skipjack tuna in 1978. This compared with a total catch in 1977 of 13,000 tonnes. In 1978, 14,518 tonnes of frozen fish was exported while the rest was processed into cans or "arabushi" at the smoking plant. Local sales accounted for 133 tonnes. The canning factory opened in 1973, produced 1,836 tonnes of canned tuna and 1,037 tonnes of smoked fish. A large cannery costing about $12 million is planned for Noro in the Western Province, with production starting in 1983.

Timber. Major timber operations are on Kolombangara Is., New Georgia, Santa Cruz, Guadalcanal and the Shortland Islands. Total output in 1978 was 275,225 cubic metres compared with 258,972 cu.m. in 1977 and 264,117 cu.m. in 1976. There are 17 sawmills operating and four main log exporting companies, Lever's Pacific Timbers, Kalena Timber Co., Allardyce Lumber Co. and Foxwood (S.I.) Timbers Ltd. Production concentrates on logs for export and in 1978, 247,331 c.m. of logs were exported valued at $6.84 million. In the same year, 2,666 cu.m. of sawn timber and 897 cu.m. of veneer were exported.

Japan and New Zealand have been assisting in timber production, the Japan Overseas Afforesting Association financing 290 ha of pulpwood planting trials at Kolombangara.

Altogether, 11,360 ha of government-owned land had been covered by a timber-replanting programme up to the end of 1977. From the early 1980s onwards much customary land will be logged and re-planted subject to suitable lease or joint venture agreements. There are plans to grow sawn timber for the country's construction industry on Guadalcanal and Malaita.

MINING. Chief interest lies in the bauxite deposits of about 30 million tonnes contained in some 65 000 ha on Rennell Island which the Mitsui Mining and Smelting Co. of Japan is keen to work in conjunction with Conzinc Riotinto of Australia, which has deposits of about 28 million tonnes on Wagina (or Vaghena) Island. After an agreement between the government and the two mining companies, a feasibility study was conducted in 1975. However, Mitsui withdrew in 1977, although the company stated that it was still interested in the project.

On the neighbouring atoll of Bellona, a tentative interest has been shown in an estimated 10 million tonnes of phosphate-bearing material, spread over about 115 ha.

There has been mineral prospecting on each main island group except Malaita. CRA Exploration has worked especially in the Gold Ridge area, and Amoco Minerals in the Poha River region.

Gold production by islanders using hand panning methods was 14,330 gm in 1977 and that of silver was 2,540 gm.

Geological mapping has continued, together with geohydrological, seismological and geothermal work. Mining activity has been regulated since 1969 by the Mining Ordinance, which is administered by the Director of Geological Surveys. Monthly maps show the current holdings of mining tenements.

MANUFACTURING. Established industries include the Solomon Taiyo fish freezing and canning facilities at Tulagi. Other production includes rattan and other furniture, fibreglass articles, clothing, boat building, batteries and spices. Hand crafted articles of wood and decoration with mother-of-pearl shell inlay, mats, baskets and shell jewellery are produced for local and overseas markets. Biscuits, tobacco, soft drinks etc. are also processed.

Overseas interests seeking to promote new industries need to assure that there will be Solomon Islander participation.

TOURISM. The number of tourists visiting the Solomons in 1979 was 10,200, in 1978 5,063, compared with 2,972 in 1977 and 2,686 in 1976. One reason for the large, and surprising increase, bearing in mind the tourism recession elsewhere, was the arrival of large parties of Japanese on 'pilgrimage' to the Pacific War battlefields. Some of the parties announced that their visit was to make amends for the war. There was, however, a drop in the number of cruise ship passengers – 8,345 in 10 ships in 1978, 8,533 in eight ships in 1977 and 13,207 in 17 ships in 1976. The Solomons also had 3,964 'other' visitors in 1978.

The Islands belong to the Melanesian Tourist Federation, as members of the "coral chain" extending from Papua New Guinea, through the Solomons to the New Hebrides and New Caledonia.

The Solomon Islands Tourist Authority in Honiara is financed by the government and has a full-time secretary.

LOCAL COMMERCE. Over a quarter of the population is now involved in the co-operative movement. This is indicated by the existence of 197 active societies at the end of 1977, with a total membership of 16,036 heads of families. Over 190 societies were primary producer-consumer co-ops, with others being savings and loan societies. The year 1977 was a good one for primary co-operatives with an estimated total turnover of $3,758,000. Capital reserves of the primary societies totalled $1,585,000.

Secondary co-operatives had a turnover in 1977 of $2,643,000, a nett surplus of $25,000 and assets of $1,214,000.

In 1978, there were 206 private companies and three public companies incorporated locally with authorised capital of $50,928,000 and $21,256,000 of paid-up capital. Public companies were Brewer Solomons Associates, SIACO Ltd. and Solomon Islands Investments Ltd. Companies incorporated overseas totalled 49 (32 private and 17 public), the majority of them (29) in Australia.

OVERSEAS TRADE. The Solomons' international trade reached record levels for 1979. Exports were worth $60.18 million giving a favourable balance of trade of nearly $9.7 million. For the whole of 1978, exports totalled $28.72 million and imports $38.88 million. Exports of frozen fish, rice, palm oil, palm kernels and timber were all up in value.

In 1979, copra exports reached 34,430 tonnes surpassing 30,000 tonnes for the first time. Earnings from copra amounted to just under $17 million of which $6 million has gone directly to the smallholder sector. Total exports of fish and fish products amounted to $17 million compared to $5 million in 1978; the volume of frozen fish exports rose from approximately 10,300 to 23,400 tonnes – an increase of 127 per cent, with earnings rising from $5 milllion to $14.6 million (up 190 per cent).

In the forestry sector, log exports increased marginally from 246 in 1978 to 258,000 cubic metres in 1979 in volume terms but in value terms exports were up from $6.8 to $14.7 million. Exports of palm oil and kernels continued to increase over the previous year, with earnings up from $5.1 to $7.2 million – value up by 47 per cent while volume was up by 20 per cent. Among other exports to show continued growth were rice and cocoa.

The rise in import levels was less dramatic but the overall increase over 1978 was more than 60 per cent. Imports of machinery and transport equipment were significantly higher than in previous years in both volume and value terms (up from $8.5 to $18.9 million) signifying a substantial increase in capital investment. The total fuel bill rose to $6.5 million, diesel fuel consumption doubling with higher levels of activity in fishing, forestry, sea and road transport and construction.

All other commodity groups also increased and within these groups certain significant individual import items were well up in volume terms. For example, imports of rice, sugar, beer, cement and iron and steel products all showed large rises.

EXPORTS AND IMPORTS
(In $'000)

	1976	1977	1978	1979
Exports	19,341	29,614	30,594	60,184
Imports	21,087	25,753	30,879	50,516

PRINCIPAL EXPORTS
(In $'000)

	1976	1977	1978	1979
Fish	6,553	8,283	7,296	16,932
Copra	3,635	7,988	7,856	16,992
Timber	6,260	7,725	6,837	15,867
Sea shells	202	179	165	278
Cocoa	162	553	596	648
Tobacco	79	117	94	67
Scrap metal	21	n.a.	n.a.	7
Total	**19,341**	**29,875**	**22,844**	**50,791**

PRINCIPAL IMPORTS
(In $'000)

	1976	1977	1978	1979
Food	3,488	4,076	5,048	6,362
Drinks & tobacco	1,003	1,220	1,466	1,906
Inedible raw materials	130	180	241	222
Oil, petrol	2,700	3,543	3,547	6,468
Animal/veg. oil	213	277	170	584
Chemicals	1,563	2,048	2,779	3,309
Manuf. goods	3,830	4,577	5,840	8,818
Mach., transp.	6,243	7,003	8,460	18,908
Misc. manuf.	1,718	2,538	3,048	3,724
Other	198	292	282	215
Total	**21,087**	**25,754**	**30,881**	**50,516**

The value of goods from the chief suppliers has been as follows, expressed in $ million:

	1976	1977	1978	1979
Australia	8.0	8.0	10.3	15.09
Japan	2.7	3.1	4.0	9.08
Britain	2.0	3.5	3.1	6.84
Singapore	2.4	3.6	3.1	6.25

The very significant increase in personal disposable incomes, largely due to smallholder copra activity, and also to increasing wages and salaries accounted for the higher demand and, therefore, larger imports of consumer goods such as rice and beer.

Traditionally Japan has been the major market for the Solomons' products (23.8 per cent 1979), taking almost all the timber and the bulk of the fish. Commonwealth countries usually take the next largest slice of goods Britain heading the list with 16.1 per cent in 1979.

Customs Tariff. The old system of Preferential Tariffs was replaced in December 1974 with a one column metricated tariff. The general rates of duty on selected imports, regardless of their country of origin, at January 1976 was as follows:

Beer (40c), spirits ($5.00) and still wines (60c) per litre; motor cars – 33 per cent for less than 1,100 cc, graduating to 70 per cent for 2,000 cc or above. Other items range from cement (3 per cent), agricultural equipment (5 per cent), fresh meat (11 per cent), to footwear and boats (28 per cent) and clothing (33 per cent). Items imported free of duty include: butter, eggs, milk, fuel oil, fertilisers, wheat flour, insecticides, canned meat and poultry, rice, medicines, surgical equipment and hand tools.

There were comparativly large increases in duty in January, 1980, to help pay for the development projects. Import duties were increased on about 40 items with the tariff on imported sweets, confectionery and soft drinks rising to 50 per cent. Other increases were: beer 3c a bottle; spirits $1.30 a litre; cigarettes 12.5c a packet of 20; sugar 6.7c a kg; petrol 1.8c a litre; diesel fuel, avgas and kerosene 1c a litre.

Copies of the tariffs are available from the Government Printer, Honiara, price $2 plus postage.

FINANCE. The Solomons' recurrent budget is balanced by a grant-in-aid from Britain, while most of the capital budget is met from United Kingdom development funds. The accompanying table shows the levels of local revenue together with total expenditure (recurrent and capital) in recent years.

REVENUE AND EXPENDITURE
(expressed in $ million)

Year	Local Revenue	Expenditure	U.K. Aid
1968	3.3	7.7	3.6
1970	4.6	9.3	4.5
1972	5.4	11.8	6.8
1973	5.7	11.1	5.1
1974	8.2	9.0	5.1
1975	7.82	9.61	6.1
1976	9.31	11.44	8.12
1977	12.09	21.78	8.2
1978	15.2	30.61	12.3

Revenue. The main sources of local revenue were: import-export duties 1977, $4.84 million; 1978, $5.89 million. Direct taxation, 1977, $2.94 million; 1978, $4.26 million. Forestry, 1977, $376,000; 1978, $33,000. Government services, 1977, $2.23 million; 1978, $2.9 million. Total domestic revenue was, 1977, $12.09 million; 1978, $15.2 million.

Aid. Under the independence settlement, Britain has promised grants in aid to the Solomons of about $40 million over the first four years from the date of independence. This is divided into $7.75 million for joint venture projects promoted through the Government Shareholding Agency, $4.65 million in special financial assistance on a gradually reduced scale for the recurrent budget and the remainder for development aid. A further allocation has been

GOVERNMENT SHAREHOLDING

The Government Shareholding Agency was involved in the following investments at the end of 1978.

Investments	Authorised Capital SI $	Issued Capital SI $	Government Holding Issued share Capital %	Cost of Investment SI $
Air Pacific	6,900,000	4,100,000	1.7	69,623
Solomon Taiyo	1,000,000	1,000,000	25.0	1
Solomon Islands Plantations	2,500,000	2,500,000	26.0	650,000
National Fisheries Development	1,500,000	1,500,000	75.0	281,250
Mendana Hotels	500,000	500,000	36.0	300,000
Pacific Forum Line	108,000	108,000	11.1	11,985
Solomon Islands International Telecommunications	800,000	800,000	49.0	392,000
Brewers Solomons Agriculture	3,000,000	3,000,000	45.0	1,350,000
Development Bank	5,000,000	1,800,000	100.0	1,800,000

made of nearly $4 million from the European Development Fund in addition to more than $10 million previously allocated from the same fund.

The Asian Development Bank in late 1978 approved technical aid of $US95,000 for preparation of the Second National Development Plan and $US81,000 for forestry development. In 1980, the ADB also approved technical assistance for a water supply project for Honiara to increase supply capacity from its present 5.9 litres a day to 10 million litres a day.

Postage stamps. Postage stamps contribute to local revenue and, by adopting a wise policy to limit issues, the Solomons' stamps are attracting the interest of philatelists from all over the world. Total stamp sales in 1976 were $445,000, in 1977 $452,000 and in 1978 $546,000.

Income tax. Individual income tax is paid on a sliding scale which was increased for higher incomes by the 1980 Budget. Under the new measures the level at which income tax becomes payable is raised from $600 to $1,200 for single persons and from $1,200 to $2,400 for married income earners. This removed the tax burden from about 7,000 Solomon Islanders and left about 2,000 nationals and 1,000 expatriates to pay income tax, which is raised to a new starting rate of 15c in the $, rising in 2c steps for each thousand to a new maximum of 45c in the $.

Income tax enquiries may be addressed to the Commissioner of Income Tax, Inland Revenue Division, Ministry of Finance, Honiara. Copies of the ordinance cost $3.95.

Banks. There are four banks, the Solomon Islands Development Bank, recently upgraded from the Loans Board, and three overseas institutions, the Commonwealth Banking Corp. of Australia, the Australia and New Zealand Banking Group Ltd. and the Hong Kong and Shanghai Banking Corp.

The three trading banks provide a full range of services with a number of savings bank agencies throughout the group. The Commonwealth Bank operates a sub-branch at Gizo in the Western District.

The Development Bank makes loans for a wide range of projects in all sectors, aiming particularly at increasing the participation of nationals in the cash economy and developing rural areas. The government plans a development finance company to channel loans to major commercial projects.

At the end of 1978, the trading banks had assets totalling $31,386,000, and the Central Monetary Authority $25,369,800.

Overseas investment. A Solomon Islands investment guide was published in March 1976, emphasising the encouragement given to joint ventures with the government or its agencies, or with local business interests.

Projects approved by the government may receive assistance over site negotiations, tax relief, import duty concessions, infrastructure, staff training and purchase contracts for outputs. The guidelines indicate preference for investment in agriculture, livestock, forestry, mining, fisheries, small manufactures, food processing, tourism and transport.

Preliminary proposals should be addressed to the Central Planning Office, Office of the Chief Minister, Honiara.

Development Plans. The National Development Plan of 1975-79 was aimed at establishing the Solomon Islands as an independent nation, no longer requiring foreign recurrent aid by 1980/81. During the plan, government spending was estimated at $50 million (recurrent), $60 million (capital) all at 1975 prices, with as much as over $200 million from the private sector if the Rennell bauxite project is undertaken.

However, the bauxite project has been pigeonholed and does not even rate a mention in the new National Development Plan 1980-84. This plan, which could depend on the General Election in August (1980) for final decision, concentrates on making the Solomons self-sufficient in food production, water resources and energy; other aims are to develop customary land tenure systems and develop the land; promote optimum use of marine resources; encourage and assist nationals to enter the commercial and industrial sectors; increase development of co-operatives and tourism; provide each island with a road system and provide a nationwide network of efficient overseas and local ports and airfields. It is also hoped to localise ownership and control of the housing industry, provide an integrated, comprehensive health system throughout the country and promote cultural development, cultural values, traditions and heritage.

TRANSPORT. Four firms lease drive-yourself cars in Honiara; taxis and taxi trucks are available in Honiara and in Auki. Scheduled bus services operate along the coast road through Honiara and the suburbs.

Roads. There are 470 km of main roads in the Solomons including 84 km of bitumen roads. A new 14.5 km sealed road was opened between Munda and Noro in the Western District in January, 1980. The urban areas of Honiara, Auki and Gizo have an additional 85 km of secondary roads. Major roads are on Guadalcanal, Malaita, Makira and at Munda in the New Georgia group.

In the rural areas there are some 1,280 km of secondary roads, of varying standard: Gurkhas and Royal Engineers have assisted in road and wharf construction.

Vehicles. Vehicle registration figures are only kept for the area around Honiara, around Auki on Malaita and for Gizo. The number of vehicles is insignificant elsewhere.

The following figures show total registrations in 1977: motor cars, 909; goods vans etc., 654; motor cycles, 358; public service vehicles, 277. Total motor vehicles registered were 2,409.

Overseas airlines. Overseas services are provided by Air Niugini flying in from Papua New Guinea,

Air Pacific operating from Fiji and Australia and Air Nauru, connecting Nauru, Australia and the northern Pacific.

Domestic airline. Internal services are provided by Solomon Islands Airways Ltd. (Solair) which operates Beechcraft Barons and Britten Norman Islander. The Seventh-day Adventist Mission and the United and South Sea Evangelical Churches are also authorised to operate non-scheduled services.

Airports. Four aerodromes are open to international traffic: Honiara (Henderson) for regional services up to BAC 1-11 and Boeing 737 standard: Munda for regional services up to F27 standard, Gizo (Nusatupe) and Santa Cruz (Graciosa) for aircraft up to HS748 standard.

In all, there are 11 government, 9 licensed and two private unlicensed aerodromes in the Solomons, excluding Kukum which is no longer in use. Domestic aerodromes are Yandina (Russell Is.), Auki (Malaita), Barakoma (Vella Lavella), Kira Kira (San Cristobal), Mono (Stirling Is.), Seghe (New Georgia), Avuavu, Marau and Ba a' akia (Guadalcanal), Paraxi (small Malaita), Rennell, Choiseul Bay, Ballalae I. (Shortland group), Graciosa Bay (Santa Cruz), Fera, Kukudu, Ringicove, Koli, Bellona and Atoifi. This list excludes the international airports.

Port facilities. Overseas shipping uses the ports at Honiara, Yandina, Gizo, Tulagi, Viru Harbour, Nila and Ringicove. It is planned to expand Noro in the Western District into a full deep-water overseas wharf. Allardyce Harbour is no longer in use and log exports have been transferred from there to Graciosa Bay in Santa Cruz. New wharfage at Auki is now available for local vessels of 36.6 m with a draught of 3 m and a new council wharf has been built in Santa Cruz.

The main port of Honiara has two wharves, the larger capable of taking vessels up to 198 m in length with a draught of 9.1 m. Three small jetties cater for local shipping.

Honiara operations are controlled by the Ports Authority. The Yandina port is operated by Lever's Pacific Plantations Ltd., with a wharf length of 53.5 m.

Island shipping also uses wharves built at various trading centres. A new government wharf has been completed at Gizo, while a wharf was planned for bauxite operations on Rennell Island.

Inter-island transport is by a fleet of about 145 craft, including private and mission vessels and about 36 operated by the government. Lagoon transport is popular, with an increasing use of outboard motors around the islands of New Georgia, Santa Isabel and parts of Malaita.

Shipping services. A consortium of Conpack, NGAL/PNGL have three container vessels operating on a 28-day turnaround from Melbourne, Sydney and Brisbane to Honiara and PNG ports supplemented by Daiwa vessels, Pacific Princess and Fiji Maru. Daiwa Line operates a container service every 30 days from Sydney to Honiara where Gizo cargoes are transhipped. The Line also operates a four-weekly service Sydney-Honiara-Guam-Taiwan-Japan. China Navigation's New Guinea Pacific Line (NGPL) operates a regular cargo service from Hong Kong, Taiwan, Manila, Port Kelang and Singapore to Honiara via PNG ports, and Kyowa Shipping Ltd. has a monthly service from Hong Kong and the Far East to Honiara through Micronesia and Daiwa a 30-day service from Japan through Tahiti, the Samoas, Fiji, Noumea and Sydney to Honiara and on to Kieta, Tarawa and Guam. Bank Line has a regular service from Honiara to New Orleans, UK and Europe, while Pacific Forum Line operates a fully containerised service (Gen/Reefer) from New Zealand ports to Honiara via Fiji and Noumea. Sofrana Unilines operates with three ships to Honiara through Vila and Santo. Bank Line runs a 28-day cargo service from Europe to PNG ports and then to Honiara and, on inducement, to Yandina.

COMMUNICATIONS. Automatic telephone services operate in Honiara, Gizo and Auki with about 2,000 subscribers and there are two international telephone circuits provided by H.F. radio via Sydney. A new company, Soltel, jointly owned by Cable and Wireless Limited (51%) and the Solomon Islands Government (49%), is proposing to operate international telephone circuits from a ground station in Honiara via the Intelsat Pacific Ocean communications satellite. There are three international telex circuits in operation via Sydney.

Telegrams within the country are passed between the main centres over a H.F. radio network. Telegrams for overseas destinations are routed through Sydney, Australia. Incoming telegrams are either telephoned to the addressee or delivered by messenger.

It is planned to expand and speed up the telegram service with the introduction of a new high-quality national trunk network.

In addition to the General Post Office in Honiara, post offices are established at Gizo, Munda, Yandina, Tulagi, Auki, Kira Kira and Santa Cruz. There are also 77 postal agencies operating throughout the country and 90 licensed stamp dealers. All mails are normally sent by air throughout the country. Where this is not possible, inter-island shipping is used.

Radio. The Solomon Islands Broadcasting Corporation, an independent statutory body, produces radio programmes every morning, noon and evening, Monday – Saturday and noon and evening on Sundays. There are 118 hours of transmission per week including programmes for schools during term time. News programmes include local and relayed overseas broadcasts, some in Pidgin.

All transmitters have an aerial power of 5 kilowatts but plans are being made, through the Australian Aid Development Bureau, to substantially increase the broadcasting range.

The work will be carried out in stages. The first phase is for higher powered transmitters to be installed near Honiara, together with two omnidirectional aerials 100 metres in height, with another transmitter at Gizo, in the Western part of the country. These transmitters will be of 10 kw capacity.

Later stages involve building new studios and offices for the corporation in Honiara tentatively for completion by October, 1980. New studios and offices will also be built at Auki on Malaita island, Kira Kira on San Cristobal, and at Mohawk Bay in the Eastern Outer Islands. It is planned to erect a 10 kW transmitter at Kira Kira to relay the Honiara signal on MF. A 2 kW transmitter will be installed at Mohawk Bay to relay the Honiara HF signal.

Films. There are two commercial cinemas in Honiara and one in Gizo.

Public information. The government's Information and Public Relations Office provides a newspaper and also information, locally and overseas, on government activity, explaining government policy and generally acts as a link between the government and the people. A daily news bulletin is provided free of charge to the local news distributors.

Newspapers are the government owned "Solomons News Drum", a weekly; the "Solomons Star", a weekly devoted to sport and owned by In Focus Promotions; the "Solomons Tok Tok" a weekly owned by the local firm, News Limited; and "Nadepa" (fortnightly), also in English, owned by the National Democratic Party and devoted to party propaganda.

The Diocese of Melanesia (Anglican) also produces a regular periodical.

WATER AND ELECTRICITY. Electricity is in continuous supply at Honiara, Auki, Gizo, Kira Kira, Santa Cruz and Tulagi, operated by the Solomon Islands Electricity Authority. Wiring rules of the Standards Association of Australia are used. Plans have been made for eventual electricity supplies at Mali'u (Malaita); Buala (Santa Isabel) and Munda (New Georgia). The supply is 230/415V at 50 Hz.

Generally good drinking water is abundant throughout the country, except in some outlying areas during extreme drought conditions. A reticulated water supply is provided in Honiara, Gizo, Auki, Malu'u, Munda, Dodo Creek, Kira Kira, Santa Cruz and Tulagi.

A number of hydro-electric projects are being investigated. One big scheme to supply electricity to Honiara and North Guadalcanal by harnessing the River Lungga is in an advanced state of preparation.

PERSONALITIES AND ORGANISATIONS

Governor-General: Sir Baddeley Devesi, G.C.M.G.

CABINET

Prime Minister: Rt. Hon. Peter Kenilorea
Deputy Prime Minister and Minister of Health and Medical Services: Francis Hilly
Minister of Finance: Benedict Kinika
Minister of Education and Training: G. Beti
Minister of Natural Resources: Paul Tovua
Minister of Agriculture and Lands: Waeta Ben
Minister of Trade, Industry and Labour: Pulepada Ghemu
Minister of Transport and Communications: Moffat Bonunga
Minister of Home Affairs: Philip Kapini
Minister of Law and Information: Lawry Wickham
Minister of Youth and Cultural Affairs: Denis Lulei
Minister of Works and Public Utilities: Tom Harehiru

MEMBERS OF THE SOLOMON ISLANDS LEGISLATIVE ASSEMBLY

West Are Are: Peter Kenilorea
West Kwara'ae: Allen Taki
North-East Guadalcanal: Waeta Ben
North Guadalcanal: Philip Kapini
Central Guadalcanal: Paul Tovua
East Honiara: Bartholomew Ulufa'alu
South Choiseul: Jason Dorovolomo
Rasnongga and Simbo: Francis Hilly
Gizo, Kolombangara: Lawry Wickham
Roviana and North New Georgia: Geoffrey Beti
Marovo: Ghemu Pulepada
East Makira: Benedict Kinika
Temotu Pele: Moffat Bonunga
North West Malaita: Leni Olea
Lau and Mbaelelea: George Suri
East Malaita: Alfred Maetia
Central Malaita: Adrian Bataiofesi
West Kwaio: Jonathan Kuka
East Kwaio: Daniel Fa'asifoabae
West Are Are: Alfred Aihunu
Small Malaita: Emmanuel Harihiru
Malaita Outer Islands: Paul Keyaumi
West Guadalcanal: Kamilo Teke
South Guadalcanal: George Mangale
East Guadalcanal: Ezechiel Alebua
West Honiara: Ben Gale
Russells and Savo: John Ngina
Rennell and Bellona: Paul John
Gela: Richard Harper
West Ysabel: Denis Lulei
East Ysabel: Michael Evo
Shortlands: Peter Salaka
North Choiseul: Allan Qurusu
Vella Lavella: George Talasasa
Vona Vona/Rendova and Tetepari: Hughie Soakai
West Makira: Solomon Mamaloni
Ulawa and Ugi: Andrew Mamau
Temotu Nende: Ataban Tropa

JUDICIARY

Chief Justice: Mr Justice F. Daly
Principal Magistrate, Honiara: K. Brown
Attorney General: Frank Kabui

HEADS OF GOVERNMENT DEPARTMENTS

Secretary for Foreign Affairs: Francis Bugotu

Secretary for Law & Information: Bobby Kwanairara
Secretary for Education & Training: Augustine Manakako
Secretary for Health & Medical Services: Eddie Nielson
Secretary to Prime Minister: Isaac Qoloni
Secretary for Works & Public Utilities: Jim Michie
Secretary for Finance: Tony Hughes
Secretary for Natural Resources: Milon Sibisopere
Secretary for Agriculture & Lands: Rusty Russell
Secretary for Trade, Industry & Labour: Philip Solodia Funifaka
Secretary for Transport & Communications: Dr Peter Beck
Secretary for Home Affairs: Wilson Ifunaoa
Commissioner of Lands: Geoffrey Moore
Solomon Islands Broadcasting Corporation, Chairman: B. Bennett
Official Administrator, Unrepresented Estates: L. M. Holt
Government Archivist: R. Chesterman
Commissioner of Labour: Christopher Cocoran
Director, Solomon Islands Centre, University of the South Pacific: Tony Austin
Principal Collector, Inland Revenue: Toby Campbell
Government Statistician: I. W. K. Taylor
Principal Collector, Customs & Excise: Charles Rafeasi
Trade Development Oficer: Sam Osifelo
Comptroller, Posts & Telecommunications: J. Simister
Chief Marine Officer: W. R. Irvine
Senior Communications Officer: G. Murray
Register of Co-operatives: W. E. Kerlx
Chief Forestry Officer: Terry Kera
Chief Geologist: Frank Coulson
Senior Fisheries Officer: R. H. James
Solomon Islands Tourist Authority: B. Buchanan
Solomon Islands Monetary Authority: Philip Coney

PUBLIC BODIES

President, Western Provincial Assembly: Francis Billy Hilly
Clerk: Martin Glass
President, Malaita Provincial Assembly: David Nanato
Clerk: David Ruthven
President, Guadalcanal Provincial Assembly: Samual Ono
Clerk: Nathnel Waena
President, Ysabel Provincial Assembly: Edward Vunagi
Clerk: Joseph Huta
President, Central Islands Privince: Unknown (elections pending)
Clerk: Rex Biku
President, Makira/Ulawa Provincial Assembly: Mathias Ramoni
Clerk: Henry Manuhea
President, Eastern Islands Provincial Assembly: Unknown (elections pending)
Clerk: Samuel Patavaqara
President, Honiara Municipal Authority: Charles Panakera
Clerk: G. Marsden

DIPLOMATIC

British High Commissioner: Gordon Slater
Australia High Commissioner: R. G. Irwin
Papua New Guinea High Commissioner: Jacob Kairi
Ambassador for South Korea: Han Lim Lee (in Australia)
Ambassador for the United States: Harvey Feldman (in Port Moresby)
New Zealand High Commissioner: Mary Chamberlin
Solomon Islands has diplomatic ties with 13 countries.

CHURCH DIGNITARIES

Church of Melanesia (Anglican): Archbishop N. K. Palmer
Roman Catholic: Archbishop Daniel Sturvenberg
Uniting Church (Methodist): Bishop John Pratt
South Seas Evangelical Church: Superintendent Jezreel Filoa
Seventh-day Adventist Church: Pastor Rex Moe
Christian Fellowship Church: Silas Eto (Holy Mama)

ASSOCIATIONS AND UNIONS

Solomon Islands Christian Associations (SICA), Secretary: Francis Lambu
Solomon Islands National Union of Workers, Secretary-General: Joses Taugenga
Chamber of Commerce, Chairman: Winsto Tshe
Youth Organisations: Boys' Brigade, Girls' Brigade, Scouts, Guides, Pathfinders and Brownies.
Solomon Island National Museum, Curator: Henry Isa

SPORTING

Honiara Golf Club, Honiara Cricket Associations, Solomon Islands Football Federation, athletics, rugby, soccer, netball, softball, tennis, skydiving and sailing, etc.

HISTORY. Archaeological research has revealed that the Solomon Islands have been occupied by man for at least 3,000 years. Material excavated on Santa Ana, Guadalcanal and on Gawa in the Reef Islands has all been radiocarbon-dated to about 1000 BC. Red pottery, thought to be related to Lapita ware, has also been found on Santa Ana, where it is estimated to have been used between 140 and 670 AD. Similar pottery has been found in the Reef Islands.

The European discoverer of the Solomons was the Spanish explorer Alvaro de Mendana, who set out from Peru with two ships in 1567 to seek the legendary Isles of Solomon, believed to lie to the west of South America, and said to have been visited by the Incas. In February 1568, after sighting Nui in the Tuvalu group and what was probably Roncador Reef, he came upon a large, mountainous island which he named Santa Isabel.

Other large islands, including Guadalcanal, Malaita and San Cristobal, were discovered over the next six months, as well as several smaller ones. Although miners from Spain were carried in the ships to seek reef or alluvial gold, it has not been revealed whether or not any gold was located on Guadalcanal. Probably it may have been found, but the discovery was kept secret.

King Solomon's "riches". The Spaniards in Peru and Chile were told of islands to the west which they assumed were the lost Islands of Solomon, and the name was mentioned in some documents between 1531 and 1539. Again, in 1565 and 1566, the Governor of Peru, Lope Garcia de Castro mentioned "yslas que llaman de Salomon" in regard to projected voyages of discovery. In a letter to the King dated June 5, 1566, the governor described the projected voyage of Mendana and said that he would be seeking the "Islands of Salomon". This name was subsequently applied to the islands that Mendana found in 1567 and added to the attraction of potential settlers when they were being recruited in 1595.

Mendana himself does not seem to have had any part in spreading these rumours. But he did succeed in persuading officialdom to provide him with the necessary ships to go on a colonising expedition to the same parts of the Pacific.

For a variety of reasons, Mendana's second expedition did not leave Peru until 1595. There were four ships and a large number of prospective colonists. After discovering the southern Marquesa Islands and losing one ship in a fog near the volcanic island of Tinakula, Mendana reached Ndeni (Ndende) Island, which he named Santa Cruz. Here a vain attempt was made to found a colony. Mendana himself and many other Spaniards died; dissension broke out among the others; and there were difficulties with the islanders. Finally, the remnants of the expedition made for the Philippines; the flagship's remaining two consorts became lost on the way although one later reached Mindanao. "The Almiranta" was lost at night in poor visibility just as the fleet reached Santa Cruz, is now known to have called at San Cristobal, where the remains of a settlement have been found.

In 1606, Pedro Fernandez de Quiros, Mendana's chief pilot in 1595, commanded a second colonising expedition to the Western Pacific. The expedition touched at Taumako Island in the Duff group, and then went on to the northern New Hebrides. It, too, was a failure, and the Spaniards thereafter lost interest in Pacific exploration.

Two Dutch expeditions were the next to visit the Solomons area. In 1616, Schouten and Le Maire discovered some low islands which seem to have been part of the atoll of Ontong Java; and in 1643 Tasman bestowed the name Ontong Java on that atoll because of the resemblance of its islands to islands of that name near Batavia.

Carteret, Bougainville. More than 120 years then passed before Europeans were again in Solomons waters. The first, in 1767, was Captain Philip Carteret who rediscovered the Santa Cruz group, including Utupua and Vanikoro, and the northern coast of Malaita. He also added the small island of Ndai, north of Malaita, to the map. About a year later, the French explorer Bougainville, coming north from the New Hebrides, passed through the waters now known as Bougainville Strait and so came upon Choiseul, which he named after a French minister. He also passed the Treasury Islands, Vella Lavella. Bougainville and Buka.

In 1769, Surville, another Frenchman, rediscovered several of the islands seen by Mendana, Carteret and Bougainville and named them Terres des Arsacides (Lands of the Assassins). Mourelle, a Spaniard, rediscovered Roncador Reef in 1781 and so named it for its 'frightful roaring'. Six years later, the American ship 'Alliance' (Captain Thomas Read) sailed along the western fringe of the islands of Tetipari and Rendova, then northwards to Bougainville.

In 1788, Lt. John Shortland, in command of the 'Alexander' and 'Friendship', two transport vessels of the First Fleet to Botany Bay, sailed along the coast of San Cristobal and Guadalcanal. From there, he coasted the largish islands in the central part of the archipelago, which he named New Georgia. Two smaller groups to the northward were given their present names, Treasury and Shortland Islands.

Accounts of the voyages of Shortland, Surville, Bougainville and Carteret led the French geographer M. Bauche to the realisation in 1781 that their discoveries had been made in the same area as those of Mendana, and that they were all part of the Solomon Islands. Most of the Solomon Islands had, in fact, been discovered by that time. But just over a century passed before all the islands were reasonably well charted.

Some important details were added to the charts in the 1790s. In 1791, Captain John Hunter discovered Sikaiana, and Captain Edward Edwards of HMS 'Pandora' became the first European to sight Anuta and Fataka. In 1792, Captain Edward Manning discovered the passage between Santa Isabel and Choiseul now known as Manning Strait. In 1793, Captain Matthew Boyd of the 'Bellona' became the discoverer of Bellona Island and probably its neighbour, Rennell Island. In 1794, Captain Wilkinson of the 'Indispensable' discovered Indispensable Strait between San Cristobal and Guadalcanal. And in 1799, Captain James Wilson of the missionary ship 'Duff', rediscovered Quiros',

Taumako and other islands in the same group and gave them the name of his ship.

La Perouse episode. The most celebrated episode in the early history of the Solomons concerned the French explorer La Perouse. In January 1788, in the ships 'Boussole' and 'Astrolabe', La Perouse had arrived in Botany Bay in the course of an extensive voyage of exploration in the Pacific. He sailed again in the following month – and was never seen again. Despite many rumours and an official search for him by the d'Entrecasteaux expedition, no positive clue to La Perouse's fate was found for almost 40 years.

The man who unveiled the mystery was an Irishman, Captain Peter Dillon, who chanced on some articles of European origin during a visit to Tikopia in 1826. The islanders told him that the articles had come from the neighbouring island of Vanikoro. Dillon visited Vanikoro in the following year and recovered numerous articles that had been washed ashore or salvaged by the islanders. He was told that La Perouse's two ships had been wrecked in a storm, one in shallow water inside the reef and one in deep water outside. The survivors had lived on shore for a time and had built a boat from local timber. They had eventually sailed away in their boat, never to be heard of again.

Several months after Dillon's visit to Vanikoro, the French explorer Dumont d'Urville recovered several cannon and other relics from the inner wreck, which was identified as the 'Astrolabe'. Numerous other relics were recovered from Vanikoro in subsequent years. However, it was not until 1962 that the remains of the 'Boussole' were found. The discovery was made by Mr Reece Discombe, of Vila, New Hebrides, after many hours of swimming over the outer edge of the reef. The 'Boussole' had come to grief in a deep, wedge-shaped chasm, about 1 km from where the 'Astrolabe' was wrecked. Several coral-encrusted anchors and cannon, many iron and lead ingots, and a number of other items were subsequently recovered.

Missionaries rebuffed. The discoveries of Dillon and d'Urville at Vanikoro focused some European attention on the Solomon Islands. But apart from occasional visits by whalers, there was little European contact with the area until the mid-nineteenth century. The first Europeans to try to establish themselves in the group were seven priests and six lay brothers of the French Marist order, under the direction of Bishop Epalle. They landed on the south coast of San Cristobal in 1845. But the bishop was murdered on Isabel within a few days, and the mission, which they established at Makira Bay, never really got going. After three more of its members had been murdered and one had died of malaria, the mission was abandoned in 1848.

Another person to lose his life in the Solomons at this time was Benjamin Boyd, an enterprising capitalist from New South Wales. In 1851, he visited San Cristobal and Guadalcanal in his yacht 'Wanderer' with the idea of forming an independent government there under his own control. However, this idea came to nothing, for Boyd was murdered by islanders when he landed early one morning to shoot birds at a place still known as Wanderer Bay on the south-west coast of Guadalcanal.

Boyd's murder and the grim experiences of the Marists may have prompted the cautious methods of the Melanesian Mission of the Church of England, which extended its work to the Solomons in the early 1850s. Instead of establishing missionaries in the group, the Anglicans persuaded young islanders to go with them for training either in New Zealand or Norfolk Island. The idea was that, on being returned to their home islands, these novices would start converting their own people. The mission ship 'Southern Cross' made regular visits to the Solomons each year. But the Anglicans made little progress until they themselves began to settle in the group in the late 1870s.

The labour recruiters. Meanwhile, labour recruiters had moved into the Solomons seeking labour for plantations in Fiji, Queensland and occasionally New Caledonia and Samoa. The first recruiting vessel appeared in 1870. Recruiting for Queensland continued until 1904 and for Fiji until 1911. Nearly 19,000 islanders are estimated to have been taken to Queensland and more than 10,000 to Fiji. Less than half of those indentured for Fiji were returned to their homes, but 14,105 are estimated to have been returned from Queensland. Descendants of those who went to Fiji live in the village of Wailoku near Suva, Fiji's capital.

Abuses committed by the labour recruiters, popularly known as blackbirders, frequently led to the murder of innocent people, particularly in the early days. Two prominent Europeans who lost their lives were Bishop J. C. Patteson, the second bishop of Melanesia, who was clubbed to death at Nukapu, Reef Islands, in 1871, and Commodore J. G. Goodenough of HMS 'Pearl', who died from a poisoned arrow wound sustained at Carlisle Bay, Santa Cruz, in 1875.

Protectorate declared. The evils of the labour trade and its consequences prompted Great Britain to declare a protectorate over the southern Solomon Islands (Guadalcanal, Savo, Malaita, San Cristobal, and the New Georgia group) in 1893. In 1898 and 1899, the islands of the Santa Cruz group, including Utupua, Tikopia, Vanikoro, and the outlying islands of Anuta, Fataka, Sikaiana, Rennell and Bellona were added to the protectorate.

There were further additions in 1900. By a treaty with Germany, and in exchange for Britain's withdrawal from Western Samoa, several islands in the north of the group that had previously come within the German sphere of influence were transferred to British administration. These islands were Isabel, Choiseul, the islands south and south-east of the main island of Bougainville, and the atoll of Ontong Java.

When the British protectorate was established, approximately four dozen European traders were resident in the group. Twelve years later, in 1905, there was a move to open up the Solomons commercially. Lever's Pacific Plantations Ltd. chartered the steam yacht 'Victoria' to visit the protectorate, and representatives of the company took up land on a large scale. Planting began almost immediately, and by 1940 the company had more than 8,000 hectares under cultivation. Two other companies that acquired interests in the Solomons early in the 20th century were Burns Philp & Co., of Sydney, and the Malaita Co. The latter sold out to W. R. Carpenter & Co. Ltd.in the 1930s.

Pacific War. The economic development of the Solomons progressed only sluggishly before World War II. After the Japanese entered the war in 1941, most of the planters and traders in the group were evacuated to Australia. Soon afterwards, the Japanese thrust southwards from New Guinea and occupied the main islands. From May 1942, when the Battle of the Coral Sea was fought, until December 1943, the Solomons were almost constantly a scene of combat.

One of the most furious sea battles ever fought took place off Savo Island, near Guadalcanal, in August 1942. Heavy losses were inflicted on both sides, but more crushingly on the Allies. Many fierce naval engagements followed before the Japanese withdrew completely from Guadalcanal in February 1943. The Allied forces later drove them from other islands, and by December 1943 they were in command of the Northern Solomons.

When civil administration of the Solomons resumed after the war, the authorities found that Tulagi, the former capital, on an islet off Florida, had been destroyed. It was decided to establish a new capital at Honiara on the north coast of Guadalcanal. This was the site of an important American wartime campaign against the Japanese, situated about 16 km west of Henderson Field, a major wartime air base. Originally, many of the buildings in use in Honiara were relics of the war, but few of these are now to be seen.

Marching Rule. Between 1946 and 1950, a good deal of official attention was devoted to a native movement known as Marching Rule, believed to be an Anglicised version of 'masina' (brotherhood). Some people thought it had its origin in the close wartime contacts between islanders and American soldiers with their seemingly limitless wealth; others looked on it as a nationalist movement that followed naturally on the profoundly disturbing effects of the war.

In a general way, the movement took the form of adherence to some chief who assumed dictatorial power, was strongly anti-European, and who led his people in a sullen defiance of governmental authority. Large numbers of people on Malaita and in other islands were affected, and there was much disorder until some of the leaders were gaoled in late 1948.

Other indigenous movements that developed later were breakaway movements from the Christian missions. In 1959-60, followers of Silas Eto, later called Holy Mama, broke away from the Methodist Mission on New Georgia. They lived in a model village called Paradise and engaged in bursts of agricultural development. In the early 1960s, the adherents of a cult called Moro collected about $8,000 to buy their freedom from the government.

Gradual changes in the system of governing the Solomons were made from the end of World War II until the early 1970s, after which changes came much more rapidly as Britain prepared to give the islanders their independence.

When civil administration was resumed after the war, an advisory council, first created in 1921, was re-established. This had originally consisted of the resident commissioner as president and four nominated members, but membership was now increased. In 1960, the advisory council was superseded by a legislative council, and an executive council was created as the policy-making body for the protectorate. Progressively the council was given more authority.

In 1970, under a new constitution, both the legislative council and the executive council were replaced by a single governing council. The constitution provided for 17 elected members and up to nine public service members, with the high commissioner holding reserve powers of disallowing legislation. The new council sat for the first time in July 1971, and five committees were subsequently set up in an interesting experiment in consensus. These committees covered Finance; Natural Resources; Communications and Works; Education and Social Welfare; and Health and Internal Affairs. Legislation was initiated by these committees, except in respect of some reserved subjects such as defence and internal security; and as every elected member belonged to one of the committees, he therefore had a direct say in framing policy.

After the governing council, with its committee system, had been in operation about 18 months, its members generally agreed that a cabinet system, under a chief minister, would be more practical.

A new constitution was adopted in April 1974. Under this, the high commissioner became governor, the chief secretary became deputy governor, the governing council became the legislative council with 24 elected members and three ex-officio, and the leader of government business became chief minister with the right to select his own cabinet. Solomon Mamaloni was appointed the first chief minister.

In mid-1975, the name Solomon Islands was officially adopted in place of British Solomon Islands Protectorate. And on January 2, 1976, the Solomon Islands became an internally self-governing state. Independence followed on July 7, 1978.

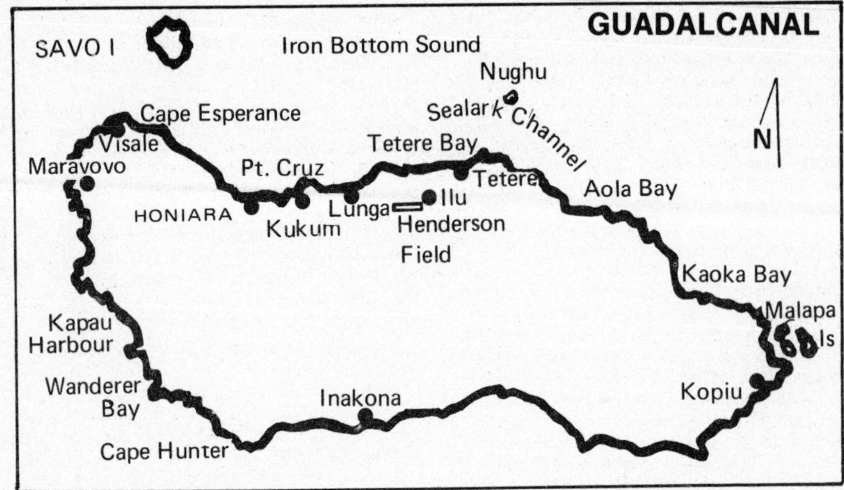

ISLANDS OF THE SOLOMONS IN DETAIL

The Solomon Islands are divided into four administrative districts, each under a district commissioner assisted by one or more district officers. These are:

Central District (headquarters: Honiara), including Guadalcanal, Savo, Florida, Russell Islands, Santa Isabel, Rennell and Bellona Islands.

Western District (headquarters: Gizo), including New Georgia, Choiseul and the Shortland Islands.

Malaita District (headquarters: Auki), including Malaita, Maramsike, Sikaiana and Ontong Java.

Eastern District (headquarters: Kira Kira), including San Cristobal, Ulawa, the Santa Cruz, Reef and Duff Islands, Tikopia, Anuta and Fataka.

GUADALCANAL

Guadalcanal, the largest of the Solomon Islands, is about 150 km long by 48 km wide. It extends from west to east. The interior is high and rugged, with many razorback mountains. Mt. Makarakombou (2,447 m) and Mt. Popomaniasu (2,440 m) are the highest points. On the northern coast, foothills descend in many places to a coastal plain of varying width. There are many coconut plantations in this area. Timber and rice are also produced, and oil palms have been planted in recent years. Most of the southern coast falls in precipitous cliffs to the sea. Strong currents, tide rips and a heavy surf make it dangerous for small ships even in moderate weather. Both the northern and southern coasts are cut by many rivers. During the rainy season, those in the south are likely to become raging torrents.

Honiara, the capital of the Solomons and main port of entry, is situated on the northern coast, about 40 km from the NW point. It is built on either side of Point Cruz where Mendana anchored in 1568. Point Cruz has a deep-water wharf which can accommodate vessels of nearly 200 m length. There are also facilities for small ships. Sheltered anchorages, except in the NW region, exist at many points along the north coast. About 16 km east of Honiara is Henderson Field, an international airport, which links the Solomons with Australia, Papua New Guinea, Nauru, the New Hebrides, New Caledonia and Fiji. It is also the hub for internal air services in the Solomons. Other airstrips on Guadalcanal are situated at Kukum, just outside Honiara, at Koli on the north coast, at Avuavu on the SW coast, and at Marau Sound at the eastern end of the island. A road about 117 km long runs along the northern coast from Lambi Bay in the west to Bokokimbo, east of Henderson Field.

Honiara is a post-war town which stands on the site of a former coconut plantation. Its name is derived from Naghoniara, meaning 'place of the east wind.' The Japanese occupied the site in 1942 and built a small base there. The Americans built a much larger one after defeating the Japanese in a bitter struggle.

The post-war civil administration of the Solomons used many of the wartime Army buildings as offices and quarters until the late 1950s and early 1960s when both the government and private enterprise carried out a vigorous building programme. The present Public Works Department and Treasury buildings, the post office, police station and the circular, air-conditioned court house all date from this period. In 1969, the reconstruction of Government House was completed at a cost of $270 000. It replaced a thatched roof construction that had been built by the Americans. Other strikingly modern buildings in Honiara include St. Barnabas Anglican Church, the Museum and the Mendana Hotel. Like the government offices, government housing built in recent years is of permanent cement construction. Most such houses are built on ridges behind the town.

Recreations available in Honiara include golf, tennis, bush walking and swimming, although there is a serious shark danger on the coast. There are a number of European and Chinese stores catering for most needs, a freezer store, and a dry cleaning establishment. Honiara has an elected town council, a public bus service, adequate taxis, and electricity and water supplies. It is the centre of a growing tourist industry and education for the Solomons.

Several places on or near Guadalcanal figured in the early history of European penetration of the Solomons. The small island of Rua Sua off the NE coast was the site of a Roman Catholic mission station in the 1840s.

Wanderer Bay on the SW coast is the spot where Benjamin Boyd, who had plans to create a private kingdom in the Solomons, went ashore from his yacht 'Wanderer' in 1851 and was never seen again.

Tetere, about 32 km east of Honiara, was the scene of the murder of five Austrian gold-seekers who landed there in 1896 and expressed a desire to climb Mt. Tatuve, despite local opposition to their plan. There is a stone memorial to them at Tetere.

SAVO

Savo, a quiescent volcano, rises abruptly from the sea about 32 km NW of Honiara. Its last known eruption took place in 1840 with considerable loss of life. Areas of boiling mud and ground temperatures of up to 84 deg. Celsius (215 deg. Fahr.) are constant reminders that the volcano is far from dead. The volcano has two craters, one inside the other, at the western end of the island. Waterfalls of almost boiling water and sulphur vents issue from the inner crater.

Savo has several peaks, the highest being 510 m. The shores of the island are steep and are infested with sharks. There is little shelter for vessels. Despite all the hazards, there is a large Melanesian population on the island in 12 villages scattered round the coast. Coconuts thrive as do fruit and vegetables. Near the village of Pamueli, the islanders maintain hatcheries of megapode eggs in the warm volcanic sands.

The waters between Savo and Guadalcanal were the scene of a disastrous naval battle for the Allies in August 1942, with many ships sunk. The sea between Savo and Honiara is now known as Ironbottom Sound as a result of the battles in that area.

FLORIDA

Florida is the name given by the Mendana expedition to a group of volcanic islands lying northward of Guadalcanal and clearly visible from Honiara. There are two large islands, Nggela (Gela) and Small Nggela. They are separated by the narrow Utaha Passage.

Olevugha, Vatilau, Hanesavo and several other small islands lie off the western extremity of Nggela. Another, Tulagi, which is about 5 km in circumference, lies off the south coast. Before World War II, this was the capital of the British Solomon Islands Protectorate. Nearby is the islet of Makambo, the pre-war head station of Burns Philp (SS) Co. Ltd. in the Solomons. Taroaniara on Nggela and Siota on Small Nggela figure prominently in the history of the Melanesian Mission in the Solomons.

Iron and nickelliferous laterites occur near Siota. Manganese has been found on Olevugha and Hanesavo. Gavutu, about 3 km south of Tulagi, has been leased to Lever's Pacific Plantations Pty. Ltd. Mandoliana Island, south of Small Nggela, was the scene of the murder of Lieut. J. St. C. Bower and several seamen of HMS 'Sandfly' in 1880.

RENNELL AND BELLONA

Rennell Island (Mu Nggava) and Bellona Island (Mu Ngiki) are two upraised coral limestone islands lying about 190 km SW of San Cristobal. They are about 24 km apart. Rennell, by far the larger, is SE of Bellona. It is about 80 km long by 16 km wide, and 150 m high. It has an extensive lake, Tinggoa, at its SE end, the largest in the South Pacific. The water of the lake is at sea level, but it is surrounded by lofty cliffs. Bellona is only about 11.5 km by 3 km at its widest. Both islands are thought to be raised atolls. Rennell is the finest example of its kind in the world.

Bellona is named after the merchant ship 'Bellona' (Captain Matthew Boyd) which passed it in 1793. But historians have yet to discover why Rennell was so named, and by whom. The significance of the two native names, Mu Nggava and Mu Ngiki, is also unknown.

Because both islands are difficult of access, the Rennell and Bellona people, who are Polynesians, were little visited by Europeans until after the turn of this century. It was not until 1939 that the islanders adopted Christianity. They have since been studied intensively by the Danish scholars Kaj Birket-Smith and Torben Monberg, and by an American linguist, Samuel H. Elbert.

Rennell Island has extensive bauxite deposits. These have been of considerable interest to the Mitsui Mining & Smelting Co. of Japan for several years. But to mid-1980, no agreement had been reached for mining to proceed. Bellona is also of interest to the mining world because of valuable deposits of phosphatic rock — some 10 million tonnes of it.

An airstrip was opened for service on Rennell in 1970.

RUSSELL ISLANDS

The Russell Islands comprise two large islands, Pavuvu and Banika, with a fringe of small ones, including Money. They lie about 40 km NW of the NW tip of Guadalcanal. Pavuvu is about 16 km from east to west, and rises to about 488 m. It is extensively planted with coconuts, as is Banika. Yandina and Lingatu Plantations on Banika are owned by Lever's Pacific Plantations Pty. Ltd. At Yandina on the eastern side of Banika is a wharf capable of accommodating overseas copra vessels, and also Renard Airfield.

SANTA ISABEL

Santa Isabel (formerly Ysabel) is a long, narrow island some 80 km northwestward of Guadalcanal. It is about 145 km long by 30 km at its greatest width. It is made up of a single chain of volcanic mountains which generally dip to a low-lying coastal strip. A complex of small islands extends off the NW end of Santa Isabel; and at the SE corner is San Jorge, about 24 km long by 14 km wide.

The leeward side of Santa Isabel is largely under coconuts, plantations having been established there from a very early date. Meringe Lagoon, formerly a port of call for ships from Sydney, extends about 13 km along the NE coast. It is formed by five islets in a semi-circle, and is a favourite watering place for inter-island vessels. Allardyce Harbour in the south-west was used until recent years for the export of timber.

There is an airstrip on Fera Island, off the NE coast.

San Jorge, which is separated from the mainland by Thousand Ships Bay, has been thoroughly investigated for minerals.

NEW GEORGIA ISLANDS

The New Georgia Islands, a group of 11 islands of moderate size and a number of smaller ones, lies to the south and SW of Choiseul and Santa Isabel. The group is separated from those islands by New Georgia Sound, otherwise known as The Slot.

The islands extend in a double chain from NW to SE over a distance of about 200 km. Those on the inner side (facing The Slot) are: Vella Lavella, Kolombangara, New Georgia, Vangunu and Nggatokae. Those on the outer side are: Ranongga, Gizo, Vona Vona, Arundel, Rendova and Tetepare.

The group has been described as among the most beautiful and picturesque in the SW Pacific. It was the scene of some fierce fighting between the Japanese and Americans during World War II. But it is still little known to Europeans, and some of its coasts have never been thoroughly surveyed. Gizo (see below), the smallest of the 11 principal islands of the group, is the administrative centre and port of entry for the Western District. The group is noted for its copra plantations. Lever's Pacific Plantations Pty. Ltd. is the biggest operator.

Details of the inner islands, from west to east, follow:

Vella Lavella, at the western end of the group, is mountainous and forest-covered, with several dormant volcanoes, fumaroles and hot springs. There are numerous trading stations on the island visited regularly by local small ships. An airstrip is situated at Barakoma (Mbarakoma) on the SE side.

Kolombangara, 21 km SE of Vella Lavella, is roughly circular in shape. It is an extinct volcano rising directly from the sea to a series of remarkable peaks up to 1,661 m high. Logs are exported by Lever's Pacific Timbers, but reafforestation work is also being carried out. A wartime airfield at Ringicove on the southern side had 834 aircraft movements in 1974. There is also an airstrip at Kukudu on the western side.

New Georgia, the largest island in the group, lies to the eastward of Kolombangara. It is separated from it by the deep waters of Kula Gulf. It was named by Lieut. John Shortland who coasted its southern side in 1788. The island is about 80 km long from NW to SE and from eight to 48 km wide. The most populated part is around the Roviana Lagoon on the SW side. The lagoon is about 40 km long by 6.5 km wide, and is sheltered by a series of flat-topped islands about 60 m high.

Roviana was one of the first places in the Solomons to attract European traders. One such pioneer, Norman Wheatley, established Lambete Plantation at the western end of the lagoon in an area known as Munda. Munda is the site of the second busiest airfield in the Solomons — after Guadalcanal's Henderson Field. It was originally built by the Japanese in 1942. A rest house at Munda provides limited accommodation for travellers. Another airfield is situated at Seghe at the SE end of New Georgia. This serves the people of Marovo Lagoon, a large expanse of water extending from the NE side of New Georgia to the northern side of the adjacent Vangunu Island. Marovo, one of the beauty spots of the Solomons, is entered through an opening in a high cliff which separates the lagoon from the sea.

Vangunu Island, roughly circular with an extremely indented coastline, is about 26 km in diameter. Besides the Marovo Lagoon on its north coast, it has another, Kolo Lagoon, on its eastern side. The island is probably the remains of a single volcanic cone whose summit reaches a height of 1,123 m and is usually lost in cloud.

Nggatokae (Gatukai) Island, about 6 km SE of Vangunu and about one-fourth of its size, is another volcanic cone. The highest point is 887 m. Mbulo Island, with steep coral cliffs, lies about 3 km NE. In 1952, a submarine volcano erupted 29 km SSW of Nggatokae.

Outer islands, from west to east, are:

Ranongga (or Ghanongga) Island is the westernmost of the outer chain of New Georgia Islands. It is about 25 km long by eight broad. About 8 km due south is Simbo Island, formerly known as the Eddystone. Simbo is about 6.5 km from north to south, and is formed of two volcanic hills joined by a low coral isthmus. In the 19th century, Simbo was a popular calling place for ships sailing northwards from Sydney to China and the Philippines. An 1863 sailing directory recommended captains to call there for pilots and interpreters, as the islanders, unlike their neighbours, were 'on friendly terms with Europeans'.

Gizo, lying about midway between Ranongga to the west and Kolombangara to the NE, is an island of coral formation. It is about 13 km long by 5 km wide, rising to a height of about 180 m. There are no prominent features. A chain of small islands extends for about 8 km off the SE extremity, from near Gizo harbour. The township of Gizo, badly damaged during the war, is on the southern side of the harbour. It has been headquarters for the Western District since 1949. In 1955, the first Gilbertese to be resettled in the Solomons were landed at Gizo, and established a village. Since then some have gone to the Shortland Islands. An airfield for Gizo is situated on Nusatupe Island to the east.

Vonavona (Wana Wana) and Arundel (or Kohinggo) Islands lie to the southward of Kolombangara. Arundel is separated from the western end of New Georgia Island by Hathorn Sound and the Diamond Narrows. Vonavona lies to the SW of Arundel. Both are flat and of coral formation.

Rendova, the largest of the outer islands of the group, lies to the southward of Roviana Lagoon. It is roughly rectangular, about 26 km long, and with a long peninsula extending from its SE corner. Rendova Peak, a volcanic cone with an extinct crater, is 1,063 m high. The US capture of a Japanese base on Rendova in 1943 was a preliminary to the recapture of the important Munda airfield.

Tetepare, SE of Rendova, is about 26 km long by 14.5 km wide. It is separated from New Georgia Island by the Blanche Channel.

CHOISEUL

This is a long, mountainous island, extending about 144 km from NW to SE, and with a maximum width of 32 km. It is on the eastern side of Bougainville Strait and northward of New Georgia Sound. Mt Maitambe (1,006 m) near the middle of the island is its highest point. Much of the interior has never been explored, and only the SW and NW sides of the island have been surveyed. Most of the people live round the coast.

Choiseul Bay, near the NW tip of the island, is the site of several coconut plantations. Taro Airfield is nearby. There are mission stations at Sasamungga on the central western coast and on Mole islet further north.

Off the eastern end of Choiseul are a number of islands, the largest of which are Rob Roy (Vealaviru), Susuku and Vaghena (Wagina). Vaghena is the site of a Gilbertese resettlement scheme dating back to 1963. The name Choiseul was given to the island by the French explorer Bougainville in 1768. There appears to be no native name for it.

SHORTLAND and TREASURY ISLANDS

The Shortland and Treasury Islands lie only a few kilometres eastward and southward of the large island of Bougainville, and are at the border of Papua New Guinea. They are westward of Bougainville Strait. The main islands in the Shortland group are Shortland and Fauro. The Treasury group consists of Mono and Stirling.

Shortland Island (native name: Alu) is the largest in the two groups. It is about 30 km by 24 km, rising to a height of nearly 200 m. Korovou, at the SE end, is the main settlement and headquarters for the district. Logging is carried on nearby.

Faisi, a small island NE of Korovou, was formerly the government station. It encloses a sheltered harbour where overseas ships can be accommodated. Faisi and surrounding foreshores are planted with coconuts. Other islands off the coast include: Magusaiai, Pirumeri, Poporang, Onua, Olofi and Aloataghala.

Fauro, about 18 km NE of Shortland, is an irregularly shaped island of volcanic origin. It is about 22 km long. Numerous small islands lie nearby. To the north are Ovau and Oema (island and atoll); to the west are Asie, Ilina, Nusave, Nielai, Nusakova, Benana and Nuhahana; to the south is Mania; and to the NE, Piru (Piedu), Obeani (Cyprian Bridge) and Masamasa.

Mono in the Treasury group lies about 32 km SSW of Shortland Island. It is oval in shape, densely wooded, and about 14.5 km long by eight broad. Its highest point is 355 m. Falamae village stands on a promontory near the island's southern extremity.

Stirling Island, off the south coast of Mono, is separated from it by Blanche Harbour. Several small islands in the harbour are planted with coconuts.

Two airfields serve these groups — one on

Mono and one on Ballalae Island between Shortland and Fauro. Both were built during the war.

MALAITA

Malaita, lying NE of Florida and Guadalcanal and SE of Santa Isabel, is separated from them by the deep waters of Indispensable Strait. It is a mountainous, densely wooded island, running roughly from NNW to SSE. It is about 165 km long by 37 km at its greatest width, with an area of about 3,840 sq km. The land rises gradually from the coast to a maximum elevation at Mt Kolovrat of 1,303 m.

There are many indentations along the coast affording shelter for coastal shipping. These are often at the mouths of fast-flowing rivers, which, together with many precipitous hills, kept tribes apart in ancient times, fostered suspicion, and favoured the survival or development of many languages and dialects. Today, however, there is a unity of purpose among the Malaita people and they are most progressive.

Because Malaita had a large population when European contact began, it was a popular rendezvous for labour recruiters from the 1870s onwards. Abuses committed by the labour traders made the establishment of law and order difficult after the Solomons became a British protectorate in 1893.

However, by the 1920s, a good start had been made from the government station at Auki on the west coast, while Catholic missionaries had made some progress from a station at Bina, south of Auki. The murder of District Commissioner Bell and some members of a police detachment in 1927 was a serious setback.

When World War II came, many Malaita men volunteered to serve with the Americans on Guadalcanal as guides, scouts and labourers. Their sudden contact with the ships, aeroplanes, bulldozers, canned food and other marvels of the Americans had an unsettling effect after the war. The Marching Rule movement, a cargo cult, was one manifestation of it. Later there was a Federal Council. Although neither Marching Rule nor the Federal Council achieved much materially, they did help bring about the unification of the Malaita people. In 1953, the first Malaita Council was formed. This and its successors have been responsible for a great deal of economic development on the island — copra, rice and cocoa growing; road-building; the establishment of schools, etc.

Auki, now the seat of administration of the Malaita District (which includes the atolls of Ontong Java and Sikaiana), is a township with modern offices and housing, a district hospital, schools, a shopping centre, harbour facilities for coastal ships, yards for boat-building, etc. There is an airfield about 2.25 km northward of the town. The longest road in the Solomons runs through Auki. Beginning at Bina, 27 km south of Auki, it extends to the northernmost point of the island and continues down the east coast to Fouia, a distance of 147 km.

Many Malaita people live on artificial islands off the coast. These are built up with coral and frequently have the appearance of forts. Sharks, which are numerous, are held to be sacred.

Maramsike, sometimes called Small Malaita, lies off the SE end of Malaita. The two islands are separated by a narrow and tortuous passage. The local council maintains an airfield at Parasi on the SW side. Maana'oba (Manaoba) is an island off the NE coast.

The population of Malaita, including Maramsike, was 60,043 at the 1976 census, the largest for any island in the group. The native name for Malaita is Mala. It was once known to Europeans as Malanta.

NDAI, RAMOS

These are two islands off Cape Astrolabe, the NW point of Malaita. Ndai, about 40 km northward, is some 8 km long by 3 km wide. It was called Gower Island by Captain Carteret in 1767.

Ramos, about 2.5 km long, is 33 km west of Cape Astrolabe. Ramos, Spanish for 'palms' as in Palm Sunday, was the name that Mendana gave to Malaita in 1568. It was mistakenly applied to the present Ramos Island by the Russian hydrographer Krusenstern in 1824.

SIKAIANA

Sikaiana, sometimes written Sikayana, is a triangular atoll lying about 177 km NE of Malaita. It takes its name from the largest of four islets on its reef, which is the site of the principal settlement. The other islets are called Matuavi, Matuiloto and Tehaolei. The inhabitants are Polynesians, probably of Tuvalu origin.

Sikaiana's reef is steep-to with tremendous depths a few metres out. This makes it dangerous to approach by night or in poor visibility as no warning is given by soundings. Moreover, lack of anchorages and a continual heavy swell make it very difficult of access. A few small trading vessels visit it occasionally to collect copra and beche-de-mer. They make use of two boat landings at either end of Sikaiana islet. The islanders are adept at building canoes and in handling them in the surf.

Of all the Polynesians in the Solomons, they are said to come nearest to the popular idea of Polynesians — carefree, laughing, 'children of nature'.

The atoll was formerly known as Stewart Island. The first European to report it was Captain John Hunter who passed it in the ship 'Waaksamheyd' in 1791. One of the best early accounts of it was given by Dr Karl Scherzer of the Austrian frigate 'Novara' which called there in 1859. It became a British protectorate on August 18, 1898.

Further information: Article by Tim P. Bayliss-Smith in 'Pacific Atoll Populations' (Vern Carroll, ed.), Honolulu, 1975.

ONTONG JAVA

Ontong Java, the northernmost island in the Solomons, lies 5 deg south of the Equator, some 250 km north of Santa Isabel. It is an atoll shaped like a boot, the toe being in the SE. It is about 72 km long from north to SE, and about 48 km at its greatest width.

There are about 100 islets on the reef, mainly on the southern and eastern sides. Luangiua, the largest, and site of the principal settlement, is at the SE end. Other sizeable islets are Pelau (site of the only other village), Avaha and Keila. All the islets are well planted with coconuts and copra production is large. There are 23 passages through the reef. Kaveiko pass, to the south of Luangiua, leads to the main anchorage.

The first Europeans to see Ontong Java were probably the Dutch explorers Schouten and Le Maire in 1616. But the name Ontong Java was applied to the atoll by Tasman in 1643. Captain Hunter named it Lord Howe's Group in 1791, and it was commonly known as Lord Howe Atoll until recent times (it is not to be confused with Lord Howe Island, off Australia's east coast). Because of its isolated position, few whalers or traders appear to have visited it before about 1875 when labour recruiters sought men there. In 1895, the E. E. Forsayth Company of New Guinea's so-called 'Queen' Emma, established a trading station on the atoll and visitors became more frequent. The population was then about 2,000. Introduced diseases caused it to drop to a record low of 588 by 1939, when the atoll was declared a closed district. Since then the numbers have gradually increased again. The islanders are Polynesians. They have the unusual burial custom of marking graves with large upright coral stones.

Further information: Article by T. Bayliss-Smith in 'Pacific Atoll Populations' (Vern Carroll, ed.), Honolulu, 1975.

SAN CRISTOBAL

San Cristobal, known locally as Makira, is about 112 km from NW to SE, with a maximum width of about 38 km. It lies about 53 km SE of Guadalcanal. A series of mountain ranges run parallel to the main axis of the island, which is densely wooded. The highest point is 1,250 m. There is a strip of level land along the north coast, but the south coast falls precipitously to the sea. Star Harbour, near the eastern end, is the best anchorage on the north coast. Others are Wanione (Wanoni) Bay, Kirakira Bay, and Wango Bay. Makira and Marunga Harbours afford the best shelter on the south coast. Makira is the site of a Catholic mission.

Kirakira, headquarters for the Eastern District, is situated on the north coast on the bay of the same name. It is a short distance eastward of Wanione Bay. It has a small hospital and an airstrip, Ngora Ngora, which links San Cristobal with Honiara.

There are several islands off the coast of San Cristobal. Santa Ana (Owa Raha) and Santa Catalina (Owa Riki) lie off the eastern end. Uki (formerly written Ugi), Bio and the Three Sisters (or Olu Malau) lie from 7 to 32 km to the northward. About 27 km northward of the Three Sisters is Ulawa. Ulawa, the largest of these islands, is about 20 km long.

All the islands produce copra. Santa Ana, a raised atoll, is particularly well planted. Both Santa Ana and Santa Catalina have been investigated for phosphates. Santa Ana was one of the first islands in the Solomons to have a resident European trader.

Pamua, on the north coast of San Cristobal, is now known to have been the site of a camp established in 1595 by the passengers and crew of the Spanish ship 'Santa Isabel'. The 'Santa Isabel' was one of the four vessels of Mendana's second expedition to the Solomons. She became separated from her companions near the volcano island of Tinakula, and was never seen again. Evidently she continued due westward to Pamua, a distance of about 440 km. Pieces of pottery from the Spanish camp were first found at Pamua in 1923, but it was not until 1970 that archaeologists identified these and other pieces, plus an iron nail, as being of Spanish-American origin and undoubtedly from the 'Santa Isabel'. The ultimate fate of the 'Santa Isabel' and her complement is unknown.

SANTA CRUZ GROUP

The Santa Cruz Group, lying some 450 km eastward of San Cristobal, consists of four main islands: Ndende (Ndeni or Santa Cruz), Utupua, Vanikoro and Tinakula.

The name Santa Cruz dates back to 1595 when the Spanish explorer Mendana tried to form a colony at Graciosa Bay. Although Peter Dillon found relics of the La Perouse expedition at Vanikoro in 1827 (see under History), the group had little continuous contact with Europeans until quite recent times.

Early this century, a trader, Captain Oscar Svensen, established a store at Graciosa Bay, and Lever's had a station there for about 16 years until just after World War I. But it was not until 1923 when the Kauri Timber Co. of Melbourne took up rights to export kauri from Vanikoro that direct British administration was extended to the group. From a district office on Vanikoro, it took about 10 years to bring law and order to all the islands.

During World War II, the Americans had an observation post on Ndende and a major naval battle was fought in Santa Cruz waters against the Japanese. The extraction of kauri from Vanikoro ended in 1964. Since then copra has been the main source of income in the group.

Ndende, by far the largest of the Santa Cruz group, is roughly rectangular in shape, about 25 km from west to east, and 17 km across. Its densely wooded hills rise to a height of about 550 m. Graciosa Bay is the principal harbour. There is an airfield nearby. Byron and Carlisle Bays on the north coast also give good shelter. Offshore islands are Temotu, at the entrance to Graciosa Bay, and Lord Howe (Tomotu Noi) on the SE side.

Utupua lies about 70 km SE of Ndende. It is roughly circular, about 11 km in diameter and with a fringing reef about 3 km wide. A passage through the reef leads into Basilisk Harbour.

Vanikoro, about 32 km SE of Utupua and somewhat larger, is ruggedly volcanic, with traces of recent lava flows still visible. A small island, Tevai, lies off the east coast. Both islands are densely wooded. The highest point on Vanikoro is 923 m. Peu is the principal harbour.

Tinakula, or Tenakula, lies about 30 km north of Ndende. It has been an active volcano for most of its recorded history. But during a lull in 1958, people from Nupani, one of the Reef Islands, planted gardens there, and in 1960 some of those islanders occupied it.

Further information on the group: Articles by William Davenport in 'Baessler-Archiv', 1968, 1969 and 1972, and that cited under Reef Islands.

REEF ISLANDS

The Reef Islands, also known as the Swallow Islands, comprise about a dozen small islands lying 60 km and more northward of Ndende. They are spread over an area of about 70 km and appear to be the remnants of a raised atoll. They are generally surrounded by fringing reefs. The men have a reputation as daring navigators.

The most distant islands from Ndende, called the Outer Reef Islands, are only a few metres above sea level. They are from west to east: Nupani, Naloko, Nukapu, Makolobu and Pileni. They are inhabited by Polynesians. Nukapu was the scene of the murder of Bishop J. C. Patteson in 1871.

The other islands, known as the Main Reef Islands, are as much as 50 metres high. They are: Nifiloli, Fenualoa, Ngabelipa, Ngagaue, Nananiebulei, Nibane Tema (or Pangani), Nibange Nede (or Pokoli) and Matema. The inhabitants are Melanesians, except on Nifiloli, the northernmost island, where they are Polynesians. The islands of Ngabelipa, Ngagaue and Nananiebulei are known collectively as Ngailo, Nevelo or Lomlom.

Further information: Article by William Davenport in 'Pacific Atoll Populations' (Vern Carroll, ed.), Honolulu, 1975.

DUFF ISLANDS

The Duff Islands, a chain of 10 small volcanic islands and pinnacles, lie about 110 km NE of the Reef Islands. The principal island, Taumako, is 365 m high. Others are Bass, Obelisk and Treasurers. They are inhabited by upwards of 400 Polynesian-speaking people who maintain close ties with the Reef Islanders. Quiros, in 1606, discovered the group. Captain James Wilson of the 'Duff' visited it in 1797 and gave the name Disappointment Island to Taumako.

Further information: Article by William Davenport in 'Baessler-Archiv', 1968.

ANUTA, FATAKA, TIKOPIA

These three islands are the easternmost outliers of the Solomons. Anuta is about 320 km due east of Vanikoro and 120 km NE of Tikopia. Fataka is 42 km SE of Anuta. Only Anuta and Tikopia are inhabited, their people being Polynesians.

Anuta is little more than 1 km from north to south. Fataka, steep and rocky, is somewhat larger. Tikopia, the largest of the three, is about 5 km by 3 km, being roughly oval in shape. It is an ancient volcano and heavily wooded. The old crater rim, which rises to a height of 366 m, encloses a lake of fresh, but murky water.

The orginal settlers of Anuta are said to have come from Tonga and Uvea (Wallis Island) about 14 generations ago. They maintain contact with the Tikopians, and some are inter-related.

Anuta and Fataka were discovered in 1791 by Captain Edwards of HMS 'Pandora' while searching for the 'Bounty' mutineers. He named them Cherry and Mitre, respectively.

Tikopia acquired some celebrity early last century as the place where Captain Peter Dillon acquired a silver sword guard engraved with a fleur-de-lis, which led him to discover the fate of La Perouse at Vanikoro in 1827. The Tikopians have been intensively studied since the 1930s by the anthropologist Raymond Firth. Because of overcrowding, some Tikopians have been resettled on San Cristobal and in the Russell Islands.

FOR THE TOURIST. The chief interest of visitors to the Solomons in recent years has been to see this major theatre of U.S. operations in World War II. Improved air links are bringing greater numbers of Japanese back to visit this area. The scene of the fiercest battles was Guadalcanal.

Entry formalities. All visitors must carry a valid passport. Entry visas are not required from British subjects or certain others such as U.S. citizens. Transit visas are issued on arrival to holders of confirmed onward travel reservations who do not intend to stay in the Solomons for more than seven days. Visitor Resident Permits may be issued for up to four months per year.

Health regulations require a smallpox certificate from all travellers except those arriving from specified neighbouring South Pacific islands. While malaria is not normally a health hazard around Honiara, visitors are nevertheless recommended to

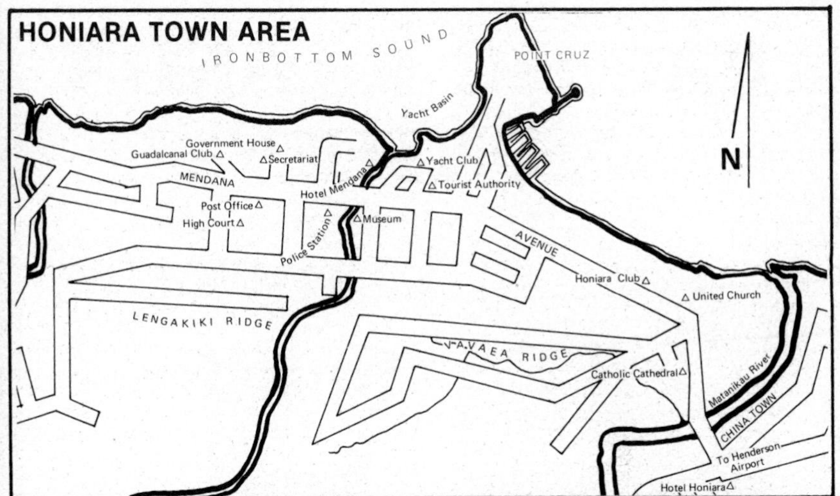

take precautions such as two anti-malarial Chloroquin 150 mg. base tablets each week of their stay and for four weeks after leaving the Solomons.

Airport tax. There is an airport tax of $S.I.2.00. Tipping in the Solomons is not encouraged.

Duty free shopping. Several shops in Honiara offer duty-free goods with delivery to plane or ship. Also on sale are local carvings, handicrafts, etc.

Sightseeing. Drive-yourself cars can be hired in Honiara and there are three travel agencies that arrange tours. Half-day tours from Honiara include Honiara and environs, with residential ridges, museum, botanical gardens, etc.; World War II battlefields inc. Henderson Field; Melanesian villages and dancing. Full day tours inc. car tour to Tambea village; boat tours to Savo Island with its megapode bird sanctuary and hot springs; boat tours to Tulagi, Marau Sound, etc.

There are war relics in and adjacent to Honiara and boards may be seen indicating major battles and incidents in the World War II Guadalcanal campaign. There is a National Museum at Honiara, and Solomon Islander Fred Kona, at Vilu Village 24 km from Honiara, has war relics in his museum. Tours of the surrounding battlefields or excursions to the other islands by boat or aircraft can be arranged.

Apart from the war debris, there are several Japanese monuments to World War II dead.

ACCOMMODATION

Honiara:

HOTEL MENDANA, on beachfront; all rooms air conditioned with private facilities; tea and coffee facilities.

HONIARA HOTEL, 2 km from town centre on airport highway; 53 rooms air-conditioned with private facilities.

HIBISCUS HOTEL central Honiara; motel-type accommodation 14 units with cooking facilities, ceiling fans.

Outside Honiara

TAMBEA VILLAGE RESORT, 45 km by road west of Honiara. Comfortably furnished 20 native-style bungalows, with private facilities, adjacent to beach. Fully licensed.

TAVANIPUPU ISLAND RESORT, 100 km east of Honiara in Marau Sound, accessible by air or island trading ships. Two fully furnished South Seas-style cottages, each with four beds, toilet and cooking facilities.

Malaita Island

AUKI LODGE, in Auki; licensed hotel with six twin rooms and dining room, glass bottom boat, car rental.

New Georgia Islands

KASOLO HOTEL in Gizo; licensed, with six air-conditioned rooms.

THE RESTHOUSE, at Munda; accommodation with meals; 3 double rooms.

Reef Islands, Santa Cruz group

NGARANDO RESTHOUSE, two fully furnished bed-sitting rooms each with three divan beds, kitchen, dining area, toilet and shower facilities.

Other

There are government rest houses that provide accommodation only at Gizo and at Kira Kira; and government rest houses with accommodation and meals at Munda and Auki. Enquiries should be directed to the District Commissioner in each location.

TOKELAU

Tokelau (formerly known as the Tokelau Islands) is a non-self-governing territory under New Zealand's administration.

The group consists of three atolls located between 8 and 10 deg. S latitude and 171 and 173 deg. W longitude, and about 483 km north of Western Samoa. Local time is 11 hours behind GMT.

The three atolls are Fakaofo, Nukunonu and Atafu. Fakaofo, the southernmost atoll is 64 km from Nukunonu, which, in turn, is 92 km south of Atafu. Each atoll has its own administrative centre.

In October, 1978, the Tokelau Affairs Office in Apia reported an estimated population of 1565 compared with the 1976 census figure of 1575 and 1900 in 1966.

Population of the individual atolls in October, 1978, was Fakaofo 605, Nukunonu 373 and Atafu 587.

New Zealand currency is legal tender but for convenience, the Western Samoan tala and sene are used.

The national anthem is "God Save the Queen" and the New Zealand flag is used.

Public holidays are those in New Zealand: January 1, Good Friday, Easter Monday, April 25 (ANZAC Day), early June (Queen's Birthday), late October (Labour Day) and Christmas and Boxing Day.

THE PEOPLE. Apart from a minority of Europeans, the people of Tokelau are Polynesians. To some extent they retain linguistic and cultural links with Samoa. This is fostered by direct contact with Samoans and through Samoan literature, radio broadcasts and church affiliations.

Nationality. Tokelauans are British subjects and New Zealand citizens.

Language. Tokelauan speech has linguistic links with Samoan. The islanders also use English.

Migration. The drop in population noted above has been due to workers and their families moving overseas. Some have gone to Samoa but many travelled to New Zealand under the Tokelau Resettlement Scheme.

Under this scheme hundreds of Tokelauans received government assistance to resettle, mostly around the Taupo-Rotorua area of the North Island of NZ. Others emigrate with the aid of their overseas relatives. Overcrowding in Tokelau has also led the New Zealand Government to encourage migration from the village at Fakaofo to a larger motu nearby. As the population stabilised, in 1976 the islanders agreed to a NZ proposal that the Tokelau Resettlement Scheme be suspended indefinitely.

Religion. Most islanders belong to the Congregational Christian Church of Samoa (70 per cent) deriving from the London Missionary Society, while 28 per cent are Roman Catholic. On Atafu all inhabitants belong to the Congregational church; on Nukunonu all are Roman Catholics, while both faiths are represented on Fakaofo. The work of both missions is directed from Western Samoa.

Lifestyle. The islands are a border area between Micronesia and Polynesia. To some extent the inhabitants retain cultural ties with Samoa but the culture is distinctly moulded by the atoll environment, which has its closest parallel with Tuvalu, with which there are also linguistic, family and cultural affinities.

The lifestyle is centred mainly on the family group. Village affairs are conducted by a council of elders consisting of representatives of the families. In this way the traditional form of patriarchal authority has been preserved.

GOVERNMENT. The basis of the Tokelau's legislative, administrative and judicial systems is the Tokelau Islands Act, 1948, and amendments enacted by the NZ Parliament. In November 1974, the administration of Tokelau was transferred from the Maori and Island Affairs Department to the Ministry of Foreign Affairs. The Seretary of Foreign Affairs is the Administrator of Tokelau and is responsible to the Minister of Foreign Affairs. The powers of the Administrator are delegated to an Official Secretary (in 1979 Simon Carlaw) in Apia. By agreement with the Government of Western Samoa, the Office of Tokelau Affairs continues to be based in Apia.

The staff of the office in Apia regularly visit the islands, making the trip by chartered ship. There is close co-operation between the Government of Western Samoa and the Tokelau Office. Officers of the Western Samoa Government, particularly medical officers and radio technicians, visit the islands regularly.

Five Tokelauan directors, also based in Apia, are responsible to the Official Secretary. In 1979 they were:

Director of Administration: Tioni Vulu
Director of Health: Dr Ropati Uili
Director of Education: Hosea Kirifi
Director of Public Works: Kima Levi
Director of Agriculture and Fisheries: Semu Uili

Tokelau is included in the South Pacific Commission area and benefits from the results of the commission's work. Delegates from Tokelau attend the annual South Pacific Conference.

Elections. The faipule (commissioner or headman) and pulenuku (village mayor) are democratically elected for three-year terms. The current faipule are:

Atafu: Amusia Patea
Nukunonu: Aloisio Kave Ineleo
Fakaofo: Itieli Pereira

The village mayors (pulenuku) in office at present are:

Atafu: Elia Tinielu
Nukunonu: Tioni Pasilio
Fakaofo: Pulu Levao

Local government. The dominant village political institution is the Council of Elders (Taupulega) consisting of the head of each family group together with the faipule and pulenuku. A faipule (who is also a Commissioner of the Court), a village mayor (pulenuku) and a village clerk (failautuhi) are responsible for the day-to-day administration on each island. An administrative officer acts in a supervisory capacity over public servants on his island. The faipule administers the law and presides over the court. The village mayor is responsible for such matters as the maintenance of good order, sanitation, cleanliness, water supplies and the inspection of plantations. The village clerk keeps the records of deaths, births and marriages.

Public service. There is a Tokelau Public Service under the control of the New Zealand State Services Commission. In 1979, there were 149 permanent employees in the Tokelau Public Service. They included doctors, nurses, teachers and tradesmen.

Tokelau public servants receive in-service training in Western Samoa under the administration's training scheme and in New Zealand under the NZ training scheme.

Justice. The High Court of Niue Islands has civil and criminal jurisdiction. The Supreme Court of New Zealand has original and appellate jurisdiction. There is provision for a Tokelauan commissioner for each of the three islands with jurisdiction to deal with certain civil proceedings and criminal offences.

Police. The police force consists of seven Tokelauan officers – three in Fakaofo, two in Atafu and two in Nukunonu. A chief policeman is in charge of each atoll. Apart from petty offences there is little crime. There are no prisons. Punishment takes the form of public rebukes, fines or labour, which is directed to assist with public work, but there is little restraint on personal conduct during the sentence.

EDUCATION. Primary education is available for all children on each island. The NZ Education Department gives the administration advisory assistance. It also provides material and equipment for the schools and carries out periodic inspections.

Three qualified New Zealand teaching couples worked in Tokelau for some years but they have now left and there are now only local teachers on the atolls. The last expatriate teachers to leave were Tom and Allison Struthers who left Fakaofo in 1976. However, an educational adviser from New Zealand, Mr Eddie McKersey, makes regular visits to Tokelau for a 3-monthly stay on each visit. At present there are 40 qualified teachers and 15 teacher-aides.

At March, 1979, Tokelau had students in New Zealand, Western Samoa, Niue, the Cook Islands, Fiji and the Solomon Islands as follows:

New Zealand: 75 students and 29 trainees
Western Samoa: 73 students and five trainees
Niue: 11 students and 2 trainees
Cook Islands: 2 trainees
Fiji: 6 trainees
Solomon Islands: 3 trainees

From the financial year 1977-78, all students have been sponsored from Tokelau.

All the primary schools are well equipped and cater for children from 5 to 15 years of age. Schooling is free and attendance close to 100%. There are also pre-school classes in each village. School equipment includes radio sets, tape recorders and slide and movie projectors. Each island has a parents' committee which raises funds and helps to organise school activities. The schools have a dual aim – to prepare the children for life in Tokelau or for a career in New Zealand.

LABOUR. Copra production and the manufacture of plaited ware and woodwork are the only industries. No supervision of employment conditions in these industries is necessary. Between trading calls, the people devote their labour to procuring food from lagoons, ocean, or plantation, to village maintenance, and to the production of woven mats, fans and curios. Many of the men also work on building projects.

Employment on the works programme has directed much of the islands' labour force from food gathering and copra production, but care is taken to limit dislocation.

Social security. There is no question of providing poor relief and it is not likely to arise while there

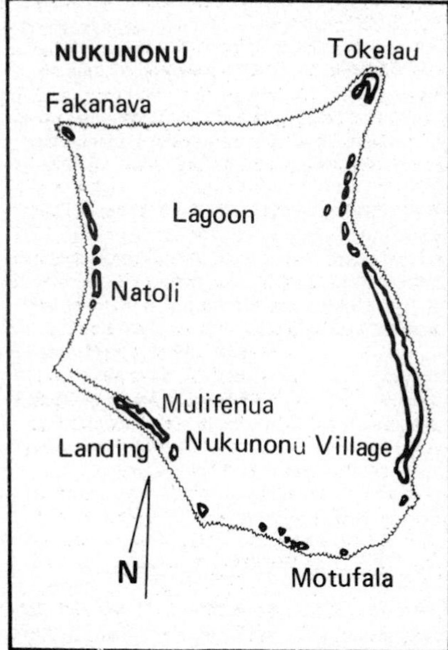

Zealand has been a partial solution. A new village has been established on a larger motu nearby, and includes the school, hospital and other facilities. Housing policy is based on the self-help principle. Materials are bought through the co-operative stores and the Public Works assists with design and construction.

THE LAND. Each atoll consists of a number of reef-bound islets (motus) encircling a lagoon. The islets vary in size from 90 m to 6 km in length. The largest atoll is Nukunonu of 540 ha. Fakaofo and Atafu are 260 and 200 ha respectively. From Atafu in the north to Fakaofo in the south, the group extends for just under 200 km. The atolls are three to five metres above sea level.

Climate. The mean average temperature is 20 deg.C. July is the coolest month and May the warmest. Rainfall is heavy but inconsistent. A daily fall of 80 mm or more can be expected at any time of the year. Severe tropical storms are rare but can cause widespread damage.

Land tenure. The shortage of natural resources has been the major factor encouraging Tokelau migration overseas. Practically all their land is held by customary title in accordance with islander customs. The Tokelau Islands Amendment Act 1967 provides

is enough land. Respect for the aged is firmly embedded in the social system. There is an accepted family responsibility to provide food and accommodation for the aged and indigent. Village women's committees, constituted mainly of married women, help the nursing staff in infant care and child welfare.

HEALTH. The medical officers from Western Samoa regularly visit Tokelau, assisting three Fiji-trained Tokelau medical officers.

Three new hospitals were completed in 1976.

On each atoll a women's committee is active in village health and sanitation.

Skin diseases, resulting from the limited supply of fresh water available for personal hygiene, are common, but are kept under control. In an effort to improve the supply of fresh water, several large water tanks have been installed.

There is some eye trouble, partly caused by irritation from sand and water, which enters the eye during fishing, and partly by the effects of glare from lagoon and ocean.

HOUSING. Most Tokelau houses are constructed of native materials, kanava and pandanus timbers with walls and roofs of plaited pandanus leaves. The villages are well laid out. The Atafu people live in one village which occupies part of a motu (islet), while at Nukunonu the village occupies about half a motu, which is connected by a bridge to a neighbouring motu where some families have settled. The village at Fakaofo is on a small but comparatively high and well-shaded motu. There are overcrowding problems at Fakaofo, although emigration to New

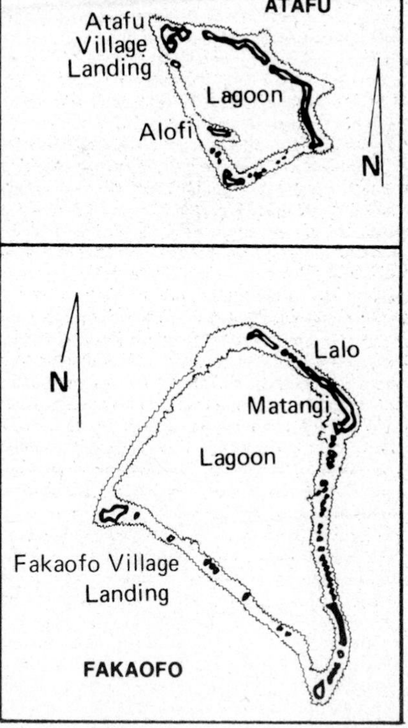

that islanders may dispose of land by custom among themselves, but may not alienate land to non-indigenes. Land holdings pass from generation to generation within families, being held by the head of a closely related family group, although some land is held in common.

PRIMARY PRODUCTION. The physical characteristics of the atolls allow very little scope for economic development and the few natural resources are sufficient only to meet the needs of the simple pattern of life followed by the people. Until recent years, there has been little demand for the material standards of more developed countries, but increasing contacts with Western Samoa and New Zealand have stimulated a desire among the people for wider opportunities to advance their living standards.

The economy is based mainly on the resources of the sea, and the coconut and pandanus palms. Most families get part of their cash income from relatives working in New Zealand. Funds are also sent by the Tokelau communities in New Zealand for village and church projects.

Crops. Apart from the manufacture of copra, agricultural products are of a basic subsistence nature. Food crops consist of coconuts, pulaka (taro), breadfruit, ta'amu, papaw, the fruit of edible pandanus and bananas. Many other seeds have been tested, but because of the poverty of the soil, very poor results were achieved. The many uninhabited islets are used as food plantations. The coconut palm, which is predominant in the atolls, provides the staple export crop of copra.

The UNDP and the USP College of Agriculture in Apia are assisting with a vegetable trial on each atoll, using carefully-selected seeds and fertilisers.

The rhinoceros beetle has infested coconuts at Nukunonu and surrounding islets, although no evidence of the beetle has been found on Atafu or Fakaofo. Because of the promising results achieved in eradication through the use of attractant traps and Rhabdion virus, it is hoped this beetle can be eliminated within a few years.

Livestock and Fisheries. Livestock consists of pigs which, except in Fakaofo, are kept apart from the village areas, and fowl. An experimental piggery has been completed in Nukunono and pig and poultry stocks are being upgraded. Ocean and lagoon fish and shellfish are available in quantity and form a staple constituent of the diet. The most common species of fish caught are tuna, bonito, trevally and mullet. Fisheries experts from UNDP/FAO and the SPC have visited Tokelau which is now participating in the SPC skipjack tuna assessment programme. The NZ Government has affirmed that the benefits of the 200-mile exclusive economic zone to be established around the group will accrue to the people of Tokelau.

Timber. Local timber is used for canoe making, house building and domestic utensils. One islet of each atoll is reserved for growing the short, stubby tauanave tree used for these purposes.

MANUFACTURING. Local industries are copra production, woodwork and finely plaited goods, such as hats, mats and bags.

TOURISM. There is no provision for tourists in Tokelau.

LOCAL COMMERCE. Each village has its own co-operative store run by a village management committee and supplied by the Office of Tokelau Affairs.

OVERSEAS TRADE. A bad drought in 1977 devastated the copra crop so that the harvest in 1978 was reduced to about 47 tonnes, well below previous harvests. Copra proceeds for the year ended March 31, 1976 (latest available figures) totalled $19,465. The only figures available for recent years are:

	1971	1974	1975	1976
Tonnes	165	51	257	110
Value $	13,995	4,813	87,154	22,658

Imports. Main items are staple foods and fuel.

Customs Tariff. Duty of 12½ per cent ad valorem is levied on all goods entering the group.

FINANCE. Total revenue and expenditure for financial years ending March 31 has been ($WS):

	1977-78	1978-79 (est)
Revenue	$248,000	$1,198,330
Expenditure	$997,167	$1,198,330

Expenditure for 1977-78 of $997,167 included administration $342,706, agriculture $93,438, communications and transport $175,196, education $127,393, health $104,439 and public works $153,995. Aid received for the same period consisted of $655,000 from New Zealand, $A500 from Australia for a project on cultural preservation and UNDP financed the purchase of electricity generators, overseas study tours and fisheries development plant including walk-in freezers, fishing gear and outboard motors.

Estimated expenditure of $1,198,330 for 1978-79 included administration $294,230, agriculture $20,500, communications and transport $280,320, education $302,080, health $112,150 and public works $116,050.

The estimated income for the same period was $180,000 from local revenue, $988,330 New Zealand aid and $30,000 grants from other sources. (All figures are in Western Samoa currency.)

Tokelau has a Copra Stabilisation Fund which is invested in New Zealand securities.

Revenue is derived chiefly from export duty on copra levied at the rate of 10 per cent ad valorem on the fob value at Apia on all copra exported from the group. Other revenue is derived from a 10 per cent export tax on handicrafts, from shipping and freight charges, the sale of postage stamps and radio and telegram services.

After discussion with the fonos, especially about the works programme, the annual estimates of revenue and expenditure are prepared by the Administrator and approved by the NZ Minister of Foreign Affairs.

Currency. New Zealand currency is legal tender in the Tokelau Islands, but for convenience, Western Samoa currency of tala and sene ($ and cents) is used. Post Office Savings Bank and commercial banking facilities in Apia are available to the Tokelau people. There are no banks in Tokelau.

Tokelau released its first coin, a souvenir dollar, in 1978. The obverse shows the effigy of Queen Elizabeth II from a drawing by Arnold Machin, RA, of London. The reverse design is by Tokelauan artist Faraimo Paulo, of Atafu. His design shows the pandanus fruit, an important food for the islanders. Paulo was the first Tokelauan artist to study in New Zealand.

TRANSPORT. The islands were without a regular shipping service after the withdrawal of the Pacific Navigation Company's 'Aoniu' from charter in 1974. The administration then arranged to charter the Nauru Pacific Line's 'Cenpac Rounder' for regular calls, generally about five times a year. A new aluminium ferry boat is being built in Apia to take schoolchildren between Fakaofo and its two islets. The craft will cost $WS13,000 and will have capacity for 45 children or 35 adults or 5 tonnes of copra. It was designed by UNDP adviser Arild Overa in Apia for work in sheltered waters and will be too small to travel between the three atolls.

Port Facilities. There are no ports. Landing conditions at the main settlements of all three atolls have required blasting of the coral at various times to provide adequate small boat channels through the reef.

COMMUNICATIONS. Radio stations at Atafu, Nukunonu and Fakaofo transmit traffic and weather reports every four hours.

Radio telephones are available at all three stations. Single sideband tele-radio equipment is installed at all stations, including Apia.

HISTORY. Nothing is known for certain about the origins of the Tokelau people. Samoa, Rarotonga and Nanumanga in the Tuvalu group are all described in the islanders' traditions as homelands, and the probability is that early settlers of the three islands came from each of those places. Atafu was the first island to be seen by Europeans. It was discovered on July 24, 1765, by Commodore John Byron in HMS "Dolphin" and named Duke of York's Island. Captain Edward Edwards of HMS "Pandora" sighted the same island in June 1791 while searching for the "Bounty" mutineers. A few days later he discovered Nukunonu, which he called Duke of Clarence's Island. Atafu was uninhabited at that time.

Although islanders were seen on the beach at Nukunonu, Edwards had no contact with them. Several whalers were in the vicinity of Tokelau in the late 1820s. But Fakaofo, the most populated island, appears to have remained unknown to Europeans until February 14, 1835, when Captain Smith of the whaler "General Jackson" of Bristol, Rhode Island, sighted it. Smith called his discovery De Wolf's Island after the owner of the ship.

First European Knowledge. The first detailed knowledge of Tokelau was obtained in 1841 when the USS "Peacock" and "Flying Fish" of the United States Exploring Expedition spent several days among the islands. Horatio Hale, the expedition's ethnologist, wrote an interesting account of the islands and recorded something of the local language. As Smith's discovery of Fakaofo was unknown to the "Peacock's" commander, he named it Bowditch Island. This name remained in use for many years. Fakaofo's population in 1841 was estimated at between 500 and 600 while about 120 people were thought to live on Atafu.

Christian Conversion. French Catholic missionaries on Wallis Island (Uvea) and missionaries of the London Missionary Society in Samoa used native teachers in various attempts to convert the Tokelauans between 1845 and 1863. By the latter year, Atafu had been entirely Christianised by the LMS, Nukunonu was entirely Catholic. Catholic teachers later established themselves on Fakaofo. As a result, that island now has both Protestant and Catholic adherents, while Atafu and Nukunonu have remained Protestant and Catholic respectively.

Slave Raids. In 1863, several Peruvian slave raiders removed about 140 people from the three islands. A dysentery outbreak at about the same time reduced the total population to barely 200. During the next few years, several beachcombers – American, Portuguese, Scottish, French and German – settled in the islands and intermarried with the local women. Some Polynesian immigrants did likewise. The present-day Tokelauans are thus 'an improbably bizarre genetic mixture', according to a recent description. One of the Portuguese settlers, a Cape Verde Islander of African descent, obtained control over large areas of land and dominated the local copra-based commerce.

British Jurisdiction. In 1877, the British High Commissioner for the Western Pacific in Fiji was given jurisdiction over British subjects in the Tokelaus, as those islands had not come within the jurisdiction of any foreign power. Twelve years later, when Britain thought the islands might prove useful as staging points for the then-proposed trans-Pacific cable, the commander of HMS "Egeria" visited each of them and formally placed them under British protection.

During the next twenty years, Britain nominally administered the islands through her representative in Western Samoa, then Tonga, and finally Ocean Island, then headquarters of the Gilbert and Ellice Islands Protectorate. In 1916, the three islands, then known as the Union Group, became part of the newly proclaimed Gilbert and Ellice Islands Colony. Administration from Ocean Island resulted in some improvement in medical care, and some Tokelauans were recruited to work that island's phosphate deposits.

Samoan Administration. However, the long distance from Ocean Island – 2,200 km – made administration difficult. In 1925, the New Zealand Government undertook to administer the islands from Western Samoa, then a mandated territory. This arrangement still persists even though Western Samoa became independent on January 1, 1962.

In 1946, the group was officially designated the Tokelau Islands under the Tokelau Nomenclature Ordinance, and the islands were included within the territorial boundaries of New Zealand by the Tokelau Islands Act of 1948. For ten years after Western Samoa became independent, New Zealand's high commissioner in Apia held the office of administrator of the Tokelau Islands. In 1976, the territory was officially re-designated Tokelau, the name used by the inhabitants.

Administration of the Tokelaus from Western Samoa has fostered ancient Tokelauan linguistic and cultural links with that country. Before 1962, it also encouraged immigration. In 1951, for example, 220 Tokelau-born islanders were living in Western Samoa, and by 1956 the number was 297. Meanwhile, the population of the three islands was also growing apace. It reached its highest known figure, nearly 2,000, in the 1960s.

Migration to NZ. The New Zealand Government began sponsoring limited immigration of Tokelauans to New Zealand in 1963. By 1965, forty islanders, all single, had become immigrants. A destructive hurricane in 1966 increased the number to 110 in that year. Thereafter, families were encouraged to migrate. By March, 1979, the Tokelau Affairs Office estimated there were more than 2,000 Tokelauans or part-Tokelauans living in New Zealand.

Further Information. Antony Hooper and Judith Huntsman, 'A Demographic History of the Tokelau Islands', Journal of the Polynesian Society, (1973), vol. 82. Gordon MacGregor, 'Ethnology of Tokelau Islands', Bernice P. Bishop Museum Bulletin 146, Honolulu, 1937.

TONGA

The independent kingdom of Tonga, a member of the British Commonwealth, consists of three main island groups and many smaller islands. They are located between 15 and 23 deg. 30 min. S. latitude and 173 and 177 deg. W. longitude. Total area is 696.71 sq. km. There are 169 islands of which 36 are inhabited.

The capital is Nuku'alofa, on Tongatapu, which is about 1,770 km north-east of Auckland. Local time is 13 hours ahead of GMT.

Tonga's currency is pa'anga ($T) and seniti.

The national anthem is "E' 'Otua Mafimafi" "O Almighty God above"; the flag is light red with a white upper left quarter which encloses a light red cross.

Public holidays are: January 1, Good Friday, Easter Monday, April 25 (ANZAC Day), May 4 (Crown Prince's birthday), June 4 (Emancipation Day), July 4 (King's birthday), November 4 (Constitution Day), December 4 (King Tupou I Day) and Christmas.

THE PEOPLE. The Tongans are Polynesians and the census in December 1976 revealed a total population of 90,128, compared with 77,429 in 1966, consisting of Tongans, 88,577; Europeans, 452; part-Europeans, 692; other Pacific Islanders, 265; all others, 142. The estimated population at the end of 1979 was about 92,000 distributed as follows: Tongatapu, 61,000; 'Eua, 4,000; Ha'apai, 10,000; Vava'u, 13,000; other islands, 4,000. The population of the capital, Nuku'alofa, in the 1976 census was 18,396, 17 per cent higher than that in the 1966 census.

Nationality. The Tongans, as citizens of an independent kingdom, have their own nationality.

Language. The islanders speak their own dialect of Polynesian and, usually, English.

Migration. Many Tongans migrate overseas, attracted by better opportunities for employment. In 1974 about 30 Tongans were migrating monthly to the U.S., mostly families with relatives there. Even more were going to New Zealand, creating a labour drain from Tonga and posing problems for New Zealand. Since 1977 Tongans needed guaranteed sponsorship for work and accommodation before they could enter New Zealand. Visas are for six months with a possible extension of five months.

Religion. The Free Wesleyan Church has the largest number of adherents and has had a profound influence in Tonga. Other churches are the Free Church of Tonga, the Anglican, Roman Catholic, Seventh-day Adventist and Mormon. Strict observance of the Sabbath precludes all work, trade, sport, taxi and bus services, etc., on Sunday.

Lifestyle. The Tongans are oriented to work either on the land or at sea. However many have settled in the urban centres, seeking work with the government, in commerce and in what little industry there is.

Recreation. The main recreations are imported – rugby, boxing, soccer, cricket and basketball. However, indigenous games and sports survive. Lafo is a game similar to carpet bowls, except that round wooden discs made from coconut shells are used instead of bowls. Hiko is a juggling game played by young girls – they juggle up to six candlenuts or oranges at a time, while they sing or recite special rhymes, using archaic words which are no longer understood. Another local recreation is "Ilo'ito" a dance in which girls sit on their heels facing each other in two rows. To the accompaniment of a chant and hand movements they hop and skip, and in their singing they refer to flowers and the names of unmarried chiefs. Every time a girl begins to tire and has to drop out, the others make fun of her, telling her she will never win a young chief. Finally, only one or two are left and they are reputedly the ones who will win a handsome chief.

GOVERNMENT. Although Tonga is a constitutional monarchy on the British model, the King in fact exercises wide influence. The government consists of the King, the Privy Council, Cabinet, the Legislative Assembly and the judiciary. The Tongan constitution was handed down by King Tupou I on November 4, 1875. The king voluntarily limited his own powers after emancipating his people from the

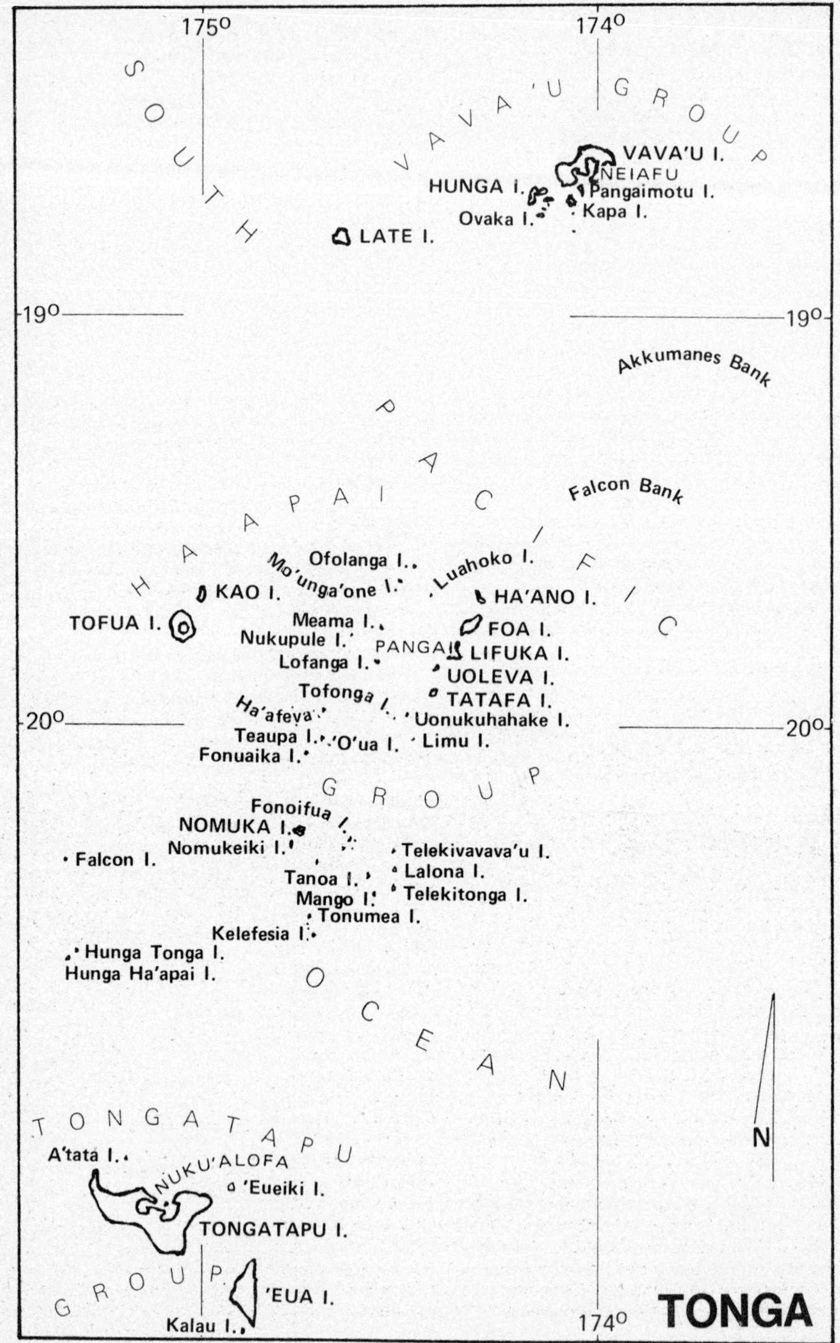

175°
174°
SOUTH PACIFIC OCEAN
VAVA'U GROUP
VAVA'U I.
NEIAFU
HUNGA I.
Pangaimotu I.
Ovaka I.
Kapa I.
LATE I.
19°
19°
Akkumanes Bank
Falcon Bank
HA'APAI GROUP
Ofolanga I.
Mo'unga'one I.
Luahoko I.
KAO I.
HA'ANO I.
TOFUA I.
Meama I.
FOA I.
Nukupule I.
PANGAI
LIFUKA I.
Lofanga I.
UOLEVA I.
Tofonga I.
TATAFA I.
Ha'afeva
Uonukuhahake I.
20°
20°
Teaupa I.
'O'ua I.
Limu I.
Fonuaika I.
Fonoifua I.
NOMUKA I.
Nomukeiki I.
Telekivavava'u I.
Falcon I.
Lalona I.
Tanoa I.
Telekitonga I.
Mango I.
Tonumea I.
Kelefesia I.
Hunga Tonga I.
Hunga Ha'apai I.
TONGATAPU GROUP
A'tata I.
NUKU'ALOFA
'Eueiki I.
TONGATAPU I.
'EUA I.
Kalau I.
174°
N
TONGA

condition of semi-serfdom in which they had lived for centuries.

Legislature. The members of the Legislative Assembly are the Speaker, members of the Cabinet, seven nobles elected by the 33 nobles of Tonga, and seven representatives of the people elected by universal suffrage of all Tongans aged 21 and over. Three of those representatives are from Tongatapu and the two Niuas, and two each from Ha'apai and Vava'u. The seven nobles are elected to represent similar areas.

The Prime Minister is head of the government and administers several departments – Foreign Affairs, Agriculture, Marine, Tourism, and Telephone and Telegraphs. He also controls district and town officers. Parliament meets about the end of May or early-June to pass the estimates before July 1, the beginning of the financial year.

Executive. The King appoints a Speaker and Cabinet which includes Ministers of the Crown and the Governors of Ha'apai and Vava'u, presided over by the Prime Minister. All the Ministers are permanently appointed by the King and retain office until retiring age. The Cabinet becomes the Privy Council when presided over by the King.

The Privy Council also sits as the Court of Appeal, with the addition of the Chief Justice of Tonga.

Local government. The only form of local government is through town and district officers. Town officers represent the government in a village. District officers have authority over a group of villages.

In addition, Ha'apai and Vava'u have their own governors.

Justice. The judicial system of Tonga is based on the British model. At the top is the Court of Appeal (the Privy Council), then the Supreme Court, the Land Court and Magistrates' Courts. In criminal cases before the Supreme Court an accused person has the right to elect for trial by jury or by judge alone. Appeals from the Supreme Court lie with the Privy Council. The Chief Justice is also the judge of the Land Court, on which he sits with a Tongan assessor, who acts in an advisory capacity. A number of Tongan magistrates preside over the Magistrates' Courts throughout the group. There are about 40 Tongan lawyers who practise under licence granted by the Chief Justice.

Police. The Tongan Police Force in 1977 had a strength of 266, which included the Minister of Police and 19 special constables, who made up the police band.

The Minister of Police is the principal Immigration Officer and is also responsible for all prisons and prisoners. Prison policy is administered by the Superintendent of Prisons. There are five prisons in Tonga – in Tongatapu, Ha'apai, Vava'u, Niuatoputapu and 'Eua.

Liquor laws. A permit is required to buy liquor from licensed retailers. Everyone is eligible for a permit, which is issued by the police. A quota is stipulated on each permit. Short-term tourists in transit do not need permits. Liquor is sold in bars, clubs, and, since 1976, in restaurants, and night clubs that offer meals.

DEFENCE. Tonga has had various defence systems. In 1954, a military training scheme, headed by a New Zealand Army officer, was instituted to train a defence force, which was known as the Tonga Defence Force. It was composed of Tongan officers and NCOs and a seconded NZ commanding officer. In 1974, the Tonga Defence Force consisted of three branches i.e. a Regular force, Infantry, Royal Guards and a Maritime Branch. The force was renamed the Tongan Defence Services. The strength of the respective branches are Infantry, 108; Royal Guards, 50; Maritime, 50 (less officers).

The role of each force, its reponsibilities and priorities are: Infantry: 1. Internal security; 2. Aid to civil authorities; 3. Technical trade training in mechanical engineering and carpentry. Royal Guards: 1. Security of the Sovereign; 2. Ceremonial Tasks; 3. Aid to civil authorities; 4. Internal security. Maritime Branch: 1. Patrolling Tongan waters; 2. Fisheries protection; 3. Sea rescue operations; 4. Aid to civil authorities; 5. Ceremonial tasks.

In January 1977, a Tongan took over as commanding officer of the Tonga Defence Force. The established posted strength is 18 officers and 390 other ranks. However, strength in February, 1979 was 17 officers and 208 other ranks.

EDUCATION. Education is free in state schools and compulsory for all Tongan children between six and 14. Students can go to the level of sitting for Australian and New Zealand university entrance examinations.

At the end of 1976 there were 116 primary schools in the kingdom, 85 of them run by the government and 31 by the church. Total enrolment was 19,260 pupils (16,566 government and 2,694 church).

At the secondary level there were 11,721 students with 1,405 in the two government schools – Tonga High School and Tonga College. At the one private school – 'Atenisi College – there were 810 students. In the remaining 43 church secondary schools there were 9,506 students. The largest church schools included: Free Wesleyan Church – Queen Salote College for girls (868 students), and Tupou College for boys (750); Roman Catholic – St. John's High School (460), and St. Mary's High School (479); Anglican – St. Andrew's School (655, co-educational); Church of the Latter Day Saints – Liahona High School (701); Seventh day Adventists – Beulah College (240); and Free Church of Tonga – three Tailulu Colleges (1,400).

Training. There is provision in the Third Five-year Development Plan for the establishment of an Agricultural Technical and Teachers' Training Institute. An expert has been seconded to the Tongan Ministry of Education from New Zealand to provide guidance in its planning. Meanwhile, the Govern-

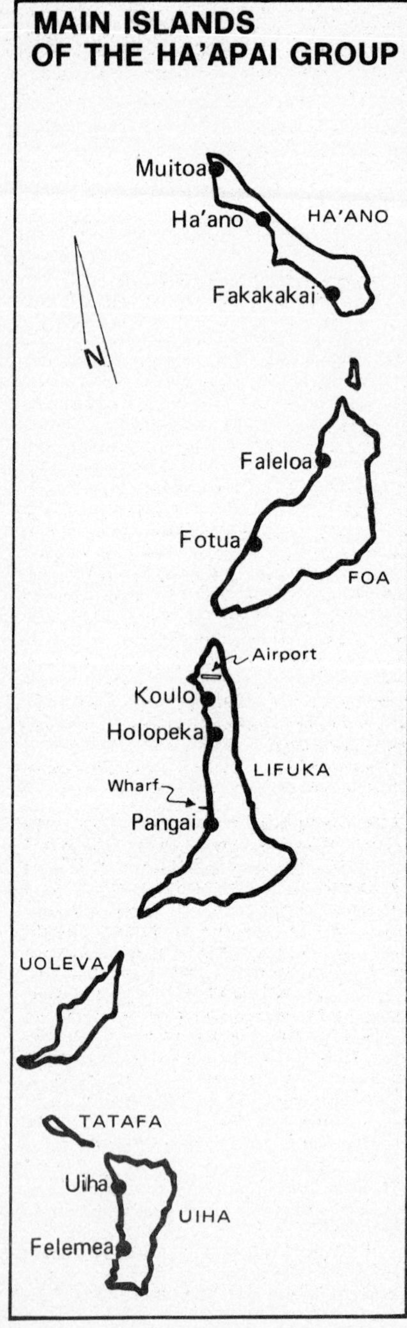

ment and Churches have other training schemes for young people and adults.

The Government provides apprenticeship training at the Ministry of Works; training of nurses at the Queen Salote School of Nursing conducted by the Ministry of Health; teacher training for primary and middle school teachers at Tonga Teachers' College conducted by the Ministry of Education; and police training at the Tonga Police Training School conducted by the Ministry of Police.

The Free Wesleyan Church of Tonga trains young men as farmers at Hango Agricultural College on 'Eua Island; and trains both men and women at Sia'atouyai Theological College. The Roman Catholic Church trains young men as farmers at Fualu Rural Training Centre.

Teacher training. The two-year course at the government Teachers' College for primary teachers had 140 enrolments in 1976.

Overseas studies. In 1976, 115 Tongans were studying overseas, mostly in New Zealand, Fiji, Australia and India.

LABOUR. There are insufficient opportunities for employment in Tonga. Of the population at December 1976 consisting of 46,029 men and 44,099 women, only 21,435 could be classed as 'economically active' (including those people partially employed). Of the people employed, 9,529 were in fisheries and forestry and 9,097 in other occupations. There is substantial under employment in agriculture and many people work only 1-2 days a week.

Outside those people categorised in the labour force, there were 68,693 Tongans. They included 14 years and under, 43,038; students (15 years and over), 6,781; physically disabled, 1,223; engaged in 'household work', 17,593; and others, 3,058.

The estimated visible rate of unemployment was about 13 per cent but if under-employment and those sporadically employed in household work had been taken into account, the rate would have been much higher.

The Kingdom, through its Five-Year Development Plans, is gradually becoming less dependent on subsistence agriculture. The economy is being diversified through industrial development and expansion of exports and the development of tourism. However, agriculture still constitutes the backbone of the economy.

Wages. Daily wage earnings of workmen range from $T2.25 for the unskilled to $T3.85 for skilled workers. A maximum wage control is enforced in Tonga.

Social security. While the decline in purchasing power affects the whole community, it is particularly hard on employees paid by the day who have no job security, sick pay, retirement benefits, etc. A feasibility study of introducing a contributory pension scheme to the Kingdom was carried out for the government in 1974 under the Australian South Pacific Aid Programme, but by 1977, none of the recommendations had been implemented.

Unions. There are no trade unions in Tonga and so far the government has done little to encourage their formation.

Overseas employment. New Zealand allows a number of Tongans to work for limited periods each year in major New Zealand cities. These men send some of their earnings back home or save for when they return.

HEALTH. For administrative purposes Tonga is divided into 10 health districts based on the location of the three hospitals and seven rural dispensaries. The hospitals are Vaiola (Tongatapu), Ngu (Vava'u), and Niu'ui (Ha'apai).

The three hospitals have 296 beds, while out-patient consultations create pressures on the hospital staffs. The seven rural dispensaries are at Mu'a, Kolovai, 'Eua, Nomuka, Ha'afeva, Niuatoputapu and Niuafo'ou. The dispensaries offer a limited range of services. Only three do not have in-patient wards or shelters.

A well-trained clinical staff caters for the needs of the public. However, there is generally a shortage of trained personnel. Health Ministry personnel in 1976 included 28 medical officers, 10 dental officers, 234 nurses, 37 public health nurses and 10 health inspectors.

Diseases. Although the general health of the community is good, the authorities wage a constant battle against several communicable diseases. The largest number of reported illnesses in 1976 were those of the influenza type with 12,982 reported. Gastro-intestinal infections (2,897) showed that there remains a need for improved hygiene and sanitation. Pneumonia and other acute respiratory infections cause many deaths among the young and the old. Reported incidence of other diseases in 1976 was: typhoid, 92; filariasis, 115 (now subject to WHO programme begun in 1976); tuberculosis 67 new cases; leprosy, 5 patients at the leprosarium, 64 receiving treatment at home, no new cases reported.

Family planning. A programme funded by UNFPA and New Zealand aid is encouraging family planning techniques. The Tongan birth rate was 13 per 1,000 in 1976, compared with 32 per 1,000 in 1964 and 25 per 1,000 in 1974.

THE LAND. The land area of 747 sq. km is in an ocean area of 259,000 sq km. There are about 150 islands, but only 45 are permanently inhabited. The largest island is Tongatapu, 260 sq. km in the south of the group.

From north to south, the kingdom extends 560 km from Niuatoputapu to 'Eua.

The highest point in the group is an extinct volcano, Kao, of 1,125m. Apart from 'Eua, the islands have no distinct mountains. Vava'u has hills of between 150 and 300m.

Climate. The climate varies, becoming cooler and drier in the south: Niuatoputapu has an average rainfall of 2,500mm, Vava'u has 2,000mm, while Tongatapu has 1,500mm. The average temperature also varies from 23.5 deg. C on Vava'u to 21 deg. C at Tongatapu (Nukualofa). Mean humidity is about 77 per cent. Hurricanes occur from time to time, and are more frequent in the northern islands.

Most of the islands are of raised coral, with an overlying soil developed from volcanic ash, which is fertile. The remainder of the islands, generally forming a western chain, are volcanic. These are relatively young islands, and soil development is still progressing.

Flora and fauna. There is a limited but interesting variety of land birds – doves, rails, starlings, kingfishers, owls, cuckoos, shrikes, bulbuls, whistlers, honey-eaters, purple swamp hens and swiftlets. On 'Eua are two of the most beautiful birds in the Pacific, the red-breasted musk parrot and the blue-crowned lory. Red-tailed and white-tailed tropic birds make their home in the cliffs.

Niuafo'ou has endemic birds including the incubator bird. Apart from the common reef heron, the shore birds in Tonga are transient. These include the golden plover, wandering tattler, long-billed curlew and bar-tailed godwit. Seabirds seen in Tongan waters include varieties of noddies and other terns, the frigate bird and the muttonbird.

Flying foxes cling to large trees in the village of Kolovai by day and fly off at night to forage for food. They are sacred and protected by custom. They may be hunted only by members of the Royal family.

The waters around Tonga are renowned for their variety of game fish. They include barracuda, tuna, marlin and sailfish.

Natural bushland consists mainly of pandanus, araucaria, etc.

Land Tenure. The Tongan system leads to many problems of land ownership and the right to land use. A Nuku'alofa seminar in September 1975 on land tenure and migration called for a Royal Commission to review the land tenure system.

The Tongan land system is, in many respects, unique. All land is the property of the Crown, but large estates have been divided among the nobles. Every Tongan, when he attains the age of 16 years and thereby becomes a taxpayer, is entitled to a bush allotment of about 3 ha and a town site of about .16 ha. He obtains the grant on application to the Minister for Lands. He pays an annual rental of T$3.20 for his allotment and no rent for his town site. The Minister grants the allotment from the estate of the noble where the applicant lives, and subject to agreement by the noble. Otherwise the grant may be made from government land if available. Provision is made in the law for eviction for non-payment of rent or for failing to comply with the planting laws. The interest of Tongans in land, whether they are the holders of hereditary estates or of tax allotments, is lifelong and alienation is expressly forbidden. Leasing, whether to Tongans or to Europeans, is subject to the consent of Cabinet. A tax allotment can be transferred to widow or heirs on death of the holder.

The law provides that a Tongan, instead of applying for a tax allotment, with its definite area, may apply for an ordinary lease. An allotment holder may also be granted a lease, and a condition precedent to any grant is a well-cultivated allotment.

Shortage of land is a major problem and a large number of male taxpayers are without tax allotments. The nobles may retain a portion of their holding for their own use, although the law does not specify the area. Since 1945, they have been able to lease only 5 per cent of their land to foreigners, the remaining 95 per cent being reserved for Tongans. This system does not apply to crown land, but all leases are subject to Cabinet approval, through the Minister's recommendation, and are reviewed by Government every five years.

Government surveyors are constantly employed – mostly in defining hereditary estates and in demarcating tax allotments.

Although the rental of allotments is very low, every year some holders are taken to court for non-payment of rent.

Of the total land area of 747 sq. km, ownership in 1976 was as follows – tax and town allotments – 66 per cent; government leases 0.9 per cent; leased by Tongans 0.6 per cent; leased by Commodity boards 0.1 per cent; government land (uninhabited islands, forest reserves etc.) 11 per cent; estates of hereditary nobles 7 per cent; foreign leases 1 per cent; charitable leases (church) 2 per cent; lakes and internal waters 4 per cent; Telekitonga and Telekitokelau Islands 7 per cent.

Although it is not always possible to provide them with land, the theory is that Tongans shall take part in agriculture, which is the basis of the economy. By law, every holder of an allotment is required to plant 200 coconuts within 12 months of acquisition, and maintain it in a weed-free condition.

PRIMARY PRODUCTION. Copra and bananas provide the basis of the economy. Both are subject to the vagaries of overseas markets. Copra growers enjoyed a good year in 1974, but in 1975 they had to export more than twice as much as they did in 1974, to earn about the same amount.

Copra. While the annual copra export figures vary considerably, the average is about 10,000 tonnes. Copra production could reach 30,000 tonnes a year, but for the many other local uses of the coconut. Copra exports in 1974 were 8,107 tonnes, but jumped to 18,407 tonnes in 1975, and accounted for 44.6 per cent of all exports.

Tonga ceased to export copra in November, 1978, since when all copra has gone to Oil Mills of Tonga Ltd at Maufanga where the oil is extracted and exported. The resultant coconut meal is used for stockfeed. The mill has crushing capacity of between 12,000 and 15,000 tonnes annually. As an incentive to planters, Oil Mills of Tonga pays 5 per cent above the world price. This is payable to the Tonga Commodities Board which, in turn, passes it on to the planters as an incentive payment.

The coconut has been subject to the depredations of the rhinoceros beetle for more than 10 years. It has been cleared from Niuatoputapu but is now on Ha'apai. It does considerable damage in Tongatapu and Vava'u.

Bananas. Banana production and earnings, except in a few isolated cases, have been declining slowly for several years. A number of catastrophes, such as hurricanes and plant disease, disheartened growers, who turned to other crops. New Zealand, the biggest market for Island bananas, is turning more to Ecuador as a supplier. Although production is below a former peak, banana exports in 1976 were 148,870 cases, compared with 116,096 cases in 1975.

Vegetables. Other crops produced for export include watermelons, tomatoes and capsicum as well as vanilla beans.

Sales of vanilla beans by co-operatives in 1977 were worth $68,000 compared with $16,000 in 1976. They were expected to exceed $100,000 in 1978. The Department of Agriculture and private individuals are curing vanilla and still more farmers are starting co-operatives and curing the beans as a group because co-operatives pay a higher price to farmers.

The kava root is also a significant export. Lime tree planting has been encouraged in preparation for a possible juice industry.

Commodities Board. Early 1974 saw the abolition of the Produce and Copra Boards and the formation of the Commodities Board to handle the marketing of local produce.

Livestock. Cattle farmers in Tonga receive a subsidy as an incentive to increase the cattle population and improve quality. The objective is to substantially reduce the imports of beef. There were 6,856 cattle in 1976.

There is also a subsidy for poultry farmers, aimed at lifting egg and poultry meat production to meet local requirements. In 1976, there were 100,107 birds and the layers provided 66,486 dozen eggs.

The subsidy for the pig industry takes the form of provision by the Department of Agriculture of building materials for piggeries, livestock, a water supply, meat meal, etc. An integrated piggery was opened at the village of Tu'anekivale early in 1979. The cost of $45,000 was provided by the Foundation for the Peoples of the South Pacific. Waste digesters will be installed to obtain methane gas from pig manure.

A census showed that in 1976 there were about 34,700 pigs.

Pigs are probably the most important livestock in Tonga. As a sucker, the pig is a traditional dish. It is estimated that 2,000-3,000 suckling pigs are slaughtered each Sunday to provide the weekly feast. On national festive occasions as many as 8,000 pigs will be cooked for a single feast attended by thousands of people.

The horse is important in agriculture, and for transport although it is rarely used for cultivation, most of which is by long-handled hoe. The 1976 census confirmed that there were more than 7,000 horses.

Fisheries. Several new projects have been started to develop deep water fisheries, mussel and oyster experiments and aquaculture. A new Fisheries Extension Centre is being established at Vava'u; Japan and Australia have provided new vessels for long line and live-bait fishing for skipjack.

In addition, fisheries survey work has been conducted under the FAO – UNDP marine resources development project. New Zealand scientists have assisted in the mussel and oyster experimental projects, while Japanese specialists have helped in pearl oyster experiments in Vava'u. Aquaculture ponds have been built for farming bait fish.

The kingdom's turtle population has declined to critical levels and stern control measures on their capture have been urged.

Total fish landings in Nuku'alofa for local consumption were estimated at 620 tonnes in 1976. Imports of tinned and processed fish that year totalled 204 tonnes, mostly from Japan. The kingdom exported 9.5 tonnes of Albacore tuna.

Whaling. Tonga is one of the few places in the world where men, from economic necessity, still hunt the humpback whale from small boats, using hand harpoons. The main whaling season is from July to October. The sight of two boats sailing into Nuku'alofa flying a black flag indicates a whale in tow, although the event is becoming rarer. People flock from all over the island to buy the meat. Every bit of the whale is eaten, including the skin and blubber.

Forestry. The Forestry Division of the Department of Agriculture has its headquarters at 'Eua Island. The government supervises the use of wood from native and planted forests and operates a sawmill at 'Eua. A sawmill for coconut timber began operating in July 1976.

MANUFACTURING AND MINING. The current development plan has emphasised the development of industries as a means of diversifying Tonga's economic activities. As an encouragement to local and overseas investors, the government is providing attractive fiscal incentives (such as a five-year tax holiday) and 'certain measures of protection' against competing imports. Several small industries have been established in recent years. A manufacturer of plastic pipes set up business early in 1976. Production now meets the country's needs. Two charcoal enterprises came into existence late in 1975. They export their product to New Zealand. Another factory rolls corrugated iron.

Other enterprises include handicrafts, industrial-type chicken-breeding, and a small canning factory.

The desiccated coconut industry is assuming greater importance and in recent years has been rivalling bananas as an earner of overseas income. Most of it is exported to New Zealand, Australia and the U.K. Fiji takes small quantities. Total exports in recent years have varied from 1,538 tonnes in 1970 to 1,100 tonnes in 1976. In 1975, exports provided 10.1 per cent of total exports.

A coir-processing plant near Nuku'alofa produces brushes and mats etc. for local consumption and export.

A foreign firm produces ferro-cement lighters and other products.

Major construction work and housing are undertaken by the Ministry of Works, which also sells concrete blocks, while the Tonga Construction Company was taken over in 1974 by the Commodities Board.

Other light processing is carried out by co-operative societies such as Tonga Feeds Manufacturing Society, providing stock feed, and the Leimatu'a Vanilla Society, curing vanilla in the Vava'u group.

In December 1977, the Asian Development Bank approved a loan for $370,000 to Tonga to provide the infrastructure for a Small Industries Centre. It is located about 1 km from Queen Salote Wharf on a 5 ha block in Ma'ufanga village on the outskirts of Nuku'alofa. About 24 industrial lots are available. The centre was opened by the King in May, 1980.

Factories already established by opening day were, knitwear, tubular furniture and bicycle assembly, wire mesh and paper products.

During 1978, 25 new companies were registered in Tonga, and brought the total number of registered companies in the kingdom to 94.

Construction of a bulk-oil storage depot in the Vava'u Islands north of the main island is expected to help increase economic activity and to end fuel shortages in the Vava'u group.

In 1978, conditional approval was granted for a number of new industries, including the manufacture of leather goods, sandals, thongs (for export) and jute/hessian bags; bareboat operations in Vavau; opal cutting; stationary products; footwear manufacture; sausage manufacture; automobile assembly, body building and fibreglass boat building; clothing manufacture and soft drink and ice cream manufacture.

Oil. The country is hoping for the discovery of oil. An exploration consortium, set up in 1970, gave up the search about two years later. Then early in 1976 the government and representatives of Webb Resources Inc, Denver, US, signed an agreement for further exploration. Early in 1977, Webb announced that drilling would begin soon.

The possible existence of manganese nodules on the seabed is also of economic interest.

A 3,700 km cruise, designed to explore Tonga's offshore resources was organised in 1976 by the Tongan Department of Lands and Survey and the Committee for the Co-ordination of Joint Prospecting for Mineral Resources in South Pacific Offshore Areas (CCOP/SOPAC). Offshore surveys continued in 1977.

TOURISM. The tourist industry is a major contributor to the Tongan economy. In 1978 earnings were estimated at more than $3.9 million compared with $3.3 million in 1977. Total visitors in 1978 were 12 090, an increase of 10 per cent on 1977.

TONGA — TOURIST ARRIVALS

	Air	Sea
1974	6,403	36,731
1975	6,770	45,824
1976	9,312	34,251
1977	11,023	28,324
1978	12,090	34,545
1979	12,126	29,990

Extensive promotion in Japan is expected to result in a large increase in Japanese tourists.

LOCAL COMMERCE. There were 28 societies on the Register of Co-operative Societies at the end of 1976 the sixth full year of co-operative development. The co-operatives include produce market/consumer, thrift and credit societies as well as manufacturing enterprises. Although agriculture is the major resource of the country, little progress has been made on the formation of co-operatives in that area, since the Commodities Board deals directly with farmers(However increasing interest has been shown in consumer co-operation.

Markets. Organised markets in Nuku'alofa: the Vuna market with its cold storage offers meat, fish and ice while Talamahu market offers the produce of local growers.

OVERSEAS TRADE. Tonga regularly has an adverse balance of trade, offset to some extent by invisible earnings from such sources as remittances from overseas, tourism, donations, gifts, etc. In 1976 the adverse balance of trade was $T8.3 million. The total value of imports and exports in recent years is shown in the accompanying table.

TONGA — OVERSEAS TRADE
(In $T million)

	1975	1976	1977	1978	1979
Imports	13.0	11.7	18.0	22.3	26.2
Exports	6.0	3.04	6.2	4.8	6.1

The EEC countries were Tonga's best customers, taking 58.1 per cent of total exports in 1976. New Zealand was next with 29 per cent and Fiji 6.5 per cent.

The level of invisible earnings in recent years was: 1970-71 $T2.2 million; 1972-73 $T3.8 million; 1974-75, $T10.7 million; 1975-76, $T8.8 million.

Tonga's main imports are flour, fresh and canned meat, canned fish, dairy products, tobacco, cotton piece goods, drapery, motor cars, motor cycles and petroleum products. Australia and New Zealand are the biggest suppliers, chiefly of food.

The values of main export commodities in recent years have been as shown in the accompanying table.

TONGA — EXPORT COMMODITIES
(in $T'000)

	1976	1977	1978	1979
Copra	1,178	3,931.4	2,980	1,687
Desiccated coconut (bulk)	356	866.9	715.7	1,050
Bananas	278	401.5	182	301.3
Watermelons	179	137.4	154.6	107.3
Vegetables	212	89.9	63.7	29.4

Customs tariff. Tonga has abolished the Commonwealth Preferential Tariff and all imports come under one rate of duty, some examples of which are given below (from May 30, 1980)

TONGA — CUSTOMS TARIFFS

	Duty
Live animals & poultry (other than Zoo animals, dogs and cats)	free
Paper & Paperboard	15%
Hand tools	free
Chassis fitted with engine and bodies	30%

Tonga increased the customs duties on luxury goods by 50 per cent in February 1976, affecting items such as beer, ale, stout, sparkling wines, cigars and cigarettes.

FINANCE. The principal sources of revenue are, import dues, port and service tax, postal and philatelic revenue, interest and rents. Poll tax was abolished on July 1, 1977 when the Kingdom adopted the PAYE tax system. Most export dues were abolished in 1975. However, about $NZ45,000 a year was expected from an airport departure tax imposed in January 1978.

Budget. Recurrent revenue and expenditure in recent years are as shown in the accompanying table.

TONGA — REVENUE AND EXPENDITURE
(In $T million)

	Revenue	Expenditure
1964-65	1.7	1.6
1970-71	2.7	3.0
1974-75	5.53	4.77
1975-76	5.05	5.87
1976-77	6.5	7.0
1977-78	8.6	8.5

External aid. Tonga receives overseas aid from Britain, New Zealand, and Australia. The Asian Development Bank has provided the following assistance since Tonga became a member in March 1972. A special funds loan of $US1.3 million for telecommunications development, $US370,000 for the Small Industries Centre, and technical assistance grants for a road improvements and maintenance study, plan preparation and project identification, the Small Industries Centre and the development of the Tonga Development Bank, amounting to $US672,000.

TREASURY INVESTMENTS: At June 30, 1977, the Treasury held investments and overseas government securities of a nominal value of $T1.2 million, and T$1.7 million at June 30, 1978. Government shareholdings were as follows:

	Value T$	
	1977	1978
Air Pacific	68,760	71,745
Pacific Navigation Co. Ltd.	765,429	—
Kintail Honey (Tonga) Ltd.	4,000	4,000
Bank of Tonga	140,000	140,000
Shipping Corporation of Polynesia Ltd	—	6,000
Pacific Forum Line Ltd	—	11,808
Tonga Development Bank	—	450,820

Development expenditure for the year ended June 30, 1978 amounted to T$1.9 million.

Currency. Tonga's currency consists of pa'anga ($T banknotes) and seniti (cents). The banknotes are in denominations of 10, 5, 2 and 1.5 pa'anga. The coins are for 1 pa'anga, 50, 20, 10, 5, 2 and 1 seniti. Tonga converted to decimal currency in 1967. Australian currency was used before the introduction of Tongan currency.

In April, 1963, Tonga issued gold coins known as "koula" (Tongan for gold), a half-koula and a quarter-koula, worth respectively £A20, £10 and £5. These were mainly collectors' items and were not in circulation. Four gold and three silver coins were minted in November 1975 to mark Tonga's centenary.

Banks. Tonga's own bank, the Bank of Tonga, opened for business on July 1, 1974. The Government Savings Bank was wound up the day before, and depositor liability was transferred to the new bank. The Bank of Tonga is owned jointly by the Government of Tonga, the Bank of Hawaii, the Bank of NZ and the Bank of NSW. Foreigners are allowed to open accounts, using a code number known only to the owner of the account and one or two bank officers.

The Tonga Development Bank was established by the government as a multi-purpose development finance institution in June 1977. Since then, the TBD has received three supporting loans from the Asian Development Bank.

During its first 11 months of business, the TDB estimated that its lending had generated the equivalent of 200 full-time jobs in agriculture and a further 242 jobs in industry and business.

The authorised capital of the TDB is $T1 million and of initial investment, the Tongan government provided $T599,000 while the Bank of Tonga provided a further $T50,000. In December 1978, the TDB received a 40 year loan from the Asian Development Bank of $US1.5 million. This was to be used for financing manufacturing industries including small-scale industries (25 per cent), service industries (20 per cent), and smallholder agricultural development projects (55 per cent). This loan was expected to provide about 37 per cent of the TDB's estimated foreign currency needs for the period 1979-81.

In the first 16 months to December 31, 1978 the bank approved 2,313 loans totalling $T1,574,616, the majority being of individual amounts no greater than $T1,000.

Overseas investment. To attract more investors, Tonga, in October 1977, adopted an industrial incentives policy with tax holidays, depreciation and accounting concessions, customs duty exemptions and repatriation of funds. Immigration assistance, promotional aid, finance through the new Development Bank and land availability are also offered. The incentives operate through licensing of both local and foreign enterprises setting up processing and assembly or tourist-related industries.

Central Planning. The Third Five-Year Development Plan (DP III) (1975-80) was prepared with technical assistance from the Asian Development Bank. Of the $T49.6m envisaged total investment expenditure of DP III, about $T31m was to be for development. A mid-term review of DP III was published in 1978 and showed a two-year development expenditure of $T11.5m. Major projects completed or progressing in January 1979 included the Small Industries Centre, an Automatic Telephone System, a Mariculture Centre, formation of the Tonga Development Bank and several agricultural improvement schemes. Projects expected to commence during 1979 include a national road-improvement programme, extensions to the main wharf and construction of a new desiccated coconut factory.

A Fourth Development Plan (1980-85) is now in the early stages of preparation.

Stamps. The Philatelic and Numismatic Section of the Tongan Treasury reports that the sale of commemorative issues of stamps and coins continues to attract considerable overseas interest and thus contribute to local revenue.

TRANSPORT. There were 300 km of formed roads throughout the country: 190 in Tongatapu, 74 in Vava'u, 20 in Ha'apai and 16 in 'Eua. One hundred and fifty-five km are classed as main road — 52 km with bitumen surface and 103 with a coral surface. The 40 km are classed as either secondary road or town bitumen and are sealed, and the remaining roads are unsealed secondary coral or earth.

Vehicles. The number of vehicles licensed in 1976 was 1,650 and included 438 private cars, 220 motor cycles and 405 trucks.

Overseas airlines. Air Pacific uses BAC 111s on flights from Suva to New Zealand, via Tonga's international airport of Fua'amotu. Air Pacific and Polynesian Airlines operate regional services with HS748s. Two Polynesian Airlines flights each week return to Apia via Niue Island.

Air New Zealand planned a new service for 1980

between Auckland and Apia via Tonga. South Pacific Island Airways operate three flights per week to Vava'u, Ha'apai, Nuku'alofa and 'Eua, they return the same day to Pago Pago.

Domestic Airline. South Pacific Islands Airways took over operations of the local air service in September, 1976, from the Tonga Internal Air Service (also known as Air Vavau) which had been operating for four years. SPIA also connects Tonga with Pago Pago (American Samoa).

Airports. There are four airfields in Tonga – Fua'amotu (Tongatapu), Vava'u, 'Eua and Ha'apai. At Fua'amotu, which is 22 km from Nuku'alofa, the main runway is sealed for 2,100 m with clearways at both ends. The Vava'u airstrip is 1,067 m and 23 m wide. The Salote Pilolevu Airfield on Lifuka Island, Ha'apai, has a 820 m coral-base runway while 'Eua has a 689 m grass runway.

International and regional flights are handled at Fua'amotu which is to be upgraded under the current Five-Year Plan.

Port facilities. Ports of entry are Nuku'alofa, Pangai, Neiafu and Niuatoputapu.

Tonga has two good harbours at Nuku'alofa and Neiafu (Vava'u). Both handle overseas ships. Nuku'alofa is enclosed by coral reefs and islands. Queen Salote wharf is 100 m long and has an apron of 10 m. There is no limit to the size of ship that can be handled as there is a depth of 13 m alongside. The current Five Year Plan provides for extensions to this wharf and construction of a slipway and docking facilities.

At Neiafu, ships drawing less than 7 m and no longer than 120 m may berth. The wharf is in the inner harbour, which is enclosed. Ships of unlimited tonnage and draught may anchor in the sheltered harbour anchorage off 'Utulei Point, which is about 2 km from the wharf.

At Lifuka, Ha'apai, large ships anchor about 1 km from the jetty.

The appointment of customs/transit agents has been urged to avoid much of the wastage due to poor port handling and storage of goods.

Shipping services. The Pacific Navigation Co of Tonga Ltd (PNT), jointly owned by the Government of Tonga and Lauritzen, operates internal and overseas shipping services. One ship runs a regular return service from Nuku'alofa to Sydney. On return voyages the ship calls at Fiji and Western Samoa and sometimes Norfolk Island. Pacific Navigation also has one ship on an Auckland-Nuku'alofa service. Warner Pacific Line uses two conventional ships to provide a service to Auckland, and one goes to Timaru-Lyttelton. The Forum Line operates between Sydney, Brisbane, Fiji, the Samoas and Tonga.

Columbus Line, of West Germany, announced in March 1980 an extension of its services to Tonga.

COMMUNICATIONS. Internal communications using telephone, telex, telegraph and data were being carried by satellite circuits, with an Earth Station operated by Cable and Wireless Ltd in Nuku'alofa. At the end of February 1979, there were 1500 automatic telephone lines which had replaced the former manual exchange.

Radio-telephone is used to communicate with the inland, from Nuku'alofa, and also overseas via Suva and to Pago Pago.

Radio. Broadcasting is administered by the Tonga Broadcasting Commission. The studio is in Nuku'alofa. The station, A3Z, is known throughout the South Pacific as the "Call of the Friendly Islands". It is one of the most powerful in the South Pacific, and may be heard in New Zealand and the nearer island groups. Programmes are devoted to the work of local artists, and include traditional Tongan music, stories and legends, public events, interviews with visiting personalities, etc. The service runs advertising in Tongan, English and Samoan. It broadcasts personal messages to areas not covered by the Telegraph and Telephone Department. Regular bulletins covering overseas and local news are broadcast in Tongan and English.

Newspapers. There is one weekly newspaper in Tonga, the "Chronicle", published each Thursday in Tongan and English. The "Chronicle" covers items of local and overseas interest, and also includes commercial advertising.

In addition, the Agriculture Department publishes a quarterly "Tokanga".

WATER AND ELECTRICITY. The electrical system is 230V AC 50 cycles, generated by diesel motors.

The water in Nuku'alofa is safe to drink. Elsewhere it should be boiled, unless advised otherwise.

The Tonga Electric Power Board and the Tonga Water Board are responsible for these two services.

PERSONALITIES AND ORGANISATIONS

GOVERNMENT

PRIVY COUNCIL

President: King Taufa'ahau Tupou IV

Prime Minister Minister of Agriculture and Marines: H.R.H. Prince Fatefehi Tu'ipelehake

Deputy Prime Minister and Minister of Lands & Survey: Baron Tuita

Minister of Works, Education and Aviation: Hon. Dr S. L. Kavaliku

Minister of Police: Hon. 'Akau'ola

Minister of Health and Acting Minister of Finance: Dr S. Tapa

Minister of Labour, Commerce & Industries: Baron Vaea

Minister for Foreign Affairs and Defence: H.R.H. Prince Tupouto'a

Governor of Vava'u: Hon. S. Ma'afu Tupou

Governor of Ha'apai: Hon. Ve'ehala

MEMBERS OF THE LEGISLATIVE ASSEMBLY

The Speaker: Hon. Ma'afu

Nobles Representatives of Tongatapu, 'Eua, Niuatoputapu and Niuafo'ou: Hons. Ma'afu, Vaha'i & Tu'ivakano
Nobles Representatives of Ha'apai: Hons. Malupo and Tu'iha'ateiho
Nobles Representatives of Vava'u: Hons. Luani and Fuliavi
Peoples Representatives of Tongatapu, 'Eua, Niuatoputapu and Niuafo'ou: Taniela Manu, Mrs Papiloa Foliaki, Tomiteau Finau
Peoples Representatives of Ha'apai: Tofa'i-mala'e'aloa Ramsay
Peoples Representative of Vava'u: Masoa Paasi, Palavilala Tapueluelu
Also includes all Privy Councillors

JUDICIARY
Judge of the Supreme Court: Puisne Judge Justice Henry Hill

CENTRAL ADMINISTRATION
Secretary to Government: Taniela H. Tufui
Deputy Seceretary to Government: Sione Kite
Private Secretary to H.M.: F. M. Tongilava
DEPARTMENTAL HEADS
Director of Agriculture: T. Simiki
Government Auditor: P. B. Collacott
Crown Solicitor: T. Tupou
Collector of Customs: S. Havea
Director of Education: S. N. Fiefia
Secretary for Foreign Affairs & Defence: S. T. T. Tupou
Secretary for Finance: O. A. Matoto
Harbourmaster: Capt. S. Fotu
Director of Health: Dr S. Foliaki
Deputy Commissioner for Inland Revenue: S. T. 'Alipate
Secretary for Labour, Commerce & Industries: S. Raghavan
Secretary for Lands, Survey & Natural Resources: S. L. Tongilava
Chief Superintendent of Police: H. H. Tonga
Chief Postmaster: A. Filimone
Chief Planning Officer: J. C. Cocker
Government Printer: V. M. Misi
Superintendent of Prisons: S. M. Fifita
Government Statistician: A. H. Gould
Superintendent of Telegraphs and Telephones: J. Durkin
Visitors Bureau Tourist Officer: R Marriot
Director of Works: D. Keith

STATUTORY BOARDS
Director, Commodities Board: S. Hurell
Manager, Tonga Broadcasting Commission: T. Fusimalohi
Manager, Tonga Electric Power Board: J. C. Bernabe
Manager, Tonga Water Board: M. C. Ramos
Manager, Tonga Development Bank: G. Johns
Manager, Oil Mills of Tonga: M. Soakai

DIPLOMATIC
Australian, High Commissioner: Miss Maris King M.B.E.
Belgium, Ambassador: M. L. Oliver (resident in Wellington, New Zealand).
Canada, High Commissioner: Mrs. I. Johnson (resident in Wellington).
Chile, Ambassador: Sergiou Fuenzalida (resident in Wellington); Charge d'Affaires Mr F. Marull.
China, Republic of, Ambassador: Cheng Kao
Denmark, Ambassador: Mr M. Warberg (in Canberra, Australia).
E.E.C. Commission delegate: Mr E. Stahn (in Suva).
Fiji, Special representative to the Prime Minister: Mr J. Cavalevu (in Suva).
France, Ambassador: M. J. Guerry (in Wellington). Honorary Consul in Tonga is Rev. Fr. George Callet.
Germany, Federal Republic of, Ambassador: Dr. H. A. Steger (in Wellington); Honorary Consul in Tonga: Mr R. Sanft.
Great Britain & Northern Ireland, High Commissioner: Mr H. A. Arthington-Davy
India, High Commissioner: Mrs S. Kochar (in Suva).
Israel, Ambassador: Mr A. Kidron (in Canberra).
Italy, Ambassador: Mr R. Gesini (in Wellington).
Japan, Ambassador: Mr H. Ohtaka (in Suva).
Korea, Republic of, Ambassador: Mr Chun S. Lee (in Wellington)
Naru, Honorary Consul: Mr C. Riechelmann
Netherlands, Royal Neth. Ambassador: Mr Kernkamp (in Wellington)
New Zealand, High Commissioner: Mr R. Gates
Papua New Guinea, High Commissioner: Dr. Ako Toua (resident in Suva).
Sweden, Ambassador: Mr G. Gunnar (in Wellington).
U.S.A., Ambassador: Mr W. Bodde (in Suva).
Tonga High Commissioner to the United Kingdom: I. Faletau, also Ambassador to France, Federal Republic of Germany, Luxembourg, Netherlands, Belgium, E.E.C. and the United States of America.
Hon. Consul to Hong Kong: Thomas Chen
Hon. Consul to San Francisco: Mr F. Kohlenburg
Hon. Consul to Australia: W. S. Waterhouse
Hon. Consul to Japan: R. Sasakawa
CHURCH DIGNITARIES
President of the Free Wesleyan Church of Tonga, and Royal Chaplain: H. Mo'ungaloa
Roman Catholic: Bishop Patelisio Finau

HISTORY. Recent archaeological research has revealed that the Tongan archipelago had its human inhabitants at least 3,000 years ago. The earliest radiocarbon date so far established is 1140 BC.

The Tongans of those days were makers of elaborately decorated Lapita pottery, like that also found in Fiji. But a few centuries later they were making only plain ware. A small amount of pottery was still in use when the first European explorers visited Tonga, but it is not certain whether it was then being made in Tonga or was imported from Fiji.

There is no doubt, however, that Tonga had a highly developed social system long before the arrival of Europeans.

Originally, the paramount ruler was called the Tu'i Tonga. The first such leader, who is estimated to have flourished about AD 950, was considered to be the son of the sun god Tangaloa. He and his successors for about 500 years had both spiritual and temporal power. But a series of murders is said to have caused the 24th Tu'i Tonga to hand over his temporal powers to his brother, and a new dynasty was created under the title of Tu'i Ha'atakalaua.

About the beginning of the 17th century, a third dynasty, with the title of Tu'i Kanokupolu (a name indicating a link with Upolu, Samoa), was created to administer the country. Thereafter, some historians say, the position of Tu'i Ha'alakalaua gradually became redundant, while the office of Tu'i Tonga became increasingly ceremonial. Thus it was that when the first Europeans became acquainted with Tonga, the most powerful person in the land was the Tu'i Kanokupolu.

Eventually, when the religious functions of the Tu'i Tonga were rendered obsolete by the adoption of Christianity, all the remaining functions of the three most important titles were merged into one, that of Tu'i Kanokupolu; and the holder of that title was the sovereign of all Tonga, as is the case today.

European Discovery. The first Europeans to sight any of the islands of the Tongan archipelago were members of the Dutch expedition of Schouten and Le Maire. They came upon the northern outliers of Tafahi and Niuatoputapu in 1616 while crossing the Pacific to the East Indies. Twenty-seven years later, in 1643, their countryman, Abel Janszoon Tasman, approached the archipelago from the south. Sailing with the ships 'Heemskerck' and 'Zeehaan', he sighted the southernmost island, Ata, before coming upon Eua and Tongatapu, which he named Middleburgh and Amsterdam respectively. Tasman spent three days at Tongatapu, and a week at Nomuka to the northward, taking in provisions. Nomuka was named Rotterdam.

In 1767, 125 years after Tasman's visit, Captain Samuel Wallis, the discoverer of Tahiti, came upon the two northern islands seen by Schouten and Le Maire. Unaware of their prior discovery, he gave the name Boscawen to Tafahi and Keppel to Niuatoputapu – names they bore on European charts for the next century or so.

Cook's Voyages. In October, 1773, Captain James Cook made the first of three visits to Tonga. Approaching the group from the Society Islands, he anchored briefly at Eua (which he recognised as Tasman's Middleburgh) before going on to Tongatapu. Five days at Tongatapu gave him and some of his companions the first opportunity to write detailed descriptions of Tongan life.

In the following June, Cook returned to Tonga and spent several days trading amicably at Nomuka.

Cook's third visit was made on his final voyage in 1777. He then spent two and a half months at Nomuka, Lifuka, Tongatapu and Eua, during which much valuable information was obtained about the inhabitants. He named the Lifuka (Ha'apai) group the Friendly Islands although, ironically, there was a plot by the Tongans to kill Cook during his sojourn at Lifuka.

In 1781, a Spaniard, Francisco Antonio Mourelle, chanced upon some of the northern islands of Tonga in attempting to sail from the Philippines to Mexico during the wrong season of the year. His landfalls included Fonualei, Late and Vavau, of which he was the European discoverer. Cook had heard about Vavau but did not see it. Mourelle spent a fortnight trading for supplies at Vavau before picking his way through the more southerly islands in the hope of finding a favourable wind.

About six years later, in 1787, the French explorer, La Perouse, reached Tonga from Samoa and touched briefly at Niuatoputapu, Vavau and Tongatapu.

In April, 1789, the celebrated mutiny in the 'Bounty' took place off the volcano island of Tofua, a few weeks after the 'Bounty' had arrived from Tahiti with a cargo of breadfruit. Her captain, William Bligh, and 18 other men were cast adrift in an open boat. They landed on Tofua in the hope of obtaining provisions. But the Tongans attacked them, killing one man, and Bligh had to head for Timor in his open boat empty-handed.

In 1791, Captain Edward Edwards, of HMS 'Pandora', who had been sent from England to find and arrest the 'Bounty' mutineers, passed through the Tongan archipelago on two occasions in the course of his search. Two years later, the French explorer, d'Entrecasteaux, visited Tongatapu seeking traces of his countryman, La Perouse, who had disappeared after leaving Botany Bay in January, 1788.

Malaspina's arrival. Barely two months after the departure of the d'Entrecasteaux expedition, two Spanish ships, 'Descubierta' and 'Atrevida', anchored at Vavau under the command of Captain Alessandro Malaspina. As Vavau was considered a Spanish possession by virtue of Mourelle's discovery, Malaspina formally annexed it and buried a message in a bottle to attest the fact. Although Malaspina and some of his officers wrote exceptionally interesting accounts of what they saw and learned at Vavau, these have never been translated from Spanish.

Malaspina was the last European explorer to visit Tonga before the arrival of the first permanent European settlers. These were six deserters from the American ship 'Otter' who went ashore at Ha'apai and Eua in 1796. A year later, the first European missionaries — 10 lay members of the London Missionary Society — were landed at Tongatapu from the ship 'Duff'. Three of these men were murdered in 1799 during a civil war between followers and opponents of the Tu'i Kanokupolu of the time. Six of the others eventually escaped to Sydney. The tenth man, George Vason, abandoned his faith and lived among the Tongans until 1804. He later published a book about his experiences.

Fighting was incessant in one or another of the Tongan islands until 1809. During this time an unscrupulous chief called Finau Ulukalala gained control over Vavau and Ha'apai, and sometimes ascendancy in Tongatapu as well.

In 1806, the Tongans cut off the English privateer 'Port-au-Prince' at Ha'apai and killed many of her crew. One of the survivors, a youth called William Mariner, lived in Tonga under Finau's protection for the next four years. His record of Tongan life, 'An Account of the Natives of the Tonga Islands', first published in 1817, is one of the classics of South Seas literature.

After Finau's death in 1809, most of the fighting stopped in Vavau and Ha'apai, although it went on spasmodically in Tongatapu. Meanwhile, the three royal titles had fallen into abeyance, and the islands were ruled by a variety of lesser chiefs.

The title of Tu'i Ha'atakalaua became vacant in 1799 after the murder of the incumbent. No Tu'i Tonga was appointed between 1800 and 1827. And even the office of Tu'i Kanokupolu was vacant for much of that period.

However, in 1820, a new star appeared on Tonga's horizon — a man who was to acquire all three royal titles and so create the modern kingdom of Tonga. This new figure was Taufa'ahau, whose father, the Tu'i Kanokupolu, died in 1820. Taufa'ahau thereupon became chief of Ha'apai.

First missionaries. While Taufa'ahau was consolidating his position in Ha'apai, several new missionaries arrived in Tonga. The first, a Wesleyan, was the Rev. William Lawry, who settled on Tongatapu in 1822 and stayed for 16 months. He was followed in 1826 by two Tahitian missionaries; then came two more Wesleyans, the Revs. John Thomas and John Hutchison.

Although all the early evangelists found much to discourage them, they and others who came later gradually persuaded some of the Tongans to take heed of their teachings. Among these was Taufa'ahau, who was baptised in 1834, a year after he had defeated and expelled from Ha'apai several chiefs, including the Tu'i Tonga, who had opposed his rule. Under Taufa'ahau's influence, the whole of Ha'apai became Christian. And when Taufa'ahau succeeded soon afterwards to the chieftainship of Vavau, the people of that archipelago followed his example also. Meanwhile, although some of the Tongatapu chiefs had adopted Christianity, there were several of considerable status who were still resolute heathens. These included Taufa'ahau's grand-uncle, the Tu'i Kanokupolu.

During the next few years, war went on almost constantly between the Christian and heathen parties. Twice Taufa'ahau successfully intervened on his grand-uncle's side, but the state of war continued. In 1840, Captain Croker of HMS 'Favourite' was killed when he tried to mediate between the two parties. However, two years later, when a party of French Roman Catholic priests established themselves on Tongatapu, many of the remaining heathens adopted Christianity — as Roman Catholics. One such convert was the Tu'i Tonga.

Rise of Tupou. In 1845, after his grand-uncle's death, Taufa'ahau was elected to the title of Tu'i Kanokupolu under the name Siaosi (George) Tupou. However, not all the chiefs were willing to accept him, and there was further fighting until August 1852. When Tupou (as he is called henceforth) finally emerged the victor, he was indisputably the most powerful chief in Tonga.

In 1862, Tupou introduced a code of laws for the whole of Tonga. Features of the code were that the chiefs and commoners were to be treated equally before the law; the commoners were freed from forced labour for, and compulsory contributions to, the chiefs; and the commoners were given control over their own property. In addition, a parliament was set up, with representatives of both the chiefs and the commoners. Another significant event occurred three years later. The incumbent Tu'i Tonga died, and Tupou was invested with all the dignities of his office, although the office itself was of little significance because of the universal adoption of Christianity.

At a meeting of Parliament in 1895, Tupou declared that the title of Tui Ha'atakalaua had also been conferred upon him. This meant that he was now the possessor of all three ancient titles. He was thus in a position to introduce a constitution for Tonga, making it a limited monarchy.

Constitution effected. The constitution became effective on November 4, 1875. It guaranteed rights to life, property and worship, it defined the form of government; and it declared that all land belonged to the king, that he could grant estates to the nobles, and that they, in turn, could lease portions of their estates to the people.

The Rev. Shirley Baker, a Wesleyan missionary, was conspicuous in advising the king about the constitution and other acts of government during this period. In the next few years, Tonga signed treaties with Germany (1876), Great Britain (1879) and the United States (1888), in all of which the kingdom's independence was recognised. A treaty of a similar character had been signed with France 30 years earlier.

After Tonga's first Premier, Tevita Uga, died in

1879, Baker resigned from the Wesleyan ministry and became Premier himself, as well as Minister of Foreign Affairs and Minister of Lands. With the king well into his eighties, Baker was soon wielding considerable influence. He quickly moved to have hereditary estates conferred on 30 nobles and six matapules, and the government took over all the primary schools from the missions, besides establishing a government college. Later, in 1885, Baker persuaded the king to establish a Free Wesleyan Church of Tonga.

Baker's great influence was resented by many Tongans, and in 1886 four escaped prisoners attempted to assassinate him, but only succeeded in wounding his son and daughter. In retaliation, Baker arranged for armies of men from Ha'apai and Vavau to attack the Wesleyans on Tongatapu; and several hundred Wesleyans were eventually exiled to uninhabited islands of Tonga. Later, Baker interfered to such an extent in the administration of justice in the Tongan courts that the British High Commissioner for the Western Pacific visited Tonga and ordered him to be deported.

As Tonga's affairs generally were in an intolerable mess, a British official, Basil Thomson, was sent from Fiji for nine months as Assistant Premier. Thomson described his sojourn in a notable book. 'The Diversions of a Prime Minister' (London 1894).

King George I dies. A year after Thomson left Tonga, King George Tupou died at the age of 96. He was succeeded by his great-grandson, as George Tupou II, who inherited an empty treasury and many other problems. As Britain feared that some other power might attempt to annex the kingdom at this stage, Basil Thomson was again sent to Tonga to negotiate a treaty of friendship with Britain. Under the treaty Tonga agreed not to make agreements with any other nation, and to transact her foreign affairs through the British Agent and Consul. The treaty was signed on May 18, 1900, and ratified on February 16, 1901. But in 1905 it was amended to give the British Consul the power of veto over Tonga's foreign affairs.

When King George Tupou II died in 1918, he was succeeded by his daughter Salote as Queen Salote Tupou III. She had married a Tongan noble, Uiliame Tungi, in 1917, and he became Premier in 1923. In the following year, a schism that had existed in church circles since Baker's time was healed when the Queen, who occupied the position of chief member of the Free Wesleyan Church, persuaded 12,000 members of that church to unite with 4,000 Wesleyans who formed the old parent church. However, some 6,000 Tongans who were unwilling to join the Wesleyans either abstained from church attendance or joined the body calling itself the Free Church of Tonga.

The Queen's consort, Tungi, remained Premier of Tonga until his death in 1941. His successor was Ata, a high chief, who was in office until his retirement in 1949. During Ata's premiership, Tonga, in close collaboration with New Zealand, formed a local defence force of 2,000 men. Some of these saw action in the Solomons against the Japanese. Meanwhile, New Zealand and American troops were stationed on Tongatapu, which became a staging point for shipping. An airfield was also built at Fua'amotu.

Ata was succeeded as Premier by Queen Salote's eldest son, Crown Prince Tungi (the present king), who had succeeded to his father's title of Tungi in 1945. As Prince Tupouto'a, he had matriculated from Newington College, Sydney, and in 1943 had taken an honours degree in jurisprudence at Sydney University. Meanwhile, his brother, Prince Sione Ngu, studied agriculture at Gatton College, Queensland, and returned to Tonga in 1944. He was later given the title of Tu'ipelehake and was made Minister of Lands and Health. The two royal brothers were married in a double wedding, an occasion for great celebration in Nuku'alofa on June 10, 1947. Crown Prince Tungi married Princess Halaevalu Mata'aho, and Prince Tu'ipelehake married Princess Melenaite Tupou-Moheofo. A son, Prince Taufa'ahau Manumataongo Tukuaho, was born to Crown Prince Tungi and his wife in May, 1948, and there were three subsequent children. The eldest is now Crown Prince under the name Tupouto'a.

Two events in 1953 brought Tonga into the world spotlight as never before. In June, Queen Salote attended the coronation in London of Queen Elizabeth II, and spent about two months in Britain during which she endeared herself to all who saw and met her. In December, Queen Elizabeth and the Duke of Edinburgh visited Tonga.

In 1958, a new treaty of friendship was signed between Tonga and Great Britain. It was ratified in May 1959. It provided for the appointment of a British Commissioner and Consul (in place of the former British Agent and Consul) to be responsible to the Governor of Fiji, who held the office of British Chief Commissioner for Tonga. In 1965, the British Commissioner and Consul in Tonga became directly responsible to the British Secretary of State for the Colonies.

On the death of Queen Salote in December 1965, Prince Tungi acceded to the throne as King Taufa'ahau Tupou IV, and his brother Prince Tu'ipelehake became Premier, Minister for Foreign Affairs, Minister of Education, and Minister of Agriculture and Works. When Tonga became completely independent of Britain on June 4, 1970, the title of Prime Minister was substituted for that of Premier. Other consequences of this development were that Britain appointed a high commissioner and a deputy high commissioner to Tonga, and Tonga joined the British Commonwealth and appointed a high commissioner in London.

Notable developments in Tonga's recent history have been government encouragement for the growth of tourism and the temporary migration of large numbers of Tongan men to New Zealand as 'guest workers'.

Tonga signed treaties of friendship with Germany (1979) and France (1980).

In 1977, Tonga became the first Pacific country to officially create marine parks and sanctuaries. There are now marine parks at Pangaimotu, Monuafe Reef, Malinoa Island and Reef and Ha'a-tafu Beach. The Pangaimotu Park is on the western perimeter of the island. The reef flat has been heavily exploited and is almost devoid of shell fish. Some attractive coral may be seen on the Piha Channel side. The area is rich in tropical fish, such as the Clown fish.

The reef at Monuafe is off the Piha Channel, about 6.5 km from Nuku'alofa. Many species of corals and their faunas are found there. The reef is ideal for snorkeling and underwater photography, but is also dangerous as it is at the confluence of channel tides. The sand flats adjoining the reef are unique as they are inhabited by sand-living univalve shells of many different families.

Malinoa island, 14.5 km north of Nuku'alofa is of great historical interest as it was there that the attempted assassins of the second prime minister of Tonga were taken in 1835 to be summarily shot. The graves are still tended. The reefs around the islands have large fish populations.

Ha'atafu Beach is on the south-west side of Tongatapu, about 22.5 km from Nuku'alofa. There are still healthy outcrops of coral despite some damage from starfish and indiscriminate coral and shell collectors. The reefs are the habitat of a variety of wrasses, butterfly fish and the Clown fish.

Further information: Noel Rutherford, 'Shirley Baker and the King of Tonga', Melbourne, 1971; Sione Latukefu, 'Church and State in Tonga', Canberra, 1974.

TONGAN ISLANDS IN DETAIL

TONGATAPU GROUP — The Tongatapu group is the most southerly of the Tongan islands and TONGATAPU ("Sacred Tonga") island is the largest in the group and in the kingdom, with an area of 257 sq km. Nuku'alofa, on the northern side of the triangular island, is the capital and chief port. Its population in early 1975 was 27,000. The harbour is protected by reefs. Just to the east of Nuku'alofa is the reef-strewn entrance to a large central lagoon that runs back behind Nuku'alofa and also towards the eastern end of the island.

The town stretches along the harbour side, most of which has a verge of green grass bordering Vuna Road. At one end of it is the Royal Palace and Chapel, set in lawns. The International Dateline Hotel is about a kilometre away from the palace and faces the harbour. The government offices, business houses, park, hospital, etc., are in streets that run back from the harbour. An increasing number of modern buildings has been built in recent years.

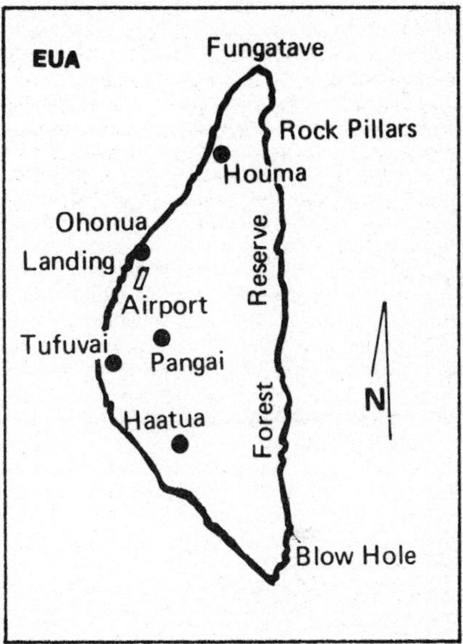

Tongatapu is of coral formation, quite flat and without running streams. It has many roads and all of the tourist sights and ancient monuments are easily accessible.

Rainfall on Tongatapu is from 1500-1700 mm per annum.

EUA lies south and east of Tongatapu and with an area of 87 sq km is the second largest of the group. It is well timbered and the source of most of the sawn local timber used in the kingdom.

Unlike Tongatapu it is hilly and rises to about 330 m. Sheep were established there years ago because of its cool climate but they finally died out due to disease. The population of Niuafoou were settled there after an eruption on their northerly island in 1946 but many returned to their home island.

Tasman sighted ATA in 1683 as he sailed from New Zealand and he gave it the name of Pylstart. The island is 136 km S.S.W. of Tongatapu. There are two peaks, the higher being 382 m, but the volcano is extinct. Ata contains deposits of guano, suitable for manure, but the lack of a harbour renders these useless commercially. The island was formerly inhabited, but in the 1860s King George Tupou I ordered the 200 inhabitants to move to Eua because the islanders were being taken away by kidnapping ships to work in the mines of Chile.

The other islands of this group are ATATA, EUAIKI, KALA'AU, KENATEA. Together they are about 1 sq km in area and the last two are uninhabited.

HAAPAI GROUP — The Haapai group is about 144 km north of Nuku'alofa by sea. The main anchorage is on the west side of the island of LIFUKA, opposite the township of Pangai. Lifuka is a low sickle-shaped island, so narrow that it can be crossed in ten minutes.

The site of the old palace of the chiefs of Haapai, the last and greatest of whom was the first constitutional King of all Tonga, George Tupou I, is a short distance from the landing place of Lifuka. The present Royal family has a summer residence there. Three kilometres along the shore from the jetty is the point where Captain Cook landed in 1777, and where, in 1806, the privateer, 'Port-au-Prince', was attacked by the Tongans. Most of the crew were massacred.

Lifuka has an area of 11.8 sq km. It has a strip for light aircraft.

The Governor of Haapai resides at Pangai. It was here that the Rev. Dr. Shirley Baker, a former Premier of Tonga, died in the early part of this century. A large monument has been erected to his memory.

The total area of the 36 islands of the Haapai Group is 118 sq km.

In the group an extinct volcano, KAO, has a perfect cone. The summit is 1,109 m high, the highest point in the Tongan group. It is easily visible from Lifuka, which is 56 km to the eastward. The island is uninhabited. It is 12.5 sq km in area.

TOFUA is a large island 558 m high, over 8 km long, and about 6 km wide. Its area is 46.6 sq km, of which over 7 sq km is the lake in the crater of the active volcano, Lofia. Smoke can often be seen issuing from the summit, but there is no record of damage in recent years. The island was once inhabited. When Captain Bligh and his loyal sailors called there for water in 1789, after the 'Bounty' mutiny, they were attacked by natives, and the quartermaster, Norton, was killed.

NOMUKA, south of the main Haapai group, was visited by more voyagers than any other island in Tonga. The large pond of fresh water from which Tasman, Cook, Bligh and others took supplies is still there. Nomuka has an area of 5 sq km.

HUNGA TONGA and HUNGA HAAPAI are sister islands north-west of Tongatapu. Both possess deposits of guano, but no anchorages. Volcanic activity has long ceased. The former is 161 m high and Hunga Haapai 131 m high. In addition to the islands mentioned above, the group has the following inhabited islands: MANGO, OUA, TUNGUA, MATUKU, HA'AFEVA, UIHA, FOTUHA'A, LOFANGA, FOA, HA'ANO and MO'UNGA'ONEO. The other uninhabited islands are: NOUMUAIKI, KELEFESIA, TONUMEA, TELEKITONGA, LALONA, TELEKIVAVA'U, TEAUPA, FETOA, UANUKUHIHIFO, UANUKUHAHAKE, TOFANGA, TATAFA, NINIVA, UOLEVA, OFOLONGA, NUKUAMU and LEKALEGA.

VAVA'U GROUP — There are, in all, 34 islands in the Vava'u group with a total land area of 115 sq km and a population of approximately 15,529 (1970), and a density of 206 to the sq km. The island of VAVA'U has a population of 11,795. The island with the biggest population density is OKOA, half a sq km, but with over 200 people. 'UTUNGAKE is 1.9 sq km in area.

The island of Vava'u is the largest (89 sq km) of the Vava'u group and is famous for its harbour. The port of Vava'u, Neiafu, is reached after steaming some kilometres up a sound of great beauty.

Vava'u was the last part of Tonga to be discovered by Europeans — by the Spaniard, Maurelle, in 1781. Twelve years later Vava'u was visited by Captain Alessandro Malaspina, Italian-born officer of the Spanish Navy.

He arrived in Vava'u in May, 1793, and established friendly relations with the Tongans, especially with a chief named Tupou, an ancestor of the present King of Tonga. On May 30, Malaspina buried a document proclaiming annexation at a secret "observation point" and had the Spanish flag raised and saluted by both the corvettes' crews and the Tongans. The Tongans raised no objection to any of it — but doubtless only because they did not know what was going on. Spain never followed up the gesture.

It is believed that the document proclaiming annexation was contained in a bottle which was buried on an islet in the harbour. Mr Stuart Inder, Editor of the "Pacific Island Monthly", visited Vavau in June 1973, and identified the islet, one of several, from drawings he had seen in the National Library of Australia in Canberra. The following September, King Taufa'ahau Tupou IV, led an expedition to the islet. A search revealed signs that a camp might have been established there. There were several holes in the coral which might have been tent post-holes but no bottle was found. The King's view, expressed to Mr Inder later, was that the Tongans on the islet would unearth the bottle as soon as Malaspina's ships had sailed.

A great attraction of Vava'u is the caves, which are reached in a short launch journey from Neiafu. The most interesting, "Mariner's Cave" — first described by William Mariner in his 'Tonga Islands' (1817) and woven by Byron into his poem 'The Island' — is only reached by diving through an underwater passage. The Swallows' Cave, which is nearer Neiafu, can be entered by boat. It is a fine cathedral-like chamber, nearly 32 m high and 65 m in circumference. The sunlight at the entrance sometimes lights up the cave in multi-colours. The "Bell Rock", nearby,

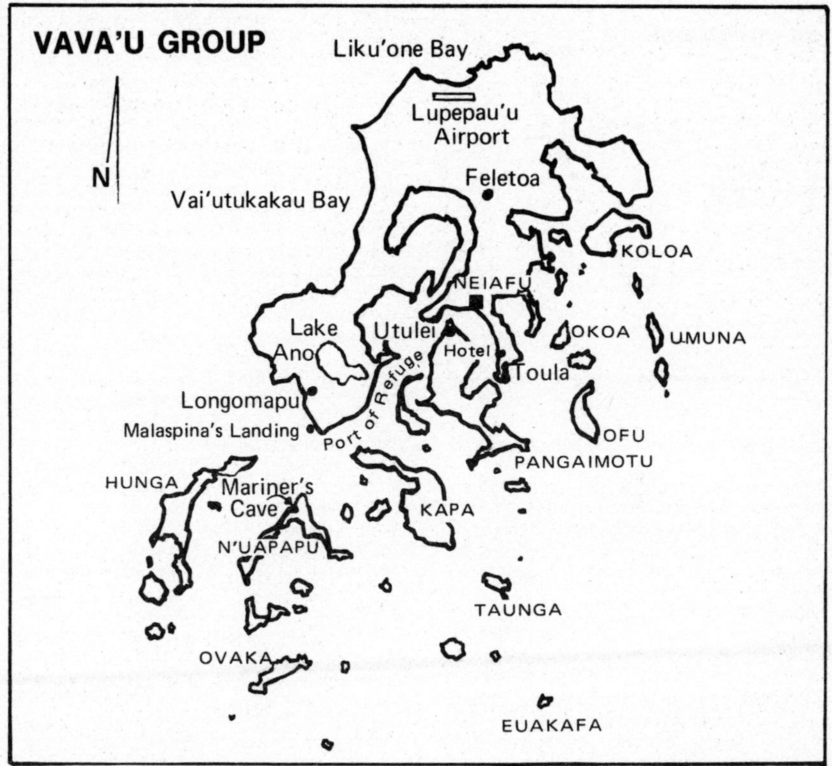

is famous for an obvious reason — when struck it rings like a bell.

There are hotels at Neiafu. The settlement also has stores, a hospital and other amenities. There is an excellent airstrip.

There is a dormant volcano on LATE which has not erupted since 1854. The island's height is 557 m and the island has an area of 15 sq km. The peak is plainly visible for 80 km on clear days, and has always been a landmark for mariners. The island, now uninhabited, is very fertile and densely wooded.

LATEIKI. In May, 1979, Metis Shoal, lying between the volcanic cones of Kao and Late in the Vava'u Group, erupted and a small volcanic island appeared for the third time in the last 100 years. The island named by the King, Lateiki ("It lies beside Late"), was 320 metres long and 120 metres wide, rising to a height of 16 metres. On July 7, 1979, the King sailed in the MV Sami to the new island, and, while His Majesty watched from the MV Sami lying off the island, His Royal Highness Prince 'Aho'eitu raised the Tongan Flag on the island and the King named it. Scientists believed that the new island, through erosion by the sea, will disappear once again.

FONUALEI is 64 km north-west of Vava'u, and is 197 m high. The Spaniard, Maurelle, discovered it in 1781, and he named it Amargura, or "Bitterness" because of his disappointment at not getting food and water there. In 1846 the volcano threw ashes over such a large area that the gardens in Vava'u were spoilt. Fonualei is uninhabited.

Other populated islands in the group are TAUNGA, OVAKA, HUNGA, LAPE, NUAPAPU, 'OTA, KAPA, PANGAIMOTU, OFU, OLO'UA, KOLOA and OKOA. Unpopulated islands not mentioned above are 'EUAKAFA, 'OVALAU, FOILIFUKA, LUAMOKO, A'A, TAPANA, 'UTUNGAKE, MAFANA, KENUTU, 'UMUNA, FAI'OA, SISIA, TU'UNGASIKA, FOEATA, 'OTO, 'EUAIKI, FONUA'ONE'ONE, FUA'AMOTU and TOKU.

NIUATOPUTAPU — Niuatoputapu, or Keppel Island, lies 240 km north of Vava'u. The anchorage on the west of the island is not good and is not a regular port of entry. Nonetheless, it is a convenient calling point for Tonga's own vessels

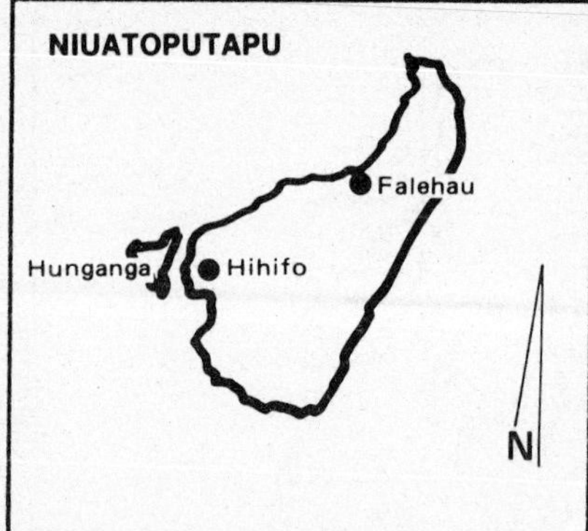

on voyages to and from Pago Pago and Apia, in the Samoas.

TAFAHI — Tafahi, or Boscawen, is about 10 km from Keppel, and reaches a height of 656 m. It is of volcanic origin. It is 3.4 sq km in area.

Tafahi was the first part of the group seen by Europeans — the Dutchmen, Schouten and Lemaire, in 1616.

NIUAFOOU — Niuafoou, which is on the outskirts of the Tongan group, is nearly 640 km from Tongatapu and west and slightly north of Niuatoputapu; it is 34.7 sq m in area and of volcanic origin, and has a long record of serious eruptions, in which parts of the island were devastated. Following a violent eruption in September, 1946, which wiped out practically the whole of the government headquarters and the villagers' homes and property, the 1,300 inhabitants were removed and eventually resettled at Eua Island, south of Tongatapu. However, many later returned.

Pre-war, its interest to tourists was its unique method of mail delivery, instituted by a European resident named C. S. Ramsay, and, because of this, the island has been nicknamed "Tin Can Island". The mail from the steamer was sealed by the ship's carpenter in large biscuit tins. The outward mail was made up ashore into several parcels and tied to the ends of sticks about one metre long. Two or three islanders usually swam out, each with a stick topped by its parcel of mail supported by poles of fau wood, of 2 m in length.

A large lake, which lies in the old crater of the island, contains islets, which themselves have craters. Hot springs are found in various parts of the lake.

FALCON ISLAND — To the westward of Haapai, and between the two ports of Nukualofa and Lifuka, is Falcon Island. Several times in the 19th century, the island was above water; at other times a shoal marks its location. Maurelle, in 1781, and La Perouse, both observed a reef there; so did H.M.S. 'Falcon' in 1865. The warship 'Sappho' in 1865, saw smoke issuing from it. In October 1885 it appeared as an island 2 km long and 50 m high but by 1894 it had "washed away". Early in 1896, the shoal suddenly erupted and cast up an island of pumice more than 320 m high. This subsided too.

In October, 1927, violent volcanic eruptions again began. As a result of this disturbance, a pumice island 118 m high and 2.4 km long was formed, but as on previous occasions the sea again gradually eroded the pumice to below sea level. It has appeared and disappeared several times since 1927, and no doubt will continue to do so.

FOR THE TOURIST. Detailed information on the main island of Tongatapu and outlying areas is available from the Tonga Visitors' Bureau in Nuku'alofa and overseas.

Travel agents in Nuku'alofa include the following: TETA Tours Ltd, Tonga Holiday Tours Ltd, Motta Tours Ltd, and South Seas Travel.

Entry formalities. Visitors staying for not more than 30 days require a valid passport, onward sea or air ticket, and proof that they have adequate funds. If they wish to extend their stay they must apply to the Principal Immigration Officer.

Valid smallpox vaccination certificates are required by all travellers, except children under six months, who have been in infected areas within 14 days of arrival in Tonga. Valid certificates showing inoculation against yellow fever are required by all travellers over one year of age who have been in an infected area before arrival in Tonga.

Airport tax. An airport tax of $NZ2.80 paid by departing passengers was imposed in January 1978.

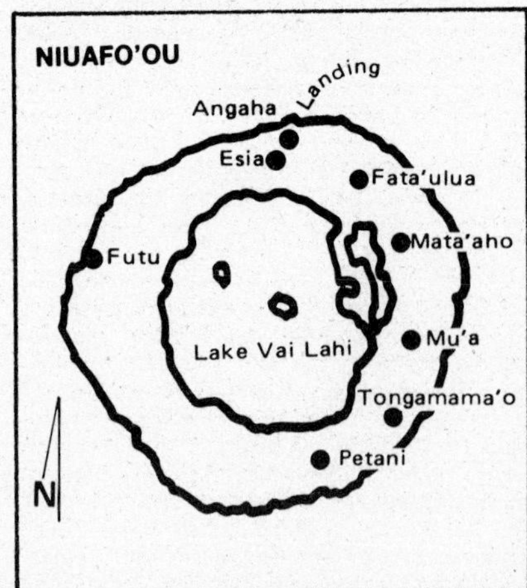

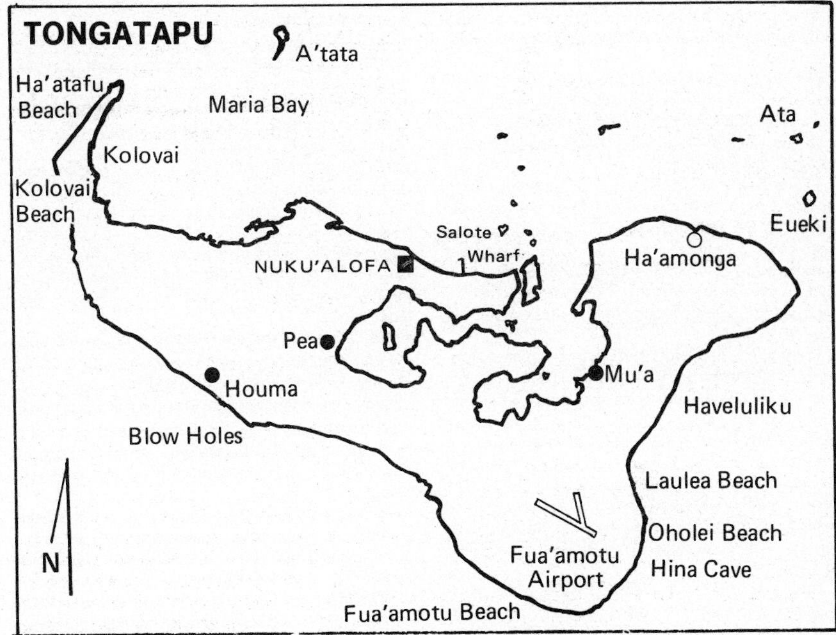

Duty-free facilities. For the shopper, Tonga is one of the most interesting places in the South Pacific for traditional handicrafts. Among the specialties are tapa cloth, finely woven mats and baskets, wood carvings, shells and beadwork.

The International Dateline Hotel and the airport at Fua'amotu offer a range of duty-free goods, such as cameras, radios, watches, perfumes, liquor and cigarettes. The Tonga Broadcasting Commission sells, duty-free, a range of radio and sound equipment.

Sightseeing. There is plenty for the traveller to see and do. In Nuku'alofa there are the Victorian white-framed royal palace and chapel, surrounded by tall Norfolk pines; the royal tombs, the burial place of Tongan royalty since 1893; Talamahu market, the major fruit and vegetable market of the kingdom, which is open every day except Sunday with a great abundance of food making a colourful picture; and the Fa'onelua tropical gardens, which contain a big variety of flora indigenous to the South Pacific.

Fourteen kilometres, from Nuku'alofa, at Houma, are the famous blow holes, where the waves send water spouting 20m into the air through coral rock for as far as the eye can see. This stretch of coastline is called Mapu'a Vaea (the Chief's Whistle) by the Tongans.

Hufangalupe (the Pigeon's Doorway) is one of the scenic areas of Tongatapu. It has three main attractions: a huge natural coral bridge under which sea water churns, towering cliffs overlooking the sea, and a beautiful beach at the bottom of a steep downhill trail.

The Ha'amonga trilithon is world renowned. It is an ancient construction built to enable the early people to identify the seasons. It consists of two upright coral stones, each about 5m high, topped by a horizontal connecting stone 6m long. Each stone weighs an estimated 40 tonnes. Ten kilometres from Ha'amonga are the terraced tombs, or "langi", built for an ancient dynasty of kings. They form quadrilateral mounds faced by huge blocks of stone rising in terraces to 4m. The stones are of coral and are extremely heavy.

At Captain Cook's landing place near Mu'a is an 'ovava tree, descendant of one under which the navigator is said to have rested while visiting that area for Tongan ceremonies.

Near the coastal village of Haveluliku, about 21 km from Nuku'alofa, are impressive underground stalactite and stalagmite caves of unknown length through which flows a deep underground river. They can be visited on a guided tour.

In the Vava'u islands, the Port of Refuge, named by an early Spanish navigator, Malaspina, is one of the most picturesque harbours in the Pacific. Panoramic drives around the main island offer spectacular views of the harbour.

Swallow's Cave, which may be entered by launches, is a sanctuary for thousands of swallows in the autumn. The fluorescent blue water, in which stalagmites grow, makes the cave an excellent swimming pool.

Not far from Swallow's Cave is the famed Mariner's Cave, a submerged grotto, about which there is a legend of a young chief and his sweetheart who used it in ancient times when feuds raged between noble Tongan families.

The entrance is below water at all times, but it may be entered with the aid of local guides if the wind is in the right direction.

At the southern end of 'Eua Island is Matalanga'a-Maui, a high natural stone bridge. Less than 1 km away are the 115m sheer cliffs of Lakufa'anga, at the base of which turtles can usually be seen.

Also on 'Eua, the clear Heike stream rushes from the hills to form a natural pool at Hafu.

In the Ha'apai islands there is a beautiful village on the historic island of 'Uiha, where visitors may stay and take part in all aspects of village life.

Pangai, in Ha'apai, is worth a visit, especially now that it is accessible by air. The royal family keeps a residence there for holidays and there is much of historic interest in the area, where the famous Rev Shirley Baker, former Premier of Tonga, is buried.

Tongan feasts. These are gargantuan affairs, with as many as 30 different dishes such as pork, fish, crustaceans, beef, fruit and vegetables. Much of the food is wrapped in banana leaves and baked in underground ovens known as "'umu".

Tourist representatives abroad. The Tongan Visitors' Bureau is represented overseas by: US, T.C.I., 700 South Flower Street, Los Angeles, California; Australia, Hutchinsons Public Relations, 107 West Street, North Sydney, N.S.W., also Captain Hugh M. Birch, 61 Cross Street, Double Bay, Sydney; NZ, Mr Ken Came, Instant Travel Marketing, Auckland.

ACCOMMODATION

Tongatapu Island

• INTERNATIONAL DATELINE HOTEL — 76 double rooms with private bathrooms and air conditioning, 4 suites in Nuku'alofa overlooking the harbour. Bar, pool, boutiques, tennis court, Tongan entertainment; 500 m from town centre, ocean views.

• MOANA HOTEL — four double Polynesian "fale" units with private bathrooms; Tongan dining room, bar and garden; 2 km from town centre, overlooking Faua Harbour.

• THE BEACH HOUSE — 10 double rooms, no private facilities, in large old wooden bungalow; unlicensed lounge and dining; 1 km from town centre, ocean view; economy standard — pure "Maugham".

• JOE'S HOTEL — 10 rooms, all private bath, 2 bars, night club; 15 min. walk from town centre, overlooking harbour.

• VETE'S WAY-IN MOTEL — 28 rooms, inc. 18 air conditioned with private bath; 10 min. walk from Nuku'alofa centre.

• SELA'S GUEST HOUSE — 5 double, 7 single rooms, sharing bathrooms, dining room, lounge, garden; 20 min. walk from town centre.

• K's GUEST HOUSE — 5 rooms, lounge, dining, kitchen; in midst of Kolofo'ou village, 20 min. walk from central Nuku'alofa.

• GOOD SAMARITAN INN — 12 Tongan fale units, shared bathroom, dining room, lounge; at Kolovai Beach, about 20 km from Nuku'alofa.

• OLOTA'ANE GARDENS MOTEL — 6 fale units, each with 2 twin rooms, lounge, dining area, kitchen, shower and toilet; self-catering; on Fangatapu lagoon, 15 min. by bus from Nuku'alofa.

• KOLO SI'I — 4 units each with one double and 2 single rooms, sharing a lounge and bathroom; 20 min. walk to Nuku'alofa centre.

• CAPTAIN COOK VACATION APARTMENTS — 6 self-contained units, each with 2 bedrooms on Nuku'alofa waterfront, 30 min. from airport, 5 min. from seaport. Swimming pool and canteen being built.

• FRIENDLY ISLANDER MOTEL — 12 modern suites with bathrooms, fully equipped, kitchen, private balcony, wall-mounted fans, radio and telephone, 3 km from downtown Nuku'alofa.

• NUKUMA'ANU MOTEL — Individual fales with one, two or three bedrooms, full kitchen facilities, hot showers, 2 km from downtown Nuku'alofa.

• RAMANLAL MOTEL — 4 modern, self-contained units with twin beds, air-conditioned, fully-furnished kitchen, refrigerator, bar, telephone, centre Nuku'alofa commercial area.

• PANGAIMOTU ISLAND — Polynesian fales, swimming and snorkelling sites, 2 km from Nuku'alofa, 15 minutes by boat, 32 acres tropical island.

• LEO'S GUEST HOUSE — 1 km from Nuku'alofa centre.

• FASI-MOE-AFI GUEST HOUSE — located beside Tourist Bureau, within 1 km of Nuku'alofa shopping centre, cafe and restaurant.

'Eua Island

• LEIPUA LODGE — 4 units each with 4 rooms, share bathroom; about 4 km from the harbour.

• HAUKINIMA MOTEL — 3 double bedrooms and 2 kitchens available, self-catering. 16 min. from Kaufana Airport, 4 km from 'Ohonua.

Vava'u Islands

• PORT OF REFUGE HOTEL — 29 units, air conditioned, all with private bath, dining room, snack bar, kiosk, freshwater pool, extensive gardens, small beach, watersport facilities; overlooking Port Refuge harbour.

• STOWAWAY VILLAGE — 4 fale units containing 4 single rooms and 8 double, each unit with private facilities, dining room, bar lounge area; overlooking old harbour.

Ha'apai Islands

GOVERNMENT GUEST HOUSE — 4 rooms, kitchen facilities.

TORRES STRAIT ISLANDS

The Torres Strait Islands are an Australian possession administered as part of Queensland.

There are more than 70 islands and islets between 11 deg. S. latitude and the Papua New Guinea mainland. They extend from 141-144 deg. E. longitude. The administrative centre is on Thursday Island and local time is 10 hours ahead of GMT.

According to the 1976 census, 9,396 Torres Strait Islanders were living in Queensland and in the islands, 6,698 of them in the Northern area which includes the Cape York Peninsula and the Torres Strait Islands.

The flag, national anthem and currency are those of Australia.

THE PEOPLE. The most heavily populated island in the group is Thursday Island, which offers some employment because it is the administrative centre and has some industry, based on marine resources, and a ship repair facility.

There is a serious sexual imbalance in the population with more women than men on every island. On Saibai, women outnumber men by as much as 80 per cent. There is a big concentration on all islands in the under-15 age group. Many of these children belong to single mothers or to parents in Australia who have sent their children home to be cared for by grandparents.

The people fall roughly into three categories. Those of the eastern group have Polynesian blood and characteristics; those in the western group tend more to be Melanesian; and in the central group there are Melanesians with an infusion of European blood. Malay, Chinese and Japanese intermingling is also evident.

However, the Torres Strait Islanders are a unified people, proud of their identity.

Language. There has recently been a revival of traditional languages. Two distinct languages are spoken. One commonly spoken in the eastern group is known as Miriam, the other is more generally spoken throughout the islands and is known as Mabuiag.

Nationality. The Torres Strait Islands are part of the state of Queensland, and the inhabitants are citizens of Australia. Of the inhabited islands, 14 are reserved for natives. Three are non-reserve and are open to visitors or intending residents without any need for permits from the Department of Aboriginal and Islanders' Advancement. Some of the reserve islands are administered by missions. Christian missions are operated by the Church of England, which succeeded the London Missionary Society in 1914, and the Roman Catholic and Presbyterian churches.

Lifestyle. The lifestyle of the islanders is changing as more "Western" type amenities are introduced. With electricity available, freezer units to store fish and other seafood awaiting transport to Thursday Island have been installed on Yorke, Coconut, Badu, Mabuiag and Stephen islands. Eventually the freezer unit system will be extended to cover Warraber, Boigu and Dauan islands and the village of Kubin on Moa Island.

The Department of Aboriginal and Islanders' Advancement is building houses of various types on several of the islands. A plumber's and carpenter's workshop, added in 1974-75 to the industrial complex on Thursday Island, helps to build modules for buildings, and to install and repair water supply and laundry/toilet facilities.

In 1979 house-building and maintenance programmes were continued with emphasis on the erection of modular-style homes. Two 3-bedroomed houses were constructed at Hammond Island, and renovations, extensions and repainting were carried out to other units. At Yorke Island, 6,000 bricks were manufactured and the foundations laid of a new brick house. Repairs were carried out to the island guest-house and to one residence. New houses were erected or are under construction at Boigu (2), Kubin Village (Moa), Saibai, Badu, Murray, Coconut, and Sue (2). Substantial renovations and extensions were also completed to houses on most islands, while at Tamwoy on Thursday Island a maintenance programme continued.

Three new houses were constructed on Thursday Island while conversion commenced on two units of the former Waiben Hospital for use as an Aged Persons' Home.

On some of the reserve islands, more than a fifth of the houses have been built over the past 20 years. Style of dwelling varies from sandfloor coconut palm houses to pre-fabricated aluminium dwellings. Some Commonwealth-supplied houses are rented for 15 per cent of cash incomes. About 50 per cent of homes have sewing machines and radios; a smaller percentage have modern cooking facilities.

A junior youth council on Hammond Island organises recreation, sports, dances, picnics and special film showings for the youth during school holidays. The young people are encouraged to give half a day a week during school holidays to community work.

The islanders' custom of accepting care of children other than their own is being practised now more than ever with the advent of legal adoption. Adoption procedures usually take about five months.

GOVERNMENT. A manager and deputy manager of the Department of Aboriginal and Islanders' Advancement are based on Thursday Island, with subsidiary staff. They are responsible to the departmental director in Brisbane.

The islands are divided into three administrative districts – Western, Eastern and Central. Each island in the three districts elects its own council.

Elections. Councils are usually elected every three years by people of 18 and over and usually consist of the most respected elders. The chairman is the candidate who won the highest vote and he has the final say on most important matters.

These councils, which meet monthly, have complete control of the domestic affairs of their own islands. They frame their own laws, and their policemen are responsible for enforcing them. The powers of the councils are very wide. They include control of the islands' revenue, the flow of non-island visitors, and exclusion of some islanders for various reasons. They are responsible to the Department of Aboriginal and Islanders' Advancement.

Three islander representatives, elected by the councillors of their groups, are responsible for the general government of their particular island group. They meet regularly on Thursday Island, and in the intervals between full conferences of councillors, determine progress and development of the island reserves of Torres Strait in consultation with officials of the Department of Aboriginal and Islanders' Advancement. These representatives regularly visit each of the islands.

The Torres Strait Islanders' Act, 1971, provides for the conduct of island reserves and the admission of those who want to live there.

Justice. Law-breakers are brought before the courts, where the councillors act as judges.

Liquor laws. Torres Strait Islanders generally enjoy all rights available to Europeans on Thursday Island. There are beer canteens on seven of the islands. Island councils help to provide reasonable drinking conditions, for example by supplying tables and chairs for the canteens. Alcohol does cause some minor problems. But it is usually consumed within a couple of days after the fortnightly shipments arrive.

International Border: Part of the Australian international border with Papua New Guinea passes through the Torres Strait region, and a border agreement between the two countries was signed late in 1978 following protracted negotiations. The border recognises cultural affinities on both sides by establishing a marine reserve in which traditional freedom of movement and sharing of economic resources is recognised. At the wish of the Islanders, three islands close to the PNG coast – Boigu, Dauan and Saibai – remain part of Australia but they are effectively island enclaves within a PNG sea.

EDUCATION. The education system caters for children at primary and secondary levels, with provision for technical education at Bamaga on nearby Cape York Peninsula, and in secondary schools in other parts of Queensland. The standard of education for the current generation is much higher than before.

Most schools are State schools, but the Roman Catholic Mission has a primary school on Thursday Island.

There are 16 primary schools in the area, administered by the Department of Aboriginal and Islanders' Advancement.

A number of new advances were made in 1979.

The Torres Strait Islands' Principal office was relocated in a new building situated in the State primary school grounds on Thursday Island, and new school buildings were erected at Dauan and Darnley, while the Badu school is currently being extensively renovated and upgraded.

Work was scheduled to commence on new schools at Yam and Boigu Islands.

Four Seminars were held to assist teachers with the Oral English course introduced in 1978.

In 1979, 450 children attended kindergartens at 22 centres in Aboriginal communities and the Torres Strait Islands.

A number of students, after completing Grade 7 in their island schools now go to mainland schools and are generally able to cope with the demands of secondary education.

High schools on Thursday Island and at Bamaga on Cape York Peninsula cater for most secondary school needs. The courses are designed to teach technical skills and crafts, and academic, commercial and industrial subjects. Children from other islands attending the Thursday Island High School either board on the island, or travel there daily by barge. Bamaga has a residential college for island students.

Supervised evening study is a feature on Hammond Island. It is done with the assistance of the sisters and teachers' aides from the Sacred Heart

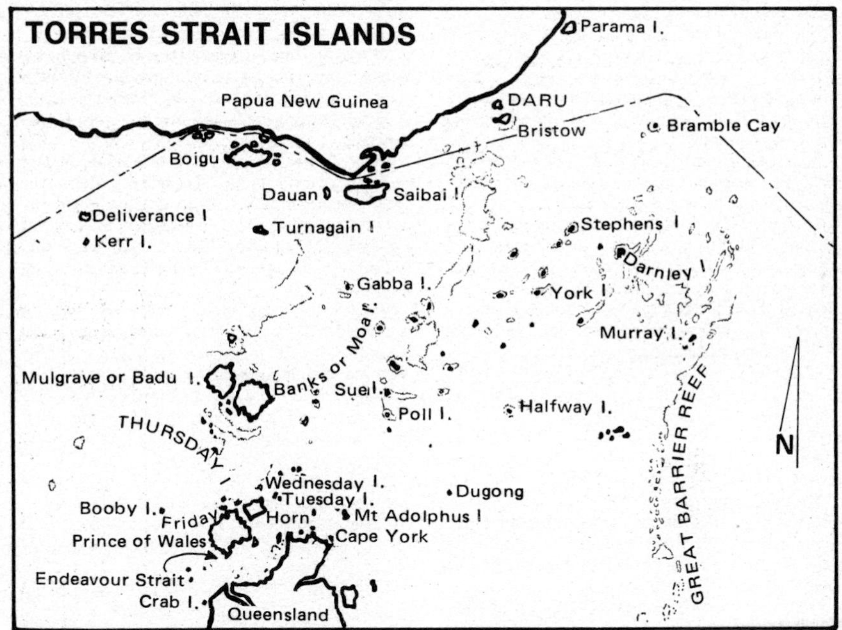

School and teachers from both the high and primary schools on Thursday Island.

A junior council on Hammond Island organised youth activities during the school holidays in 1979 which included a half-day per week community work. The annual sports day of the Sacred Heart school on Thursday Island was held at Hammond Island and was one of the major events of the year.

The interest of parents and island councils in the education of young children is growing. The development and expansion of libraries is being fostered by principals, and the local parents and citizens' associations are active in raising additional funds for school amenities.

Ten Island teachers enrolled in 1979 for the special training course at the North Brisbane College of Advanced Education which also places emphasis on the Oral English programme. A further six island teachers were enrolled for their diploma at Townsville and Adelaide.

During 1979, the Murray Island Deputy Chairman, Mr George Passi, became one of the first Torres Strait Islanders to graduate from an Australian University when he received his Arts degree from the Queensland University.

Three-teacher and four-teacher schools in the Torres Strait standardised on an intake of Year 1 children every second year but, despite this innovation, enrolments throughout the region remained stable.

LABOUR. As the Torres Strait area is more than 90 per cent open sea, the islands do not lend themselves to widespread agricultural or pastoral activities. Employment centres mainly on marine industries. Some islanders are employed as crew and divers on pearling and fishing ships.

A number of Torres Strait men have developed technical skills in such trades as carpentry and marine and mechanical engineering which have helped them to find lucrative employment on the mainland.

In 1971, according to the census of that year, there were 1,842 of them working in Queensland, in trades, primary industry (chiefly fisheries), service industries, transport and communications. With a continuing migration to Australia, the number of islanders working throughout the country is now much higher than in 1971.

On the mainland many of them work on mining and development projects in Queensland, the Northern Territory, and elsewhere. Torres Strait Islanders are believed to have set a world record for speed in laying railway tracks for a mining development in Western Australia.

In 1979 Hammond Island residents found employment with the Sacred Heart Mission in clerical and manual positions on Thursday Island and in maritime occupations further afield. At Weipa South, Hammond Island residents were employed in the mining industry, while a number of residents obtained lucrative returns from cray-fishing on a part-time or full-time basis.

The government department is the largest employer in the Torres Strait area, providing work for 262 persons. Other employment opportunities were provided by the Islands Industries Board, Applied Ecology Pty. Ltd., Commonwealth-sponsored projects and the marine industry and other branches of private enterprise.

With the opening of the Yorke Island fish processing plant, self-employment opportunities on this and neighbouring islands expanded.

Aborigines and Islanders have been affected by the high level of unemployment in the general community, and the majority of regional and detached offices have reported increased unemployment amongst the Aboriginal and Islander population.

A statutory body known as the Island Industries Board, which is established under the provisions of the Torres Strait Islanders Act, has continued to be in many cases the only retail outlet of consumer items in the many remote and isolated areas of far north Queensland. It is mandatory that any profits of the Island Industries Board be applied only to the general welfare of the Islanders.

The trading enterprise of the Board is also responsible for the grading, packing and sale of mother-of-pearl, trochus and miscellaneous shell, following purchase from Torres Strait Islander luggers and then marketed by the Board.

The department's training ship, 'Kuzi', in addition to its regular work of training young men in seamanship and fishing techniques, has also taken part, together with the Department of Primary Industries, in a survey of the breeding habits of prawns. The knowledge thus gained was made available to all who seek a livelihood from the sea in the Torres Strait area.

Social services. The social services section of the Department of Aboriginal and Islanders' Advancement on Thursday Island acts as an agent for Queensland Government departments not represented there. The section advises and assists the islanders on all aspects of social security and repatriation benefits.

The section is also responsible for the administration of estates of deceased islanders. The section's liaison officers actively participate in education, employment, housing, health and many other activities, including community and group affairs. One officer is permanently employed to promote football and other sports on Thursday Island.

There are three liaison officers and an assistant liaison officer, who is a Torres Strait Islander.

The people, under the Aborigines' and Torres Strait Islanders' Affairs Act of 1965, have special status. They are eligible for Commonwealth social services, pensions, etc., and have a vote in Australian Federal and State elections.

A savings bank, operated by the Department of Aboriginal and Islanders' Advancement, is the only method available to Torres Strait Islanders for safe deposit of their money, combined with ready access to it, not only in their own islands, but also in towns of reasonable size in Queensland.

HEALTH. Health services are maintained by the Department of Aboriginal and Islanders' Advancement in conjunction with the Thursday Island Hospital authorities and the Royal Flying Doctor Service.

There is a medical aid post on each island, in most cases staffed by fully qualified nursing sisters, who are stationed at centres where airstrips provide direct access to professional assistance for both routine and emergency situations. There is daily radio contact between the sisters and nurses at smaller medical centres.

Bamaga Hospital is administered by the Thursday Island Hospital Board and is staffed by a resident medical officer and four sisters, supported by locally recruited nursing aides and domestic staff.

Hammond Island was visited fortnightly in 1979 by a sister to conduct a clinic, while the island council supervised normal health regulations under instruction from a health inspector.

Medical services in the Torres Strait have greatly improved since the posting of eight trained sisters throughout the islands. This move has also led to Islander nurses receiving a higher standard of training.

Close liaison is maintained with Thursday Island hospital and the Government Medical Officer to ensure maintenance of standards. Two outbreaks of malaria were quickly recognized and contained due to improved surveillance methods.

Child and maternal welfare was further extended, and the liaison officers of the Department, in conjunction with the Aboriginal Health Team, screened a number of educational films at the Thursday Island outpatients hostel.

Thursday Island Hospital, where many patients are transferred from Bamaga, lacks specialist support and equipment in certain fields. Thus, some patients must be taken south for adequate treatment. Urgent transfers to Thursday Island from other islands are made by light aircraft, speedboat or hovercraft.

Expert medical advice is available by radio. Many diagnoses are carried out in this way and patients are treated at home.

Airstrips have been made on most inhabited islands to provide for air evacuation of patients.

Sisters based on Yorke Island frequently travel over long distances of open sea to visit such islands as Coconut, Warraber, Stephen, Yam, Darnley and Murray.

Generally, the health of the islanders is good. The area is free from many diseases common to tropical areas.

But there is a fairly high incidence of diseases such as tuberculosis and venereal disease. VD is hard to control because of the unnatural imbalance between the numbers of men and women, and frequent contact with the crews of fishing boats. The greatest incidence of these diseases is on Thursday Island.

THE LAND. The islands range in size from a few sq km to 180 sq km. Prince of Wales Island is the largest in the group. Some peaks on this island are about 250 m high.

The land area ranges from small cays, barely visible above sea level, to coral and volcanic islands, and high rocky islands, sparsely covered with vegetation.

The islands' tropical climate is modified by trade winds. The annual rainfall on Thursday Island is 1,500mm.

Rainfall is restricted for much of the year, leading to water shortages at various times on some islands.

A natural rock well on Booby Island holds more than 30,000 litres of water and never runs dry.

PRIMARY PRODUCTION. Most industry is based on marine resources such as pearl culture, barramundi, trochus, turtle, skipjack, sardines, mackerel and crustaceans. Prawns are processed on Thursday Island.

The pearl culture industry flourished in the early 1960s, employing about 200 men. But in 1970, the live shell was attacked by disease and most farms had to close. Employment fell to less than 40. Although the situation has improved somewhat, it is too early yet to predict if the industry will fully recover.

A pilot fishing scheme for Yorke Island was launched in 1979. The fish processing and freezing plant, developed at a cost of $175,000, was designed to handle fish fillets and lobster tails caught by island fishermen for the commercial market. Production commenced in March 1979, with catches exceeding expected levels and returning Islander fishermen approximately $1,000 net per week.

Apart from providing a basis for an expanded fishing industry in the Torres Strait, the project generated a local source of income for residents on Yorke and neighbouring islands. It is hoped to expand this project with the provision of fish dories under the control of a freezer supervisor and island chairman and available for hire to island fishermen.

Development of the Yorke Island facility has also encouraged cray fishing on adjacent islands with over 1,800 kg supplied by the Sue, Yam and Coconut island freezers collectively.

The turtle farming scheme, a centre of a political conflict in the mid-1970s, was a failure and closed in 1980.

There is a ship repair yard at Thursday Island.

The Queensland Island Industries Board, established on Thursday Island as a bulk distribution centre, retail outlet and office, distributes to 22 retail outlets as far north as Saibai and Boigu and as far south as Weipa.

TRANSPORT. There are made roads, sealed with bitumen, on Thursday Island. Vehicles are also used on one or two of the other islands.

Air services. The airport for Thursday Island is on nearby Horn Island. Connections are made by launch. Ansett Airlines maintains a Fokker Friendship service, four times a week, from Weipa to connect Thursday Island with the mainland. The flight time between Horn Island and Weipa is 45 minutes. Bush Pilots Airways operates a Cessna from Cairns and Bowen to Jacky Jacky airstrip, near Bamaga. There are airstrips on the islands of Horn, Yorke, Saibai, Badu, Yam, Murray and Sue (Warraber). Work began in 1980 on an airstrip on Boigu. When this is completed, no inhabited island in Torres Strait will be more than 40 km from an airstrip.

Local vessels. Two ships, the 'Stephen Davies' and 'Melbidir' deliver food and building materials, and carry people who have to travel for medical and dental checks and school interviews.

The Queensland Coast and Torres Strait Pilot Service consists of 40 master mariners who provide a pilotage service from the western approaches of the Torres Strait to ports on the east coast of Australia, as far south as Sydney, and to Papua New Guinea by the Great North-East Channel. None of the pilots has his home on Thursday Island. Most live in Brisbane and Sydney, and commute by air to the islands as required. There are some pilots at all times on Thursday Island. There is a base for them in Sydney, which is actually their control centre, and from which instructions are issued to them to join ships. The service also provides a shipping mail exchange, medical aid and stores and police services, if required by ships.

Thursday Island has the best anchorage between the Australian mainland and PNG.

COMMUNICATIONS. each island has a radio transmitting and receiving set. These operate in conjunction with a "mother" station at Port Kennedy (Thursday Island). This gives most islands quick communication with the outside world. Equipment for the VHF radio used for Thursday Island harbour is housed in one of the underground chambers of a large old fort high on the island.

Reception of radio broadcasts from the mainland is generally poor. There is a weekly news sheet produced by a local resident.

HISTORY. Because it is a navigable passage, though a perilous one, between Australia and New Guinea, the discovery, exploration and history of Torres Strait is overwhelmingly a maritime story. All information about the natives of the innumerable islands and their way of life came from navigators and the survivors of shipwrecks, until the arrival of missionaries in 1871. All communication between the islands was by sea until the recent building of airstrips on the more important islands, and most economic activity has been pearl-shelling and other maritime occupations.

The first European knowledge of Torres Strait dates from 1606, when Captain Luis Baez de Torres took a month to work his way through the maze of islands and reefs, finally passing through Endeavour Strait into the open waters of the Arafura Sea. An imaginary strait had been shown on some charts before 1600, drawn at about 21 deg. S. latitude (instead of between 9 and 11 deg. S.) in order to separate the known land of New Guinea from the mythical and undiscovered continent of Terra Australis Incognita.

Torres' report. Torres' report to the King of Spain did not become generally known, and lay buried in the archives until 10 years after the strait had been rediscovered by Cook in 1770. The story that a copy of the report was found in Manila in 1764 by Dalrymple is quite untrue, though it has been repeated by writers from Flinders in 1814 to the most recent history books. Dalrymple was sent a copy from Spain in 1780, and translated it himself for publication in 1806, just 200 years after the voyage of Torres.

The report was a very brief one, but a much fuller account came to light in 1929, written by a noble passenger who travelled with Torres, Captain Don Diego de Prado y Tovar, who also drew the charts of their discoveries. From Prado's narrative we can work out that they anchored off at least 10 islands, though they did not land on them all, and often when they did land the natives had taken off to other islands, or had hidden in the bush. The islands involved were Parama, Bristow, Dungeness, Turtle-backed, Cap, Gabba, Long, Mount Ernest, Twin and Prince of Wales. The last anchorage, in Endeavour Strait, was two miles south of Cape Cornwall, and here Torres' ship, 'San Pedro', bumped on the bottom during the night on a five-metre shoal. His consort, the launch 'Los Tres Reyes', though anchored closer to the shore, did not bump, and next day, October 4, Torres made the latitude 11 deg. at noon, before leaving the strait.

He had been in sight of the Australian coast for about two days, but did not know it was the continent he had been searching for in the Pacific, and in the Coral Sea, but thought it was just an extensive group of islands.

Jansz's voyage. He was actually preceded in the sighting of this part of Australia by the Dutchman Willem Jansz in the small vessel 'Duyfken', who landed near the present port of Weipa, followed the coast south to Cape Keer-Weer, and then returned northwards. He passed up the western side of Torres Strait, and landed on Prince of Wales Island, which he named Hoogh Eylandt (High Island), and returned to Banda in the East Indies.

A fine chart of his discoveries was made, but no journal or log-book of the voyage exists, so we do not know the details or dates of his contact with Australia, which were probably in March or April, 1606, and therefore six months before Torres. To Jansz the strait appeared to be a large shallow bay or bight, so he and his successors, including Tasman, assumed that Cape York Peninsula was a part of New Guinea, despite the vague reports that Torres had sailed through a strait in the area.

Although Prado's charts of the southern coast of New Guinea were sent to Spain, they were later lost, and we only have a few rare hand-drawn copies which vary widely in their details and place names. To navigators using the strait, the islands and their warlike and cannibal natives were regarded as part of the hazards of navigation, and of no particular importance or interest in themselves.

The islands. The islands of Torres Strait are of all sizes, and of two kinds, high and rocky, and low and coralline. There are about 100 of each, if you count the smallest rocks and sand-cays, but only about 30 are inhabited.

Australia and New Guinea are joined over hundreds of kilometres by the continental shelf, and in Torres Strait this becomes a shallow bank of less than 17 m depth. If the sea level fell by that amount we could walk across without getting our feet wet at any state of the tide. Fortunately for navigation, the sea level has remained constant for at least the 370 years since Torres' visit, but there is no doubt that in prehistoric times there was a land bridge right across the strait, especially during the Ice Ages. The last of these was at its height about 50,000 years ago, when man first came into the area, and the strait would have been dry for thousands of years after that, possibly until 10,000 years ago.

To the east the shallow waters of the strait are flanked by the Great Barrier Reef, which extends to the edge of the continental shelf. To the west the shallows merge gently into the Arafura Sea, though the shoal water follows the coast of Irian Jaya for hundreds of kilometres further.

From the earliest days of contact the natives of the strait were known as fierce warriors, with fleets of large canoes for raiding neighbouring islands and the adjacent coast of New Guinea, where the population was very sparse. In spite of a brisk trade for canoes, bows and arrows with villages near the Fly River, the islanders regarded the New Guineans as permanent enemies.

After 1606 there were several Dutch expeditions to the western side of the strait, including Tasman's in 1644, but no one approached the eastern side until Cook left himself with no choice but to find a way through the strait in August, 1770. He had no contact with the natives, but sighted a few with bows and arrows while he was taking possession of "the east coast of New Holland" on Possession Island, a few kilometres west of Cape York.

Bligh's visits. The next visitor to pass through the strait was Captain William Bligh in the 'Bounty' launch in June, 1789. He also passed close to Cape York, but missed Endeavour Strait, thinking it was a bay, and made his way through Prince of Wales Channel, which is today the main shipping channel. Bligh named Wednesday Island, setting the fashion for later navigators to name Tuesday Islets, and Thursday and Friday Islands, all in the Prince of Wales group.

During 1791 a boatload of escaped convicts from Sydney, including Mary Bryant, worked their way right up the east coast, through Torres Strait and on to Timor, but the long arm of the law was not far astern. In August HMS 'Pandora' was wrecked trying to enter Torres Strait near Raine Island; many lives were lost, including some of the mutineers of the 'Bounty', who had been arrested in Tahiti.

Captain Edwards sailed the ship's boats through the strait to Timor, where he was able to add the escaped convicts to his prisoners, all bound for the hangman's noose in England. On reaching Java, Captain Edwards met the 'Resolution', a small vessel built by the mutineers at Tahiti, but manned by some of the 'Pandora' crew before leaving Tahiti. They had also sailed through the strait in 1791, making it a busy thoroughfare for distressed mariners.

The next visitor was again Captain Bligh, this time with two ships carrying breadfruit plants from Tahiti to the West Indies, HMS 'Providence' and 'Assistant'. This time Bligh avoided the Barrier Reef by entering the strait near the coast of New Guinea, believing that Torres had taken a northerly track in better waters. He sailed down what is now called the Great North-east Channel, then through Basilisk Pass, and passed Gabba Island before being blocked by extensive coral reefs, as Torres had been in the same area. Bligh worked his ships down towards Banks Island, and then escaped to the open sea through Bligh Channel on September 18, 1792.

Next year two ships, the 'Shah Hormuzeer' under Captain Bampton, and the whaler 'Chesterfield', Captain Alt, also looked for a passage in the northern part of the strait and after following the tracks of Torres and Bligh, pushed on through the shoals, keeping close to the New Guinea coast. The two ships took turns in running aground and in helping each other off, and it was a whole month before they finally cleared the shoals near Deliverance Islet on August 29, 1793.

Flinders' charts. The strait remained largely uncharted, despite these perilous passages by different ships, and Flinders made a chart of all the tracks followed for his book in 1814. He had passed through the strait three times himself, first as a midshipman under Bligh in 1792, then in command of HMS 'Investigator' in October, 1802, and finally in the much smaller HMS 'Cumberland' in October, 1804. On the two latter occasions he used Prince of Wales Channel, and therefore did not add much to our knowledge of the rest of the strait.

There is no foundation for the many reports of unknown Spanish galleons being wrecked in the strait. The finding of stray Spanish dollars on the islands would be due to the fact that these were common currency in Sydney in the early years, being imported by Governors Macquarie and Brisbane to overcome the shortage of coinage in the colony. Many ships were wrecked in the strait and in the approaches through the Barrier Reef, and many boats' crews were attacked by natives. The warriors of Turtle-backed Island (Yam or Yama), tried to capture Torres' launch, but were repelled by firearms. Torres named the island "Caribes" or "Cannibals", being impressed by the collection of skulls and bones found in the village where he landed. He also saw masks and figures made from turtle-shell, similar to those seen in museums today. He also remarked on the very strong bows of bamboo, and clubs with heavy stone heads. Their canoes were later reported to be over 18 m in length.

Naval surveyors. The fullest accounts of the natives of the Torres Strait Islands were written by various naval surveyors who charted the area between 1819 and 1875. Their ships included the 'Fly', 'Rattlesnake', 'Bramble' and 'Basilisk' (Captain Moresby). In 1844 a beacon, almost 20 m high, was erected on Raine Island to mark an entrance through the Barrier Reef for ships making for Torres Strait.

An unofficial "post office" came into use at Booby Island, and here a supply of provisions was left for wrecked crews making their way towards Timor. The post office was unmanned, and consisted of a cave in which bundles of letters were left for other ships to pick up and deliver. The cave is also an archive of inscriptions made by passing ships and boatloads of survivors of wrecks and massacres.

In October, 1849 men from HMS 'Rattlesnake' picked up a white woman, Mrs Barbara Thomson, on Prince of Wales Island. She was the sole survivor of the cutter 'America', wrecked nearby about four years before. She had been taken to wife by the chief, Boroto, and renamed Gi'Om after a dead girl of the tribe.

During her stay she had met the infamous runaway convict named Wini, who had become the war chief of Badu, or Mulgrave Island, where he led the locals into killing all white men who came near their island. He was finally shot by a punitive expedition from the settlement founded at Somerset in Albany Passage in 1864, only nine kilometres south-east of Cape York. It was under the charge of John Jardine, with a garrison of 25 marines, and formed a harbour of refuge for castaways. During the next 11 years there were 14 wrecks recorded, and it was an important port for ships working in Torres Strait.

Modern period. The year 1871 marked the beginning of modern history in the strait, with the arrival of the first missionaries, and the development of fishing for beche-de-mer, pearl shell and trochus shell. By 1877, when the settlement was moved to Thursday Island, there were 16 firms in the trade, employing 109 vessels, 50 Europeans and about 700 natives. The area being worked covered 4,800 sq. km, and the value of pearl shell was £200 a ton. The value of pearls found in the shells amounted to only a third of the value of the shell. The trade went through many vicissitudes through the following decades, and finally stopped about 1940, when the settlement at Thursday Island fell into decline.

Thursday Island's native name was Wyben; it used to be referred to as Port Kennedy. The island was fortified about 1880 to defend the navigational passage. The first nine official pilots were licensed in 1884 by the Queensland Government, and the service still flourishes as the "Torres Strait and Queensland Coast Pilot Service", and numbers about 35 pilots, all experienced master mariners. Their services are not compulsory to passing ships, but most large ships use them to pass safely through the dangerous waters of the strait, and of the Great Barrier Reef.

The Anglican Cathedral at Thursday Island was originally built as a memorial to the 173 souls lost in the wreck of the steamer 'Quetta', which struck an uncharted pinnacle of coral near the Albany Passage on February 28, 1890. The 109 souls saved included an unidentified baby girl, later named Quetta Brown. Perhaps the luckiest survivor was a teenager named Emily Lacy, who was picked up nearly 36 hours after the wreck; she was later married in London, and her son, Dyson Hore-Lacy, was well known in New Guinea.

Bathurst Bay disaster. Another disaster occurred in 1899, when the pearling fleet from Thursday Island was struck by a hurricane in Bathurst Bay; about 50 vessels were lost, and about 300 lives, with only three pearling luggers left afloat.

Perhaps the best-known massacre of castaways occurred on Aureed Island in 1834, after the wreck of the barque 'Charles Eaton'. Five survivors in a boat reached Timorlaut, and four young boys were spared from death by the natives. Two of these survived, to be picked up by a punitive party in the schooner 'Isabella' in 1839, and the skulls of the victims were brought to Sydney for burial.

The pearling firms at Thursday Island employed divers of many races, so the population of Thursday Island came to include Aborigines, Kanakas, Polynesians, Malays and Japanese, the last-named in overwhelming numbers in the last 70 years of the industry. The other islands often had a white resident of unknown origin, some being escaped convicts from New Caledonia, and others escaping from the world or from the law of various countries.

The last 100 years have seen a steady spread of administration and education throughout the islands of Torres Strait, the schools being mostly run by the missions, so that the islanders have become citizens of Queensland, receive social benefit payments, and are free to travel and work in Australia. Hundreds of them are now living on the mainland, including a settlement at Bamaga in the far north, which was first peopled by natives from Saibai Island who needed more land for development.

The history of Torres Strait has continued to be mostly maritime, and the developments of the last 100 years belong to the subjects of administration, missions and education, communications, and finally navigation, which can be taken to cover the improvements in charts of the area, and the provision of navigational lights and facilities. The recent development of aviation between the islands has lessened dependence on launches and luggers for inter-island services, though they will continue to be used for all forms of exploitation of the waters in the strait.

ISLANDS IN DETAIL

The individual islands have often had more than one name, even in the native languages, and although none of the names given to them by Europeans in 1606 has survived, some given in 1770 and later are still in use. In 1977 the Queensland Department of Lands was trying to establish the preferred names of the islands, whether native or European, to form an official list for general use and for mapping purposes. A list of past and present names for 124 of the islands is given at the end of this section. Only 17 have permanent inhabitants. Islands which are official reserves are divided into four groups.

Eastern: Stephen, Darnley, Murray. These are small and steep with rich volcanic soil and dense tropical vegetation. Surrounding waters are deep, and fish are plentiful.

Central: Warraber or Sue, Coconut, Yorke. Small and flat, with coral base and less tropical vegetation. Waters are shallower, fish are plentiful.

Western. Badu, Mabuiag, Moa, Dauan, Yam. Larger and elevated, rocky soil with only bush and scrub. Water shallow, suitable for pearl diving.

North-western: Saibai, Boigu. Large and low-lying swamps and mangroves. Little marine life. In the southern part is the island of Hammond, administered as a reserve by the Catholic Mission, and the three non-reserve islands of Prince of Wales, Thursday and Friday. Some other islands in this Prince of Wales Group are inhabited sporadically by fishing parties, and this also applies to many of the other islands in the Strait.

THURSDAY ISLAND the administrative and business centre of Torres Strait, has a harbour and a wharf, and is surrounded by seven islands of the Prince of Wales Group. It measures 2.4 km by 1.2 km, and has the main radio station, hospital and hotels. It is nearly surrounded by seven other islands — Horn, Tuesday, Wednesday, Goode, Hammond, Friday and Prince of Wales. Ships pass through a passage with Friday and Prince of Wales on one side, and Goode and Hammond Islands on the other to reach Thursday Island's harbour.

FRIDAY ISLAND, about 1.6 km long, and 3.2 km south-west of Thursday Island, is a resort area for Thursday islanders. It has attractive beaches and low sand dunes, and the beaches are a natural breeding ground for green turtles. There are some week-end houses, and there were some pearl-culture enterprises.

PRINCE OF WALES is the largest of the Torres Strait islands with an area of 180 sq. km, and peaks up to 250 m high. It houses a number of permanent families, and week-end cottages cater for many visitors. The island has never been exploited to any extent, as it lacks a good anchorage on the northern side, is very rugged, except for a small area of cultivable land, and has no permanent fresh water supply. It is little more than 1 km from Thursday Island at the nearest point.

TUESDAY, WEDNESDAY, GOODE. Tuesday islets, named by Flinders in 1802, are small and rocky. Wednesday, named by Bligh in 1789, has some week-end cottages. Goode Island, with a lighthouse, is 2.5 km wide. It was actually named Good's Island by Flinders in 1802.

MOA, originally called Banks by Bligh in 1792, is about 48 km north of Thursday Island. The native community, with a few European missionaries, live at Kubin village, a government reserve, and at St. Paul's Anglican Mission reserve. Both communities are interested in the possible mining of wolfram (tungsten).

BADU, is just north-west of Moa, and is a fertile island. It is also known as Mulgrave.

MABUIAG, just north of Badu, is small, but has traditionally provided the best sailors for pearling luggers, as well as one of the two main languages for the Strait. The natives are largely engaged in the modern crayfish trade. It is also known as Jervis Island.

MURRAY. This is near the northern end of the Great Barrier Reef, and with Darnley and Stephen, has supplied many men for work on the mainland. They mostly return to the islands in their old age.

DARNLEY is noted for its unusual fish traps, which completely encircle the island. They are made of huge boulders, and their origin is a mystery.

YORKE, known best for its colourful history. Many early ships frequented the area, some sailing past, and others coming to grief on reefs in the area. Relics of these wrecks, in the form of cannon, guns, swords and old coins are still being found today.

Yankee Ned was an American sailor who deserted his ship, settled on Yorke Island, amassed a fortune in pearls and reputedly married eight wives, leaving many descendants. He was nearly 90 when he died about 1920.

SAIBAI, DAUAN, BOIGU. These are the islands mainly affected by the bid to move the Australian border further away from the New Guinea coastline.

In addition to the islands in the Strait, many islanders have moved to the mainland to the west of Cape York, where they live with some aborigines on reserves called Bamaga, Cowal Creek, New Mapoon, Umagico and Red Island Point. The area has a water supply used for domestic purposes and irrigation. The community is self sufficient in meat, grows fruit and vegetables, and operates a timber mill. There is also a small airstrip. Most of the islanders came from Saibai, owing to shortage of cultivable land there.

TORRES STRAIT ISLANDS

Alphabetical list of names, including alternative and obsolete names from old charts. Current official names are given in capitals, but are liable to change in accord with custom. Names of very small islands close to the coasts of New Guinea and Australia are omitted. To help in locating an island on a map the Strait is here divided into six areas, and each name is followed by initials representing the area in which it may be found; C.Y. for Cape York area north of 11 deg. S. latitude; E. for eastern islands; C. for those in the centre of the Strait; B-M for the Badu-Moa group; P.O.W. for Prince of Wales Group area; N. for the northernmost islands.

Aada = HAMMOND ROCK P.O.W.
AKONE ISLAND C.Y.
ALBANY I. C.Y.
AUKANE I. E.
AURID = Aureed I. E.
BADU = Mulgrave I. B-M
Banks I. = MOA B-M
Barn I. = Tarrau C.Y.
BARNEY I. B-M
BELLE VUE Islands B-M
BET Islet = Burrar C.
BOIGU = Talbot's I. N.
BOND I. B-M
BOOBY I. P.O.W.
BOURKE I. E.
BRAMBLE Cay = Massaramcoer E.
Brothers I. = GABBA C.
BROWN I. B-M
Burke I. = SUARJI, Suaraji C.
Burrar = BET Islet C.
BUSH Islet C.Y.
CAMPBELL I. = Tappoear E.
CANOE ISLET E.
CAP ISLET = Muquar, Moquar C.
Caribes = YAM, Yam, Turtle-backed
CASTLE I. B-M
CLARKE I. B-M
COCONUT I. = Parremar E.
CRAB I. C.Y.
Cuddalug = TUESDAY Islets P.O.W.
DALRYMPLE I. = Damuth E.
DARNLEY I. = Errub E.
DAUAN I. = cornwallis N.
DAYMAN I. C.Y.
DELIVERANCE I. N.
Djuna = ENTRANCE I. P.O.W.
Double I. = TWIN I., Nelgee
DOVE I. = Utta E.
DUGONG I. E.
DUNCAN I. B-M
Dungeness I. = Jeaka, ZAGAI C.
DUMARALUG Islet P.O.W.
EAST STRAIT I. P.O.W.
EBORAC I. C.Y.
Eegarba = MARSDEN I. E.
Eet = western side of MOA B-M
ENTRANCE I. = Djuna P.O.W.

Mt. ERNEST I. = Nagheer C.
Errub = DARNLEY I. E.
FAREWELL Islets B-M
FLAT I. B-M
FRIDAY I. = Jealug P.O.W.
GABBA = Brothers I. C.
Garboy = ARDEN Islet E.
GETULLAI = Pole I. C.
GOODE I. = Goods I. P.O.W.
GREAT WOODY I. P.O.W.
GREEN I. B-M
HALFWAY I. E.
HAMMOND I. = Kerriri P.O.W.
HAMMOND ROCK = Aada P.O.W.
HAWKESBURY I. B-M
HIGH I. C.Y.
HIGH I. B-M
Hogar = STEPHENS I. E.
Homogar = KEATS I. E.
Hoogh Eylandt = P.O.W.
HORN I. = Laforey, Narupai P.O.W.
IDA I. C.Y.
Jeaka = Dungeness, ZAGAI C.
Jealug = FRIDAY I. P.O.W.
KABBIKANE I. E.
KAPUDU I. P.O.W.
KAUMAG I. N.
KEATS I. = Homogar E.
KEATINGE I. C.Y.
Kei Cuddalug = No. 3 of the TUESDAY Islets, P.O.W.
Keriri = FRIDAY I. P.O.W.
KERR I. N.
Kodal in YORKE Islets E.
KUNAI I. P.O.W.
LACEY I. C.Y.
Laforey's. I. = HORN I., P.O.W.
LITTLE WOODY I. P.O.W.
LITTLE ADOLPHUS I. C.Y.
Long I. = SASSIE C.
LOWRY I. C.
MABUIAG = Jervis I. B-M
Maer, Mer = MURRAY I. E.
MAI Islet C.Y.
MARSDEN I. = Eegarba E.
Masig, Massig = YORKE Is. E.
Massaramcoer = BRAMBLE Cay E.
Mauar = RENNEL I. E.
Maururra = WEDNESDAY I. P.O.W.
MEDDLER I. C.Y.
MEIPA I. near Jervis I. B-M
Mer, Maer = MURRAY I. E.
Moquar = CAP Islet C.
MOA = Mua, Banks I. B-M
Monserrat I. = Mt. ERNEST I. C.
MORILUG Islet C.Y.
Mt. ADOLPHUS I. C.Y.
Mt. ERNEST I. = Nagheer C.
Mt. Cornwallis = DAUAN E.
Mua = MOA, Banks I. B-M
Muggi Cuddalug = No. 2 of the TUESDAY Islets P.O.W.
Muralug = PRINCE OF WALES I.
MURRAY I. = Maer, Mer E.
Muquar = Moquar, CAP Islet
Nagheer = Mt. ERNEST I. C.
Narupai = HORN I. P.O.W.
Nelgee = TWIN I., Double I.
NEPEAN I. = Attogoy E.
NICKLIN Islet P.O.W.
NORTH I. B-M
NORTH POSSESSION I. B-M
PACKE I. P.O.W.
Parilug = GOODE I. P.O.W.
Parremar = COCONUT I. C.
PASSAGE I. B-M
PEENECAR C.
Perros = Dungeness, ZAGAI C.
PHIPPS I. B-M
Pole I. = GETULLAI C.
POLL Islet C.
PORTLOCK I. B-M
POSSESSION I. = Bedanug C.Y.
PRINCE OF WALES I. = Muralug P.O.W.
QUOIN I. C.Y.
RAINE I. (on edge of Barrier Reef)
RED I. C.Y.
RED WALLIS I. C.Y.
RENNEL I. = Mauar E.
ROBERTS I. E.
ROUND I. P.O.W.
ROUND I. B-M
SADDLE I. C.
SAIBAI I. N.
SALTER I. C.Y.
SASSIE = Long I. C.
Six Sisters, sand cays, E.
SOUTH I. B-M
SPENCER I. B-M
SAURJI = Suaraji, Burke I. C.
SUE Islet = Warraber C.
Talbot's I. = BOIGU N.
Tappoear = CAMPBELL I. E.
Tarrau = BARN I. C.Y.
Three Sisters = BET, SUE, POLL C.
TERN I. C.Y.
THURSDAY I. = Wai-ben, Wyben P.O.W.
TOBIN Cay E.
TOBIN Islet B-M
TRAVERS I. B-M
TREE Islet B-M
TREE Islet C.Y.
TROCHUS I. C.Y.
TUDU I. = Warrior I. C.
TUESDAY Islets (4) C.
TURNAGAIN I. N.
TURTLE I. near ENTRANCE I. P.O.W.
TURTLE I. & TURTLEHEAD I. C.Y.
Turtle-backed I. = YAM, Yama C.
TWIN I. = Double I., Nelgee P.O.W.
UNDERDOWN I. E.
Uttu = DOVE I. E.
Wai-ben = THURSDAY I. P.O.W.
WAI-WEER I. P.O.W.

Warrior I. = TUDU, Tutte C.
WEDNESDAY I. = Maururra P.O.W.
WEST I. B-M
WHALE I. B-M
WILSON Is (2) B-M
WOODY WALLIS I. P.O.W.
Wyben = THURSDAY I. P.O.W.
YAM = Yama, Turtle-backed I. C.
YORK I. C.Y.
YORKE Islets, Kodal & Masig E.
ZAGAI = Dungeness, Jeaka C.

The three main islands belonging to Papua-New Guinea are not given above, but are:— PARAMA or Bampton, Bobo or BRISTOW and DARU, the last-named being a government station.

FOR THE TOURIST. The islands with their beaches offer a fascination for a particular type of tourist who enjoys getting away into a rugged and remote environment.

Accommodation facilities on Thursday Island include the Rainbow Motel with about a dozen units and a restaurant, and hotels such as the Federal and the Grand.

Thursday Island has a bowling club with a licensed bar, plus a tennis court. The island also offers water sports.

A guest house, completed in 1974-75, on Yorke Island, caters for the increasing number of people requiring accommodation while en route to other islands.

TRUST TERRITORY OF THE PACIFIC ISLANDS

Encompassing more than 2,000 islands in three major archipelagoes – the Marianas, Carolines and Marshalls – the Trust Territory is a United Nations trust area administered by the USA. It is located between the equator and 22 deg. N. latitude and from 130 to 172 deg. E. longitude. In 1976, the Northern Marianas were administratively but not technically separated from the Trust Territory with Saipan as that group's capital. Other changes followed in 1979 in anticipation of the scheduled termination in 1981 of the 1947 Trusteeship Agreement, with the delegation of limited authority to the three political subdivisions of the remainder of the Trust Territory – the Federated States of Micronesia, embracing Yap, Truk, Ponape and Kosrae, the State of the Marshall Islands and the State of Palau.

Until termination of the Agreement, the three states, and the Northern Marianas, are limited to internal self-government, including legislative and judicial functions.

Kolonia, in Ponape, was named as the administrative centre for the Federated States of Micronesia, but at the beginning of 1980, almost all administrative departments were still in Saipan.

Majuro is the administrative centre of the Marshall Islands and Koror the administrative centre of Palau.

The four member states of the Federated States of Micronesia are also separate internal self-governing countries, each with its own parliamentary body or council.

Majuro is about 2,285 nautical miles west of Honolulu, Siapan 3,550, Koror 4,152 and Kolonia 2,839.

Local time is 10 hours ahead of GMT.

Palau's flag shows an adze and 16 stars on a red and blue ground. The stars represent the territory's 16 municipalities, and the adze, a traditional tool of local craftsmen, symbolises the importance of labour in government.

The flag of the Marshall Islands is dark blue with rays of orange and white extending from the lower left corner to the upper right corner. A 24-point white star is at the upper left side, the points representing the 24 municipalities with the four longer points signifying Majuro, Wotji, Jaluit and Kwajalein. Blue is the ocean and the rays represent the equator and extend upwards as symbols of the increase in vitality and growth of life in the Marshalls. The four longer points of the star also represent the four ends of a cross signifying Christianity in the new state.

The flag of the Federated States of Micronesia consists of four white stars, representing the four member states, on a field of light blue. The only difference between this flag and the official Trust Territory flag is that the latter has six white stars, representing the six districts which remained after the seventh, the Northern Marianas, changed its political status. The FSM motto is "Peace, Liberty, Unity".

Ponape, one of the member states of the Federated States of Micronesia, has also decided to fly its own flag along with the flag of the FSM. The flag is similar to the official TT flag except that its six white stars represent the six islands of Ponape – Kapingamarangi, Mokil, Ngatik, Nukuoro, Pingelap and Ponape Island proper. It also displays a half-coconut shell, symbolising the sakau (kava) cup and coconut palm leaves on a white background indicating Ponape's dependence on coconut resources.

Each territory has its own special holidays but the Trust Territory holidays common to all are: January 1 (New Year's Day); February 20 (President's Day); May 29 (Memorial Day); July 4 (Independence Day); July 12 Micronesia Day (celebrating the first Congress meeting); September 4 (Labor Day); October 9 (Columbus Day); October 24 (United Nations Day); November 11 (Veterans' Day); last Thursday in November (Thanksgiving Day); December 25 (Christmas Day).

United States currency is used in all the Micronesian states.

THE PEOPLE. The people of the Marianas, Carolines and Marshalls are Micronesians but they differ in physical characteristics, customs and

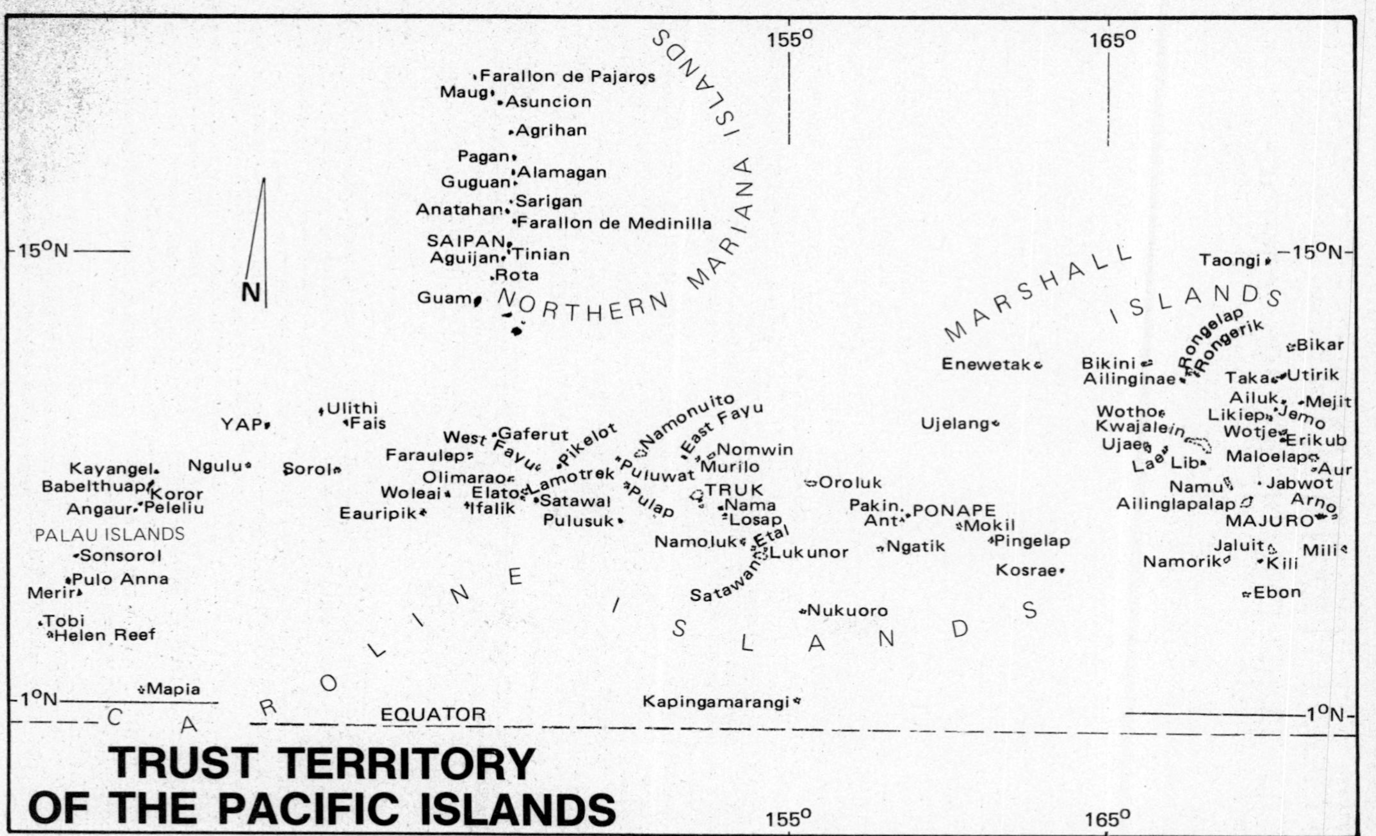
TRUST TERRITORY
OF THE PACIFIC ISLANDS
NORTHERN MARIANA ISLANDS
MARSHALL ISLANDS
CAROLINE ISLANDS
PALAU ISLANDS
EQUATOR
15°N
1°N
155°
165°
N
Farallon de Pajaros
Maug
Asuncion
Agrihan
Pagan
Alamagan
Guguan
Sarigan
Anatahan
Farallon de Medinilla
SAIPAN
Tinian
Aguijan
Rota
Guam
Ulithi
Fais
YAP
Ngulu
Sorol
West Fayu
Gaferut
Pikelot
Faraulep
Olimarao
Lamotrek
Elato
Satawal
Woleai
Ifalik
Eauripik
Namonuito
East Fayu
Nomwin
Murilo
Puluwat
Pulap
TRUK
Nama
Losap
Pulusuk
Namoluk
Etal
Lukunor
Satawan
Oroluk
Nukuoro
Kapingamarangi
Pakin.
Ant
PONAPE
Ngatik
Mokil
Pingelap
Kosrae
Kayangel
Babelthuap
Koror
Angaur
Peleliu
Sonsorol
Pulo Anna
Merir
Tobi
Helen Reef
Mapia
Taongi
Bikar
Rongelap
Rongerik
Utirik
Taka
Bikini
Ailinginae
Mejit
Ailuk
Jemo
Likiep
Erikub
Wotje
Wotho
Kwajalein
Ujae
Lae
Lib
Maloelap
Aur
Jabwot
Namu
Ailinglapalap
Arno
MAJURO
Jaluit
Mili
Kili
Namorik
Ebon
Enewetak
Ujelang

languages and, to an extent, the division of the three groups into districts recognises these differences.

Generally, the closer the islands are to the Philippines and the Asian mainland (i.e. the Marianas), the closer the people resemble Filipinos and Asians; the closer the islands are to Polynesia (i.e. the Marshalls and Eastern Carolines), the closer they resemble Polynesians.

While all of the people are Micronesians, and are collectively referred to as such, locally they are called Marshallese, Palauans, Trukese and so forth. The people of the Mariana Islands are called Chamorros.

Traditional customs differ as the scattered and isolated islands have produced local adaptations and inventions but there is a basic similarity in general cultural characteristics such as class distinctions, the making of artifacts, kinship ties, ancestor cults and political loyalties. There are differing degrees of lifestyle, however, depending on the people's contacts with Spanish, German, Japanese and American cultures.

Language. There are wide differences in language, although each islands dialect has a common Malayo-Polynesian source. The nine major languages spoken in the Trust Territory all belong to the Malayo-Polynesian family. Chamorro and Palauan are classed as Micronesian: the languages of Yap, Ulithi, Truk, Ponape and Kusaie as Malaysian; that of Kapingamarangi and Nukuoro as Polynesian; and that of Sonsorol and Tobi, in the S-W of Palau District, different from all others although with some relationship to Trukese and the Ulithi dialect.

The Chamorro language especially shows the influence of Tagalog from the Philippines and big incursions of Spanish.

The Chamorro people of Rota are believed to speak a purer form of their language and to have retained more remnants of pure Chamorro culture.

Where there were large Japanese populations and Japanese was taught in the schools, many of the older people can speak conversational Japanese.

English is widely spoken.

Census. A census was scheduled for September, 1980, but figures were not available. The previous census was in 1973, all figures issued since then being estimates. The census of September 18, 1973 showed the total population as 114,973, of whom 110,805 were Trust Territory citizens, but excluded the population at Kwajalein Missile Range (4,467).

The estimated mid-year population of the Trust Territory, including the Northern Marianas, in 1978, was 113,480, of whom 51,240 were aged up to 14 years, 57,550 from 15 to 64 years and 4,690 aged 65 and over.

Citizenship. The islanders are "citizens of the Trust Territory of the Pacific Islands" but are, in fact, regarded internationally as US protected persons. They travel abroad on Trust Territory passports, but under the diplomatic protection of the US.

Population distribution. In 1980, the estimated population including the Northern Marianas, was 136,500 and was divided as follows:

Truk	38,650
Marshalls	29,670
Ponape	23,140
Palau	14,800
Yap	9,320
Kosrae	4,940
N. Marianas	15,970

About 25,000 Micronesians, or about 18 per cent, live in outer islands, accessible only by field trip vessels, the rest, generally, living within a day's journey of district centres.

Migration. Migration trends in recent years have shown a growing tendency for young Micronesians to go overseas for further education. In addition, significant numbers of Palauans and Saipanese have moved to Guam, Hawaii and the US mainland to work. In 1976, some 3,000 residents of Ebeye Island in Kwajalein Atoll were asked to return to their home islands. This was to reduce overcrowding on Ebeye.

The people of the Marshall atolls of Bikini and Enewetak, who were displaced in 1947 when the United States conducted atomic tests there, were still waiting in 1980 to return to their homes. Attempts have been made to return the people to their atolls but those who had gone back, Bikinians from Kili and Enewetakans from Ujelang, had to be re-evacuated because the test sites were still dangerously radioactive. It was announced late in 1980 that Enewetakans could return home for a trial period of three months.

Religion. In 1973 there were 56,287 Protestants, 51,890 Roman Catholics, 3,290 who followed a traditional religion, 1,511 "other" religion, and 2,273 without religion or religion not stated.

In the Marianas, the majority of Chamorros are practising Roman Catholics.

Lifestyle. The people of the Marianas have suffered almost complete culture change as a result of contact with outsiders. Their background is similar to that of other ex-Spanish colonial peoples in such places as the Philippines and Mexico. Early Spanish Catholicism has given them their basic patterns of conduct, overlaid with US influence. However, they have retained some of the old Chamorro techniques of a subsistence existence.

The people of Yap, in the Carolines, by contrast, still retain much of their old culture. They still have a largely subsistence economy of fishing and gardening, can still build their houses and their canoes without use of nails; and, away from the district headquarters, wear native dress. This consists of a loin-cloth (called a thu) for men and a thick, full grass skirt for women.

The people of Kapingamarangi and Nukuoro

atolls are Polynesian. These atolls are the most southern in the Ponape District of the Carolines and are isolated from the rest of the Trust Territory – they are, in fact, a great deal closer to New Hanover and New Ireland, in Papua New Guinea.

Recreation. Popular activities include skin diving, fishing and trail hiking.

GOVERNMENT. With the exception of external affairs, which are still handled by Washington, all the territories are now self-governing in the three departments, executive, legislative and judicial but the power of veto of any decision by the respective governments still rests with Washington through the High Commissioner appointed by the US President, whose decision is subject to confirmation by the US Senate. Presumably, at least in some of the countries of Micronesia, the power of veto will be curtailed and exercised only where defence policy is concerned when the Trusteeship Agreement ends. In all the discussion with the United States on the political status of the Micronesian territories, the former has always stressed that it wanted control of defence.

Though the four newly-autonomous groups, the Marshalls, the Federated States of Micronesia, Palau and the Northern Marianas, have their own administrative centres, the overall administration under the Trusteeship Agreement, is conducted from Saipan in the Marianas.

The negotiations between Micronesians and the United States have been lengthy and, at times, acrimonious, but, by the middle of October, 1980, agreement over the compacts of free association, which will govern the status of the Marshalls, the FSM and Palau after the Trusteeship is terminated, was in sight. The Marianas' future political status had been agreed three years ago and commonwealth status assumed in January, 1978.

Following further negotiations on Guam and at Kona on Hawaii in October US Ambassador Peter R. Rosenblatt, President Carter's personal representative at the negotiations, announced that compacts of free association between the United States and the FSM and Palau could be initialled before the US Presidential election in November. The compact with the Marshall Islands had been initialled earlier but may be re-initialled in accord with the FSM and Palau.

The Palauan Constitution, which had been approved by the Palauans, was opposed by the United States, and by the Palau Political Status Commission, because it 'ran counter to United States' global strategic interests, preventing the United States from carrying out its defence role'. The Palauans had included in the draft Constitution a provision banning nuclear substances in Palau and another provision defining Palau's territorial waters according to the archipelagic baseline principle, the United States regarding the waters as open territorial waters. Both these provisions were unacceptable to the Americans.

It was expected, however, at the time, that agreement on these two matters was not far distant.

American aid. By October, 1980, the United States had apportioned monetary aid for the three political entities. Full details were not available at that time but the Federated States of Micronesia is expected to receive $US151 million over the next 15 years – $60 million over the first five years; $51 million over the second five years and $40 million over the third five years. At least 40 percent of the financial aid must be used for economic development.

In addition, smaller grants, to be divided between the FSM, the Marshalls and Palau, will include $1 million a year for marine surveillance, a one-time payment of $2 million for the initial costs of mounting the surveillance, $2 million a year for health services and $3 million a year for scholarship aid.

The United States Federal Government's services including the Post Office weather services, disaster relief, airline administration and regulations and the construction of airports, which have been available for the Trust Territory Government, will be continued for the three countries.

Other aid for the FSM includes seven TT Government ships and two fishing vessels.

In December, 1978, the United States agreed to give the Micronesians $12.6 million as payment for the use of their lands by the US military forces after the Pacific War. The Micronesians are also claiming compensation from the United States and Japan for destruction of property during the war.

Legislatures. All the Micronesian states have their own separate legislatures with members elected by popular vote except in Palau which also has a House of Chiefs. As well as sending representatives to the central government of the Federated States of Micronesia, the four partners, Truk, Ponape, Yap and Kosrae elect their individual legislatures, while the Marshall Islands have their Nitijela (Parliament) and district legislatures or councils, as has Palau though Palau in October, 1980, was still awaiting formal approval of its new political status. The apparatus for internal self-government was functioning, however. When Palau does become a republic, it will have 16 municipalities which will be known as states.

All three political groups have elected their governors and lieutenant-governors, and all the governors, including the governors of the Northern Marianas and Guam have joined the Association of Pacific Basin Chief Executives.

TRUST TERRITORY GOVERNMENT

This government continues in office until the Trust Territory Agreement is terminated. Termination is scheduled for 1981 but there are indications that it might be postponed as some representatives of territories have suggested postponement on the grounds that they are not fully prepared for new status.

High Commissioner: Adrian P. Winkel

Deputy High Commissioner: Juan A. Sablan
Administrator, Dept. of Administrative Services: N. Neiman Craley
Administrator, Dept. of Development Services: Lazarus E. Salii
Administrator, Dept. of Community Services: Resio Moses
Attorney-General; Daniel High
Director, Office of Planning & Statistics: Michael Rody
Director, Program & Budget: Haruo Willter
JUDICIARY
Chief Justice: Harold W. Burnett
Associate Justice: Mamoru Nakamura
Associate Justice: G. F. Gianotti

MARSHALL ISLANDS

On May 1, 1979, the Marshall Islands became the first of the three political entities to declare self-government under its own constitution, the President, Cabinet and members of the Nitijela being sworn in by the High Commissioner of the Trust Territory, Mr Adrian P. Winkel.

GOVERNMENT

President: Amata Kabua
Speaker: Atlan Anien
Vice-Speaker: Namo Hermios
Cabinet
Minister of Finance: Atjang Paul
Minister of Internal Security: Ataji Balos
Minister of Internal Affairs: Wilfred Kendall
Minister of Public Works: Kunar Abner
Minister of Social Welfare: Jina Lavin
Minister of Health: Henry Samuel
Minister of Education: Tom Kijiner
Minister of Resources & Development: Kessai Note
Minister of Transportation & Communication: Ruben Zackhras
Nitijela
Majuro: Amata Kabua, Wilfred Iroaki Kendall, Jina J. Lavin, Henry Samuel, Toke Sawej
Kwajalein: Ataji L. Balos, Imada Kabua, Jolly L. Lokjar
Arno: Kanchi Ibino, Katip Mack
Ailinglaplap: Atjang Paul, Ruben R. Zackhras
Jaluit: Carl Heine, Evelyn Konou
Jabat: Kessai H. Note
Mili: Alee Alik
Ebon: Ekpap Silk
Lib: Pijja Jerwan
Namdrik: Andrew Hisaiah
Maloelap: Namo Hermios
Wotje: Litokwa Tomeing
Likiep: Tom Kijiner
Ailuk: Luckner K. Abner
Aur: Beasa Peter
Namu: Atlan Anien
Wotho: Mwejar Mathusla
Enewetak/Ujeland: Ismeal John
Kili/Bikini: Henchi Balos
Rongelap: Jeton Anjain
Mejit: Report E. Emmius
Utrik: Donald Matthew
Lae: Jimmy Jimi Akeang
Ujae: Calep Rantak
JUDICIARY
Presiding Judge: Kabua Kabua

The Marshalls is being paid by the United States for the latter's use of Kwajalein as a missile testing range. It was announced in November, 1979, that the United States would pay $6 million in 1980 for use of the atoll and, after the termination of the Trusteeship Agreement, would pay $8 million a year.

It has been suggested that the Marshalls change its name to Ralik Ratak.

FEDERATED STATES OF MICRONESIA

The FSM, consisting of the states of Truk, Ponape, Yap and Kosrae, came into being on May 10, 1979 with ceremonies at Kolonia, Ponape. The first President, Tosiwo Nakayama, was inaugurated on May 15, 1979, by the High Commissioner, Mr Adrian P. Winkel. The ceremonies included the presentation of Yapese stone money by the Community College of Micronesia on Ponape. The stone money, weighing more than 227 kg, represented Yap's pledge of loyalty to the new government.

The new congress is a 14-member unicameral body which was still choosing its permanent departmental heads in October, 1980.

GOVERNMENT

President: Tosiwo Nakayama
Vice-President: Petrus Tun
Speaker: Bethwel Henry
Vice-Speaker: Joab Sigrah
Chief Clerk: Nishima Siron
Assistant Chief Clerk: Tadeo Sigrah
Floor Leader: Luke Tman
Ways & Means Committee, Chairman: Raymond Setik
Resources & Development Committee, Chairman: Sasauo Haruo Gouland
Health, Education & Social Affairs Committee, Chairman: Hirosi Ismael
External Affairs, Chairman: Bailey Olter
Members: Peter Christian, Elias Thomas, Koichi Sana, Julio M. Akapito, Kalisto Refalopei, Masachiro Christlib, John Hagelgam

FSM STATE GOVERNMENTS
Kosrae:
Governor: Jacob Nena
Lt. Governor: Vacant
Speaker, Kosrae Legislature: Gaius Nedlic
Presiding Judge: Linus George
Ponape:
Governor: Leo A. Falcam
Lt. Governor: Strik Yoma

Speaker, Ponape Legislature: Edwel Santos
Presiding Judge: Carl Kohler
Truk:
Governor: Erhart Aten
Lt. Governor: Hans Wiliander
Speaker, Truk Legislature: Tadashi Wainit
Presiding Judge: Soukichi Fritz
Yap:
Governor: John A. Mangafel
Lt. Governor: Hilary Tacheliol
Speaker, Yap Legistature: Joseph Ayin
Presiding Judge: Joseph Marnifen

PALAU

Palau's Constitution, which was approved by the majority of Palauans in a referendum in October, 1979, following several technical and legal manoeuvres to alter the original draft constitution, was still facing opposition from the United States and Palau's own Political Status Commission in October, 1980. Originally, the new state Constitution would have been inaugurated on January 1, 1980.

When the constitution becomes legal, the Government of the Republic of Palau will have executive, legislative and judicial branches. Parliament known locally as 'Olbiil era Kelalau', will be bicameral, with an elected House of Delegates, one from each of the 16 states, and a Senate. The President, elected for a four-year term and limited to two terms, will head the executive branch, and a council of traditional head chiefs from each of the 16 states will advise the President of traditional laws and customs.

The judicial branch will have a Supreme Court with a Chief Justice and from three to six associate justices. There will be a national court and inferior courts.

Palauan and English will be the official languages. Koror is the temporary capital but the permanent capital must be established on Babeldaob Island (Babelthuap) within 10 years. Palau will become Belau on January 1, 1981.

GOVERNMENT

President: Haruo Remeliik
Vice-President: Alfonso Oiterong
SENATE
Kuniwo Nakamura, Johnson Toribiong, Joshua Koshiba, Edward Temengil, Moses Uludong, Kaleb Udui and Peter Sugiyama (Koror State); Hank Takawo and Olkeriil Rehuher (Kayangel and Ngerchelong); John Tarkong and David Ngirmidol (Ngaraard); George Ngirarsaol and Seit Andres (Ngiwal, Melekeok and Ngchesar); Baules Sechelong (Airai); Masami Siksei and Lucius Malsol (Imeliik, Ngetpang, Ngeremlemgui and Ngerdmau); Miichungi Solang (Peleliu); Abel Suzuki (Ngeaur, Tobi and Sonsorol).
HOUSE OF DELEGATES
Kambalang Olebuu (Kayangel); Johnny Reklai (Ngerchelong); Laurentino Ulechong (Ngaraard); Hideo Termeteet (Ngiwal); Kazuo Asanuma (Melekeok); Ignacio Anastacio (Ngchesar); Mengiraro Ngiratechekii (Airai); Tem Obakerbau (Imeliik); Demei Otobed (Ngetpang); Blau Skebong (Ngeremlengui); Akiko Sugiyama (Ngerdmau); Santos Olikong (Koror); Takeshi Kintol (Peleliu); Carlos Salii (Ngeaur); Mariano Carlos (Sonsorol); and Pablo Kyoshi (Tobi).

Local government. The municipality is the basic unit of local government. Its responsibilities include safety and public welfare, licensing of retail and service businesses, excise, head and property taxes, streets, roads and docks, law enforcement not otherwise provided for, and support functions for courts, education, and public health.

Municipalities may be chartered or unchartered, with varying proportions of elected and appointed officers. The chief executive of a municipality is known as magistrate or mayor.

Traditional rulers. In some states, hereditary position or rank has been extremely important. The growth of the elective process coupled with increasing demands of office has prompted some chiefs not to run themselves as magistrates but rather support younger men better educated in modern government.

Justice. The judicial authority in all states is independent of the other two branches of government and is vested in the Territory High Court and other courts. The Chief Justice and three associate justices of the High Court are appointed by the Secretary of the Interior.

Courts. Apart from the High Court, there are state courts and community courts.

The High Court is the highest judicial authority, with appellate and trial divisions. The appellate division has jurisdiction to review, on appeal, decisions of the trial division in the following instances: (1) All cases tried originally in the High Court; (2) All cases decided by the High Court on appeal from a district court or a community court.

The trial division has original jurisdiction in all civil and criminal cases, including probate, admiralty and maritime matters and land titles, and reviews appeal decisions of the state courts and community courts from which no appeal is made.

The Chief Justice has two Associate Justices responsible for Truk, Ponape and Marshall Islands and one Associate Justice responsible for Palau and Yap.

Selected opinions of the High Court are published in Trust Territory Reports.

The state courts are restricted to certain maximum limits in civil and criminal cases. They may also review decisions of community courts.

All state court judges are Micronesians, appointed by the High Commissioner.

The community courts are restricted to minor civil and criminal matters.

All the courts continue to function as in the past until the Marshalls, the FSM and Palau have each established their own courts, and have had the approval of the Chief Justice of the High Court of the Trust Territory. Application for approval has to be made by the chief judicial officer of each country to the Chief Justice. Any cases pending at the time will be transferred to the new courts but strict supervision will be exercised to protect the legal rights of the parties in litigation.

Appeals from the courts of the three countries will be to the High Court of the Trust Territory, the ruling of which will be final and binding. In May, 1980, FSM President Nakayama nominated Mr Edward C. King of Maryland in the United States as Chief Justice of the FSM Supreme Court.

Police. The Micronesia police are divided among districts, each having a district chief of police. Detachments cover law and order, local defence, criminal investigation, fire-fighting, service of legal processes and administration of district gaols. Police are trained in the Public Safety Academy. The Attorney General is the security officer of the territory and supervises administration and operation of the Bureau of Public Safety.

Police strength in 1977 totalled 234 all ranks plus 68 in the Northern Marianas.

Liquor laws. There is no commercial manufacture of alcoholic drinks in the Trust Territory.

Importation of beer, wine and spirits is permitted and occurs in all districts.

A visitor Drinking Permit, costing a few dollars and valid for 30 days is required in Ponape, Truk and Palau. Municipalities have a "local option" under which residents may vote to decide whether to allow alcohol to be sold or not. In January 1978, Moen municipality in Truk introduced total prohibition on alcoholic drinks within the municipal area. This was to reduce "alcohol-related" crimes. Sizeable tax revenue results at both the territorial and district level from the importing and sale of liquor which is through bars, by the glass, and stores, by the bottle or can.

DEFENCE. The Trust Territory is of strategic importance to the US, and negotiations towards a free association of the various districts with the US have involved arrangements for granting facilities for defence to the US. These include retention of the lease of parts of Kwajalein atoll, in the Marshalls, for the US missile range established there. In March 1976, a new five year lease was signed between the Micronesians and the US Government for use of the range's mid-atoll corridor islands.

In 1980, the Marshalls received $6 million for the use of Kwajalein. Payment will rise to $8 million a year after termination of the TT Agreement.

The US Armed Forces occupy various areas of what is called 'retention land' for defence in Micronesia. These lands include about 3,640 hectares on Tinian, or about one third of that island in the Marianas, and nearly 2,000 hectares, including the airport, on Saipan. This land was leased in July and August 1944 for an indefinite period at the rate of $99 per hectare, paid into a trust fund.

The covenant to establish a Commonwealth of the Northern Marianas will result in some changes to the Marianas defence land situation. The covenant provides for a long-term lease for 7,203 hectares on Tinian, 82 hectares at Tanapag Harbour, Saipan, and 83 hectares at Farallon de Medinilla Island, encompassing the entire island. It is agreed that the retention land not included in these leases will be returned to the Government of the Marianas.

Currently the military has no plans of setting up military installations on Saipan or Tinian, but funds will be used to improve Tinian harbour and airport.

The Department of Defence also intends to negotiate with the Trust Territory about utilisation of the Kwajalein missile range, and will seek to lease about 16 hectares of submerged land in the port of Malakal in Palau and 809 hectares on the west coast of Babelthuap, Palau. It would also want to use 12,140 hectares on Babelthuap for military manoeuvres, although the land could also be used by the local population.

EDUCATION. Education is free in public schools and compulsory between six and 14 years of age or until graduation from secondary school. In the 1973 census, 90 per cent of children 6 to 16 attended school. Administratively education is in the charge of a territorial Director of Education, and District Directors of Education.

Elementary schools. Primary schools begin at grade one and go as high as grade eight. Secondary schools go from grade nine to grade twelve. In 1977, there were 239 primary schools in the territory with an enrolment of 27,085 and 25 secondary schools with an enrolment of 6,632. There is one vocational school (Micronesian Occupational College) located in the Palau district with an enrolment of 314. The Community College of Micronesia, two-year post secondary education, is located in Ponape with 406 students enrolled.

In 1980 it was planned to spend $5.4 million for new buildings and facilities. Another 1,226 students were abroad attending post secondary schools.

Private schools. Private schools may be established only with the approval of the High Commissioner and on the recommendation of the Director of Education. The charters of each school must be renewed every three years. Under the law, students in private schools receive from the Trust Territory the same benefits enjoyed by public school students such as transportation, insurance, medical services, textbooks and meals. Enrolments in private elementary schools have been declining.

In 1977, there were 17 private elementary schools in the three political territories and one in the Northern Marianas and 11 private secondary schools and one in the Northern Marianas.

Vocational and technical education. Vocational

courses are offered at all territory secondary schools, all of which also offer agricultural courses. Two main institutions offer fulltime vocational instruction – the Micronesian Occupational College on Koror and the Ponape Agriculture and Trade School. In 1975, 318 students attended courses at Koror, and 171 at Ponape.

The MOC pays the salaries of vocational education supervisors in each district, who are responsible for the development of the programme in district elementary and secondary schools.

Both institutions take pupils from all districts.

Tertiary education. There is no tertiary instruction within the territory. In 1976, 1,091 students were receiving post-secondary education abroad, mainly in the US. Most of these were in receipt of scholarships from the government and the Congress of Micronesia.

Teachers. In 1977, there were 1,992 teachers in the territory – 998 in FSM, 403 in the Marshalls, 329 in Palau and 262 in the Northern Marianas. Of the total, 1,718 were Micronesians. There were 1,320 in the public elementary schools and 383 in the public secondary schools. The major establishment for teacher training within the territory is the Community College of Micronesia, Kolonia Town, Ponape. It has a two year training course and 1975-76 enrolment was 171. There are teacher-training centres in the district centres of Ponape, Palau, Truk and the Marshall Islands, providing fulltime courses for 106 students, with 147 attending part time.

LABOUR. Of an estimated population of 113,400 in 1978, of whom about half were below the age of 14, about 15,000 were employed. In 1976, there were 13,501 wage earners, 6,611 Micronesians employed by the government, 577 expatriates in government employ and 6,313 people employed in private enterprise.

It is estimated that the number of people of working age was 55,600 in 1977, and will increase to 80,600 in 1988. Present unemployment rate is 13 percent. Over the next 10 years, about 15,000 people will be entering the labour force. This number, plus the estimated unemployed population of 7,200, means that over 22,000 jobs are needed to absorb these workers.

However, because the labour force is scattered, the number available for employment in any one location is very small. Limited numbers live on individual islands and many prefer to follow the traditional practices of food-growing and fishing. The government is also inclined to skim the cream off the workforce, and there is a shortage of skilled workers in the private sector, particularly in construction, and labour has to be imported in many instances.

Because of the subsistence economy no reliable statistics of the total available work force are available, but the proportion of the work force employed by the government has been criticised by the last two UN visiting missions as being too high. Private employers have also complained of a shortage in private enterprise of skilled manpower in managerial, professional and middle-level skills, due to high rates of pay for the public service.

Peace Corps. An important contribution to work in the Trust Territory is being made by the American Peace Corps, which has been operating in the Territory since 1966, mainly in the field of education, but they are gradually being withdrawn. In 1976 there were 240 Peace Corps volunteers in the territory, but by mid-1979 the total had dropped to 147, including those in the Northern Marianas.

Wages. The government's rate of wages and conditions for its employees are regarded as the pattern for the private sector but in most skilled jobs the government rate exceeded that of the private sector. In 1979, the government rate was a minimum of 80 cents an hour, but from July 1, 1979, the minimum wage for Micronesians employed by the government at the TT headquarters on Saipan was increased to $1.35 an hour.

A wages survey in April, 1976, showed the following average hourly wage for selected positions in both sectors:

	Private Sector	Government Sector
Clerk	**$ .74**	**$1.14**
Accountant	**2.24**	**2.56**
Labourer	**.83**	**1.14**
Heavy Equipment Operator	**1.43**	**1.83**
Auto Mechanic	**1.38**	**1.71**
Carpenter	**1.11**	**1.71**
Electrician	**1.00**	**1.71**
Mason	**1.40**	**1.41**
Plumber	**1.13**	**1.71**
Cook	**.98**	**1.22**
Janitor	**.64**	**1.14**

Social security. The Trust Territory social security scheme is patterned on the US social security programme, with employees and employers contributing. Benefits and contributions are based on the territory's economy.

All employees working for government or private are covered under Trust Territory Social Security System unless the employee and employer are subject to the US Social Security system or another recognised social security programme. All employers are required to withhold one and one half per cent of the employee's salary and contribute an equal amount. Total taxable wages per quarter in 1978 were $1,200.

Revenue for social security from both government and the private sector in 1976 totalled $876,000 excluding the Marianas' contributions, and benefit payments amounted to $239,000.

Credit unions. At December 31, 1978, there were 37 credit unions in the Trust Territory, six fewer than in 1977, but assets increased by 15 per cent over the 1977 valuation to $7.5 million and members' savings increased by 14 percent to $6 million.

Co-operative societies. There were 73 co-operative societies in the three political groups in 1976 but only 31 supplied statistics showing a total membership of 12,558; dividends paid $56,500; total sales revenue $11,527,500; net earnings $521,400; total assets $4,961,000; share capital $1,090,700. As most major societies sent in statistics, the figures represent more than 80 percent of the financial activity.

Trade unions. There are no trade unions in the Trust Territory but there is no official government opposition to trade unions and no prohibition against them.

HEALTH. The Director of Health Services administers health care facilities which provide for more than 80 per cent of the people to have direct access to a fully equipped state centre hospital, or be within one day's travel of one. In each state there is a Director of Health Services (a Micronesian medical officer) who is also responsible for direct administration of state hospitals, etc.

The Marshalls Government negotiated an agreement in 1979 with the Seventh-day Adventist Church for the latter to operate the Health Department, the Administrator of which is F. Schlehuber.

November, 1979, saw the opening in Yap of a new 50-bed hospital costing $54 million. The hospital is the biggest building in Yap.

Medical staff. The medical staff is part of the public service. There are no private doctors other than those at the dental clinic at Saipan run by the Seventh-day Adventist Mission and a dentist who practises in the Ponape state. There are 56 doctors in the Department of Health Services, 54 doctor's assistants, 421 nurses and 215 health assistants. There are 24 government dentists, 34 dental nurses and 29 dental auxiliary personnel providing dental health care throughout the islands. These figures include the Northern Marianas.

In 1976, 115 students were attending medical and paramedical courses outside the Trust Territory.

Medical facilities. There are hospitals in each district and a 30-bed rehabilitation centre has been annexed to Majuro Hospital. There are more than 170 dispensaries, mainly on the outer islands remote from district centres.

The outer islanders receive additional health services when regular field trip ships visit their islands, and by aircraft or special trips in emergencies. More than 200 small radio stations outside district centres offer communication for health workers.

Some health services are free, such as immunisation and treatment for communicable diseases; otherwise there are fee schedules.

There were 21,692 admissions to TT hospitals in 1977, 4,197 in N. Marianas, 10,118 in FSM and 4,761 in the Marshalls. Outpatients treated totalled 151,312. Of 3,975 live births, 721 were in the home.

Medical research. Medical research is carried out mainly through special projects sponsored by outside agencies. A team of Atomic Energy Commission scientists, including medical specialists, continues long-range follow-up work on the effects of the 1954 radiation fallout on the residents of Rongelap and Utirik in the Marshalls.

Diseases. Major causes of deaths in the last 25 years have been respiratory infections, but this situation is improving. Although influenza is no longer a major cause of death it is still the most common disease. Cases of venereal disease have declined.

THE LAND. The Trust Territory, including the Northern Marianas, extends over eight million square kilometres in the western Pacific Ocean. There are more than 2,000 islands and islets grouped in three major archipelagoes – the Carolines, the Marianas and the Marshalls. Hence the name Micronesia, meaning 'tiny islands'.

Total land area is 1,833 sq km. Only 96 islands are inhabited.

The largest islands are Babelthuap, Palau and Ponape.

The territory extends about 2,200 km from north to south, that is from the northernmost uninhabited island of the Marianas to Kapingamarangi atoll in the south of Ponape. From east to west, the islands extend 3,700 km from Majoro atoll in the Marshall Islands to Koror in Palau.

The Mariana Islands, consist of 16 islands, including a group of three tiny islands, known collectively as Maug. The total land surface of the group is approximately 471 square kilometres, two thirds of which form the three principal islands, Saipan, Tinian and Rota. Headquarters is on Saipan. For further details, see Northern Mariana Islands.

Palau is the westernmost state of the Caroline Islands. It consists of a main group of islands known as the Palau group and four small coral islands scattered between the Palau group and the north-eastern islands of Indonesia. The Palau group consists of more than 200 islands, some volcanic and others of coral limestone composition extending over an area about 200 kilometres in length by 40 kilometres in width. Only eight of the islands are permanently inhabited. The total land area of the state (460 square kilometres) consists mainly of the island of Babelthuap (404 square kilometres), the largest in the territory. The state capital is located on the island of Koror. Most of the population lives on Koror, and the second major population group is on Babelthuap.

Yap State, in the eastern Caroline Islands, consists of the Yap group, where the district centre, Colonia, is located, and 15 other islands and atolls scattered to the east for a distance of approximately 1,120 kilometres in a band 257 kilometres wide. The Yap group is made up of four major high islands separated by narrow passages and surrounded by barrier reefs. With one exception, the outer islands are low, most of them lagoon-type atolls. The area of Yap proper is almost 100 square kilometres and the combined land area of the outer islands is 21.2 square kilometres. The population is widely scattered, although most live on Yap.

Truk State lies roughly in the centre of the long, east-west chain of the Caroline Islands. It consists of 15 island groups with a total land area of 118 square kilometres scattered over an ocean area some 480 kilometres by 960 kilometres. Truk proper is a complex atoll composed of 14 mountainous islands of volcanic origin, with a combined area of 72 square kilometres, surrounded by a great coral ring which forms a lagoon of over 2,000 square kilometres. The outer islands of the district are all low islands or atolls. Moen, Tol, Dublon, Fefan and Uman are the most populated islands of Truk Atoll. State headquarters is on Moen Island.

The two self-governing states of Kosrae (pronounced Co-shy) and Ponape, members of the Federated States of Micronesia, were formerly the Ponape district with a total land area of 488.2 sq.km. They lie in the Eastern Caroline Islands and consist of the two main land masses, which are volcanic, and eight widely-scattered atolls. Ponape Island rates second and Kosrae fourth in land area among the islands of the Trust Territory. Kolonia town, on Ponape Island, is the capital of FSM. Most of the population lives on Ponape.

The Marshall Islands, the easternmost of the Trust Territory's states, comprises 29 coral atolls and 5 low coral islands with a total land area of about 180 square kilometres scattered over approximately 970,000 square kilometres of ocean. State headquarters is located on Majuro Atoll, which has the major population.

Elevations in the Trust Territory range from about 2 metres on a coral atoll to 965m on Agrihan Island, Marianas.

Terrain ranges from substantial volcanic islands to tiny coral islets. Most islands in the Eastern Carolines and the Marshalls are of coral formation. The Marianas and Western Caroline Islands are formed of remnants of a vast undersea volcanic ridge, stretching south from Japan.

Flora and fauna. Vegetation varies considerably from high islands to low atolls, although coconut and breadfruit trees are common to both. The high volcanic islands usually have mangrove swamps on the tidal flats, and mixed forest growth on the uplands.

Native land animals are represented only by two species of insect eating bats and two species of fruit bats. Introduced animals include water buffalo, goats, an oriental shrew, and deer. In Palau there are crocodiles, and most of the islands have snakes, including highly venomous sea snakes in the Marshalls and Palau. A large monitor lizard, up to 1.8 m long, is found on many islands.

Marine and shore birds abound, including freshwater ducks and cormorants. A rich marine fauna also includes porpoises and the protected dugong, or sea cow. There are more than 7,000 species of insects in the territory.

Soil. The soil suffers leaching and erosion through heavy rainfall. It is generally made up of decomposed volcanic or coral rocks. Valleys and alluvial plains towards the coasts are moderately fertile.

Climate. Temperatures generally range from about 23 deg. C. to about 30 deg. C. and are relatively uniform. Humidity averages 80 per cent, while annual rainfall varies greatly among the islands, ranging from as high as 5,000 mm in parts of Ponape to as low as 250 to 400 mm in some of the northernmost Marshalls. Most islands have pronounced wet and dry seasons.

The territory is in an area of the western Pacific where major ocean storms develop and typhoons strike.

Land tenure. Land ownership is restricted to indigenous people, except for land held before World War II. The only land owned by non-indigenous people to any extent is in Ponape, where a Belgian family holds a substantial area, after settling there about the end of the 19th century.

Customary land tenure varies greatly from district to district, and even on an island there may be as many as five distinct local land tenure systems. These traditional practices have been modified by court decisions, and by the use of money for land sales made under US administration.

Land disputes are fairly common in the Marshalls, Truk and Palau, and to a lesser degree in Ponape. Principal cause is the lack of written records.

Territory citizens are allowed to settle on undeveloped areas of public land and obtain ownership through development.

PRIMARY PRODUCTION. Copra and fish are the two most important exports. Land under cultivation for various crops including coconut, banana and breadfruit totalled 31,008 ha excluding the Marianas. More than a third of the land under crops was in the Marshalls. Forests of hardwood and mixed timbers covered 27,418 ha, including the Marianas, and there were 8,772 ha of mangrove forests. There were 24,029 ha of grazing land and 43,461 ha of unused arable land, including 27,829 ha in the Marianas.

Crops. Most volcanic and atoll islands, where people live, have swamp areas where taro is grown as a staple food. Some alluvial plains and gentle slopes near the coast are used to grow coconut palms, breadfruit, bananas, cacao, yams, dry land taro, sweet potatoes, and other vegetables. Small quantities are exported.

Produce marketed in the Trust Territory (excluding the Marianas) in 1977 included 12,428 tonnes of copra, 116.3 tonnes of fruit, 154.8 tonnes of staple crops, 79.4 tonnes of vegetables and 3.4 tonnes of pepper.

Copra. Copra is the only important cash crop in the territory. In the fiscal year 1977, coconut oil valued at $4 million was exported to the United States and copra cake, valued at $500,000 was exported to W. Germany. It is anticipated that by 1982 nearly 8,000 ha of new land will be under coconut increasing output by 40 percent. There is a $3.7 million copra mill in Palau which processes copra for most of the territory.

Livestock. The principal livestock are pigs and poultry. Cattle, goats and carabao (water buffalo) graze on the high islands. In 1976 the territory had 7,325 cattle, of which 7,196 were in the Marianas.

In 1977, the territory (excluding the Marianas) had 200 cattle, 1,475 goats, 102 carabao, 19,326 pigs, 39,400 chickens, 40 turkeys and 775 ducks.

To encourage farming, the TT Government has two breeding herds of Santa Gertrudis cattle, one in Ponape and one in Palau and an experimental chicken broiler unit in Truk.

The TT Agriculture Division maintains a staff at the TT headquarters on Saipan and a field staff in extension, entomology, plant pathology, veterinary services, conservation and forestry. There are development stations and sub-stations in each of the six states covering all aspects of agricultural development, including development of new commercial crops and improvement in production and marketing of existing crops.

Fisheries. Fish is the second largest export commodity. Live bait pole-and-line fishing for skipjack and tuna is conducted. Exports in the year ended September 30, 1977 amounted to 6,989.6 tonnes of tuna valued at $3,518,300 and 50.8 tonnes of other marine products valued at $73,900.

Micronesia's huge stretch of ocean and hundreds of square kilometres of fringing reef and lagoons hold opportunities for development of inshore fisheries, shark, oyster and pearl culture, trepang, mother-of-pearl, turtle, crocodiles, clams, crabs, reef fish etc. All the states will have a declared fisheries zone, but at present, offshore resources are being exploited by Japan and other countries.

An American firm has developed a skipjack tuna fishery in Palau and between 3,000 and 5,000 tonnes of fish are landed there every year making Palau the largest producer of island-caught skipjack in the Pacific, surpassing Hawaii, Tahiti, Fiji and other highly-developed areas. There is also scope for fishery development in the other five states.

The inshore resources offer great opportunities for fish farms in the lagoons with cultivation of oyster, shrimp and trepang. An experimental farm has been opened in Palau and young turtles are being raised at the mariculture centre there.

Foreign investment is welcomed in joint ventures in inshore fishery. A local company has established a plant to smoke and dry tuna (arabushi) for Japan. Production in 1975-76 was 45,442 kg. The company was using three vessels.

TOURISM. Tourism has third priority in the territory's development programme and attempts are being made to increase production in agriculture and manufacture to serve the tourist industry's requirements, as emphasis is being laid on the use of locally-produced goods.

Tourism has grown at more than 20 per cent a year over the last few years and the territory (excluding the Marianas) is anticipating more than 40,000 visitors in 1980. The Northern Marianas, which attracts more than twice the number of visitors as the rest of the territory, passed the 50,000 mark in 1977. This total is more than twice the number of visitors to the FSM, the Marshalls and Palau. However, the total of 20,579 in 1977 represented a 35 per cent increase over the 1976 total. Visitors' spending also increased from about $1.6 million in 1976 to about $2.16 million in 1977. Whereas, in the Northern Marianas, Japanese visitors outnumbered the rest in 1977, visitors from the United States made up 56 per cent of the total in the rest of Micronesia with 21 per cent from Japan and the remaining 23 per cent from the Philippines and elsewhere.

In 1977, there were 530 hotel rooms in the Northern Marianas and 447 in the rest of the territory, with another 50 rooms under construction.

LOCAL COMMERCE. Merchandising through the islands is generally conducted by one to three large enterprises in each district, operating as 'General Import-Wholesale-Retailer'. Many smaller retailers are dependent on them for supplies.

For local produce, corpra is marketed by a Trust Territory incorporated company under contract to the Copra Stabilization Board.

All district centres, except the Marshalls, have public farmers' markets.

MINERALS. There are scattered mineral deposits in Micronesia but they are believed to be of limited value. Exploitation cannot be attempted, however, until determination of land ownership in some areas has been made. Because of a shortage of land, exploitation would require expensive reclamation to avoid displacing people from their homes.

Reef and offshore areas are known to contain geological structures that are gas and oil bearing, but the great depth of the waters in Micronesia would make exploration and subsequent exploitation difficult and costly.

MANUFACTURING. Small-scale local industries include handicrafts, bakeries, boat building, fish-processing and bottling, as well as two copra crushing mills. There are about 12 medium to large construction firms, but their activities depend on the degree of hotel construction and military installations, though approaching changes in political status is giving impetus to the building of administrative and service centres.

OVERSEAS TRADE. The estimated value of imports and exports in recent years expressed in $million was as in the accompanying table.

	1972	1973	1974	1975	1976	1977
Imports	26	26	NA	38	38	40
Exports	2.6	1.9	8	7	5	10

The decrease in exports for 1972 and 1973 was due to a drop in copra prices.

Exports. Commodity exports reached a record high in the fiscal year 1974. The value was $8 million, compared with $1.9 million in the previous year. The dramatic increase was due primarily to an increased fishing catch and increased copra exports under the influence of high world prices. Commodity exports for 1976 were about $5 million. A new record was created in 1977, again because of increased fishing catches and copra exports.

US TRUST TERRITORIES — EXPORTS (In $'000)

	1974	1976	1977	1979
Copra & oil	4,400	1,617	4,000	22,992
Fruit/vegs.	159	n.a.	800	—
Beef/pork	222	—	—	—
Fish (tuna)	2,964	3,079	3,518	4,090
Reef fish	—	11	74	35
Handicrafts	n.a.	101	248	825
TOTAL	**8,038**	**4,809**	**10,124**	**28,299**

Copra exports are sent to USA and Japan while beef, pork and vegetables go to Guam. Fish goes mainly to the US although smoked arabushi goes to Japan.

Imports. The territory relies heavily on imports of consumer and investment goods. The value of imports tripled in the five-year period 1966 to 1971.

The main suppliers to the territory are the US and Japan.

US TRUST TERRITORY — IMPORTS 1975-76 (In $'000)

	USA	Japan	Total
Rice	1,821	—	2,962
Flour	642	1	700
Sugar	609	33	924
Canned meat	1,192	37	1,403
Canned fish	292	681	1,009
Building materials	1,820	836	3,093
Beverages	4,771	168	5,217
Tobacco	1,468	61	1,529
Clothing, textiles	723	524	1,886
Machinery	637	1,487	2,156
Boat parts etc	130	67	218
Total	**24,380**	**8,091**	**38,395**

Customs tariff. Customs duties, known as import taxes, are imposed on a range of goods, although at a very low rate, especially for foodstuffs. Cigarettes, perfumery and alcoholic liquor attract higher rates. In addition, an excise tax is levied on consumption of gasoline and diesel fuel.

FINANCE. Transfers from the US Government provide almost all the economic base of the Trust Territory. Budget funds in recent years are shown in the accompanying table.

SOURCE OF BUDGET (In $'000s)

	1977	1978	1979
Local revenue	3,431.9	3,800	4,433
Direct US approriation	1,357.1	1,778	1,307
Grants from US Congress	71,176.6	95,151	113,397
Unobligated funds brought forward	2,665.4	8,024	17,598
TOTAL	**78,613.0**	**108,753**	**136,735**

Tax system. Taxing authority is exercised by the three levels of government — territorial, state and municipal.

The territorial government has exclusive control of import, export and income taxes. In 1979, its taxes were: Excise taxes on motor vehicle fuel; Income taxes; Taxes on gross revenue of business; General import taxes.

The State administrations control liquor licences and taxes on copra and scrap metal exports, alcoholic beverages, licences for wholesale business other than financial concerns, and sales taxes.

The municipal councils control licences for retail businesses and head taxes.

Income tax. Income tax is the most important source of tax revenue. It is 3 per cent on the first $11,000 and 5 per cent on wages in excess of $11,000. It brought in more than $5 million (excluding the Marianas) in FY 1977. The business tax varies in the States but, generally, is $40 plus 1.5 per cent of revenue over $10,000 for the territorial tax, $40 plus 1.5 per cent over $10,000 for state surtax and $80 plus 3 per cent over $10,000 for composite tax.

Currency. The Trust Territory does not have its own currency. All foreign exchange transactions are in US currency, which is also the local legal tender.

Banks. Residents have access to banks in Guam, Hawaii and the US mainland. The Bank of America had branches in Saipan, Truk and Majuro, and a facility on Tinian but these have been acquired by the Bank of Guam. The Bank of Hawaii has branches at Kolonia, Ponape, Koror, Palau, Colonia, Yap, Saipan and Kwajalein. The branches make small loans to individuals and private business firms.

There is a Micronesian Development Bank, established under authority of the Congress of Micronesia because of the shortage of investment capital in the territory.

Foreign investment. Applications for investment in the Trust Territory may be submitted by investors from any nation. Economic Development Boards in each state have been considering business permit applications under guidelines established by the territory's Foreign Investors Business Permit Act, but as each state assumes more responsibility for its own affairs, the appropriate ministries are dealing with investment. Since June, 1979, the Secretary for Resources and Development in the Marshalls has been dealing with applications in that state and permits are issued by the President. The same situation was to apply to the FSM in 1980.

The critera by which investment applications are reviewed and should be covered in the investment proposals are:

1. Economic need for the service or activity to be performed;

2. Extent to which the operation results in a net increase in exports or a net decrease in imports;

3. Extent to which the operation will deplete the island's natural resources or adversely affect the island's economy;

4. Extent of ownership management and employment of Trust Territory citizens;

5. Extent the operation will enhance the overall economic well-being of the state without adversely affecting the existing social and cultural values and ethnic conditions of the state.

There can be three kinds of private corporations in the territory – foreign corporations, those wholly-owned by Micronesians and those owned by Micronesians and non-citizens.

Overall investment assets increased from $47.6 million in 1973 to $97 million by the end of 1975, with tourism and wholesale/retail trade absorbing most of the increase. Since then, separate statistics have been produced for the Marianas and the rest of the territory. In 1976, investment in the Marshalls, FSM and Palau totalled $15,343,000; in 1977 $18,073,000 and in 1978 $18,730,000. Agriculture and marine manufacturing industries attracted more than a third of the total and half is invested in Palau.

Development plan. A Trust Territory development plan was drawn up in 1976 and is being put into effect. It is to concentrate on fisheries, tourism, rice and general agriculture in a bid to bring the territory towards self-sufficiency.

TRANSPORT. The territory's roads range from concrete and macadam through coral finished surface to dirt roads that are little more than footpaths. Main thoroughfares are confined to state centres.

All-weather roads link airports, docks, markets, administrative centres and hospitals in all states, and Majuro (Marshalls) and Saipan (Marianas) boast a paved road to all important points. Other state roads are being paved gradually under the capital improvements programme. At September, 1977, there were 64 kilometres of paved roads in the territory (excluding the Marianas) and 471 kilometres of unpaved roads. The Marshalls had 51.2 kilometres of the paved roads. Kosrae, Ponape and Yap had none.

Vehicles. Government and private buses totalled 107 in 1977, divided among the states as follows: N. Marianas 37, Yap 7, Truk 21, Ponape 19, Palau 12, Marshalls 7, Kosrae 4. The number of vehicles registered at September, 1977, was 7,223 including 273 trucks, 2,038 pickups, 4,002 sedans/station wagons, 335 jeeps and 468 motor cycles and scooters.

Overseas airlines. Two international airlines, with scheduled stops, and three international airlines with unscheduled stops, service the Trust Territory. The airlines with the scheduled stops are Continental/Air Micronesia and Air Pacific International (not the Fiji-based Air Pacific) and Japan Airlines. The airlines which make unscheduled visits are Pan American and Air Nauru.

Domestic airlines. The Trust Territory is well served with internal air services. Air Micronesia, which was formed by Continental Airlines, Aloha Airlines and the United Micronesian Development Association, operates Boeing-727 to all districts and the Northern Marianas including Rota and Tinian.

Charter flights are operated between Guam and the Marianas by Air Pacific and Island Aviation.

Intra-state scheduled and chartered air services were being operated in late 1979 by the following: Pacific Missionary Aviation in Yap, Kosrae and Ponape; Ponape Air Services Inc. in Kosrae and Ponape; Aero Belau in Palau; Caroline Air Service Inc. in Truk; Trans Micronesian Airways in Yap and Guam. Others were operating in the Marianas.

In May, 1980, a new airline, Airline of the Marshall Islands, owned by Marshall Islands Development Authority, the government's economic arm, began to operate in the Marshalls with one 12-seater Nomad. A second plane was scheduled for delivery in September, 1980.

Airfields. All airport development projects planned for the Trust Territory are expected to be completed by the end of 1981. There are international airports at Majuro, Ponape, Truk, Saipan, Rota (Marianas) and Yap. Work began in 1979 on paving the existing 1,829 metre runway at Ponape and constructing an unpaved, unlighted 1,829 metre runway at Kosrae, and in January, 1980, on construction of a 2,193 metre runway for Babelthuap/Koror Airport. The airport at Truk will be extended to 2,103 metres by 1981. There are also internal airports at Koror (Palau) and Tinian (Marianas) and an important airfield at Kwajalein.

Port facilities. There are eight commercial docks on eight major inhabited islands. Saipan has a 152m dock with an alongside depth of 8.8m.

Tinian has a 610m long dock with an alongside depth of 9.8m.

Koror, Palau District, has a 155m long dock, drawing 8.8m alongside.

Takatik, Ponape District, has a 283m dock drawing 8.8m.

Kosrae has a 36.6m long dock with an alongside depth of 8.2m.

Colonia, Yap District, has a 70m dock with an alongside depth of 4m.

Moen, Truk District, has a 91m dock, with an alongside depth of 9.8m.

Majuro, Marshalls District, has a 55m dock, with an alongside depth of 10.4m.

New docks and port facilities for the Marshalls and Yap were to be completed by mid-1980, and construction was in progress in 1979 on a new dock and port development in Truk. Several channels in the outer islands in Ponape and Truk have been widened and deepened.

'Super'-port plan. It was agreed in 1976 for a Japanese feasibility study for reconstruction of a large port complex on Kossol Reef, Babelthuap, Palau, equipped with vast oil storage facilities and capable of berthing super-tankers. The tankers would bring oil in bulk from the Middle East, and it would be broken up on Palau and shipped in smaller tankers to consumers in Asia and the Pacific whose ports were not equipped for the larger tankers. The port would be supported by facilities such as power plants and housing. The feasibility study can be made by the Nissho-Iwai Co. of Japan and the Industrial Bank of Japan.

Opposition to the super-port has been voiced by environmentalists and no further developments were reported by mid-1980.

Shipping services. Shipping services are provided by a number of overseas lines. By 1980, the states were served by nine shipping lines: United Micronesia Development Association (Tiger Line), Saipan Shipping Company, Palau Shipping Company, Oceania Line Inc., Matson Navigation Company, Daiwa Navigation Company, Nauru Pacific Line, Philippines , Micronesia and Orient Navigation Company (PM&O Lines) and Kyowa Shipping Line. The first four companies listed are Micronesian-owned and operated.

An extensive fleet of government-owned inter-island ships operates from districts centres to outer islands. These ships carry out both administrative and commercial transport services and guarantee a regular 45-day service to all inhabitated islands.

Private companies carry out stevedore, terminal and warehousing functions at district and sub-district ports.

Seven new inter-island ships built in Japan plus two landing craft vessels have been distributed among the various states along with seven LCU (Landing Craft Utilities) which were acquired from the United States Army surplus in Okinawa, Japan.

In July, 1979, the management authority and operations of sea transport activities were transferred from the Trust Territory Government to the Marshall Islands Government together with ships, functions and resources. Similar transfers were to take place later in respect of sea transport operating in the other states.

COMMUNICATIONS: There are post offices in all state centres.

An extensive communications system, using high frequency, independent sideband equipment, provides a telephone service between state centres and the major relay centre on Saipan. From there, connections are made to worldwide systems, including telephone and teletypewriter services. These utilise the "Peacesat" satellite and radio telephones. A new satellite DISP (Department of Interior Satellite Project) is being introduced. In 1979 there were 19 satellite terminals throughout Micronesia including Guam.

There are about 200 local radio transceivers.

Each district centre can also communicate directly with aircraft, shipping and government stations in the outer islands. All keep a continuous watch on a number of frequencies, including international distress.

Some missionary groups and construction firms operate their own inter-island networks.

Radio. There are six government-owned radio broadcasting stations in the Trust Territory. They broadcast 18 hours a day. In addition to English, the stations broadcast in one or two local languages. The main content of the programmes comprises music, local and world news and public service programmes. In Ponape, news is broadcast in four languages.

Television. Television was introduced in October, 1969, when WSZE opened in Saipan. Now, all states except Truk and Kosrae have television. Cable television started in Majuro in February, 1975 and is also now operating on Saipan, Yap and Palau.

Newspapers. Privately-owned newspapers in the territory are the 'Marianas Variety', published weekly in the Northern Marianas and the 'Marshall Islands Journal', which was previously known as the 'Micronesian Independent' and is published weekly in Majuro. A fortnightly publication is the 'Truk Chronicle'.

Government publications from the Trust Territory Public Information Office on Saipan are 'Highlights', issued monthly and containing a digest of TT news and 'Micronesian Reporter', a quarterly.

The government also operates a daily news distribution system, the Micronesian News Service, transmitted locally and overseas.

WATER AND ELECTRICITY. There is diesel-generated electricity at all state headquarters and in some other areas. Voltage in all cases is 110 volts.

Central piped water systems are found in state centres and in some villages. Some supplies are obtained from wells drilled into the fresh water lens of the volcanic islands.

HISTORY. The islands of the three archipelagoes that technically still comprise the United States Trust Territory of the Pacific Islands despite granting of separate status to the Northern Marianas, the Marshall Islands, the Federated States of Micronesia (Truk, Ponape, Yap and Kosrae) and Palau, had no common history until the end of the

19th century. The history of each archipelago is therefore treated in detail in its own section. The history of Guam, the largest of the Marianas, but an outright possession of the United States since 1898, may also be consulted because it is intimately linked with that of the Marianas, which is also listed separately under Northern Marianas.

In brief, it may be said that all three archipelagoes of the Trust Territory became known to Europeans in the early 16th century. Magellan discovered Guam, Saipan and Rota in the Marianas in 1521; and some of the islands of the other archipelagoes were sighted – and found to be dangerous to navigation – in the next few years. The Spanish explorer Villalobos took possession of the Marianas for the Spanish Crown in 1565; and after the galleon trade between Mexico and the Philippines was inaugurated, the galleons made their westward voyages in the latitude of those islands to avoid the troublesome Marshalls and Carolines. In 1668, Spanish missionaries, supported by a small garrison, landed on Guam, and after many setbacks and much fighting, the local inhabitants, the Chamorros, were Christianised and subdued. In 1695, all Chamorros in the Marianas who had survived the fighting and the lethal diseases that the Spaniards had introduced, were persuaded to move to Guam. The other, northern Marianas were thereafter deserted for many years.

Spanish missionaries made two unsuccessful attempts to take Christianity to islands in the Carolines in the early 18th century. Otherwise, both the Carolines and Marshalls were little disturbed by Europeans until the late 18th and early 19th centuries. American whalers began frequenting the two archipelagoes in the 1820s, and by the 1860s American, British and German traders had established themselves there. American Protestant missionaries were also in residence. In 1885, Germany took the question of sovereignty over the Caroline Islands to the Pope for arbitration. Although the Pope ruled in Spain's favour, the Germans were given the right to trade there and establish coaling stations and settlements. In 1886, by agreement with Great Britain, Germany established a protectorate over the Marshall Islands.

Sold to Germany. After Spain's defeat in the Spanish-American War of 1898, she sold both the Caroline archipelago and Marianas (except Guam) to Germany. Guam was excluded from the sale, as that island, like the Philippines, had been captured by the Americans during the war, and was ceded to them in the peace settlement. The outcome of the war thus gave Germany control over all islands of the three archipelagoes of the present Trust Territory. However, the Germans retained possession only until the Japanese captured and occupied them soon after the outbreak of World War I. In 1921, the League of Nations mandated the former German colonies to Japan which administered them as an integral part of the Japanese empire. Key islands in each group were strongly fortified and provided with sea and airport facilities after Japan withdrew from the League of Nations in 1935. These islands were used as bases for Japan's expansionist thrusts into the Philippines, South-East Asia and South Pacific in World War II. Guam was naturally one of the first islands to fall into Japanese hands.

American forces bombarded and captured many of the Japanese bases in Micronesia from February 1944, and used them for their final onslaught on Japan itself. From then until July 18, 1947, the islands were under military government, administered by the US Navy.

US Strategic Trust Territory. The military government ended with the US President's approval of a trusteeship agreement between the United States and Security Council of the United Nations, which designated the islands a strategic Trust Territory of the United States. Under the agreement, the Americans were granted authority to fortify the area; to apply such laws to the area as might be deemed appropriate; and to secure veto power over any proposals to alter, amend or terminate the trusteeship agreement. In return, the United States, among other things, bound herself to act in accordance with the Charter of the United Nations to foster the development of self-government or independence in accordance with the wishes of the peoples concerned.

The US President delegated authority for the civil administration of the territory to the Secretary of the Navy on an interim basis. Subsequently, Admiral Louis E. Denfeld was commissioned as the first US High Commissioner of the Trust Territory (with headquarters in Hawaii) and Rear-Admiral Carleton H. Wright was appointed Deputy High Commissioner (with headquarters in Guam). On July 1, 1951, administration of the territory passed from the Navy to the US Department of the Interior and Mr Elbert D. Thomas became the first civilian high commissioner. But in 1953 all islands in the Marianas, except Rota, were returned to the control of the Navy Department for a special security purpose. This situation prevailed until mid-1962 when control reverted to the Department of the Interior and the northern Marianas became the Mariana Islands District of the Trust Territory. At the same time headquarters for the entire territory were transferred from Guam to Saipan. Besides the Mariana Islands, five other districts were established – Palau, Yap, Truk and Ponape (Carolines) and the Marshall Islands.

Congress of Micronesia. The Micronesians were given a voice in their own government in January 1965 when the first elections were held for a bicameral Congress of Micronesia, consisting of a House of Representatives and a Senate. The Congress held its first meeting in the following July. In 1967, the Congress established a Future Political Status Commission, comprising six of its members (later increased to 10), to investigate ways in which the territory might develop politically. The commission visited Washington and Puerto Rico in 1968 and American and Western Samoa, Fiji and Papua New Guinea in 1969, besides studying the political systems in the Cook Islands and Okinawa. When it eventually reported to the Congress of Micronesia, the commission recommended that the territory should either become a self-governing state in free association with the United States, or it should have complete independence. The United States, for its part, offered the territory commonwealth status, like that of Puerto Rico. Originally located in Saipan, the Congress moved to Kolonia, Ponape in 1977.

Talks between United States representatives and the commission in 1970 and 1971 resulted in impasse. But in 1972 there was a breakthrough when the United States agreed to guarantee the four basic requirements of the Micronesians. These were: the right of self-determination; the right to decide their own constitution and laws; the right to control their own land; and the right, unilaterally, to terminate any compact with the United States. However, the 1972 negotiations did not cover the future status of the Marianas which, it was agreed, should be decided through direct dialogue between Marianas leaders and the United States.

Commonwealth status. By May 1973, a preliminary agreement was reached that commonwealth status should be the goal of the Mariana District; and on June 17, 1975, about 80 per cent of the people of the Marianas voted in favour of this proposal.

The Northern Marianas officially assumed commonwealth status on January 9, 1978, but decisions by the legislature were subject to review by the United States in its capacity of trustee. More talks followed between the political status commissions of the remaining districts and the United States and further fragmentation of what was expected to be a sovereign state embracing the rest of Micronesia was ensured with the holding of a referendum on the proposed Constitution of the Federated States of Micronesia on July 12, 1978, The Marshalls and Palau voted against it, the votes being cast as follows: Marshalls, yes 3,888, no, 6,217; Palau, yes 2,720, no, 3,339; Ponape, yes 5,970, no, 2,020; Truk, yes 9,762, no, 4,239; Yap, yes 2,359, no, 168; Kosrae, yes 1,188, no, 704.

The Marshalls and Palau negotiated with the United States each for separate status while Truk, Yap, Ponape and Kosrae continued to combine to negotiate for status as the Federated States of Micronesia.

Voters in the Marshall Islands ratified their constitution in a referendum held on March 1, 1979, and first elections for the Federated States of Micronesia Congress were held on March 27, 1979. The Marshalls elected their Nitijela (Parliament) under the new constitution in April, 1979, and on April 25, 1979, the United States Secretary of Interior Cecil Andrus signed the order recognising 'governmental entities under locally-ratified constitutions in the Trust Territory of the Pacific Islands'.

The new Marshalls Government was inaugurated on May 1, 1979, and the new Government of the Federated States of Micronesia was inaugurated on May 15, 1979.

The referendum for the Palauans was held on July 9, 1979, and an overwhelming majority voted for the constitution but the United States and members of the Palauan Political Status Commission objected to clauses governing Palauan territorial water limits and the entry of nuclear material into the country. An amended constitution was put to the people's vote in October, 1979, and defeated. The position had not been resolved by November, 1980, but agreement was thought to be near. The agreements between the United States and the FSM and the Marshall Islands were initialled at the end of October, 1980, the chief US negotiator, Mr Peter Rosenblatt stating at the time that it was expected an agreement between the United States and Palau would be initialled before the end of November, 1980.

CAROLINE ISLANDS HISTORY. From the little that is yet known of the prehistory of the Caroline Islands, it appears that some parts of the archipelago have been inhabited for more than 2,000 years. The chief archaeological work carried out so far has been in Palau, Yap, Ponape and the Polynesian outlier, Nukuoro. Excavations in Palau have revealed extensive agricultural terraces, trade beads, pottery and shell artifacts resembling those of the Marianas. The trade beads indicate links with South-East Asia dating back some 200 years before the Christian era. On Yap two types of pottery have been discovered, the earlier of which is thought to have been in use from at least the second century to 847. On Ponape, stone structures with walled and unwalled burial sites have been investigated as well as stone and coral platforms. The chief artifacts found have been of shell. Radio-carbon dates obtained have ranged from AD 1180 to 1430. At Nukuoro, excavations have suggested human occupation since about AD 1300. Early in 1979, an ancient living site was found on Mt. Tonnaachau overlooking Truk Airport on Moen. Tradition has it that the great leaders Soukachaw and Souwooniiras had a meeting-house on the mountain.

The history of European contact with the Carolines has much in common with that of the Marshalls. After some of the islands had been discovered by the first European navigators to cross the Pacific in the 16th century, the archipelago remained largely unvisited until the end of the 18th century. Ulithi and Fais, in the north-western corner of the group, are thought to have been the first islands to be discovered, as their description seems to match that of the Spanish explorer Villalobos in

1543. On his way from Mexico to the Philippines, Villalobos called at two islands which he named Matelotes (Sailors) and Arrecifes (Reefs).

Galleon trade. After the galleon trade between Acapulco and Manila began in the mid-1560s, the captains of the galleons were instructed to cross the Pacific from east to west in the latitude of the Mariana Islands and they thus avoided both the Marshalls and Carolines. However, occasionally a galleon would be driven out of its way and some new island would be discovered. Thus, in 1686, Francisco Lazeano, commanding a westbound galleon, chanced on the high island of Yap, which he called La Carolina, after the Spanish king of the time. The name was later applied to the archipelago as a whole. Another island, Faraulep, was discovered by a Manila ship in 1696. It was at about that time that the Spaniards were also made aware of the existence of the Carolines by the arrival of islanders in the Philippines and Guam who had drifted from there in storms. In 1710, the Spaniards made an exploratory voyage to the archipelago which resulted in the disc|very of Palau and Sonsorol. Two years later, a second ship went to Palau and Ulithi; and in 1731 yet another Spanish ship went to Ulithi with a party of missionaries headed by Juan Antonio Cantova. Although Cantova had taken a close interest in the welfare of some Carolinians who had drifted to Guam several years earlier, he and his party were murdered within three months, apparently in retaliation for some imagined misdeeds. This setback dissuaded the Spaniards from any further efforts to Christianise the Carolines for the time being.

Wreck of the 'Antelope'. In 1783, an event occurred which was to bring the Palau islands to the notice of people in Europe for the first time. This was the wreck of the East India Company ship 'Antelope' at Palau, and the subsequent escape of the crew to the Philippines in a much smaller vessel which they built there. The crew took with them the second son of the island's principal chief – a young man of 20 who eventually reached London where he was much feted as Prince Lee Boo of the Pelew Islands. A book compiled by one G. Keate from a journal kept by the 'Antelope's' commander, Captain Henry Wilson, was one of the most popular books on the Pacific of the late 18th century.

A few British ships sailing to China from New South Wales began passing through the Carolines in the 1790s. At about the same time, an occasional Spanish ship also ventured there en route from the Philippines to Peru. Almost every voyage resulted in the discovery of new islands. Captain James Wilson of the 'Duff' discovered Satawal, Lamotrek, Elato, Ifaluk and Woleai in 1797. Juan Ibargoitia discovered Pulusuk, Puluwat and Oran in 1800, and his countryman, Juan Baptiste Monteverde, added Nukuoro to the charts in 1806. Meanwhile, in 1804, Luis de Torres, vice-governor of Guam, paid a visit to several of the Carolines in the American ship 'Maria' of Boston.

Trading posts. A surveying voyage by the French exploring vessel 'Coquille' under Captain L. I. Duperrey in 1824 greatly increased European knowledge of the Carolines; and the Russian explorer Lutke in the ship 'Seniavine' added further details to the charts in 1828. At about this time, American whalers and traders began frequenting the archipelago; and by the middle of the century the high islands of Palau, Yap, Ponape and Kusaie were all known. However, evangelists' visits to Truk were uncommon until the 1880s. Protestant missions were established on Ponape and Kosrae by American evangelists in 1852; and in the next few years British, American and German companies established trading posts there and elsewhere and became rivals in the copra trade. One of the leading figures was David O'Keefe, an American, who built up a trading empire on Yap.

In 1869, Germany acquired 1,215 ha on Yap for use as a way station between Samoa and Cochin to serve as a centre for her Caroline-Marshalls-Marianas trade. Later, Germany's increased presence in the area was seen by Spain as a threat to her interests in the Philippines. In 1873, Spain demanded that all merchant ships bound for the Carolines should stop in the Philippines to receive permission to trade there and to pay customs and licensing fees for the privilege. The Germans refused to comply, and Britain later took Germany's side. Both nations declared that they did not recognise Spanish sovereignty over the Carolines because the islands had never been occupied by Spain.

Spanish sovereignty. In 1885, Spain sent a warship to take possession of Yap. But the Germans anticipated it and ran up the flag first. When the Germans also occupied Truk, Ponape, Kosrae and some of the lesser islands, Spain protested, but later agreed that Pope Leo XIII should arbitrate in the matter. On October 22, 1885, the Pope declared in favour of Spain; but Germany was given liberty to trade and fish in the area, and to establish settlements and coaling stations. Spain thus gained sovereignty over the archipelago with all the attendant expenses and responsibilities, while Germany was given privileges without responsibilities.

In 1886, Spain sent two warships to the Carolines to raise the flag and bring the islands under the control of the Philippines government. Ponape was made the administrative centre and an agency of the administration was opened at Yap. At the same time, Capuchin priests established missions and schools in Yap, Ponape and Palau. The arrival of the Spaniards at Yap produced little change; but difficulties arose on Ponape. A Protestant missionary, E. T. Doane, was arrested and sent to Manila in June 1887; native Protestant teachers were removed; and the islanders generally were forced to work like convicts. In an uprising against the Spaniards, the governor and some of his men were killed and the priests fled. Three Spanish warships later called at Ponape and arrested a few islanders, but on being tried in Manila they were acquitted. Another party of Spaniards was killed on Ponape in 1890. When news of this reached Madrid, a punitive expedition was sent to the island. But the transport vessel carrying the Spanish troops ran aground on a reef and the Ponapeans killed 1,500 men.

During the Spanish-American war in 1898, Germany made a secret provisional agreement with Spain whereby it secured a lien on Kosrae, Ponape and Yap in any future disposal of Spain's insular possessions. Later that year, Spain agreed to give Germany the right to purchase all the Caroline and Mariana Islands, other than Guam, which the Americans had captured. A German-Spanish treaty of 12 February, 1899 transferred the Carolines and Marianas to Germany for 25 million pesetas.

German administration. With the establishment of German administration in the Carolines, German Catholic missionaries arrived to replace the Spanish Capuchins, and German Protestants moved into the islands where American Protestants had been working. The Germans governed the eastern Carolines from Ponape and the western Carolines, including Palau, from Yap. Relations between the islanders and the German administration were mainly peaceful. However, in 1910, a German overseer was killed after striking an islander with a whip, and when the governor hastened out to restore order he was shot dead. The ringleaders in this incident were later executed and 200 islanders were deported to Angaur to work in the phosphate deposits.

The Japanese, who had had commercial interests in the Carolines, from 1893 onwards, were quick to occupy the islands in World War I. Having declared war on Germany on August 23, 1914, the Japanese captured Yap on October 7, and less than three weeks later all islands in the Carolines were under their control. The islands were mandated to Japan by the League of Nations in 1921 and administered from 1922 as an integral part of the Japanese empire. Administrative headquarters were at Koror on Palau, and there were district offices at Yap, Truk and Ponape. Following the arrival of the Japanese civilian administrators, Spanish Jesuit missionaries replaced the German Catholics and pastors from the Congregational Church of Japan replaced the German Protestants.

As in the other islands of its Micronesian territory, Japanese policy was to develop the resources of the Carolines to the full. Japanese immigration was encouraged. Harbour facilities were developed in Palau; production was stepped up from the Angaur phosphate deposits; the copra industry was expanded; and the growing of tapioca, rice and oil palms was introduced to some islands. After Japan withdrew from the League of Nations in 1935, Palau and Truk were developed for military purposes and other islands were fortified. When Japan entered World War II, Palau was used as a base to attack the Philippines and Netherlands East Indies, and Truk was a key to the Japanese thrust into the South Pacific.

World War II. American fleet aircraft attacked Truk early in 1944 and destroyed 23 ships and 201 planes at a cost of 17 American planes. However, Ulithi Atoll was the only island in the Carolines to be occupied by the Americans before the Japanese surrendered in September 1945. After the Caroline Islands became part of the United States Trust Territory of the Pacific Islands in 1947, the archipelago was divided into four districts – Palau, Yap, Truk and Ponape – with headquarters for each district on the islands named.

MARSHALL ISLANDS HISTORY. No archaeological work has yet been conducted in the Marshall Islands so that little is known about the pre-history of the group. European contact with the islands began when the first Spanish ships were groping their way across the Pacific in the early 16th century, but there was no continuous contact until the third decade of the 19th century.

Taongi, the northermost atoll, was the first island to be discovered by Europeans. This was a landfall of the Loaisa expedition in 1526. In the following year, three ships under Alvaro de Saavedra, sent from Mexico to seek news in the Moluccas of the Magellan and Loaisa expeditions were also among the Marshalls. Two of them were subsequently lost. The next visitors were the four ships of the Legaspi expedition, proceeding to the Philippines in 1565. One of them was almost wrecked in the group. A year later, some of the crew of the ship 'San Jeronimo,' which was taking supplies to Legaspi, staged a mutiny while among the Marshall Islands. The pilot, Lope Martin, and two dozen fellow conspirators were marooned on an atoll that has since been identified as Ujelang. They were never seen again, although the Spanish explorer Mendana touched at a nearby atoll in 1568 following his discovery of the Solomons.

Two centuries then passed before the next Europeans were among the Marshalls, as the Spanish galleons sailing from Mexico to the Philippines were instructed to proceed to the northward of these dangerous low-lying islands. In 1767, Captain Samuel Wallis, the discoverer of Tahiti, chanced on Rongerik and Rongelap in sailing northward to reach Tinian in the Marianas. Twenty-one years later, the 'Scarborough' (Captain John Marshall) and 'Charlotte' (Captain Thomas Gilbert) sighted Mili, Arno, Majuro, Aur, Maloelap, Erikub and Wotje Atolls in proceeding to China from Botany Bay. The name Marshall Islands was later applied to the group as a whole by the Russian hydrographer A. J. Krusenstern. In 1792, Captain E. H. Bond sighted Namorik in the British ship 'Royal Admiral'. The Russian explorer Otto von Kotzebue made an extensive examination of the group in 1817 and gave the names Ralik and Ratak to the western and eastern chains respectively. He revisited the Ratak chain on his second voyage to the Pacific in 1824. His accounts of the Marshalls are easily the most comprehensive of the early 19th century.

From the 1820s onwards, the Marshalls were visited by American whalers seeking food and water. Some of these occasionally left men ashore to become beachcombers and, later, traders. American and Hawaiian Protestant missionaries arrived in the group in the 1860s, sent by the Hawaiian Evangelical Association, an auxiliary of the American Board of Commissioners for Foreign Missions. About this time, J. C. Godeffroy und Sohn, of Samoa, established trading stations on Mili, Aur, Jaluit, Ebon and Namorik. A few years later, two other German companies, Hernsheim & Co. and A. Capelle & Co., were also in business there. Copra was their principal interest.

In 1878, Germany secured a coaling station on Jaluit by a treaty negotiated with the island chiefs during a visit by a German warship. A German consul was appointed to Jaluit in the same year. In 1886, by agreement with Great Britain, the Marshall Islands became a German protectorate. Later, the Germans formed the Jaluit Gesellschaft which bought out two foreign competitors based in San Francisco and Auckland. However, Burns Philp & Co. of Sydney, which had been trading in the group for some years, continued to do so, sending a ship there once every two months. This prompted the Germans to charge discriminatory port dues, but the Sydney company remained in the group until World War I.

In 1906, the German Government took over the rights of the Jaluit Gesellschaft (which had expanded into the Carolines) to strengthen its position in the South Seas. From that year, the Marshalls were administered from Rabaul, capital of Germany's colony in New Guinea. This situation continued until the outbreak of World War I when the Marshalls, like the Marianas (except Guam) and the Carolines, were occupied by the Japanese. After the war, the Marshall Islands were mandated to Japan by the League of Nations, together with the other occupied islands. The group was administered as a separate district. The Marshallese were given little voice in their own government; but the copra industry was left in their hands. However, the copra had to be exported to Japan at a price fixed by the Japanese.

From 1935, when Japan withdrew from the League of Nations, the Marshalls, like the other mandated archipelagoes, were fortified and provided with facilities for Japan's adventure in the Pacific in World War II. It was from there that the Japanese attacked and invaded Nauru, Ocean Island and Kiribati (Gilbert Islands). The Allies were unable to launch a counter-attack on the area until strategic islands in Kiribati had been occupied in late 1943. Kwajalein Atoll was the first island to be captured – in February 1944. The concentration of fire directed at Kwajalein exceeded any artillery barrage in the two World Wars.

The Marshall Islands became part of the United States Trust Territory of the Pacific Islands in July 1947, following three years of American military administration. Meanwhile, in 1946, the Americans had used Bikini Atoll for atomic bomb tests, having resettled its inhabitants on Rongerik. Isolated Enewetak Atoll was chosen for further tests in December 1947, and its 146 people were provided with new homes on Ujelang. The first United States hydrogen bomb was exploded at Enewetak on March 1, 1954; two others were detonated in the following few weeks. Further tests were carried out in 1956, 1958 and 1962. Meanwhile, the United States spent billions of dollars developing Kwajalein as an anti-missile base, and many Marshallese were attracted to work there by the high wages. Bikini Atoll was announced to be fit again for human habitation in August 1968, and by 1971 two of its islets had been cleared of debris and preparations were underway for the Bikinians (who had latterly been living on Kili) to be resettled there. Enewetak Atoll was formally handed back to its original inhabitants in September 1976, and the US authorities undertook to carry out a $20 million clean-up and rehabilitation programme over the ensuing three or four years.

However, tests conducted at Bikini in 1977 revealed that despite a $3 million decontamination project, Bikini groundwater was still too radioactive for human consumption, as were the coconuts, fruit and vegetables grown in Bikini soil. As a result, early in 1978, the U.S. Department of the Interior asked Congress for $15 million to resettle the Bikinians once again. The proposed site was said to be Enyu atoll, about 15 km from Bikini.

In an attempt to dispose of radioactive debris, the Americans dug a huge pit on the islet of Runit on Enewetak in 1980. They burried 84,150 cubic metres of radioactive sand and debris mixed with cement and over the crater built a concrete dome 113 m in diameter, 7.6 m high and nearly 0.5 m thick. Nuclear scientists say the contents of the pit will remain radioactive for 25,000 years.

It was also revealed at the same time that inhabitants of Rongelap and Utirik, more than 160 km from Bikini, were developing thyroid problems as a result of the 1954 explosion, and an additional $600,000 was requested as compensation for present and future people who develop tumours

As with the Japanese, the Americans have administered the Marshalls as a separate district of their Micronesian territory. Headquarters are on Majuro. This atoll has been an increasingly important focal point for tourists to the district in recent years, with Air Micronesia jets flying in from Honolulu. Air Nauru also links the group with the South Pacific from Nauru.

Until 1974, the Marshall Islands were quiet politically. In that year separatist tendencies flared when the Marshallese voted to begin their own talks with the United States on their political future. This followed a decision by the Congress of Micronesia (the legislative body for the Trust Territory) to defer action on a revenue-sharing bill that would have returned to the districts a greater share of their income tax monies.

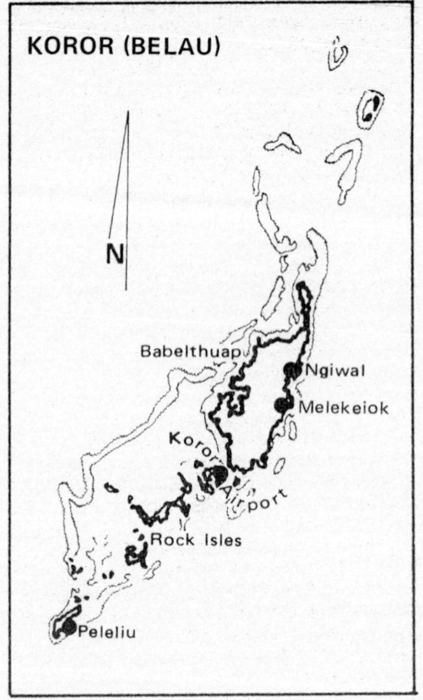

ISLANDS IN DETAIL

CAROLINE ISLANDS lie in a vast chain, just north of the equator, extending from the Palau (Pelew) group in the extreme west at 130 deg. E. long, through four self-governing states Palau, Yap, Truk and Ponape to Kosrae (formerly Kusaie Island) at 163 deg. E. long. There are 963 islands which include every kind — coral and volcanic ranging from fairly large territories, with mountains and streams, to tiny, palm-clad islets and coral reefs, just above sea-level. Their land area is 2,150 sq. km.

PALAU (Pelew) GROUP forms the western end of the Caroline chain. It contains about 200 islands, of which Babelthuap (formerly called Palau) is the largest. This island is about 43 km long by 13 km across. It is fertile, well-wooded and produces every kind of tropical fruit and vegetable. There are interesting ruins of ancient fortifications.

Spain did little in her 300 years of nominal ownership and the people's real contact with European ideas started only during the German era in 1898. The Germans tried not to disturb the cultural patterns but applied pressure to the chiefs to increase copra production, brought in other Micronesians to work the phosphate on Angaur and tried to introduce some public health measures.

The Germans had scarcely established themselves when the Japanese arrived and under their rule, every economic resource was exploited — but for the Japanese not the Palauans. There were about 12,000 Japanese in the district at the beginning of World War II and about 8,000 Palauans.

The Palauans went some way with the Japanese concept of westernisation and although anti-foreign feeling developed among them during the war they were eager to accelerate the process of economic change when the United States took over. Palauans have become enthusiastic entrepreneurs and superficially they appear very westernised.

The Japanese placed their administrative centre, for the whole Territory, on Koror, a small island off the southern coast of Babelthuap. In the war, the Americans devastated it with bombs, but the U.S. Trust Territory government has partially restored it for use as its administrative headquarters of the Palau District.

A large barrier reef surrounds most of the Palaus. South of Koror, in this chain, are Malakal (Koror's seaport) and Ngerkabesang; both are connected to Koror by causeways. Ulebsehel, south-west of Koror, helps to enclose an "inland sea" studded with raised coral islands; an artificial canal separates Ulebsehel from Ngarmalk (on which there is a tidal brackish lake).

Other islands in the chain are: Ngarekelau and Ngaregur (in the north), Eil Malk, Ngeregong, Ngurukdabel (the largest purely limestone island in Micronesia), Ngaiangas and Ngeremeyaos. Peleliu, at the southern end of the reef, has been mined for phosphate. North-west of it are the Ngemelis "string" of small islands.

Outside the main barrier reef, in the north, are Kayangel (Ngaiangl) Atoll (four small islets) and Ngaruangl nearby; in the south are Angaur, Sonsorol, Fauna, Pulo Anna, Merir, Tobi (westernmost island of the Trust Territory) and Helen Reef (two small uninhabited islets).

On Angaur there were important phosphate deposits which provided the Territory with its largest export industry until 1954. The reserves were exhausted in 1955. Recently the most valuable export from Palau has been scrap metal and supplies of this are now diminishing.

The Palauans are expected to change the name of their state to Belau.

YAP ISLANDS consist of nine inhabited atolls, two single islands and four normally uninhabited islands and atolls.

Yap is a group of four islands (Yap, Map, Rumung, Gagil-Tomil), separated by narrow channels. It is hilly and covered with magnificent forests of coconut and areca palms, bamboos and crotons, and is one of the most beautiful and picturesque of the Caroline Islands. Although all tropical fruits and vegetables are grown there is mainly a subsistence economy augmented by some copra production.

Yap is known as "the land of grass skirts and stone money". The men wear very little; the women, bulky grass skirts, although Western clothing is now worn when visiting the District centres. Betel-chewing is widespread.

The famous stone money — huge discs hewn out of coral stone with holes through their centres — were brought by sea from Palau, and represent hoarded wealth. The Germans built stone paths, causeways and retaining walls around these islands. They also dug the Tageren canal, which bisects the main island in the north-east.

The Americans cleared Yap harbour of coral heads, so seaplanes could use it. Roads extend several kilometres north of Colonia along the east coast of the main island and are being improved continuously. The road from the airport to the Coast Guard station at Loran is good but some parts of the island are accessible only on foot.

It was on Yap that an American named O'Keefe set up an extensive trading organisation in the late-Spanish and early-German eras. He understood and was respected by the Yapese and was able to encourage them to increase their production of copra, and to fish large quantities of beche-de-mer which O'Keefe schooners traded as far as Malaya. O'Keefe was finally lost while aboard one of his schooners in Micronesian waters. He is best remembered today because of the cinema film, "His Majesty O'Keefe". However, the movie was not shot in Yap but in Fiji.

After the Germans bought the Caroline Islands from Spain in 1898 they set about making Yap the centre for three undersea cables and this Pacific cable system was a matter of dispute between Japan and the United States from 1919-1921.

Yap island is in the north-west section of the District; it has been subject to heavy erosion and there has been much subsidence. Highest point is Mt. Tabiwol (178m) in the north-centre of the main island. Southwards, about 200 km from Yap, lies Ngulu Atoll (a string of 12 islets, some inhabited).

North-east of Yap are Ulithi (with nearly 40 islets, it has the largest land area of any atoll in the Carolines — 8 sq. km) and Fais, south-east

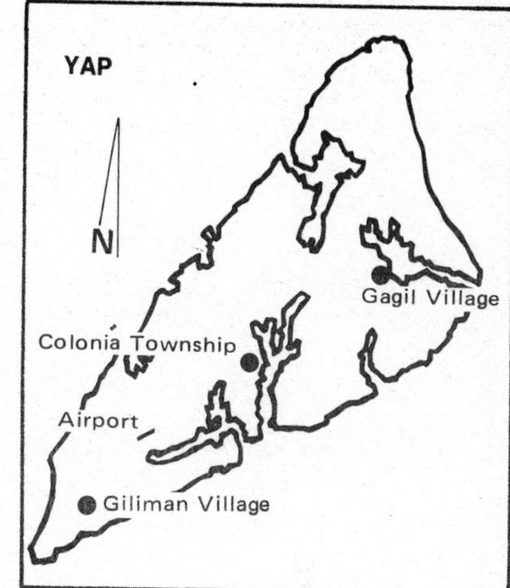

of Ulithi, an inhabited raised atoll with some phosphate deposits. Sorol, with five other islets in an elongated grouping of two clusters is well south of Ulithi. The only island in Yap captured by the Americans before the surrender of Japan in 1945 was Ulithi which subsequently was used by Allied naval forces as a staging area.

Although in pre-European times the peoples of Ulithi and Woleai were vassals of the Yapese, they differ in several respects, including language. The atoll people are generally lighter skinned and look more like Polynesians.

These atolls like all of Yap district, are subject to typhoons and severe storms.

Between Sorol and the boundary of Truk District are a dozen small groups of atolls and islets, the only one of importance being Woleai, where the Japanese had an airfield.

TRUK GROUP, about 1,440 km east of Yap, consists of nearly 90 islands — 50 of them on a great encircling reef with the enclosed lagoon having a radius of 48 km. Within this great lagoon is the Truk cluster of large, high islands. The largest from east to west are:

NAME	ALTERNATIVE NAME	HEIGHT (metres)
Moen	Wena	376
Dublon	Tonoas	353
Fefan	Aki	313
Uman	Fuyu	288
Udot	Getsuyo	242
Fanapenges	Tuesday	113
Tol	Ton	435

This large cluster is not an atoll; the islands are

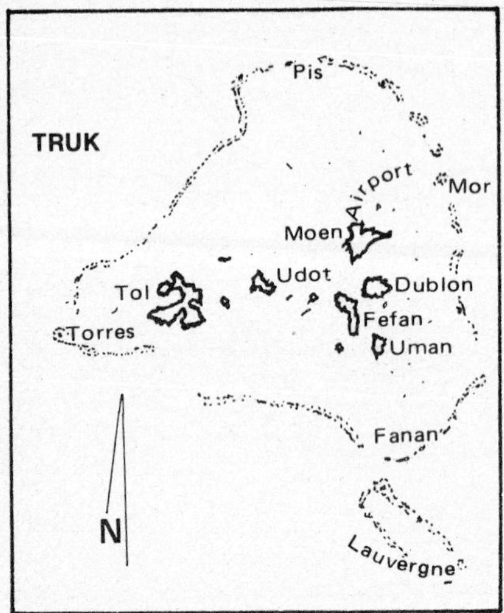

high and broad, and situated in the middle of the great lagoon.

According to some authorities the Trukese acted as predators on Polynesians who moved along this corridor and into Polynesia proper. The first European sighting is credited to Alvaro Saavedra in 1528. The Dublon lagoon did not become known until the early 19th century when the navigator Dublon visited it in 1814. Duperry mapped the lagoon island of Truk in 1824, but Dumont d'Urville, 14 years later, was the most thorough explorer of Truk.

After the Germans acquired the area they established trading stations and encouraged the people to plant more coconuts and produce more copra. The Japanese who followed invested large sums in commercial fisheries and plant for drying the fish. Early in World War II there were 35,000 Japanese (including Okinawans) on Truk.

The Japanese chief port and administrative centre was on the eastern side of Dublon. The American headquarters, are on Moen.

Most people live in small villages scattered along the shores of all the green islands, which are in an area about 48 km by 19 km.

Most northerly atoll of the district is triangular Namonuito (the world's second largest atoll), with 10 small islets. Eastwards lie East Fayu and the Hall Islands (Nomwin and Murilo).

Westwards from Truk are Pulap and Puluwat; while directly south is Kuop (Royalist) Atoll, with its four islets. Continuing south are Nama, a single low island and Losap, a small atoll with a narrow reef. Laol, Pis and Talap, the largest of its eight islets, are populated.

To the south-east, near the district boundary, are Namoluk Atoll (triangular, with a reef opening in the south-east) and the Mortlock (or Namoi) Islands. They consist of some 100 islands arranged in three groups — Etal, Lukunor and Satawan.

PONAPE the most eastern of the Carolines, consists of two high volcanic islands, Ponape and Kosrae (formerly Kusaie) and eight atolls. Kosrae is now a state in its own right.

PONAPE (OR ASCENSION) the main island is surrounded by a barrier reef and by more than 25 small islands, half of them volcanic.

It is 19 km long and 37.6 km wide with Mt. Totolom (791m) being the highest peak. The three main coastal towns are: Kolonia or Ponape (in the north), Metalanim (south-east) and Rohnkiti (south-west).

This island is fertile with luxuriant forest covering the gentle slopes that rise from the beaches to the mountain tops. There are many freshwater streams, some of considerable dimensions. The people live in ease and comfort on the coastal lands — the interior which is practically uninhabited, is notable for the large number of ruins of an ancient civilisation.

In prehistoric times Ponape was ruled by the Saudeleurs, chieftains who lived on Nan Madol, a group of more than 80 partly man-made islands off the S.E. coast of the island near Metalanim. Ruins of the canals, mighty temples and walls, some made of enormous crystals of basaltic rock 6 m long, may still be seen and are of considerable interest to archaeologists.

German traders operated in the Ponape area while it was still nominally Spanish and during

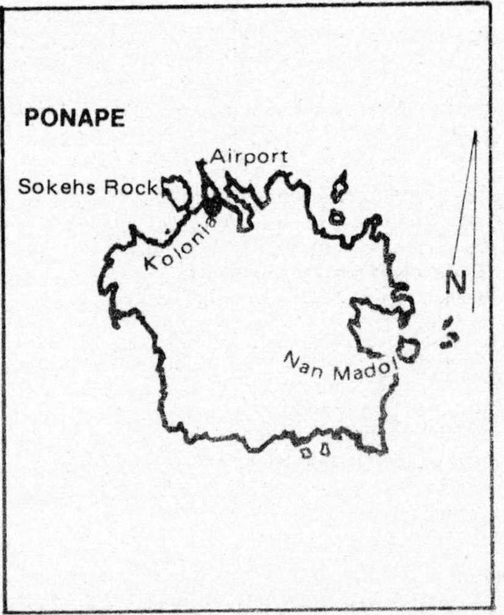

this time Protestant missionaries also established themselves. However, after the Papal decision in favour of Spanish sovereignty, the Spanish built a walled town in the Bay of Ascension (Kolonia) and dislodged the Protestants. The town was named Kolonia by the Germans who reorganised the copra industry. Later, the Japanese actively colonised Ponape. They had a manioc flour-processing plant at Metalanim and planted sugar-cane in the hitherto unused upland. A sugar mill was completed just before World War II and the cane was used to make alcohol for military use.

Near Ponape are the small islands known as the Ants, and Pakin Groups and Ngatik (or Raven's Island). The Ants, 19 km west of Ponape, consists of two large and 12 small islands. Ponape, Ant and Pakin are collectively known as Senyavin Islands after the "Senjanin" in which Lutke, a Russian surveyed the Carolines in 1828.

OROLUK, isolated in the north-west, has a large lagoon but its islets are very small. Except for a handful of people on Oroluck island in the atoll's north-west corner, the atoll is uninhabited.

About 160 km south-east of Ponape is the Mokil Group — Urak, Manton and Mokil. There are several hundred on these islands, and the main village is on Mokil. The islands, though small, are well-wooded and very beautiful.

South-east from the Mokils is the Pingelap group — three small islands (Pingelap, Takai and Tagulu) close together on the one reef. The land area is about 715 ha and population is heavy.

Kosrae (formerly Kusaie, Strong Island or Ualan) is one of the most beautiful islands in the Pacific and is the farthest east of the Carolines. It has an area of 109.6 sq. km and is hilly and broken, but possesses four good harbours — Okat in the north-west and Lelu on the east coast and Taf and Utwe in the south. It is forest-clad, well-watered and is so fertile that almost any tropical product can be grown there. It is noted for valuable timbers which are used for shipbuilding and similar work. The large population of pre-European discovery times, dwindled to 200 by 1880. It is now increasing — 4,780 est. in 1979.

Highest peak, Mt Crozer or Finkol (634m) is near the centre of the island; others are Matunte (583m) on the north east. Tafeayat and Wakapp. A fringing reef surrounds and is narrow and close to the shore in places.

The charm of life on Kosrae has been described by well-known Pacific writers including Louis Becke. With others, he added much to the atmosphere of romance which surrounded Pacific Islands in the early part of the 20th century. The harbour of Lelu was once a notorious rendezvous for American whaling ships and wild orgies took place there among the natives. Lelu,

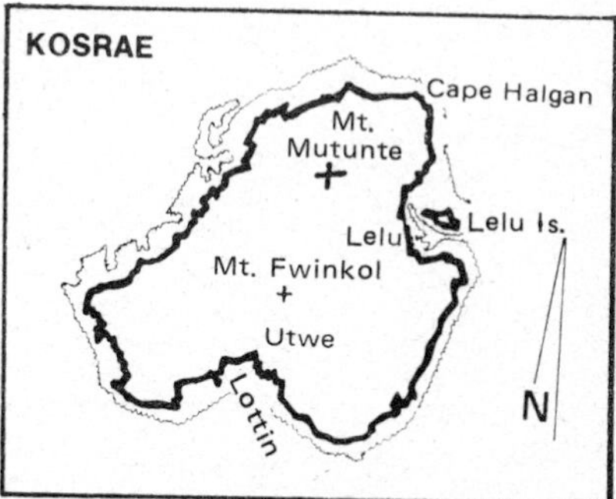

also, was notorious in 1874 as the base of the piratical "Bully" Hayes, who was one of the last of the Pacific Ocean buccaneers. Hayes lost his vessel on the reefs in this vicinity, and settled in Kosrae with his swashbuckling crew of Ocean and Gilbert Islanders. They brewed large quantities of the very intoxicating coconut toddy, and spent their time alternately drinking and fighting. They were eventually chased away by a British warship.

Remarkable ruins of an unusual character are found near Lelu.

POLYNESIAN COMMUNITIES

Two small isolated atolls, Kapingamarangi and Nukoro, in the south-east corner of Ponape District, are inhabited by people whose physical type, language and culture are Polynesian — this is the farthest west that Polynesians have been found.

Kapingamarangi (known also as Greenwich) is 1 deg. North of the equator, on 154 deg. East longitude; it has about 30 islets, all on the east of the pear-shaped atoll. The population of 389 (1979) is mostly confined to the tiny islet of Touhou, although a few people live on Werua and Taringa, flanking islets separated by narrow water channels.

Three hundred and twenty kilometres to the north-east is Nukuoro Atoll, on 155 deg. E. long. It is nearly circular, with a completely enclosed reef, and has 40 islets, on each side except the west.

MARSHALL ISLANDS are a double chain of coral atolls (34 islands and 870 reefs) which lie between 5 deg. and 15 deg. N. lat and 162 deg. and 173 deg. E. long. Probably, they were visited by Alvaro de Saavedra in 1529. Captain Wallis was at Tongerik in 1767; and in 1788 Captains Marshall and Gilbert explored this and the neighbouring Gilbert Group very thoroughly.

For one hundred years this group was a happy hunting-ground for all kinds of adventurers. Ger-

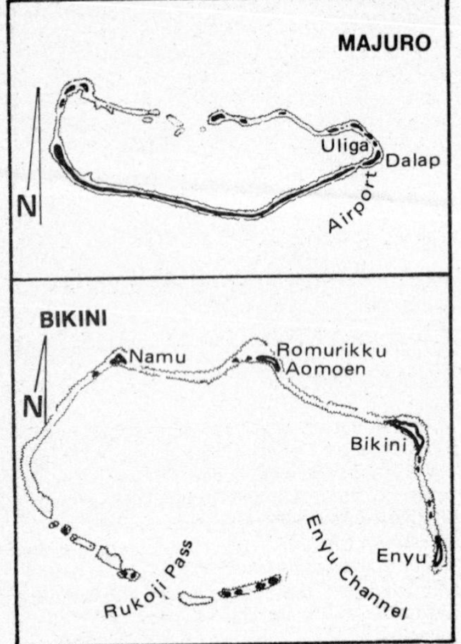

many annexed the group in 1885 and tried to establish a colony there, but had little success.

The islands were occupied by the Japanese (as Britain's ally) when World War I began in 1914; it became part of the territories given into Japanese administration in 1920 under League of Nations mandate. The Japanese administered the Group, as a Mandated Territory, until 1935; then they left the League of Nations and claimed absolute sovereignty. They then constructed many naval and air bases in the islands, especially in the eastern Carolines and the Marshalls; they excluded all Europeans and exiled many of the half-German half-Marshall Islanders into the British Gilberts so that details of their military preparations remained restricted.

The islands are in two chains, about 208km apart — the Rataks ("Sunrise") Chain, to the east and the Ralik ("Sunset") group to the west.

None of these islands is more than a few feet above sea level. The total area of the group is 171 sq km and there are at least a dozen islands of about the same dimensions. The chief island is Jaluit, where there is a good port, but the administrative centre of the group is Majuro.

During the past 46 years the Marshall Islands population has increased from 9,900 (in 1934) to 29,670 in 1980.

JALUIT LAGOON is triangular in shape, about 48 km long by 19 km wide. There are three deep passages through which vessels of any size can pass to a safe anchorage of 45-55 m depth. It has more than 80 islets.

Vessels of considerable size may anchor safely in the Jaluit Lagoon.

Ebon (or Boston) atoll. This is the most southerly of the group and also contains a large and safe anchorage. Ebon was the best-known port of the Marshalls in the early part of the 19th century, when these islands were freely used as a wintering ground by whalers, etc. who roved the South Pacific from the 1820s to 1870s.

The islets of importance are called Jurijer, Enijarmek, Ebon, Dereg, Enijadok, Guamagumlap, Euer, Munjak, Taka, Enlio, Jio, Met. Ebon forms the south and south-east side of the atoll. It is 8 km long and is the largest and most important of the atoll islets.

Kwajalein and Majuro. As a result of war operations, two other atolls, Majuro and Kwajalein, became well known. Both have good accommodation for shipping; Majuro is now the state's administrative centre. There are some 60 islets.

Ujelang is the westernmost island of the Marshalls; narrow, with 27 scattered islets it became home for the population of Enewetak (to the north) when that island was used for nuclear bomb tests. Bikini (east of Enewetak) is large with 36 islets and wide ship-passages to the south, was uninhabited until 1968. Its people were transferred to Rongerik to the north, of the Ralik Chain before the first nuclear explosions in 1946. Later they were moved to Kili in the extreme south of the chain.

Ailinglapalap, and nearby Namu (each with 50 islets) are inhabited. Namorik is small with an enclosed angular reef, and has a land area of 2.5 sq km.

Best known of the other Ratak chain are: Likiep, which has the highest point in the group, only 10 m above sea level; 72 islets mostly on the straight north-east side, Arno (large, bib-shaped, with reef openings near the middle: land area of 8 sq km); and Mille (south of Arno, has 90 islets extending for 51 km).

Kwajalein consists of some 90 islets along a reef which encloses the largest lagoon in the world with an area of 1,684 sq km. There are excellent anchorages for ships, and runways for aircraft (on both Kwajalein islet and on Roi). The best anchorage is between Rol and Namur, in the north.

Kwajalein was the first island in the Territory to be captured by American forces during World War II. Kwajalein islet in the extreme southern point of the triangular atoll, is now a top-secret anti-missile base for the United States and is under the control of the U.S. Navy. Missiles are fired from California and other missiles are fired from Kwajalein to intercept. Entry to the area is prohibited to unauthorised people.

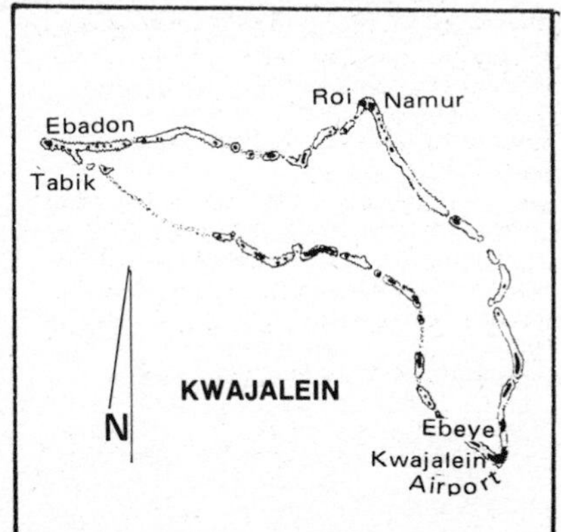

Billions of dollars have been spent on the installations and building them created a considerable demand for labour that paid better-than-normal rates. As a result Micronesians crowded into Ebeye, the next islet on the atoll which until recently was used as a dormitory for workers. More than 3,000 of these people were persuaded to leave Ebeye voluntarily in 1976.

FOR THE TOURIST. From exploring the battle-scarred relics on land and in the lagoon to discovering jungle waterfalls or spear fishing in the lagoon, the tiny islands of the Northern Marianas offer new attractions for the adventurous traveller who is prepared to endure occasional inconvenience.

The scenic beauty of the islands, with the unaffected culture of their people is combined with historic battle sites.

Information is available from the tourist commission in Saipan and especially from the offices of Continental Airlines operating with Air Micronesia.

Tour operators include Micronesia Tours, Inc. and Saipan Kanko Service, in Saipan (Marianas).

Entry formalities. United States citizens need proof of citizenship to visit the territory, such as a driver's licence. No visa, passport, or advance entry permit are needed unless the stay is for longer than 30 days, or the visit is for some purpose, other than tourism, in which case a Trust Territory entry permit is required in advance.

Citizens of countries other than the US require a passport, a round trip or onward air ticket and a visa to enter their next destination (if necessary). Smallpox immunisation is required unless the visitor starts from the US or one of its territories or possessions. Cholera and yellow fever immunisation are required if the visitor is from an infected area. Typhoid, para-typhoid and tetanus shots are recommended.

Recreation. There is keen interest in diving in such districts as Truk and Palau, which attract several thousand diving tourists each year. Fully equipped shops rent out all the gear necessary for a diving expedition. Portable decompression chambers are installed in Truk and Palau hospitals. Game fishing for marlin and large tuna offers some potential in Palau and the Marshall Islands.

Sightseeing. Among the main attractions for tourists are:

PALAU: The Rock Islands, Peleliu, the Cave Inn.

YAP: O'Keefe's Oasis, Gagil or Giliman village, stone money.

TRUK: Japanese lighthouse, sunken Japanese ships, Dublon Island.

PONAPE: Ruins of Nan Madol, old Spanish fort, Sokehs rocks.

MAJURO: Atoll touring, outrigger sailing.

ACCOMMODATION

MARSHALL ISLANDS

Ebeye:

EBEYE HOTEL — 14 rooms.

Majuro:

EASTERN GATEWAY HOTEL — 16 rooms.

HOTEL MAJURO — 11 rooms, dining room, bar.

AJIDRIK HOTEL — 9 twin rooms.

PONAPE

Kolonia:

BLUE ROSE MOTEL — 4 singles, 2 doubles.

CLIFF RAINBOW HOTEL — 10 twin cottages, 20 rooms

HIFUMI INN — 10 twin rooms.

KAWAII INN — 10 rooms.

HOTEL NAN MADOL — 20 twin rooms

HOTEL POHNPEI — 11 cottages.

SOKEHS DIAMOND HEAD HOTEL — 11 rooms.

SOUTH PARK HOTEL — 10 twin rooms, 5 single rooms.

THE VILLAGE HOTEL — 15 cottages.

TRUK

Moen:

BAYVIEW HOTEL — 4 twin rooms.

CHRISTOPHER INN — 21 twin rooms, 3 doubles, 3 triples, 4 suites.

TRUK CONTINENTIAL HOTEL — 54 twin rooms.

MARAMAR HOTEL — 16 twin rooms

YAP

Colonia:

ESA HOTEL — 12 twin rooms.

RAI VIEW HOTEL — 10 rooms.

PALAU

Koror:

BARSAKESAU HOTEL — 8 rooms.

NEW KOROR HOTEL — 6 rooms.

ROYAL PALAUAN HOTEL — 21 twin rooms.

PALAU CONTINENTAL HOTEL — 56 twin rooms.

PARADISE HOTEL — 5 single rooms.

Peleliu:

NGERCHONG BOAT-TEL — 6 single rooms.

PELELIU INN — 4 rooms.

WINTY'S INN — 4 rooms.

TUVALU

Tuvalu became an independent constitutional monarchy, with Britain's reigning monarch as its head, on October 1, 1978. Until October, 1975, when it became separated from the Gilbert Islands (now Kiribati) and adopted the name Tuvalu (meaning Eight Standing Together), the group was known as the Ellice Islands and was part of the British Colony of the Gilbert and Ellice Islands. There are nine atolls or coral islands, only eight of which are permanently inhabited. They are located between 5 and 10 deg. S. latitude and 176 and 179 deg. E. longitude. The capital and main island is Funafuti about 1,100 km north of Suva, capital of Fiji. Local time is 12 hours ahead of GMT.

Australian currency is still legal tender.

Local public holidays are January 1, second Monday in March (Commonwealth Day), Good Friday and Easter Monday, early June (Queen's Birthday), August 4 (National Children's Day, 1980), October 1 and 2 (Tuvalu Days 1980), day appointed in November (Prince Charles' Birthday, Nov. 10, 1980), Christmas Day and Boxing Day.

THE PEOPLE. The islanders of Tuvalu are Polynesians, unlike their former partners, I Kiribati, who are Micronesians.

A census was held on 27/28 May, 1979. Preliminary results indicate a total population of something over 9,000, mainly Polynesians, made up of 7,357 living within Tuvalu; some 800 in Kiribati, just under half of whom were on Banaba; 724 on Nauru; about 300 employed as seamen, plus a number of students overseas.

Funafuti is now the most heavily populated island with 2,191 inhabitants, followed by Vaitupu (1,269), Niutao (866) and Nanumea (842). At the previous census in 1973 Nanumea had the most with 977, followed by Vaitupu (948), Niutao (907) and Funafuti (871).

Nationality. Almost all the inhabitants are Tuvaluans. The 1979 Citizenship Ordinance lays down the registration qualifications for Tuvalu citizenship.

The qualifications for naturalisation are:

(a) That the applicant has been ordinarily resident in Tuvalu for the seven years immediately prior to the date of his application for naturalisation; (b) that he intends to make Tuvalu his permanent home; (c) that he will remain financially self-supporting now and in the years to come; (d) that he is familiar with the laws and customs of Tuvalu; (e) that he is of good character and free from communicable disease; (f) that he qualifies in accordance with any such other matters as the Citizenship Committee may consider material.

Language. The Tuvalu language is a Polynesian tongue closely related to Samoan. A Gilbertese dialect, introduced by invaders several hundred years ago, is spoken on Nui. English is also used throughout the islands.

Migration. Tuvaluans move out of their islands to find employment. Most of those living overseas do so because of their own or their families' employment. One source of employment, Banaba (Ocean Island) where more than 600 Tuvaluans were employed in the phosphate industry, is now closed, the phosphate petering out late in 1979.

Religion. The Church of Tuvalu, derived from the Congregationalist foundation of the London Missionary Society, embraces about 97 per cent of the population and small communities from the Seventh-day Adventists, Bahai and others comprise the remainder. The Church of Tuvalu is headed by a chairman. With the aid of the Bible Society in the South Pacific, it was responsible for the publication, in 1977, of the first book in the Tuvalu language – a translation of the New Testament. A translation of the Old Testament is to follow.

Lifestyle. Although many Tuvaluans earn wages from employment, or receive income from the sale of copra, the cultivation of gardens in the sparse soil and fishing are still fundamental to the Tuvaluan way of life.

Recreation. The islanders' favourite recreations are singing and dancing at the "feast and fatele". The Tuvalu Amateur Sports Association plays an important part in organising other sporting activities, including volleyball (played by both men and women) and cricket. In 1979, a team was sent to the

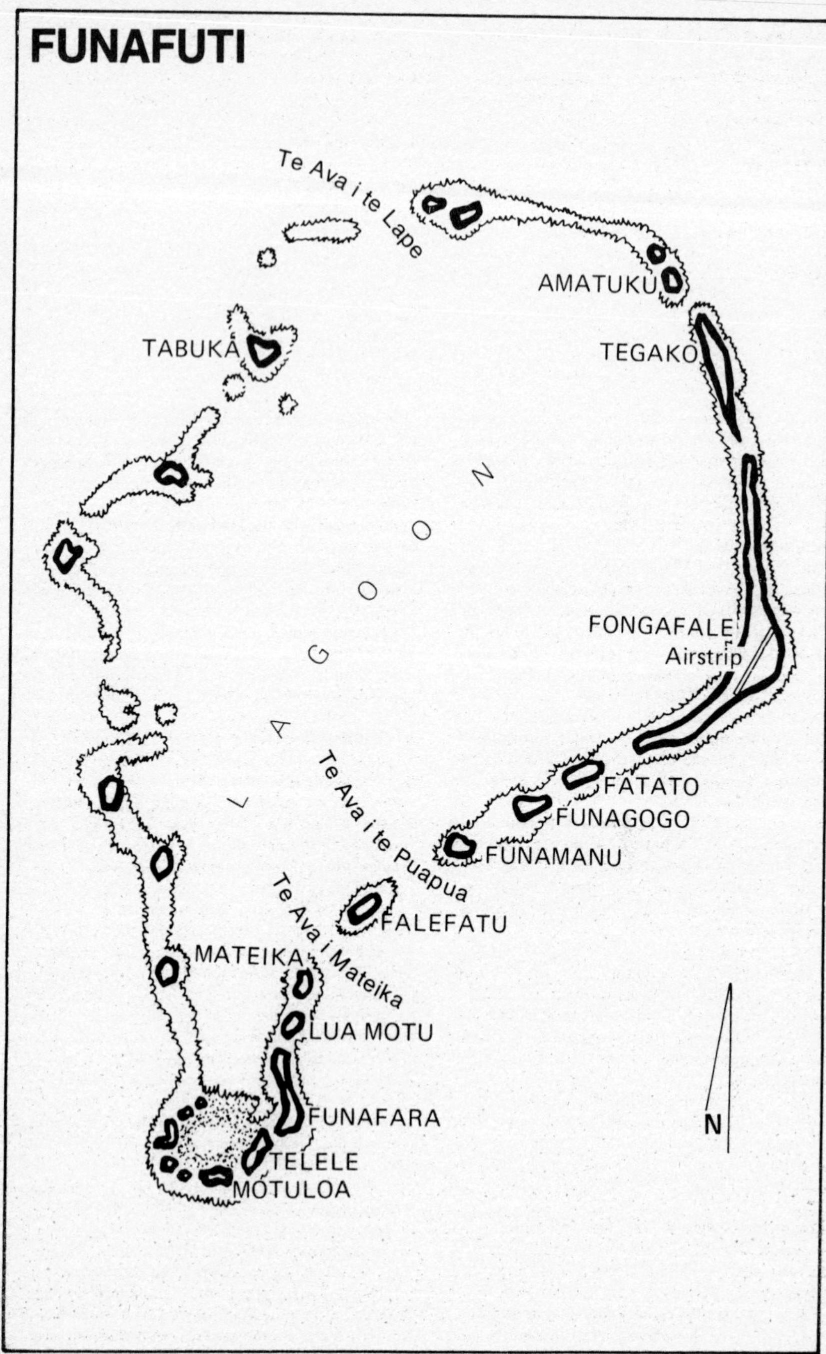
FUNAFUTI
Te Ava i te Lape
AMATUKU
TABUKA
TEGAKO
LAGOON
FONGAFALE
Airstrip
FATATO
FUNAGOGO
FUNAMANU
Te Ava i te Puapua
Te Ava i Mateika
FALEFATU
MATEIKA
LUA MOTU
FUNAFARA
TELELE
MOTULOA
N

6th South Pacific Games in Suva but no medals were won.

GOVERNMENT. Tuvalu is an independent constitutional monarchy, the thirty-eighth member of the Commonwealth, with the Queen as Head of State, represented in the islands by a Tuvaluan Governor-General. The country achieved its Independence on October 1, 1978.

Previously known as the Ellice Islands, from 1916 to 1975 it formed part of the British Gilbert & Ellice Islands Colony. Following overwhelming support for separation in a referendum among Tuvaluans in 1974, the territory was legally separated from the Gilbert Islands on October 1, 1975, and formal separation took effect from January 1, 1976.

Legislature. The Tuvalu Parliament consists of a single chamber with 12 members. Four islands (Nanumea, Niutao, Vaitupu and Funafuti) each return two members (for electoral purposes Niulakita is regarded as part of Niutao) and the others one each. A speaker, elected by members of Parliament, presides at sittings. The normal life of Parliament is four years, the first General Election being held in August 1977. The Attorney-General attends the sessions.

Executive. The Cabinet consists of the Prime Minister and four other ministers. The Attorney-General attends Cabinet meetings.

The power to summon, prorogue and dissolve Parliament rests with the Governor-General, acting on the advice of the Prime Minister.

Elected Chief Minister in October 1975 and confirmed in that office following the general election in 1977, Mr Toalipi Lauti became the country's first Prime Minister at Independence. Mr, later Sir, Fiatau Penitala Teo was chosen to be the country's first Governor-General.

Overseas relations. Apart from its ties with other members of the Commonwealth Tuvalu has established diplomatic relations with the following countries: Belgium, Republic of China, France, West Germany, Japan, South Korea, Turkey and the United States. It is represented in Suva by a High Commissioner, who also acts as Tuvalu's High Commissioner to Papua New Guinea. There are Tuvalu Consulates in New Zealand and Australia.

Tuvalu was the 10th country to join the South Pacific Commission and among other organisations belongs to the S.P.E.C. and W.H.O.

Electoral system. Voting is on a common roll, restricted to citizens of Tuvalu aged 18 or over. A person must be 21 before being eligible to stand for Parliament.

Local government. There is a Town Council on Funafuti and Island Councils on the seven other main islands, each consisting of six elected members including a president. These councils are designed to accept responsibility for and to finance local services required at the island level.

Members of Parliament, medical officers and medical assistants are ex-officio members of Island Councils. The Minister for Works and Local Government, after consultation with a council, may appoint additional persons, but the number of nominated members shall in no case exceed one third of the number of elected members.

Justice. There is a High Court of Tuvalu provided for in the constitution, with a judge appointed from among judges in neighbouring territories. In 1979 there was an agreement with the Government of the Solomon Islands for the office to be filled by the Chief Justice of the Solomons. Appeals lie to the Court of Appeal which, until otherwise resolved, is the Fiji Court of Appeal. From there there is a further right of appeal to the Privy Council. The High Court is to apply the Law of England and Island laws.

Serious crime is rare in the islands. The majority of offences are minor, being of assault or infringements of the traffic ordinance or drinking laws. Civil litigation is negligible apart from land and other customary rights and divorce cases.

Island courts, presided over by Tuvaluans, operate on the eight islands with limited jurisdiction in criminal and civil matters.

The chief of police and 24 officers and constables are all Tuvaluans.

Liquor laws. There are several public bars and a government-owned hotel on Funafuti. Except for Niutao and Nukufetau all other islands are "dry".

There are no discriminatory liquor laws in force and licensing hours for a public bar are normally from 11 a.m. to 3 p.m. and 6.30 p.m. to 10 p.m.

EDUCATION. All children in Tuvalu go to school in primary schools, one of which exists on each of the eight inhabited islands. Primary school enrolments in 1978 were 1,338 (742 boys, 596 girls). The estimated total in 1979 was 1,392. Children enter school at the age of six and those selected transfer to the secondary school at ages 11 to 13. The primary schools consist of nine classes and are each staffed by trained teachers, the teacher-pupil ratio being 1:35.

Secondary education is provided at Motufoua School on Vaitupu Island to School Certificate level. Students attending in 1978 (the latest for which figures are available) totalled 236. In 1976, 50 students were attending secondary schools outside Tuvalu and 54 were attending tertiary courses outside Tuvalu – 18 at the Marine Training College at Tarawa, 12 on technical courses, 16 on diploma courses and eight at university.

Maritime Training School. Tuvalu now has its own maritime training school. Built with finance from the Australian Government, the school was opened in 1979 on the Funafuti islet of Amatuku. The intention is to train up to 60 young men each year, principally for posts with overseas shipping companies.

LABOUR. The active workforce in Tuvalu is estimated to be 3,000. In 1973, the latest year for available accurate figures, of the 3,569 inhabitants aged 15 years and over, 2,317 were active in the village economy and 449 in the cash economy. This last group consisted of one employer, 3 self-employed, 2 unpaid family workers and 443 employees. About 300 seamen are away at a time working on overseas ships while other Tuvaluans are employed in the phosphate industry on Nauru. The last of the Tuvaluans working on Banaba were due to return home at the end of 1979.

In 1977, for the first time, agreement was reached for 12 Tuvaluans to take up short-term employment in New Zealand but the project only lasted for a year. The agreement with the New Zealand Government is still in force with the total increased to 20, but opposition by trade unions in New Zealand to Tuvaluans occupying the positions prepared for them has caused suspension of the scheme.

HEALTH. The Princess Margaret Hospital at Funafuti was opened in 1978. It has 30 general beds in two wards, 4 maternity beds and 2 private wards. There is an operating theatre, a dental centre, x-ray unit, a laboratory and a rapidly-expanding family planning unit. Each island has a resident dresser, a state-registered nurse and a maternity-child health nurse.

THE LAND. The total land area of the islands is 25.9 square kilometres. The largest island is Vaitupu of 5.6 square km. The main island, Funafuti, has an area of 2.8 sq. km; the smallest of the nine atolls, Niulakita, is only 50 ha. The other islands are Nanumea, Nanumanga, Niutao, Nui, Nukufetau and Nukulaelae. The territory encompasses 1.3 million sq. km of sea.

The atolls extend over 560 km in a winding line from Nanumea in the north to Niulakita in the south. They are no more than 5 metres above sea level.

Climate. The climate is not unduly trying, particularly during the season of the north-easterly trade winds (March-October) but becomes enervating during the season of rains and westerly gales (November to February). The temperature varies from 22-38 deg. C. in the shade, but usually between 26 and 32 deg. C.

Rainfall varies considerably, not only between the islands but also from year to year. In an average year, the annual rainfall extends to 3,000 mm in the islands farthest to the south.

Because of the atoll terrain, there are no rivers, Nanumanga, Niutao, Vaitupu and Niulakita are reef islands. Vaitupu has a closed-off lagoon, and there is a brackish lake on Niutao.

Fauna and flora. Local vegetation is limited to plants such as coconuts, bananas, breadfruit etc. The only animal wildlife is the Polynesian rat. There are only 22 known species of moths and butterflies. Australia has 12,000.

Land tenure. Most land is owned by islanders in small holdings. Land is also held communally and jointly. With the limited resources available, one problem is the repeated splitting of holdings for next-of-kin upon the death of a land owner.

PRIMARY PRODUCTION. Copra production averaged about 420 tonnes a year in the Ellice Islands through the 'sixties, with little or no investment taking place. In addition, subsistence production of coconuts is estimated at least to equal these figures. In the absence of other cash crop opportunities and with the necessity to feed the increasing population, the chief objective in agriculture is to increase coconut production.

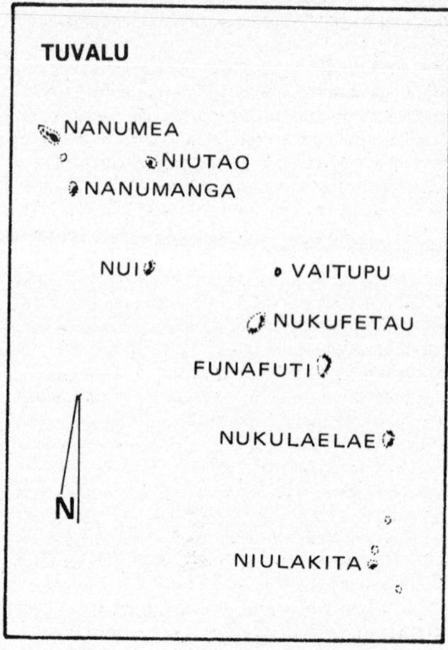

Actual commercial production of copra has varied in recent years according to such factors as hurricane damage, fluctuations in world prices and the availability of income from employment and remittances.

As the table below demonstrates, Tuvalu's copra production was hit badly by hurricane Bebe in October, 1972.

COPRA PRODUCTION
(in tonnes)

1971	1972	1973	1974	1975	1976	1977	1978
468	104	66	566	122	61	139	233

The Tuvalu Copra Co-operative Society assumed responsibility in 1978 for the production and marketing of copra. Production in 1979, January-July, amounted to 285.51 tonnes and copra exports to Fiji in the same period totalled 373.47 tonnes.

Agriculture. The headquarters of the Agricultural Division is on Vaitupu where a poultry and livestock officer are stationed. Lack of suitable grass prevents the grazing of cattle but efforts are being made to increase the numbers of pigs and poultry to help reduce import requirements. Imported meat, dairy products and eggs cost $175,768 in 1978. An experiment with goat rearing has shown initial success and a number of rabbits have been brought in to breed for food. However, they show no signs of flourishing.

Fisheries. A fisheries development station was established on Funafuti in 1970 but it was seriously hampered by hurricane Bebe which sank two deep sea fishing boats and damaged the mother ship. The South Pacific Commission, however, carried out a skipjack tuna survey in Tuvalu waters from June 25 to July 4 in 1978 and later reported that bait fish was plentiful, that an average of one school of tuna was sighted for every hour of searching time and that "the location of Tuvalu close to the equator would suggest that skipjack should be abundant year-round and the excellent seasonal catches taken by the Japanese distant water fleet in this area endorse optimism for the establishment of some type of skipjack fishery in Tuvalu". Prime Minister Toalipi Lauti said in 1979 that with four ships – two on-line and pole skipjack fishing and two on long line fishing for albacore and yellow and blue fin tuna – Tuvalu could earn more than $US9 million in four years. At present, fishing is confined to local catches in and around Funafuti. The government is also seeking to persuade other countries to take out licences for fishing in Tuvalu's territorial waters. In 1979, two foreign fishing vessels were detained at Funafuti and the ships' masters fined heavily for illegal fishing in Tuvalu waters.

Beche-de-mer exports from Nanumea, Nukufetau, Funafuti and Nukulaelae provide a useful source of revenue through markets in Fiji and Hong Kong.

LOCAL COMMERCE. A co-operative wholesale society is established on Funafuti to carry out importation for the co-operative societies, one of which is retail trading on each island. The few small businesses on Funafuti include grocery, baking and building.

TOURISM. Because of its remoteness and the infrequency of air flights, Tuvalu has not attracted tourist traffic and visitors have numbered less than 100 a year. But, since independence, the country has been thinking more seriously of tourism as a money-raiser. Air Pacific, Fiji's regional airline flies through Funafuti to Tarawa once weekly and, fortnightly, visitors can disembark at Funafuti on the flight to Tarawa, stay overnight at Funafuti and join the flight the following day on its return to Suva from Tarawa. Arrangements have been completed for the opening of an amphibious air service from Funafuti to the other islands in the group.

OVERSEAS TRADE. Copra exports were, until a few years ago, almost the only overseas earner Tuvalu had but sales of stamps to overseas philatelists now bring in a comparatively large income. In 1977, Tuvalu's exports, apart from the sale of handicrafts which did not rate a mention in statistics, totalled $60,940 made up of copra, 217 tonnes valued at $46,401, scrap copper, 807 g valued at $20 and re-export of cinema films (after showing) valued at $14,519. In 1978, 153 tonnes of copra, valued at $35,551, was exported.

The latest available returns for 1979 show that copra exports for the first eight months of the year were valued at $205,000. This figure was exceeded by philatelic sales. The Philatelic Bureau, a joint venture between the Tuvalu Government and the

IMPORTS: JULY 1976 TO DECEMBER 1978

	July-Dec 1976		Year 1977		Year 1978	
	Value	Proportion	Value	Proportion	Value	Proportion
	$	%	$	%	$	%
Food and live animals chiefly for food	217 627	29.95	432 691	34.70	572 708	36.41
Beverages and tobacco	43 411	5.97	52 174	4.18	120 157	7.64
Crude materials, inedible, except fuels	37 035	5.10	85 061	6.82	59 778	3.80
Mineral fuels, lubricants and	39 947	5.50	66 477	5.33	172 847	10.99
related materials	1 558	0.21	1 562	0.13	2 209	0.14
Animal and vegetable oils and fats						
Chemicals	23 099	3.18	64 602	5.18	91 729	5.83
Manufactured goods classified chiefly by material	212 568	29.25	260 297	20.88	257 099	16.35
Machinery and transport equipment	60 210	8.28	136 867	10.98	132 821	8.45
Miscellaneous manufactured	82 296	11.32	128 238	10.28	147 762	9.40
articles	8 997	1.24	18 893	1.52	15 645	0.99
Special transactions not classified according to kind						
TOTAL IMPORTS	726 748	100.00	1 246 862	100.00	1 572 755	100.00

British firm, Philatelists Ltd, of Bristol, with the company providing a European adviser and a European bureau manager, reported that the government's share of stamp sales for 1979 totalled $300,000. The bureau is the largest employer of labour with a local staff of from 50 to 90.

Customs tariff. A new tariff, based on the Customs Corporation Council Nomenclature came into effect on January 1, 1980.

Imports. With inflation overseas affecting landed prices in Tuvalu, the import bill has risen steadily over the past few years – from $1,246,862 in 1977 to $1,572,755 in 1978 with another increase expected for 1979. The table below has been prepared by the United Nations Development Advisory Team (UNDAT) which has its headquarters in Suva, Fiji.

In the food division in 1978 Fiji was Tuvalu's biggest supplier with a total of $236,783, followed by Australia with $207,006 and New Zealand $103,812. Other importing countries were well below these totals. Overall, however, Australia topped the list of importers for 1978, its share of the total of $1,572,755 being $552,219 (33.11%). Fiji was next with $447,469 (28.45%) and New Zealand came third with $216,946 (13.79%).

FINANCE. The estimates of revenue and expenditure for Tuvalu for 1979 provided for a budget of $2,019,817 of which $1,269,817 was to be raised locally and $750,000 was to be a grant-in-aid from the British Government which, as an independence settlement, contributes £2.5 million ($A5 million approx.) as a development aid grant and £2.6 million ($A5.2 million approx.) as a special development fund grant. Personal tax was expected to raise $85,000, customs duties $370,000 and philatelic sales $200,000.

The main expenditure heads were:

	$
Commerce and Natural Resources	86,392
Communications and Transport	482,766
Social Services	549,151
Finance	134,701
Pensions and Gratuities	42,410
Works and Local Government	286,250
Office of Governor-General	34,750
Office of Prime Minister	239,224
Office of Principal Auditor	21,590
Police and Prisons	102,387
Parliament	40,196

The Development Fund estimates for 1979 were to be derived entirely from grant and loan funds amounting to $2,570,412 cash payments and $817,171 in services etc, to be spent on the new deep sea wharf on Funafuti (Australian-financed), a community vocational training school on Vaitupu, an internal seaplane service (installations financed by New Zealand), expansion of Motufoua Secondary School, overseas training and scholarships.

A United Nations Development Programme (UNDP) is spending $US1,140,000 between 1977 and 1981 to improve Tuvalu's broadcasting system and communications and for marine and administration training courses.

Investment. In February, 1979, Prime Minister Toalipi Lauti went to the United States and invested $554,380 with Blue Chip Realty Investment of California at interest of 15% a year. In December, 1979, Tuvalu received $31,560.50 interest on its investment but in December, 1979, Parliament was told that the investment was to be withdrawn from Blue Chip Realty and reinvested in a joint venture with Barclays Bank which has reached agreement with Tuvalu to establish a bank at Funafuti. Tuvalu's equity at the outset will be 25% with Barclays holding the balance but long-term plans provide for a full Tuvaluan takeover.

Currency. Australian currency is legal tender but Tuvalu also has its own coins in circulation. One Tuvalu dollar equals one Australian dollar.

TRANSPORT. All islands have tracks or feeder roads to give access to cultivated areas but Funafuti alone has a network of roads of impacted coral to serve the capital.

Vehicles. There are several cars, tractors, trailers, light lorries and a 15-seater bus on Funafuti. The only other four-wheeled vehicles in the country are a lorry and tractor on Vaitupu. There are a few motor cycles in use on most islands.

Airlines. Funafuti is served by Air Pacific which operates a service between Fiji and Kiribati through Funafuti. It is expected that Tuvalu will have a seaplane service operating between Funafuti and the other islands in the group with the exception of Nanumanga, Niutao and Niulakita which are islands of raised coral without lagoons to provide suitable landing facilities for an amphibious aircraft. The Auckland firm Sea Bee Air Ltd will provide the aircraft and operate weekly flights. Houses, hangar and maintenance facilities have been constructed on Funafuti and the New Zealand Government has made a grant of $55,000 for the provision of air/ground communication equipment and radio beacons. Two Tuvaluans have been taking a course in New Zealand in connection with the maintenance of the aircraft, a Grumman Goose.

Port facilities. Port of entry is Funafuti which has a deep-water lagoon 20 km by 16 km with three entrance passages. Ships can anchor safely between 400 m and 800 m from the shore according to draft and are served by ships' boats and mobile pontoons to a boat-jetty equipped with a mobile 5-tonne crane. Work was continuing early in 1980 on a deep-water wharf which will allow ships drawing up to 5 m to come alongside. The cost, $1,360,000 is being defrayed by Australia.

Shipping. Tuvalu has only one small freighter, the 'Nivanga', which was formerly owned by the GEIC. It was handed over to Tuvalu as its sole share of colony assets when it parted company with Kiribati. Its absence undergoing overhaul and survey at Suva in 1979 caused supply difficulties in Tuvalu's outer islands, some of which ran out of imported food.

The Pacific Forum Line calls about once a month

from Australia and Fiji and there are periodic calls by ships of the Nauru Pacific Line and occasional visits by private or chartered vessels.

COMMUNICATIONS. There is an efficient telegraph service, supplemented by single-channel speech telephone, between all islands in the group and connecting with the international network via Suva. In addition, there is telegraphic communication with Kiribati and Nauru.

Radio. Radio Tuvalu broadcasts for three hours daily from Funafuti on 621 kHz. The programmes are mainly in Tuvaluan with English news broadcasts.

Newspapers. There is a fortnightly government publication – The Tuvalu News Sheet.

WATER AND ELECTRICITY. As there are no streams or catchment areas, water supplies come from roof catchments that run into household tanks. Electricity is 240 volt 50 cycle. There is a limited supply on Funafuti installed for the operation of the SPATC meteorological station, providing power for the broadcasting station, hospital, hotel and some domestic consumers on a restricted basis. Work was proceeding in 1980 to improve and enlarge the existing system, the first part of the scheme being completed at the end of 1979 by a team of British Army engineers. On Vaitupu there is a limited electricity supply to the Motufoua Secondary School.

PERSONALITIES

Governor-General: His Excellency Sir Fiatau Penitala Teo GCMG, ISO, MBE

CABINET

Prime Minister: Hon. Toalipi Lauti

Minister for Commerce and Natural Resources: Hon. Tomu Sione

Minister for Communications and Transport: Hon. Ilaoa Imo

Minister for Social Services: Hon. Taui Finikaso

Minister for Works and Local Government: Hon. Maheu Naniseni

MEMBERS OF PARLIAMENT

Speaker: Hon. Elia Tavita

Nanumea: Maheu Naniseni, Motufoua Feso

Nanumanga: Ilaoa Imo

Niutao: Tomu Sione, Tepepe Papua

Nui: Lale Seluka

Nukufetau: Meauma Moeanga

Vaitupu: Taui Finikaso, Dr Tomasi Puapua

Funafuti: Toalipi Lauti, Elia Tavita

Nukulaelae: Henry Naisali MBE

Secretary to Government: Ionatana Ionatana OBE

Attorney-General: Vacant.

PRESIDENTS OF ISLAND COUNCILS

Nanumea: Malaelu Peni

Nanumanga: Fataoto Munua

Niutao: Soaloa Tiloua

Nui: Lale Seluka

Nukufetau: Nelesone Apelano

Vaitupu: Selu Fangalele

Funafuti: Tapu Levi BEM

Nukulaelae: Tinilau Loni

MINISTRY OF COMMERCE AND NATURAL RESOURCES

Secretary: Feue Tipu

Coconut Production Officer: Ken Trewren

Fisheries Officer: Elisala Pita

Livestock Specialist: G. J. Jack

Fish Processing Officer: K. Machell

Manager Tuvalu Co-operative Wholesale Society (TCWS): J. Warren

MINISTRY OF COMMUNICATIONS AND TRANSPORT

Secretary: Kitiseni Lopati MBE

Broadcasting/Information Officer: Faimalanga Luka

Broadcasting/Information Adviser: A. G. M. Slatter

Postmaster: Vaea Sakale

Manager, Philatelic Bureau: F. Hoy

MINISTRY OF SOCIAL SERVICES

Secretary: Silinga Kofe

Senior Medical Officer: Dr Falesene Salesa

Senior Education Officer: Laloniu Samuelu

Captain Superintendent, Maritime Training School: K. J. Barnett

MINISTRY OF FINANCE

Secretary for Finance: Tauaasa Taafaki

MINISTRY OF WORKS AND LOCAL GOVERNMENT

Secretary: Saufatu Sopoanga

Lands Officer: Siniala Auega

Superintendent of Public Works: B. J. Hall

Government Auditor: Loto Ala

Chief of Police: Saloa Tauia

Secretary Supernumerary: A. McDonald

Planning Officer: M. D. Abbott

TUVALU HIGH COMMISSION IN FIJI:

(P.O. Box 46, Suva, Fiji)

High Commissioner: Kamuta Latasi

U.S. Ambassador to Tuvalu: W. Bodde, (Embassy, Suva, Fiji)

P.N.G. High Commissioner to Tuvalu: Dr Ako Toua (in Fiji)

Australian High Commissioner to Tuvalu: Mr. R. Greet, (in Suva).

HISTORY. Although the name Tuvalu is a local word meaning 'eight standing together', there are nine islands. The southernmost of the nine in the group, Niulakita, stands apart from the others and is not permanently inhabited. The old name Ellice commemorates a nineteenth century English politician, Edward Ellice, MP for Coventry and owner of the ship 'Rebecca' in which Captain Arent De Peyster discovered Funafuti Atoll in 1819. De Peyster named Funafuti in Ellice's honour, and this name was later applied to the whole group by the English hydrographer A. G. Findlay.

The people of Tuvalu are of Polynesian origin. But many now have some European blood, derived from beachcombers and traders who settled in the group in the nineteenth century. On Nui, there is a strong Gilbertese component. The local language has affinities with Samoan and Tongan. Most traditions refer to Samoa as the islanders' original home. But there are also stories of marauders from the Gilberts and Tonga. Many of the early settlers were no doubt castaways who drifted northwards and westwards before the south-east trade wind.

First Europeans. The first of the Tuvalu Islands to become known to Europeans was Nui. This was sighted by the Spanish explorer Mendana on his first voyage to the Pacific in 1568. He sighted another island, Niulakita, on his second voyage in 1595.

However, Mendana's discoveries had been forgotten by the time the next European was in Tuvalu waters almost two centuries later. This was the Spaniard Francisco Mourelle who came upon the northern atolls of Nanumanga and Nanumea in the frigate 'Princesa' in 1781.

The other islands were not discovered, or rediscovered, until the end of the first quarter of the nineteenth century. Captain De Peyster discovered two – Nukufetau and Funafuti – in 1819. Captain George Barrett, of the Nantucket whaler 'Independence II', discovered Nukulaelae and rediscovered Niulakita in 1821. Four years later, another whaler, Captain Obed Starbuck, of the 'Loper', came upon Niutao and Vaitupu, while Captain Eeg of the Dutch ship 'Pollux' rediscovered Nui after a lapse of more than 250 years.

From the date of Captain Barrett's voyage in 1821 until about 1870, the waters in the vicinity of Tuvalu were frequented by whalers operating in what became known as the 'on-the-line-grounds'. Seamen from these ships occasionally deserted and settled ashore, while some of the more adventurous islanders shipped as crewmen. Some of the European beachcombers became traders and agents for firms in Australia, Germany and the United States. They organised the export of coconut oil and later copra.

In the early 1860's, 'blackbirders' carried off about 400 islanders from Funafuti and Nukulaelae to work in Peru. None of them returned. Others were later recruited for plantations in Fiji, Samoa and Hawaii. European diseases introduced at this time caused many deaths among the islanders.

Christianity arrives. Another innovation was Christianity. This was first adopted in Tuvalu in 1861 after some adherents of the London Missionary Society on Manihiki, Cook Islands, drifted to Nukulaelae in a canoe. In May 1865, the Rev. A. W. Murray visited the group from Samoa and placed Samoan pastors on the various islands. The pastors were soon exercising considerable sway; the new faith was universally adopted, and all aspects of island life that did not conform with it were abandoned.

In 1877, British subjects in Tuvalu were brought formally within the jurisdiction of the High Commissioner for the Western Pacific in Fiji. Fifteen years later, following the establishment of a protectorate over the Gilbert Islands, Captain E. H. M. Davis of HMS 'Royalist', visited the group to ascertain whether the inhabitants also wished to come under the British flag. After Davis reported affirmatively on this matter, Captain H. W. S. Gibson of HMS 'Curacoa' was sent to Tuvalu to raise the flag at each island. This was the origin of the Gilbert and Ellice Islands Protectorate. It became the Gilbert and Ellice Islands Colony in 1916.

For most of the colonial period, the Ellice Islands consisted of a single administrative district with its headquarters at Funafuti which was also a port of entry. During World War II, Tuvalu remained outside the immediate war zone. However, the Americans established a base on Funafuti in 1942, and it was from there that the colony was administered until the Japanese were driven from the Gilberts in November 1943. The Americans cut down coconut trees to build airstrips on Funafuti, Nukufetau and Nanumea. All areas were replanted after the war but in the early 1960s the Funafuti runway was again cleared when a commercial airstrip was required. A Fiji Airways aircraft used the strip for the first time in July 1964.

Migration. After World War II, many Tuvalu people migrated to Tarawa, capital of the Gilbert and Ellice Islands Colony, because it offered more and better opportunities for education and employment.

Partly because of the pre-war standards attained at the Ellice Islands School, partly because Ellice schools had continued during the War, and partly because the Ellice Islanders capitalised more quickly on the opportunities available, these Islanders soon found employment opportunities far exceeding their numbers. This led to rivalries within the civil service and an assertion of Gilbertese rights. In an attempt to protect their identity, as well as their future well-being against a perceived Gilbertese threat, the Ellice Islanders sought secession when Britain began to prepare the colony for self-government.

A British commissioner, Sir Leslie Monson, held an inquiry into Tuvaluan attitudes in 1973. This was followed in 1974 by a referendum in which the Tuvaluans could opt to remain with the Gilberts or secede from them. They were told beforehand that, if they voted to separate, they could expect no share in the colony's royalties from Ocean Island phosphate or other assets apart from one ship. Despite this, 3,799 islanders voted to secede, only 293 voted against secession, and there were 40 spoilt papers.

Separation. A year later, on October 1, 1975, the Gilbert and Ellice Islands were legally separated, the latter became Tuvalu, and a new constitution was proclaimed for the group. Toalipi Lauti was elected the first Chief Minister. However, to make the changeover smooth, Tuvalu continued to be administered from Tarawa until January 1, 1976 when Funafuti became the administrative centre. Efforts were then directed to establishing an administration in Tuvalu by people who, in some cases, had spent a lifetime in Tarawa. All this became necessary because it was decided that Tuvalu would gain independence on October 1, 1978.

Independence. Tuvalu formally achieved independence on October 1, 1978, but ceremonies were marred by the non-appearance of the Queen's sister, Princess Margaret, who was confined to bed on the New Zealand frigate, *HMNZS Otago*, at Funafuti, with a high temperature. The official 'handing over' of independence from Britain was performed by Lord Napier.

Early in 1979, Tuvalu signed a treaty of friendship with the United States. Under the treaty, the United States agreed to drop its claims, based on the Guano Act, to four of Tuvalu's nine islands, Funafuti, Nukufetau, Nukulaelae and Niulakita. The treaty calls for consultations between the two partners to the agreement on security and marine resources matters.

ISLANDS IN DETAIL

NANUMEA. Nanumea, the most northerly and most populous of the Tuvalu group, has two main islets, Lakena and Nanumea. They are about 5-6 km apart. There is an unsheltered anchorage off the NW end of Lakena, and landing is made on the western side of the other islet, Mourelle, in 1781, named Nanumea San Augustin. It was occupied by American armed forces during World War II as is attested by landing craft still visible on the reef. The population in 1979 was 842.

NANUMANGA. This island is only 2.5 by 1.5 km. There is no lagoon and no anchorage, and landing is difficult. In 1781, Mourelle named the island Isla del Cocal because it was covered with coconut trees. This was later converted to Gran Cocal. Captain William Hudson of the United States Exploring Expedition surveyed the island in 1841 and it was subsequently known as Hudson Island. The author Louis Becke lived for about a year on Nanumanga in the eighties of the last century. Population in 1979 was 605.

NIUTAO. Niutao is roughly triangular in shape and a little over 1.5 km at its widest. It is heavily wooded with coconuts, and has a tiny lagoon in its centre. Its European discoverer, Captain Obed Starbuck, named it Loper's Island after his ship in 1825. It has also been called Lynx and Sepper. In 1973, this was the most densely populated island and residents were given the right to occupy and exploit Niulakita. Present population is 866.

NUI. Nui is a crescent-shaped island running north and south, 16 km long with two islets, one at each of its horns. New Zealand engineers completed work in September, 1979, on blasting the reef to widen the 122 m boat passage into the lagoon. Attempts have been made to construct a safer anchorage and also to clear a lagoon site for the amphibious aircraft which will link most of Tuvalu's islands in 1980. The people, numbering 546 in 1979, are Gilbertese (I Kiribati) in appearance and are closely affiliated with the Gilbertese in language and culture.

Mendana sighted Nui in 1568 and called it 'Isla de Jesus'. When Captain Eeg of the Dutch ship 'Pollux' rediscovered it in 1825, he called it 'Nederlandsch Eiland' (Netherlands Islands).

VAITUPU. This is a pear-shaped island, about 5.5 km long by 3.25 km at its greatest width. It is completely surrounded by a fringing reef, much of which is dry at low water. There are two lagoons, but only one practicable entrance for boats, and then only at high tide. There is an anchorage in seven fathoms off the village.

Vaitupu has rather better soil than most coral islands and, although small, it is the second most populous island in the group with 1246 residents. Fearing overcrowding, its inhabitants bought Kioa Island, Fiji, in the 1940s, and about 150 islanders went to live there.

The writings on the culture of Vaitupu by D. G. Kennedy, one-time headmaster of the local school, have made the island better known than most of the other Tuvalu islands. He originally established it on Funafuti but after a brief period, moved his Ellice Island's School to Vaitupu in the 1920s. It is now at Motufoua on Vaitupu.

Vaitupu is shown on some maps as Oaitapu or Tracy Island. The latter was the name given to

The Islands of Tuvalu — Areas and Distances

Area (ha)	Distances (Nautical Miles)								
361	Nanumea								
310	40	Nanumanga							
226	77	63	Niutao						
337	144	77	73	Nui					
509	188	160	118	93	Vaitupu				
307	197	164	132	90	36	Nukufetau			
254	254	220	188	151	74	64	Funafuti		
166	317	283	248	208	124	120	70	Nukulaelae	
41	367	329	308	254	204	180	137	85	Niulakita
2 511									

it by Captain Obed Starbuck, its European discoverer, in 1825.

NUKUFETAU. This is an oval-shaped atoll, about 38 km in circuit, with 37 islets on its reef. Ships may enter its large lagoon through a channel on the western side. The lagoon was once suggested as a base for flying boats. The island was previously known as De Peyster's Group, after the captain of the ship 'Rebecca' who discovered it in 1819. A wartime strip is a reminder of US occupation.

FUNAFUTI. Funafuti is a pear-shaped atoll enclosing a lagoon about 18 km long by 20 km wide at its widest. There are about 30 islets on the reef. On the eastern (windward) side, the islets form an almost continuous line, but on the western side there are many gaps. Only three entrances into the lagoon can be safely used, and then only with local knowledge. They are Te Ava i Mateika, Te Ava i Te Puapua and Te Ave i te Lape.

Funafuti is the capital of Tuvalu. The administration offices, a hotel, gaol and hospital are all located at Fongafale on the largest and easternmost islet, Funafuti, which gives its name to the whole atoll. The airstrip is also situated on that islet. The atoll is the only port of entry for Tuvalu.

The population was about 300 in the 1860s but in 1866, Murray found only 100 people after the island had been raided by Peruvian slavers. Recovery was assisted by migration from other Ellice Islands and from Samoa, Tokelau and Manihiki. There were 200 people on the island by the 1880s and 250 by 1900. At the 1979 census there were 2191.

Captain De Peyster who discovered Funafuti in 1819 named it Ellice's Group. In 1897-98, Professor (later Sir) Edgeworth David, of Sydney University, bored through the coral to a depth of about 330 metres to substantiate Darwin's theory on the origin of coral reefs. Edgeworth David made another expedition about 1911, as he had sunk his bore on one of the islands at the edge of the atoll, which did not satisfy some scientific critics of Darwin's theory. So the second time David had to sink his bore in the centre of the atoll, where the critics claimed he would find a rocky volcanic peak. He fond only sand and coral as before. David's wife published a book, 'Funafuti, or Three Months on a Coral Island: An Unscientific Account of a Scientific Expedition', still the only popular account of life in Tuvalu.

NUKULAELAE. This is an atoll with about two dozen islets, of which the two largest are on the eastern side. The reef on the western side is largely submerged. There is no entrance into the lagoon. Work was begun on a new sea wall in 1976 and almost completed by the end of 1979.

The atoll was discovered by Captain George Barrett of Nantucket in 1821 and named Mitchell's Group. The native name is shown on some maps as Nukulailai.

About 200 of the atoll's 300 inhabitants were kidnapped by Peruvian slavers in the 1860s. None returned. The population numbered 348 in 1979.

NIULAKITA. This island, sometimes called Nurakita, is slightly higher than the others in the group. It is about 5.5 km in circumference and thickly wooded with coconut palms. Landing is difficult except in canoes. There is an anchorage off the SW side.

Mendana in 1595 called it La Solitaria. Captain George Bennett, a Nantucket whaler, who rediscovered it in 1821, named it Independence Island after his ship. It has also been called Sophia and Rocky.

The American trader Harry S. Moors, of Samoa, exploited its guano deposits late last century. It later passed into the control of Burns Philp & Co. Ltd., of Sydney, who sold it during World War II to the Western Pacific High Commission on behalf of the Ellice Islanders. It is now occupied and worked by people from Niutao. The population in 1979 totalled 64.

FOR THE TOURIST. The capital has one hotel, the Vaiaku Langi Hotel, which has seven double rooms, four with private facilities, and it is planned to add six more rooms. Daily rates in 1979 were from $15.50 to $19.50, meals included. The hotel is 10 m from the lagoon where there is safe bathing, and a two-minute walk from the airport. Facilities include dining-room and liquor bar and there is a public tennis court a short walk away. It is the only hotel in the group. There is a co-operative store and a number of small shops. It is expected that the other islands will be offered as a tourist attraction some time in 1980 when the seaplane service is opened. A weekly air service operates between Fiji, Tuvalu and Kiribati. At infrequent intervals, small water craft leave Funafuti for the other islands where life has changed little over the years.

No visa is needed for entry to Funafuti (the only port of entry) but visitors must have a passport or similar identity papers and possess on-going travel tickets or proof of the existence of such tickets.

VANUATU

Vanuatu, known until attainment of independence on July 30, 1980, as the New Hebrides, is a double chain of 80 islands located between 12 and 21 deg. S. latitude and 166 and 171 E. longitude. It was jointly administered by France and Britain as a condominium from 1906 until independence. Its new name of Vanuatu, meaning The Land, was given to the group by the Vanuaaku Party (formerly the New Hebrides National Party) which became the government on independence. The new, independent state has a president and is a full member of the Commonwealth of Nations and of the French cultural organisation, the Association de Co-operation Culturelle et Technique.

The main island, Efate, with the administrative centre Port-Vila, is about 2,250 km north-east of Sydney, Australia.

Estimated population in January, 1979, was 112,596, an increase of 34,608 over the total of 77,988 calculated in May, 1967, in the only census held in the country. The totals include "locals" and expatriates. Local time is 11 hours ahead of GMT. The currency is both Australian dollars and New Hebrides francs, but a new national currency will be introduced from January 1, 1981.

THE PEOPLE. The indigenous people are of Melanesian stock, speaking a variety of Melanesian dialects with Bislama as the lingua franca. They are now known as ni-Vanuatu

Population estimates at the end of various years have shown the urban/rural distributions on the accompanying table.

	1967 census	1970	1972	1975
Urban Vila	7,738	10,600	12,700	16,604
Urban Santo	2,564	3,400	3,900	4,954
Rural	67,686	69,600	72,400	74,974
Total	77,988	83,600	89,000	96,532

It was decided in 1979 not to give estimates for rural and urban populations until more reliable data is available.

Results of the May 1967 census showed the following ethnic breakdown:

Vanuatuan	72,244
French subjects	3,840
British subjects	1,631
Foreigners	273
Total	77,988

Nationality. The new Constitution, adopted at independence, frames the regulations for citizenship. Automatic citizenship is bestowed on all persons with four grandparents belonging to a tribe or community indigenous to Vanuatu; on a person of Vanuatuan ancestry who has no citizenship, nationality or the status of an optant. The latter class is given a three-month period (from Independence Day) in which to claim citizenship. Anyone born after Independence Day may become a citizen if at least one parent is a citizen. Nationals of a foreign state or stateless persons can apply for naturalisation after 10 years residence in the Vanuatu. Dual nationality will be banned.

Language. The new Constitution declares the national language of the republic to be Bislama, the Vanuatu pidgin (Bichelamar in French). The "official" languages are Bislama, English and French and the principal languages of education are English and French. The Constitution also lays it down that "The Republic shall protect the different local languages which are part of the national heritage and may declare one of them as a national language."

Migration. Until recently, the only movement of Vanuatuans in and out of the country was to work in the nearby French overseas territory of New Caledonia, but an increasing number of students are entering the University of the South Pacific in Fiji and French universities. However, with the downturn of prosperity in the New Caledonian nickel industry, the steady stream of Vanuatuans into New Caledonia is becoming only a trickle. In 1974, 600 Vanuatuans went to New Caledonia and 631 came back, in contrast to 1972 figures of 1,371 departures to New Caledonia and 1,550 arrivals back in

Vanuatu. With independence, fewer exchanges between Vanuatu and New Caledonia are expected.

Religion. The 1967 census indicated that 84 per cent of the population professed Christian faith, the others following indigenous custom. The largest group was Presbyterian (40%), followed by Roman Catholic (16%) and Anglican (14%), with Seventh-day Adventist, Church of Christ and French Protestant also represented.

Lifestyle. Seventy per cent of the islanders live in rural communities, some of them quite isolated from life in the two towns of Vila and Santo. Chief activity for the rural dwellers is their traditional subsistence agriculture, while those in the towns have greater opportunities to share in the diversions of a cash economy.

Recreation. Soccer is the main sport, although there is a thriving cricket league on Efate, including school teams. Other activities are golf, yachting, boxing, basketball and rugby union.

GOVERNMENT. The condominium was set up by a convention of October 1906, the terms of which were later superseded by the Anglo-French Protocol of 1914. It saw only occasional, minor modifications until talks in the early 1970s between French and British government officials in London and Paris resolved upon giving greater legislative voice to the local population. This change was the most important since the 1914 Protocol.

While the condominium had shown that two Powers could govern a small and isolated community in amity, it won few praises, and much criticism. It appeared in many ways ridiculous, because of the amount of expensive governmental machinery – mostly more decorative than useful – required to administer the affairs of 4,000 French nationals, 2,000 British and more than 90,000 Melanesians.

Legislature. Voting for the first Representative Assembly by universal suffrage took place in November 1975. Prior to this there had been an Advisory Council, established in 1957 and enlarged in 1969 to 30 members of whom 14 were elected.

The new Representative Assembly provided 42 seats, of which 29 were for members elected in Vila, Santo and rural electorates while 4 were reserved for indigenous chiefs and 9 represented economic interests.

The 1975 elections led to victory for the National Party, which sought independence within two years.

In February 1977, the Vanuaaku Party (formerly the National Party) members refused to sit again while the House included special members representing the Chamber of Commerce which, the party claimed, was undemocratic. The Assembly was then dissolved and a seven-man provisional council was formed to advise the Resident Commissioners until new elections were held based entirely on universal suffrage.

The elections were held on November 29, 1977, throughout the country but they were boycotted by the Vanuaaku Party, which, as the National Party had won 17 of the 29 "people's" seats in the 1975 elections. The boycott was imposed on a number of grounds, including the fact that six seats in the Representative Assembly were simply filled without election from the chambers of commerce, a practice branded by the Vanuaaku Party as undemocratic. Despite the fact that no seats were contested in the 1977 elections, a Representative Assembly was declared elected with George Kalsakau as Chief Minister. The Vanuaaku Party took itself out of the conventional political system and declared a Provisional People's Government of its own with powers to raise taxes, etc., in areas under its control. November 29, 1977, was marked by civil disturbances in Port-Vila as rival political factions confronted each other, and the Vanuaaku Party attempted to raise its PPG flag.

The era of self-government was proclaimed on January 11, 1978. Almost a year later, on December 21, 1978, the Vanuaaku Party having decided on a dissolution of the PPG, a Government of National Unity was proclaimed with the Vanuaaku Party holding five ministries and non-VP representatives another five. The casting vote was with the non-VP Chief Minister, Roman Catholic priest Father Gerard Leymang.

On February 7, 1979, as a gesture of goodwill and reconciliation, the Anglican priest Fr Walter Lini, president of the VP and Deputy Chief Minister in the Government of National Unity, handed over to the government a cheque for $A6,852, representing taxes raised by the PPG during the period of its existence. After lengthy sessions, September 17-19, 1979, a constitutional conference produced a constitution for an independent Vanuatu, providing for a republican form of government with a single-chamber parliament, which has a life of four years.

General elections on November 14, 1979, resulted in the Vanuaaku Party winning 26 of the 39 seats in the Representative Assembly. In the regional assemblies on Santo and Tanna, provided for in the new Constitution, the VP also won a majority – eight seats out of 15 in both cases. For three days later in the same month, groups opposing the VP roamed Luganville streets, threatening people who had come from other islands and telling them to get out. Many hundreds fled.

Fr Walter Lini was elected Chief Minister of the new government on November 29, 1979 and he named a ministry of nine, all VP members. The assembly session was boycotted by seven non-VP members from Santo and Tanna, who alleged irregularities in the November polling.

Talks followed in Paris and London in March, 1980, covering the local political scene and economic, budgetary and development issues. The New Hebrides Government asked Britain and France to contribute $A6 million each to the anticipated budgetary deficit as well as providing generous grants for new economic development.

In the Paris talks, the French Government linked the nature and volume of its future aid to New Hebrides Government assurances of protection for French interests in various fields after independence.

As late as October, 1980, the issue of French aid, by that time complicated by the fact that the Vanuatu Government had just declared 110 French nationals 'prohibited immigrants' in the wake of the Santo revolt, remained unresolved.

Despite a revolt by French expatriates and locals led by Jimmy Stevens, independence was attained on the appointed date, July 30, 1980, and Fr. Lini became Prime Minister.

The former Deputy Chief Minister George Kalkoa was elected president in July, 1980. He took the title Ati George Sokomanu, the last name being a traditional chiefly title in his family. He is generally known as President Sokomanu.

Subsequently, the Representative Assembly elected Maxime Carlot as Speaker. Mr Carlot will act as president in the absence from the country of President Sokomanu.

A further move in consolidating the parliamentary structure of the new nation occurred in October when Vincent Boulekone was named Leader of the Opposition.

Head of State. The President of the Republic is elected by secret ballot by an electoral college of Parliament and the Presidents of the Regional Councils, and the office, which has a term of five years, is open to any indigenous Vanuatu citizen qualified to be elected to Parliament. The President can only be removed from office for gross misconduct or incapacity on a motion introduced by at least one-third of the members of the electoral college and approved by at least two-thirds of the members when at least three-fourths of the members including at least three-fourths of the Presidents of the Regional Councils are present. In the absence overseas of the President or his incapacity, his duties will be taken over by the Speaker of Parliament. The President can refer to the Supreme Court any regulation which he considers to be inconsistent with the Constitution.

The Executive. Executive power is vested in the Prime Minister and Council of Ministers which shall consist of the Prime Minister and other ministers, the number of which, including the Prime Minister, shall not exceed a quarter of the number of parliamentary members. Parliament elects the Prime Minister by secret ballot from among its members. The Prime Minister and the Council of Ministers cease to hold office if Parliament passes a motion of "no confidence" in the Prime Minister. The motion must be signed by at least one-sixth of the MPs and supported by an absolute majority. The Prime Minister chooses his own ministers.

The National Council. The Constitution also provides for a National Council of Chiefs composed of custom chiefs elected by their peers sitting in District

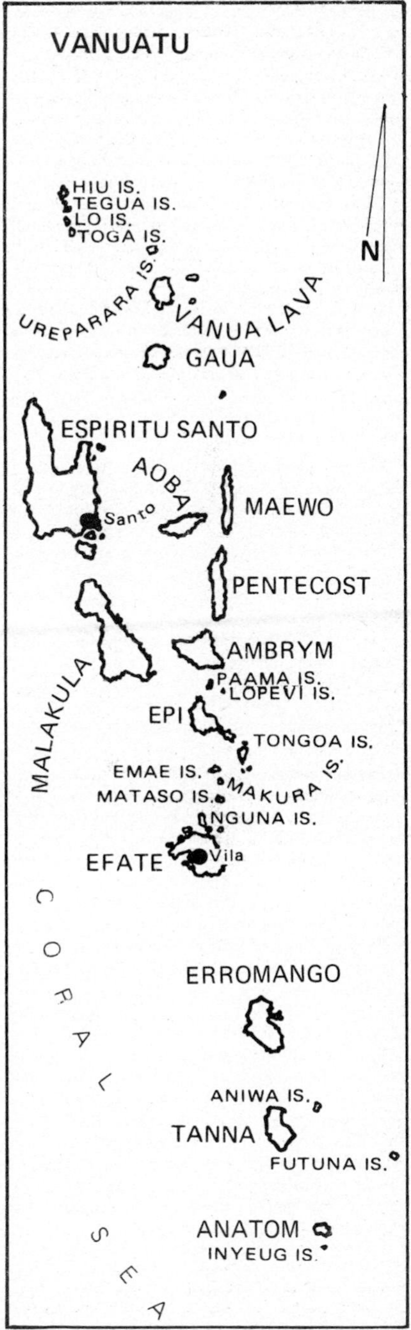

Councils of Chiefs. The National Council meets at least once a year and further meetings may be held at the request of the National Council, Parliament or the government. The council, which will elect its own president, will discuss all matters relating to custom and tradition and can make recommendations for the preservation and promotion of Vanuatuan culture and languages. It can also be consulted on any question, particularly any question relating to tradition and custom in connection with any bill before Parliament. The organisation of the National Council and, in particular, for the role of chiefs at the village, island and district levels will be determined by Parliament.

Members of the National Council, like Members of Parliament, will be protected against arrest or prosecution in respect of opinions given or votes cast by a member in the council in exercise of his office. No member, like MPs, can be arrested or prosecuted for any offence during a council session without the council's authorisation.

Regional councils. Stressing the "importance of decentralisation to enable the people fully to participate in the government of their regions", the Constitution provides for the establishment of regional councils. Each region may elect a regional council which shall, in particular, provide for the representation of custom chiefs in the regional council.

Local government. Municipal councils on the French "commune" principle were established at Vila and Santo in August, 1975, as part of the political evolution agreed on by France and Britain. There is no mention of municipal councils in the new Constitution.

The Ombudsman. The Constitution provides for the appointment of an Ombudsman, who has a five-year tenure and is appointed by the President after consultation with the Prime Minister, the Speaker, leaders of parliamentary parties, President of the National Council of Chiefs, Presidents of the Regional Councils, Chairmen of the Public Service and Judicial Service Commissions. His rights and duties are akin to those of similar officials elsewhere.

Public service. In 1978, the staff of the British Administration was 575 – 115 overseas officers, 443 Vanuatuans, 17 other Pacific Islanders and one temporary officer.

The National Government, in 1978, employed 368 permanent staff of whom 269 were Vanuatuans or "long-time" resident expatriates. There were also 62 contract officers and 37 seconded officers. The total does not include daily-rated employees.

In the joint service an attempt was made to keep a rough balance between French and British personnel – for example, if the head of the Treasury was French, his deputy may be British.

Appointments to the joint service were made by the RC's jointly. In recent years many of the appointments were secondments from British and French overseas civil services.

Justice. The system of justice under the Constitution is similar to that in other countries like Fiji. The Chief Justice is appointed by the President after consultation with the Prime Minister and the Leader of the Opposition. The puisne judges (limited to 3) are appointed by the President, one being nominated by the Speaker of Parliament, one by the President of the National Council of Chiefs and one by the Presidents of the Regional Councils.

The Judicial Service Commission consists of the minister responsible for justice, as Chairman, the Chief Justice, the President of the Public Service Commission, a judge appointed for three years by the President of the Republic, and a representative of the National Council of Chiefs appointed by the Council.

The Judicial Service Commission is not subject to the direction or control of any other person or body in the exercise of its functions.

Parliament provides for appeals from the original jurisdiction of the Supreme Court and may provide for appeals from such appellate jurisdiction as it may have to a Court of Appeal constituted by two or more judges of the Supreme Court sitting together.

Parliament may provide for the manner of the ascertainment of relevant rules of custom, and may, in particular, provide for persons knowledgeable in custom to sit with the judges of the Supreme Court or the Court of Appeal and take part in its proceedings.

Parliament also provides for the establishment of village or island courts with jurisdiction over customary and other matters and defines the role of chiefs in such courts.

Acting on the advice of the Judicial Service Commission, the President appoints the Public Prosecutor and the Public Solicitor. The latter's function is to provide legal assistance for needy persons.

Public Service Commission. The Public Service Commission controls the Public Service and appointments to it, and only citizens of Vanuatu can hold the appointments. Membership of the commission is limited to five who are appointed for a three-year term by the President after consultation with the Prime Minister. The commission has no authority over the judiciary, the armed forces, police and the teaching services.

Police. The policing of the Group is carried out by the Vanuatu Constabulary. Before independence there were British and French divisions, each division consisted of about 150 Vanuatuans under the command of a national Commandant, supported by British officers on the one hand and members of the Gendarmerie Nationale on the other. The headquarters of each division was located in Vila with smaller stations on Tanna, Malakula and Santo.

Plans were in hand to unify the police into a single force under the control of the Vanuatu Government. The authorities have also used French "gardes-mobiles", riot squad gendarmes flown in from Noumea.

Prisons. The government maintains a central prison in Vila. In addition, each District Agency has a prison in which those under short sentences are confined. There is little serious crime.

Liquor laws. Liquor is sold in bars and restaurants, seven days a week from daybreak to 11 p.m.; from off-licences it is sold from 7.30 a.m. to 9 p.m.

EDUCATION. Originally, the main initiative in education was taken by the various missions. Since 1959, the British Administration co-ordinated most of these facilities to provide six years of primary education in the English medium. From the early seventies the French Administration began building schools for French-language education.

Schools. The first Institution for higher education was Kawenu Teacher Training College which the British opened outside Vila in 1962. Secondary education first became available locally with the initial intake in 1966 of students to the British Secondary School in Vila. The Teacher Training Institution and the British Secondary School were amalgamated to become Malapoa College from January, 1977.

Non-Government English-medium primary schools which fulfil certain requirements were grant-aided by the British Administration.

There are five English-medium secondary schools (four of them operated by church bodies) and 161 English-medium primary schools in the group. In 1978, there were 10,873 primary pupils enrolled and 1,042 secondary pupils.

In 1978, there were 115 French primary schools, of which 72 were organised by the French Education Department and 43 by churches, mainly the Roman Catholic Church. The total number of pupils in French-language schools was 12,781 in 1978. This total is made up of 6,524 pupils in government schools and 5,016 pupils in private schools. At the secondary level there were 958 pupils in the Vila Lycee (Grammar School), and 283 pupils at the Lycee d'Enseignement Professionnel (Technical Grammar School).

About 40 students were enrolled in teacher training courses at Cours Normal in 1978.

Overseas studies. Technical education and commercial training, apart from the LEP (above) is provided in regional institutions, in the English-medium mainly at the Honiara Technical Institute in the Solomons, or through apprenticeships in Fiji, New Zealand and Australia. For French-medium technical and secondary education, students have been going to New Caledonia, after four years at the Lycee. Tertiary education is provided at the University of the South Pacific in Suva, the University of Papua New Guinea, the Fiji School of Medicine and other tertiary institutions in Australia, New Zealand and the United Kingdom. Provision was made for francophone agriculture students in Tahiti, and for university students in France.

LABOUR: The labour force in Vanuatu is estimated at approximately 40,000 persons, of whom 32,000 are involved in traditional agriculture and over 8,000 in various salaried jobs as well as commerce and service industries. An employment survey carried out by the Condominium Bureau of Statistics in September 1973 showed a total of 8,530 workers (excluding plantation and indigenous agriculture and stock raising, local fruit retailing and private domestic service). These workers comprised 5,089 salaried employees, 3,024 wage earners and 417 working proprietors and unpaid family helpers. Workers were further divided between 5,716 in the private sector and 2,814 in the government service. The majority of workers were Melanesian Vanuatuans (5,703), with 1,699 Europeans and 1,128 others. Since the 1973 Manpower Survey, the economic recession has caused some redundancy, particularly in building and construction.

Wages. There is no obligatory minimum wage in Vanuatu. An indication of wage movements may be seen from the accompanying table of rates paid to unskilled plantation workers, payments being expressed in NH francs:

	1970	1972	1974
Monthly salary at year's end	5,500	6,900	8,900
Corresponding hourly wage	31.4	39.4	50.8

In 1977 a minimum monthly wage for an unskilled worker was about $A50. A clerical officer or a police constable received from $2,292-$3,156 a year.

Unions. Industrial relations have remained tranquil and machinery for the peaceful settlement of industrial disputes, as provided in the Joint Labour Regulations, is rarely needed. There are 16 registered trade unions and six employers' associations. These cater for most sectors of industry.

Foreign labour: The French authorities, prior to World War II, introduced into Vanuatu over 1,000 Tonkinese labourers from French Indo-China to work French plantations, on five-year contracts. After the war diplomatic difficulties prevented their repatriation to their homeland – Vietnam – until mid-1963 when all but a few left.

This left a temporary shortage of skilled building workmen in the group, partly made up by the introduction of a limited number of tradesmen from Fiji. This has led to the introduction of Wallis Islanders, Tahitians and I Kiribati (Gilbertese) for agricultural work. However, there are not more than a few hundred of them at any one time. Labour shortages and the high costs of what labour exists contribute to the decline in European planting of all sorts. The situation was made even worse in the early 1970s when Vanuatuans were in demand as labourers in the nickel industry in New Caledonia where wages are high.

The small number of Vietnamese in the group are

mostly in small businesses, which they run themselves.

Work permits are needed under the terms of Joint Regulation No. 28 of 1977.

HEALTH: Recent years have seen increased expenditure by both British and French in upgrading hospitals and medical centres throughout the group. The British Service includes expatriate medical officers as well as graduates of the Fiji School of Medicine. The French Service has medical officers seconded from the French Military Overseas Medical Service.

Medical facilities are also staffed by Protestant mission workers and the R.C. Sisters of Mary.

There are some 20 government, private and mission doctors and a British and a French dentist in Vila and Santo.

Hospitals. There are two hospitals in Vila – the Georges Pompidou Hospital (French) completed in 1974, and the Vila Base Hospital (British) to replace the old Presbyterian John G. Paton Memorial Hospital. Vila Base Hospital has 100 beds and Georges Pompidou Hospital has 150 beds.

On Tanna, the British National Service built a complete new hospital at Lenakel with 52 beds. There is also a French hospital at Whitesands.

On Santo there are the French Government hospital and the Seventh-day Adventist hospital at Aore, but the latter has now been down-graded to a dispensary.

On Malakula there are hospitals at Norsup and Lamap run by the French Government plus dispensaries and clinics.

On Aoba there is the Godden Memorial Hospital at Lolowai, run by the Anglican Diocese of Vanuatu. The Nduindui Hospital on West Aoba is a 60-bed, well-equipped institution run by the Churches of Christ. There are Presbyterian mission hospitals on Epi and at Tongoa, both in the Southern District.

Several small clinics and dispensaries manned by trained dressers offer basic facilities on the other islands.

Diseases. In Vila and Santo, the only urbanised areas, conditions are not unhealthy provided that precautions are taken against malaria and fly-borne infections and diet is adequate. Hookworm is not prevalent in the urban areas, though fairly common in rural areas.

Generally, malaria, tuberculosis, hookworm, skin infections, gastro-enteritis and infantile diarrhoea are the major problems. Dental caries is on the increase.

So far as general health is concerned, however, Vanuatu compares favourably with other countries in the South Pacific.

THE LAND: The total land area of the group is 11,880 square kilometres with the largest single island being Santo, 3,947 square km, while the Efate, with the capital Vila, is 915 sq km. Some 80 islands and islets in the group are spread in the shape of a Y extending about 800 km from north to south.

The largest island, Santo, is 145 km from north to south and 65 km from east to west. The island of Efate extends about 45 km from east to west and 30 km from north to south.

The largest islands of the group are: Santo Malakula, Aoba, Maewo, Pentecost, Ambrym, Epi, Efate, Erromango, Malo, Tanna and Anatom (formerly Aneityum)

Vanuatu also includes the Banks group a few kilometres due north and the Torres group, 60 km north-west of the Banks group.

The highest peak in the group is Mt. Tabwemasana of 1,877 m, on the island of Santo, while Mt. Lairiri or Santo Peak reaches 1,652 m.

While half the islands are simply islets and rocky volcanic outcrops, the other half are also punctuated by numerous peaks in a terrain dominated by mountains and plateaux with only limited coastal plains.

Natural features: Within the Vanuatu Group there are a number of active volcanoes. Yasur (Yahuwei) crater on Tanna, continues to produce periodic ash showers. Two volcanoes on Ambrym emit showers of ash also and occasionally this is accompanied by lava. Lopevi (Ulveah) a cone-shaped island south of Ambrym, has erupted intermittently, and Mt Garet, on Santa Maria, in the Banks Group, and Suretimeat on Vanua Lava, both erupted in August, 1965.

Sometimes lakes are maintained in volcanic depressions as on Santa Maria and Aoba.

Soil: Besides the timber it supports, the soil contains mineral deposits such as the manganese at Forari on the island of Efate. Prospecting has been conducted for nickel, copper and bauxite.

Climate: The south-east trade winds prevail, with frequent calms which are often followed by winds from the north and east which bring rain.

At Vila the average year-round humidity is 83 per cent. Average rainfall is about 2,300 mm; the average at Luganville is 3,100 mm.

In the southern hemisphere winter the southern Vanuatu islands, including Efate, can experience quite cool weather; and in the summer, December-April, all islands of the group can experience cyclones.

Flora and fauna: The tropical rain-forests abound with a thick undergrowth of ferns and vines as well as tall trees, common also to the Solomons, such as Barringtonia and Eugenia.

Land tenure: The question of land rights has stimulated considerable debate in recent years, particularly concerning the large tracts of land held by British and Australian interests as well as the French traders SFNH. This has led to extensive parcels of land being handed back to the local people.

However, the new Constitution rules that "all land belongs to the indigenous custom owners and their descendants". Only indigenous citizens, who have acquired their land in accordance with a recognised system of land tenure shall have perpetual ownership. All alienated land will be repossessed and compensation paid to the former owners and a system of leasing may enable expatriate occupiers to remain on the land. All land transactions, including leases, must have government consent. The government may own land acquired by it in the public interest.

Land Developers. About 1967 a new phase of land development commenced in Vanuatu. This was the subdivision of large blocks of freehold land by private individuals for sale to overseas buyers. The three largest subdivisions were on Santo – Hog Harbour, Palikulo and Cape Queiros (formerly Quiros) – and about 4,000 lots were sold, sight-unseen, mostly to Americans for building lots. Some people envisioned American communities of thousands springing up in these areas, which in fact never happened.

These subdivisions and prospective colonies were not viewed favourably by the governments or by the Vanuatuans. In August, 1971, an "added value" tax of 50 per cent was imposed by Joint Regulation, to be paid by developers at the time they registered subdivided land that they had sold.

About the same time the immigration laws were tightened to make it more difficult for outsiders to settle permanently.

PRIMARY PRODUCTION. The production of copra, frozen fish and beef are the three most important industries, while the bulk of the population is engaged in some form of agriculture.

There is now little replanting of European coconut plantations. However Vanuatuans have replanted extensively and now produce about 60 per cent of the copra exported.

Yield is low, however, in comparison with other copra-producing countries because of poor methods of husbandry.

The bulk of copra is still smoke dried and there is not much incentive to improve on this method while there is a ready market for low-grade copra in Marseilles where it is used for soap. Japan also takes a small quantity.

In 1979, 40,000 tonnes of copra was exported, earning about $A18.3 million.

Cocoa. The Department of Agriculture tries to encourage Melanesian production of cocoa on a family basis but output suffers from a labour shortage and sometimes from climatic setbacks. European planters produce about half the exports. Most goes to France and about 20 per cent to Australia.

Coffee. Coffee growing, mainly by European planters, has declined considerably:

The accompanying table shows copra, cocoa and coffee exports in recent years have been as follows:

Agricultural Stations. The main agricultural station is at Tagabe near Vila and there are smaller ones at Luganville (Santo), Lakatoro (Malakula), Isangel and Middle Bush (Tanna).

A coconut Research Station has been set up in Santo. Coconut oil is also processed at Luganville in Santo.

Livestock. Conditions in Vanuatu are suitable for cattle grazing and are free from diseases. The French Government especially has favoured this industry which is largely in French hands and can contribute towards feeding the military and civilian population of nearby French territory New Caledonia, as well as Tahiti. Another outlet can be through the New Hebrides Abattoir Ltd., provided that health regulations can be satisfied.

Cattle herds have grown from an estimated 73,000 head in 1969 to a 1978 total of about 130,000 of which 60,000 are on the island of Santo. There are also large herds on Efate and Malakula. Breeding is with French Charolais and Limousin stock.

Chief problems facing exports of chilled and canned beef are the inadequacy of transport facilities and the irregularity of the Caledonian market which is influenced by the level of local slaughtering and competition from Australian beef exports.

Meat exports in recent years, including canned, chilled, offals and salted meat have been as follows:

MEAT EXPORTS (tonnes)

1973	1974	1975	1976	1977	1978
657	430	n.a.	346	486	848

Other Livestock. Vanuatu is not self-sufficient in eggs and poultry, largely because poultry food has to be imported for efficient production. The Dept. of Agriculture operates a poultry unit with the idea of improving local stock and has a piggery at Tagabe. Pigs are important to Vanuatuan life where they are used in wild or domesticated state for ceremonial as well as food.

EXPORTS (tonnes)

	1973	1974	1975	1976	1977	1978
Copra	22,200	35,700	27,000	34,228	44,304	46,960
Cocoa	828	509	n.a.	649	855	1,096
Coffee	2	n.a.	36	25	51	22
Coconut oil	—	—	—	—	86,339	87,818

Tuna Fishing. This industry was established in 1957 at Palikulo south-east Espiritu Santo, by the South Pacific Fishing Co., with Japanese and Australian shareholders. The company has a freezing depot and uses a fleet of some fifty fishing vessels, manned by Asian seamen. About 100 workers prepare the fish which is frozen and exported mainly to the U.S.A. and Japan as well as Europe.

EXPORTS — FROZEN FISH

	1975	1976	1977	1978
Tonnes	5,218	6,091	9,997	9,182
Price (FNH million)	258	514	1,060	972

Oyster farming. The enterprise at Port Sandwich on Malakula was destroyed by a cyclone.

Shell. Trochus and green-snail shell is collected from local reefs for export but although once an important source of cash for Vanuatuans the value now is small. In 1977 120 tonnes of trochus was exported and 281 tonnes in 1978.

Forestry. Aerial surveys have shown useful timber stands only on Erromanga, Efate and Anatom. There are good stands of kauri and callophyllum on Erromanga but good anchorages for shipping logs are a problem. A French company, "Agathis", a subsidiary of "Rougier et fils", after working there since 1969 decided in 1974 gradually to cease operations due to the reduction in kauri. The company had been shipping logs to France and sawn timber to New Zealand. The more easily accessible kauri on Anatom has already been exploited in the past. Softwoods are imported.

TIMBER EXPORTS (tonnes)

	1974	1975	1976	1977	1978
Logs	1100	n.a.	275	1500	3,658
Sawn timber	400	n.a.	213	642	211

MANUFACTURING AND MINING. With the exception of the small meat canneries and fish freezing works, secondary industry is on a small scale catering almost exclusively for local consumption. It includes a soft drinks plant, printery, building materials, furniture manufacturing and aluminium manufacturing which includes boat building and building accessories.

Manganese, an essential element in steel production, has been mined at Forari, on the east coast of Efate, since July, 1961. The mine was operated by the Cie, Francaise des Phosphates de l'Oceanie, the company that exploited the phospate deposits at Makatea in French Polynesia. The first ore was shipped to Japan in January, 1962, and exports for that year totalled 15,206 tonnes and reached a total of over 75,480 tonnes in 1967. However market difficulties then arose and the mine ceased operations at the end of 1968. There were no exports in 1969 but late that year a new company "Le manganese de Vate" with French and Australian capital (Southland Mining Ltd.) took over the mine and exports began again in mid-1970. However, the enterprise is not now carried on on such a large scale as it was originally. All the manganese goes to Japan.

The manganese is shipped direct from Forari where there are special loading installations.

MANGANESE EXPORTS

	1975	1976	1977	1978
Tonnes	46,520	43,831	27,533	24,739
Price (FNH million)	68	78	63	61

Managanese activity fluctuates with world prices, but further deposits have been confirmed on Erromango. Early in 1976 the company viewed future production as parallel with the extraction of pozzalan (volcanic ash) used in making cement.

Other Minerals: Conzinc Riotinto Explorations of Australia applied, in 1966, to start investigations on Efate, Santo, Malakula, Pentecost and Maewo for copper, manganese, bauxite, etc. The British government, financed a geological survey of the group in the mid-1960s.

Surveys continued with further leases being granted in the early 'seventies for nickel, copper and bauxite exploration

TOURISM. Tourist development is one of the great hopes of Vanuatu. The industry has sprung into significance since the opening of Le Lagon Hotel resort outside Vila and, more recently in 1975, the opening of the Intercontinental Island Inn.

Hopes for future development rest upon improved regional air links through UTA and Air Pacific, including the Tokyo-Noumea link which opened at the end of 1974 as well as Air Nauru which provides links to Hong Kong, Japan and New Zealand.

LOCAL COMMERCE. Economically the French were dominant in Vanuatu until the British instituted liberal legislation for company registration in 1971 which led to the country being regarded as a "tax haven". This attracted the setting up of many new banks, trust funds, etc.

But local trade is still dominated by two large companies, the "Comptoirs Francais de Nouvelles-Hebrides" (CFNH) and Burns Philp (NH) Ltd., a subsidiary of the big Australian firm of island merchants.

Co-operative Societies. Co-operative societies were provided for under Joint Regulation and have proved popular. In practice the work is delegated to an Administrative officer and financing the movement in its initial stages was from national rather than condominium funds.

At the end of 1977 there were 211 registered societies (the number in 1966 was only 40) the majority of them under British supervision. Most of the societies are consumer/marketing – i.e. selling copra and running a trade-store. Co-operatives through their secondary organisation, Vanuatuan Co-operative Federation Ltd, sell copra in large quantities to the

VANUATU TOURISTS

	1976	1977	1978*	1979
Air travellers	17,929	24,545	27,579	30,454
Cruise passengers	48,742	40,412	29,105	n.a.

* Air travellers total is for first 8 months and cruise passengers for first six months.

IMPORTS AND EXPORTS
(FNH-million)

	1975	1976	1977	1978
Imports	2,622	2,628	3,145	3,690
Exports	790	1,285	2,535	2,618

big trading firms. Other societies are organising and selling local artefacts and garden produce through another marketing subsidiary, Syndicat des Co-operatives Autochtones. Others again are savings and loan societies.

OVERSEAS TRADE. Up until 1969 Vanuatu enjoyed a favourable trade balance, because of the fishing and manganese industries. However the decline in manganese exports, coupled with increased imports due to development projects, produced the trade deficit of recent years.

Major Customers. These are France and the USA depending on the relative size of purchases of frozen fish by the US while most copra, cocoa and coffee goes to France. Third major client is Japan with its purchases of copra, frozen fish and manganese.

Chief suppliers. Principal source of imports in 1975 was Australia, providing 33 per cent, compared to 44 per cent in 1969. France continued in second place with 15 per cent (previously 13 per cent) together with Japan 15 per cent (9 per cent). Other significant suppliers were New Zealand with 7 per cent, Hong Kong, New Caledonia and Singapore, all 4 per cent, and Britain 3 per cent.

Customs Tariff. The Brussels Nomenclature classification of commodities is used. The average rate of import duty is 18 per cent and 5 per cent for exports.

EXPORTS
(FNH-million)

	1975	1976	1977	1978
Copra	338	521	1107	1162
Cocoa	41	65	168	175
Coffee	n.a.	n.a.	16	3.8
Beef	63	86	75	150
Fish, frozen	258	514	1060	972
Manganese	68	78	63	61
Timber	2	5	35	16
Coconut oil	—	—	2535	2681
Others	45	46	10	16
TOTAL	815	1315	5069	5236.8

IMPORTS*
(FNH-million)

	1973	1974	1975
Food, live animals	516	831	480
Beverages, tobacco	173	229	141
Mineral fuel	153	344	279
Chemicals	126	177	121
Manuf. goods	529	809	447
Machinery, transp.	462	678	644
Misc. manuf. goods	253	351	264
TOTAL	2,448	3,796	2,754

* cleared for home consumption, classified by UN S.I.T.C. code

Import totals for the years since 1975 were not available.

FINANCE. Three budgets have been out simultaneously in Vanuatu: The Condominium Government budget and one budget each for the British and French national governments. Condominium revenue was derived mainly from import and export duties. But independence brings only one budget.

Each national government raised its own revenue for its own purposes. The British national government received some revenue from the registration of companies under the 1971 Company Regulations and from other minor sources but most of its revenue was from grants from the United Kingdom.

The French financed their national government expenses partly by a tax on Certificates of Origin which allowed exports such as copra and frozen fish to enter France or French overseas possessions duty-free. However, direct contributions were also received from France, in the form of FIDES development funds and payments for the civil service.

Only one budget, the national one, was presented at the beginning of 1980. Total expenditure estimated to be 2,600 million FNH of which 45 per cent are grants from Britain and France. The budget made financial provision for condominium government services during the transitional period to independence. The import duty on petrol was raised in the 1980 budget by 2FNH a litre plus 10 per cent ad valorem as an energy-conservation measure, a total increase of 5FNH a litre but duty on diesel vehicles was cut by 25 per cent. Other increases were 100FNH on a medium-sized bottle of whisky (¾ of a litre), 80FNH on a normal-sized bottle of gin, 10FNH on 20 cigarettes, 9FNH on a can of Australian beer and 8FNH on a small bottle of Dutch beer. The duty on solar heaters for domestic use was removed. Of the budget total of 2,600 million FNH, 45 per cent was for social services, mainly education and health, 18 per cent for communications, transport and works and 16 per cent for administration. A surplus of about 600,000 FNH was budgeted for.

Since 1973, loan money became a significant part of the condominium budget.

The budget of the Joint Administration in recent years is summarised in the accompanying table.

Additional expenditure was undertaken through the British and French special budgets as well as through their respective development grants. However, the variations in accounting systems used, concerning the input in terms of metropolitan public servants' salaries as well as credits which were carried forward from year to year without being used, made it hard to publish comparative statements.

Tax system. Vanuatu has no personal income tax nor tax on company profits. Main tax revenue is derived from duty imposed on imports and exports which provided 60 per cent of condominium tax revenue in 1975. An "added value" tax of 50 per cent was introduced by Joint Regulation in 1971 to be paid by developers when they registered subdivided land that they had sold.

Property tax was introduced by the municipalities in September, 1977. Assessment is based on rental value.

In addition there are business licence fees, stamp duty and various minor indirect taxes.

Banks. While there is only one French bank operating in Vanuatu, the 1971 British legislation creating a local "tax haven" resulted in an influx of new banks between 1971 and 1973.

The French bank, the Banque de l'Indochine, was amalgamated with the Banque de Suez in 1975, thus becoming the Bank of Indo-China and Suez. It has a branch in Vila and one at Santo, with an agency at Norsup, on Malakula and Lenakel on Tanna.

The other banks are:

Australia and New Zealand Bank (Vila); Bank of New South Wales (Vila); Barclays Bank International (Vila and Santo); Commercial Bank of Australia (Vila); Hong Kong and Shanghai Banking Corporation Ltd (Vila); National Bank of Australasia (Vila) and the Bank Gutzwiller, Kurz, Bungener (Overseas) Ltd. There is also a local bank, the Vanuatu Co-operative Savings Bank.

Finance Centre. A Finance Centre Association is now in existence and is composed of international banks, 6 of which provide a full range of banking services within the country, 5 fully-licensed trust companies, 5 firms of international affiliated chartered accountants and 4 firms of solicitors. The association has promoted Vanuatu as an international finance centre.

The government has announced that the Finance Centre (tax haven) will continue to operate after independence.

Inflation in 1979 was running at about 8 per cent.

Currency. A new national currency will be introduced on January 1, 1981. In the interim, the French Government is supporting the New Hebrides Franc to guarantee that it will remain "pegged" against the metropolitan French Franc at the exchange rate ruling at the beginning of 1980. After January 1, 1981, the new currency will be

Vanuatu Government Budget
(FNH—million)

	1974	1975	1976	1977	1978
Revenue	985	702	872	1,033	1,401
Expenditure	819	865	927	829	1,191

backed by a Monetary Authority or Central Bank which will be set up.

Investment incentives. Certain tax exemptions covering import duties and export duties may be granted to new enterprises. Encouragement is given to industries involving fishing, processing of agricultural or marine products, tourist industries and other spheres, with minimum levels of investment stipulated.

Other incentives include ready availability of credit and subsidies for hotel companies operating under French law.

Development Plan. The Joint Office of Development Planning was transferred to the Chief Minister's Office in January, 1978, under the name of Planning Office. It was charged with the preparation of recommendations to the Vanuatu Government concerning investment and development strategies and with the preparation of the Transitional Development Plan which charted the transition of Vanuatu to full independence in 1980. This Transitional Development Plan was approved by the Representative Assembly in its 2nd extraordinary session in July, 1978. Finance for this plan was sought almost equally from France, Britain and Australia. Assistance is also provided by multilateral agencies such as European Development Fund or United Nations Development Fund. New Zealand and Canada also provide aid. The Vanuatu Government provides an amount of 2.3% of total contribution to the Transitional Development Plan.

The Transitional Development Plan provided for a balanced and co-ordinated programme of development. It listed the projects through which government aimed to prepare for independence. That aim would be reached by:

–unifying government services;
–distributing economic opportunities;
–encouraging the participation of local communities in National Development;
–improving communications between the islands;
–expanding and diversifying productive activities;
–strengthening the balance of payments;
–reducing dependence on foreign aid for the Government Recurrent Budget.

The Transitional Development Plan envisaged a total expenditure of 2,554,560,000 FNH or $A31,932,000.

TRANSPORT. The island of Efate (Vate) has about 150 km of all-weather roads, and Espiritu Santo about 100 km. There are also roads on Tanna, Tongoa (Kuwae), Pentecost, Ambrym, Aoba (Omba) and Malakula.

Vehicles. New motor registrations have shown a steady increase in recent years. Vila, the capital, has the largest population of all government centres and had registered at the end of March, 1979, 5,735 vehicles.

Overseas airlines. International air services through Vanuatu are provided by UTA French Airlines, Solair, Air Nauru, and Air Pacific. UTA introduced a 737 jet aircraft on charter from Air Nauru in February, 1976, to fly between Vila and Noumea, Solair operates a weekly flight between Honiara and Santo.

Air Nauru began a service early in 1980 linking Nauru with Honiara, Vila and Auckland.

Air Pacific uses BAC 111 flying from Nadi (Fiji), Honiara, Port Moresby and Brisbane. Air Pacific flies 3 times a week to Fiji and Brisbane and one direct flight between Vila and Brisbane.

Domestic airline. Internal services are provided by Air Melanesiae, formed by the 1966 amalgamation of New Hebrides Airways Ltd (British) and Hebridair (French). Shareholders include Qantas, and UTA. Britten-Norman Islander aircraft and a Twin Otter 300 turbo-prop are used. Air Melanesiae flies from Vila to Anatom, Dillon's Bay, Ipota, Lamap, Lamen Bay, Longana, Lonorore, Norsup, Santo, Sola, Tanna, Tongoa, Valesdir, Craig Cove, Emae, Redcliff and Walaha.

Airfields. The main international airport is Vila, several kilometres out of town and called Bauerfield, after a US Air Force commander in World War II. A new terminal building was opened in 1971, run by the Vila Chamber of Commerce. The strip is 2,231 m long. Extensions are planned at a cost of 30 million FNH.

Santo's airport is at Pekoa, a reconditioned wartime strip. The runway was sealed in 1976 to take F-27 and B-737 aircraft in all-weather conditions.

Other airfields in Vanuatu are located, from north to south, at Sola, on Vanua Lava in the Banks; Longana, Redcliff and Walaha on Aoba; Lonorore on S. Pentecost; Norsup and Lamap on Malakula; Lamen Bay and Valesdir on Epi; Tongoa; Quoin Hill, Efate; Dillon's Bay and Ipota on Erromango; Burton Field near Lenakel on Tanna and at Anatom.

Port Facilities. Ports of entry are Vila and Luganville (Santo) plus Forari with prior radio permission. A new deep sea wharf was completed at Pontoon Bay, Vila in 1972. It is 228 m long with 11 m alongside. The wharf at Santo can accommodate vessels of 156 m with a draught of 10 m.

Shipping services. Cruises including Vanuatu are operated by companies such as Sitmar Line, P & O and Royal Viking Line, all sailing out of Sydney. Cargo services are operated by the French companies Sofrana Unilines and Compagnie Generale Maritime. Others are the China Navigation Co., the Daiwa Line, the Kyowa Line and the Bank Line.

COMMUNICATIONS. There are automatic telephone exchanges in Vila and Santo. The opening of the new Post Office at Vila in 1974 helped improve local telephone services. There is internal radiophone between Vila, Santo and district headquarters; and a teleradio network of more than 100 stations, including plantations, missions, etc.

Overseas radio telephone service is available to Australia, Fiji, New Caledonia and Hong Kong using direct circuits. These may be extended to most places in the world by satellite links.

A government Coast Station at Vila provides public telephone and telegraph services to ships; there is also a privately operated service at Palekula.

The Meteorological Dept. provides weather information from six reporting stations and transmits to Fiji as part of the Western Pacific meteorological network.

Telex. Telex services were introduced at the beginning of 1973. There are direct links to Sydney, Noumea and Hong Kong and these may be extended to most countries.

Broadcasting. Radio Vanuatu now broadcasts seven days a week, and offers programmes in Bislama (the New Hebrides pidgin), English and French. Mid-day programmes and news begin at 11.30 a.m. and finish at 1.15 p.m. Evening programmes, from 4 to 9 p.m. include a variety of music and information. There is no local television.

Newspapers. There are several small publications produced by political parties, schools and churches, but no regular newspapers. "Nabanga", a weekly publication is produced by the French Residency Information Service in Vila with local news in French and Bislama. British Residency Information Department, until early 1979, published, fortnightly, "New Hebrides News" in English and Bislama. Talks were also held for the government to have its own newspaper. A new weekly newsmagazine "Nasiko", which is trilingual, made its appearance early in 1980.

WATER AND ELECTRICITY. A private undertaking, Union Electrique d'Outre Mer, (UNELCO) has a Condominium contract for the generation and supply of electricity in Vila. Voltage is 240. A private company in Santo supplies a limited area of the town. Cost of electricity from both systems is high.

The Public Works Department provides reticulated water supplies to Vila, Santo, Isangel (Tanna), Lakatora and Norsup (Malekula).

PERSONALITIES AND ORGANISATIONS

President: Ati George Sokomanu.

The Vanuatu Government

Prime Minister and Minister of Justice: Walter Lini.

Deputy Prime Minister and Minister of Home Affairs: Fred M. Timakata.

Minister of Education: Donald Kalpokas.

Minister of Finance: Kalpokor Kalsakau.

Minister of Primary Industries: Thomas Reuben Seru.

Minister of Health: George Augustus Worek.

Minister of Transport, Communications and Public Works: John Naupa.

Minister of Social Affairs: Willie Korisa.

Minister of Lands: Sethy Regenvanu.

Representative Assembly

Speaker: Maxime Carlot.

Banks and Torres: Norman Roslyn, George Augustus Worek.

Aoba and Maewo: Onneyn Tahi, Thomas Tungu, Judah Vira.

Santo, Malo and Aore: Jole Antas, Harry Karaeru, Alfred Maliu, War Nalan, Thomas Reuben Seru.

Luganville: Georges Cronsteadt, Kalmer Vocor.

Malakula: Gerard Leymang, Aime Malere, Keith Aisen Obed, Sethy Regenvanu, Jimmey Simeon.

Ambrym: Amos Andeng, Jack T. Hopa.

Pentecost: Vincent Boulekone, Samuel Bule, Walter Hedye Lini.

Paama: Edward Harris.

Epi: Jack Taritonga.

Shepherd: Kenneth Tariliu, Fred Maraki Timakata.

Efate: Manus Albert, Ati George Kalkoa, Donald Kalpokas.

Port Vila: Kalpokor Kalsakau, Albert Sande, Maxime Carlot, Guy-Michel Prevot.

Tanna: Willie Korisa, John Louhman, Charley Nako, Gideon Nampas, (one vacancy).

Other Southern Islands: John Naupa.

MAYORS

Mayor of Vila: Remy Delaveuve.

Mayor of Santo: Michel Noel.

Chairmen: Mal Fatu Mauri (Council of Chiefs) Chief Willie Bongmatur.

CHURCH LEADERS.

Anglican Bishop: Rt. Rev. Derek Rawcliffe.

Assist. Bishop: Rt. Rev. Harry Tevi.

Roman Catholic Bishop: Rt. Rev. F. Lambert.

Moderator, Presbyterian Church: Pastor R. Makikon.

DIPLOMATIC POSTS

Australian High Commissioner: Mr. M. Ovington.

BUSINESS ASSOCIATIONS.

Chamber of Commerce, Vila. Association of Tourism of Vanuatu, Vila.

SERVICE CLUBS.

Rotary, Kiwanis.

SCIENTIFIC INSTITUTIONS.

Museum and Library in Vila Cultural Centre.

SPORTING FACILITIES.

Vila Tennis Club, Golf Club (9-hole at Le Lagon Hotel), water sports from hotels.

CULTURAL GROUPS.

Art studio of N. Michoutouchkine, Pango Road, outside Vila, Nasara Art Gallery; Joe Barrett's Art Gallery; Association; Vietnamienne de Port Vila (Vietnamese Association).

VILA BUSINESS DIRECTORY

Airlines
See transport section.
Architects
Geoffrey Feast, Box 200.
Galimmard, J. M., Box 238.
Mme J. Laurens-Shanuy, Box 256.
Banks
See finance section.
Chartered Accountants
Marquand & Co., Box 257.
Peat Marwick, Mitchell & Co., Box 212.
Mackintosh & Barrett, Box 240.
Price Waterhouse & Co., Box 234.
Coopers & Lybrand, Box 231.
Moore & Priestly, Box 249.
Dental Surgeon
M. Collard.
Electric Supplies
SOCOMETRA, Box 6.
SOCONAIR, Box 191.
Vate Electrique, Box 629.
N. H. Motors.
Dien Van Phu.
Building Materials
A. Bohl, Box 555.
R. Brand, Box 205.
S.M.E.T., Box 70.
S.N.A.B., Box 42.
Import-Export Merchants
Agathis S. A. Box 171.
Au Bon Marche, Box 64.
Barrau S. A., Box 173.
Bourgeois et Cie, Box 28.
Burns Philp, Box 27.
C.F.N.H., Box 30.
Fung Kuei, Box 51.
Sullivan C. (Internat.) Ltd., Box 244.
Tropex Internat. Ltd., Box 139.
SIDIV.
Lawyers
Mr. A. de Preville, Box 14.
H. Wilshire Webb, Son & Doyle, Box 166.
Turner Hopkins & Partners, Box 225.
Hudson & Co., Box 7.
Real Estate Agents
C. Mitchell, Pacific Real Estate, Box 67.
Property & General Ltd., Box 360.
Ste 2B Services, Box 28.
Cabinet d'Affaires Cornette, Box 112.

SANTO BUSINESS DIRECTORY

Construction
Jean Desplat.
Roberto Durati.
Antonio Martinez.
Albert Perronnet.
Jean Pierres.
Food and General
Magasin Arstel.
Burns Philp (NH) Ltd.
Comptoirs Francais des N.H. (CFNH).
Cinema Bidal.
Creugnet Freres (butchers).
Tintin (customs agent).
South Pacific Fishing Co.

HISTORY. The islands of Vanuatu have been inhabited by man for several thousand years. Archaeology in the group is still in its infancy, but some useful clues to the past have already been obtained. Pottery has been found on many of the northern and central islands, namely Espiritu Santo, Malo, Aore, Aoba, Malakula, Makura, Tongoa and Efate. However, little has been found on the southern islands of Erromanga, Tanna, Anatom (Aneityum), Aniwa and Futuna (Erronan).

The making of pottery appears to have died out in all the islands except Espiritu Santo (where it is still made on the west coast) between A.D. 1300 and 1400. A French archaeologist, Jose Garanger, believes that this may have been due to the arrival of conquerors from the south, headed by a chief known in tradition as Roymata. At Eretoka (Hat) Island, off the coast of Efate, Garanger has excavated Roymata's elaborate burial site, complete with human sacrifices. The site has been dated at A.D. 1265.

A feature of archaeological research in Vanuatu is the similarity from island to island of shell and stone artefacts. The earliest radiocarbon date so far established for settlement in the southern islands is 420 B.C. on Tanna. A site on Aore in the northern part of the group yielded a date of 1300 B.C.

First European. The first European to see Vanuatu was the Spanish explorer Pedro Fernandez de Quiros. He sighted several islands in the Banks Group and Maewo on April 25, 1606. About a week later, he anchored in a large bay at an island which he called Austrialia del Espiritu Santo, now known simply as Espiritu Santo or Santo. To the large bay, he gave the name of St. Philip and St. James, and in its south-eastern corner, he planned a future city to be known as La Nueva Jerusalem and located on the banks of the River Jordan. Officials with high-sounding titles were appointed as civic dignitaries but as there were no women aboard the expedition ships, the proposed settlement remained a dream. A stockade fortified with 'sturdy stakes and earthworks with loopholes' was built there. There were fireworks, religious processions, high masses, and much beating of drums. After two vain attempts to explore the eastern coast of the island, which Quiros believed to be the Southern Continent, the strong easterly winds which prevented exploration also negated attempts by the mariners to regain their former anchorage near the Jordan River. On the stormy night of June 11, Quiros in his flagship was forced from his anchorage and sailed northward, deserting his two consorts. They finally left the bay on June 26 under command of Torres, after a total stay of 55 days.

Bougainville and Cook. Nothing more was heard of the group until 1768, more than 160 years later, when the French navigator Bougainville passed between Maewo and Pentecost, landed on Aoba, and continued on between Santo and Malakula. It remained for Captain Cook to discover and chart the greater part of the group. In 1774, he entered the Vanuatu area from the north, and, in sailing southward, he discovered most of the southern islands. It was he who gave the name New Hebrides to the islands.

In 1789, William Bligh sighted several of the islands of what he called the Banks Group during his open boat voyage following the mutiny in the 'Bounty'. The Torres Islands, north-west of the Banks Group, were among the last islands in the Pacific to be discovered by Europeans. They may have been seen by Captain R. L. Hunter of the British merchant vessel 'Marshall Bennett' in 1835. But the first positive report of them was by Captain J. E. Erskine of HMS 'Havannah' in 1850.

Sandalwooders. The Irish seaman Peter Dillon found sandalwood at Port Resolution, Tanna, in 1825. This led to the development of a trade in sandalwood on both Tanna and Erromango. The unscrupulous methods of the sandalwooders resulted in numerous bloody affrays with the islanders. These, in turn, led to the massacre at Erromango in 1839 of the first European missionaries to try to land in the group – the Revs. John Williams and James Harris, of the London Missionary Society.

However, in the following year, the Rev. T. Heath, of the LMS, sailed from Samoa with several Samoan teachers, of whom he left two at Tanna, two at Aniwa and two at Erromango. Futuna and Anatom each got two Samoan teachers in 1841, and in the same year the LMS sent the Revs. George Turner and Henry Nisbet to Tanna. All these early missionaries had little success, and by 1845 only the two Samoans at Anatom remained.

In 1848, the Samoans at Anatom were joined by the Rev. John Geddie, of the Presbyterian Church of Nova Scotia. Another Presbyterian, the Rev. John Inglis, arrived in 1852. By 1856, all but 200 of the 3,000 to 4,000 Anatomese were under Christian instruction. During the next few years, Anatom was a base from which Presbyterian missionary influence spread to the islands as far north as Espiritu Santo.

Meanwhile, the Church of England (Melanesian Mission) had entered Vanuatu through New Zealand with visits to the northern islands of the group by Bishop George Augustus Selwyn. In 1859, after many setbacks, Selwyn established headquarters for the Melanesian mission at Mota in the Banks Group. Selwyn had a great colleague in John Coleridge Patteson. Patteson reduced the Mota language to writing, made it the lingua franca of the mission, and used it as a medium for training native teachers.

In 1860, the Presbyterians in the southern islands suffered a severe setback when a measles epidemic broke out, killing thousands of islanders. The survivors blamed the missionaries for the epidemic and revolted against them. Two European missionaries were killed on Erromango and two were attacked on Tanna. The two islands were then abandoned. However, new recruits arrived in 1863 and the station at Erromango was reopened. Other missionaries were sent to Efate, Futuna (Erronan) and Aniwa.

Blackbirding. The first recruitment of native labour was made by whaling ships from Twofold Bay, N.S.W. in 1847. They were used as shepherds on Ben Boyd's sheep properties in the Monaro district. Captain Kirsopp obtained 65 men from Tanna and Erromango and landed them at Twofold Bay on April 9, 1847. The natives found the Monaro far too cold and the experiment was not a success. Then some sandalwood cutters began to recruit native labour for the cotton plantations in Fiji and the cotton and sugar plantations of Queensland. The first shipload of islanders left Tanna for Fiji in 1864. Others soon followed. At first, this labour trade was orderly and humane. But within a few years there were abuses.

Protests, particularly from missionaries, about "blackbirding" from Vanuatu and other islands forced the British Parliament to pass the Pacific Islanders Protection Bill in 1872.

Under this law, cases of actual kidnapping became rare in Vanuatu. But a Royal Commission in 1883 found that misrepresentation and cajolery by recruiters were virtually universal. By 1876, Vanuatu had provided over 7,200 labourers for Queensland; about 4,500 went to Fiji between 1868 and 1878; and about 2,000 were taken to New Caledonia around the same time. Mortality among them was heavy. For instance, of 600 Erromangans recruited between 1868 and 1878, only 200 returned to their homes. Those who did return frequently brought diseases with them that killed many who had stayed at home. European traders also brought decimating diseases.

Against this sombre background of depopulation, the missionaries continued to extend their work of teaching, preaching and pacification. By 1885, most of the islands had their missions. Meanwhile, the number of European traders and planters in the islands was increasing, particularly on Ambrym, Aoba and Efate.

Most of these settlers were either British or French, who bought large areas of land from the islanders. One of the biggest land-buyers, however, was not a settler but a speculator. This was John Higginson, a British-born naturalised Frenchman of New Caledonia, who asked the French to annex Vanuatu. His request was refused. About the same time, a French plan was put forward to allow liberated convicts from New Caledonia to settle in the group. The Presbyterian missionary J. G. Paton organised a protest movement in Australia against this plan, and so began an Australian agitation for annexation. The French Government countered in 1878 suggesting to the British Government an agreement to respect the independence of Vanuatu.

Birth of the condominium. Eight years of proposals, counter-proposals, gunboat diplomacy and alarms in Australia followed, during which Higginson formed a company in Noumea which claimed to buy almost all the land in the group.

In 1886, Britain and France agreed to set up a Joint Naval Commission for safeguarding order in Vanuatu. A convention to this effect was signed a year later – on November 16, 1887. A declaration, signed in Paris on January 26, 1888, settled the details of the Joint Naval Commission.

The commission was charged with the protection of the lives and property of the subjects of Britain and France. It was composed of two French and two British naval officers from warships in Western Pacific waters, and was presided over alternately by the British and French commanders. But the commission did not work, as there was no civil law to enforce any kind of contract. Finally, in 1906, while German interests were trying to gain a foothold in Vanuatu, the British and French Governments agreed to establish a condominium in the group.

In Queensland, economic pressure for repatriation of Islands labour went on for many years and the first Australian Federal Government accelerated it by imposing an excise duty of 3 per ton on all sugar produced, with a rebate of 2 per ton on sugar produced by all-white labour. By 1906 virtually all islanders had been returned home, but recruiting of labour for New Caledonia went on for several more years.

After World War I, the continuing de-population of the group, begun in the mid-19th century, created a serious labour shortage. The French met this by introducing labourers from Tonkin (now Vietnam) on five-year indentures. Later, during the depression of the 'thirties, the French planters received bounties which kept them out of financial difficulties.

British planters, on the other hand, could not import Asian labour and were not allowed to employ indentured Tonkinese until the late 'thirties. Also, they received no financial help during the depression. They thus either lost their copra trade to the French or were forced to take French nationality to stay in business.

World War II. In July 1940, after France fell in World War II, the Frenchmen in Vanuatu, under Resident Commissioner Henri Sautot, were the first of their nation in overseas territories to rally to the Free French flag of General de Gaulle.

After Japan entered the war at the end of 1941, Vila and Santo became huge forward bases for the Americans. They built roads, airfields and wharves in the greatest burst of activity Vanuatu had ever seen. The country enjoyed a brief period of dollar prosperity which, with the end of the war, petered out.

Many of the roads, bridges, wharves, and airstrips became overgrown or fell down. A few wartime relics still survive. But much of the American war material, including trucks, bulldozers and other mechanical equipment, was dumped in the Segond Channel before the Americans withdrew.

John Frum Movement. A native movement that began on Tanna in 1940-41 became more firmly entrenched after the arrival of the Americans and their obvious material possessions. Its followers believed that a figure known as John Frum would deliver them from the influence of missionaries and Europeans generally, and that he would bring with him great wealth in the form of refrigerators, trucks, canned food, cigarettes and so forth. The appearance of these goods along with the open-handed Americans convinced the Tannese that these things were freely available in the outside world and that they had been kept from them by the Europeans for ulterior motives.

At one period during the War it appeared that the movement would erupt into violence, but this was averted when the leaders were gaoled. The movement has had a number of crises since then – usually when some man has announced that the mantle of John Frum has fallen on him. At its most rabid periods, the movement has been anti-missionary, anti-government and anti-white. In 1976, many Tannese were still adherents, but they were exclusive and non-cooperative rather than actively hostile.

Nagriamel. A movement of another kind, the first political organisation in Vanuatu, came into being in the late 1960s. Called Nagriamel, it was said in 1969 to have about 10,000 followers, mainly in the northern islands. Its leader is a man of mixed ethnic origins, Jimmy Tupou Patuntun Stephens, also known as Chief President Moses. The organisation has a settlement on French company land at Vanafo, near Luganville.

Originally, Nagriamel's aim was confined to obtaining rights over what its followers described as 'dark bush' – land owned by Europeans but never developed by them. In more recent years, Nagriamel has become increasingly involved in politics. In 1971, Nagriamel presented a petition to the United Nations asking for 'an act of free choice' on the issue of independence in Vanuatu. Britain and France refused to discuss the matter at the time. But the French subsequently set out to influence Stephens. In 1975, for example, he was taken to Paris and presented to President Giscard d'Estaing. Later that year, Stephens demanded independence for the island of Santo and an end to the British presence in the territory. This resulted in a declaration by the British and French Resident Commissioners that, under the 1914 Protocol, neither power would withdraw from the territory without the other.

The existence of Nagriamel, the establishment of

three or four other political parties from 1971 onwards, and disruptive tactics by the Advisory Council were among the factors that led the British and French Governments to agree on some constitutional reforms for the condominium in 1974-75. These included the establishment of municipal councils in Vila and Santo, and the replacement of the Advisory Council with a Representative Assembly.

Representative Assembly. Elections for the municipal councils were held in August 1975. A pro-French alliance of three parties won 15 of the 16 seats in Santo, while the pro-French UCNH (Union des Communautes des Nouvelles Hebrides) won 18 of the 24 seats in Vila. The remaining six seats in Vila went to members of the New Hebrides National Party, a strongly pro-New Hebridean movement now called the Vanuaaku Party, which aimed for independence in 1977. By contrast, elections for the Representative Assembly in November 1975 resulted in a triumph for the National Party. This party won 17 of the 29 'people's' seats, against 10 for the UCNH and two for an alliance of Nagriamel and the Mouvement Autonomiste des Nouvelles Hebrides. The Assembly elections were accompanied by demonstrations, accusations of bribery and corruption, and even a home-made bomb. Thirteen other seats in the Assembly were filled from the Chamber of Commerce (six seats), Co-operative Federations (three) and customary chiefs (four).

When elections were held on November 29, 1977, there was a boycott by the majority of the Vanuaaku Party. This resulted in the Assembly being representative mainly of pro-French groups, and to be seriously lacking moral and political authority.

Agreement was reached between all parties in 1978 and a Government of national Unity was formed with the Vanuaaku Party holding five of the 10 seats including that of Deputy Chief Minister (Walter Lini), the Chief Minister being Fr. Gerard Leymang, who had the casting vote.

A general election followed on November 14, 1979, and resulted in the Vanuaaku Party winning 26 of the 39 seats. Fr. Lini was elected Chief Minister by the new Representative Assembly on November 29, 1979.

'Moderate' party representatives on the northern island of Santo and the southern island of Tanna refused to accept the results, alleging Vanuaaku party irregularities in the polling. They declared 'independence' of the two islands in February, 1980, with Santo being renamed 'Vemarana' and Tanna 'Tafea'.

A second declaration of secession by 'Vemarana' was made on May 28, but, despite attempts by the secessionists to delay the granting of independence to Vanuatu, including attacks on police posts and some looting, Independence was declared on July 30. There were further outbreaks of violence, which resulted in the death on Tanna of a Member of the Assembly, Alexis Yolou, and the death on Santo of a son of Nagriamel's leader Jimmy Stephens.

Asserting its authority in the face of inaction by the British and French forces, the newly-independent government applied for help to the Papua New Guinea Government, which sent troops to Santo. All resistance by the secessionists collapsed when the PNG troops captured the secessionists' headquarters at Fanafo outside Santo town on August 31.

Further information. No comprehensive history of Vanuatu has yet been published. However, Dorothy Shineberg's 'They Came for Sandalwood', Melbourne, 1967, gives an account of the sandalwood trade in the territory, and Deryck Scarr's 'Fragments of Empire', Canberra, 1967, gives details of Anglo-French involvement there from the establishment of the Western Pacific High Commission in 1877 to 1914. The most accessible source for events since 1930 is the 'Pacific Islands Monthly'. In 1980, the Institute of Pacific Studies in Fiji published 'Vanuatu' a history of the country in 21 chapters written by Vanuatu citizens including Prime Minister Walter Lini.

VANUATU ISLANDS IN DETAIL

BANKS AND TORRES GROUPS. The Banks Islands are a scattered group lying 80 km north-east of Vanuatu proper. The islands include Vanua Lava, Gaua, Mere Lava (or Star Peak). Ureparapara, Mota (or Sugarloaf), Mota Lava, or Valuwa, Vatganai (Vatu Rhandi), Merig and the Reef Islets. Vanua Lava and Gaua are each about 24 km long and 20 km across.

The group is of volcanic origin, and extremely fertile. It enjoys a good annual rainfall and vegetation is luxuriant.

The islanders of the Banks Group are Melanesian in appearance. They have been educated by the missions and in the census of 1967 numbered 3,500. Many others live in Santo.

Vanua Lava was first explored by Bishop Selwyn, who located the excellent harbour of Port Patteson, and named it after the man who became the first Bishop of Melanesia. There is a good anchorage also at Vuras Bay. The Melanesian Mission has a school at Pt. Patteson. Mt. Suretimeat is an active volcano. It is also the highest peak on the island, 950 metres, and has extensive deposits of sulphur which were worked at one time by a French company.

Gaua is very broken. Mt. Garet is an active volcano. Highest point on the island is 700 metres. There is a crater lake about 6 km long.

Ureparapara appears to be the top of an old volcano, one side of which has disappeared. Thus a fine harbour has been created, which can accommodate large ships. The island lies 12 km north-west of the Reef Islets (three low, wooded islands on a reef about 8 km north of Vanua Lava) and rises to a height of 742 metres.

The Torres Islands, which lie to the north-west of the Banks Group, consist of a chain of small high, islands — Hiu, Metoma, Tegua, Loh and Toga. Hiu is the largest, about 16 km long by 3 km across. A once considerable population has dwindled now to a little more than 200.

ESPIRITU SANTO. Known locally as Santo, this is the biggest island, being 112 km long and 72 km wide. It has a mountain range along the western division, with a peak, Mt. Tabwemasana, rising to 1880 metres. It is heavily wooded, and there are many streams. There are some good harbours, and in the north is the great Bay of St. Philip and St. James.

At the southern extremity, between Santo and Aore Island, is the Segond Channel where most of the European population of the island is congregated, with Luganville the next biggest European settlement to Vila. (There is some confusion in the use of "Luganville" and "Santo"; both usually refer to the settlement that has developed out of the former US base on the Segond Channel, although Santo can also refer to the whole island of Espiritu Santo.)

The population of Santo according to the 1967 census was approximately 10,400, Luganville, on the Segond Channel, had a population of 2,500. It was estimated at 5,000 in 1975.

Santo has a place in Pacific history as it was there, at the head of St. Philip and St. James Bay, known locally as Big Bay, that the Spanish navigator Quiros built a short-lived settlement in 1606. (See history section.) A low wall, containing two embrasures and the remains of a third, was found at the site of the settlement in January 1967.

As well as a plantation industry, Santo has a growing interest in cattle raising. A small meat cannery in Luganville takes care of surplus beef. A new abattoir built to conform to international standards was being constructed in 1977.

A tuna fishing industry, based at Palikulo, south-east Santo, was established in 1957.

There is an hotel at Luganville, most of the amenities of a small tropical town and an airport a few kilometres out.

Since 1967 three large land subdivisions have taken place on Santo.

Aore, 24 km in circumference, lies in the narrow strait between Santo and Malo, forming one side of the Segond Channel.

Small islands off the east coast of Santo are Lathi (Sakeo), Dolphin, Elephant, Pilot, Pilotine, Mavea and Aese. Off the south coast are Araki, Tangoa, Aore, Tutuba and Malo. Tangoa should not be confused with Tongoa, south-east of Epi.

MALO. This is 55 km in circumference, is very fertile and almost all cultivable, as there is only

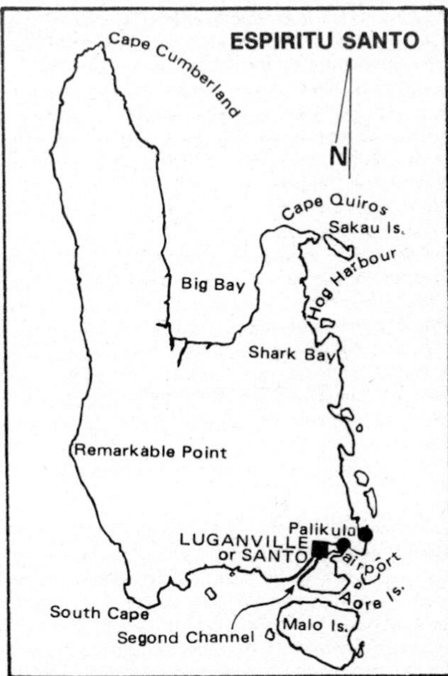

one high point (Mt. Mbwelinmbwevu, 346 metres) on the island. There are several European planters on Malo and some of the plantations are up to 2,000 hectares. The Presbyterian Church of Vanuatu has a bible college at Tangoa, South Santo.

Malokilikili, Malotina, Maloveleo, Amalo Vorivori, Asuleka and Ratua are small islets off the coast of Malo.

AOBA. This island is 38 km long by 14 km across, and rises in places to about 1,220 metres. There are lakes in the interior. The Melanesian, Roman Catholic and Church of Christ Churches are established on the island. The Melanesian Church has its headquarters for the group at Lolowai (the only good harbour, at the eastern end of Aoba). There are three airstrips on the island.

Aoba is pronounced both Oba and Omba.

MAEWO (or Aurora) is 46 km long and 6 km broad. It has a 610 metres central range, which probably accounts for the fact that it has the highest rainfall in the group. There are numerous streams — a large one (north-west coast) that falls over the cliffs at Lakarare, was for many years known as a favourite place at which wandering vessels obtained freshwater supplies. The island is well wooded and fertile, but the Melanesian population has dwindled considerably.

PENTECOST is 61 km long and 12 km wide. There is a central range, with numerous fertile valleys and many permanent streams on the western side. The islanders on the northern part take a keen interest in the condition of their villages. They are expert in various handicrafts, particularly in the braiding of mats and in carving. The Anglican Diocese of Vanuatu, the Churches of Christ and the Roman Catholic Church have stations on this island.

The native name for the island is Raga. A central peak rises to a height of 934 metres.

The islanders were once noted for their large canoes. Since the 1950's they have been better known for their so-called land-diving ceremonies. In these, men leap head-first from towers built of bush timber and vines up to 25 metres high. Bush vines are tied to their ankles and tethered to the tops of the towers. The vines are just short enough and springy enough to break their fall.

There is an airstrip at Lonorore on south Pentecost.

MALAKULA is the next largest island after Santo, being 88 km long and, in parts, 24 km across. A broken range runs the length of the island, rising in one place to form Mount Penot, 892 metres. The western portion is somewhat inaccessible, but the long eastern coast is broken by numerous harbours and bays, with fair-sized streams running back through undulating, well-wooded country — a fertile and beautiful region, where many settlers have made their homes.

The French know this island as Mallicolo.

There is a fine, land-locked harbour, Port Sandwich, on the south-east corner, and along the coast are Bushman Bay and Port Stanley, both well sheltered.

The interior of Malakula is not very well known, and the islanders may sometimes be unfriendly — it is the home of the people called Big Nambas. The coastal islanders however, have long been in contact with Europeans. The native population of the island 12,000 (est., 1971) makes it the most heavily populated island in Vanuatu.

Off the north-east coast of Malakula are the islands of Vao, Atchin, Wala, Rano, Norsup and Uripiv.

Off the south coast are Tomman, Lanur, Akhamb, and the Maskelyne Islands, the chief of which are Vulay, Khuneveo and Sakao.

There are airstrips at Norsup and Lamap.

AMBRYM, 38 km long by 25 km broad, is notable as the scene of more than one eruption by Mt. Marum (1336 metres), an active volcano which dominates the island. There was a severe eruption on December 6, 1913, accompanied by a great earthquake, and much of the fertile island was laid waste. Streams of lava ran down into the sea, wiping out numerous coconut plantations. Hundreds of the islanders were rendered homeless, but there was little loss of life.

Mount Benbow, near Mount Marum, erupted in 1929, wiping out several mission stations. There was an eruption in 1946 which considerably altered the landscape. In 1950 after another eruption, 300-400 islanders were resettled on Efate. The two volcanoes still emit periodic ash-showers and occasionally lava.

PAAMA. A densely wooded, volcanic island with peaks up to 550 metres high, Paama lies between the south coast of Ambrym and the north coast of Epi. The nearest parts of Ambrym and Epi are about 6 km away. There is a good anchorage on the western side of Paama. The Presbyterian Church has a station at the village of Liro.

LOPEVI. About 5 km east of Paama, is a volcanic cone rising to 1456 metres with a small crater at its summit. An eruption of some magnitude occurred in 1883 and there have been many lesser eruptions since. The Anglican Diocese of Vanuatu has a station on the island.

EPI is a very fertile, well-watered island, about 43 km long and 17 km wide, on which there were once some fine plantations which since have deteriorated. It is mountainous — its highest peak is 851 metres. The main port is Ringdove Bay. Formerly the island was called Tasiko, also Volcano. There are two airstrips.

A Presbyterian Church hospital is situated at Vaemali on the north coast of Epi. There is also a Presbyterian Church station at Lamen, a small island off the north-west coast. Namuka is a small island off the southern coast. Tefala and Tefala Kiki are islands off the east coast.

SHEPHERD ISLANDS, so named by Captain Cook, are a volcanic group consisting of seven islands and several islets off the south-eastern extremity of Epi.

Tongoa (not to be confused with Tangoa) is the largest in the group. It is about 12 km in circumference, with several cone-shaped peaks up to 510 metres high. The island is heavily wooded and densely populated. There is a Presbyterian Church station on the island, and an airstrip.

The other islands in the Shepherd Group are Buninga, Tongariki, Falea, Ewose, Laika and Tevala.

EMAE. This island is about 16 km in circumference and lies about 22 km due south of Epi. It has three thickly-wooded mountains, the highest of which is 662 metres high. The Presbyterian Church has a station and sub-station on the island. The native population in the 1967 census was 550.

About 8 km south of Emae is a small, steep island, Makura; and 9 km south of Makura is Mataso Island, which has a sharp peak 510 metres high.

EFATE ISLAND, 41 km by 22 km, possesses the two finest harbours in the group — Vila and Havannah. Vila is the administrative and commercial centre of Vanuatu. It has hotels, shops, transport facilities and all the amenities of a small but growing tropical town. Population (est. 1975) is 16,600 in Vila.

Vila Harbour is picturesque and within it are two islets — Fila, inhabited by local Vanuatuans, and Iririki, the site of the British Residency. A French Administration block was built in 1963 on the mainland overlooking the harbour.

New buildings constructed in recent years include banks; private office blocks; the Condominium office block on the main street, Rue Higginson; hotels; a post office; stores. Reclamation work has extended and beautified the waterfront area, and there have been extensive housing developments, particularly near Erakor lagoon.

On the waterfront is the Vila Cultural Centre, erected with funds provided by the British and French Governments to mark the jubilee of the condominium in 1956. The centre houses a free library of English and French books and magazines, and a museum of native artifacts, stuffed birds of the group, geological specimens, etc.

Despite the condominium and the mixed population of French, British, Vanuatuans, Vietnamese and Chinese, Vila is predominantly a French town in appearance and habits.

There are a number of European-owned plantations on Efate and a growing interest in beef breeding with stud herds of Charolais and Limousin cattle.

Bauerfield, the country's main international airport, is a few kilometres out of Vila. It can take jet aircraft.

The island of Efate is rugged and covered with tropical rain forest. There are some useful stands of commercial timber and sawmills cut for local consumption.

There are about 150 km of all-weather roads on Efate, which link Vila and Forari, on the east coast of the island, and Onesua, west. Forari is the site of a manganese mine.

Hat, Lelepa, Moso (Verao), Nguna (9 by 6 km), Pele, Kakula and Emao are small islands off the northern coast of Efate. Emao should not be confused with Emae south of Epi.

ERROMANGO, 56 km long by 40 km broad, is well watered and extremely fertile. There are various interior ranges, rising to Traitor's Head, 915 metres high. There are no good harbours, but various bays provide safe anchorages — notably, Dillon's Bay, in the north-west; Elizabeth Bay, in the north; Narevin and Cook Bay, in the east. There are a number of large, permanent streams on the east coast. It is an island of great possibilities, handicapped by lack of shipping facilities.

Many missionaries were killed in the early days by the islanders. The Martyrs' Memorial Church at Dillon's Bay has tablets to the memory of missionaries who died on the island.

Sheep were once successfully raised on

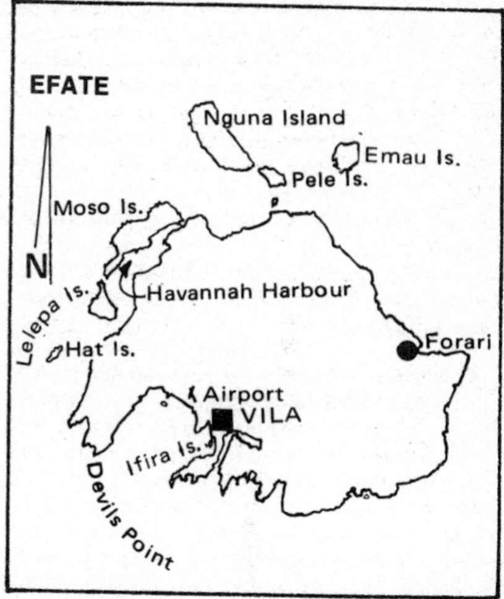

Erromango, and good prices obtained for their wool, but the former sheep station on the island has been abandoned for many years.

There is an airstrip on the east coast, and another on the west coast.

Goat Island is a small island off the north-east coast.

ANIWA is 11 km by 3 km, mostly coral, and has no harbour. There is good anchorage, however. It is a fertile place. Dr. John G. Paton, a notable Presbyterian missionary, settled there in 1866. The island is sometimes referred to as Nina (or Immer). It is noted for its oranges. It has a small airstrip. Aniwa rises to 40 metres and it lies 20 km north-east of Tanna.

TANNA, 51 km long by 24 km across, is probably the most fertile and attractive island in the group. Its southerly position gives it an equable climate. It is exceedingly well watered and well wooded. There are various ranges, and the highest rises to Mount Melen, 1,043 metres.

The rainfall is heavy but there are dry periods, sometimes lasting two to four months. The soil will grow most tropical produce. The 1967 census showed a population of 10,976.

About 50 years ago some cotton was grown in the north.

One of the most accessible active volcanoes in the world is situated 4 km from Port Resolution and 1.5 km from Sulphur Bay. This is Mt. Yasur. The crater may be reached by an hour's walking. The volcano is constantly active, and the caldera may be viewed from the crater rim.

There has been no serious eruption on Tanna since 1878 when the south-eastern end of the island was raised and Port Resolution became inaccessible to deep-water ships. It also lifted 20 metres into the air an isolated pinnacle with a flat top known as "Cook's Pyramid". It is said that it was originally at water level, and that Cook used it as a point for taking observations when he was charting the group on his second voyage.

There is a government station at Isangel; at White Sands there is a French hospital with a European medical officer in charge and a mission station. The British Hospital is at Lenakel.

There is a regular air service between Vila and Tanna. There is a store and tourist cabins near Lenakel airfield.

ANATOM, formerly Aneityum, 56 km in circumference, is the most southerly of the group. Mountains rise in the interior to 850 metres, but the valleys and the flat lands along the shore contain much fertile land, which easily supports a small population. All forms of tropical and subtropical fruits and vegetables grow luxuriantly and there is abundant timber including some kauri pine. This has not been exploited in recent years. There are some permanent streams and a fine harbour, Anelghowhat, on the south coast. An airstrip has been built on Inyeug, a small island opposite Anelghowhat.

The climate of Anatom is very pleasant, the mean shade temperature being 24.5 deg. C, and ranging between 15 and 26 deg. C.

About 120 years ago, the native population was estimated at between 3,000 and 4,000 but a disastrous measles epidemic in 1860, followed by an outbreak of dysentery, wiped out more than 1,000 people. Since then the native population has declined and in the 1967 census was only 340.

For many years, Anatom was a base for sandalwooders and whalers. It was also the centre from which missionary influence spread throughout Vanuatu.

FUTUNA (which should not be confused with the Futuna near Wallis Island) is a small island which lies about 72 km east of Tanna. It runs up to a 388 metre peak in the centre. It is a fertile, well-watered, attractive island, and its native population call the island Erronan.

FOR THE TOURIST. The official tourist promotion body is the Chamber of Commerce in Vila where Mr Joe Mulders enthusiastically helps those seeking information about the islands.

Vanuatu has much to offer – the racial mixture of the people, both French and British institutions, good climate in the winter months and unique attractions like the land-divers of Pentecost Is. and the volcanoes of Tanna.

Travel arrangements can be made by the Vila offices of Air Melanesiae, Air Pacific, UTA as well as Burns Philp, Hibiscus Tours, Island Holidays, CFNH and Coral Tours.

Rental cars are available from Avis and Hertz in Vila and Santo.

Entry formalities. These have been altered since independence. Previously French and British nationals, including Australians, Canadians and New Zealanders did not require visas. This still applies but others exempt are nationals of all European Common Market Countries, Switzerland, Scandinavia, Hong Kong, Singapore, Malaysia, South Korea, Japan, the Philippines, the Cook Islands, the Solomon Islands, Papua New Guinea, Fiji, Tonga, Nauru, Tuvalu, Kiribati and Niue. For others not included in the list, including nationals of the United States, a visa is still required. All visitors must have a valid passport, onward ticket and sufficient funds for their stay. The waiving of visa requirements is granted for a maximum of 30 days.

For those requiring a visa, it can be obtained from their nearest British, French or Australian consulate.

Airport tax. There is an export tax of 400 FNH for passengers travelling by Air Pacific and 200 FNH for passengers travelling by UTA.

Duty-free facilities. Shops in Vila and Santo offer tourist-orientated goods such as electronics, photographic equipment, jewellery, perfume, precious stones and metals, ornaments at duty-free prices. Apart from the British and French stores, the Vietnamese and Chinese shops are well worth exploring. Local handicrafts are in wood and mother-of-pearl.

Sightseeing. Although outside the main stream of tourism, Vanuatu is geared to provide the tourist with an abundance of attractions, some of which can be found nowhere else. As, for instance, the mixture of Melanesian, French and British cultures, with, in the restaurants, a flavour of Chinese and Vietnamese cuisines. Each island has something different, with Tanna offering volcanoes, Efate and Santo modern facilities and Pentecost and Malakula the fascination of a people with a living culture and customs. Vila, the administration centre, has some excellent restaurants, interesting shops, an interesting waterfront, a Cultural Centre, library, museum, six nightclubs or discotheques and two cinemas.

The Melanesians sell their produce in the open air while all manner of goods from the Orient are offered in stores owned by settlers from China and Indo-China.

For divers there is a rare combination of tropical fish, corals and spectacular wrecks in the clear, calm waters of the lagoon. One of the most interesting wrecks is the "President Coolidge", sunk during World War II and now lying on her side, 30 m from the shore of Santo Island at a depth of 20 to 80 m.

Every island in the archipelago has its own characteristics and distinct Melanesian customs. For more information see the Islands in Detail section.

ACCOMMODATION

Vila

HOTEL LE LAGON COUNTRY CLUB D'ERAKOR — 105 rooms and 25 bungalows, all air-conditioned with private facilities; snack bar, dining and grill rooms; swimming pool also water sports, tennis and 9-hole golf course; on 30 ha of land at edge of Erakor Lagoon, 4 km from Vila.

INTER-CONTINENTAL ISLAND INN — 166 rooms, all air-conditioned; 2 restaurants, cocktail lounge with outdoor terrace, pool snack bar, swimming pool, tennis, 9-hole golf, water sports; situated in 8 ha land on lagoon front, 6 km from Vila.

HOTEL ROSSI — 30 rooms, some air-conditioned and with bath; French restaurant, terrace bar with harbour views; on waterfront in town centre.

SOLAISE — 16 rooms; bar, restaurant, garden, pool; in town.

KAIVITI HOTEL — 15 rooms, 13 bungalows, air-conditioned, bar, restaurant, swimming pool.

CENTER POINT MOTEL — 19 rooms, bar.

HOTEL OLYMPIC — 16 rooms, air-conditioned, restaurant, bar.

THE GUEST HOUSE — 6 rooms.

Outside Vila

HIDEAWAY ISLAND RESORT — 10 bungalows, half with private facilities; restaurant, bar, water sports; located on own island, 10 min. from airport, 15 min. from Vila.

MANURO CLUB — 6 rooms, 6 self-contained bungalows, bar, at Manuro Point, Forari, on the east coast of Efate Is.

TAKARA BEACH — 6 bungalows, restaurant, bar; at North Efate.

MARINA MOTEL — 13 units, air-conditioned, swimming pool.

VILA CHAUMIERES — 4 bungalows, swimming pool, bar. On Forari Road, 5 km from Vila.

Santo

HOTEL SANTO — 22 rooms, all air-conditioned; in town centre, dining room, bar.

ALBERT GODDYN GUEST HOUSE — 4 rooms; in town, dining room, bar.

ASIA HOTEL — 11 rooms, in town. Dining room, bar.

RELAIS BOUGAINVILLE — 18 bungalows, dining room, bar, swimming pool.

Tanna Island

TANNA BUNGALOWS — 7 self-contained bungalows; outrigger canoes; guided tours to Yasur volcano; vehicles with chauffeur to rent; shops, markets.

Vanua Lava Island

SOLA HOTEL — 7 self-contained bungalows; plantation store; beaches, horses, hot springs; 5 min. from Sola airfield, 130 km from Santo.

Erromanga Island

DILLON'S BAY — 1 bungalow.

WAKE ISLAND

Wake Island, located in 19 deg. 18 min. N. lat. and 166 deg. 35 E. long., is midway between Hawaii and Guam. It is an atoll with a land area of about 650 hectares. There are three islets – Wake, Peale and Wilkes. Mendana is credited with discovering the island in 1568. It received its name from Captain William Wake of the British schooner 'Prince William Henry' who rediscovered it in 1796. The United States Exploring Expedition under Commodore Wilkes fixed its position in 1840. Mariners of the 19th Century also knew the island as Halcyon or Helsion.

Today it is an American possession. The United States annexed Wake Island for a cable station in 1899. It established an important naval and air base there in 1939-41. However, on December 24, 1941, having bombed Pearl Harbour and seized Guam, the Japanese captured Wake Island and occupied it. The Americans did not return there until September 4, 1945, following the Japanese surrender.

In the post-war years, Wake Island was developed to provide commercial and military aircraft with a stopover and fuelling station between Honolulu and Tokyo and Honolulu and Guam. Since 1974 the island has been used mainly as an emergency stopover. The U.S. National Weather Service has personnel and a weather station on Wake. For a time the US Federal Aviation Administration had administrative jurisdiction over the island, but this is now the responsibility of the US Air Force. Wake is a contingency base and, except for emergency landings, prior permission must be obtained from U.S. Air Force headquarters on Hawaii before landing.

Bridges and roads connect the three islets but most of the development has been on Wake. Peale is used as a recreation area. Wake is linked to Honolulu and Guam, by an underwater cable which was completed in 1964.

Rainwater is caught in two huge water catchments and is supplemented by a distillation plant capable of producing 680,000 litres a day. The population consists of five U.S. Air Force personnel who manage the base and some 200 civilians who work at base. Another 200 civilians operate the various functions of the base and a branch of the National Oceanographic and Atmospheric Administration. They live in modern bungalows and quarters and have all normal amenities.

In 1975, some 15,000 Vietnamese refugees stayed at Wake for four months while awaiting transportation to the United States.

Wake is occasionally battered by a typhoon.

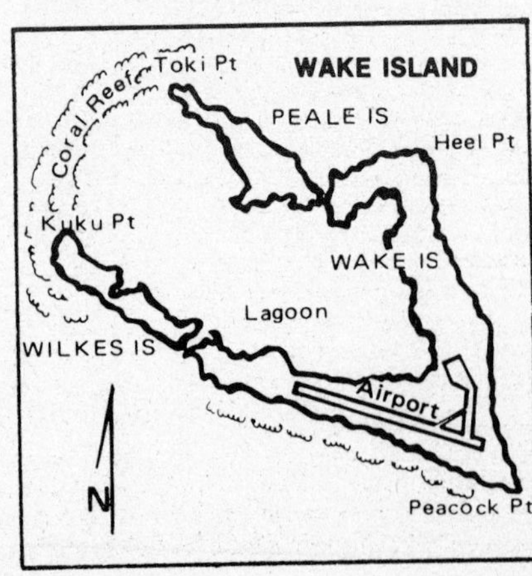

WALLIS AND FUTUNA

Wallis and Futuna, an overseas territory of France, consists of two main islands nearly 200 km apart. They extend from 13 deg. 20 min. S. to 14 deg. 21 min. S. latitude and from 176 deg. 10 min. to 178 deg. 10 min. W. longitude. Futuna is about 240 km north-east of Vanua Levu on Fiji. The capital is Mata Utu on Wallis Is.

Estimated population at the beginning of 1979 was about 10,000.

The national anthem and flag are those of France and currency is the French Pacific franc (CFP) worth CFP18.18 to the French franc in 1980.

Public holidays are New Year's Day, Easter Monday, May 1, (Labour Day), Ascension (39 days after Easter Sunday), Monday after Pentecost (about 10 days after Ascension), July 14 (Bastille Day), August 15 (Assumption), November 1 (All Saints), November 11 (Armistice Day) and Christmas Day.

THE PEOPLE. The islanders are Polynesians. At the census in March 1976, the territory had a population of 9,192 (including 168 Europeans). This compared with 8,546 in 1969. The total Wallisian population in the territory and in New Caledonia was 18,763 in 1976 (14,766 in 1969). In 1976-77, unlike other years, an increasing number of Wallisians who had emigrated to work in New Caledonia came home. However, they were not replaced.

The average household in the territory in 1976 was 7.2 people. The Wallis population of 6,019 was distributed between the central district of Hanake (2,006), Hihifo (1,472) in the north; and Mua (2,541) in the south. The 3,173 inhabitants of Futuna included: western district of Singave (1,389); and Alo (1,784) in the east.

The islanders have French nationality.

Their language is Wallisian but French is used in administrative services.

Through the work of French missionaries, the islanders are all Roman Catholic.

They live very much by subsistence agriculture, their main means of obtaining cash goods being through the funds sent home by islanders working abroad and government work. Favourite recreations are feasting and dancing which includes a spectacular sword dance performed with a spinning cane-knife.

GOVERNMENT. The territory is administered by a French Administrateur Superieur, who is stationed in the chief town, or capital, of Mata Utu, on Wallis. He is assisted by a Territorial Assembly, in addition to the traditional king of Wallis, the two kings of Futuna, and the principal chiefs. The assembly, together with a deputy to the French Parliament in Paris, are elected locally by a common roll. A senator is elected by the Territorial Assembly.

For administrative purposes, the territory is divided into three districts corresponding to three ancient kingdoms, Wallis, Alo and Singave.

EDUCATION. Educational facilities in the territory include seven primary schools conducted by the Catholic missions. They are supervised by the State which finances their operation. On Wallis, primary schools are at Hihifo, Hanake, Tepa, Mu'a and Malaetoli. On Futuna they are at Singave and Kolopelu. A state junior high school with over 200 students is at Lano, Wallis, where the church operates boarding facilities. Annexes to Lano H.S. are at Malaetoli and at Salauniu, Singave.

LABOUR. The active population was estimated at about 4,000 in 1979, with about 3,400 engaged in agriculture and fishing. About 600 worked for the public service, in commerce or handicrafts, receiving regular cash income.

Wages. The minimum rate was set at CFP54 on July 1, 1976. It was increased to CFP62 from January 1, 1978.

HEALTH. Facilities include two dispensaries in Futuna and a modern hospital at Sia, on Wallis. There are three doctors in Wallis, one on Futuna. The principal local diseases include filariasis and ailments related to the inadequate hygiene and sanitation, and the easy access of pigs and other animals to habitations.

THE LAND. Wallis and Futuna consist of two separate groups nearly 200 km apart. They are west of Samoa and north-east of Fiji.

Wallis Island (also called Uvea) is located at 13 deg. 20 min. S. latitude and 176 deg. 10 min. W. longitude.

Futuna, and its smaller neighbour, Alofi, are between 14 deg. 11 min. and 14 deg. 21 min. S. latitude and between 177 deg. 55 min. and 178 deg. 10 min. W. longitude. Futuna is about 160 km south-west of Wallis Island and 240 km north-east of Vanua Levu, Fiji.

Wallis consists of one major island surrounded by a barrier reef with about a dozen islets. Together, they extend for 21 km and are 16 km at the greatest width. The main island, Uvea (not to be confused with Ouvea in the Loyalty Islands), has an area of 6,000 hectares. It is of volcanic origin, but its highest point is only about 143 metres above sea level. Its chief islets are Nukuatea, Nukuafo, Nukufetao, Faioa, Fenuafoou, on the south; Nukulufala, Luaniva, Fungalei, on the east; and Tukuaviki, Nukuteatea, Nukuloa and Nukutapu, on the north.

Futuna and Alofi are both of volcanic origin. Each is surrounded by a fringing reef. The only anchorage for Futuna is Singave Bay on the south-west side.

Futuna is 13 km long and 8 km at its widest. It has an area of about 6,400 hectares. Mountains run the length of the island, reaching a height of 760 metres.

Alofi is about 9.5 km long east and west and about 5 km at its widest. Its area is 2,954 hectares. Alofi's highest point is about 365 metres above sea level. Alofi is separated from Futuna by the Sain Channel, about 3 km wide.

Futuna and Alofi are sometimes called the Hoorn Islands.

Futuna should not be confused with an island of the same name in Vanuatu.

PRIMARY PRODUCTION. Agricultural material is distributed by the "Societe mutuelle pour le developpement rural des iles Wallis et Futuna", S.M.D.R.

Local crops in decreasing order of production are taro, yam, banana, breadfruit, tapioca and copra. Most are grown for local consumption, and sales are minimal.

Copra. Out of some 4,000 ha. of coconut trees on the islands, only half have their copra collected. On Wallis this is used, like tapioca, to feed the pigs. The only exports are from Futuna (usually 100 tonnes a year). The campaign against the rhinoceros beetle has been successful and little damage is now caused to the coconuts by this pest.

Livestock. There are about 100 cattle at the Catholic mission and the experimental station on Matalaa peninsula. There are also about 10,000 pigs, and several thousand fowls. Table birds still need to be supplemented by imports. Several thousand day-old chicks are usually imported each year, as well as about 100 tonnes of frozen and canned meat.

Fisheries. Pirogues, about 100 with motors, are used in the lagoon. Beyond the reefs larger dories are used for tuna fishing. They are built at Mata Utu. A workshop on Futuna can perform minor ship repairs.

The application of the 200-mile limit has given the territory an area of about 300,000 square kilometres of ocean believed to be rich in tuna which could attract Korean or Japanese fishing boats.

Forestry. Timber might possibly be used to greater advantage on Futuna. Reafforestation began in 1973 when Caribbean pine was planted on the central plain of Toafa, on Wallis. There are now over 80 ha. planted. Local tamanou timber is used for building. A wood-based product which finds ready sale overseas is "tapa", decorated with paintings. These are sold by co-operatives in the centres of Apago, Ha'atofo and Lavegahau, and by church schools at Sofala, Mata-Utu and Mu'a.

TOURISM. A small hotel operates on Wallis with five bungalows and a central block. There are several restaurants in Hihifo and Hanake on Wallis, and a small one in Singave, Futuna.

LOCAL COMMERCE. There are several stores, including Ballande.

OVERSEAS TRADE. Due to the near absence of exports, the territory's trade deficit each year tends to equal the imports.

The variation in imports is due partly to the amount of heavy equipment needed for public works, but must be coupled with the effects of inflation.

WALLIS AND FUTUNA — IMPORTS (In CFP millions)

	1974	1977(i)	1976(i)
Food	83	85	73
Textiles, clothing	14	5	12
Petrol, products	20	24	22
Raw & ind. material	57	64	59
Machines, transport	42	56	43
Others	44	25	8
Total	**260**	**259**	**217**

(i) Additional imports (55 tonnes in 1976) arrive by air and include medicine and spare parts.

Customs Tariff. The French system is used, generally giving preference to goods from France and the EEC, although many basic foods are imported from Australia and New Zealand.

The three categories of tax on FOB import prices are: (1) customs duty, usually 3 per cent on foreign goods except basic essentials; higher rates on luxury goods and alcohol (10-45 per cent), tobacco (100 per cent); (2) general import tax on all but a few basics, mainly 6 per cent but up to 30 per cent on tobacco; (3) sales tax, up to 25 per cent on alcohol and CFP100 per hectolitre of fuel.

FINANCE. Revenue for the territorial budget is derived mainly from import tax and French Government subsidies. Separate French Government funds are allotted to supporting the administration and capital works.

WALLIS AND FUTUNA — TERRITORIAL BUDGET (In CFP million)

	Local Revenue	Loans	Expenditure
1975	44	1	110
1976	58	-	117
1977 est.	69	35	194

External aid. This includes grants and loans from France and the EEC. About half the total aid consists of accounts paid outside the territory e.g. transport, and administrative services rendered in New Caledonia. Some of these funds are included as "Loans" in the territorial budget.

EXTERNAL AID (In CFP million)

	French Public Service	Other	Total
1975	338	181	519
1976	374	161	535
1977 est.	343	136	479

Tax system. There is no income tax and business licence fees are low. There is a "solidarity contribution" equivalent to 48 hours work, which alternatively may be paid in cash.

Banking, currency. The first bank, a branch of the Banque de l'Indochine et de Suez, BIS, opened in mid-1977. Local currency is the Cours du Franc Pacifique (CFP), with notes and coins from New Caledonia. The exchange rate is CFP18 = FF1 (French Franc).

TRANSPORT. There are some sealed roads in the centre of Mata-Utu. Other roads are of coarse coral sand.

Air services. Through its airport at Hihifo, Wallis is linked to Noumea by a two-hour flight using a Boeing 737 chartered by UTA from Air Nauru. Air Nauru also puts down there between Apia and Nauru. In addition, irregular flights are made from New Caledonia by the French fleet air arm (aeronavale). An inter-island service operated by UTA Britten-Norman links Wallis and Futuna (Pointe Vele). South Pacific Island Airways will provide charter flights to Wallis-Futuna from Pago Pago. The flight time is 1 hr 45 min.

Shipping. On Wallis, there is a wharf at Mata-Utu, and at the village of Halalo there is a jetty ending in a slipway which permits the unloading of heavy trucks, etc. At Singave, on Futuna, there are berthing facilities.

The islands are serviced on a 45-day basis by the CCC shipping company (Compagnie des Chargeurs Caledoniens) which operates from Noumea out of Sydney and Auckland.

The islanders have formed their own stevedoring co-operative, WAFU.

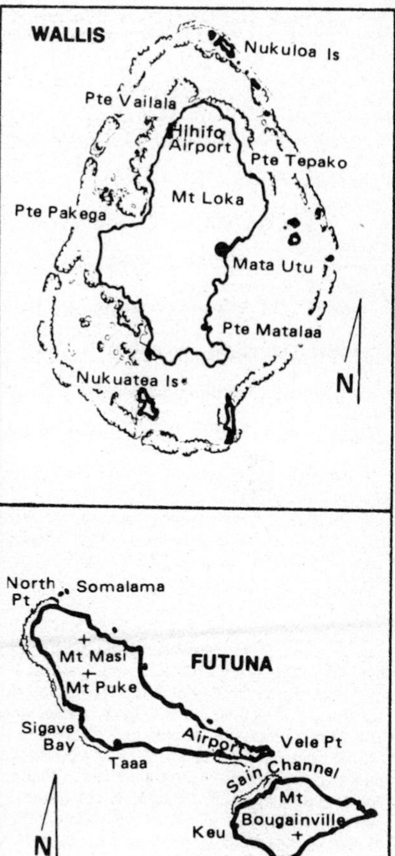

An oil storage depot with a tank capacity of 1,614 cubic metres was built by Total in 1979.

COMMUNICATIONS. The only radiotelephone link is with Noumea and the Nadi airport in Fiji. The overseas arm of the French government radio FR3 opened its transmission station for public broadcasting in mid-1979.

There are no local newspapers, but there is the government gazette, the "Journal Officiel", published monthly.

WATER AND ELECTRICITY. On Wallis, tap water was available for most of the island by the end of 1979. On Futuna, there is no lack of water with either tap supplies or numerous small steams and wells.

Electric current is available 24 hours a day only in the central district of Hanake on Wallis. It is available as far north as Vailala and south to Malaetoli.

Since January 1, 1976, the French company UNELCO has had a 25-year licence to provide this electricity.

PERSONALITIES

Administrator: M. Pierre Isaac

King of Wallis: the Lavelua, M. Tomasi Kulimoe-toke

King of Alo, Futuna: the Tui Agaifo, M. Nopeleto Tuikalepa

King of Singave, Futuna: the Tui Sigave, M. Nasalio Keletolona

Senator: M. Sosefo Makape Papilo

Deputy: M. Benjamin Brial

Economic and Social Counsellor: M. Basile Tui

President, Territorial Assembly: M. Manuele Lisiahi

Vice-President, Territorial Assembly: M. Lafaele Malau

Roman Catholic Bishop: Mgr. Laurent Fuahea

HISTORY. Tradition suggests that Wallis Island was colonised from Tonga about A.D. 1450 or 1550 and that contact with Tonga was maintained at fairly frequent intervals thereafterwards. Until the early nineteenth century, there were constant struggles between rival chiefs for supremacy over the whole island.

The island's European name is that of its discoverer, Captain Samuel Wallis, who came upon it in HMS 'Dolphin' in 1767 following his discovery of Tahiti. Apart from Mourelle (1781) and HMS 'Pandora' (1791), there seem to have been no other European visitors until the mid-1820s. In 1837, some Marist priests visited the island, and one of them, Father (later Bishop) Pierre Bataillon, remained. After many difficulties, Bataillon converted the native king and all the islanders adopted Christianity. In 1842, the king petitioned France for protection. However, Wallis did not become a French protectorate until 1887.

In 1909, Wallis was given an autonomous budget in conjunction with Futuna. It was declared to be a colony of France in 1913, but this declaration was not ratified. During World War II, Wallis was an American military base, although it was outside the area of active hostilities. Airfields were built at Hihifo in the north of Uvea and at Lavengaou in the south. The Hihifo airstrip has since been improved to take jet aircraft.

Following a referendum in 1959, Wallis and Futuna together became an overseas territory of France.

Further information: Alexandre Poncet, 'Histoire de l'ile Wallis,' vol. 2 (Paris, 1972). Vol. 1 had not been published by May 1976.

Futuna and Alofi. The early history of Futuna and Alofi is obscure. The first settlers in the Tua district of Futuna are said to have come from Samoa. There is also a well-known tradition about the arrival of a 'Chinese' ship – possibly a vessel from the Marshall Islands – whose crew left numerous descendants. And there are traditions about Tongan invaders who were generally repelled.

The first European record of the two islands dates back to 1616 when the Dutchmen Schouten and Le Maire discovered them. They named them the Hoorn Islands, after a town in Holland. Whalers put into the island for provisions and refreshment from the 1820s onwards. Some seamen deserted there and became beachcombers.

Father Pierre Chanel, a Marist, was the first European missionary to settle in the group. He was murdered in 1841 at the instance of the native king, but many of the people accepted Christianity soon afterwards. The chiefs asked for French protection in 1842. Thereafter, the political history of the group ran parallel with that of Wallis Island.

In 1976 the relics of the canonised St. Pierre Chanel were flown from France to be enshrined on Futuna.

Further information: 'Journal de la Societe des Oceanistes,' Paris, vol. 19, 1963.

WESTERN SAMOA

Western Samoa consists of two large islands and several small ones with an area exceeding 2,900 sq. km. They are located between 13 and 15 deg. S. latitude and 168 and 173 deg. W. longitude. Western Samoa is an independent state and a member of the British Commonwealth. The capital is Apia on Upolu where local time is 11 hours behind GMT. The islands are about 3,700 km south-west of Hawaii and 2,900 km north-east of Auckland.

Its closest neighbours are American Samoa, Tonga, Wallis and Tokelau.

Western Samoa gained its independency from New Zealand in 1962, being the first South Pacific island nation to become independent, to be a member of the United Nations and to be considered a Third World non-aligned state. An estimated 151,000 people live in Western Samoa, the overwhelming percentage of them being pure-blood Samoans.

The two main islands of Upolu and Savai'i are about 3,700 km south-west of Hawaii and 2,900 km north-east of Auckland.

The national flag is red with five white stars representing the Southern Cross on a blue background in the top, left quarter. Currency is the tala($) composed of 100 sene.

Holidays include New Year, Easter and Christmas, Anzac Day (April), White Sunday (early October), Arbor Day (November) and Independence (the first three days of June). The national anthem is "The Banner of Freedom".

THE PEOPLE. According to the 1976 census, Western Samoa had a population of 151,982 – 109,764 in Upolu and 42,218 in Savai'i. The Samoan population in New Zealand was estimated in 1979 to be about 30,000, about half being New Zealand born.

Nationality. The people are Western Samoan subjects. The prerequisites for citizenship are (a) to be born in the country; or (b) to have five years residence, land to live on and a job. Citizenship is not automatic for non-Samoans, and can only be granted at the discretion of the Minister of Immigration.

Language. The Samoan language is a Polynesian tongue, but English is widely spoken although rural Samoans do not always speak it that well, and, generally, older Samoans cannot speak English. English is the language used in conducting business in government departments and the commercial sector. Samoan is used for conducting the proceedings in the Fono (parliament) with simultaneous translation into English over an internal headphone system.

Migration. In recent years, large numbers of Western Samoans have migrated to New Zealand. Since 1970, this migration has provided an outlet for the surplus workforce but recently New Zealand has insisted on a severe reduction in the numbers of migrants. This was causing increasing unemployment in Samoa in 1977.

An undetermined number of Western Samoans were migrating to American Samoa and from there to Hawaii and California. The remittances received at home from New Zealand and the U.S.A. form an important source of revenue for the nation.

According to a survey made of occupations in Hawaii in 1977, there were only 781 Samoans working in the six major islands of that state but it is estimated that the Samoan population, both American and Western, of the United States is around 90,000. Many Western Samoans are in jobs in the two fish canneries in Pago Pago.

Because of the New Zealand restrictions on migration and the trend for cheaper airfares between American Samoa and the United States, the latter is expected to become an increasingly popular destination for Western Samoans.

Religion. "Fa'avae i le Atua Samoa". Those words, "Samoa is Founded on God", are part of the crest of Western Samoa, and indicate the strength of the Christian Church in the nation. Religion is today embodied into the traditional life of Samoa, and is very much part of daily life. The population is 49 per cent Protestant and 45 per cent Roman Catholic. Each church is usually represented in each village with a large locally-built and funded church.

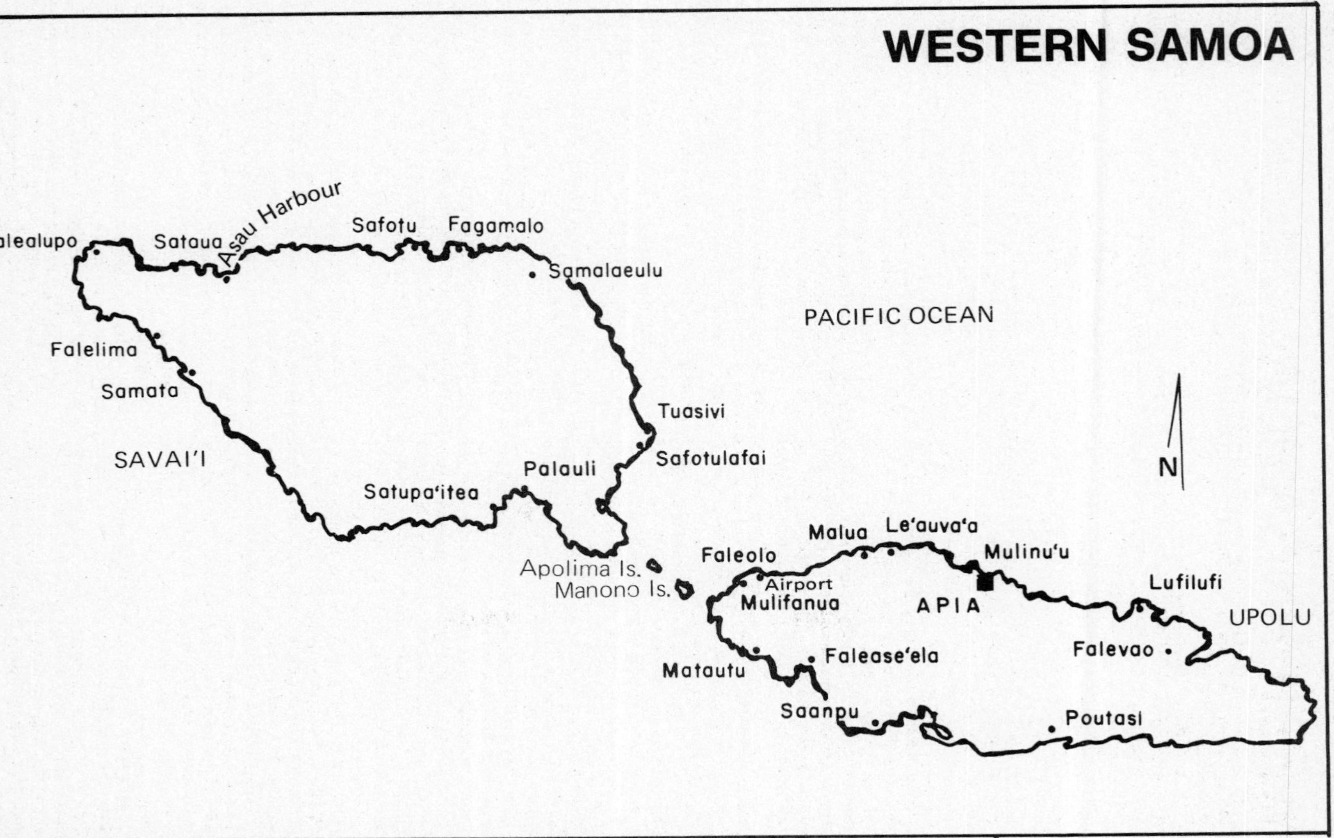
WESTERN SAMOA
Falealupo
Sataua
Asau Harbour
Safotu
Fagamalo
Samalaeulu
PACIFIC OCEAN
Falelima
Samata
Tuasivi
SAVAI'I
Safotulafai
Palauli
Satupa'itea
N
Malua
Le'auva'a
Faleolo
Mulinu'u
Apolima Is.
Manono Is.
Airport
Mulifanua
APIA
Lufilufi
UPOLU
Falease'ela
Falevao
Matautu
Saanpu
Poutasi

Some villages, especially on Savai'i are "one-religion" villages.

Western Samoans take seriously the celebration of the Sabbath, and Sunday is reserved for church services, and little else.

White Sunday, "Lotu Tamaiti", which is on the first Sunday in October is probably the most important religious and social day in Samoa, even including Christmas. It is a day in honour of children and features church services where the children are in all white, and feasts where the children are served by the adults, a reverse of the normal order.

Religion arrived in Samoa in July, 1830, when the ship *"Messenger of Peace"* carrying Reverend John Williams of the London Missionary Society arrived off Sapapali'iein Savai'i. In a relatively short time the church became established and later became known as the Congregational Christian Church of Samoa. It now sends missionaries to other parts of the Pacific and Africa. It has the largest number of adherents in the country.

The capital, Apia, gives its name to the Roman Catholic See, the Bishopric of Apia established in the 1960s when the Pope set up a hierarchy among the South Pacific Islands. The present incumbent is also a Cardinal. Other groups are the Church of the Latter Day Saints (Mormon) and the Seventh-day Adventist Church.

Lifestyle. The "faa Samoa" or traditional Samoan way, remains the central force in Samoan life. The "aiga" or extended family is the critical unit in the fa'a Samoa. The head of the aiga, which may include several Western-style families, is the "matai". The matai has "pule", or authority, over the traditional lands associated with that aiga.

The clan, whose head is called the matai, owns all the lands, and parcels it out to the members as necessity arises. All produce of the soil is theoretically the property of the matai in trust for the community, but in modern days it is becoming increasingly common to allow the actual cultivator to retain for his own use the fruits of his labour.

Each matai has his place in the village council, or fono, the governing authority in each "nu'u" or parish. The village council has wider powers than Western style local government.

There are two main forms of matai title. One is the "ali'i" or high chief title, the other is the "tulafale" or orator title. Some titles are more important than others, and each title ranking and history is contained in the "fa'alupega", which is the spoken history of the titles in that district, and is repeated at significant occasions.

The delivery of the "fa'alupega" is considered important, and in recent times chiefs, orators and scholars have been helped by the regular publication of *"O le Tusi Fa'alupega o Samoa"*, a publication listing titles.

The four highest titles in Samoa are known as the "tama aiga". They are Malietoa, Tupua Tamasese, Mata'afa and Tuimaleli'fano. Each aiga decides on its own matai, usually by talking until a consensus is reached. Titles do not automatically go from father to son.

Occasionally, a title becomes the subject of a dispute, a frequent event with tama aiga titles. Families then have recourse to the Lands and Titles Court. This court, which is headed by the Chief Justice, usually defines who may be involved in deciding on a title. It then instructs that group to consider the issue within a certain time to select a holder, and if it fails to do so, the court then selects a holder.

Factors taken into consideration are many and varied, but the wishes of the previous holder, the candidate's knowledge of "fa'a Samoa", his contribution to village welfare, whether he is resident in the village and his acceptability to the aiga are factors. All titles are registered by the court, and court approval must be given before a "saofai", or traditional ceremony of bestowal, can be held.

It is unconstitutional for foreigners to be given titles, although in recent times the practice of giving "honorary" titles has arisen. Such titles have no significance. Only matai can vote in general elections in Samoa.

Samoan etiquette. The matai are held in high respect in Samoa. A matai is addressed by his title name, and only if a person is on close and familiar terms can a person use the Christian name of a person.

For example, Western Samoa's Prime Minister is known as Tupuola Efi. The first is his matai title, the second is his Christian name. Mr is not necessary in Samoa. There are Samoan honorifics and these are Afioga, Susuga, Tofa and Masiofo. Each applies for certain titles, for example Susuga Malietoa Tanumafili (the Head of State) or Faumuina Fiame Mata'afa Mulinu'u (late Prime Minister) Masiofo is reserved for the wives of tama aiga.

Samoan children usually have a christian name, and a surname that is the christian name of their father.

For the visitor the ritual of Samoa can appear complex, and it can be relatively easy to break conventions without knowing it. For example it is impolite to address hosts in their "fale" (houses) while standing. All important conversations, both in business and at home, are carried out sitting. In the fale it is usual to sit cross-legged on the floor. It is rude to stretch one's legs out, unless they are covered by a mat. Sympathetic hosts usually understand the plight of stiff-legged foreigners and provide mats for this purpose.

Visitors should not walk around villages unescorted. Although the fale are open-sided, privacy is maintained by the convention of not looking into fales. People should only enter fales if invited.

Visitors may be invited to drink 'ava (kava). This traditional drink is quite safe, although it may taste unusual. When drinking in the 'ava ceremony, first tip a little out of the cup onto the ground in front of you and say "Manuia" (good fortune). The contents of the cup (made of half a coconut) should be downed in one gulp. For very important persons (usually heads of states or governments and high titles) a village will host the impressive Royal 'ava ceremony.

Most villages impose "curfews". A vespers curfew is held in the early evening for prayers, and at around 10 p.m. During curfew people should avoid making a noise, and stay in the fale. Curfew customs are observed in some parts of Apia. Flowers are not worn inside a church and heavy manual work should not be undertaken on Sundays.

Out of respect for the elders, passers-by should walk quietly past an open fale when chiefs are holding a fono (meeting) inside.

GOVERNMENT. The Constitution provides for a Head of State, called in Samoan, O le Ao O le Malo, to be elected by the Legislative Assembly for a term of five years.

However, in the first instance, it was decided that the two High Chiefs, who had been titled the Fautua (Tupua Tamasese and Malietoa Tanumafili II), should become joint Head of State and have a lifetime tenure of office unless they resigned or were removed from office by the Assembly. Moreover, if one predeceased the other, the survivor continued as sole Head of State during his lifetime – subject to resignation or removal from office. (On April 5, 1963, the death occurred of Tupua Tamasese; the sole Head of State thereafter was Malietoa Tanumafili II).

There is nothing in the Constitution to prevent others being elected to office but it was recommended at the time of the Constitutional Convention that the Head of State always be chosen from the "Tama-a-aiga" or Four Royal Sons, or families.

EXECUTIVE. The function of the Head of State is similar to that of a Constitutional Monarchy as in Britain – rules but does not govern. The Head of State acts on the advice of the Prime Minister and the Cabinet of eight and, with the Prime Minister and members of the Cabinet constitute the Executive Council.

All legislation passed by the Legislative Assembly must be assented to by the Head of State who must act on the advice of the Executive Council. The Head of State has power to grant pardons and reprieves, or may suspend or commute any sentence by any court, tribunal or authority. He can use this power only with the approval of Cabinet.

The Head of State appoints as the Prime Minister the member who, in his opinion, enjoys the confidence and support of the majority of the members of the Legislative Assembly. This is determined by a secret ballot of members following a general election.

The Prime Minister selects his own cabinet, which is considered to be the executive government and, traditionally is regarded as secure in office for each three-year term. Although it has not yet been tested, it is considered that, if the Prime Minister or a cabinet measure fails to gain approval in the Legislative Assembly (even on fiscal bills) this does not signal the collapse of a government.

Council of Deputies. The Constitution provides for a Council of Deputies, which virtually holds the powers of a deputy head of state. The thinking behind it is that one of the four tama aiga would be Head of State, while the other three would be on the Council. In recent times only Tupua Tamasese Lealofi IV has been on the council and respective governments have given no indication on when the other two positions provided for will be filled.

A member of the council cannot be a member of the Legislative Assembly, and its function is to act in place of the Head of State if a vacancy exists in that office, or the holder is overseas or incapacitated. The council also performs useful ceremonial functions for the government.

For a short period in 1978 neither Malietoa nor Tupua Tamasese was in Samoa, and the functions of Head of State were conducted by the Chief Justice.

Legislature. The "fono", or Legislative Assembly, is composed of 47 members, including a Speaker elected by the members. Of these, 45 members are elected by matai suffrage. There are about 10,000 people on the Matai Roll. The other two members are elected by universal suffrage from an individual voters' roll of 1600 people. Entry on to that roll is complex, and, usually, only naturalised Samoans qualify. If a person becomes a matai he cannot stay on that roll, and must go on to the traditional roll.

Elections are held every three years, the last being in February 1979.

The proceedings are broadcast by the Samoan Broadcasting Service in Samoan on one channel, and English on another.

The "Maota Fono" or Parliament Buildings, a modern building, of unusual design opened in June, 1972, is at historic Mulinu'u, a piece of land that juts out from Apia.

DIPLOMATIC. Western Samoa maintains a High Commission office in Wellington, New Zealand, and a Consul-General in Auckland, New Zealand. The office of the permanent Western Samoan representative to the United Nations in New York is also the country's Ambassador to the United States, and High Commissioner to Canada.

Western Samoa has diplomatic relations with Great Britain, France, the Federal Republic of Germany, Yugoslavia, the Soviet Union, China, Israel, Egypt, India, Thailand, North and South Korea, Japan, the Philippines, Indonesia, Australia and Chile.

As a member of the South Pacific Forum it enjoys close links with its fellow Pacific states.

New Zealand and Australia both maintain High Commissions in Apia while China maintains an

Embassy. There are also honorary representatives of the United States, France, the Federal Republic of Germany, South Korea and Nauru. The United Nations Development Programme (UNDP) also has an office in Apia, responsible for programme activities in Samoa, Tokelau, Niue and the Cook Islands.

Local government. On the island of Savai'i there are representatives of the Prime Minister's and other departments, a police station, court house, hospital, school, etc.

Administrative districts, based mainly on geographical regions, were established at the end of 1956, and are used in the operation of Government services such as health, education, police, agriculture, etc.

However, the Samoans have mainly kept local government in its traditional form based on the matai system, and the meeting together of these family heads in the village fono.

In 1977, the pulenu'u system was reorganised to improve government technical help to villages.

Public Service. There are more than 4,000 permanent and temporary officers in the Public Service, with a Public Service Commission responsible for appointments and transfers.

Volunteers. There are about 115 US Peace corps volunteers in Samoa, about 40 members of NZ Volunteer Service Abroad, and 10 members of the Japanese Overseas Volunteer corps. Most volunteers fill secondary teaching posts.

Courts. There are four types of Court: Magistrate's Court, Supreme Court, Appeal Court and Lands and Titles Court.

The Magistrate's Court is presided over by the senior magistrate, who is a qualified lawyer; or by the two Senior Samoan Judges/Fa'amasino Fesoasoani; or by the five other Samoan magistrates.

The Senior Magistrate/Fa'amasino Fesoasoani sit alone on the bench; the other Samoan magistrates sit in pairs.

The three grades of cases that they can hear are as follows: the magistrate can hear any criminal case involving imprisonment up to three years or any case involving a fine only. The two Senior Samoan Judges/F.F., can hear cases involving imprisonment for one year (although they cannot imprison anyone for more than 6 months). The other Samoan magistrates hear cases where imprisonment is not involved and can impose lesser fines.

Appeals from the Magistrate's Court go to the Supreme Court.

The Constitution provides for a Chief Justice of the Supreme Court and any other Judges as become necessary.

Provision is also made for a Judicial Service Commission consisting of the Chief Justice as President, the Attorney-General (or, if he is unable to act, the Chairman of the Public Service Commission); and some other person nominated by the Minister of Justice.

A Court of Appeal of Western Samoa was also set up after independence (appeals previously going to the Supreme Court of NZ). It must consist of three judges, who can be the Chief Justice or Judges of the Supreme Court; any other active or retired British judge; or a person possessing the qualifications required for appointment as a Judge of the Western Samoa Supreme Court.

English is the official language of the court but both Samoan and English are used. Interpreters have to be fluent in both languages.

Court procedure in the Supreme Court is that followed in most British courts; Samoan custom is taken into consideration in certain cases.

The only other legally constituted judicial body in the State, is the Land and Titles Court which has jurisdiction in respect of disputes over Samoan land and succession to Samoan titles. The Chief Justice presides over this court or he can appoint a Deputy President from either the Puisne Judge or the two senior Samoan magistrates to act in his place.

The State is, in general, orderly by Western standards and major crimes are rare – the principal offences brought before the courts are petty theft, assault, disorderly conduct, trespass, "home brewing" and traffic violations.

Police. Most crime is confined to Apia and its environs. There are three police outposts on Upolu and three on Savai'i and they have little to do because the matai system keeps its own order.

The Department of Police and Prisons, headed by a Commissioner, with a Police Force of about 200, maintains law and order.

Liquor laws. The sale of liquor in clubs and hotels is prohibited on Sundays. Hotel guests, however, are allowed drinks on a room service basis. In recent years there has been a considerable relaxation in Samoa's liquor laws, and liquor is now freely available. Only the government may import liquor.

DEFENCE. The Treaty of Friendship signed by Western Samoa and New Zealand in August 1962 symbolises a high degree of co-operation and association. In particular, New Zealand has agreed to "consider sympathetically requests from the Government of Western Samoa for technical, administrative and other assistance," and, on request, to act as the agent of Western Samoa in its dealings with other countries and international agencies.

As a Third World state Samoa is not aligned to any of the existing defence pacts in the region. Samoa does not maintain any military force, and security of nationhood is based on the universal and uncontested right of sovereignty, and the notable lack of any perceived threat.

In civil emergencies, such as search and rescue, previous experience has shown that Samoa can call on the assistance of regional powers such as Australia and New Zealand, and even the United States.

The port of Apia has been host to military vessels of many nations on the basis of "goodwill visits", and not as part of military exercises. Military aircraft from any nation are usually granted diplomatic clearance to use Faleolo Airport if necessary.

EDUCATION. Education is the responsibility of the government through the Department of Education, but several missions also operate schools and, though they are not grant-aided, the mission schools work in close co-operation with the government schools.

The education system is in three divisions as far as the schools are concerned, primary, intermediate and secondary. All are based on the New Zealand system.

Primary schools take children from the primer classes to Standard IV, from the ages of 5½-7 to 12 on the average. Instruction is in Samoan, but there is a strong programme of English to prepare children for the Intermediate stage.

In the Intermediate schools the instruction is in English with the vernacular taught as a leading subject to preserve the importance and value of the native tongue. Children attend these schools for two or three years, i.e. from 12 or 13 to 14 or 15.

The Secondary school is entered at 15 and a pupil may then continue to 19 or 20, though there is selection at the end of the second and fourth year for continued attendance at school in accordance with ability.

In 1977 there were 28,644 pupils at government primary schools, and 4,738 at mission schools. At government intermediate schools there were 6,639 students, and at mission intermediate schools 1,259. Government secondary schools in 1977 had 5,215 pupils and mission secondary schools, 3,872.

A total of 231 pupils attended various vocational courses, including teachers training college.

USP School of Agriculture. In 1975 the former Alafua Agricultural College became the Samoa campus of the University of the South Pacific, specialising in agriculture and offering a degree course in agriculture. The college aims to produce well-trained field officers and to undertake agricultural research and economic planning appropriate to the region.

LABOUR. With changing emphasis in Samoa from village agriculture to migration to Apia and overseas, the demand for employment has increased. Unemployment has become a factor in Apia. The government has attempted to overcome the problem by making farming a more profitable activity for villagers, and by providing increasing employment opportunities.

The 1976 census revealed an economically-active population of 38,249 people. Of these people 23,373 were engaged in agriculture, forestry and fishing. Numbers in other sectors were manufacturing, 712, electricity and water, 468, construction 1,813, transport 2,058 and financing, insurance and real estate 322. There were 4,492 government employees, excluding casuals.

Wages. There is a surplus of labour in the unskilled and semi-skilled fields. Wages are low, and the minimum adult basic wage by law is 10 sene per hour. The average wage is around $1,600 a year.

Overseas work. Until the recent reduction in the number of migrants permitted to enter New Zealand, many semi-skilled Samoans went there. They felt that there were better opportunities for advancement and education. However, the trend has changed and there is more movement to American Samoa, Hawaii and California.

Social Security. The National Provident Fund was introduced in 1973 as a source of social benefit to workers. The funds involved are also lent out to finance development projects. Constributions to the Fund come from employers who pay out about 10 per cent on top of their wages and salaries bill. Part of this contribution can be recouped from employees earning over a minimum rate. The sums paid are placed at the credit of each individual as the basis of lump sum payments and pensions payable on his reaching retirement age.

In 1977, an Accident Compensation Bill was introduced to the Fono. This provides for payment on a "no fault" basis for all people injured in motor and industrial accidents in Samoa. It also provides for payments to dependants where death occurs.

The legislation calls for establishment of an Accident Compensation Board designed to calculate a system of payments, and to promote safety in industry and on the roads. The scheme will be financed by a 1 per cent payroll tax on employers and an extra 5 sene added to the price of each gallon of petrol.

HEALTH. The Department of Health is under the control of the Minister of Health. He receives advice from the Director of Health who is the technical head of the department. The country has 14 health districts in which a District Medical Officer is responsible for all health activities in his district. The DMO is assisted by one or two district nurses who are working closely with women's committees. The district hospital or rural health centres are administered by the DMOs.

The Apia National Hospital (298 beds) is the main hospital of the country with a specialists' centre and teaching facilities for the Apia Nursing School. This hospital was being reconstructed in 1977. There are also 10 district hospitals on Upolu with a total of more than 200 beds; the six hospitals on Savai'i have 172 beds.

The Dental Division of the Health Department has a dental clinic in the National Hospital grounds and two dental stations are attached to rural hospitals.

Diseases. The main cause of death in 1976 was from influenza and other respiratory diseases. Diarrhoea was also significant. There were 616 deaths in 1976. Venereal disease has increased and in 1978 there were 237 cases of gonorrhoea reported.

THE LAND. Western Samoa has a land area of

2,934 sq. km. The two main islands are the most highly populated Upolu (1,100 sq. km) and Savai'i (1,820 sq. km).

The island of Upolu extends about 72 km from east to west and up to 24 km from north to south. Savai'i is also about 72 km across but is 35 km wide.

The islands have numerous volcanic peaks, the highest being Mt. Mata'aga of 1,850 m on Savai'i, and Mt. Fito of 1,100 m on Upolu.

Savai'i has a central core of volcanic peaks surrounded by a ring of lava-based plateaux, then lower hills and coastal plains. Upolu has a chain of volcanic peaks running from one end of the island to the other, with hills and coastal plains on either side.

Climate. The south and south-east windward areas receive from 5,000 to 7,000 mm of rain annually. On the leeward side, the islands receive from 2,500 to 3,000 mm of rain. There is however a marked dry season, from May to August. The average rainfall for Apia is 3,000 mm a year.

The islands' volcanic origins have produced a terrain with abundant streams and waterfalls. At sea, the coral reef is broken in many places, thus exposing the lagoon.

Flora. The rain forests produce dense growth with Barringtonia and other tall trees as well as luxuriant ferns and vines. The volvanic soil is rich and fertile.

Land reclamation. About 15 hectares of land was reclaimed in the central waterfront area of Apia, for recreational use, when over 600,000 cubic metres of material was dredged out of the harbour in a project to ensure adequate depth for ships.

Land tenure. All land in Western Samoa since the end of 1961 is legally:

(a) Customary land, held from the State in accordance with Samoan custom – i.e., land traditionally vested in matai (chiefs) who hold the land in trust for their aiga (family group). Customary land can be leased but not purchased. The Lands and Titles Court settles land disputes arising mainly out of badly defined boundaries and from conflicting claims of individual matai.

(b) Freehold land (meaning alienated land) which is held from the State of Western Samoa in fee simple; and (c) Government land which is free from customary title and from any estate in fee simple.

In earlier times, the Berlin Act of 1889 provided for a commission to settle all alien land titles, with instructions that there should be disallowed all claims to land based upon "the consideration of a sale of firearms or munitions of war, or upon the consideration of intoxicating liquors" – a shrewd hint of the origin of some of the claims put forward. This was the first attempt to examine and record in a central registry the European lands in Samoa, and the decisions then made are still the root of the titles to such land.

The intervening years saw some modifications to the registration system under German and New Zealand administration.

There were no changes in land tenure after Independence except that land formerly called Crown Land, and vested in Queen Elizabeth, became vested in the Sovereign State of Western Samoa.

By 1970, Samoan land was divided as follows: Customary land (almost 80 per cent), Government land (just over 10 per cent), Western Samoa Trust Estates Corporation and freehold land (held by persons of European status and by missions) both about 4 per cent each.

Trust Estates Corporation. After World War I, New Zealand Trust Estates took over former German plantations and worked them. In all these, total land involved amounted to about 36,800 ha. All but 12,800 ha of this was subsequently passed back to the Crown.

In 1957 the New Zealand Government passed over to the Samoan people all the land and assets of reparation estates. They then became known as Western Samoa Trust Estates Corporation. The corporation is run by a board of directors.

PRIMARY PRODUCTION. Western Samoa is dependent largely on three agricultural crops – coconuts, cocoa and bananas – for exports and for its internal needs. In order to diversify output, the country is developing other produce such as macadamia nuts, annatto (dye), timber and cattle. In December 1977, the Asian Development Bank approved a $3 million loan to finance a WSTEC development project, including an agricultural research station and general upgrading of copra, cocoa and meat production.

Copra. A major element of recent development plans has been the upgrading of old coconut plantations. In 1970, about 22,000 ha of coconuts were in full bearing but the majority of these trees were 60 years old or more and had a low or declining yield. By 1975, the replanting programme was left only 2,800 ha short of the planned target of 35,120 ha. In 1976, 259,300 seedlings were planted in 2,097 ha. Results of the replanting will not be felt until the 1980s.

Production of copra rises and falls according to prevailing price. When the price is high more people are encouraged to cut it; when it is low they don't bother.

Prices were at record high levels over the 1977-8 period, but with a small drop in prices in 1979, production fell slightly.

Recent copra production figures have been as follows:

Copra	**1976**	**1977**	**1978**	**1979**
('000 tons)	13.69	16.93	13.29	19.4
Value ($'000)	1,313	2,793	2,232	6,203

According to estimates published in January, 1980, Western Samoa had an excellent year for copra in 1979, exporting 18,500 tonnes worth more than $8 million. The estimates in any year do not tell the full story as a large proportion of the crop is consumed locally. The export pattern may change, however, as Western Samoa moves away from the export of unprocessed copra to that of coconut oil.

The WSTEC Mulifanua coconut plantation, claimed to be the largest copra plantation in the Southern Hemisphere, is 40 km west of Apia. It is the base for a joint WESTEC and Department of Agriculture "cattle under coconuts" project designed to make more intensive use of plantation lands.

Cocoa. Although cocoa was originally grown on the big private plantations, Samoan small-holders now grow a large proportion of it.

Total area planted with cocoa is about 5,000 ha. Samoan cocoa is much in demand as a high-grade product: it is used particularly for blending. The locally-developed hybrid "Lafi-7" was first grown at the Central Group Cocoa Plantation of the WSTEC, which may be seen 5 km inland from Apia.

Marketing of the beans is handled by the Cocoa Board which is endeavouring to establish new sales outlets through membership of the International Cocoa Organisation. A record 5,363 tonnes were exported in 1962, but since then export figures have gradually declined.

A new cocoa development project estimated to increase production to 8,000 tonnes a year by 1990 was opened at Nuu in December, 1979. Australia financed the buildings, vehicles and equipment.

	1976	1977	1978	1979
Cocoa (tonnes)	1,416	1,565	1,082	2,000

An estimate published in January, 1980, showed that 1,400 tonnes of cocoa worth $3,500,000 had been exported in 1979 and the crop forecast for 1980 was for 2,200 tonnes worth $5 million.

Bananas. Once the country's main export, bananas are no longer of major significance in the country's export industry. Disease, hurricane damage, intense competition from South America and poor shipping have virtually killed the banana export market. A growing population and the popularity of bananas as a staple food mean that growers can obtain satisfactory prices at local markets without the fuss of exporting them, but some shipments are made to American Samoa. New Zealand was the biggest market for Samoan bananas but the market has been taken over by Ecuador.

However, banana exports for 1979 (provisional) of 34,343 cases worth $266,000 were nearly treble the 1978 total – 12,903 cases worth $108,000. In 1958, Western Samoa exported 884,000 cases.

Livestock. Efforts are being made to build up the existing cattle industry with aid received from such bodies as the Asian Development Bank. The country is estimated to have about 20,000 head of cattle, about half of which are kept by the Trust Estates. The WSTEC actually supplies most of the cattle killed locally for meat. Besides their beef value, the cattle keep down grass that grows on plantations.

Other livestock in the country are estimated to include 40,000 pigs and 500,000 fowls. Horses are used as pack animals for transporting produce. In 1978, 3,688 cattle were slaughtered and in 1979, 3,748.

Fishing. With Japanese assistance, commercial fishing has undergone considerable development in Samoa. A fisheries training centre has been built in Apia, and a fisheries training boat provides training in long line techniques.

A Food and Agriculture Organisation boat building project has provided almost 400 twin hulled fishing boats to villages around the country. Refrigeration and regular collection has meant that any surplus fish in the villages can be sold in Apia. A bait breeding project was also launched in 1978.

The United States agreed in September, 1979, to fund a fisheries project for Upolu as part of a small self-help programme which will also include the training of students in agricultural produce marketing. Fresh fish caught in 1977 under the village fisheries programme amount to about 1,700 tonnes compared with 1,400 tonnes in 1976.

Timber. There are very valuable stands of timber in Western Samoa, particularly on Savai'i. Timber has assumed greater importance in the Samoan economy since a timber industry began on Savai'i when the United States company, Potlatch Forests Inc., obtained extensive timber leases in 1968. The company has now pulled out and the government and Standard Sawmilling of Australia are partners in the operation, with the government holding 80 per cent of the shares.

Exports of tropical hardboard and other timber earned more than $403,000 in 1974 but the value of shipments declined steadily and is only now recovering. Timber exports for 1977 were worth $185,000; for 1978, $142,900; for 1979, $291,000.

MANUFACTURING. Most light industries established are concerned with supplying the local market and thus contribute to import substitution. Local plants produce concrete products, industrial and household gases, paints, and sundry building materials. Good manufactured for export include clothing, canned fruit, processed food and handicrafts marketed by the Western Samoa Handicrafts Corporation.

Western Samoa Breweries Ltd, a new company owned by the Government of Western Samoa, the DEG (German Development Corporation), Brauhausse (the brewers) and Breckwoldt (a trading company) was registered in Apia in 1976. Tariff protection has been given to the new company together with a five-year tax holiday and maximum import tax concessions of $7.4 million.

The brewery has become the country's biggest industry producing more than 30,000 hectolitres of beer a year under the "Vailima" label. Other major developments undertaken by WESTEC include a stockfeed mill financed under the NZ Bilateral Aid Programme and opened in February, 1979, and a soap factory at Vaitele. Both will sell locally and, if possible, export.

Under the New Zealand Pacific Islands Industrial Development Scheme, a leather-goods factory and a tobacco factory have been opened. The former, which is operated by J. Wiseman South Pacific Ltd and makes women's handbags and other leather goods, made its first shipment to New Zealand in December, 1977. The tobacco factory, belonging to Rothmans Industries NZ, employs a workforce of 40.

Another newcomer to the industrial scene is the Western Samoa Match Co., which has a factory at Vaitele and plans to produce 25 million boxes of matches a year.

TOURISM. Enthusiasm to encourage tourism was only aroused about 1965 and then with emphasis placed on preserving Samoan traditions.

New hotels have been built since the late 1960s under the first Five-Year Development Plan. This has resulted in a slow increase of visitors. From 1969, when there were 14,584, the number has risen to 33,776 in 1976.

WESTERN SAMOA — TOURISTS

1976	1977	1978	1979
33,776	21,792	37,814	49,866

In 1975 and 1976, the largest number of tourists came from American Samoa (23 per cent) followed by the U.S.A. (20 per cent) and New Zealand (16 per cent).

Fourteen cruise ships brought 10,972 passengers to Apia in 1977 and another 11,400 arrived by air in the nine months of 1977 to September 30. No further figures were available. Tourist development and publicity is supervised by the Department of Economic Development. Western Samoa's tourist industry representative in Australia is Pacific Area Promotions of 95/99 York Street, Sydney (telephone 2902844; telex AA27585).

LOCAL COMMERCE. Island produce is sold in the local markets. Handcrafted goods are handled by curio stores, Apia Agencies and Burns Philp, as well as the Western Samoa Handicrafts Corporation, which is government-sponsored.

OVERSEAS TRADE. Western Samoa has faced significant trade deficits over recent years, only compensated by aid from such sources as New Zealand and the remittances to Samoan families from workers in New Zealand.

WESTERN SAMOA — EXPORTS AND IMPORTS (in $ million)

	1975	1976	1977	1978	1979
Imports	23.1	23.6	28.0	40.5	60.9
Exports	4.5	5.4	10.8	8.4	15.3

Copra and cocoa were responsible for the big drop in exports in 1978 but the first nine months of 1979 showed a recovery with total exports increasing by 68 per cent over the 1978 total. Imports also increased over the same period at an annual rate of 24 per cent to a total of $36 million for the nine months. The resulting trade deficits, according to Finance Minister Vaovasamanaia Filipo in his budget speech for 1980, were large offset by receipts from tourism and other services accounts together with private and official transfers which included grants and soft term loans. The value of major exports in recent years is detailed in the following table:

Customers. Western Samoa's major trading partner is New Zealand which, in 1978 took goods worth $2.8 million, followed by West Germany ($1.7 m), Netherlands ($0.75 m), American Samoa ($0.53 m), Japan ($0.5 m), U.K. ($0.38 m), India ($0.34 m), U.S.A. ($0.30 m), Belgium ($0.22 m) and Australia ($0.21 m).

WESTERN SAMOA — MAJOR EXPORTS (in $'000)

	1976	1977	1978	1979*
Copra	1,873.8	4,607.9	3,535.9	8,018.4
Cocoa	2,220.6	5,875.1	2,637.8	3,468.4
Bananas	144.3	61.3	108.0	266.1
Taro, ta'amu	363.5	336.5	993.7	1,512.2
Timber	64.6	185.4	142.9	291.0
Coconut cream	204.4	187.2	251.1	427.2
Soft drinks	4.2	3.0	n.a.	2.4
Annatto seeds	32.2	18.2	20.9	7.8
Handicrafts	31.0	15.7	35.0	48.6
Hardboard	—	n.a.	2.6	0.2
Textiles (piece goods)	26.2	9.0	23.8	20.8
Apparel	195.6	2.3	6.9	n.a.

* Provisional

Imports. Imports have been expanding at about 20 per cent annually, despite relatively high average import duties, the introduction of selected controls and only nominal growth in national income.

Imports spiralled in 1978, however, expanding by more than 40 per cent over the 1977 figure.

Of total imports, 80 per cent are for commercial channels, with this share remaining relatively constant during the last four to five years. Basic food commodities represent one quarter of commercial imports. Another quarter is liquor, tobacco, clothing, vehicles and petrol. Efforts are being made to limit the annual growth of imports to 15 per cent.

Suppliers. Imports in 1978 came mainly from New Zealand ($12.8 m), Japan ($7.4 m), Australia ($5.9 m), U.S.A. ($3.6 m), Singapore ($2.1 m) and Fiji ($1.7 m).

Customs tariff. Western Samoa has been struggling over the past decade to reduce its trade deficit, one method being the raising of customs duties. There was a big rise in 1975 and for the 1980 budget increases of up to 100 per cent were imposed on alcoholic liquor and tobacco, but these rises were also seen as a protective tariff as the country is now making its own beer and cigarettes. Heavier taxes were also imposed in 1980 on electricity-powered stoves and turbines and the duty on airconditioners was increased by 18 per cent to 60 per cent. High-powered motor cycles also attracted a heavier duty but, in an attempt to conserve fuel, the duty on bicycles was cut from 48 per cent to 10 per cent.

FINANCE. Import and export duties remain the chief source of the country's income and in 1978 it was estimated that nearly 50 per cent of revenue ($10.92 m) would come from customs duty and inland revenue would provide 14.6 per cent ($3.25 m).

The 1980 budget, presented by Finance Minister Vaovasamanaia Filipo in November, 1979, provided for total expenditure of $60.2 million. The main items in the budget were: Local current revenue $31.4 million; current expenditure $22.7 million; statutory expenditure $3.1 million; estimated operating surplus $5.6 million; development expenditure $34.4 million.

Of the development expenditure, $7.7 million would be provided locally from the operating budget surplus ($5.6 million), a locally-raised loan ($2 million) and $210,000 from grants. Other contributions would come from foreign capital project assistance of $15.1 million and from soft term loans of $11.6 million. Total planned expenditure in 1979 was $49.2 million.

The government legislated in late 1979 for a loan of $7 million to come from various sources including $105,000 from the Bank of Western Samoa, $880,000 from borrowings from local or overseas sources up to December, 1979, $US100,000 from OPEC Special Fund, 591,000 German marks from Western Germany (repayment over 15 years at 8.5 per cent interest), $2 million loan on the security of public revenues (repayment over 20 years) and $US2 million from any source on terms which the minister could arrange. A state lottery with a first prize of $10,000 was launched in 1978.

External aid. Western Samoa receives a comparatively large amount in aid from developing countries and, recently, West Germany has displayed great interest in aiding the Samoans, one example being "Forum Samoa", a cargo ship which was launched in Hamburg late in 1979 as part of a German aid programme for Western Samoa. New Zealand bilateral aid to the Samoans in the last few years has amounted to $3.543 million in 1977-78 and $3.3 million in 1978-79. Australian aid includes $30,000 in 1978-79 for a vehicular ferry and recent American aid has totalled more than $400,000.

A second important area of funds from abroad is the high volume of transfers, a large part of which is accounted for by remittances from Samoans working in New Zealand and the U.S.A. During the five years of the plan, these transfers are expected to grow from $6.8 to $11.9 million per annum by 1979.

Currency. Western Samoa uses the tala (dollar) divided into 100 sene (cents). A new set of coins was introduced in 1975, depicting the country's agricultural projects. These are for 1, 5, 10, 20 and 50 sene and one tala. Bank notes are in denominations of 1, 2 and 10 tala. Western Samoa issued its own coinage for the first time when the changeover was made to decimal currency in July 1967; there was also a new bank note issue for the occasion.

The Western Samoa tala (dollar) was devalued by 15 per cent on June 20, 1979, and tariff rates on 11 basic food items were reduced, in some cases by 33.3 per cent. Trading banks increased deposit and lending rates of interest.

Western Samoa's gross international reserves amounted to $4.3 million at October 31, 1979, and were expected to increase to $5 million by the beginning of 1980.

The rate of inflation dropped from 9 per cent in 1977 to about 3 per cent in 1978 but rose to about 16 per cent in 1979 due to big increases in the price of oil and imported food.

Banks. The Bank of Western Samoa was established on April 1, 1959 with 55 per cent of capital provided by the Bank of New Zealand which conducted former operations, and 45 per cent from the Government of Western Samoa. The bank has a board of four directors appointed by the Bank of NZ and the Samoan Government. The Joint Management Committee operating the bank also has Samoan and New Zealand members.

In a joint operation between the Bank of New South Wales and the Bank of Hawaii a new commercial bank, the Pacific Commercial, has been established in Apia. It offers similar services to those currently available from the Bank of Western Samoa.

The Development Bank of Western Samoa became independent in October 1974, evolving out of what was until then the Development Department of the former bank.

The Bank of Western Samoa made an after-tax profit in 1977 of $170,309. In 1979, the European Economic Community made a loan of $980,000 to the bank for lending to small and medium-sized enterprises.

Investment incentives. Extensive provisions have been made to encourage foreign investment that will develop the West Samoan economy. Regulations are contained in the Enterprise Incentives Act, 1965, with amendments. Further facilities are provided under the Industrial Free Zone Act, passed in December 1974. Investors who wish to establish an industry in Western Samoa under benefit of the Incentives Act must submit their applications to the Department of Economic Development, with final decisions being made by Cabinet.

Detailed information on this subject is available in a useful document the "Summary of Industrial Investment Incentives in Selected Pacific Islands" by I. J. Fairbairn, South Pacific Commission, Noumea, New Caledonia, 1975, and also from the Department of Economic Development, Apia.

Development plan. The country's Fourth Five-Year Development Plan for 1980-84 is the most ambitious yet. The 1975-79 plan was committed to spending $44.4 million, most of it raised overseas, but the current plan is expected to cost much more. The 1980 budget planned to spend $34.4 million on the plan. Major emphasis has been given in the plan to those projects capable of enhancing the productive base of the economy, strengthening exports, promoting import replacement activities, creating employment and greater economic diversification. With these aims in view, high priority has been given to projects in agriculture, fisheries, forestry, industry, electric power generation and related infrastructure items.

Stamps and coins. The sale of postage stamps is also considered a valuable source of revenue for the country, together with the sale of coins, such as a new set issued in 1975.

TRANSPORT. There are more than 1,800 km of roads on the two large Samoan islands of which just over 100 km are sealed. To enable more areas of Samoa to be cultivated, large-scale road-building projects have been initiated under the Rural Development Programme.

In Apia, rental cars and taxis are available as well as public buses. There is a timetable for buses serving the villages and districts but visitors are advised to consult the traffic policeman on duty at the old market bus stand for full particulars.

Vehicles. There were 3,613 motor vehicles registered in 1976 including: private cars, 951; pick-ups, 1,574; taxis, 428; trucks, 338; buses, 152; motor cycles, 120. New registrations in that year were 374.

Overseas airlines. Western Samoa's own Polynesian Airlines flies two return flights a week between Western Samoa and New Zealand, with stop-overs at Tonga. A chartered 108 seat Boeing 737 is used. Polynesian also uses its two Hawker Sidley 748 prop-jets on a weekly return service from Western Samoa to Rarotonga via Niue. Services also include weekly flights to Tonga, and three return flights a week to Fiji.

The HS 748 and the airline's 14 seater Nomad fly a number of daily flights between Western and American Samoa, linking with Air New Zealand, Pan American and UTA.

Air New Zealand calls twice a week at Western Samoa on flights from Auckland, via Suva using a Boeing 737.

Air Pacific has two flights a week between Suva and Western Samoa using a BAC 1-11. There is also a same-day Faleolo-Auckland service via Fiji operated by Air Pacific.

Air Nauru, using a Boeing 737, operates a weekly Nauru-Western Samoa service.

The Pago Pago-based South Pacific Island Airways flies between the two Samoas every two hours using a Twin-Otter.

Major changes to the airline scene came with the arrival in the second half of 1979 of Continental Airlines, which operates low-budget fares on flights from Los Angeles to Sydney and Auckland through Honolulu and Pago Pago. There are twice-weekly flights, from Los Angeles via Honolulu and Pago Pago to Sydney, and via Honolulu, Pago Pago and Nadi to Sydney, and thrice-weekly via Pago Pago to Auckland.

Polynesian Airlines has obtained rights to fly to Tahiti for 12 months beginning on March 1, 1980. Under the deal, the French carrier UTA charters PAL aircraft for the service between Rarotonga and Papeete on Saturdays.

Domestic air services. These are operated by Polynesian Airlines using a Nomad, two nine-seater Britten-Norman Islanders and a four-seat Cessna. There are a number of flights daily between Upolu and Savai'i.

Airports. The country's international airport is at Faleolo, about 40 km from Apia. The new runway and terminal opened in mid-1972, plus reconstruction of the road to the capital, were financed largely by a loan from the Asian Development Bank.

There is also a 623 m strip for light planes at Fagali'i, about 4 km east of Apia wharf. The airstrips on the island of Savai'i are located at Asau on the north coast and near Salelologa in the southeast. The Savai'i airstrips take planes of the Britten-Norman Islander class.

Port facilities. Ports in Western Samoa are administered by the Marine Department. At Apia there is a deep-water wharf, 198 m in length, with a low water depth of 12 m alongside. Facilities include large goods sheds, a mobile crane, forklifts and other modern cargo-handling equipment. The

Vacuum Oil Co. Pty Ltd has a bulk oil terminal at Sogi, near Apia.

At Asau, on the north coast of Savai'i, a deepwater wharf was completed in late 1966. However it was not until five years later that the necessary access channel had been blasted through the coral reef to allow shipment of timber exports.

Outport harbour facilities are usually jetties adjacent to convenient reef passages. Ferry terminals at Mulifanua and Salelologa link Savai'i and Upolu.

Shipping services. The Pacific Forum Line is headquartered in Apia, and the line has regular fortnightly services between Samoa, other Pacific islands and Australia and New Zealand.

Samoa Shipping Services owns a large modern containership which is operated by PFL.

China Navigation Co. vessels operate a regular cargo service from Hong Kong via Pacific ports.

The Daiwa Line runs a monthly cargo service from Japan via Pacific ports.

Pacific Navigation Co. Ltd operates a monthly cargo service between Tonga, Apia and Sydney.

Union Steamship Co. of New Zealand operates a fully-containerised service from Auckland through Apia every 14 days.

Pacific Islands Transport operates a five-six weekly cargo service from North American west coast ports.

Kyowa Line runs a monthly service from Asian ports to those in the Pacific including Apia.

Karlander operates monthly from Australia, to Tonga, Apia and the US West Coast.

Warner Pacific Line operates from Onehunga and Timaru every 21 days. Nauru Pacific Line runs a five times a year charter service between Apia and Tokelau.

The Western Samoa Shipping Corporation operates weekly services using the vehicular ferry Queen Salamasinia between both American and Western Samoa, as well as between Savai'i and Upolu.

Inter-Island Shipping Company runs similar motor launch services.

COMMUNICATIONS. The Postal and Radio Department looks after all internal and external communications, maintaining 21 sub-post offices under the control of the Director of Post Office and Radio at Apia. Eight radio out-stations staffed by trained Samoan operators serve Upolu and Savai'i.

In the last three years Western Samoa has seen considerable improvements to internal and international communications.

Apia is now served by an automatic telephone exchange, while the telephone services operated by a manual exchange are being extended to villages in Savai'i and Upolu. In 1977, there were 3,685 telephone connections.

Internationally, the number of telephone channels between New Zealand and Samoa, using a radio link, have been increased and the Post Office operates an on-demand no-delay international telephone service. The quality of the reception has been improved by new transmitters and receivers.

Under the Lome Convention, the EEC in 1979 granted a loan of $WS2.5 million to Western Samoa for the supply and installation of an Intelstat standard B earth station plus a spur system from the satellite earth station to the Samoan central telephone exchange as well as gateway telephone exchange facilities. Interest on the loan is 1 per cent over 40 years with 10 years grace.

The installation will allow direct dialling from Western Samoa to Australia, New Zealand and many other countries via a satellite over the Pacific without the use of an operator. The station will be operating from the end of 1980. The telex system will also reach international standards.

A telex service is also being considerably upgraded, and there are about 30 telex subscribers in Western Samoa.

Marine Radio services have been upgraded.

All services are operated 24 hours.

Apia Radio is the main connecting link for overseas communications. The out-stations communicate with Apia Radio by radio-telephone and telegraph in daily schedules. There is overseas radio-telephone to most overseas countries. Most local ships are now fitted with radio.

A continuous watch is kept on the international distress frequencies for ships at sea. A continuous radio link is also maintained with Faleolo airport.

Western Samoa updated ship-to-shore radio communications in 1979. Apia Radio's coast station 5WA was completely re-equipped, new HF and VHF transmitting and receiving stations being built with remote control exercised from the communications centre in Apia.

Ship-to-shore telegrams are accepted from any vessel at 16c a word, the minimum charge being $1 for seven words. For radio telegraphy, Apia Radio keeps a 24-hour watch on 500 KHz. The working frequency is 483 KHz and 512 KHz is also available. For HF radio telephony, Apia Radio maintains a 24-hour watch on 2182 KHz and 621 KHz. Vessels calling on these frequencies are replied to on the same frequency as that on which they call. These frequencies are for distress and calling purposes only and may not be used for passing traffic or radio-telephone calls. Apia Radio is equipped to connect radio telephone calls into the local telephone network. Charges are $1 a minute (minimum three minutes). A new station for VHF radio-telephone has been built on Mount Fiamoe in the centre of Upolu Island at about 914 m from which height the estimated range is about 129 km.

For navigation, the new HF transmitting station is at 13° 40′55″ S and 171° 49′46″ W. The Fiamoe VHF station is at 13° 55′S and 171° 47′45″ W. Antennas at both stations are fitted with red aircraft obstruction lights and should be visible for a considerable distance. On leaving port, all ships should call Apia Radio, preferably on Channel 16VHF to advise their T/Rs.

Radio. Known widely throughout the Pacific as 2AP, the Voice of Western Samoa, the local broadcast station began operations in 1948 and is government owned.

Broadcasts are in Samoan and English and consist mainly of entertainment, news, news reviews, farm and rural broadcasts, schools programmes and Legislative Assembly meetings.

The station accepts advertising and also broadcasts telegrams for the Post Office to listeners not served by telephones and in isolated villages where broadcasting is the only source of daily information.

The broadcasting service operates from 6 a.m. to 5 p.m. on one AM channel, and from 5 p.m. to 11 p.m. on two AM channels, one in each language.

The American Samoan station WVUV and the American television station, KVZK-TV are well received in Western Samoa. Radio Australia is the best received of the shortwave stations, with the BBC and Voice of America being clear at certain times. Radio New Zealand is poorly received. Reception of 2AP is fair in neighbouring islands such as Fiji and the Cook Islands.

Newspapers. Western Samoa has several low-budget newspapers, the two main weekly newspapers being "The Samoa Times", which was established in 1967 (as an amalgamation of a long-established weekly "Samoa Bulletin", "Samoana" and a third newspaper) and "The Observer", which was established in 1978. Others include "The Samoa Weekly", "South Seas Star" and "O le Tusitala Samoa".

The Prime Minister's Department produces two editions, one Samoan and one in English, of "Savali", a fortnightly which carries government notices and news, much of it dealing with the progress of government schemes. The Samoan language edition is delivered free to the villages. Churches also publish small newspapers.

WATER AND ELECTRICITY. An area exceeding 50 sq. km around Apia is served by combined hydro-electric and diesel-electric installations.

There are still ample hydro resources to be utilised in Samoa but lack of funds is restricting investigations of future sites.

Rural electrification commenced in 1967 with the construction of a 22,000 volt distribution line from Apia.

A number of small private and village-owned electrical schemes using diesel generators operate, somewhat erratically, in the outlying districts.

Apia has the only rated water supply although about 40 per cent of rural areas have piped supply of water but arrange their own maintenance and finance.

PERSONALITIES AND ORGANISATIONS

Head of State: His Highness Malietoa Tanumafili II

Member of the Council of Deputies: Tupua Tamasese Lealofi IV
Chief Justice: Mr Bryan Nicholson

CABINET MINISTERS

Prime Minister: Tupuola Efi
Finance: Vaovasamanaia Filipo
Economic Development: Letiu Tamatoa
Health: Faumuina Anapapa
Lands and Broadcasting: Autagavaia Tisena
Education: Fuimaono Mimio
Justice: Asi Eikeni
Works: Seuamuli Kurene
Agriculture: Seumanu Aita Ah Wa

MEMBERS OF PARLIAMENT

Speaker: Tu'u'u Faletoese
Deputy Speaker: A'e'au Taulupo'o
Samoan Members
Aana Alofi No. 2: Tupuola Efi
Aana Alofi No. 3: Tuigamala Saofaiga
Aiga-i-le-tai: Mulipola Leva'ula
Alataua-i-Sisifo: Nonumalo Faiga
Aleipata Itupa-i-Lalo: Letiu Tamatoa
Aleipata Itupa-i-Luga: Taua Latu
Anoamaa East: Faamatuainu Tala Mailei
Anoamaa West: Leota Leulua'ialii Ituau Ale
Faasaleleaga No. 2: Asi Eikeni
Faasaleleaga No. 3: Toleafoa Talitimu
Faasaleleaga No. 4: Aiiloilo Sua
Falealupo: A'e'au Taulupo'o
Faleata East: Faumuina Anapapa
Faleata West: Toi Aukuso
Falelatai ma Samatau: Aumua Ioane
Gaga'emauga No. 1: Sala Suivai
Gaga'emauga No. 2: Faasootauloa Semu Pualagi
Gaga'emauga No. 3: Seuamuli Kurene
Gagaifomauga No. 1: Lavea Lio
Gagaifomauga No. 2: Mala'itai Magasiva
Gagaifomauga No. 3: Tauaanae Fatu
Lefaga ma Falease'ela: Mamea Ropati
Lepa: Fatialofa Momo'e
Lotofaga: Laulu Fetauimalemau
Palauli le Falefa: Mapuilesua Pelenato
Palauli West: Vaovasamanaia Filipo
Palauli: Autagavaia Tisena
Safata: Pule Lameko
Sagaga-le-Falefa: Nonumalo Leulumoega Sofara
Sagaga-le-Usoga: Taliaoa Maoama
Salega: Leilua Manuao
Satupa'itea: Asiata Solomona
Siumu: Tu'u'u Faletoese
Vaa-o-Fonoti: Ulualofaiga Talamaivao Niko
Vaimauga East: Fuataga La'ulu
Vaisigano No. 1: Vaai Kolone
Vaisigano No. 2: Lesatele Rapi
(Two members in each of the following)

Aana Alofi No. 1: Leaupepe Pita and Leaupepetele Taoipu
Faasaleleaga No. 1: Seumanu Aita Ah Wa and Tofilau Eti
Falealili: Fuimaono Mimio and Tuatagaloa Fetu
Vaimauga West: Toomalatai Siaki and Tofaeono Tile
Individual Voters: Ronald Berking and George Lober

HEADS OF GOVERNMENT DEPARTMENTS

Agriculture, director: Tauiliili Uili
Attorney-General: Neroni Slade
Broadcasting, director: Jim Moore
Cabinet, secretary: Saena Tupai
Customs, comptroller: Papali'i Alec Stanley
Economic Development, director: Hans Kruse
Education, director: Perefoti Tamati
Financial Secretary: Alister Hutchinson
Fisheries: Alfonso Philips
Government Information: Tanumafono A. Aiavao
Government Statistician: F. E. Betham
Health, acting director: Solia Tapeni
Immigration: Faleafaga Tinoa
Inland Revenue, commissioner: James Marriage
Lands and Titles Court, registrar: Tuiletufuga Enele
Marine, harbourmaster: Capt Robert Mair
Observatory: Chris Hewson
Post Office, director: E. D. Williams
Police, commissioner: Sonny Schuster
Prime Minister's Dept., secretary to government: Vitolio Lui (Acting)
Printing, government printer: Douglas Slade
Public Works, director: Ufi Tone
USP College of Tropical Agriculture, principal: Prof. Felix Wendt

DIPLOMATIC CORPS

New Zealand High Commissioner: Douglas Law
Australia High Commissioner: Allan Deacon
People's Republic of China Ambassador: Chang Chan-wu
United States Consular Agency: V. McKenzie

DIPLOMATIC REPRESENTATIVES OVERSEAS

High Commissioner to New Zealand: Fe'esago S. Fepuleai
Consul-General in Auckland: Vaimasanu'u Niko Apa
Permanent Representative to the United Nations, Ambassador to the United States and High Commissioner to Canada: Maiava Iulai Toma

APIA BUSINESS DIRECTORY

Airlines
Air New Zealand
Air Samoa Ltd
Polynesian Airlines Ltd
Banks
Development Bank of Western Samoa
Bank of Western Samoa
Pacific Commercial Bank
Breweries
Western Samoa Breweries Ltd
Cocoa producers
Western Samoa Trust Estates Corp
Coffee producers
WSTEC
Copra producers
WSTEC
O. F. Nelson & Co Ltd
Customs & Shipping Agents
Peter Meredith & Co Ltd
WSTEC
Food Processors
Samoa Tropical Products Ltd
General Merchants
I. H. Carruthers Ltd
Chan Mow & Co Ltd
E. T. Oldehaver Ltd
A. M. Macdonald Agencies Ltd
Burns Philp (South Sea) Co Ltd
Match Manufacturers
Western Samoa Match Co
Motor repairs
Apia Motors Service Station
Rental Cars
Apia Rentals Ltd
Rentway Rentals Ltd
TV Service
Apia TV and Electronics
Smallgoods Manufacturers
Pacific Meat-packing Co Ltd
Shipping
R. V. Meredith
Pacific Forum Line
Timber & Sawmiller
New Samoa Industry Ltd
Samoa Forest Products
Tours
Samoa Scenic Tours & Charter Services Ltd
Wholesalers
Buyrite Wholesalers Ltd

SCIENTIFIC INSTITUTIONS

The Nelson Memorial Library is located on the Apia waterfront and is under the control of the Education Department. The library was donated by the Nelson family, the late Mr O. F. Nelson who was both an influential merchant and one of the leaders of Samoa in the 1920s and 1930s. Working in conjunction with the library are two bookmobiles which were the Independence gift of the United States. A microfilm reader was presented to the library from the people of Kalmar, Sweden, birthplace of the founder of the Apia business of O. F. Nelson. The Apia Observatory is situated near the extreme end of Mulinu'u Peninsula, on the island of Upolu. It is about 3 km from Apia town centre. The observatory was founded in 1902 by the Society of Natural Sciences of Gottingen (Germany), for the purpose of taking observations simultaneously with those of an Antarctic Expedition. The results were of such value that the observatory was made permanent and its scope was extended to include more detailed observations in magnetism, meteorology, seismology and related subjects.

The observatory carries out research in meteorology, terrestrial magnetism, seismology and oceanography and provides a radio time service.

A seismograph station operated by the observatory was established in 1957 at Afiamalu, not far from Apia. This station was chosen by the US Coast and Geodetic Survey to be included in their world-wide standardised seismograph network.

Western Samoa was included in the International Seismic Seawave Warning System in 1963. A visual seismograph at the observatory provides the earthquake readings and a tide gauge in Apia Harbour provides remote recording at the observatory.

The meteorological office of Apia Observatory was taken over by the Government of Western Samoa in 1964, and became completely staffed by Samoan personnel.

SPORTING FACILITIES

These include opportunities for spear-fishing; snorkelling and powered fishing boats for hire for deep-sea fishing; the golf course of the Royal Samoa Country Club; Apia Park, used for rugby union matches during March-June; Apia Bowling Club; tennis courts; horse-racing several times a year; boxing contests from July to December.

HISTORY. The history of Western Samoa concerns the history of the Samoan Islands as a whole, and for a better understanding it should be read in conjunction with the history of American Samoa.

Little is known of the group in pre-European times. Fijian conquerors are said to have established themselves in Manu'a in the dawn of known Samoan history, and to have received tribute from all Samoa. There are many Samoan legends which have as heroes and heroines princes and princesses of Fiji – legends which show ancient knowledge of the Fijian people and customs and indicate intercourse between Samoa and Fiji.

Later, the Tongans, probably after many raids, established themselves on Savai'i, crossed to Upolu, and were eventually beaten from the group by the first Malietoa, who arranged between Tonga and Samoa a treaty of peace.

Early visitors. The first European navigator to visit Samoa was Jacob Roggeveen, on his voyage round the world in 1721-1722. He located the group somewhat inaccurately, called several of the islands by names now unused, and sailed away without landing.

Over forty years later, in May 1768, Bougainville passed through the group, in the course of his voyage round the world. Seeing many canoes moving along the shores of the islands, he named the group Navigators' Archipelago. He did not land either.

La Perouse was the next visitor. He called there in 1787 and fixed the position of the various islands. During his stay, a shore party for water from both of his ships was attacked near Asu, on Tutuila (American Samoa), and Commandant Vicomte de Langle and 11 others were killed.

The first British ship to have visited the group was H.M.S. 'Pandora', in 1791. It was not, however, until 1830 when the pioneer missionary, John Williams, of the London Missionary Society, landed at Sapapali'i, on Savai'i, that much was learned about the group. John Williams makes mention of several white men whom he found living among the Samoans at the time of his arrival. Two important events around this time were that in 1834 the Samoan language was reduced to print in tracts compiled by the missionaries, and that in 1838 the captain of H.M.S. 'Conway' concluded a commercial treaty with the leading chiefs.

This agreement marked the first important step taken by Europeans towards established government. The agreement, between Captain Bethune and the chiefs, established a code of "Commercial Regulations" by which, in consideration of the ships paying harbour dues when using the ports, foreign interests should be protected.

The following year there arrived the United States Exploring Expedition, under Commander Charles Wilkes, specially equipped for the expedition and survey of the then little-known islands of Polynesia. This American expedition did useful work in a number of Pacific groups, and in its published records are the first descriptions of the flora and fauna of Samoa, while its Samoan surveys are the foundation of practically all Samoan land measurements. Wilkes made an agreement with the chiefs similar to that made by Captain Bethune, and these two sets of regulations represented the first formal recognition of the Europeans by the Samoans.

Consuls appointed. White immigration and settlement proceeded steadily. In 1847, G. Pritchard (a former L.M.S. missionary, who had been British Consul in Tahiti) was appointed first British Consul in Samoa. His son, W.T. Pritchard, in 1847, established the first permanent European store in Samoa, and succeeded his father as consul in 1856; and, in 1853, the first United States Commercial Agent was appointed.

Between 1840 and 1880, the Europeans settled in Apia formed a sort of protective society, and administered a code of laws, with the approval and consent of the native chiefs. It was based on the

Conway-Wilkes "Commercial Regulations" of 1838-39, added to and amended as required.

The old system of native government continued in the districts beyond Apia. The consuls had supreme authority within Apia districts, but in the districts outside the Samoans did not always accept European orders, and there were occasional "incidents" – especially as inter-tribal wars were frequent, and European adventurers often became advisers to the various contending chiefs.

There was an important commercial-political development when, in 1856, August Unshelm arrived in Apia. Unshelm came from Valparaiso as the representative of Johann Cesar Godeffroy und Sohn, of Hamburg. Unshelm was immensely impressed by the possibilities of trade in Polynesia, and decided to remain in Apia and extend the operations of his firm. Within five years he had greatly extended operations, and opened trading stations in Fiji, and at Vavau, in Tonga. Thus was born German commercial activity in the Pacific Islands – the actual and direct forerunner of the German colonies and protectorates established during the ensuing 50 years.

Theodor Weber, a Godeffroy man, was appointed German consul in Apia in 1861, and when, in 1864 August Unshelm was drowned, Weber took control of the company and in a few years he had extended the trading business all over the Central and Western Pacific.

He had traders on hundreds of islands, each a centre for the spreading German influence. He had agencies in Fiji, Tonga, Niue, Futuna and Wallis Islands, the Tokelaus, Ellice and Gilbert Groups, Northern Solomons, New Hebrides, New Britain, New Ireland, and Nauru; and they were so firmly established in the Caroline-Marshall-Mariana Archipelagoes that they bought 1,200 ha of land at Yap and established a great station, to be the centre of their activities in the north-west Pacific, and a half-way place between Samoa and Cochin.

Weber acquired some 30,000 ha of the best land on Samoa's best island, Upolu; and he had prepared a gigantic colonisation plan, to be operated by Germany in the Pacific Islands. Between 1850 and 1870, Germany was being swept by a fever for world colonisation; and Weber's Pacific Islands plan was welcomed and supported by many influential people in Germany. In 1870, the Pacific Islands belonged to anyone who cared to raise a flag.

The Franco-Prussian War in 1870, ruined Weber's far-flung plans. Godeffroy's home port, Hamburg, was blockaded; and the economic dislocation, plus unwise speculation in some countries, brought Godeffroy and Son to bankruptcy. The colonisation plan was put aside. When it was revived, ten years later, the same chances for German settlement did not exist. Nonetheless, large German colonies were formed in the Pacific Islands.

Godeffroy's place was taken by the famous company "Deutsche Handels und Plantagen Gesellschaft der Sudsee Inseln zu Hamburg", known for the next 40 years as "D. H. & P. G.", or, more simply, "the Long-Handle Firm".

International rivalries. By 1870-80, conditions in Samoa were becoming more settled, but an international rivalry, between Britain, the United States and Germany, was beginning to arise. This rivalry, which at one stage was heated and dangerous, became entangled with native disputes.

Samoa was divided into four districts, ruled by five chiefly families. These five great names, or titles, either ruled alone, or made unions to rule over combined districts, or became completely united in one family, in which event Samoa had an overlord or king, Tupu-o-Samoa. After bitter wars, Malietoa Vaiinupo of Savai'i became king in 1830, and held office until his death in 1841.

There followed 25 years of squabbling and fighting between the chiefly families. In 1867, thousands of men were under arms – half, in support of one "king", to the east of Apia, and the other half, urging the claims of another "king", in the west. Thus they remained for nearly two years, getting poorer and poorer, bartering their possessions, and selling their lands to the whites, to get food and arms.

In 1872, when U.S.S. 'Narragansett' visited Pago Pago, the high chief of Tutuila sought United States protection, and offered in return the exclusive right of establishing a naval station in Pago Pago. The United States took no action.

At this stage, in the early 'seventies, Britain and the United States were using all their influence to secure a peace in Samoa; and there then entered the picture Colonel A. B. Steinberger, special agent of the United States Government.

The consuls, aided by Steinberger, arranged a formal peace, in April, 1873. Malietopa Laupepa became king, and a constitution for Samoa, functioning as an independent state on the European model, was drafted, and finalised in 1875.

Steinberger then severed all official connection with the United States and settled down among the Samoans at Samoan headquarters, at Mulinuu (in Apia). He was instrumental in drafting a "Declaration of Rights", in the name of the people of Samoa, and in finalising a constitution of 32 sections, providing for a limited monarchy and two Houses of Parliament. He soon became Premier of Samoa, under King Malietoa; but he was the virtual dictator of Samoa. He was accepted by the Samoans and his influence was so great that he prevented a developing war by inducing the Samoans to accept another claimant to the kingship – Tupua Pulepule. Malietoa and Tupua were to reign alternately, each for four years.

The consuls did not like Steinberger – neither his methods nor his growing power.

The United States consul finally acted. At his request, conveyed through the British consul, Captain Stevens, of H.M.S. 'Barracouta', arrested Steinberger in February, 1876, and deported him to Fiji. Steinberger returned to America, and sued the British Government for damages in an action which was settled by compromise. Britain reprimanded Captain Stevens, and the United States recalled the American consul.

The elaborate Samoan Government collapsed after Steinberger departed; and, as the position deteriorated into factional fighting, the consuls of the three powers seemed to be always engaged in intrigue, supporting this or the other chief, in the hope of getting a political or commercial advantage.

A delegation of Samoans went to Fiji (now a British colony) early in 1877, to seek British protection. Britain declined. The delegation then visited the USA seeking American protection; but Washington did nothing but accept the right to establish a naval station at Pago Pago in Tutuila. Next year, 1879, Samoa gave Germany and Britain similar permission to establish naval stations.

The Municipality of Apia was established in 1879 by the British High Commissioner for the Western Pacific (Sir Arthur Gordon) – an international settlement where European law was supreme, and where native fighting must not take place. It was governed by a board consisting of the three consuls, each appointing one assessor.

Every year of the next 20 years was noted for "incidents" arising out of the ceaseless struggle of the high chiefs for power, out of trade rivalries, and the jealousies of the consuls. The latter, in the eighties, were supported by the warships of their respective nations.

Hurrican disaster. Just when the situation was particularly tense, there came the hurricane of March 16, 1889, and seven warships were trapped in Apia Harbour because they were watching each other so closely they were reluctant to leave, when the storm warnings flew.

The Germans lost the 'Adler', 'Eber' and 'Olga'; the Americans the 'Vandalia', 'Trenton' and 'Nipsic'; but the only British warship there, the 'Calliope', under Captain Kane, fought her way out in the teeth of the hurricane, and was undamaged. Two of the ships were later refloated. The Germans lost 92 men and the Americans 54.

This tragedy effectively dampened the powers' inclination towards war over their interests in Samoa, and there was a temporary settlement of their differences in the Berlin Treaty of 1889.

This treaty was between Britain, the USA and Germany, under which an independent government was set up in Samoa under King Malietoa Laupepa, and the three consuls given authority to supervise the Apia Municipal Council.

This treaty marked the end of German intrigue and aggressiveness in Samoa, which had caused friction and difficulties there for 30 years. But, within five years, Mataafa was challenging the kingship of Maleitoa, the Powers again were taking sides, and again the Samoans were fighting throughout Samoa.

In 1890, Robert Louis Stevenson arrived in Samoa and settled in Vailima. His stay was brief, however, for he died suddenly on December 3, 1894. He was buried on Mount Vaea, overlooking Apia where his tomb is still to be seen above his old home, which is now a State house.

Stevenson was very interested in the Samoan wars and the reasons for them, and in 1892 published an account called "A Footnote to History: Eight Years of Trouble in Samoa". It includes a dramatic account by eye-witnesses of the hurricane of 1889, and the loss of the ships.

In 1899, treaties were drawn between the three powers, under which the Berlin Treaty was completely annulled; Germany was permitted to annex Western Samoa; the United States was permitted to exercise sovereignty over Eastern Samoa as a territory under naval control; Britain renounced all claims in relation to Western Samoa.

In return for British withdrawal from Samoa, Germany surrendered all her rights in the Tongan Islands (including Vavau), in Niue (Savage Island), and all the Solomon Islands east and south-east of Bougainville.

German control. Thus in 1899, Western Samoa became a German colony. In February, 1900, Dr Solf, who was at the time President of the Municipality of Apia, was appointed Governor.

In 1908, Samoans saw the beginning of a long history of resistance to colonial overlords. The Mau of Pule was established, a movement based in Savai'i and resistant to German rule. Then, in March, 1909, tensions grew so intense the Germans had to exile the movement leaders to the Marianas, and take punitive measures against their supporters.

On August 29, 1914, with the outbreak of World War I a force of New Zealanders annexed Western Samoa without a shot being fired. The New Zealand military occupation continued under Colonel Logan until April 30, 1920. Logan's rule was marked by an appalling error which saw the deaths of 8,500 people, or 22 per cent of Western Samoa's population. Through carelessness Logan had allowed a ship into Apia, known to be carrying Spanish influenza. And even when the disease was causing many deaths and illness, Logan refused much needed medical assistance from American Samoa. The disease was never introduced into American Samoa because of tough quarantine regulations.

A 1948 United Nations report on Western Samoa said of the Samoan epidemic: "It ranks as one of the most disastrous epidemics recorded anywhere in the world during the present century, so far as the proportion of deaths to population is concerned."

By the Treaty of Versailles, Western Samoa became a "C" class mandate of New Zealand.

The Mau. New Zealand's early years were marked by endless political trouble. Basically, the Samoan traditional leadership did not accept the need for foreign overlords, and the New Zealand administration was unprepared and ill-suited for running other people's countries. The epidemic had caused considerable discontent.

Furthermore the New Zealand administration was led by military officers, and the officers had no understanding of Samoa's national feeling or pride. To them, the Samoans were simply stupid natives led by agitators.

By the 1920s, the Mau movement had grown. The word "mau" means testimony and was used to indicate that the movement represented a particular body of opinion critical of the New Zealand authorities.

The Mau was a non-violent passive resistance movement, which included leading Europeans, especially Mr O. F. Nelson, a wealthly and influential man. Judge Gurr, an American, and Mr A. G. Smyth, a leading merchant, were also active.

The New Zealand administrators feared the growth of the Mau, and on various occasions had the three Europeans exiled.

The Samoans abandoned any hope of receiving any consideration from New Zealand. They became uncooperative – they would not in any way assist the administration and they refused to pay taxes.

One of the deported Europeans, Mr Smyth, returned to Samoa after three years banishment on December 28, 1929. Members of the Mau marched through Apia, in procession, to greet Smyth. Outside the administration building a group of armed policemen attempted to grab some men known to be wanted by the police. A fight ensued and several shots were fired by the police. This was followed by the firing of a police machine gun directly into the unarmed Mau.

Eleven people died that day, including a Mau leader, Tupua Tamasese Lealofi III who was hit as he tried to calm his followers.

New Zealand sent a warship to Samoa and banned the Mau. Most of the nation's men went into the bush to resist arrest. The time was extremely tense and the Mau remained a movement engaged in non cooperation and hostility.

New Zealand responded with raids on Samoan houses in attempts to find the men.

In 1936, New Zealand elected a new Labour Government which cancelled the order of banishment against the leaders, and sent them back to Samoa.

Relations between the Samoans and the New Zealand administration improved slowly, but the obvious incompetency of the administrators resulted in continued frustration and bad feeling.

By World War II, Samoa reached a turning point. United States Marines were stationed on Upolu and they constructed roads and an airport. Today their influence is felt to have been considerable, and a watershed between an old Samoa, and a developing Samoa.

After the war Samoa became a trustee of the United Nations, administered by New Zealand. But, by this time, New Zealand had begun to prepare Samoa for self-government, which was to come in 1962.

Preparation for self-government. A Council of State was established in 1947, consisting of the NZ High Commissioner (president) and the two Samoans holding office as Fautua (leading chief). Under the Samoan Amendment Act 1947, the High Commissioner had to consult the Council of State in the exercise of those powers about which he was not bound to consult the Executive Council. A Legislative Assembly was also set up.

New Zealand suggested in 1953 that a Constitutional Convention, representing all sections of the West Samoan population, be set up to consider proposals for future political progress. The Convention met at the end of 1954.

The New Zealand Parliament in October, 1957, passed the Samoa Amendment Act, 1957. The most important provisions of this were to redefine the functions of the High Commissioner, redefine and enlarge the membership of the Executive Council, provide for the appointment of a Leader of Government Business, reconstitute official and increased Samoan membership, provide for a Speaker, redefine the Assembly's privileges and powers and abolish the Fono of Faipule, which was a Samoan advisory body.

The Executive Council became "the principal instrument of policy". The 1957 Act provided that members, other than the High Commissioner and the Fautua, should be designated Ministers.

A Prime Minister, in place of the Leader of Government Business, was appointed in September, 1959, and by the end of 1960 a Samoan Constitutional Convention had approved a draft constitution for an independent State of Western Samoa. Prime Minister Fiame Mataafa took the proposals to the United Nations in January, 1961. This led to a United Nations supervised plebiscite of May 9, 1961, wherein all adult citizens of Samoa were asked whether (a) they approved the Constitution; and (b) whether they wanted independence on Janaury 1, 1962.

The affirmative vote on both clauses was a foregone conclusion – the only unique feature about the plebiscite was that it was the first time that people of Samoan domestic status voted according to adult universal suffrage and not on the matai system.

The Constitution of Western Samoa became "the supreme law of Western Samoa" at independence on January 1, 1962.

The constitution provides for a Head of State, called in Samoan, O le Ao O le Malo, to be elected by the Legislative Assembly for a term of five years.

However, in the first instance, it was decided that the two High Chiefs, who had been titled the Fautua (Tupua Tamasese and Malietoa Tanumafili II), should become joint Head of State and have a lifetime tenure of office unless they resigned or were removed from office by the Assembly. If one predeceased the other, the survivor continued as sole Head of State during his lifetime – subject to resignation or removal from office. On April 5, 1963, the death occurred of Tupua Tamasese; the sole Head of State thereafter was Malietoa Tanumafili II.

Western Samoa joined the United Nations in 1976.

Further reading: For a detailed look at the emergence of Western Samoa as an independent state, particularly the making of the constitution, see J. W. Davidson, "Samoa mo Samoa", Melbourne, 1967. David Pitt's "Tradition and Economic Progress in Samoa", Oxford, 1970, and Brian Lockwood's "Samoan Village Economy", Melbourne, 1971, are also detailed, but technical works on the grass roots of Samoa; for lighter reading there are George Irwin's, "Samoa: A Teacher's Tale", London, 1965, and G. C. Marsack's "Samoan Medley", London, 1961. See also the reading list under American Samoa.

FOR THE TOURIST. General visitor information is provided by the Department of Economic Development, Apia. In addition, an information centre is operated near the Handicraft Corp. in Apia, by the Western Samoa Travel and Holiday Association (See also sections on the people, Samoan etiquette and transport).

Entry formalities. No entry permit is required if stay in Western Samoa does not exceed 7 days. For a longer stay, apply direct to the Immigration Division, Prime Minister's Department, Apia, or through a New Zealand diplomatic post or British Consular office. Visitors staying more than three months require an exit permit from Immigration Office before departure. Visitors must possess an international Certificate of Health showing valid smallpox vaccination.

Airport tax. An Airport Departure Tax of one tala (WS$1.00) per person is levied to help pay for new airport and passenger terminal.

Sightseeing: Numerous scenic drives can be made by tourist coach or rental car. These include plantations, lush rainforests, waterfalls and freshwater bathing pools of the inland or coastal villages and their fine sandy beaches.

Apia itself has much of interest. Set on the water's edge, the town straggles casually along the beach, and its architecture no less than its disposition embodies its history.

Perhaps the feature of Apia first to catch the eye from the deck of an incoming ship is the series of denominational churches, in villages along the shore line. Shade trees dot the main street, following the curve of the harbour front; and behind the town rise wooded hills and shaded valleys. On the western horn of the half-moon bay stands the observatory at Mulinu'u; at the eastern end is Matautu and its wharf.

Visitors who arrive by air get their first introduction to Western Samoa coming in from the airport, which is 40 km from Apia. The road skirts the shore and meanders through Samoan villages – usually situated near a freshwater creek, and with the public lavatory built out over the sea at the end of a rickety jetty. Each village has a church and some have more than one – some very modern in design, some massive with cupolas and turrets, some whitewashed, some picked out in multi-colours that make them look like Indian temples. The number of churches is surprise number one for visitors.

Some village houses are of European materials but traditional Samoan is still the style in the majority of cases. Round or oval shaped, thatched roof supported by closely spaced posts and walls of mat blinds that are pulled up except when it rains, these houses are cool but also give the passerby a close-up view of village life.

Some of the recommended excursions are as follows:

To Falefa Falls, about 30 km east of Apia, then over the Mafa Pass and another 35 km to the Aleipata District on the south-east corner of Upolu. On the way you see the Fuipisia Falls which have a drop of nearly 60 m.

About 40 km west of Apia (beyond the airport) is the West Samoan Trust estates coconut plantation of Mulifanua which is said to be the largest single coconut plantation in the Southern Hemisphere. At the extreme point of this west coast road is Lefatu Cape. There are some delightful beachside picnic spots here – and a close-up view of the small islands of Manono (claimed to be the inspiration for James Mitchener's "Bali Hai") and Apolima which lies between the big islands of Upolu and Savai'i.

A scenic drive round the whole island of Upolu can be made as a day excursion. The cross-island road at the western end of Upolu branches off some miles from Faleolo, on the north coast, and connects with Lefaga on the south coast, scene of the film "Return to Paradise".

Closer to Apia is Papaseea, or sliding rock, where the visitor can slide down a natural rock slide into a freshwater pool. This is about 8 km out and can be reached by car.

For the vigorous there is Lake Lanoto which is 17 km from Apia and at an elevation of 600 m. A car can get half way there, after which it is a matter of walking or riding a horse.

Directly above Apia is Mt Vaea, at top of which is Robert Louis Stevenson's grave. The trail that leads to the summit begins at Vailima, the final home of RLS which is now the residence of the Western Samoan Head of State. The house is about 7 km from the waterfront. It can be visited only with permission from the Prime Minister's office.

At Mulinu'u, a taxi ride from the centre of Apia, are the traditional burial grounds of Samoan royalty and the Legislative Assembly building, styled after a Samoan "fale". Adjacent are the "malae" grounds for national celebrations. Also at Mulinu'u, or along the road leading to it are a number of monuments

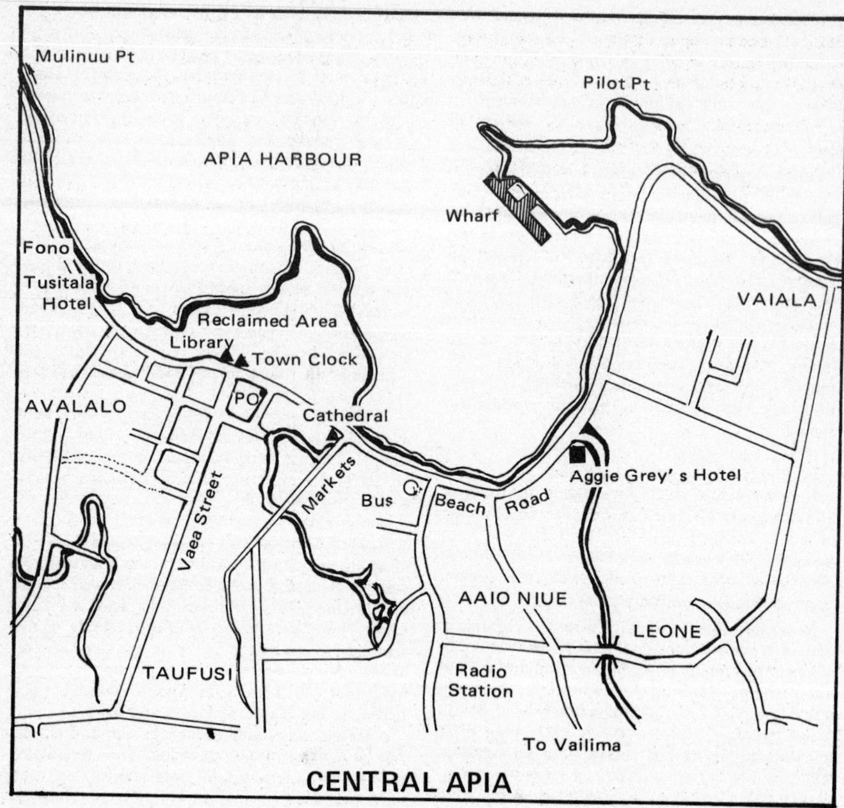

dating from the 19th century when the Samoans were engaged in civil wars and Britain, Germany and the United States were rivals for power in the area.

Visitors who want to go further afield can take the launch or a Samoan long-boat from Manonouta, near Cape Lefatau, and visit the small island of Manono; or cross to the other island of Savai'i.

The larger island of Savai'i remains untouched by outside influence in many parts and is believed to still contain secrets awaiting the archeologist concerning the origins of Polynesia. Here are old man-made rock formations including an old Samoan fort and other historical relics dating back thousands of years.

Tourist representatives abroad: Pacific Area Promotions, 95/99 York Street Sydney; tel. 290 2844; telex AA27585.

Western Samoa Trade Commissioner in New Zealand, Mr E. Stehlin.

ACCOMMODATION

AGGIE GREY'S HOTEL — 115 rooms, all with electric fans, some rooms fully air-conditioned, shower with hot water and toilet; situated at the eastern tip of Apia near Coronation Bridge on the waterfront. There is a large swimming pool, a Samoan-type building suitable for conferences or entertainments, a patio bar, extensive lawns and a tropical garden. Daily tariff includes all meals and varies according to the type of room occupied.

HOTEL TUSITALA — 96 double rooms, each with carpets, air-conditioning and patio; swimming pool, dining room, cocktail lounge, bowling green; close to golf course and tennis courts; occupies site of former old Casino Hotel in downtown Apia. Named after famous writer Robert Louis Stevenson whom Samoans called "Tusitala" (Teller of Tales).

TIAFAU HOTEL — 34 rooms all with private balcony overlooking Apia harbour, private baths and air-conditioning; dining room, lounge and bar; modern hotel on sea front, half km from town centre.

MAOTA O LE ALOFA — a couple of rooms are available for rent in this Western Samoa National Women's building which also houses private offices, a hall and restaurant; situated in town centre.

PARADISE OF ENTERTAINMENT — a newly opened club, with separate bungalows along the seafront; bungalows rented without meals.

Other accommodation on Upolu Is: Samoan Hideaway Resort Hotel – 9 duplex bungalows plus additional unit of 12 rooms, all with private facilities including fans and small refrigerators; situated at Mulivai Beach on edge of jungle stream, about 45 minutes by car from Apia; restaurant, snack bar, bar.

Accommodation on Savai'i Is: Savaiian Guest Fale – big thatched "fale" house; suitable for the hardy and adventurous, who would like to experience Samoan open-house living; situated on south-east coast at Lalomalava, close to airport; tariff includes all meals, licensed.

OBSOLETE AND ALTERNATIVE NAMES FOR THE PACIFIC ISLANDS

Most of the islands of the Pacific Ocean have been known by at least two names, and sometimes by as many as six, during the past two centuries or so. There are simple historical reasons for this. First, the European explorers were wont to bestow their own names on the islands regardless of the indigenous names; and sometimes the same islands were "discovered" by more than one explorer. Later, the native names tended to supersede those of the explorers, but because many years elapsed before the spelling of such names became standardised, Europeans frequently spelt the names in a variety of ways. As a result, modern readers of Pacific literature of the 18th and 19th centuries are apt to be confused by such antique names as Todos Santos, Cherry and Bligh's Lagoon, or by obsolete spellings such as Niaur, Aborima and Ticumbia. The gazetteers appearing in the following pages should help to alleviate these difficulties.

The gazetteers were compiled by the Pacific Manuscripts Bureau, Research School of Pacific Studies, Australian National University, Canberra, and are reproduced by permission from the bureau's newsletter, **Pambu,** No. 42, Jan.-Mar. 1976. The principal reference works used in their compilation were: Alexander G. Findlay, **A Directory for the Navigation of the North Pacific Ocean,** 2nd edn (London, 1870); Alexander G. Findlay, **A Directory for the Navigation of the South Pacific Ocean,** 3rd edn (London, 1871); Edwin H. Bryan, Jr., **American Polynesia and the Hawaiian Chain** (Honolulu, 1942); Naval Intelligence Division, **Pacific Islands,** 4 vols (Cambridge, 1943-45); Andrew Sharp, **The Discovery of the Pacific Islands** (Oxford, 1960); H. E. Maude, **Of Islands and Men** (Melbourne, 1969); and Judy Tudor **(ed.)**, **Pacific Islands Year Book,** 11th edn (Sydney, 1972).

The first gazetteer lists obsolete/alternative names for the islands with their current equivalents; the second the current names with their obsolete/alternative equivalents.

No attempt has been made to list all known alternative spellings — merely to give enough clues to enable a researcher to establish an island's most commonly used current name in the English-speaking world. The current name is not necessarily that used by the islanders themselves. For example, one of the islands of the northern Cook Group is still better known to outsiders by its European name, Penrhyn, than by its local name, Tongareva. On the other hand, the local name for another such island, Pukapuka, has now completely superseded the European name, Danger Island, by which the island was long known. In some cases, arbitrary decisions had to be made on which of a pair of names is now the more current one.

Users of the gazetteers should bear in mind that some islands discovered by 16th century explorers were not correctly identified by 19th century hydrographers. Thus, for example, the 16th century Spanish name Arrecifes seems, correctly, to belong to Ulithi Atoll in the Carolines whereas 19th century hydrographers identified it as Ujelang Atoll in the Marshalls. Because such connections as Arrecifes/Ujelang became accepted, these cases of mistaken identity have been perpetuated in the gazetteers. It should also be borne in mind that:

- In current **Fijian** orthography, **b** is pronounced **mb** as in member; **c** is **th** as in than; **d** is **nd** as in friend; **g** is **ng** as in hang; **q** is **ng** as in finger.

• In **Samoan** orthography the **g** is sometimes used to represent **ng** as in singer and sometimes the **ng** spelling is used. Thus, an island in the Manua group is sometimes spelt Olose**g**a and sometimes Olose**ng**a.

• In **Tongan** orthography **b** and **p,** and **g** and **ng** were used indiscriminately until about 30 years ago when the use of **p** and **ng** became official.

• In a number of Islands' languages, the **t** and **k,** and the **l** and **r** are, or were, frequently confused.

Abbreviations used in the gazetteers, with "I" standing for Islands, are:

AI	=	Austral
BI		Bonin
Car.		Caroline
CI		Cook
Gal.		Galapagos
GI		Gilbert
Haw.		Hawaii
JF		Juan Fernandez
KIR		Kiribati (formerly Gilberts)
KI		Kermadec
LI		Line
MI		Mariana
Marq.		Marquesas
Marsh		Marshall
NC		New Caledonia
NH		New Hebrides
PNG		Papua New Guinea
PI		Phoenix
RI		Ryuk
SI		Society
Sol.		Solomon
TA		Tuamotu Archipelago
Tok.		Tokelau
Tuv.		Tuvalu (formerly Ellice I.)
Van.		Vanuatu (formerly New Hebrides)
VI		Volcano
W & F		Wallis and Futuna

OBSOLETE/ALTERNATIVE NAMES with Current Equivalents

ABGARRIS	Nuguria	PNG
ABINGDON	Pinta	Gal.
ABORIMA	Apolima	Samoa
ADAMS	Nukuhiva	Marq.
ADAMS	Uapou	Marq.
ADMIRAL CHICHAGOV	Faaite	TA
ADVENTURE	Motutunga	TA
AGRIGAN	Agrihan	MI
AILINGLABELAB	Ailinglapelap	Marsh.
AIMEO	Moorea	SI
ALAMAGUAN	Alamagan	MI
ALBEMARLE	Isabela	Gal
ALICE THORNDIKE	Kingman	LI
ALLEN	Butaritari	Kir.
AMARGURA	Fonualei	Tonga
AMAT	Tahiti	SI
AMBOW	Bau	Fiji
AMBRIM	Ambrym	Van.
AMOTA	Mota	Van.
AMSTERDAM	Tongatapu	Tonga
ANAMOOKA	Nomuka	Tonga
ANATAJAN / ANATAXAN	Anatahan	MI
ANDEMA	Ant	Car.
ANEITEUM	Anatom	Van.
ANGATAU	Fangatau	TA
ANIMAS	Amanu	TA
ANIR	Feni	PNG
ANNATOM	Anatom	Van.
ANNE	Vostok	SI
ANONIMA	Namonuito	Car.
ANONIMA	Onon	Car.
ANTHONY CAEN / ANTHONY KAAN	Tanga	PNG
APAIANG	Abaiang	Kir.
APAMAMA	Abemama	Kir.
API	Epi	Van.
APIA	Abaiang	Kir.
APOUCAROUA	Pukarua	TA
APPALLO	Kabara	Fiji
ARAKCHEEV	Fangatau	TA
ARAKTCHEEFF	Maloelap	Marsh.
ARHNO	Arno	Marsh.
ARMSTRONG	Rarotonga	CI
ARORE	Arorae	Kir.
AROSSI	San Cristobal	Sol.
ARRAGH	Pentecost	Van.
ARRECIFES	Ujelang	Marsh.
ARROWSMITH	Majuro	Marsh.
ARTHUR	Enewetak	Marsh.
ARZOBISPO	Bonin	BI
ASAUA	Yasawa	Fiji
ASCENSION	Ponape	Car.
ASSUMPTION	Asuncion	MI
ATOOI	Kauai	Haw.
AUGIER	Tatakoto	TA
AURA	Kaukura	TA
AURH	Aur	Marsh.
AURORA	Maewo	Van.
AURORA	Makatea	TA
AUURA	Kaukura	TA
AVONDSTOND	Apataki	TA
OCEAN	Banaba	Kir.
BARCLAY DE TOLLY	Raroia	TA
BARING	Namorik	Marsh.
BARREN	Starbuck	LI
BARRINGTON	Santa Fe	Gal.
BARROW	Vanavana	TA
BARSTOW	Morane	TA
BARTOLOME	Pulusuk	Car.
BARTHOLOMEW	Malo	Van.
BARWELL	Tikopia	Sol.
BASS	Marotiri	AI
BASSE DES FREGATES FRANÇAISES	French Frigate Shoal	Haw.
BASS REEF-TIED	Maloelap	Marsh.
BATOU-BARA	Vatuvara	Fiji
BAUX	Nukuhiva	Marq.
BEDFORD	Vahanga	TA
BEDRIEGLYKE	Tikei	TA
BENGA	Beqa	Fiji
BERTERO	Maria	TA
BIGAR	Bikar	Marsh.
BIGINI	Rongelap	Marsh.
BINDLOE	Marchena	Gal.
BIRD	Farallon de Medinilla	MI
BIRD	Nihoa	Haw.
BIRD	Reitoru	TA
BISHOP	Tabiteuea	Kir.
BISHOP JUNCTION	Erikub	Marsh.

OBSOLETE/ALTERNATIVE NAMES with Current Equivalents

BISHOP OF OSNABURG	Mururoa	TA
BIVA	Viwa	Fiji
BLAKE	Moturiti	Marq.
BLIGH	Ureparapara	Van.
BLIGH'S LAGOON	Tematangi	TA
BOLABOLA	Borabora	SI
BONA VISTA	Tinian	MI
BONHAM	Jaluit	Marsh.
BONIN	Ogasawara	BI
BORDELAISE	Oroluk	Car.
BOSCAWEN	Niuatoputapu	Tonga
BOSTON	Ebon	Marsh.
BOUCHER	Tiga	NC
BOUDOIR	Mehetia	SI
BOUKA	Buka	PNG
BOW	Hao	TA
BOWDITCH	Fakaofu	Tok.
BRATTLE	Tortuga	Gal.
BRITANNIA	Mare	NC
BRITOMART	Hereheretue	TA
BROOKE	Jarvis	LI
BROOKS	Midway	
BROWN	Enewetak	Marsh.
BROWN	Lae	Marsh.
BUENA VISTA	Tinian	MI
BUEN VIAJE	Butaritari	Kir.
BUGA BUGA	Toga	Van.
BUKA	Toga	Van.
BULLOO	Ovalau	Fiji
BUNKER	Jarvis	LI
BUTTON	Utirik	Marsh.
BYAM MARTIN	Ahunui	TA
BYRON	Nikunau	Kir.
CADMUS	Morane	TA
CAINGA	Taenga	TA
CALVERT	Maloelap	Marsh.
CANTAB	Kadavu	Fiji
CARLSHOFF	Aratika	TA
CARTERET	Kilinailau	PNG
CARTERET	Malaita	Sol.
CARYSFORT	Tureia	TA
CASBOKAS	Ujelang	Marsh.
CASOBOS	Ujelang	Marsh.
CATHARINE	Kwajalein	Marsh.
CAVAHI	Kauehi	TA
CHABROL	Lifou	NC
CHAIN	Anaa	TA
CHANAL	Hatutu	Marq.
CHARLES	Floreana	Gal.
CHARLOTTE	Abaiang	Kir.
CHATHAM	Erikub	Marsh.
CHATHAM	San Cristobal	Gal.
CHATHAM	Savaii	Samoa
CHAVES	Santa Cruz	Gal.
CHERRY	Anuta	Sol.
CHICHAGOV	Faaite, Tahanea	TA
CHICHIA	Cicia	Fiji
CHICOBEA	Cikobia	Fiji
CHRISTIANA	Tahuata	Marq.
CLARK	Caroline	LI
CLARKE	Butaritari	Kir.
CLARKE	Tatakoto	TA
CLERK	Onotoa	Kir.
CLERMONT DE TONNERE	Reao	TA
COCKBURN	Fangataufa	TA
COCOS	Niuatoputapu	Tonga
CONSOLACION	Niuafo'ou	Tonga
CONSTANTIN	Kapingamarangi	Car.

CONTRARIETE	Ulawa	Sol.
CONVERSION DE SAN PABLO	Hao	TA
PABLO	Hao	TA
COOK	Tarawa	Kir.
COQUILLE	Jaluit	Marsh.
COQUILLE	Pikelot	Car.
CORAL QUEEN	Starbuck	LI
COUNT ARAKCHEEV	Fangatau	TA
COUNT HEIDEN	Likiep	Marsh.
COUNT WITTGENSTEIN	Fakarava, Toau	TA
COVELL	Ebon	Marsh.
CRESCENT	Temoe	TA
CROKER	Haraiki	TA
CUATRO CORONADOS	Actaeon	TA
CUMBERLAND	Manuhangi	TA
DAGENRAAD	Ahe, Manihi	TA
DANGER	Pukapuka	CI
DANGEROUS	Tuamotu	TA
DANIEL	Arno	Marsh.
DAUGIER	Tatakoto	TA
DAVID CLARK	Tatakoto	TA
DAWAHAIDY	Ravahere	TA
DAWSON	Bikar	Marsh.
DEAN	Rangiroa	TA
DECEPTION	Moso	Van.
DE PEYSTER	Nukufetau	Tuv.
DISAPPOINTMENT	Napuka, Tepoto	TA
DISAPPOINTMENT	Taumako	Sol.
DOG	Pukapuka	TA
DOMINICA, DOMINIQUE	Hivaoa	Marq.
DOUBTFUL	Tekokoto	TA
DOUGLAS	Parece Vela	Japan
DRUMMOND	McKean	PI
DRUMMOND	Tabiteuea	Kir.
DUKE OF CLARENCE	Nukunono	Tok.
DUKE OF CUMBERLAND	Manuhangi	TA
DUKE OF GLOUCESTER	Paraoa	TA
DUKE OF YORK	Moorea	SI
DUNCAN	Pinzon	Gal.
DUPERREY	Mokil	Car.
D'URVILLE	Losap	Car.
EAP	Yap	Car.
EAST DANGER	Enewetak	Marsh.
EBRILL	Fakahina	TA
EDDYSTONE	Simbo	Sol.
EDGECUMBE	Utupua	Sol.
EGERUP	Erikub	Marsh.
EGMONT	Vairaatea	TA
EIMEO	Moorea	SI
ELIZA	Beru	Kir.
ELIZA	Hiti	TA
ELIZA	Onotoa	Kir.
ELIZABETH	Henderson	Pitcairn
ELIZABETH	Jaluit	Marsh.
ELIZABETH	Toau	TA
ELLICE	Funafuti	Tuv.
ELLICE	Tuvalu	Tuv.
ENDERBY	Enderbury	PI
ENDERBY	Puluwat	Car.
EOOA	Eua	Tonga
EOURYPYG	Eauripik	Car.
EROMANGO	Erromango	Van.

OBSOLETE/ALTERNATIVE NAMES with Current Equivalents

ERRONAN	Futuna	Van.
ESCHSCHOLTZ	Bikini	Marsh.
FAARAVA	Fakarava	TA
FAGATAU	Fangatau	TA
FAITE	Faaite	TA
FALCON	Fonuafo'ou	Tonga
FANGAHINA	Fakahina	TA
FANOUALIE	Fonualei	Tonga
FAREWELL	Cikobia	Fiji
FARROILEP / FATTOILAP	Faraulep	Car.
FATUUHU	Hatutu	Marq.
FEAD	Nuguria	PNG
FEDERAL	Nukuhiva	Marq.
FEEJEE	Fiji	Fiji
FETUKU	Fatuhuku	Marq.
FLORA	Florida	Sol.
FORAULEP	Faraulep	Car.
FORTUNA	Futuna	Van.
FOTUNA	Erronan	Van.
FOUR CROWNS	Actaeon	TA
FOURTEEN	Ebon	Marsh.
FRANCIS	Beru	Kir.
FRANKLIN	Motuiti / Nukuhiva	Marq.
FRASER	Ant	Car.
FREEMANTLE	Eiao	Marq.
FRIENDLY	Tonga	Tonga
FURNEAUX	Marutea	TA
GALLIPAGOES	Galapagos	Gal.
GAMBIER	Mangareva	TA
GARDNER	Faraulep	Car.
GARDNER	Maria	AI
GARDNER	Tabar	PNG
GASPAR RICO	Taongi	Marsh.
GELA	Florida	Sol.
GENERAL OSTEN-SAKEN	Katiu	TA
GENTE HERMOSA	Swain	Samoa
GEORGIAN	Society Islands (Windward Group)	SI
GERRIT DE NIJS / GERRIT DENYS	Lihir	PNG
GILLESPIE	Butaritari	Kir.
GILLET	Rabi	Fiji
GLOUCESTER	Paraoa	TA
GOEDE HOPE	Niuafo'ou	Tonga
GOEDE VERWAGHTING	Rangiroa	TA
GOOD HOPE	Rekareka	TA
GORO	Koro	Fiji
GOULOU	Ngulu	Car.
GOW	Gaua	Van.
GOWER	Ndai	Sol.
GRAF OSTEN-SACKEN	Katiu	TA
GRAN COCAL	Nanumanga	Tuv.
GRAND DUKE ALEXANDER	Rakahanga	CI
GREAT GANGES	Manihiki	CI
GREENWICH	Kapingamarangi	Car.
GREIG	Niau	TA
GRENVILLE	Rotuma	Fiji
GRIGAN	Agrihan	MI
GROENE	Green	PNG
GUAHAN / GUAJAN	Guam	MI
HABAI	Haapai	Tonga
HADOW	Munia	Fiji
HAGEMEISTER	Apataki	TA
HALCYON	Wake	
HALGAN	Ouvea	NC
HALL	Maiana	Kir.
HANCOCK	Hatutu	Marq.
HARPE	Hao	TA
HARVEST	Namoluk	Car.
HASHMY	Namoluk	Car.
HAT	Eradaka	Van.
HENDERVILLE	Aranuka	Kir.
HERGEST	Motu-iti	Marq.
HERO	Starbuck	LI
HERVEY	Cook	CI
HIAU	Eiao	Marq.
HIGH	Raivavae	AI
HINCHINBROOK	Emau	Van.
HIRST	Caroline	LI
HOGOLEU	Truk	Car.
HOLLAND	Howland	PI
HOLT	Taenga	TA
HOOD	Espanola	Gal.
HOOD	Fatuhuku	Marq.
HONDEN	Pukapuka	TA
HOORN	Futuna	W & F
HOPPER	Aranuka	Kir.
HORN	Futuna	W & F
HUDSON	Nanumanga	Tuv.
HULL	Maria	AI
HUMPHREY	Manihiki	CI
HUNTER	Kili	Marsh.
HURD	Arorae	Kir.
IBARGOITIA	Pulusuk	Car.
IBBETSON	Aur	Marsh.
IFALIK	Ifaluk	Car.
ILE DE PINS	Isle of Pines	NC
IMMER	Aniwa	Van.
INATTENDUE	Ndai	Sol.
INDEFATIGABLE	Santa Cruz	Gal.
INDEPENDENCE	Caroline	LI
INDEPENDENCE	Malden	LI
INDEPENDENCE	Niulakita	Tuv.
INDUSTRIEL	Vairaatea	TA
IRELAND	Raraka	TA
ISLA DEL COCAL	Nanumanga	Tuv.
JABWAT	Jabwot	Marsh.
JAMES	San Salvador	Gal.
JEFFERSON	Uapou	Marq.
JERVIS	Rabida	Gal.
JESUS	Nui	Tuv.
KADOOLAWE / KADULAUI	Kahoolawe	Haw.
KANDAVU	Kadavu	Fiji
KANTAVU	Kadavu	Fiji
KARLSHOFF	Aratika	TA
KATA	Puluwat	Car.
KAVEN	Maloelap	Marsh.
KAWAHE	Kauehi	TA
KEMIN	Gardner	PI
KEPPEL	Tafahi	Tonga
KILI	Hunter	Marsh.
KING	Taiaro	TA
KING GEORGE	Takapoto / Takaroa	TA
KING GEORGE III	Tahiti	SI
KINGSMILL	Southern Gilberts	Kir.
KNOX	Eiao	Marq.

OBSOLETE/ALTERNATIVE NAMES with Current Equivalents

KNOX	Tarawa	Kir.
KONGELAB	Rongelap	Marsh.
KOUTOUSOFF	Makemo	TA
KORDIUKOFF	Rose	Samoa
KRUSENSTERN	Ailuk	Marsh.
KRUSENSTERN	Tikehau	TA
KUNIE	Isle of Pines	NC
KUTUSOFF	Utirik	Marsh.
KUTUSOV-SMOLENSKI	Makemo	TA
KWADELEN	Kwajalein	Marsh.
KYLI	Jaluit	Marsh.
LACONA	Gaua	Van.
LADRONES	Mariana	MI
LAGOON	Vahitahi	TA
LAGOON (Bligh's)	Tematangi	TA
LAKOON	Gaua	Van.
LAMBERT	Ailingalapalap	Marsh.
LAMOLIORK	Ngulu	Car.
LAMULIUR	Ngulu	Car.
LANCIERS	Akiaki	TA
LANGDON	Hatutu	Marq.
LATTE	Late	Tonga
LAURU	Choiseul	Sol.
LAZAREV	Matahiva	TA
LEGIEP	Likiep	Marsh.
LEOPOLD I	Nukutavake	TA
LEPERS	Aoba	Van.
LETTE	Late	Tonga
LIEUTENANT-GENERAL YERMOLOV	Taenga	TA
LIFU	Lifou	NC
LINNEZ	Ebon	Marsh.
LINCOLN	Onotoa	Kir.
LITTLE GANGES	Rakahanga	CI
LOMO-LOMO	Lomaloma	Fiji
LOO-CHOO	Ryukyu	RI
LOPER	Niutao	Tuv.
LORD EGMONT	Vairaatea	TA
LORD HOOD	South Marutea	TA
LORD HOWE	Ontong Java	Sol.
LORD HOWE	Mopelia	SI
LORD HOWE	Vavau	Tonga
LORD NORTH	Tobi	Car.
LOSTANGE	Nengonengo	TA
LOUASAPPE	Losap	Car.
LOUGOUNOR	Lukunor	Car.
LOW	Starbuck	LI
LUANIUA	Ontong Java	SI
LU-CHU	Ryukyu	RI
LUGUNOR	Lukunor	Car.
LUTKE	East Fayu	Car.
LYDIA	Ujae	Marsh.
LYNX	Niutao	Tuv.
MAATAAH	Makatea	TA
MACASKILL	Pingelap	Car.
MACKENZIE	Ulithi	Car.
MACQUEMO	Makemo	TA
MADISON	Nukuhiva	Marq.
MAE	Emae	Van.
MAETEEA	Makatea	TA
MAGDALENA	Fatuhiva	Marq.
MAI	Emae	Van.
MAITEA / MAITIA	Mehetia	SI
MAIWO	Maewo	Van.
MAKIN	Little Makin	Kir.
MAKIRA	San Cristobal	Sol.
MALA	Malaita	Sol.
MALANTA	Malaita	Sol.
MALAYETTE	Malaita	Sol.
MALLICOLLO	Malekula	Van.
MALOELAB	Maloelap	Marsh.
MANDEGHUGHUSU	Simbo	Sol.
MANGEA	Mangaia	CI
MANNICOLO	Vankioro	Sol.
MAN-OF-WAR ROCK	Gardner Pinnacles	Haw.
SYDNEY	Manra	PI
MANUAE	Fenua-Ura	SI
MARAKI	Marakei	Kir.
MARALABA	Mera Lava	Van.
MARCHAND	Uapou	Marq.
MARGARET	Nukutipipi	TA
MARGARETTA	Namu	Marsh.
MARIA	Beru	Kir.
MARINA	Espiritu Santo	Van.
MARQUE(E)N	Tauu	PNG
MARTIN DE MAYORGA	Vavau	Tonga
MARTIRES	Tekokoto	TA
MARUA	Maupiti	SI
MARY	Kanton	PI
MARY BALCOUT	Kanton	PI
MASSACHUSETTS	Eiao	Marq.
MASSE	Eiao	Marq.
MAOUNA	Tutuila	Samoa
MATAA / MATEA / MATHEA / MATIA	Makatea	TA
MATILDA	Mururoa	TA
MATORIKI	Moturiki	Fiji
MATTHEW	Abaiang	Kir.
MATTHEW	Marakei	Kir.
MATY	Woodlark	PNG
MAU	Emau	Van.
MAURA	Maupiti	SI
MAUITI	Maiao	SI
MAUTI	Mauke	CI
MBAU	Bau	Fiji
MBENGA	Beqa	Fiji
MEDURO	Majuro	Marsh.
MEERDER ZORG	Arutua	TA
MELBOURNE	Maturei Vavao	TA
MELVILLE	Hikueru	TA
MERLAV	Mera Lava	Van.
MIADI	Mejit	Marsh.
MIDDLE	Tegua	Van.
MIDDLEBURGH	Eua	Tonga
MIDDLETON	Rose	Samoa
MILLE	Milli	Marsh.
MILORADOVICH	Faaite	TA
MINERVA	Reao	TA
MINTO	Tenarunga	TA
MITCHELL	Nassau	CI
MITCHELL	Nukulaelae	Tuv.
MITIERO	Mitiaro	CI
MITRE	Fataka	Sol.
MOERENHOUT	Maria	TA
MOKOGAI / MOKUNGAI	Makogai	Fiji
MOLLER	Amanu	TA
MOLLER	Laysan	Haw.
MONTAGU	Nguna	Van.
MONTEVERDE	Nukuoro	Car.
MOPIHAA	Mopelia	SI
MOROTOI	Molokai	Haw.
MORTLOCK	Nomoi	Car.

OBSOLETE/ALTERNATIVE NAMES with Current Equivalents

MORTLOCK	Tauu	PNG
MORUROA	Mururoa	TA
MOTA LAVA	Valua	NH
MOTANE	Mohotani	Marq.
MOTU ITI	Tupai	SI
MOUMOLU-NAUNITU	San Jorge	Sol.
MOURILEU	Murilo	Car.
MOWEE	Maui	Haw.
MULGRAVE	Mili	Marsh.
MU NGGAVA	Rennell	Sol.
MU NGIKI	Bellona	Sol.
MURUA	Woodlark	PNG
MUSGRAVE	Pingelap	Car.
MUSKILLO	Namu	Marsh.
MUSQUILLO	Ailinglapelap	Marsh.
NAIRSA	Rangiroa	TA
NAMO	Namu	Marsh.
NAMARIK	Namorik	Marsh.
NAMUKA	Nomuka	Tonga
NANOUKI NANOUTI	Nonouti	Kir.
NARCISO	Tatakoto	TA
NARIK	Knox	Marsh.
NATLOP	Valua	Van.
NAVIGATORS	Samoa	Samoa
NAWODO	Nauru	
NDENI	Ndende	Sol.
NDUKE	Kolombangara	Sol.
NEDERLANDSCH	Nui	Tuv.
NEOW	Gau	Fiji
NEU MECKLENBURG	New Ireland	PNG
NEU POMMERN	New Britain	PNG
NEVILLE	Tobi	Car.
NEW HANOVER	Lavongai	PNG
NEW NANTUCKET	Phoenix	PI
NEW YEAR	Mejit	Marsh.
NEW YORK	Eiao	Marq.
NEW YORK	Washington	LI
NEXSEN	Hatutu	Marq.
NGARYK	Ngatik	Car.
NGGELA	Florida	Sol.
NHOW	Gau	Fiji
NITENDI	Ndende	Sol.
NIAU	Greig	TA
NIAUR	Angaur	Car.
NIUA	Aniwa	Van.
NIEUE	Niue	
NIGURIA	Nuguria	PNG
NIHERA	Nihiru	TA
NINE	Kilinailau	PNG
NINGONINGO	Nengonengo	TA
NISSAN	Green	PNG
NIUAFU	Niuafo'ou	Tonga
NIUATABUTABU	Niuatoputapu	Tonga
NOOAHEEVAH	Nukuhiva	Marq.
NORBARBAR	Ureparapara	Van.
NORTH	Hiu	Van.
NORTH	San Alessandro	VI
NOUGOUORE	Nukuoro	Car.
NOUVELLE CYTHERE	Tahiti	SI
NUKULAILAI	Nukulaelae	Tuv.
NUKUNONU	Nukunonu	
NUKUNAU	Nikunau	Kir.
NURAKITA	Niulakita	Tuv.
NURORUTU	Maria	AI
NUSI	Tench	PNG
NUTLOFF	Valua	Van.
OAHTOOHA	Upolu	Samoa
OAITUPU	Vaitupu	Tuv.
OBA	Aoba	Van.
OBALAUO	Ovalau	Fiji
OBELISK	Elina	Sol.
OGASAWARA	Bonin	BI
OHETEROAH	Rurutu	AI
OJALAVA	Upolu	Samoa
OLOSENGA	Swain	Samoa
OLOSINGA	Olosenga	Samoa (Manua Group)
OMBA	Aoba	Van.
ONALAU	Ovalau	Fiji
ONAVERO ONEEHEOW	Nauru	
ONEEOW	Niihau	Haw.
ONUTU	Onotoa	Kir.
OPARO	Rapa	AI
OPOLOO	Upolu	Samoa
OPOUN	Manua	Samoa
ORAISON	Manua-Tele Tanga	PNG
ORISEGA OROSENGA	Olosenga	Samoa
ORONA	Hull	PI
OSNABURG	Mururoa	TA
OSNABURGH	Mehetia	SI
OSTEN-SAKEN	Katiu	TA
OTAHA	Tahaa	SI
OTAHEITE	Tahiti	SI
OTDIA	Wotje	Marsh.
OTOOHO	Tepoto	TA
OUAHOUKA	Uahuka	Marq.
OUMAITIA	Makatea	TA
OVOLAU	Ovalau	Fiji
O WAHI OWHYHEE OWHYHI	Hawaii	Haw.
OWA RAFA	Santa Ana	Sol.
OWA RAHA	Santa Ana	Sol.
OWA RIKI	Santa Catalina	Sol.
PAANOPA	Banaba	Kir.
PAGON	Pagan	MI
PALAOS	Palau	Car.
PALLISER ISLANDS	group: Apataki Arutua Kaukura Toau	TA
PARRY	Eniwetok	Marsh.
PARRY	Mauke	CI
PASCUA	Easter	
PATERSON	Namu	Marsh.
PAUM	Paama	Van.
PAUMOTU	Tuamotu	TA
PEACOCK	Ahe	TA
PEDDER	Arno	Marsh.
PEGUENEMA	Pakin	Car.
PELEW	Palau	Car.
PENTECOTE	Pentecost	Van.
PEROAT	Beru	Kir.
PERU	Beru	Kir.
PESCADORE	Rongelap	Marsh.
PHILIP	Makemo	TA
PHILIP	Sorol	Car.
PHILLIP	Makemo	TA
PHOEBE	Phoenix	PI
PIC DE LA BOUDEUSE	Mehetia	SI
PITT	Little Makin	Kir.
PITT	Vanikoro	Sol.

OBSOLETE/ALTERNATIVE NAMES with Current Equivalents

PLATTE	Manono	Samoa
PLEASANT	Nauru	
POLLARD IS. } POLLARD ROCK }	Gardner Pinnacles	Haw.
POLOAT	Puluwat	Car.
POMOTU	Tuamotu	TA
POREEMO	Apolima	Samoa
PORTLAND	Tingwon	PNG
POULOUSOUK	Pulusuk	Car.
PREDPRIATIE	Fakahina	TA
PRINCE DE JOINVILLE	Taenga	TA
PRINCE GOLENITSCHEV-KUTUZOV-SMOLENSKI	Makemo	TA
PRINCE OF WALES	Manihi	TA
PRINCESS	Lib	Marsh.
PRINCESSA	Jabwot	Marsh.
PRINCE VOLKHONSKI	Takume	TA
PRINCE WILLIAM HENRY	Nengonengo	TA
PROBY	Niuafo'ou	Tonga
PROSPECT	Washington	LI
PROVIDENCE	Ujelang	Marsh.
PUKARARO } PURARUNGA }	Vairaatea	TA
PUYNIPET	Ponape	Car.
PYLSTAART	Ata	Tonga
QUATRE FACARDINS	Vahitahi	TA
QUEEN CHARLOTTE	Nukutavake	TA
QUIROS	Swain	Samoa
RADOKALA	Rongerik	Marsh.
RAEVSKI	Eliza } Tepoto }	TA
RAGA	Pentecost	Van.
RAIROA	Rangiroa	TA
RAMBI	Rabi	Fiji
RANAI	Lanai	Haw.
RANBE	Rabi	Fiji
RAPA-ITI	Rapa	AI
RAPA-NUI	Easter	
RATAK	Radak	Marsh.
RECHERCHE	Vanikoro	Sol.
RECREATION	Makatea	TA
REEF	Rowa	Van.
REID	Tuanake	TA
REINE LOUISE	Pinaki	TA
REIRSON	Rakahanga	CI
RESOLUTION	Tauere	TA
RIMATERA	Rimatara	AI
RIMSKI-KORSAKOFF	Rongerik	Marsh.
RIOU	Uahuka	Marq.
ROAHOUGA	Uahuka	Marq.
ROBERTS	Eiao	Marq.
ROCKY	Niulakita	Tuv.
ROGER SIMPSON	Abemama	Kir.
ROMANZOFF	Wotje	Marsh.
ROMANZOFF	Tikei	TA
ROOAHOOGA	Uahuka	Marq.
ROOK(E)	Umboi	PNG
ROSS	Namu	Marsh.
ROTCH	Tamana	Kir.
ROXBURGH	Rarotonga	CI
RUK	Truk	Car.
RUMANZOFF	Tikei	TA
SACKEN	Katiu	TA
SADDLE	Valua	Van.
ST. ANDREW	Sonsorol	Car.
ST. BARTHOLOMEW	Malo	Van.
ST. CLAIRE	Merig	Van.
ST. JANS } ST. JOHN }	Emirau	PNG
ST. MATTHIAS	Mussau	PNG
ST. PAUL	Hereheretue	TA
SAKEN	Katiu	TA
SALT	Lo	Van.
SAN AGUSTIN	Nanumea	Tuv.
SAN AGUSTINO	Oroluk	Car.
SAN CHRISTOVAL	San Cristobal	Sol.
SAN CRISTOBAL	Mehetia	SI
SAN DIONISIO	San Augustino	VI
SANDS	Maria	AI
SANDWICH	Efate	Van.
SANDWICH	Hawaiian Is.	Haw.
SAN JUAN	Hikueru	TA
SAN JULIAN	Tahanea	TA
SAN MARCOS	Mera Lava	Van.
SAN MIGUEL	Vairaatea	TA
SAN NARCISO	Tatakoto	TA
SAN PABLO	Hereheretue	TA
SAN PABLO	Pukapuka	TA
SAN PEDRO	Mohotani	Marq.
SAN QUINTIN	Haraiki	TA
SAN SIMON Y JUDAS	Tauere	TA
SANSORAL	Sonsorol	Car.
SANTA CRISTINA	Tahuata	Marq.
SANTA CRUZ	Ndende	Sol.
SANTA GERTRUDIS	Isabela	Gal.
SANTA MAGDALENA	Fatuhiva	Marq.
SANTA MARIA	Floreana	Gal.
SANTA MARIA	Gaua	Van.
SANTA POLONIA	Vairaatea	TA
SANTA ROSA	Raivavae	AI
SANTA YSABEL	Santa Isabel	Sol.
SANTIAGO	San Salvador	Gal.
SANTO	Espiritu Santo	Van.
SARIGUAN	Sarigan	MI
SARPAN	Rota	MI
SATOUWAN	Satawan	Car.
SAVAGE	Niue	
SCHADELYK	Takapoto	TA
SCHANTZ	Wotho	Marsh.
SCILLY	Fenua-ura	SI
SEAGULL	Raevski	TA
SENIAVINE	Ponape	Car.
SEPPER	Niutao	Tuv.
SERLE	Pukarua	TA
SETUAHAL	Satawal	Car.
SEU	Hiu	Van.
SEYPAN	Saipan	MI
SHANZ	Wotho	Marsh
SIEW	Hiu	Van.
SIR CHARLES HARDY	Green	PNG
SIR CHARLES MIDDLETON	Lomaloma	Fiji
SIR CHARLES SAUNDERS	Maiao	SI
SIR HENRY MARTIN	Nukuhiva	Marq.
SMALL MALAITA	Maramsike	Sol.
SMITH	Butaritari	Kir.
SMYTH	Taongi	Marsh.
SOLA	Ata	Tonga
SOLITARIA	Niulakita }	Tuv.
SONDERGRONT	Takapoto } Takaroa	TA
SOOUGHE	Pulusuk	Car.
SOPHIA	Niulakita	Tuv.
SOUWOROFF	Suwarrow	CI

OBSOLETE/ALTERNATIVE NAMES with Current Equivalents

SOUWOROFF	Taka	Marsh.
SPENCER KEYS	Ngulu	Car.
SPIRIDOFF	Takapoto	TA
SQUALLY	Emirau	PNG
STAR PEAK	Me a Lava	Van.
STARVE	Sta buck	LI
STAVERS	Vostok	LI
STEEP-TO	Jemo	Marsh.
STEWART	Sikaiana	Sol.
STORM	Emirau	PNG
STRONG	Kusaie	Car.
SUGAR-LOAF	Mota	Van.
SUK	Pulusuk	Car.
SULPHUR	Volcano	VI
SUNDAY	Raoul	KI
SURRY	Hereheretue	TA
SUVAROV	Suwarrow	CI
SWALLOW	Canton	PI
SWALLOW	Reef	Sol.
SYDENHAM	Nonouti	Kir.
TAAPOTO	Takapoto	TA
TAAROA	Takaroa	TA
TABUTHA	Tuvuca	Fiji
TACUME	Takume	TA
TAGAI	Taka	Marsh.
TAHAURAWEE	Kahoolawe	Haw.
TAHOORA	Kaula	Haw.
TAHOOROWA	Kahoolawe	Haw.
TAKOTO	Tatakoto	TA
TANA	Tanna	Van.
TANNOA	Tangoa	Van.
TAPAMANOA	Maiao	SI
TAPUTEOUEA	Tabiteuea	Kir.
TARITARI	Butaritari	Kir.
TCHITCHAGOFF	Tahanea	TA
TEAPY	Easter	
TEBUT	Jabwot	Marsh.
TEHUATA	Rekareka	TA
TEMO	Jemo	Marsh.
TETHUROA }		
TETUAROA }	Tetiaroa	SI
THORNTON	Caroline	LI
THREE HILLS	Emae	Van.
THRUM CAP	Akiaki	TA
TICUMBIA	Cikobia	Fiji
TIKA	Tiga	NC
TIMOE	Temoe	TA
TIN CAN	Niuafo'ou	Tonga
TINDAL & WATTS	Ailuk	Marsh.
TIOKEA	Takaroa	TA
TODOS SANTOS	Anaa	TA
TONGAREVA	Penrhyn	CI
TOOTOOILAH	Tutuila	Samoa
TORGA	Toga	Van.
TOUCHING	Butaritari	Kir.
TOWER	Genovesa	Gal.
TRACY	Vaitapu	Tuv.
TRAITORS	Tafahi	Tonga
TRAVERSEY	Aur	Marsh.
TREVENEN	Uapou	Marq.
TROMELIN	Fais	Car.
TSCHITSCHAGOFF	Erikub	Marsh.
TUBAI	Tupai	SI
TUBUAI MANU	Maiao	SI
TUCKER	Satawal	Car.
TUCOPIA	Tikopia	Sol.
TUGA	Tegua	Van.
TUPUAEMANU	Maiao	SI
TURTLE	Vatoa	Fiji
TUSCAN	Hikueru	TA

TWO BROTHERS	Motuiti	Marq.
TWO GROUPS	Marokau }	
	Ravahere }	TA
TWO HILLS	Mataso	Van.
UALAN	Kusaie	Car.
UDIA-MILAI	Bikini	Marsh.
UDIRICK	Utirik	Marsh.
UEA	Uvea	NC
UEA	Wallis	W & F
UGI	Uki	Sol.
UJILONG	Ujelang	Marsh.
ULIATEA	Raiatea	SI
ULIE	Woleai	Car.
ULIETEA	Raiatea	SI
UNION	Tokelau	
URACAS	Farallon de	
	Pajaros	MI
UVEA	Ouvea	NC
UVEA	Wallis	W & F
VAGHENA	Wagina	
VALIENTES	Ngatik	Car.
VANIKOLO	Vanikoro	Sol.
VAN SHIRNDING	Cikobia	Fiji
VANUA-VALAVO	Vanuabalavu	Fiji
VATE	Efate	Van.
VATIU	Atiu	CI
VATU-RERA	Vatuvara	Fiji
VATU RHANDI	Vatganai	Van.
VAVITAO	Raivavae	AI
VERKWIKKING	Makatea	TA
VERRADERS	Tafahi	Tonga
VINCENNES	Kauehi	TA
VITI	Fiji	Fiji
VLIEGHEN	Rangiroa	TA
WAIHU	Easter	
WARREN HASTINGS	Meru	Car.
WASHINGTON	Uahuka }	
	Uapou }	Marq.
WATEEOO	Atiu	CI
WATERLANDT	Ahe	
	Manihi	TA
WELLINGTON	Mokil	Car.
WENOOAETE	Takutea	CI
WEST DANGER	Eniwetok	Marsh.
WHITSUN	Pentecost	Van.
WHITSUN }		
WHITSUNDAY }	Pinaki	TA
WHYTOOTACKEE	Aitutake	CI
WILLIAM THE FOURTH	Ant	Car.
WILSON	Ifaluk	Car.
WILSON	Manihi	TA
WOAHOO	Oahu	Haw.
WOLEA	Woleai	Car.
WOLKONSKY	Takume	TA
WOODLE	Kuria	Kir.
WORTH	Howland	PI
WOTTHO	Wotho	Marsh.
WRIGHT'S LAGOON	Maria	TA
WYTOOHEE	Napuka	TA
YERMOELOFF	Taenga	TA
YSABEL	Santa Isabel	Sol.
ZARPANE	Rota	MI
ZEALANDIA ROCKS	Farallon de	
	Torres	MI
ZONDERGRONDT	Takaroa }	TA
	Takapoto }	

CURRENT NAMES with Obsolete / Alternative Equivalents

ABAIANG	Apaiang	Kir.
	Apia	
	Charlotte	
	Matthew	
ABEMAMA	Apamama	Kir.
	Roger Simpson	
ACTAEON	Cuatro Coronados	TA
	Four Crowns	
AGRIHAN	Agrigan	MI
	Grigan	
AGUIJAN		MI
AHE	Dagenraad	TA
	Peacock	
	Waterlandt	
AHUNUI	Byam Martin	TA
AILINGINAE		Marsh.
AILINGLAPALAP	Ailinglabelab	Marsh.
	Lambert	
	Musquillo	
AILUK	Krusenstern	Marsh.
	Tindal & Watts	
AITUTAKI	Whytootakee	CI
AKIAKI	Lanciers	TA
	Thrum Cap	
ALAMAGAN	Alamaguan	MI
ALOFI		W & F
AMANU	Animas	TA
	Moller	
AMBRYM	Ambrim	Van.
ANAA	Chain	TA
	Todos Santos	
ANATAHAN	Anatajan	MI
	Anataxan	
ANATOM	Aneiteum	Van.
	Annatom	
ANGAUR	Niaur	Car.
ANIWA	Immer	Van.
	Niua	
ANT	Andena	Car.
	Fraser	
	William the Fourth	
ANUANURARO	Duke of Gloucester	TA
ANUANURUNGA		
ANUTA	Cherry	Sol.
AOBA	Lepers	Van.
	Oba	
	Omba	
APATAKI	Avondstond	TA
	Hagemeister	
APOLIMA	Aborima	Samoa
	Poreemo	
ARANUKA	Henderville	Kir.
	Hopper	
ARATIKA	Carlshoff	TA
	Karlshoff	
ARNO	Arhno	Marsh.
	Daniel	
	Pedder	
ARORAE	Arore	Kir.
	Hurd	
ARUTUA	Meerder Zorg	TA
ASUNCION	Assumption	MI
ATA	Pylstaart	Tonga
	Sola	
ATAFU	Duke of York	Tok.
ATIU	Vatiu	CI
	Wateeoo	
AUR	Aurh	Marsh.
	Ibbetson	
	Traversey	
BABELTHUAP		Car
BAKER	New Nantucket	PI
	Phoebe	
BALTRA		Gal.
BANABA	Ocean	Kir.
	Paanopa	
BANKS		Van.
BAU	Ambow	Fiji
	Mbau	
BELEP		NC
BELLONA	Mu Ngiki	Sol.
BEQA	Benga	Fiji
	Mbenga	
BERU	Eliza	Kir.
	Francis	
	Maria	
	Peroat	
	Peru	
BIKAR	Bigar	Marsh.
	Dawson	
BIKINI	Eschscholtz	Marsh.
	Udia-Milai	
BIRNIE		PI
BONIN	Arzobispo	BI
	Ogasawara	
BORABORA	Bolabola	SI
BOUGAINVILLE		PNG
BUKA	Bouka	PNG
BUNINGA		Van.
BUTARITARI	Allen	Kir.
	Buen Viaje	
	Clarke	
	Gillespie	
	Smith	
	Taritari	
	Touching	
CANTON	Mary	PI
	Mary Balcout	
	Swallow	
CAROLINE		Car.
CAROLINE	Clark	LI
	Hirst	
	Independence	
	Thornton	
CHESTERFIELD		NC
CHOISEUL	Lauru	Sol.
CHRISTMAS		LI
CICIA	Chichia	Fiji
CIKOBIA	Chicobea	Fiji
	Farewell	
	Ticumbia	
	Van Shirnding	
CLIPPERTON		
COCOS		Costa Rica
COOK	Hervey	CI
CULPEPPER		Gal.
DUFF		Sol.
EASTER	Pascua	
	Rapa-Nui	
	Teapy	
	Waihu	
EAST FAYU	Lutke	Car.
EAURIPIK	Eaurypyg	Car.

CURRENT NAMES with Obsolete/Alternative Equivalents

EBON	Boston	Marsh.
	Covell	
	Fourteen	
	Linnez	
EFATE	Sandwich	Van.
	Vate	
EIAO	Freemantle	Marq.
	Hiau	
	Knox	
	Masse	
	New York	
	Roberts	
ELATO		Car.
ELINA	Obelisk	Sol.
EMAE	Mae	Van.
	Mai	
	Three Hills	
EMAU	Hinchinbrook	Van.
	Mau	
EMIRAU	Squally	PNG
	Storm	
ENDERBURY	Enderby	PI
ENEWETAK	Arthur	Marsh.
	Brown	
	East Danger	
	Parry	
	West Danger	
EPI	Api	Van.
	Tasiko	
ERADAKA	Hat	Van.
ERIKUB	Bishop Junction	Marsh.
	Chatham	
	Egerup	
	Tschitschagoff	
EROMANGO	Erromanga	Van.
ESPANOLA	Hood	Gal.
ESPIRITU SANTO	Marina	Van.
	Santo	
ETAL	Mortlock	Car.
EUA	Eooa	Tonga
	Middleburgh	
EWOSE		Van.
FAAITE	Admiral Chichagov	TA
	Faite	
	Miloradovich	
FAIS	Tromelin	Car.
FAKAHINA	Ebrill	TA
	Fangahina	
	Predpriatie	
FAKAOFU	Bowditch	Tok.
FAKARAVA	Count Wittgenstein	TA
	Faarava	
FANGATAU	Angatau	TA
	Arakcheef	
	Count Arakcheev	
	Fagatau	
FANGATAUFA	Cockburn	TA
	Grimwood	
FARALLON DE MEDINILLA	Bird	MI
FARALLON DE PAJAROS	Uracas	MI
FARALLON DE TORRES	Zealandia Rocks	MI
FARAULEP	Farroilep	Car.
	Fattoilap	
	Foraulep	

	Gardner	
FATAKA	Mitre	Sol.
FATUHIVA	Magdalena	Marq.
	Santa Magdalena	
FATUHUKU	Fetuku	Marq.
	Hood	
FENI	Anir	PNG
	St Jans	
	St John	
FENUA-URA	Manuae	SI
	Scilly	
FERNANDINA	Narborough	Gal.
FIJI	Feejee	Fiji
FLINT	Viti	LI
FLOREANA	Charles	Gal.
	Santa Maria	
FLORIDA	Flora	Sol.
	Gela	
	Nggela	
FONUAFO'OU	Falcon	Tonga
FONUALEI	Amargura	Tonga
	Fanoualie	
FRENCH FRIGATE SHOAL	Basse des Fregates Francaises	Haw.
FUNAFUTI	Ellice	Tuv.
FUTUNA	Erronan	Van.
	Fotuna	
FUTUNA	Hoorn	W & F
	Horn	
GAFERUT		Car.
GALAPAGOS	Gallipagoes	Gal.
GARDNER	Kemin	Pi
GARDNER PINNACLES	Man-of-War Rock	Haw.
	Pollard Is.	
	Pollard Rock	
GAU	Neow	Fiji
	Nhow	
GAUA	Gow	Van.
	Lacona	
	Lakoon	
	Santa Maria	
GENOVESA	Tower	Gal.
GILBERT	Kingsmill (Sthn Gilberts)	Kir.
GREEN	Groene	PNG
	Nissan	
	Sir Charles Hardy	
GUADALCANAL		Sol.
GUAM	Guahan	MI
	Guajan	
GUGUAN		MI
HAAPAI	Habai	Tonga
HALL		Car.
HAO	Bow	TA
	Conversion de San Pablo	
	Harpe	
HARAIKI	Croker	TA
	San Quintin	
HATUTU	Chanal	Marq.
	Fatuuhu	
	Hancock	
	Langdon	
	Nexsen	

CURRENT NAMES with Obsolete/Alternative Equivalents

HAWAII	O Wahi	Haw.
	Owhyhee	
	Owhyhi	
HAWAIIAN ISLANDS	Sandwich	Haw.
HENDERSON	Elizabeth	Pitcairn
HEREHERETUE	Britomart	TA
	St Paul	
	San Pablo	
	Surry	
HERVEY	Manuae	CI
	Te Au-o-Tu	
HIKUERU	Melville	TA
	San Juan	
	Tuscan	
HITI	Clute	TA
	Eliza	
HIU	North	Van.
	Seu	
	Siew	
HIVAOA	Dominica	Marq.
	Dominique	
HOWLAND	Holland	PI
	Worth	
HUAHINE		SI
HULL	Orona	PI
HUNTER		NC
HUON		NC
IFALUK	Ifalik	Car.
	Wilson	
ISLE OF PINES	Ile des Pins	NC
	Kunie	
ISABELA	Albermarle	Gal.
	Santa Gertrudis	
JABWAT	Jabwot	Marsh.
	Princessa	
	Tebut	
JALUIT	Bonham	Marsh.
	Coquille	
	Elizabeth	
JARVIS	Bunker	LI
	Brooke	
JEMO	Steep-to	Marsh.
	Temo	
JOHNSTON		near Haw.
JUAN FERNANDEZ		JF
KABARA	Appallo	Fiji
KADAVU	Cantab	Fiji
	Kandavu	
	Kantavu	
KAHOOLAWE	Kadoolawee	Haw
	Kahulaui	
	Tahaurawe	
	Tahoorowa	
KAPINGAMARANGI	Constantin	Car.
	Greenwich	
KATIU	Gen. Osten-Saken	TA
	Sacken	
	Saken	
KAUAI	Atooi	Haw.
KAUEHI	Cavahi	TA
	Kawahe	
	Vincennes	
KAUKURA	Aura	TA
	Auura	
KAULA	Tahoora	Haw.
KERMADEC		KI
KILI	Hunter	Marsh.
KILINAILAU	Carteret	PNG
	Nine	
KINGMAN	Alice Thorndike	LI
KIOA		Fiji
KNOX	Narik	Marsh.
KOLOMBANGARA	Nduke	Sol.
KORO	Goro	Fiji
KURIA	Woodle	Kir.
KOSRAE	Strong	Car.
	Ualan	
KWAJALEIN	Catherine	Marsh.
	Kwadelen	
LAE	Brown	Marsh.
LAKEBA		Fiji
LAMEN		Van.
LAMENU		Van.
LAMOTREK		Car.
LANAI	Ranai	Haw.
LATE	Latte	Tonga
	Lette	
LAU		Fiji
LAVONGAI	New Hanover	PNG
LAYSAN	Moller	Haw.
LELEPA		Van.
LIB	Princess	Marsh.
LIFOU	Chabrol	NC
	Lifu	
LIHIR	Gerrit de Nijs	PNG
	Gerrit Denys	
LIKIEP	Count Heiden	Marsh.
	Legiep	
LINE		LI
LITTLE MAKIN	Makin	Kir.
	Pitt	
LISIANSKY		Haw.
LO	Salt	Van.
LOMALOMA	Lomo-Lomo	Fiji
	Sir Charles Middleton	
LORD HOWE		Aust.
LOPEVI		Van.
LOSOP	D'Urville	Car.
	Louasappe	
LOYALTY	Loyaute	NC
LUKUNOR	Lougounor	Car.
	Lugunor	
	Mortlock	
McKEAN	Drummond	PI
MAEWO	Aurora	Van.
	Maiwo	
MAIANA	Hall	Kir.
MAIAO	Mauiti	SI
	Sir Charles Saunders	
	Tapamanoa	
	Tubuai Manu	
	Tupuaemanu	
MAJURO	Arrowsmith	Marsh.
	Meduro	
MAKATEA	Aurora	TA
	Maataah	
	Maeteea	
	Mataa	
	Matea	
	Mathea	
	Matia	
	Oumaitia	

CURRENT NAMES with Obsolete/Alternative Equivalents

	Recreation	
	Verkwikking	
MAKEMO	Koutousoff	TA
	Macquemo	
	Philip	
	Phillip	
	Prince Golenitschev-Kutuzov-Smolenski	
MAKOGAI	Mokogai	Fiji
	Mokungai	
MAKURA		Van.
MALAITA	Carteret	Sol.
	Mala	
	Malanta	
	Malayette	
MALDEN	Independence	LI
MALAKULA	Mallicollo	Van.
MALO	Bartholomew	Van.
	St Bartholomew	
MALOELAP	Araktcheef	Marsh.
	Bass Reef-tied	
	Calvert	
	Kaven	
	Maloelab	
MALOLO		Fiji
MANGAIA	Mangea	Ci
MANGAREVA	Gambier	TA
MANIHI	Dagenraad	TA
	Prince of Wales	
	Waterlandt	
	Wilson	
MANIHIKI	Great Ganges	CI
	Humphrey	
MANONO	Platte	Samoa
MANRA	Sydney	PI
MANUA		
MANUA-TELE	Opoun	Samoa
MANUAE		CI
MANUHANGI	Cumberland	TA
	Duke of Cumberland	
MARAKEI	Maraki	Kir.
	Matthew	
MARAMSIKE	Small Malaita	Sol.
MARCHENA	Bindloe	Gal.
MARCUS		near Bl.
MARE	Britannia	NC
MARIA	Gardner	AI
	Hull	
	Nurorutu	
	Sands	
MARIA	Bertero	TA
	Moerenhout	
	Wright's Lagoon	
MARIANA	Ladrones	MI
MAROKAU	Two Groups	TA
MAROTIRI	Bass	AI
MARQUESAS		Marq.
MARSHALL		Marsh.
MARUTEA	Furneaux	TA
MARUTEA (Sth)	Lord Hood	TA
MAS-A-FUERA		JF
MAS-A-TIERRA		JF
MASKELYNE		Van.
MATAHIVA	Lazarev	TA
MATASO	Two Hills	Van.
MATTHEW		NC
MATUREI VAVAO	Melbourne	TA
MAUG		MI
MAUI	Mowee	Haw.
MAUKE	Mauti	CI
	Parry	
MAUPITI	Marua	SI
	Maura	
MEHETIA	Boudoir	SI
	Maitea	
	Osnaburg	
	Pic de la Boudeuse	
	San Cristobal	
MEJIT	Miadi	Marsh.
	New Year	
MERA LAVA	Maralaba	Van.
	Merlav	
	San Marcos	
	Star Peak	
MERIG	St Claire	Van.
MERIR	Warren Hastings	Car.
MIDWAY	Brooks	
MILI	Mille	Marsh.
	Mulgrave	
MITIARO	Mitiero	CI
MOHOTANI	Motane	Marq.
	San Pedro	
MOKIL	Duperrey	Car.
	Wellington	
MOLOKAI	Morotoi	Haw.
MOOREA	Aimeo	SI
	Duke of York	
	Eimeo	
MOPELIA	Lord Howe	SI
	Mopihaa	
MORANE	Barstow	TA
	Cadmus	
MORTLOCK		Car.
MOSO	Deception	Van.
MOTA	Amota	Van.
	Sugar-loaf	
MOTUITI	Blake	Marq.
	Franklin	
	Hergest	
	Two Brothers	
MOTU-OA	Lincoln	Marq.
MOTURIKI	Matoriki	Fiji
MOTUTUNGA	Adventure	TA
MUNIA	Hadow	Fiji
MURILO	Mourileu	Car.
MURUROA	Bishop of Osnaburg	TA
	Matilda's Rocks	
	Moruroa	
	Osnaburg	
MUSSAU	St Matthias	PNG
NAMA		Car.
NAMOLUK	Harvest	Car.
	Hashmy	
NAMONUITO	Anonima	Car.
	Onon	
NAMORIK	Baring	Marsh.
	Namarik	
NAMU	Margaretta	Marsh.
	Muskillo	
	Namo	
	Paterson	
	Ross	
NANUMANGA	Gran Cocal	Tuv.
	Hudson	
	Isla del Cocal	

CURRENT NAMES with Obsolete / Alternative Equivalents

Current name	Obsolete / Alternative	Location
NANUMEA	San Agustin	Tuv.
NAPUKA	Disappointment	TA
	Wytoohee	
NASSAU	Mitchell	CI
NAURU	Nawodo	
	Onavero	
	Pleasant	
NDAI	Gower	Sol.
	Inattendue	
NDENDE	Ndeni	Sol.
	Nitendi	
	Santa Cruz	
NECKER		Haw.
NENDO	see Ndende above	
NENGONENGO	Lostange	TA
	Ningoningo	
	Prince William Henry	
NEW BRITAIN	Neu Pommern	PNG
NEW CALEDONIA		NC
NEW GEORGIA		Sol.
NEW GUINEA		PNG
NEW IRELAND	Neu Mecklenburg	PNG
NGATIK	Ngaryk	Car.
	Valientes	
NGULU	Goulou	Car.
	Lamoliork	
	Lamuliur	
	Spencer Keys	
NGUNA	Montagu	Van.
NIHIRU	Nihera	TA
NIHOA	Bird	Haw.
NIIHAU	Oneeheow	Haw.
	Oneeow	
NIKUNAU	Byron	Kir.
	Nukunau	
NIUAFO'OU	Consolacion	Tonga
	Goede Hope	
	Niuafu	
	Proby	
	Tin Can	
NIUATOPUTAPU	Boscawen	Tonga
	Cocos	
	Niuatabutabu	
NIUE	Nieue	
	Savage	
NIULAKITA	Independence	Tuv.
	Nurakita	
	Rocky	
	Solitaria	
	Sophia	
NIUTAO	Loper	Tuv.
	Lynx	
	Sepper	
NOMUKA	Annamooka	Tonga
	Namuka	
NOMOI	Mortlock	Car.
NOMWIN		Car.
NONOUTI	Nanouki	Kir.
	Nanouti	
	Sydenham	
NORFOLK		Aust.
NUGURIA	Abgarris	PNG
	Fead	
	Niguria	
NUI	Jesus	Tuv.
	Nederlandsch	
NUKUFETAU	De Peyster	Tuv.
NUKUHIVA	Adams	Marq.
	Baux	
	Federal	
	Franklin	
	Madison	
	Nooaheevah	
	Sir Henry Martin	
NUKULAELAE	Mitchell	Tuv.
	Nukulailai	
NUKUMANU		PNG
NUKUNONO	Duke of Clarence	Tok.
NUKUORO	Monteverde	Car.
	Nougoure	
NUKUTAVAKE	Leopold I	TA
	Queen Charlotte	
NUKUTIPIPI	Duke of Gloucester	TA
	Margaret	
OAHU	Woahoo	Haw.
OENO		Pitcairn
OFU		Samoa
OLIMARAO		Car.
OLSOENGA	Olosinga	Samoa
	Orisega	
ONON	Anonima	Car.
	Namonuito	
ONOTOA	Clerk	Kir.
	Eliza	
	Lincoln	
	Onutu	
ONTONG JAVA	Lord Howe	Sol.
	Luaniua	
OROLUK	Bordelaise	Car.
	San Agustino	
OUVEA	Halgan	NC
	Uea	
	Uvea	
OVALAU	Bulloo	Fiji
	Obalauo	
	Onalau	
	Ovolau	
PAAMA	Paum	Van.
PAGAN	Pagon	MI
PAKIN	Peguenema	Car.
PALAU	Palaos	Car.
	Pelew	
PALMERSTON		CI
PALMYRA		LI
PARAOA	Duke of Gloucester	TA
	Gloucester	
PARECE VELA	Douglas Reef	Japan
PEARL & HERMES REEF		Haw.
PENRHYN	Tongareva	CI
PENTECOST	Arragh	Van.
	Pentecote	
	Raga	
	Whitsun	
PHOENIX		PI
PIKELOT	Coquille	Car.
PINAKI	Reine Louise	TA
	Whitsun	
	Whitsunday	
PINGELAP	MacAskill	Car.
	Musgrave	
PINTA	Abingdon	Gal.

CURRENT NAMES with Obsolete / Alternative Equivalents

Current name	Obsolete / Alternative	Location
PINZON	Duncan	Gal.
PITCAIRN		Pitcairn
PONAPE	Ascension	Car.
	Puynipet	
	Seniavine	
PUKAPUKA	Danger	CI
PUKAPUKA	Dog	TA
	Honden	
	San Pablo	
PUKARUA	Apoucaroua	TA
	Serle	
PULO ANNA		Car.
PULUSUK	Bartolome	Car.
	Ibargoitia	
	Poulousouk	
	Sooughe	
	Suk	
PULUWAT	Enderby	Car.
	Kata	
	Poloat	
RABI	Gillet	Fiji
	Rambi	
	Ranbe	
RABIDA	Jervis	Gal.
RADAK	Ratak	Marsh.
RAEVSKI	Hiti	TA
	Tepoto	
	Tuanake	
RAIATEA	Uliatea	SI
	Ulietea	
RAIVAVAE	High	AI
	Santa Rosa	
	Vavitao	
RAKAHANGA	Grand Duke Alexander	CI
	Little Ganges	
	Reirson	
RALIK		Marsh.
RANGIROA	Dean	TA
	Goede Verwaghting	
	Nairsa	
	Rairoa	
	Vlieghen	
RAOUL	Sunday	KI
RAPA	Oparo	AI
	Rapa-iti	
RARAKA	Ireland	TA
RAROIA	Barclay de Tolly	TA
RAROTONGA	Armstrong	CI
	Roxburgh	
RAVAHERE	Dawahaidy	TA
	Two Groups	
REAO	Clermont de Tonnere	TA
	Minerva	
REEF	Matema	Sol.
	Swallow	
REITORU	Bird	TA
REKAREKA	Good Hope	TA
	Tehuata	
RENNELL	Mu Nggava	Sol.
RIMATARA	Rimatera	AI
RONGELAP	Bigini	Marsh.
	Kongelab	
	Pescadore	
RONGERIK	Radokala	Marsh.
	Rimski-Korsakoff	
ROSE	Kordiukoff	Samoa

Current name	Obsolete / Alternative	Location
	Middleton	
ROTA	Sarpan	MI
	Zarpan	
ROTUMA	Grenville	Fiji
ROWA	Reef	Van.
RURUTU	Oheteroah	AI
RUSSELL		Sol.
RYUKYU	Loo-choo	RI
	Lu-chu	
SAIPAN	Seypan	MI
SALA-Y-GOMEZ		Chile
SAMOA	Navigators	Samoa
SAN ALESSANDRO	North	VI
SAN AMBROSIO		Chile
SAN AUGUSTINO	San Dionisio	VI
SAN CRISTOBAL	Chatham	Gal.
SAN CRISTOBAL	Arossi	Sol.
	Makira	
	San Christoval	
SAN FELIX		Chile
SAN JORGE	Moumolu-Naunitu	Sol.
SAN SALVADOR	James	Gal.
	Santiago	
SANTA ANA	Owa Rafa	Sol.
	Owa Raha	
SANTA CATALINA	Owa Riki	Sol.
SANTA CRUZ	Chaves	Gal.
	Indefatigable	
SANTA FE	Barrington	Gal.
SANTA ISABEL	Santa Ysabel	Sol.
	Ysabel	
SARIGAN	Sariguan	MI
SATAWAL	Setuahal	Car.
	Tucker	
SATAWAN	Satouwan	Car.
SAVAII	Chatham	Samoa
SEYMOUR		Gal.
SHEPHERD		Van.
SHORTLAND		Sol.
SIKAIANA	Stewart	Sol.
SIMBO	Eddystone	Sol.
	Mandeghughusu	
SOCIETY		Si
SONSOROL	St Andrew	Car.
	Sansoral	
SOROL	Philip	Car.
SOTOAN	Mortlock	Car.
SOUTH MARUTEA	Lord Hood	TA
STARBUCK	Barren	LI
	Coral Queen	
	Hero	
	Low	
	Starve	
SURPRISE		NC
SUWARROW	Souworoff	CI
	Suvarov	
SWAIN	Gente Hermosa	Samoa
	Olosenga	
	Quiros	
TABAR	Gardner	PNG
TABITEUEA	Bishop	GI
	Drummond	
	Taputeouea	
TAENGA	Cainga	TA
	Holt	
	Lieutenant-General Yermalov	

CURRENT NAMES with Obsolete/Alternative Equivalents

Current name	Obsolete/Alternative	Location
	Prince de Joinville Yermoeloff	
TAFAHI	Keppel	Tonga
	Traitors	
	Verraders	
TAHAA	Otaha	SI
TAHANEA	Chichagov	TA
	San Julian	
	Tchitchagoff	
TAHITI	Amat	SI
	King George III	
	Nouvelle Cythere	
	Otahiti	
TAHUATA	Christiana	Marq.
	Santa Cristina	
TAIARO	King	TA
TAKA	Souworoff	Marsh.
	Tagai	
TAKAPOTO	King George	TA
	Schadelijk	
	Sondergrondt	
	Spiridoff	
	Taapoto	
	Zondergrondt	
TAKAROA	King George	TA
	Sondergrondt	
	Taaroa	
	Tiokea	
	Zondergrondt	
TAKUME	Prince Volkhonski	TA
	Tacume	
	Wolkonsky	
TAKUTEA	Wenoaette	CI
TAMANA	Rotch	Kir.
TANGOA	Anthony Caen	PNG
	Anthony Kaan	
	Oraison	
TANGOA	Tannoa	Van.
TANNA	Tana	Van.
TAONGI	Gaspar Rico	Marsh.
	Smyth	
TARAWA	Cook	Kir.
	Knox	
TATAKOTO	Augier	TA
	Clarke	
	Daugier	
	David Clark	
	Narciso	
	San Narciso	
	Takoto	
TAUERE	Resolution	TA
	San Simon y Judas	
TAUMAKO	Disappointment	Sol.
TAUU	Marque(e)n	PNG
	Mortlock	
TE AU-O-TU		CI
TEGUA	Middle	Van.
	Tuga	
TEKOKOTO	Doubtful	TA
	Martires	
TEMATANGI	Bligh's Lagoon	TA
	Lagoon	
TEMOE	Crescent	TA
	Timoe	
TENARARO		TA
TENARUNGA	Minto	TA
TENCH	Nusi	PNG
TEPOTO	Disappointment	TA
	Otooho	
TEPOTO	Eliza	TA
	Raevski	
TETIAROA	Tethuroa	SI
	Tetuaroa	
TIGA	Boucher	NC
	Tika	
TIKEHAU	Krusenstern	TA
TIKEI	Bedrieglyke	TA
	Romanzoff	
	Rumanzoff	
TIKOPIA	Barwell	Sol.
	Tucopia	
TINGWON	Portland	PNG
TINIAN	Buena Vista	MI
TOAU	Count Wittgenstein	TA
	Elizabeth	
TOBI	Lord North	Car.
	Neville	
TOGA	Buga Buga	Van.
	Buka	
	Torga	
TOKELAU	Union	Tok.
TONGA	Friendly	Tonga
TONGATAPU	Amsterdam	Tonga
TORRES		Van.
TORTUGA	Brattle	Gal.
TRUK	Hogoleu	Car.
	Ruk	
TUAMOTU	Dangerous	TA
	Paumotu	
	Pomotu	
TUANAKE	Reid	TA
TUPAI	Motu-iti	SI
	Tubai	
TUREIA	Carysfort	TA
TUTUILA	Masuna	Samoa
	Tootooilah	
TUVALU	Ellice	Tuv.
TUVUCA	Tabutha	Fiji
UAHUKA	**Massachusetts**	**Marq.**
	Ouahouka	
	Riou	
	Roahouga	
	Rooahooga	
	Washington	
UAPOU	**Adams**	**Marq.**
	Jefferson	
	Marchand	
	Trevenen	
	Washington	
UJAE	**Lydia**	Marsh.
UJELANG	**Arrecifes**	Marsh.
	Casbobas	
	Casobos	
	Providence	
	Ujilong	
UKI	**Ugi**	**Sol.**
ULAWA	**Contrariete**	**Sol.**
ULITHI	**Mackenzie**	**Car.**
UMBOI	**Rook(e)**	**PNG**
UPOLU	**Oahtooha**	**Samoa**
	Ojalava	
	Opoloo	
UREPARAPARA	**Bligh**	Van.
	Norbarbar	
UTIRIK	**Button**	Marsh.
	Kutusoff	
	Udirick	
UTUPUA	**Edgecumbe**	**Sol.**
VAHANGA	**Bedford**	**TA**

CURRENT NAMES with Obsolete/Alternative Equivalents

Current name	Obsolete/Alternative	
VAHITAHI	Lagoon	TA
	Quatre Facardins	
VAIRAATEA	Egmont	TA
	Industriel	
	Lord Egmont	
	Pukararo	
	Pukarunga	
	San Miguel	
	Santa Polonia	
VAITUPU	Oaitupu	Tuv.
	Tracy	
VALUA	Mota Lava	Van.
	Mottlap	
	Natlop	
	Nutloff	
	Saddle	
VANAVANA	Barrow	TA
VANIKORO	Mannicolo	Sol.
	Pitt	
	Recherche	
	Vanikolo	
VANUABALAVU	Vanua-Valavo	Fiji
VANUA LAVA		Van.
VATGANAI	Vatu Rhandi	Van.
VATOA	Turtle	Fiji
VATUVARA	Batou-Bara	Fiji
	Vatu-rera	
VAVAU	Lord Howe	Tonga
	Martin de Mayorga	
VIWA	Biva	Fiji
VOLCANO	Sulphur	VI
VOSTOK	Anne	LI
	Stavers	
WAKE	Halcyon	
WALLIS	Uea	W&F
	Uvea	
WASHINGTON	Prospect	LI
	New York	
WENMAN		Gal.
WEST FAYU		Car.
WOLEAI	Ulie	Car.
	Wolea	
WOODLARK	Murua	PNG
WOTHO	Schantz	Marsh.
	Shanz	
	Wottho	
WOTJE	Otdia	Marsh.
	Romanzoff	
WUVULU	Maty	PNG
YAP	Eap	Car.
YASAWA	Asava	Fiji

Index

OF ISLANDS AND CHIEF CENTRES

Abbreviations used in this index are:

Am.S	American Samoa	NMA	Northern Marianas
CI	Cook Islands	Norf	Norfolk Island
FrP	French Polynesia	Og	Ogasawara Islands
Gal	Galapagos	PNG	Papua New Guinea
GI	Gilbert Islands	Pit	Pitcairn
Haw	Hawaii	Sol	Solomons
Ir.Jaya	Irian Jaya	Tok	Tokelau
Jap	Japan	Torres	Torres Strait Islands
JF	Juan Fernandez	TT	Trust Territory of the Pacific Islands
KI	Kermadec Islands		
Kir	Kiribati (Gilberts)	Tuv	Tuvalu
LI	Line Islands	Van	Vanuatu (New Hebrides)
Ld Howe	Lord Howe		
NC	New Caledonia	W&F	Wallis and Futuna
NH	New Hebrides	WS	Western Samoa

Page numbers set in bold type indicate a major entry under that heading.

A

B

F

G

H

I

J

K

L

M

N

O

P

Q

R

S

T

U

V

W

Y

Advertisers' Index